DVD DELIRIUM
VOLUME 2 REDUX

This revised and updated second edition of DVD Delirium Volume 2 published March 2011
by FAB Press Ltd.

DVD Delirium Volume 2 was first published by FAB Press, December 2003

FAB Press Ltd.
2 Farleigh
Ramsden Road
Godalming
GU7 1QE
England, U.K.

www.fabpress.com

Edited by
Nathaniel Thompson

A CIP catalogue record for this book is available from the British Library.

ISBN 978-1-903254-63-9

DVD
DELIRIUM

The International Guide to Weird and Wonderful Films on DVD & Blu-ray
Volume 2 Redux

edited by
Nathaniel Thompson

CREDITS

Editor:
Nathaniel Thompson

Reviews:
Nigel Burrell, Tim Greaves, Tim S. Greer, Bruce Holecheck,
Kim Newman, Edwin Samuelson, Brad Stevens, Nathaniel Thompson.

Picture Research and Additional Information:
Francis Brewster

Copy Editing, Design and Layout:
Harvey Fenton

DVD cover designs are copyright © the respective DVD companies,
and the covers are reproduced here in the spirit of publicity.

Picture credits:
ABC DVD, Acme, ADV, Alpha Video, Anchor Bay Entertainment, Anchor Bay UK,
Arrow, Artedis, Artificial Eye, Artisan, Artsmagic, Astro, Atlantic, Barrel Entertainment,
BBC, BFI, Blue Underground, Boudicca, Buena Vista, Carlton, CasaNegra, CDA,
Chimera, Ciné-Tamaris, CMV Laservision, Columbia, CP Digital, Criterion, Cryptkeeper,
Cult Epics, Cutthroat, Dark Sky, Dark Vision, DEI, Delta, Digital Entertainment,
Direct Video, Discotek, Divisa, DreamWorks, Eastern Star, Elite Entertainment,
Encore, Entertainment In Video, Eros International, Eureka Video, Exploitation Digital,
Fantoma, Film 2000, First Run Features, Fox Video, FrightFlix, Hardgore,
Home Vision Entertainment, Hong Kong Legends, Icestorm, Icon, Image, Italian Shock,
J. & B., Kino, Kinokuniya, Lionsgate, David Lynch, Madman, Malibu Bay Films, Manga,
Marketing-Film, Media Blasters, Mediacs, Medusa, Metrodome, MGM, MGM-ILC, MK2,
Momentum, Mondo Macabro, Mondo Mini Shows, MPI, Network, New Concorde,
New Line, New Video, NoShame, Odyssey, Omega, Optimum, Paradiso, Paramount, Pathé,
Pathfinder, Planet X, Platinum, Plexifilm, Pro Fun, Retromedia, Rhino, Rise Above,
The Roan Group, Salvation, Screen Edge, Screen Entertainment, Second Sight, Severin,
Shadow Warrior, Shameless, Shriek Show, Simitar, Something Weird, Sony, Spectrum,
Spinning Our Wheels Productions, Strand, Studio Canal, StudioWorks, Sub Rosa,
Svensk Filmindustri, Synapse, Tartan, TF1 Video, Tip Top, Tokyo Shock, Touchstone,
Trimark, Troma, Twister, Unearthed Films, Universal, Universe, VCA, VCI, VCL,
VCX, Velocity, Ventura, Video Film Express, Warner Bros, Wellspring, Westlake,
Wicked Pixel, Worldtrade.
Any omissions will be corrected in future editions.

INTRODUCTION

It's hard to believe that more than seven years have passed since *DVD Delirium Volume 2* was originally published. In that time fans of strange and unusual films have had to become more resourceful than ever to find their latest fix, with new companies springing up to replace ones that have vanished into the ether and online purchasing now accounting for a larger percentage of sales than ever. Meanwhile studios have tried new formats including digital downloads (sometimes included as bonus discs with DVDs), Blu-rays (which are noted in here where appropriate), and on-demand DVD burning thanks to the experimental Warner Archive program, which has unleashed many obscure titles back onto the market. Naturally, you'll read about a few of those long-desired titles within these pages along with the more widely available roster of titles ranging from vintage exploitation to modern horror to far-out art house fare, all of which have many rewards to offer the open-minded.

Each review listing here begins with technical and talent notes to provide some additional information: "Colour" or "Black and White" ("**B&W**"), the year of film's original release, the running time in minutes (**m.**), the major **director** and **actors**, the name of the DVD company or studio releasing the disc, the video standard (**PAL** or **NTSC**) and region coding ("**R**"), widescreen ("**WS**") format where applicable followed by the aspect ratio (often with **16:9** enhancement, the common industry standard, for higher resolution on widescreen monitor playback), and audio format for multi-channel releases (most often Dolby Digital – "**DD**" – or sometimes "**DTS**"). Multi-region and multi-standard players are also popular across the globe, so hopefully this guide will help all our readers to determine whether they should spend their money on an import in preference to their own region's edition.

This *Redux* edition of *DVD Delirium Volume 2* can certainly be enjoyed on its own and provides a valuable snapshot of the state of unusual genre entertainment at the start of the format's second decade. If you enjoy it, I would urge you to seek out the other three volumes in this series, which are also loaded with unique and valuable information about titles you may have missed while perusing your favourite store or online retailer. *DVD Delirium Volumes 3* and *4* are still in print and available direct from the FAB Press web store (**www.fabpress.com**), or from all good book retailers. *Volume 1* is currently out of print, but at the time of writing it is due to be issued as one of the first FAB Press ebooks, so seek it out if you've taken that leap and joined the world of the iPad, Kindle or Sony Reader. Regardless of exactly how you choose to enjoy the *DVD Delirium* series of books, may you have many hours of happy reading and video hunting ahead!

Here you'll find marvellous work by additional writers whose hours in front of the television paid off with the prose you'll find in these pages. Kim Newman ("**KN**"), Tim Greaves ("**TG**"), Brad Stevens ("**BS**"), Bruce Holecheck ("**BH**"), Tim S. Greer ("**TSG**"), Nigel Burrell ("**NB**"), and Edwin Samuelson ("**ES**") will also be your guides for this dizzying trip into the cinematic unknown, so keep a seatbelt handy. Whether you're a cinematic novice or a hopeless round-the-clock movie junkie, you'll hopefully find all of this informative and, above all, entertaining. Happy viewing!

Nathaniel Thompson
Editor

A

À MA SOEUR! (FAT GIRL)

Colour, 2001, 85m. / Directed by Catherine Breillat / Starring Anaïs Reboux, Roxane Mesquida, Libero De Rienzo / Criterion (US R1 NTSC), Tartan (UK R0 PAL), Montparnasse (France F2 PAL) / WS (1.85:1) (16:9), Winson (HK R3 NTSC) / DD2.0

After the controversial "anti-porn film" *Romance*, many wondered how director Catherine Breillat could possibly top herself. Though technically less explicit than its predecessor, *À ma soeur!* is an even darker and more startling film as it explores the murky terrain of adolescent sexuality from two different, equally disturbing vantage points. During a country holiday with their parents, 15-year-old Elena (Roxane Mesquida) and 12-year-old, overweight Anaïs (Anaïs Reboux) decide to pass the time talking about and finding boys to strike up a summer romance. Elena hooks up with an older law student, Fernando (Libero De Rienzo), who steals all of Elena's attention away from her sister. Fernando even sweet talks her into having sex while Anaïs lies awake in the same room; though Elena believes she is falling in love with Fernando after giving up her virginity, a nasty surprise awaits after he offers up an engagement ring. With the holiday over, the girls head back for home with their mother during one of the most jolting, horrific road trips ever committed to film.

Deliberately confrontational, Breillat's film presents the sexuality of female teenagers as an inevitable but delicate force. While Elena's vulnerability may be a subject already well explored in such fare as *Sweet Talk*, the dangerous combination of fantasy, delusion and carnal longing within Anaïs is certainly a cinematic first. The sex scenes are intense and fairly explicit (albeit with some prosthetic aid, later riffed upon by Breillat in *Sex Is Comedy*), though they don't cross the line into hardcore territory, as already explored in *Romance*. For many viewers the harsh, slasher-style ending comes out of left field, though the vicious, bleak tone it imposes on the rest of the film in retrospect is essential to understanding Breillat's *modus operandi*. How successful she was in the end will be a matter of taste; it's not an easy film to watch, much less like, but it certainly leaves its mark and is essential viewing for devotees of both provocative art house fare and twisted sleaze.

Yet another Tartan title to fall victim to the scissors of the BBFC, *À ma soeur!* lost 88 seconds of footage from a pivotal but not terribly graphic rape scene at the end of the film. Considering that images of urination, erect members, and underage sodomy remain intact, one has to marvel at this kind of logic. In any case Tartan is upfront about the censorship in its packaging, and otherwise the disc is a worthy presentation. The anamorphic transfer looks quite nice with optional English subtitles (as opposed to the theatrical prints they usually transfer). The disc also contains trailers for *Lovers of the Arctic Circle*, *The Red Squirrel*, *Turkish Delight*, *Thesis*, *Dead or Alive*, and *Freezer*.

An uncensored French DVD is also available, albeit without English subtitles, while a Hong Kong disc with English subtitles is uncut but cropped, with a decidedly bleary-looking transfer. However, the most satisfying release came on the heels of the others courtesy of Criterion, whose uncensored transfer is the best of the lot with improved English subtitles as well. Extras include a marginally-changed alternative ending and a video interview with Breillat, who explains the film's English and French titles as well as her various travails with the actors.

ABANDON

Colour, 2002, 99m. / Directed by Stephen Gaghan / Starring Katie Holmes, Benjamin Bratt, Tony Goldwyn, Charlie Hunnam, Melanie Lynskey, Fred Ward / Paramount (US R1 NTSC), Touchstone (UK R2 PAL) / WS (2.35:1) (16:9) / DD5.1

While toiling over her marketing thesis, pretty college student Katie (*Dawson's Creek*'s Katie Holmes) is more than a little distracted when troubled cop Wade Handler (played by Benjamin Bratt) shows up inquiring about Katie's boyfriend, Embry (Charlie Hunnam), who disappeared without a trace two years before. Unfortunately the police and her shrink (Tony Goldwyn) don't prove to be much comfort when Embry shows up again, stalking and threatening Katie in dark and isolated locations. While Katie and Wade begin to form a tentative romantic relationship, another disappearance on campus puts them both in danger.

A rising TV writer, Stephen Gaghan rose to the big time with his 2000 Oscar win for penning the wildly over-praised *Traffic*. Given enough cachet to both write and direct, he turned out this asinine thriller which, to put it simply, is a clumsy imitation of Pete Walker's *Schizo* without the gore or entertainment value. The requisite "big twist ending" is so obvious that Bratt's cop character, already hobbled by a cardboard performance, seems so incapable he should be bagging groceries instead. The talented Hunnam, best known for the original *Queer as Folk*, is wasted in a ridiculous part that leaves him to act with his unruly hair, and the hot/cold cinematography (cribbed from *Traffic* apparently) simply comes across as pretentious. It isn't all a lost cause; Holmes continues to indicate she has more talent to give than her roles deserve; the criminally underused Melanie Lynskey (*Heavenly Creatures*) has some great moments as Holmes's bitchy academic rival; the always watchable Fred Ward turns in another good turn as Bratt's superior; and best of all, Clint Mansell (*Requiem for a Dream*) provides a terrific score, complete with a *Rosemary's Baby*-style lullaby from Holmes, that should have been saved for a better film.

Paramount's fairly generous DVD of this Super 35 title is available in both an anamorphic transfer (kind of dark and murky, but that's how the film's supposed to look) and an opened-up full frame edition. Compositionally the former is more satisfying, though either way it mostly looks like a long music video. The 5.1 sound mix is fairly good, though limited mostly to the score; split surrounds are minimal throughout. Extras include a surprisingly critical commentary from Gaghan and cinematographer Matthew Libatique, with the former criticizing many of his own choices and those of the studio. Also included are a typical interview-filled 22-minute featurette, "A Look at the Dark Side: The Making of *Abandon*", six disposable deleted and extended scenes, and the overheated theatrical trailer. A no-frills U.K. disc is also available.

A

ABHAY

Colour, 2001, 177m. / Directed by Suresh Kirshna / Starring Kamal Hassan, Raveena Tandon, Manisha Koirala / DEI (India R0 NTSC), Tip Top (UK R0 PAL) / WS (2.35:1) (16:9) / DD5.1

While it's fairly common knowledge that lots of Bollywood movies swipe their plots from big budget Hollywood hits, there is nothing – *nothing* – even remotely like *Abhay* elsewhere in the cinematic universe. In the action-packed opening sequence, rogue commander Major Vijay Kumar (Kamal Hassan) and his handful of agents infiltrate a snowy mountain cabin where a group of terrorists are holding Americans hostage. After much gunplay, the good guys and the hostages take out most of the villains and escape; however, Vijay corners the evil leader in the cabin, graphically nail guns the baddie's hands to the floor while strapping a bomb to his chest, and

A

leaps out to safety just before the structure explodes! Afterwards Vijay returns to his newscaster girlfriend, Tejaswini (Raveena Tandon), to whom he is engaged; naturally they celebrate at a bar by performing a lavish musical number about the power of laughter, complete with nonsensical quasi-dirty jokes. Unfortunately Vijay has one nasty skeleton in his closet; his bald, psychotic brother, Abhay (also Hassan), is in the loony bin for killing their mother. For some reason Vijay and his relatives have been trying to secure Abhay's release, despite the fact that the courts and asylum heads agree that Abhay is a walking, talking menace to society. Vijay and his lady love go to visit Abhay in the institution, which triggers a murderous rage after Abhay recognizes Tejaswini as the embodiment of his evil mother. Before long Abhay has broken out and, with the help of drugs, is bumping people off in a rage of hallucinations and flashbacks. Of course, like any good maniac, his murderous visions involve singing and dancing, menacing Ronald McDonald clowns, a kung fu-kicking *Matrix* babe leaping out of a *Ladyhawke* poster (!) in front of a movie theatre, and rapid-fire animation sequences filled with fighting and gore. Then there's the big theatrical musical number with chanteuse Manisha Koirala in a kinky tiger outfit, a high-speed car chase, and the ultra-violent finale with the two brothers squaring off in a cartoonish battle involving high buildings and a hot air balloon. You won't believe your eyes.

The multi-talented Haasan does an especially good job of portraying both the hero and villain of the piece; amazingly, he also wrote the film's source novel and has made something of a cinematic specialty out of performing dual roles. Obviously the completely unhinged Abhay is the more memorable of the two portrayals, and this Bollywood rendition of a dangerous criminal is really something to behold. The film itself defies categorization, wavering between serial killer horror, knockabout action, and flat-out surrealism; the multiple

animated scenes spring out of nowhere and simply add to the peculiar brew. Finally, no discussion would be complete without a little quotation from the DVD packaging, typos intact: "*Abhay* is a novel written by Kamal Hassan many years ago is a precursor of Thomas Harris's *Silence of the Lambs*. Thank goodness or else our well informed scribes would have screamed plagiarism." Of course, the storyline obviously bears no resemblance to the Harris book in any shape or form, but that's beside the point.

Both digital presentations are on par with Bollywood product of this vintage; the anamorphic transfer looks quite good for the most part except for fairly weak blacks, and the optional English subtitles are always legible and, for the most part, coherent. Not surprisingly, the 5.1 mix is extremely aggressive from start to finish with an abundance of exaggerated split surround effects. The DEI disc also includes the original Hindi trailer, which barely captures the insanity of the feature itself. Unfortunately many DEI discs have since proven to be defective, often locking up halfway into the feature or simply dying completely a few months out of their packaging; good luck finding a functioning version!

ABSOLUTION

Colour, 1978, 95m. / Directed by Anthony Page / Starring Richard Burton, Dominic Guard, Billy Connolly, Dai Bradley / Westlake (US R1 NTSC), Showbox (UK R0 PAL), Cheezy Flicks (US R0 NTSC)

 The late Anthony Shaffer was a master of puzzle plots, ranging from the drawing room gamesmanship of *Sleuth* to the pagan shenanigans of *The Wicker Man*. Made five years after those films but not released in many territories until Richard Burton's death ten years later,

Absolution forms something of a trilogy with its predecessors, mixing wry black humour with blood-freezing terror where you least expect it. Riding in on a motorcycle, a roving Scottish man named Blakey (stand-up comic Billy Connolly) sets up his tent in the woods outside a remote Catholic boys' school. Meanwhile the students are preparing a comical stage production, much to the displeasure of domineering Father Goddard (Burton). One of the more mischievous students, Benjamin (*Picnic at Hanging Rock*'s Dominic Guard), becomes fast pals with Blakey, and Goddard's pet pupil, the limping Arthur (Dai Bradley), begs to go along for the decadent ride. Goddard is infuriated by Benjamin's growing corruption, but then the boy slips into the confession booth and tells Goddard that he has murdered Blakey, burying the body in the woods. Sealed by the oath of confession, the priest himself goes alone to the woods and finds himself the butt of a vicious prank. But soon after Benjamin returns to the confessional, saying that this time he really has committed a murder...

Laced with an eerie folk score by Stanley Myers and an appropriately broody, Gothic setting, *Absolution* is the sort of film that would really appeal to horror and thriller fans if they knew what it was really about; unfortunately the whiplash plot reversals of the second half prevent a more thorough summary. Bear in mind, however, that the story climaxes with a truly shocking moment of gore, plenty of Burton hamminess, and a deliciously sick twist ending, and it's easy to see why the art house crowd went dashing for the exits. Shaffer brilliantly manipulates the viewer's sympathies, which shift from one character to another with sometimes alarming frequency. (This would make a terrific double feature with *The House that Screamed*, which pulls the same trick and has no compunction about bumping off its characters.) Continuing the tense subtext of religion versus sexuality explored in *The Wicker Man*, Shaffer makes Goddard an even more repressed, emotionally tangled protagonist than that film's Sergeant

Howie; Burton's well-calibrated performance uses silence to great effect, and when Goddard first appears with eyes flaring at schoolboys preparing for an opera in drag, you know this isn't going to be a pleasant ride.

Shot open matte with TV-safe compositions by the competent but unremarkable Anthony Page, *Absolution* (known as *Murder by Confession* on U.K. television) first appeared on laserdisc courtesy of TransWorld. That transfer wasn't any great shakes, and the film now screams out for an updated presentation. Unfortunately you won't get that with the Westlake DVD, which appears to be a direct port of the laserdisc, but inexplicably featuring far more washed out colours. Darker scenes also tend to clog up rather badly, with blocky artefacting often in evidence. It's watchable overall but far from impressive, befitting its bargain bin status. However, the film itself is more than worth the effort of tracking down, and until a decent licensor gives this the treatment it deserves, the disc earns a spin for the quality of the title, not the product itself. The front cover inexplicably boasts this is based on a true story, which seems highly unlikely to say the least. A subsequent edition in the U.K. and a U.S. reissue from bootleg outfit Cheezy Flicks look even worse and can't be recommended at all.

AENIGMA

Colour, 1987, 87m. / Directed by Lucio Fulci / Starring Jared Martin, Lara Naszinski, Ulli Reinthaler, Milijana Zirojevic / Image (US R1 NTSC), Hardgore (UK R2 PAL) / WS (1.85:1), Raro (Italy R2 PAL), Minerva (Italy R2 PAL) / WS (1.85:1) (16:9) / DD5.1

"How does a young girl who's braindead experience a violent emotion?" Made a good five years after Fulci's burst of genuine if cracked creativity within the horror genre, this is

the one in which a sleeping girl is smothered by a slimy mass of snails. It's actually a variation on *Patrick* (a big hit in Italy, remember) and of course *Carrie*, littered with silly hallucinations that wind up with nasty characters meeting ridiculous fates. In the opening scene, scored with an especially sappy ballad from the depths of the worst decade ever for pop music, Kathy (Milijana Zirojevic), plain Jane daughter of the cleaner at an exclusive Boston school, is made up (hideously) for a date with the hulking gym teacher. This turns out to be a set-up for her humiliation by most of the pupils at the school, which is populated by hateful bitches with too much hairspray, and she winds up in a coma on life-support, tended by caring, curly-haired Dr. Robert Anderson (Jared Martin). Eva (Lara Naszinski), new in school, is semi-possessed by Kathy, as indicated by much pouty staring, but the psychically-gifted patient seems to be able to wreak her revenge from bed by making her tormentors have hallucinations: one girl keeps finding the headless and bleeding body of her boyfriend everywhere, another is attacked by a marble statue while prowling a museum late at night. Eva-or-Kathy begins a relationship with the doctor but supernatural influence prompts a nervous breakdown and the faithless hero moves on to another girl (Ulli Reinthaler), the Sue Snell figure who has expressed guilt over the initial prank. Eva escapes from a sanatorium and goes after her rival, cornering her in the hospital morgue and threatening her with a Fulci-esque eye-gouging averted at the last moment, and Kathy's mother puts an end to the goings on when she mercy-kills her daughter by pulling out all her life-supports.

Set in Massachusetts but shot in the then-Yugoslavia, this isn't as frankly inept as the efforts Fulci would turn out for the rest of his career (*Ghosts of Sodom*, *Cat in the Brain*, etc.) but is an entirely conventional, unfelt entry in a cycle that had come and gone before the end of the 1970s. None of the Euro-model actresses are credible as school-age girls, probably a mercy given the young-middle-aged hero's tendency to seduce them. The dubbed dialogue is thuddingly bad, and the synthesized drone of Muzak is worse.

Hardgore's DVD is an improvement over video releases: the transfer shows up moderate grain in the original materials, but is letterboxed to a sliver less than 1.85:1 without 16:9 enhancement. Every detail of the snail scene is in sharp, glistening focus. The extras are an image gallery (five video sleeves), a Fulci filmography and trailers for other Hardgore titles (*I Spit on Your Grave*, *Demonium*, etc.). The Image DVD contains no bonus features and, like most English language versions, is missing a fleeting flashback snippet inexplicably present in Italian and Japanese versions. The best and priciest option is to buy an Italian DVD (either incarnation), both of which boast a slick anamorphic transfer, audio options in English, French, and 5.1 or mono Italian (with optional subtitles in English as well), a bogus stills gallery, and the Italian theatrical trailer. The Raro edition also includes an audio commentary with Antonio Tentori, who covers the basics of filming (in Italian only) with anecdotes about the various actors.
– KN

ALI: FEAR EATS THE SOUL
Colour, 1974, 93m. / Directed by Rainer Werner Fassbinder / Starring Brigitte Mira, El Hedi ben Salem / Criterion (US R1 NTSC), Arrow (UK R0 PAL)

Decades before Todd Haynes dissected '50s soaper deity Douglas Sirk in *Far from Heaven*, Rainer Werner Fassbinder already did the trick for European cinema with several of his melodramatic character studies. The most obvious Sirkian project is clearly *Ali:*

Fear Eats the Soul (Angst essen Seele auf), a dazzling reinterpretation of *All that Heaven Allows* that throws age and racial differences into the already volatile story of love ripped apart by class divisions. Fassbinder's most unorthodox leading lady, Brigitte Mira, takes centre stage as Emmi Kurowski, an ageing cleaning woman with two grown children. She begins an affair with Ali (El Hedi ben Salem), a much younger Arab whose fractured German proves to be only one of his traits which others find unacceptable. Convinced they are in love, Emmi and Ali decide to get married, much to the distress of her friends and family. Much drama and tragedy ensues.

Despite their reputation as austere and often difficult to enjoy, Fassbinder's films are actually quite engaging and rewarding as long as one doesn't necessarily expect a traditional Hollywood ending. One of his most accessible films, *Ali* benefits from extremely rich and realistic characters whose plight elicits a number of powerful emotional responses. The spectacular two lead performances are the greatest assets; amazingly, Mira would go on to nearly equal her work here one year later in *Mother Küsters Goes to Heaven*. As usual Fassbinder's use of the camera to frame his characters and their striking, angular environments is without peer, and here we really see him developing the dynamic, stylized use of colour which would explode in later films such as *Lola* and *Querelle*. Whether seen as a tearjerker, social statement, or artistic experiment, Fassbinder's masterpiece works perfectly and remains sadly relevant, regardless of the passage of time or the country of origin.

Criterion's beautiful presentation ranks with the best of the much-needed Fassbinder restorations. Colours are rock solid and beautifully saturated; the red-lit Arab bar where Emmi and Ali repeatedly return to dance could pass as a set from Dario Argento's *Suspiria*. Detail is exceptionally clear and crisp, with no digital problems in sight. The optional English subtitles are well translated and always legible. As with most Fassbinder titles, this was shot at the standard Academy ratio of 1.33:1 but, for widescreen TV owners who prefer filling up their frame, it blows up to 1.78:1 quite nicely. Criterion's double-disc set pays lavish tribute to this landmark film; the first disc contains the film along with the original German trailer. Disc two contains a wholly appropriate interview with Haynes, who discusses his film school exposure to Sirk, outlines the Sirk influence on both quasi-remakes, and defends a genre once spat upon by cineastes. A 2003 short film entitled "Angst isst Seele auf" (a more grammatically correct version of the film's title) takes place entirely from the point of view of a dark-skinned Arab in Germany, encountering violent neo-Nazis before stepping into a live theatrical production of *Ali* with Mira reprising her role. The short is presented in anamorphic widescreen, framed at 1.78:1. Mira also turns up for a new 22-minute video interview in which she comes across as extremely sharp and witty; she makes for charming, candid company and discusses how Fassbinder's approach revolutionized her acting career. Long-time Fassbinder editor Thea Eymèsz also appears for a separate interview, running for 21 minutes, in which she discusses the professional working relationship she cultivated with the director and traces how his approach evolved over time before his premature death. "Signs of Vigorous Life: New German Cinema" is a 32-minute BBC program from 1976 which offers an overview of the rising directorial talents in Germany; Fassbinder doesn't really enter the picture until halfway through and is covered mainly through stills and second hand narration, while Werner Herzog is interviewed and receives the lion's share of screen time. The final extra is a snippet from Fassbinder's earlier *The American Soldier*, in which a character quickly relates the story of Emmi and Ali with a far more brutal conclusion than the one Fassbinder ultimately chose.

A subsequent U.K. special edition features the same transfer and a completely different set of extras: the 50-minute "Fassbinder in Hollywood" documentary, "Life Stories: A Conversation with Rainer Werner Fassbinder" (50 minutes as well), Fassbinder's "The City Tramp" short, a Todd Haynes interview about Fassbinder, the trailer, and liner notes by Julian Savage. The disc is also included as part of the second volume of Arrow's Fassbinder Commemorative Collection 73-82 line (which also includes *Chinese Roulette*, *The Marriage of Maria Braun*, *Effi Briest*, *Fox and His Friends*, *Fear of Fear*, *Satan's Brew*, and *Mother Kusters Goes to Heaven*).

ALUCARDA

Colour, 1978, 77m. / Directed by Juan López Moctezuma / Starring Tina Romero, Claudio Brook, Susana Kamini, Tina French / Mondo Macabro (US R0 NTSC, UK R0 PAL) / DD2.0

 A long way from those K. Gordon Murray Mexican horrors for the kiddies, *Alucarda* is one of the more striking and shocking south of the border Gothic fests from the golden age of cinematic sleaze. Replete with nuns, devil worship, blood baths, and sadistic religious fanaticism, this is one drive-in jewel ripe for rediscovery. In the 1800s, young orphan Justine (Susana Kamini) arrives at a repressive convent where Alucarda (Tina Romero) has spent her life since infancy. They become fast friends and, while frolicking in the woods, encounter a sinister gypsy (Claudio Brook) who warns them about a nearby cemetery, the devil's stomping ground. After unleashing a malevolent power inside one of the tombs, Alucarda proves to be the most susceptible upon returning to the convent. The gypsy then magically reappears and initiates the girls into the ways of the horned one, courtesy of a blood rite and a sylvan orgy. Potentially bisexual Sister Angelica (Tina French) realizes something's amiss and decides to stage an exorcism, though the ceremony of tying the girls naked to crosses proves to have disastrous results. The local physician, Dr. Oszek (also Brook), finds himself unable to explain away the bizarre deeds occurring within the convent walls, which escalate when Justine seems to be killed... or does she?

Though shot on a low budget in obviously limited sets, *Alucarda* is a thematically fascinating response to the increasingly depraved Italian nun antics being churned out around the same time. Even during its most outlandish moments, Juan López Moctezuma rarely seems to be pandering to the audience's baser instincts; instead his use of bare flesh and blood feels poetic and organically linked to the story, which never loses focus on the emotions and motivations of the characters. The story construction also makes effective use of Hitchcockian doubling motifs, including casting both Romero and Brook in dual roles. The last third of the film contains a number of intriguing narrative reversals which further this technique, and the finale presents a more intricate view of the relationship between good and evil than one normally expects in a nunsploitation effort. Of course, the standout scene here – a character rising nude from a blood-filled coffin and going on a murderous rampage – is quite difficult to forget, but Moctezuma imbues even the quieter scenes with a palpable sense of unease and menace. The woodland orgy is a particularly effective demonstration of his command of the cinematic medium, evoking Terence Fisher's *The Devil Rides Out* with a few erotically charged twists of its own.

One of the earliest U.K. releases from Mondo Macabro, *Alucarda* served as the first American title in the line as well. Image quality is excellent for the most part, with the upgraded U.S. disc gaining the edge as it was transferred directly from the original negative and sports only minor scratches and damage. Colours are wonderfully saturated, and while the detail is sometimes almost too sharp (revealing some of the more cost-cutting measures in the otherwise impressive production design, and also exposing some of the inferior stock used for a handful of shots), there's little quibbling to be done with this stellar presentation. The actors performed in English, resulting in an audio track which synchs up with their lip movements even though several voices appear to be looped later. Brook's voice is definitely his own, and it's interesting to see this veteran actor (who also appeared in Moctezuma's fascinating *Mansion of Madness* and, much later, the 007 actioner *Licence to Kill*) tackling two very different personae. The stereo audio track limits most of the ambient separation effects to the low-key electronic score, which sounds like a sparser cousin to Tangerine Dream's soundtracks of the period. For some reason a persistent, bass-filled hum is barely audible throughout the English track; those with a sensitive sound system can minimize this background droning by cranking up the treble. A dubbed Spanish audio track is also included. The U.S. disc contains the lurid theatrical trailer under the original title (though tapes have circulated under such other names as *Innocents from Hell*, *Sisters of Satan*, and *Mark of the Devil 3*), as well as a 15-minute featurette on Moctezuma including tantalizing snippets from his other, earlier work and several useful bits of biographical information like his relationship with peer Alejandro Jodorowsky. The U.K. disc instead contains a 22-minute episode on Mexican horror from the excellent Mondo Macabro television series; perhaps for legal clearance reasons this couldn't be ported over directly to the American version. The package is rounded out with a Moctezuma filmography and text interview as well as a 7-minute video interview with director Guillermo del Toro (*The Devil's Backbone*), who speaks appreciably of the film and its creator with a number of humorous interjections. He also discusses his working relationship with the late Brook, who appeared in del Toro's *Cronos*. The final extra is a stills gallery, rounding out an admirable tribute to one of the more outlandish entries in Mexi-horror.

THE AMAZING TRANSPLANT

Colour, 1970, 71m. / Directed by Doris Wishman / Starring Juan Fernandez, Linda Southern, Kim Pope / Image/Something Weird (US R0 NTSC), Odeon (UK R0 PAL)

Percy did it funnier, *Sex and Zen* did it sexier, but *The Amazing Transplant* did it first, and in the exploitation biz that's all that really matters. In 1970 lunatic artiste Doris Wishman decided to tackle the sensational concept of the penis graft, and while the results aren't nearly as scandalous as the sordid subject matter would suggest there's still an abundance of deliriously dished-out depravity for admirers of her reckless charms to cherish.

Right from the beginning you can tell this ain't your usual case of penis envy. Uninhibited Mary is relaxing in bed practicing her zither (look it up) when she unexpectedly receives a phone-call from ex-beau Arthur. He desperately wants to visit, and despite her initial assertions against the meeting ("It's Saturday, and the only day I'll have to shop") she eventually relents. Bad move. Arthur comes over, and after confessing his love and offering a marriage proposal proceeds to tear Mary's clothes off and strangle her. In a matter of minutes the entire city somehow knows of the murder (probably due to the hilariously informative radio newscasts that make sure they repeatedly point out Mary was

A

nude), and Arthur is nowhere to be found. His Uncle Bill, conveniently a cop, pleads and grovels to be put on the case ("He's my dead brother's kid!") and is granted 24 hours to uncover his whereabouts. Wasting no time, he immediately begins seeking out and questioning the women in Arthur's little black book (including NYC skin-flick vet and future porn gal Kim Pope), and they all have an incredibly similar story to tell. It seems dear shy Arthur wasn't all that shy, and after working his way into each of the women's homes he exploded in a carnal frenzy, forcing himself upon them, regardless of their not-so-convincing struggles ("Stop, you're mad... you're tearing my clothes"). So why is reclusive Arthur, who was previously quite unlucky when it came to the opposite sex, now a rape-happy psycho? It seems he so admired his friend Felix's prowess with the ladies that when a "deadly virus" suddenly knocked him off, Arthur blackmailed the family doctor (who's an illegal abortionist on the side) into performing a previously unheard-of procedure ("I want you to put Felix's penis on me!"). Unfortunately the stiff's stiffy not only granted Arthur the sexual suaveness he craved but also brought Felix's freaky fetish into play ("Whenever he saw a girl wearing gold earrings he would get terribly excited"). So who is truly at fault for Mary's death? It all ends with a shot that'll make you throw your remote at the TV. Seriously.

With the exception of the titular operation, the bulk of the film seems to be inspired by the then-current Boston Strangler case; yet for a motion picture so rife with rape, *The Amazing Transplant* remains astonishingly inoffensive. Perhaps it's due to Doris's patented filmmaking formula, which transforms even the seediest concept into a non-stop barrage of groovy lounge tunes, horrendous fashion and laughably dubbed conversations. With a more accomplished director in charge we could have ended up with another sadistic endurance test à la *I Spit on Your Grave*, but instead *Transplant* is about as good as can be expected for a movie where the actors' lips rarely match their dialogue. Most exploitation fans will already know what to expect, as Wishman's cinematic excursions are the absolute definition of "love-it-or-hate-it" cinema, with both factions usually citing identical reasoning behind their stance. The total avoidance of synch sound (which results in endless camera shots of feet, plants and various other inanimate objects, conversations where the *listener* is focused on, etc.) and the refusal to play by the basic rules of filmmaking will have her followers jumping for joy. Contrarily, gorehounds looking for some mondo-styled surgery footage will be disappointed, as Doris didn't try her hand in *that* field until she made *Let Me Die a Woman* eight years later.

Theatrically this outing found distribution with Jerand Film Distributors, who had previously handled the chore for Wishman's *Indecent Desires* and *Too Much, Too Often*. On home video, Electric Video unzipped their VHS of *The Amazing Transplant* in 1981, attempting to pass it off as a Jack the Ripper-inspired slasher flick – a ruse that undoubtedly melted the mind of any teenager expecting to rent something akin to *Friday the 13th*. The title quickly disappeared from sight and wasn't heard of again till exploitation heroes Something Weird Video came to the rescue with a much-needed reissue. While their original VHS was a bit dull and washed out, on DVD *Transplant* looks better than it has any right to. Transferred directly from the original negative, colours are bright and vibrant (essential for the kitsch '70s décor) and the image is as crisp and sharp as frequent collaborator Chuck Smith's haphazard photography permits, allowing every scar, zit and cellulite dimple to be examined with utmost clarity. Although some slight print damage is noticeable throughout it only becomes bothersome for a 15-minute stretch starting about 23 minutes in, when a collection of thin white vertical lines appear and run rampant. It's not the end of the world, but it's worth noting. The mono audio track is basic but clear, with the occasional crackle and pop giving away the film's age. Before you go rushing to the store, however, you may want to know that SWV's release is, well... circumcised. The disc's 71m 16s running time is almost seven minutes shy of Electric Video's 77m 53s length, and upon comparison several set pieces are either shortened, wholly missing or presented in alternative versions! The cuts actually start pretty early on, during the opening sex murder of Mary Thorne that thrusts the plot into motion. What sex you ask? Exactly. The entire forced fornication and the majority of the strangulation is missing from the DVD, which in turn eliminates the motive for the killing itself ("Poor sick Arthur..." "I'm not sick! I'm like other men!"). The next omission is a lesbian interlude that takes place before Uncle Bill delivers a mislaid package to Arthur's upstairs neighbour, though when reinstated this bit actually destroys the subsequent scene's punchline! The third deletion involves some bewilderingly casual chitchat unfolding during the operation, eliminating close-ups of the plainly visible penis. While Arthur and Bill are talking on the steps the fourth chop is made, completely getting rid of a flashback sequence where Arthur and his perpetually off-screen boner donor Felix talk about the worries of impregnating girls, during which the secret side-job of Dr. Meade is revealed. Lastly, the threesome near the end contains some additional sexual grinding on the tape. Strangely this *ménage a trois* unfolds in black and white on disc, but in sepia-tone and colour on Electric's release. Apparently at some point after the film's theatrical release, Doris got a hold of her negative and trimmed out these sections for reasons known only to herself. It's a shame complete elements weren't located for a definitive DVD presentation, since the segments should be intact for a true appreciation of the film.

Keeping with tradition, Something Weird Video has thrown a few thematically related supplements into the mix. In addition to the original trailer for the main feature (which offers brief snippets of the missing moments), you can find theatrical previews for several other Doris-directed oddities. Represented are her Chesty Morgan breasterpieces *Deadly Weapons* and *Double Agent 73*, their pseudo-sequel *The Immoral Three* and a marvellously trashy *The Love Toy* spot (which features several of the same cast members as *Transplant*). Two short subjects are onboard as well; a Navy scare film titled "Sex Hygiene", which warns seamen about the perils of unprotected sex (approach with caution: it contains enough STD-ravaged genital manhandling to keep even the most jaded viewers squirming in their seats), and "Penis Facts 1952", a ragged-looking curio documenting the different forms of the male sex organ. Nice to see I'm average. Finishing things off is a slideshow of Wishman pressbook and poster art, scored with fabulous '70s radio advertisements for lurid attractions like *Grimm's Fairy Tales for Adults*.

A subsequent U.K. release from Odeon castrates an additional 12 minutes from the entire disc, trimming three of the assault scenes as well as numerous shots from the trailers and shorts.

– BH

ANACONDA

Colour, 1997, 86m. / Directed by Luis Llosa / Starring Jennifer Lopez, Jon Voight, Eric Stoltz, Ice Cube, Jonathan Hyde, Danny Trejo, Owen Wilson, Vincent Castellanos / Sony (DVD & Blu-ray) (US R1 NTSC, UK R2 PAL) / WS (2.35:1) (16:9) / DD5.1

A small documentary film crew led by Dr. Steven Kale (Eric Stoltz) ventures into the Amazon jungle in the hope of locating and capturing footage of the long-lost tribe of the Shirishama Indians. A short way up river they rescue snake hunter Paul Serone (Jon Voight) from his stricken boat. Almost immediately the bullish Serone exerts his forceful personality on the group, clashing swords with docu-director Terri Flores (Jennifer Lopez), cameraman Danny Rich (Ice Cube) and whinging presenter Warren Westridge (Jonathan Hyde). Kale is left comatose after a large insect lodges itself in his throat and Serone commandeers the boat, leading the group into perilous conflict with the object of his obsession – a huge, man-eating anaconda.

After some brief factual blurb clueing you in as to how big and how nasty anacondas can be, director Luis Llosa lurches headlong into the action with an assault on Danny Trejo (*From Dusk Till Dawn*) by an unseen menace. Llosa isn't one of those directors who keeps you in suspense for long though, and in no time at all the immense star makes its on-screen debut, turning a marauding panther into light lunch. Playing the trump card so soon could have paid off had it been a winner, but in the case of *Anaconda* it isn't. A combination of full size live action animatronics and primitive computer generation, it's unconvincingly maladroit in the former mode and swifter than the Road Runner on acid in the latter. In either guise though, the mean-tempered, yellow-eyed critter livens up the proceedings whenever it gets peckish, consuming its prey in a couple of gulps; there's a marvellous moment when the screaming face of a recently munched-up victim is outlined through the outer wall of the creature's gut. Yet for all its purported threat it's the scaly beastie's smaller cousins that are most likely to give snake-phobics the shudders. The moment when a cantankerous nipper latches onto Jonathan Hyde's finger and refuses to let go is a real (pardon the pun) squirm-inducer. Still, phony-looking monster or otherwise, Llosa manages to scare up a few suspenseful scenes with a mid-way attack on the crew

(in which Owen Wilson provides the late-night snake snack), Hyde's waterfall demise, and a dynamite climax with Lopez drenched in monkey blood and pursued at breakneck pace round an abandoned mill by the ravenous reptile. When he runs out of ideas Llosa isn't adverse to filching from acknowledged monster classics, the most obvious example being *Jaws*: Serone is fishing for the anaconda and, after a few suspect clicks, his reel bursts into life as the hooked serpent takes off. The moment is capped off with the famous Spielberg/Scheider tracking shot as Lopez gets her first sighting of the fork-tongued fiend. Jon Voight manages to steal the movie from under the nose of his gargantuan adversary with an unbelievably over-the-top performance – all sneers, grimaces and threats hissed through clenched teeth – and it's worth the price of admission just to see him firing on all burners. Not to mention his juicy comeuppance when the snake opens its gullet, sucks him in and, shortly afterwards, regurgitates the partially digested corpse into Lopez's lap. J Lo herself is actually somewhat vapid, but rapper Ice Cube, who one doesn't expect so much of, is surprisingly proficient and ultimately the hero of the day. Jonathan Hyde is a touch irksome but he nabs the script's funniest line as he coldcocks Voight with a golf club: "Arsehole in one!" Vincent Castellanos, who got a bullet through the head in David Lynch's *Mulholland Dr.*, fares even worse here as skipper Mateo, noshed down by the snake in one of the film's better sequences. Make sure to keep your eyes peeled for the reprised shot of the boat arriving in the cove, played in reverse to make it look as if it's leaving and resulting in the world's only gravity-defying waterfall in the process. As freaks of nature monster movies go *Anaconda* is pretty standard fluff, no better or worse than the imitations that followed; for fanged fodder with the same flavour check out the likes of *King Cobra* and *Python*.

Hardly worthy of special edition treatment, it's nevertheless disappointing that Columbia didn't see fit to add any additional incentive to their DVD release of *Anaconda*. If they'd only gone as far as to include the trailer, brief cast and crew interviews and photo gallery that comprised the film's multimedia press kit it would have been something. As it is, their Region 2 disc – and its Region 1 counterpart – is as empty as a freshly shed snakeskin. On the plus side the English 5.1 Dolby Digital (and optional English Dolby Surround) sound provides plenty of atmosphere, with the noises of the jungle enveloping the listener in a melee of chattering monkeys and incessant birdsong. Subtitling is provided in English, Polish, Czech, Hungarian, Icelandic, Hindi and Hebrew. The movie is divided by 19 chapter marks. *Anaconda* was also released as a movie only Superbit release with 5.1 and DTS sound, or in a box set with its much cheaper sequels, *Anacondas: The Hunt for the Blood Orchid*, *Anaconda: The Offspring* and *Anacondas: Trail of Blood*. A Sony Blu-ray is also available in an improved (but not drastically so) hi-def transfer and surprisingly spry lossless surround mix, albeit again with no extras.

– TG

ANGEL

Colour, 1984, 94m. / Directed by Robert Vincent O'Neill / Starring Donna Wilkes, Cliff Gorman, Dick Shawn, Susan Tyrrell, Rory Calhoun, Steven Porter, John Diehl

AVENGING ANGEL

Colour, 1985, 93m. / Directed by Robert Vincent O'Neill / Starring Betsy Russell, Rory Calhoun, Barry Pearl

ANGEL III: THE FINAL CHAPTER

Colour, 1988, 100m. / Directed by Tom DeSimone / Starring Mitzi Kapture, Mark Blankfield, Anna Navarro, Tawny Fere, Maud Adams, Richard Roundtree / Anchor Bay (US R1 NTSC) / WS (1.85:1) (16:9)

After exploitation legend Roger Corman bailed from New World Pictures for greener pastures, the studio was left to contend with the 1980s, arguably the strangest decade in film history. The beloved women-in-prison and low budget sci-fi epics from the drive-in days weren't enough to sustain the exec's lunch tabs, so what was left? Enter Robert Vincent O'Neill, the director of oddball sleaze titles like *The Psycho Lover* and *Blood Mania*. More importantly, he had just written the terrific cable favourite *Vice Squad* and had tweaked that film's guns and hookers formula with a brand new twist – *Angel*, whose posters summed it up perfectly: "High school honor student by day. Hollywood hooker by night." Released in the cold days of January 1984, the film became a surprise box office hit, thanks mainly to its tantalizing poster featuring 25-year-old star Donna Wilkes as both squeaky-clean teen and slutty tramp (which is actually the closest thing to leering teen porn connected to the film).

Abandoned Molly (Wilkes) lives alone in a Hollywood apartment where she pretends to care for an ailing mother. She spends her days at high school, keeping away from the other kids but earning decent grades, while her evenings are spent as "Angel", strolling Hollywood Boulevard looking for tricks. (Those familiar with L.A. geography will note that her high school is only a few blocks from her place of employment, so one can only wonder why it takes so long for her peers to catch on.) Angel spends most of her time with a colourful crew of characters, including sassy drag queen Mae (Dick Shawn), her butch landlord Solly (Susan Tyrrell), washed up cowboy actor Kit Carson (Rory Calhoun, fresh from *Motel Hell*), and Chaplin impersonator Yo-Yo

A

Charlie (Steven Porter). She also becomes a personal crusade for a tough-as-nails police officer, Lieutenant Andrews (Cliff Gorman), who gradually uncovers the truth about Molly/Angel. As if that weren't enough, Angel's fellow ladies of the night are being carved up by a raving nutball (*Miami Vice*'s John Diehl) who naturally sets his sights on Angel.

Angel is pure trash heaven, of course, though it isn't quite the trash many would expect. Wilkes stays clothed throughout the film (apart from one quick, discreet scene changing into her skivvies), and her encounters with johns are always interrupted by minor distractions like hidden police radios or dead bodies. The T&A factor is instead provided by incongruous shots of suspiciously mature-looking "high school girls" taking showers, which have no connection to the plot whatsoever. The tasteful treatment of Wilkes doesn't extend to the action quotient, however, with the film tossing her into an insane climax that finds the hooker-garbed teen tearing down Hollywood Boulevard wielding a mean pistol. Of course, that's nothing compared to a raving-mad, shaved-scalped Diehl in Hare Krishna garb fighting to the death with Shawn in full drag, or Diehl disrupting a police line-up by holding one of the cops hostage. However, the biggest jaw dropper is saved for the big scene when Wilkes's extracurricular activities finally become the talk of the school: "I can't believe she's a whore", one girl mutters. "That's too bad, I really liked her!" Or the class nerd running up and asking Molly on a date: "Here's 25 dollars; it's all I could save. Is that enough?" As our heroine runs off in tears, few viewers are likely to share the same reaction. Fast-paced, utterly ridiculous, and irredeemably junky, *Angel* benefits the most from its canny supporting casting, with Shawn turning a poorly written character into a memorable tour de force. None of the script's "witty" comebacks are clever at all, but old pro Shawn still makes them sound

like Oscar Wilde. (Poor Wilkes doesn't fare as well; her retorts to the school jocks are verbal lead balloons all the way.)

With *Angel* a certified hit, New World released a virtual remake (albeit with a much older lead), Ken Russell's *Crimes of Passion*, later the same year. It wasn't until the next year that an actual sequel hit the screens, starring a *younger* actress, Betsy Russell (*Tomboy* herself), as the now-collegiate Molly. Now a track runner and aspiring law student, Molly is pulled back to her old stomping grounds when Lieutenant Andrews is mowed down on the job by a stray bullet. Back on Hollywood Boulevard, Angel hooks up (err, sorry) with Solly and Yo-Yo Charlie, who help her spring Kit Carson from a nursing home. Solly's also a new mother (don't ask), which allows lots of baby close-ups for an extra dose of the cutes. New blood is provided by the questionable Johnny Glitter (Barry Pearl), a very dated attempt to replace the absent Mae. Shootouts and heavy doses of neon lighting ensue. Far more genteel than its predecessor, *Avenging Angel* is good cable fare but lacks the weird edge of the original. Russell's a much sweeter (and blander) version of Molly, and the loss of the whole high school hooker angle makes this a much plainer outing. At least most of the original cast is back, providing a much-needed shot in the arm whenever things get too pedestrian. And bonus points for the goriest use of a Bronski Beat song in movie history.

Unfortunately the merits of the first two films were mostly thrown out for the third instalment, *Angel III: The Final Chapter*, starring the improbably named Mitzi Kapture as yet another version of Molly. Apparently no longer interested in that whole lawyer business, she's now a professional photographer. Her deadbeat mother, Gloria (Anna Navarro), comes back into her life and reveals that Molly has a sister, Michelle (Tawny Fere), who's now trapped as a hooker for drug-and-skin peddler Nadine (Maud Adams). Proving that the series had finally resorted to remaking Pam Grier films, Angel goes undercover as a high-class call girl to foil Nadine's nefarious crime trade. For no discernible reason, Richard Roundtree also pops up as the obligatory police officer to offer a moral counterbalance. Directed by sleaze favourite Tom DeSimone (*Hell Night*, *The Concrete Jungle*), this final entry in the saga (not counting 1993's unrelated *Angel 4: Undercover*, which is not included in this set) feels more like a contractual obligation than a spirited exploitation romp. Adams is enjoyable to watch as always, but she's drastically underused and never gets to be really nasty. Instead we get lots of padding and the usual cable-friendly chases and shootouts, with comedian Mark Blankfield (of *Fridays* and *Jekyll & Hyde... Together Again* fame) offering some mild relief as a male hustler/ice cream vendor named Spanky. Kinda says it all, doesn't it?

While some of Anchor Bay's New World transfers have been shaky at best, these three titles get the first class treatment and look much better than those endless late night cable screenings might suggest. Colours are bright in that day-glo '80s way we all know and love (especially the second film), while black levels are generally fine depending on the quality of the photography. The third film looks the slickest of the bunch, but it's also rather bland; the grit and grime visible in the elements for the first one in particular really enhance the mood. Audio is straight mono here with no bells and whistles; those synth-heavy theme songs come through loud and clear, and dialogue is always intelligible. *Angel* features three brief deleted scenes, all presented silent with subtitles to fill in the dialogue. The biggest one is an extension of the diner scene with Angel and her pals; the others show Angel gambling and leaving with a john. Also included are two trailers; the second is the one most will recognize from theatrical play. Strangely, the alternative footage from the syndicated TV version (notably a different, extended ending) is not included.

Avenging Angel includes two trailers and a gallery of posters and stills. *Angel III* features only a trailer. (Oddly, DeSimone contributed a commentary to Anchor Bay's *Hell Night* but not to this.) The fold-out, triple-disc packaging also includes a booklet with thorough liner notes by Jay Marks, who provides a good accounting of the development of everyone's favourite jailbait hooker with a gun. A lovably disreputable box set all around.

ANGEL EYES

Colour, 1993, 82m. / Directed by Gary Graver / Starring Monique Gabrielle, John Phillip Law, Rachel Vickers [Raven], Robert Quarry, Erik Estrada / Retromedia (US R1 NTSC) / WS (1.66:1)

Having spent several years in a mental institution for murdering her mother, Angel (Monique Gabrielle) is released and immediately seeks sanctuary with her ex-stepfather Stephen (John Phillip Law). Stephen's partner Michelle (Rachel Vickers) believes that Angel is trying to come between them and makes it clear the girl is an unwelcome house guest. What neither of them realises is that Angel's period of incarceration has failed to cure her and she's a Grade A psychotic time-bomb waiting to go off.

Where to begin? Well, let's call a spade a spade: it's a bad sign indeed when the only recommendation one can offer for watching a film is to see its leading lady disrobe. Not that this is a liability per se when Monique Gabrielle is the leading lady in question, but with *Angel Eyes* that really is the sole benefit of sitting through its eighty-something minute running time. Directed from his own story by Gary Graver – a protégé of Z-grade celluloid prince Fred Olen Ray (who co-executive produced

A

here) – although the excess of exposed flesh will be the main draw for many in the first place, the more discerning will be irked to discover that's basically all there is. The plot – barely substantial enough to supply a synopsis for the disc sleeve, and with a script whose dialogue is so leaden it'd sink in zero gravity – is little more than a channel for a series of simulated (but sometimes only just!) sex scenes featuring B-movie favourite Gabrielle and porno starlet Raven (aka Rachel Vickers), alone, together and with leading man John Phillip Law. A subplot concerning a loan shark (*Count Yorga, Vampire*'s Robert Quarry) and his flunky (Erik Estrada) chasing Law for monies owed should have added a little meat to this bare bones affair and yet it's a tedious, cheap distraction which will have you reaching for the fast forward button on your remote. While Estrada was probably never destined for anything higher than this on the entertainment ladder, it's a shame to see Law reduced to its like. Though initially his presence imbues the film with a glimmer of must-see value, the sight of his undulating buttocks as he flounders around with Raven devalues his talent pretty sharpish. More interesting, surprisingly enough, is Miss Gabrielle, who with everything stacked against her proves to be more than just a body to ogle, even though that's her primary *raison d'être*. At her authentic best when she wigs out and has a tea party with her dolls (one of which she force-feeds when she believes it's refusing to eat), she really hits her stride when she loses control and perforates a sexual conquest with a pair of fireside tongs.

Released on Region 1 DVD by Retromedia Entertainment in Fred Olen Ray's Nite Owl Theater series, *Angel Eyes* is a pretty grotty-looking piece of software, the 1.66:1 matted, 9-chapter-encoded movie debilitated by a murky, underlit and irritatingly soft picture that's devoid of the crispness one has every right to expect from the format. To highlight the deficiencies

further, the disc includes a trailer that's brighter and more colourful than the feature itself. Some on-screen waffle from Ray that bookends the film bumps the 82 minute running time up by some 6 minutes, but doing the maths that still falls short of the 90 minute claim on the sleeve. As if it really mattered. Along with a small slideshow format stills gallery and around a minute's worth of bloopers from *Angel Eyes* itself – if this is all that went wrong Graver must have saved the backers a fortune in film stock! – there are promotional trailers for a small handful of other Nite Owl releases and some outtakes of Ray messing up his intro.
– TG

APARTMENT ZERO

Colour, 1988, 117m. / Directed by Martin Donovan / Starring Colin Firth, Hart Bochner, Liz Smith / Anchor Bay (US R1 NTSC) / WS (1.85:1) (16:9), Platinum (US R0 NTSC) / DD2.0

 A twisted, gender-bending thriller for film buffs, *Apartment Zero* plays like what might have happened if Roman Polanski had been assigned to adapt *Kiss of the Spider Woman*. Set in a dreamy Buenos Aires where dusk seems to last for hours, this deliberately paced but rewarding psychological exercise has built up a substantial cult following over the years and, while flawed, offers enough unpredictable delights to still grip an audience's imagination. Due to the increasingly dwindling audiences at his posh art house movie theatre, twitchy and withdrawn cineaste Jack Carney (Colin Firth) decides to rent out the room of his now institutionalized mother – the titular apartment 0 – to a charming stranger, Adrian (Hart Bochner), who becomes a favourite with all of the building's eccentric

tenants. Meanwhile a series of gruesome, politically-motivated murders in the city leads Jack to believe that Adrian's suave veneer might be concealing a dangerous beast beneath, and the psychological tension between them begins to mount.

Co-written by the always interesting David Koepp (*Stir of Echoes*), who later spun off many of the same themes in his memorable *Bad Influence*, *Apartment Zero* is an efficient, tightly wound thriller which largely dispenses with showboating theatrics in favour of a chilling slow turn of the screws. The always-excellent Firth carries the burden of the film on his shoulders, and while he subsequently softened his image by appearing as the (often cuckolded) lead in a string of increasingly innocuous romantic farces, here he proves that he can go off his rocker with the best of them. Boiling with a mixture admiration, jealously, lust, and fear, he's the perfect counterpoint to Bochner's Brando-styled ideal, a pearly-toothed, potential wolf in leather clothing. Fans of British sitcoms should also look for *The Vicar of Dibley*'s delightful biddy, Liz Smith (*The Cook, the Thief, His Wife & Her Lover*), as one comical half of a pair of nosy, elderly sisters. Add to that the perfectly utilized settings and a vertigo-inducing score by Elia Cmiral (*Ronin*), and you've got one of the more memorable nail-biters of the 1980s.

Following its small but profitable theatrical run, the 124-minute film was retooled by director Martin Donovan, who trimmed out seven minutes for all video and television editions. Consisting of mostly Bertolucci-style edits (i.e., dropping entrances and exits from rooms, conversation bridges, etc.), the revised cut also lost a few little character bits including an odd moment with a shirtless Bochner erotically sniffing his sweaty T-shirt.

The budget-priced bare bones release from Platinum ports over the Academy video transfer but looks notably sharper than the U.S. laserdisc release. Shot almost open matte, the film looks okay but could use a bit of letterboxing to focus the framing. The stereo soundtrack is rendered well enough, sounding clear and free of distortion. However, fans should be more pleased with the Anchor Bay edition, which presents the longer cut of the film with an improved anamorphic transfer, a punchier 5.1 mix, and an audio commentary track with Donovan, Koepp, and the always enthusiastic Steven Soderbergh.

THE APE MAN

B&W, 1943, 64m. / Directed by William Beaudine / Starring Bela Lugosi, Wallace Ford, Louise Currie, Minerva Urecal, Emil Van Horn, Henry Hall, Ralph Littlefield / Delta (UK R0 PAL), Slingshot (US R1 NTSC), Alpha (US R0 NTSC)

 One of nine Bela Lugosi vehicles produced by Monogram Pictures in the early 1940s, this has been a PD title for years, turning up on tape in a variety of blurry, battered editions. This DVD "special edition" continues the tradition; it boasts that it's "digitally mastered from the best available sources and presented in Standard Speed (SP) for the highest quality possible" but still looks like an old 16mm copy projected onto a sheet at two-thirty in the morning in some side-room during a science fiction convention. Like Delta/Laserlight's low-quality releases of Boris Karloff in *The Ghoul* and Lon Chaney in *The Hunchback of Notre Dame*, *The Ape Man* is prefaced by an introduction from an oddly-selected Tony Curtis, who reveals that his personal connection to the star was that his parents were from Hungary too and his father sounded like Lugosi. Curtis gives a précis of the Lugosi career and sets up a PD *Dracula* trailer then promises to talk to us again after the feature, though he doesn't.

A

The film itself is typical Monogram Lugosi; it's a very loose reprise of a Karloff vehicle, *The Ape*, only this time the mad scientist is turned part-gorilla by his experiments rather than just wearing a gorilla suit and he commits spinal fluid-draining murders not to cure a little girl but so that he can stand up straight. It opens with wartime topicality as hardboiled newsman Jeff Carter (tubby Wallace Ford) sees off his long-time photographer sidekick as he joins the signal corps, which means he has to take on a girl (Louise Currie) replacement. The script is peppered with references to the draft, gasoline rationing and women taking the jobs of men away in the services, but we're supposed to believe that the disappearance of eccentric scientist James Brewster (Lugosi) and an interview with his ghost-hunting sister Agatha (Minerva Urecal) would be big news. Brewster, far from missing, is holed up in his mansion, sometimes sharing a straw-filled cage with a big gorilla (Emil Van Horn in a familiar suit) and whining about his unhappy condition (he has shaggy hair, a Neanderthal beard and bad posture). When a colleague (Henry Hall) won't commit murder to gain spinal fluid that might cure him, Brewster and his gorilla buddy (they seem unnaturally close – one of the more perverse touches in a film full of them), Brewster sulkily kills the man's butler, after which he is temporarily able to walk like a man (though he's no less hirsute). The beast flesh comes back, of course and it all winds up with the heroine menaced and the cops crashing the mansion. In a memorable final bit, Zippo (Ralph Littlefield), a weird creep who has been peeking through windows and popping up throughout, admits that he's "the author of the story ... screwy idea, wasn't it?" Indeed.

The opening titles are window-boxed, but most of the film just has a sliver of lower matte and a black bar across the top. The print shows an enormous amount of wear and tear, and ends abruptly in the middle of fade-out music. Then again, maybe it's

appropriate the DVD transfer has been handled with all the care shown by director William Beaudine, who knocked this one out with as few set-ups as possible. Lugosi, who could never be accused of walking through anything, gives his all in truly wretched circumstances. The odd poignancy this approach sometimes yields (such as the "hunted ... despised" scene of *Bride of the Monster*) never applies here; James Brewster spends so much time pleading for sympathy while acting like a selfish, immature jerk that one wonders why his devoted sister (who enables his criminal activities) or even the shaggy gorilla bother to put up with him.

– KN

APOCALYPSE NOW REDUX / THE COMPLETE DOSSIER

Colour, 1979/2000, 202m. / Directed by Francis Ford Coppola / Starring Marlon Brando, Martin Sheen, Robert Duvall, Dennis Hopper, Laurence Fishburne / Paramount (US R1 NTSC), Buena Vista (UK R2 PAL) / WS (2.1:1) (16:9) / DD 5.1, Lionsgate (US R1 NTSC) (Blu-ray & DVD) / WS (2.35:1) (16:9) / DD5.1

All the world knows, thanks to the documentary *Hearts of Darkness* and several books (notably Eleanor Coppola's *Notes*), of the epic struggles Francis Ford Coppola went through getting his Vietnam-set epic reimagining of Joseph Conrad's novella *Heart of Darkness* completed. Captain Willard (Martin Sheen) and his patrol boat crew voyage upriver, encountering perils and adventures, towards the compound of Colonel Walter E. Kurtz (Marlon Brando), a U.S. officer accused of insane crimes who just might be the first American to understand the Vietnam War. The film's eventual commercial, critical and cult success came only after a lot of people had accused Coppola of being as jungle-mad as his Kurtz. He now claims he felt pressure to make *Apocalypse Now* into a straight-ahead action/war movie, but always had in mind something more surreal, more political and more weird. In 2000, he went back to the raw material, not simply cutting in deleted scenes but reassembling the whole film from scratch on an even more epic scale.

The first thing: *Apocalypse Now* is as good as ever. Cinematographer Vittorio Storaro and sound designer Walter Murch, deployed by mad general Coppola, create effects that will stay with you forever, from the haunted tropical hotel room where Willard is found having a breakdown through the Wagner-scored helicopter attack led by Colonel Kilgore (Robert Duvall) on the surf-friendly riverhead occupied by the VC to the atrocity-filled encampment where a photojournalist (Dennis Hopper) scuttles as acolyte to the ambiguous monster whose name comes half from (Walter Elias) Disney and half from Conrad's Mr. Kurtz. In any version, this is one of the defining films of its generation, coming precisely at that point when the radical, exciting, opposi-tional, visionary American cinema of the 1970s was about to be superseded by the soulless blockbuster mentality of the '80s and beyond. Originally scripted by John Milius as a project for George Lucas, it is the twisted doppelganger of the *Star Wars* series as a hero goes on a quest to face a father figure "gone over to the dark side" – compare the finales of *Apocalypse* and *Return of the Jedi* to see how thorny material can be tamed and packaged.

But what about the hour of "new" material? It's all good but there are niggles; when Willard rags Kilgore by stealing his surfboard, it deepens the characters and establishes a nice rapport between the hit-man and the PBR crew that sets up the disintegration of the relationship upriver, but the extra footage blunts Duvall's great exit line ("some day this war's gonna end"). The *Playboy* bunny scene, set in a rain swept abandoned hospital, has its moments but feels unfinished and a crucial segment with Laurence Fishburne losing his virginity is still MIA. The long French plantation sequence with its dinner table arguments about Indochinese history has weird echoes of Sid James and company taking tea during battle in *Carry On Up the Khyber*, but the first ghostly appearance of the colonials in the mist is a magical moment. A bit in the Kurtz compound with Brando reading articles aloud makes this a more specific film about this particular war, but is literal editorialising. *Redux* is a slower film, with a little more intellect and sentiment, but the added time to think might well undercut the still-pretty-overwhelming impact of the movie. Sadly, the only extra on the DVD is a trailer.

The DVD of the 1979 *Apocalypse Now*, which completists won't want to get rid of, includes an original release trailer, a reproduction of the program distributed for 70mm showings of the film (which had no end credits) and the 35mm release end credits which run over footage of an air strike destroying the Kurtz Compound (a significant plot event we never see in *Redux*). Coppola even contributes a commentary over these alternative credits, though sadly not for the whole film. The big draw of the *Redux* disc is the transfer, which offers the next-best thing to a theatrical experience. The anamorphic widescreen, a sliver off from 1.85:1, is a slight reduction of the 2.35:1 theatrical framing, which can be assessed in the trailer, but this never seems to compromise the compositions. Storaro's smoky visuals must be a nightmare for any DVD authoring process, and the *Redux* transfer sometimes seems less rich than the original – though it is never less than wholly satisfying, and the intimate home medium brings out every drop of sweat and makes Brando's bald pate seem like a moon in eclipse. Murch's sound design, one of the great achievements in the field, benefits enormously from the 5.1 process, with helicopters that seem to fly through

A

your skull, Sheen's sonorous narration (scripted by Michael Herr), many shots and explosions and the myriad tiny sounds of the jungle contributing as much as the imagery to the impact of the film.

Both versions of the film can be accessed in the more elaborate The Complete Dossier, which adds Coppola commentary for both cuts, an outtake of Brando reading T.S. Eliot's "The Hollow Men", additional deleted segments familiar to anyone who's seen the various long bootlegs floating around, a "Then and Now" retrospective featurette, the "PBR Streetgang" supporting cast reunion, "The Color Palette" featurette, four post-production featurettes (prominently featuring Coppola and Storaro), and four audio-visual featurettes (basically one long piece chopped up) covering the sound mix and camerawork. A subsequent reissue from Lionsgate (who nabbed the Zoetrope library rights) reinstates the original aspect ratio along with the expected perk of a new HD transfer; the carried-over extras are augmented by the inclusion of the essential *Hearts of Darkness* with a commentary by both of the Coppolla spouses but, curiously, nothing with its actual directors, George Hickenlooper and Fax Bahr.
– KN

ASWANG

Colour, 1994, 82m. / Directed by Wrye Martin & Barry Poltermann / Starring Norman Moses, Tina Ona Paukstelis, Flora Coker, Mildred Nierras, John Kishline / Mondo Macabro (US R0 NTSC) / WS (1.66:1) (16:9) / DD5.1

Ever wonder how *Mystics in Bali* would have turned out had it been made by a gang of American Midwesterners? Well, wonder no more; the utterly mad *Aswang* lifts that Indonesian film's most celebrated foetus-feeding scene and stretches it out for an entire feature, along with touches lifted from sources as disparate as Filipino horror, *The Evil Dead*, and *The Texas Chain Saw Massacre*. Obviously, you've never seen anything like it. Against the wishes of her mopey boyfriend, pregnant Kat (Tina Ona Paukstelis) goes to the office of an ageing lawyer and enters into a complex legal agreement with the Null family, a clan of orchard growers in the country. In exchange for payment, she agrees to pose as the wife of the male head of the household, Peter (Norman Moses), who must produce an heir to maintain the family wealth, and then offer up her unwanted baby upon its birth. Soon Peter spirits her away to the family home, where she meets his ageing mother (Flora Coker) and the creepy, quiet housekeeper (Mildred Nierras). While strolling outside, the not-so-affectionate couple bumps into a trespasser, Dr. Harper (John Kishline), who has come across strange, cocooned remains in the woods. Kat invites the doctor for dinner, much to Peter's displeasure, and that evening Harper learns the Filipino legend of the Aswang, a vampiric creature that feeds on unborn children. Later that evening, Harper is attacked by a long, slimy tongue which wraps around his throat, and Kat is soon plunged into a gruelling night of terror including chainsaw mayhem, spade attacks, dismemberment, baby slurping, and other antisocial behaviour.

Completely lost in the dying gasps of the home video horror wave in the mid-1990s, *Aswang* was a surprising entry in the Sundance Film Festival (where it played to a full house at midnight) before it was picked up by Prism, who retitled it *The Unearthing*, trimmed out several seconds of bloodshed, and barely released it on VHS with a shoddy cover and substandard transfer (replicated on a scarce Image laserdisc). Too bad, as the film itself is worth seeing despite some shortcomings. The isolated, rural atmosphere is well maintained, with the unfamiliar Wisconsin settings (previously the stomping grounds of *The Giant Spider Invasion*'s Bill Rebane) lending the film an off-kilter sensibility from the opening frames. Though the film isn't exactly frightening in the traditional sense, it does boast a number of memorable, grotesque set pieces, particularly one elaborate sequence in which the family matriarch uses her Aswang tongue to assault the heroine before winding up dangling outside the house from a slammed window. The actors range from adequate (Paukstelis, Coker) to substandard; unfortunately the weakest link is Moses, who contributes a wildly uneven, stagey performance complete with hammy, eye-bugging theatrics that don't translate well for the camera at all. The sick twist ending may not come as a huge shock, but it's pulled off with panache and is a logical, nasty product of everything that's come before

Mondo Macabro's DVD offers what appears to be the best possible transfer of a difficult title; the cheap film stock results in an erratic, cheesecloth-style texture at times, with dark scenes ranging from moody and well-lit to downright murky. All things considered, the anamorphic presentation looks satisfying all around; note that the 1.66:1 compositions will appear a bit vertically cropped on many widescreen monitors (which adjust automatically to 1.78:1); this noticeably cramps the framing in a number of early scenes. Audio is presented in both the theatrical 2.0 stereo mix and a remixed 5.1 option; the former is by far the most effective, as the 5.1 version features extremely muffled dialogue and almost nonexistent sound effects with an overamped music track. Two audio commentaries are offered, with the two one-shot directors first up at bat. Moderated by Mondo Macabro head Pete Tombs, their track is generally engaging if a bit on the sedate side; they explain the genesis of the film (including the rationale for doing Filipino horror in Wisconsin) and relate how the project was financed, cast, produced, and distributed. The second track

is a bouncier chat with Moses, Paukstelis, and Kishline; it appears Moses was recorded separately with each actor, as he introduces himself twice and seems to be existing in two different places at once (a very disorienting but appropriate experience). The genial Paukstelis gets the best moments, from her opening recollections of shooting the nude opening credits sequence (during which her male co-star got overexcited) to dealing with the complex, often icky special effects. Moses hams it up just as much on the commentary track, but he's much easier to take out of character. The participants turn up again for "Different than Hollywood", an engaging 27-minute documentary covering the making of the film including audition and rehearsal footage, interviews, and other odds and ends. The directors also explain the fundraising demo trailer they concocted for the film, which is duly included on the disc along with two more traditional trailers for the final product, under its original and alternative video titles. (You'll also get a fun, nostalgic look at Prism's VHS ballyhoo tying *The Unearthing* in with some other barely remember straight-to-video schlockers.) Kishline turns up again to read a lengthy deleted prologue, scripted but never filmed, which explains in greater detail how his character became involved with the Aswang (and which also goes some way to explaining his character's peculiar longevity). Other bonuses include two audition tapes, an extensive stills gallery, and a little hidden goodie as well.

ASYLUM OF SATAN
Colour, 1971, 78m. / Directed by William Girdler / Starring Charles Kissinger, Carla Borelli, Nick Jolley
SATAN'S CHILDREN
Colour, 1974, 84m. / Directed by Joe Wiezycki / Starring Stephen White, Kathleen Archer, Joyce Molloy, Eldon Mecham, Bob Barbour, Rosemary Orlando, Robert C. Ray II / Something Weird (US R0 NTSC)

The debut feature of the short-lived William Girdler (*Three on a Meathook*, *Day of the Animals*, *The Manitou*), *Asylum of Satan* is a low-rent paranoia thriller, which combines the sane-person-in-a-madhouse and Satanic conspiracy themes. Lucina Martin (Carla Borelli), a timid young concert pianist whose name is pronounced "Lucinia", is confined to Pleasant Hill Hospital after a minor breakdown and groomed for sacrifice by Dr. Jason Spector (Charles Kissinger), who not only sports a stick-on evil goatee but also shows up in transparent disguise as a butch female nurse or a dim-witted gardener. Because there's not really enough plot in the menacing of the heroine, the film takes time out to deliver a few other patients to set piece deaths (a wheelchair-bound woman gassed and bugged, an annoying guy burned by robed cultists, a blind girl attacked by snakes in a swimming pool), trot through makeshift nightmares (it's a moot point as to whether the fright-masked creature who pursues Lucina in one scene is real or not) and have the girl's short, homely boyfriend (Nick Jolley) sleuth around in eye-offending plaid outfits and the director's yellow Porsche. It winds up with a lengthy, not-terribly-exciting basement ritual attended by a demon in a goofy horror mask apparently modelled on the *Night of the Demon* demon but with the ping-pong eyes of a Larry Buchanan fiend. Upset that the promised virgin sacrifice has been deflowered along the way, the demon turns its smoking wrath upon Spector. Nothing is very impressive about this Kentucky-accented quickie, though connoisseurs might note a death-by-toy-bug sequence even more ridiculous than the one in *The Beyond*, humorously wooden dialogue delivery and goofy monster outfits. SWV's "digitally remastered" transfer is pretty good; the cinematography by William L. Asman (*Speed*) has the odd decent set-up (the silent, wheelchair-bound, white-robed patient/cultists feature in several creepy scenes) but is murky throughout until it cuts loose with red filters for the infernal finale. Print quality is well above average for these early 1970s rescue jobs – the film didn't get much theatrical play, so there's less damage than you'd expect. The extras are seven minutes of on-set footage showing cast, crew and Satan dawdling about and a give-it-all-away trailer ("murdered by reviling reptiles drenched in a pool of her own blood!"). A commentary track from Jeffrey C. Hogue of Majestic International Pictures and Girdler's enthusiastic, clear-eyed biographer Patty Breen (who also contributes an essay insert) makes for good company, with lively, often amusing analysis ("every scene with Nick leaves me quivering in polyester ecstasy") and background material (detailing the involvement of the Church of Satan).

Something Weird double-bills *Asylum* with an even more obscure exploitation item, Joe Wiezycki's Florida-shot *Satan's Children*. Not quite a horror picture (though it perhaps takes its villain's name from *Simon, King of the Witches*), this is incidentally a rare male rape-revenge movie but chiefly a ludicrous attempt to show a Satanic cult as a long-haired counterculture gang along the lines of the bikers of *The Wild Angels* or the commune of *Alice's Restaurant*. Gangly teenage loser Bobby Douglas (Stephen White) is sexually taunted by his stepsister (Joyce Molloy) while his oppressive Dad (Eldon Mecham) makes him do chores around the garden. When the sister tells Dad about his dope stash, Bobby runs away from home and is picked up by Jake (Bob Barbour), a macho guy in a diner. Though Jake sneers at the ageing "queer" who has tried to chat up Bobby, the brute pulls a knife and invites over a gang of like-minded thugs whose idea of a "good-ass hell party" is to subject Bobby to extensive humiliation. White's awkward performance almost becomes convincing in one lengthy scene in which he is naked, tied up and stretched in a car, doused with beer and taunted by good ole gayboys. Raped, beaten and dumped, Bobby is found by a bunch of flower-children who turn out to be the Satanist commune, temporarily run by Sherry (Kathleen Archer) while the real leader is away. Sherry, who's warding off a lesbian (Rosemary Orlando) with a crush on her, takes in Bobby and sleeps with him, though there is a sense among the others that Satan doesn't like "victims". When another faction within the cult makes a power play, Sherry has them hanged, which brings back the real leader, Simon (Robert C. Ray II), an interestingly conservative, homophobic Satanist. The only supernatural touch is that the lesbian chokes on blood when she lies to Simon about her inclinations, but there's plenty of sadism as Sherrie is buried up to her neck and smeared with syrup for ants to crawl over. Bobby, in white underpants which soon get filthy, makes an escape bid through swampland and Simon sends thugs to track him down. As much through accidents involving an electric fence and quicksand as his own efforts, Bobby sees his pursuers dead. He returns home, muddy and bloody, and smashes in his Dad's head with a bottle. He shotguns Jake and his beer buddies and shows up back at the commune, offering Simon a bagful of rapists' heads and the slutty stepsister, who is clumsily crucified for a freeze-frame ending that lingers for several footage-expanding minutes.

Though action-packed in synopsis, *Satan's Children* is cheapskate and clumsily directed; the revenge rampage near the end is conveyed with a few slo-mo shots of the thugs taking shotgun blasts and the actors who die in quicksand have to work hard to seem imperilled. The script is vehemently if peculiarly homophobic ("You go making

sacrifices seeking dispensations for a queer and you'll bring down Satan's wrath all right, you'll unleash all the demons of hell on this place"), but the camera spends a lot of time leering at Stephen White's barely-clad, sometimes trussed-up body. The performances are amateurish and unenthused, especially from pouting leading lady Archer and short, unsinister Ray. A devil worship movie made by people who have no idea what Satanism is all about – though the vision of in-fighting and oppression even within an alternative lifestyle rings weirdly true.

The transfer is what you'd expect, a ragged print of a movie that probably never looked great. The traditional SWV "full supporting program" of extras includes the b&w burlesque short "Satan's Dance", with Lorraine Lane decorously sporting with a fake Satan head next to her own in front of two chairs, and the half-hour colour featurette "The Soul Snatcher", a 1965 effort from director H.L. Zimmer with Ed Wood-style narration ("Kathy again found it wasn't what you happened to know but whether you were willing to play their little games that counted") and a lot of tame cheesecake as an unsuccessful model (Diane Webster) who gets ahead by wearing magic shoes given her by a balding, bearded "stranger" with a cloak and goatee but then loses her soul. Plus trailers for *Horror High*, *Dr. Tarr's Torture Dungeon* ("so shocking that it will never appear on television"), *The House of Missing Girls*, *Don't Look in the Basement*, *The House That Vanished*, *The Murder Clinic* ("the more beautiful they were the better their chance to wake up and die"), *Mansion of the Doomed* ("They told us that death was the ultimate horror ... they were wrong") and *House of the Damned*; and the now-familiar "ghastly gallery of ghoulish comic cover art with music by the Dead Elvi" (as seen on several other SWV discs).

– KN

A

ATOMIC WAR BRIDE

B&W, 1960, 75m. / Directed by Veljko Bulajic / Starring Anton Vrdoljak, Ewa Krzyzewska

THIS IS NOT A TEST

B&W, 1961, 72m. / Directed by Fredric Gadette / Starring Seamon Glass, Thayer Roberts / Something Weird (US R1 NTSC)

 "It's an Atomic Bomb Bonanza with this Duck & Cover Double Feature!" boasts the strapline for SWV's *Atomic War Bride*/*This Is Not a Test* Special edition. A valuable bill of Cold War rarities, the disc is satisfyingly bulked out with a full program of short subjects. *Atomic War Bride* – not to be confused with *Atomic War Brides*, the film being shot in *Hollywood Blvd* – is a dubbed and trimmed U.S. release print of the Yugoslav *Rat (War)*. Set in an imaginary country – in the dubbing, characters are given names like "Jack Jackson", "Addy Addison" and "Pete Peters" – it's an odd mix of the grimly realist and the satirical as the wedding of handsome John (Anton Vrdoljak) and pretty Maria (Ewa Krzyzewska) is interrupted by the outbreak of war. Many events are deliberately absurd, though no more so than the advice given in the civil defence shorts: the army hand out anti-radiation ponchos to citizens who squat in the streets wearing them (the hero's doesn't work so he tries to squeeze into someone else's) and a platoon of soldiers are taught to flex their trigger fingers in the air before being let loose on the rifle range. When war comes, John is instantly conscripted and dragged away from Maria only to meet her again in a public shelter. "The President of the Republic" appears on a huge television screen to announce a first atomic strike against the enemy (prefiguring the Gulf War, images are transmitted from cameras in the noses of missiles), prompting John to lead an uprising. A crowd marches singing out of the shelter to protest against the war and ringleader John is dragged off to be executed by firing squad. Maria intervenes, but the hero is saved by a victory that comes as suddenly and inanely as war. The forces of repression still want to make an example of the young lovers and total destruction of the enemy still doesn't prevent their missiles wiping out the city, reducing the pompous president to crawling in the rubble and the militarist martinets to panicking fools. In the final, post-Armageddon minutes, the tattered lovers move into the ruin that was to be their house, where Maria dies and John is left howling in grief.

Rat was written by the Italian Cesare Zavattini (*Bicycle Thieves*), and has aspirations to making big pacifist statements aimed at both sides. By using a made-up country with elements of both capitalist (consumer goods bought on an instalment plan) and communist (summary conversion of civilian population to a war footing) societies, the film can afford to be much harder on politicians and generals than most nuclear war films – it's a rare movie which depicts what should notionally be "our side" as an aggressor who makes first use of atomic weapons. It's hard to judge what the original might have been like from this version. The tone veers wildly and, thanks to the dubbed-in-a-vacuum effect, it's often impossible to tell whether any given scene is being played for laughs, cynicism or melodrama. Shot in Totalscope, it's presented in standard framing that serves to make what was a healthily-budgeted movie made with a surprising amount of assistance from Marshal Tito's army seem like a quickie. The image is a tad soft but the print has very little damage; the flat, dubbed soundtrack, however, is in poor shape, with a constant background hiss and crackle.

This Is Not a Test is one of the cheapest American Awful Warning movies. At four in the morning, state trooper Dan Colter

(Seamon Glass) sets up a road block in a mountain area and waylays a group of randomly-selected citizens, who include a jive-talking hipster fresh from a big score and a clean-cut hitch-hiking kid who happens to be a hysterical serial killer. Word comes through that a missile attack is imminent, and the rest of the brief film unfolds in real time as the trooper insists the variously-stunned or uncomprehending folks convert a large truck into an impromptu shelter. Romances flare up, various people venture half-baked theories about nuclear war and the cop goes beyond doing his civil defence duty as he turns into a ranting madman who throttles a poodle to conserve air. Looters show up and a young couple head for an abandoned mine where they *might* have a better chance of making it. The finish is among the first to use the *Two-Lane Blacktop* trick of burning the film to suggest a holocaust, and is far more despairing than almost all 1950s nuke movies – the end title isn't The Beginning but a whiteout on Colter hammering desperately to get back into the truck which probably won't offer any protection at all. It's an awkwardly-acted film with a tin ear for dialogue and hokey bits like the cool cat losing his faith in cash by using his hundred-thousand-dollar wad as a fan when the atmosphere in the truck gets too stuffy, but it has a potent sense of the chaos liable to follow the titular announcement and the inconsistency of its characterisations and plot makes a horrible sort of sense. After a battered set of credits, with some names clipped a letter or so by the standard frame presentation, the transfer is well above average for a micro-budgeted effort of this vintage, with deep noirish shadows.

Rounding out the themed package are a host of "Isotopic Extras:" a couple of Fallout Shelter TV spots ("It's my fault and responsibility to protect my family – that's why I have one"); *You Can Beat the A-Bomb* (19m.), RKO's public service announcement ("Yessir, even if a bomb

blew the house over, we'd have a pretty good chance here in the basement"); *Survival Under Atomic Attack* (9m.), a similar public information effort ("Let us prepare for survival by understanding the weapon that threatens us"); *Duck and Cover* (9m.), familiar from *The Atomic Cafe*, and starring the survivalist cartoon character Bert the Turtle (who "was very alert"); *Medical Aspects of Nuclear Radiation* (20m.), in blurry Technicolor amid so much grey and grainy black and white, with cartoon illustrations of how radiation affects the body ("If you had some plutonium inside you, you wouldn't make any plans to celebrate the event"), frank talk about baldness and sterility, and a jaw-dropping theory that atomic mutation of your offspring might be a good thing (!); *One World Or None* (9m.), a rare exercise in peacenik scare-mongering backed by the National Committee on Atomic Information which dares to suggest that it might be a good idea to avoid atomic war altogether by having international controls on nuclear weapons; and *Atomic Blonde in Action* (2m.), a silly bit of burly-cue.

The government-backed shorts are at once terrifying and bland, reassuring dollops of propagandist misinformation essentially designed to sell the lie that our side could win an atomic war. Full of calm, responsible citizens and well-behaved children who are far less convincing than the looters, hysterics and incipient megalomaniacs of *This Is Not a Test* and many another nuclear war film, these offer tips for surviving an atomic attack and imply than an unquestioning subservience to the duly-constituted authorities is your only option if the worst comes. "Older people will help us as they always do" smarms the narrator of *Duck and Cover*, which must have made even crew cut '50s kids muse that older people were likely to be the ones that got civilisation into this mess in the first place.

– KN

ATTACK OF THE 60 FOOT CENTERFOLD

Colour, 1995, 86m. / Directed by Fred Olen Ray / Starring J.J. North, Raelyn Saalman, John Lazar, Jay Richardson, Tim Abell, Tammy Parks, Michelle Bauer, Russ Tamblyn, Tommy Kirk, Ross Hagen, Peter Spellos, Forrest J. Ackerman, Jim Wynorski, Nikki Fritz / New Concorde (US R1 NTSC)

Eager to scoop the title "Centerfold of the Year", but insecure about her looks, Angel Grace (J.J. North) has signed up with Dr. Lindstrom (John Lazar) for an unorthodox miracle beauty enhancement program designed to increase her assets dramatically. Angel inadvertently overdoses, creating a hormonal explosion that causes her to grow to 60 feet tall. With the scent of money nipping at their nostrils, magazine publisher Bob Gordon (Jay Richardson) and photographer Mark (Tim Abell) conspire to prevent Angel from acquiring the antidote. But contest rival Betty (Tammy Parks) gets hold of the growth formula and the scene is set for a battle of the giants in the middle of bustling Hollywood Boulevard!

Did you ever wonder why, when *Attack of the 50 Foot Woman*'s Allison Hayes spurted up to over eight times her normal height, her outfit grew with her? So did Fred Olen Ray. Thus, outdoing Hayes by an extra 10 feet, when J.J. North does her incredible expanding woman act, off comes the clothing and she's left cowering behind a coastal outcrop in the altogether. A sexed-up spoof of the aforementioned 1958 B-movie played 100% for laughs, *Attack of the 60 Foot Centerfold* – it may be singular on the packaging, but it's plural on the movie itself – makes for far more tolerable viewing than the straight-faced 1993 Daryl Hannah remake. That said, when director Ray accelerates into out and out farce it does threaten to jump the rails; just when you think it can't get any dafter, he shamelessly produces a man in a giant rat suit! J.J. North emerged at the tail end of the "Scream Queen" cycle and so failed to make as great an impact as some of her predecessors, which is a pity because (unlike many of said predecessors) she actually harboured a modicum of talent beyond the ability to look fetching with no clothes on. With a notable flair for comedy she deserved to proceed to better things. Not so Tammy Parks, who's plain awful, with a breast implant job as offensive as her annoyingly truant acting skills. *Attack of the 60 Foot Centerfold* sells itself as a titillating flesh parade, but there's more to it than that. The funnies come thick and fast – some of them so dreadful that you can't help but admire Ray's nerve for trying it on – and the characters are mostly a pleasure to spend time with, particularly Jay Richardson in a wickedly funny affectionate parody of millionaire *Playboy* chieftain Hugh Hefner. The "giant" effects are achieved economically by simple forced perspective, and yet they work, proving that in an age where CG technology can accomplish anything the mind can imagine, the old tricks still sometimes serve to get the job done. Ray regular Michelle Bauer manages to keep her clothes on as a research scientist, and there are cameos from Russ Tamblyn, Tommy Kirk, Ross Hagen, Peter Spellos, Forrest Ackerman and Jim Wynorski (who bags the immortal line, "Oh my God, look at the size of those tits!"). Undemanding sweetmeats for an undemanding audience.

New Concorde short-change their punters once again. Here's what you don't get on their U.S. Region 1 DVD of *Attack of the 60 Foot Centerfolds*: test effects footage with Michelle Bauer, an archive of over 200 production stills, a trailer, and a commentary from Ray and big-breasted bit-part actress Nikki Fritz. What am I talking about? Well, all of this material appeared in the supplementary section of the film's Image Entertainment laserdisc presentation several years back. All that the DVD has to offer by comparison is brief cast and crew bios and the money-raking trailering of other New Concorde product. To add insult to injury the picture throughout the full screen presentation (punctuated by 24 chapter stops) is slightly soft, with flesh tones that occasionally border on bright orange! Though this gives the movie a very fitting surreal comic-book appearance, it's not right and will have even the least finicky viewer fiddling with his colour control to try and correct it.

– TG

AU PAIR GIRLS

Colour, 1972, 81m. / Directed by Val Guest / Starring Richard O'Sullivan, Gabrielle Drake, Nancie Wait, Astrid Frank, Me Me Lai, Geoffrey Bayldon, Harold Bennett, John Le Mesurier, Trevor Bannister, John Standing, Johnny Briggs, Milton Reid, Ferdy Mayne, Marcia Fox / Salvation (UK R0 PAL), Image (US R1 NTSC)

 A quartet of young women arrives in London seeking work as Au Pairs. Danish Randi (Gabrielle Drake) is immediately stranded when her employer's son has car trouble and they get caught in a rainstorm. German girl Christa (Nancie Wait) is very prudish at first but the daughter of the house introduces her to London's swinging nightlife and she loses her virginity to a doped-up rock star. Sweden's Anita (Astrid Frank) gives her would-be seducer the push in favour of a wealthy sheik and ends up joining his harem. Chinese Nan (Me Me Lai) finds employ in a wealthy household and falls in love with an emotionally retarded pianist. For all of them it's but a day in the life of an Au Pair girl.

An extremely odd, episodic little film populated by rather unappealing characters in situations which aren't nearly as amusing as the premise might suggest, nor that the names associated with it might lead one to expect. Geoffrey Bayldon, Harold Bennett, John Le Mesurier, Richard O'Sullivan, Trevor Bannister, John Standing... stalwarts of British TV sitcom every one, but you can bet they all wished they hadn't blighted their CVs with *Au Pair Girls*. Watch out too for appearances by Johnny Briggs (*Coronation Street*), Milton Reid (*The People That Time Forgot*), Ferdy Mayne (*The Fearless Vampire Killers*) and Marcia Fox (*Creatures the World Forgot*). Yet in spite of all the talent to hand, it's a rather sad and sorry tale that director Val Guest weaves them into. The frothy theme song which launches and closes the proceedings lends it an air of frivolity that it doesn't deserve, for after a fairly lightweight opener with Gabrielle Drake's segment the proceedings plummet through an array of uneasy smiles before skydiving into poignant circumstance. Where Drake and Frank are given the more comic scenarios – not that they're particularly funny mind you – Lay's and Wait's chapters (the latter in particular, as she realises her sexual awakening and virginity have been squandered on a worthless creep) are tragic and vaguely depressing. In actual fact, be it willingly or otherwise, all the girls are exploited at some point by dissolute individuals with the solitary aim of getting them to drop their panties, which leads in turn to the requisite nudity but very little sexplay. This is almost certainly a reflection of Guest's ill ease with the project, a feeling you also get from his hugely successful but ultimately drab Timmy Lea entry, *Confessions of a Window Cleaner*. Indisputably a master of his craft, with the subject matter here one gets the distinct impression that Guest is swimming out of his depth; he flounders around trying to make something meaningful and artistic, patently embarrassed that he also has to cater to the raincoat brigade at whom the financiers were obviously pitching. The results are an uninspired curate's egg of a film. So why did the man who gave the

A

world minor classics like *The Quatermass Experiment* and *The Day the Earth Caught Fire* allow himself to be manoeuvred into directing this guff anyway? Even stranger, the David Adnopoz/David Grant screenplay is based on Guest's own story. It would seem he liked the idea but ultimately didn't know how to execute it. As a less than fragrant sniff of a seedy yet overwhelmingly alluring era of British cinema long outmoded by political correctness, *Au Pair Girls* functions well enough one supposes. And its value to fans of Gerry Anderson's cult TV show *UFO* is immeasurable, giving them the opportunity to inspect Gabrielle Drake's charms from top to toe. Expect no more than this and you won't come away too disappointed.

The DVD releases of *Au Pair Girls* offer up a fairly respectable number of additional features, rather surprising given the negligible value of the film itself. There's a suitably grubby looking trailer and a number of galleries encompassing original press release materials, stills and lobby cards. The 16-chapter fullscreen feature itself may be no great shakes, but it's unlikely to ever look any better. As if anyone cared enough to even want it to.

– TG

THE AVENGERS

Colour, 1998, 89m. / Directed by Jeremiah Chechik / Starring Ralph Fiennes, Uma Thurman, Sean Connery, Jim Broadbent, Fiona Shaw, Patrick Macnee (voice), Eileen Atkins, Nicholas Woodeson, Keeley Hawes, Shaun Ryder, Eddie Izzard / Warner (US R1 NTSC, UK R2 PAL) / WS (1.85:1) (16:9) / DD5.1

The Prospero research facility, the site where a defensive weather shield was being developed, has been destroyed by a look-alike of former project leader Dr. Emma Peel (Uma Thurman).

Ministry chief Mother (Jim Broadbent) orders top agent John Steed (Ralph Fiennes) to team up with the real Peel to expose the true culprit. The trail leads them to Sir August de Wynter (Sean Connery), who has harnessed control of the weather and plans to blackmail the governments of the world into paying him for clement conditions. If his demands aren't met he will wreak havoc with rapid and diverse climate changes that could wipe out entire continents...

Given that this is Tinseltown's take on something of a British institution, remarkably enough director Jeremiah Chechik's movie succeeds in bottling a lot of the quintessential off-kilter eccentricity of its cult '60s TV show source of inspiration. Where it unsurprisingly flounders is in the absence of Patrick Macnee from the role of John Steed; the ladies came and went, but Macnee was a constant and, no matter how hard they might try to convince you of otherwise, it isn't *The Avengers* proper without him. With this insurmountable handicap in mind, it was brave of Ralph Fiennes to even attempt to fill Macnee's immaculate pinstripe suit. He tries hard to walk the walk of the cucumber cool Steed but the results are stilted and contrived. To be fair he doesn't carry the can alone. Uma Thurman's interpretation of Emma Peel, stepping in for Diana Rigg, is even worse. Her wardrobe – which affords a costume change every ten minutes – endows her with plenty of visual panache, but her attempts at an upper crust British accent are about as convincing as Johnny Depp's cockney in *From Hell*. To be fair, Don Macpherson's script doesn't help matters, laden as it is with double entendres that paint Steed as a bit of a lech and Peel as a babbling idiot. And having the pair lock lips at the film's climax was a serious breach of protocol. Paying tribute to the archetypal baddie he fought as the spy that time refuses to let him shake off, former 007 Sean Connery is unable to restrain himself; his performance leans more towards Dr. Evil than Dr. No. Jim Broadbent gives us a congenial, nicotine-fuelled turn as Mother, though it's tainted by memories of the late Patrick Newell in the TV series. The duplicitous Father (Fiona Shaw, replete with an Elsa Lancaster *Bride of Frankenstein* white stripe in her hair and Claude Rains *Invisible Man* sunglasses) is a nice addition to the fold. Mention of the Invisible Man leads one to note that Patrick Macnee does get a cameo of sorts; he supplies the voice of invisible ministry archivist Colonel Jones. Of the supporting cast, it's swings and roundabouts: Where there are lively turns from Eileen Atkins, Nicholas Woodeson and Keeley Hawes (TV's *Ashes to Ashes*), there's less likely casting in the shape of Shaun Ryder (who's squandered) and Eddie Izzard, the latter serving only to lower the tone of the film by uttering its completely unnecessary single word expletive (which, incidentally, was snipped from British prints). The conspicuous and misguided underuse of the classic theme music further deprives the piece of *Avengers*-esque mood (Joel McNeely's score isn't very memorable), although there's an appropriate Grace Jones number, "Storm", grafted on to the closing credits. As if there weren't enough problems with the film anyway, post-production truncation saddled it with jarring continuity problems. Yet for all its shortcomings, *The Avengers* is certainly pretty to look at, thanks in no small part to spiffing production design and plenty of CG effects work; the gallery of miniaturized weather systems at the Wonderland Weather showroom provides a particular standout moment, as does the finale in which de Wynter visits a meteorological pounding upon London (blowing up Big Ben in the process). The best sequence in the movie, however, belongs to the swarm of outsize mechanical radio-controlled hornets that pursue Steed and Peel through the English countryside. Fans will doubtless find plenty to get excited about in the myriad of little touches unique to the world of John Steed – from the cups of tea served from a faucet in the dashboard of his bottle green Bentley to the ministry's mobile HQ in a double-decker London bus,

from swashbuckling umbrella swordplay to machine-gun-toting old ladies – and if nothing else this is the only chance you'll ever get to catch Sir Sean Connery wearing a giant teddy bear costume. But there's no disguising the fact that *The Avengers* is as great a failed transition of small screen show to big screen extravaganza as were *Lost in Space* and *The Saint* before it.

If ever a disc needed a making-of documentary, *The Avengers* was it. It was almost essential that some of the butchered footage be reinstated too, or at least presented in a gallery of deleted scenes. This may yet come about at some future juncture, but for now the Regions 1 and 2 platters from Warner Brothers are rather threadbare affairs. The feature itself, with 31 chapters, is presented with a choice of English or French sound and subtitles. Be aware that the British release is missing the aforementioned Izzard cuss. Beyond this, however, the only inclusion of interest is the theatrical trailer, mostly due to the fact that it includes a few snatches of excised material. Some textual blurb on the film and the show that spawned it, plus a handful of trailers for other Warner's product (including one for *Batman and Robin*, which doesn't even appear on that movie's own disc!) fills out a typically slender WB offering. – TG

THE BABY OF MÂCON

Colour, 1993, 122m. / Directed by Peter Greenaway / Starring Julia Ormond, Ralph Fiennes / New Vision (Australia R4 PAL), Atlantic (DVD & Blu-ray) (Sweden RB/R2 HD/PAL) / WS (2.35:1) (16:9) / DD2.0

Designed as a play within a play, this calculated outrage begins with the birth of a beautiful baby to the ugliest woman in the town of Mâcon. The woman's chaste

daughter (Julia Ormond) swiftly passes off the child as her own, a miraculous virgin birth. Most of the town falls for the ruse and hails the child as a provider of miracles, but the scientifically inclined bishop's son (Ralph Fiennes) is not so convinced. When he decides to put the girl's virginity to the test, horrific and possibly supernatural events are set in motion.

The Baby of Mâcon marked something of a departure for director Peter Greenaway, who had just achieved art house success with *The Cook, the Thief, His Wife and Her Lover* and *Prospero's Books*. Devoid of the technological Paintbox gimmickry that marks his more recent films, this stylized exercise in theatricality takes place entirely onstage with one of the spectators, a rotund Cosimo de Medici, even taking part in the action. Ultimately the film blurs the line between real life and theatre until one cannot tell whether the actors are truly being killed or simply acting; in any case, the notorious mass rape near the end of the film is excruciating to behold (though very little is actually shown), followed by an act of dismemberment which kept this firmly out of American movie houses. The film also marked Greenaway's first feature without the involvement of composer Michael Nyman, and the loss is sorely felt; here we have only traditional classical tracks, which make little to no impression. Celebrity skin fans will also note that both of the now-famous leads expose a considerable amount of themselves, though not in a very erotic context.

The first DVD from Australia is a compromised but welcome presentation of Greenaway's rarely seen film, which was previously available only on U.K. VHS and Japanese laserdisc (with optical censorship). The disc plays at a squeezed 1.85:1 aspect ratio on 4:3 players (no downconversion here), but when adjusted on a 16:9 television, it plays out at the correct 2.35:1 framing. Image quality is significantly improved over prior versions, though black levels are lacking and have a tendency to turn bluish.

Detail is on the soft side, but colours are strong (especially the omnipresent reds). The surround audio is effective, with audience applause often rising from the rear speakers. No extras. A much later version from Sweden (also carried in Finland) features a correctly framed and noticeably superior HD transfer that particularly sparkles on the Blu-ray version. Audio is in English with removable subtitles in Swedish, Danish or Finnish. If you're a Greenaway fan, it's easily worth the trouble of hunting down.

BAD TIMING

Colour, 1980, 117m. / Directed by Nicolas Roeg / Starring Art Garfunkel, Theresa Russell, Denholm Elliott, Harvey Keitel / Criterion (US R1 NTSC), Network (UK R2 PAL) / WS (2.35:1) (16:9), Carlton (UK R2 PAL) / WS (2.35:1)

After coaxing strong performances from pop music personalities, firstly in 1970's collaboration with Donald Cammell, *Performance* (Mick Jagger) and then in 1976's *The Man Who Fell to Earth* (David Bowie), director Nicolas Roeg found his next leading man in the unlikely form of Art Garfunkel, whose previous headlining experience was limited to two excellent Mike Nichols projects (*Catch-22* and *Carnal Knowledge*). Both men got far more than they bargained for with *Bad Timing*, a notoriously troubled film which pushed all of its primary talent into very dangerous personal and professional territory. Reviled by its distributor, critically lambasted, and so extreme that both of its leads were desperate to be released from their contracts, this largely off-the-cuff study in sexual obsession pushes Roeg's trademark time-fractured editing to nearly unbearable extremes, creating a film still capable of wildly polarizing viewers.

Skipping back and forth through time, we begin as psychiatrist Alex Linden (Art Garfunkel) accompanies the nearly dead Milena (Theresa Russell) in an ambulance to the hospital. Catatonic from an overdose, Milena undergoes a tracheotomy and other medical ministrations while Alex looks on and recalls their stormy relationship, which began with a chance meeting at a party and soon degenerated into a series of psychologically violent games with sex and power becoming interchangeable. Two other men are also involved: Milena's much older husband, Stefan (Denholm Elliott), and during her operation, the investigating police officer (Harvey Keitel) who tries to account for over an hour of lost time between Milena's overdose and Alex's telephone call for help.

The beginning of *Bad Timing* features one of the finest opening credits sequences ever filmed, as Roeg's gliding scope compositions capture Garfunkel and Russell studying Gustav Klimt paintings to the accompaniment of Tom Waits's "An Invitation to the Blues". This powerful curtain raiser has nothing to do with the film proper on a narrative level, but it perfectly sets the aesthetic tone; the images of male forms caressing slumbering women trapped in lavish, ornate fabrics are echoed in Roeg's own visual scheme (relying heavily on Klimt-like golds and browns) and the infamous final revelation (incorrectly referred to as necrophilia by many sources, though the distinction here is pretty thin), a truly startling sequence for two mainstream actors. The fact that Roeg and Russell actually fell in love during filming and were married shortly afterwards is rather staggering considering what his leading lady endures here; Russell was never this powerful on film again, though the two certainly tried several more times. Garfunkel is adequate enough in the lead, with his eyes communicating a great deal during his more introspective moments, though one can only wonder

what a more seasoned actor like, say, Robert De Niro could have accomplished with the role. Interestingly, *Bad Timing* could be considered the first sexual warfare film to explore the concept of two people literally exhausting themselves to death (or at least coming perilously close); while *Who's Afraid of Virginia Woolf?* and its like depicted relationships as a battle, Roeg's film creates a new terrain in which love is a consuming, destructive, time-swallowing force when the partners are essentially incompatible. One need only look at the following year's more overtly horrific *Possession* to see the difference (that film also uses the split of Communist and Western urban culture as an emotional mirror), or later studies in sexual/emotional exhaustion such as *Bitter Moon* and *Crash*, where empty thrills must consume a couple when their hearts have long since stopped beating.

Barely released on video in the U.K. and completely unavailable on home video in the U.S. for decades (with only occasional TV screenings late at night), *Bad Timing* (subtitled *A Sensual Obsession* in American theatres) nevertheless built up a strong cult following thanks to the video grey market. Unfortunately its astonishing scope framing was always subjected to clumsy panning and scanning, though DVD finally corrected that long-standing injury. Though regrettably non-anamorphic, the first disc out of the gate from Carlton features optional English subtitles which also identify the dizzying array of pop, classical, and world music selections on the soundtrack (some of which, such as The Who's "Who Are You", could account for this feature's home video tribulations). The film's running time has been the subject of speculation for years, with press materials listing it at 124, 122 and 117 minutes depending on the venue. The 117-minute length has been the standard one for years and is represented on both DVDs, but the Criterion edition – along with a better

B

anamorphic transfer – resolves the mystery of the missing footage by presenting some deleted scenes which, along with adding some extra nudity, present a few interesting little character shadings. Other extras on the Criterion disc include a hilariously candid video interview with Russell, a video chat with Roeg and producer Jeremy Thomas, the trailer, behind-the-scenes and production photos, and liner notes by Richard Combs supplemented with a Garfunkel text interview. A subsequent U.K. reissue from Network carries over the trailer and deleted scenes along with an additional teaser, a different illustrated booklet, pdf versions of the press notes and pressbook, and a stills gallery.

BADLANDS

Colour, 1973, 95m. / Directed by Terrence Malick / Starring Martin Sheen, Sissy Spacek, Warren Oates / Warner (UK R2 PAL, US R1 NTSC, Holland R2 PAL) / WS (1.85:1) (16:9) / DD5.0

Arguably the most romanticized film about serial killers ever made, this debut feature from the not-terribly-prolific Terrence Malick joined *The Honeymoon Killers* as a high profile independent film made in reaction to *Bonnie and Clyde*. A barely fictionalized account of the Starkweather/Fugate killings during the late 1950s, Malick's film concentrates on stunning visuals to convey the sensibility that led to the crimes; the explicit particulars are left mainly to the audience's imaginations, making this a rare true crime film which can be shown unedited on television. In her first lead role, Sissy Spacek more than holds her own against the more established Martin Sheen; she is Holly, an impressionable South Dakota teen given to delusional fantasies, while he is Kit Caruthers, her older, bad boy

suitor who winds up killing her disapproving father (Warren Oates). Together they embark on a crime spree across middle America, hiding from the law while taking out the occasional interloper.

Though relatively linear in comparison to Malick's later films, *Days of Heaven* and *The Thin Red Line*, this is obviously the work of the same man. The elaborate, painterly visuals are never less than hypnotic, while the integration of source music (often classical) lends a dreamlike air enhanced by the naturalistic performances. Of course, this also established Malick's fondness for narration as his primary narrative glue; fortunately Spacek makes for better aural company than the verbal historians in Malick's other two films. Her perspective also helps make sense of the film, which deliberately plays out like the distorting visions of a young girl unable to see the true horror erupting around her and instead focuses on the love she imagines blossoming with a man who can do her no good.

All DVD editions from Warner boast a pleasing anamorphic transfer. Like many films of the period, *Badlands* was shot with a deliberately gritty and grainy appearance at times; fortunately the texture has not been smoothed away by digital technology. The colourful outdoor shots look as vivid and impressive as they do on the big screen, while the spacious surround remix makes the most of the often quiet, subdued sound mix. All discs also include the theatrical trailer, but the U.K. and Dutch discs easily trump their U.S. counterpart with the inclusion of "Absence of Malick", a 23-minute documentary from Blue Underground. Sheen and Spacek are both on hand to discuss the film, which had an immeasurable impact on both of their careers and still holds a place dear to their hearts. Obviously the camera-shy Malick does not participate, a potential liability which the doco instead turns to its advantage quite cleverly.

BANGKOK HAUNTED

Colour, 2001, 131m. / Directed by Pisut Praesangeam, Oxide Pang / Starring Pete Thong-jeur, Pramote Sangsorn / Tartan (UK R0 PAL), Panik House (US R0 NTSC) / WS (1.85:1) (16:9) / DD 5.1

 A rather old-fashioned omnibus spooker on the *Dead of Night* model, *Bangkok Haunted* is framed by scenes in which three young, apparently modern Thai women sit in a deserted cafe on a rainy night and tell each other their own ghost stories. Oddly, they don't cut in until after the first story has been told, a disorienting effect that also means the movie has to open with a TV-style teaser in which a hobo in the back of a truck is spooked by a white-faced, long-fingerknived lady ghost.

"Legend of the Drum" is closest in style to traditional Far Eastern horror, with Jieb, an antique dealer, troubled by a drum that seems to invoke the spirit of Paga, a dancer who disappeared eighty years ago after befriending and then rejecting a hooded, disfigured outcast. Given that this is already a three-story film, it's slightly awkward that this tale should be told through intercut parallel modern and 1913 narratives, though the collision of the two strands is artfully unsettling. "Black Magic Woman" is a more lurid tale in sleazy style, about Pan, a girl who uses an extract of corpses as an aphrodisiac perfume with unpleasant consequences for her lovers, who have spells of vomiting demon possession or become psychotic ghosts. Oxide Pang, co-director of *The Eye*, takes over from Pisut Praesangeam for the final episode, "Revenge", about a cop called Nop (Pete Thong-jeur) who investigates the death-by-hanging of Gunya, a young woman with whom he was involved, and learns nasty things in the process, leading to a dramatisation of the old puzzle about a suicide who uses ice blocks to blur cause of death and suggest murder.

Each forty-five minute story is overextended (you might ponder the relevance of the walk-on security guards discussing bets on English football in the first scene of "Black Magic Woman", for instance), but the film has its share of genuinely creepy moments, ranging from delicate ghost scares to splatter grue. However, the stories are presented with such elliptical style that it's hard to get involved with them, or even to work out which characters we're supposed to be afraid for and which afraid of. This isn't through any deep moral ambiguity, but because everyone is ill-defined and yet given undue attention as the restless camera hops about within the narrative while the directors overcomplicate the basic anecdotes. All the stories are at once simple and hard to pin down, which might have been the intention – though *The Eye*, for instance, works much better for being more straightforward in sticking with one haunted viewpoint character. Pang's "Revenge", with its mystery plot, is the most straight-ahead of the tales here, though also the least scary in that the cruel "haunting" is set off while the dead woman is alive and her occasional ghostly appearances don't really add much to it. Oddly, the most engaging moments come in the interstitial snippets, thanks to some bright spark squabbling – the women disagree about the ending of "Legend of the Drum" while the punchline of "Black Magic Woman" is followed by a listener suggesting it ought to have been titled "Horror Sex on a Horrific Night" – and the subtle depiction of an ordinary setting as somehow ghostly that pays off with a not-unexpected Amicus-style revelation, though the guessable twist is followed by a more satisfying couple of surprises.

Tartan's Asia Extreme DVD showcases an anamorphic widescreen transfer with optional English subtitles: the image is a little soft (maybe deliberately), which helps with the eerie feel (and blends in some subtle CGI

B

trickery with more traditional ghost effects) and the 5.1 audio delivers a symphony of creepy, half-heard sounds and ominous music licks. The extras are the trailer, director filmographies, a 25-minute puff clips-and-talking-heads promo (evidently made for television, with a pink-tinged and -flecked video look), impressive promotional art, skimpy notes by Justin Bowyer and a trailer reel. The later American release from Panik House features the 5.1 track along with DTS and Dolby Stereo, with optional English and Spanish subtitles. The transfer looks a bit more robust and also doesn't suffer from PAL conversion; the same extras are carried over along with production notes, a poster gallery, and essays about the Pang Brothers and Thai cinema.

– KN

BATMAN

Colour, 1966, 105m. / Directed by Leslie H. Martinson / Starring Adam West, Burt Ward, Cesar Romero, Frank Gorshin, Burgess Meredith, Lee Meriwether, Alan Napier, Madge Blake, Neil Hamilton, Stafford Repp / Fox (Blu-ray & DVD) (US RA/R1 HD/ NTSC, UK R2 PAL) / WS (1.85:1) (16:9)

 When the inventor of a revolutionary dehydration device is kidnapped, Batman (Adam West) and Robin (Burt Ward) conclude it to be the work of not one but four of their deadliest foes: Joker, Riddler, Penguin and Catwoman. As the dynamic duo race against time to solve the crime, it becomes apparent that the fearsome foursome are intent on dehydrating and holding to ransom the entire Security Council at Gotham City's United World headquarters.

After the huge success of the indefensibly silly *Batman* TV show in 1966, 20th Century Fox rushed a movie-length adventure into production. For anyone unfamiliar with the show, the tone is established early on when Batman is assailed by a shark which attaches itself to his leg and refuses to let go; a series of punches on the snout fail to dislodge the beast, so he disposes of it with a handy atomizer filled with – what else? – Shark Repellent Bat-spray.

Adam West and Burt Ward reprise their small screen roles and the show's most popular super-criminals are drafted in, that's Cesar Romero's Joker, Frank Gorshin's Riddler, Burgess Meredith's Penguin and Lee Meriwether (standing in for an unavailable Julie Newmar) as Catwoman. Alan Napier is on hand as faithful retainer Alfred and Madge Blake is Aunt Harriet, with Neil Hamilton and Stafford Repp as the worryingly inept Commissioner Gordon and Chief O'Hara respectively. Taking up the reins on Lorenzo Semple Jr.'s screenplay was veteran TV director Leslie H. Martinson, who'd just managed a Penguin episode in the show's first season.

All the anticipated finery is on display, and our heroes get a few more toys to play with too; along with the turbo-charged Batmobile there's a helicopter, a motorcycle-sidecar combo and a high-power boat. The other requisite facets that made the TV show such a hit are also firmly in place – the skewed camera angles whenever there's villainy afoot, the "Zap" and "Ker-Pow" cartoon captioning when a fight breaks out, and the writing that made "Holy" the most overworked adjective in script history – and Martinson ladles on the buffoonery with a Bat-shovel. Where other than in *Batman* would you find submarines with penguin flipper propulsion, flying jetpack umbrellas and porpoises willing to lay down their lives to save those of our befuddled crime fighters... and accept it all without question? For those who love the show, this is an extended slice of revelry with even more ludicrous than usual plotting. The methods employed by Batman and Robin to tackle crime beggar belief, with clues solved via the most hilariously contrived scripting imaginable. And although it inevitably takes a couple of rounds of fisticuffs to bring the baddies to justice, perpetual bickering and an inability to collude in harmony has more to do with their downfall than anything the costume-clad chumps manage to orchestrate. The giddy highlight comes when the caped crusader dashes along a pier trying desperately to dispose of a smoking bomb, only to be foiled at every attempt by the presence of nuns, a Salvation Army band, mothers pushing prams – even a family of ducks! – prompting the immortal, exasperated line "Some days you just can't get rid of a bomb." Neither Romero's jocular, white pancake-plastered Joker or Meredith's cantankerous, putty-nosed Penguin are particularly intimidating, and Meriwether's Catwoman evokes more desire than danger. Only Gorshin's Riddler conveys the feeling that there just might be something dangerous lurking behind the manic cackling. The whole concoction functions of course because no matter how fatuous the dialogue, no matter how demented the situations they become embroiled in, the cast never play it less than 100% straight. When *Batman* re-emerged on the screen in the late 1980s in a revamped, darker mode it was highly successful in its own right, yet ironically when the franchise lightened up and attempted to emulate the campiness of *Batman* circa 1966 it fell flat on its cowl. Thirtysomethings who remember this one with misty-eyed affection will probably cringe with embarrassment at the shenanigans. Yet in spite of the decline and abrogation of the series – which put pay to any chance of a sequel – this film is as joyous a chunk of kitsch escapism as you'll find, and approached entirely in that spirit it's as fresh and as much fun today as it was almost forty years ago.

"Holy interactive menus Batman!" "Precisely, Robin. It must be some sort of modern navigation device. How clever!" So goes the exchange between Adam West and Burt Ward in their specially recorded introduction as the opening menu pops up on 20th Century Fox's *Batman* DVD, which sets the mood for a fun package with a super collection of Bat-extras. The feature itself is presented in 1.75:1 matted ratio with 32 chapter breaks and has never looked this good before, its soaring prismatic colours and boisterous stereo sound flowing intoxicatingly out of your TV set. The sound is also available in English mono or French mono. The movie even opens with the original (now rather antiquated looking) Fox logo – a welcome retention. There is an accompanying commentary provided by West and Ward, who are also the focus of a 17-minute retrospective featurette. In addition to this there's a short devoted to Batmobile designer/builder George Barris, two stills galleries and three trailers (one with Spanish sound). Tagged on the end is a superfluous preview for Fox's 1967 *Planet of the Apes*. Fox released it twice in the U.K., with a "special edition" reissue in 2005 in a deluxe cardboard box and a Batman light keyring.

Newcomers and staunch Batfans may be most tempted by Fox's Blu-ray edition, which features a boisterous (and thankfully film-like) HD transfer and a more powerful uncompressed DTS mix (and, amazingly, an isolated score track for Nelson Riddle's infectious music). Several new extras are added including four HD featurettes: "Batman: A Dynamic Legacy", "Gotham City's Most Wanted", "Caped Crusaders: A Heroes Tribute", and "The Batmobile Revealed". Semple, Martinson and Meriwether pop up here along with a lot of unrelated admirers, though this time the two leads are nowhere to be found. Interactive "Mapping the Movie" and "Tour with the Batmobile" features are also provided with a focus on locations used for the film.

– TG

BATMAN

Colour, 1989, 126m. / Directed by Tim Burton / Starring Michael Keaton, Jack Nicholson, Jack Palance, Kim Basinger, Michael Gough, Pat Hingle, Billy Dee Williams, Jerry Hall, Robert Wuhl / Warner (Blu-ray & DVD) (US/UK RA/R1 HD/NTSC/PAL) / WS (1.85:1) (16:9) / DD5.1

Under the flaccid protection of a sadly corrupt police department, Gotham City is in danger of becoming easy prey to the criminal element, none more powerful than the syndicate governed by Carl Grissom (Jack Palance). When his chief enforcer, Jack Napier (Jack Nicholson), is disfigured during a shoot-out in a chemical factory, he returns as The Joker to wreak havoc and destruction upon the City. In the guise of masked sentinel Batman, millionaire Bruce Wayne (Michael Keaton) must contend with The Joker's insane schemes while staving off the attentions of prying photojournalist Vicky Vale (Kim Basinger), who is intent on uncovering the true identity of the sombre vigilante.

As much of a pleasure as it was to learn that the slapstick approach of the 1960s TV show would play truant in the 1989 relaunch of the caped crusader's career, the announcement that Michael Keaton (a questionable choice, as up to that point he was renowned primarily for light comedy) was to take on the role of Bob Kane's seminal antihero was met with trepidation by Bat-fans around the globe. Nevertheless as soon as he appeared in that armoured suit and spoke his first line in a harsh whisper, it was obvious that director Tim Burton had got it right. Keaton's Batman proved to be a breath of fresh air. Gone was Adam West's care-free, indefatigable Bruce Wayne, in his place a very troubled human being, tortured by the memory of his parents' murder,

tormented by doubt over the double life with which kismet has saddled him. The story takes a while to warm up, but once Jack Nicholson has been transformed into the Satanic Joker, the ball really gets rolling. Could anyone else have seriously been considered for this part? He chews up the scenery and spits out the blackened remnants with his customary screen assurance. Nicholson not only thieves the show, his name also appears before Keaton's on the credits and as much, if not more time is devoted to the scourge of Gotham City as to the Dark Knight. He provides all the devilish black humour and things sizzle whenever he's on screen, which has the unintentional adverse effect of rendering the film so much less interesting when he isn't. Kim Basinger is bearable as Vicky Vale, in spite of a hairstyle that changes in every scene, but her character is sorely underwritten. *Horror Hospital*'s Michael Gough – who went on to appear in three Bat-sequels – delivers a wonderfully understated performance as faithful butler Alfred, the rock to whom Wayne's sanity is anchored. Pat Hingle is Commissioner Gordon, *The Empire Strikes Back*'s Billy Dee Williams is DA Harvey Dent (replaced by Tommy Lee Jones for *Batman Forever*). Jack Palance teeters on the edge of OTT as mob boss Grissom, while Jerry Hall as Joker's moll Alicia is so annoyingly bland that you can understand why the clown prince of crime throws a fit and douses her in acid.

Production Designer Anton Furst's sets – a beguiling blend of 1920s meets 21st Century – are as integral a part of Burton's Gothic fantasy as his principal characters. Having been fortunate enough to walk through the Gotham set at Pinewood Studios before it was torn down, I can attest first hand to its awe-inspiring elegance.

Highpoints? So many. The armour-clad Batmobile tearing through the night, spewing up leaves in its wake, is a standout. As is the wonderfully indulgent moment when the Batwing sails up through the clouds to be silhouetted against a bright full moon. And let's not forget the striking, if all too brief, climactic face-off in the bell tower of Gotham Cathedral. All said and done it would be fatuous to suggest that *Batman* is without fault; in fact as exercises in style over substance go this is up there with the best of them; where Burton has an unequalled eye for visual genius, storytelling is not his forte. The film is also at least a quarter of an hour too long and Robert Wuhl's annoyingly cartoonish reporter Knox is the most noteworthy of several definite misfires in Sam Hamm's less than suspenseful script. Regardless, Tim Burton's *Batman* haemorrhages élan from every frame and, until Marvel came along with *Spider-Man* more than a decade later, it held the sceptre as most polished screen adaptation of a comic book creation to date.

After a lacklustre no-frills DVD that sat on shelves for years, Warner finally stepped up with a worthy special edition featuring a sparkling transfer from hi-def and a solid roster of extras. Tim Burton appears for another one of his, ahem, deliberately-paced commentary tracks, while the second disc packs in the lions' share of the extras including the Batman overview "Legends of the Dark Knight" (40 mins.), "On the Set with Bob Kane", the three-part "Shadows of the Bat" (with Keaton, Burton, Nicholson, and more talking about the making of the film), the innocuous pair of "Batman: The Heroes" and "Batman: The Villains", the six-part behind-the-scenes "Beyond Batman", a deleted storyboard sequence for an appearance by Robin, and three amusingly dated Prince music videos. The same extras were subsequently carried over to Blu-ray with the expected bump in image and audio quality; it was originally issued as part of a *Batman Motion Picture Anthology* (containing the entire Burton/Schumacher cycle) and then released separately with Digibook packaging containing an extensive booklet packed with photos and notes.
– TG

BATTLE ROYALE

Colour, 2001, 121m. / Directed by Kinji Fukasaku / Starring Tatsuya Fujiwara, Aki Maeda, Takeshi Kitano, Taro Yamamoto, Masanobu Ando, Kou Shibasaki / Arrow (Blu-ray & DVD) (UK R0 HD/PAL), Tartan (UK R0 PAL, UK R0 NTSC), Anchor Bay (Blu-ray & DVD) (US RA/R1 HD/NTSC), Warner (France R2 PAL) / WS (1.85:1) (16:9) / DD5.1, Universe (HK R3 NTSC) / WS (1.85:1) / DD5.1

Japan, during the early 21st Century. As a reaction to ever rising levels of unemployment and juvenile delinquency, the government has passed an act allowing for the staging of Battle Royale, whereby an entire class of 14-15 year-olds chosen by lottery are transported to a remote island, fitted with explosive collars that can be triggered by remote control, given weapons and allowed three days to kill each other off until only one survivor remains. The latest class of 42, supervised by embittered ex-teacher Kitano (Takeshi Kitano) and a cadre of soldiers, includes two "transfer students", previous BR winner Kawada (Taro Yamamoto) and psychopathic volunteer Kiriyama (Masanobu Ando). During the screening of an instructional video that explains the rules, Kitano kills a girl for talking out of turn and detonates the collar of a class troublemaker who once assaulted him. Over the three days, the body count rises: some opt to commit suicide rather than become killers, Kiriyama obtains an automatic weapon and hunts for sport, and class bitch Mitsuko (Kou Shibasaki) becomes a serial killer. Shuya (Tatsuya Fujiwara) and Noriko (Aki Maeda) stick together and form an alliance with Kawada, who claims to know a way that more than one can survive the battle.

With a cast of thirty-five-year-old cowboys, soldiers or gangsters, *Battle*

Royale would be no more shocking than any other post-Peckinpah action bloodbath, and many violent dystopian satires, from Peter Watkins's *Punishment Park* through *Turkey Shoot* and *No Escape* to *Series 7: The Contenders*, have covered roughly the same ground. However, making the killers and victims schoolchildren in their mid-teens demonstrates that it is still possible to be transgressive, as roughly forty uniformed, apparently ordinary kids are murdered in familiar, blood-bursting action picture manner: riddled with bullets from automatic weapons, throats slashed or blasted out, stabbed, shot with arrows, jumping from great heights, decapitated with a samurai sword, blown up, gruesomely poisoned. As in *Lord of the Flies*, an obvious precedent, we are in the territory of allegory rather than a study of real-world child violence. Based on a best-selling novel by Koshun Takami, the film skips over the set-up and introduces Class B on the bus as they are supposedly taken on a school trip, establishing that they are neither particularly innocent nor especially deserving of this punishment. Most films in this sub-genre are satires at the expense of crass media, and early on we do get a hilariously perky instructional video for mass murder by a pouting Japanese MTV-type hostess, but this is not an avenue the film chooses to explore. Though monitored by a sad-eyed but brutalised Takeshi Kitano, the kids are on their own, with no rules and only their own characters. An especially horrific aspect of the premise is that the point of BR is not to entertain sadistic mobs, but to teach children a lesson.

The film has to keep a count of who has died, with printouts on screen and regular announcements, and with so many characters it can't get close to them all. The central figures, meek Noriko and numb Shuya, are less vivid than some shorter-lived characters, and the most effective moments are vignettes: the take-charge head girl type cheerfully organising her clique to survive, but everything going wrong as girls with ordinary grievances ("Why do you have to be the leader all the time?") reach for guns; contrasting moments as boys approach girls upon whom they have crushes, with one trying to bully a girl into liking him through death threats and another being shot dead by the girl he has just confessed his love to ("but you never even spoke to me"); the revelation that Kiriyama, who sports a sharp suit and Johnny Rotten hair, has entered the contest for fun; teen bitch Mitsuko's assumption of the role of serial murderess, paying back all the real and imaginary sleights she has suffered in school ("I didn't want to be a loser any more"). Perhaps because it's impossible to rationalise the situation as credible and perhaps because taking it seriously would make the film unwatchably grim, veteran director Kinji Fukasaku (*The Green Slime*, *Virus*, *Tora! Tora! Tora!*) plays a vein of very black humour, with the wry, impassive, hard-to-fathom Kitano acting as if this were a normal school activity, as classical music is played over the tannoy and updates on the class's progress are read out. As the scrambling of character name and actor suggests, Kitano is our anchor, a familiar presence with an inimitable stance, and his poised, perfect death scene tells us we must take *Battle Royale* seriously but not literally.

Universe released the film in Hong Kong as a purely functional non-anamorphic disc featuring a 1.85:1 transfer of the standard theatrical print, which ran to exactly 113 minutes. Tartan first released this cut of the film as a no-frills film-only DVD, which despite being a massive hit in Japan and surprisingly successful in the U.K., was held off the American market for complex reasons. This was superseded by a high-definition NTSC disc, which only included the film's trailer as an extra, and finally they also produced a two-disc PAL Special edition which showcases a slightly longer cut of the film (running to 121m), with a few more extended flashbacks showing the normal, pre-BR lives of the class (delivering one or two major revelations) and an extended off-the-island finish. As with many Tartan Extreme Asia titles, the transfer on this release is okay rather than outstanding (though improved over the first PAL edition). There is moderate grain throughout and a touch of blurriness in the darker, busier scenes, but the muted colours, mostly island greens, are attractive, with gushers of distinctively red, red blood. Sealed in a nice-looking tin, this set also includes a frame taken from a theatrical print in a presentation card, an insert with brief notes about Fukasaku and Takeshi and a chapter listing sheet that features a map of the island. Disc Two highlights a fifty-minute "making of" that confirms suspicion that the young cast had the time of their lives during the shoot ("I'm extremely honoured to be killed by Mr. Takeshi", claims one girl). Early on, Fukasaku claims he can't remember being the age most of his cast are, but later he tells sobering tales of his experiences at the end of the Second World War that visibly impress and move the children he is directing. A word of comfort for parents worried that their kids like this 18-certificate film too much: after watching the special edition, they'll talk about what they'd do if forced to play the game but what they'll really want is to have been cast in the film, which must have been the best-ever summer camp/school play experience of their lives. This is augmented by a variety of bits and pieces: a videotaped nine-minute press conference with Fukasaku, Takeshi and some of the kids (in bloodied costume); a gag version of the BR instructional video made for the director's seventieth birthday; audition and rehearsal footage; snippets of effects scenes, showing the elements used; footage of Fukasaku and the cast (some noticeably older than in the film) introducing a Tokyo film festival screening; a twelve-minute promotional featurette; raw behind-the-scenes footage of the initial shooting and the 'special edition' reshoot (a basketball game flashback that reunited the cast five months later); three trailers

(one including a tiny recommendation from Quentin Tarantino); a director's statement; and filmographies for Takeshi and Fukasaku.

In an odd commercial move following Fukasaku's death (he passed away in 2003), the film was announced as a likely target for the pre-*Avatar* 3D conversion process which was also being tested on the *Star Wars* films. This plan was eventually realised years later under the supervision of the director's son, Kenta Fukasaku, though die-hards will probably want to stick with the original. The 3D version was enough of an impetus to trigger an incredibly belated North American deal with Anchor Bay, marking a full decade for the film to officially reach US shores. They also acquired the rights to the middling sequel, which has a much smaller fan base than the original.

Almost simultaneously, Arrow Films in the UK stole a bit of their thunder by announcing a massive limited (10,000 piece) Blu-ray set containing three discs: both cuts of the film in new HD transfers with optional English subtitles, the theatrical trailer, and a horde of video features, many longer or repurposed from the previous editions but with some new goodies as well. You get the "Experience of 42 High School Students" featurette, "Conducting *Battle Royale*" (devoted to the orchestra performance of the score), the Quentin Tarantino TV spot (which ties in with his love for the film and explains why he prominently cast one of its actors in *Kill Bill: Volume 1*), a Kitano interview, two looks at the preparation and unveiling of the special edition, a Tokyo International Film Festival presentation, opening day coverage from the Maru No Uchi Toei theatre, "The Slaughter of 42 High School Students", a press conference from the premiere, "The Correct Way to Fight" featurette, rehearsal and composer conducting footage, a special FX comparison piece, on-set production footage, more TV spots and commercials, bonus Fukasaku trailers, and a 32-page comic and 36-page booklet including notes by Asian film scholar Tom Mes, a Fukasaku interview, excerpts from the source novel, bonus notes by Jay McRoy (only in the limited set, though a stripped-down version is also available with fewer extras), conceptual art and postcards, a fold-out poster, and material from the original press kit. In typical Arrow fashion, this one truly goes all out to deliver everything you could ask for.

– KN

BEAST OF BLOOD

Colour, 1970, 90m. / Directed by Eddie Romero / Starring John Ashley, Celeste Yarnall, Eddie Garcia, Lisa Belmonte, Bruno Punzalan, Beverly Miller / Image, Alpha (US R1 NTSC), Cinema Club (UK R2 PAL)

 Uniquely in the loose series of Filipino-made "Blood Island" horror pictures, this is actually a sequel to an earlier entry, *Mad Doctor of Blood Island*. It picks up where that left off, with "Don Ramon" – the chlorophyll monster – struggling ashore and a bit of plot-tidying as an explosion sinks a ship and kills off the unseen heroine of *Mad Doctor* but leaves hero Bill Foster (John Ashley) alive and traumatized.

Eddie Romero directed this one without input from Gerardo De Leon, his partner on earlier "Blood Island" movies, and it's a notably less eccentric picture. Partnered with a *Gilligan's Island*-type skipper (Beverly Miller, who also scripted), Bill returns to Blood Island and slogs through the jungle after Myra (Celeste Yarnall), a nosy journalist with a vibrant pink outfit, who has been kidnapped by the usual swarthy, machete-wielding extras. Dr. Lorca (Eddie Garcia, replacing Ronald Remy) has survived being burned to death and admits that he's "madder than ever" (with facial scars, too), experimenting on islanders who sprout green patches. Don Ramon's living

severed head occasionally growls vindictively from its bowl, while his hulking body strains straps on the operating table as Lorca fails to attach a new, more biddable head. Though there's amusing mad lab business, with Lorca ranting about his vague but impressive scientific plans, much of the film is low-rent action-cum-melodrama with stuntmen popping off rifles and burning down huts while Ashley turns down a willing island girl (Lisa Belmonte), saving himself for a topless grapple with Yarnall.

The fourth in Image's "Blood Collection" series, with another installment (53 minutes' worth) of Sam Sherman's autobiography via commentary track, this presents a pinkish, muddy, scratched-up standard-frame transfer (one blatant bit of day-for-night has been "corrected" and looks very, very blue). Carrying over the Eddie Romero interview and trailers familiar from the other discs in the collection, it adds a few other extras: footage originally intended to play under the credits (eventually replaced with hokey animation) and a nine-minute on-camera chat between Sherman and Yarnall. Cinema Club's U.K. disc has the same transfer but without the added material, while the full extras were carried over for a bargain U.S. issue from Alpha with less consistent encoding.

– KN

BEAUTY AND THE BEAST (LA BELLE ET LA BÊTE)

B&W, 1946, 93m. / Directed by Jean Cocteau / Starring Jean Marais, Josette Day, Marcel André, Mila Parély / Criterion (US R1 NTSC), BFI (UK R2 PAL)

 The greatest fairy tale film ever made, Jean Cocteau's *Beauty and the Beast* (*La belle et la bête*) is both an ideal introduction to the world of foreign cinema and a perfect

encapsulation of a daydream on film, with enough artistic flourishes to fill a dozen other screen fantasies. Influencing projects as diverse as the Disney animated production of the same and *Bram Stoker's Dracula*, Cocteau's masterpiece retains its ability to inspire wonder and delight the viewers' senses even after countless viewings. Everyone knows the basic story, but for the record our heroine is Belle (Josette Day), a sweet-natured and dutiful daughter to her father (Marcel André) despite the scorn of her two wicked sisters. With the vain and boorish Avenant (Jean Marais) hovering over her, Belle's prospects seem dim indeed. One day while riding in the woods, her father is caught in a windstorm and takes refuge at a mystical castle where he plucks a single rose to take home to his daughter. Unfortunately the owner, the Beast (Marais again), demands the man's life but offers to take one of his daughters in exchange. Belle is appalled by the thought of sacrificing her father and goes to the Beast's castle, where she becomes a reluctant guest and tries to look past the master's bestial nature.

For the first 15 minutes or so, viewers may wonder what all the fuss is about. Cocteau begins the film in a deliberately flat style, with static compositions flooded with sunlight. However, as with his *Orpheus*, once we pass through the figurative looking glass into the Beast's palace, the film assumes a life of its own and unspools one remarkable sequence after another. The disembodied arms wielding candles, the Beast's hands smoking after killing a deer, the transformation of Belle's tears into diamonds, and Belle's dreamlike floating through the palace hallways are all images impossible to forget; equally effective is the dreamy Georges Auric score, which wafts through the film like a silvery whisper.

The first film to be issued twice on DVD by the Criterion Collection, *Beauty and the Beast* made its digital bow in an edition that was considered at the time to be the best the film could possibly look. Though filled with scratches, visible tape splices, and other debris, the overall quality was satisfying enough (and also turned up on a similarly appointed U.K. DVD). However, Criterion's expanded reissue lays that transfer to waste with an impeccably smooth, wonderfully clean image; you'd have to stare long and hard to find a flaw, amazing for a film once thought to be damaged forever. The audio sounds exceptionally clear and rich, with the music rendered far better than before. The disc also includes a Dolby Digital 5.1 presentation of Philip Glass's opera written for the film, originally performed at live presentations of the film itself. The dialogue is sung in French with Glass's music and stays more or less in sync with the actors throughout. It's a beautiful piece of work and fares better overall than his hypnotic but disconcerting accompaniment to the 1931 *Dracula*. Fans of the film will also be delighted to know that, for the first time in an English-speaking home video format, the original and utterly charming opening titles have been restored, with Cocteau drawing the main credits on a blackboard in a classroom full of students.

Both DVD versions contain an informative audio commentary by film historian Arthur Knight, in which he catalogues Cocteau's influences and innovations while making the film and places it within its correct cinematic context. The reissue adds on a second commentary by writer and cultural historian Sir Christopher Frayling, which focuses more on the fine art and literary aspects of the film and discusses the contributions of everyone involved in a more humanities-related fashion. Both discs contain a text version of the complete original fairy tale by Mme. Leprince de Beaumont and some informative liner notes by Cocteau biographer Francis Steegmuller; after that the supplements part company. The original (discontinued) disc contains a sole documentary, "Angel of Space and Time", produced for the 1970s cinema appreciation program, *Cinematic Eye*. Though it's an interesting novelty, the information contained in this film is covered elsewhere in the reissued disc so its loss will be minimal to all but die hard completists. The upgraded DVD adds on a wealth of extras, the most immediately appetizing of which is the film's original French theatrical trailer hosted by Cocteau himself. It's a wonderful promo, with tributes to everyone in front of and behind the camera. A French trailer for the restored edition was also concocted for the theatrical reissue and is included here as well. A 1995 half hour documentary, *Projection au Majestic* (*Screening at the Majestic*) returns to several of the original filming locales and features interviews with some of the principals, including a snowy-bearded Marais and one of the wicked sisters, Mila Parély. A nine-minute interview from 1995 with cinematographer Henri Alekan for French television is also included, while the film's make-up artist, Hagop Arakelian, gets the spotlight in *Secrets Professionel*, a delightful eight-minute, black and white special produced in 1964. Last of all is an extensive stills gallery, which features several valuable images documenting the creation of Marais's Beast appearance. A subsequent BFI reissue utilizes the same restored transfer along with the Frayling commentary and a different 30-page collector's booklet including an essay by Marina Warner. An absolutely essential part of any fantasy film or family video library.

THE BEDROOM

Colour, 1992, 63m. / Directed by Hisayasu Sato / Starring Kiyomi Ito, Momori Asano / Screen Edge (UK R0 PAL) / WS (1.66:1)

One of the more accomplished artists within the Japanese "Pink" cinema genre, Hisayasu Sato, unleashes a torrent of sexual unease in *The Bedroom* (*Shisenjiyou no Aria*), an interesting precursor to metaphysical, violent women-as-object studies like *Audition*. Here

our heroine, Kyoko (Kiyomi Ito), works at a fringe club called the Bedroom, where the girls dose up on "hallusion", a drug which leaves them practically comatose as they experience intense trips. In this delusional state, men come into the rooms and take advantage of these oblivious women. Unfortunately some of the staff are turning up dead, horribly mutilated, and Kyoko believes her boyfriend may be the culprit.

A strange mix of industrial age erotica and *giallo* aesthetics, *The Bedroom* is a typical Pink film in spirit but boasts some interesting artistic flourishes. The camera's treatment of the female body as a blank canvas upon which men sculpt out their own fantasies is a fascinating concept, and ultimately the depiction of flesh as material to be broken up and mutilated reflects the increasingly fractured nature of the story. Sato earlier explored much of this territory in his gay variation on the same theme, *Muscle*, which would make a good companion feature with this. Image quality is mediocre, thanks to a combination of low budget photography and a dodgy compression job, though it's still watchable and, thanks to the 35mm stock, a bit sharper than its 16mm Pink counterparts. The burned-in English subtitles can be difficult to read against white backgrounds.

THE BELIEVERS

Colour, 1987, 114m. / Directed by John Schlesinger / Starring Martin Sheen, Helen Shaver, Harley Cross, Jimmy Smits, Robert Loggia / MGM (US R1 NTSC, UK R2 PAL) / WS (1.85:1) (16:9) / DD2.0

Touted as the heir apparent to *The Exorcist* in the religious horror sweepstakes, this flawed but effective chiller stars a pre-*West Wing* Martin Sheen as Dr. Cal Jamison, whose trauma over the death of his wife is one-upped when he learns of a sinister variation on the ancient religion of Santeria. As people in his life fall prey to mishaps, he realizes that his own son (Harley Cross) may be a primary target.

Late, genre-hopping director John Schlesinger displays a sure hand for grisly horror, coupled with the feeling of urban unease generated in his earlier *Marathon Man*. The galvanizing opening and a handful of other showstoppers (including Helen Shaver's spider-related complexion problem) provide the necessary violent spikes for audience appeal, but more subtle sequences create disquiet through the manipulation of framing and sound. In particular, the fates of co-stars Jimmy Smits and Robert Loggia invoke a nasty, lingering chill, with the viewer's mind filling in some of the nastier details. One significant flaw is the racism inherent in the story, which fails to distinguish between positive Santeria and its corrupt variation through white culture; a sequence in which Sheen apologizes for firing his protective, Santeria-practicing housekeeper was nixed at the last minute, and this scene desperately needs to be restored at some point as it would significantly balance out what is now a painfully lopsided narrative. However, the sinister presence of magic can be felt throughout the film, from the paranoid urban blight to the creepy-crawly J. Peter Robinson score (complete with obligatory choir). Interestingly, according to rumour this film has since been embraced by certain communities as a demonstration of how to wield magical power, which makes the cinematic experience even more frightening. *The Believers* has also proven to be surprisingly influential over the years, obviously inspiring sequences in *The Devil's Advocate* and a host of more recent Japanese horror films.

MGM's DVD looks attractive, certainly better than the earlier pallid HBO transfer, with welcome anamorphic enhancement. Some darker scenes have

that bleary mid-'80s feel (think *Fatal Attraction*), which in this case is wholly appropriate as the whole visual scheme is awash in eerie shades of grey and brown. Surround audio is fine; a trailer is the only extra. The British version (which is carried over in most other European countries as well) adds on no substantial extras but does feature a wider array of language options including audio and subtitles in English, French, German, Italian, and Spanish, with additional subtitles in Dutch, Swedish, and Greek.

BELOW

Colour, 2002, 105m. / Directed by David Twohy / Starring Bruce Greenwood, Olivia Williams, Scott Foley, Jason Flemyng, Matthew Davis, Holt McCallany, Zach Galifianakis, Nick Chinlund / Buena Vista (US R1 NTSC, UK R2 PAL) / WS (1.85:1) / DD5.1

 During World War II, a distress signal from a torpedoed medical ship sends a U.S. sub on a rescue mission which salvages three survivors, including an English nurse called Claire (*The Sixth Sense*'s Olivia Williams). The commanding officer on the ship, Lieutenant Brice (Bruce Greenwood), has recently taken over for the deceased captain and doesn't take kindly to Claire's attempt to smuggle a German patient on board. However, bigger problems are in store as the submarine appears to be haunted; the men become more nervous by the moment and the sub shows signs of steering itself to a sinister destination, as the late captain's presence becomes something very alarming indeed.

A reasonably accomplished fusion of *Das Boot*-style thrills and old-fashioned ghost story, *Below* marked the troubled third feature of director David Twohy, who previously helmed the promising *Pitch Black* and *The Arrival*. Due to a lack of name stars and clashes with the studio, the film was briefly dumped into theatres and barely promoted, leaving it to the mercy of word of mouth. A cult reputation soon built around it as a horror yarn that deserved much better, and while the praise is mostly justified, it's not quite the unsung classic some have claimed. Good points first: the actors are uniformly good-to-excellent, with solid turns from the two leads as well as Scott Foley (TV's *Felicity*), the always busy Jason Flemyng, and Cary Elwes look-alike Matthew Davis (*Legally Blonde*), whose role takes an unexpected turn. The requisite submarine situations are handled skilfully, with some new twists on the usual "we're trapped and bombs are falling on us" scenario; as for the ghostly scenes, the first half crackles with some fine little visual fillips, including one soon-to-be-classic bit involving a reflection with a mind of its own. On the downside, the opening few minutes are rather chaotic and do a shaky job of establishing the characters, but worse, the film utterly slides downhill in its final act. The decision to turn the villain into one of the humans on board is a lousy call, made worse by the inexplicable decision to pilfer the already mediocre ending of Brian De Palma's *Snake Eyes* almost shot for shot. The soggy climax then fizzles out to a presumably open-ended coda (was there really a ghost on board...?), though all the screaming, apparitions and violent deaths tend to make such ambiguity a moot point.

Buena Vista's nicely appointed DVD treats the film like a blockbuster regardless of its performance. The video and audio aspects are all up to reference standards, with plenty of fancy split-surround effects and exquisite integration of live action and CGI to keep fx hounds happy. An audio commentary is provided by Twohy, Greenwood, Davis, and other cast members Holt McCallany, Zach Galifianakis and Nick Chinlund. Obviously recorded near the film's theatrical release, the discussion is lively and surprisingly cleanly edited for so many participants; for some reason Twohy ignores the screenwriting contributions of director Darren Aronofsky, who receives credit on the finished film; it would be interesting to compare their script drafts. Other extras include three deleted scenes (with optional Twohy commentary), all expendable, a theatrical trailer, and a 12-minute featurette, "The Process", a better-than-average behind the scenes look focusing on the methods used to go from page to screen.

BENT

Colour, 1997, 108m. / Directed by Sean Mathias / Starring Clive Owen, Lothaire Bluteau, Mick Jagger, Brian Webber, Nikolaj Coster-Waldau, Ian McKellen, Jude Law, Rachel Weisz, Rupert Graves, Sadie Frost, Paul Bettany / Park Circus (UK R2 PAL) (MGM (US R1 NTSC) / WS (1.85:1) (16:9), Cinema Club (UK R2 PAL) / WS, Salzgeber (Germany R2 PAL) / WS (1.66:1) / DD2.0

Bent is a harrowing adaptation of the late 1970s stage favourite from Martin Sherman that begins like an unholy collision of Tinto Brass and Luchino Visconti, as the camera records events at a nocturnal German bash where club owner "Greta" (Mick Jagger) floats down on a swing singing a torch song while the partygoers carouse and make love. Among the revellers are well-to-do Max (*Children of Men*'s Clive Owen), his irritated lover Rudy (Brian Webber), and a handsome Nazi, Wolf (*Nightwatch*'s Nikolaj Coster-Waldau), who becomes Max's conquest for the night. Unfortunately this turns out to be the Night of the Long Knives, and soon Wolf's on the wrong end of a bayonet while Max and Rudy are on the run. After a failed attempt at help from Max's flamboyant uncle (Ian McKellen), the men are packed onto a train to Dachau with Rudy meeting a chilling fate along the way. En route Max meets the gay Horst (Lothaire Bluteau), who becomes emblazoned with the infamous pink triangle, but Max strikes a deal to be designated with a yellow Star of David at the camp instead to ensure a greater probability of survival. At the camp he and Horst, both assigned to move heavy rocks from one place to another with no apparent purpose, never touch and rarely even look at each other but form a tentative bond which allows them to live with dignity in the most horrific of environments.

A film with an impressive pedigree, *Bent* was several years in the making despite its stage success (a theatrical breakthrough for actors as diverse as McKellen and Richard Gere). A lush Philip Glass score (alas still unreleased), beautiful photography and committed performances do what they can, though the staginess of the material and heavy-handed symbolism in the second half dilute what could have been an overwhelming cinematic experience. The curtain raiser is also so startling that there's really no way the film can top it, and while the attempt to split the experience between the sensory and the emotional is noble (a feat achieved far better in *Irréversible*), the end result doesn't quite come off; the ending, meant to be a devastating punchline and the ultimate gesture of defiance, instead feels more like a writing stunt. That said, the entire cast is astonishing, with a surprising roster of talent in supporting roles, including Jude Law, Rachel Weisz, Rupert Graves, Sadie Frost and Paul Bettany.

Inexplicably slapped with an NC-17 rating in the U.S. (the sex is confined to the opening few minutes and isn't all that explicit), *Bent* was later circulated in both edited and uncensored editions. All DVDs represent the complete cut of the film and have their own individual strengths. The U.S. disc features an excellent anamorphic transfer, with strong surround presence from the Glass score; the only extra is a theatrical trailer (accompanied by Jagger's "The Streets of Berlin"). The German DVD contains a flat 1.66:1 transfer with noticeably weaker black levels, though with wider framing at the top and the bottom looks a bit roomier than the U.S. compositions. Extras on the German disc include the German trailer, bios and a photo gallery. The film was purportedly trimmed down after its premiere at Cannes, though the excised footage (all expository) has yet to resurface. A subsequent dual-format DVD/Blu-ray version from Park Circus features a remastered anamorphic transfer along with the trailer, interviews with the cast (Owen, McKellen, Bluteau, Jagger, Sherman, and Mathias), on-set footage, and Mick Jagger's "Streets of Berlin" music video.

BETTY

Colour, 1992, 99m. / Directed by Claude Chabrol / Starring Marie Trintignant, Stéphane Audran, Jean-François Garreaud / MK2 (France R2 PAL), Kino (US R1 NTSC), Artificial Eye (UK R2 PAL) / WS (1.66:1) (16:9)

 An updated compilation of ideas from past Chabrol films, Betty returns to themes from the suspense master's more famous works as found in *Les biches* and *La rupture*, to cite two of the more obvious examples. Marie Trintignant plays the fragile lead, Betty, first seen in a drunken haze staring off into space at a local dive called the Hole. She's taken home for the night by the older Laure (Stéphane Audran), who spends the night in the next room making love with the bar's owner, Mario (Jean-François Garreaud). Over the course of the following day, Betty reveals her tragic secret; her in-laws forced her to give up her baby after she was caught in a compromising position, and now

she is sinking into self-destruction. However, beneath Betty's seemingly damaged exterior, all is not as it seems.

A rich adaptation of a novel from French mystery great Georges Simenon, *Betty* is primarily a vehicle for its powerhouse female leads. Trintignant (Jean-Louis's daughter) suggests endless depths of sorrow and pain through a simple glance, while Audran is still captivating and sexy even in her golden years. The film also features flashier visuals than usual for Chabrol; the often-excerpted image of Betty staring through an aquarium is almost Argento-like in its intensity.

MK2's disc is the ideal way to experience the film at home, thanks to a lustrous transfer with dead on black levels (essential for the shadowy photography in this film). The disc features optional English subtitles as well as French language extras (Chabrol commenting on video about three scenes, a video intro from Joel Magny, and numerous Chabrol trailers). The same disc was later ported over for American consumption by Kino (who also included it in their Chabrol "Tales of Deceit" box set with *The Color of Lies*, *L'enfer*, *Inspecteur Lavardin*, and *Cop au vin*) as well as Artificial Eye in the U.K., whose disc appears to boast heightened (colour timed) warmness and artificial sharpness.

LES BICHES

Colour, 1968, 95m. / Directed by Claude Chabrol / Starring Stéphane Audran, Jean-Louis Trintignant, Jacqueline Sassard / Pathfinder (US R1 NTSC), Artedis (France R2 PAL), Arrow (UK R0 PAL) / WS (1.66:1) (16:9)

Following his groundbreaking New Wave films in France and a failed bid to gain the acceptance Hollywood studios with 1966's *The Champagne Murders*, Claude Chabrol entered new directorial terrain with *Les biches*, an elegant, erotically charged thriller honed as sharp as a diamond. The clear blueprint for his work over the next decade, this exercise in suspense and bisexual chic remains one of his more popular films and has lost little of its allure. In her breakthrough role, Stéphane Audran stars as rich and pretentious socialite Frédérique, who encounters street artist Why (*Accident*'s Jacqueline Sassard) in Paris. The two begin an affair and take off for the winter in St. Tropez, where handsome architect Paul (Jean-Louis Trintignant, briefly Audran's husband in real life) shows an interest in both women. They invite him to move in with them, igniting a vicious game of psychological manipulation and homicide.

Les biches (whose title literally means "The Does", taken from Why's peculiar line, "I like drawing does, but I prefer kissing men") proved to be an international success, helped along by the forbidden allure of the subject matter and some juicy alternative titles (*Bad Girls* and, under the banner of drive-in king Jack H. Harris, *The Heterosexual*). Deliberately ambiguous, the film keeps the eyes and ears occupied without ever nailing down the characters' motivations, a tactic which ultimately works in its favour as the inevitable tragic finale approaches. If cinema is indeed a history of men looking at women and vice versa, then this is one of the most astute examples around. Also on display here is Chabrol's often overlooked sense of humour; the characters often say and do outrageously funny things, aided by a snappy gay couple who have the perfect response for everything.

Pathfinder's DVD was the first option on the market with English subtitles, while both the U.S. and French discs contain a very attractive anamorphic transfer with only the mildest of distractions (reel change markers, bits of dirt here and there). Much of the soft, powdery lighting is intentional; that's not a transfer or compression problem. The U.S. disc also contains the English and Spanish dub tracks, a French trailer (no subs), and a surprisingly listless commentary by critics Wade Major and F.X. Feeney, both of whom seem to have gotten a little tired of wading through their Chabrol discussions by this point. A subsequent release from Arrow in the U.K. is a significant step down with a drastically inferior transfer from a battered print with burned-in English subtitles; it was also included in their eight-disc Chabrol box, but it's worth the effort of hunting down the U.S. disc instead.

BIG WEDNESDAY

Colour, 1978, 120m. / Directed by John Milius / Starring Jan-Michael Vincent, William Katt, Gary Busey, Patti D'Arbanville / Warner (UK R2 PAL, US R1 NTSC, Italy R2 PAL, Australia R4 PAL) / WS (2.35:1) (16:9) / DD2.0

While documentarian Bruce Brown had been exploring the beauty and aesthetics of surfing for years in films like *The Endless Summer*, it wasn't until 1978 that a narrative feature finally took the sport to a level above the usual Frankie-and-Anette fare. Coming off the epic *The Wind and the Lion*, director John Milius plunged headfirst into the surf, so to speak, by allowing his camera to linger for minutes on end at the poetic beauty of wave riding, coupled with a Vietnam Era-storyline similar to the following year's *Hair* (another box office failure soon to become a cult classic). The storyline is strictly bare bones: three friends, Matt (Jan-Michael Vincent), Jack (William Katt), and Leroy (Gary Busey) spend over a decade growing up near the beach, with surfing serving as a metaphor for the free, youthful spirit they hope to keep for their entire lives. When not on the water,

they also have to face real life intrusions such as employment, alcoholism, and come-and-go girlfriends, including a young Patti D'Arbanville. Eventually the boys face "the big wave" and come up against the threat of mortality during the spectacular finale, which closes on an appropriately mythic note.

At first glance, *Big Wednesday* seems a bit out of step for Milius, better known for his macho spectacles like *Conan the Barbarian* and *Red Dawn*. However, the theme of male camaraderie proves to be a perfect fit for the Malibu-raised director, who exhibits an astonishing flair for capturing the pulse and feel of the ocean waves. Milius also deserves a huge pat on the back for offering music scoring duties to his former film school buddy, composer Basil Poledouris, who went on to become one of the soundtrack greats. His score here is never less than amazing; its sweeping, emotional arcs easily compensate for the absence of any real surf rock tunes on the soundtrack.

All of the DVD editions feature a spectacular, colourful anamorphic transfer; this is a film to be experienced in its original Panavision dimensions or not at all. The surround audio is surprisingly aggressive and dimensional for a non-Dolby title; the crashing waves and music often make striking use of split channel effects. The U.S., U.K. and Australian DVDs include the theatrical trailer and a terrific Milius commentary (in which he discusses surf culture and the film's literary and cinematic influences, among many other topics), but the U.K. and Aussie discs also include an impressive (but all too short) 14-minute featurette, "Capturing the Swell", produced by Blue Underground. Milius appears again to offer a more linear account of the film and a few amusing anecdotes, the best involving a point-sharing agreement between himself, George Lucas, and Steven Spielberg that some parties have lived to regret.

BITTER MOON

B

Colour, 1992, 139m. / Directed by Roman Polanski / Starring Peter Coyote, Hugh Grant, Emmanuelle Seigner, Kristin Scott Thomas / New Line (US R1 NTSC), Arrow (UK R0 PAL) / WS (1.85:1) (16:9), Manga (Spain R2 PAL) / WS (1.85:1) / DD2.0

Trust Roman Polanski to take the tired erotic thriller subgenre and turn it into something absolutely wonderful. In this twisted variation on his *Knife in the Water* scenario, Polanski casts his own wife, Emmanuelle Seigner, as damaged temptress Mimi, who meets vacationing but troubled couple Nigel (a pre-stardom Hugh Grant) and Fiona (a pre-dye job Kristin Scott Thomas). Also aboard is Mimi's wheelchair-bound husband, Oscar (Peter Coyote), who delights in regaling Nigel with the story of his and Mimi's highly unorthodox courtship while Fiona's either traipsing around the ship or tranquilizing herself for seasickness. In flashback we learn how psychological cruelty and sexual gamesmanship turned the relationship between Mimi and Oscar from a loving Parisian fling into dark, dangerous warfare of the soul. Nigel shows more than a passing interest in taking Mimi to bed after Oscar's stories are through, but a few unexpected surprises are await him before the cruise is over.

A hysterical black comedy and vicious send-up of the sexy shockers popular at the time, *Bitter Moon* ruthlessly dispenses with clichés right and left as it explores the emotional complexities of each character. Fiona might seem to be getting short shrift through most of the running time, but Thomas's portrayal pays off with a crackerjack finale that casts an entirely new light on everything that preceded it. Bearing an alarming and probably intentional resemblance to John Cassavetes in *Rosemary's Baby* (in terms of both appearance and mannerisms), Coyote steals all of his scenes as he transforms from a naïve, boyish American in Paris with writer's block into a creepy, sneering lech with bad teeth. And then there's the often derided Seigner, giving unquestionably her best performance, who can be either heartbreakingly vulnerable or damn frightening when she's dressed in nothing but a black leather slicker and wielding a razor. Ideally suited for repeated viewings, *Bitter Moon* is a wonderfully decadent treat of a film whose lengthy running time flies by with surprising ease. Add to that some gorgeous photography and a haunting score by Vangelis (tragically still unreleased), and you've got a kinky cult item in the making.

Bitter Moon first surfaced on DVD in Spain courtesy of a mediocre presentation, which appeared to be culled from the U.S. laserdisc. Much more satisfying is the New Line DVD, which features a new anamorphic transfer and a spacious surround soundtrack that makes full use of the electronic score and constantly splashing waves. The added clarity also makes some of the nudity even more explicit than it was in the theatre; we'll leave you celebrity skin fanatics to your own devices to figure out the details on that one. Extras are minimal, consisting of the U.S. theatrical trailer (which blows far too many plot points late in the film, so approach with caution), as well as trailers for Polanski's *Death and the Maiden*, Werner Herzog's *Invincible*, *The Invisible Circus*, and *The Sleeping Dictionary*. The cover art (which tries to pass this off as a romantic comedy) is absolutely atrocious. A 2009 edition in the U.K. from Arrow corrects the dearth of extras elsewhere by adding a solid commentary track with producer Timothy Burrill and writer John Brownjohn as well as a video interview with Coyote.

BLACK DRAGONS

B&W, 1942, 62m. / Directed by William Nigh / Starring Bela Lugosi, Clayton Moore, Joan Barclay / Alpha (US R1 NTSC), Elstree Hill (UK R0 PAL)

Even in the company of Monogram's other 1940s B horrors, *Black Dragons* is undeniably demented. Admittedly, it consists mostly of drab actors in drabber suits standing about in underfurnished rooms chatting, but the stream-of-consciousness plot manages to combine post-Pearl Harbor scare-mongering and a glowering Bela Lugosi as a plastic surgeon/serial killer with a sideline in hypnosis and perhaps ventriloquism. In its fervour to depict the Japanese as fiendishly treacherous, the film makes America seem like a nation of clueless losers whose highest-ranking industrialists and dignitaries are all fifth columnists working to wreck the war effort. And what's worse, the fanatics aren't caught by the plodding, clueless official investigators (4F-looking Clayton Moore and frankly plain Joan Barclay) but by a vengeful Nazi renegade. If the world had been produced by Sam Katzman, the Allies would have lost the War.

Given the lunatic premise, the movie is still a dullish plod. The mysterious Monsieur Colomb (aka Dr. Melcher) doesn't even try to conceal his guilt, as if Lugosi knew he was the whole show and was determined to give value for money by lacing the most banal lines ("Who knows in this crazy world") with odd double meanings and rather strangely making time with the undercover heroine. The murders drag on for nearly an hour, with victims left clutching giveaway Japanese daggers, until a hooded figure is introduced to narrate an explanatory flashback that William Nigh directs a little better than the bulk of the film and then reveals a hideously deformed face (or Monogram approximation

of the same). Even Lugosi laughs at that. Rubbish, of course – but much-loved.

Alpha Video's print of this PD title is splicy, scratchy, and given to flaring whites and sounds as if there's a constant rainstorm on the soundtrack. As usual, the sleeve pointlessly lists a longer running time of 69 minutes. The later U.K. version is only a marginal step up as it's at least more competently encoded.

– KN

BLACK ROSE MANSION

Colour, 1969, 90m. / Directed by Kinji Fukasaku / Starring Akihiro Maruyama, Eitarô Ozawa, Masakazu Tamura / Chimera/ American Cinematheque (US R1 NTSC), Tartan (UK R0 PAL) / WS (2.35:1) (16:9)

Often relegated to the sidelines of the entertainment industry, female impersonators sometimes find that big break to catapult them into the spotlight. Divine and RuPaul spring to mind, of course, but other countries got there much earlier and cultivated this fascinating form of celebrity before most Americans even knew what "drag" meant. Case in point: Akihiro Maruyama, the glamorous star of *Black Lizard* and *Black Rose Mansion*, a pair of campy cult items from the late Kinji Fukasaku. In these vehicles designed to exploit the star's unearthly charisma, Maruyama segues from femme fatale to comic foil with bewitching ease, making these curios even more beguiling today now that audiences have learned to swallow postmodern winking without any protest. Darker and much more Gothic than its companion film, *Black Rose Mansion* centres entirely around Ryuko (Maruyama), a nightclub performer whose signature black rose pops up in every performance. Wealthy Kyohei (*The H-Man*'s Eitarô Ozawa)

arranges a gathering at his private mansion to celebrate his beloved star, but trouble begins when a strange variety of other men turn up and vie for Ryuko's affections. Among them are the millionaire's son, Wataru (Masakazu Tamura), and more than a few criminals; amidst hallucinatory flashbacks and fantasies, the mansion soon turns into a feeding ground of lust and murder.

The fractured structure of *Black Rose Mansion* extends from the plot itself to the editing of the film, rife with freeze frames, colour tinting, distorted lens effects, and bizarre mood lighting. As usual Fukasaku manipulates the scope image extremely well; a genre-hopping chameleon best known for directing *The Green Slime*, *Virus*, the Japanese segments of *Tora! Tora! Tora!*, a slew of outrageous yakuza films, and the incredible cult favourite *Battle Royale*, Fukasaku rarely bores his audience even when the story might not quite make sense. Such is the case here, as style overtakes any kind of rational behaviour on the part of the characters. When two men wind up wriggling bloody on the floor and clutching at the white fabric of Ryuko's dress, it's just another soapy chapter in this strange time capsule from an era long gone.

As with other entries in the Chimera/American Cinematheque/Vitagraph Japanese series, *Black Rose Mansion* has been treated to a splendid special edition. The anamorphic transfer looks quite colourful and rich, with dead-on black levels (vital for this film in particular) and clear mono audio. The theatrical trailer is included, along with five other trailers from the collection, as well as a spotlight on the Egyptian Theater (home of the American Cinematheque) and a 20-minute video interview with Fukasaku, who sheds light on the production's history, recalls working with his gender-sliding star, explains the role (or lack thereof) of writer Yukio Mishima in the two films, and recalls the Japanese studio system of the late 1960s. A subsequent 2008 release from Tartan as part of their "Fukasaku Collection" boxed

set (along with *Blackmail Is My Life* and *If You Were Young: Rage*) features a somewhat problematic PAL conversion from the same NTSC master and eschews all of the previous extras. Perhaps better enjoyed by seasoned veterans of Japanese cult cinema than newcomers, *Black Rose Mansion* is an often confounding but eye-catching oddity rescued from oblivion; share it with someone you want to corrupt.

BLACK SCORPION

Colour, 1995, 92m. / Directed by Jonathan Winfrey / Starring Joan Severance, Bruce Abbott, Casey Siemaszko, Garrett Morris / New Concorde, Buena Vista (US R1 NTSC)

In the wake of her father's murder, undercover Angel City cop Darcy Walker (Joan Severance) is kicked off the force amidst accusations of police brutality. Frustrated by what the law won't allow her to do by day, she resolves to do without a badge beneath the shadow of night. Lacing herself into a skin-tight, black vinyl leotard and concealing her identity beneath a mask, as Black Scorpion she takes to the streets to deal out justice in her own way. Intolerant of vigilantism, the police chief assigns detective Michael Russo (Bruce Abbott) the task of tracking down and arresting her. But when a madman known as The Breathtaker (Casey Siemaszko) sabotages the City's new ionization towers, intent on asphyxiating the entire populace, it looks as if Black Scorpion is the only one equipped to stop him.

Kicking off like a million and one other renegade cop thrillers, thirty minutes into *Black Scorpion* things take on a distinctly comic book flavour and, after the introduction of robotic supervillain The Breathtaker, it never looks back. What Craig J. Nevius's script lacks in originality is compensated for with robust dialogue, relatively interesting characters and oodles of panache. Director Jonathan Winfrey, who has an evident fondness for automobile mayhem – which he stages regularly and efficiently – defies his budget by piling on the eye candy and keeping the action moving at a super-swift gallop. Winfrey, who puts in a fleeting onscreen appearance, would return along with his leading lady for the following year's inferior sequel. Drawing parallels with *Batman*, both the '60s TV show and the latter-day films, is unavoidable; aside from the facets that slap an "adults only" label on what might otherwise be family entertainment (i.e. bad language, nudity and bursts of violent bloodshed), *Black Scorpion* is the female answer to the *Dark Knight* in every respect, right down to the plot to gas innocent citizens, plucked straight out of Tim Burton's first Bat-movie. Kevin Kiner – who scored mainly for TV and whose work includes *Superboy*, *The Invisible Man* and Joan Severance's *Love Boat: The Next Wave* – brings to the party some classy, dramatic and occasionally haunting themes. Severance is excellent in the title role, if perhaps a little older than the character she's meant to be playing; offering up a nicely rounded Plain Jane performance as Darcy Walker, when she climbs into the slinky Black Scorpion outfit she's hotter than a jalapeno pepper in a sauna. Charismatic Garrett Morris provides the comic relief as Argyle, the dodgy car dealer who soups up Walker's orange Corvette with gadgetry that would turn 007 green with envy; it can morph into a sleek black munitions-laden Porsche at the flick of a switch. A lovable rogue who bends his rules to help a cop because "the streets aren't even safe for criminals any more", Argyle quickly becomes the consummate scene-stealer of the piece. Abbott (*Re-Animator*) is in top form as resident tough cop/love interest, while Siemaszko (*Storm of the Century*) makes for a suitably over the top baddie. Interestingly enough, six years later when *Black Scorpion* became a short-lived TV series (with Michelle Lintel donning the PVC outfit

for the title role), none other than Adam West stepped into the shoes of The Breathtaker for several episodes, with Frank "The Riddler" Gorshin also dropping in for a piece of the action. In the annals of countless costumed crime fighting capers there have been few with quite the same allure as *Black Scorpion*. Seek her out and see for yourself.

New Concorde's Region 1 DVD (repurposed almost identically by Buena Vista when they temporarily got the rights to Corman's later catalog) is a nice, if unassuming little package, comprising a clean, 24-chapter punctuated, full screen print of the film, along with a smattering of supplemental treats. Although a trailer for the movie itself is regrettably absent, a small selection of previews for other New Concorde product does include the trailer for *Black Scorpion II: Aftershock*. Joan Severance contributes quite heavily to the disc, submitting an 18-minute on-camera retrospective (in which it's apparent that she has fond memories of the film) and a zesty commentary, although two-thirds of the way through the movie she runs out of things to say, bids the listener happy viewing and, rather disappointingly, takes her leave.
-TG

BLACK SCORPION II: AFTERSHOCK

Colour, 1996, 85m. / Directed by Jonathan Winfrey / Starring Joan Severance, Whip Hubley, Stoney Jackson, Sherrie Rose, Jeannie Millar, Garrett Morris, Matt Roe, Stephen Lee, Terri J. Vaughn, Laura Harring / New Concorde (US R1 NTSC)

Darcy Walker, aka Black Scorpion (Joan Severance), returns to continue her nocturnal skirmishes with villainy on the streets of Angel City. Dealing with a crime wave instigated by the insane Gangster Prankster (Stoney Jackson) is trouble enough, but when former scientist gone bad Dr. Ursula Undershaft (Sherrie Rose) – now known to the world as Aftershock – sets about mercilessly obliterating the City using a machine with immense destructive capabilities, Scorpion's ingenuity is put to the ultimate test.

In the wake of such an interesting start the previous year, how could things go so wrong with this sequel? Same director, same star, but woefully dismal results. Like a walking advertisement for products from a bondage catalogue, Joan Severance returns as Black Scorpion for a follow-up to 1995's original that plunders new dimensions of substandard. Director Jonathan Winfrey and scripter Craig Nevius slip up badly by focusing too much on the everyday trials and tribulations of Darcy Walker to the detriment of her Black Scorpion alter ego, who gets less screen time than she did in the original. What on earth were they thinking? Severance in her shiny PVC outfit thwarting diablerie is surely what people are tuning in for. The camp quotient is intensified with an even more garish wardrobe, asinine dialogue, idiotic sound effects and fight sequences that are TV's *Batman* in all but the "Zap" and "Pow" bubble captioning. As before there's an infusion of adults only material – Jeannie Millar as Prankster sidekick Giggles removes her top for no other reason than to add some bare flesh to the brew, plus there's an explosively grisly decapitation – but combined with cartoonish characters and infantile humour that even children would deem childish the outcome leaves you wondering just what age group *Black Scorpion II: Aftershock* was supposed to appeal to. In spite of the fact there's actually some semblance of plot lurking beneath all the witlessness, it's gossamer thin and for the most part it meanders aimlessly.

Whip Hubley supplants Bruce Abbott as Russo, the apple of Walker's eye, but there's an injurious dearth of chemistry between them. The new villains on the block – Stoney Jackson as Harvey Dent/Joker hybrid Gangster Prankster, and Sherrie Rose's Aftershock – are more irritating than intimidating. Severance (who's always watchable) apart, there are plenty of hang-overs from the first film to hand, including Garrett Morris as Scorpion's lone confidante cum mechanic Argyle, Matt Roe as crooked Mayor Artie Worth, Stephen Lee's brusque Captain Strickland and Terri J. Vaughn as Walker's sassy girlfriend Tender Lovin'. Director Winfrey again does a Hitchcock (this time as a cop) while Laura Harring (*Mulholland Dr.*) is the Mayor's dumb secretary. Although Kevin Kiner's score is a worthy addendum to his original opus, the rock heavy soundtrack (most of it co-penned by actor Stoney Jackson) is obnoxious. As a stand-alone effort Winfrey might just have got away with it. But coming after the frothy *Black Scorpion*, this sequel is a bitter pill to swallow and delivered a rabbit punch to the prospect of a continuing film series before it even had the chance to gather momentum. Amazingly however, the seed of an idea to bring the character to TV was sewn in Roger Corman's mind and in 2001 Michelle Lintel took on the role for a short-lived series of adventures.

New Concorde's DVD release, much like its predecessor, includes a small collection of extra materials. Joan Severance's input is regrettably absent this time round; since she is obviously quite proud of the original, it would have been interesting to hear her opinion of this abomination. The film itself is a fullscreen affair, divided by 24 chapter stops. The previews section duplicates the content of the earlier disc exactly, but this cost-cutting measure is compensated for by the inclusion of four TV spots for the show spawned by the movies, each highlighting a supervillain (Adam West's Breathtaker, Marty Kove's Firearm, Lisa Boyle's Medusa and Alison Armitage's Stunner). There's also a 21-minute documentary hosted by former Batman, Adam West. Entitled "The Making of *Black Scorpion*: Behind the Sting", it's a relatively fun peek behind the cameras, which unfortunately suffers from cheaply shot camcorder interviews and wildly disparate sound levels.

– TG

BLIND TARGET

Colour, 2000, 89m. / Directed by Jess Franco / Starring Rachel Sheppard, Oliver Dennis, Tatiana Cohen, Lina Romay, Linnea Quigley / Sub Rosa (US R1 NTSC) / DD2.0

Better known for his forays into sexual delirium and violence, Jess Franco cannot claim to be anyone's idea of an action director. However, he has veered towards the genre at times in such diverse films as *Angel of Death*, *Pick-Up Girls*, and *Dark Mission*, while occasionally staging a mean chase sequence in one of his *Most Dangerous Game* riffs like *The Perverse Countess* or *Tender Flesh*. His closest attempt to a legit action film, *Blind Target*, is one of his later period shot-on-video projects and, despite a slow and disorienting first act, offers a few wild moments to appease his followers while keeping unsuspecting babes 'n' bullets fans utterly baffled.

As part of a publicity tour, successful writer Maria Baltran (*Vampire Blues*'s Rachel Sheppard) returns to the South American country of San Hermoso, from which she fled as a young girl. Her latest work is a scathing indictment of the corrupt politics in her homeland, and no sooner does she arrive than mysterious threats are delivered at knifepoint from a gang of black-hooded secret police (whose female leader bears a very familiar, thick Spanish accent). Of course, that doesn't stop Maria from enjoying some lesbian lovin' in her hotel room with her best friend, Beatriz (Tatiana Cohen), who's promptly kidnapped for her

trouble. In a hotel bar Maria runs into two very different scream queens, Tora (Lina Romay) and TV personality Serena (Linnea Quigley); unfortunately it's not long before our heroine winds up bound naked to a table, getting poked and prodded by Tora before being blackmailed into assassinating an enemy of the San Hermoso dictator. Yep, with a rifle now forced into Maria's hands, Franco turns this into a kinky copy of *La femme Nikita*! Can the plucky novelist find a way out of committing cold-blooded murder? Will resourceful, kickboxing CIA agent Greg (Oliver Dennis) find her in time? Will Lina ever give a believable line reading? Watch and find out!

As with most of Franco's other "commercial" projects like *Faceless* and *Count Dracula*, this is one odd mongrel of a movie. While Franco peppers the beginning with a gratuitous towel-draped girl-on-girl encounter and some mild bloodshed, his trademark mania doesn't really kick in until the always-reliable Lina struts her stuff during the torture and blackmail sequences. From that point *Blind Target* is low rent, guilty fun, with a thoroughly ludicrous climax packed with awkward gunfire and flying feet. The hyperactive digital editing effects which cluttered some of his other recent work are thankfully kept in check here, but the sound editing is still touch and go at best; Sheppard's disorienting delivery in particular ranges from her almost indecipherable on-set voice to dubbed dialogue seemingly recorded by two different performers. Perhaps it's Franco's Buñuelian ploy to underscore the duality of Maria's personality... or maybe not.

As with other Franco video features, *Blind Target* looks good overall but is wholly dependent on the erratic nature of the format, which can be grainy or muddy at times. Daylight scenes are consistently clear; however, note that there isn't digital artefacting during those driving scenes – it's just dust on the camera lens. As usual Sub Rosa and One Shot have thrown in a bounty of extra goodies, including a clip from the dubbed Spanish version (Linnea's scene only), a "making of" featurette showing Franco at work, excised footage with commentary by producer Kevin Collins, and a stills gallery.

BLOOD CASTLE
(SCREAM OF THE DEMON LOVER)

Colour, 1970, 98m. / Directed by José Luis Merino / Starring Erna Schürer, Carlos Quiney, Agostina Belli / Retromedia (US R1 NTSC) / WS (1.85:1), Triton (US R0 NTSC)

Better known to late night television fanatics as the more lurid *Scream of the Demon Lover*, this by-the-numbers Gothic potboiler is a barely disguised rehash of Antonio Margheriti's splendid *Virgin of Nuremberg* with a few dashes of *Jane Eyre* thrown into the second act for good measure. A Spanish-Italian co-production, *Blood Castle* crams in plenty of spooky atmosphere, torture chamber nightmares, a Roger Corman-style climax with fistfights and a raging inferno, and a marauding, disfigured monster, but don't expect anything out of the ordinary for European horror fans.

Beautiful blonde Ivanna (*Strip Nude for Your Killer*'s Erna Schürer) arrives by carriage at the forbidding estate of Janos Dalmar (Carlos Quiney) to lend her biochemical aid to his recent experiments. The staff at the castle proves less than forthcoming with details about the Baron, who wanders around with large guard dogs and dodges the subject of the gruesome murders of local town girls. Meanwhile the maids scamper around in a variety of sexual shenanigans, and Ivanna suffers from nightmares in which a scarred visitor gropes her nightgown and ties her naked to a rack. As Ivanna and the Baron fall in love, she begins to suspect that perhaps he may not be the only man roaming around their home at night...

Perhaps due to its Spanish origins, the explicit horror content of *Blood Castle* is fairly low compared to its Italian brethren of the same period; the film runs considerably longer than average and seems padded with lots of extraneous dialogue and shots of characters wielding candelabra wandering down hallways. Director José Luis Merino (who re-teamed with Quiney for the more effectively paced *The Hanging Woman*) at least realizes he has a commercial project on his hands and sees that an actress loses her top every ten minutes or so to keep the audience's interest. (One of the lovely ladies includes '70s cheesecake starlet Agostina Belli, who went upmarket, sort of, with *Bluebeard*, *Revolver*, and *Profumo di donna*.)

Retromedia's DVD has been transferred from a fairly battered but colourful print, with black levels ranging from satisfactory to wildly unstable. At least it's vastly superior to the earlier DVD double feature from Triton, which paired this up (under the *Demon Lover* title in a hideous, almost colour-free transfer) with Mario Bava's *Hatchet for the Honeymoon*. Framing-wise the two DVDs are fairly similar; the Retromedia disc is barely windowboxed and skims off a little extraneous information from the top and bottom, while the full frame Triton transfer is slightly squeezed. Both contain nudity and mayhem shorn from other video versions, which ran as short as 76 minutes. The Retromedia disc includes a combo trailer (when New World paired this up with *The Velvet Vampire*) and solid liner notes by Mirek Lipinski.

THE BLOOD DRINKERS

Colour Tinted, 1966, 86m. / Directed by Gerardo De Leon / Starring Ronald Remy, Amalia Fuentes, Mary Walter, Eddie Fernandez, Eva Montes / Image (US R1 NTSC), Cinema Club (UK R2 PAL)

"Padre, my sister is a living corpse and she feeds on blood." Based on a Filipino comic strip and influenced by Universal horror films (especially *Son of Dracula*), this bizarrely-hued effort (aka *The Vampire People*) mixes many distinctive ideas and national quirks with its familiar vampire plotting. The flamboyant villain is Dr. Marco (Ronald Remy), a bald vampire who looks like a slimmed-down Colonel Kurtz and switches between a traditional Dracula-like cape-and-tailcoat ensemble and a succession of mod, pop-art outfits (cool wraparound shades, black polo-necks, a black kimono with white circles). At the end, the villain gets away clean – suggesting sequels were planned (maybe the comic was still running?) but Marco sadly didn't return in the same team's thematically-similar 1970 effort *Blood of the Vampires*. Arriving in a small, jungle-bounded community, Dr. Marco is accompanied by a doting vampire girl/masochist lover (he whips her and drinks from the weal raised on her arm), a snaggle-toothed hunchback minion (unusually, the good guy priest also has a deformed sidekick), a nasty dwarf and Basra the glowing-eyed bat (to whom he addresses several funny speeches). Marco wants to revive his comatose blonde beloved Katrina (Amalia Fuentes) and needs the heart of her dark-haired sister Cherito (also Fuentes) to manage the trick (sources vary as to the spelling and pronunciation of the girls' names). While working on his grand scheme, enlisting the aid of the twins' mother (Mary Walter), Marco is responsible for the usual vampire depredations, which stirs handsome good guy Victor (Eddie Fernandez) and a wise elderly priest-narrator to take countermeasures. Mixing ancient and modern – Marco's two-vehicle cortege consists of a horse-drawn hearse and a sleek black automobile – the film stresses the religious angle with a great deal of cross-wielding and praying but takes odd detours into science as Marco uses a whirring, flashing-light-studded blood transfusion machine to keep Katrina alive and the heroes employ flare-guns to harry the light-phobic vampires.

Perhaps too slowly-paced for its own good, with absurdities that tend to stay too long on screen like that bloody bobbing plastic bat, *The Blood Drinkers* remains a fascinating, eerie, romantic and perverse effort. Its most unusual gambit, prompted by budgetary and film stock access limitations, is its mix of lovely pastel-coloured footage with monochrome sequences that mostly use a rich blue or a cherry-crimson tint but sometimes blend like a Mario Bava lighting scheme. Full colour represents daylight normality or evening idyll (as when the heroine is being serenaded) and even Marco's bucolic fantasy of normal life with his revived sweetie. The tints stand for various nighttime moods: blue when the vampires are offscreen or quiescent; red when they are attacking or impassioned. For a cash-saving measure, it's carefully thought-out and this release even corrects processing errors in earlier versions by making sure all the tints are as director De Leon intended.

Image's DVD, first in its "Blood Collection", uses the original elements for a new, standard frame transfer. There's some very slight speckling, but the film looks better than it ever has. In common with the rest of the collection are a clutch of trailers, a non-specific but illuminating interview with filmmaker Eddie Romero (conducted by Pete Tombs) and a "rarely seen" *House of Terror* live horror show promo that can't count as rare any more. Specific to this release is the hour-long first part of a commentary by Samuel L. Sherman that stretches over the whole Blood Collection, covering his involvement with Hemisphere and Independent International Pictures rather than this film in particular. More interesting are twenty-five minutes of trims, outtakes, deleted scenes and alternative footage (presented silent): evidently, the original intention was to make more of the jealousy of Tanya (Eva Montes), Marco's long-suffering minion-lover, to the extent of having her try to stake Katrina, a set-up for her suicide when abandoned in the finished film. The U.K. disc, in Cinema Club's Cult Collection, uses the same great-looking transfer but its extras are limited to couple of trailers; come on, guys, would it have broken the bank at least to include the deleted scenes?

– KN

BLOOD HARVEST

Colour, 1985, 86m. / Directed by Bill Rebane / Starring Tiny Tim, Itonia Salochek, Ed Bevin, Lori Minnetti, Peter Krause, Frank Benson / BCI (US R1 NTSC) / WS (1.78:1) (16:9), Retromedia (US R1 NTSC)

 Jill Robinson (Itonia Salochek) returns from college to the small farming community of Winchester to discover that her home has been daubed with obscenities and her mother and father have disappeared. Rekindling a friendship with her childhood sweetheart Gary Dickinson (Ed Bevin), who lives with his retarded brother Mervyn (Tiny Tim) in a neighbouring property, Jill begins to suspect she's being watched. The local constabulary proves less than helpful in her plight. But she isn't imagining things. There's a killer on the prowl and he's obsessed with Jill...

A veteran of clunkers such as *Monster a-Go-Go* and *The Giant Spider Invasion*, Bill Rebane co-wrote and directed *Blood Harvest* in 1985, though it didn't see video distribution until 1987, and even then only sparsely. His final fabrication (to date), it's one of those movies that stretches ten

minutes worth of plot to almost an hour and a half and is too lazy to try to disguise the fact. There are numerous scenes where there's virtually nothing happening, and the thinly drawn heroine, Jill, behaves so irrationally as to beggar belief. After an initial show of concern over her missing parents she seems to forget about them, sweetly oblivious to the fact that everyone around her is being slain as she mooches aimlessly around the house or sits on her bed talking to a teddy bear. Compounding its problems, the bloodshed is far too modest when compared to similar offerings of the period; Lori Minnetti gets her hand pierced by an arrow before having her throat cut, while *Six Feet Under*'s Peter Krause is strung up and left to bleed out into a bucket like a slaughtered pig. It reads a lot nastier than it plays. Not only does our killer dispatch Jill's friends and family, he also has a nasty habit of breaking in while she's asleep, drugging her and then fondling or undressing her to snap a fistful of keepsake Polaroids. Despite a half-hearted effort to point the finger of suspicion at backward man-child Mervyn, it's patently obvious from the outset who the perpetrator is and seasoned slasher fans won't be even mildly surprised by his final unveiling.

This is movie making at its least inspired, made none the easier to swallow by poor performances all round, weak dialogue and mediocre cinematography. Yet for all its shortcomings it's more than worth catching for the only headlining dramatic performance by ukulele strumming Herbert Khaury – better known as Tiny Tim – whose deliriously falsetto '60s rendition of "Tiptoe Through the Tulips" still gets air play today. Much like famed uke-tickler George Formby before him, Tim looked like he'd taken a severe beating from the ugly stick, but possessed a warm sincerity and compelling charm that deservedly escorted him to the heights of stardom. *Blood Harvest*, however, is not among his most auspicious moments. He plays the aforementioned Mervyn, adopting the persona of The Marvellous Mervo, hiding behind creepy clown's greasepaint and given to unpredictable bursts of childlike behaviour for reasons that are never satisfactorily resolved. The singularly oddball Tim displays a complete inability to act but compensates for it with charisma by the bucketload and by trilling a couple of songs. To be fair, the dearth of acting prowess extends to the entire cast, who fail to scare up a convincing performance between them. Itonia Salochek is very attractive, but a hopeless actress. One wouldn't have been surprised to see her cropping up frequently in other films based solely on her physical attributes, but it wasn't to be and this represents her only known role. Ed Bevin proves mortifyingly talentless, and the less said about Frank Benson as the local sheriff the better. With no real redeeming qualities whatsoever, *Blood Harvest* is an embarrassment for all concerned. Which, in a fittingly skewed way, makes it a fiercely irresistible curio.

Some considerable effort appears to have gone into forging a worthwhile package for the Retromedia DVD release of the film. It's just a shame that the quality of the feature and the fact that it's cut (omitting much throat-slitting footage) undermine the good intentions of everyone involved. This platter delivers the director's cut (under Rebane's preferred – but insipidly routine – title *Nightmare*) in a full screen transfer punctuated by an insubstantial 7 chapter marks. The opening and closing credits sequences have been freshly generated specifically for this release. The movie starts with an apology for any audio and video imperfections caused by the age of the material (which was sourced from the director's own shabbily preserved video master), but this doesn't even begin to prepare you for the appalling quality of the print that follows. The film has always been hindered by amateurish production values. On VHS it barely got away with it, but the DVD platform only serves to heighten its imperfections, with faces often bleached out and conspicuously impaired sound. Then again, since these problems seem to have been inherent since day one, it's never going to get any better than this. In addition to the feature there's a messily constructed 15-minute documentary, "The Incredible Tiny Tim Sideshow", which treats the film with more reverence than it probably deserves. It includes an unrelated interview with Tim (circa 1985), retrospective cognizance from director Rebane (circa 2002) who confesses that the star had problems learning lines and so most of his material was improvised (he ain't kidding!), low grade behind the camera footage of the making of *Blood Harvest*, a performance of "Tiptoe Through the Tulips" by Tim (lifted from a 1992 children's TV show), and a large number of production stills. There's also a separate slideshow presentation of images which, by comparison, is positively stingy. For some reason Itonia Salochek is titles credited (and referred to by Rebane in the documentary) as Cari Salochek. The film later popped up completely uncut in BCI's "Crypt of Terrors" box set (alongside some unrelated Euro horrors including two versions of *Black Candles*, *Evil Eye*, and *Stigma*), in anamorphic widescreen to boot, but this was yanked out of circulation after a few weeks on the market and quickly became a hot collector's item. The cut, cruddy old *Nightmare* master was then trotted out by BCI as part of their "Psychotic Tendencies" four-film set (along with *Mole*, *Cut*, and *The Stranger*) but hardly seemed worth the trouble.

– TG

BLOOD OF FU MANCHU

Colour, 1968, 92m. / Directed by Jess Franco / Starring Christopher Lee, Richard Greene, Tsai Chin, Howard Marion-Crawford, Maria Rohm, Shirley Eaton / Blue Underground (US R0 NTSC), Optimum (UK R2 PAL) / WS (1.66:1) (16:9)

In competition with the growing Hammer Films franchise in the 1960s, producer Harry Alan Towers devised a series of Fu Manchu films starring Christopher Lee as the fiendish Asian genius who is determined to wreak havoc across the globe. Things started off well enough with Don Sharp's *The Face of Fu Manchu* and *The Brides of Fu Manchu*, then stepping down a gear with *The Vengeance of Fu Manchu*. However, things took a turn for the bizarre when Towers became aligned with Jess Franco for a brief but wonderful period in which the pair cranked out a series of lush, loopy spectacles including *Count Dracula*, *Eugenie*, *Venus in Furs*, *99 Women*, and *The Bloody Judge*. Usually regarded as the least of this collaboration are Franco's pair of Fu Manchu offerings, of which *Blood of Fu Manchu* was the first. Often screened in woefully abbreviated versions (with shoddy quality, to boot), the film is an amusing and often stylish diversion peppered with more than its share of perverse moments, all shot through with Franco's obvious affection for the cliffhanger tradition.

In a South American jungle, Fu Manchu and his equally nefarious daughter, Lin Tang (Tsai Chin), devise a plot to conquer the world. Ten women are injected with deadly poison that will kill anyone they kiss, so naturally the beauties are sent off on their deadly errands post haste. Fu Manchu's frequent nemesis, stuffy Nayland Smith (Richard Greene), falls prey first but simply goes blind for a little while. He tracks down the villain to his lair with the aid of Dr. Petrie (Howard Marion-Crawford), stopping along the way for some campfire mayhem involving a topless native girl. The two foes clash again in a battle to the almost-death, leaving Fu Manchu to once more warn the world that they will hear from him again.

Lifting its central "ten angels of death" gimmick straight from Ian Fleming's *On Her Majesty's Secret Service*, Franco's film is great fun but could have exploited the deadly kiss angle a bit more thoroughly. Fortunately he explored the possibilities with more perverse results a few years later with *The Demons*, but this film is certainly worth watching as an evolutionary step in the director's career. Filled with stylish lighting effects, the production makes good use of its limited means and comes off as a respectable entry in the cinematic history of Sax Rohmer's enduring antagonist. Unfortunately many people resent the film for its stream-of-consciousness plotting and, even worse, the fact that they were often duped into seeing it more than once; among its variant titles are *Against All Odds*, *Kiss and Kill*, *Fu Manchu and the Keys of Death*, and *Kiss of Death*, among many others. When Republic issued the film on U.S. video, fans were startled to see the rear sleeve adorned with a photo of a topless Maria Rohm being tortured; sadly, the actual scene was apparently never shot, or discarded, and has yet to turn up in a finished print. In any case, Blue Underground's DVD is a sight for sore eyes, restoring bits of excised footage including some nudity usually removed to make this more family-friendly. Image quality is spot-on from start to finish, and the English dialogue (the language in which it was shot) sounds just fine. Extras include "The Rise of Fu Manchu", an elaborate featurette containing interviews with Lee, Chin, and Towers (as well as a brief word from Shirley Eaton, whose footage from another Franco project was hijacked here). A trailer, photo and stills gallery (including the notorious Rohm imagery), bios, and liner notes round out the package. A later U.K. double feature from Optimum pairs this up with *Castle of Fu Manchu* without any extras, but it is incredibly cheap.

BLOOD OF THE VAMPIRES
(CURSE OF THE VAMPIRES)

Colour, 1970, 82m. / Directed by Gerardo De Leon / Starring Eddie Garcia, Amalia Fuentes, Romeo Vasquez, Mary Walter / Image (US R1 NTSC), Cinema Club (UK R2 PAL)

 Four years after *The Blood Drinkers*, director Gerardo De Leon (and female stars Amalia Fuentes and Mary Walter) returned to the vampire genre with this effort, originally released as *Curse of the Vampires* (or *Creatures of Evil*) and retitled on video to fit with Image's "Blood Collection". It lacks the comic strip elements and distinctive colour gimmicks of the earlier film, though De Leon again uses lighting changes to convey the encroachments of the vampires on normality. The plot is a blend of traditional bloodsucking and family soap: the veneration of the Virgin Mary used by the religious good guys against the vampires is paralleled by a tender feeling towards motherhood in general that paradoxically ensures the spread of the curse through the noble Escudero family.

Melting heroine Leonor (Walter) and her sleek, moustachioed brother Eduardo (Eddie Garcia) return to their family estate in a remote area to discover that their supposedly dead mother (Walter) is a vampire kept chained in the cellar by a patriarch who can't bring himself to destroy his wife (though he does regularly whip her). By the time the father does his duty and stakes the harridan, it's too late – she has bitten Eduardo and transformed him into a vampire. Escudero Senior dies of grief and Eduardo takes over the estate, his plans blighted only by a provision of the will insisting he burn down his hacienda. More trouble arises because Eduardo bites (and apparently rapes) a neighbour who becomes his smitten vampire minion, ramping up enmity between the monster and his girlfriend's brother Daniel (Romeo Vasquez), who happens to be in love with Leonor. Being transformed into a superhuman vampire still doesn't give Eduardo the stones to trounce upright Daniel in a fair fistfight, so the battered baddie reacts like many a cowboy heavy taken down by a good guy in a bar fight and sabotages the hero's carriage. The local priest forms the expected lynch mob and Leonor is visited by her lover's ghost, which sets up an ending that can only be construed as happy in that hero and heroine are reunited after death.

Mixing action with atmosphere, the film is slightly too square in its morality to be really engaging: the conflicted villain characters are far more interesting than the supposed good guys, and as usual the cross-wielding religious figure seems a bullying spoilsport. Quite a bit of the film, especially the sub-plot with Leonor and Daniel, is vintage melodrama, scored with syrupy strings and played with near-laughable earnestness. Also hard to take is the minstrel-show blackface make-up sported by the family servants Eduardo transforms into his minions. Nevertheless, the perverse, incestuous elements ("Eduardo, I'm your sister", pleads the heroine as the vampire struggles with unspeakable urges and is pestered by the harp-accompanied ghost) are provocative and, as in *The Blood Drinkers*, Walter is an unusual monster figure, a middle-aged bloodsucker who is alternately witchlike and pathetic.

Image's Blood Collection DVD offers a standard-frame transfer which has its fair share of white flecks but wonderfully preserves the colour scheme; De Leon is fond of tricks like lighting separate faces in shadow with different gels, and this release is the first to bring out his considered use of colour. Extras familiar from the series are a clutch of trailers, an Eddie Romero interview, some stills and the last 45 minutes of Sam Sherman's five-part (!) ego trip commentary (spread over the various releases in Image's collection) which delves deep into his own

career but barely mentions the film he is talking over except to promise ten minutes of fascinating outtakes (along with his own short student film) that aren't included in the final release. Given the choice, you're as well-off with the frills-free U.K. R2 "Cult Collection" release from Cinema Club that uses the same transfer. A substandard version was briefly released in the U.S. by Retromedia but quickly withdrawn due to legal considerations.
– KN

BLOOD OF THE VIRGINS

Colour, 1967, 73m. / Directed by Emilio Vieyra / Starring Ricardo Bauleo, Susana Beltran, Rolo Puente, Walter Kliche, Gloria Prat / Mondo Macabro (US R1 NTSC, UK R0 PAL)

 This reduces the horror movie formula almost to its essentials: it opens with a Gothic anecdote about a buxom blonde (Susana Beltran) forced into a marriage and bitten by the vampire she really loves, then has a striking animated credit sequence and launches into the Down Argentine Way equivalent of a sexploitation romp as a bunch of pretty young people cut loose while on a modelling assignment in an Andean ski resort (dancing topless on bars, etc.). The youngsters' car breaks down and they wind up in an old dark house where an undead Beltran lingers and her vampire lover starts licking his fangs at the sight of an almost-as-bosomy brunette (Gloria Prat). Though there are romantic and horrific elements, and a tacked-on police investigation to bring it up to feature length, not a lot happens beyond the striking of horror movie poses and girlie footage of the leads.

Referred to in the extras as Argentina's first vampire movie (though the documentary oddly also includes a clip from a 1952 item called *El vampiro negro*), this isn't quite as demented as Vieyra's *Placer sangriento* (aka *Feast of Flesh* or *The Deadly Organ*) or *La venganza del sexo* (*The Curious Dr. Humpp*), as if the filmmaker were trying hard to abide by genre rules he didn't quite understand. It has situations rather than plot elements, but is liberal with flesh and blood until a finish which stutters to a dead stop rather than wind anything up. Beltran and Prat are pouting presences with Russ Meyer silhouettes, but none of the male characters – including the regulation cloaked Latin vampire – can really compete.

Mondo Macabro's DVD is well up to the company's high standard. The standard frame transfer is gorgeous, with rich ruby reds (for the tinted shots of vampire gulls and spurting blood), sumptuous fleshtones (for the voluptuous cheesecake) and velvety black (for the shadows of the old dark house). The useful extras are an episode of MM's late-night TV series covering Argentinean exploitation (built around interviews with sprightly pioneer Vieyra and sexpot Isabel Sarli) and "Gauchos Go Gear", an essay by Pete Tombs on Vieyra's horror films in general and *Blood of the Virgins* in particular. The American edition tosses in a welcome sampler of Vieyra trailers as well.
– KN

BLOOD RELATIVES

Colour, 1978, 90m. / Directed by Claude Chabrol / Starring Donald Sutherland, Lisa Langlois, Aude Landry, Donald Pleasence, David Hemmings, Laurent Malet / Carlton (UK R2 PAL)

 Director Claude Chabrol's few English language thrillers often have a strange, otherworldly feel alien to his more familiar French suspense exercises; just check out *The Champagne*

Murders, Ten Days' Wonder, or this Canadian-lensed whodunit, adapted from one of mystery writer Ed McBain's popular 87th Precinct novels.

Donald Sutherland plays McBain's recurring investigator hero, Inspector Carella, who must solve a vicious sex crime involving the death of young Muriel (*The Nest*'s Lisa Langlois). Her cousin, Patricia (Aude Landry), was present at the attack and survived, albeit covered in blood. Her testimony leads Carella through an odd gallery of suspects, including recurring child molester Doniac (Donald Pleasence), well-to-do Armstrong (David Hemmings), and even Patricia's brother, Andrew (*Querelle*'s Laurent Malet). The young girl's unreliable account of the crime proves to be a major stumbling block as the suspects mount, but thanks to expert sleuthing, Carella finally reveals the shocking truth.

Visually stark and grimy, this bid for mainstream distribution from Chabrol never really took off but became a regular home video staple. It's too sleazy and gruesome for most murder mystery readers but not quite graphic enough for *giallo* fanatics; however, Chabrol addicts and strong-stomached thriller buffs will be more receptive. Sutherland plays his role very seriously but seems distracted at times; also, the decision to relate so much of the plot in flashback causes some major pacing problems in the second half, which are fortunately countered with a solid shock finale.

Carlton's budget-priced DVD, which was issued as part of their interesting "Silver Collection" looks a bit better than a VHS tape, but not by much; detail is soft and sometimes smeary, though black levels look acceptable. The mono audio is occasionally muffled, though all home video versions have sounded this way. Thankfully there are optional English subtitles, which help out during some of the quieter scenes.

BLOOD SIMPLE

Colour, 1983, 96m. / Directed by Joel Coen (& Ethan Coen, uncredited) / Starring John Getz, Frances McDormand, M. Emmet Walsh, Dan Hedaya / Universal (US R1 NTSC, UK R2 PAL), MGM (US R1 NTSC) / WS (1.85:1) (16:9) / DD 2.0

Most movie mysteries are told from the inside. We, the audience, along with a detective character, are confronted with baffling circumstances and gradually piece together the clues, finally learning the truth just as the hero or heroine does and walking away unscathed from the last-reel revelations. *Blood Simple*, the debut feature of the Coen Brothers, is not like that. For a change, we're in a privileged position, always knowing more than the characters we're following, understanding their wrong-headed thought processes, appreciating the ironies they miss, seeing where a slightly different action or assumption would have saved lives or led to happier endings.

Typical of the Coen approach is the handling of a traditional thriller gimmick (e.g., the finale of *Strangers on a Train*) of the incriminating item left at the scene of the crime, which forces the killer to return and imperil himself to cover up. Murderous private eye Loren Visser (M. Emmet Walsh) leaves his distinctive Man of the Year cigarette lighter under a clump of fresh-caught fish in the office where he has put a bullet into bar-owner Julian Marty (Dan Hedaya), and later assumes lovers Abby (Frances McDormand) and Ray (John Getz) know he is a killer because they have this vital clue. But the lighter remains unnoticed under the fish throughout the film, and Visser isn't even the killer, having left Marty wounded only for Ray to come along and, under the impression Abby has tried to do away with her husband, finish him off by

B

burying him alive. At every turn of this complex plot tangle, we know what's going on – but none of the characters ever get the big picture, except (perhaps) Visser on the point of death after he has been shot by Abby under the mistaken impression that he is her husband. "I'm not afraid of you, Marty", she says. Chortling, Visser responds. "Well, ma'am, if I see him, I'll sure give him the message."

The title, an expression the Coens found in the stories of hard-boiled writer Dashiell Hammett, refers to a state of mind whereby a person is so caught up in the need for violence – or sex, money, revenge, status – that he or she loses his or her wits and is destroyed. The setting is Texas, but not the wide-open state of numberless westerns. This is a world of dark, dark desert nights, where unlit roads cross empty spaces. Marty, proprietor of a bar named Neon Boots, has hired Visser to prove that his wife is an adulteress, though it's possible that it's only this paranoia that drives her to get together with dim-bulb bartender Ray. Humiliated when Abby breaks his "pussy finger" (more relevantly, his trigger finger) and walks out, Marty hires Visser to kill the lovers, but the PI opts for the lower-risk strategy of collecting the fee and shooting Marty. When Ray thinks Abby has shot her husband, he makes a botch of cleaning up the blood with his windbreaker and can't even bury the corpse without imperilling himself as the dying Marty points a gun out of his grave. An alleged theft, a doctored photograph in a safe, tensions between the lovers and suspicions that won't go away complicate an intricate but always clear pattern.

Less obviously comic than the Coens' subsequent films, this has a degree of beyond-black humour but is mostly a study of the way things always go wrong when people don't use their heads. "Who looks stupid now?" is an appropriate send-off line delivered by a murderer to a victim, as all the dumbness naturally leads to death. The last reel, with Abby attacked by a man she doesn't know for reasons she can't understand, is a great monster-and-the-girl face-off, as M. Emmet Walsh in a career-best performance as the sweaty thug in a yellow leisure suit and huge straw cowboy hat shoots holes through a wall to free his knife-pinned hand. It's a cruel picture, in which all four main characters get to be possible or actual murderers or murder victims and anyone is capable of doing the worst to anyone else. Later, in *Fargo*, the Brothers would add a humane, caring figure, promoting McDormand to detective, and set this murderous anthill in context; but here, at the beginning, they were more ruthless.

Universal's DVD isn't touted as a special edition, but Joel and Ethan Coen did overhaul the picture for re-release, allegedly trimming some very minor bits of business and, most importantly, digitally sprucing up the image. The anamorphic widescreen transfer looks a lot better than almost any other low- or even medium-budget picture of its vintage. It's especially important that the blacks be deep and the neon vibrant, and cinematographer Barry Sonnenfeld's work is showcased wonderfully. Given that the trims made in the 1983 release version for this redo are apparently as minimal as the shots of haircuts or salad included as "deleted scenes" on the DVD of *The Man Who Wasn't There*, it's a shame they weren't slipped in somewhere – though it's entirely possible that rather than cutting anything, the Coens just told people they did and simply fiddled with a few rough edits. The restoration is touted by a pompous, mock-introduction by "Mortimer Young" of "Forever Young Films", who talks about the sorry state of cinema in 1983 ("unfortunately, filmographic techniques were in their infancy"). The commentary track by "Kenneth Loring" is an extended put-on, perhaps written but certainly not read by a Coen; the dry Englishman blathers blandly throughout the film, spreading misinformation (identifying a real dog as an animatronic) and taking off on bizarre tangents. When Universal lost

the rights to the film, the same transfer was later ported over (minus the commentary and some of the other minor extras) and reissued by MGM, though the Universal disc can still be obtained second-hand fairly easily.
– KN

BLUE SUNSHINE

Colour, 1976, 89m. / Directed by Jeff Lieberman / Starring Zalman King, Richard Crystal, Robert Walden / Synapse (US R1 NTSC), Another World (Denmark R2 PAL) / WS (1.85:1) (16:9) / DD5.1

 Horror fans raised during the slasher glut of the '80s and afterwards can find adapting to the socially twisted terrors of the 1970s an uphill battle. The decade really kicked in with the 1973 domestic, commercialized terrors of *The Exorcist* before plunging into the dangerous territory of David Cronenberg's early works (specifically *Shivers*, *Rabid*, and *The Brood*) and Philip Kaufman's astonishing 1978 reinvention of *Invasion of the Body Snatchers*, films which pondered whether all of these psychoanalytic, hot-tubbing, free-wheeling, substance-abusing lifestyles might have some nasty consequences down the road. In real life they did, of course, as the early 1980s proved, and *Blue Sunshine* now feels prophetic in its depiction of a post-1960s culture ripping apart at the seams as it tries to dissolve back into normal, capitalist society. As a horror film there isn't much aggressive shock material on display; the unease of *Blue Sunshine* lies instead in its queasy sense of the mind and body breaking down without any control, all accompanied by a nerve-jangling score that sounds exactly like a musical nervous breakdown.

In an eerie opening montage, a group of young adults find their hair falling out and their behaviour becoming more aggressive and jittery. The first major warning sign comes at a small party out in the woods, where a crooning party clown, Frannie (played by Billy Crystal's brother, Richard), loses his wig to reveal a bald dome underneath, then promptly goes berserk and kills those around him by stuffing them in the fireplace. Good guy Jerry (future *Red Shoe Diaries* producer Zalman King) chases the lunatic into the road, where he's promptly run over by a truck, leaving Jerry with all of the blame. Now a man on the run, Jerry consults a friendly doctor (Robert Walden) and follows a trail of clues to track down a chain of potential murderers, all bred from a nasty batch of experimental LSD taken by Stanford college students years before. Jerry also learns that the man responsible for this chemically-induced madness might also be a prominent, respectable politician; even worse, the decade time bomb embedded in the drug means a whole slew of new killings are set to begin.

Director Jeff Lieberman apparently felt the urge to provide his own twist on various exploitation genres during his early career, starting with rampaging nature (worms, in his case, courtesy of *Squirm*) and continuing with this, a response to the drugsploitation films of the late '60s. He finished his drive-in trilogy five years later with the *Deliverance*-inspired wilderness terror outing, *Just Before Dawn*, before settling into more routine cable and home video fare. *Blue Sunshine* is arguably the slickest and certainly the strangest of the bunch, with bizarre tonal shifts and strange plot U-turns comparable only to Larry Cohen's *God Told Me To*. As usual King's acting ability ranges from mannequin-style passivity to shrieking overacting (no wonder he decided to move behind the camera), but the approach here is almost appropriate as the film builds to its fever-pitched, department store finale. The visuals of grimacing bald people running around with butcher knives and plunging off buildings offer some palpable chills,

B

and Lieberman throws in stylish flourishes like a discotheque attack sequence later aped in *Scream 2* of all things.

An early home video staple courtesy of Vestron, *Blue Sunshine* disappeared for several years (how appropriate) before resurfacing courtesy of Synapse's deluxe, digitally scrubbed edition. Taken from the best surviving 35mm print, the transfer looks quite nice overall, with rich colours and a faint sheen of film grain to remind you that this did indeed play movie houses. Scratches and scuffs have all been carefully removed, as demonstrated by a nice restoration demo piece on the DVD. The original mono mix is included, but those looking for some audio-related thrills will get a kick out of the 5.1 mix. Almost absurdly aggressive, this is demo material as all five speakers get a workout throughout most of the running time. Even the innocuous sound of a crackling fireplace is dramatically foregrounded in an early scene, bursting from the front speakers with unnerving impact. Lieberman contributes a number of extra features, beginning with an audio commentary in which he discusses with moderator Howard Berger the ins and outs of low budget shooting, the obstacles posed by the production, and the problems associated with putting multiple bald people on screen. An early Lieberman short film, "The Ringer", is a stylized parody of *Afterschool Special*-style alarmist educational films, complete with dizzying close-ups and stern monologues. Then he turns up again for "Lieberman on Lieberman", a half hour career overview in which he discusses everything from his big break to his most recent activities. The disc is rounded out with a stills gallery and the creepy theatrical trailer, which must have turned a few heads at the drive-ins. The first pressing of the release includes a second disc, the complete music score on CD, which is guaranteed to disrupt the happy mood at any party. Another World Entertainment issued a later PAL edition, which is basically identical to the US single disc (without the bonus music CD), but with subtitle options in Danish, Norwegian, Swedish and Finnish, plus an AWE trailershow and a 4-sided booklet written by Mikkel Svendstrup.

BODY DOUBLE

Colour, 1984, 114m. / Directed by Brian De Palma / Starring Craig Wasson, Melanie Griffith, Gregg Henry, Deborah Shelton, Dennis Franz, Barbara Crampton, Brinke Stevens / Columbia (US R1 NTSC) / WS (1.85:1) (16:9) / DD5.1, Columbia (UK R0 PAL) / WS (1.85:1) (16:9) / DD2.0

With his love life and career in tatters, struggling actor Jake Scully (Craig Wasson) is pleased to be offered the chance to stand in as housesitter in a luxury home currently being looked after by casual acquaintance Sam Bouchard (Gregg Henry). Before leaving on business, Bouchard introduces Scully to the fringe benefits: Every night in a nearby house a beautiful woman performs a striptease – and Bouchard just happens to have a telescope to hand. Over the next few evenings Scully becomes captivated by the woman, eventually engineering an awkward meeting at which he learns her name: Gloria Revelle (Deborah Shelton). While watching her house that evening Scully witnesses a break-in by an Indian with pockmarked skin and gold-capped teeth. He's unable to intervene in time and the intruder subsequently murders Gloria. Viewed with suspicion by police for his voyeuristic preoccupation with Gloria, Scully begins to suspect that there's a lot more to the murder that it first seemed and decides to investigate for himself. The trail leads him into the world of adult movie making, an encounter with lithe artiste

Holly Body (Melanie Griffith), and an impending date with death.

Body Double was released to the clamour of press reports about the potential outrage it could spur among women's groups. This of course was nothing new for writer/director Brian De Palma, whose *Dressed to Kill* travelled the same road four years earlier. The primary target of indignation this time was the grisly set piece in which Shelton is perforated by an electric drill, every bit as nasty as the straight-razor slaying of Angie Dickinson in *Dressed to Kill*. Shot from behind the killer, the drill descends on Shelton from between his legs like a whirling, razor-sharp, death-dealing phallus; jaws hit floors and accusations of misogyny were fired off in all directions. De Palma probably couldn't have been more pleased, the ire of the outspoken minority generating the sort of publicity you can't buy, though a generally lukewarm critical reception was less helpful.

The director's oft-remarked upon appreciation for the films of Alfred Hitchcock has never been more apparent than here; devout Hitch aficionados will be none too happy at the assertion that gratuitous fare such as this should be likened to the Master's work, but there's no escaping the fact that in essence this movie is pure Hitchcock. De Palma borrows from themes in *Rear Window* (the nocturnal neighbour-watching) and *Vertigo* (Scully suffers from debilitating attacks of claustrophobia), and if *Frenzy* was any evidence of Hitch's appetite for pushing the boundaries, then *Body Double* is precisely the sort of film he'd have been making had he been shooting in the more liberated climate of the mid-1980s.

Although Craig Wasson doesn't immediately strike one as an ideal leading man, and hardly the first choice for a film such as this, he's actually perfect as the ineffectual wimp for whom everything goes wrong. He's the unlikely hero; he could be you, me, any one of us. You chuckle as he starts to get flustered watching the striptease – after all, you're watching too, and if you've got blood in your veins you're probably feeling the same. Only when Scully's actions take a less savoury path do you find yourself disassociating with him; watching a woman foolish enough to dance about naked in a brightly lit room with no curtains is one thing, but sneaking a peek at her trying on panties in a boutique changing room and then, not very surreptitiously, pocketing the discarded pair she's been wearing departs voyeur-ville and crosses the county line into sleazeball-city. Regardless, Wasson rides out superbly the chain of events that sees him conquering his own insecurities and emerging from the ordeal with job reinstated and a new girlfriend in tow. That said, the verity of Scully being the everyman, so carefully established by De Palma and co-scripter Robert J. Avrech, is almost eradicated in a ridiculous scene where Shelton, grateful to him for retrieving her purse from a thief, allows him to embrace and half undress her in public. Not so much of an everyday occurrence methinks.

Griffith is adorable as flaky porn starlet Holly Body, and her staccato-paced, deadpan delivery to a bemused Scully of the kinks she refuses to perform is hugely comical: "I do not do animal acts. I do not do S&M or any variation of that particular bent. No watersports either..." (This dialogue was cut from the original British release by humourless BBFC meanies.) Deborah Shelton, familiar to TV soap viewers for her stint on *Dallas*, is extremely easy on the eye, but her (dubbed) performance is adequate at best. To remark too much upon Gregg Henry would spoil a few neat plot twists; suffice to say he's excellent for the short time he's on screen. Dennis Franz – formerly in De Palma's *Dressed to Kill* and *Blow Out* – is on fine form as the uptight director of Scully's latest degrading film, *Vampire's Kiss*. Watch out too for cameos by cult movie queens Barbara

Crampton as Scully's adulterous girlfriend and Brinke Stevens in a lesbian interlude in the trailer for faux porn flick *Holly Does Hollywood* (which Scully nips out and buys from an all night sale at Tower Records).

Overlooking the slightly weak denouement, some dodgy back-projection – budgetary constraints, or another homage to Hitch? – and an out of place sequence on a porno movie set with band Frankie Goes to Hollywood performing their hit "Relax", *Body Double* is essential De Palma. He even throws in an amusing codicil as the end credits scroll, epitomizing the stimulus for the movie, which was conceived on the set of *Dressed to Kill* while employing a double for Angie Dickinson's shower scene. Accompanied by a typically intoxicating Pino Donaggio score, *Body Double* pushed the limits of R-rating acceptability as far as was possible for its era. And though it may all taste like fast food compared to the more refined piquancy of *Carrie* or *The Untouchables*, even the most ardent gastronome craves a double cheeseburger with extra relish now and again.

Columbia's first R1 platter was one of their earliest releases on the DVD format and bears little in the way of bonus goodies, in fact only the seductive teaser trailer (with John Barry's music from *Body Heat*) has been included. The disc itself is a double-sider, offering the uncut film in both 1.85:1 theatrical ratio and full screen formats, with a 28-chapter split. The sound is in unremarkable English 2-channel Dolby Surround or French, with subtitling in the same two languages. The subsequent special edition ditches the nice teaser trailer, alas, but upgrades the transfer considerably with a crisper, fresher-looking facelift from hi-def, plus a solid Laurent Bouzareau documentary (chopped into little featurettes, as usual for union regulations) with De Palma, Griffith, Henry, Franz, and Shelton talking about the film from its inception to its rocky theatrical release.

– TG

LE BOUCHER

Colour, 1969, 88m. / Directed by Claude Chabrol / Starring Jean Yanne, Stéphane Audran / Artedis (France R2 PAL), Pathfinder (US R1 NTSC), Arrow (UK R0 PAL) / WS (1.66:1) (16:9)

Schoolteacher Hélène (played by Stéphane Audran) lives a quiet if not quite fulfilled existence In a remote French village, whilst recovering from a nasty break up. During a wedding she meets the local butcher, Poupal (Jean Yanne), who has returned from fifteen years of military service. This pair of psychologically wounded souls forms an immediate connection despite their intellectual and social differences. Meanwhile a series of brutal murders causes shocks in the countryside, including one gruesome discovery during a picnic with the schoolchildren. Hélène begins to suspect that her new friend may be the one responsible for the carnage, leading to a suspenseful finale when she's trapped at home in the middle of the night.

One of director Claude Chabrol's most well known and widely acclaimed films, *Le boucher* looks better and better with each passing year. Though low on traditional suspense mechanisms (no elaborate chases or brutal murder set pieces here), it's a searing experience all the same due to a pair of exceptional lead performances, a wonderfully uneasy music score, and a haunting final act featuring some of the director's most innovative visual concepts. The opening credits over Cro-Magnon paintings quickly establish the story's tension between society and man's irrepressible bestial nature, but surprisingly it also turns into a deeply affecting love story between two people who deserve better than the miserable hands they've been dealt. For those seeking an ideal introduction to Chabrol, look no further.

The French DVD of *Le boucher* pairs the film with Chabrol's *La femme infidèle* (*The Unfaithful Wife*), while the U.S. disc is a single feature. Both transfers look very similar; the film's colour scheme is intentionally subdued, filled with greys, golds and browns (and occasional splashes of red), but the anamorphic transfer looks fine. The American edition suffers slightly in comparison due to some PAL-conversion anomalies (occasional streaking during fast movement, some clogging during darker scenes) but overall looks quite watchable and pleasing. The French disc includes a reprocessed surround track ("Arkamys Sound Process", according to the packaging), which sounds surprisingly good, while the U.S. disc is in mono. Both feature optional English subtitles, while the U.S. disc also contains English and Spanish dubbed audio. In terms of extras Pathfinder's release easily trumps the no-frills French version, as it includes the French trailer (no subs), a stills gallery, bios for Chabrol and the leads, and an audio commentary by screenwriters and Chabrol fans Howard Rodman and Terry Curtis Fox, both of whom offer good insights into the character development and the film's place within the director's impressive body of work. A later U.K. release from Arrow in 2004 goes back to PAL again for a better visual presentation but has no extras; it's also included in their eight-film Chabrol box set.

BOY MEETS GIRL

Colour, 1994, 89m. / Directed by Ray Brady / Starring Tim Poole, Danielle Sanderson, Margot Steinberg / Unearthed (US R1 NTSC), Boudicca (UK R2 PAL)

 Hiding under this generic title is one of the nastier British films from the post-Video Nasty era, the inaugural effort from indie filmmaker Ray Brady, whose subsequent work like *Love Life* and

Kiss Kiss Bang Bang is certainly quirky but not remotely as vicious. A sort of Jacobean revenge drama with all the motivation sapped out of it, this stripped-down torture tale begins with randy Tevin (Tim Poole) hooking up for the evening with Anne Marie (Margot Steinberg), only for him to pass out watching porn films at her apartment before they can consummate their one-night tryst. Next thing he knows, he wakes up in his skivvies and tied to a dentist's chair, with Anne Marie and her cohort, Julia (Danielle Sanderson), informing him that he's simply the latest in a line of men broken at the hands of these two women, who intend to undercut and destroy the male psyche and body with every blow captured on video. Gradually Tevin's considerable transgressions come to the surface under pressure, while the women subject him to an outlandish array of horrors involving a microwave, a cigarette chamber, maggots, and amateur surgery.

Not terribly explicit in the traditional sense, *Boy Meets Girl* doesn't even try to compete with entrail-laden geek shows like the *Guinea Pig* series. Instead the focus is more on a progressive sequence of psychological terrors, with the characters interacting in a series of complex debates about gender, violence and society as Tevin's physical and mental resources are stripped away one by one. Despite the obviously limited budget, it's shot with all the elegant veneer of a Peter Greenaway film; the horrific, candlelit climax is almost seductive in its imagery but shattering in its implications. The snarky intertitles used to comment on the action come off like a twisted nod to Woody Allen, which would be appropriate under the circumstances, and the skilful manipulation of both film and video footage is handled in a smooth, professional manner that sidesteps the gimmickry usually found in such exercises

Not surprisingly, *Boy Meets Girl* was received with less than open arms by the British censors after its limited theatrical showings and was prohibited from a video release for years. The eventual DVD goes a long way to putting this film in context as a deliberate shot fired at the BBFC, with a number of acts (sexual assault, mutilation, etc.) specifically designed to confront the hard and fast rules concerning gender-related violence. In this respect Brady's feature-length commentary is an essential listen (after viewing the film normally, of course) as he proves to be an articulate, thoughtful guide through this moral minefield. Not surprisingly, the BBFC has caved in considerably since this film's release; it would make a perfect co-feature with the similar *Audition*, which was passed uncut and became a critical darling. Video and audio quality on the DVD are adequate but obviously limited to the original source material, which is deliberately scrappy at times. Other extras include a stills gallery and an interesting comparison between rehearsal footage and the finished product for a quartet of scenes.

THE BRAIN EATERS

B&W, 1958, 61m. / Directed by Bruno VeSota / Starring Edwin Nelson, Jack Hill, Leonard Nimoy / Direct Video (UK R2 PAL)

 Among the most marginal invasions of the 1950s, this microbudget quickie was thrown together by Bruno VeSota and Edwin Nelson – actors who had appeared in enough creature features to think they could do as well themselves. An unauthorised adaptation of Robert A. Heinlein's novel *The Puppet Masters*, which would get a more elaborate and official film version four decades later, it uses narration to paper over cracks in the story and is lackadaisical when it comes to minor things like giving characters proper introductions or explaining how the heroes make so many correct assumptions about the parasite creatures.

A giant metal cone appears in a rural area and scientist Dr. Kettering (Nelson) erects scaffolding to study the apparent spaceship (it turns out that the monsters come from underground rather than another planet) while Washington sends in bullying politician Walter K. Powers (Jack Hill) who keeps gruffly insisting on things and stressing his middle initial. It's a shame that the parasites are so feeble (pipe-cleaner antennae attached to fur offcuts) and so much action unfolds in *précis* (even a fight scene has a voice-over explanation) since Heinlein's *Body Snatchers* premise is workable. The creatures attach themselves to the backs of human hosts and take over (rather than eat) their brains, sensibly co-opting the town Mayor and cops first, cutting off the community from the outside (as in *Invasion of the Body Snatchers*, they get the telephone switchboard operators early on). VeSota's direction is intermittently effective, using James Whale-style skewed angles to work up unease and making early use of the subjective camera as parasites creep towards victims (incidentally keeping bad effects offscreen). The zombified hosts are creepy, dazed by their take-over, staggering into gunfire, with writhings under their shirt collars. Oddest in the cast is a white-bearded, long-haired human collaborator ("we have learned patience in two hundred million years") played by a young Leonard Nimoy (billed as Nemoy) in old-age make-up.

Too brief to be dull, it's one of those films that seems unfinished – as if the budget ran out before vital sequences could be shot. Direct Video's DVD shares its extras (trailers, an audio lecture) with the rest of the company's "Samuel Z. Arkoff Collection". The transfer looks like a straight port from a video master and isn't quite broadcast standard, though it has solid black and white contrasts and is probably as adequate as the film deserves.

– KN

THE BRIDE AND THE BEAST

B&W, 1958, 78m. / Directed by Adrian Weiss / Starring Charlotte Austin, Lance Fuller / VCI (US R1 NTSC) / WS (1.78:1) (16:9), Retromedia (US R0 NTSC)

For years critics argued about the popular auteur theory, which cites a strong director as the primary author of a film – its true cinematic voice, as it were. Sure, directors like Truffaut, De Palma, Scorsese, Chaplin, Welles, and Hitchcock are often used as proof, but then on the other side of the coin we have Ed Wood Jr., whose undeniable stamp appears on both his films as director and his works as a screenwriter for hire. For those in doubt, check out such celluloid atrocities as *The Love Feast*, *One Million AC/DC*, *Orgy of the Dead*, or this little number, all of which were penned by Wood but directed by other men whose artistic instincts were obviously swallowed whole by Eddie's peculiar obsessions.

Hopelessly dull Dan (Lance Fuller) and his clueless new bride, Laura (Charlotte Austin), arrive at hubby's sprawling estate where he keeps a pet gorilla, Spanky, who greets the new lady of the house by peeking up her skirt and pawing her dress. Naturally Dan responds by shooting the poor fellow dead. Soon Laura's having strange dreams involving rampant jungle stock footage and the worship of gorillas, and through hypnosis, it turns out in a past life she was once an ape queen. Dan's less than thrilled with the prospect of his wife being groped by someone else's hairy paws, especially when they're attached to a monkey suit, but Laura finds the tug of nature too strong to resist... especially when they head back out to the jungle (or at least a backlot facsimile), where all hell breaks loose.

While most monster movies of the period still remained coy by fading away as the damsel in distress was carried off, *The Bride and the Beast* makes few attempts to disguise what's really on the frisky gorillas' minds. Unbelievably kinky for its vintage, this one probably slipped by the censors thanks to the script's loopy distractions like hypnosis, jittery natives, and goofy costumes, all of which make the bestiality a bit more palatable for matinee audiences. While more than two decades passed before *Humanoids from the Deep* finally showed the monsters going all the way, Wood's script still packs a twisted wallop if you're really paying attention. And who would've thought decades later Nagisa Oshima would remake this film as *Max mon amour*?

Retromedia's transfer appears to be lifted from an old one-inch master someone had lying around from the early video days; while the print itself is free from damage, resolution is soft and hazy for the most part with weak contrasts. It's still a doozy of a movie, though; until a glossy restoration comes along, this is at least a viewable option. The mono audio is a bit on the murky side, but at least you can make out the catchy jungle-lounge score by Les Baxter (which was later recycled and adapted on some of his albums). The disc comes with a handful of extras, including a spicier theatrical trailer, a stills gallery, and three godawful video shorts revolving around David "The Rock" Nelson: a video interview, "Mummy A.D.", and "The Man from Plan 9", all of them negligible. The package is rounded out with "Beach Blanket Bloodbath", a rough clip from Retromedia maven Fred Olen Ray featuring *Famous Monsters* legend Forrest J. Ackerman. Also available from VCI as a 2007 reissue paired up with *The White Gorilla* (both matted to 16:9) with a commentary track by monster movie expert Tom Weaver alongside Austin, Bob Burns, and Trustin "Slick Slavin" Howard, as well as trailers, cast bios, and surviving footage from 1927's serial *Perils of the Jungle*.

BRIDES OF BLOOD

Colour, 1968, 97m. / Directed by Gerardo De Leon and Eddie Romero / Starring John Ashley, Kent Taylor, Beverly Hills [Powers], Eva Darren, Mario Montenegro / Image, Alpha (US R1 NTSC), Cinema Club (UK R2 PAL)

Second (after the dour *Terror Is a Man* aka *Blood Creature*) of the loosely-connected Blood Island quartet of Filipino horrors, *Brides of Blood* was followed by *The Mad Doctor of Blood Island* and *Beast of Blood*. On his obligatory commentary track, U.S. distributor Sam Sherman owns up that he was the one who insisted on the current title, overruling the original *Brides of Blood Island* (he lost out on *Mad Doctor*, but ensured there'd be no *Beast of Blood Island*). This grindhouse/drive-in chestnut has also been released as *Blood Brides* (for an all-"blood something" bill and on U.K. video) and *Island of Living Horror* (for TV markets that wouldn't broadcast anything with 'blood' in the title). The film arrives on DVD as the second instalment of Sherman's "Blood Collection", which brackets the three colour Blood Island pictures with a brace of Filipino vampire movies from director Gerardo De Leon and the American-made offshoot *Brain of Blood* (which never, even tentatively, was called *Brain of Blood Island*). Under any title, it's a guilty pleasure: a ridiculous 1930s-style jungle horror picture with chanting "natives" sacrificing maidens to "the Evil One", a radioactive mutant out of the 1950s (it bears more than a passing resemblance to the infamous killer tree of *From Hell It Came*) and some extreme-for-1968 sex and gore.

Scientist Kent Taylor, with dyed hair and moustache, visits Blood Island along with his blonde sexpot wife (Beverly Hills, aka Beverly Powers) and youthful volunteer Ashley, to assess the after-effects of nearby A-bomb tests, which entail strange specimens among the local fauna (a horned nasty butterfly) and fauna (lots of strangling creepers). While John Ashley falls for a sarong-filling local lass (Eva Darren), Hills fails to get a rise out of her aged husband and is smitten with slick-haired, virile-seeming, young-looking-for-his-years landowner Esteban Powers (Mario Montenegro). Of course, Esteban – who lives in a hacienda staffed by pygmies who can barely reach the tables they are supposed to wait on – has been genetically scrambled, periodically transforming into the shambling, fang-faced, neckless thing who "satisfies himself" by rending topless native girls limb from limb. It takes a long time for anyone to work out who the guilty party is, whereupon an elaborate if hokey Wolf Man-style transformation sequence prompts a brisk run-around that sees some major characters ripped up and yields some sort of an ending. It's nonsense, of course, and the first hour is draggy as bad actors recite worse dialogue; but the finish is at least lively as it serves up serial-style thrills with a modicum of sleaze.

Image's standard frame DVD uses a print that is in surprisingly good shape – certainly an improvement on many releases and re-releases of variously-titled versions that habitually used elements that look as if they've been dragged across the floor of every projection booth in the mid-West. The extras are familiar from the rest of the Blood Collection; one of Sherman's hour-long, marginally relevant commentaries, an interview with co-director Eddie Romero (who obviously prefers his war films) and a batch of entertaining trailers. Specific to this title are a Beverly Hills pin-up gallery and a silly promo spot hawking "genuine imitations of wedding and engagement rings worth $500" handed out to unmarried women who attend screenings. The U.K. release has the same transfer but none of the extras except the trailer, while the budget reissue from Alpha in the U.S. features the same extras with significantly worse compression on the feature itself. – KN

THE BRIDES WORE BLOOD

Colour, 1972, 84m. / Directed by: Robert R. Favorite / Starring Dolores Heiser, Chuck Faulkner, Paul Everett, Bob Letizia / Retromedia (US R1 NTSC)

With the help of dubious female fortune teller Madam Von Kirst, rich old eccentric Carlos De Lorca (Paul Everett, sporting bushy eyebrows that put both Fuad Ramses and Dennis Healey to shame) lures a quartet of young women to his Florida mansion in an attempt to cure his nephew Juan (Chuck Faulkner) of a malediction, the "De Lorca curse", hanging over them. The idea is to get one of the girls pregnant, which will break the cycle of inherited vampirism. Needless to say, things don't work out too smoothly along the way... Old man De Lorca's household comes over like a low rent redux of the Addams Family, with a skulking mute butler called Perro (Bob Letizia), and a scab-faced hooded ghoul prowling the basement, not to mention Juan's unhealthy predilections. Soon several of the women have fallen victim to Juan's bloodlust, one is walking around with plastic fangs bulging from her gob, and the one survivor, Yvonne (Dolores Heiser), is locked up in solitary confinement as her belly swells with its unwanted occupant. Mucho bloodshed results in this Florida-shot shocker, right up to the genuinely unsettling twist ending.

Hardly anyone seems to have a kind word to say about this grisly obscurity (which is ignored totally by most reference books), but *The Brides Wore Blood* (great title!) ain't that bad. It's refreshing to watch a film packed with good old fashioned gore effects and no computer generated graphics to be seen anywhere. Then again Florida is a long way from L.A., a good thing too in this case. Indeed the acting is largely poor (but not as bad as some reviewers would have it), but so what? This film was designed to play at drive-ins as a bottom-of-the-bill filler, not win Oscars, and it's better than most H.G. Lewis or Andy Milligan flicks (not a difficult achievement). Plenty of gloopy poster paint gore is spilled, with stake-impalements, throat-gashings and a machete in the head. Parts of the plot recall the (better) Spanish film *The Dracula Saga*, but the ultra-gory ending, with a pregnant woman impaling her distended belly with a shard of broken glass, apes an oft-censored scene from David Durston's demented *I Drink Your Blood*. There's a dime-store re-run of the final moments of Terence Fisher's Hammer *Dracula*, complete with neat meltdown effects, too! People with a dread of having injections will flee the room during the protracted, close-up shots of a needle being pushed into an arm vein, blood being drawn and then re-injected... it's almost pornographic in its detail. All the music seems to be stock library cues, including one very long excerpt that some viewers will recognise from *Night of the Living Dead*! Derivative, nasty, sick and a little boring in places, this is also rich with that great early '70s ambience which cannot be faked now and which leaves one pining for more and more with each inane Hollywood abortion foisted on its audience.

Another cheapo release from Fred Olen Ray's Retromedia company (and more fun than any of his own films), this full-frame DVD looks really nice for most of the time, though it's obviously just been lifted from a grainy old video master. Extras are nonexistent, not even a trailer! We could do without the naff intro by some dork in a cloak and topper calling himself "Son of Ghoul", who spends most of his slot humiliating his dwarf sidekick by pouring toothpaste and mouthwash into the little fella's mouth... when he's not fluffing his lines that is. Despite this lapse, the DVD is still recommended for those with a hunger for low-budget '70s schlock. Also available as a subsequent Retromedia double feature with *Mark of the Witch*.

– NB

BROTHER (BRAT)

Colour, 1997, 96m. / Directed by Aleksei Balabanov / Starring Sergei Bodrov Jr., Viktor Sukhorukov, Svetlana Pismichenko, Mariya Zhukova, Yuri Kuznetsov, Vyacheslav Butusov / Tartan (UK R0 PAL), Kino (US R1 NTSC) / WS (1.78:1) (16:9), Ruscico (US R1 NTSC) / WS (1.66:1) / DD2.0

The American gangster movie, from *The Public Enemy* through *King of New York*, has always been as much a portrait of its time as an action-character piece. *Brother* sees post-Soviet Russian cinema pulling the same gambit, using the trajectory of a hit man's career to explore 1990s St. Petersburg, a city that hasn't yet got used to not being Leningrad but is a-buzz with criminal, entrepreneurial and media activity. Baby-faced Danila (Sergei Bodrov Jr.), a veteran of the Chechen conflict who claims he spent his military service at a desk job, drifts to "Peter" and follows older brother Viktor (Viktor Sukhorukov) into the underworld. An apparent innocent whose most prized possession is a walkman on which he constantly plays the music of slightly naff Russian rock band Nautilus (by now Russian kids prefer American disco techno, which Danila despises), Danila is also a cool, professional killer. Aleksei Balabanov shows preparations for a hit in fetishist detail, as Danila modifies household commodities into weaponry, and suggests that the protagonist's total cool is also a deadness of soul that will eventually make him into a monster. Viktor is already totally corrupt, committing the ultimate transgression of betraying his brother – for which Danila shockingly forgives him at the shrug of a climax. All the characters are slightly too emblematic of modern Russian types: a leather-jacketed good time girl (Mariya Zhukova) who hustles for drugs and cash in McDonald's; a female tram driver (Svetlana Pismichenko) who becomes Danila's girlfriend but ultimately prefers to stay with an abusive husband; a philosophical tramp-trader of German descent (Yuri Kuznetsov).

The most interesting aspect of Danila's self-contained personality is a strain of patriotism that must once have been formed by Young Pioneer communism and is on the point of turning into Russian nationalism: he values Nautilus over "Don't Have Sex with Your Ex" because they sing in Russian and have a musical idiom rooted in Russian culture; at a rave, he smilingly harangues an "American" (not realising the man is French) about how his country will soon collapse too (in the sequel, Danila heads for Chicago). He values blood ties and loyalties in a way that sits ill with the brutally cynical cross-and-double-cross world of feuding criminal gangs; a strange, weirdly effective moment has him abandon a tense situation in which he is supposed to menace some shady characters because his idol (Vyacheslav Butusov, who plays himself and provided the music score) comes to the door asking for directions to a party in the same block of flats, whereupon Danila crashes the gathering of musical folk and is distracted by a visit to a different world as the situation downstairs spirals out of control.

Tartan's DVD is an excellent presentation of an interesting film; it has a Russian-language soundtrack with optional English subtitles, and the letterboxed transfer reproduces faithfully the sepia-orange-brown tones of the film (the colours are so muted video releases seem to be tinted monochrome). The extras are notes from David Parkinson, a music video, the trailer and a "world cinema trailer reel". The sleeve promises an interview with Bodrov and a trailer for *Brat 2*, but they seem to be missing in action. The same transfer was later issued in the U.S. from Kino, while the first (discontinued) NTSC version from Ruscico features a non-anamorphic transfer with optional English subtitles and a music video.
– KN

B

THE BROTHERHOOD
Colour, 2000, 85m. / Directed by David DeCoteau / Starring Nathan Watkins [Samuel Page], Josh Hammond, Bradley Stryker, Elizabeth Burderman / DEJ Productions (US R1 NTSC), Liberation (US R1 NTSC) / WS (2.35:1) / DD2.0

THE BROTHERHOOD II: YOUNG WARLOCKS
Colour, 2001, 81m. / Directed by David DeCoteau / Starring Sean Faris, Stacey Scowley, Forrest Cochran / DEJ Productions (US R1 NTSC) / WS (2.35:1) / DD2.0

THE BROTHERHOOD III: YOUNG DEMONS
Colour, 2002, 82m. / Directed by David DeCoteau / Starring Kristopher Turner, Paul Andrich / DEJ Productions (US R1 NTSC) / WS (2.35:1) / DD2.0

THE FRIGHTENING
Colour, 2001, 86m. / Directed by David DeCoteau / Starring Matt Twining, James Foley, Brinke Stevens / DEJ Productions (US R1 NTSC) / WS (2.35:1) / DD2.0, Prism (UK R2 PAL)

While Hollywood studios cashed in on the quickly diminishing *Scream* craze, prolific B-movie maestro David DeCoteau, the man behind such cable favourites as *Creepozoids* and *Dr. Alien*, rode the teen horror wave in a quite unexpected fashion with a quartet of home video cult favourites which quickly found an audience, though perhaps not the one originally intended. While the "hot, young line-up" ad art looks like your average Dimension Films horror knockoff, these are peculiar puppies indeed and guaranteed to live on in the pantheon of off-kilter cinema.

A vampire film more by suggestion than action, *The Brotherhood* tosses in some riffs on the old Dorian Gray story and sets it all at a sunny college campus. Newbie Chris (soap actor Samuel Page, acting here as "Nathan Watkins") winds up sharing a dorm room with twitchy Dan (Josh Hammond) but catches the eye of frat boy Devon (Bradley Stryker), who tries to lure him into going Greek. Looking like refugees from an Abercrombie & Fitch photo shoot, the frat boys make Chris feel welcome but have darker designs in their nasty, beer-guzzling hearts; namely, they're a bunch of immortal bloodsuckers who need to find new blood and new bodies keep going through the centuries. Meanwhile pretty coed Megan (Elizabeth Burderman) and Dan try to uncover the mysteries of this infernal youth order, while Devon initiates Chris with one of the more perverse three-way scenes in horror history. While most teen horror efforts (at least in the '80s, not the neutered '90s) focused on young women running around in their undies or nothing at all, *The Brotherhood* turns the formula on its head by stripping all the guys to their white boxer briefs for the last third of the film instead. It's a fairly amusing conceit actually and makes the film seem a lot more perverse than it really is; the actual gore content is kept to a minimum and there's no nudity per se. It's still demented enough to keep an adventurous horror fan's attention, however, and it looks and sounds great. Acting is less impressive, thanks mainly to the stilted script and wafer-thin characters, but sometimes you can't have everything.

A sequel in name and underwear only, *The Brotherhood II: Young Warlocks* hops over to an upmarket private academy where John (Sean Faris) suffers daily torment from a gang of preppy bullies, who are apparently jealous of the attentions given to him by pretty Mary (Stacey Scowley). During a nocturnal swimming pool bash, a strange buffed outsider, Luc (Forrest Cochran), offers John and two of his buddies a chance at untold power by joining an ancient sect of warlocks, who cast black magic in their skivvies and walk around the campus wearing black shades. Thanks to a more intricate plot and slightly improved acting, this follow-up is a generally more confident piece of work, while the characters are better defined and have more complex motivations than the previous film's *Lost Boys*-style plotting. The blood quotient is also upped, thankfully, and the atmosphere actually gets moderately creepy from time to time thanks to some surprisingly accomplished camerawork. Despite the numbering of the titles, newcomers may want to start out with this one instead; it's arguably the best of the series and will probably appeal to fans of *Buffy the Vampire Slayer*, too.

So, from vampires and warlocks we then move to the much messier *The Brotherhood III: Young Demons*, a sort of soft-focus slasher film spiced up with would-be supernatural elements. A group of teens breaks into their school for some weekly game-playing in which they assume roles and act them out, with one of them romping around in a medieval knight suit. They run up and down dark hallways a lot. Much fog ensues. Meanwhile Lex (Kristopher Turner) surveys it all from his library headquarters, and eventually the nitwits summon up genuine forces of darkness from a book of spells. Or do they...? Unfortunately, with this outing DeCoteau decided to go artsy by filming almost the entire film at dutch angles, with the camera slowly swaying

back and forth. Grab some Dramamine; you're gonna need it. While the previous two films were unrated but fairly tame in content, this one somehow squeaked by with a PG-13 despite a killer who seems to force (offscreen) oral sex on his victims. There's also a laughable shower scene that must be seen to be believed, and it all ends with an anti-climax that should have most patrons hurling their remotes at the TV.

A more appropriate third instalment for the series would have been *The Frightening*, paired up as a DVD double feature with *The Brotherhood III*. This amusing high school yarn begins with a single mom (the always watchable Brinke Stevens) bringing her teen son, Corey (Matt Twining), to a new town after a tragic mishap at his old school (involving wrestling, believe it or not). However, something's amiss at the new school. Students are dying in a horribly sadistic fashion, and a mysterious clique of teens appears to have its eye on Corey. Released the same year as the markedly similar but far less entertaining *Soul Survivors* (itself a thinly disguised teen rip-off of *The Sixth Sense*), this sole film in the batch to bear a legitimate R rating is the most traditional horror venture but shares the ogling sensibility of the first two *Brotherhood* films. The exaggerated, colourful bloodshed is fairly strong for a teen market title these days, and as with the other movies, it's all shot extremely well and moves along nicely. Don't expect any dense narrative layering or emotionally sensitive direction; it's pure popcorn fare and gets the job done well enough.

Shot in Los Angeles and Canada, these inaugural efforts for DeCoteau's film company, Rapid Hearts, look and sound considerably more impressive than his previous horror work. From the sleek widescreen compositions to the thunderous surround mixes, they should keep home video tech buffs happy. While the insert for the first *Brotherhood* disc states all these titles were anamorphically shot at 2.35:1, the framing looks a little more complicated than that. The first two titles were released in bleary-looking, full frame editions, with weak colours and distracting cropping in almost every shot. Borderline unwatchable, they at least indicate the films were shot in some variation of Super 35, with the actual 35mm negative shot somewhere around 1.85:1 but framed for scope presentation, as demonstrated by the ample dead space usually visible at the bottom of the frame. The double feature discs, all framed at 2.35:1, benefit from more satisfying compositions, which add substantially to the sides but lose that extraneous vertical information. Ditto for the second pairing of *The Brotherhood III* and *The Frightening*, both of which are graced with the scope presentation lacking on the VHS and stand-alone DVD releases.

Ah, and then there are the extras. DeCoteau provides commentary for all four films and is joined on the first by Bradley Stryker. While all are entertaining and worthwhile, the dual commentary is the best of the bunch as the two riff off each other throughout the film. DeCoteau tries to downplay the homoeroticism angle, not too convincingly, by arguing that he simply wanted to provide a novel twist on the usual horror formula. True enough, but anyone who's seen his wacko softcore work like *Petticoat Planet* and particularly *Naked Instinct* should know that he's always been one to give a little something to every segment of his audience. Each title contains its own trailers and photo galleries, while the second disc includes a healthier dose of goodies including *Brotherhood III* cast auditions and behind-the-scenes footage (most of it raw but fairly interesting; the former consists of cast members reading out lines from *The Frightening*, since the movie didn't yet have a finished script at the time). *The Frightening* only includes a lengthy, silent raw footage excerpt from the first film's memorable *ménage a trois*, with DeCoteau providing commentary again. The first Brotherhood film was subsequently

reissued with the same transfer by Liberation, who also distribute DeCoteau's more recent fare including a string of wild Edgar Allan Poe "reimaginings". *The Frightening* was released as a fullscreen bare bones edition in the U.K. by Prism.

BRUTES AND SAVAGES

Colour, 1977, 107m. / Directed by Arthur Davis / Starring Arthur Davis, Richard Johnson (narrator) / Synapse (US R1 NTSC)

 As most sleaze fans know, the filmmakers of Italy and America have done more than their share of imitating each other since the days of neorealism; however, despite their worldwide success, Italy's unique Mondo, nunsploitation, cannibal, and Nazi-porn innovations remained largely confined to Europe throughout the 1970s. One oddball exception is the American *Brutes and Savages*, an absolutely ridiculous *Mondo Cane* knockoff complete with a disco-inflected score by the previous hit film's composer, Riz "More" Ortolani.

The film's director and "star", Arthur Davis, takes the audience on a whirlwind and highly dubious tour through the world's "primitive" jungles, where natives apparently spend their time putting on face paint, carrying around spears, hunting animals, and engaging in various sexual rituals. Some of the atrocity footage is hilarious in its ineptitude, such as one native falling prey to a group of alligators that leave floating limbs bobbing in the water. Unfortunately, the animal-on-animal gore appears to be completely real and coldly staged for the camera; bunnies, armadillos, and snakes fall prey to bigger predators, though the nastiest highlight comes when a big jungle cat is attacked by gators in what appears to be a real life, violent feeding frenzy. Ah, and let's not forget the ritualistic, native llama sacrifice, which is up there with the turtle scene from *Cannibal Holocaust* on the unwatchable scale. Fortunately Davis had the sense to end his film with the most ludicrous bit, which is best experienced with no warning beforehand; let's just say that if you thought Anchor Bay's *Mountain of the Cannibal God* restoration was over the top...

Too addle-brained and sloppy to even be considered harmfully racist, *Brutes and Savages* trades in all the Mondo conventions without a single clue as to what makes them work. That's part of its lurid charm, of course, as the film lurches from one vignette to the next with no rhyme or reason. Look, it's natives scampering up and down a riverbank! Ah, now it's time for erotic sculpture! Oh no, here comes a hungry eagle! Oops, now it's time for some graphic brain surgery! As if that weren't odd enough, the whole enterprise is narrated by a hopefully well-paid and obviously unbilled Richard Johnson (*The Haunting*), who turned up shortly thereafter in Lucio Fulci's *Zombie*. For better or worse, you've never seen or heard anything like it... and of course, it comes fully endorsed by the Institute for Primitive Cultures.

As much as one can fault the film, no quibbles can be had with Synapse's DVD. The original 1.33:1 aspect ratio is maintained with a bit of windowboxing on the sides, which will most likely not be visible depending on the overscan settings on one's TV. Image quality is superb, with rich, film-like colours and very crisp detail; it's highly doubtful the theatrical prints circulated by Aquarius looked even remotely this good. As an added bonus, this transfer from the original negative is sourced from a longer cut (labelled *Uncivilized*) complete with 15 minutes of additional footage; this will come as a nice surprise for owners of the long discontinued MPI VHS edition. Unfortunately that also means more llama mayhem, so consider yourself warned. (And whatever you do, don't watch it on a double bill with *The Emperor's New Groove*.) Extras include an Arthur Davis "diary" containing many extracts from a *Brutes and Savages* tie-in book and excellent, no-punches-pulled liner notes by Chris Pagialli.

BULLDOG DRUMMOND ESCAPES

B&W, 1937, 67m. / Directed by James Hogan / Starring Ray Milland, Heather Angel, Porter Hall, Sir Guy Standing, Reginald Denny, E.E. Clive

BULLDOG DRUMMOND'S SECRET POLICE

B&W, 1939, 54m. / Directed by James Hogan / Starring John Howard, Heather Angel, H.B. Warner, Leo G. Carroll, Reginald Denny, E.E. Clive / Image (US R1 NTSC), Classic Entertainment (UK R0 PAL)

None of the film adaptations present Sapper's two-fisted hero Captain Hugh Drummond (aka "Bulldog") as the anti-Semitic upper-class thug of the novels, opting instead to make him a debonair, usually pencil-moustached gentleman adventurer with a knack for getting into "scrapes". Image's double-feature disc bills two installments from a series of Drummonds put out by Paramount in the 1930s. Though different stars (Ray Milland, John Howard) take the lead and the key supporting character of Inspector Nielsen of Scotland Yard is played by Sir Guy Standing and H.B. Warner (John Barrymore played Nielsen in between these films), some key cast members are held over: Heather Angel as the heroine who becomes engaged to Drummond at the end of the first film and (continuing a running joke of the series) just fails to marry him in the second feature, Reginald Denny as Drummond's slapstick silly-ass pal Algy Longworth (annoying comic relief) and the droll E.E. Clive as Drummond's Jeeves-like resourceful manservant.

Bulldog Drummond Escapes is a brisk attempt at reintroducing the character in a B context. It's not quite a remake of the Ronald Colman *Bulldog Drummond*, in that it assumes the hero is an established sleuth and has his key sidekicks in place, but it does replay the fateful meeting between imperiled heroine and her valiant rescuer, with the reliably scurvy Porter Hall aptly filling the role of "bearded scoundrel". Milland's 'tache-free reading of the role involves a great many teeth-bared grins, but the picture moves like a rocket and it has a nice sense of its own absurdity.

Strangely, the late-in-the-series *Bulldog Drummond's Secret Police* (a meaningless title) is even more fun. On the eve of his much-delayed marriage, Drummond opens up his family manor just as a cold-blooded killer (Leo G. Carroll) shows up disguised as the new butler, and an eccentric professor blathers about a Royal Stuart treasure concealed from Cromwell in a maze of tunnels under the house. An unusual touch is a dream sequence mingling a slapstick bungled wedding with flashbacks to earlier adventures, but the real thrills come when the secret passageways are opened up and Drummond and pals chase the villain and the abducted heroine through impressive cobwebbed sets, with a fine staging of the traditional lowering-ceiling-of-spikes trap. Carroll, a butler whose guilt is established early, is a fine, semi-maniacal killer and Howard's Drummond a more genuinely likeable sort than Milland's.

Those used to seeing 1930s B thrillers in the appalling state offered by most DVD and video distributors of such material will be pleasantly surprised at Image's crisp transfers of broadcast-quality prints. Neither of these pictures is anything more than pulp fun, but they look suitably shadowed and sinister. The first film in the set was later issued as part of a different Drummond package (along with *Bulldog Drummond's Bride* and *Bulldog Drummond Comes Back*) from the UK's Classic Entertainment label.

– KN

BURIAL GROUND: THE NIGHTS OF TERROR

Colour, 1980, 85m. / Directed by Andrea Bianchi / Starring Karin Well, Gianluigi Chirizzi, Mariangela Giordano / Shriek Show (US R1 NTSC) / WS (1.85:1) (16:9), VIPCO (UK R2 PAL), Italian Shock (Holland R2 PAL) / WS (1.55:1)

Released under a bewildering number of titles but shot as *Le notte del terrore*, this is the most minimally-plotted of the early 1980s rash of Italian *morti viventi* movies. In an isolated region, a wild-haired professor somehow awakes the Etruscan dead; a small party of friends turn up at the academic's house for a weekend break and are gruesomely murdered by shambling, clay-faced, entrail-fondling, snaggle-toothed zombies. Some of the freshly killed return to eat their friends and relations (including one bit of incestuous nipple-biting that remains the film's most memorable moment), and a nearby community of monks are also converted into monsters, showing an unusual streak of cunning by doing their best to seem normal until looked at cowl-on. Of course, this may have more to do with setting up a shock effect than suggesting a flicker of intelligence in the zombies.

Essentially mean-spirited nonsense, this is one of the few horror movies that really is structured like a porno movie with atrocities substituted for hardcore action. After a sketchy premise and the shuffling onscreen of a group of minimally-detailed characters, the only thing the film has on its mind is mayhem. The zombies, with ridiculously large teeth and bulbous potato heads, don't look like the monsters in any of the films being imitated (though they do echo de Ossorio's Templars in some scenes) but act in the expected Fulci-via-Romero manner, stumbling slowly towards victims who could easily run away, invincible unless their heads are blown off or battered in, and occasionally prone to catching fire. The human characters have little to distinguish them, though horror diva Mariangela Giordano and her strange-looking son (a tiny adult playing a child) work up an odd, smothering relationship that is all build-up for the mammary mutilation punchline. The script is haphazard at best, Andrea Bianchi's direction functional, the pacing lead-footed and the grue looks like splatters of red paint over butcher's leavings. Many of its highlights are cribbed, like a face-to-window impalement modelled on the eye-puncturing from *Zombi 2*, and the enigmatic final caption gets more laughs than shudders thanks to misspellings in the English version ("the profecy of the black spider"). But if you've watched your discs of *Nightmare City* and *Hell of the Living Dead* so often you can recite the dialogue back at the screen you'll want to own this too. However, the back cover claim that this edition "is sure to attract a new legion of horror-crazed fans and solidify the film's reputation as the next *Rocky Horror Picture Show*" is just desperate.

The film first appeared on DVD as a Region 2 disc from Holland, under the oft-used alternative title *Zombie 3*. A trailer and slideshow are the only extras. VIPCO issued the film in the U.K. with similar specifications, and decided to re-title it 'The Zombie Dead'! Shriek Show's Region 1 DVD looks better than any previous release. An anamorphic transfer of an English-dubbed print (as usual, it's a shame an Italian track isn't included) bears the onscreen title *The Nights of Terror*, which has always seemed too blandly generic for all these goings-on. It's a washed-out looking film, except for the vividly scarlet gore, and the night scenes especially show a great deal of grain – but what do you expect for something shot quickly by limited-talent hacks? The special features are a trailer, a "gallery of the undead" (stills, publicity materials), recent shot-on-video interviews with producer

Gabriele Crisanti and Giordano (neither of whom seem to believe the interviewer's assertion that the film is lastingly popular around the world), and coming attractions for other Shriek Show Italian releases (*Zombie Holocaust, House on the Edge of the Park, Spasmo, Eaten Alive!*).

Indefensible, but a generation of fans who came to the genre through terrible video dupes in the early '80s love this picture and its like the way Depression kids revere Bela Lugosi's Monogram pictures or baby boomers adore Sam Arkoff presentations.
– KN

BY BRAKHAGE: AN ANTHOLOGY
Colour/B&W, 2003/2010, 243m. / Directed by Stan Brakhage / Criterion (Blu-ray & DVD) (US R1 NTSC)

Anyone who attended film school during the 1970s or later will surely recognise Stan Brakhage as the creator of *Dog Star Man*, a 75-minute avant-garde master-piece created between 1961 and 1964. An avalanche of cinematic technique using wild colours, endless superimpositions, and only traces of realistic footage (showing Brakhage and a dog trudging through the snowy wilderness, for example), this experimental epic influenced generations of artists and filmmakers while Brakhage himself remained on the fringes, turning out over 400 films of varying lengths before his death in 2003. Twenty six representative Brakhage films were chosen for this double-disc set, which offers an almost chronological tour through his pioneering techniques. As most of the films are silent, this may be tough going for avant-garde newcomers; keep some CD accompaniment handy just in case.

The first disc contains only four films, but they're among his most widely recognised and significant works. "Desistfilm" (1954) is an early study of light and shadow, buildings and the human form, which foreshadows in six minutes the visual obsessions he would explore over the next decade. The haunting and visually powerful "Wedlock House: An Intercourse" uses eerie black and white photography to depict a couple (played by Brakhage and his wife at the time, Jane) coming to terms with each other at an isolated house, interspersed with negative footage of their rather explicit sex life. The aforementioned *Dog Star Man* comes next, accessible as either a complete film or divided into its original five segments ("Prelude", "Part 1", "Part 2", "Part 3", "Part 4"). Last is easily the most notorious Brakhage film of them all, 1971's "The Act of Seeing with One's Own Eyes" (a literal translation of the word "autopsy"), an unflinching and utterly clinical look at the autopsy process shot at a Pittsburgh morgue. Forget *Faces of Death*; this one will clear the room within seconds at your next dinner party, but it's also strangely gripping and beautiful if you're in a receptive frame of mind. Not surprisingly, Criterion has posted a prominent content warning before the start of the film.

The other 22 films are collected on the second disc and most have little to no traditional representational content. "Cat's Cradle" (1959) is a beautiful 6-minute light study using fabric, sunlight, a cat, and a young couple; "Window Water Baby Moving" (1959, 12 mins.) is a 16mm art film using footage of the birth of Brakhage's first child; the oft-screened "Mothlight" (1963, 3 mins.) is an abstract experiment using celluloid and light, as are "Eye Myth" (1972, 9 seconds!), "The Wold Shadow" (1972, 2 mins.), and his nature study/Bosch homage, "The Garden of Earthly Delights" (1981, 1 min.). Other films include "The Stars Are Beautiful" (1974, 18 mins.), "Kindering" (1987, 3 mins.), "I... Dreaming" (1988, 6 mins.), "The Dante Quartet" (1987, 6 mins.), "Nightmusic" (1986, 32 seconds),

"Rage Net" (1988, 52 seconds), "Glaze of Cathexis" (1990, 3 mins.), "Delicacies of Molten Horror Synapse" (1991, 8 mins.), "Untitled (for Marilyn)" (1992, 10 mins.), the ominous "Black Ice" (1994, 2 mins.), the even more ominous "The Dark Tower" (1999, 2 mins.), "Study in Colour and Black and White" (1993, 1 min.), "Stellar" (1993, 2 mins.), "Crack Glass Eulogy" (1996, 6 mins.), "Commingled Containers" (1997, 2 mins.), and "Love Song" (2001, 10 mins.).

Apart from three 35mm films ("The Dante Quartet", "Nightmusic", and "Rage Net"), all are transferred from the original 16mm elements and look exactly as they should, with grain and rough splices intact. The image quality is quite good (certainly better than any of those film school prints) with robust colours. Brakhage and his estate were extensively involved in the creation of the disc, and the man himself appears in five video "encounters" which chronologically cover his filmmaking career and the effect it had on his personal life (and vice versa). Filmed in 1996, the discussions provide some much-needed context for many of the films, as do the written forewords that accompany each title. Also included is a thick annotated booklet with further liner notes and a handy essay by writer Fred Camper, all elegantly designed around individual frames from the films.

The identical package was later issued on Blu-ray with fresh HD transfers of each film alongside a second disc of additional Brakhage short films spanning 1955 to 2003 including "The Wonder Ring" (1955, 5 mins.), "The Dead" (1960, 10 mins.), "Two: Creeley/McClure" (1965, 3 mins.), "23rd Psalm Branch" (1967, 63 mins.), "Scenes from under Childhood, Section One" (1967, 23 mins.), "The Machine of Eden" (1970, 10 mins.), "Star Garden" (1974, 20 mins.), "Desert" (1976, 10 mins.), "The Process" (1972, 8 mins.), "Burial Path" (1978, 8 mins.), "Duplicity III" (1980, 22 mins.), "The Domain of the Moment" (1977, 14 mins.), "Murder Psalm" (1980, 16 mins.), "Arabic

12" (1982, 17 mins.), "Visions in Meditation #1" (1989, 16 mins.), "Visions in Meditation #2 (Mesa Verde)" (1989, 16 mins.), "Visions in Meditation #3 (Plato's Cave)" (1990, 16 mins.), "Visions in Meditation #4 (D. H. Lawrence)" (1990, 17 mins.), "Unconscious London Strata" (1982, 22 mins.), "Boulder Blues and Pearls and..." (1992, 22 mins.), "The Mammals of Victoria" (1994, 34 mins.), "From: First Hymn to the Night – Novalis)" (1994, 2 mins.), "I Take These Truths" (1995, 17 mins.), "The Cat of the Worm's Green Realm" (1997, 14 mins.), "Yggdrasill: Whose Roots Are Stars in the Human Mind" (1997, 16 mins.), "...Reel Five" (1998, 14 mins.), "Persian Series 1–3" (1999, 5 mins.) and "Chinese Series" (2003, 2 mins.).

THE CABINET OF DR. CALIGARI

Colour Tinted, 1919, 72m. / Directed by Robert Wiene / Starring Werner Krauss, Conrad Veidt, Friedrich Feher / Eureka Video (UK R2 PAL), Kino (US R1 NTSC), Image (US R1 NTSC)

This is the keystone film of a notable strain of bizarre, fantastical cinema that flourished in Germany in the 1920s and was linked, somewhat spuriously, with the Expressionist art movement. If much of the development of the movies in the medium's first two decades was directed towards the Lumiere-style "window on the world", with fictional or documentary stories presented in an emotionally stirring manner designed to make audiences forget they were watching a film, *Dr. Caligari* returns to the mode of Méliès by constantly presenting stylised, magical, theatrical effects that exaggerate or caricature reality. Here, officials perch on ridiculously high stools, shadows are painted on walls and faces, jagged cut-out shapes predominate in all the sets, exteriors

are obvious painted and unrealistic backdrops and performances are stylised to the point of hysteria.

Writers Carl Mayer and Hans Janowitz conceived the film as taking place in its own out-of-joint world, and director Robert Weine and set designers Hermann Warm, Walter Roehrig and Walter Reimann put a twist on every scene (and even inter-title) to insist on this. Controversially, Fritz Lang – at an early stage attached as director – suggested that the radical style of the film would be too much for audiences to take without some "explanation". Lang devised a frame story in which hero Francis (Friedrich Feher) recounts the story – of sinister mesmerist mountebank Dr. Caligari (Werner Krauss), his zombie-like somnambulist slave Cesare (Conrad Veidt) and a series of murders in the rickety small town of Holstenwall – and is finally revealed to be an asylum inmate who, in *Wizard of Oz* style, has imagined a narrative that incorporates various people in his daily life. This undercuts the anti-authoritarian tone of the film as Caligari, in the main story an asylum director who has become demented, is revealed to be a genuinely decent man out to help the hero. Indeed, by revealing its Expressionist vision to be that of a madman, the film could even appeal to conservatives who deemed all modernist art demented nonsense.

Wiene, less innovative than most of his collaborators, makes surprisingly little use of cinematic technique – with the exception of the flashback-within-a-flashback as Krauss is driven mad by superimposed words and letters ordering him to become Caligari, the film relies entirely on theatrical devices. The camera is fixed centre stage to show off the sets and it is down to the actors (especially Veidt) to provide movement. Lang's input did serve to make the movie a strange species of amphibian: it plays as an art movie to the high-class crowds who appreciate its innovations, but it's also a horror movie with a gimmick. With its sideshow ambience, hypnotic mad scientist villain and leotard-clad, heroine-abducting monster, *Caligari* is a major early entry in the horror genre, introducing images, themes and characters that became fundamental to the Universal monster cycle of the 1930s and almost every subsequent horror film.

Eureka Video's DVD of this important title is a solid job of work. The source print displays quite a bit of damage and has a distracting black watermark-like line at the top of the frame for 90% of the running time, but a 1996 restoration has added the correct tinting, English intertitles in the jagged style of the sets and an evocative orchestral score by Timothy Brock. The film runs at the correct projection speed and is afforded 20 chapters. The extras are some promotional artwork, a detailed academic commentary from expert Mike Budd (author of *The Cabinet of Dr. Caligari: Texts, Contexts, Histories*) and a very brief fragment from another Weine effort (*Genuine: Tale of a Vampire*, in which a femme fatale steps out of a painting to seduce a young man).

– KN

[The U.S. Kino disc finally gets rid of the horizontal line throughout the film, which also plagued the Image DVD. – ed.]

CAMPFIRE TALES

Colour, 1991, 88m. / Directed by William Cooke and Paul Talbot / Starring Gunnar Hansen, David Avin / Sub Rosa (US R1 NTSC), Cryptkeeper (UK R0 PAL)

 The American South has a strange history with horror movies. North Carolina had its day in the sun with all those Dino De Laurentiis/Stephen King projects (not to mention *Hellraiser III*), while Georgia had *Squirm* and *Kiss of the Tarantula*. And let's not even get into Florida, which spawned the H.G.

Lewis gore trilogy, and Texas, what with its chain saw massacres and S.F. Brownrigg. But what about South Carolina? Yes, they got their turn as well with *Campfire Tales*, a direct-to-video horror anthology featuring Gunnar "Leatherface" Hansen as a bearded coot telling scary stories to a handful of kids around a fire.

The first yarn is another retelling of that popular urban legend, "The Hook", except this time the kids wind up getting gutted in juicy detail instead of driving off. The second, "Overtoke", is a silly tale about a couple of stoners who pick up some really good weed... that turns them into a gory mess. Things pick up considerably with "The Fright Before Christmas", a *Tales from the Crypt*-style holiday yarn about a young man who offs his mother by tossing her down the stairs, only to be confronted with Santa—err, Satan Claus, an axe-wielding ghoul with his own gruesome form of Yuletide cheer. Finally we close with the most elaborate story of the bunch, "Skull and Crossbones", a pirate romp that starts off like a retelling of Edgar Allan Poe's "The Gold Bug" but soon turns into a swashbuckling zombie fest!

Despite the immediate presence of Hansen, *Campfire Tales* may be a bit difficult for jaded horror fans to warm up to; the first half hour or so is standard zero-budget fare with only an unusual amount of gore to distinguish it. Stick with it, though, and you'll be well rewarded; the last two stories really pay off with a fine mix of storytelling, grue, and sick laughs, coupled with some atmospheric camerawork and nifty monster effects. Directors William Cooke and Paul Talbot show a definite flair for pulling chills from a threadbare budget, and their affinity for horror anthologies continued in 1995 with the less satisfying but interesting *Freakshow*, reuniting them with Hansen. Here's hoping they team up behind the camera again, as these guys could easily become the Amicus of our digital video generation.

In visual terms, Sub Rosa's DVD is barely an improvement over those old VHS tapes found in mom and pop video shops; probably culled from the same master, the picture looks very soft with indistinct colour and pasty black levels. It's watchable in a throwback sort of way but nothing to get excited about; considering the film was shot cheaply and shuffled straight to video anyway, it's difficult to assess whether it could possibly look any better. Audio is also coherent but very limited. However, fans and casual interested parties will still prefer the DVD for the audio commentary by journalist Mike Watt, who discusses the creation of the special effects, the stories behind the various non-professional actors, and various anecdotes about the shooting. Also included is an unrelated black and white short, "Tenants", sort of a Gothic character piece with optional commentary from its directors as well. If you don't care about the extras, the U.K. disc offers the same lacklustre transfer.

CANNIBAL APOCALYPSE

Colour, 1980, 96m. / Directed by Antonio Margheriti / Starring John Saxon, Elizabeth Turner, John Morghen [Giovanni Lombardo Radice], Tony King, Cinzia De Carolis, Wallace Wilkinson / Image (US R1 NTSC), Optimum, Cinema Club (UK R2 PAL) / WS (1.66:1) (16:9)

 An anything-goes entry in the early 1980s cycle of extreme gore movies, this scrappy picture riffs at once on *Apocalypse Now* (its original title is *Apocalypse domani*), *Rabid*, *Dawn of the Dead* and the Italian cannibal cycle, staking a mild claim for originality by getting in early on the rampaging-Vietnam vet trend that would be properly triggered by *First Blood*. It opens in a Vietnam War that consists of grainy stock footage and fiery action staged in anonymous woods, as Green Beret Norman Hopper (John Saxon) leads a raid to rescue GIs Charlie Bukowksi (John Morghen) and Tommy Thompson (Tony King) only to discover the POWs have resorted to cannibalism while penned in a hole. Bitten by Tommy, Hopper wakes up from this nightmare next to his understanding but shut-out wife (Elizabeth Turner) back home in suburban Atlanta. It is a movie convention that people dream accurate flashbacks, but how many times have you? Hopper finds himself strangely tempted by the bizarrely-dressed nymphet next door (Cinzia De Carolis) not in the obvious way but by an urge to lift her jumper and bite her tummy. Meanwhile, Bukowski is just out of the asylum and not even struggling with his urges: peeping on a couple making out during a matinee showing of Umberto Lenzi's *From Hell to Victory* (also from producer Edmondo Amati), he bites the girl and is pursued by the cops and a grudge-holding bike gang into a local flea-market where a siege develops that brings Hopper onto the scene. Charlie is returned to a prison-like mental hospital where Tommy is also confined, but the vets' bites have spread the cannibal infection to a cop and a nurse, leading to more carnage. "What I don't understand is how a social phenomenon such as cannibalism can become a contagious disease", whines the heroine, but the infected flesh-eaters are already on the streets (and, eventually, in the sewers) gruesomely slaughtering all who get in their way as the authorities equally gruesomely track them down.

In apparent tribute to Arthur Kennedy's *Let Sleeping Corpses Lie* copper Sgt. McCormick, Wallace Wilkinson plays Captain McCoy – a weary, bigoted redneck who turns up at the siege demanding, "Is he a subversive, a queer, a black, a commie or a Moslem fanatic?" There is an odd attempt at sensitivity in Saxon's performance, which evokes the bewilderment of the monsters in *Dead of Night* and *Rabid*, and the finale features a couple of tactful offscreen gunshots as a suicide pact almost ties up the epidemic problem. However, though Antonio Margheriti competently stages most of his on-location stuntwork, the money shots are all in Gianetto De Rossi's splatter effects: the POWs tucking into the burnt flesh of a Vietnamese woman who has been grilled by a flame-thrower (while wearing a huge amount of visible padding under white pyjamas), the nurse french-kissing a doctor and biting out his tongue, the cannibals taking a circular-saw to the leg of a murdered garage attendant, a biker having his eye not gouged out but pushed in and, most memorably, Charlie shotgunned through the midriff so his intestines fall out and the camera lowers to do a complex rack-focus that shows the attacking cops through the bloody hole in his torso.

Classed as a video nasty in an uncut through horribly panned-and-scanned U.K. release, this has had quite a few separate incarnations under different titles; the gory U.S. theatrical version was *The Cannibals Are in the Streets* while the dreadful-looking and very cut U.S. video release from Almi Films was called *Invasion of the Flesh Hunters*. Image's disc is certainly the best this film has ever looked – considering the sort of theatres it would have played in on its original release, it probably never looked that great projected on a stained screen. The opening sequence might make you misjudge the quality of the transfer in that very bad scratches are visible on all the attack helicopter shots, but a closer look shows that when the main titles are imposed on the picture the scratches run under the pristine lettering, revealing the problem to be inherent in the stock footage rather than this presentation. The pristine transfer of a sometimes makeshift-looking movie is in an approximately 1.66:1 ratio, with twelve chapter stops and an acceptable DD Mono mix of the English language soundtrack (the absence of an Italian option is regrettable for

purists, but the film seems to have been shot with the cast speaking English on set). Quite lengthy cues from Alexander Blonksteiner's score play over the menus. To illustrate not only how badly cut some other versions have been but also how awful they have looked, the extras include the first seven minutes of *Invasion of the Flesh Hunters* in their grotty-looking, splicy, muddy-coloured, gore-trimmed, tinny-sounding glory. Also among the "sewer-dwelling special features": "Apocalypse in the Streets", a brief tour of the Atlanta locations as they look today; a battered but bloody European theatrical trailer and a murky but tempting Japanese teaser trailer; selected filmographies for the director and stars; specific notes on the cuts made in earlier versions but not here; and an insert-booklet with an essay by Travis Crawford; not to mention Easter egg trailers for *Cannibal Holocaust*, *The Girl Who Knew Too Much* and *Cannibal Ferox*.

In the overlong but interesting retrospective documentary *Cannibal Apocalypse Redux*, Margheriti, Saxon and Radice all try politely to summon up 54 minutes of enthusiasm for a film they plainly don't rate among their best work and sometimes change the subject to cover other aspects of their careers. Curiously, Margheriti and Radice get to explain in detail their choices of the names Dawson and Morghen, but Carmine Orrico is never asked how he became John Saxon. The documentary does explain the uneven tone of the film, evidently made by professionals who gave it a fair 75% of their talents but never tried to solve the problems inherent in Dardano Sacchetti's script. Margheriti and Saxon admit in different ways that this wasn't their idea of a good time, but are prompted perhaps to overvalue the picture now because someone has sat them down to do a DVD supplement about it (Saxon amusingly has to be reminded what happens in the end); while the engagingly realist Radice manages to be amused and appalled by the whole experience. The documentary has twelve chapter-stops, as many as the main feature. A subsequent U.K. release from Optimum (carrying over from the identical discontinued Cinema Club version) has no extras at all but, more surprisingly, is also missing a shot of a flaming rat during the finale per BBFC regulations.

– KN

CANNIBAL TERROR

Colour, 1981, 90m. / Directed by Allan W. Steeve [Alain Deruelle], Julio Pérez Tabernero / Starring Sylvia Solar, Gerard Lemaire / Hardgore (UK R2 PAL) / WS (1.85:1) (16:9)

 One of a handful of Eurociné efforts from the turn of the '70s/'80s that seem like sun-drenched, watery imitations of far more full-blooded Italian films, this doesn't even have any bizarre auteur interest in that it wasn't directed by someone like Jess Franco (who made the similar *Cannibal* and *The Devil Hunter*). Presumably set in cosmopolitan South America, it's an almost comically listless melodrama that occasionally throws in scenes of blatantly Caucasian cannibals (some have sideburns or neatly-trimmed moustaches under the face-paint) pawing at raw animal organs fished out of fake human torsos to justify the title (*Terreur cannibale* on this print).

It begins in a marina with an extremely loud and funky music track by Jean-Jacques Lemètre and a gang of foul-mouthed crooks deciding on the spur of the moment to kidnap the tiny daughter of a luxury car tycoon whom one of the villains happens to have had a talk with in the street. The film omits any exciting scenes of the kiddie-snatching and cuts to later on when the girl, who rarely complains and hugs her dolly, is in the hands of the crooks and the wealthy parents are vowing to get her back. The crooks go through a border in some grasslands, though their lady driver is hauled off and eaten by the local flesh-eaters, then hole up with a local don, who is teed off when the most uncontrolled of the baddies rapes his teasing wife. The don leads the rapist into the jungle on the pretence of a hunting expedition and leaves him tied to a tree for the cannibals. Despite offending a border guard by calling him a cunt, the father shows up with his wife and some gun-toters. They pursue the remaining kidnappers, who are dragged off and eaten while the little girl plays with cannibal children – a Franco or a Fulci would not have been able to resist a final kicker showing the little civilised girl with bloody mouth having become a cannibal herself, but Alain Deruelle and/or Julio Pérez Tabernero just turn up the music again and assume a happy ending.

Hardgore's DVD has a small image gallery, mostly of old video covers, and some trailers for their other product. The transfer is anamorphic widescreen and looks about as good as this title is ever going to, though there is a mild amount of damage to the source print. This is the English language dub, which adds a more surreal feel to the enterprise as flat line readings cover hysterical performances even during the worst atrocities and falls back on the strange old convention of having a child played by an adult woman putting on a squeaky voice.

– KN

[Note: a very different edition of this film was later issued in the U.S. and is covered in depth in DVD Delirium Volume 4. – ed.]

THE CASE OF THE BLOODY IRIS

Colour, 1971, 91m. / Directed by Giuliano Carnimeo / Starring Edwige Fenech, George Hilton, Paola Quattrini, Ben Carra / Blue Underground, Anchor Bay (US R0 NTSC), VIPCO (UK R0 PAL) / WS (2.35:1) (16:9)

Among the bizarre, wordy titles associated with Italian '70s thrillers, few can compare with *What Are Those Strange Drops of Blood on Jennifer's Body?* (or in Italian, *Perché quelle strane gocce di sangue sul corpo di Jennifer?*), sensibly issued on DVD under its more terse (but less colourful) export title, *The Case of the Bloody Iris*. Better known for his spaghetti westerns, director Giuliano Carnimeo attempted a single dip in the *giallo* pool with this marvellous, utterly irredeemable trash-fest starring the photogenic male and female leads more often associated with director Sergio Martino.

The lovely Edwige Fenech stars as Jennifer, a fashion model living in a high rise apartment building populated by an array of beautiful, sexually voracious women who spend their days either posing in front of the camera, turning tricks, or beating up men in nightclub performances. Unfortunately said women are also being bumped off one by one by a mysterious killer, who attacks them in the elevator and the bathtub. Jennifer and her roommate, Marilyn (Paola Quattrini), are a bit concerned they might be next (since one of the victims had lived in their new apartment) and try to narrow down the list of suspects. Could it be the landlord (and Jennifer's current beau), Andrea (George Hilton)? Or Jennifer's freakish ex-husband, Adam (Ben Carra) who has a proclivity for mystical orgies? Or that slinky lesbian next door? Or the strange, mentally challenged guy with a domineering mother down the hall?

Utterly devoid of any social significance, character development, or stylistic innovation, *The Case of the Bloody Iris* is pure *giallo* fun stripped down to its basics. Set in a bizarre universe where everyone acts suspiciously and speaks in some weird form of dubbed double-talk, the film exists to propel the viewer from one tableaux of menaced, scantily clad females to another; not surprisingly, the final revelation is absolutely absurd, piling on Catholic guilt as some sort of motivational device for mass slaughter.

As usual Fenech and Hilton make a great pair, compulsively watchable in any setting and giving the circuitous storyline their all. Another Martino veteran, composer Bruno Nicolai, pops up again to deliver one of his best *giallo* scores, a catchy bit of slasher pop even better in its stereophonic glory on Digitmovies's wonderful CD release. Western cinematographer Stelvio Massi chips in with colourful, nicely balanced scope photography, ensuring that any pan and scan versions on home video are absolutely worthless. Eurocult fans should also note that the story was concocted by the amazingly prolific Ernesto Gastaldi, who penned most of Martino's best films as well as a slew of classic '60s Gothic shockers. Sheer decadent fun, with no apologies necessary.

Initially available only as a bonus feature in Anchor Bay's "The Giallo Collection", this was certainly a fine incentive to pick up the whole set before it went out of print. The transfer looks very good overall, though some slight water damage is evident on the left third of the screen during a handful of darker scenes. The English dubbing is significantly worse and sillier than usual, but it sounds fine; for years viewers had to settle for non-subtitled Italian prints, so this is a great step up. Extras include the European trailer, an alternative version of the elevator stabbing, and a director filmography (under his most common screen name, "Anthony Ascott"). The same disc was later issued as a standalone release by America's Blue Underground in 2008, and in the interim VIPCO provided it to U.K. audiences in 2003 with their attractive but extras-free disc.

CASTLE OF BLOOD

B&W, 1964, 89m. / Directed by Antonio Margheriti / Starring Barbara Steele, Georges Rivière / Synapse (US R1 NTSC) / WS (1.66:1) (16:9)

Made at the peak of the Italian Gothic horror boom, *Castle of Blood* remains one of the most highly regarded films by the often fascinating but erratic director Antonio Margheriti, usually credited as "Anthony M. Dawson". Passed off as an Edgar Allan Poe adaptation, presumably to cash in on the Roger Corman/ Vincent Price hits from AIP, Margheriti's film (titled *Danse macabre* in Europe) packs in all of the elements one might expect from the period: ghostly apparitions, a dunderhead hero, a few tasteful dashes of bloodshed, cobweb-laden castle corridors, and a little sexual titillation for the continental crowd. The result is a classic of the genre that bears admirable comparison to the similar works of Mario Bava.

While staying at an inn, travelling bachelor Alan Foster (Georges Rivière) listens to bloodcurdling tales of horror told in a tavern by Poe himself. The men there begin to discuss the nearby Blackwood Castle, which is reputed to be haunted by ghosts on this very night, All Soul's Eve. Alan accepts a wager that he'll be willing to spend the entire remainder of the evening inside the castle, after which the men will come to collect him in the morning. Once inside Alan explores the desolate halls and encounters a variety of peculiar characters, including the beautiful and mysterious Elisabeth (Barbara Steele), who seems to be murdered by a psychopathic muscleman. Further apparent murders pile up as a mysterious blonde also drifts through the castle, and meanwhile Elisabeth reappears and kindles a romance with Alan – though she refuses to leave the castle grounds. Will Alan unravel the castle's deadly mysteries and survive until dawn?

A film comprised of 90% atmosphere and 10% plot, *Castle of Blood* utilizes its moody black and white photography to the hilt as the camera morbidly caresses each dusty corner of the haunted building and fixates on the always fascinating Steele, whose ability to simultaneously convey romantic attraction and sinister lust pays off during the memorable finale (and the startling twist ending, which can still draw gasps from theatrical audiences). Fresh off the success of *Mondo Cane*, composer Riz Ortolani pulls out all the stops with a rapturous score based upon a particularly haunting love theme. Amazingly, one of the film's writers was spaghetti western maestro Sergio Corbucci (*Django*), a reputable genre stalwart in his own right. Oddly enough, Margheriti remade this film a mere six years later (in colour, alas) as the inferior *Web of the Spider*, featuring Tony Franciosa and Klaus Kinski, with Ortolani returning for musical chores. Margheriti and Steele also collaborated the same year as *Castle of Blood* on the equally effective companion piece, *The Long Hair of Death*, though this remains their most famous piece of work together.

A familiar staple of public domain horror dealers, *Castle of Blood* has usually been seen via dupey, spliced 16mm transfers, which obscure much of the sensitive camerawork. To make matters worse, the notoriously scissor-happy U.S. distributors, Woolner Brothers, made the film more family-friendly by trimming out most of a homoerotic murder tableaux between two women and a brief topless scene. Also scissored was a great deal of Poe's dialogue (including the bulk of his opening story) and a few other random lines here and there.

Synapse's DVD originates from the longest possible variant, the French *Danse macabre* print, with the English soundtrack married to the image wherever possible.

The effect is fairly similar to Anchor Bay's bilingual *Deep Red* disc, though the shifts in dialogue occur here less frequently. The French passages are accompanied by optional English subtitles, or the entire French soundtrack can be accessed (with no subtitles except for the restored footage). The mono soundtrack is extremely good for a film of this vintage, certainly preferable to the scratchy, muddy audio most horror fans have grown to, well, tolerate. The anamorphic transfer from 35mm looks quite good overall, with nicely rendered black levels and detail. Some blooming in overly white areas (usually when an actor passes under a light source) is sometimes evident, but this appears to be a flaw in the original elements. The print contains the original French opening titles, which contain a completely different set of names for most of the crew! Obviously the chance to finally see the full, uncut version of *Castle* in English is the big draw here, and Synapse has pulled it off with great panache. Extras accessible from the elegantly designed menus include the alternative U.S. opening credit sequence (over a silhouette of the London cityscape), a gallery of rare photos and stills from the collection of the late Alan Upchurch, and the highly emphatic American trailer ("A night of horror!").

CASTLE OF FU MANCHU

Colour, 1969, 92m. / Directed by Jess Franco / Starring Christopher Lee, Richard Greene, Günther Stoll, Maria Perschy, Tsai Chin / Blue Underground (US R0 NTSC), Optimum (UK R2 PAL) / WS (1.66:1) (16:9)

Hot on the heels of Franco's idiosyncratic *Blood of Fu Manchu* came this widely reviled final entry in the series. During the highly disjointed opening, the megalomaniac sinks an ocean liner by melting an iceberg, courtesy of blue-tinted *Titanic* footage from *A Night to Remember*. Now located in Istanbul, he's still cooking up nasty plots with his daughter, though this time their plan is rather dubious: gain world domination by freezing bodies of water. To save the life of the ailing genius who holds the key to bringing this scheme to fruition, Fu Manchu elicits the enforced aid of Dr. Curt Kessler (Günther Stoll) and his shapely right arm, Ingrid (Paul Naschy regular Maria Perschy). Once again it's up to Nayland Smith (Richard Greene) to put a stop to all these shenanigans, leading to a typical nonsensical climax.

With Blue Underground's DVD, this cut rate climax to the Fu Manchu saga at least moves up a few notches from "unwatchable tedium" to "eye-catching timewaster". Defaced for years thanks to murky transfers saturated in ugly browns and greys, the film at last looks more like a regular Franco/Towers collaboration filled with gaudy, colourful lighting and cockeyed camerawork. Unlike the previous film, this was intended as an all-ages adventure romp and doesn't have any saucy outtakes lying around, at least as far as anyone knows.

Picking up from the previous disc, the main extra is "The Fall of Fu Manchu", in which Christopher Lee, Tsai Chin, Harry Alan Towers, and Franco offer their thoughts about the making of the final film. Also included are the trailer and a stills gallery. The disc is also available with its predecessor as well as *Circus of Fear* and *The Bloody Judge* in a four-disc boxed set (limited to 7,500 copies) from Blue Underground, promoted as *The Christopher Lee Collection*. While this is probably the least of the entries in that set, it's still an item of interest for Lee and Franco fans; it's also available as a bare bones disc in the U.K. paired up with *Blood of Fu Manchu* if you don't feel like spending extra for all the bells and whistles.

THE CAT AND THE CANARY

B&W/Tinted, 1927, 81m. / Directed by Paul Leni / Starring Laura La Plante, Creighton Hale, Tully Marshall / Kino, Image (US R1 NTSC) / DD2.0

Cognoscenti are often heard to speculate on how the horror genre might have developed if Lon Chaney had lived long enough to take the title role in *Dracula*. Less often considered and even more tantalising is the probability that had Paul Leni not died at 44 in 1929, he would have been Universal's first choice to direct the breakthrough vampire movie. With a German Expressionist anthology (*Waxworks*) and a Chaney-style historical grotesque (*The Man Who Laughs*) on his resume, Leni was well on his way to cornering the market in Hollywood horrors, but his most important credit is this 1927 adaptation of John Willard's comic-horrific Broadway hit, which is perhaps the most influential of all silent American horror films. Leni uses clutching hands that evoke *Nosferatu* and a sinister doctor who resembles Dr. Caligari, but his creaky mansion Gothic, with a broad edge of eccentric humour amid the shadowed sets, is very much his own creation and served as the template for James Whale's *The Old Dark House* and many, many other films.

A symbolic opening finds dying millionaire Cyrus West imagining his grasping heirs as giant cats attacking him as he struggles inside a huge medicine bottle, then leaps twenty years to the reading of his will. The fortune and his decaying mansion go to his most distant like-named relative Annabelle West (Laura La Plante), on the condition that she be judged sane – with a mystery second heir named in case she goes mad. A brutal-looking asylum attendant shows up to inform the unhappy relatives that a homicidal maniac known as the Cat has escaped and is probably somewhere on the grounds or inside the house's traditional secret passageways. Lawyer Crosby (Tully Marshall) is about to reveal the name of the most likely culprit to the heroine when a hairy clawed hand drags him into the wall, and the hand reappears throughout at the most terrifying points, snatching a valuable locket from the sleeping heroine's neck or creeping round corridors. The leading man is a chubby, slightly overage Harold Lloyd-style comedian (Creighton Hale), who overcomes his traditional cowardice to get into an enthusiastic fistfight with the slouch-hatted, bug-eyed, weirdly-fanged Cat at the finale. The villain is unmasked as the most cheerful prospective heir by the memorable touch of his false eye falling to the floor and staring up. Already archetypal, the reading-of-the-will plot is lightly sent up, but the film still goes all out to deliver genuine scares – more, indeed, than most 1930s Universal horrors. Among the many frills introduced here and reused later are the twin pencil-lights to make eyes glow, as seen in *Dracula* and used for comic effect in this film, making Hale's eyes glow as he hides under a bed while the daffy second female lead and her shrieking old maid aunt undress as he tries not to look – the younger woman's roll-top stockings were considered very racy in 1927.

Image's DVD of this important title is given very respectful treatment, with the monochrome image tinted various shades throughout and the original 1927 music/effects track compiled by James Bradford performed with spirit by Eric Beheim and "The Cyrus West Players". The 2005 remastering (the first version on video from 35mm) is especially fine; this version gives you a far more effective idea of why 1920s audiences were so excited by Leni's style than the various untinted, blotchy grey market video releases that have hitherto represented the movie. Whale-watchers will note that *The Old Dark House* recreates one of this film's most memorable sets and set-ups: a long corridor lined with thin windows, the curtains blowing in like ghostly shrouds.

A nice extra is the 1920 Harold Lloyd short "Haunted Spooks", in which a suicidal young man is married to a girl he's never met so she can inherit a Southern mansion while her nasty uncle fakes a haunting in an attempt to drive her off – its best comic scene is Lloyd's fumbled attempt to kill himself. There's some now-embarrassing business which reminds you that "spook" was in the 1920s a mildly derogatory term for African-Americans, with terrified Negro servants fleeing from shrouded figures and a little black boy (Ernest Morrison) dunked in flour and mistaken for a ghost.

Silent horror specialists Kino chimed in with their own 2007 version, "The Photoplay Restoration" (from an original nitrate print), which offers something of an improvement on its already solid predecessor in terms of detail but also betrays some peculiar conversion anomalies due to either noise reduction or PAL conversion (though nowhere nearly as disastrous as Milestone's *Phantom of the Opera*). A photo gallery is the only extra on this version.
– KN

CAULDRON OF BLOOD

Colour, 1970, 94m. / Directed by Edward Mann [Santos Alcocer] / Starring Boris Karloff, Viveca Lindfors, Dianik Zurakowska, Jean-Pierre Aumont, Rosenda Monteros / Cryptkeeper (UK R0 PAL)

 A Spanish production filmed mostly in 1967 as *El coleccionista de cadáveres* and released in the U.S. as *Blind Man's Bluff*, Cauldron of Blood is an odd melodrama with a cosmopolitan setting. Boris Karloff, replacing an ailing Claude Rains, is Franz Badulescu, a blind

sculptor manipulated by his strange, leather-miniskirted wife (Viveca Lindfors) into using human skeletons as armatures. Dianik Zurakowska, a familiar face from '70s Spanish horror (*The Vampires Night Orgy*, etc.) is a bikini babe obviously on the victim list. A great deal of footage is taken up by Jean-Pierre Aumont as a suave French journo and a white-capped Rosenda Monteros poking around the edges of the mystery with a surprising lack of urgency. For a movie with so little going on, it's rather intricate, with a lot of characters and backstory.

It's a dull, uninvolving little picture, though flashes of ambition suggest it was as interested in evoking *Laughter in the Dark* or *Suddenly Last Summer* as *House of Wax* or *Color Me Blood Red*. The cobwebby basement where corpses are rendered down to skeletons is a horror movie locale, but the rest of the film takes place in a lively Spanish resort with picturesque but sinister gypsies, drunken revellers and masked festivals. Karloff shambles through, in better shape than he would be in his Mexican movies and with a little more meat to his part, but the whole production has clearly been arranged to put as little strain as possible on the veteran star. The climax is a hilarious serial-style fistfight between Aumont and a villain, accompanied by an ultra-jazzy score, with Karloff smashing the lights to even things up as he sets out to get his revenge on Lindfors, who is memorably shocked to death when her arm is plunged into her own acid pit and skeletonised.

The sort of marginal effort it's surprising to find on DVD at all, this doesn't get a great showcase from The Cryptkeeper's Collection. The credits, which feature colourful expressionist images and form titles from cartoon bones, are letterboxed, but the bulk of the film is fullscreen – which clips the beginnings and ends off English subtitles for a scene with Spanish-speaking characters. The print is in rough shape at the outset, but improves considerably thereafter; though there's

always a great deal of grain, the colours are vivid, as befits the mix of Bava-lit Gothicisms and swinging sixties fashions on view. Besides trailers for *Voodoo Woman* and *A Bucket of Blood* (selling its beatnik angle more than the horror or comedy), the disc also contains "The Silver Curtain", a twenty-five-minute episode of the Karloff-starring *Colonel March of Scotland Yard* TV series from 1954. With Anton Diffring as a scoundrelly murder victim and a very young Arthur Hill (*The Andromeda Strain*) as an American abroad patsy, it's not as ingenious in its plot as author Carter Dickson [John Dickson Carr] was capable of, and is directed flatly by Bernard Knowles (Terence Fisher worked on the series). However, a sprightly Karloff – one of the first major stars to master television as a medium – is great fun as the eyepatched Scotland Yard man who heads "The Department of Queer Complaints".
– KN

LE CERCLE ROUGE

Colour, 1970, 140m. / Directed by Jean-Pierre Melville / Starring Alain Delon, Yves Montand, André Ekyan, Gian Maria Volonté, André Bourvil, François Périer / Criterion (US R1 NTSC), BFI (UK R2 PAL), Studio Canal (DVD & Blu-ray) (France, UK, Germany R2/RB PAL/HD) / WS (1.85:1) (16:9)

With his pivotal *Le samouraï* in 1967, French cinematic crime specialist Jean-Pierre Melville began pushing his stories of cops and robbers into increasingly stylized territory, culminating in his penultimate film, the operatic *Le cercle rouge*. Once again starring Alain Delon, this razor-sharp heist film (a probable influence on Michael Mann and Walter Hill, not to mention the self-admitted

John Woo) operates like an existential primer on fate and morality, as indicated by the mystical title (from a fabricated Buddhist quote cited in the first scene).

Recently released from prison, Corey (Delon) decides to exact a little retribution against his boss, Rico (André Ekyan), who also swiped Corey's girl. To restore himself financially and professionally, Corey embarks on a carefully planned jewel heist with the aid of escaped convict Vogel (Gian Maria Volonté), who slips into Corey's car by chance after a daring train escape, and a boozing ex-cop/marksman, Jansen (Yves Montand). Meanwhile, cat-happy Commissioner Mattei (André Bourvil) is none too pleased about Vogel's escape and, while tracking him down, learns of details involving the impending robbery at a Place Vendôme shop.

Skilfully balancing gangster chic (the typical fedoras, trenchcoats, and ever-burning cigarettes are all in abundance) with beautifully executed suspense sequences, *Le cercle rouge* (shown in a shorter, English language variant as *The Red Circle*) is certainly one of Melville's finest achievements, though its exact placement in his pantheon will be mostly a matter of viewer preference. The mammoth running time allows plenty of room for the characters to breathe and exude squinty-eyed moral complexity, while the occasional flashy flourishes (such as a swinging nightclub run by *Nights of Cabiria*'s François Périer and a memorable DT-inspired vision involving spiders) make this satisfying as a piece of Eurocult thrillmaking as well.

Delon has rarely been better; deglamorized a bit here, he manages to keep attention anchored on his criminal pursuits whenever the film threatens to spin off on another tangent. From a technical standpoint Melville's directorial style remains fresh and immediate; the soggy, autumnal woods where Corey meets his old boss make for a surprising change from the norm, and the robbery itself allows for some striking use of cinematic space and movement to generate tension both in the viewer and between the archetypal characters.

Criterion's double-disc set presents the film itself on the first DVD in an immaculate widescreen transfer. Detail and colour look excellent, and the optional subtitles are easy to read, which is a welcome relief after years of bad video copies. The second disc boasts a wealth of Melville-related extras, including half an hour of on-set footage from the making of this movie in which the director, Delon, Montand, and Bourvil are seen at work and stop to speak to the camera. Also included is a lengthy segment from *Cineastes de notre temps: Jean-Pierre Melville*, an older French TV documentary in which the director discusses his craft and is seen hard at work on production.

Other extras include the original and reissue trailers (pretty much the same except for a "John Woo Presents" tag and different title cards), an extensive gallery of production and publicty stills and art, and a thick booklet containing liner notes by Michael Sragow (who draws numerous parallels between Melville and his literary namesake), excerpts from a text interview with Rui Nogueira in the book "Melville on Melville", a recollection by composer Eric Demarsan, ruminations on the title's meaning by Chris Fujiwara, and a brief text appraisal by John Woo. Nogueira also turns up for a video interview in which he discusses the film's placement in Melville's filmography and examines some of its prominent themes, while Melville's assistant director, Bernard Stora, appears in a separate video interview in which he tackles the film from a more technical standpoint.

Subsequent DVDs from the BFI and Studio Canal ignited some debate about this film's intended colour scheme, which looks earthy on the Criterion disc but chillier and bluer on the others. The BFI disc includes an audio commentary and video intro with French film professor Ginette Vincendeau and an interview with director's assistant

Bernard Stora; Studio Canal's DVD is light on extras but far heavier in its much later Region B Blu-ray version (distributed by Optimum in the U.K.) which carries over the video intro and Stora interview but also adds "Code Name: Melville" (Olivier Bohler's 76-minute documentary covering Melville's entire career) and additional interviews with writers Jose Giovanni and Rui Nogueira. The Blu-ray (which contains subtitle options in English, French, and German) falls somewhere between the Criterion and BFI versions in terms of colour but is also considerably more detailed and impressive, so fans would probably be best directed to that option if they can play Region B titles.

UN CHANT D'AMOUR

B&W, 1950, 26m. / Directed by Jean Genet / Starring André Reybaz, Lucien Sénemaud / Cult Epics (US R0 NTSC), BFI (UK R2 PAL) / DD2.0

Though best known as a novelist, the notorious Jean Genet also made a brief foray into filmmaking with a silent short film, *Un chant d'amour*, which was originally produced for the Parisian stag film underground. Though it doesn't feature any sex per se, the film plays like an eroticized ode to the films of Jean Cocteau; from the quaint chalkboard credits to the surreal use of disembodied hands and torsos, the film clearly sprang from the same soil as *Orpheus* and *Beauty and the Beast*. However, Genet also included elements that populated his written work: shared tobacco, flowers, prison walls, voyeurism, nature worship, flowers, and victimization, to name but a few. Genet later denounced the film when his career began to ascend, but it was eventually reclaimed by the art house community and hailed as a groundbreaking classic. Without this film, the films of Todd Haynes and Derek Jarman would have had a much tougher road to follow.

The "story" takes place at an unnamed stone prison where a guard sees two male arms swinging a floral branch out of a barred window. He enters the prison and looks into each cell, observing the inmates in a state of extreme sexual agitation. Two prisoners share a cigarette by blowing smoke back and forth through a straw, forced through a hole in the wall (an image more memorably lewd and poetic than any of the film's more notorious nudity). The prison guard eventually enters one of the cells and indulges in a lengthy S&M fantasy climaxing with an image later replicated in *Beyond the Valley of the Dolls*, before the day finally closes.

More often discussed than actually seen, *Un chant d'amour* (translation: *A Love Song*) is a fairly tough sit for those not already disposed to avant garde filmmaking; even more challenging is the lack of a soundtrack. While some critics came up with elaborate symbolic explanations for the film's silence, the truth is that it's quite sleep inducing when viewed without any music. Luckily the worthwhile but wildly overpriced BFI disc (which flies in the face of Genet's wishes to never have the film commercially released) adds a score by regular Jarman composer Simon Fisher Turner, and the percussive music suits the film well; it's an appropriately stark and sparse composition similar to his work on *Edward II*. Image quality is extremely good; every awkward splice and scuff is still in place, but the level of detail is astonishing for a 35mm film usually seen in muddy 16mm copies or bootleg tapes. Extras include a commentary by writer Jane Giles and director Richard Kwietniowski (*Love and Death on Long Island*) which elaborates on the film's history, its place in Genet's highly unique artistic canon, and its influence on gay culture over the years. There are also text bios of Genet and Turner.

More affordable, and offering a completely different set of extras, is the two-disc American set from Cult Epics, which presents a similar transfer but without a music score; get a CD handy to play while watching it. This time the audio commentary comes from none other than Kenneth Anger, who goes into great detail about the film's origins, Genet's intentions, and the state of experimental filmmaking at the time. In addition the first disc has an introduction by Lithuanian avant garde director Jonas Mekas, who sits way, way too close to the camera as he talks for eight minutes about the film's origins and its importance in underground film culture.

Disc two features two documentaries, starting with Antoine Bourseiller's "Genet" (52 minutes), a very candid 1981 talk with the cigarette-puffing author outside a country home in which he talks about his prison experiences, his sexuality, his novels, and lots, lots more. The following year's "Jean Genet" (46 minutes) by Bertrand Poirot-Delpech is another interview (indoors this time) with a more theoretical and academic examination of his writing technique. Both are worth viewing; if you're really a completist, also be sure to track down the South Bank Show episode devoted to him as well, which is floating around among video traders. Overall, both discs are valuable additions to the Genet legacy and feature no overlap whatsoever, making each a unique and recommended purchase.

CHARLES MANSON SUPERSTAR
Colour, 1989, 107m. / Directed by Nikolas Schreck / Starring Charles Manson / Screen Edge (UK R2 PAL)

This is a ragged-looking documentary that consists mostly of an interview with "Charlie" Manson conducted in prison in the late 1980s, with a minimum of narrated contextualising material.

Author of *The Satanic Screen*, Nikolas Schreck is especially interested in the "magical" elements of Manson's belief system and attempts to draw links between the Family and various factions, including Anton LaVey's Church of Satan and sundry extremist political parties. Mostly he just lets Manson speak, drawing him out but not needling him – tellingly, the film uses edits to truncate the passages when the articulate Manson loses any argument he might be making and sidesteps into verbal (and physical) bebop. Demystifying the image of a hippie Rasputin, the film shows a self-styled child of the forties whose musical influences might as well be Hoagy Carmichael as The Beatles and who can be candid and evasive in a way shaped by a lifetime lived mostly behind bars. Manson's look, accent, manner, shallowness and tendency to shrug off responsibility are a surprising dead ringer for Angel Martin, the ex-con con-man played by Stuart Margolin on *The Rockford Files*.

Screen Edge's DVD does what it can with something never intended to look slick. The interview footage is fuzzy video, like a dupe from a cable access TV show, though there are some more appealing visuals in a tour of the abandoned ruins of the Death Valley hideout where the Family lived. Shot cheap and without access to news footage – a PD trailer clip from *I Drink Your Blood* does get in, though – it has to film grainy newsprint to document its points. Manson clearly likes, or claims to like, his interviewer/director and is still playing directly to the camera, but his various ramblings are suggestive not of a coherent spiritual or political philosophy but rather of an old lag trying to keep himself entertained with the sound of his own voice.

The only extras are a director biography and some pictures. However, there's a fairly astonishing insert essay from Schreck, which repudiates the thesis of the film that Manson was an outlaw and suggests that he was in fact "a government infiltrator of counter-culture circles", more involved than is believed in the actual murders and part of a vast conspiracy to discredit various non-conformist 1960s factions. Very decently, Schreck also adds some notes correcting factual errors in the film – though his conspiracy theory interests have evidently yet to extend to the probability that the prisoner who died in Spandau and with whom Manson claims some kinship wasn't actually Rudolf Hess.

– KN

CHILDREN OF THE STONES

Colour, 1976, 174m. / Directed by Peter Graham Scott / Starring Gareth Thomas, Peter Demin, Iain Cuthbertson, Freddie Jones / Second Sight (UK R0 PAL), Acorn (US R1 NTSC)

 A seven-part children's serial, made by HTV during the long hot summer of 1976 and telecast early in 1977, this taps into many of the concerns found in Nigel Kneale's 1970s work (*The Stone Tape*, *Quatermass*). A tweed-jacketed scientist (Gareth Thomas) and his sandwich-addicted teenage son (Peter Demin) arrive in the village of Milbury (played by Avebury in Wiltshire) to study the standing stones. A mystery develops in that most of the village children are maths geniuses with mindlessly sunny dispositions ("Happy Day!") and the local squire (Iain Cuthbertson) is up to something odd involving computers and a black hole, which seems to replicate an ancient ritual.

Over the somewhat attenuated course of the seven episodes, the Stepford-like effect knocks off various supporting cast members who are invited to dinner at the big house and emerge as smiling zombies and the boffin and his son realise that it's impossible to leave the circle. Cuthbertson is an impressively smug, patriarchal villain and a burst of Welsh eccentricity is provided by the wonderful

Freddie Jones as a mad poacher. Scripted by Jeremy Burnham and Trevor Ray, it offers enough eerie touches to linger in the memories of children who saw it at the time, though it's slightly too mild-mannered even for the *Goosebumps* generation. The last episode tries to have it both ways by delivering a very downbeat finish as the villagers are turned to stone and then shifting the leads into a parallel time track where things aren't so bad but the whole cycle is poised to start again.

Shot on 16mm for the location work and '70s quality video for the studio scenes, *Children of the Stones* comes to DVD after several video editions: it has a slightly soft, greenish look that, like some of the more strident performances, seems crude now but was pretty much the standard for U.K. children's TV at the time. Sidney Sager's Penderecki-inspired "Neolithic choral" score is especially memorable, though perhaps overused. Second Sight's disc has a nice smattering of extras: comprehensive notes and filmographies, a picture gallery and fifteen-minute interviews (by an unseen Nigel Algar) with star Thomas and producer-director Peter Graham Scott (*Headless Ghost*), both of whom remember the production in detail. The same transfers and extras were later issued by Acorn in the U.S. as well.

– KN

CHINESE TORTURE CHAMBER

Colour, 1995, 92m. / Directed by Bosco Lam / Starring Lawrence Ng, Yvonne Yung, Julie Lee, Siu-Kei Lee, Ching Mai, Elvis Tsui / Discotek (US R0 NTSC) / WS (1.85:1) (16:9), MO Asia (Holland R0 NTSC) / WS (1.85:1)

Originally entitled *Man qing shi da ku xing* and also known as *Chinese Torture Chamber Story*, this is Hong Kong Category III nonsense in the *Sex and Zen* style, combining the familiar Chinese period/martial arts mode with elements from *Ilsa*-like torture exploitation, Chaucerian bawdiness and the sort of sex-com lo-jinx endemic in British, Italian and German softcore of the '70s.

The framework is a trial at which innocent heroine Little Cabbage (Yvonne Yung) and her chaste married lover (Lawrence Ng) are subjected to indignities by a tyrannical, ranting magistrate ("Hit her ass twenty times!") – walking on knees over broken plates, fingers crushed in a vice, etc. Flashbacks establish the decency of these characters, but reveal that the scholar hero's wife (Ching Mai) and her brutally lecherous partner (Elvis Tsui) have contrived to have their victims suffer the harshness of the legal system to conceal their own adultery. It's the sort of film remembered for scenes rather than overall story: a pair of naked kung fu heroes who really do give a flying fuck; the elaborate use of the "four lustful instruments" to spice up Ng's marriage; Yung married off to a nice guy with a freakishly large penis which (in separate scenes involving a Chinese arrangement of "Unchained Melody") explodes first in a hosepipe-like gusher of semen and (after a poisoned aphrodisiac has been used) a cloud of blood; the villainess punished on a wooden horse that impales her on a dildo saddle; a supporting nanny enduring a painful ancient Chinese breast-enlargement therapy. Yung manages to seem fresh and innocent throughout, despite the extremes she is involved in, but the performances are one-note shrill, and the anything-goes see-sawing between sex, sadism and slapstick means that no particular audience is liable to come away satisfied.

MO Asia's disc has a Cantonese dialogue track with optional subtitles in English or Dutch. The transfer is letter-boxed widescreen and not anamorphically enhanced; on 16:9 monitors, the subs tend to bleed off the bottom of the screen, though the film is easy to follow with only half the dialogue translated. The sole extras are a trailer and awkwardly-translated notes on Ng and Yung. A better option is the American release from Discotek, which features a remastered anamorphic transfer, much improved English subtitles, and a trailer and similar talent notes.

– KN

THE CHRISTMAS SEASON MASSACRE

Colour, 2001, 69m. / Directed by Jeremy Wallace / Starring D.J. Vivona, Jason Christ, Eric Stanze, Joy Payne, Chris Belt, Julie Farrar / Sub Rosa (US R1 NTSC) / DD2.0

To paraphrase an oft-quoted line from *This Is Spinal Tap*, there's a thin line between clever and stupid. Of course, the line is even thinner when you're trying to be stupid, which is precisely the aim of this whacked-out spoof of '80s slasher films. No, no, this isn't like *Scream*; no postmodern winking here or hot teen stars flouncing around. Instead we've got oceans of ridiculous gore, utterly gratuitous nudity, Christmas slasher antics clearly shot during the height of summer, strip Trivial Pursuit, and an over the top gag ending. If you aren't already brain damaged going into this one, you very well might be on the way out.

In the hilarious opening monologue, a randy bad boy named Boom Boom (*Scrapbook* director Eric Stanze) comforts his jittery date in a car by relating the tragic tale of Tommy "One Shoe" McGroo, a little victimized boy who turned into a maniac after receiving an eyepatch for Christmas (don't ask). Still trudging around with only one shoe and the pirate accessory over his eye, Tommy stalks the woods and, of course, quickly makes gory work of this necking couple. Since Tommy's intent on striking down more of his classmates every Christmas, the last batch of survivors holes

up in a house near his stomping grounds (of course), essentially making themselves easy targets. In the meantime they indulge in loads of thickheaded debauchery, all the while acting out the typical '80s body count stereotypes. Will anyone survive? Will anyone get laid? And most importantly, will Tommy ever get his shoe back?

The biggest problem with *The Christmas Season Massacre* is that the opening fifteen minutes are so jaw-dropping in their goofiness that the ensuing antics can't help but look milder in comparison: Tommy's curtain-raiser (flinging innards at the camera), the aforementioned monologue, and a couple using a watermelon piñata as a sexual accessory underneath a Christmas tree. Though extremely prolonged and lingering, none of the murders can be taken seriously except for one mean-spirited bit involving a woman tied to a tree, which really belongs in a different movie. The usual band of Sub Rosians is on hand, including Jason Christ as the requisite nerd (named Dorcas, har har), main bully Ernie (D.J. Vivona), and the busty Abbey (Joy Payne), among others. Most of the dialogue is deliberately bad and hokey, with one ad-libbed guitar serenade earning a few genuine chuckles as well. (Check out the alternative versions in the extras section for kicks, too.)

As usual Sub Rosa ladles on the gory goodies with their DVD, which features video and surround sound quality comparable to their other shot-on-video releases. The rock songs are actually well used, including a memorable closing ditty accompanied by loopy outtakes. There are two commentary tracks, both rather brief (due to the short running time of the feature itself, naturally). Director Jeremy Wallace takes the honours first and proves to be as genial and jokey as you might expect, while the mic for track two goes to actors Jason Christ, Chris Belt, and Julie Farrar, all of whom recount the standard obstacles of zero budget filmmaking. Also included are seven minutes of behind the scenes footage and trailers for this movie, *Insaniac, The Undertow, I Spit on Your Corpse – I Piss on Your Grave*, and hidden away, *Scrapbook, Ice from the Sun* and *Savage Harvest.* Further hidden extras are two Stanze music videos, "I Lost My Innocence to the Industrial Age" and "Put Your Feet in the Wedding Cake" by Hotel Faux Pas. However, the award for the strangest extra goes to the short film presentation, Chris Grega's "Frank Wang: The Vengeance". Running over half an hour, this goofball B&W nod to martial arts should satisfy anyone in the mood for stickfights and bowling ninjas after watching an hour of slasher gore. Chow down!

CIRCUS OF FEAR

Colour, 1966, 94m. / Directed by John Llewellyn Moxey / Starring Christopher Lee, Klaus Kinski, Skip Martin, Margaret Lee, Suzy Kendall, Leo Genn / Blue Underground (US R0 NTSC), Cinema Club (UK R2 PAL), Kinowelt (Germany R2 PAL) / WS (1.66:1) (16:9)

 Often confused with the far more sensational *Circus of Horrors*, this subdued but moderately engaging crime thriller features a drive-in hound's dream cast and a handful of oddball twists, geared more for the Edgar Wallace crowd than the blood and gore set. Beginning in heist film territory, the plot follows a cache of stolen money from the hands of Manfred (Klaus Kinski) and his gang to a nearby circus, where one of the criminals is murdered and a combination whodunit/who-got-it ensues. Among the suspects are the always-masked and heavily-accented Gregor (Christopher Lee), suspicious dwarf Mr. Big (Skip Martin), and a handful of beauties including Gina (*Venus in Furs*'s Margaret Lee) and lion tamer Natasha (*Torso*'s Suzy Kendall). Weaving through a network of lies and greed, intrepid Inspector Elliott (Leo Genn) has little time to waste before the killer strikes again.

While director John Llewellyn Moxey (*City of the Dead*) does a professional job of keeping the film on track with such an elaborate cast of characters, the end result is neither fish nor fowl; it isn't witty enough to qualify as a real English mystery, and it's not Gothic or surreal enough for German *krimi* fans. The decision to keep the violence mostly offscreen means we must be engaged enough in other proceedings, but the viewer's interest is only fully captured in fits and starts. At least Lee finally removes his mask for the final act of the film, and his repeated tendency to make sudden, dramatic entrances even in the most mundane of circumstances provokes a few welcome chuckles.

Fortunately it's a gorgeous film to look at, thanks to Blue Underground's meticulous restoration from the original negative. Released in some territories by AIP in black and white (robbing the film of one of its greatest assets, the striking colour photography) under the title *Psycho-Circus*, the film has been restored back to its original running time and then some; an additional eight minutes of snooping and sleuthing from an early cut has been reinstated. Moxey turns up for an audio commentary with David Gregory, who keeps the proceedings flowing with a steady stream of solid questions and comments. You'll learn about the international conditions that facilitated the film's production, where it was shot, and how all the bestial performers (no, not the actors) were kept in line. Other extras include the British and American trailers in both their monochrome and colour variants, as well as Lee and Kinski talent biographies and an extensive stills and art gallery. Nice job on the atmospheric menu design, too.

Two subsequent discs appeared on the market from the UK's Cinema Club (no extras, standard cut) and Germany's Kinowelt, which adds on an alternative B&W German version (in full frame for some reason) as well as German language text extras and pdf notes, though the compression to smash all this on a single layer results in a very problematic presentation.

CITY OF LOST SOULS

Colour, 2000, 105m. / Directed by Takashi Miike / Starring Teah, Michelle Reis, Patricia Manterola, Mitsuhiro Oikawa / Chimera/ American Cinematheque (US R0 NTSC) / WS (1.85:1) (16:9) / DD5.1, Tai Seng (US R0 NTSC), Mei Ah (HK R0 NTSC) / WS (1.85:1) / DTS/DD5.1, Tartan (UK R2 PAL) / WS (1.85:1) (16:9) / DD2.0

 Following the atypical *Audition*, the obscenely prolific Takashi Miike returned to the stomping grounds of his classic crime favourites (*Fudoh*, *Dead or Alive*) with *City of Lost Souls* (*Hyôryuu-gai*), his take on the familiar criminal-lovers-on-the-run subgenre. Of course, this being a Miike film, that also means spastic editing, outrageous violence, and enough energy to fuel a dozen American action knockoffs.

Writing to her mother, pretty Kei (Michelle Reis) enthuses about her wonderful Brazilian boyfriend, Mario (Teah), who's then seen blasting away some adversaries, Sergio Leone-style, in a dusty border town. Mario proceeds to hijack a helicopter so he can rescue Kei from a deportation bus, instigating an elaborate chain of events involving a feud between the Yakuza and the Chinese mob, a mysterious young girl, and Mario's ex, Lucia (Patricia Manterola), whose help may come at a high price. Then there's Kei's former flame, pretty boy gangster Ko (Mitsuhiro Oikawa), who's after the lovers with an axe to grind, literally.

Spiked with bizarre touches like the now infamous CGI cockfight (a *Matrix* spoof, believe it or not) and a sadistic showdown straight out of a Russ Meyer film, *City of Lost Souls* largely avoids the gruesome excesses of *Dead or Alive*, though you do get the occasional bad taste hiccup like a man's face plunged into a bloody toilet. The focus here is on action, pure and simple, with lots of macho gun-toting, pursuits, double crosses, and international intrigue to keep the proceedings speedy even when they don't always quite make sense. None of the characters are really sympathetic, but Miike does manage to pull off an effective love story nonetheless, which at least makes one wish the couple would steer away from their rollercoaster ride straight to hell.

The U.S. DVD presented under the auspices of the American Cinematheque is a tremendous leap over the earlier non-anamorphic, no-frills Tai Seng disc. The transfer looks excellent and, in a rarity for a Japanese title, appears to be freshly struck for Western NTSC standards with dead-on black levels. The explosive 5.1 soundtrack keeps the rear channels active through most of the running time (dig those opening credits!). Also included are detailed liner notes by the Cinematheque's Chris D. (in which he places the film in context both as Hong Kong entertainment and Miike's stab at film noir), a reel of rough behind-the-scenes footage showing Miike at work during three of the action sequences, a demo of the video game *Escape from Tokyo*, and a huge array of alternative trailers and TV spots, with additional trailers for other titles in the series like *Black Rose Mansion*. Incidentally, the DVD kicks off with the full red-band U.S. trailer for *Audition* before the menu screen, so prepare to settle back for a few minutes.

The PAL disc from Tartan does not stand up favourably next to its NTSC counterpart, having a lacklustre 2.0 soundtrack and an image that lacks contrast and has a compara-tively muted colour scheme. Extras include a 10-minute Takashi Miike interview, notes by Tom Mes, the film's trailer and a Tartan/ Miike trailer reel for *Shinjuku Triad Society*, *Rainy Dog*, *Ley Lines*, *Audition*, *Dead or Alive* and *Dead or Alive 2*.

CLEOPATRA'S SECOND HUSBAND

Colour, 1998, 92m. / Directed by Jon Reiss / Starring Paul Hipp, Rhada Mitchell, Bitty Schram, Boyd Kestner, Radha Mitchell / First Run (US R1 NTSC) / WS (1.85:1) / DD2.0

Best known for making the widely acclaimed rave culture documentary, *Better Living Through Chemistry*, director Jon Reiss cut his teeth on music videos and first tackled narrative film a year earlier with his own twisted contribution to the well worn "cuckoo in the nest" thriller genre. Though not overly graphic in the traditional sense, *Cleopatra's Second Husband* is packed with enough implied perversion, dysfunction, and psychological torture to fuel a dozen late night cable TV heavy breathers, few of which would dare to enter the territory explored during this sick puppy's third act.

Robert (Paul Hipp), a submissive photographer enduring an oppressive relationship with his wife, Hallie (Bitty Schram), plans to go off with her for a country vacation. They arrange for two strangers, Zack (Boyd Kestner) and Sophie (*Pitch Black*'s Radha Mitchell), to housesit in their absence but find the situation far out of control upon their early return to Los Angeles. The housesitters ask to stay on while they find an apartment, and soon Robert's life becomes consumed by these intruders whose charisma may mask a darker purpose. Hallie finds herself unable to cope with the mind games, but Robert has an entirely different approach to the situation.

A direct descendant of chamber work horrors by the likes of Claude Chabrol and Roman Polanski, this indie shocker takes its time to build up a full head of steam but more than pays off in the end with a succession of morbid twists and turns. Many viewers may be put off by some of the more uncomfortable propositions raised by the ultimate direction of the story, but at least it's more interesting and unpredictable than junky, silly, major studio exploiters of marital trauma like *The Hand That Rocks the Cradle* and *The Tie That Binds* (remember those?). The film isn't an unqualified masterpiece by any means; some of the stylistic flourishes call attention to themselves at the wrong time, and the script could have used a little tightening in the first half. However, the actors remain nimble and convincing in their tricky roles, and overall the film is executed with enough visual invention to prevent the claustrophobic setting from becoming too limited or stagy.

Regrettably not 16:9 enhanced (rare for a title this recent), First Run's disc of *Cleopatra's Second Husband* (whose title suggests an oblique parallel between Robert and Rome's Mark Antony) looks colourful but definitely on the soft side, while the surround audio track remains active throughout. Detail is wanting in many of the darker shots and dark areas tend to smudge, though this may be a shortcoming inherent in the original film considering the large number of trick shots, filters, and diffused lighting effects on display. A full length commentary track features Reiss and journalist David Williams, in which they discuss everything from the film's genesis (a real life experience of the director's) to the technical and financial pluses and minuses of shooting indie 35mm projects within a limited space. Other extras include a gallery of photographs featured within the film, talent bios, and a purposefully vague theatrical trailer (as well as trailers for a handful of other First Run titles).

COLD HEARTS

Colour, 1999, 90m. / Directed by Robert A. Masciantonio / Starring Marisa Ryan, Robert Floyd, Amy Jo Johnson, Christopher Wiehl, Christian Campbell, Robert A. Masciantonio / Synapse (US R1 NTSC) / WS (1.66:1), Bigben (UK R2 PAL) / DD2.0

 When this film was first released, in the immediate wake of Anne Rice, Buffy, and countless direct-to-video "erotic thrillers", the vampire subgenre appeared to have finally run out of ideas. A teen-friendly, indie-style updating of '80s vamp romps like *Near Dark* and the more watered-down *The Lost Boys* (minus the homoerotic subtext), *Cold Hearts* begs the obvious question of why it was made in the first place; while the proceedings are handled professionally enough, the prevailing attitude seems to be that of a film that wants to lunge for an easy demographic without fussing itself over such things as tastelessness or invention.

A band of seaside vampires prey on the tourist trade by night (cue the amusement park music), though the bloodsuckers experience some animosity between badass loner Viktoria (Marisa Ryan), her blood-abstaining and self-destructive best friend Alicia (former Power Ranger Amy Jo Johnson), and the dominating, stalker-prone Charles (Christopher Wiehl). Into this unhappy clan comes the mysterious Seth (Robert Floyd), a seemingly nice schmuck who brings out Viktoria's long dormant better instincts. Charles and his cronies, including sidekick Christian Campbell (Neve's brother and star of *Trick*), don't take kindly to Seth's intrusion but face a number of unexpected surprises during their final showdown.

Shot like an Aaron Spelling TV show with a little blood thrown into the mix, *Cold Hearts* constantly teeters on the verge of becoming something outrageous, wild, or kinky, but unfortunately it keeps reeling the excesses back in. The flimsy acting and erratic special effects (supervised by Tom Savini's disciples) don't really help matters either, though director Robert Masciantonio (who also pops up in a minor role) tries to keep things interesting with lots of moody neon lighting and a handful of shock set pieces; unfortunately even one promising and well-handled bit at a waterslide backs off from exploring the full horrific, comic, or erotic potential of its set up. The gimmicky twist ending would have also probably packed a much stronger punch if HBO's *Tales from the Crypt* hadn't already used the same exact device in a more imaginative fashion. Horror fans will probably find it all mildly diverting, and overall the finished product is certainly competent, but one can only wonder how much more powerful it could have been.

First released on a gritty-looking British DVD with Johnson receiving top billing, *Cold Hearts* fares better via Synapse's special edition. The licensor could only provide a non-anamorphic widescreen transfer, but that one obvious caveat aside, the film looks good considering its minuscule budget. The grainy night scenes still have a film-like look that avoids any distracting pixilation and other compression problems, and the limited surround audio is fine given the rather basic original mix. Masciantonio contributes a solid commentary track in which, par for the course for recent independent budget horror efforts, he covers the professional challenges of mounting a production on this scale. He seems to keep the film in perspective most of the time, revealing himself to be more of a craftsman than a nervy artist. The disc also includes a promotional trailer used to push the film at festivals, an oddball short film by the director entitled "Jerks", a stills gallery, and raw footage of original cast audition tapes which appears to be lifted from better than average VHS.

THE COLLECTOR

Colour, 1965, 119m. / Directed by William Wyler / Starring Terence Stamp, Samantha Eggar / Columbia (US R1 NTSC) / WS (1.85:1) (16:9)

After winning a small fortune in the football pools, a lonely bank clerk and butterfly collector (Terence Stamp) decides to make his life complete by wooing lovely art student Miranda (Samantha Eggar). To accomplish his goal, he purchases a nice house in the country, kidnaps Miranda, and keeps her confined to a secret room until she decides to fall in love with him. Horrified by her situation, Miranda must engage in a series of mind games with her captor before he will fulfil his promise to eventually release her.

One of the greatest psychological horror films ever made (though rarely classified as such due to its pedigree), *The Collector* marked a radical change of pace for director William Wyler, previously known for such Hollywood favourites as *Ben-Hur* and *Wuthering Heights*. Adapted as well as possible from John Fowles's tricky novel (which takes turns with its two main characters as narrators), the film is a model of narrative economy and character development, slowly drawing the viewer into the psyche of both kidnapper and captive while keeping them firmly established as flawed, believable human beings. Both leads are exceptional, with Stamp's simultaneous vulnerability and icy coolness making him an ideal psychopath in the making; the gorgeous Eggar matches him each step of the way, often conveying volumes with a simple gesture or flicker of the eyes. The soon to be popular Maurice Jarre also contributes a terrific, haunting music score, utilizing harpsichord to nerve-jangling effect. Though mainstream audiences had some difficulty embracing such a dark, troubling film, *The Collector* earned many admirers (critical and otherwise) and fuelled countless imitations, ranging from the sublime (*Tie Me Up! Tie Me Down!*) to the ridiculous (*Boxing Helena*).

Columbia's DVD accurately replicates the look of the theatrical prints, all bathed in delicate autumnal hues and occasional bursts of colour reflecting the central butterfly collection. While the earlier laserdisc tended to be oversaturated with orange and yellow, here the hues seem just right with accurate fleshtones. The film was shot open matte and exhibited at 1.85:1, as seen here; the laserdisc wound up exposing more of Ms. Eggar than was originally intended during the fireside seduction scene, but her modesty is kept intact here. The only extra is the theatrical trailer, which does an efficient job of selling the film as a major prestige product.

COLOR OF NIGHT

Colour, 1994, 139m. / Directed by Richard Rush / Starring Bruce Willis, Jane March, Kathleen Wilhoite, Scott Bakula, Lance Henriksen, Brad Dourif, Lesley Ann Warren, Kevin J. O'Connor, Ruben Blades / Buena Vista (US R1 NTSC), UFA (Germany R2 PAL) / WS (1.85:1), Studio Canal (France R2 PAL), Cecchi Gori (Italy R2 PAL) / WS (1.85:1) (16:9), Fox (UK R2 PAL) / DD2.0

Indisputably the most trashy movie ever financed by Disney, this Americanized *giallo* tribute from decidedly non-prolific director Richard Rush (*The Stunt Man*) tried to cash in on the erotic thriller craze of the mid-'90s but is in fact a much stranger beast. Though heavily publicized due to the amount of nudity and the studio's decision to truncate Rush's 140-minute cut down to a streamlined two hour running time, *Color of*

Night failed to stir up much box office interest but attracted more attention with home viewers who were understandably stopped in their tracks.

A heavily toupeed Bruce Willis stars as Dr. Bill Capa, a psychologist whose disturbed patient, Michelle (a cameo by *ER*'s Kathleen Wilhoite), tosses herself out of his office window and leaves a bloody mess on the pavement below. Traumatized, Capa becomes instantly colour blind and cannot sense the colour red. Some time later he's summoned to Beverly Hills by his successful colleague Bob (Scott Bakula), who allows Capa to crash out at his lavish estate. Unfortunately Bob gets slashed to ribbons in his office (a *Tenebrae*-inspired scene), leaving Capa to take over Bob's group therapy sessions which include a variety of neurotics: a crooked cop (Lance Henriksen), a twitchy nerd (Brad Dourif), an omnisexual slut (Lesley Ann Warren), a kinky artist (Kevin J. O'Connor) and a withdrawn teen named Richie. Meanwhile a nosy cop (Ruben Blades) snoops around the deceased doc's house and cracks bad jokes. Things get even more complicated when Capa's involved in a fender bender with the beautiful and mysterious Rose (Jane March), who keeps reappearing at odd times and turns the bemused shrink's life into a sexual free-for-all on the dining table, in the swimming pool and in a bathtub. On top of that, the mystery killer – now evidently one of the group session members – decides that Capa is getting too close to the truth and tries to kill him by dumping a car off a parking structure (!). When another gruesome murder finally occurs, Capa realizes that his days may be numbered.

An outrageous greatest-hits package of exploitation, Rush's film packs in gory slasher murders, lesbianism, sweaty sex scenes, deafening suspense music from *The Outer Limits*'s Dominic Frontiere, the William Castle-style colour gimmick (everything red turns grey from Willis's POV), a double-twist ending, graphic nail gun mayhem, bondage, multiple personalities, a rattlesnake in a mailbox, and much more. Apparently this was all too much fun for some critics, who dismissed the film outright as a misfired attempt to emulate the box office returns of *Basic Instinct*. However, this is one delirious thrill-ride from start to finish even if it can't be classified as a traditionally "good" film. As far as Paul Verhoeven films go, this really has much more in common with *Showgirls*. Fresh off her saucy turn in *The Lover*, March gets naked a lot once again but does well in her tricky role(s); too bad her distinctive choppers give away an important plot point earlier than they should. Everyone else overacts all over the map, with Willis actually looking subdued in comparison to the loonies surrounding him. One can only wonder how Rush kept everyone under control on the set, but the results speak for themselves.

In its theatrical incarnation *Color of Night* clocked in at 117 minutes; while the popular consensus tends to rate director's cuts as the best option around, this film joins such diverse company as *Dressed to Kill*, *Blade Runner* and *The Lawnmower Man* as a film which actually works well in its original, studio-altered form. While Bruce Willis's infamous full frontal shots were the most notorious trims from the shorter cut, other removals included all of the Warren/March lesbian antics, most of Henriksen's wholly irrelevant character background, and extensive comic relief footage with Blades. The result was a tighter, trimmer film that moved like a bullet; the restored narrative tangents of the director's cut add character weight but also bog down the story. Now consumers are left with no less than three different versions of the film, two of them on DVD (with only the U.K. disc offering a now infamous open matte transfer with even more genitalia on display); the worthy but decidedly padded "director's cut" is available only on U.S. DVD. This much-publicized American edition may indeed restore Rush's original narrative intentions, but it's hardly the most complete version around; the other

European DVD editions run about a minute and a half shorter but boast a significant amount of alternative footage. Chief among these is even more explicit footage of little Willis floating in the pool, a sequence in which Willis and March play naughty footsie under the table, and numerous alternative and extended shots during their sex montage. Some bits from the American cut are missing in exchange (namely a slower, more revealing intro shot during the bathtub scene), so neither one can really be considered definitive. The best of the European DVDs are the anamorphic Studio Canal and Cecchi Gori releases; the former features French or English audio and a French theatrical trailer. As with many French DVDs, subtitles *en français* are supposed to be mandatory during playback of the English track but didn't consistently appear on two players used to audit the disc. The Italian disc (with very spicy cover art) features the English track and a gimmicky Italian 5.1 dub track, with subtitles in Italian or English, as well as the Italian trailer. Both transfers are excellent, while the non-anamorphic U.S. disc looks decidedly drab and soft in comparison. The German DVD of the European cut is flat as well and only contains a German language audio option.

.COM FOR MURDER

Colour, 2002, 97m. / Directed by Nico Mastorakis / Starring Nastassja Kinski, Nicolette Sheridan, Roger Daltrey, Jeffrey Dean, Huey Lewis, Mindy Clarke, Julie Strain / Omega (US R1 NTSC) / WS (1.85:1) (16:9) / DD5.1

A slick exercise in updated Hitchcockery, with a villain who smugly tells the menaced heroine that he's seen *Rear Window* too and has surge protectors in his night-vision goggles

so her flashbulbs won't blind him. Like a lot of Nico Mastorakis's movies, it's a glossy stalker picture with high-tech elements.

Wheelchair-bound Nastassja Kinski is left to her own devices in a huge mechanised luxury L.A. home by her architect boyfriend (Roger Daltrey) and logs onto a sexy chatroom under his user-name, which leads her to ticking off a Goethe-loving, computer-superliterate serial killer (Jeffrey Dean). With her sister (Nicolette Sheridan) as sidekick, Kinski tries to sic the FBI on the murderer, who kills a girl and netcasts it to his next intended victims. Of course, the ranting madman and his gadgetry invade the home and a face-off ensues, with a ticking clock as Sheridan slowly bleeds to death and the Bureau's cybercrime experts (Huey Lewis, Mindy Clarke) dash about the city trying to locate the scene of the action.

A standard lady-in-peril shocker, with a lot of repetition in order to prolong the agony, this doesn't make especially good use of Kinski – though Lewis and Clarke make a surprisingly smart pair of cynical feds, while Dean overdoes the fiendishness with his eye-make-up, red-lit keyboard, Buffalo Bill nightshades and a suitcase full of neat tricks. Of course, Kinski has a lot of tech at her disposal too, and taps away at her keyboard or patters into her voice-recognition mike as she electrifies the doors.

Mastorakis's own Omega Entertainment produced the DVD, distributed through Image Entertainment, and so this marginal title comes with a modest but worthwhile package of extras. "The Making of *.com for Murder*" is a fairly substantial effort hosted by the genial do-everything Mastorakis himself; he says he won't comment about "how good or bad it is" working with the leading lady (though he has kind words for stripper Julie Strain) and Kinski notably isn't interviewed. Also included: unedited interviews with guest stars Daltrey and Lewis; music cues (not pop videos, but three tracks from Ross Levinson's score over montages of scenes from the movie and pages from the script);

scope trailers for *.com for Murder* and other Nico movies from his glossier, high-tech B period (*In the Cold of the Night*, *Skyhigh*, *Bloodstone*, *Blind Date*) rather than the grottier extremes of *Island of Death*; biographies-filmographies (skimpy for the cast, extensive for Mastorakis); photo gallery; tracks in English and Spanish; subtitles in Greek, French, German and Russian.

– KN

LA COMUNIDAD

Colour, 2000, 112m. / Directed by Alex de la Iglesia / Starring Carmen Maura, Eduardo Antuña, Jesús Bonilla, Maria Asquerino / Lolafilms (US R1 NTSC), Manga (Spain R2 PAL), e-m-s (Germany R2 PAL) / WS (2.35:1) (16:9) / DD 5.1

 A delirious, dark comic thriller, *La comunidad* takes one of the primary themes of Preston Sturges – great fortune dropped at random on an unsuspecting or undeserving individual – and gives it a sadistic twist that seems equal parts Hitchcock and Buñuel.

Carmen Maura (*Women on the Verge of a Nervous Breakdown*) is a hapless temp working for a real estate agency sent to show a furnished flat in a building occupied by a host of tenants, each of whom seem to have hurtled into this Polanski-flavoured edifice from a Fellini film. When one of said tenants, a lottery winner, turns up dead, Maura finds herself in a battle with the remaining occupants for the millions of pesos the dead man left behind in his water-logged, dilapidated flat. And, as they say, hilarity ensues, along with more suspense and gore than is to be found in any Hollywood thriller of recent memory. Maura's life-and-cash struggle with the crazed inhabitants – especially the creepy mastermind/building manager (Jesús Bonilla) and a maniacal housewife (Maria

Asquerino) – is a jumping off point for director de la Iglesia (*800 Bullets*, *Day of the Beast*) to pay ingenious homage to movies as diverse as Argento's *Deep Red* and *The Matrix*, not to mention a hilarious *Star Wars* reference that's the prime reason American viewers will probably never discover this ingenious film *en masse*.

The DVD editions feature a sharp widescreen transfer of the film, with especially good resolution in darker areas of the frame. The full-bodied soundtrack is presented in Dolby Digital 5.1 and succeeds in conveying the claustrophobic aspects of the dank apartment building, as well as providing an optimum way to experience the Herrmann-on-crack ebullience of Roque Baños's terrific musical score. The Spanish version boasts an entire second disc of extras including a "Making-of" featurette, deleted scenes, the teaser trailer, Goya awards footage, a great de la Iglesa short film ("Mirandas Asesinas"), and text bonus features which, without English subtitles, were sadly of little use to this reviewer, for whom Spanish is still a work-in-progress. The German release is also a two-disc Special Edition, while the one-disc American version ports over the featurette, deleted scenes and short film.

– TSG

CONTAMINATION

Colour, 1980, 95m. / Directed by Luigi Cozzi / Starring Marino Masé, Louise Marleau, Ian McCulloch / Blue Underground (US R0 NTSC), Anchor Bay (UK R0 PAL) / WS (1.85:1) (16:9) / DTS-ES 6.1, DD-EX 5.1

 When an unmanned cargo vessel drifts into New York Harbor, Police Lieutenant Tony Aris (Eurotrash perennial Marino Masé) hops aboard to see just what exactly is going on.

Joined by a health inspector and related personnel, he soon stumbles upon the severely shredded carcasses of several crewmembers along with some green, pod-like objects. Baffled as to what could've happened and perplexed by the mysterious, pulsating bursas he's discovered, Tony gets all the answers he needs when one of the sacs erupts, dousing his companions with a viscous fluid that causes them to promptly swell up and explode in gloriously gory slo-mo! Enter Colonel Stella Holmes, a callous ice queen from the Internal Security Department who's convinced these vesicular organisms were imported from outer space, and Hubert, an assumedly daft Mars-mission astronaut (the typically ingratiating Ian McCulloch) who's dealt with this situation before. Together, the intrepid trio traces the otherworldly shipment back to a Colombian coffee farm and, in an attempt to save the world, makes the jaunt to South America. However, they quickly find their intergalactic foes still have a few surprises waiting for them.

Originally envisioning a simple *Alien* rip-off, director/co-writer Luigi Cozzi (under his "Lewis Coates" Anglicisation) managed to incorporate the bankable elements his producers demanded (bursting bodies and extraterrestrial eggs) into a stripped-down mishmash of sci-fi conventions that somehow stands on its own two feet. Most fans tend to only discuss the outrageously splashy explodo-torsos (by Giovanni Corridori), but Cozzi is a talented director and they're only part of the reason *Contamination* is so much fun. To Luigi's eternal credit he sustains viewer interest, even when someone isn't blowing up, through good use of the scenic tropical vistas and several humorous character asides (with some of the goofiest dialogue this side of *Cannibal Apocalypse*). The cast is definitely up to the challenge, remaining straight-faced no matter how ridiculous a situation they find themselves in, plus it's always nice to see the underused Ian McCulloch chewing up the scenery. Another major point of interest is Goblin's outstanding score. Consisting of a few recycled cues from D'Amato's *Beyond the Darkness* along with some freshly written material (which Bruno Mattei's *Hell of the Living Dead* later appropriated), their excellent soundtrack has understandably become a fan favourite over the years. The out of print 1992 SLC CD release from Japan fetched some major bucks until Italy's Cinevox reissued it (with additional tracks) in 2000. Those who like their movies fun and trashy without taking things too seriously will find plenty to enjoy here.

Scripted under the moniker *Alien Arrives on Earth* (not to be confused with Ciro Ippolito's "spelunkers-go-splat" outing, *Alien 2: On Earth*), a money-man wisely switched the film's handle to *Contamination* during pre-production. Budgeted at about $225,000 with a shooting schedule of five weeks (including location footage filmed in New York and Colombia and interiors at De Paolis Studios in Rome), Cozzi's outing was a total bomb during its Italian theatrical run. Regardless, Menahem Golan's Cannon Releasing Corporation acquired the film for Stateside distribution in 1981. Reworked to delete some explicit gore for an R rating and retitled *Alien Contamination*, it was this compromised edition that was later issued on VHS by Paragon Video. A more complete option was made available in Canada with Lettuce Entertain You's *Toxic Spawn* release (issued as a cheapo EP-speed tape domestically by Saturn Productions), which was essentially an unauthorized bootleg of the British pre-cert VIP release (which itself was banned as part of the "Video Nasties" upheaval). Unfortunately, while the gore scenes were finally intact the print itself looked dupey and detail was horrendously difficult to make out – not to mention that two dialogue scenes were chopped to eliminate a romantic subplot. A better alternative was to import the complete Japanese Nikkatsu VHS, but after the letterboxed opening credits this version reverted to a cropped, panned and scanned presentation! What's a fan to do? Eventually *Contamination* made its DVD debut in Germany, released by CMV Laser Vision as *Astaron – Brut des Schrekens* (*Astaron – Brood of the Frights* (?)) and later issued again under this title by Marketing Film, but the lack of an English language track on either disc really hampered their value.

Thankfully, Blue Underground once again comes to the rescue and their U.S. DVD release is easily the last word on the subject. Restored from its original negative elements, the 1.85:1 transfer looks flawless. The picture is sharper than ever imagined with dead-on colours and no damage or technical flaws in sight. Those accustomed to seeing the film's previous incarnations will revel in newly uncovered details, especially during the opening venture through the ship's hull and the basement-bound climax, both of which previously played out in blurry darkness. For once you can actually see the "Alien Cyclops!" Not to be outdone on the audio front, Blue Underground pulled out all the stops and included a DTS-ES 6.1 track. The dialogue remains clear and centred throughout, with most of the directional effects being used for various gunshots, car movement, ambient background noise, etc. As could be expected, the Goblin score is appropriately cranked up and really shakes the foundations when necessary. Other listening options include an EX 5.1 mix, a 2.0 stereo track and the original mono for you purists out there.

In case the amazing remastering of the main attraction wasn't enough, Blue Underground has loaded their DVD with supplements. First up is a well-made 17 1/2-minute interview featurette with director Luigi Cozzi in which he expresses regret about changes imposed by the producers, comments on casting choices and generally reveals quite a bit about the production. Second is a real curio – a 23-minute behind-the-scenes documentary assembled during the movie's shooting. Filmed on what appears to be either Super8 or 16mm, this makes a nice companion piece to the newer chat and showcases Cozzi directing the actors along with several special effects sequences. Next up is a European theatrical trailer, which almost serves as a sort of music video for Goblin's "Connexion" track. It's well worth checking out, but watch the film first. We're then given two separate stills galleries; the first is a 66-item presentation of lobby cards, posters and box art mixed with many on-set photographs from the director's personal files, while the second is a 25-image collection of original concept art. Wrapping things up, for those with DVD-ROM capabilities there's a 54-page graphic novel adaptation translated into English for the very first time. This B&W comic (which originally appeared as an insert to an Italian magazine) reinstates several small bits that were nixed from the finished film, including a brief prologue and some nudity. The U.K. version from Anchor Bay is essentially the same aside from dropping the mono track and tacking on additional step-through liner notes.

– BH

CONTEMPT (LE MÉPRIS)

Colour, 1963, 103m. / Directed by Jean-Luc Godard / Starring Brigitte Bardot, Michel Piccoli, Fritz Lang, Jack Palance / Criterion (US R1 NTSC), Studio Canal (Blu-ray) (US, UK, France, Germany, Australia, Denmark, Spain, Sweden R0 HD), Momentum (UK R2 PAL), Surf (Italy R2 PAL) / WS (2.35:1) (16:9)

Still able to beguile mainstream audiences today, *Contempt* (*Le mépris*) glosses its acidic message in such sensory delights as sun-dappled South of France beachscapes, a ticklish collection of international personalities, and the sultry, often undraped form of Brigitte Bardot. One of the finest films about filmmaking, this is an ideal introduction to both the French New Wave and the possibilities of cinema in general; just don't mistake it for your average Jean-Luc Godard film.

During a splashy cross-continental production of *The Odyssey* in Capri, Paul Javal (Michel Piccoli) toils on the screenplay for director Fritz Lang (playing himself) and a boorish American producer, Jeremy Prokosch (Jack Palance, in a role purportedly based on actual producers like Joseph E. Levine and Carlo Ponti). When Paul sends his luscious wife, Camille (Bardot), to ride with the leering Prokosch upon their arrival at the Cinecittà studios, her respect and love immediately transform to, yes, contempt. At first baffled by her change of heart, Paul gradually comes to understand how his simple gesture has caused a permanent rift in the lives of this once-happy couple.

Often cited as one of the most skilful displays of Cinemascope framing, *Contempt* is awash in gorgeous Technicolor hues, which belie the ugly, raw emotions squirming beneath the characters' sleek facades. While Godard fanatics will delight in his trademark distancing techniques, beginning with the haunting opening sequence in which a shot of Piccoli and Bardot in bed is manipulated with a variety of tints and gels, the film offers other riches as well, most notably the opportunity to witness Lang in the last phase of career. (There's even a cheeky reference to his pair of masterful Indian adventure films, *The Indian Tomb* and *The Tiger of Eschanpur*.) Adding to the dreamy atmosphere is Georges Delerue's monothematic score, a piece so achingly beautiful Martin Scorsese used it to kick off his *Casino* over thirty years later. One of the more prestigious titles in the restored Rialto series which ran in art theatres and found its way to DVD courtesy of Criterion, *Contempt* spent a couple of years in transit from its 35mm revival to (amazingly enough) its first

presentation in Franscope on home video, but the efforts involved more than paid off. The transfer is an absolute knockout, with beautifully rendered colours and detail. The striking compositions of Bardot's burnished blonde hair composed in relief against the azure seascapes are breathtaking, and there's nary a print flaw in sight. If ever there was a title that screamed out to be viewed on a 16:9 monitor, this is it. The audio is presented in 2.0 stereo, though the film is mostly dialogue-driven and offers little in the way of fancy separation effects. It does sound robust and crystal clear, however.

The first half of Criterion's double-disc set is dedicated to the film itself, with commentary by film scholar Robert Stam. Obviously this was a fairly intricate shoot, with an iconoclastic director accommodating commercial demands in the most non-commercial terms possible while juggling an international cast. He efficiently dissects Godard's directorial quirks, which are very much in evidence here, right from the spoken word opening credits (which probably had more than a passing influence on the equally colour-coded *Fahrenheit 451* by François Truffaut).

Disc two contains a host of goodies beginning with "The Dinosaur and the Baby", an hour-long discussion between Godard and Lang in which they consider a variety of art forms, the role of the cinema, their collaboration together, and much more. Godard turns up again in a 9-minute interview segment from 1964, in which he chats about his attitude towards critics, his filming style, and more. Two films shot on location, "Bardot et Godard" (8 minutes) and "Paparazzi" (22 minutes), offer on-the-fly coverage of the film's location shooting, with the latter depicting Bardot as the most desirable trophy for a seemingly insatiable pack of publicity hounds. Interestingly, all of the aforementioned supplements are in black and white, which stands in stark contrast to the final product. Image quality is good to excellent throughout, though "Paparazzi" looks like it was shot on short ends and has suffered a bit through the following decades. Moving on, we have a half-hour interview with the legendary cinematographer Raoul Coutard, who also lent his incomparable eye to Truffaut, Demy, and many other vanguards of the French New Wave. Then comes a five-minute demonstration of the ravages inflicted on *Contempt* through television cropping, with a mobile grey box passing over the image to reveal just how much information was lost from each shot. Finally comes the brilliant theatrical trailer, a mysterious and beautiful piece of work that has been imitated repeatedly since (most recently by *The Rules of Attraction*).

If you've been scared off by Godard's reputation, this DVD is the perfect place to start; on the other hand, if you've only seen this film on television, prepare yourself for an entirely new experience. The two main location shorts and trailer are carried over to the U.K. edition, while die-hards who don't mind a lack of English subtitles may also enjoy the Italian DVD, which contains both the original French cut (with optional Italian subs) and the drastically shortened and reworked Italian theatrical release version, *Il disprezzo*, which features an alternative (rather good) jazz score by Piero Piccioni.

Contempt turned out to have a little more controversy under its belt when an announced Blu-ray from Criterion was suddenly withdrawn when Studio Canal decided to rescind rights to much of its catalogue to form an international brand of its own. Their efforts resulted in much immediate scorn when they forced Criterion to discontinue their versions of films like *The Third Man* and *Ran* only to have them replaced on the market by Studio Canal's substantially inferior versions. The reissue of *Contempt* (distributed in the U.S. by Lionsgate and the U.K. by Optimum) fares a bit better, though the jump to HD doesn't quite result in the dazzler one might expect. The film looks surprisingly blown out and gritty in many shots, and film damage is apparent throughout; it's still a significant boost in terms of detail, but anyone who expected the warm Technicolor bath afforded by the HD version of Godard's *Pierrot le Fou* is going to be disappointed. The nearly hour-long "Once Upon a Time There Was... Contempt" features Godard covering the entire making of the film and is nearly worth the price tag by itself, but you also get the half-hour "Contempt... Tenderly" (a study of its adaptation from the source material and location shooting), two film conversations with Fritz Lang ("The Dinosaur and the Baby", "Conversation with Fritz Lang"), and an intro by Colin McCabe. Die-hard fans will probably want to grab both versions as there's no overlap at all in the excellent sets of supplements, while casual cineastes should find either more than satisfactory.

CONTRABAND

Colour, 1980, 97m. / Directed by Lucio Fulci / Starring Fabio Testi, Marcel Bozzuffi, Ivana Monti, Ajita Wilson, Romano Puppo / Blue Underground (US R0 NTSC), Another World (Denmark R2 PAL) / WS (1.85:1) (16:9), Italian Shock (Holland R0 PAL) / WS (1.85:1)

Meet Luca Di Angelo (Fabio Testi from *The Heroin Busters*): loving husband and father by day, Naples's premier cigarette smuggler by night. Having worked his way up from the ghettos of Milan, his life is one of peace and prosperity until the police unexpectedly raid his trafficking operation and cause the loss of several million bucks worth of merchandise. Convinced he was ratted out by a jealous rival, things violently escalate when his brother Mickey is shot to death in a roadside ambush and his wife is abducted by an unknown assailant. It soon becomes apparent there's a new heavy in town and he's knockin' off bosses left and right in an effort to enter the narcotics trade, but this time he picked the wrong family to mess with. In a vendetta-fuelled rage Luca launches an all-out assault to eradicate his enemies, and he definitely isn't taking any prisoners.

Fulci's sole crime actioner eschews the traditional cops vs. criminals set-up and instead spins a gruesome mobsters vs. mobsters scenario. Fabio Testi may be our hero, but he's also a ruthless killer who lays waste to several folks throughout the flick. Relying on the old "honour among thieves" credo, followers of spaghetti westerns, samurai epics and Hong Kong "heroic bloodshed" gun-fu slaughterthons will find a comfortable familiarity with the general tone. Testi's good looks and cool demeanour add credence to his performance, and it's easy to believe someone with his charm could effortlessly climb the underworld ladder. The role occasionally harks back to the skills he honed as a stuntman, forcing Fabio to really earn his paycheck by ably jumping out windows and swingin' from ropes, among other things. The supporting cast also presents a few surprises, with Euro-sex superstar Ajita Wilson popping up as a slutty gangster groupie and all-around badass Romano Puppo portraying a particularly mean-spirited hitman who wipes out half the cast. Lucio Fulci's workmanlike direction lacks the energetic staging someone like Enzo Castellari or Umberto Lenzi would have brought to the table and he instead relies upon his customary forté: wholesale carnage. That's right, gang, *Contraband* ranks right up there alongside Tulio Demicheli's *Ricco* as the goriest, most ruthless *poliziotteschi* Italy has to offer. Bellies are blown open, heads are demolished by gunfire and, in one of the more excruciating scenes in Fulci's *oeuvre*, a woman's face is blistered off with a Bunsen burner. Weak stomachs beware.

Shot from the end of November through December 1979 on location in Naples with some interior work done at De Paolis Studios in Rome, Fulci's effort started life under the title *Vicious* and was filmed as *Mean Blood* before eventually settling on *Luca il contrab-bandiere* (*Luca the Smuggler*). Distributed overseas as *The Smuggler* and *The Naples Connection* (presumably to capitalize on Marcel Bozzuffi's similar role in *The French Connection*), the outing was skipped over for domestic theatrical dates and didn't see U.S. shores until Mogul Communications's 1987 VHS release as *Contraband*. A nice rarity for collectors, the tape itself left a lot to be desired with its cropped and fuzzy transfer. Additionally, the entire opening sequence was blacked out to showcase cheesy, computer-generated credits! The determined could acquire better-looking, more complete VHS editions from either Japan, the U.K. or Holland, but *Contra*-fans really rejoiced in 2000 when Holland's Shock Distribution announced their intentions to debut the film on DVD. Accolades soured quickly, though, when it was noticed that many of the film's blood-splatterin' bullet hits were mysteriously missing from the decent, but non-anamorphic, release. Blue Underground's U.S. disc thankfully rectifies this situation with a complete, uncut print that easily eclipses the import's presentation. Letterboxed at 1.85:1, their transfer represents Sergio Salvati's unusually subdued and slightly soft-focus photography as accurately as can ever be expected. By no means a vibrant movie, there are still several colourful interludes (like the discotheque sequence) that reinforce what a nice makeover the film received here. A few instances of brief print damage still pop up, but they float right by and aren't worth fussing over. The mono soundtrack, while obviously limited, is also free of any problems and the noticeable hum that plagued other issues is mercifully absent.

There's nothing out of the ordinary as far as extras go, but that shouldn't deter anyone from giving *Contraband* a chance. Included is a theatrical trailer which, amazingly for a

Fulci effort, *doesn't* give away all the goriest moments. Still, enough characters' demises are shown to warrant skipping until viewing the film proper. We also have a pair of talent bios for Fabio Testi and Lucio Fulci, although most of this DVD's target audience will have already read them on other releases. The Fulci-holics at the Scandinavian label Another World eventually took their own crack at this one with an uncut anamorphic transfer in English, three gallery slideshows, a "Tempus Fugit" featurette (23 mins.) about the making of the film (in Italian with optional English subtitles), and a slew of trailers.

– BH

CONVERSATION PIECE

Colour, 1974, 121m. / Directed by Luchino Visconti / Starring Burt Lancaster, Helmut Berger, Silvana Mangano, Claudia Marsani, Stefano Patrizi, Dominique Sanda, Claudia Cardinale / Arrow (UK R0 PAL) / WS (2.35:1) (16:9)

 Emphasis on the word "conversation" in the title here, as veteran director Luchino Visconti explored his twilight years with a drawing room black comedy after the orgiastic excess of *Ludwig*. For the last time he composed a tragic ode to his muse, Helmut Berger, with whom he shared a more than slightly complicated relationship off-camera; in many respects this could represent the director coming to terms with society and the film world advancing without him, reflected in the central character of the Professor (Burt Lancaster) who just wants to be left alone with his books and art relics. The Professor owns an ageing house in Italy with an expansive upper floor he plans on converting into a library; unfortunately his world is torn asunder with the arrival

of a pushy, bourgeois Marchesa, Bianca (Pasolini goddess Silvana Mangano), who insists on leasing out the floor for one year as an apartment. However, the rental turns out to be for her pouting kept boy, Konrad (Berger), though it's occupied just as often by her daughter, Lietta (Claudia Marsani) and her milquetoast boyfriend, Stefano (Stefano Patrizi). Much to the Professor's irritation, the family bustles to and fro, carrying out unauthorized alterations to the apartment (complete with water leaks and knocked-down walls), and generally makes a nuisance of itself. However, after nasty start, the Professor and Konrad reach a tentative understanding when the latter is attacked and left bloody in the middle of the night. Unfortunately the Professor soon realizes that life has passed him by, leaving some rich, spoiled brats to take over the world.

Though filmed with his usual immaculate eye for décor and composition, the first half of *Conversation Piece* (*Gruppo di famiglia in un interno*) is unusually spry and funny for a Visconti film. Lancaster's flustered reactions and Berger's profane telephone threats make for great trash viewing, and the story really kicks into gear one hour in with a kinky plot twist that really could have been elaborated further. After this high point, the film unfortunately loses its footing as it struggles to a tragic climax; devotees of melodrama will no doubt enjoy the climactic dinner party, which finds everyone screaming at the top of their lungs about politics and Berger eventually shunned because, apparently, he leans a little to the left. The last few minutes are pretty standard Visconti in his *Death in Venice* mode, with characters wistful about the tragedy of their lives, but it doesn't really live up to the earlier proceedings.

Of course, when a film looks this gorgeous, flaws like these hardly matter. The scope framing is never less than stunning, often turning confined spaces into elaborate visual vistas worthy of a David Lean epic. The performers and settings alike are never less than ravishing, and the ear candy musical score nicely balances classical music with some sparing dollops of Euro-pop. Pan and scan video transfers of this film are completely unwatchable, so Arrow's DVD is really the only way to go outside of a movie theatre; the 16:9-enhanced framing seems correct, and colours look beautiful throughout. The film was shot in English (with Marsani and Patrizi later looped by other actors), so the audio track here is appropriate. For some reason Arrow's cover art devotes most of its space to a shot of Dominique Sanda, who pops up for a few seconds in a flashback as the Professor's mother; likewise, look hard for a cameo by Claudia Cardinale in another flashback as his wife.

COUNTESS DRACULA

Colour, 1970, 89m. / Directed by Peter Sasdy / Starring Ingrid Pitt, Nigel Green, Sandor Eles, Lesley-Anne Down, Maurice Denham, Peter Jeffrey, Patience Collier, Nike Arrighi, Andrea Lawrence / Carlton, Network (UK R2 PAL) / WS (1.78:1) (16:9), MGM (US R1 NTSC) / WS (1.66:1)

In a fit of rage, ageing and embittered Countess Elizabeth Nadasdy (Ingrid Pitt) viciously lashes out at her maid and by chance discovers that the girl's blood has properties that can restore her youthful appearance. She then has the innocent girl slain and uses her lifeblood to regress to less than half her true age, so the Countess assumes the persona of her own daughter Ilona, who has been away for some years at school. She also embarks on an affair with handsome young solider Imre Toth (Sandor Eles), but as time passes it becomes apparent that the regenerative effects of bathing in the blood of young girls is transitory. Worse yet, with each reversion

to her haggard self she becomes increasingly decrepit and mentally unhinged. Intent on marrying Imre, she charges her devoted comrade Captain Dobi (Nigel Green) with the task of ensuring that a steady supply of peasant women are available for sacrifice.

Based with a degree of poetic licence upon the legendary crimes of the Hungarian Countess Erzsébet Bathory, star Ingrid Pitt often spoke of her disdain for *Countess Dracula*, in particular director Peter Sasdy's softly-softly approach to the bloodletting. Given the potential sanguinary latitude offered by the subject matter, it is indeed a relatively coy production, more costume drama cum romance with sinister overtones than traditional blood'n'guts Hammer horror. That said, Sasdy does stitch in some efficient nastiness – the gypsy girl's jugular spray, the slit wrists of the tavern strumpet – to prevent it from being a wholly anaemic affair. The shortfalls of Jeremy Paul's over-talky, under-eventful script are fortuitously all but buried by the striking presence of Ingrid Pitt, better still than she was in the same year's *The Vampire Lovers*, sensuously provocative as the younger Countess, a convincingly sadistic crone (beneath the ever more ugly layers of Tom Smith's outstanding make-up) in her older guise. The sequences in which the harridan Countess frantically paces her room, wailing and wringing her hands in frustration as she descends into the mouth of madness, are disturbing and yet tinged with an innate sadness. It was an odd decision to dub Pitt's aptly accented voice in post-production, but the actual harm it does to what is possibly her finest screen performance is pretty negligible.

Less than engaging input from Sandor Eles (*Evil of Frankenstein*) and Lesley-Anne Down (as the real Ilona) are compensated for with laudable character turns from Nigel Green (in his last screen role) as spurned suitor Captain Dobi, Maurice Denham as the scholarly Master Fabio (who discovers the Countess's secret and dangles from the end of a rope as a consequence), Peter Jeffrey as the requisite none-too-sharp police captain and birdlike Patience Collier as devoted nanny Julie. Nike Arrighi (*The Devil Rides Out*) is the virgin gypsy prophetess who's drained to provide the Countess with a quick makeover, and Andrea Lawrence (*Frankenstein and the Monster from Hell*) is Ziza, the whore with the heart of gold, whose "tainted" plasma isn't up to the task.

Harry Robinson's atmospheric score gradually supplants the gaiety of recaptured youth and the flush of new-found romance with an aura of impending doom as Toth discovers what's going on and is blackmailed into marriage with the artful Countess anyway. In spite of its few shortcomings – and an extraordinarily misleading title, which would have audiences believe that Nadasdy is a vampire – *Countess Dracula* is an elegant fairytale which, though not as fertile as some of Hammer's finest, is an estimable enough specimen of proof as to how they remained masters of their game for so long.

In Britain *Countess Dracula* was first available on DVD as part of a three-film boxed set from Carlton that also includes *Twins of Evil* and *Vampire Circus*. The 1.78:1 anamorphic feature is divided into 8 chapters, with subtitles and soundtrack in English. The picture is given to infrequent (and fortunately brief) moments of soft haziness, though it doesn't harm one's enjoyment of the overall presentation, which is otherwise rich in colour and definition. The Region 1 U.S. release from MGM (one side of a "flipper" disc, paired with Hammer's *The Vampire Lovers*) is a 1.66:1 non-anamorphic print with an audio commentary by Ingrid Pitt, Peter Sasdy and Jeremy Paul. The picture looks 'squeezed' in comparison to the British disc, with faces unnaturally thin, though the amount of picture information on these discs appears identical. The film's original theatrical trailer is also included on both editions. A subsequent U.K. reissue from Network features a comparable anamorphic

transfer as well as a different, rather saucier Pitt commentary track with Kim Newman and Stephen Jones, a TV interview with Pitt and brief news item on Hammer, a Nigel Green episode from 1970's *Conceptions of Murder* entitled "Peter and Maria", and a one-hour episode of Brian Clemens's *Thriller* (a spectacularly good show available in its entirety separately from Network), "Where the Action Is", with Pitt involved in a plot to lure former teen idol Edd Byrnes into a high-stakes game of murder; it's a fairly good episode despite the leading man's half-hearted performance, and a better-than-usual showcase for Pitt's acting skills.

– TG

CQ

Colour, 2001, 88m. / Directed by Roman Coppola / Starring Jeremy Davies, Angela Lindvall, Gérard Depardieu, Giancarlo Giannini, John Phillip Law, Billy Zane, Elodie Bouchez, Jason Schwartzman, Dean Stockwell, Sofia Coppola / MGM (US R1 NTSC) / WS (1.85:1) (16:9) / DD5.1

 Set in Paris in 1969, *CQ* tells the story of Paul Ballard (Jeremy Davies), film editor by day, aspiring director by night. His personal project is an art house documentary about his own life, while his day job finds him working on a crummy science fiction adventure film, set in the year 2001, entitled *Codename: Dragonfly*. Its director, the temperamental Andrezej (Gérard Depardieu) is booted off the production by producer Enzo (Giancarlo Giannini) for failing to meet his demands, and the task of finishing it is handed to Paul. Infatuated with the film's star Valentine (Angela Lindvall), Paul becomes so preoccupied with his new role that he starts daydreaming himself into the movie.

C

CQ is an odd but endearing first time directorial offering from Roman Coppola, son of Francis Ford. Sister Sofia had already stepped out from her father's shadow to helm 1999's *The Virgin Suicides* (on which Roman served as second unit director, having earlier performed the same duties on dad's *Bram Stoker's Dracula*), so it wasn't entirely unexpected when Roman took up the reins of his own project. In essence an affectionate homage to a period of movie-making long since past, Coppola clearly harbours a passion for the era and took his real-life experiences growing up in the company of filmmakers and fashioned them into something uniquely stylish and highly accomplished. Set in a world where shooting movies is second only to breathing, as the '60s dissolve into the '70s reality and fantasy interweave for young Paul. *Codename: Dragonfly*, the film-within-the-film that offers him his big break, is a *Barbarella/Diabolik* hybrid, this intention affirmed through the casting of John Phillip Law, who starred in the Vadim and Bava pictures; Coppola even pilfers the shower scene and bed of money sequence from the latter cult favourite.

Dragonfly (played by actress Valentine, played by Angela Lindvall) is a 21st Century spy working for an organization dedicated to freeing the world of crime, and she operates out of a lair-cum-spaceship perched high atop the Eiffel Tower. Her latest assignment is to recover a top-secret weapon from Mr. E (Billy Zane), who has taken refuge with a band of revolutionaries in a secret base on the Moon. It's a highly stylized slice of kitsch – it even snows on the Moon! – that would sit comfortably alongside any one of the films on which it's based. Certainly if you've a fondness for either *Barbarella* or *Diabolik*, then *CQ* is essential viewing. But there's much more to it than that. Jeremy Davis is splendid as "serious" filmmaker Paul, struggling to complete the lowbrow exploitation extravaganza by day while earnestly working on

his highbrow piece of *cinéma vérité* by night: "But what if it's boring?" remarks his live-in girlfriend Marlene (Elodie Bouchez), innocently damning his dream project in one matter-of-fact swipe. Coppola's cousin Jason Schwartzman amuses as pretentious and egotistical director Felix de Marco. Giancarlo Giannini effortlessly hogs the screen every time he's on as volatile Italian producer Enzo Di Martini. Special mention too for Dean Stockwell who cameos as Paul's father in one of the best-played scenes in the movie. The real revelation though is model Angela Lindvall in a screen debut that grants her the opportunity to toy with two starkly contrasting characters, plain-Jane actress Valentine and glittering action-babe Dragonfly; she handles both with aplomb. Threatening to upstage the players at every turn, however, are *Codename: Dragonfly*'s flamboyant outfits and tawdry set designs, mirroring with astute precision the look of the future as so many films of the time envisioned it. *CQ* is a beautifully crafted nostalgia trip invested with plenty of interesting, mostly likeable characters living out their lives in an era whose like we'll not see again. Absolutely unmissable.

MGM's Region 1 disc of *CQ* is a double-sided affair. Side A contains two faultless transfers of the 32-chapter encoded movie itself, one full screen, the other in its 1.85:1 theatrical ratio. Subtitle choices are provided in English, French and Spanish, and there's an optional commentary from Roman Coppola and cinematographer Robert D. Yeoman. Side B meanwhile houses the disc's special feature offerings, of which there are many. There's a trailer, a meaty photo-gallery, footage from a live concert by soundtrack artistes Mellow (including a rendering of Dragonfly's theme song performed by Alison David), five featurettes focusing on different aspects of the production and a quartet of diverse mini-documentaries, one by Coppola's sister Sofia (who cameos in *CQ* as Enzo's mistress), and another by his mother Eleanor. The most intriguing feature

– and the one you're most likely to want to return to time and again – is the option to watch *Codename: Dragonfly* (broken into segments throughout *CQ* itself) not only in its 15-minute entirety but also in two different versions, Andrezej's incomplete rough-cut and Paul's finished masterpiece. The latter offers optional commentary from Angela Lindvall. There's also a featurette on the making of the film-within-a-film segments and even a mocked-up trailer for the movie, all of which leaves one thirsting for a 90-minute version of the greatest exploitation romp there (n)ever was! And as if all this weren't enough, there are several hidden pages (accessed by highlighting the "Personal Documentaries" title bar, clicking up to highlight the poster art and pressing enter), which comprise a fistful of behind the scenes snippets and a deleted scene.

– TG

CRY OF THE BANSHEE
Colour, 1970, 88m. / Directed by Gordon Hessler / Starring Vincent Price, Essy Persson, Elisabeth Bergner, Patrick Mower / MGM (US R1 NTSC), Optimum (UK R2 PAL) / WS (1.85:1) (16:9)
MURDERS IN THE RUE MORGUE
Colour, 1971, 93m. / Directed by Gordon Hessler / Starring Jason Robards, Herbert Lom, Christine Kaufmann, Lilli Palmer, Adolfo Celi, Maria Perschy, Brooke Adams / MGM (US R1 NTSC) / WS (1.85:1) (16:9)

 Combining two Gordon Hessler restorations on one disc, this MGM drive-in pairing of often neglected AIP latter-day horrors serves to rectify years of damage wrought by censorship, recutting, and sloppy video presentations. Up first is the original U.K. cut of *Cry of the Banshee*, starring Vincent Price in *Witchfinder General*/Prince Prospero mode as Lord

Whitman, a domineering patriarch prone to slaughtering guests and family members who displease him. His latest wife, Patricia (*I, a Woman* star Essy Persson), doesn't take kindly to her husband's homicidal ways, but her protests fall on deaf ears. Things go from bad to beastly when Whitman decides to wipe out the local coven and disrupts the ceremony of Oona (Elizabeth Bergner), who sends a half-man/half-demon named Roderick (Patrick Mower) to pick off members of the offensive clan.

Typical of its AIP brethren at the time, *Cry of the Banshee* tries to evoke the spirit of Roger Corman's Poe films while also doling out sex and violence on a stronger scale. Unfortunately this resulted in a massive recutting of the film for the U.S. market, and this version (rescored by Les Baxter, with nudity eliminated and the mid-film coven attack becoming a prologue) has been the one most often seen in circulation. The original U.K. version is a much stronger affair (and boasts Terry Gilliam animated credits, too!); the more subdued Wilfred Josephs score and additional cheesecake shots put this closer to Hammer territory than expected, and the film is all the better for it. It's still no master-piece to be sure; the low budget and wildly uneven pace see to that. However, this is at least a noble and often fascinating addition to the Price and AIP legacy, which is more than could be said for it before.

A much more extensive reappraisal is due for Hessler's *Murders in the Rue Morgue*, made the following year. One of the wildest AIP Poe adaptations, this convoluted experiment in the fantasy vs. reality school of cinema stars Jason Robards (in a rare genre turn) as Cesar Charron, the owner of a Parisian theatrical troupe whose wife, Madeleine (Christine Kaufmann), is suffering from dreams which may be connected to her husband's grisly Grand Guignol productions. To make matters worse, a scarred, masked lunatic named Rene (Herbert Lom in a return to *Phantom of the Opera* territory) is stalking and disfiguring

C

the actors. Featuring a significant amount of restored footage (including snippets with familiar genre faces like *The House That Screamed*'s Lilli Palmer, *Diabolik*'s Adolfo Celi, Paul Naschy favourite Maria Perschy, and a very young Brooke Adams), this far more coherent cut of Hessler's film also removes the annoying colour tints imposed by AIP on the numerous dream sequences, as well as restoring the original, more satisfying twist ending.

Derived from the original, pre-release negatives, both films look simply terrific. Framing, colours and detail are beautiful and wipe away any comparisons to the old HBO and Vestron tape editions (not to mention the mutilated theatrical screenings). The double-sided disc includes theatrical trailers for both features as well as a Hessler interview divided into two featurettes, "A Devilish Tale of Poe" and "Stage Tricks & Screen Frights". Amiable and candid, Hessler discusses his difficulties with the studio at length and goes into detail about the casting and location shooting processes. (*Cry of the Banshee* is also available separately from Optimum in the U.K. with only the trailer as an extra.) Very highly recommended for fans of '70s Gothic horror, and a vital revisionist chapter in horror cinema history to boot.

THE CURSE OF FRANKENSTEIN

Colour, 1957, 83m. / Directed by Terence Fisher / Starring Peter Cushing, Hazel Court, Christopher Lee, Robert Urquhart / Warner (US R1 NTSC, UK R2 PAL) / WS (1.78:1) (16:9)

 The first horror outing in colour for Hammer Studios seemed like a gamble at the time. Universal had already exhausted the classic literary monsters by sinking them into the world of parody, and science fiction had taken hold of youthful imaginations at matinees around the world. So they revived Mary Shelley's literary chestnut about playing God, pumped it up with gory Technicolor, brought aboard the relatively unknown Terence Fisher to direct, and cast two non-marquee character actors, Peter Cushing and Christopher Lee, as Baron Victor Frankenstein and his monstrous creation, respectively. The rest, as they say, is history. Telling his life story to a priest while in prison, privileged Baron Victor Frankenstein explains how he was determined from youth to push the limits of society and scientific discovery. Franken-stein recruits his friend and former tutor, Paul (Robert Urquhart), for a little dabbling with the dead, to the ignorance of both his lovely cousin, Elizabeth (horror icon Hazel Court), and also the sultry housekeeper with whom he's having an affair. First the men reanimate a small puppy and then decide to take a crack at a human body, stealing the body of a criminal from the gallows. The resulting creature proves to be an unstable and violent entity though nowhere near as dangerous as its Machiavellian creator, who even resorts to murder to accomplish his questionable ends.

The Curse of Frankenstein is really Cushing's show all the way, and his forceful characterization would determine all of the future Hammer titles in this series as well. While each subsequent film offers a somewhat different slant on this scientist determined to tread into a forbidden domain, this first offering is a far cry from the well-meaning but doomed protagonist of Shelley's novel. Though his role is bereft of any dialogue, Lee cuts an imposing figure as the monster and offers the film's unquestionable showstopper involving a strategically aimed bullet. This moment remains shocking today and no doubt had audiences reeling in the days before *Blood Feast*. Cushing's surgical procedures are also far grislier than the sanitized antics of Colin Clive in the Universal days, and of course with Court on hand the sex appeal is amped up as well. That said, the film now seems much more quaint than its standard companion piece, *Horror of Dracula*, and the pacing occasionally lags a bit longer than it should. Great fun all the same, but it's really a primer for Cushing's more outrageous sequels before Fisher finally gave the Baron his swan song in the delirious *Frankenstein and the Monster from Hell*. It's also worth noting the participation of screenwriter Jimmy Sangster, who became a frequent Hammer scribe and was responsible for some of their most memorable titles, such as the often-overlooked masterpiece, *Scream of Fear* (and where's that DVD, Columbia?). Skilfully mounted and sporting attractive period detail, *The Curse of Frankenstein* is a visually enjoyable film but looks restrained compared to Fisher's more confident Technicolor splashings of *Horror of Dracula* and *The Hound of the Baskervilles* (or the even more striking chromatic fiestas of *The Mummy*). For some reason all of the Frankenstein films tend to have a more subdued palette; here everything is predominated by shades of blue, green, and grey. The occasional splash of red turns up here and there, of course, but it's a visually odd film which substandard video transfers have managed to render almost monochromatic (e.g., the pasty-looking widescreen laserdisc from many years ago).

The elements used for the Region 1 disc under review look clean enough, while the anamorphically enhanced, widescreen framing keeps the crucial details in check but may irritate viewers used to the more generous vertical framing of previous video editions. Headroom is more spacious than on *Horror of Dracula*, however, and even blown up to a 1.85:1 ratio it registers well. Unfortunately the only extra is the theatrical trailer, which looks like it has seen better days. The British DVD is only currently available as part of a three-film box set, which also contains *Horror of Dracula* and *The Mummy*.

CUT AND RUN

Colour, 1985, 90m. / Directed by Ruggero Deodato / Starring Lisa Blount, Willie Aames, Michael Berryman, Leonard Mann, Richard Lynch, Karen Black / Anchor Bay (US R1 NTSC) / WS (1.85:1) (16:9)

 Developed (as *Marimba*) by Wes Craven and released outside Italy by New World, this is a budgetary step up from the average Italian jungle cheapie – which means Ruggero Deodato has access to a few recognisable name actors (even if one of them is Willie Aames) and a few more helicopters and planes than usual. It's still a ridiculously-plotted melodrama, melding elements of the Italian jungle terror genre with a story that loosely derives from *Heart of Darkness* (well, *Apocalypse Now*) along with an opportunist appropriation of the true-life Jonestown Massacre to cover the tabloid exploitation bases.

It opens with a snarling Michael Berryman exploding out of the water like a *Jaws* imitation as he leads a tribe of machete-wielding South American Indians against a cocaine factory. The drugs war spreads to Miami, and involves an intrepid TV newslady (Lisa Blount) who winds up in the Colombian jungles with her cameraman (Leonard Mann) doing regular live satellite feeds for the station back home. The aim of the expedition is to secure an interview with Colonel Horne (Richard Lynch), architect of the Jonestown suicides, but the station manager also hopes this will lead to the rescue of his missing son (Aames), who is coincidentally a slave prisoner of the very same band of obscure killer Indians. The film is none too clear on many of its plot details, but stops every few minutes for crowd-pleasing gore footage as various characters are hacked, disembowelled, ripped apart, beheaded, crippled and raped in the service of underlining Horne's case that all people are rotten.

Cut and Run – filmed as *Inferno in diretta* – is an extraordinarily '80s film, from the puffy clothes and haircuts sported by the supposedly civilised cast (Aames wears a non-authorised Mickey Mouse shirt throughout) to the mostly synthesised drone of Claudio Simonetti's score. Deodato, never especially in control of his cast, is fortunate that Blount plays it straight, Berryman has an iconic presence and Lynch delivers a performance beyond the demands of the screenplay – since everyone else is all over the place (Karen Black, in particular, is bewildering) and too many characters tend to get mixed up.

Anchor Bay's "uncut and uncensored" DVD presents a nice-looking (if '80s-style bland) transfer of an anamorphic widescreen print, with Italian and English language options though no general English subtitles. Some scenes, mostly with violence, are in subtitled Italian. "Uncut and Run", a sixteen-minute documentary, reveals that these scenes are mostly the gruesome alternative material shot for markets which demanded violence; in the documentary, we glimpse the tamer versions (with clothed female corpses) seen in previous English-language releases, but it's a shame for completists that these scenes weren't included in their entirety as an extra. Besides the documentary, the extras are the trailer and a Deodato bio.
– KN

DANCE OF DEATH

Colour, 1968, 73m. / Directed by Juan Ibáñez and Jack Hill / Starring Boris Karloff, Julissa, Andrés García / Acme (US R1 NTSC)

One of four films made by Boris Karloff shortly before his death in 1968, with his scenes shot (by uncredited co-director Jack Hill) in Hollywood, the rest of the picture being filmed by Juan Ibáñez in Mexico. None are great, even by the standards of cheap late-'60s horror, but all manage a distinctive blend of old-fashioned pulp thrills with new-fangled semi-sleaze. *Dance of Death*, which claims spuriously to be based on an Edgar Allan Poe story, was made as *Serenata Macabra*, and has also been released as *House of Evil*; this version, which has burned-in video generated beginning and closing titles over dialogue and action and a 1987 copyright, seems to have suffered further trims since it runs nearly a quarter of an hour shorter than the commonly-listed 88 minute running time (though no plot seems missing).

It opens with the discovery of one of a series of eyeless corpses in the vicinity of Morhenge Mansion in 1900, then goes into the old dark house for some *Cat and the Canary* grasping heir business that sets up a premise not unlike several Charles Band films made decades later. It is also the only film in the quartet that suggests the script input of Hill, in that it shares several thematic threads and a sly streak of black humour with his masterpiece, *Spider Baby*.

Matthias Morteval (Karloff) is the elderly head of a family with a streak of inherited madness that might take the form of gouging out the eyes of strangers and a tradition of making and supernaturally-manipulating toys and automata. Karloff's character has scenes at the beginning and then apparently dies, letting the no-name Mexican cast take the weight until a finale where he shows up again, makes a hash of explaining the plot and plays the pipe organ as Corman-style flames consume the mansion. Among the more interesting moments are attacks by toy cannons and lifesize dolls of a dancing sheik and a platoon of toy soldiers, played by extras in playroom costumes with sewing machine whirring on the soundtrack to suggest their mechanical works.

Acme Video, an imprint of Rhino Home Video, offers a standard frame transfer with no frills. The print is in a pretty ropy state, with plenty of damage and fading, but – though the cover claims otherwise – it is in colour.

– KN

DANGEROUS GAME

Colour, 1993, 104m. / Directed by Abel Ferrara / Starring Harvey Keitel, Madonna, James Russo, Nancy Ferrara, Richard Belzer / MGM (US R1 NTSC) / WS (1.85:1) (16:9), Universal (UK R2 PAL) / DD 2.0

 Filmed as *Snake Eyes* before Brian De Palma used the title, this wound up getting saddled with a title that suggests an identikit cable TV "erotic thriller". Actually, it's another in director Abel Ferrara's series of plunges into Hell in search of Redemption, a draft of themes he would develop further in *The Blackout*.

Eddie Israel (Harvey Keitel), a New York-based film director, arrives in Los Angeles to make *Mother of Mirrors*, a movie about the disintegrating relationship of an agonised swinger and his born-again wife. Casting TV star Sarah Jennings (Madonna) and old friend Frank Burns (James Russo) turns out to be a problem since Burns is unable to play an abusive drunk without actually becoming one, and Sarah keeps reaching out to her director and co-star as a subtle way of taking over the scene. Given that Israel is so mixed up with Ferrara that the wrong name sometimes appears on the clapperboard and Israel's wife is played by Ferrara's, it's impossible not to assume that there are autobiographical elements involved, though Keitel throws in his own breed of agony to make this one long male howl. Towards the end, when the crises of the film start manifesting themselves in Israel's life, you even expect Ferrara to

intervene in the frame and explain things to Keitel, just as Israel compulsively breaks into scenes of Mother of Mirrors to sort out Russo and Madonna.

As movies about moviemaking go, this is uncommonly concerned with accuracy: the film-within-a-film is shot out of sequence, the sets are crowded with extraneous and unexplained personnel, and we see a lot of the footlings around waiting for things to happen. Keitel, following up his work on Ferrara's *Bad Lieutenant*, gives another stretching performance, coming over as together at the outset but gradually working his way towards a memorable farewell shot that finds him slumped by a vomit-spattered toilet bowl. Madonna, looking unglamorous, actually subdues herself to the material and gives the best screen acting performance of her career, suggesting in the intense off-set arguments the sort of sequences that must have been snipped out of *Truth or Dare* (*In Bed with Madonna*). Russo, overpowered by Keitel, has the misfortune to end up at the bottom of the food chain, representing Keitel in the fake movie as Keitel represents Ferrara, but nevertheless pulls out all the intensity stops.

The problem is that, since both *Mother of Mirrors* and *Dangerous Game* are constantly being interrupted by shifts of reality, it's hard to really get involved in either story, no matter how brilliant the performances are. It goes on too long and turns strangely soapy in its last quarter, but for followers of Ferrara's extraordinarily naked and urgent *oeuvre* it's still a gruelling, rewarding, shocking, and moving experience.

Universal's DVD presents the film in standard 4:3 frame, which seems appropriate for the compositions (some snippets appear to have been shot on video), while MGM's offers both full frame and matted (anamorphic) options; the transfers do what they can with the rough edges expected of a Ferrara film, though note the subtle differences between the various levels of reality and the director's habit of privileging performance moments over academically perfect images, a Ferrara trait not shared by Eddie Israel in that the *Mother of Mirrors* extracts we see have a far more conventional style than the framework film. The only extras are a trailer that sells the director over the star and, in the Universal release only, an insert booklet with a cursory note by the director that sounds like a blurb to drum up financing. Watch out for a funny one-scene bit by Richard Belzer of TV's *Homicide: Life on the Street*.

– KN

DARK CITY

Colour, 1998, 96m. / Directed by Alex Proyas / Starring Rufus Sewell, Kiefer Sutherland, William Hurt, Jennifer Connelly, Ian Richardson, Richard O'Brien, John Bluthal, Melissa George, Colin Friels / New Line (Blu-ray & DVD) (US RA/R1 HD/ NTSC) / Entertainment In Video (UK RB/ R2 HD/PAL) / WS (2.35:1) (16:9) / DD5.1

 An apartment block in the middle of the night. John Murdoch (Rufus Sewell) wakens in the bathtub, disoriented, frightened and unsure who he is. The phone rings. Murdoch answers it and a voice on the end of the line warns that people are coming for him. He flees, tripping over the mutilated body of a woman on the living room floor. With police inspector Frank Bumstead (William Hurt) on his trail for the murder of several prostitutes, and pursued by a sinister group of shadowy figures who seem to want him dead, Murdoch embarks on a voyage of self-discovery which leads him into conflict with a hive of telepathic alien beings who inhabit a subterranean world... and who appear to control the destiny of everyone in the City.

A jewel of visual wonderment, Alex Proyas's *Dark City* is one of the most original, fascinating and thought provoking pieces of science fiction to emerge from the 1990s or indeed any other decade. Brewing up a moody blend of dreamlike fantasy and classic film noir, Production Designers Patrick Tatopoulos and George Liddle have taken their cues from the likes of *Metropolis*, *Blade Runner* and Tim Burton's *Batman* to create a City like no other you've ever seen. The story unfolds in an unspecified era; the clothing, architecture and vehicles indicate early 20th Century yet the aura of a period in time as yet unreached pervades every frame. But it's perpetually night time and at regular intervals everyone in the City is rendered comatose by the aliens beneath. New buildings sprout from the ground, existing edifices shape-shift, and fresh identities and memories are implanted in selected citizens as they sleep. The premise is established in an impressive early sequence when the lowly dwelling of a working class husband and wife is transformed into a regal abode. With new memories implanted, they wake and go about their lives as if this is how it has always been. Travelling beyond the City boundaries to the fabled Shell Beach appears to be an impossibility, prompting Murdoch to try and find out what lies on the other side; what he eventually discovers is beyond imagination.

Rufus Sewell's Murdoch is the nucleus of the action, struggling to comprehend the meaning of a fragmented childhood memory while learning to cope with his own burgeoning telepathic abilities. Kiefer Sutherland is Dr. Daniel Schreber, a snivelling, creepy Peter Lorre clone, claiming to have betrayed mankind by assisting the dying race of outsiders, who use their combined telepathic energy to refine and revise the lives of their unwitting guinea pigs in a quest to learn to what extent the human animal is the product of its own recall. Schreber concocts new memories in fluid form beneath his microscope, employing lethal looking hypodermic syringes to plant them, and Sutherland's impassioned delivery of the beautifully written speech that explains the impetus of these experiments is a pointed highlight of the film. By contrast William Hurt's accordion-playing cop is slightly bland, underwritten to the point he's almost superfluous to the furtherance of the plot. Jennifer Connelly (*Phenomena*) is Murdoch's wife – or is she? – a sultry nightclub singer as non-plussed by what's happening as is Murdoch himself. The bald-headed, ashen-faced members of the hive are all so similar as to be almost indistinguishable, although chieftain Mr. Book (Ian Richardson) and the menacing, sadistic Mr. Hand (*Rocky Horror Picture Show* creator Richard O'Brien) are memorably evil candidates in the annals of sci-fi villainy. There are several extended cameos worth waiting for – for variant reasons – from John Bluthal (*Vicar of Dibley*'s Frank Pickle) as Uncle Karl, Melissa George (*Mulholland Dr.*) as a harlot tortured and murdered by O'Brien, and Colin Friels (*Darkman*) as round-the-twist conspiracy theorist Detective Walensky.

Though special effects are in evidence on a wall-to-wall basis, director Proyas is smart enough to use them to strengthen the story, not substitute it. The final staggering revelation of the City's true location is one of the most awe-inspiring moments in fantasy cinema, topping itself minutes later with an incredible panoramic shot of the sun rising over the skyscrapers in Murdoch's reshaped world. With a complex, but nevertheless coherent plot, Proyas's film is an atmospheric, nigh on flawless masterpiece of Gothic cinema and – hang onto your hat, here comes the contro-versial bit – superior to the over-praised *The Matrix*, which followed on the tail of *Dark City* and borrowed more than a brick or two from its foundations.

The initial Region 2 DVD from Entertainment In Video includes just a five-minute promo featurette and a theatrical trailer, with sound and subtitling in English alone. The Region 1 disc in New Line's Platinum series is a little more impressive,

offering up two commentaries, trailers, set designs, and an interactive game to locate Shell Beach, to accompany both full screen and widescreen versions of the movie. In 2008 director Proyas revisited the film to create a director's cut, and in this case, the results are all laudable refinements that enhance an already impressive jewel. The omission of a spoiler-laden introduction, the reinstatement of some valuable additional snooping footage with Hurt, and the thankful restoration of Connelly's original, far more fragile vocals to "The Night Has a Thousand Eyes" are just a few of the wise tweaks here, though for completists, the Blu-rays include the original theatrical cut as well via seamless branching. The Blu-rays also include a Proyas intro, an interesting making-of featurette called "Memories of Shell Beach", a production gallery, an "Architecture of Dreams" spotlight piece, a Neil Gaiman review, a director's cut fact track, the trailer, and multiple audio commentaries featuring Proyas, Roger Ebert, writers David S. Goyer and Lem Dobbs, cinematographer Dariusz Wolski, and production designer Patrick Tatopoulos. HD purists balked at a few scenes betraying a slightly overzealous application of noise reduction (though nowhere near the severity of New Line's treatment of *Pan's Labyrinth*), but to all but the most finicky, this *Dark City* really delivers.

– TG

DARK NIGHT OF THE SOUL

Colour, 1998, 97m. / Directed by Ron Atkins / Starring John Brodie, Helena Vaughn / Cutthroat (US R1 NTSC) / DD2.0

 It's not often you see a guy in a skull mask pontificating about the raptures of Satanic worship while flanked by naked, drug-huffing college students being brainwashed into the joys

of occult philosophy, all in a fog-enshrouded graveyard. But then you don't see too many movies like *Dark Night of the Soul*, either. Lensed in Florida and openly dedicated to that low budget cemetery romp, *Children Shouldn't Play with Dead Things*, this oddball concoction bears some visual resemblance to Alan Ormsby's classic but tosses in some distorted drug trip sequences, a shaggy-haired and topless priestess of evil, a couple of plaster sphinxes, and some poetic touches worthy of Jean Rollin for good measure.

The plot is as skimpy as can be: ostracized cult leader Shawn (the aforementioned masked man) and his zombie sidekicks preside over dark ceremonies in a graveyard, where a passing quartet of brainless, homophobic students fall into his clutches. The skulled one seems to control their gradual initiation into depravity, with tarot cards used as repeated symbolic illustrations for good measure, but his conspirators may have a few surprises in store themselves.

Though virtually devoid of bloodshed, *Dark Night of the Soul* compensates with plenty of bare flesh (including a brunette who, according to the supplements, became an Internet porn starlet) and the ripest dialogue this side of an Andy Milligan rant. The nonexistent budget undercuts the filmmakers' attempts at times, particularly during some ill-advised solarized footage, but surprisingly enough, the tinted trip sequences are oddly effective and eyeball-punishing. A handy abandoned monastery serves as the primary set apart from the graveyard, and the director milks it for all the atmosphere it's worth. As with Rollin, forward narrative propulsion isn't much of a priority here, but there are other rewards to be found. Bonus points for the continuously droning, eerie electronic score (courtesy of "The Unquiet Void"), which is reminiscent of the old Bob Clark days and keeps those surround speakers constantly humming.

An under the radar release from fledgling company Cutthroat Video, this film has been given a relatively lavish two-disc treatment. Taken from what purports to be the only surviving element, the transfer looks watchable enough despite some colour bleeding that seems to be inherent in the original photography. On the other hand, even the darkest scenes were lensed skilfully enough to keep detail visible and clear. Don't expect the clarity to approach anything resembling slick. Bonus goodies include a trailer, four teasers, an interview with director Ron Atkins (who was apparently so shattered by the film's tortuous production and subsequent reception that he virtually disowned it for a long period afterwards), and a 50-minute documentary covering the making of the film.

DAY OF THE DEAD

Colour, 1985, 102m. / Directed by George A. Romero / Starring Lori Cardille, Joseph Pilato, Antone DiLeo, Richard Liberty, Howard Sherman / Anchor Bay (Blu-ray & DVD) (US R0 HD/NTSC) / WS (1.85:1) (16:9) / DD5.1/DTS-ES, Arrow (Blu-ray & DVD) (UK R0/R2 HD/PAL), Force (Australia R4 PAL), Astro (Germany R2 PAL) / WS (1.85:1) / DD2.0, JVD (Japan R2 NTSC), Fravidis (France R2 PAL)

A few years after the global zombie siege of *Dawn of the Dead*, mankind is making its final stand against the walking dead. An irate band of survivors are holed up in an underground compound in Florida. They are now down to twelve in number, consisting of a volatile mixture of military, scientific and blue collar denizens. Tough as nails Sarah (Lori Cardille) fights for the rapidly declining sanity of her lover, soldier Miguel (Antone DiLeo), who serves under the brutal grip of psychopathic Captain Rhodes (Joseph Pilato). Meanwhile Dr. Logan (Richard Liberty), nicknamed "Dr. Frankenstein" by the increasingly agitated military, attempts to prove his theories of undead behaviour conditioning with his favourite guinea pig, Bub (Howard Sherman), a zombie who develops a love for Beethoven. Tensions mount, body parts are severed one by one, and eventually human weakness leads to a brutal face-off with the zombies ambling in wait outside.

In 1984, director George A. Romero faced a quadruple threat while mounting the third instalment in his landmark "Dead" trilogy of socially relevant zombie films (a subgenre he pioneered and now occupies almost entirely by himself). First and foremost, he had to compete with his own two previous films, *Night of the Living Dead* and *Dawn of the Dead*, both milestones in the depiction of onscreen violence and the use of satire and bleak political content within a pulp horror framework. Second, the market for unrated horror had changed drastically due to the highly arbitrary stranglehold the MPAA held (and continues to hold) on the depiction of violence onscreen, a situation that had already hobbled the *Friday the 13th* series. Next, the attitudes to screen horror were shifting to a jokier, more mainstream sensibility (borne out by the increasingly cartoony *Nightmare on Elm Street* sequels, *Gremlins*, *Fright Night*, and *Re-Animator*, to name just a few). And finally, *NOTLD* scribe John Russo was busy with his own postmodern sequel, *Return of the Living Dead*, destined to be released head to head with Romero's effort. As it turns out, the MPAA ratings factor wound up causing the most trouble, as financiers refused to cough up over $7 million for a title with such limited commercial prospects. Romero refused to adhere to the limits of an R rating and decided to scale down his sprawling, epic-length screenplay, entitled *Day of the Dead*, to a more manageable length with

nearly half the budget. To compensate, *Dawn*'s FX maestro, Tom Savini, came back on board and outdid himself with an avalanche of gory showstoppers, climaxing in a half-hour climactic siege with wall-to-wall grue. The resulting film was dismissed by audiences and critics as too repellent and downbeat, and it quickly died at the box office before shuffling off to home video heaven.

In retrospect, it's difficult to imagine how horror fans could have failed to see the value in Romero's film; it certainly played well with many audiences back in '85 and elicited all the raucous shouts, laughter, and cheers one would expect. In any case, the film was simply too good to disappear and built a solid fan base over the years, helped in no small part by fervent fanzine props from the likes of *Deep Red* magazine. And so, thanks to cable and VHS, *Day* belatedly took its deserved place in the pantheon next to its predecessors and is now usually ranked as one of Romero's five best movies. While Romero's prior zombie films were cutting edge commentaries on the Vietnam and consumer generations, *Day* is a striking shift in direction and tone. The sympathetic minority leads (black, female, etc.) are still here, but a tremendous misanthropic stance has taken over. It's no accident that this film followed on the heels of *Creepshow*, as this is also an extended E.C. Comics yarn, filled with nasty, hateful, backbiting characters who get their just deserts in a variety of ghastly, ironic set pieces. Many viewers rankled at the foul-mouthed, angst-ridden interaction between the characters, but that's precisely the point; this is a civilization finally coming completely undone, and in the best horror comics tradition, people who can't play nicely are going to get what's coming to them. Continuing the '50s influence, Romero incorporates those familiar tropes from drive-in era horror and sci-fi films, the military and scientific characters who clash over what to do with that awful menace lurking outside their door. The first half of the film is proudly in keeping with the dramatic layout established in *The Thing (from Another World)*, before Romero finally pulls out the bottom from his house of cards and lets Savini strut his stuff. The performers seem to be aware of this stylized approach with their histrionic, often hammy performances; Pilato in particular rarely delivers a line lower than a bellow. Special kudos also goes to Sherman, creating perhaps the screen's most memorable zombie; while Bub could have easily been risible comic relief, a dialogue-free Sherman imbues him with surprising layers of depth, humour and pathos. (Romero tellingly refers to Bub as "mainstreamed" elsewhere on the DVD, a sly commentary on his own perspective concerning the direction of screen horror.)

As effective as it is, *Day* is still not without its flaws. Romero was also busy kicking off his *Tales from the Darkside* television series, and a certain awkward, cheapjack quality from that show filters over here on occasion; some of the dialogue comes off a little too arch and pedantic, as if it was written for a half-hour TV show rather than a film. Another surprising liability is the score by John Harrison, whose stellar work on *Creepshow* remains one of the best electronic contributions to the genre. While the score to *Day* works on occasion (and sounds just fine on its own terms as a soundtrack album), the wonky tone more often grates against the action and cheapens the effect of several key dramatic scenes. Goblin and Romero's familiar library music tracks are sorely missed.

Anchor Bay originally released *Day of the Dead* on DVD as a two-sided disc, featuring the film in a non-anamorphic 1.85:1 transfer on one side with a trailer and half an hour of behind-the-scenes footage on the other. (Ditto for the various international discs, which are either full frame or non-anamorphic rehashes of pre-existing

masters.) The presentation was barely adequate for its time, and not surprisingly their upgraded "Divimax" presentation is a significant improvement. Colours are richer, restoring the full *Creepshow*-style blue and red glow to several shots during the climax, and overall this is a more vivid and satisfying look than the film even had in first run theatres. Just check out that fluorescent crimson when the operating table zombie's innards splash out onto the floor near the beginning; it's enough to make a gorehound cry. More significantly, the older disc had muddy black levels and gritty artefacting, which clogged up detail during several darker scenes; here the problem is completely absent, with crisp detail throughout. There has always been a bit of grain to the original photography (especially the opening Laurel title card), and it's still here and accounted for. The widescreen framing differs slightly between the two, with the 16:9 transfer adding some information to the right and lower edges of the frame while losing the same amount from the left and top. Compositions don't seem affected either way (and both were always preferable to the distracting open matte version on tape and cable). The Dolby Digital Surround EX and DTS-ES tracks sound crisp and clean, but there's isn't much in the way of surrounds; this was originally a mono film, and while there is some ambient support from the front and rear speakers (mostly the score and occasional moans and gunshots), this still sounds predominantly like a mono track with dialogue front and centre. Don't expect much in the way of showy split surrounds or gimmicky rechanneling; this is extremely faithful to the original design of the audio mix, and works just fine. For some reason the original mono version isn't included, though considering the limited nature of the remix, the loss isn't that grievous. (A stereo track is also included.) More perplexing is the presence of a few minor bits of alternative looped dialogue and clipped sound effects; though barely noticeable and certainly not obvious to casual viewers, this anomaly still should have been caught. (For example, when Sarah finally sees where the doc has really been getting his zombie chow for Bub (at 1:11:13), she turns away and utters "Oh, Jesus" in the standard print, while here she's looped in a different voice with "I don't believe...") The changes are extremely minimal, but their presence will no doubt stir debate for years now just like the hybrid cut of *Dawn of the Dead* and the frame trims from *Tenebrae*.

How many extras are there? You'll "choke on 'em!" Along with the feature, disc one contains a pair of audio commentaries. The first is an extremely lively and inform-ative chat with Romero, Savini, Cardille ("Ah, to have a young butt again"), and production designer Cletus Anderson (who kicks off by explaining how he achieved that amazing opening jolt). Everyone recalls the film with exceptional detail, and the track nicely balances the anecdotal with the technical. A very valuable and enjoyable listening experience worth repeated visits.

Unfortunately the same can't be said for the second commentary from director Roger Avary (*The Rules of Attraction*), who abruptly starts several minutes into the feature and, apart from raving about his favourite gore effects, doesn't contribute much notable about the film itself. Most likely he would have had far more to contribute on a *Dawn* commentary since he drafted his own variant on the Romero mythos and seems to reference it as much here as the film at hand. The only real nuggets of insight gleaned are that Avary was stoned when he first saw the film, he "pissed himself" over each gore effect, and as he points out over and over, he bought the *Dawn of the Dead* board game when it came out. Okay, you just saved 100 minutes of your life. Moving on...

The feature-laden second disc begins with "The Many Days of *Day of the Dead*", a 39-minute documentary featuring the participants from the commentary track along with Pilato, Sherman, producer David Ball, FX artist Greg Nicotero, and Christine Romero. Here we learn much more about Romero's original vision of the film, a factor barely touched on in the commentary, and everyone gets plenty of time to offer their own memories of shooting in dark mines for months on end (where they would cough up dark residue on a daily basis, a detail more disturbing than anything in the movie). Savini's effects receive a great deal of attention, including a welcome look at how he pulled off that jaw-dropping arm amputation via machete, while the actors all seemed to have an enjoyable experience. Sherman gets some of the best moments discussing his own mindset while portraying "the smartest zombie, which is slightly above a very dumb dog." Romero still refers to this as his favourite film in the trilogy and makes a few intimations about a fourth instalment (with Savini also expressing interest in continuing the series) which eventually morphed into *Land of the Dead*, and some interesting theories are given about the torrent of profanity in almost every scene in the film. "*Day of the Dead*: Behind the Scenes" spends 31 minutes exclusively with Savini, who is seen at work executing his gruesome prosthetic effects, which still put any CGI dismem-berment to shame. The late Liberty is represented by a 15-minute audio interview in which he talks about his portrayal of the mad doc, while a mid-'80s 8-minute promotional short for the Wampum Mine where the film was shot takes the cake as the strangest archival extra. The theatrical trailer from the prior DVD is carried over here, but the real doozy is a jokey second trailer in which an actor in Bub make-up manages to clear out an audience trying to watch Romero's film. A shorter third trailer offers a minor re-edit of the first one. Also included are TV spots, copious production stills, behind-the-scenes photos, posters, ad art, memorabilia photos, a zombie make-up gallery, and continuity snapshots; prepare to spend a lot of time shuffling through these. A Romero bio/filmography closes out the traditional extras on the second disc, all of which is thankfully 16:9 encoded and, like the feature itself, closed captioned. But there's yet more to come, and it's possibly the most valuable extra on the disc; though the packaging only vaguely promises a "DVD-Rom Original Screenplay & Production Memos", this section actually contains Romero's entire 166-page initial draft (in PDF format) with all of the characters and locations scissored out for budgetary concerns. Especially interesting are the changes to the characters of Rhodes and Miguel, while the (significantly less profane) dialogue touches on some major religious and sociological concerns jettisoned in later rewrites. Referred to as *"Raiders of the Lost Ark"* with zombies" by Romero elsewhere on the disc, this is a highly recommended reading experience and worth the expense of time and printing paper. The somewhat flimsy packaging features flip-open Velcro art of Bub which holds together the two discs, with an adhesive mini-legal pad (which might be a bitch for some collectors to store) containing liner notes along with some strikingly gruesome sketch art by Rob B. Webb.

Anchor Bay's single-disc Blu-ray version reinstates the uncensored dialogue track for the mono option (but not the 5.1 track) but unfortunately suffers from some excessive noise reduction, though nothing on the scale found on their wholesale destruction of the *Evil Dead II* Blu-ray. The Arrow Blu-ray looks considerably less processed and is also uncensored, while also adding a different commentary track (with FX artists Howard Berger, Greg Nicotero, Everett Burrell and Mike Deak), a wonderful 51-minute featurette called "Joe of the Dead" following Mr. Pilato from then till now, a "Travelogue on Tour"

for the film's re-promotion in Scotland, a 40-minute "The Many Days of the Dead" featurette with Savini and crew members reminiscing about the film's inception, half an hour of behind-the-scenes footage, a 15-minute audio interview with Liberty, and the Wampum Mine promo. In typical Arrow fashion, the packaging is also a fan's delight, with reversible cover art, a hefty liner notes booklet, a poster, and lobby cards. If you're a Romero fan, well, you really need both.

THE DAY THE WORLD ENDED

B&W, 1956, 78m. / Directed by Roger Corman / Starring Richard Denning, Lori Nelson, Mike Connors, Paul Birch, Adele Jergens, Paul Blaisdell / Lionsgate (US R1 NTSC) / WS (2.35:1), Direct Video (UK R2 PAL)

 The archetypal after-the-bomb AIP exploitation movie, this gathers together a cross-section of American society in an undevastated valley amid a ruined post-war world. "Cheap hood" Mike Conners sneers at straight-arrow geologist hero Richard Denning, survivalist Paul Birch witters ominously about the effects of radiation, and Lori Nelson (good girl) and Adele Jergens (stripper) compete to be the new Eve. Meanwhile, Nelson's hideously mutated three-eyed fiancé (an incredible Paul Blaisdell suit) lurks in radioactive fogs beyond the valley. It's hard to tell whether the film is being sloppy or clever in that it never has the heroine tumble to the reason why the telepathic mutant is pestering her, expressing vague sympathy for the creature and looking from time to time at a photograph of the pre-mutated version (Roger Corman himself) but never coming out and recognising who he used to be. However, it's a nice, self-amused touch to admit that while mutant skin looks like rubber, it's "tough as steel".

It's a mix of hokey old melodramatics, with characters snarling hard-bitten wisecracks at each other as civilisation crumbles, with then-new post-nuclear plot devices that have subsequently grown up to be clichés of their own. It relies on off-the-peg characterisations, but at least understands that we need to be interested in all the sub-plots – as opposed to many '50s monster movies that just trudge through the character scenes to get to the creature attacks. For instance, Jergens borrows from Claire Trevor in *Key Largo* and has a poignant moment as she runs through her old dance routine, explaining the effect she used to have on audiences, and then breaks down in a despair at once personal (she's older) and science-fictional (all those men are dead). Shot inside a week, this is watchable where other science fiction films of its time have turned into bores because Corman insists on keeping things going at a hectic, one-damn-thing-after-another pace. Though the mutant features prominently in the ads and the trailer, the film itself holds it back for the finale, setting its arrival up with shadows, out-of-focus glimpses, the odd claw and rustling undergrowth, then giving it a nighttime entrance before affording a full daylight look at the beast. It's not remotely convincing as a mutation, despite tiny vestigial extra arms and three eyes; in fact, it looks more like a fairytale creature from some Eastern European children's film. But it's striking and iconic.

Sadly, this is the worst-looking item in Direct Video's "Arkoff Film Library". The opening credits and the end title – of course, it starts with "The End" and ends with "The Beginning" – are windowboxed to show the full SuperScope image, but everything in between is cropped annoyingly to standard framing. This film was shot in a process (essentially identical to the later Super 35) which enabled a 1.66 film to be cropped and screened at 2.35. The version on the DVD is, however, panned-and-scanned, which means that an incredible 75 percent of the image

has been eliminated! If the director were Edward L. Cahn or Bert I. Gordon, whose AIP pictures rely on getting characters into the middle of the frame and getting their dialogue over with, this wouldn't matter so much, but Corman was already making full use of widescreen. A chat between the two women as they lie in twin beds is cropped in this version so we can't see either of their faces but get a good look at the bedside table, and almost all interiors are compromised by edging one or more characters into the dark.

The extras are identical to those on the other Arkoff releases: see *Earth vs the Spider* for details. The American disc presents the film in non-anamorphic "Superscope" in an adequate transfer (basically laserdisc-like in texture) as a double feature with a full frame version of *The She Creature*.

– KN

DEAD AGAIN

Colour, 1991, 107m. / Directed by Kenneth Branagh / Starring Kenneth Branagh, Emma Thompson, Derek Jacobi, Andy Garcia, Hanna Schygulla, Campbell Scott, Robin Williams / Paramount (US R1 NTSC, UK R2 PAL, Germany R2 PAL, Australia R4 PAL) / WS (1.85:1) (16:9) / DD5.1

In 1949, European émigré composer Roman Strauss (played by Kenneth Branagh) is executed by the State for the brutal scissors murder of his wife, Margaret (played by Emma Thompson, Branagh's spouse at the time). In present day Los Angeles, a nameless amnesiac (Thompson again) staying at a Catholic orphanage suffers nightmarish flashbacks to the Strauss affair. The nuns hand her off to one of their former pupils, low rent private eye Mike Church (Branagh again), who reluctantly agrees to investigate the woman's past. A charming and decidedly mercenary antique dealer (Derek Jacobi) dabbling in hypnosis offers his services to Church, and gradually the sessions reveal that Church and his charge may be the star-crossed reincarnations of Strauss and his wife. Unfortunately, as the truth behind the murders becomes clearer, their murderous history may be doomed to repeat itself.

Two years after the release of his wildly acclaimed debut film, *Henry V*, British directing/acting tyro Branagh made the leap to big budget Hollywood in what appeared to be a bid to cover his artistic bases as thoroughly as mainstream Shakespeare adapters Orson Welles and Laurence Olivier before him. The resulting film was *Dead Again*, an unabashed love letter to the Selznick-era films of Alfred Hitchcock: *Spellbound* (the Dali-inspired visual motifs, an amnesia-stricken and possibly murderous protagonist whose mind is unlocked through hypnosis), *Rebecca* (a romance overwhelmed by the lingering presence of the dead, a Gothic mansion, the ability of a long-suppressed crime to upend the present), and *Notorious* (an often disoriented heroine trapped between two men, a mother-dominated villain driven by love). (*The Paradine Case* apparently wouldn't fit into the already crowded grab bag of references.)

Though obviously a showpiece for Branagh's virtuoso staging and editing, much of the credit for *Dead Again*'s effectiveness can be attributed to the serpentine but always engaging script by Scott Frank, who lent his skills to such similarly disorienting whodunits as *Malice* and *Minority Report*. Separated by over four decades, the two storylines dovetail beautifully throughout thanks to the wise decision to lens the Roman/Margaret segments in beautiful black and white; the alternating chromatic schemes are far more than a technical stunt and pay off in a powerhouse dual climax which adds flourishes from sources as disparate as *Dial "M" for Murder* and *Tenebrae*. The film's reputation has diminished slightly in the wake of Branagh's highly uneven subsequent work, though his off-centre portrayal of the too-Americanized Church (complete with stilted accent) may also be to blame. Otherwise the film is pitch perfect, with Thompson making a wonderful Hollywood-style heroine (or two, to be precise) and Jacobi milking his part for all it's worth. The supporting cast offers a truly eclectic display of faces, including Andy Garcia (looking every bit a '40s star apart from a brief but distracting foray into old age make-up), Fassbinder staple Hanna Schygulla, and solid cameos from Campbell Scott and Robin Williams, whose affinity for hammy bit parts works well here but paid far fewer dividends in Branagh's *Hamlet*.

One of the earliest special editions from Paramount, this DVD is a generally attractive showcase for Branagh's baroque visuals but is mildly plagued by that odd, gritty-looking texture found on some of their maiden 16:9 transfers like *Grease* and *Rosemary's Baby*. The widescreen framing looks dead on and is essential to enjoying the film, whose opening newspaper headline was memorably chopped down to "URDER!" in its earlier pan and scan incarnations. The 5.1 audio is boosted almost entirely by Patrick Doyle's magnificent score, still among the composer's best-ever work, while split surrounds are limited mainly to the occasional crackle of thunder. Unfortunately the striking original poster art was nixed in favour of a terrible quadrant design, but the bonus features make up for this lapse. The bombastic theatrical trailer is an obvious extra, but the real bonus here comes in the form of multiple commentary tracks. First up is Branagh, who contributes a mostly technical and slightly aloof track that's filled with information but a rather odd lack of passion about the finished product. More engaging is the second commentary, featuring Frank and producer Lindsay Doran. They go into great detail about the elaborate process of bringing the project to life, from initial conception to carrying it out with the right creative team.

DEAD MEN WALK

B&W, 1943, 62m. / Directed by Sam Newfield / Starring George Zucco, Mary Carlisle, Nedrick Young, Dwight Frye

THE MONSTER MAKER

B&W, 1944, 63m. / Directed by Sam Newfield / Starring J. Carrol Naish, Ralph Morgan, Tala Birrell, Wanda McKay, Glenn Strange / Roan (US R0 NTSC)

Number 8 in the Roan Group's "Horror Classics" series, this flipper disc presents two quickies from Sam Newfield, brother of PRC honcho Sigmund Neufeld. Both have features of interest, almost by accident, but are also the usual derivative B nonsense.

Dead Men Walk is a New England-set vampire movie, with the gimmick that PRC's frequent star George Zucco plays both the vampire and his vampire-hunting twin brother, with or without a wig to differentiate the roles (which means it can't make much of the usual *Black Room* business of the bad twin impersonating the good one). Dwight Frye, Lugosi's old cringing minion, has a late, entirely stock role as a vampire-toadying hunchback with a weird name (Zolarr) and most of the script consists of offcuts from Universal's Dracula pictures. Zucco is always value for money, and it's nice to see him equally stereotyped as the benign academic and his Satanic sibling, but even at a lick over an hour, these dead men walk slowly.

The Monster Maker has a more unusual premise, though it "borrows" heavily from the Lugosi-Karloff *The Raven* in making the villain (J. Carrol Naish) a mad genius medico obsessed with a young woman (Tala Birrell) who resembles his idealized lost love (in this instance, a dead wife). Like Lugosi, Naish goes after the unwilling heroine by torturing her father – here, injecting a genial concert pianist (Ralph Morgan) with a fluid that causes the deforming condition acromegaly (forever

associated in the minds of B horror fans with Rondo Hatton). There are a few effective moments, such as when the heroine hears music coming from her father's darkened study and rushes in thinking he has stirred from his misery only to find the now-deformed pianist listening in depression to one of his old records. By PRC's standards, which usually stretched barely to cardboard Devil Bats, the make-up effects are surprisingly good, and Morgan tries harder than many a lazy horror star would have done to make the "monster" pathetic. But all the characters are stock, and the ending is extremely flat.

Both features have been PD eyesores for years; Roan's transfers are above average for the materials.

– KN

DEAD OF NIGHT

B&W, 1945, 103m. / Directed by Charles Crichton, Alberto Cavalcanti, Basil Dearden and Robert Hamer / Starring Michael Redgrave, Mervyn Johns

QUEEN OF SPADES

B&W, 1949, 95m. / Directed by Thorold Dickinson / Starring Anton Walbrook, Edith Evans, Yvonne Mitchell / Anchor Bay (US R1 NTSC), Studio Canal (France R2 PAL), Optimum (UK R2 PAL)

While the real life horrors of World War II ensured that true horror films took a backseat to reassuring, safe fare like the Universal monster sequels and comedies, occasional genuine frights managed to slip through during the latter half of the decade. Britain in particular opened the floodgates with *Dead of Night*, one of the finest horror anthologies (though hardly the first, despite its reputation). Many of the genre's conventions were explicitly spelled out here; one need only look at the handful of Amicus anthologies like *Dr.*

Terror's House of Horrors and programs like *The Twilight Zone* and *Tales from the Crypt* to see the influence. Of course we also have this film to thank for the numerous evil ventriloquist/dummy films and TV programs (*Magic*, *Devil Doll*, et al), not to mention the trend of using big ensembles of actors to boost the marquee value. The often imitated framing device begins when a nervous guest (Mervyn Johns) arrives at a country home for the weekend and immediately experiences overpowering déjà vu. The guests are intrigued by his claim and begin to relate their own stories of brushes with the paranormal, including a car racer's eerie dreams foretelling of misfortune, a ghostly encounter at a children's Christmas party, an antique mirror exerting a malefic influence on a young couple, a pair of golfers feuding beyond death for the love of a woman, and a ventriloquist (Michael Redgrave) whose dummy seems to be getting a bit out of control.

Though not all of the stories are classics (e.g., the golfer episode, which was trimmed from the original U.S. prints along with the wonderful Christmas yarn), *Dead of Night* rises above any such flaws due to the sheer force and commitment of the material and execution. Normally such a hodgepodge of directors and styles would be a detriment, but here the framing device is so chilling and wonderfully conceived (with Johns making bizarre predictions which have a habit of coming to pass) that it makes the strongest moments seem even more bloodcurdling in context. The mirror and ventriloquist stories still pack a sizeable punch, and the nightmarish finale, which ties all of the loose ends together, could hardly be more effective. Mandatory viewing for any horror fan, this is still one of the greats.

The Studio Canal transfer released under their own banner in France and by Anchor Bay in the U.S. is an attractive presentation, with far better contrast and detail than the earlier tape and laserdisc editions. The sound is still on the shrill and tinny side, which is unfortunate. Extras include a behind the scenes stills gallery (including some nice cast shots) and various international posters and stills. This edition is now out of print, though a later U.K. disc by Optimum popped up in 2006 sadly looking much the worse for wear, apparently yanked from an old one-inch master and actually sounding far more muffled.

Paired up with the U.S. disc is a far more obscure English ghost story, *Queen of Spades*, a cult item known mostly to viewers through late night television screenings. Based on a story by Alexander Pushkin (and later adapted into a Tchaikovsky opera, also available on home video), the film chronicles the sinister misadventures of Herman Suvorin (Anton Walbrook from *The Red Shoes*), a down on his luck Russian officer desperate to join the lucrative gambling craze sweeping the country. Through a series of clues he learns that Countess Ranevskaya (*The Importance of Being Earnest*'s Edith Evans) sold her soul to the devil years ago in exchange for the secret of winning at cards. He worms his way into the confidence of the Countess's beautiful ward, Lizaveta (*Demons of the Mind*'s Yvonne Mitchell), with horrific results for all concerned. Elegantly mounted and played to perfection, *Queen of Spades* is a class act all the way, aided in no small part by stylish direction from Thorold Dickinson (who made the British, pre-MGM version of *Gaslight*, also starring Walbrook) and excellent cinematography by Otto Heller (*Peeping Tom*). As if that weren't enough of a pedigree, the film's composer was Georges Auric and the associate producer was Jack Clayton, both of whom went on create one of the screen's greatest ghost stories, *The Innocents*.

For all of its effectiveness and historical importance, *Queen of Spades* may suffer a bit with modern viewers expecting a full throttle tale of terror. More than an hour of the film is a simple character study of Herman, a thoroughly unsympathetic character whose conniving and whining makes the payoff a bit difficult to reach. Once he finally confronts Evans in her home, the film takes flight with a series of beautifully mounted set pieces climaxing with a memorable showdown at the card table.

Anchor Bay's DVD features a nice though unspectacular transfer; it's doubtful the film could look much better without an expensive restoration. The mono audio sounds fine, with excellent bass. Extras include the theatrical trailer (which plays up the role of producer Anatole de Grunwold and ignores the horror aspects), a fun gallery of candid shots behind the scenes, and a poster and stills gallery. A U.K. release on Optimum in 2010 (following theatrical screenings for the first time in 60 years) includes a filmed introduction by Martin Scorsese, two audio interviews with Thorold Dickinson from 1951 and 1968, an analysis of the film by Philip Horne, and the original trailer.

DEAD OF WINTER

Colour, 1987, 100m. / Directed by Arthur Penn / Starring Mary Steenburgen, Roddy McDowall, Jan Rubes / MGM (US R1 NTSC) / WS (1.85:1) / DD2.0

 A bizarre change of pace for Arthur Penn (the director of *Bonnie and Clyde*), this Gothic melodrama lifts several plot points from the excellent, though little-seen 1945 thriller *My Name Is Julia Ross* but fashions a creepy mood all its own.

Responding to a trade magazine call for acting jobs, Katie McGovern (Mary Steenburgen) is approached by a twitchy casting representative (Roddy McDowall) who offers her a job in upstate New York. Soon she finds herself in the snowy wilderness, staying at an isolated mansion with a vaguely creepy casting agent (Jan Rubes) who videotapes her delivering a sinister monologue about attempted murder. After finding the contents of her wallet burning in a fireplace and the phone lines cut, Katie realizes that a murderous plot is underway, with her audition tape as the centrepiece.

Despite a few sadistic concessions to the slasher craze of the time, the traditional old dark house approach ironically keeps the film from feeling dated. Steenburgen contributes no less than three performances, even battling herself as both heroine and villainess in one memorable showdown, though her turn as Katie is the most effective and one of her best showcases to date. McDowall is watchable as always, building up a menacing characterization slowly enough to be believable. The climax sags somewhat with a silly showdown in which the able-bodied Steenburgen is menaced by a very, very slow opponent, and cutaways to the standard boyfriend-to-the-rescue are distracting; despite these flaws, *Dead of Winter* remains a crackerjack suspenser worthy of a larger fan base. Since every director seems obligated to make his own "Hitchcock film", here you'll find nods to such classics as *Vertigo* and *Rear Window*. Though exactly who is responsible for these touches is not entirely clear, as it should be noted that most of this film was actually directed by Marc Shmuger (a friend of Arthur Penn's son) under Penn's supervision. The decision to give Penn the director credit appears to have been made at the last minute, presumably for commercial reasons.

MGM's DVD offers both full frame (open matte) and letterboxed transfers; the latter simply appears to be black mattes slapped over the former, with no 16:9 enhancement. Inexplicably, the open matte version looks a bit sharper and makes for more satisfying viewing. Surround audio is fine for a mid-'80s title; the music receives most of the audio separation along with the occasional howling wind sound effects. A theatrical trailer is the sole extra.

D

DEAD OR ALIVE

Colour, 2000, 105m. / Directed by Takashi Miike / Starring Riki Takeuchi, Sho Aikawa, Renji Ishibashi / Tartan (UK R0 PAL), Kino (US R1 NTSC) / WS (1.85:1) (16:9)

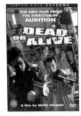

Takashi Miike has made so many films that it'll take more than the sampling so far released outside Japan to get a handle on him. It might also not help that most non-Japanese started on his *oeuvre* with *Audition*, which seems to be atypically controlled, rather than one of his many, many scrappier efforts. This lively, absurd yakuza movie may well be the entry-level Miike: a very familiar plot about a hood and a cop whose lives unfold in parallel until a stand-off at the end is the springboard for wild style, strange comedy and dollops of unusual milieu. It has set piece opening and closing sequences, with a confusing, makeshift middle, working on a scene-by-scene basis but never quite connecting the dots, with a lot of characters who buzz through without making enough of an impression to keep the interest.

The opening is almost like a trailer or MTV clip, with pounding music and a lot of intercut vignettes – a naked woman falling out of a building clutching a bag of cocaine, a suited doper snorting the world's longest line off a bar, a traditionally-dressed hit man stabbing a gay thug who is having sex in a toilet (a spray of arterial blood soaks his boyfriend), etc. Then, we are in the world between the Chinese triads and the Japanese Yakuza, with the main crook characters unusual in that they are in-betweens, ethnic Japanese left on the Chinese mainland after the war but returned to be outsiders in Japan (however, they are all a lot younger than this would suggest). Crook Ryuichi (Riki Takeuchi) has a disapproving brother and a mob of youngish punks, some of whom are hard to keep in line, while cop Jojima (Sho Aikawa) has an ailing daughter and an awkward marriage.

There's a strange bit of trickery early on with a knife-throwing act in a gay circus, and a joke about bestiality porn as a visitor to a photographer is asked to stimulate a dog to erection before a shoot can continue, but these sexual frills mingle with typical sub-John Woo gunplay and brooding, until the deliberately ridiculous finish, prefaced with the line "here comes that scene." If you've never seen the film, skip the next sentence as a spoiler; if you have you still won't believe the director actually shot a finale in which the protagonists blow up each other's cars but pass into a cartoonish world where the wounded cop can rip off his arms and pull a bazooka out of his jacket and the gangster extracts a glowing ball from his heart that blows up all of Japan. It's incredible, but a tad desperate, though tame compared to the excesses of Miike's subsequent *Ichi the Killer*, a film that seems calculated to make this seem conventional.

Tartan's DVD looks fine, considering Miike mixes scenes shot with care and deliberation with connective material that might have been thrown together as an afterthought. It has a Japanese language soundtrack, with optional English subtitles. Besides trailers and filmographies, the extras are extensive notes by Chris Campion that put the film in some sort of context and an interesting if enigmatic chat with the very busy (some years, he makes seven or eight films) Miike, who conveys a bit of background but also the sense that he can't quite remember which of his projects this was.

– KN

DEAD OR ALIVE 2

Colour, 2000, 95m. / Directed by Takashi Miike / Starring Sho Aikawa, Noriko Aota, Riki Takeuchi / Tartan (UK R0 PAL), Kino (US R1 NTSC) / WS (1.85:1) (16:9) / DD2.0

An off-the-cuff Japanese gangster movie with an absurdist streak that shades into surrealism, *Dead or Alive 2* isn't thrown by its brief to sequelise a film which ended not only with the deaths of its lead characters but also the destruction of Japan. This follow-up, aka *Dead or Alive 2: Birds*, brings back the stars of the first film but gives them fresh roles and relationships though it does spring a few gag-references that refer back to *Dead or Alive*, such as when characters pull brieze-blocks out of the backs of their shirts or wear cardboard cyborg arms to evoke gimmicks that pleased crowds first time round. Miike spins off another strange shaggy dog tale that starts out with a Yakuza vs. Triads gang war in the offing, then sidesteps into Beat Takeshi territory as a couple of hit-men who meet when they turn up for the same assassination turn out to be childhood friends and enjoy a nostalgic wallow as they return to the orphanage where they originally met, re-encounter other old pals and stand in for some injured actors putting on a play for the children. White-suited and terminally ill Shu Sawada (Riki Takeuchi) and bleached blond and Hawaiian-shirted Mizumi Otamoko (Sho Aikawa) get back to gunplay, committing contract murders and funnelling the profits into third world charities, which earns them occasional angel-wings or transformations back into innocent children. In constant danger of collapse, the film keeps pulling surprises: txt msg-addicted killers, a *Godfather*-style intercutting of the kiddie play with a high body-count gang war back in the city, an animated diagram of bullet trajectories through an unfortunate dwarf's brain.

The first film blew up the country because it couldn't think of an ending, and this also has a lot of trouble signing off, with protracted deaths and redemptions for the heroes. Miike alternates clumsiness and confusion with exciting and powerful cinema, and here manages a few stretches of affecting, nothing-in-particular-happening male bonding and nostalgia as he is distracted from the carnage by a method of eating tofu soup or gaining sexual satisfaction from poles.

Tartan's DVD is anamorphic widescreen with a Japanese language track and optional English subtitles. Besides filmographies and trailers familiar from the distributor's other Miike releases, there are some pertinent notes by Sloan Freer. The later Kino release from 2003 follows suit with a similar transfer and the trailer as well as bonus promos from their other Japanese titles.

– KN

DEATH AND THE MAIDEN

Colour, 1994, 103m. / Directed by Roman Polanski / Starring Sigourney Weaver, Ben Kingsley, Stuart Wilson / New Line (US R1 NTSC) / WS (1.85:1) (16:9) / DD2.0

Roman Polanski had his work cut out for him with this film. Adapting a prize-winning Ariel Dorfman play about the aftershocks of political torture in South America, the resourceful director employed a capable but decidedly non-Latino cast and a story which rigorously resisted any kind of cinematic "opening up" to conceal its stage origins. Yet somehow the entire project works and packs an emotional wallop, thanks to the ingenious decision to treat this as another of Polanski's chamber dramas exploring the process of madness, in the same vein as *Repulsion*, *The Tenant*, and *Rosemary's Baby*. Set entirely during a stormy night in a remote house, the film takes on an oppressive, chilling air in which viewer sympathies shift every five minutes with disturbing ease.

Left alone at home, former activist Paulina Escobar (Sigourney Weaver) is a bundle of nerves by the time her politically ambitious husband, Gerardo (Stuart Wilson), arrives home after being delayed by a flat tyre. However, Gerardo didn't come home alone; he was driven by Dr. Miranda (Ben Kingsley), whose voice Paulina recognises from years earlier as the man who brutally tortured and molested her to the strains of Schubert's "Death and the Maiden". Much to her husband's horror, Paulina takes their guest hostage in an attempt to force him to admit the truth; Miranda steadfastly denies that he was ever involved with her torture, while Gerardo is forced to determine whether his wife is delusional or truly seeking justice for an unimaginable crime.

Despite the grim subject matter, *Death and the Maiden* is an involving and surprisingly cathartic viewing experience, leaving the viewer on a far more hopeful (though still tremulous) note than expected. As with *Bitter Moon*, Polanski drifts away from the more pessimistic, darkly humorous finales of his earlier films and towards a sort of survivor's stalemate, an approach he would explore further with *The Ninth Gate* and particularly *The Pianist*, for which this film feels like an emotional dry run.

New Line's DVD features much deeper and more appropriate black levels than their earlier laserdisc, though that edition's 1.66:1 framing has been cropped in a bit to 1.85:1 for the DVD. The tighter compositions don't affect the film much one way or the other (it usually screened at 1.85:1 theatrically in any case), and overall the presentation is quite fine. Surround audio is fairly limited except for the occasional thunderclap, Wojciech Kilar's beautiful score, and the crashing of ocean waves during the climax. The disc also includes the U.S. theatrical trailer, probably the only time "Nietzsche!" has ever been used as major punctuation in big studio marketing.

DEATH BED: THE BED THAT EATS

Colour, 1977, 77m. / Directed by George Barry / Starring Demene Hall, Rusty Russ, Julie Ritter, Linda Bond, Patrick Spence-Thomas (voice), Rosa Luxemburg, Dave Marsh / Cult Epics (US R1 NTSC)

Just when you thought you'd seen it all – murderous houseplants, elevators, computers, even tomatoes – along comes *Death Bed: The Bed That Eats*, which is certainly stranger and more worthwhile than the title might lead you to expect. It's also become quite a popular punchline as part of a routine by comic Patton Oswalt, which has kept its profile much higher than many of its fellow indie horror brethren.

A dreamlike and often amusing bit of Gothic surrealism, the film takes place mainly within the confines of a stone crypt, the only remains of a demonic house once constructed around a voracious four-poster created by a tree demon to seduce a human woman. Unfortunately the bed took things a bit too far and swallowed her whole, with the ghost of Victorian illustrator Aubrey Beardsley trapped in the same room within a hanging portrait. The first victims are a horny young couple who stumble through the woods and seek shelter for the night on the devilish mattress, which first gobbles up an apple, a bottle of wine, and a bucket of fried chicken before turning the randy pair into a bloody mess. Later, three young girls arrive and reckon with the evil powers of the bed, which decides one of them is too beautiful and alluring to wind up as demon chow. We also see flashbacks explaining the bed's history, including a stint with a quack doctor and a disastrous romp through New York.

Though most obviously a horror film (with nods to all the familiar trappings, including ghosts and flesh-eating), *Death Bed* also fits snugly within the experimental conventions of the late '70s; in particular, one-shot director George Barry nicely evokes the whimsical, slightly perverse tone of arty underground filmmaker James Broughton, whose memorable 1968 short, *The Bed*, must have been a strong influence. In the best Doris Wishman style, dialogue is looped after the fact with the actors doing their best to keep their lips either away from the camera, in the dark, or out of frame to minimise production costs. That's fine, really, as this is virtually a silent film in approach, using visual humour and shocks instead of rational plotting and dialogue exposition. The bed's activities are cheaply but effectively conveyed by showing a yellowish bubbling emerging from the mattress as an object or person sinks in, with a cutaway to the honey-coloured, liquid interior where food and flesh are consumed. Incidentally, a not-bad 2002 film with the same title ("presented" by Stuart Gordon) ran with the same idea from a possession angle, adding kinky sex to the mix but decreasing the weirdness and comic value considerably. Try 'em both on a double feature for maximum effect.

Never really released after its lengthy tenure in post-production, *Death Bed* languished in the vaults after American distribution plans went belly up and a possible British distributor took off with a pirated copy. Fortunately for horror fans, said pirate distributed the film on video in the U.K., allowing word of mouth about this endearing oddity to spread through the horror underground grapevine. Eventually the fanzine reviews led to a burgeoning interest in the project, which boasts only the director's name among its credits. Luckily Barry was still around to participate in a DVD and theatrical renaissance for his film, which has been treated to a brand spanking new transfer. Exterior scenes tend to look grainy and a little peculiar due to some strange day for night

tinting, but the rest of the film looks quite crisp and colourful, among the best new 16mm transfers out there.

Barry turns up for a new video introduction in which he lays out the story behind the film's creation, disappearance, and resurgence, a history reiterated in detail in a solid four-page insert with liner notes by *Nightmare USA* author Stephen Thrower. For any fan of unsettling, semi-comic '70s horror cinema (admirers of *Children Shouldn't Play with Dead Things*, you know who you are), this comes highly recommended.

DEATH SMILED AT MURDER

Colour, 1973, 84m. / Directed by Joe D'Amato / Starring Ewa Aulin, Klaus Kinski, Sergio Doria, Angela Bo, Luciano Rossi, Giacomo Rossi Stuart / Italian Shock (Holland R0 PAL) / WS (1.85:1)

The first major solo effort in the director's chair for the infamous Joe D'Amato is a far cry from the sleaze in which he was destined to wallow. Best known for low budget horror films like *The Grim Reaper* and a bevy of soft and hardcore adult films, D'Amato began his career as a cinematographer before embarking on this peculiar film, a throwback to the Italian Gothic tradition of the 1960s laced with some commercially viable helpings of nudity and gore. The "plot" is so fragmented as to be nearly meaningless, but generally it concerns a beautiful young woman, Greta (*Candy* herself, Ewa Aulin), who suffers a nasty case of amnesia after a carriage crash which leaves her driver impaled on a broken wheel. She's taken in by a well-to-do couple, Sergio Doria and Angela Bo, and attended to by the curious Dr. Sturges (Klaus Kinski in a glorified cameo), who treats her condition by ordering her to strip and then plunging a needle into her eye! While Greta seduces her hosts, the doctor returns to his nocturnal practices of reviving the dead only to wind up murdered for his trouble. Meanwhile Greta's lunatic, hunchback brother (Luciano Rossi) skulks around in flashbacks and may be responsible for a series of killings, including the facial shotgunning of a lesbian maid who's been watching Greta. And then there's Walter (*Kill Baby Kill*'s Giacomo Rossi Stuart), Greta's lover seen mostly in flashback, who's also experimenting with corpse reanimation. Throw in a couple of masked balls, an extended homage to Poe's "The Black Cat", and Aulin repeatedly returning from the dead as an avenging angel to wipe out most of the cast, and you've got the recipe for a very strange hour and a half.

Not surprisingly, D'Amato's strong cinematography background serves him well. The eerie opening sequence, which finds Rossi grieving over Aulin's body, is a beautiful intro aided by Berto Pisano's haunting and ravishing score, easily the film's strongest asset. As the story lurches from one vignette to another, D'Amato's succession of fetching images and the accompanying music will keep avid Eurocult fanatics glued to the screen even when they don't know what the hell is going on. The film's legacy wasn't helped much when it went straight to American TV courtesy of Avco Embassy, who hacked it down to 70 minutes to fit an hour and a half time slot. This also meant removing all of the plentiful gore from the rousing finale, which features the world's only flying killer kitty bouquet.

A long-time staple of the bootleg video market, *La morte ha sorriso all'assassino* (translated on European prints as *Death Smiles at Murder* (the title on the DVD print, though the cover substitutes "Smiled" in place of "Smiles") but shown in America under the more literal title of *Death Smiles on a Murderer*) has fared poorly on VHS, with the colourful but awkwardly cropped Greek VHS standing as the most watchable option. The Dutch region free DVD offers a solid widescreen transfer of the uncut European version and, most importantly, finally restores the original letterboxed framing. The transfer still has some problems, namely a few odd digital glitches in the upper letterbox band during the first five minutes and some wildly inconsistent black levels, but it's vastly preferable to any other option out there. Unfortunately the audio suffers from consistent crackling and noise during quieter dialogue scenes, but at least the score comes through well enough. Just don't play it too loudly through your receiver. The disc also includes the European theatrical trailer, a gallery of stills, and surprisingly insulting liner notes which, apart from some glaring factual errors, knock the film before offering a half hearted apology.

DEATH WALKS ON HIGH HEELS

Colour, 1971, 105m. / Directed by Luciano Ercoli / Starring Susan Scott [Nieves Navarro], Frank Wolff, Simón Andreu

DEATH WALKS AT MIDNIGHT

Colour, 1972, 101m. / Directed by Luciano Ercoli / Starring Susan Scott [Nieves Navarro], Simón Andreu, Luciano Rossi / NoShame (US R0 NTSC) / WS (2.35:1) (16:9), Mondo Macabro (UK R0 PAL) / WS (1.85:1) (16:9)

As the Italian *giallo* craze took hold in the early 1970s, a number of directors tried their hand at offering new twists on what was already a firmly established formula. Though he only directed three titles that really qualify, Luciano Ercoli acquitted himself well enough in the arena of black-gloved killers and damsels in distress to justify a double-feature box set that shows off two twisted gems in the best light possible.

Following his interesting 1970 thriller, *Forbidden Photos of a Lady above*

Suspicion, Ercoli turned out two Italian-Spanish shockers in quick succession utilizing most of the same cast and personnel, with Susan Scott (a.k.a. Spanish-born Nieves Navarro) taking honours in both as leading scream queen. In 1971's *Death Walks on High Heels*, she stars as Parisian nightclub performer Nicole Rochard, whose wild routines consist of blackface, gold wigs, and garish backgrounds straight out of an LSD trip. After her jewel-thief father turns up knifed in the throat on a train, she becomes the next target of a threatening man in black whose only attribute is his piercing blue eyes. Creepy phone calls and an intense interrogation at knifepoint make her more than a little nervous, especially when a pair of strategically placed blue contact lenses reveal the culprit could literally be anyone. Is it her booze-swilling boyfriend, Michael (Simón Andreu)? Or how about a British doctor (Frank Wolff) prone to sending her flowers and skulking around her dressing room? One thing's for sure; when Nicole agrees to accompany the latter for a getaway to an isolated village on the coast, her ordeal is far from over.

Slick, nicely shot, and boasting a wonderfully catchy score by Stelvio Cipriani, this engaging thriller packs in one hell of a plot twist a little over an hour into its running time and manages to generate thrills without diving into the sleaze department. Sexuality is more implied than depicted, though Scott's backside gets more than its fair share of camera attention. Likewise, the bloodshed is restrained to a couple of savage knifings and some brutal fisticuffs, a combination Ercoli repeated in his next film, 1972's *Death Walks at Midnight*.

This time Scott returns as the more demurely clothed Valentina, a fashion model who takes an experimental hallucinogenic drug at the behest of reporter Gio (Andreu). Faster than you can say Blood and Black Lace, she witnesses a gory murder with a woman's face punctured by a spiked metal glove. Did it really happen outside the window across the street, or did she imagine the whole thing? When Gio's story hits the street, sinister threats indicate that she really did see far too much and might be next on the madman's list.

A much slower burner than its predecessor, *Death Walks at Midnight* stalls out a bit after its surreal opening sequence but manages to rebound in the last half hour, with the plot suddenly swerving in several different directions that will keep even the most adept mystery buff scrambling to keep up. Once again the story climaxes in a nasty, punch-driven showdown, though this time Ercoli stages the action atop an apartment building with an engaging sequence that would do John Woo proud. Again the entire film is beautifully shot, this time accompanied by a delicious (and far more readily available) score by Gianni Ferrio. (The lush "Valentina" theme song is especially noteworthy.)

Both films look magnificent in NoShame's editions, which present the films with their English and Italian soundtracks (complete with optional subtitles). Surprisingly, both films were almost completely shot in Italian and work far better that way, and the mono audio sounds nice on each option. *Death Walks at Midnight* was previously released on DVD in the United Kingdom from Mondo Macabro in a soft, compromised transfer that cropped the compositions to just under 2.00:1; here the full scope ratio is preserved, and the extra breathing room helps considerably. Also, the U.K. DVD used a rather inorganic stereo version of the main theme over the opening titles, while the NoShame disc retains the original mono mix, which blends in more smoothly.

Both films are housed in a three-disc package dubbed "The Luciano Ercoli Death Box Set", which adds on a very welcome collection of rare Cipriani music entitled *The Sound of Love & Death*. Though no music from these films is present, Euro music fans will delight at the 18 tracks showcased here including a pair of cues from *What Have They Done to Your Daughters?* as well as groovy selections from *The Night Child, Evil Eye, Cara sposa, La polizia ha le mani legate, Nightmare City, Dedicato a una stella,* and more. The DVD for *Death Walks on High Heels* also includes a poster and stills gallery, plus the very wild trailer in its English and Italian incarnations. The *Death Walks at Midnight* disc includes another gallery, plus a very odd bonus feature, the (letterboxed but non-anamorphic) TV cut of the film, which features an additional four minutes of footage, mainly more cop padding. Last but not least is a thick illustrated booklet featuring liner notes by Chris D. as well as bios for Ercoli, Scott, Wolf, and actor Luciano Rossi.

DEATH WISH II

Colour, 1982, 92m. / Directed by Michael Winner / Starring Charles Bronson, Jill Ireland, Robin Sherwood, Thomas Duffy, Kevyn Major Howard, Stuart K. Robinson, Laurence Fishburne, E. Lamont Johnson, Silvana Gallardo, Melody Santangello, Jim Begg, Vincent Gardenia, Anthony Franciosa, Charles Cyphers / Columbia (Australia R4 PAL, Spain R2 PAL, UK R2 PAL) / WS (1.85:1) (16:9), Columbia (Brazil R4 NTSC), MGM (US R1 NTSC)

Paul Kersey (Charles Bronson) has moved from New York to Los Angeles with his daughter who is still recovering from a dreadful assault four years earlier in which she was raped and her mother murdered. But history repeats itself when a gang of punks he's innocently fallen foul of raid Kersey's house, raping and murdering his housemaid and kidnapping Carol. When the girl dies while trying to escape, Kersey is pushed over the edge. Pulling out his handgun he

resolves to track down the gang members and mete out death penalties in his own indomitable style.

You have to feel bad for Paul Kersey; fate sure hasn't given him an easy ride. In *Death Wish* his wife and daughter were assaulted, the former left dead, the latter rendered a vegetative shell of her former self. Despite the fact he turned vigilante on the streets of New York, Kersey never saw the gang responsible brought to justice. In *Death Wish II* (four years later narratively, closer to eight in actuality) he's moved to L.A. but finds himself facing off against the miscreants who've taken his daughter's life. Director Michael Winner paints the pond scum – Nirvana (Thomas Duffy), Stomper (Kevyn Major Howard), Jiver (Stuart K. Robinson), Cutter (Laurence Fishburne) and Punkcut (E. Lamont Johnson) – as the vilest bunch of deviants imaginable. And to ensure that the audience is rooting for Kersey when he sets out to nail them, Winner piles on the adversity; first the gang harasses him and steals his wallet, then the thugs show up at his home to viciously rape and murder his housekeeper Rosario (Silvana Gallardo), ultimately kidnapping his daughter Carol (Robin Sherwood, substituting the original's Kathleen Tolan), who's subsequently impaled on metal railings after being violated by Jiver. If you thought the assaults in *Death Wish* were unpleasant, Winner ups the ante in *Death Wish II* by staging what is arguably one of the nastiest, most vivid depictions of gang rape in screen history, the camera unflinchingly capturing every harrowing moment of terror and humiliation on Rosario's face. Not content with that, he tops things off with one of the most distasteful, as the retarded Carol is defiled. Deigning that tracking down those responsible for these atrocities isn't sufficient to keep our anti-hero occupied, writers David Engelbach and Brian Garfield throw in plenty of subsidiary mayhem. This includes Kersey interrupting an attempted rape –

with an amusing coda in which the grateful almost-victim and her husband purposely feed police misleading descriptions of their saviour – and a rip-roaring shoot-out with a gang of arms dealers.

Neither Charles Bronson nor his wife Jill Ireland (playing Kersey's girlfriend, radio newshound Geri Nichols) were likely to win any awards for thespian talent here, though that's partially the fault of stilted dialogue. They do, however, play off each other with a nice familiarity born of their real-life propinquity and are adequate enough to carry the tale through to its rather cynical conclusion. Vincent Gardenia returns from the first film as New York police detective Frank Ochoa, suspicious that Kersey has resumed old habits and determined to call a halt to it. There are smaller roles for Anthony Franciosa (*Tenebrae*) and Charles Cyphers (*Halloween*). Much as Jeff Goldblum's career got off the ground playing a mugger in *Death Wish*, so *Death Wish II* marks an early turn by Laurence Fishburne (credited here as Laurence Fishburne III). The score by Led Zeppelin's Jimmy Page occasionally feels a touch mismatched to the material, but not to the point where it does it any harm.

The movie has a chequered history of cuts and re-edits and has proven, not without good reason, the most controversial and drastically censored entry in the series, with few countries seeing an uncut print. In England (both theatrically and for home viewing) it lost almost three minutes to the BBFC's shears, specifically from the rape of Rosario and her subsequent death on the sharp end of a crowbar, but also – with some re-editing of events to cover for lost footage – from the violation of Carol. It has to be said that in its uncensored form it's a pretty gruelling trip. Three further sequels ensued, each less involving than the last. If energetic vigilante flicks float your boat, stick with the original and Part II and you won't go too far wrong.

The Region 4 NTSC disc out of Latin America (under the title *Desejo de Matar 2*) offers up the film as a fine quality full screen presentation with 28 chapter points. A revelation for viewers who've only ever seen it in its severely butchered form will be how uncomfortably protracted and explicit the rape sequences actually are. Although to all intents and purposes this disc represents an uncut print, it can't be credited as fully so since it's missing a small amount of (not particularly significant) covering footage that was used to paper over the cracks in otherwise messy re-edits of the assault on the housemaid. The sound is in English with subtitling provided in Portuguese, Chinese, Spanish and English. Minor irritation arises from a burnt-in caption – the Spanish translation of the film's title – that appears at the foot of the screen on the opening credits. There are no movie specific supplements included, but the disc does carry previews for a quartet of other Columbia releases. The content of the actual film notwithstanding, somewhat startling in itself is that such a brutal exploitationer – and make no mistake, it is excessively so – should, in Latin America, carry a certificate that indicates one only has to be over 14 years old to legally watch it! The Australian release is also uncut, and the anamorphic widescreen print is partnered with the original *Death Wish* in a double pack. All other versions are cut to varying degrees; the U.K. disc reflects the BBFC-mandated edition missing those three minutes, while MGM's American disc is the even more drastically censored R-rated cut which might as well just be avoided entirely by this point.

– TG

THE DEATHMASTER

Colour, 1972, 84m. / Directed by Ray Danton / Starring Robert Quarry, John Fiedler, LeSesne Hilton, Bill Ewing, Bobby Pickett, Brenda Dickson / Retromedia (US R0 NTSC) / WS (16:9) / DD5.1

Most commentators tend to characterize this Ray Danton-directed vehicle for Robert Quarry, briefly hot from the Count Yorga films and credited here as co-producer, as a Manson exploitation movie. This is fair enough as far as it goes, but it feels more like a Californian riff on Jean Rollin's vampire movies, albeit with a PG level of sex (even among hippie free spirits there's no nudity except from the back).

In a wordless opening, recorder-playing mute Barbado (LeSesne Hilton) charms a coffin out of the sea and strangles a surfer. From the coffin emerges Khorda (Quarry), a vaguely Indian, ancient vampire who dresses in guru chic and insinuates himself as the guiding light of a castle-commune. The first to succumb are a biker chick and a hairy guy, who soon sprout fangs. Khorda has a few of the usual vamp licks (supernaturally cracking a mirror that doesn't reflect him) as well as some odder ones (his face goes white when he shows fangs). The rather unlikeable hero Pico (Bill Ewing) is a semi-Hispanic kung fu kid with an American Indian hairdo, who escapes from chains in the castle's dungeons and dips his hands in a bowl of leeches, seeing off Barbado using the unique method of tracing a cross in blood on his cheek. Pico hooks up with head shop owner "Pop" (character actor John Fiedler, mildest of the *Twelve Angry Men*), who plays the wise elder Van Helsing role in a snappy knitted waistcoat. There are folk songs from Bobby "Boris" Pickett (who gets vampirized), a lot of stoned chatter ("Hey, man, don't split, we groove on what you say"), fabulous hippie fashions, and a deal of philosophic maundering ("The nights of our lives are always filled with meaningless screams"). As usual with these things, the counterculture is in the end associated with supernatural evil – though a biker's iron cross momentarily spooks the vampire.

The ending mixes cynical licks from several then-recent films, but not the memorable twist of *Count Yorga*. Pico makes the mistake of staking Khorda's coffin before opening it and finds he has skewered nice old Pops, whereupon Khorda shows up for some cackling and gloating and gets the leeches thrown in his face. He bleeds a lot and trips onto the stake, his death causing all his acolytes to crumble to dust. Discovering his girl Mona (Brenda Dickson) decaying among the dead, Pico goes mad, prompting a high-angle frame of him screaming (à la *Witchfinder General*) and a cut to symbolic shattered glass (à la *The Trip*). The horror scenes rely on dark facial close-ups of snarling with hand-held judder and ducking, and most of it takes place inside the underlit real-life castle. It's a slight picture, less distinctive than other Danton horrors (*Young Hannah: Queen of the Vampires*, *Simon King of the Witches*, *Psychic Killer*) but its flavour-of-the-times feel commands attention and the script comes up with a few new-ish or unusual variants on the vampire theme.

Considering that this rarely-revived title was only available for some years as a low-quality grey market video release, Retromedia's "Deluxe Wide Screen Edition" is a major improvement. The framing is a little tight, slicing the tops of some heads, the often-seen full moon and a couple of the credits, but the transfer is good-looking, reproducing that slightly hazy early 1970s look but with solid, stable blacks for the many night and dungeon scenes (it was an early credit for cinematographer Bill Butler, who later shot *Jaws*, *Grease*, some *Rocky* sequels and *Frailty*). The 5.1 surround sound remix is fine, albeit with a degree of hiss and crackle under the dialogue and the music (by Bill Marx and Ray Coniff). Though some of the posters call the film *The Deathmaster*, the onscreen title lacks the definite article. Extras: theatrical trailer; very rough-looking trailers; radio spots for *Count Yorga, Vampire* and *Sugar Hill* (both with Quarry); galleries of stills from the film and Quarry's extensive career; commercials with Quarry (a black and white effort for Lucky Strike cigarettes – in a modern-day context, the most shocking thing on the disc) and Fiedler (a Frankenstein-themed spot for Shasta soda). In conversation with Fred Olen Ray, Quarry delivers a candid, amusing, informative commentary track and is far more engaged with his work than many other veterans hauled out to talk over films they're embarrassed to find on their résumés. Ray slips in wondering why a cavern fight scene reminds him of *Hannah* (not remembering that Danton also directed that), though he adds a lot to the conversation with memories of the drive-in era and a light-hearted analysis of vampire film conventions.

– KN

DEATHWATCH

Colour, 2002, 94m. / Directed by Michael J. Bassett / Starring Jamie Bell, Laurence Fox, Torben Liebrecht, Andy Serkis / Asia Test (HK R3 NTSC), Pathé (UK R2 PAL), Lionsgate (US R1 NTSC) / WS (2.35:1) (16:9) / DTS/DD5.1

 The second of two duelling British ghost stories which involve British vs. German armed forces during a world war (following 2001's *The Bunker*), this is a fog-drenched morality tale that earned most of its press as the follow-up feature for Jamie Bell, the young lead of *Billy Elliot*. Best described as a big budget *Twilight Zone* episode stretched out to feature length, this odd and occasionally effective spooker boasts some splashy gore effects and strong atmosphere despite a few missteps from its first time director.

A terrified, young Charlie Shakespeare (Bell) is forced by his superiors to cross over into enemy lines during a fierce World War I battle. Eight other soldiers follow him through the mist and mud. After wading through mist and mud, their leader, Captain Jennings (Laurence Fox), takes them into a trench which they occupy by killing all but one of the German soldiers (Torben Liebrecht). As the men are beaten down and scared out of their wits by being trapped in unknown territory, they're also bumped off one by one by an unseen force with a penchant for barbed wire. The German survivor intones that an evil force already inhabits the trench, and the interlopers may be next on its list...

A dark and largely humourless affair, *Deathwatch* (which really could have used a better title) effectively evokes those hellish tableaux readers often imagine while reading *All Quiet on the Western Front*. The injection of horror elements seems only a minor step away from the already nightmarish setting, and the film is at its best when the camera is simply allowed to prowl around the evocative sets, juxtaposing the actors' sweaty, bug-eyed faces against layers of wire mesh and splintered wood. In narrative terms it has all been done before, and most will probably approach this as *Event Horizon* in combat gear with a better twist ending. Much of the scenery chewing comes courtesy of Andy Serkis, now famous as Gollum from *The Lord of the Rings*; here he veers into sheer loony territory, ranting and raving at the camera until he finally gets his big scene in the spotlight. Gorehounds will get a kick out of the second half, when most of the murders finally kick in; the grue isn't layered on non-stop but is undeniably effective when it does appear. However, one major debit for the music score, written by no less than three composers; it's a pompous mess that should have been scuttled in favour of something far more subtle.

At least the score sounds great, as do the explosions, on the DTS and 5.1 mixes. This is powerhouse audio material all the way from the opening credits, and you'll be constantly looking over your shoulder with a well-calibrated surround system. Anamorphic image quality is quite good, nicely rendering the scope compositions throughout.

The Hong Kong disc is bare-bones (and has a couple of glaring digital pops on the soundtrack), but the British and American editions pack in some deleted scenes and two commentary tracks, one with Serkis and the other with Bell, Fox, and Michael J. Bassett, all of which are rather flat and on the sparse side but most likely of interest for fans of the film. The more value-friendly British disc (whose transfer looks appreciably sharper and with clearer blacks) also adds a separate Bassett commentary, cast interviews, and a making-of featurette.

DEEP IN THE WOODS

Colour, 2000, 84m. / Directed by Lionel Delplanque / Starring Clotilde Courau, Clément Sibony / Tartan (UK R0 PAL), Artisan (US R1 NTSC) / WS (2.35:1) (16:9) / DD5.1

Filmed as *Promenons-nous dans les bois*, this was the first commercially successful French horror movie in decades, and it cleared the way for a mini-revival of the genre on its home turf. However, the only unusual thing about this solidly average slasher film is that it comes with subtitles, which lends it a certain rarefied air but doesn't make it any less ordinary – like a *Scooby-Doo* episode done in the style of Claude Chabrol.

A troupe of good-looking young actors who specialize in school performances are hired by a sinister, paralyzed aristocrat to perform their "Little Red Riding Hood" at his remote mansion as a birthday treat for his strangely silent grandson. The film works best in the early stages, when it

piles on the omens and disturbing touches, with unsettling by-play between host and guests as he stuffs them with vodka-drenched tripe, the little boy breaking up his party by stabbing his hand with a fork, and an unseen noisy helicopter heralding the arrival of a strange-looking red herring cop on a hunt for an escaped psycho rapist. The extended finale is more conventional, featuring familiar demises for most of the cast as someone predictable dressed in the Big Bad Wolf costume stalks them with a spear gun and acid, and overkill animal snares set by the perverted gamekeeper snap into action.

The attractive victims bicker and get naked just like in a rubbish American movie, and the genre's usual square morality means victims pay heavily for infractions ranging from dope-smoking through infidelity to attempted rape. However, a Hollywood horror might think twice about having the leading lady/likely survivor be a lesbian in a blue dress – though her mute bisexual cheating girlfriend is an early casualty. The willowy Clotilde Courau, most familiar as the young Anne Parillaud in *Map of the Human Heart*, is wasted in the nothingy heroine role, with an early girl-girl sex scene that could stand as a working definition of gratuitous, but various mad people provide some fleeting entertainment value. The linkage of fairy-tale with slasher movie, through the Red Riding Hood theme and the use of strange childhood imagery (a burning doll), is perhaps overly obvious, but adds some texture to the basic whodunit.

Though one of the lesser releases in the "Tartan Terror" line, *Deep in the Woods* may be the best-looking disc the sometimes-careless company has issued. The 2.35:1 transfer is lushly dark but never indistinct, showing off the excellent cinematography and set decoration, with a layered 5.1 soundtrack full of unsettling noises. The transfer is so sharp that the unusual use of CGI for explosions, smoke and fog is exposed – the owners of the impressive mansion location didn't want physical effects damaging their home. English subtitles are optional, and the only extras are a list-of-titles-from-the-IMDb filmographies for director and two stars, a brief essay by Alan Jones, a trailer and a trailer reel for the TT line.

– KN

[The U.S. disc contains the same technical specs along with an atrocious English language dubbed track. – ed.]

THE DEER HUNTER

Colour, 1978, 183m. / Directed by Michael Cimino / Starring Robert De Niro, Christopher Walken, John Savage, Meryl Streep, John Cazale, Shirley Stoler / Optimum (Blu-ray & DVD) (UK RB/R2 HD/PAL), Warner (UK R2 PAL), Universal (US R1 NTSC, Italy R2 PAL, Germany R2 PAL), On-Air (Denmark R2 PAL) / WS (2.35:1) (16:9) / DD2.0

 By the late 1970s, it seemed the world was finally ready for films that confronted the difficult topic of the Vietnam War. Still a fresh wound in the public psyche, the costly and demoralizing experience was the most prominent sore spot in a decade already filled with debacles like Watergate. While the same year's *Coming Home* took an intimate, emotional approach to the Vietnam experience and its aftermath, director Michael Cimino – who only had one previous film under his belt, the skilful but politically sticky *Thunderbolt and Lightfoot* – had an entirely different kind of treatment in mind. The now legendary perfectionist and budget-blaster compiled a startling roster of talent to craft a three hour study of America's involvement in the war as represented by a handful of friends, with the powerful (and fictional) metaphor of Russian roulette destined to become associated forever with the historical conflict.

In Pennsylvania, three young friends enjoy their mundane lives in a small steel town. Michael (Robert De Niro), Nick (Christopher Walken), and Steven (John Savage) are all drafted to fight in Vietnam, and Steven's wedding proves to be a final hurrah for them all. Meanwhile Michael and Nick are both infatuated with Linda (Meryl Streep), a situation unresolved by the time of their departure. Overseas the men are all captured and held in a makeshift camp, where they are forced to engage in brutal rounds of Russian roulette against each other. In the final movement of the film, the survivors' homecoming proves to be complicated and emotionally shattering, as each man tries to exorcise his demons and deal with the aftermath of a conflict that has scarred them forever.

During the 1970s, Hollywood seemed to crown a new golden boy director every year: William Friedkin, Francis Ford Coppola, Peter Bogdanovich, Steven Spielberg, and George Lucas were all hailed as new saviours of cinema, and apart from Lucas, each eventually crashed at the end of the decade with a costly or high profile bomb. Thanks to *The Deer Hunter*, Cimino was also hailed as a genius, at least until the debacle of the expensive but fascinating *Heaven's Gate*. In retrospect he has been charged repeatedly with racism, a claim which may have some validity in the wake of *The Year of the Dragon* and *The Sicilian*; his treatment of the Vietnamese here doesn't exactly look politically correct now, but at least it's preferable to the video game-style ethnic cleansing of *Rambo: First Blood Part II*. Otherwise *The Deer Hunter* has stood up admirably over the years, offering screen time to several performers at their peak; while De Niro and Streep seemed to bounce from one career high to another, the rest of the cast is also outstanding. Walken's award-

145

winning turn is still a textbook example of harrowing character development, while the excellent John Cazale (who sadly died the year of the film's release) is too often overlooked as a guilt-ridden friend who stayed at home. And sleaze fans, keep an eye out for the unmistakable Shirley Stoler (*The Honeymoon Killers*) as Savage's mother.

The first DVD on the market came from Universal's U.S. division in a surprisingly shoddy transfer; the non-anamorphic video quality was a sub-par representation of the film, with harsh aliasing and digital grain throughout. A variety of anamorphic upgrades of varying merits soon appeared in Europe; best of the initial lot is Warner's two-disc U.K. set (in conjunction with Canal Plus). The transfer reveals more picture information on all sides and, apart from some noticeable fading on the far right side of the frame during some dark scenes, looks quite impressive. Surround audio is limited on all editions, with Stanley Myers's fine score getting most of the benefits from surround playback. The U.K. set contains the entire film on the first disc along with an informative Cimino commentary; he discusses the immense difficulties encountered in getting the picture produced at the time and elaborates on the various historical and fictional influences woven together for the final product. The second disc features an array of supplements produced by Blue Underground (who also handled the commentary). "Realising *The Deer Hunter*" returns to Cimino for an informative documentary featuring a chronological account of the film from pre-production through its release. "Shooting *The Deer Hunter*" turns the focus on legendary cinematographer Vilmos Zsigmond, who discusses the difficulty of reconciling Cimino's tyro directorial practices, the variety of improvised acting styles, and the complex scope compositions in a number of different settings. "Playing *The Deer Hunter*" features John Savage, who

becomes visibly distraught talking about the film, its place in American history, and its importance to the rest of his life. Other extras include a photo gallery, the theatrical trailer, and a DVD-Rom pressbook. The same package was then carried over to Optimum when Studio Canal asserted its rights again in the U.K., and their Blu-ray features an HD transfer that obviously ranks as the best of the lot. It's considerably more detailed and features more filmic grain, and along with the same extras, it also adds another 48-minute documentary, "Vietnam War: Unknown Images". The Region B release comes with lossless DTS audio in English (at a higher pitch than the previous version, oddly enough), German, French, Italian, Spanish, and German, with subtitles in the same languages as well as Danish, Swedish, Finnish, Dutch, Norwegian, Turkish, and Japanese.

A watchable American version finally came with Universal's "Legacy Series" release, containing the anamorphic upgrade, an audio commentary with Vilmos Zsigmond and journalist Bob Fisher, and a shockingly sparse second disc containing a trailer, some "deleted and extended scenes" (just longer alternative takes of little consequence), and some text notes. Presumably Universal didn't want to pony up any money to carry over the Warner extras, à la *Flash Gordon*.

DELIRIUM

Colour, 1972, 102/85m. / Directed by Renato Polselli / Starring Mickey Hargitay, Rita Calderoni / Blue Underground, Anchor Bay (US R1 NTSC) / WS (1.85:1) (16:9)

In 1972, the maverick director Renato Polselli launched himself from workmanlike director of Gothics like *The Vampire and the Ballerina* to full-fledged cinematic madman with a pair of freakish, stream-of-consciousness Italian sleaze classics, *The Reincarnation of Isabelle* and *Delirium* (originally released as *Delirio caldo*). Both films star Mickey Hargitay (the former Mr. Jayne Mansfield) and the stunning Rita Calderoni, but the similarities hardly end there; both movies also share a predilection for rampant nudity, dream sequences slip-sliding into reality, and a refusal to play by the normal rules of narrative storytelling. While fans continue to debate which film is "better", *Delirium* is a film which, once seen, cannot be forgotten.

Essentially Polselli's response to the escalating *giallo* cycle begun in the mid-1960s, our story begins with doctor Herbert Lyutak (Hargitay) picking up a sweet young thing at a small bar while they hang around the jukebox. During their ride home, he chases her off into the woods and brutally murders her while splashing in a river. Back home he enjoys the company of his beautiful wife, Marcia (Calderoni), though his impotence keeps them from consummating their relationship. Nevertheless she stands by her man, even after she deduces that he's the mad sex killer running across the countryside, and the plot quickly thickens as the police become involved. Then while Herbert is in custody, the murders continue... so who's the new psycho in town?

While the storyline sounds hopelessly stupid on paper, Polselli keeps things percolating by injecting the film with plenty of perverse murders (including one bathtub scene involving a knife that would have the BBFC spitting nails). The final ten minutes are soap operatic trash at its finest, with an escalating series of hysterical encounters that would make Pedro Almodóvar proud. The groovy music score is also an asset, and Hargitay wanders through the film in a manner similar to his earlier, barechested turn in *Bloody Pit of Horror*. While Calderoni has some juicy material to work with, she doesn't look quite as lustrous as her appearances in *Isabelle* or the notorious *Nude for Satan*; however, her performance is one of her best as she oscillates between misguided sympathy to full-fledged lunacy.

The distribution history of *Delirium* is a nightmare of complications, with variant editions floating around in Italy, America, and France. The first two are preserved on Anchor Bay's DVD, with the longer European cut (containing optional English subtitles) offering the finest-looking presentation of the film to date. Colours are bold and a delight to behold, while the print material itself is in excellent condition. The dramatically different U.S. cut was cobbled together from a moderately damaged 35mm print with segments from a Danish video release added to fill in the gaps (easily identified as the picture quality becomes smudgy, and the English dialogue features Danish subtitles). Aside from dropping nearly 20 minutes from the narrative, the second version also tacks on a wholly unnecessary opening and closing Vietnam sequence which was later aped in *Jacob's Ladder*, of all things. The third version from France featured some alternative, borderline hardcore insert footage during the murder and sex scenes but has been omitted from Anchor Bay's disc; however, it's difficult to quibble with the already stuffed package on hand. Also included is a 14-minute featurette, including interviews with Polselli and Hargitay reminiscing about shooting the film on a fairly rushed schedule. Blue Underground later reissued the same package, though the Italian audio is only carried over for the international cut. Given the lack of subtitles either way, it's not much of a loss.

DELIRIUM

Colour, 1987, 92m. / Directed by Lamberto Bava / Starring Serena Grandi, Daria Nicolodi, Karl Zinny, George Eastman [Luigi Montefiori], Vanni Corbellini, David Brandon / Shriek Show (US R0 NTSC) / WS (1.85:1) (16:9)

Some audiences felt the *giallo* films of the '60s and '70s were more than a little absurd, but nothing could have prepared them for the direction the genre took in the '80s. While *Miami Vice* and MTV swallowed up pop culture, directors scrambled to make their sexy murder mysteries ever more hip, flashy, and senseless, resulting in the conclusion of Al Festa's unbelievable train wreck, *Fatal Frames*. Lamberto Bava helped with a few detours along the way such as the eccentric *Body Puzzle* and his slaphappy *Le foto di Gioia*, released on video and DVD as *Delirium*.

Busty Tinto Brass starlet Serena Grandi (*Miranda*) is Gloria, a skinflick star and model whose porn magazine business is disrupted by dirty prank calls from a wheelchair-bound teen fan (Karl Zinny) and the mysterious murders of her models. *Blood and Black Lace* this ain't, however. One of the models – in one of the oddest killings you'll ever see – is stung to death by a swarm of bees inside her house. The bodies are then arranged stylishly in front of – you guessed it – giant pictures of Gloria. Meanwhile we occasionally jump to the killer's psychotic perspective as each model assumes a surrealistic appearance, ranging from a giant eyeball head to a big beehive. Could the killer be Gloria's piggy former flame, Alex (Joe D'Amato favourite George Eastman)? Or how about her impotent brother, Tony (Vanni Corbellini)? Or how about her sadistic lead photographer, Roberto (*Stagefright*'s David Brandon)? Eventually there's a ridiculous finale best seen without any prior warning.

Despite his technical proficiency, Lamberto Bava seems unable here to generate the commercial project for which he was so clearly aiming. Instead what we have is a truly cockeyed mishmash of sexploitation and audience friendly horror; devoid of the perverse sense of sadism that distinguishes Dario Argento's *gialli*, this is instead a strangely benign and inoffensive film that has

already dated far more than its predecessors. That doesn't mean there isn't plenty of fun to be had, however; Grandi is always highly entertaining to watch as she and her breasts heave their way from scene to scene, and the delicious supporting cast includes a number of familiar Italian horror vets such as Daria Nicolodi (in what amounts to a glorified cameo). On the other hand you'd be hard pressed to nail the soundtrack as the work of Simon Boswell, who went on to great mainstream success but provides little more than suspenseful Muzak here.

Whatever dubious merits the film itself may possess, *Delirium* has been given the red carpet treatment on DVD. Along with a vibrant anamorphic transfer (marred only by the annoying inherent fuzziness – oops, "stylishness" – of late-'80s cinematography), the disc contains fine video interviews with Bava and Brandon, both of whom put the film in perspective with their careers at the time and seem to have warm memories of working on the project. Though no trailer for this film seems to be floating around, the disc does include promos for other Shriek Show Euro horror titles. Curiously, the theatrical prints carrying the *Gioia* title boasted a Dolby Stereo credit, but all video transfers – including this one – have been in mono.

DEMONS OF THE MIND

Colour, 1971, 89m. / Directed by Peter Sykes / Starring Robert Hardy, Paul Jones, Patrick Magee, Michael Hordern, Gillian Hills, Shane Briant, Kenneth J. Warren, Yvonne Mitchell / Anchor Bay (US R1 NTSC), Optimum (UK R2 PAL) / WS (1.85:1) (16:9)

This late Hammer Film unusually blends their familiar Mittel European sets with a plot that applies primitive psychiatry to demonology in order to take slightly more seriously many of the clichés of Gothic horror. It comes from a period when Hammer (and their competitors) were casting around for various ways of keeping the product up to date, most obviously through added explicit sex and violence but also through a modish, almost cynical rethink of the basic premises. The convention of the village mob bearing torches as they attack the castle and the Van Helsing-style scientific-religious savants usually played by Peter Cushing are put through the ringer, so that the villagers are chanting throwbacks as happy with rituals of petty sadism involving burned scarecrows as with murdering monsters, while the savants are represented by Patrick Magee as a cracked mesmerist failing to help anyone and Michael Hordern as a ranting, mumbling itinerant priest.

There's a curse on the House of Zorn. Baron Friedrich (Robert Hardy, with sidewhiskers) is torn between accepting a supernatural explanation and trying for a scientific cure for the hereditary madness that is afflicting his strange children, Elisabeth (Gillian Hills) and Emil (Shane Briant). Sundry village girls are murdered and sunk in the lake by a devoted servant (Kenneth J. Warren) and a long-haired scholar (Paul Jones) tries to get involved with Elisabeth, who occasionally escapes from the supervision of her father and her unusual aunt (Yvonne Mitchell). Christopher Wicking's literate script builds slowly into a credibly messy horror finale involving multiple tragedies and a huge burning cross, while director Peter Sykes takes the proceedings unusually seriously, getting close to striking faces. Shot by Arthur Grant, it has a paler colour scheme than most contemporary British horror films, with drabber decor but more striking props and costumes – like Briant's odd orange blouse and Magee's purple dressing gown, or the sadistic period medical gadgets and Magee's glass-tubes-and-liquids mesmeric apparatus. Hardy's rather stiff central performance lacks the nuance

that his co-stars uniformly bring to their roles, but he still convinces as a rigid man close to cracking up.

Anchor Bay's DVD showcases a superb transfer of a film that must have required a lot of care in colour-timing. Besides a theatrical trailer, the sole extra is a busy, probing commentary track with a lot of good detail from Sykes and Wicking and looser anecdotalising from actress Virginia Wetherell, who plays the most prominent village girl victim. Wicking and Sykes clearly put a lot of extra effort into this movie, and they credit veteran producer Frank Godwin with pushing Hammer into new areas; perhaps because of its lack of "cult" stars and perhaps because it mounts something of an attack on its genre, it has never quite managed to secure its reputation. This release, however, serves nicely to boost its position. Later reissued in the U.K. from Optimum in 2007 with the same transfer and extras.

– KN

DERANGED
Colour, 1974, 82m. / Directed by Jeff Gillen & Alan Ormsby / Starring Roberts Blossom, Robert Warner, Leslie Carlson, Micki Moore, Marion Waldman, Pat Orr / MGM (US R1 NTSC), Universum (Germany R2 PAL) / WS (1.85:1) (16:9)
MOTEL HELL
Colour, 1980, 101m. / Directed by Kevin Connor / Starring Rory Calhoun, Paul Linke, Nancy Parsons, Nina Axelrod, John Ratzenberger / MGM (US R1 NTSC) / WS (1.85:1) (16:9) / DD2.0, ILC Prime (UK R2 PAL)

 Unable to cope with the death of his mother, a year after her passing simpleton Ezra Cobb (played by Roberts Blossom) digs up her corpse and brings it home to his isolated farmhouse.

Attempting to restore the rotting cadaver to its former glory, it occurs to Ez that only real flesh will do the job. So he begins plundering the graves of freshly departed souls, starting off with his old Sunday School teacher. As his unsociable nocturnal habits send him further into a fantasy world which robs him of all sense of moral right and wrong, Ezra shifts his ghoulish gaze towards the living...

Based on the misdeeds of the notorious Ed Gein, to enhance its docu-drama veracity the early part of *Deranged* is encumbered with an on-screen narrator (a suitably sombre Leslie Carlson: "Nothing has been left to the imagination"). Although a minor distraction, it does achieve what it sets out to do and adds an edge of unnerving authenticity to the story's true crime roots. Jack McGowan's photography of the chill winter landscapes and Carl Zitter's pipe-organ score (in particular the frequent recurrence of "The Old Rugged Cross") further imbue the proceedings with a bleak malaise. Co-directed by Jeff Gillen and Alan Ormsby from the latter's own screenplay, *Deranged* is brimming with the stuff of nightmares, much of the grislier stuff courtesy of f/x maestro Tom Savini; from the sequence in which Ez force-feeds his dying mother pea soup (which she promptly regurgitates, mixed with a measure of blood, while Ez tries in vain to ladle the mess back in again) to the old ladies tea party at which he proudly introduces the terrified apple of his eye (Micki Moore) to his collection of putrefied corpses, the film heaves with imagery that's tough to shake off. And, just when you think you've seen it all, Gillen and Ormsby spring a final heinous evisceration upon you in a sequence that caused the film classification difficulties in the U.K.

There are some nicely understated performances by the largely unknown supporting cast, with only Marion Waldman being familiar (from *Black Christmas*) as Maureen Selby, victim of Ez's calamitous attempt to find a sweetheart – he ends up shooting her through the head. But this is

well and truly Roberts Blossom's show and he affords us a tour de force portrait of insanity, topped with a stare that could loosen your bowels at a hundred paces; you're never quite too sure what's going on behind those eyes. That he's also a bit of a pitiable old geezer who has no real comprehension what he's doing is wrong – so never makes a secret of it – adds a tasty frisson of wicked black humour to the mix. He even tells friends from a neighbouring farm what he's up to, but they laugh it off as eccentric old Ez spending far too much time alone. Blossom's guttural chuckle as the film comes to a close is guaranteed to linger with you long after the credits have rolled.

If you think *Deranged* is twisted, *Motel Hell* is a double twist with a backflip, although it's nowhere near as much fun. Anyone checking into the backwoods Motel Hello run by Farmer Vincent Smith (Rory Calhoun) and his demented sister Ida (Nancy Parsons) is assured never to check out. Instead they're drugged, have their vocal chords cut out, and find themselves planted up to their necks in the back yard. When "ripe" they're uprooted, slaughtered, then carted off for smoking and curing to bolster Vincent's stock of world famous meat products: "It takes all kinds of critters to make Farmer Vincent's fritters." All is running smoothly, with the local populace having become willing (albeit unwitting) cannibals, until Vincent takes a fancy to one of his potential fresh meat packages (Nina Axelrod) and decides to keep her alive...

Motel Hell is one for must-see-everything die-hards only. Best described as a pauper's *Texas Chain Saw Massacre* with much more humour but far less interesting freaks, it does boast some highly original ideas, foremost the trussed-up "livestock" planted like cabbages in Vincent's secret garden. Regrettably it's little more than a ten-minute concept stretched to feature length and the premise quickly goes off the boil with the introduction of an unconvincing subplot which finds Vincent wooing a girl half his age; not only does she fall for his cornball schmaltz, she also doesn't seem to notice that everyone around him, from sister Ida to kid brother Bruce (Paul Linke), who also happens to be the town sheriff, is crazy as a box of arseholes. They say love is blind, but this is ridiculous!

The setting for the madness is Motel Hello (except the "o" has burned out, hence Motel Hell – geddit?). The late Rory Calhoun, best known for an endless string of B-westerns, earlier touched base with the genre for *Night of the Lepus*, the so bad it's dreadful killer rabbits flick. The more recently departed Nancy Parsons will always be remembered as Beulah Balbricker in *Porky's*, but she's on fine form here as a middle-aged nutball with the mind of a five year-old. John Ratzenberger (of *Cheers* renown) pops up as the drummer of a rock band who wind up chin-deep in fertilizer; bet he rues the day he signed up for this one. It's hard to believe that this slice of schlock came from Kevin Connor, the British director of family fantasy fare the like of *People That Time Forgot*, *At the Earth's Core* and *Warlords of Atlantis*. Although there is little here that is overtly ghastly, for its anthropophagic themes alone those with weak stomachs are probably best advised to give it a wide berth. That said, just in case you were in any doubt that Connor had his tongue wedged firmly in his cheek, he closes with C&W toe-tapper "You're Eating Out My Heart and Soul". And if nothing else *Motel Hell* can hold its head high as the only film to feature a crazed country hick wielding a chainsaw while wearing a freshly slaughtered pig's head and chasing a cretinous cop around a smokehouse. A recommendation? Depends how you look at it, as cheap and effectively nasty victuals for the undemanding and easily pleased.

British devotees of the deliciously nasty *Deranged* will be fairly pleased with MGM's Region 1 "Midnight Movies" double feature disc, although it does play Indian giver. Eclipsing the former U.K. VHS release from Exploited, the print utilized is in reasonably good shape and includes the climactic hack-job on Sally (Pat Orr) that's missing from the tape, blood trickling over bare breasts having been a definite no-no in the hallowed halls of the BBFC at the time of that release's classification. However, it's still devoid of a gross sequence in which Ezra spoons the brains out of a disembodied head (included previously only on the Moore U.S. VHS, as it never existed in theatrical prints and had to be salvaged from the cutting room floor). The 16-chapter punctuated presentation offers English language sound only, but there's a choice of Spanish, French or English subtitles to accompany it, and the disc is rounded out with the inclusion of the theatrical trailer.

The German release carries over the MGM transfer and splices in the dupey-looking deleted brains scene (apparently lifted from the VHS tape) while adding the Moore Video's short retrospective documentary featuring scarce behind the scenes footage, "The Ed Gein Story" (an on-location chat with producer Tom Karr), an extra teaser, and the infamous "Ed Gein: American Maniac", a half-hour look at the murder with real photographs from the crime scene. The lesser half of the MGM bill is *Motel Hell*. A clean transfer, broken by 16 chapter stops, it's available for consumption with language and subtitle choices in English, French and Spanish. As with its co-feature, a trailer is the only additional sweetmeat. *Motel Hell* is also available in the U.K. as a stand-alone release featuring a full screen transfer.

– TG

THE DEVIL AND DANIEL WEBSTER

B&W, 1941, 107m. / Directed by William Dieterle / Starring Edward Arnold, Walter Huston, James Craig, Anne Shirley, Jane Darwell, Simone Simon / Criterion (US R1 NTSC), Eureka (UK R0 NTSC)

A film as famous for its tumultuous production and distribution history as its overall quality (which is considerable), this magnificent horror/fantasy adaptation of the classic Stephen Vincent Benet story offers a twist on the durable Faust saga with a distinct twist of Americana. The storyline is simplicity itself but filled with memorable flourishes; New England farmer Jabez Stone (James Craig) makes a deal with the devil, offering to sell his soul in exchange for a good luck streak. Sure enough, a tobacco-puffing Old Scratch (Walter Huston) appears in the barn doorway and offers seven years of good fortune. His family, including wife Mary (Anne Shirley) and mother (Jane Darwell), benefits from the results, but Jabez notes a few odd occurrences over the next few years, such as the supernatural arrival of sexy nanny Belle (*Cat People*'s Simone Simon), one of the devil's more attractive minions. When the deadline for payment finally closes in, Jabez panics and solicits the aid of legendary lawyer Daniel Webster (Edward Arnold), who accepts the case under extremely perilous circumstances: if he loses the case before a jury of famous damned men, both the lawyer and his client lose their souls to Old Scratch.

The Devil and Daniel Webster was released the same year as *Citizen Kane* and in many respects is the horror/fantasy equivalent to that legendary film. Like a colonial etching sprung to life, this is a visual marvel with expert use of light and framing; the device of streaming light as a harbinger of evil is a terrific reversal of expectations (and technically more accurate in theological terms), while the pacing and performances are honed to perfection. Huston and Arnold get the juiciest dramatic moments, of course, but the charming Simon also makes a searing impression in her limited screen time. Like *Kane* (which shares

the same composer, Bernard Herrmann), this is great filmmaking but also more than a bit chilly and austere at times; director William Dieterle later imbued a bit more passion in the sloppier but more heartfelt *Portrait of Jennie*. However, that's a minor quibble with what is absolutely essential viewing for lovers of *film fantastique*.

Financed as an independent production and subjected to endless recutting and retitlings, *The Devil and Daniel Webster* (widely shown as *All That Money Can Buy*) became something of a critical cause for film restoration during the early 1980s. Eventually Criterion restored the film to an approximation of its original condition with a welcome laserdisc in the company's early days, the 85 minutes of pristine material were fleshed out with recovered 16mm footage of the excised scenes, resulting in a patchwork of a vital cinema classic. The DVD goes one better, with a transfer as close to immaculate as this film will probably ever be; while the restored footage is still identifiable by a very slight image softness, the results are much smoother and cleaner. Element damage is extremely minimal; there's a barely visible hairline scratch during the extended opening sequence, but for the most part this is a very satisfying presentation similar to the restoration done on Warner's *The Thing (from Another World)* disc. Carried over from the laser is an excellent audio commentary by film historian Bruce Eder and author/Herrmann expert Steven C. Smith; it's an extremely fast-paced and informative talk, still one of the finest in the Criterion canon. The reasons for the film's troubled history are laid out in detail, with much attention paid to the use of historical details (both visual and musical). The rest of the supplements, amusingly tucked away as a "Scratch's Notebook", kick off with a video comparison between the finished product and an alternative preview version entitled *Here Is a Man*. The editing differences are fairly minor, but it's an instructional look at the tweaking done to a film on its road to release. In a nice companion piece to the commentary, Herrmann's music score is analyzed on a cue-by-cue basis; written comments are provided for each composition, after which one can skip to many of the musical highlights of the film. Other goodies include a radio production by the Columbia Workshop (with Herrmann music), an extensive gallery of behind-the-scenes photos and promotional materials, a written essay by author Tom Piazza, and most interestingly, a reading of the original story by Alec Baldwin, whose own production of the same tale encountered even more drastic difficulties before its eventual completion.

A later 2009 disc issued by Eureka in the U.K. utilizes the same transfer and replaces the Baldwin reading with an actual reprint of the story in the sizeable (60-page!) insert booklet which also contains wood etchings from the first edition, on-set production photos, and a Stephen Vincent Benét appraisal of the film. The only significant video extra is a useful comparison between the finished film and an early preview version under the title *Here's a Man*.

DEVIL DOLL

B&W, 1964, 81m. / Directed by Lindsay Shonteff / Starring Bryant Haliday, Yvonne Romain, Sandra Dorne, William Sylvester / Image (US R1 NTSC), Cinema Club (UK R2 PAL) / WS (1.66:1) (16:9)

The producer of this film, Richard Gordon, cannily retained all the rights to his independent output and is thus in a position to ensure titles that might otherwise be shoddily treated as minor releases come to DVD with due care and attention. Following good-looking if no-frills discs of *Horror Hospital* and *Tower of Evil*, straight ports from a double-bill laser in releases of *The Haunted*

Strangler and *Corridors of Blood* and a Criterion edition (!) of *Fiend Without a Face*, Gordon's essay in the "ventriloquist's dummy" horror sub-genre is here afforded deluxe treatment. Like Image's edition of *The Flesh and the Fiends*, the *Devil Doll* DVD offers a double feature of the familiar UK-US print and a spicier export version. For the record, the continental release offers one additional sequence as a shy girl is hypnotised into performing a striptease on stage (unthinkable then but it's the sort of thing that shows up on cable these days), very slightly more explicit nudity for Sandra Dorne as she exposes a nipple while tossing and turning in bed before she's murdered, and an alternative take of one bedroom scene in which a bit-part girl seen in scanties in the U.K. version is bare-breasted. On his commentary track, Gordon says he prefers the regular version but these sensational bits don't really detract from the mood of the piece. Though the striptease sequence (which can be glimpsed on the menu) seems a little silly, it makes some sense in showing that the grimly lecherous Great Vorelli (Bryant Haliday) carries his nasty, exploitative sexual attitudes into his onstage act as well as exercising them in private. Even the milder cut seems frank for 1964: the heroine (Yvonne Romain) unmistakably has sex with the hero (William Sylvester) in a car (a Rolls Royce borrowed from producer Kenneth Rive) and is later mind-controlled by Vorelli into being his sex slave without having to commit suicide (or otherwise being written out of the picture) afterwards.

Obviously inspired by the climactic sequence of *Dead of Night*, to the extent of reusing the name "Hugo" for the sinister dummy, this is actually a reversal of most ventriloquist movies and TV shows in that the dour, false-bearded Vorelli is the evil dominant partner and the living dummy is a put-upon victim forced to do the villain's bidding. Director Lindsay Shonteff, a protégé of Sidney J. Furie (originally set to helm the film), concentrates on the character

D

interplay, with Haliday an unusually joyless master fiend whose lecherous perfidies never prompt him to crack a smile and whose hypnotist/ventriloquist stage act is an especially harsh little exchange of ill-humoured glowering and bullying. Romain, beautiful but stiff in most roles, unbends a little, doing a mean twist (under hypnosis) and playing a rare sexually active good girl in early '60s cinema; usually called on only to pout, she here gets to smile and look like a different, more interesting person. The cinematography by the talented Gerald Gibbs is moody and evocative, and the editing employs some unusual techniques like brief freeze frames and negative images to convey supernatural forces – though low budget shows through in the use of the same few shots of the same audience members as cutaways in scenes that are supposed to take place on different nights.

Both prints are in great, restored shape, with lovely rich shadows; it's possible that the export version just has the edge in picture quality, but neither have anything to be ashamed of when compared to the grey-look many contemporary black and white pictures have on disc. The 1.66:1 framing loses a little off the top and bottom through the 16:9 enhancement, but this is only notable in that it cramps the credits: otherwise, the matting probably makes the claustrophobic air of perversion and terror even more unhealthy. In addition to two versions of the film, you get a ballyhoo American trailer (among the odder claims, "for maximum Shock Sock, see it from the beginning!") and an extensive gallery of stills, on-set shots and promotional material. Gordon and historian Tom Weaver provide a commentary for the non-export version, with the producer's reminiscences prodded by Weaver's useful info-dumps about the actors involved or the various drafts adapted from Frederick E. Smith's short story "The Devil Doll". The insert includes an interesting memoir/comment from Smith (*633 Squadron*), who sold his story outright to *London Mystery Magazine* for £10 and wasn't even told it had been made into a movie until it was on release. The later U.K. release is a bare bones presentation of the same U.K. version.

Devil Doll is a good little late-night effort, certainly far superior to the same team's follow-up (*Curse of Simba*); it would be stretching things to hail it as a classic, but it is an effective, low-key sleeper.

– KN

THE DIABOLICAL DR. Z

B&W, 1965, 83m. / Directed by Jess Franco / Starring Estella Blain, Mabel Karr, Antonio Jiménez Escribano, Jess Franco, Daniel White, Howard Vernon / Mondo Macabro (US R1 NTSC) / WS (1.66:1) (16:9)

Following the success of his debut horror film, 1962's *The Awful Dr. Orlof*, Jess Franco continued his string of kinky, black and white Gothics with memorable variations on the same theme: *The Sadistic Baron von Klaus, Dr. Orloff's Monster*, and the greatest film of his early period, *The Diabolical Dr. Z* (also shown in Europe under the more appropriate title of *Miss Muerte*, as Dr. Z exits the film ten minutes in). With this film Franco established many of the themes and obsessions which would continue through his colour films of the '60s and '70s, including erotic stage shows with mannequins, beautiful women programmed to kill, a bereaved loved one avenging a tragic death, and fetishised body appendages used to kill. An ideal starting point for newcomers terrified of Franco's reputation, this beguiling mixture of drive-in sleaze and European art film remains one of the director's most purely enjoyable and accessible efforts.

During a thunderstorm, the soon-to-be-executed Woodside Strangler attacks his guard and escapes from prison, only to arrive barely conscious at the estate of bespectacled Dr. Zimmer (Antonio Jiménez Escribano), a disciple of the late Dr. Orlof. At the insistence of his daughter Irma (Mabel Karr), the doctor tries out his new mind control experiments on the convict thanks to his latest contraption, a robot-armed mechanism complete with spikes which puncture the patient's spinal column. Zimmer presents his findings at a scientific conference, but the hostile reception from his colleagues drives Zimmer to a fatal heart attack on the spot. To cope with her grief, Irma goes to a jazz club where the beguiling Miss Death (Estella Blain) performs a bizarre stage routine involving a huge spider web. Consumed by the need to continue her father's experiments, Irma runs over a sexy blonde hitchhiker but winds up horribly scarred while disposing of the body. When the doctor's female assistant rebels, Irma uses the Strangler (now her mind-controlled servant) to subdue the rebellious woman and turn her into a servant, too. Together they set out after Miss Death (real name Nadia) in order to create a killing machine capable of striking down the men responsible for Zimmer's death. The method is simple; with her long, poisonous fingernails, Miss Death can seduce her prey in any location without being caught, and soon this instrument of terror sets out after the three guilty parties with the police gradually closing in.

The subject matter is top grade lurid Franco, complete with nasty surgical procedures, jazz fugues, and even appearances by Franco and composer Daniel White as police inspectors. Even Dr. Orlof himself, the always reliable Howard Vernon, pops up in two scenes as the ill-fated Dr. Vicas, who meets his fate aboard a speeding train in one especially peculiar set piece. As the beautiful Nadia, Blain has some of the film's most memorable moments and effectively carries her scenes largely through facial expressions. Her capture at Irma's hands while wearing a skin-tight spider outfit is one of

the film's more eye-catching moments, but here Franco keeps the cinematic virtuosity coursing throughout the narrative without losing sight of his story. The climax is one of his best, with a bravura castle fistfight, which begins with a smashing tracking shot down a stony hallway, intercuts a brilliant series of punches, and climaxes with a staircase sword duel. Despite one phoney-looking shot of a scalpel slicing Irma's face and Miss Death's skimpy costumes, this is also a rare Franco film able to be shared with younger or more squeamish horror fans who might want to see what all the fuss is about. More seasoned Franco viewers will be curious to see his first run through a plotline (itself inspired by Cornell Woolrich's *The Bride Wore Black*) later revisited and revised in such films as *She Killed in Ecstasy* and *Eugenie de Sade*, while the visual parallels to the next year's *Succubus* and even his controversial shot-on-video projects like *Tender Flesh* and *Mari-Cookie and the Killer Tarantula* should be glaringly obvious.

After years of ignominious public domain treatment, *The Diabolical Dr. Z* comes to DVD in high style courtesy of Mondo Macabro. The anamorphic transfer looks smashing, with excellent contrast and detail. Element damage is almost nonexistent, and the source (taken from the original French-language edition) betters all previous versions. A handful of shots near the beginning display some minor blurring and streaking in the forest sequence, but this may be a fault of the original film processing. The disc contains both the English and French language versions; both were looped in keeping with Franco's filming tradition at the time, but since this version runs slightly longer than the U.S. English language cut, the English track includes a bit of French dialogue (with optional subtitles) to keep the flow intact. The French version from start to finish is really the classier and smoother of the two options and comes highly recommended. The packaging indicates a stereo soundtrack, but it sounds like plain old mono, albeit very crisp and clear. As for extras, the disc includes the U.S. title sequence (not significantly different from the European one, but a nice extra all the same), the U.S. theatrical trailer, a still and poster gallery, and talent bios. Perhaps the most worthwhile but peculiar bonus is "The Diabolical Mr. Franco", a 15-minute featurette in the vein of the *Mondo Macabro* TV show containing Franco interview footage interspersed with comments from the likes of Peter Blumenstock (co-author of the out of print book *Obsession: The Films of Jess Franco*). For some reason Caroline Munro pops up for a half-sentence cameo that looks like an editing error. The disc comes with a cover built around the original French poster art and contains some nifty animated menus, all of which revolve around a spider web motif, of course.

DIE ANOTHER DAY

Colour, 2002, 127m. / Directed by Lee Tamahori / Starring Pierce Brosnan, Halle Berry, Toby Stephens, Rosamund Pike, Rick Yune, Madonna / MGM (Blu-ray & DVD) (UK RB/R2 HD/PAL, US RA/R1 HD/ NTSC) / WS (2.35:1) (16:9) / DD5.1

 A badly compromised mission behind enemy lines lands James Bond (Pierce Brosnan) in a North Korean prison cell for 14 months. Upon his release he defies orders from his superiors and sets out on a personal mission to discover the identity of the saboteur. His investigation takes him from Hong Kong to Cuba and on to Iceland where it transpires that treacherous entrepreneur Gustav Graves (Toby Stephens) plans to utilise a state-of-the-art satellite weapon named Icarus to decimate the earth.

The twentieth (official) movie, the fortieth year of production, and producers Michael G. Wilson and Barbara Broccoli, along with director Lee Tamahori (*The Edge*) and scribes Neal Purvis and Robert Wade concocted a 007 blockbuster which divided audiences like no other in the franchise before it. Many claimed it to be the best ever, equally as many dubbed it the worst. In actual fact it's neither, slotting in instead somewhere in the middle. As the most fantasy-oriented instalment since 1979's oft-vilified *Moonraker*, *Die Another Day* pays homage to the Bonds of yesteryear by sprinkling in dozens of references to previous entries in the series, from the patently obvious (Halle Berry doing an Ursula Andress by strolling out of the sea in a bikini with a knife strapped to her thigh, and the upgraded Aston Martin with ejector seat and motion-activated machine guns) to the slightly more obscure (rotating mirrors that echo a scene in *The Man with the Golden Gun*, and Bond pilfering a grape from a clinic patient's fruit bowl, as he did in *Thunderball*). Pierce Brosnan, arguably the best Bond since Sean Connery turned in his toupee, is near pitch perfect, strolling impeccably through the mayhem, bedding CIA agent Jinx (Berry) and MI6 ally Miranda Frost (Rosamund Pike) with enviable ease, while locking horns with plenty of that insidious variety of villainy indigenous to the James Bond universe. Yes, indeed, the women are vivacious and the villains as despicable as ever, and few will be disappointed on that score. Gustav Graves, the sociopath of the moment, is all sadistic threats and arrogant sneers, but he's upstaged by one of the most effective Bond baddies in years, Zao (Rick Yune), a bald-headed albino henchman with a diamond-studded face. David Arnold's score is zippy enough (though he fails to top his work on *The World Is Not Enough*), and here's something no one ever expected to hear in a Bond flick – The Clash's "London Calling!" Madonna's widely reviled theme song meanwhile fits Daniel Kleinman's classy fire and ice titles sequence quite satisfactorily. In addition to her contribution in the music department, Madonna chips in with an uncredited (and unremarkable) turn as a fencing instructress at Graves's plush London club. This sets the scene for one of the best action sequences in the film, a frenetic fencing bout between Bond and Graves that begins as an animus-fuelled wager and mutates into a furious duel to the death.

Tamahori stokes up the fires and stages exciting set piece after exciting set piece, many of which are right up there with the most memorable in the series; there's a balletic car chase across a frozen lake, an explosive pursuit through a minefield on hovercrafts, and a punch-up in a lab amidst a zigzagging mesh of laser beams. Not everything works so well, however. Some truly dreadful double-entendres slip through the net and the Aston Martin's invisibility function is up there with some of the worst one-vodka-martini-too-many-at-the-script-conference misfires in the entire series. And one action sequence in particular – in which Bond paraglides to safety across the crest of a tidal wave festooned with icebergs – is marred by cheap-looking CG work that renders our man as a stick figure out of a Playstation game, worsened further by unconvincing inserts of Brosnan acting his shoulder-holster off against a back-projected rush of water. All said and done, *Die Another Day*, though unquestionably highly entertaining, lacks the replay factor of the older Bonds and will be far less memorable forty years down the line than *Dr. No* is today. Oh, and it does no harm to reveal that not only does 007 triumph against all odds in the end, but the final credit roll reprises the promise of almost every film's conclusion to date, too: "James Bond will return." We expected nothing less.

MGM pulled out all the stops for their initial two-disc DVD of *Die Another Day*, using it as a platform for their first series of double-disc Bond releases. Disc #1 houses the film itself in its 2.35:1 theatrical ratio with 36 chapter divisions. An extra feature offers one the option of watching it through with a host of integrated behind the scenes segments stitched in, or alternatively with one of two commentaries (the first from director Lee Tamahori and producer Michael G. Wilson, the second from players Pierce Brosnan and Rosamund Pike). The sound on the British R2 release is in English Dolby Digital Surround EX and English DTS and there are also subtitles provided in English and Dutch. Disc #2 comprises a trove of supplementary features. "Inside *Die Another Day*" is a meaty look at the production of the film, with a running time a little over half the length of the feature itself. A second, shorter documentary, "Shaken and Stirred", delves into the problems – and they were manifold – of shooting a car chase on ice. Then there are storyboard/final shot comparisons on several scenes, multi-angle presentations for key action sequences, a look at the construction of the titles sequence, some CG presentations detailing the film's gadgetry quotient, a huge step-frame gallery of still images, before-and-after comparisons of digitally enhanced footage, Madonna's rather violent music video and a short look at its making, several TV spots, and three trailers (though the British version of the second teaser – including a raunchy shot of Bond and Jinx getting intimate that had to be substituted for something milder for the U.S. market – is absent). Rounding things off there's a trailer and featurette promoting a Bond computer game. An Easter egg feature offers an additional treat, the chance to ogle Halle Berry emerging from the ocean from a variety of different camera angles; you'll find it by accessing the stills gallery, selecting the "Sets and Locations" sub-section, stepping through to the first shot of Berry in her orange bikini and hitting Enter.

As if all this wasn't enough, the U.K. R2 disc release cocks a snook at its R1 U.S. counterpart by throwing in an additional 50-minute documentary, "From Script to Screen", possibly the most candid supplementary component to feature on any 007 title to date. Bond buffs beware: Although the American R1 disc could be considered mildly inferior due to the absence of the R2 exclusive features, it becomes extremely inferior when you realise the film itself is cut! The R1 disc is missing several seconds of steamy passion when Bond first beds Jinx in a Cuban hotel room, while the R2 disc presents the sequence intact.

Perhaps to avoid cutting into sales, the reissued version of this film in MGM's much later remastered collections features a "Lowry restoration" that can't improve much on the already near-perfect first issue, then drops the second disc in favour of a completely different, rather inferior bonus platter – meaning Bond buffs have to hang on to both editions. Extras on this one include the "From Script to Screen" (carried over from the U.K. disc), "Shaken and Stirred on Ice" (a featurette on the ice palace sequence), an image gallery, and some more minor featurettes ("Just Another Day", "The British Touch", "On Location with Peter Lamont"). The Blu-ray versions are essentially identical, presenting the full version of the film with all of the extras from the first DVD but none from the bonus disc. However, the boost to HD-level image and (especially) audio makes for a fairly rousing home theatre experience even when the narrative comes up short.

– TG

DIE, MONSTER, DIE!

Colour, 1965, 79m. / Directed by Daniel Haller / Starring Boris Karloff, Nick Adams, Suzan Farmer, Freda Jackson, Terence De Marney, Patrick Magee / MGM (US R1 NTSC, UK R2 PAL) / WS (2.35:1) (16:9)

Even Roger Corman couldn't keep AIP satisfied when it came to his flow of 1960s product, driving the company to various attempts at expanding the producer-director's Vincent Price-Edgar Allan Poe franchise. Corman had already tapped H.P. Lovecraft for the ostensibly Poe-based *The Haunted Palace*, actually taken from *The Case of Charles Dexter Ward*. In backing *Die, Monster, Die!* (aka *Monster of Terror*), AIP probably had visions of Daniel Haller, Corman's art director, launching a parallel series of Boris Karloff-Lovecraft pictures. An old dark house take on "The Color Out of Space" (later remade, even less well, as *The Curse*) filmed in England, the film was evidently disappointing enough commercially to rule out more of the same, though the Karloff-starring *Curse of the Crimson Altar* (an uncredited adaptation of "Dreams in the Witch House') and Haller's *The Dunwich Horror* are almost follow-ups.

The film opens eerily, though shockingly for HPL purists, as trench-coated Yank Steve Reinhart (Nick Adams) wanders around the small English village of Arkham (played by a familiar Avengers location near Shepperton Studios) asking unfriendly, terrified locals for directions to "the Witley place". The next reel is almost a remake of Corman's *Fall of the House of Usher* as Steve walks through a desolate landscape scarred by a meteorite impact and finds the crumbling family mansion. Mad scientist Nahum Witley (Boris Karloff) tries to scare Steve off paying a visit to his college girlfriend, Nahum's Marilyn Munster-type cheery daughter (Suzan Farmer). Nahum is struggling with the heritage of his warlock father (represented by another *Usher* plagiarism, a weird portrait of Karloff) by dedicating himself to science rather than sorcery.

However, with a missing mutated maid, a wife (Freda Jackson) transforming into a leper-like monster behind bed-curtains and a servant (Terence De Marney) who drops inconveniently dead, Nahum reassesses his rational worldview. He has been experimenting with a glowing meteorite that gives off strange, mutagenic radiation, though he comes to believe that the substance originates not from outer space but from hell.

In one genuinely unsettling sequence, the hero and heroine explore a greenhouse full of mutant flora and fauna, which is all the more effective for leaving some of its monsters unnoticed in the background, but too much time is spent on characters whining or acting illogically as the older cast members turn into monsters and attack people. A frail Karloff, in one of his wheelchair roles, does little to distinguish Nahum from his many similar characterisations, while Adams – after neat opening banter with a cabbie about American tailoring standards that cuts off cold when he mentions where he wants to be taken – is an unlikeable, undistinguished good guy. The best work comes from solid British pros in tiny roles: Jackson, De Marney, and Patrick Magee (as an embittered local doctor). A final rampage by a silver-faced Karloff stand-in echoes the actor's meteor mutation back in *The Invisible Ray*, and is standard stuff but for buzzing, electrical sound effects.

MGM's DVD uses a slightly damaged print, but has subtle, creepy colours and the full 2.35:1 image. It offers English and French Mono soundtracks, with English closed captions and French and Spanish subtitles. The only extra is a supposed "original theatrical trailer", actually a spoiler-filled montage of clips without narration or ballyhoo. Released in the first wave of MGM's Midnite Movies collection, before the company hit on the brilliant idea of issuing its genre catalogue in themed double-bills, *Die, Monster, Die!*

might have been more appealing as part of a Haller-Lovecraft dual with *The Dunwich Horror*. The later U.K. version is even less appointed, dropping the faux trailer.
– KN

DJANGO, KILL!
(IF YOU LIVE SHOOT!)

Colour, 1967, 117m. / Directed by Giulio Questi / Starring Tomas Milian, Marilù Tolo, Milo Quesada, Ray Lovelock, Piero Lulli, Roberto Camardiel / Blue Underground (US R0 NTSC), Argent (UK R2 PAL), X-Rated (Germany R2 PAL) / WS (2.35:1) (16:9)

 Filmed as *Se sei vivo spara* and then retitled internationally to tag onto the success of Sergio Corbucci's *Django* and its many spin-offs, this is overrated in some quarters but is a twisted, gruesome, sometimes amusing, sometimes silly Italian-Spanish western Guignol. It opens with two Indians (obviously Europeans in wigs) discovering a nameless half-breed (Tomas Milian) buried alive at a massacre site, then has elliptical flashbacks about the ambush of a U.S. army gold shipment and the murder of the Mexican bandits by the Anglo members of the gang – which aptly leaves the half-breed half-dead. During the shootings, a desperate victim cripples or drives off the horses, leaving the killers to trudge wearily through the desert to the nearest town. The half-breed and his devoted Indians, who want news from him about the afterlife, are on their trail, the hero's gun loaded with golden bullets made from his share of the loot ("bullets made of gold are better than lead, they go deeper"). However, by the time the avengers get to town, the gold has changed hands and is a matter of dispute between various significantly-named factions: saloon-keeper Templar (Milo Quesada), who has a grasping

young mistress (Marilù Tolo) and a strange teenage son (Ray Lovelock); pillar of respectability Alderman (Piero Lulli), with a supposed mad wife stashed in the attic; and burly rancher Zorro (Roberto Camardiel), who commands a gang of black-shirted, pouting catamites ("my muchachos") and a parrot who's just as avaricious as he is.

The plot follows roughly the template of *A Fistful of Dollars* and *Django* as the stranger in town tries to protect the few token innocents by playing off the various baddies against each other. As in the earlier films, he is martyred at one point – hung up in a cruciform pose – but recuperates enough to see all his enemies dead. The most potent of many images of bizarre death (evoking *Diabolik*, and reused as recently as *Goldeneye*) is of the man trying to rescue his stash of gold from a burning building only to be coated with the molten metal and die as a gilded statue. While this certainly has the cartoonish social comment and political bitterness its admirers claim, so do most spaghetti westerns. Its surreal touches are also not rare in the genre, and it never tries to break out of its format the way Giulio Questi's thriller follow up *Death Laid an Egg* does. It's a mostly good, horrid melodrama with some '67 hippie-ish touches (like Milian's headband) and many of the usual spaghetti drawbacks (stick figure characters) rather than an attempt to compete with Pasolini or Bertolucci, and should be judged as such.

Blue Underground's DVD is a major upgrade on all previous video editions of this title, with a smart-looking, anamorphic widescreen transfer of a near-pristine print. A few vertical scratches are noticeable in the opening reel, but it's otherwise in excellent shape. Two brief, violent sequences – fingers digging gold bullets out of a dying outlaw and the close-up scalping of one of the Indians – have not previously been included in English-language releases and so are only presented in subtitled Italian; visually, they are slightly brighter than the rest of the film, with lashings of blood that looks exceptionally like red paint. The soundtrack options are Italian or English, with optional English subtitles. The Italian track sounds a little tinnier than the English, and it's a safe bet that few of the actors speak with their own voices on either version. The subs, incidentally, reproduce the English dialogue rather than translate the Italian, losing some of the more picturesque snarled insults and making trivial errors in naming characters ("Lori" for "Flory").

The extras are: "Django, Tell" (an informative little documentary with input from Questi, Milian and Lovelock), a trailer that consists entirely of animated gunfighters and looks like a titles sequence, and an extensive poster/stills gallery. An insert booklet has liner notes by William Connelly, which are fine as far as they go but make the common spaghetti western fan mistake of seeing a far greater break with American westerns than was actually the case. Connelly claims that it's radical to have a bandit hero or to present townsfolk as hypocritical, which suggests he's missed numberless Billy the Kid movies and a whole raft of 1950s pictures that came out after *High Noon*. An Easter egg accessible by clicking on the half-buried hand on the menu gives access to some amusing anecdotes from Milian and Lovelock about their attempt to form a rock band, The Tomas Milian Group. NB: in a rare instance of carelessness from Blue Underground, the back jacket copy twice misspells the director's first name.

The X-Rated Kult release includes German, English and Italian soundtrack options, and four trailers, while the U.K. disc from Argent has an enthusiastic Alex Cox video intro, Lovelock and Questi interviews, and the trailer (plus more spaghetti western trailers including *Django* and *Keoma*), though it only includes the English track with the brief Italian inserts (with subtitles).

– KN

DO OR DIE

Colour, 1991, 97m. / Directed by Andy Sidaris / Starring Pat Morita, Erik Estrada, Pandora Peaks / Malibu Bay Films (US R0 NTSC), Laser Paradise (Germany R2 PAL)

After hissing his way through Andy Sidaris's *Guns*, Erik Estrada apparently enjoyed the surf and babes so much he reunited with the director one year later for *Do or Die*. However, despite Estrada's apparent new willingness to do softcore love scenes with silicone-enhanced pin-ups, he's overshadowed by a new twist: Mr. Miyagi goes evil! That's right, Pat Morita of *The Karate Kid* fame takes over villain duties as Kane, a crime boss prone to speechifying in front of palm trees. This insidious foe has lined up a team of assassins to take down jacuzzi-lovin' spies Donna and Nicole, who spend much time running around in bikinis. That's about it for plot, except that Estrada plays helpful, gun toting agent Richard Estaban, who comes to the girls' aid with an array of ridiculous gadgets. Add to that the usual story-stopping sex scenes, sport boating, late hour Russ Meyer starlet Pandora Peaks, and a lot of Vegas and Louisiana bayou scenery, and you've got the usual recipe for surefire entertainment that won't tax your brain.

The transfer quality is up to par with other Sidaris titles, meaning it's eye candy of the first order with lots of super saturated hues; those tropical sunsets never looked so good. The standard extras are also on hand, with a Sidaris/Julie Strain intro, commentary by Andy and Arlene Sidaris, a locations featurette, an "Andy Sidaris Film School" featurette (also repeated on later titles), cast interviews, a stills gallery, trailers from the entire collection, and a fold-out illustrated booklet.

The U.S. disc is quite hard to come by now, but a solid backup option is Germany's 10-disc Sidaris box set, which contains all of his American DVD releases (including, inexplicably, a heavily cut version of *Guns*); the commentary is dropped, but the featurette footage is cut up differently: a Sidaris and Strain interview, two "Film School" tutorials, and three location featurettes ("Sedano", "Playboy", and "Parachute").

DOCTOR GORE

Colour, 1972, 83m. / Directed by J.G. Patterson Jr. / Starring J.G. Patterson Jr., Jenny Driggers, Roy Mehaffey

HOW TO MAKE A DOLL

Colour, 1968, 78m. / Directed by Herschell Gordon Lewis / Starring Robert Wood, Bobbi West, Jim Vance / Something Weird (US R1 NTSC)

Something Weird Video has made a fine art out of reviving obscure and otherwise forgotten exploitation movies for the digital era; through value-for-money double-billing of films that might struggle to rack up sales as singletons and the judicious addition of a generous array of extras, they have managed to make worthwhile releases of films of only marginal interest. This package consists of footnotes to the career of Herschell Gordon Lewis, one film in his tradition made by a former associate, and another by Lewis himself but different in tone from his best-known work. The bill also presents distinct variations on the *Bride of Frankenstein* theme, with scientists creating female love objects and learning hard lessons.

Bearing the onscreen title *The Body Shop* – with an opening theme that burbles a repeated phrase from "My Favourite Things" – *Doctor Gore* is a gruesome, amateur hour *Frankenstein* knock-off written and directed by J.G. "Pat" Patterson, who also takes the lead role under the name of the character he plays, Don Brandon. Bereft at the loss of his beloved wife, Dr. Brandon sets out to replace her with a perfect woman assembled from the choicer parts of various hypnotized North Carolina cuties who are messily dissected in his laboratory. Assisted by Gregory (Roy Mehaffy), a minion who has trouble getting his lab-coat over his enormous hunch, Brandon has a lot of Universal-look sparking mad science equipment in the basement of his castle, though the emphasis on surgical gore is closer in tone to the Hammer Frankensteins. Among many questions not addressed by the film is why Brandon – a homely fellow with a dreadful comb-over who somewhat resembles an uncharismatic Geoffrey Rush – needs to create a mate when he can mind-control a selection of reasonable-looking women.

It takes about an hour to raise Anitra (Jenny Driggers), the patchwork girl, from the lab table, and the remainder of the film is so garbled (including the most blatant left-in clapperboard in cinema) as to lend credence to the theory that the film was never properly completed. The doctor and his creation frolic through a montage, carving messages of love on trees, accompanied by a saccharine country song ("Lovin' Tree") from Bill Hicks (not the comedian), and Brandon educates his manufactured mate in everything from basic spelling to drinking a glass of water, all the while indoctrinating her in the differences between men and women and the duties of a woman to love her (or any) man. She learns the lesson too well, and Brandon is so enraged to find her giving the hunchback a hug that he turns on the loyal boob by tossing acid in his face, chopping into his hump with a machete and pitching him into the lab's Hammer-style acid bath. Brandon ends up in an insane asylum, while Anitra takes off across country in a bikini, hitchhiking and putting out for any many who catches her eye.

Patterson fumbles all three of his jobs, with some filmmaking gaffes even Lewis would have avoided. A sequence in which

the Sheriff comes to the door to investigate consists of a shot of the Sheriff in an open field stumbling through his dialogue intercut with shots of Brandon holding the door open a crack to keep up his end of the conversation – the cop is dissuaded from investigating rumours of horrors at the castle with absurd ease, but the real reason he doesn't enter is that the actor obviously never got near the location. Towards the end, key plot scenes seem never to have been filmed – but the early stretches are padded with a visit to a club to take in a magic act and another lachrymose song from the untalented Hicks ("A Heart Dies Every Day").

The SWV print is in great shape compared to many films of this vintage, perhaps because the movie was barely released and so it hasn't been ground through a thousand drive-in projectors. It has solid blacks and vivid colours, especially the scarlet paint-look blood, so the fact that the movie looks dreadful throughout is all down to Patterson's original lapses rather than any dereliction of the transfer. Among the extras is an alternative titles sequence with the *Doctor Gore* label followed by an introductory talk from H.G. Lewis shot for a video release in the mid-1980s – Lewis, who is here rather an awkward public speaker, honestly admits "you may not like the acting, you may not like the direction, you may not like the gore, but you won't forget the movie." A commentary track with producer Jeffrey C. Hogue and film historian Cynthia Starr-Soroka rarely touches on the movie itself, which he acquired well after its production, supervising the Lewis-introduced version. The talk ranges throughout the broadly Arkansan Hogue's interesting career in production, exhibition and distribution.

How to Make a Doll, included on the disc as an "extra added attraction", is an insufferable sex comedy from H.G. Lewis, distantly derived from the *Dr. Goldfoot* movies. Percy Corly (Robert Wood), a virginal 32-year-old genius, lives with his smothering Mom and knows "all about the relationship between a and b but nothing about the relationship between b and g." He drives about in his snazzy little red car and hooks up with Dr. Hamilcar West (Jim Vance), a computer genius who has spent ten years creating a device which will whip up living beings – the test subject is a rabbit, but he's really interested in turning out beautiful, compliant bikini babes who can have sex with lonely bachelors and then be disappeared ("instant women, and no morning after"). Oddly for such a pointless and derivative film (Corly's home life seems modelled on Seymour's in *The Little Shop of Horrors*), it dabbles in concepts that would be cutting edge cyberpunk stuff in the 1990s, though one suspects Lewis and producer David Chudnow were dimly recalling *Donovan's Brain* rather than breaking new ground. During his first heavy petting session with a creation, West dies of a heart attack but his entire personality is uploaded into a computer and he lives on, able to interface with reality when Corly sits under a hair-dryer which enables the disembodied West to relive his disciple's fleshy experiences with an assortment of love dolls. Eventually, Corly rebels against his disembodied, sexist master ("Enough already, this isn't living – I'm just feeding the memory banks of that dirty-minded computer"). The computer sets a horde of bikini zombies chanting "we love you" on him and, in an odd variant on HAL's shutdown in *2001: A Space Odyssey*, Corly defeats the computer by reprogramming him "from AC to DC", whereupon West's voice gets gayer as Corly manipulates the machine. Predictably, Corly meets grad student Agnes (Bobbi West) who is bespectacled and has an unflattering hairstyle but otherwise looks exactly like his favourite doll. The science fiction plot is over, but the film has another twenty excruciating minutes to run in order to make it to feature length as the two ugly ducklings cope with their annoying parents as they get together

for a date and a happy ending that undoes the vaguely moralistic real-women-are-better-than-screwbots theme by having Agnes magically transformed into a bikini babe with bunny ears and a tail.

It would seem to be a nudie cutie, complete with boinggg-heavy comedy soundtrack and one of those fantastical get-random-babes-on-screen premises, but none of the girls appear nude and the sexual hijinx consist of nothing more than passionate kissing. The performances are down to the standard of the average Lewis film, but since these actors are trying for comic effect without funny dialogue or amusing situations (a supposed humour highlight is a lengthy conversation about how possible it is to cut one's ear while shaving) there isn't even the sidetrack into unintentional humour that makes the auteur's gore films occasionally watchable. The flatly-shot and makeshift sets are dressed with quite a lot of now-antique, then-sophisticated computer gear, augmented by low-rent items like the brain-transference hairdryer or the corrugated iron "materialization chamber". The transfer of this extremely negligible item is more than acceptable, with garish red-dominated sets and healthy bikini fleshtones, though there is the expected amount of print damage. The image is presented fullscreen, though this crops the V of the intermittent SWV logo in half and trims the opening credits to render the director's name as "Herschell Gordon Lew". Hollow-sounding dialogue scenes and overstressed comedy music are presumably a fault of the original soundtrack. As an "extra", it's probably a useful item for Lewis completists; on its own, it's just rubbish.

Also in the package: wild ballyhoo trailers for *Dr. Black Mr. Hyde* (with a rap narration that bears repeating, "shot full of lead and he still ain't dead ... don't give him no sass or he'll kick your *ass*!"), *Boots and the Preacher*, *The Curious Dr. Humpp* ("from every act of pleasure comes an equal act of perversion"), *The Doctor and* the *Playgirls*, *The Gruesome Twosome*, *The Wizard of Gore*, *The Awful Dr. Orlof* ("such carryings-on, such carryings-out!"), *The Wacky World of Dr. Morgus*, *Professor Lust*, *Monstrosity*, *Fanny Hill Meets Dr. Erotico* and *I, Marquis de Sade*; trailers for *Doctor Gore* (including yet another clapperboard with yet another title – *Anitra*) and the Patterson-produced *Axe* are Easter eggs, accessible by clicking on bloodstains; two short subjects, "Quest of the Perfect Woman – The Vampire of Marrakesh" (a 1930s antique that is arguably Hammer Films's first vampire movie, though it's essentially a travelogue using *National Geographic*-style native nudity as a lure) and "Maniac Hospital" (not a horror movie but a sore-heavy, slightly surreal venereal disease warning film); and a "ghastly gallery of ghoulish cover art" accompanied by The Dead Elvi. Another oddball Easter egg is a snippet from Lewis's *Just for the Hell of It*, in which a blind Patterson gets beaten up by delinquent teens; if you access this after watching *Doctor Gore*, you'll cheer the thugs.

– KN

DR. JEKYLL AND MR. HYDE

Colour tinted, 1920, 79m. / Directed by John S. Robertson / Starring John Barrymore, Martha Mansfield, Nita Naldi / Dark Vision (UK R0 PAL), Kino (US R1 NTSC), Image (US R0 NTSC)

Robert Louis Stevenson's *Strange Case of Dr Jekyll and Mr Hyde* had been filmed over a dozen times before this lavish John Barrymore vehicle, but this first surviving feature-length version inaugurated the tradition that the dual role was more likely to be played by respected actors – from Fredric March through Spencer Tracy to John Malkovich – than

horror "names", though Boris Karloff and Christopher Lee have also had stabs at what is always a bravura acting work-out. The scenario makes changes to the novel that had precedents in earlier stage and film versions and which would become the norm: this Jekyll is a handsome young idealist rather than an ageing hypocrite, the two sides of his personality are mirrored by two women (Jekyll's pure fiancée and Hyde's slutty mistress) and the selling point set pieces are the transformation scenes.

Influenced by actors like the Victorian Richard Mansfield, Barrymore does as much of the metamorphosis as possible through distorting his features, though film trickery and make-up additions do come into play. As so often, the stiffness of Jekyll is exaggerated to make Hyde more hideous, and John S. Robertson rings the good doctor with a shining aura to emphasise the depths to which he falls. A year before *Nosferatu*, Barrymore delivers arguably the cinema's first truly great monster performance (it's likely that Murnau and Max Schreck were influenced by his Hyde). With a balding dome head the shape of his battered hat, teeth that get more misshapen with each transformation and claw-like finger extensions, this Hyde is certainly an impressive visual grotesque, but Barrymore's scuttling, grinning, impish, malevolent performance animates the creation. In one symbolic scene, the sleeping Jekyll is approached by his alter ego in the form of a phantom giant spider that crawls up on his bed and sinks into him. Stevenson's Hyde isn't the roaring giant ape of some film versions, but a nasty little monkey who only lashes out at those weaker than himself: Barrymore catches perfectly the mix of meanness and terror in his nature as a crowd gathers after he has impulsively trampled a child. In a wonderful death sequence, Hyde poisons himself and slumps in a chair only for the legendary great profile to re-emerge.

For a 1920 film with theatrically static camera and mostly gesticulative supporting performances, *Dr. Jekyll and Mr. Hyde* holds up surprisingly well. The titles are melodramatic but have a touch of wit, courtesy of dollops of *The Picture of Dorian Gray* aptly stirred into the mix. Nita Naldi shines in the role of the dancer who excites Jekyll's lusts and is later abused by Hyde, though this character is only a rough draft of the role played by Miriam Hopkins in the 1932 version. It's one of the first films to make much of the Victorian era as a period that should be recreated in movie adaptations of novels of that vintage; most Sherlock Holmes films had contemporary settings until well into the talkie era, for instance. The production offers smart evening dress for the uppercrust drawing room characters and makes atmospheric capital of the smoky dives and music halls Hyde frequents. Of course, it's possible that Americans thought Britain was still like that.

Dark Vision's print is very slightly letterboxed, and mostly tinted in sepia or blue as appropriate, with an organ-dominated score that switches to the piano for the heroine's clunky parlour recitals. The expected amount of print damage is evident throughout, and the sepia scenes seem a little too brightly exposed with the loss of detail on faces regrettable in that this is a movie you go to for the performances. The title has been around for years in variant editions: this isn't quite the longest available, though it does contain the often-omitted Borgia poison ring historical flashback and has the original wonderfully-illustrated purple prose title cards ("Nature took her hideous revenge – and out of the black abyss of torment sent upon him the creeping horror that was his other self"). Competing U.S. releases from Kino and Image offer variant prints, each with snippets absent from the other, and have different sets of extracts from various other silent versions of the story sadly absent from the U.K. edition, which has a few filmographies and three video cover images as the sole extras.
– KN

DR. JEKYLL VERSUS THE WEREWOLF

Colour, 1972, 83m. / Directed by León Klimovsky / Starring Paul Naschy, Jack Taylor, Shirley Corrigan / Mondo Macabro (UK R0 PAL) / WS (1.85:1) (16:9)

D

Isolated Hungarian towns known for their werewolf population usually don't make the best honeymoon spot, but that doesn't stop young married Justine (*The Devil's Nightmare*'s Shirley Corrigan) from journeying to this land of perpetual fog for some fun in the graveyards. Soon a group of bandits offs her husband and prepares to debase poor Justine, but she's saved at the last minute by everyone's favourite barrel-chested werewolf, Waldemar Daninsky (Paul Naschy), who returns her to the local castle. Quickly overcoming her grief, Justine falls for the hirsute one and persuades him to return with her to London for treatment (with angry villagers nipping at his heels). Back home she introduces Waldemar to her pal, Dr. Jekyll (Jess Franco favourite Jack Taylor), who foolishly injects the hapless werewolf with a serum that transforms him into that murderous cad, Mr. Hyde. Now loose in a city filled with swinging '70s clubs and nubile innocent women, this schizo monster must fight to resist his homicidal urges and return to the woman he loves.

This utterly mad fifth instalment in the Waldemar werewolf saga (following *Mark of the Wolfman*, *Nights of the Werewolf*, *Assignment Terror* and *Werewolf Shadow*) gives Naschy the chance to ham it up as two classic monsters for the price of one. Whether growling into the camera or wielding a mean cane, he's consistently great fun to behold, and keeps the film lively through some of the slower spots.

Mondo Macabro's beautiful DVD presents an immaculate, extremely colourful presentation of the film, which usually looked tattered and heavily cropped from other companies. Gone is the risible "cor, blimey!" English dub track; here we have the more aurally pleasing Spanish audio with optional subtitles, which makes the film easier to sit through if no less amusing. Like the U.K. disc of *The Vampire's Night Orgy*, this is the "clothed" version of the film; some scenes were shot twice, with women bare-breasted or covered up by blouses, hands, or undies, and this is the latter. Contrary to the "stereo" claim on the packaging, this is in standard mono like the original prints. Extras include a 20-minute Naschy interview (quite charming and entertaining as usual), thorough bios for the main stars and director, and a text essay on the history of Spanish horror.

DOG SOLDIERS

Colour, 2001, 105m. / Directed by Neil Marshall / Starring Sean Pertwee, Kevin McKidd, Liam Cunningham, Emma Cleasby, Darren Morfitt / Artisan (US R1 NTSC), First Look (Blu-ray & DVD) (US RA/R1 HD/NTSC), Pathé (UK R2 PAL) / WS (1.85:1) (16:9) / DD5.1

A small squadron of soldiers are deposited in the remote terrain of the Scottish highlands to undertake a training exercise. When they happen across the shredded campsite of a Special Forces unit and learn from the sole survivor that they're in the domain of a pack of werewolves, routine manoeuvres turn into a live combat predicament. As darkness falls the reality of the situation is proven. Pursued through the forest, they're rescued from certain massacre by a local woman who drives them to a nearby farmhouse where they take refuge for the night. But the circle of ravenous werewolves is closing in...

Predator meets *Evil Dead* meets *Night of the Living Dead*... with werewolves as houseguests. *Dog Soldiers* is a multi-flavoured adrenaline rush that grabs you by the throat and drags you through a tempest of brutal violence and gung-ho military antics. Kicking off almost documentary style, it wastes no time in giving the audience a short, sharp introduction to the squaddies they'll spend the next ninety minutes watching get torn to shreds. We meet, among others, the good-humoured Sergeant, his hard-nosed, no-nonsense right hand man, the resident whinger, and the one who'd rather be home watching the football. On face value they're a likeable, if apparently slightly undisciplined assembly, but from the second the chips tumble they pool together as an efficient close-knit crew, the sort of guys you'd be grateful to have in your corner in a scuffle. Sean Pertwee (*Event Horizon*) is the refractory Sergeant Wells, almost immediately put out of action when the claws of a flesh-ripping beast pluck out his lower intestines, yet resolutely refusing to lay down and die. Liam Cunningham (*First Knight*) is Captain Ryan, the malicious survivor of the Special Ops team whose werewolf-inflicted lesions are healing with worrying rapidity. Pertwee and Cunningham aside, the film is inhabited by a relatively unrecognisable cast which works well in its favour, and to the one they equip themselves superbly. To single out a particularly fine performance look no further than *Trainspotting*'s Kevin McKidd as Scottish bruiser Cooper, whose mission it becomes to try and keep the platoon alive till dawn. Emma Cleasby is Megan, the mysterious woman who knows more about the human identities of the creatures than she first lets on.

After a campfire spook story with a punchline guaranteed to have you out of your seat, first-time feature writer/director Neil Marshall (who also edited the film) and his f/x team splash out with the claret, ensuring that the cast kiss goodbye to a variety of limbs and vital organs at regular intervals and in the messiest ways possible. Marshall litters his script with some nice little nuggets of black humour too, though he's smart enough to keep it on a well-tethered leash and never once permits whimsy to supplant drama. Genuine wit is born of an unyielding defiance to the bitter end on the part of the unit, as witnessed when Private Wither-spoon (Darren Morfitt) spits in the face of the animal about to devour him, and later when Cooper finds a recently transformed adversary bearing down on him. There's also a lovely skin-crawling moment of juxtaposed sound when an amorous camper undoes the zipper on his lover's jeans only to realise that the zip-fastener on the tent flap is sliding open in tandem. The in-your-face heroics are accentuated by a rousing score from Mark Thomas, and it's a true mark of Marshall's talent as a filmmaker that into the middle of all the testosterone-fuelled mayhem he successfully stitches a chic moment of introspective respite, with Cleasby at the piano playing Debussy's "Clair de Lune".

Described by Marshall as a soldier movie with werewolves, not a werewolf movie with soldiers, *Dog Soldiers* is a competent hybrid, if perhaps a touch too predictable. It's also nice to see a British horror film that doesn't pander to American sensibilities (even more laudable given that it had American co-producers) and, with the possible exception of *An American Werewolf in London*, it's just about the most gripping movie of its ilk you'll encounter. Hyperbole? Give it a whirl and judge for yourself.

Artisan's U.S. Region 1 DVD offers viewers the option of enjoying the film in either 1.85:1 theatrical ratio or fullscreen pan & scan (which crops the image both left and right, while adding nothing extra to the top and only a sliver to the tail). The feature has been afforded 24 chapter stops and has both 5.1 Dolby Digital sound and 2.0 Dolby Stereo; with the rattle of copious discharged bullet shells ricocheting around your speakers, the former is the princely

option. Subtitling is provided in Spanish alone. Supplemental inclusions are a 19-minute featurette (which, among much else of interest, gives one a closer look at the werewolves that, in the movie itself, remain mostly only glimpsed), a commentary from the film's American producers and two trailers. More laden than a lycanthrope's larder, the British Region 2 release from Pathé offers an additional commentary from the director and members of the cast, a blooper reel, four trailers, a selection of storyboards, a handful of deleted scenes and an early Marshall short entitled *Combat*. On the other hand, the U.S. reissue from First Look (on both DVD and Blu-ray) offers no extras and, even worse, sports an insultingly bad transfer with very weak contrast, black levels that never go deeper than a soft pale grey, and an overall soft appearance thanks to a mushy collision of overzealous noise reduction and tricky film stock. Stick with the special edition DVDs at all costs.
– TG

DOLLS

Colour, 1987, 77m. / Directed by Stuart Gordon / Starring Stephen Lee, Guy Rolfe, Carrie Lorraine, Ian Patrick Williams, Carolyn Purdy-Gordon, Hilary Mason / MGM (US R1 NTSC) / WS (1.85:1) (16:9), Hollywood (HK R0 NTSC) / DD2.0, Dragon (Germany R0 PAL) / DD5.1

During his tenure at Empire Pictures, Stuart Gordon took time out from his delirious H.P. Lovecraft adaptations (*Re-Animator* and *From Beyond*) to make this twisted, comparatively low-key fairy tale for adults, which bears a closer resemblance to *The Company of Wolves* than a standard '80s gorefest. Fans tend to be split down the middle over this one, but horror buffs willing to savour atmosphere and well crafted special effects should find more than enough to enjoy.

On a dark, spooky night, little Judy (Carrie Lorraine) rides in a car with her spineless father, David (Ian Patrick Williams), and his nasty new wife, Rosemary (Carolyn Purdy-Gordon, the director's wife). An automotive mishap sends them seeking shelter at the isolated home of the Hartwickes, Gabriel (Guy Rolfe, *Mr. Sardonicus* himself) and Hilary (*Don't Look Now*'s Hilary Mason). Soon more stragglers appear, namely man-child Ralph (Stephen Lee) and an obnoxious group of punks who decide to rummage the place for possible loot. However, the Hartwickes are also compulsive dollmakers and collectors, and those hundreds of creepy-looking dolls have a very nasty tendency to come to life at night.

Skilfully shot, scored, and edited, *Dolls* is easily one of the classiest films from the Empire canon; in fact, the mixture is so successful that many of the effects crew went on to shine in the similar *Puppetmaster* series from the next incarnation of Empire, Full Moon Pictures. The sly casting of old pros Rolfe and Mason works wonders, as the couple projects a potent combination of suppressed menace and twisted attentiveness that carries the story through some of its slower patches. Running less than 80 minutes, this feels like more of a sketch than a fully developed film, but it accomplishes what it sets out to do and demonstrates a director as comfortable with slowly mounting, psychological terror as overt bloodshed. However, Gordon does deliver a handful of brief but nasty, E.C. Comics-style moments worth mentioning, including a nasty bit of ankle violence and the screen's most unusual firing squad.

As with other Empire titles, *Dolls* suffered from a smeary, colourless transfer from Vestron Video in both its VHS and laserdisc incarnations. Though not perfect, the first DVD edition from Hong Kong offers a far more colourful appearance.

Some compression problems are evident in a few of the darker scenes, and detail tends to clog up badly during the night exteriors; however, this was by far the best the film had looked on home video to date. The open matte compositions appear to be fine, though some matting would have focused in several of the more imaginative visual set ups. The audio is a bit more disappointing; though technically it is a 5.1 mix, dialogue is shoved off to both of the front speakers with some minor musical bleed-through to the rears. It's a distracting mix, and frankly listening to the film through a television monitor provides a more balanced audio experience. The disc, bargain priced by import standards, features optional English or Chinese subtitles.

The film is also available in an attractive digipak edition from the German company Dragon, but the last version out of the gate to date, from MGM, is the best; the sparkling anamorphic transfer is a much-needed improvement, and the low-priced title packs in some surprising value with two commentaries (Gordon and writer Ed Naha on the first, pretty much the entire cast talking sporadically on the second), a gory trailer, a gallery, and a storyboard comparison.

DON JUAN
(OR IF DON JUAN WERE A WOMAN)

Colour, 1973, 95m. / Directed by Roger Vadim / Starring Brigitte Bardot, Jane Birkin, Mathieu Carrière / Home Vision Entertainment (US R1 NTSC) / WS (1.66:1) (16:9)

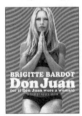

The final pairing of director Roger Vadim and bombshell Brigitte Bardot (after *...And God Created Woman* and *The Night Heaven Fell*) is a peculiar '70s updating of the Don Juan story, casting France's favourite animal rights activist as a female version of the legendary lothario.

Aboard her lounge-cum-submarine, Jeanne (Bardot) confesses her sins to a young priest (Mathieu Carrière), which involves numerous vignettes in which she seduces and abandons any men she can lay her talons on. One of her conquests also happens to be Clara (chanteuse Jane Birkin), the frustrated wife of a successful businessman, with whom she has a heated encounter in blue jeans. Unfortunately her naughty ways get the best of her in a fiery finale, which updates the familiar story with an ironic little twist.

Boasting Vadim's typical visual flair, this film (actually titled *Don Juan 73*, a name obviously not suited for today's commercial purposes) features a fair amount of bare flesh but is hardly your standard softcore yarn. Vadim seems more interested in exploring the décor and tweaking his story for the age of feminism than turning on his audience, which may be why the film died a fairly quick death overseas. As a pop art artefact it's more than satisfying, with enough wild set design and groovy pop music to ensure a place in the Eurocult time capsule. The undraped pairing of Bardot and Birkin, two of music legend Serge Gainsbourg's music protégées, doesn't hurt either.

The essentially no-frills disc from HVE features an appropriately colourful transfer that eclipses all past video versions (including one dubbed incarnation under the title of *Ms. Don Juan*). For the record you do get a Bardot filmography and some trailers (the other Vadims plus *Plucking the Daisy*, aka *Mademoiselle Striptease*).

DONNIE DARKO

Colour, 2001, 113m. / Directed by Richard Kelly / Starring Jake Gyllenhaal, Jena Malone, James Duval, Drew Barrymore, Noah Wyle, Katharine Ross, Patrick Swayze / Fox (Blu-ray & DVD) (US RA/R1 HD/NTSC), Metrodome (Blu-ray & DVD) (UK RB/R2 HD/PAL) / WS (2.35:1) (16:9) / DD5.1

October, 1988. While sleepwalking, neurotic teenager Donnie Darko (Jake Gyllenhaal) has a dreamlike encounter with a large, reptilian-faced rabbit named Frank (James Duval). Warned that the world will end in 28 days, 6 hours, 42 minutes, and 12 seconds, Darko wakens and returns home to find that his absence has allowed him to escape death, for a displaced airplane jet engine has crashed through the roof into his bedroom. With the clock ticking, dreams and reality merge into one for Darko as Frank urges him into ever more rebellious and destructive acts against the Establishment.

Psychological thriller, off the wall horror, science fiction fantasy, teen angst/coming of age drama... the fabric of *Donnie Darko* is so blurred at the seams, such a convergence of genres, that it's impossible to categorize succinctly. Its view of the world is occasionally so dexterously skewed that you wouldn't be surprised to discover that David Lynch had had a hand in its production. But he didn't. Instead this is the brainchild of first time writer/director Richard Kelly. An exhilarating trip through the shadows of dreams – maybe even dementia – and building to a distressingly downbeat climax that throws everything Kelly has shown you into question, *Donnie Darko* will leave you pondering and debating its myriad of nooks and crannies long after the credits roll. The brilliant script also bristles with 24-carat laugh out loud exchanges; a discussion over the sexual orientation of Smurfs is particularly amusing. Discard any notion you may have that the introduction of a giant rabbit is in any way an homage to Jimmy Stewart's genial pal Harvey. Darko's compatriot is a very different bunny. The sequence in which Frank joins Darko in the empty auditorium of a theatre during a screening of *The Evil Dead* is a disturbing standout moment among many, with Frank revealing the mutilated face beneath his mask, a chilling portent of events yet to happen. At regular intervals on-screen captioning reminds us that the moment of Armageddon is creeping ever nearer.

Kelly's casting is pitch-perfect. Watch out for Jake Gyllenhaal (Darko) and Jena Malone (his girlfriend Gretchen); they're destined for big things. Both are genuine revelations, effortlessly carrying the film despite the littering of star turns nipping at their heels. It's somehow fitting that a film as quirky as *Donnie Darko* should take actors who in most other films would command the spotlight and relegate them to supporting roles; beautifully drawn supporting roles to be sure, but supporting roles just the same. Drew Barrymore (who co-executive produced) and *ER*'s Noah Wyle are both splendid as teachers at Darko's school, and Katharine Ross – who we just don't see enough of these days – is excellent as the lad's psychiatrist. But the loudest applause should be directed towards Patrick Swayze for daring to take a risk with the most atypical role of his career thus far. As self-help guru Jim Cunningham – whose brainwashing, quasi-religious life coaching seminars are merely a front for his paedophile activities – he's filth incarnate.

Steven (*Dead and Buried*) Poster's lavishly saturated cinematography brings an edge of surrealism to the show. Peppered with the sounds of the '80s, including classic numbers from Joy Division and Echo & The Bunnymen, the haunting rendition of the Tears For Fears hit "Mad World" that brings the film to its downbeat denouement makes the hairs on the back of your neck stand on end. But a trip down the memory lane of pop music does not a good score make and the more discerning will be awed by Michael Andrews's impressively brooding work. As original and inspired a piece of work as you're likely to encounter in a life-time of chasing good movies, there's never been anything quite like *Donnie Darko*. It'll make you laugh. It might even make you weep. But above all it will make you think. And regardless of any conclusions you may reach, rest assured that it will leave its mark upon you long after the projection lamp flickers out and goes cold.

From the outset, Fox treated *Donnie Darko* to a Region 1 DVD release that exceeds expectation. The 2.35:1 widescreen feature is broken by 28 chapter stops and faithfully recreates the theatrical look of the film. There's a choice of two commentaries with which to enhance the viewing experience, one from Kelly and Gyllenhaal, the second from other assembled members of cast and crew. Sound provisions on the feature are English 5.1 Surround and English or French Dolby Surround, while subtitling is in English and Spanish. The bonus materials encompass 20 extended and/or deleted scenes (with optional commentary), the "Cunning Visions" infomercial as seen briefly in the film (again with optional commentary), a music video for Gary Jules's take on "Mad World", a trailer, five TV spots, a gallery of stills and artwork, plus text sections that include cast and crew information, pages from the film's Internet website and liner notes from the soundtrack album. Hidden features include an additional deleted scene (find it by locating the circle on "Appendix A" amongst the special features) and a second trailer (find it by locating the black arrow on "Appendix B" amongst the special features). The pick of the crop though is a selection of pages from one of the film's key props, the book "The Philosophy of Time Travel", which rounds out what can only be classified as a genuine "must have" addition to your collection.

The British R2 release from Metrodome is equally desirable. It includes most of the R1 extras with the exception of the Gary Jules video, adding to them with a large number of interview clips with key cast and crew, filmographies, plus several minutes worth of B-Roll and out-takes. There's also a featurette entitled "They Made Me Do It" in which a number of artists are given 6 hours, 42 minutes and 12 seconds to create imagery inspired by the film, the results having gone on display in London for 28 days. The Jules song plays out over this sequence. For some reason 4 of the 20 deleted/extended scenes (including the more graphic version of Darko's ultimate demise) have been relocated as hidden features; 2 can be found by selecting the "Special Features" header on the main menu and clicking right, 2 others under the "Commentaries and Subtitles" section (select Spanish subs, click right and hit enter when the small rabbit lights up in Jim Cunningham's eye). The Region 1 disc's hidden features (the alternative trailer and extra deleted scene) are not included. The section devoted to the book "The Philosophy of Time Travel" has also been gingered up for R2, presented in animated form as flipping pages or a more legible text only version. The quality of the 2.35:1 ratio picture is noticeably better than on the R1 disc with more vibrant colours. The sound is in English (5.1 or 2.0), with subs in English and Spanish.

The surprising popularity of the film on home video spurred Kelly and the studio to revisit it with a "Director's Cut" that, for better or worse, alters several song choices and attempts to clarify the story by restoring much of the omitted footage. While some characters (Barrymore's and Ross's in particular) benefit, the overall film loses much of its punch, and several of the song switches (particularly for the opening credits) are ill-advised. (even Kelly himself still acknowledges the theatrical cut as his preferred one.) The transfer is still a replication of the hazy, soft original look, and the 5.1 sound mix seems much more modern. Kelly and Kevin Smith offer a new commentary, and other extras include a 52-minute "Production Diary", a clumsy "Cult of Donnie Darko" featurette, a reissue trailer, a storyboard-to-screen comparison, and the amusing "#1 Fan: A Darkumentary" piece that's best seen without any prior warning.

Both versions of the film are available on Fox and Metrodome's Blu-ray editions (timed in with the release of the ill-advised video sequel, *S. Darko*), which again do what they can with a problematic film shot through with gauzy textures and a deliberate lack of precise detail; all the substantial extras (the three commentaries, the featurettes, etc.) are carried over, dropping only the TV commercial and music video for some reason. While the picture quality may only represent a minor step up, the audio is considerably more powerful and shakes the room like DVD never could.

– TG

DON'T PANIC

Colour, 1987, 86m. / Directed by Rubén Galindo Jr. / Starring Jon Michael Bischof, Gabriela Hassel, Juan Ignacio Aranda / Dark Vision (UK R0 PAL), BCI (US R1 NTSC)

This unassuming south of the border concoction is an addition to a brief run of Ouija board-based horror flicks kick-started by 1985's *Witchboard* and including Roberta Findlay's grisly but inept *The Oracle*. Despite the fact that *Don't Panic* (*El secreto de la Ouija*) is set in Mexico City you wouldn't have known it without the voice-over that fills you in; all the high school kids in this film look like regular WASP teenagers (and are just as irritating) and the central character, Michael Smith (Jon Michael Bischof) has been moved from Beverly Hills down to Mexico by his alcoholic mother. It's pretty obvious that the film is supposed to slot in seamlessly with the mid-80s "teens in peril" stalk 'n' slashers so popular at this time. Throw in some gory hallucinations and a wisecracking crusty-faced demonic killer *á la* Freddy Krueger, and you have one made-to-measure horror hit. At least that's what the film's producers must have hoped. Sadly for them *Don't Panic* was rapidly consigned to the cobwebbed far reaches of the local video stores' shelves; there was to be no *Don't Panic 2*, no rich concessionary vein to be mined...

Actually it's hard to actively dislike *Don't Panic*, though the plot can be summed up in a few sentences. Teenagers mess around with a Ouija board at Michael's birthday party, and his best friend Tony (Juan Ignacio Aranda) gets possessed by his spirit guide Virgil, becomes crusty-faced, develops a bog-standard gruff demonic voice, and takes to carving up various female classmates. Michael begins to have precognitive visions of the killings, but no one will believe him, especially his gin-pickled mother. Finally gaining an uneasy ally in the brother of one of the butchered girls, Michael sets off to find Tony, who through Virgil is bumping off all the kids who were present at the Ouija session. All of them, bar Michael and his girlfriend Alexandra (Gabriela Hassel), are killed brutally by Virgil (who wields a vicious ceremonial dagger) before the big climactic battle.

Storywise this is nothing particularly noteworthy, but there are a few interesting touches like a sentimental conceit involving a red rose given in love and several pretty neat scenes involving Tony's limbo-held spirit bulging forth from various TV sets to issue warnings (obviously inspired by Lamberto Bava's *Demons 2*). Director Rubén Galindo Jr. was also responsible for the entertainingly dumb Hugo Stiglitz-starring zombie flick *Cementerio del terror* (*Cemetery of Terror*), and an in-joke has a couple of jittery *Don't Panic* cast members watching a scene from it on TV as they wait for Tony/Virgil to return home. With the help of Screaming Mad George, some righteously spouting splatter is served up as Virgil slices and dices his way through the cast with gusto, the show-stopper being a knife thrust up through the chin and tongue of one unfortunate victim just like in Dario

Argento's *Opera*! There are some unintentionally funny scenes, as when Michael rides his pushbike through the night-time city streets in a vain attempt to save a classmate at the city hospital, and then wonders why people think he's crazy! It has to be said though that Virgil's cut-price facial job is beyond a joke, looking like a kid's rubber Halloween mask, and as for that dire end credits song (courtesy of Bischof himself), perhaps unsurprisingly called "Don't Panic", the least said the better.

Though by no means an essential film, *Don't Panic* is a harmless enough way to spend 86 minutes of your time. Thanks to ultra-cheapo U.K. DVD label Dark Vision you can now experience the fully restored uncut version of this Mexi-Chiller on a PAL region free disc (some of the brief graphic violence was trimmed off for the original U.K. video release on Colourbox). Not only do you get a luridly packaged, good-looking full-frame transfer of the film itself (far better than any video print), but also filmographies of the director and various cast members and a video-art gallery. Worth looking out for, especially as this disc can be picked up for peanuts. The same transfer was later used for BCI's American "Crypt of Terror – Horror from South of the Border Vol. 1" set, which only stayed in print for about a year; it also includes several other delirious '80s Mexi-horrors including *Vacation of Terror 1 & 2*, *Hell's Trap*, *Cemetery of Terror*, *Grave Robbers*, and *The Demon Rat*.
– NB

DRACULA VS. FRANKENSTEIN
Colour, 1971, 91m. / Directed by Al Adamson / Starring Lon Chaney Jr., J. Carrol Naish, Russ Tamblyn, Regina Carrol, John Bloom, Zandor Vorkov, Anthony Eisley, Shelly Weiss, Forrest J. Ackerman, Angelo Rossitto / Troma (US R0 NTSC), Cheezy Flicks (US R1 NTSC), Cinema Club (UK R2 PAL)

Though not free of the deadwood diversions that make many Adamson pictures endurance tests, this bizarre mélange ranks among the most entertaining items in the Independent International catalogue. The "Deluxe Collector's Edition" also has enough contextualising material to make it a worthwhile purchase for old-time horror fans with an interest in the byways of 1970s sleaze. Originally entitled *The Blood Seekers* or *Blood Freaks*, the first draft of the film was built around J. Carrol Naish and Lon Chaney Jr., cast as sideshow entrepreneur-mad scientist Dr. Duryea and his minion Groton the Mad Zombie, with *Satan's Sadists* veteran Russ Tamblyn as a gang-leader and "freak out girl" Regina Carrol as a Vegas headliner searching for her sister among the hippies and bikers of a California beach. The film was rethought in production by writer-producer Sam Sherman to bring on bigger horror names, revealing that Duryea is actually the last of the Frankensteins, additionally tossing in his rubberfaced monster (John Bloom) and a blue-lit, Frank Zappa-look-alike Dracula (Zandor Vorkov). This version was retitled *Blood of Frankenstein* but still needed tampering – in order to justify the socko *D vs F* title, the original ending in which Dracula zaps the monster's heart with his magic ring and hero Eisley shoves the vampire against a protruding pipe was junked (and Anthony Eisley's character casually killed off) to make way for a *Frankenstein Meets the Wolf Man*-type slugfest that finds Dracula rending the monster (Shelly Weiss taking over from Bloom) limb from limb but turned to a skeleton by sunrise. The big loser of this endless rethinking is Chaney, whose Lennie-like star turn as a puppy-loving halfwit periodically turned into an axe-wielding killer is reduced to a virtual cameo while Vorkov (hitherto a stockbroker named Roger

Engel) is perhaps the screen's worst Dracula and middle-aged hipster Eisley models a sharktooth-necklace and polo neck ensemble that enlivens otherwise dreary romantic and counterculture sleuthing angles.

Though there are discs from other companies on the market, the one to go for is the Troma release, which offers a standard-frame transfer that highlights the many flaws of the original elements: out-of-focus shots, mismatched scenes from the various incarnations (note the ridiculous variations of Vorkov's make-up), scratched-into-the-emulsion optical effects, and just-plain-ugly cinematography. That the print is in excellent shape and carefully transferred probably makes the film seem even more inept. Throw in stock music (the *Creature from the Black Lagoon* theme blares over the climax), bad line readings of unspeakable dialogue, Forrest J. Ackerman as a victim (Forry gave the film an award in *Famous Monsters*; in repayment, his name is misspelled in the credits), Angelo Rossitto dropped face-first onto an axe, Carrol doing an amazingly tacky Vegas number and later sampling a drink spiked with LSD, a scene reuniting the stars of *The Incredible Two-Headed Transplant* and Kenneth Strickfaden's old lab equipment. It's rubbish, but you wouldn't want it any other way.

The disc includes a ton of extras: one of Sherman's better commentary tracks, with a lot of background information (he also does an on-camera introduction); alternative scenes from the original version of the film; 8mm location scout footage; Ackerman and Sherman introducing a deleted Ackerman-Dracula scene, but missing the point of why it was cut (it sets up the way Dracula kills the Monster in the unused ending); a TV segment on the I-I gang called "Producing Schlock!"; an easter egg containing a stumbling outtake from Sherman's introduction; trailers for this and other "Al Adamson Collection" titles (*Man with the Synthetic Brain*, *Angels Wild Women*, etc.); a text about the distinctive Dracula ring; on-set photos.

– KN

THE DREAM OF GARUDA

Colour, 1994, 54m. / Directed by Takahisa Zeze / Starring Takeshi Ito, Saki Kurihara, Shirô Shimomoto / Screen Edge (UK R0 PAL) / WS (1.66:1)

 A rather dark example of Japanese Pink Cinema, *The Dream of Garuda* (*Karura no yume*) takes its title from a mythical Hindu god, a half man/half bird whose evil deeds led the path to its redemption. The creature figures prominently in both Eastern and Western culture (and was used to memorable effect in China Miéville's epic novel, *Perdido Street Station*), though its role here is more symbolic.

Freed from prison after serving a lengthy term for rape, the delusional Ikuo (Takeshi Ito) seeks vengeance against his victim, Mieko (Saki Kurihara), now working as a prostitute for her former boyfriend, Tomimori (Shirô Shimomoto). Ikuo seeks her out in the soaplands, an area of Japan where the illegal act of prostitution is justified by having the girls bathe their clients, with sex thrown in as a bonus. Of course, things do not go as planned...

As much an experimental film as a piece of erotica, this film fractures its narrative through artistic cutaways and disjointed storytelling that plays disturbingly against the extended sequences of Meiko and her cohorts seductively washing the flesh of men. There's also more direct violence than usual for a Pink entry; rape has always played a significant role in many of these films, but here it's more of a plot device than a titillation ploy and hovers uncomfortably over the rest of the film. Unfortunately much of its artistry is hampered by the lacklustre technical limitations, ranging from cut-rate film processing to a murky transfer job that looks little better than a bootleg tape. Perhaps the smeary appearance was an artistic choice, but this seems unlikely. Audio is adequate, considering, and the English subtitles are burned onto the print. The disc contains a Pink overview and trailers for *Pervirella* and *Tandem*.

DROWNING BY NUMBERS

Colour, 1988, 118m. / Directed by Peter Greenaway / Starring Joan Plowright, Joely Richardson, Bernard Hill, Juliet Stevenson / Film Four (Australia R0 PAL) / WS (1.66:1), Kinokuniya (Japan R2 NTSC) / WS (1.66:1) (16:9), Culture (Japan R2 NTSC)

 Following his pair of despairing urban studies, *A Zed and Two Noughts* and *The Belly of an Architect*, director Peter Greenaway returned to the sardonic countryside of *The Draughtsman's Contract* for another tongue-in-cheek murder yarn, *Drowning by Numbers*. Easily his most playful film in every sense of the term, this tricky and often charming film boasts some of his wittiest dialogue and makes for an ideal introduction for newcomers compared to his more experimental works.

In the middle of the night, ageing Cissie Colpitts (Joan Plowright) watches her drunken, adulterous husband frolicking in a tin bath with a naked woman. Cissie calmly decides to drown him and turns to the local coroner, Madgett (*The Lord of the Rings*'s Bernard Hill), convincing him to pass off the death as a heart attack. The lovelorn and game-obsessed Madgett reluctantly agrees, but trouble brews when the neighbours begin to suspect something is amiss. To make matters worse, Cissie's daughter (Juliet Stevenson) and niece (Joely Richardson), both named Cissie as well, decide to drown their own husbands too, with Madgett's aid, promising sexual favours but delivering little. Meanwhile Madgett's peculiar son, Smut, develops an unhealthy fixation with the constellation-counting girl next door, leading to a climax filled with ironic tragedies.

One of the most sumptuous English films around, *Drowning by Numbers* revels in sun-dappled fields, moonwashed forests, and rippling bodies of water. All of the performers rattle off their tricky patter perfectly, and Greenaway loads the movie with an encyclopaedic collection of games, both literal and psychological. This work also features his most audacious and entertaining visual gimmick, outdoing the sequential drawings of *Draughtsman* or the colour-coded rooms of *The Cook, the Thief, His Wife and Her Lover*. Here the numbers 1 to 100 are contained within the film, in order, hidden somewhere from the first scene to the last; thus, viewers can either focus on the plot or simply have fun playing numeric hide and seek. This William Castle-style device is also thematically appropriate, drawing the viewer into playing along with the characters and firmly announcing when the game is finally over. The trademark Greenaway nudity is still in abundance, with the shapely Richardson getting most of the attention, but the sexual and violent content is extremely mild (even borderline mainstream) compared to his subsequent work. Sonically this may be his richest film as well thanks to Michael Nyman's astonishing score, partially derived from Mozart and filled with moments of musical brilliance. A wonderful treasure of a film well worth exploring.

All of the early video editions of *Drowning by Numbers* were quite a mess. The attractive but full frame and optically censored Japanese laserdisc and DVD from Culture offered a compromised version of the film, while the uncensored U.S. laserdisc was horrendously cropped on all four sides and suffered from a bright pink tinge over the entire film. The Australian DVD improved things a bit, but it's still on the soft side; at least it offers more accurate fleshtones than the earlier editions. The

film contains a Dolby Stereo tag on the end credits, and while the U.S. laser had muddy sound with often indecipherable dialogue, it was barely stereo; the two early DVD editions are mono, which makes no sense. The Australian DVD promises a theatrical trailer, which would be fine except it's really promotional trailers for *Raining Stones* and *Bhaji on the Beach*.

More expensive but vastly preferable is the 2007 Japanese reissue, which is not only correctly framed at 1.66:1 (at least, you can spot all the numbers onscreen) but, thanks to drastically relaxed Japanese content restrictions, also completely uncensored with all of the frontal nudity intact. The Dolby Stereo audio also sounds infinitely better, with crystal clear dialogue and rich multi-channel activity for Nyman's score. This time the promised theatrical trailer is the genuine article as well.

D-TOX (EYE SEE YOU)

Colour, 1999, 92m. / Directed by Jim Gillespie / Starring Sylvester Stallone, Robert Patrick, Dina Meyer, Charles S. Dutton, Christopher Fulford, Robert Prosky, Kris Kristofferson, Polly Walker, Tom Berenger / Universal (UK R2/R4 PAL), Columbia (US R1 NTSC), First Look (US R1 NTSC) / WS (2.35:1) (16:9) / DD5.1

On the trail of an elusive serial killer, the pursuit becomes personal for FBI agent Jake Malloy (played by Sylvester Stallone) when the hunted rounds on the hunter and targets Malloy's girlfriend (Dina Meyer). Turning to the bottle, and subsequently attempting suicide, Malloy suffers a complete breakdown. His boss (Charles S. Dutton) packs him off to a Wyoming rehabilitation institute that specializes in treating burned out cops. When a snowstorm cuts the place off and his fellow patients start turning up dead, Malloy has to face up to the possibility that the killer has somehow tracked him down, infiltrated the clinic and wants him dead.

Here's a formulaic stalk'n'slash flick for the multiplex crowd with big league Hollywood player Sylvester Stallone pitched against a maniac with a penchant for testing power tools on the eyes of his randomly selected victims. No great actor, Stallone is also getting a little long in the tooth to be dallying with the same sort of adrenaline-pumping vehicle he was driving during his '80s prime, but to be fair he was still in pretty good physical shape at the time this was made, and much like Bruce and Arnie, has the balls to pull it off. Just.

Director Jim Gillespie conjures up plenty of atmosphere and tension, the eerie setting itself giving him a strong head start; a vast, tundra-wreathed ex-army bunker turned asylum, it's more akin to a prison than a clinic and, with the perpetual howling of the wind echoing round its oppressive metal walls, you have to wonder how many more suicides than recuperative cases would be prompted by an enforced stay in such an establishment. In terms of blizzard-blown isolation, it certainly gives *The Shining*'s Overlook Hotel a run for its money. Accepting that there's nothing new the slasher sub-genre can throw at you, success must be gauged by how well the familiar facets are juggled. In the case of *D-Tox* the result isn't too shabby. Most of the staff, as well as Stallone's fellow inmates – who include Christopher Fulford, Robert Patrick and Robert Prosky – are such an unpleasant bunch of low-lifes that the identity of the killer is barely predictable. Tempers run high, disputes erupt and every time you find yourself thinking, "Yes, it's definitely him", your suspect winds up next on the chopping block. On the down side, whenever the action moves outside into the raging snowstorm it's often difficult to ascertain who's doing what to whom. Of course, this is all familiar

ground for Gillespie (who directed *I Know What You Did Last Summer*) and he follows the standard slasher trail right down to the climax in which the killer makes an unlikely return from the brink of death to vex our hero one last time and earn himself a final, even more fittingly violent demise.

Kris Kristofferson is the grizzled ex-cop who runs the clinic, Polly Walker is the nurse who teams up with Malloy to expose the killer, Tom Berenger plays the shifty caretaker and Dina Meyer appears briefly as Malloy's girlfriend before getting her eyes drilled out. The real treat though is watching Robert Patrick firing on all thrusters as a no-nonsense, hard-nosed bully whose craven personality is exposed when he's reduced to a blubbering wreck at the prospect of his impending execution.

D-Tox was shot as *Eye See You*, a superior title derived from the characters I-C-U, tauntingly marked by the killer on the inside of a victim's eyelids as his calling card. Unfortunately the film spent a prolonged stopover in post-production limbo, and then received the sparsest of theatrical engagements before quietly being filtered out for home viewing. It's evident from its running time that the old garden shears have been working overtime, but this isn't necessarily a bad thing. In an era when movies often outstay their welcome by upwards of half an hour, substantial judicious pruning here has resulted in a film that nips sprightly along and never loses your interest for a moment. And that has to be a bonus.

Although *Eye See You* eventually appeared on Region 1 DVD, Britain beat it off the starting blocks by some nine months, when it was released as *D-Tox* on a joint Regions 2 & 4 PAL disc from Universal. Presented in its 2.35:1 theatrical ratio, the 16-chapter punctuated movie looks very clean, with only minimal traces of grain in the darkest scenes. Subtitles are provided in English alone. Also included by way of a bonus is a little over 12 minutes of deleted and extended footage (inferior quality and with running time-codes), though there was even more shot and omitted than that on offer here as is evidenced in the trailer, which includes snatches of material in neither the feature nor this outtakes supplement. Additionally there is a "Wrap Reel" – basically an extended barrage of rapid-fire shots from the film, played out against a jarringly annoying music track. In America, the DVD was reissued via First Look in a steelbox collector's case, for those intent on gathering every title with that heavier packaging. With so much potential for a Director's Cut, don't be too surprised if *D-Tox* surfaces as a revamped reissue somewhere down the line.

– TG

THE EARLY FILMS OF PETER GREENAWAY 1

Colour/B&W, 1969-1978, 87m. / Directed by Peter Greenaway

THE EARLY FILMS OF PETER GREENAWAY 2

Colour, 1978/1980, 224m. / Directed by Peter Greenaway / bfi (UK R2 PAL), Zeitgeist (US R1 NTSC)

Before launching on a career as one of Britain's most consistent cinematic provocateurs, Peter Greenaway created a series of short films (and in one case,

an extremely long film that feels like a series of shorts strung together) in which his experience as a painter and documentary editor collided with often amusing, tantalizing results. He first began dabbling with film in the 1960s, but it wasn't until the late 1970s that the Greenaway style began to truly

take shape. This pair of DVDs compiles the highlights of his pre-1982 career, culminating in what many still consider to be his masterpiece, *The Falls*.

The first volume contains six short films, with only one black and white project, 1969's *Intervals*. This six-minute look at wintertime Venice focuses on repeated footage with different musical accompaniment (lifted from Vivaldi), producing a distinctly new mood each time. The more overtly humorous *Windows* (1974) features narration (provided by Greenaway) over four minutes of shots depicting an English countryside in which 37 residents felt compelled to commit "defenestration", i.e., falling out of windows. The first of Greenaway's lavish "fictional histories", this is a good primer for newcomers and features effective use of Jean-Philippe Rameau on the soundtrack. Greenaway returned to the same location in 1976 for the sunnier *H is for House*, one of his notorious listing exercises, in which similar narration provides a deadpan 9-minute listing of absurdly juxtaposed items beginning with the letter "h" while a mother plays with her young daughter. The same year Greenaway also directed *Dear Phone*, running 17 minutes, in which common telephone boxes take on a ridiculous meaning when used to illustrate a rambling narrative (shown as bits of written text) about men whose initials are "HC" trying to reach a woman named Zelda. The whimsical, 11-minute *Water Wrackets* from 1978 presents a series of beautifully filmed lake shots (both vistas and shimmering close-ups) while narrator Colin Cantlie (who also did services on numerous other Greenaway shorts) describes a distant future in which five lakes have been artificially created by the military. Featuring lush photography and elegiac music, this is a stylistic forerunner to the director's first mainstream film, *The Draughtsman's Contract*. However, the highlight of the set is certainly 1978's *A Walk Through H*, which introduces several elements destined to figure prominently in future work: music by composer Michael Nyman (who provided most of his feature scores through *Prospero's Books*), the enigmatic character of Tulse Luper (who became the protagonist of the sprawling *The Tulse Luper Suitcases* multimedia series), and the obsessive use of the number 92, represented here by a series of maps referred to by an ornithologist across Europe. Even at 41 minutes it's a densely packed ride, throwing the viewer through a museum's gallery and into a bizarre world entirely of Greenaway's creation, all accompanied by Nyman's marvellous, hypnotic score.

Disc two begins with another 1978 short, the 41-minute *Vertical Features Remake*. Lampooning film criticism of the period, Greenaway depicts four attempts to reconstruct an unfinished film by Mr. Luper, *Vertical Features*, which pathologically fixates on vertical objects (telephone poles, trees, sticks, etc.). None of the academics involved can agree, however, which results in a *Rashomon*-style diversion of styles each time. That's just an appetizer for *The Falls*, a sprawling, three-hour examination of the effects caused in the future by a Violent Unknown Event ("VUE") involving birds, which has affected the lives of 92 people (whose last names all begin with "Fall") now affiliated with our feathered friends in one form or another. Along the way we meet an elegant performer attempting to sing with bird noises, a man whose body is remodeling itself one organ at a time to conform to avian standards, and other eccentric personalities who provoke amusement and bewilderment, usually at the same time. Throw in a few jokey nods to Hitchcock's *The Birds*, and you've got a piece of celluloid truly unlike any other. How willing viewers will be to sit through the entire running time depends entirely on one's tolerance for Greenaway's flights of fancy, but it's a creative, often dazzling experience for those willing to put in the hours. Again both films contain exceptional Nyman scores, offering a taste of things to come.

Both DVDs feature the best possible transfers one could expect for these works, which are in good shape albeit limited by technical conventions of the time. *The Falls* was released in a softer-looking VHS edition in the U.K., while *Dear Phone*, *A Walk Through H*, and *Water Wrackets* were issued on a tape compilation, both under the Connoisseur banner. The DVDs make for a more compact and obviously longer experience, and fortunately Greenaway's extensive participation in the discs puts these exercises in a much more accessible context. Apart from contributing new liner notes to both sets, Greenaway also appears for a series of video introductions, which can be played straight through or chopped up as separate intros for each film; his comments are placed in Paintbox-style fashion over montages from the films, similar to the approach used in *A TV Dante*.

Other extras on both discs come in the form of two galleries, "Artworks" and "Archives", which present sketches, paintings, written plans for unmade films, and other assorted bits and pieces from this time period. The packaging also promises hidden features, which must be uncovered in typical Greenaway gamesman fashion. It's also worth noting that, despite Greenaway's reputation, both discs come with PG ratings and are mostly suitable for any viewers, though it's doubtful children will get much out of these; apart from a bit of nudity in *The Falls*, his trademark "excesses" are kept in check here. The same discs were later issued in the U.S. and, apart from some minor PAL conversion glitches, are comparable in presentation and value.

EARTH VS THE SPIDER (THE SPIDER)

B&W, 1958, 72m. / Directed by Bert I. Gordon / Starring Ed Kemmer, Gene Persson / Direct Video (UK R2 PAL), Lionsgate (US R1 NTSC)

"Somewhere in that hideous carcass are the genes which control organic growth. Man had better find out what made it grow so big and pretty fast, or we'll be in trouble." This big bug s-f monster movie opens well, with a motorist gruesomely lashed across the face by a giant black pipe-cleaner, then proceeds to hit all the generic bases as small town teens are menaced in an eerie cave, and the local authorities try to track down and kill the arachnoid beast. The giant spider, whose presence is never explained, is apparently vanquished early and put on display at the nearby high school, but a local band rehearsing for the sock hop revives it and, as infuriated as any other '50s adult would have been, it goes on a rampage.

With no acting to speak of and lots of ominous if half-assed scientific talk ("Insects have a pretty simple nervous system, Sheriff; you can plug holes in one all day and never hit a vital spot"), this came from Bert I. Gordon, the producer-director who also delivered *The Cyclops* and *Beginning of the End* and was still pulling the same trickery during the 1970s in *Empire of the Ants*. Made around the same time as AIP's *How to Make a Monster*, it's among the first self-referential monster movies, with posters and publicity for Gordon's *The Amazing Colossal Man* and *Attack of the Puppet People* on display at the local moviehouse and a copy of the first issue of *Famous Monsters* on view in a teenager's room. Gordon was known for his DIY monster effects, here superimposing a real spider over desert townscapes or directing the bug through air draughts shot out of straws to crawl over miniature sets that consist of cut-up photographs of Carlsbad Caverns. It makes the elementary mistake of staging its best scare scenes early and dawdling through the climax with teens-lost-in-a-cave business before the monster is defeated by an electric arc. However, in a low-key way, some earlier scenes are rather effective and the monster-revived-by-rock 'n' roll is one of the great archetypal moments of the '50s creature feature cycle.

Though Direct Video's DVD sleeve sells the film as *The Spider*, the on-screen title shrieks *Earth vs THE SPIDER*. The transfer is adequate, a generation or so cleaned-up from murky video releases, with deep blacks and very occasionally blooming whites. Actually, the upgrade of the image makes the use of card-mounted photographs in the effects scenes all the more obvious – though the trick is less imperfect here than in *Beginning of the End*. Part of the "Arkoff Film Library", the disc shares extras with the other titles in this range (*War of the Colossal Beast, How to Make a Monster, Day the World Ended, The Undead, Blood of Dracula, The Brain Eaters, The She-Creature, Voodoo Woman, Reform School Girl*): trailers for the whole series, a batch of postcards featuring wonderfully lurid poster images, and an audio interview with Samuel Z. Arkoff augmented with photographs. A partial record of Arkoff's Guardian lecture at the National Film Theatre, the talk features polished and amusing anecdotes, but (like his autobiography and the privileging of his name on the packaging) is part of the late studio head's late-in-life campaign to rewrite his reputation as a maker of movies rather than deals. Though he doesn't hog all the credit that should accrue to his partner James H. Nicholson, his assumption of the title of producer does minimise the contributions of men like Roger Corman, Herman Cohen, Alex Gordon and Bert I. Gordon – who actually line-produced (and sometimes directed) these movies. The subsequent U.S. release contains the same transfer (oddly encoded so it zooms from open matte to 1.78:1 framing on widescreen televisions) as a no-frills double bill with *War of the Colossal Beast*.

– KN

EAT THE RICH

Colour, 2000, 87m. / Directed by Ron Atkins / Starring Terry King, Garvin Lee / Cutthroat (US R1 NTSC) / DD2.0

 Well, there aren't really any rich people to be found, but you do get lots of cops and cannibals in this sick, slaphappy DV riff on the *Texas Chain Saw Massacre* cycle. Boasting more elaborate sets, locations, subplots, and gore effects than your average underground project, *Eat the Rich* (subtitled *The Cannibal Murders*) hops along briskly and, despite its technical shortcomings, makes for rousing party viewing.

In the prologue, our not terribly efficient FBI chief (who has a taste for loose women) and one of his underlings analyze the human remains from the latest in a series of cannibal killings. The lawman dismisses the flesh-eating scenario: "Maybe they just got in a fight and bit each other." Nevertheless, one intrepid agent begs to go out alone undercover and, while exploring a drainage sewer, winds up running into a ferocious killer. It turns out there's a clan of depraved goons living in the Nevada sewers: one tubby guy who takes to wearing a war helmet and sometimes a bag over his head (to disguise the scars from his mama whackin' him with an iron a few too many times), a drawling goofus with a painted-on moustache, and a third wearing a gas helmet who enjoys disembowelling his prey. Meanwhile the donut-scarfing officials slowly close in on the perpetrators, who continue to inflict all sorts of mayhem on the locals.

Apart from a few hair-raising set pieces (particularly the first sewer excursion, which is borderline nightmarish), *Eat the Rich* skews more towards broad, gore-soaked spoofery, with some funny dialogue passages that come out of nowhere (including one riotous scene with a necking couple in a car that nearly stops the movie in its tracks). The editing is also surprisingly ambitious, and if it weren't for some sloppy sound editing that renders the odd line of dialogue unintelligible, this would be a prime example of how to pull off a horror movie on a minimal budget.

Continuing the double-disc treatment of director Ron Atkins's other titles, *Eat the Rich* is given its own entire platter for the film itself. Transfer quality is par for the course, about as sharp as the original material probably allows. The surround audio is extremely active throughout, and the electronic music is well-mixed and effective. The second disc contains a video interview with Atkins, a trailer, six alternative teasers spoofing *The Blair Witch Project*, and a whopping 20 minutes of deleted footage, containing a startling amount of sadistic sex and violence trimmed from the final cut.

EATEN ALIVE! (MANGIATI VIVI!)

Colour, 1980, 87m. / Directed by Umberto Lenzi / Starring Ivan Rassimov, Janet Agren, Mel Ferrer, Robert Kerman, Gerald Grant, Me Me Lai / Shriek Show (US R1 NTSC) / WS (1.85:1) (16:9), VIPCO (UK R2 PAL), EC (Holland R2 PAL), Spike Adventure (Japan R2 NTSC) / WS (1.85:1)

 A year before Blake Edwards used archival clips and outtakes to help create the bizarre patchwork that is *The Trail of the Pink Panther*, the beloved Eurohack Umberto Lenzi pulled the same trick with *Eaten Alive!* (*Mangiati vivi!*), a grisly greatest-hits package cobbling together clips from the likes of *Jungle Holocaust*, *The Man from Deep River*, and *Mountain of the Cannibal God* by way of a new storyline inspired by the

Jim Jones tragedy at Guyana. Fast-paced and wholly derivative, this is unrepentant trash filmmaking at its most resourceful and astonishing.

As with Lenzi's subsequent atrocity, *Cannibal Ferox*, this jungle romp begins in New York where crime is running rampant. In this case, however, the culprit is a mysterious evildoer running around shooting soporific darts into innocent victims, who are then spirited away to the jungle. One unfortunate's sister, Sheila (Janet Agren), takes a canister of suspicious film footage to a local professor (Mel Ferrer), who points to New Guinea as the primary site for these nefarious activities. Apparently Jonas (*giallo* favourite Ivan Rassimov), a powerful cult leader, has led his followers to this emerald hell and is drawing in outsiders to feed his bloodlust. After hopping onto a plane, Sheila hooks up with military deserter Mark (*Cannibal Holocaust* star and porn legend Robert Kerman), who assembles some local guides to wade through hungry cannibals and seemingly endless stock footage of animals dismembering each other. Eventually they reach Jonas's deadly camp, where Sheila is reunited with her sister but finds the adventure is just beginning.

So devoid of logic that it could be termed dreamlike if it were more technically proficient, *Eaten Alive!* heaps on the gory goods and even offers some skin from Ms. Agren, something of a fanboy favourite from her Lucio Fulci days. The usual klutzy dubbing provokes a few laughs as well (don't miss the dodgy southern accents), and *Ferox* fans will find much of the music score strangely familiar. As usual Rassimov looks sinister and magnetic, even though his motives rarely make any sense, while Agren fans will delight in her nude recreation of Ursula Andress's famous body painting scene. While Ruggero Deodato's *Cannibal Holocaust* found an excuse for its ragged

16mm appearance, you'll find no such justifications here (except for that can of 8mm film at the beginning); Lenzi shot this one on the fly, loose and quick, so it's a credit that, repugnant animal atrocities aside, the results turned out to be this fast-paced and entertaining. (A side note to Radley Metzger fans: look for *Score*'s Gerald Grant as a badly dubbed cop in the opening ten minutes.)

After circulating seemingly in every country in the world on VHS, *Eaten Alive!* first appeared on laserdisc and two (!) DVD editions from Holland's EC Entertainment. The second DVD was an anamorphic upgrade and looked passable given the condition of the elements, while Britain later chipped in with VIPCO's heavily scissored DVD (running a scant 81 minutes), which renders the film even more senseless. The American disc from Shriek Show is anamorphic and looks strikingly good, considering the hodgepodge mixture of 35mm and 16mm stock. Even the recycled footage looks better and more seamlessly integrated here than before, aside from the Me Me Lai "hot coals" bit from *Jungle Holocaust* which sticks out like a sore thumb. The U.S. disc includes the usual batch of trailers and a trio of interviews, with the show easily stolen by the gregarious Robert Kerman's lengthy interview. Happily discussing his legit and more, ahem, exotic film roles, he offers a candid assessment of his work in Italy's most notorious trio of cannibal films and even offers a misty recollection of a more recent fan convention experience. Umberto Lenzi (in Italian with English subtitles) and Ivan Rassimov (in his own voice, finally!) have much shorter interviews and sketch out their own approaches to the film and the state of exploitation filmmaking in Europe during the early 1980s. The colourful packaging (which doesn't list the interviews for some reason) is polished off with R. Ian Jane's brief liner notes.

ED WOOD

B&W, 1994, 121m. / Directed by Tim Burton / Starring Johnny Depp, Martin Landau, Sarah Jessica Parker, Lisa Marie, George "The Animal" Steele, Vincent D'Onofrio, Patricia Arquette, Jeffrey Jones, Bill Murray / Buena Vista (UK R2 PAL, US R1 NTSC, Denmark R2 PAL, Australia R4 PAL, Korea R3 NTSC, Italy R2 PAL) / WS (1.85:1) (16:9) / DD5.1

 This is the second of the many collaborations between director Tim Burton and actor Johnny Depp, a bittersweet biopic (with its artistic licence protruding proudly from its breast pocket) about the life and work of the legendary Edward D. Wood Jr. Set around the period of his life when he shot some of his most significant trash classics, including *Glen Or Glenda?* and *Bride of the Monster*, it also focuses on Wood's transvestitism – he had a penchant for wearing Angora sweaters – and his moving relationship with ageing and unemployed horror movie star Bela Lugosi. The film concludes with the unleashing of his infamous and much celebrated clunker *Plan 9 from Outer Space*: "This is the one I'll be remembered for!" exclaims Wood excitedly. How right he was, albeit not for the reasons he might have hoped.

One of Tim Burton's finest films, *Ed Wood* is a splendid wallow through the seedy hinterland of Z-grade movie-making in Hollywood. Look-alikes are the order of the day here, and we're treated to some uncanny resemblances to their real-life counterparts by Lisa Marie as Vampira and George "The Animal" Steele as Tor Johnson. Even Johnny Depp as the titular Wood himself occasionally passes as a dead ringer for the incontrovertible king of '50s trash cinema. Top honours, however, go to Martin Landau (in a marvellous Rick Baker make-up job) for his performance as washed-up horror

icon Lugosi, justifiably scooping the Oscar for Best Supporting Actor for his troubles.

Ed Wood focuses on a seven-year period during which the man and his extended family of misfits made some of their most renowned films. Though it may be a tad loose with the truth, Wood's inextinguishable enthusiasm – which keeps him smiling in the face of all the punches Tinseltown can throw at him – ensures the feel-good factor is fully charged and operational throughout the two hours plus running time. That the film ever got made at all, let alone in period-establishing black & white, is quite amazing, but there couldn't have been a finer choice than Tim Burton to do it. He may pull out the artistic licence and play liberal by sacrificing historical accuracy – Wood's meeting with Orson Welles (a staggering resemblance in the form of Vincent D'Onofrio), or Lugosi's habit for turning the air blue with foul language – but such indulgences can be forgiven by virtue of the delightful varnish such frivolity adds to the story. Depp's Wood, with his wide-eyed eagerness to succeed, earns him instant audience allegiance and we root for him to make it... even if we're already aware of the tragic route fate had mapped out for the real Ed. Stepping into the shoes of the colourful, amiable kooks with whom Wood surrounded himself are Sarah Jessica Parker (later in Burton's *Mars Attacks!*), Patricia Arquette, *Beetlejuice/Sleepy Hollow* Burton disciple Jeffrey Jones (as "clairvoyant" Criswell) and Bill Murray. If you're familiar with Wood's story then Burton's film will prove irresistible. For everyone else, seek it out and prepare to be educated in the most delightful way. And just remember, with more direct to video crud on the shelves than ever before, Wood's title as "worst director of all time" has been appropriated many times over by directors whose non-efforts make *Plan 9 from Outer Space* look like a work of art.

After numerous delays on the road to DVD, *Ed Wood* made its debut on Region 2 format from Touchstone, then much later on Region 1. And what a joyous bag of tricks it proved to be. After the lack of supplementary materials on the otherwise very pleasing NTSC laserdisc, Touchstone has done the DVD proud, the only minor gripe being an ill judged layer change that results in the loss of a fragment of Depp's dialogue on the U.K. release. The feature itself, divided by 28 chapter marks, offers up a choice of English or Spanish sound, with subtitle options in English, Spanish, Swedish, Norwegian, Danish and Finnish. A Tim Burton commentary heads up a nice collection of bonus features, which also include the theatrical trailer and a "music video" (in fact a model dolled up as Vampira, dancing around a graveyard set to the strains of Howard Shore's titles theme). There are also five featurettes of mixed worth. The first, an above average production piece, is bookended by Depp in drag addressing the audience. There follows a chat with Rick Baker and Landau about bringing Lugosi back to the big screen. Next up is a fascinating short on the use of the Theramin electronic instrument in the film's score, followed by a very fulfilling look at the production designs of Tim Duffield. Finally there's a relevant but rather misplaced item about cross-dressers. Although menu screens are often cleverly conceived, it's rare that I would deign to mention them, but in *Ed Wood*'s case I must make an exception. Viewed from behind an audience watching a movie screen, when you make your selections the film slips in the gate and appears to break down, prompting the audience to jeer loudly and hurl popcorn at the screen. It makes for an amusing opener, which sets the tone perfectly for a hugely entertaining disc.

The road to American DVD proved a bit bumpier, with over a year of delays halting its release after the initial announcement and no less than two recalled versions that barely touched a store shelf before being shuffled back off to the warehouse. The officially available version now on the market carries most of the British extras (apart from the transvestism short, which isn't missed, and the "When Carol Met Larry" featurette, which is on both recalled versions as well as the international discs) and contains six deleted scenes (one accessible only via Easter egg on that relevant Special Features menu screen). If you have the current U.S. and U.K. versions, that really covers all the material you might want on the film; however, if you have to make a choice, the appetizing deleted scenes on the U.S. disc should be enough to sway most collectors.

– TG

THE EDUCATIONAL ARCHIVES 3: DRIVER'S ED
THE EDUCATIONAL ARCHIVES 4: ON THE JOB
THE EDUCATIONAL ARCHIVES: RELIGION
THE EDUCATIONAL ARCHIVES: PATRIOTISM
Fantoma (US R0 NTSC)

The most familiar genre of educational films is indisputably the driver's ed training film, which can cover anything from learning to obey stop signs to avoiding the evils of drunk driving. *Volume Three: Driver's Ed* features some of the more memorable entries while avoiding the more notorious, gore-drenched classics like "Red Asphalt". There are quite a few grim surprises in store, though, so take care. A wonderfully droll James Stewart narrates "Tomorrow's Drivers", a surprisingly fun little B&W short which makes the point that teaching responsible automotive behaviour to young kids will result in better future drivers. The real fun lies in watching little kindergartners smack the daylights out of each other while riding toy cars through playground scale replicas of Main Street

USA. Then we switch to colour for the more sombre "Joy Ride", in which a pair of '70s teens jack a car for some freewheeling fun and pay the consequences in high tragic style. (The music is pretty groovy, though.) The amusing "Alco Beat" proves its pre-MADD point by showing a bunch of Average Joes on a driving course both before and after they've been thoroughly liquored up; a valid point conveyed in fine tongue-in-cheek style. Then cold reality takes over for a similar message in "The Bottle and the Throttle", in which a careless high-schooler downs a few two many brewskis and winds up on the nasty end of a manslaughter charge. "The Talking Car", a bizarre colour cartoon, features yapping automobiles chastising a kid for acting like he owns the neighbourhood streets. Then we hit paydirt with "The Last Prom", an incredible 1980 update of the old black and white chestnut about the ultimate bad date. Obviously made in the wake of *Carrie* and *Suspiria*, this one outdoes its predecessor in every way and leaves a lingering, creepy feeling long after the final 22nd chilling minute has passed. Pretty young Sandy looks forward to her prom date with Bill, and they decide to double date in his van with two friends, Jim and Judy. Accompanied by a gradually darkening choir score, we follow Sandy's preparations for the big night. After some dancing and laughter, they decide to go for a drive and crack open the beers... The message here may be familiar stuff, but you can't say the same thing for the execution. Though the crash aftermath footage features some gruelling gore effects (with that freaky music again), the real highlight is the big crash itself, featuring a haunting freeze frame that would do Dario Argento proud. One of the last truly great scare films, this was still terrorizing classrooms well into the late '80s before 16mm projectors were widely retired. Then it's back in time again with "Safety Belt for Susie", an early '60s classic teaching in no uncertain terms the high cost of driving kids around without

seatbelts. The more benign "I Like Bikes, But..." preaches tolerance between car and bike operators via montages and cartoons depicting folks of all wheeled persuasions. In "Highball Highway", which bears more than a weird passing resemblance to *Scream and Scream Again*, a drunken jock smashes up his car (with his best buddy inside) and wakes up in the hospital less complete than he used to be. Finally we hit borderline avant-garde territory with "The Crossroads Crash", a government-sponsored project in which crash test dummies and test cars careen, collide, and collapse in fetishistic detail. David Cronenberg would love this one.

 We move to less violent territory with *On the Job*, aka *Volume Four*, which is thankfully a lot more fun than those soul-deadening training videos so commonplace in fast food joints, temp agencies, sexual harassment seminars, and a certain reactionary video store chain. "Promotion By-Pass" depicts a manager torn over a promotion decision between a promising newer employee and his more seasoned counterpart, and his foibles are meant to illustrate what not to do during that final "big talk" in the office. Then it's slapstick time with "Down and Out!", sort of a workers' comp nightmare reel in which a poor schmo bangs and bruises himself by slipping on everything in sight. Enjoy a look at decidedly non-chic fashion with "Barbers and Beauticians", a tribute to those hardworking folks who wield blowdryers and scissors day by day. The Orwellian "You and Your Work" espouses the virtues of toiling day to day in retail with no hope of advancement; approach as irony, not fact! The interesting pre-Women's Lib artefact, "The Trouble with Women", offers a fairly progressive argument against unfair attitudes towards female employees, with one jerk

manager shouldering all of the blame here. The bleak "When You Grow Up" is more or less a kiddie sized, updated version of "You and Your Work", offering a not terribly persuasive argument for becoming a worker ant and riding along with the status quo. "The Grapevine", a '50s artefact if ever there was one, rails against gossiping at work without pointing out that it's one of the few things that makes a long day at a desk tolerable. That familiar "ephemeral films" gruesome edge creeps in a bit during "Shake Hands with Danger", a workers' safety film cautioning the perils of dealing with farm equipment. It's bracing stuff and will certainly make you think twice before approaching a large piece of machinery. It's back to brainwashing again with "How to Keep a Job", a quaint black and white collection of homilies blaming disgruntled, irresponsible employees for problems in the post-WWII workforce. Told as a moral fable to a potential slack-off employee, it's short, concise, and rather creepy. The most interesting narrative of the bunch, "Purely Coincidental" offers an O. Henry style examination of two employees, one at a pet food factory and the other at a baby food company, whose paths cross in a most unexpected fashion. Things get more political with "Hidden Grievance", about an ingrate worker who goes complaining to the union every time he has a problem despite the best efforts of his bosses. Nice to see things haven't changed much since the '50s. Finally we close with the oddest entry, "All Together", in which crooner Lou Rawls does some Navy recruiting narration for black citizens stuck in dead end jobs who might fulfil their dreams in the military.

Volumes five and six dispense with the numbering system, but the graphic design still dovetails with other entries in the series. For the most part, *Religion* plays it safer than one might expect; the films on view are mostly clean-scrubbed, sincere, but ultimately dubious attempts to link God and apple pie with modern progress. "The Door to Heaven" takes a live storybook approach as it depicts actors on cardboard sets representing all of the virtues necessary to get into heaven, not to mention the nasty baggage sure to keep unlucky souls out. The twinkly star sets must have been a huge influence on Rogers & Hammerstein's *Carousel*, too. Next up is "Carnivorous Plants", a bizarre, colourfully illustrated analogy between vicious Venus flytraps and the perils of man forgetting who put him here in the first place. Somehow a circa-Disney Fred MacMurray got roped into popping by for a few minutes in "Atomic Energy Can Be a Blessing", which features grey-haired Father James Keller extolling the virtues of atomic experimentation (the non-bomb kind, of course) as a necessity for advancing the lives of good Christians everywhere. The bizarre, Euro-'60s curio "Stalked" features a Dutch man going face to face with Jesus when he decides to bail out of the wax museum biz. In "Turn the Other Cheek", witness the bizarre collision of homespun '50s suburbia and pacifism as a young girl tries to cope with life's nasty problems. The Mormons go up to bat with "Of Heaven and Home", a guide to friendly behaviour and social conduct, Utah-style. "Getting Ready Morally" is a prep film for soldiers about to encounter a host of nasty temptations and bad influences, often in the form of their fellow troops! "New Doorways to Learning" features elaborate recreations of Biblical scenes to illustrate the power of actors to convey religious lessons; one recreation of the Three Wise Men's journey is especially vivid. "Teenage Challenge" follows a youth overcoming his peers' sceptical attitude towards his faith, with everyone turning out just fine in the end. For Gen-X viewers, the real gold here will be "Youth Suicide Fantasy", a perfect encapsulation of the logic-free heavy metal hysteria that shook parents in the 1980s.

Shot on video, this half-hour jawdropper presents two brothers plugging their book, Why Knock Rock, while bashing such acts as Motley Crüe, Prince, KISS (whose name gets a funny explanation here countering the usual Knights In Satan's Service myth), AC/DC, the Rolling Stones (with a young, crotch-grabbing shot of Jagger offered as proof of his decadence), and several no-name bands. Of course, it's all really a platform to attack such diverse targets as bondage, homosexuality, and pornography; the last of these gets the silliest attacks, with these guys claiming the most popular commercial erotica these days involves abused children and animals. The mind reels.

Patriotism is a look at flag-waving education from the '40s through the '70s, beginning with a fairly innocuous black and white short, "Despotism", that lays out some basic political science definitions in easy to understand terms. The very scratchy "Great Rights" is sort of a dry run for the *Schoolhouse Rock* template, with animation depicting the words of the Bill of Rights. "A Day of Thanksgiving" (which also appears in a more perverse context on Something Weird's *Blood Freak* disc) lays out all the reasons Americans should commune once a year around a big roasted turkey, without all those pesky political issues to get in the way; courtesy of the folks who brought you *Carnival of Souls*. In "Patriotism", a soon-to-be-late Bob Crane teaches a classroom the meaning of pride in one's country. Of course, almost everyone has at least seen snippets of "Duck & Cover", presented here in all its lunatic glory as cartoons and live action demonstrations prove you can avoid nuclear annihilation by getting close to the ground, just like a turtle. A host of Hollywood stars clutters up "You Can Change the World", an early '50s look at social activism with Irene Dunne, a fleeting Bob Hope, Loretta Young, William Holden, and a reprise from Father Keller. Of course, things weren't so cut and dry when teens took this film at its word in the next decade. And speaking of counterculture, "200" offers a trippy look at animated American pride. "Getting Ready Emotionally" is something of a companion piece to the *Religion* disc's "Getting Ready Morally", laying out the reasons grown-ups are always right and know what's best for your emotional welfare, even when it involves being sent off to war. "In Our Hands" reveals the necessity of industry and commercialization for an efficient society, with the old pre-technology days held up as a horrific example of where we'd all be otherwise. The unsettling "Freedom Comes High" is a WWII-era short explaining why a few deaths in the family are all really for the good of the country, so don't question it. It's doubtful this was shown much twenty years later. Things get a bit lighter again with "Mission Sonic Boom", in which the necessity for sonic reverberations during military tests is explained as a natural part of the order of things. Just take care of those eardrums, okay? Then things escalate considerably with the all-time champ of paranoid propaganda films, "Red Nightmare" (later expanded to a terribly padded one-hour version hawked on VHS as *The Commies are Coming! The Commies are Coming!*). Like the priceless *Invasion U.S.A.*, this pre-*Red Dawn* vision of America under Red control comes off like an amusing relic now, with *Dragnet*'s Jack Webb thrown in for further weirdness value. And it's from the director of *The Wolf Man*, too! The disc closes off with a little cool-down, "Pledge of Allegiance", which is a fairly self-explanatory look at the obligatory recitation and what it all really means.

As with the previous two volumes, picture quality varies from film to film but overall looks fine, scratches and all. The discs come with illustrated liner notes by avgeeks.com's Skip Elsheimer and a great extra wrinkle on the audio tracks: "The

Classroom Experience", which is essentially a secondary 5.0 audio stream filtering the movie through the echoing sound of a rattling projector, complete with 16mm film humming, clacking, and shaking as the celluloid passes between the reels.

EIGHT LEGGED FREAKS

Colour, 2002, 99m. / Directed by Ellory Elkayem / Starring David Arquette, Kari Wuhrer, Doug E. Doug, Eileen Ryan, Scarlett Johansson, Scott Terra, Tom Noonan, Rick Overton / Warner (US R1 NTSC, UK R2 PAL) / WS (2.35:1) (16:9) / DD5.1

 A chemical spill on the outskirts of the backwater town of Prosperity in the Arizona desert results in an infestation of out-size mutant spiders. Upon his father's death Chris McCormick (David Arquette) has returned after an absence of several years to take over the family mining business. Chris attempts to kindle a romance with Sheriff Sam Parker (Kari Wuhrer), and when the "arach attack" begins, the pair of them team up with paranoid, conspiracy theory obsessed radio show host Harlan (Doug E. Doug) to defeat the beasts as swiftly and as messily as possible!

Giant insect movies are hardly a new concept, with spiders alone having had their fair share of outgrowing the web, whether it be Leo G. Carroll battling the *Tarantula*, Steve Brodie and Barbara Hale coping with *The Giant Spider Invasion*, or Jeff Daniels suffering from *Arachnophobia*. Coming from Roland Emmerich and Dean Devlin, the duo behind the overhyped and underwhelming *Independence Day* and *Godzilla*, you may find yourself approaching *Eight Legged Freaks* with trepidation. Fortunately the lads are in producer mode only, with the directorial chair falling to co-writer (with Randy Kornfield and Jesse Alexander) Ellory Elkayem. And although the resulting movie is very much a paint-by-numbers affair, it's more fun than the aforementioned Emmerich-Devlin efforts combined. Baited for chortles rather than chills, the proof rears its head early on when the textbook smart kid character alerts Arquette to the imminent mutant spider problem and concludes his improbable story with the words "...but you're not going to believe me because I'm the kid and they never believe the kid." If you were in any doubt after this that Elkayem is targeting your chuckle muscle, he cements the tone with the eight legged freaks themselves which, though ferocious enough critters to look at, are given to farcically vocal mutterings that range from disgruntled hisses to gurgles of bewilderment. John Ottman's score, however, is a light-hearted leap too far; when, at key points, its should be conveying a degree of suspense, it's often just saying, "Hey, folks, isn't this all a jolly good jape?" Hard to believe this is the work of the same man whose score helped elevate *The Usual Suspects* from fantastic to astounding. Joey Deluxe's take on "Itsy Bitsy Spider", which plays out over the end titles, is a keeper though.

Feeling like a hybrid of Jeff Lieberman's *Squirm* and Chuck Russell's remake of *The Blob* – with a soupcon of Joe Dante's *Gremlins* and *Small Soldiers* – *Eight Legged Freaks* is worth a look for the marvellous CG spiders alone, which react to bullet hits with a spectacularly squishy explosion of green intestinal fluids. Unfortunately Elkayem drops the ace from his sleeve a touch too soon, with some fast-paced broad daylight mayhem as a swarm of giant hopper spiders pursue youths on dirt-track bikes across the rocky desert terrain. Nothing that follows manages to match this pulse-racing sequence and the momentum is lost when night falls and the action spirals into a humdrum series of chases through dark, disused mineshafts.

David Arquette lends to McCormick his well-meaning clown who comes good in the end routine. Laugh out loud when his Aunt Gladys (Eileen Ryan) recommends he lose his face fuzz because it "looks like a stripper's crotch." Laugh even louder when he takes on the mean, mammoth Queen arachnid armed only with an ineffectual looking scent atomizer. Kari Wuhrer, who'd already had a shot at tackling nature gone wacky in *Anaconda*, is the spunky Sheriff cum long-suffering mother of Ashley (Scarlett Johansson from *Ghost World*) and Mike (Scott Terra). Watch out for an uncredited Tom Noonan (the original and best Tooth Fairy in *Manhunter*) as Joshua, proprietor of an exotic spider farm, who's set upon, cocooned and eventually ingested by an army of his scuttling exhibits. By no means a four-course meal of a movie, if you're in the mood for brain cell-void popcorn entertainment then *Eight Legged Freaks* is guaranteed to fill the gap.

Punctuated by 29 chapter stops, Warner's Region 1 DVD release is a reasonably generous offering. The 2.35:1 ratio presentation of the feature itself – with language choices in English and French, plus subtitling in the same plus Spanish – can be viewed with an audio commentary from director Elkayem, producer Devlin and stars Arquette and Rick Overton (dippy Deputy Pete). Bonus features comprise eleven deleted and/or expanded sequences of lesser quality and with unfinished effects, being largely character exposition and hardly the "spine-tingling additional scenes of the spiders in action" that the packaging promises. There's also a theatrical trailer, some textual blurb on cast and crew and a summary of mutant spider movies across the decades. The highlight for this viewer is the thoughtful inclusion of Elkayem's 14-minute 1997 b/w film *Larger Than Life*, an affectionate tribute to creature features of the '50s and '60s (with a

verbatim replay of the climactic spider battle from *The Incredible Shrinking Man*) and the direct inspiration for *Eight Legged Freaks* itself. It's a quivering barrel of fun and a welcome addition to the package.
– TG

8 WOMEN

Colour, 2002, 113m. / Directed by François Ozon / Starring Catherine Deneuve, Fanny Ardant, Virginie Ledoyen, Isabelle Huppert, Ludivine Sagnier, Danielle Darrieux, Emmanuelle Béart, Firmine Richard / Universal (US R1 NTSC) / DD5.1, Momentum (UK R2 PAL), Paramount (France R2 PAL) / WS (1.85:1) / DTS/DD5.1

A mind-boggling array of French actresses populates *8 Women* (*8 femmes*), a stylized combination of murder mystery, pop musical, and drawing room comedy adapted from a play by thriller writer Robert Thomas (*Trap for a Lonely Man*). Continuing his apparent desire to explore every film genre imaginable, director François Ozon perfectly captures the look of a '50s Technicolor opus from Hollywood while instilling the film with a cockeyed sense of class and humour that's unmistakably continental.

One snowy morning, young Suzon (*La cérémonie*'s Virginie Ledoyen) returns to her isolated family estate for Christmas to join her mother Gaby (Catherine Deneuve), her aunt Augustine (Isabelle Huppert), little sister Catherine (*Water Drops on Burning Rocks*'s Ludivine Sagnier, almost unrecognisable), and her father, who is inconveniently discovered murdered in his bed. With the phone lines cut and the car unable to start, the women find themselves trapped in the house and playing detective. Others in attendance include the wheelchair-bound grandmother (Danielle Darrieux), two secretive maids (Emmanuelle Béart and Firmine Richard), and arriving suspiciously late on the scene, the deceased's black sheep sister, the free-spirited and sultry Pierrette (Fanny Ardant). While not busy puzzling over the crime, each woman pauses for her own musical reverie to express herself, but that's not enough to prevent a string of catfights, lesbian clinches, and dramatic revelations, all of which culminate in a final, tragic twist ending.

8 Women will be of great amusement to fans of French cinema who rarely get the opportunity to see these legends assembled in the same room, doing what they do best. Huppert has the juiciest role as the repressed, tweed-clothed spinster, who naturally undergoes a crowd-pleasing transformation in the third act. Fortunately each performer gets the spotlight at least once, with the always-beguiling Béart performing a saucy rendition of the '80s pop standard, "Pile ou face (Heads or Tails)". In fact, each musical number originated as a familiar ballad or pop song from the '60s or '70s, which makes this something of a stylistic cousin to *Moulin Rouge* (and in visual terms, *Far from Heaven*).

Exploding with colour from the (literally) flowery opening credits, this is a rich visual experience that surprisingly loses little in the transition to DVD. In fact, the anamorphic transfer looks even more vivid than the theatrical prints (saddled in the U.S. with an inexplicable R rating) and stands up to the best of Warner's MGM musical restorations. Every shot in the film is designed with immaculate care (think *The Umbrellas of Cherbourg* married to *All That Heaven Allows*), and the aesthetic scheme often threatens to completely obliterate the plot chugging along in the background. The 5.1 audio isn't as showy, mostly channelling the music to the front speakers with mild bleed-through to the rears. While the American disc from Universal looks top notch and affords the only opportunity to watch the film on DVD with English

subtitles, it's depressingly devoid of extras aside from a serviceable American trailer. It's a pedestrian package considering the high retail price, and even worse, the large yellow subtitles are burned in; if you want to watch the musical numbers without subs or have a 4:3 set and wish the subtitles were in the lower letterbox band, well, you're out of luck.

In France the film exists in no less than two DVD editions, a double-disc set and a four-disc set. Disc one includes the movie itself (in DTS or 5.1), along with an audio commentary (in French only) with Ozon, Ardant, Sagnier, script supervisor Agathe Grau, and producer Dominique Besnehard. On the second disc, the centrepiece is a one hour documentary that begins with the elaborate set construction and goes through the filming process. Even for those who can't speak a syllable of French, the doco offers some nice moments of levity including Ozon's deer wrangling during the opening shot, Deneuve and Ardant passively puffing on ciggies while watching the stunt doubles for their big catfight, and other sundry behind the scenes bonbons. Also included are eight video interviews with the actresses, screen tests (which play more like fashion demos), a deleted opening scene with the two maids discussing the members of the household, footage from the film's premiere, a press conference with the cast and director at the Berlin International Film Festival, a lengthy promo reel designed for international sales, an elegant teaser (scored with John Zorn music!), a delicious gallery of poster art, and two music videos, Deneuve's "Toi jamais" and a remix of Sagnier's "Papa, t'es plus dans le coup". Perhaps best of all is a riotous outtake reel, which finds the actresses repeatedly flubbing their musical numbers. It's strange and somehow reassuring to see such class acts as Deneuve and Huppert tripping over their lines while remaining thoroughly poised. So, that's it for the two-disc set. In the quadruple platter edition (housed in a fuzzy

E

pink and red slipcase, of course), the third disc kicks off with a 130-minute version of the original play recorded onstage and broadcast on French television in 1972. The program's vintage results in a bland and often smeary appearance, but it's interesting to compare the original (non-musical) work to the Ozonified film, which added all of the kittenish (bi)sexuality and camp elements. For French pop nuts there's a terrific selection of six of the song's earlier versions, mostly lifted from French TV programs. For the record, the songs are Françoise Hardy's "Message personnel", an amazingly kitschy disco version of "A quoi sert de vivre libre" by Nicoletta, Dalida's "Pour ne pas vivre seul", Jane Mason's "Toi jamais" (excerpted from a film), Georges Brassens's "Il n'y a pas d'amour heureux" (which incidentally was later covered by Hardy, twice!), and the most memorable of the batch, a disco version of "Pile ou face" by Corinne Charby. The disc is rounded off with a French TV interview with Deneuve, Ardant, and Ozon for a local news program. The fourth disc is the soundtrack CD, which contains all of the songs along with Krishna Lévy's appropriately lush music score.

EL TOPO

Colour, 1970, 119m. / Directed by Alejandro Jodorowsky / Starring Alejandro Jodorowsky, Mara Lorenzio, Brontis Jodorowsky / Anchor Bay (US R1 NTSC), Tartan (UK R2 PAL) / DD5.1, Raro Video (Italy R0 PAL), SPO (Japan R2 NTSC)

Philosophy-spewing freaks, rivers of blood, gunfights, gay banditos with a shoe fetish, passive-aggressive prostitutes, and sandy tableaux of human and animal carcasses populate the world's greatest spiritual western, El Topo. Still holding its place in history books as the first acknowledged "midnight movie", Alejandro Jodorowsky's film (whose title means "The Mole") virtually passed into oblivion thanks to the efforts of its American rights owner, '60s rock guru Allen Klein, to keep it off the market following a violent dispute with the notoriously eccentric director. Fortunately Japanese home video and the ensuing grey market kept its reputation alive throughout the decades, with new generations of viewers discovering its crackpot charms and passing word of mouth on to friends. One can only imagine its impact in 1970, when *2001: A Space Odyssey* and *Fantasia* had brought head culture cinema into the mainstream; El Topo extends beyond these studio efforts and drags the viewer's consciousness on a whirling rollercoaster ride of violence, religious theory, and stunning imagery that only coalesces together in the realm of dreams.

Clad in black leather, self-absorbed loner El Topo (Jodorowsky) rides into the desert with his naked son, Brontis, ordering him to bury his toys and a portrait of his mother so that he may become a man. Afterwards they encounter the slain residents of a nearby village, inspiring El Topo to hunt down and kill the perpetrator, the Colonel. El Topo ditches his little boy to ride off with the Colonel's woman, Mara Lorenzio, who encourages him to wipe out the Four Masters who control this forbidding territory. One by one he encounters the Masters, who demonstrate different abilities and philosophical viewpoints before their showdowns. At this point the film takes a bizarre, pre-*Mulholland Dr.* plot turn involving a time jump, subterranean freaks, and the grown Brontis, leading to an appropriately grim and transcendent finale.

Despite the hordes of peculiar characters on display, *El Topo* is Jodorowsky's show all the way. Apart from acting, directing, and writing this opus, he served as production designer and composed the evocative, Morricone-inspired score, which was even given a deluxe vinyl release from Klein's Apple Records. The film isn't really so different from Jodorowsky's previous film, *Fando and Lis*, but the addition of colour brings an increased sense of immediacy by contrasting the profuse, ultra-red blood with the vivid blues in the skies. Obviously the disconnected narrative and parade of surrealistic imagery will prove tough going for cult movie newcomers, but for those interested in checking out Jodorowsky's work, this is a solid place to start along with his more linear *Santa Sangre*.

El Topo first hit DVD in Italy in a highly problematic release. Hues looked far less vivid than the Japanese release, and excessive sharpness enhanced an already damaged print. The Italian disc had two major factors in its favour though: the original Spanish-language soundtrack (with optional subtitles in English or Italian) and the absence of those fuzzy Japanese censorship blobs, which blocked out the frontal nudity. The disc presentation is similar to that of Raro's *The Holy Mountain*, with text-related Jodorowsky supplements including a filmography, reviews for the film (featuring an amusing mixed response from Vincent Canby) and an academic discussion by Massimo Monteleone, which focuses on the origins of the film and its symbolic references.

Luckily these various incarnations were finally rendered obsolete many years into the DVD era when Jodorowsky and Klein belatedly arrived at a much-needed truce allowing the legal availability of these films once again. Jodorowsky supervised new transfers, in some cases correcting colour schemes seriously botched on the original prints. The results are nothing short of stunning throughout. The framing on *El Topo* still seems a little peculiar; while it often screened at academy ratio in theatres, the opening titles don't quite fit comfortably even with the complete absence of overscan. Fans of the film's English and original Spanish audio tracks get both options here,

in mono or in surprisingly spacious and natural-sounding surround mixes, with the experimental music scores and bizarre sound effects bound to get viewers looking over their shoulders on more than a few occasions. Jodorowsky also contributes an audio commentary which continues in his often inscrutable style; his verbal flights of fancy (thankfully in Spanish with optional English subtitles) make for an interesting companion to the films, though it's best sampled in small doses rather than a marathon of Jodorowsky-isms, which could inflict massive brain damage.

Jodorowsky returns in front of the camera for a baffling English-language video interview on *El Topo*, complete with flashy editing tricks that make it even more of a chore to endure. Fortunately this is the only underwhelming supplement; other goodies include the great slideshow-style theatrical trailer, a stills gallery, and the original script.

Both this movie and its successor are available separately, but the Jodorowsky box set editions in the U.S. and U.K. sweeten the deal by adding his sought-after short film, "La Cravate", a funny bit of surrealist whimsy about a man who decides to change his head at an oddball store but finds the bargain more dear than he imagined. This film is presented on a separate disc in the U.S. edition, while the U.K. set pairs it up with *Fando & Lis* (another separate disc on the U.S. set), the director's first film, which was previously available from Fantoma (and reviewed in *DVD Delirium Volume 1*). The flat, barely letterboxed transfer is similar to the lacklustre prior edition but at least is free of those distorting crosstalk waves that made the Fantoma version so difficult to watch. Also carried over is the prior disc's Jodorowsky commentary and endearingly oddball documentary, *El Constellation Jodorowsky*. Finally, the set is rounded out with two CDs marking the digital debuts of *El Topo* (a fine and melodic score previously available only on vinyl from Apple Records) and, in its world soundtrack debut, *The Holy Mountain*, which is certainly good for reaching an enlightened state at home but absolutely not recommended for lengthy auto commutes.

EMANUELLE IN AMERICA

Colour, 1977, 100m. / Directed by Joe D'Amato / Starring Laura Gemser, Gabriele Tinti, Lorraine De Selle / Blue Underground (US R0 NTSC), Stormovie (Italy R2 PAL) / WS (1.85:1) (16:9), Astro (Germany R0 PAL) / WS (2.00:1)

 "You are evil!" snarls a young man as he points a gun to the head of lovely Emanuelle (Laura Gemser). "You stimulate the basest, most inhuman instincts in people. Sex! Shame! Hell and damnation!" Well, if purgatory is anything like the visions concocted by Gemser and her director, the late sex-and-horror maven Joe D'Amato, expect to throw plenty more souls on the fire after viewing this madcap mixture of softcore sleaze and now-legendary shock tactics including hardcore snippets, bestiality and quasi-snuff antics. (According to one of the more popular horror anecdotes, David Cronenberg was even inspired by this film to create *Videodrome*; may the exploitation gods be praised.)

After tabloid/nude model photographer Emanuelle escapes from the aforementioned gun-toting puritan (who's trying to reverse the corruption of his model girlfriend) by offering to orally satisfy him ("An executioner should know his victim before he kills her!"), she goes back to her usual shutterbug routine investigating reports of deviant activity around the world, all the while tossing out such *bon mots* as "Don't you think that a hot bath is as nice as a lover's caress?" Whispers of a modern harem lead her to a remote ranch where the girls wander around topless and indulge in lesbian gropes in the swimming pool... but that's just the beginning. Upon hearing a horse whinny nearby, one of the courtesans comments about her animal-lovin' co-worker, "She just can't help it, poor kid! Since she met that Pedro she's lost her head." Indeed, Pedro turns out to be a stallion (literally) who gets manually aroused by his human bedmate; fortunately D'Amato cuts away before things get too, err, out of hand. As with the other girls, Emanuelle is known only by her astrological sign ("Virgo"), which makes for some bizarre encounters including a lesbian clinch with sleaze veteran Lorraine De Selle (*Cannibal Ferox*) in a steam room. Then it's off to a Venetian mansion where Emanuelle kick-starts a three-way with frequent co-star Gabriele Tinti (Gemser's late husband) and his wife, a pair of decadent souls who get off on throwing massive parties where the guests watch a girl burst out of a cake and then lick the sugary debris off her body. Equipped with her nifty little gold camera, Emanuelle's off again to witness more sexual antics at an island where rich women pay for the services of willing men. Cue the hardcore *ménage a trois*, a red-headed women arousing herself while watching a hairy male stripper dressed as Zorro, and possibly more disturbing, a snuff movie. That last item triggers Emy's curiosity and leads her to a prominent senator, who tries to arouse her by pulling out a handy reel of film depicting snuff atrocities including breast-slicing, rape, and one seriously nasty use of a butcher's hook. Understandably the film has nowhere to go from there, leading to a strangely jokey wrap-up.

While the content alone would be enough to earn this one a secure slot in the grindhouse pantheon, the most shocking thing is its casual, lighthearted tone. In fact, the majority of the running time feels no different than any other Black Emanuelle film (or any other '70s soft-sex title); in this context, the sudden graphic detours induce a truly nasty feeling of cinematic whiplash. This is a film best experienced full strength or not at all, and fortunately Blue Underground's

DVD has somehow gotten this forbidden gem out to an unsuspecting public in its first legal, English-language digital incarnation. The hardcore footage has always seemed strangely placed in the film; though it was obviously performed by the actors hired for the film, it's edited in with little rhyme or reason and doesn't, shall we say, function in the same way scenes of this kind usually do. As usual Gemser doesn't partake in any of the non-simulated footage, but she's still game for just about anything else; her fans will be more than pleased, and newcomers will be dashing out to find more titles starring this enigmatic starlet of '70s sleaze.

Previously released on a decent-looking, non-anamorphic German DVD from Astro (which was slightly overmatted at about 2.00:1 and had no English audio track), the Blue Underground DVD looks as fine as one could expect for this movie. Certain exterior scenes were obviously shot using a zoom lens, which means the grain tends to amplify significantly at the expense of detail, but the majority of the film looks terrific. Colours are strong for the most part (though not as vivid as the knockout menu design – kudos on those loungy visuals!) while detail is sharp throughout. Playback in 16:9 is highly recommended as it boosts the resolution for this title even more than usual, for some reason. Toss out those bootleg tapes now! The dubbed dialogue (which matches the performers' lip movements as with other entries in the series) sounds clear and well recorded throughout, but more importantly, that delirious music score by Nico Fidenco comes through loud and strong. Prepare to hum "Goodbye and Farewell" and "Celebrate Myself" for days after viewing. French and Italian audio tracks (also in mono) are included, with no subtitle options.

With most of the participants either deceased or in seclusion, the potential for extras here was minimal at best. Add to that the fact that the film's content kept it out of circulation in many countries (precluding the inclusion of even a trailer), and you've got to admire the fact that Blue Underground turned up as much as it did. The biggest extra is a 13-minute extract from *Joe D'Amato Totally Uncut*, a documentary also released as a standalone VHS feature in Europe and included as a bonus on Astro's DVDs of *Emanuelle in America* and *Porno Holocaust*. Fortunately this version is subtitled, with Blue Underground's trademark slick editing thrown into the mix, making for a nice featurette in which the cheerful D'Amato reminisces about working with Gemser and other exploitation icons of the period. An 11-minute vintage audio interview with Gemser (circa the mid-'90s) is accompanied by a gallery of stills and posters; it's a rare opportunity to hear her talk openly about her career and the peculiar European phenomenon she inspired. "The Unofficial Emmanuelle Phenomenon" traces the character's history from the Sylvia Kristel hit through such ignominious lowlights as *Carry On Emmanuelle* and the *Emmanuelle in Space* TV series. It's fairly sketchy at times but makes for a nice intro for the uninitiated, and as usual for movie scribe David Flint, is well-written and hilariously opinionated. Excellent Gemser and D'Amato biographies round out this sinfully tasty package.

Die-hards can also seek out a later two-disc edition from Italy, which carries over the same transfer and also the Gemser interview as well as the full version of *Uncut*. Unfortunately there aren't any English subtitles, while the feature itself can be played in Italian, English, French, or German, with the Italian mix presented in a wholly unnecessary 5.1 remix. The only exclusive extra is "Remembering a Friend", a little memorial for the late D'Amato. While it's still a mystery who this film was originally made for (as the porn and gore audiences would have both no doubt reacted in horror), this astonishing confection has lost none of its capacity to shock and amaze over the years. Look for it on shelves at an oblivious store near you.

ENEMY GOLD

Colour, 1993, 90m. / Directed by Drew Sidaris / Starring Bruce Penhall, Julie Strain, Rodrigo Obregón, Suzi Simpson / Malibu Bay Films (US R0 NTSC)

Inspired by the home video success of Andy Sidaris and his wife/producer Arlene, their son Drew decided to get in on the action in 1993 with *Enemy Gold*, a sleek entry in the same vein of boobs and bombs which could probably pass itself off as an Andy film without much difficulty. A bit more plot heavy than most of his parents' fare, this one recruits many of the usual suspects (including the hard-working Julie Strain and another *CHiPs* vet, Bruce Penhall) for an espionage yarn in which three intrepid agents stumble upon a gold cache from the Civil War tucked away in the Texas bayous during a leave from work. Their arch-enemy, nefarious drug lord Carlos Santiago (Rodrigo Obregón), turns out to be after the same stash, and much Leone-style double-crossing and gunfire ensues.

The real attraction here is Greek centrefold Suzi Simpson, who dominates most of the scenery as daring agent Becky Midnite (a Bondian name if there ever was one). The Civil War angle provides an odd wrinkle in the usual Sidaris formula (think of it as *The Good, the Bad and the Ugly* in fashionable swimwear), and while the pace tends to lag more than customary for Sidaris product, fans will still find plenty here to enjoy.

The tutti-frutti colour schemes are vintage Sidaris and look dazzling on this DVD, which also includes the Sidaris family's input about the film on the commentary track, video intro and featurette; other features include the standard gallery and trailer collection.

THE ENTITY

Colour, 1981, 119m. / Directed by Sidney J. Furie / Starring Barbara Hershey, Ron Silver / Fox (UK R2 PAL, Australia R4 PAL), Anchor Bay (US R1 NTSC) / WS (2.35:1) (16:9) / DD4.1

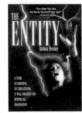

Pleased by the book sales of his two "real life reincarnation" *Audrey Rose* thrillers, Frank De Felitta returned to similar but "sexier" territory with his novel, *The Entity*, inspired by the story of a California housewife terrorized and sexually molested by a poltergeist in her home. Not surprisingly, Hollywood took notice and decided to mount a slick ghost story which made more explicit the rape implications of films such as *The Legend of Hell House*. Here the unfortunate heroine is Carla Moran (Barbara Hershey), struggling to raise her kids and earn a meagre living. Suddenly she's attacked in bed by an unseen assailant, with only her traumatic children around to watch the horrific aftermath. Her friends unsurprisingly find the story difficult to believe, and soon Carla's in the office of Dr. Sneiderman (Ron Silver) seeking aid for what he diagnoses as a psychological disorder. As the brutal attacks continue, Carla turns to other, more unorthodox means to regain control of her life.

Competently directed by jack of all genres Sidney J. Furie (*The Ipcress File*), whose love of scope framing is well in evidence here, *The Entity* rises above the level of pandering junk thanks mainly to Hershey's committed, multi-layered performance. Not afraid to appear unsympathetic (or potentially silly as her prosthetic, Stan Winston-engineered breasts are groped by a ghost), Hershey turns Carla into one of the more intriguing '80s horror heroines, both strong and terrified at the same time. On the other hand, Silver has little to do besides bullying Hershey out of her third act paranormal solution, a narrative tactic that unfortunately leaves the film painted into a corner with a disappointing cop-out at the end.

The DVD editions nicely preserve the original widescreen framing of the film, which is crucial to understanding exactly what's going on through the *Demon Seed*-style climax. Furie uses every inch of the frame, so this is really the only way to go outside of a theatre. The surround audio is extremely loud and punchy, with plenty of jolting sound effects and a very aggressive Charles Bernstein score. The identical British and Australian DVDs (rated 18 in the U.K. for "horror, sexual assault") only contain the U.S. trailer as a bonus, while the later Anchor Bay release adds a new documentary, " The Entity Files", covering the factual basis of the case and its adaptation into the source novel.

ERASERHEAD

B&W, 1977, 88m. / Directed by David Lynch / Starring Jack Nance, Charlotte Stewart / David Lynch (US R1 NTSC), Subversive (US R1 NTSC), Comstock/ Beam (Japan R2 NTSC), Paramount (France R2 PAL), Scanbox (UK R2 PAL), Umbrella (Australia R4 PAL) / WS (1.85:1) (16:9) / DD2.0, Universal (UK R2 PAL) / DD2.0

 A key player in the midnight movie revolution of the 1970s, the surreal and often inscrutable *Eraserhead* marked the feature film debut of David Lynch, aided by an American Film Institute grant and a squad of fearless, possibly insane cinematic conspirators. Lensed in gloomy black and white, the film today works best as a surprisingly thorough primer in the visual motifs that would come to dominate Lynch's later films and television work.

After an extended prologue in which a series of cosmic mechanisms mimic the process of birth (complete with monstrous spermatozoa), the fragmented storyline begins in a nameless town smothered in industrial grime and smog. Dumpy and socially afflicted Henry (the late Jack Nance) comes home to his dingy apartment, where his busty neighbour peers at him continuously from a half-closed door. At night he goes to the house of his girlfriend, Mary (Charlotte Stewart), where her parents engage in fractured conversation and serve him a twitching, bleeding chicken for dinner. As it turns out, Mary has been impregnated by Henry and given birth to a scrawny, malformed infant, so naturally mother and child move in with him. Thanks to sleepless nights spent with his twitching common law spouse and the mewling baby, Henry soon drifts off into a fantasy world governed by a platinum-haired, plump-cheeked, singing lady who lives in his radiator.

Best viewed late at night in a hazy state of mind, *Eraserhead* brims with unsettling images of bodily assault and decay, sexual revulsion, unidentifiable mechanical constructions, and shadowy hallways staggered with malfunctioning elevators and bizarre plant life. Though still off-putting to many viewers, this is in many respects a keystone to future science fiction, horror and avant-garde filmmaking; there simply wouldn't be a *Delicatessen*, *Se7en*, *Brazil*, *Combat Shock*, or *Irreversible* without it. The film's most lyrical and chilling moment, a performance of the eerie "In Heaven, Everything Is Fine", foreshadows Lynch's Roy Orbison microphone reveries in *Blue Velvet* and *Mulholland Dr.*, while the audacious cosmic finale was later repeated (in different contexts) in *The Elephant Man*, *The Straight Story*, and the opening of *Dune*. Finally there's the groundbreaking sound mix, a disconcerting mixture of low rumblings, metallic scraping, and industrial chugging, which anticipates the sonic experimentation of *Lost Highway* and other industrial music-related projects. A must for Lynch fans and curious viewing for almost anyone else, *Eraserhead* is an experience few genuinely enjoy but none ever forget.

David Lynch's decision to create and distribute *Eraserhead* on DVD by himself is something of an industry anomaly, particularly considering the film's rabid cult following. It debuted in the U.K. as a full-screen edition from Universal. Subsequent release in France and Japan contained watchable and sometimes-impressive widescreen transfers, certainly leagues above the muddy Columbia tapes and bootlegs which afflicted viewers' eyes for years. Lynch's DVD, cleaned up frame by frame from an interneg transfer, looks exceptionally good and wonderfully film-like. Apart from the inherent graininess of some outdoor daylight shots, there's nary a quibble to make with the transfer. The 2.0 surround audio (listed as uncompressed PCM in the notes, though it registers as Dolby Digital) delivers an admirable sonic presentation of the film, and while it's not quite as aggressive as the surround mix on the Japanese laserdisc, it's more than enough to convey the film's sonic palette and sounds remarkably textured. Housed in an oversized box (emblazoned with "DVD 2000" for some reason), the disc comes with an illustrated booklet containing poster reproductions, an outline excerpt, a storyboard page, and several stills. The supplements (accessible from rather long menus of Nance's shoes tied to the dead cat) include the oft-seen theatrical trailer and, more importantly, an 84-minute documentary (simply titled "Stories"). Shot in full frame black and white, this behind the scenes retrospective features Lynch at his familiar microphone in front of curtains (as seen in his *Short Films* DVD) reminiscing about the making of the film, from its inception in the early '70s through the entire shooting process. Accompanied by a continuous windy sound effect and a barrage of still photos, he provides a consistently interesting tour of the

film's history. Some grainy video footage of the shooting is also included, along with a thumbnail sketch of various deleted scenes scrapped either during shooting or the final assembly. Assistant director Catherine Coulson also chimes in via speakerphone for a lengthy conversation with Lynch in which they discuss such subjects as the effect of Nance's bizarre haircut on his everyday life. It's a pricey package to be sure, but Lynch fans won't hesitate to add this oversized oddity to their digital collections. Lynch's website ceased selling the DVD in 2005, at which time the film and extras were licensed for distribution in the U.S. by Subversive, who issued *Eraserhead* in a standard sized box. Identical editions, in PAL format, followed from Scanbox in the U.K. and Umbrella in Australia.

EUGENIE... THE STORY OF HER JOURNEY INTO PERVERSION

Colour, 1969, 83m. / Directed by Jess Franco / Starring Marie Liljedahl, Jack Taylor, Maria Rohm, Christopher Lee / Anchor Bay (UK R2 PAL), Blue Underground (US R1 NTSC) / WS (2.35:1) (16:9)

In the late 1960s, prolific auteur Jess Franco was working with the international producer Harry Alan Towers and had access to luxuries like widescreen cinema-tography, the occasional "name" actor outside his usual stock company and delirious bossa-styled jazz scoring from the likes of Bruno Nicolai. Of all the presold subjects Franco made with Towers (who wrote and produced under his "Peter Welbeck" pseudonym), *Eugenie* might have been the most personal – he has remade it more than once with varying degrees of explicit sex and perversion. It still boils down to a pretty-looking softcore picture with *longueurs* between seductions, but it's certainly less unwatchable than many efforts from the lower depths of its maker's career and, on balance, plays better than other Towers-backed Christopher Lee-starrers like *Castle of Fu Manchu* or *Count Dracula*.

It's not a period adaptation of the novel *Philosophy in the Boudoir* but an update to the fab-fashioned 1960s with the decadent villains members of a cult who seem to worship de Sade, though their antics might also owe something to *Rosemary's Baby*. Sweet Eugenie (Marie Liljedahl, fresh from *Inga*) is an innocent invited for a weekend to the island retreat of Madame de St. Ange (Maria Rohm) and her stepbrother/ lover Mirvel (Jack Taylor), who set about seducing her with drugs ("This cigarette tastes funny"), caresses and other funny business. Eugenie goes through an orgy that climaxes with whippings that turn out to be fake so the hostess can claim it was just a dream. A body turns up hanging from beams, Eugenie is manipulated into murdering Mirvel and it seems the girl is due for more extensive torture until the cult's presiding genius Dolmance (Christopher Lee, in his Sherlock Holmes smoking jacket) pulls a quite logical reversal that manages to be at once titillating, moralist and silly. After this twist, there's a wild bit with Liljedahl rolling naked down a sand-dune and another, *Dead of Night*-style recurring dream kicker.

The film has been distributed under a great many titles, and the print sourced by Anchor Bay bears the onscreen card *Marquis de Sade's "Philosophy in the Boudoir"*. The letterboxed transfer is pristine, with gorgeous colour to show off the occasional red lighting effects and healthy skin-tones, though occasional shots are slightly out of focus. Some of these are among the most explicit moments, suggesting a censored print has had material from a slightly degraded source spliced in, but a few appear to be deliberate attempts at dreaminess. The extras include a long trailer, an extensive stills gallery, a Jess Franco biography, and "Perversion Stories",

an interesting interview-based featurette with input from the twinkling Franco, a reserved Towers, a solemn Liljedahl and a slightly embarrassed Lee.

– KN

EUREKA

Colour, 1983, 129m. / Directed by Nicolas Roeg / Starring Gene Hackman, Theresa Russell, Jane Lapotaire, Rutger Hauer, Mickey Rourke, Joe Pesci / MGM (US R1 NTSC, UK R2 PAL) / WS (1.85:1) (16:9) / DD2.0

What do hot voodoo, a gory blowtorching and a decapitation, world-weary whores, and a hysterical court trial have in common? They're all elements in *Eureka*, one of the maddest studio films ever made. Somehow after the troubled releases of *The Man Who Fell to Earth* and *Bad Timing*, Nicolas Roeg still managed to get major financing for a (comparatively) star-studded production, loosed based on Marshall Houts's celeb-studded true crime book, *Who Killed Sir Harry Oakes?* Here the world-weary zillionaire is fictionalized as Jack McCann (Gene Hackman), a single-minded prospector whose years in the tundra finally pay off when he strikes gold. Years later, his wealth has brought him little happiness as the one goal in his life has been accomplished; even his wife (Jane Lapotaire) and daughter, Tracy (Theresa Russell), offer little solace. Harry is deeply disturbed by Tracy's romance with suave playboy Claude (Rutger Hauer), whom the protective dad sees as a possible usurper to McCann's fortune and very soul. Meanwhile thug heavies D'Amato (Mickey Rourke) and Mayakofsky (Joe Pesci) lean on Harry for a piece of the action, leading to a gruesome evening that leaves our characters either dead, guilty of murder, or stuck in a courtroom.

From a visual and editing standpoint, *Eureka* is really the last great Roeg film. The opening hour is a frenzy of beautifully jagged cuts, stylized camera zooms, and visual free association that rivals the best of his earlier films. Hackman's snowy ordeal at the beginning is a particular marvel, integrating a gunshot suicide, a heavenly chunk of ice, and a prophetic, dying prostitute into a series of bizarre tableaux better seen than described. Russell and Hauer's romance is no less surreal, with the aforementioned voodoo orgy stopping the film in its tracks for a good five minutes as the viewer is assaulted with snakes and writhing bodies. Then we have the aforementioned murder, which won't be much of a shock for anyone who pays attention to the source novel's title; it's a prolonged, nasty piece of business that could have stepped out of Lucio Fulci's *Contraband*. Unfortunately the trial business is something of a letdown, with Russell's heartfelt but utterly mad climactic speech provoking more head scratching than the soapiest Douglas Sirk dialogue. A one-of-a-kind experience, to be sure.

After sitting on the shelf for three years, *Eureka* was finally released by United Artists on the heels of a later and far more genteel Roeg film, *Insignificance*. It languished on home video in a rather dull transfer for years, but the widescreen DVD makes up for it with a brilliant, colourful transfer (complete with that beloved early '80s grain, though it's fairly mild). The surround audio also serves the movie well, especially Stanley Myers's beautiful, evocative score. The only extra on both MGM releases is the U.S. theatrical trailer, which tries to sell the film as best it can.

EVIL DEAD TRAP 2

Colour, 1991, 102m. / Directed by Izô Hashimoto / Starring Shoko Nakajima, Rie Kondô, Shirô Sano / Unearthed (US R0 NTSC), Japan Shock (Holland R0 NTSC) / WS (1.66:1), Artsmagic/Shadow Warrior (UK R2 PAL) / WS (1.66:1) (16:9) / DD2.0

Inexplicably passed off as a sequel to the slasherfest *Evil Dead Trap*, this Asian response to the Crazy Fat Ethel films of the 1980s plumbs the nasty depths of a young woman's psyche with typically gory results. If the first film was an homage to the films of Dario Argento, this one owes everything to Jörg Buttgereit.

City girl Aki (Shoko Nakajima) works as a projectionist at a small Japanese theatre and doesn't have much of a social life, apart from self-absorbed former classmate Emi (Rie Kondô), now a reporter. At least Aki does have some other use for her time: prowling the streets at night and carving up innocent women. Things get more complicated when Emi, who's busy covering the brutal crimes, tries to fix up Aki with a married man, Kurahashi (Shirô Sano). Meanwhile Aki's murderous instincts are propelled by visions of a creepy young boy, Hideki (the sole reference to the first *Evil Dead Trap*), leading to a typically nasty denouement.

Loaded with gore and stylish visuals, *Evil Dead Trap 2* (originally *Shiryo no wana 2: Hideki*) is more erratically paced than its companion film and feels a bit closer to art house territory. The performers are all good despite the sketchy nature of their characters, and director Izô Hashimoto (the man behind one of the *Guinea Pig* films, *Lucky Sky Diamond*) displays a solid sense of how to execute a gore scene for maximum impact.

The U.S. disc from Unearthed offers a serviceable widescreen transfer, which captures the low-budget, grimy look of the film adequately enough. Colours veer towards the rusty side, which appears to be the intended colour scheme of the film. Optional subtitles in English are the clearest around for this title. The U.K. DVD offers 16:9 enhancement, though the image quality isn't much of an improvement and, as with a couple of other Asian faux-anamorphic jobs, may just be a blow-up from a similar master. The Dutch edition looks the worst of the bunch, with extremely soft detail and washed out blacks. None of the discs are extras-laden, featuring the theatrical trailer and little else.

EVIL OF DRACULA

Colour, 1974, 83m. / Directed by Michio Yamamoto / Starring Mori Kishida, Toshio Kurosawa, Kunie Tanaka, Mika Katsuragi, Katsuhiro Sasaki / Artsmagic/Shadow Warrior (UK R2 PAL) / WS (2.35:1)

This is the third (and last) of Toho studio's "bloodthirsty" trilogy of hybrid East-West vampire movies, which was originally entitled *Chi o suu bara* and also known as *The Bloodthirsty Roses*. It brings back star Mori Kishida from *The Bloodthirsty Eyes* but offers an unconnected storyline. Drawing heavily on the imagery of Hammer Films and Roger Corman, with some scenes restaged from Terence Fisher's filmography, this still offers a unique take on the vampire sub-genre.

A new teacher (Toshio Kurosawa) arrives at an isolated school for mature-looking girls and is immediately suspicious of the pale-faced Principal (Kishida), who wears a distinctive white scarf instead of the traditional cape and keeps the corpse of his recently killed wife (Mika Katsuragi) in the basement. After an encounter with the vampire wife, the hero settles into his job, becoming the subject of several schoolgirl crushes, and the Principal spreads the curse throughout the school population. A bizarre flashback traces the trouble to a bearded Western castaway who was forced to reject Christianity and drink his own blood while wandering in a desert and then subjected a local girl to vampire attack; it turns out that this interloper has either been possessing a

series of principals down through the years or, as his wife/original victim does with a pupil, slicing off and wearing their faces. There are peculiar, surreal/romantic touches: the Renfield character is a Beaudelaire-quoting decadent schoolmaster (Katsuhiro Sasaki), and much symbolic business is made of the vampire's white roses which turn red when the recipient of the flower's scratch finally dies. Nevertheless, it ends in approved Hammer fashion with the impaled vampire lovers holding hands as they age rapidly and dissolve to messy skeletons.

Artsmagic's DVD is on a par with their releases of the other "bloodthirsty" films (under the titles *Legacy of Dracula* and *Lake of Dracula*): a letterboxed Japanese-language transfer with optional subtitles that appear below the frame. Not augmented for 16:9, widescreen playback occasionally lops a line off the subtitles and presents a slightly rough image. The picture mostly has a murky green look, though occasional solid reds suggest directorial choice rather than a transfer problem. The extras are a brief Kishida bio, a useful portrait gallery that identifies the cast, five stills, artwork for the series and promotional material for other "Shadow Warrior" releases.

– KN

EVIL TOONS

Colour, 1990, 83m. / Directed by Fred Olen Ray / Starring David Carradine, Monique Gabrielle, Madison Stone, Stacey Nix, Suzanne Ager, Arte Johnson, Dick Miller, Michelle Bauer / Retromedia (US R1 NTSC) / WS (1.66:1)

Megan, Roxanne, Jan and Terry (played by Monique Gabrielle, Madison Stone, Stacey Nix and Suzanne Ager respectively) arrive at a run down old house to spend the weekend cleaning up. Unperturbed by warnings from jovial neighbour Mr. Hinchlow (Arte Johnson) that the house is a dangerous place to spend the night, the girls set to work. But when they pry open an old trunk buried in the basement they inadvertently unleash a cartoon demon with a taste for human flesh.

Who could resist a movie that opens with David Carradine quarrelling with a talking book (mimicking the flesh-bound tome of *The Evil Dead*), and then promptly hanging himself to escape its evil powers? With Fred Olen Ray's name above the title, if nothing else you're assured the ride is going to be fun. This is Fred doing what Fred does best. Gourmet meals were never a part of his menu, but if plenty of T&A filling sandwiched between layers of unimaginative comic horror sounds appealing then you won't come away too disappointed. Written by Ray under the nom de plume Sherman Scott, the title *Evil Toon* (singular) would have been more appropriate, since there's only one and it enjoys less screen time than some of the cameoing players. A Tasmanian Devil look-alike, it was created for the film by late *Deep Red* magazine editor Chas. Balun, but the effects are poorly executed. For example, when the Toon attacks Madison Stone and rips off her brassiere you can clearly see the wire doing the work. The cartoonish tang is carried through to the live action too, with daft sight gags – at one point Monique Gabrielle gets scared and her ponytail springs up on end – and Tom & Jerry sound effects.

The quartet of female leads are adequate in respect of what's required of them, which amounts to little more than discarding their clothes and running round the house screaming their lungs out, but there's no evidence of anything that remotely touches upon acting ability. Could this have something to do with the fact that two of them had stepped straight off the set of their latest porno movies? Madison Stone is better known by her Christian name only and Stacey Nix will be familiar to some

as Barbara Dare. A slightly bewildered looking David Carradine doesn't appear to be too certain where he is and his wrap-up monologue, intended to enlighten viewers as to what's been going on, is likely to leave them even more perplexed. Dick Miller meanwhile gets a scene where he's watching his old Roger Corman movie *A Bucket of Blood* on TV: "How come this guy never won an Academy Award?" he grumbles. Later, he excitedly prepares to receive the blowjob of a lifetime from Stone, but things turn nasty as she sprouts fangs and gnaws off his manhood – cue exaggerated expression of painful surprise. Michelle Bauer cameos as Miller's wife and, despite being on camera for less than 20 seconds, still manages to expose her breasts.

Even allowing for the fact that one man's gooey fish crud is another's best beluga caviar it's difficult to be benevolent towards *Evil Toons*; as Thora Birch's character in *Ghost World* might opine, "This is so bad it's gone past good and back to bad again." Strictly entertainment for the indiscriminate or inebriated, Ray knows it, embraces it and flaunts it shamelessly. Can't blame him for that I suppose.

One can't be too disgruntled that the promising sounding "Making of *Evil Toons*" documentary on Retromedia's Region 1 DVD comprises little more than a static camera aimed at Fred Olen Ray as he discusses the film's genesis. The man speaks with such gusto and childlike enthusiasm for his work that he packs more information into its 11-minutes than other "making-ofs" manage in double the time. Presented as part of his "Nite Owl Theater" series, the disc contains a colourful, if occasionally rather grainy looking widescreen presentation of the feature, divided by a stingy 7 chapter breaks. There's also some dumb, unrelated Ray filler on either end of the feature but he compensates for this by also including a sizeable stills gallery and some snippets of footage prior to the overlay of the cartoon monster. As well as a trailer for *Evil Toons* itself, there are grotty, sub-VHS quality teasers (complete with flecks of ex-rental dropout) for other Ray clunkers *Hybrid* and *Dark Universe*. Presented back to back, it's impossible to access the trailers individually. Not that you're likely to want to. A 2010 "20th Anniversary Edition" from Retromedia is essentially the same package, except it also adds on a pretty funny, self-deprecating director's commentary track.

– TG

EXORCIST II: THE HERETIC

Colour, 1977, 118m. / Directed by John Boorman / Starring Linda Blair, Richard Burton, Louise Fletcher, Max von Sydow, Kitty Winn, Ned Beatty, James Earl Jones / Warner (US R1 NTSC, UK R2 PAL) / WS (1.85:1) (16:9)

After the success of *Deliverance*, director John Boorman was given carte blanche to run rampant through the science fiction genre with *Zardoz* and the horror genre (ostensibly at least) with *Exorcist II: The Heretic*, perhaps the most unorthodox sequel of the 1970s. Deliberately eschewing all of the commercial elements that made the 1973 William Friedkin film a box office smash, this follow-up contains nary a blasphemous utterance or subliminal Satanic image. Instead the story treads into the far more puzzling terrain of metaphysical spirituality where good and evil coexist in a kind of uneasy balance within each person, with some chosen as earthly purifying agents once they have overcome their demons, so to speak.

Afflicted with nightmares and sleepwalking spells years after her possession, teenager Regan (Linda Blair) receives help from paranormal researcher Dr. Tuskin (Louise Fletcher), while perpet-ually intense Father Lamont (Richard Burton) stops by to watch and observes that Tuskin's latest gadget, a strobe light patched to Regan's forehead, has "proved scientifically that there's an ancient demon locked within her." Lamont and Regan get "in synch" through the machine and travel back in time to witness the African exorcism which nearly killed Father Merrin (Max von Sydow *sans* make-up), spurring Lamont to follow in his predecessor's footsteps.

Rife with absurd dialogue, haphazard editing, and a surfeit of characters who serve no narrative purpose whatsoever (particularly Kitty Winn and Ned Beatty), *Exorcist II: The Heretic* is one of the most astonishing bad films ever made. In visual and narrative terms it's the closest thing to an American Jess Franco film, filled with dreamlike camerawork that drifts through glittering artifices and dives within elaborate, orange-bathed sets. Unfortunately the dialogue sinks an already wobbly ship, with Burton and Blair woefully unable to pull off a single scene together convincingly. Coupled with bouncing locusts, James Earl Jones in a parade of degrading costumes, a dazzling but wholly misused Ennio Morricone score, and an unbearably stupid, money-wasting finale, Boorman's film was damned before it ever got off the ground. The exhibition woes of *Exorcist II* became legendary upon its release, as rumours persisted that Boorman was hacking his original three-hour version down to a workable length until the last minute. The resulting 118-minute cut was jeered off the screen, causing an immediate withdrawal of the film, which was later given a general release at 110 minutes (the version most commonly available on VHS for years). Rather than a simple pared-down variant, the reissue cut is a wholly different animal, featuring different music cues, a completely revamped editing scheme, an additional prologue summarizing events from the previous film coupled with new footage of Lamont surmounting a flight of stone steps, and an alternative finale in which Lamont perishes to leave Regan staring angelically at the camera. Though a great deal of footage was excised (most memorably Regan's early "Lullaby of Broadway" tap-dance rehearsal), the short cut also added a few other odds and ends of additional footage, including the film's only genuine gore effect, a close-up of the Georgetown cab driver's head speared onto a spiked fence.

While fans of delirious schlock should be thankful Warner felt the urge to release this on DVD at all, the end result is only halfway satisfying. Boorman's premiere cut is presented in a highly attractive, colourful transfer, with magnificent shades of gold and bronze often flooding the screen. The anamorphic framing looks ideal, trimming a bit of spare headroom from prior versions while adding a sliver to the sides. The disc includes the alternative opening, but alas, other material from the general release cut is not included; the "tragic" ending would have been a more valuable bonus at the very least. Perhaps someday they'll revisit the title and include all three versions, at least if some home video executive has a truly depraved sense of humour. Two trailers are included, both of them fascinating. The general release trailer (also included on *The Exorcist: 25th Anniversary Edition* DVD) is a marvellous piece of work, furiously edited to Morricone's "Magic and Ecstasy" (a cue heard only in the revised cut, ironically enough). The teaser contains no footage from the actual film, instead using surreal artwork to tease the viewer while attributing the script to William Goodhart, whose work was largely jettisoned when Boorman brought in his regular collaborator, Rospo Pallenberg, to overhaul the entire story. While one can only ponder what the result might have been with the original (and purportedly far more coherent) Goodhart conception, the film itself is certainly capable of making a strong impression, though not quite the one its creators intended.

EXPOSÉ
(THE HOUSE ON STRAW HILL)

Colour, 1975, 80m. / Directed by James Kenelm Clarke / Starring Udo Kier, Linda Hayden, Fiona Richmond, Brian Smedley-Aston, Karl Howman, Vic Armstrong / Odyssey (UK R2 PAL)

 Having hit the bestseller list with his first novel, Paul Martin (Udo Kier) hires secretary Linda Hindstatt (Linda Hayden) to assist him by holing up in a remote country cottage to thrash out his follow-up. Suffering from writer's block (hardly surprising since it transpires the first book was plagiarized) and hindered by terrifying nightmares and sundry other distractions – not least of which is discovering Linda fondling his girlfriend, Suzanne (Fiona Richmond) – Paul's ability to focus becomes ever more erratic. To add to his problems, Linda appears to be harbouring a deadly secret, and Paul's good fortune is about to depart him...

Vampyres producer Brian Smedley-Aston (who cameos in flashback sequences as the dead author of the novel Kier appropriates) and director James Clarke (who wrote the score for *Vampyres*) teamed up to make this low budget little number as *The House on Straw Hill*. The title was altered to *Exposé* just prior to release to entice audiences with a hint of juicy promise for what was primarily a launch vehicle for up and coming adult magazine icon Fiona Richmond. As such, and given the sunny location of the little cottage – idyllically situated amidst fields of golden corn – the events that unfold couldn't be more contrary to expectation. It's obvious from the get go that one-time Baron Frankenstein Udo Kier is a bit of a mixed up individual – though quite why he wears surgical gloves during sex is never elaborated upon – but this still doesn't prepare those who turned up specifically to glimpse Richmond's unclad curves for the catalogue of nastiness that ensues; rape, mutilation and murder are all waiting in the wings for our trio of protagonists. The characters are pretty thinly drawn and there's a distinct slenderness of plot too, not to mention an absence of any real intrigue as to the identity of the killer. And the finale, involving the reappearance of a character believed to have been dead for several days, stretches suspension of belief to breaking point. But somehow everything gels and *Exposé*, if not quite up there with the best 1970s Brit-exploitation, is an efficient and relatively enjoyable chiller.

Kier's escalating paranoia is extremely convincing, reaching its apex in abject terror as a shotgun-toting Hayden pursues him out of the cottage and across the fields. The sex scenes probably came as second nature to Amazonian Richmond, who performs her duties adequately enough within the boundaries of expectation, but beyond that she offers little that is ever likely to convince the world she's a competent actress. Hayden, though comparatively skilled at her craft, seems out of her depth with the more salacious material, be it pawing at herself or negotiating her way around Richmond's erogenous zones. In an interview some years back she made known her disregard for the film, intimating that footage of which she had no knowledge was added after she'd finished shooting; quite what this might have been – so dreadful that it should cause her to disown the film, when relatively graphic scenes of rape, lesbianism and masturbation were lensed with her participation – God only knows. It's most probably a case of retrospective regret, for if any of this mythical footage to which Hayden alluded ever really existed it has yet to surface in any known print. Watch out for appearances from TV's Karl Howman and stuntman (later second unit director on the Bond movies) Vic Armstrong as a couple of reprobates who pay the price for assaulting Hayden's fruit-loop floozy. The climactic slaying of Richmond is rather gratuitous, as is the early rape scene involving Hayden, but neither stopped the

film receiving some good notices at the time of its original release and it certainly deserved better than the fate which befell it; a 1984 ban on video in the U.K. remained in force until a censored reissue surfaced in 1997.

With its history in home viewing form all too familiar among the film's devotees, no one was naive enough to expect that any U.K. disc release of *Exposé* would be uncut. And sure enough, absent from Odyssey's R2 DVD are the rape of Linda in the cornfield (and the grisly retribution that follows), and Suzanne's bloody demise. What is a surprise, however, is that a couple of extra seconds are missing from the former sequence compared to its 1997 VHS incarnation from Siren Video. If nothing else this loss serves to tidy up an excision that previously resulted in a messy jump on the soundtrack, but it's still rather odd. The transfer itself is reasonably good given the movie's age and cheapie origins. The 4:3 full screen offering is presented with mono sound and divided by 14 chapter stops. There's some brief textual matter on the film and its stars thrown in and a step-through photo gallery so sparse that they may as well not have bothered; it comprises just five images, one of which isn't even from *Exposé* anyway.

– TG

THE EYE

Colour, 2002, 95m. / Directed by Oxide Pang Chun and Danny Pang / Starring Lee Sin-Je [Angelica Lee], Lawrence Chou, So Yut-Lai, Chutcha Rujinanon / Tartan (UK R0 PAL), Panorama (HK R0 NTSC), Palm (US R1 NTSC) / WS (1.85:1) (16:9) / DD5.1

Blind since the age of two, twenty-year-old Mun (Lee Sin-Je) is given the chance of restored sight when she undergoes a corneal transplant. The operation is an apparent success but it quickly transpires that it's anything but a blessing, for her surgery has opened up a portal into the parallel world of the dead, a realm populated by bitterly malcontent souls. Resolved to reveal the identity of the deceased cornea donor, Mun and her doctor, Wah (Lawrence Chou), travel a terrifying road of discovery that leads to a cataclysmic conclusion.

Every so often a film comes along that has the power to refresh the palate of even the most jaded cineaste. *The Eye* (shot as *Jian gui*) – written, directed and edited by brothers Oxide and Danny Pang – is just such an accomplishment. With the principal character burdened by an ability to see the restless spirits of the dead, comparisons with M. Night Shyamalan's *The Sixth Sense* have been rife – but that's where the similarity ends. One might as well liken it to *Final Destination 2*, *Stir of Echoes*, *The Eyes of Laura Mars*, or even *Dragonfly*, for *The Eye* discharges flavours of all these films throughout its running time. But make no mistake; it has its own very distinct piquancy and blisters with a surfeit of perturbing imagery and sound. Being able to see things that no one else can is hardly an original premise but the Pangs have managed to craft a cocktail of chills that ranks their film up there among the best genre fare to emerge from Hong Kong in the last decade. At first we see the spirits only through Mun's eyes, which, immediately post-op, renders them unfocussed and blurry, no different to everyone and everything else she sees. Yet even at this point, through the penetrative use of camera and sound, we're unnervingly aware that something isn't right. As Mun's sight improves, so the clarity of these manifestations becomes ever more distinct. From her encounter with a disgruntled spectre in the hospital and the ghastly vision in her calligraphy class, through to a poignant meeting with a recently departed friend and the unexpectedly devastating coda, *The Eye* is by turns creepy, moving and truly shocking. A standout sequence in which Mun is

trapped in an elevator with the deformed figure of an old man makes palpable Wally Campbell's facetious claim in *The Cat and the Canary* that "...even my goose pimples have goose pimples!" Yet it's the scene in a diner involving a distended purple tongue languidly lapping at a piece of meat that holds the most unforgettably disturbing image in the film for this reviewer. When they're not busy scaring the pants off you the Pangs extend their writing skills to a different form of emotion, but they hold a tight enough rein that the scenes between Mun and the hospitalized Ying Ying – which might seem out of place and could so easily have descended into mawkish sentiment – are a natural facet of the story and genuinely touching. To sustain edge of the seat tension from end to end is a pretty tall order, but the brothers take up the challenge with gusto. And when the story threatens to sag a little during the mid-section, these fellows are savvy enough to change gear and limber up for a climax that delivers one of the most spectacularly harrowing scenes of mass quietus ever put on film. But it's not just the big budget trappings of this small budget film that leave a lasting impression. *The Eye* boasts a strong narrative, beautiful cinematography and convincing performances all round. Key players Lee Sin-Je as Mun, Lawrence Chou as Wah, little So Yut-Lai as tragic brain tumour patient Ying Ying, and Chutcha Rujinanon as Ling, the former owner of Mun's corneas, are all quite excellent. The Pangs also serve up some memorable effects – for example the rapid travelling shot through an electrical system between an ignition switch and the point at which the charge flashes across the sparkplug – and they wisely employ these to enhance their story, not carry it. The fabulous score by Orange Music heightens the tension during Mun's encounters with revenants and imbues her relationship with Ying Ying with acute sadness. When we reluctantly part company with Mun at the wholly satisfying conclusion, we do so filled with felicitous optimism that ephemeral vision has been cathartic, bringing peace and contentment to her darkened world.

In Britain *The Eye* is available as an irresistible Region 0 DVD from Tartan, issued under their Asia Extreme banner. The film is presented in 1.85:1 ratio with a 16-chapter divide. The sole language option is its original Cantonese, but there are English subtitles provided. The quality is exceptional, with a scintillating colour palette and plenty of eerie effects emanating from the Dolby Digital soundtrack. Of the supplementary offerings the "Making of *The Eye*" featurette and a slightly longer piece about the Pang brothers (relating specifically to their work on this film) are the highlights. There are also three trailers, a slender step-frame gallery of promotional artwork and flyers, selected cast and crew filmographies and a short essay about the film. Rounding things off there are a handful of trailers for other titles in Tartan's Asia Extreme collection. The Region 0 Hong Kong disc from Panorama Entertainment is a movie only release with Cantonese 5.1 DTS Surround sound and a choice of English or Chinese subs, while the U.S. Palm release splits the difference by carrying only the featurette and a trailer.

– TG

EYEBALL

Colour, 1974, 91m. / Directed by Umberto Lenzi / Starring John Richardson, Martine Brochard / Marketing-Film (Germany R0 PAL) / WS (2.35:1) (16:9)

 The final *giallo* from the prolific Umberto Lenzi (director of *Paranoia* and *Spasmo*) is widely considered to be the weakest of his murder mystery output, primarily because most viewers have only seen the butchered U.S. version, which circulated on countless double bills in the '70s. With its abundance of empty-headed suspects and victims, thumping Bruno Nicolai score, and trendy lesbianism, this would make an excellent double bill with its mid-'70s kin like *Case of the Bloody Iris* and, on its own trashy terms, makes for energetic and often amusing viewing.

A busload of American tourists enjoying the sights of Spain finds trouble when two of their party (one of them riding through a spook house attraction) run afoul of a knife-wielding killer with a penchant for plucking out eyeballs. Our hero, Mark (John Richardson), deduces that his wife may be connected, since she was found months ago lying by a swimming pool with a bloody orb nearby. In classic fashion, each person who finds a vital clue winds up under the blade of the red-gloved maniac, but that doesn't stop the tour from pressing on.

Originally known under the more poetic title of *Gatti rossi in un labirinto di vetro* (*Red Cats in a Glass Labyrinth*), this ludicrous, slash-happy outing was released in Europe as *The Secret Killer* and *Wide-Eyed in the Dark* before landing its most famous title courtesy of Joseph Brenner. Newcomers to the genre would be better off starting somewhere else, as *Eyeball* is padded out with an ungodly amount of filler, mainly travelogue footage and conversations in which characters stand around speculating about the killer's motives. The cheeky Nicolai theme tends to blast forth whenever things get too slow (whether the film calls for music or not), and the always reliable Richardson (*Torso*) somehow keeps a straight face even during the OTT finale.

Viewers tired of fuzzy bootlegs and those awful, bloodless Prism videotapes will be pleased with this German DVD, titled *Labyrinth des Schreckens* (that's *Labyrinth of Frights* to non-Teutonics). Featuring the full-length opening credits sequence (with the *Secret Killer* title) and every gory knife slash intact, this presentation is even more valuable because it finally preserves the original scope compositions with anamorphic enhancement to boot. Some compression problems pop up during darker scenes and the black levels look a bit pasty, but this is by far the best this film has looked on home video. The dubbed German track is presented in a gimmicky 5.1 mix (which at least utilizes Nicolai's stereo music tracks); it's distracting but fares better than Marketing-Film's earlier job on *All the Colors of the Dark*. A German mono track is also included, but most viewers will want to opt for the original English track, which is looped of course (this is an Italian horror film after all) and features the usual dubbing crew we've come to know and love. Extras include a newly constructed and fairly respectable trailer (though the catchy U.S. one is worth tracking down, too). The disc also contains a gallery and a batch of promo spots for other titles in the series, most of them shot on video and, by all appearances, pretty dire.

THE FACELESS MONSTER (NIGHTMARE CASTLE)

B&W, 1965, 100m. / Directed by Mario Caiano / Starring Barbara Steele, Paul Müller, Rik Battaglia, Helga Liné / Retromedia (US R1 NTSC) / WS (1.66:1), Madacy (US R0 NTSC)

 One of the more widely seen Euro horrors from the golden age, *Amanti d'oltretomba* has circulated for years under a variety of titles, most commonly in a drastically truncated version entitled *Nightmare Castle*. Though no great shakes as a horror film, this Gothic conflation of Italian horror tropes is a smorgasbord of delights for Barbara Steele fans.

After falling out of love with her money-grubbing, disinterested scientist husband, Stephen (Paul Müller), raven-haired Muriel (Steele) dallies in the greenhouse with the studly groundskeeper, David (Rik Battaglia). Unfortunately the doc catches them in the act, chains them to a wall, and begins torturing them to death, pausing only momentarily when Muriel claims she's revised her will, leaving her fortune to her goody-goody sister, Jenny (Steele again). Stephen follows through by electrocuting the lovers, surgically slicing out their hearts, and burning the remains. While not busy transfusing experimental serums into his haggard maid (Helga Liné), Stephen woos the mentally unstable Jenny and makes her his wife. However, she's soon suffering from bizarre dreams involving a stocking-faced killer in the greenhouse; will Jenny catch on to the murderous plot in time, or are supernatural forces also conspiring to unmask the villainous doctor?

Thanks to the workmanlike direction of genre-hopping director Mario Caiano, this Steele vehicle goes through the motions without ever tapping into the darker, visually arresting territory of *Black Sunday* or *The Horrible Dr. Hichcock*. What we get instead is a kinkier version of those old Boris Karloff potboilers like *The Black Room*, filled with plenty of wandering around dark castles, murders for profit, and scheming baddies who get theirs in the final reel. The real appeal here is watching Steele strut her stuff, both dark-haired and blonde, in roles ranging from tortured victim to terrorized innocent to vengeful, disfigured ghost. The black and white cinematography is serviceable, as is the loud, organ-filled Ennio Morricone score (interesting as a precursor to his work on *Bluebeard*, at the very least).

Clocking in just under 80 minutes, the standard short cut of *Nightmare Castle* has long been a home video mainstay thanks to its public domain status. Madacy issued this version on DVD in a murky, sorry-looking edition paired up with the fascinating *Track of the Vampire*, while those seeking the longer cut often had to make do with the English language, Japanese VHS release, *Night of the*

Doomed. Retromedia's DVD of the complete cut, bearing the title of *The Faceless Monster*, looks significantly rougher than the Japanese transfer, with loads of digital glitches cluttering up the image. A loud, digital hissing sound is also evident for the first five minutes, then mercifully disappears. Part of the problem lies with the brightness level, which can be rectified with a little player or TV adjustment to get the black levels back to normal. However, it's reasonably priced and complete, and it's certainly an improvement over most other home video options. Extras are limited to a meagre Steele gallery of stills, which will be of interest to her fans at least. A no-frills version of the same transfer was later reissued by Retromedia as part of its "Euro Fiends from the Grave" release, packed in with *Satanik* and a new-to-DVD release of the Renzo Russo's 1971 necrophilic oddity, *The Red-Headed Corpse*, starring Farley Granger and Erika Blanc. Note: An authorized, remastered version under the *Nightmare Castle* title has since been released as a wholly separate edition by Severin and is covered in-depth in *DVD Delirium Volume 4*.

FAMILY PLOT

Colour, 1976, 119m. / Directed by Alfred Hitchcock / Starring Barbara Harris, Bruce Dern, Cathleen Nesbitt, William Devane, Karen Black / Universal (US R1 NTSC, UK R2 PAL) / WS (1.85:1)

Strangely ignored to this day, Hitchcock's final film received a lukewarm response upon its release (no doubt as it came on the heels of the far more vicious *Frenzy*) and seemed somewhat out of step at the time, closer to a light Disney adventure than more modern shockers like *Taxi Driver* and *Jaws*. On its own terms, this is a sweet and gentle swan song, a whimsical romp with some nice directorial flourishes and committed performances. The biggest scene stealer is Barbara Harris as Madame Blanche, a phoney psychic (of course) whose latest customer, Julia Rainbird (Cathleen Nesbitt), is tormented by sleepless nights and constant guilt over her family's rejection of her sister's illegitimate child. Offered a $10,000 payment for information leading to the now grown son, Blanche enlists the aid of her irritable cab driver boyfriend, George Lumley (Bruce Dern), to do her legwork. Meanwhile scheming jeweller Arthur Adamson (William Devane) and his conflicted, often bewigged girlfriend Fran (Karen Black) pull off a series of high profile abductions in exchange for valuable diamonds, cleverly tucked away into Adamson's chandelier. George's investigation overlaps with the villainous pair's latest plot involving the Bishop at St. Anselm's Cathedral, and soon the two plot strands come together with clues involving a fatal fire, a phoney tombstone, and a boy named Eddie Shoebridge once thought dead.

Apart from a few hypodermic syringe jabs, a comical car chase and some mildly racy banter between Harris and Dern, *Family Plot* is extremely benign fare carried along by the breeziness of its execution. Apart from an oddly lethargic middle third, which leaves everyone but Dern spinning their wheels offscreen, the story affords some delicious interplay between all four leads. Devane never seems all that menacing despite his gleaming teeth and moustache; it's hard to imagine this con man actually following through on his threat to kill one of his captives. The charming enterprise is also helped by a bouncy score from John Williams, at the time two films into his relationship with Steven Spielberg.

Universal's DVD improves considerably on overly bright prior transfers, which exposed the already shoddy rear projection during the nocturnal driving scenes to the point where everyone suffered from distracting blue halos around their heads. These bits still look clumsy but are at least properly colour timed and watchable on this widescreen presentation, which adds some much needed breathing room to the sides of the frame. The transfer still looks grainy, even more so than usual due to the increased resolution. The biggest extra is a 48-minute documentary, "Plotting *Family Plot*", from the reliable Laurent Bouzareau. Assistant director Howard Kazanjian takes most of the discussion chores here, relating in especially fascinating detail the short tenure of Roy Thinnes in the Adamson role before Devane took over. Much-needed attention is also paid to the development of the screenplay, originally entitled *Deceit*, from its more sober literary source, Victor Canning's *The Rainbird Pattern*. Dern, Black and Devane appear for new interview footage (where's Harris?) in which they fondly chat about their tenure with Hitch during his final years. John Williams even pops up to mention how he got his composing gig. Two rough-looking theatrical trailers are included, along with car chase storyboards, a photo and poster gallery, and production notes and cast bios. A subsequent reissue as part of Universal's Hitchcock remasters even manages to look a bit crisper and more colourful in comparison but doesn't warrant an upgrade as much as other titles in the collection.

THE FAN

Colour, 1981, 95m. / Directed by Edward Bianchi / Starring Lauren Bacall, James Garner, Michael Biehn, Maureen Stapleton / Paramount (US R1 NTSC) / WS (1.85:1) (16:9)

Inspired by the success of independent fright flicks like *Halloween*, major studios wanted to capitalize on the growing trend by cranking out horror films of their own. Having the successful formula down, Paramount retooled an already finished thriller by adding exploitative elements such as graphic gore scenes that would hopefully attract the ever-growing horror audience of the day (as well as the mainstream crowd), but the resulting film didn't fare well in either group. *The Fan* stars Lauren Bacall as Sally Ross, an older actress about to make her debut on Broadway in a new musical. While prepping for her show-stopping role, she finds herself the target of an obsessive young fan (*The Terminator*'s Michael Biehn) who bombards her with letters professing his extreme love for her. These letters are intercepted by Ms. Ross's personal assistant (Maureen Stapleton), who tries to calm the situation, but when the fan doesn't get the responses he wants, he goes wacko, bent on killing Ms. Ross and her friends.

It's still hard to believe that a big-budget exploitation film like *The Fan* was made by a major studio with A-list stars, considering its extreme subject matter. Even more mind-blowing is the fact that actors like Lauren Bacall and James Garner would appear in a huge sleazy mess like this. Bacall might have signed on because it allowed her the opportunity to sing and dance to musical numbers written by famed composer Marvin Hamlisch. Seeing her sing "Hearts Not Diamonds" is a campy highlight, as she doesn't display too much talent as a song and dance personality. James Garner as Bacall's two-timing husband is wasted in a part that's so underwritten he immediately fades from memory. As the deranged fan, Biehn (in his first role) is semi-convincing, but the script doesn't given any reason why he is so obsessed with the ageing starlet and what makes him tick. However, the biggest problem is the studio's interference in trying to make the movie something it isn't. *The Fan* was based on a book by Bob Randell that was originally written as a suspense piece, a series of letters between stalker and victim. The movie was to be a vehicle for Elizabeth Taylor with Jeff Lieberman directing, but when the project was delayed, both left the picture. Enter Lauren Bacall and Edward

Bianchi, who filmed this as a straight thriller; however, when horror films became popular, it was reshot to add some gore to appeal to the horror audiences of the day. The finished movie was scheduled for an early 1981 release, but it suffered another blow when John Lennon was assassinated. The ending had to be completely reworked and reshot yet again. As you can imagine, this makes the film a real mix and match job, alternating between scenes that try to look pretty classy while others are repugnant and sleazy (e.g., the swimming pool scene and the throat-slashing outside a gay bar). Add to that extremely tacky musical numbers and uncomfortable-looking actors, and you've got a real mess on your hands with no target audience.

The film is given an anamorphic transfer, and unfortunately it doesn't appear that much work was put into locating decent elements. Colours are slightly faded with quite a bit of dirt and wear on the print. The mono soundtrack is about on par with the video. Dialogue is sometimes really hard to make out, as the track sounds very tinny. Nothing extra is included, not even a trailer; it would be fascinating to see how they sold this, especially after all the retooling.

– ES

FAR FROM HEAVEN

Colour, 2002, 108m. / Directed by Todd Haynes / Starring Julianne Moore, Dennis Quaid, Dennis Haysbert, Patricia Clarkson, Viola Davis, James Rebhorn, Celia Weston / Universal (US R1 NTSC), Entertainment In Video (UK R2 PAL), Video Film Express (Holland R2 PAL) / WS (1.85:1) (16:9) / DD5.1

 In the 1950s, sheltered New England housewife Cathy (Julianne Moore) discovers her husband (Dennis Quaid) is, in the parlance of the period, a homosexual, and finds solace in the company of her overqualified gardener (Dennis Haysbert), who happens to be black, to the shock and dismay of both her best friend (Patricia Clarkson) and her tightly-knit community. But this simple synopsis is merely the jumping-off point for Todd Haynes's loving homage to the cinematic melodramas of Douglas Sirk and, to a lesser extent, Max Ophüls.

Utilizing both the language of words and the camera of Sirk's films, Haynes creates a stylized world that miraculously amplifies and, more importantly, humanizes the characters as they struggle within the confines of the restricted society of 1950s American life. Moore is simply brilliant as Cathy Whitaker, making this seemingly-conventional character real and heartbreaking. It helps that Moore is supported by actors who are also more than up to the challenges of delivering the script's intentionally stilted dialogue in a naturalistic manner. Haysbert (of television's *24*) brings a warmth and intelligence to his part that easily makes it possible for Cathy to consider leaving the safety of her world ("I have to get back", she explains to him at one point, even though she's just stepped around the corner of her house) for his company. To say that Quaid's performance as Cathy's husband is a revelation would be to ignore the obvious quality of his underrated work in previous films, but his performance here will come as a surprise to those who have never considered him a "serious" actor. Clarkson is particularly fine as Cathy's best friend, and deservedly won praise for her layered portrayal. Rarely has a movie been so ideally cast; even in smaller roles, actors like Viola Davis, James Rebhorn and Celia Weston make indelible impressions.

Far from Heaven complements the brilliance of its casting with rich and carefully-composed cinematography by Edward Lachman, using a saturated colour palette that evokes the Technicolor topography of Sirk without drawing undue attention to itself. Unlike recent period fare such as *O Brother, Where Art Thou?*, there is no digital grading (computerized colour adjustment) of the photography in *Far from Heaven*, instead relying on carefully placed expressionistic lighting (the artificial blue of the "moonlit" shots) and happy coincidence (the sun coming out on Moore as she stands outside a clinic) to achieve its effect. Underlining everything is a beautiful romantic score by Elmer Bernstein, most helpful in bringing the tragedy of Quaid's character to the surface, since his Whitaker is a man whose language has no words for the situation in which he finds himself.

Universal's Region 1 and Entertainment In Video's Region 2 DVDs of *Far from Heaven* feature a crisp transfer of the film, commentary by director Haynes, a short "making-of" featurette, an episode of the Sundance channel show "Anatomy of a Scene" focusing on the filming of the party scene, and a brief clip of director Haynes and star Julianne Moore speaking about the film to a gathering of film students. For real completists, the two-disc Dutch release carries over everything (apart from the talent notes) along with exclusive extras including 11 minutes of B-roll footage, additional soundbite interviews with the cast, "selected clip" highlights, and an additional European trailer. Ignore the terrible yellow and brown cover art of the U.S. disc, which strangely obscures the vibrant nature of the film it is supposed to be promoting.
– TSG

FASSBINDER'S BRD TRILOGY: THE MARRIAGE OF MARIA BRAUN

Colour, 1978, 120m. / Directed by Rainer Werner Fassbinder / Starring Hanna Schygulla, Klaus Löwitsch, George Byrd / Criterion (US R0 NTSC), Arrow (UK R2 PAL) / WS (1.66:1) (16:9)

LOLA

Colour, 1981, 113m. / Directed by Rainer Werner Fassbinder / Starring Barbara Sukowa, Armin Mueller-Stahl, Mario Adorf / Criterion (US R0 NTSC), Artificial Eye (UK R2 PAL) / WS (1.66:1) (16:9)

VERONIKA VOSS

B&W, 1982, 104m. / Directed by Rainer Werner Fassbinder / Starring Rosel Zech, Hilmar Thate, Annemarie Düringer / Criterion (US R0 NTSC), Artificial Eye (UK R2 PAL) / WS (1.66:1) (16:9)

Finding a thematic link between many of Fassbinder's intensely personal films can be tricky, but this splendidly appointed four-disc set from Criterion ties together three of his studies on post-war German culture. Dubbed the "BRD Trilogy" (that's "Bundesrepublik Deutschland", by the way), the films all focus on one strong woman building a life after the war; often combining comedy, tragedy, and eroticism within the same story, these movies dovetail nicely with each other and form a sort of loose study in the director's evolving but always distinct style.

The most internationally famous of the three, *The Marriage of Maria Braun* (*Die Ehe der Maria Braun*), stars Fassbinder's frequent muse Hanna Schygulla as the title character, a woman married during the turbulent final days of Allied bombing in Germany. Her soldier husband, Hermann (Klaus Löwitsch), is separated in the chaos after one day of wedded bliss and trots off to Russia; soon Maria is cozying up to American soldiers to learn her spouse's whereabouts. News of his death sends her into the arms of another man, a soldier named Bill (George Byrd) who falls in love with her. Unfortunately their liaison is interrupted by Hermann's unexpected return, the consequences of which swiftly result in Hermann being carted off to prison. Always resourceful, Maria goes to work earning money to have a comfortable life ready when he finally gets out. However, the temptations of power, money, and other men prove to be a strain on her loyalty, and her plan works out far differently than she had imagined.

Featuring a powerhouse lead performance and studied, well-composed camerawork, this remains one of the director's more accessible films; while the theme of emotional deadening and financial corruption might not sound like much fun, Fassbinder keeps the story moving briskly with a wry sense of humour about our heroine's need to get along in a society where political winds shift on a daily basis. For the groundlings there's enough titillation in the form of Maria's amorous encounters over the years, but the sex really takes a backseat to the elaborate plot machinations which function as a satire on the corrupt development of Germany in the aftermath of war.

Substantially lighter, at least on the surface, is the wild fantasia of *Lola*, whose title immediately announces its intentions as a riff on Josef Von Sternberg's *The Blue Angel*. Here our capitalistic siren, played by Barbara Sukowa (*M. Butterfly*), is a nightclub performer and whore in the service of wealthy, cheerfully decadent Schukert (*The Bird with the Crystal Plumage*'s Mario Adorf), with whom she has a child out of wedlock. Enter morally pure Von Bohm (Armin Mueller-Stahl), a building commissioner who threatens Schuckert's financial grip on the city. On a bet with her patron, Lola plays innocent and sets out to seduce Von Bohm, who falls in love with her. However, the interplay of emotions and money prove to be more complicated than either of them imagined.

Unlike its predecessor, there's nothing naturalistic about *Lola* at all. Shot through with glowing primary colours that make Dario Argento and Pedro Almodóvar look restrained in comparison, this is a stylist's dream come true. Characters are constantly bathed in particular shades to emphasize their moral condition: Lola equals red, Von Bohm equals blue, and so on. Scene transitions are usually accomplished with elaborate dissolves in and out of focus, and the constant flow of cigarette smoke provides an appropriately gauzy visual texture. For some reason Sukowa remains one of the less internationally renowned actresses, which is a shame; she really cuts loose here with a magnetic performance, including one musical freak-out that gives Ann-Margret a run for her money. In a twisted sense, this is also one of Fassbinder's most cheerful films; the characters celebrate their corruption and infidelities, and as the seemingly incorruptible hero finds his scruples eroding with Lola's influence, the film closes on an ironic "happy" note whose consequences are left to be addressed in the viewer's mind.

The visual and thematic opposite of *Lola*, *Veronika Voss* finds its fallen heroine in a black-and-white Germany whose appearance resembles the glittering surfaces of a Von Sternberg film; unfortunately something is very rotten underneath. A former UFA cinema star, Veronika (Rosel Zech) runs into reporter Robert (Hilmar Thate) during a rainstorm and, after a reluctant bus ride, accompanies him home for a half-hearted tryst. Her star rapidly falling, Veronika has not fared well since the war and, even worse, has become addicted to morphine thanks to the questionable medical practices of her physician, Dr. Katz (Annemarie Düringer). Unfortunately Veronika's attempts at a comeback do not fare well, and Robert's earnest quest to end the corrupt doctor's plans also encounters a few nasty snags.

While these films could most obviously be read as a parallel to the experience of post-war Germany epitomized as three women (or, if you prefer, one woman under three different names), they could also easily be read as a sardonic commentary on the role of success and celebrity in a more disillusioned era. The first film follows a rise to power, a capitalist climb with an ultimate disillusionment; the second depicts the height of excess and success, an orgy of colour and corruption; the third, sapped of colour, casts a mirror back at the past and follows the decline of fame and fortune. Of course, the parallels to Fassbinder himself are unmistakable; *Maria Braun* found him at the peak of critical acclaim, a rising force in the film world with a stable of actors. *Lola* finds him indulging in gleeful directorial excess of the highest order, like Douglas Sirk on acid. By the time of *Veronika Voss*, his penultimate film, his drug addiction was about to claim his life. Each film also offers the opportunity to witness the Fassbinder crew at various stages, particularly composer Peer Raben; his triptych of works represents a beautiful contrast in styles, integrating Germany's music hall and theatrical heritage into a beautiful group of orchestral scores.

All three transfers look magnificent, framed at 1.66:1 with anamorphic enhancement. Playback in 16:9 (which tends to mask off to 1.78:1 on many monitors) may result in some peculiar framing during the opening credits for each film; Fassbinder uses the odd device of repeating the names numerous times across the screen in linear strips, with portions of information deliberately running off the screen. Naturally *Lola* is the most dramatic piece of the set; its ultra-gaudy colours look magnificent and certainly surpass the smeary VHS transfers found in Europe. Inexplicably, the Criterion release is the film's first-ever appearance on American video.

Each disc comes with its own audio commentary featuring different participants. *Maria Braun* finds cinematographer Michael Ballhaus and director Wim Wenders discussing the film in great detail; a few bits of Ballhaus's talk cover information from his earlier *Whity* commentary, but for the most part this is a fresh and new experience. Also included are video interviews with Schygulla (who looks great and fondly recalls her projects with the extremely prolific director) and Fassbinder scholar Eric Rentschler, who puts the film in context within the volatile chronology of the filmmaker's life. For *Lola*, commentary duties go to Fassbinder biographer and friend Christian Braad Thomsen; it's an extremely factual and

structured talk, with very few conversational asides, and offers some good insights into the visual construction of the film despite Thomsen's notably strong accent. (This commentary works best in separate chunks than a continuous experience.) Sukowa turns up for a welcome video interview in which she charts the elaborate process of how she came to work for Fassbinder in *Berlin Alexanderplatz* and how *Lola* came to be. Fassbinder co-writer Peter Märthesheimer appears for a separate video interview, explaining his own collaborative experiences. *Veronika Voss* features a commentary with Fassbinder scholar (how many are there anyway?) Tony Rayns, who covers the latter stages of the director's life and discusses the various cultural influences on the film. A fine companion piece to the commentary (best viewed afterwards) is a one-hour documentary, *Dance with Death* (*Tanz mit dem Tod*), about the life of UFA actress Sybille Schmitz (*Vampyr*), whose tragic life was more or less the inspiration for this movie. Video conversations with Zech and editor Juliane Lorenz also cover the making of the film, focusing on how the amazing period look and feel was created through performance and pacing.

If that weren't enough, a fourth disc of supplements is also included. The 90-minute *I Don't Just Want You to Love Me* is an astoundingly rich documentary covering all things Fassbinder from his scrappy early days through his lavish final works. Most of the more unsavoury aspects of his life are acknowledged but not dwelled upon, with his colleagues offering a mostly positive perspective on a man who was either blazingly brilliant or impossible to be around, depending on his mood. The man himself appears in a rare 45-minute German TV interview for *Life Stories*; apparently he was good friends with the interviewer and agreed to discuss his creative process in far more depth than usual. More video interviews are included with Fassbinder cinematographer Xaver Schwarzenberger (whose work on *Veronika Voss* is never less than breathtaking), Fassbinder scholar Laurence Kardish (yes, another one!), and editor Juliane Lorenz. Finally, each film's theatrical trailer is included; all of them are in very good shape, and the promo for *Maria Braun* is the most striking thanks to some fancy explosion-style transition effects. Set aside a few days for this one; the time spent is well worth it.

In the U.K., licensing issues prevented the films from being grouped together; *Maria Braun* is out from Arrow in a slimmer package (also included in their "Fassbinder Commemorative Collection 73-82 Volume 2" box set with seven other films) which features a half-hour "Fassbinder Frauen" overview of his heroines, an interactive guide to his regular acting troupe, a 35-minute featurette with Florian Hopf covering his filmography, Fassbinder's "The Little Chaos" short film, the trailer, and liner notes by Jim Clark. The other two BRD films are available in stripped-down editions from Artificial Eye, split into the first and second volumes of their own Fassbinder four-film box set releases.

THE FEAR CHAMBER

Colour, 1968, 87m. / Directed by Juan Ibáñez and Jack Hill / Starring Boris Karloff, Julissa, Charles East, Isela Vega, Yerye Beirute / Elite (US R0 NTSC) / WS (1.85:1) (16:9), Retromedia (US R0 NTSC) / WS (1.85:1)

Of the four Mexican films for which Boris Karloff shot scenes in the last months of his life, this is the only one to abandon period Gothic settings for a contemporary sci-fi look. It's an evil blob movie, with some overtones of Karloff's *The Sorcerers* and quite a surprising amount of go-go sleaze.

Dr. Carl Mandel (Karloff) supervises a program of experimentation on a living rock found near the centre of the Earth; this creature feeds on a substance generated by fear in the female brain, leaving young chicks shrivelled into dead old women when its rocky tendril siphons the stuff. In a scene that seems as if Karloff shot it for yet another movie, Mandel dresses up as a devil-worshipper and presides over one Satanic ceremony to scare a test subject, but then reverts to fatherly and decent for the rest of the film (he doesn't even die at the end). Helga (Isela Vega, the only other "name" in any of the four films), Mandel's lab assistant, takes over as abductor and torturer of young women, aided by Roland (Yerye Beirute), a diamond-obsessed Lenny-like minion who thinks the rock thing is his friend and will make him "king of the world". Like all of these Ibáñez-Hill collaborations, the film consists of self-contained weird sequences strung together with only Karloff's exposition to tie up the plot, and a few chunks of the star's dialogue post-dubbed by someone who sounds nothing like him. It's sort of fun but makes no sense.

Retromedia's Drive-In Theater DVD is introduced by company head Fred Olen Ray and sidekick Miss Kim. Ray admits "the print's all scratchy and beat-up, the colour turning pink", but actually the release looks better than either Something Weird Video's *Snake People* (a co-feature with *Rattlers*) or Acme Video's *Dance of Death* (*Alien Terror*, the fourth in the batch, has yet to turn up on DVD). The transfer is letterboxed and colourful, offering credits in Spanish (*La camara del terror*) and the real names of filmmakers mangled or Anglicised on the other releases. The packaging promises "exclusive stills gallery" and "vintage drive-in spots", but the special features wouldn't access on the disc under review. However, the definitive (to date) presentation of the film comes courtesy of Elite's later (2005) version, which features a more robust and finely detailed anamorphic transfer, 5.1 and mono

F

options in English, and a typically fast-paced and entertaining Jack Hill commentary track as well. For some reason the film's most risqué scene (a topless girl ageing rapidly while doing a go-go routine) is presented as an extra here but is part of the regular feature on the Retromedia disc.

– KN

FELIDAE

Colour, 1994, 78m. / Directed by Michael Schaack / Mediacs (Germany R2 PAL) / WS (1.85:1) (16:9) / DD5.1

 Adapted from the first in a highly successful series of mystery novels by Akif Pirinçci, this gruesome mixture of Walt Disney and Italian *giallo* has the distinction of being populated almost exclusively by cats. Traditionally animated with a beautiful palette of blinding colours, this is certainly not kiddie fare and much more likely to please horror buffs with a perverse edge. Or as the hero observes at one point, "It became obvious I wasn't watching something out of *The Aristocats*." No kidding!

Our story begins when furry puzzle solver Francis moves into a new neighbourhood with his crime writer owner. While prowling the neighbourhood he meets foul-mouthed, one-eyed Bluebeard, who shows him the latest gruesome casualty in a series of brutal kitty sex killings. That's right, these tomcats were all "excited" at the moment of death when their throats were sliced open. When a sweet blind cat named Felicity turns up decapitated, Francis takes the murders personally and vows to unmask the culprit. Along the way he stumbles upon the Claudandus cult, led by the imperious Joker, a sect of kitties devoted to electro-shock rituals, and uncovers a terrible secret involving animal experimentation.

Stealing the crown from *Watership Down* as the most brutal all-animal cartoon feature, *Felidae* is both impeccably mounted and consistently shocking. Even years after Ralph Bakshi, it's jarring to behold cute cats swearing and slashing. The film also refuses to anthropomorphise its hero; Francis makes gory work of mice and has savage, neck-biting sex with passing females – hardly typical behaviour of a screen detective. The film also contains a number of bravura artistic sequences, including a breathless, highly suspenseful rooftop pursuit and a shocking, Gerald Scarfe-style dream sequence with hundreds of disembowelled cats dancing on puppet strings.

The German DVD features a terrific anamorphic transfer with nary a print flaw in sight. The German soundtrack is presented in both 5.1 and 2.0 surround, with optional German subtitles; this track is primarily of interest for its celebrity voices, including Klaus Maria Brandauer as the elderly Pascal, Mario Adorf (the cat-nivorous artist from *The Bird with the Crystal Plumage*) as Bluebeard, Fassbinder regular Wolfgang Hess as Kong, and Ulrich Tucker (Soderbergh's *Solaris*) as Francis. English-speaking viewers will probably have more use for the English dubbed track (in 2.0 surround), which is a little shaky at times but faithfully translates the German version right down to Francis's off-handed, randy narration. (No English subtitles for purists, alas.) The disc contains a bounty of German-only extras: an audio commentary from director Michael Schaak (whose later *Käpt'n Blaubär* is also trailered on this DVD) and co-writers Veit Vollmer and Komplettes Hörbuch; a half-hour documentary featuring studio recordings of the actors, footage of the artists at work, and an interview with Pirinçci; storyboards and paintings; a cruddy-looking trailer; and a complete audio version of the novel divided by chapter selections. The disc is also available in a limited boxed set edition with a paperback of the second instalment in the series, *Francis: Felidae 2*.

FEMME FATALE

Colour, 2002, 116m. / Directed by Brian De Palma / Starring Rebecca Romijn-Stamos, Antonio Banderas, Eriq Ebouaney, Edouard Montoute, Peter Coyote, Gregg Henry, Rie Rasmussen / Warner (US R1 NTSC, UK R2 PAL), Paradiso (Holland R2 PAL) / WS (1.85:1) (16:9) / DD5.1

 When a jewel heist at the Cannes Film Festival flounders, Laure Ash (played by Rebecca Romijn-Stamos) double crosses her accomplices (Eriq Ebouaney and Edouard Montoute) and makes off with the booty. Hiding out in Paris, she's presented with a golden opportunity to assume another woman's identity and leave the country. Several years on, however, her past catches up with her when she returns to Paris and paparazzo photographer Nicolas Bardo (Antonio Banderas) snaps her picture. Cover blown, Laure's unforgiving ex-compatriots move in to execute their revenge.

With a couple of exceptions, anything bearing director De Palma's name is worth investigating; if his story-telling technique might on occasion be questionable, there's still plenty to admire in the works of the king of operatic thrillers. With a fistful of frustratingly under-explained plot turns, *Femme Fatale* is an erotic cat and mouse thriller that is neither particularly erotic nor especially thrilling. What it is, however, is thoroughly enthralling viewing. De Palma casts his eye over that age old "What if?" scenario, how a split-second decision can potentially determine one's fate for better or worse. Where it would be churlish to reveal too many of the film's secrets here, it's fair to warn those who have yet to dip into its treasures that attentiveness and patience have never been more paramount in enjoying a De Palma epic. For although there are countless hints as to what might

really be unfolding beyond the obvious – clocks reading the same time, characters popping up as different people in different places, etc. – many of those hints are conveyed almost too subtly to be noticed. After a protracted opening the director builds upon each strata of *Femme Fatale*'s mildly perplexing plot until it towers beyond all reasonable understanding. Yet he's master enough of his medium that every small detail is adequately resolved before he rolls the credits. It helps to have an affinity for foreign language films too. Shooting entirely in Paris, De Palma stays true to reality and instead of having his actors speak English with dodgy French accents, over the half the dialogue in the film is delivered *en français* (with subtitles provided).

De Palma usually stitches a couple of captivating set pieces into his films, often dialogue-light and carried along purely by visual intrigue and a seductive Pino Donaggio composition; in *Dressed to Kill* it was the museum courtship ritual between Angie Dickinson and Ken Baker, in *Blow Out* John Travolta racing to save Nancy Allen from the sharp end of John Lithgow's icepick, in *Carrie* Sissy Spacek's prom night retribution. *Femme Fatale* opens with just such a set piece, a hypnotic effusion of equivocal events that are part of an elaborate diamond theft, audaciously improbable yet sizzling with tension for all that. Here, however, the set pieces are coupled with a lush score by Ryuichi Sakamoto – something akin to Donaggio by way of Ravel – and the experience is intoxicating.

With limited film experience under her belt, Rebecca Romijn-Stamos (*X-Men*) is no earth-shaking actress but carries the weight of the film on her slender shoulders superbly. As the anything-for-cash photographer who comes good in the end, Antonio Banderas plays it nicely low-key with one exception, a dreadful scene (which should never have got past the cutting room) in which he feigns fey to charm his way into a hotel room. Peter Coyote (*Bitter Moon*) and Gregg Henry

(*Body Double*) have less pivotal involvement than one might expect, but both are on top form. Eriq Ebouaney – looking as if he's been prepped to enter a Samuel Jackson look-alike contest – is the mean, if slightly under-used heavy who gets a deliciously nasty send-off. Rie Rasmussen sets pulses racing as victim in the heist and, necessity being the mother of invention, relishing a tussle as Stamos's slinky Sapphic squeeze.

Furbished with plenty of the slightly outmoded but undeniably gorgeous dioptre split-screen effects that are his trademark, *Femme Fatale* is De Palma's homage to the bad girl classics of his boyhood (it opens with a TV screen showing Barbara Stanwyck and Fred MacMurray going through their paces in *Double Indemnity*), traditional film noir themes woven into a modern age thriller. The result in assessment may be something of a fractured masterpiece, but if nothing else it almost (that's almost) wipes out bitter memories of the director's previous offering, possibly his most disappointing work to date, the horrible *Mission to Mars*. And where its unoriginal "cop-out" twist at the eleventh hour will probably irritate the devil out of many, it's followed by such a wholly satisfying wrap-up in which all the threads he's fed his audience finally converge (prompting a reassessment of the entire film) that even the least forgiving will feel obliged to concur that De Palma deserves his crown. Perhaps just that bit too esoteric for a broad audience, *Femme Fatale* is nevertheless essential viewing for those who like their cinematic cuisine with a little more meat on its bones.

Warner's Region 1 and 2 DVDs deliver the film in a 1.85:1 matted theatrical ratio with 29 chapter marks. Picture and sound are as clean as you'd expect from such a recent production. Language options are English and French, with subtitling in English, French and Spanish. Supplementary materials comprise of four featurettes with a total running time of just over 40 minutes (though it's heaving with spoilers, so anyone new to *Femme Fatale*

is advised not to touch any of this material before watching the film itself), cast and director filmographies and two different trailers. The somewhat more elaborate Dutch release (with removable subtitles in French and Dutch) splits the extras differently, offering an 11-minute B-roll reel of behind-the-scenes footage, a four-minute making-of featurette, the French trailer, and eight cast and crew interviews each clocking in under five minutes each. This version also offers a slightly punchier DTS track that should thrill Sakamoto enthusiasts.

– TG

LA FEMME INFIDÈLE (THE UNFAITHFUL WIFE)

Colour, 1969, 98m. / Directed by Claude Chabrol / Starring Stéphane Audran, Michel Bouquet, Maurice Ronet / Artedis (France R2 PAL), Pathfinder (US R1 NTSC), Arrow (UK R2 PAL) / WS (1.66:1) (16:9)

Beginning with this film, French director Claude Chabrol and his then-wife, Stéphane Audran, embarked on their remarkable "Hélène cycle" of suspense thrillers, known as such because the actress shares the same character name in each film. (The subsequent titles are *Le boucher*, *La rupture*, *Just Before Nightfall*, and *Without Apparent Motive*.) Here she's Hélène Desvallées, a housewife and mother married to businessman Charles (Michel Bouquet). On the side she's also having an affair with Victor (Maurice Ronet), a bohemian writer, and the suspicious Charles hires a private detective to confirm the awful truth. With evidence in hand, the cuckolded husband decides to confront the writer with a payment offer to stay away from his wife, but things do not go as planned... and murder ensues.

One of Chabrol's finest "domestic thrillers", this psychological study really comes to life with the pivotal confrontation scene between the two men and its violent aftermath. The elaborate manipulations of the central characters form an unexpected emotional quandary in the final movement of the film, which finds Hélène's love for her husband reawakening in a most unexpected fashion. An excellent and often underrated actor, Bouquet has one of his best roles here and makes the most of the legendary final shot, one of the greatest in cinema history.

The film is available as a beautiful anamorphic transfer from France (with a reprocessed "Arkamys sound process" surround track) paired up with *Le boucher*, and there is also a far less attractive flat edition from Pathfinder, riddled with digital noise and pasty black levels. Both feature optional English subtitles. At least the Pathfinder disc contains the original French trailer, while the French DVD is limited to just the feature itself. Best avoided entirely is the U.K. release from Arrow, also available in their eight-title Chabrol set, which is taken from a faded print with clearly substandard compression and a squished aspect ratio that squeezes the image halfway to scope with silly-looking results. Incidentally, Chabrol's film was later remade by Adrian Lyne, in 2002, as the surprisingly good *Unfaithful*.

FIANCÉE OF DRACULA

Colour, 1999, 91m. / Directed by Jean Rollin / Starring Cyrille Iste, Thomas Smith, Jacques Régis, Thomas Desfossé, Magalie Aguado, Brigitte Lahaie / Shriek Show (US R1 NTSC), Redemption (UK R0 PAL) / WS (1.85:1) (16:9)

A virtual catalogue of the images and themes which marked his 1970s vampire films, Jean Rollin's *La fiancée de Dracula* (*The Bride of Dracula*, regrettably translated for DVD as *Fiancée of Dracula*) is a more confident and typical outing for the director than the intensely personal *Two Orphan Vampires*. The grandfather clock from *Shiver of the Vampires*, those omnipresent beach and cliffside scenes, copious nudity, and a romantic sense of melancholy clearly indicate Rollin had lost none of his artistic obsessions over the years, and while it's strange to see his trademark imagery carried over into a milieu outside of the '70s, his surrealist sensibility remained a force to be reckoned with throughout his career.

The film opens in a graveyard, of course, where a vampire expert professor (Jacques Régis) instructs young Thibault (Thomas Smith) in the ways of bloodsucker surveillance and destruction. In a serial-style narrative, the disciples of the presumably deceased Count Dracula lead the men to a nearby convent where the sultry Isabelle (Cyrille Iste) seems to be held in the sway of a diabolical power related to the still-living Dracula (Thomas Desfossé). Meanwhile a number of other supernatural entities roam the countryside. Scheming, devilish nuns hold sway at the convent, while a man-eating ogress (Magalie Aguado) scarfs down her prey in a nearby cave. And let's not forget the malefic jester dwarf, a horseback-riding vampiric aide (Brigitte Lahaie), and a handful of witches for good measure. The smitten Thibault attempts to stop Isabelle from going to meet her betrothed, who pops from one location to another through a magical clock, before the characters finally face off at dawn for a beachside finale.

Guaranteed to provoke bewilderment from newcomers, this film is best recommended to those already well-versed in all things Rollin. The actors behave in a typically somnambulist fashion, and while the story produces an occasional romantic frisson, this isn't meant to be a particularly terrifying film. The low budget production is more of an inconvenience than usual in Rollin's films; the glossy sheen present in even his earliest, unpolished efforts has been dulled somewhat by flat, 1990s-style cinematography. However, his eye for unusual and psychologically piercing visuals remains intact, with the melancholy finale offering a nice updated twist on his aquatic resolutions from *Shiver of the Vampires*, *Lips of Blood* and *The Demoniacs*.

Shriek Show's transfer is a considerable improvement over the misfire of *Two Orphan Vampires*, though the limited lighting and filming conditions don't result in the most ravishing visual experience. Some compression artefacts are visible in dark scenes but overall it's a pleasant enough presentation. Mercifully the only option is the original French soundtrack with optional English subtitles. Apart from the usual gallery of Shriek Show trailers, the only extra is a nine-minute interview with Rollin in which he discusses his influences and the casting procedure for the film. Several years later, in 2009, Redemption issued a U.K. version on disc with a different, 20-minute video conversation with Rollin about his overall career, plus the trailer, a lengthy gallery of production and promotional photos, and additional Redemption promos.

FIRST MEN IN THE MOON

Colour, 1964, 103m. / Directed by Nathan Juran / Starring Edward Judd, Martha Hyer, Lionel Jeffries / Columbia (US R1 NTSC, UK R2 PAL) / WS (2.35:1) (16:9) / DD4.0

Sometimes, an objective view isn't possible. This was the first film I ever saw, and the memories of that theatrical experience overlay every subsequent viewing and in all probability my entire sensibility. It remains a lively, imaginative and colourful picture, wrestling an intrac-

table novel into kiddie matinee shape, but perhaps the spiky H.G. Wells was no more comfortable a source for a Ray Harryhausen Dynamation matinee than Jonathan Swift (*The Three Worlds of Gulliver*). A straight-ahead adventure man like Jules Verne (*Mysterious Island*) was much more congenial, though note the carry-over of certain anti-war cynicism from the earlier films into this spectacle.

It opens wonderfully in the then-near future with a UN space mission touching down on the moon to worldwide acclaim, only to discover a tattered Union Jack and a scribbled note dated 1899 claiming the satellite in the name of Queen Victoria. Harassed officials track down Arnold Bedford (Edward Judd in flaky old age make-up) in a nursing home and he recounts his involvement with Professor Cavor (Lionel Jeffries), inventor of an anti-gravity paint (Cavorite) that enables a trip to the moon in an upholstered sphere that tumbles through space. Also included on the crew, thanks to complex but irrelevant plotting, is Bedford's fiancée, an American miss (Martha Hyer) who insists on packing an elephant gun, some live chickens and a pre-mixed bottle of gin and bitters. On the moon, screenwriters Nigel Kneale and Jan Read try to reconcile 1964-vintage scientific knowledge with Wells's 1901 vision as the surface is a pitted, airless desert while a thriving insect civilisation of Selenites toils in caves and tunnels below. It may be that the semi-fascist insects of the moon owe something to the Martians of Kneale's *Quatermass and the Pit*, though the notion of aliens who represent an exaggerated version of human failings dates back to Wells.

As with many Harryhausen films, a lot of disparate elements are tossed together and scrambled, with the effects man doing more to qualify as auteur of the piece than the competent traffic cop entrusted with the job of direction (Nathan Juran is a dependable hand, but no Cy Endfield). The earthly scenes are hectic with slapstick comedy and an all-over-the-place performance from Jeffries, though there's an interesting depiction of Judd as a grasping reprobate of a hero, going along on the voyage only because he's been told the moon is studded with gold nuggets and prone to bursts of violence, irresponsibility and sulking. In outer space and on the moon, the film comes up with one crisis after another to fill the screen with wonders and a traditional monster in a giant caterpillar replaces Wells's "mooncalf". Cavor's exhilaration ("hello moon", he bellows upon emerging from the sphere) is carried over into the film's breathless pace as we hurry through encounters with the Selenites, the Grand Lunar and their *This Island Earth*-style civilisation. A punchline, adapted from *War of the Worlds*, is surprisingly bleak: staying behind to reason with the Selenites, who are alarmed by Bedford's two-fistedness, Cavor passes on a cold which wipes out the entire race.

Columbia's Ray Harryhausen Signature Collection presentation is optimal. The sole Dynamation adventure in 2.35:1 Panavision, the film looks magical, showing off imaginative art direction and lighting – especially in the pastel-glowing sub-lunarian sequences that might be influenced by the 1959 film of "Journey to the Centre of the Earth". The anamorphic transfer is so perfect that it becomes slightly too apparent that the Selenites are more often small people in rubber suits than proper Harryhausen-animated creations. The extras are familiar from other releases in this series: the "This is Dynamation" featurette and the "Harryhausen Chronicles" documentary, plus trailers, a photo gallery and optional subtitles in a clutch of languages. Those who list *John Carpenter's Vampires* or *Wes Craven Presents Dracula 2000* under J or W might consider the onscreen title to be *H.G. Wells's First Men in the Moon*.

– KN

FLASH GORDON

B&W, 1936, 245m. / Directed by Frederick Stephani / Starring Larry "Buster" Crabbe, Charles Middleton, Frank Shannon, Jean Rogers, Priscilla Lawson, Jack "Tiny" Lipson, Richard Alexander, James Pierce, Glenn Strange / Image (US R1 NTSC), Delta (US R0 NTSC, UK R0 PAL)

The distant planet of Mongo is on a collision course with Earth. After a chance meeting with maverick scientist Dr. Hans Zarkov (Frank Shannon), who is planning a voyage to the planet in his specially constructed rocketship, Flash Gordon (Larry "Buster" Crabbe) and Dale Arden (Jean Rogers) find themselves headed into deep space. But upon arriving on Mongo they discover its rogue trajectory is no natural phenomenon, for the black hearted Emperor Ming (Charles Middleton) has adopted a hostile attitude to Earth and its inhabitants.

Originally seen as part of the Saturday morning children's shows of the 1930s, I first encountered Larry Crabbe's episodic *Flash Gordon* escapades some 40 years on from their premiere, unspooling when BBC television screened them – one episode each morning – over Christmas 1976. Corny as they were, it was easy to see how each 20-minute instalment of the series would have captivated baying audiences with its awe-inspiring blend of spaceships, ray guns, monsters, death-defying feats of bravery and the most dramatic cliffhanger conclusions imaginable. How often would we see Flash hurtling towards destruction in a rocketship with no controls, the curtain falling as the ship exploded against a cliff face? How could he possibly have survived? No problem for filmmakers with no consciences; at the beginning of the next episode they'd simply splice in a previously unseen shot of Flash producing a handy parachute and bailing out seconds before impact. You'd think there'd have been a collective cry of "Cheat!" throughout theatres across the land, but this was all rousing stuff back in the '30s and the pace was far too rapid to allow such inconsistencies to be dwelled upon; Flash had survived to fight another day, that was all that mattered.

Based on Alex Raymond's comic strip, the 13-part Universal serial tells of the intergalactic trek that brings about the first clash between hunky all-American hero Flash Gordon and the sinister Emperor Ming. Assisting bleached-blonde Crabbe (who later played Buck Rogers) in the fight against evil are beautiful Jean Rogers as Dale Arden and grizzled Frank Shannon (who, someone should have informed him, simply didn't have the legs for pantaloons!) as Zarkov. Charles Middleton (always to be remembered fondly for his attempts to drill some discipline into Laurel and Hardy in *Beau Hunks*) is the epitome of dastardly boo-hiss villainy as Ming the Merciless, bent on annihilating both Gordon and the Earth with the aide of his spoilt bitch daughter Princess Aura (Priscilla Lawson), who has somewhat more lascivious designs on the latter. Incidentally, Crabbe, Middleton and Shannon reprised their roles for two further series – both inferior in this reviewer's opinion – *Flash Gordon's Trip to Mars* (1938 – 15 episodes) and *Flash Gordon Conquers the Universe* (1940 – 12 episodes). Rogers (also in Universal's *Night Key*) returned for *Mars* only, replaced on the third jaunt by Carol Hughes. There's functional support here from Jack "Tiny" Lipson, Richard Alexander and James Pierce as Princes Vultan, Barin and Thun respectively. Prolific Glenn Strange (the Frankenstein monster in *House of Frankenstein*, *House of Dracula* and *Abbott & Costello Meet Frankenstein*) puts in several appearances as a soldier, a robot and the dinosaur-dragon Gocko. Universal buffs will undoubtedly recognise props and sets from, among others, *The Mummy*,

Frankenstein and *Dracula's Daughter*, while most of the score is lifted from other Universal output, notably W. Franke Harling's *The Invisible Man*.

The serial is built, as were all those of the era, on a formulaic succession of punch-ups, captures, escapes and recaptures, and if the plot becomes increasingly lame as it trots along at least it's all good clean fun. In its day, at a reported $350,000, *Flash Gordon* was the most expensive serial ever made – by Universal or anyone else for that matter. The story has been refashioned twice over the years since, once as the porno spoof *Flesh Gordon* in 1973, then later for Mike Hodges's camp replay *Flash Gordon* (1979). Not likely to appeal to everyone – or indeed be something that even the keenest will necessarily want to return to with frequency – in spite of its cheap effects and stereo-typed dialogue the 1936 serial is a genuine diamond in film entertainment.

At one time fashioned into an eighty-something minute feature under the title *Rocketship*, the U.S. Region 1 DVD from Image Entertainment is fortunately the full enchilada, presenting the 13-episode serial uncut under its collective title *Flash Gordon: Space Soldiers* (so re-named in the early 1950s to avoid confusion with a short-lived Gordon TV show). Previously available as a lavish 3-platter laserdisc box set, remarkably the entire series is housed on one side of a single DVD – the wonders of technology, eh? Each instalment – intact with splashy credits sequences and opening "story so far" scroll (mimicked by George Lucas for his *Star Wars* saga) – is an individual chapter with no additional inter-episode chaptering. The image quality is about what you'd expect from something fast approaching its 70th birthday, but this is the best it's ever likely to look. The sound is mono. There are no supplementary materials. A considerably less carefully encoded version for a bargain basement price is also available from Delta, but you get what you pay for.

– TG

FLASHBACK

Colour, 2000, 96m. / Directed by Michael Karen / Starring Valerie Niehaus, Xavier Hutter, Elke Sommer / Trimark (US R1 NTSC), Cinema Club (UK R2 PAL) / WS (1.85:1) (16:9) / DD5.1

"We've had some more sad news this Wednesday evening", intones a local radio newsman. "Another ghastly murder has caused a stir in our town. A man in woman's clothing was spotted; that's probably the only clue!" With this opening, *Flashback* proves that Americans aren't the only ones who can churn out idiotic slasher films. Saddled with a plot packed with gobsmacking story holes and a distracting music score that should have *Scream*'s Marco Beltrami consulting his lawyers, this senseless mixture of slashes and misfired black humour is one of the oddest genre efforts in recent memory.

Subtitled *Mörderische Ferien* (or "Murderous Vacation"), our story ramps out the clichés from the opening sequence in which a necking couple on a train falls prey to a killer in little old lady drag. Next up is a married couple whose young daughter, Jeanette (Valerie Niehaus), survives the attack but spends the next several years in an asylum packed with *Star Wars: The Phantom Menace* fanatics. (A fate worse than death!) Jeanette's shrink decides she's fit for society and sends her off to the mountains as a private French tutor for a trio of spoiled teenage brats. With only the cranky housekeeper (Elke Sommer) to keep them in line, the hormone-riddled pupils are soon teaching their instructor the joys of pool parties and horror films. Meanwhile a killer in drag is stalking the countryside, and Jeanette struggles to remember the entire event from her childhood before she winds up next on the chopping list.

Adapted from an unproduced script by Hammer scribe Jimmy Sangster, the narrative itself feels like an especially late addition to the string of '70s *Psycho* imitations like *Schizo* and *Die! Die! My Darling*, but the necessity to inject gory killings results in some astonishing lapses in logic that rival *I Know What You Did Last Summer* for sheer stupidity. For example, just try to figure out how a traumatic practical joke late in the film negates everything that happened earlier in the story. Even worse, all of the young characters start out as truly loathsome and vicious, then skid downhill from there; you'll be pining for the good old days of those sweet natured, horny kids at Camp Crystal Lake. That said, if you want some undiscriminating gore, the film does deliver a few sick thrills like a body shredded through a mower, a number of sickle attacks, and a surprisingly high body count during the last ten minutes that rivals *Tenebrae* for sheer decimation of its actors. Just don't go in expecting it to make any sense at all.

The Trimark DVD courtesy of Lionsgate contains an immaculate anamorphic transfer of the film. Though lacking in any striking visual style, it all looks fairly attractive and colourful with some beautiful exterior shots to keep things interesting. The surround audio is consistently active but not all that interesting, with synthesized moans and jolts tossed into the rear speakers to goose up some of the slower scenes. The original German track can be played with optional English subtitles, but the dubbed English track is a real laugh riot, packed with canned voices reciting ludicrous dialogue in the most off-handed manner possible. A trailer is also included. The U.K. disc has no extras at all and only contains the dubbed version.

FLAVIA THE HERETIC

Colour, 1974, 101m. / Directed by Gianfranco Mingozzi / Starring Florinda Bolkan, Anthony Corlan [Anthony Higgins] / Synapse (US R1 NTSC) / WS (1.78:1) (16:9), X-Rated (Germany R2 PAL), Shameless (UK R0 PAL) / WS (1.78:1)

Arguably the most notorious entry in Italy's nunsploitation cycle of the 1970s, *Flavia the Heretic* is a charged combination of art house politics and grindhouse sleaze, the exact combination that makes current distributors run screaming. Often released on video in watered-down editions, this nasty concoction is best experienced full strength and gains much of its power by developing dynamic, interesting characters whose grisly fates pack more of a punch than a dozen slashers.

After seeing her would-be lover decapitated by her overbearing father, Flavia (Florinda Bolkan) is packed up and sent to a remote convent where she lives a humdrum, hypocritical existence under the thumb of a fiendish Mother Superior. Flavia decides to leave the church for greener pastures and makes the acquaintance of a Hassidic scholar, but soon she winds up back under the fiendish lash of her holy sisters. Salvation seems to arrive in the form of a Muslim sect, the Tarantulas, with whom Flavia becomes an emancipated leader in a violent revolt. Drawn in by the sect's charismatic leader (*Vampire Circus*'s Anthony Corlan, aka Anthony Higgins), Flavia chops off her hair and embarks on a tragic journey that leads from hunger for power to gruesome agony.

Capped by a now legendary final scene of unbearable sadism, *Flavia* looks for all the world like a respectable film for the most part... except for those startling detours into animal castration, mass slaughter, disembodied head hoisting, and a Jodorowsky-style sequence in which a naked woman clambers in and out of a giant, hollowed-out animal carcass. Bolkan's magnetic presence keeps the viewer's eye riveted to the screen even during her long non-verbal sequences; even when our heroine descends into pure, bloodthirsty madness, her plight is compelling enough to make the unavoidable ending all the more painful.

Shot in lush, earthy tones, the film is also a feast for the eye, with the camera wandering down medieval hallways and gracing golden meadows occasionally tainted by splashes of blood; the ear is also kept enthralled by a wonderful score from Nicola Piovani (*The Perfume of the Lady in Black*), with one of those gorgeous, haunting main themes that often makes a perfect counterpoint to the gruesome goings-on.

Those who have suffered the agony of non-subtitled Italian tapes or the heavily censored Redemption tape and VCD versions of *Flavia* will find Synapse's DVD a long overdue revelation. Image quality is razor sharp with excellent black levels and a lush, bronzed colour scheme that often saturates the screen. Darker scenes tend to get a little grainy, which is how this has always looked, but it's never distracting. The long-censored gore and nudity remain quite strong by today's standards, with some very convincing special effects (apart from some overtly latex-enhanced breast mayhem) and rampant full frontal nudity making this a potent reminder of how dizzying Eurosleaze viewing can be. Like many European films of the period, this was shot with the major actors speaking English and later looped in the studio, so the English track is for all intents and purposes the legitimate one. The disc also includes a stills gallery and a video interview with Bolkan, who proves to be quite intelligent and articulate. The sound quality (recorded in a restaurant) can be a little distracting at times, but it's worth the effort to hear what she has to say. The German release is a non-anamorphic 2 disc set which includes a soundtrack CD, while the much later (2008) Shameless disc is also non-anamorphic (but boasts a 16:9 claim on the box) and fills out the rest of the disc space with the usual reel of cross-promotional trailers.

THE FLY

Colour, 1958, 94m. / Directed by Kurt Neumann / Starring Al Hedison, Patricia Owens, Vincent Price, Kathleen Freeman, Herbert Marshall / Fox (US R1 NTSC, UK R2 PAL) / WS (2.35:1) / DD4.0

THE RETURN OF THE FLY

B&W, 1959, 80m. / Directed by Edward L. Bernd / Starring Vincent Price, Brett Halsey, David Frankham, Dan Seymour / Fox (US R1 NTSC, UK R2 PAL) / WS (2.35:1)

François Delambre (played by Vincent Price) is shocked to receive a telephone call informing him of the death of his brother Andre (Al Hedison), worse still discovering that the cause was having his head and arm crushed flat in a hydraulic press at their co-owned electronics plant. It seems inconceivable that Andre's wife Helene (Patricia Owens) could have done it, yet she calmly admits responsibility. As François gently coaxes the truth out of her, he learns of a scientific experiment gone hideously wrong. Having designed a device for the instantaneous transmission of solid matter from one place to another, Andre had been on the verge of completing his work. Unperturbed by a disastrous attempt to disintegrate and reintegrate the family cat, he subjected himself to the process, unaware that he was sharing the chamber with a common housefly. The reintegration left him with the clawed arm and bulbous head of a giant fly!

Utter the words "Help me!" in a squeaky voice wherever a bunch of movie buffs are gathered together and there won't be one among them unable to identify its source. An acknowledged genre classic, *The Fly* is more famous than anything for the disturbing shot of the miniaturized screaming head of Al Hedison grafted onto the body of a fly that's about to be consumed by a voracious garden spider. The look of disbelieving revulsion on Vincent Price's face as he realizes Helene's story was true makes the hairs on the back of your neck bristle. The film is among the best of several morality fables of the era that underscored the folly of tampering with science. In the wake of the calamitous experiment, Andre's need for Helene to capture the fly with the "funny white head and a sort of white leg" (so that he may repeat the process in the vain hope of unscrambling the mish-mash of molecules that has rendered him mutant) becomes the lynchpin for high tension. Director Kurt Neumann ekes it out to the point that you find yourself holding your breath for fear that exhalation will disturb the fly Helene is on the verge of snaring. Of course, the fact that the opening scenes have already spelled out Andre's fate dissipates the tautness a tad, but waiting round the corner is a wickedly outlandish sting in the tail. With his head mostly covered by a black cloth, the early glimpse of Hedison's clawed arm builds up a degree of expectation for what's lurking beneath that cloth. But, as is usually the way, it's what you think you're going to see as opposed to what you eventually do see that conjures up the most effective chills. The actual revelation is a bit of an anti-climax.

Al Hedison (later known as David, star of TV's *Voyage to the Bottom of the Sea* and the only actor to play James Bond's buddy Felix Leiter twice – in *Live and Let Die* and *Licence to Kill*) performs well enough given the restrictions of his fuzzy overhead mask with its large golden compound eyes and twitching proboscis. The scenes where, unable to eat solid foods, he sucks up milk laced with rum, are distinctly disquieting. And there's a nice bit of business when he struggles to control both the pincered arm and his rapidly deteriorating grasp of reason. Patricia Owens conveys the desperation of the situation convincingly as Helene, while Vincent Price as François pleases as only Vincent Price ever could. Of the remaining cast only Kathleen Freeman (veteran of over 2000 film and TV performances, but most

F

familiar as a regular Jerry Lewis stooge in the likes of *The Nutty Professor*, *Who's Minding the Store* and *The Disorderly Orderly*) as fly-swatting housemaid Emma and British actor Herbert Marshall as Inspector Charras are recognisable. The 1986 remake from David Cronenberg, though brilliantly staged with a far more graphic transformation (of Jeff Goldblum) from man into insect, is nowhere near as gripping as Neumann's original, which is as efficient a piece of fiction now as it was way back in 1958.

Fifteen years after the death of his father, Philippe Delambre (Brett Halsey) tries to convince his Uncle François (Price again) to help him pick up where Papa nearly succeeded – in perfecting a process for matter transference. Fearful of the inherent dangers, François relents, but only to protect his nephew from the consequences of blind ambition. However, there's a rotten apple in the barrel; Philippe's friend and laboratory assistant Alan Hinds (David Frankham) is really crooked refugee from the British justice system Ronald Holmes, in cahoots with mortician Max Berthold (Dan Seymour) to sell the secrets of molecular transmission for their own financial gain.

In actual fact this is *Son of the Fly*, since the downbeat conclusion of the first movie precluded Al Hedison's comeback. Opening with the funeral of Helene Delambre (which also ruled out the return of Patricia Owens) this direct sequel, made just a year after *The Fly*, focuses on grown-up son Philippe and his own insectile mishap. Director Edward L. Bernd wisely retained the Cinemascope picture but the retrograde step from colour to black & white is inevitably a step down. David Frankham is suitably oily as Holmes, the traitor who imprisons Philippe in the transmission chamber, casually drops in a fly, and presses go! When a detective chasing Holmes for his past misdemeanours catches up with him, the hapless gumshoe receives the same treatment, except that his travelling companion across the ether is a hamster. The moment when he integrates as half man-half rodent, complete with giant paws (while the hamster reappears with human hands), is in itself reason enough for tuning in. The fly mask was redesigned for this one, being far bulkier than in the original and less effective for it. But Philippe's squeals – "Cecile! Help me!" – echo Andre's in the original and still send a tingle up your spine. A chirpier ending this time round too, with the relevant scoundrels dead and Philippe restored to his human self by the time the curtain drops. That said, the wrap-up does raise the question of whether jumping back into the disintegrator with the fly and crossing your fingers would really suffice for successful reintegration. Drastic situations call for drastic measures one supposes. A second sequel, the British made *Curse of the Fly* (without Vincent Price) followed in 1965.

20th Century Fox's initial Region 1 disc, which pairs *The Fly* and *Return of the Fly*, was an essential acquisition for monster fans and was later repurposed a bit for a more elaborate boxed set containing all three films in the initial trilogy. (A full rundown on *Curse of the Fly* can be found in *DVD Delirium Volume 3*). The definition on the colourful 2.35:1 ratio image of *The Fly* is simply breathtaking: The resplendent greens in the Delambre garden, the silky red of François's robe, the burnished highlights in Helene's auburn hair... the film has simply never looked so gorgeous. Language options on the 24-chapter presentation are English stereo, English 4.0 surround and French mono, with subtitling in English and Spanish. The 20-chapter-encoded *Return of the Fly* also gets a beautiful 2.35:1 transfer, with cleanly defined blacks and whites rendering it the finest version for home viewing you're likely to see. Language choices here are less generous, with only English mono or stereo, though subtitles are again provided in English and Spanish. The half-dozen trailers are repeated on both sides. They comprise a scratchy original for *The Fly* (with specially shot footage of Price stepping up to camera and addressing the audience) and *Return of the Fly*, plus those for the Cronenberg remake, its own sequel (*The Fly II*, with Eric Stoltz getting a buzz out of molecular transference), and '60s fantasies *Voyage to the Bottom of the Sea* and *Fantastic Voyage*. The Region 2 disc is essentially the same as its NTSC counterpart, with trailers for the two main features only, but subtitle options in eleven different languages.

The versions in the box set look similar (though the first film features somewhat livelier colours), but the extras are the real selling point here. Hedison and David Del Valle offer a chatty commentary track for the first film, and along with the usual stills galleries and trailers, you get a bonus disc featuring "Fly Trap: Catching a Classic" (a fan-heavy piece about the making of the film with an emphasis on Price adoration) and the full 1997 A&E *Biography* Vincent Price special.

– TG

FRANKENSTEIN ISLAND

Colour, 1981, 97m. / Directed by Jerry Warren / Starring Cameron Mitchell, John Carradine, Robert Clarke, Katherine Victor / Retromedia (US R1 NTSC)

Poor Jerry Warren. While Ed Wood is now regarded as the king of lovable Z-grade schlock, the equally stupefying output of Warren is marginalized by those who can't see the cracked entertainment value in drive-in gems like *Man Beast*, *Teenage Zombies*, and *The Wild World of Batwoman*. Fortunately DVD has rescued a few of his gems from home video oblivion, and one of the beneficiaries is his final cinematic opus, *Frankenstein Island*, released after Warren spent a whopping fifteen years away from the cameras.

Thanks to a hot air balloon snafu that leaves them stranded on a remote island, a doctor (Robert Clarke) and his band of cohorts (including "Melvin the dog") wind up sharing company with a tribe of Amazonian she-babes (who obviously discovered the wonders of modern cosmetics instead of fire). Unfortunately there's also a nearby castle, and a babbling prisoner (Cameron Mitchell) warns them of the unspeakable evils being conducted on the premises. As it turns out, the guilty party is platinum-haired Sheila Frankenstein (Warren regular Katherine Victor), who's carrying on the family tradition by churning out mutants, keeping her father's decrepit assistant alive with blood experiments, and fiddling with electrical gadgets. Oh yeah, and John Carradine shows up as a rambling superimposition for some reason, and a bolt-necked monster does finally appear in the final few minutes to shamble through the lab set.

As surreal as they come, *Frankenstein Island* firmly belongs in the company of such other rambling non-movies as *The Beast of Yucca Flats* and *Glen Or Glenda?*, though its relatively late vintage of 1981 makes this one the arguable swan song of old school Z-grade exploitation. The precious minutes of Mitchell and Carradine footage weren't much of a selling point by the time this was unleashed on drive-in audiences, but it is an oddly nostalgic reminder of those days when a quick appearance from the likes of Boris Karloff or Peter Lorre would be enough to land any cut-rate quickie a spot on the silver screen. Then there's that priceless Warren dialogue, which meanders around every single point and uses ten sentences to convey what normal people would express in three words.

Retromedia's *Frankenstein Island* DVD is tough to evaluate, given that the film was apparently shot for about five dollars on cheapo film stock. The appearance isn't much above what you'd expect from a standard one-inch video master, with soft colours and detail, but God only knows how pristine this could ever look. A long reel in the middle suffers from a slight horizontal jitter, but otherwise print damage is kept to a minimum. Colour saturation looks fine, but the black levels tend to be flat and washed out – again, perhaps a flaw with the original film processing. The DVD (which top-bills Carradine on the cover) features a stills gallery and a five-minute interview with Victor, who paints Warren as an affable con man who didn't always treat his actors with the utmost respect. A shame, as even here those pros gave him more than his directorial abilities really deserved.

FREEWAY

Colour, 1988, 93m. / Directed by Francis Delia / Starring Darlanne Fluegel, James Russo, Billy Drago, Richard Belzer, Clint Howard / Anchor Bay (US R1 NTSC) / WS (1.85:1) (16:9) / DD2.0

 Though technically a theatrical release, this baby has straight to video stamped all over it. A rote "suspense thriller" that feels like a slightly nastier offshoot of *Homicide* or *Law & Order*, this look at California's idea of mania circa 1988 follows off-his-rocker road-rager Heller (home video staple and psycho specialist Billy Drago) on a murderous rampage in which he blasts away at hapless commuters while cruising around in his *eeeevil* black car. Of course, he also snags his fifteen minutes of fame by calling up radio host Dr. Lazarus (Richard Belzer, who appropriately went on to both of the aforementioned TV shows); this stunt also catches the ear of a nurse named Sunny (Darlanne Fluegel), whose husband was killed by the maniac a year ago. While Sunny pesters the cops for hints, a mysterious man named Frank Quinn (James Russo) turns up and, while not busy bedding Sunny and taking off quietly in the morning, comes up with a plan to trap the killer.

Basically a remake of the wacko made-for-TV classic *Death Car on the Freeway* (starring proto-Fluegel Shelley Hack) dressed up in symbolic religious drag, this darkly lit, by-the-numbers exercise is one of those films that actually seems to evaporate before your eyes while watching it late at night. Apart from some of Drago's nuttier dialogue, the characters fail to register as anything deeper than cardboard, and while the climax contains one or two excessive touches that should please action fans, it still unfolds with all the predictability of a cake recipe. In keeping with the director's earlier experience on TV's *Crime Story* (with Ms. Fluegel, natch), the film is perfectly glossy, professional, and competent, with slick neon-and-rain photography straight out of the Michael Mann playbook and a hard-working score by Abel Ferrara composer Joe Delia. Be prepared to feel hungry for something of substance when the end credits roll, but at least *Evilspeak*'s Clint Howard pops up as a good-natured perv... so ya know it can't be all bad.

In keeping with Anchor Bay's other New World transfers of this vintage, the souped-up digital treatment can only go so far to correcting a film saddled with that grainy, mushy '80s look. Blacks range from deep to pasty, but colours are reasonably saturated and defined. The widescreen framing looks fine, though the open matte presentation seen on TV was also acceptable. The 2.0 stereo track captures the music adequately and features a few nice directional effects, mainly via gunshots and screeching tyres. Don't expect a great deal, but it gets the job done. Not much to speak of in terms of extras; you get a theatrical trailer, a static menu, and chapter stops. A must for '80s cable freaks, but a cheap rental for anyone else.

FREEZER (FREEZE ME)

Colour, 2000, 102m. / Directed by Takashi Ishii / Starring Harumi Inoue, Naoto Takenaka, Shunsuke Matsuoka, Shingo Tsurumi, Kazuki Kitamura / Tartan (UK R0 PAL), Tokyo Shock (US R1 NTSC) / WS (1.85:1) (16:9) / DD2.0, Edko (HK R3 NTSC) / WS (1.85:1) (16:9) / DD5.1

Freezer is a glossy and well-acted rape/ revenge-cum-*Repulsion* style picture, effectively suspenseful but with little new to add to its limited subgenre. Chihiro (played by Harumi Inoue), a bright young woman who has moved from the provinces to Tokyo, is engaged to a fellow office worker (Shunsuke Matsuoka) and has a good job, though she shows a slight neurotic twinge as she flinches from an unexpected caress or ritualistically locks up her apartment. Into her life come three contrasting men, a trio who gang-raped her in her hometown and then distributed a video of the crime; the flashy, white-suited Kojima (Shingo Tsurumi), a swaggering yakuza-type, invades her apartment and life, coerces her sexually and threatens to make public her old ordeal, announcing that he has arranged a reunion of the "video stars". After the humiliation of losing her fiancé and job, Chihiro snaps and attacks Kojima as he takes a bath, battering him to death with a bottle of water, then stuffing his corpse in the fridge. Hirokawa (Kazuki Kitamura), the second rapist, arrives and is initially a contrite salaryman though he becomes abusive when drunk, blaming the woman for the rape, and is also killed. Chihiro has to move apartments to a tiny place, buy two large freezers for the preserved corpses and take a menial job to get by, and soon enough the third rapist shows up, ex-con Baba (Naoto Takenaka), who also assumes he can become her master and order her to wait on him hand and foot. When he is killed, Chihiro faces a bizarre situation in that the power in her new flat cuts out if she overloads it with appliances, so that she can only use hot water or the air conditioning if she turns off one of the three freezers. The last reels as Chihiro tries to sustain some sort of lifestyle with the responsibility of maintaining the frozen rapists edge even further into deep black comedy, but climax inevitably in tragedy.

Takashi Ishii (*Gonin*) gets fine performances from his heroine and her tormentors, though the situations are always stylised rather than credible. The problem of telling essentially the same anecdote three (indeed, four) times is solved by making each of Chihiro's abusers a different type and framing the build-up to their inevitable deaths in varying manners. Though there is plentiful nudity, it's surprisingly restrained in its explicit horrors, preferring to tighten the psychological screws and establish an oppressive atmosphere by emphasising the effect the weather (snow for the initial rape, a great deal of sloshed-about water for the bathroom killings, a feverous heat-wave for the finale, the stench of decay in the flat) has on the plot and the characters. Tartan Asia Extreme's DVD offers a fine-looking anamorphic transfer with Japanese audio and optional English subtitles; the image sometimes seems fogged by so much water, rain, snow and blood, but it's not grainy or blurry. The extras are brief notes on the film and its director by Justin Bowyer, a stills gallery, the trailer (and a trailer reel for the line), and filmographies for the director and some of the cast.

– KN

FRIDAY THE 13TH PART VII: THE NEW BLOOD

Colour, 1988, 88m. / Directed by John Carl Buechler / Starring Kane Hodder, Lar Park Lincoln, Susan Blu, Terry Kiser, Heidi Kozak, Elizabeth Kaitan / Paramount (US R1 NTSC, UK R2 PAL) / WS (1.85:1) (16:9) / DD5.1

Tina Shepherd (Lar Park Lincoln) arrives on the shores of Crystal Lake with her mother (Susan Blu) and private psychoanalyst Dr. Crews (Terry Kiser). It seems that Tina has psychic abilities that enable her not only to move objects at will but which have also given her the power of a seer. When a surge of energy caused by her pent up frustration inadvertently resurrects Jason Voorhees (Kane Hodder) from his dormant state at the bottom of the lake, he rises and before long the bodies are stacking up.

Poor old Jason. Through half a dozen pictures he's been mutilated in every way imaginable. He's been shot, chopped, stabbed, sliced, drowned, electrocuted, strangled, torched, blown to smithereens... and yet the greatest hurt of all was appearing in *Friday the 13th Part VII: The New Blood*. Actually *The No Blood* would have been a more appropriate title, for the MPAA mercilessly disembowelled this entry in the ongoing Voorhees chronicles, rendering it the tamest in the entire series. Worse still the cutaways are so blatant that the whole show invokes boredom. Where a little more in the way of gruesome effects work wouldn't have managed to dredge this up from the bottom of the *Friday* barrel, it might at least have rescued it from a debilitating case of blandness. Transcending awful, it's a despicable misuse of studio funding, screaming sub-mediocrity from every frame. With special effects veteran John Carl Buechler at the controls fans had every right to expect big things, but he let them down seriously. The campsite slaughter formula having been drained to the point of anaemia, at least Buechler was smart enough to try something different, but somewhere between good intention and final result things went astray. After most of the lookalike characters have been wiped out, it's Jason vs. Carrie in all but name as

Lincoln's brains take on Hodder's brawn with the predictable result that our machete-wielding anti-hero ends up back in the lake where he started. The irony in all this is that the excellent make-up effects on Jason himself provide audiences with one of his best incarnations of all; emerging from the lake where the fish appear to have had a good old nibble at him, his ribs and spine are now partially exposed through tattered garb and when the moment of unmasking arrives we get to see hideous disfigurement, oozing pus and chronic dental problems like never before. In light of this it's a crime that Buechler fails to mine even the most rudimentary levels of suspense from the plot. He even resorts to that lowest of low pranks for an easy audience jolter, having a cat leap out of a closet. The killings – a party blower through the eye, two bisected faces, a ripped out heart, a slice'n'dice with a rotary hedge trimmer and a body in a sleeping bag smashed against a tree (the latter replayed to comic effect in *Jason X*) – are substandard in both inventiveness and execution, and, as already noted, occur largely off-screen anyway. There is a nice parody of the attack on Susan Backlinie in *Jaws*, with a POV shot as our killer rises up through the water beneath skinny-dipping Heidi Kozak, however it's but a single moment smothered by the apathetic ambience of the film as a whole.

On the plus side we have Kane Hodder in the lead for the first of four appearances as Jason to date and he acquits himself well with the requisite emotionless intensity and, even out in the middle of nowhere, appears to have a finer array of pointy stabby things to hand than your local B&Q. Lar Park Lincoln is a charismatic and attractive enough leading lady, though her performance is purely perfunctory. Terry Kiser is nice and oily as the duplicitous psychiatrist, purportedly out to help Lincoln but actually intent on exploiting her powers. The remainder of the cast are pretty much unknowns, although fans of that dubious guilty pleasure *Slave Girls from Beyond Infinity* might want to tune in to see Elizabeth Kaitan getting naked. The next instalment in the series, *Jason Takes Manhattan*, made for a mild recovery. But only just.

By the time this entry first reached DVD it appeared as if Paramount had lost interest. Here was the golden opportunity to restore the long absent footage, if not in the film itself then in a supplementary section, and what did they do? They released the same old R-rated cut and enhanced it with precisely nothing. There's not a single bonus item accompanying the 15-chapter encoded, 1.85:1 matted feature, unless you count the sleeve listed special features, which include subtitles and sound... don't get me started! At least the earlier DVD releases were accompanied by a basic trailer. The transfer is clean, even if the colours are a little soft, and the sound is presented in an unremarkable English 5.1 surround mix and French mono, with subtitles available in English only. Its subsequent inclusion in Paramount's "From Crystal Lake to Manhattan" box set only marks a marginal improvement thanks to a frank commentary track with Buechler and Hodder, a few appearances on the featurette overviews on the special features disc ("Secrets Galore behind the Gore"), and the film's splattery excised footage presented as an outtake reel, apparently sourced from a VHS tape. Paramount's third trip to that bloody well came with their 2009 Deluxe Edition, part of their double-disc versions for each of the series titles in their library, and the transfer actually shows some marked improvement with a much fresher appearance and surprisingly vivid colours. More importantly, the special features deliver the goods with 10 more minutes of deleted footage (in addition to the 6 carried over from the prior release) with a new Buechler intro, "Mind over Matter" (a superfluous but interesting seven-minute overview of telekinesis), and a different commentary with Hodder, Buechler and

Lincoln, plus a goofy "Makeover by Maddy" sketch. For some reason the trailer for this particular entry has yet to surface on any of the three discs, but it's easily obtainable online. F13 fans will probably want the box set version for the original commentary and the additional chit chat for the first round of deleted scenes, but for thoroughness, the third time's easily the charm here.

– TG

FRIDAY THE 13TH PART VIII: JASON TAKES MANHATTAN

Colour, 1989, 100m. / Directed by Rob Hedden / Starring Jensen Daggett, Kane Hodder, Alex Diakun, Peter Mark Richman / Paramount (US R1 NTSC, UK R2 PAL) / WS (1.85:1) (16:9) / DD2.0

 Rennie (Jensen Daggett) is one of a class of graduating students on a cruise to New York. Unfortunately there's an uninvited passenger aboard in the shape of masked maniac zombie Jason Voorhees (Kane Hodder), freshly reborn and primed for a massacre. After the irreversible damage inflicted upon the franchise by *Part VII*, all but the most dedicated stayed away from *Friday the 13th Part VIII: Jason Takes Manhattan*. And who could blame them? It proved to be the lowest grossing entry in the series to that point and firmly nailed the lid on Paramount's interest in continuing the saga. In actuality it's by no means the worst of the *Friday*s, but it's far from the best. You can't help but wonder if the idea of transporting Jason from the sleepy shores of Crystal Lake to the thriving metropolis of the Big Apple was ever really deigned to be a smart one. Given that someone must have thought so, the problem of getting him from A to B was solved by having him stow away on a

privately chartered passenger liner full of students bound for NYC, killing off most of the kids and crew en route.

Director Rob Hedden managed to put together a couple of violent episodes – the dearth of which in *The New Blood* contributed to its undoing – but he failed to raise the level above the by-the-numbers plotting technique of his predecessor in the directorial seat, John Carl Buechler. There's little here you've not seen before, though Jason does get a few new utensils to toy with, including sauna coals, a hypodermic needle and an electric guitar. Hedden does extract a minor degree of tension from the claustrophobic setting aboard ship, though the question of why the disappearing students and increasing pile of corpses remains unnoticed for so long in such a relatively confined space is conveniently overlooked.

The story picks up with Jason resurrected from beneath the remains of the jetty where he was consigned by Tina Shepherd at the end of *The New Blood*, a surge of electricity from a power cable snagged by a boat anchor jolting him back to life. More ubiquitous than ever before – sometimes appearing to be in two or three places at the same time – he gets aboard ship and we're off down slaughter street once again. Kane Hodder gets to expand on his interpretation of Jason, eclipsing the relatively emotionless stalker of past outings with a raging, unstoppable machine, his seething hatred discernible even from behind the benignly expressionless hockey mask. That said, where the previous film gave us the most malevolent make-up job in the series, this one's the most feeble, the final unveiling revealing something akin to a blob of toasted marshmallow. Have they not heard the adage if it ain't broke don't fix it? Change for change's sake doesn't wash, and even more baffling is the fact that our killer now sports black leather gloves straight out of a Dario Argento *giallo*; where Jason acquired these is anyone's guess. Serial-Killers-R-Us, perhaps.

Jensen Daggett is an acceptable enough heroine as Rennie, emotionally scarred by a childhood encounter with the drowned boy Jason out in the middle of the lake. And in an attempt to capture the flavour of the early entries in the series we get a Crazy Ralph clone in the form of a paranoid deck hand (Alex Diakun) who slinks about proffering such comforting nuggets as "This voyage is doomed!" The only other noteworthy turn comes from Peter Mark Richman as Rennie's starchy Uncle Charles, whose cruel shock tactics in trying to coax the frightened child Rennie to swim earn him audience disdain and, eventually, a headfirst dip in a vat of toxic sludge.

Somewhat mystifying is the substitution of Harry Manfredini's classic sounds – as integral a part of Jason's world as the hockey mask itself – in favour of a score by Fred Mollin, whose nondescript offering is disappointing and ill fitting. The biggest brain-bender of all though is saved for the climax in a sewer brimming with toxic waste, which first melts Jason and then appears to purify his soul, returning him to the form of a small boy in swimming trunks. No, really! How did the serial killer equivalent of the indestructible Scratchy return from childhood regression in a New York sewer at the end of *Part VIII* to his fully grown self, maiming and killing back in Crystal Lake at the opening of *Part IX*? Somewhere between Paramount 1989 and New Line 1993 it was obviously decided it was a question best left unaddressed.

What a shame that Paramount didn't see fit to include the amusing, specially shot teaser trailer for *Jason Takes Manhattan* on their Region 1 DVD release. It's indicative yet again of the short shrift they've paid the latter entries in the series. Sure, the film itself is disappointing, but does that really have to result in less diligence in the preparation of its DVD presentation? These are the chances to add enticement value to otherwise less than essential purchases. Regardless, the 17-chapter feature is bright and colourful,

matted to 1.85:1 with 16:9 enhancement. The sound is available in English Dolby Digital or French mono. Subtitling is in English alone. The subsequent "From Crystal Lake to Manhattan" set (which pairs this film up on a dual-layer disc with *The New Blood*) adds on a Hedden commentary track (which addresses the film's budgetary constraints head-on) and a few comments from Hodder elsewhere on the separate special features disc, which thankfully does contain the original trailer. The third Paramount edition, a double-disc affair in line with their other series revamps, chucks out the commentary track but compensates with plenty of new material including a new transfer (slightly more picture info and a bit less edge enhancement, but very close all the same), a terrific new featurette called "New York Has a New Problem" (with virtually everyone seen in the film chipping in), 12 minutes of good-looking and sometimes very gory deleted footage, a gag reel (featuring a very funny and raunchy punchline at the end), and a new commentary with Hodder (via phone), Daggett, and Reeves. The film may have been overlooked at the time, but its time in the spotlight certainly arrived here.
– TG

FROM HELL

Colour, 2001, 122m. / Directed by The Hughes Brothers / Starring Johnny Depp, Heather Graham, Ian Holm, Robbie Coltrane, Katrin Cartlidge, Susan Lynch, Paul Rhys, Jason Flemyng / Fox (Blu-ray & DVD) (US R0/R1 HD/NTSC, UK R2 PAL) / WS (2.35:1) (16:9) / DD5.1

 During an opium haze, Victorian-era police inspector Fred Abberline (played by Johnny Depp) witnesses a vision of Jack the Ripper in the act of performing his handiwork on an unfortunate prostitute. Using his precognitive abilities as an aid in crime detection, Abberline decides to expose the culprit, much to the displeasure of his superiors. His interrogations lead him to the extremely clean and healthy-looking Mary Kelly (Heather Graham), a gold-hearted hooker concerned about her murdered co-worker's vanished baby. Abberline also seeks advice from the former royal physician, Sir William Gull (Ian Holm), who points the inspector in the direction of Freemasons and a possible royal conspiracy.

An elaborately mounted fantasia only partially revolving around Ripper lore, *From Hell* jumps off from the same speculations which produced Bob Clark's more successful *Murder By Decree*, lifting characters and events but not the full scope or focus from the Alan Moore/Eddie Campbell comic serial. Neither of the leads is really up to the task, saddled with unworkable accents (Graham fares the worst) and largely unfocused characterizations that lead to a finale that should be overwhelmingly emotional but instead produces a minor shrug. Far more successful is the sterling supporting cast, including Holm, Robbie Coltrane, the late Katrin Cartlidge, Susan Lynch, Paul Rhys, and an especially memorable Jason Flemyng as the Ripper's sinister coachman. The direction by The Hughes Brothers (Albert and Allen) ranges from breathtaking (most of the murders, each different from the last, and some eye-popping cityscape shots) to pedestrian, a flaw in their earlier films as well (including *Menace II Society* and *Dead Presidents*). Apart from the memorable image of a group of sleeping whores roped together for an evening by the police, their stated attempts to bring a new streetwise sensibility to the setting never really comes off. It doesn't help that the political angle results in a wholly unbelievable reaction from Queen Victoria, and a last minute victim switch is pilfered directly from Nicholas Meyer's *Time After Time* without the emotional payoff.

Fox has released *From Hell* in two versions, a double-disc edition and a single-disc variant (containing only the first disc). The feature disc includes a magnificent anamorphic transfer, with especially rich hues of absinthe greens bathing the horror sequences. The 5.1 mix is also state of the art, with Trevor Jones's melancholy score and the clattering of carriages on cobblestones keeping those rear speakers constantly busy. The Hughes Brothers appear for a busy commentary track with cinematographer Peter Deming, screenwriter Rafael Yglesias, and Coltrane; it's a largely technical track, focusing on the creation of the film's visual look and how they tried to capture all the little period details. 21 deleted, alternative or extended scenes are included with a novel twist; the footage from the final film before and after each is presented in black and white for proper context. The much-touted alternative ending is nothing special, offering a more exotic take on Abberline's eventual fate; more rewarding is the attention devoted to Flemying, whose masturbatory habits are chronicled with an especially sick punch line.

Disc two contains a routine 15-minute HBO featurette, "A View from Hell", hosted by a very wooden Graham and sporting some of the lousiest editing ever seen in a professional promo piece. Better are "Jack the Ripper: 6 Degrees of Separation" (an educational featurette with archival Ripper footage and trivia titbits accessible via pop-up magnifying glass), a "Production Design" featurette with Martin Childs, and a "Tour of the Murder Sites" with the Hughes Brothers taking a modern stroll round the Ripper murder locations. Also included is a look at the original Moore and Campbell graphic art, with some surprisingly hardcore sexual imagery for a studio DVD. The history of absinthe is covered in "Absinthe Makes the Heart Grow Fonder" (which could have wound up on Fox's *Moulin Rouge* DVD as well), while other bonuses include the gory/grungy theatrical trailer and, for no apparent reason, a promo for Adrian Lyne's *Unfaithful*. The subsequent Blu-ray release features the expected bump in picture quality (the omnipresent lime hues in particular look much more accurate and striking) and ports over the extras from the standard first disc, prompting collectors with that bonus disc to hang on to their standard def editions a little longer.

FUDOH: THE NEW GENERATION

Colour, 1996, 98m. / Directed by Takashi Miike / Starring Tôru Minegishi, Riki Takeuchi, Shosuke Tanihara, Marie Jinno, Miho Nomoto / Artsmagic (UK R2 PAL), Tokyo Shock (US R1 NTSC) / WS (1.85:1) (16:9), MO Asia/Japan Shock Video (Germany R2 PAL, Holland R2 PAL) / WS (1.85:1)

Here's another in the ten-year wave of Takashi Miike movies that hit the DVD market in a flood that made him seem even more prolific than he actually is. Its concept is deliberately provocative yet ridiculous: ten years after the decapitation of an errant yakuza soldier by his own father (Tôru Minegishi), the victim's younger brother Riki (Shosuke Tanihara), a military-uniformed schoolboy, trains his angelic-seeming classmates to carry on a gang war against the rival clan.

The plot is typical tit-for-tat killing-and-betrayal gangster stuff, but the Miike touch ensures many memorable scenes and characters: a schoolgirl-dressed stripper (Miho Nomoto) who fires darts out of her vagina and through the head of a victim in the audience (this character later turns out to be a hermaphrodite), a cup of complementary coffee that makes an arrested gang boss fountain blood inside a police car, cheerful infants training to take down full-grown gangsters or playing football with the English teacher's head, a tattoo made with the blood of the murdered brother as ink that only appears when the body warms up in a shower or during sex, a hulking giant "pupil" who winds up as a near-cyborg, substitute teachers who are mini-dressed sexpots or yakuza hit-men. Familiar player Riki Takeuchi is the gym teacher-cum-assassin, Riki's unacknowledged half-brother – who takes the generational feud to another level in an open freeze-frame ending.

Impossible to take seriously and yet treated with a solemnity that becomes bizarrely amusing, *Fudoh* was the first of Miike's films to get a theatrical release – he had previously toiled in direct-to-video action – and has the feel of something that is straining for its effects with studied weirdness, but the intricate family squabble that underpins the splattery action and the unusual location (the Southern island of Kyushu, far from the familiar Tokyo underworld of most yakuza movies) suggest a seriousness of purpose that would become more evident with later films.

Artsmagic's 'eastern cult cinema' DVD isn't as kitted out with extras as Tartan's Asia Extreme releases of Miike titles, but showcases a fine anamorphic widescreen transfer of one of the director's slicker-looking films. The audio track is Japanese language, with optional English subs. The supplements are limited to biographies, filmographies, stills and cross-promotional trailers. Unfortunately this release has suffered from BBFC-enforced cuts totalling 21 seconds. The NTSC format release from Tokyo Shock is uncut and carries English subtitles, but be careful as their first release presents an unimpressive transfer of the feature and has no extras. However, their subsequent "Deluxe Edition" is anamorphic, looks infinitely better, and also features a 40-minute, typically fractured interview with Miike and a Tanihara interview, as well as a subtitled, sporadic commentary with both. There are two PAL editions from MO

Asia / Japan Shock Video, neither of which carries English subtitles; the Dutch edition is uncut, but the German release has had two scenes censored.

– KN

THE GHOST AND MRS. MUIR

B&W, 1947, 104m. / Directed by Joseph L. Mankiewicz / Starring Gene Tierney, Rex Harrison, Natalie Wood, George Sanders / Fox (US R1 NTSC, UK R2 PAL) / DD2.0

Widowed and living with her boorish in-laws, young Lucy Muir (Gene Tierney) decides to take her young daughter, Anna (Natalie Wood), to a new home by the sea. Against the advice of her real estate agent she settles on Gull Cottage, the haunted former residence of a sea captain (Rex Harrison) who may have committed suicide. However, the captain's gruff ghost still prowls the premises and even appears in the flesh (more or less) to Lucy one dark and spooky night. The two reach a tentative understanding to live under the same roof, and when money begins to run low, he even comes up with a plan to help her out. However, trouble brews when a children's author, Miles (George Sanders), arrives on the scene and begins to court Lucy away from her ghostly companion.

The inspiration for a far more frivolous television show as well as countless supernatural romances, *The Ghost and Mrs. Muir* remains one of the finest and most delicate of all screen fantasies. Mixing whimsical humour with an almost overwhelming sense of melancholy and loss, the film's plaintive mood is difficult to shake and builds to a transcendent finale capable of wringing tears from the hardiest of viewers. Tierney has never look more radiant or been more charming, while Harrison matches her every step of the way as the blustery

Captain Gregg. They're helped considerably by a wonderfully literate script (which humorously has to sidestep the captain's salty language), razor sharp direction by Joseph L. Mankiewicz (*All About Eve*), and best of all, one of Bernard Herrmann's richest and most haunting music scores. A perfect juggling act of tone and style, the film somehow avoids dipping into sentiment or silliness, instead serving as a simple and moving story of two souls caught in highly unusual circumstances. Ghost story fans with a romantic streak could hardly do better.

Fox's Studio Classics edition is something of a step down from the pristine work they performed on other titles in the line, like The *Day the Earth Stood Still* and *All About Eve*. Visual debris is still in evidence, and many shots have a slight softness, which likely was not a factor in the original presentation. It's certainly a huge step up from their murky laserdisc, but for a top-of-the-line title, a little more work would have helped. The audio is also surprisingly mediocre; the rechanneled stereo track is a warbly mess best avoided, while the original mono track sounds fine for the most part but is occasionally muffled (including part of the pivotal final scene, unfortunately). The film is strong enough to still work with these debits, but a nice HD overhaul at some point would be appreciated. At least the disc doesn't disappoint in terms of extras (in America anyway, as the U.K. counterpart is bare bones for some reason); the theatrical trailer is included along with promotional art and stills, as well as the hour long A&E *Biography* episode, "Rex Harrison: The Man Who Would Be King". A hefty audio commentary comes courtesy of Greg Kimble, Christopher Husted, Jeanine Bassinger and Kenneth Geist, with Makiewicz receiving the lion's share of discussion time among the countless trivia titbits about the production. The film comes highly recommended, of course, and despite the technical shortcomings, so does the disc itself.

GHOST SHIP

Colour, 2002, 90m. / Directed by Steve Beck / Starring Julianna Margulies, Desmond Harrington, Gabriel Byrne, Ron Eldard, Karl Urban / Warner (Blu-ray & DVD) (US R0/ R1 HD/NTSC, UK R2 PAL) / WS (1.85:1) (16:9) / DD5.1

 Receiving a tip-off about a large vessel spotted adrift in the Bering Sea, a salvage boat captain, Murphy (played by Gabriel Byrne), takes a small crew out to find her. They locate the ship, which, to their disbelief, is the rusting hulk of the Italian ocean liner Antonia Graza, which vanished mysteriously back in 1962. Ascertaining that she's damaged, the team map out a plan of action as to the best way to patch up and salvage her before she sinks. But they haven't been aboard long before it becomes apparent that paranormal forces are at work...

Dubbed by lead actress Julianna Margulies as "*The Shining* meets *Dead Calm*", Steve Beck's *Ghost Ship* could more accurately be described as a hybrid of *Event Horizon* and *Virus*. It kicks off in 1962 with a jaw-droppingly grisly bit of hocus-pocus as dozens of passengers partying aboard the Antonia Graza are murdered in the blink of an eye when a high tension steel cable, primed by an unseen assailant, whiplashes across the deck and slices them all in two. The blend of CGI and live action effects work in this sequence is superbly mounted as bodies all too convincingly fall in half before your eyes, leaving displaced and dying upper torsos flailing around helplessly on the floor. How could the rest of the movie possibly live up to such a shocker of an opening you might ask? It couldn't. And it doesn't. As we move forward forty years to the present, *Ghost Ship* adopts the routine frippery of a haunted house movie located on the briny. Fate sets up the protagonists so the Antonia Graza can knock 'em down in a variety of not particularly inventive ways; one's blown up, one's impaled, one's drowned, and another meets a demise that's dismissed untold.

From the same team that served up technically superior but efficaciously inferior revisions of William Castle classics with *House on Haunted Hill* and *Thir13en Ghosts*, you won't find a great deal here that you haven't seen a dozen times before. But director Beck delivers the frights adequately enough and there's a refreshing absence of padding as he keeps events moving along at a fair old clip. Once Murphy and his crew make an unexpected discovery in the cargo hold, and the truth about what happened forty years earlier is revealed as the spirits of long dead passengers start showing up, it becomes a fight for survival against an all powerful demon. A graduate from the Sigourney Weaver/Ripley school of action heroines, Margulies's Epps is tougher than all the men on the team put together and, unsurprisingly, it is she who survives to sail another day. The film boasts outstanding production values with some superb full size sets, and even though there's a slight over-reliance on CG to pull off some of the more outlandish demands of the script, there's plenty of eerie atmosphere; one particularly inspired touch is the ever present reflection of rippling water – even when there's no water around – dappling the walls and ceilings aboard the ghost ship. On the down side, some of the writing is irritatingly patronising. For example, to draw a comparison with their discovery, Murphy relates the story of the Marie Celeste to a captivated crew who've never heard of her. It's doubtful that even the most historically ignorant landlubber hasn't heard of the Marie Celeste, and the suggestion that a bunch of versed mariners would be unaware of the legend is facile. Equally annoying is the closing scene,

which makes no sense whatsoever and appears to be tagged on only to pander to formulaic twist ending expectations of modern audiences. In summation *Ghost Ship* is a cliché-driven opus for the MTV generation – a tenet cemented in by some of the ostentatious editing and auricle-assaulting score – but it's a bundle of fun with a sufficient enough infusion of bumps and jumps to keep most viewers entertained for its duration. Also starring Desmond Harrington (TV's *Dexter*), Ron Eldard (*Black Hawk Down*) and *Lord of the Rings*'s Karl Urban. An oddly conceived marketing campaign might have had you believe that the film was called *Sea Evil*, words which appear at the foot of promotional materials in a font size that dwarfs the movie's actual title.

Warner continues to vex collectors with a "one or t'other" option as *Ghost Ship* drops anchor in the home viewing forum on both a 1.85:1 matted disc and a full screen alternative. The picture is crisply rendered, even in darker scenes – and there's a lot of dark in the bowels of the Antonia Graza – with some nice, if sparingly applied surround sound effects. It's divided into an ample 28 chapters. The supplementary freight is made up of an unremarkable 15-minute behind the scenes puff piece, a trio of short f/x segments, a time-wasting interactive puzzle which accesses four segments revealing key plot twists (best to save this until after you've watched the feature), a trailer, a music video (which proves not to be any such thing, rather a rapid-fire cut together of clips from the film set to Mudvayne's noisy "Not Falling"), brief cast and crew bios and some DVD-ROM nick-nacks. The sound is in English and French, with subtitling in the same plus Spanish. The much later HD rendition on Blu-ray is, not surprisingly, a substantial step up in terms of clarity if a bit limited by the dark, dingy nature of the original photography, while the same extras are carried over as well.

– TG

GHOSTS OF MARS

Colour, 2001, 94m. / Directed by John Carpenter / Starring Ice Cube, Natasha Henstridge, Joanna Cassidy, Jason Statham / Sony (Blu-ray & DVD) (US R0/ R1 HD/NTSC, UK R2 PAL) / WS (2.35:1) (16:9) / DD 5.1

At the same time that David Cronenberg was easing into art movie mode, Tobe Hooper sank to direct-to-video and George Romero fell sadly silent, John Carpenter remained the only 1970s horror auteur still toiling away in the genre and getting his pictures on the big screen before their video/DVD releases at the turn of the new millennium. The bad news is that – following *Village of the Damned*, *Escape from L.A.* and *Vampires* – this is another disappointment, a thrown-together scramble of action, horror and science-fiction that ought to be a lot more fun than it is, with the added sadness that it's a pillaging of Carpenter's earlier, stronger work *Assault on Precinct 13*.

In 2176, Mars is partially terraformed and run by middle-aged lesbians. Cop Ballard (Natasha Henstridge) gives testimony to a board convened to inquire into the failure of her simple mission to bring in a captured serial killer called Desolation Williams (Ice Cube) from a frontier outpost. In an unbelievably complex but essentially pointless series of interlocked flashbacks-within-flashbacks, we learn the truth – that Williams is innocent and the atrocities were committed by miners possessed by ancient Martian spirits unleashed from an archaeological site by academic Whitlock (Joanna Cassidy). The possessees all adopt pierced goth-punk looks (as in *Vampires*, Carpenter seems to think that a head villain should look like Marilyn Manson on steroids) and besiege a small group of cops and crooks in the town jail, forcing Ballard and Williams to bond in order to survive – though the fact that the whole supporting cast gets needlessly killed suggests neither of our heroes are much good at it.

Obviously, something like this doesn't require David Mamet to do a dialogue polish, but *Ghosts of Mars* suffers from a script that gets laughs in all the wrong places, with duff lines given to performers who can't do anything with them (Brit hardman Jason Statham probably comes off worst). A more serious problem is that all the suspense-action-horror scenes are badly mistimed, with mêlées of stunts and decapitations that look like a rough cut of a filmed rehearsal rather than the razor-sharp set pieces of even Carpenter's previous lesser works.

As with *Vampires*, Sony has done a fine job of presenting this disappointment on DVD and its even more polished Blu-ray overhaul. An anamorphic widescreen transfer does what it can, presenting the many muddy red tones perfectly, with a 5.1 mix that punches up Carpenter's rock-beat score. Besides filmographies and the trailers, the extras run to three featurettes – a video diary of the shooting ("Red Desert Nights"), an inside-look at some effects shots and some B-roll in the studio with members of Buckethead and Anthrax laying down the score – and a lively, teasing commentary track with an impish Carpenter and straight person Henstridge.
– KN

GHOSTWATCH

Colour, 1992, 91m. / Directed by Lesley Manning / Starring Michael Parkinson, Sarah Greene, Craig Charles / BFI (UK R2 PAL)

Originally telecast as a Halloween special, *Ghostwatch* was the BBC's entry into the mock-documentary field pioneered by the Orson Welles radio play *War of the Worlds* in 1938 and later revived by *The Blair Witch Project*. Staged as a live TV "event", the drama features all the paraphernalia of issue-led documentary television: a familiar face (Michael Parkinson) in the studio flanked by experts and minions, taking phone-in calls from viewers and trying to keep everything calm, while an outside broadcast unit fronted by presenters Sarah Greene and *Red Dwarf*'s Craig Charles report from a house in North London that is supposed to be haunted. Over the course of an hour and a half, a back-story for the house is pieced together *Quatermass and the Pit*-style as bits of information are volunteered that might suggest the identity of the bald, robed ghost some claim to have seen. Meanwhile, in the house, a hoax is exposed and a deeper, upsetting truth revealed with an unsettling climax as the audience at home are roped in on what is referred to as a huge séance, perhaps liberating the malign spirit into the airwaves to spread chaos throughout the land.

At the heart of the gimmickry is a nasty little ghost/horror story which provides some genuine chills and shocks after the camp elements have been pruned away. While it is always difficult to pull off the levels of performance required to present "real" people on TV, this manages for the most part to suggest the levels of discomfort felt on camera by presenters who see their control slipping away and the genuinely terrified parties who come to feel that the camera is intruding upon their supernatural sufferings. A great deal of the power of the piece comes from the illusion that it is being transmitted "live", with events unfolding rapidly and crucial developments delivered by viewers phoning in to complain that the broadcast has triggered poltergeist phenomena in their own homes. Nevertheless, though the conventions of mock-doc have developed in the decade since transmission, this still manages the kind of creepiness found in latter-day, internet-based descendants like *My Little Eye*. Like *The Stone Tape*, this piece remained in the minds of those who saw it when it went out, making it a highly anticipated DVD release.

As with *The Stone Tape*, the BBC passed on releasing the property themselves and the BFI took up the slack with a disc in their Archive Television series. The smart transfer reproduces the look of the broadcast work, which sometimes plays clever tricks to add ambiguity to the images. The package includes: an essay by this reviewer on the production and reception of the piece; a very lively commentary from producer Ruth Baumgarten, director Lesley Manning and writer Stephen Volk, which points out the various "appearances" of the ghost on screen as well as delving deep into the making of the piece and the subsequent storm-in-a-teacup media controversy; Manning's "Shooting Reality", an audio essay over script pages, stills and newspaper pieces; and DVD-ROM features presenting Volk's original treatment and finished screenplay.

– KN

GRAND SLAM

Colour, 1967, 119m. / Directed by Giuliano Montaldo / Starring Janet Leigh, Robert Hoffmann, Klaus Kinski, Jorge Rigaud, Riccardo Cucciolla, Aldofo Celi, Edward G. Robinson / Blue Underground (US R0 NTSC) / WS (2.35:1) (16:9)

 An elderly schoolteacher hatches an elaborate plan (30 years in the making!) to filch a precious diamond cache from a Rio de Janeiro vault during the yearly carnival. With the help of an old Mafioso chum he gathers four specialists – an electronics expert, a womanizer, a safecracker and a militant chieftain – to bring his long-gestating scheme to fruition. While at first everything goes exactly as scripted, matters are soon

complicated by The Grand Slam 70 – an unbeatable, sound-sensitive super-alarm that threatens the entire operation. With the clock ticking and pressure building our Euro-centric A-Team quickly becomes susceptible to bickering and infighting, but can they still pull off the job?

Undoubtedly influenced by earlier caper flicks like *Rififi* and *Topkapi* as well as the then-popular *Mission: Impossible* television series, *Grand Slam* is a fun ride and a real surprise. Competently directed by Giuliano Montaldo, the plot does away with any irrelevant trivialities and concentrates solely on the intricate theft itself. Generally light in tone with a peppy score composed by Ennio Morricone, the film quickly moves down the expected route culminating with some very startling twists, turns and old-fashioned detours in the final quarter. The international cast – which includes Eurotrash standbys Jorge Rigaud, Riccardo Cucciolla, Robert Hoffmann, Aldofo Celi and the always-psychotic Klaus Kinski alongside American notables Janet Leigh and Edward G. Robinson – is up to par and each actor pulls off their role with the appropriate verve. Eagle-eyed credit-hounds will also spot *giallo*-man Massimo Dallamano listed as "general administrator", whatever that means. Smartly filmed on location in New York, Rome, Spain, London and Rio, the wide array of local colour and travelogue footage helps the production appear much more lavish than it actually was. Heist film devotees need to seek this one out, though it's recommended to fans of Eurospy pix and James Bond outings as well.

Originally titled *Ad ogni costo* (which translates as *At All Costs*), this Italian/German/Spanish co-production was distributed overseas as both *Top Job* and *Diamonds a Go-Go*. Stateside, Paramount Pictures snapped it up for a run as *Grand Slam* starting 20 February 1968, garnering favourable reviews from mainstream heavyweights like Leonard Maltin and Roger Ebert and reportedly performing quite

nicely. Yet for such a well-received film it strangely wasn't sold to television and was never afforded a domestic home video release – meaning Blue Underground's DVD is the first chance that folks will have to view *Grand Slam* in almost 35 years! (The more resourceful got hold of a rare Dutch VHS, but who buys tapes anymore?) Letterboxed at 2.35:1, BU's disc sports a nice, sharp transfer that especially comes to life during the colourful Rio de Janeiro festival segments. Some minor nicks and scratches show up on occasion, but nothing distracting. (It's worth noting that the optical FX shots do appear a bit grainy, due to the dated process used and not a transfer issue.) The mono soundtrack presents no problems, remaining clear for the duration.

Extras are a bit sparse, but given the previous unavailability of the title and lack of a built-in audience they're more than acceptable. We first get a mediocre and semi-misleading trailer, which spells out a little too much of a plot that's centred around surprises. Next we're treated to a 41-image stills collection consisting of various promo photos, lobby cards and soundtrack sleeve art. – BH

GRAVE OF THE VAMPIRE

Colour, 1972, 90m. / Directed by John Hayes / Starring William Smith, Michael Pataki, Kitty Vallacher / Alpha, Retromedia (US R1 NTSC), VIPCO (UK R0 PAL)

 One of the more memorable revisionist vampire outings of the early '70s (along with *The Dracula Saga*, *Daughters of Darkness*, and *The Velvet Vampire*, among many others), this drive-in favourite treads some novel cinematic ground (vampiric childbirth and rape by vampire, among others) but doesn't particularly feel like an exploitation film. In

the unforgettable opening, a young necking couple near a graveyard is interrupted when bloodsucker Croft (genre regular Michael Pataki) kills off the boyfriend and rapes the girl, Leslie (*Deathmaster*'s Kitty Vallacher), in an open grave. Months later she gives birth to a baby with a thirst for blood, which she quenches with her own breast and then a blood supply fed through a baby bottle. Soon the half-vamp grows up to be James (William Smith, Arnold's dad in *Conan the Barbarian*), a college student determined to hunt down and destroy his father, now posing at the school as Professor Lockwood, and having a penchant for holding séances.

Grim and bloody, *Grave of the Vampire* would be worthwhile enough just for the sheer oddness of its concept. Fortunately it also has plenty of wonderful atmosphere in the same style of its contemporaries like *Death Dream*; a sense of unease permeates even through the daylight scenes, and the actors all acquit themselves well. It's certainly significant enough to earn a special edition DVD treatment, though you won't find it on Alpha's budget priced disc. It appears lifted from a VHS source, with occasional dropout lines and all. For spare change you could do a lot worse, but hopefully this release won't deter the real rights owners from issuing a respectable version someday. A slightly more expensive option is Retromedia's "Blood Flood" release, which appears lifted from the letterboxed Showtime broadcast version prepared by MGM. It's in much better shape and has some extra gore (notably the hammer killing), though two explicit shots (some entrails during the hooker murder and a bit of bloody neck-slobbering) present only in the German tape editions are still understandably AWOL. The VIPCO release in the U.K. is another dupey-looking rehash of the standard cut. Eagle-eyed viewers with access to a channel like MGM HD or some of its international affiliates might be lucky enough to stumble across their hi-def transfer of the film, which is obviously a good sight better than any of the DVD options out on shelves.

GUINEA PIG: DEVIL'S EXPERIMENT / ANDROID OF NOTRE DAME

Colour, 1988/1989, 105m. / Unearthed (US R1 NTSC), Devil Pictures (Germany R0 PAL)

GUINEA PIG: MERMAID IN A MANHOLE / HE NEVER DIES

Colour, 1991/1992, 105m. / Unearthed (US R1 NTSC), Devil Pictures (Germany R0 PAL)

GUINEA PIG: FLOWER OF FLESH AND BLOOD / MAKING OF GUINEA PIG

Colour, 1985/1986, 89m. / Unearthed (US R1 NTSC), Devil Pictures (Germany R0 PAL)

As the horror genre was cannibalizing itself almost to death in the wake of the slasher genre, cinematic gore was being pushed around the world to lengths that would eventually culminate in the '90s in Peter Jackson's unbelievably soggy *Dead-Alive* (*Brain Dead*). Before that a strong contender for the heaviest onscreen splatter was the Japanese *Guinea Pig* series, a low-budget string of shot-on-video exercises in sadism which earned considerable fanfare after an apocryphal story circulated involving actor Charlie Sheen, who supposedly mistook one entry for a real snuff film and contacted the FBI. Repellent and tasteless though they may be, the *Guinea Pig* videos almost seem inevitable in the evolution of horror and, at least in hindsight, can comfortably be viewed as pure fiction. Thankfully the enhanced clarity of DVD makes the illusions even easier to sit through, as each ripped shred of latex and pulled punch can now be exposed without the foggy haze of a third generation VHS dupe. However, even time cannot dull the impact of the films, which purportedly inspired at least two copycat crimes, were banned in their native country, and have now become almost tame compared to the excesses of subsequent real-life psychopaths (such as the infamous Hello Kitty murder).

Usually referred to simply as *Guinea Pig*, the first instalment, *Devil's Experiment*, is a plotless study in sadism, which finds three unidentified Japanese youths abducting a woman and torturing her. And, well, that's about it. She's tied up, spun around, burned, poked, prodded, kicked, pelted with maggots and animal guts, forced to listen to deafening music, and generally mistreated until the showstopping finale, arguably the most repellent act of eyeball violence ever filmed. While movies like *I Spit on Your Grave* divide viewers who can passionately argue the viewpoints of characters or the sociological and gender-political implications of torture, no such depth can be found here. Sick, extreme, and highly disturbing, this remains fascinating in that something so stylized (filled with arty cutaways and POV shots) and cheaply produced could provoke an even more violent reaction than the animal killings in Italian cannibal epics. Even more perplexing is what the first two *Guinea Pig* films say about Japanese pop culture at the time; until the late 1990s, pubic hair could never be shown on film while any kind of atrocity could be committed without fear of censorship. Thus we have manga in which schoolgirls are violated in graphic detail by tentacled demons, "pink" films in which women are subjected to any depravity the director can dream up, and finally the logical conclusion, the *Guinea Pigs*. As with most extreme entertainment (to use the term loosely, of course, as most will find these unwatchable), this series

gained a massive cult following through the bootleg video market even without subtitles. Not surprising, as the dialogue is largely irrelevant.

The most notorious episode, *Flower of Flesh and Blood*, instigated the aforementioned apocryphal Sheen/FBI incident and spurred on a memorable Chas. Balun article in *Deep Red*; this is really video-driven sadism boiled down to its most visceral elements, a quasi-snuff sketch in which a grunting brute in a samurai costume kidnaps a young girl, ties her to a mattress, sacrifices a chicken, then carves up his victim for the remainder of the film while delivering giddy monologues about flowers directly to the camera. Though filled with spewing bodily fluids, screaming, and shaky, faux-realistic videography, this is less harrowing than its predecessor mainly because of the sheer hyperbole of the effects (in which every chop and hack seems to unleash torrents of blood) and the killer's bizarre appearance, which is probably meant to be some sort of commentary on feudal-ism's lingering fallout in Japan. Or maybe not. Adventurous viewers may want to pair this up with the earlier Japanese abduction/limb-removal study, *Blind Beast*, for a particularly harrowing double feature. Appropriately, the U.S. disc of *Flower* is packaged with *The Making of Guinea Pig*, a clinical behind-the-scenes chronicle of the extremely wet latex effects required to pass off each dismemberment and disembowelment. Even after this hour long documentary became an official part of the series on the video grey market, stories lingered for years about the verisimilitude of certain sequences.

Fortunately this speculation tends to be dispelled for most viewers upon watching the third *Guinea Pig* film and its successors, all of which are more cartoonish and wildly varying in quality. The third released entry, *Android of Notre Dame*, is a much "safer" viewing experience. Sort of a post-splatter remake of *The Brain That Wouldn't Die*, this follows the misadventures of a demented dwarf scientist (Toshihiko

Hino) who conducts experiments involving the yammering, rotting severed head of an extortionist to save the life of his stricken sister. He then kidnaps a woman and performs some perfunctory gore procedures on her before the morose finale. Filled with ranting, raving, and ludicrous gore FX (including a disembowelling that's more silly than it is sickening), this is an odd and frequently perplexing piece of cartoonish grue, to say the least.

The cinematic equivalent of a kid gleefully showing off his chewed-up food, *Mermaid in a Manhole* strives for a combination of poetic, *Night Tide*-style fantasy and stomach-churning goo, with the latter ultimately winning out. Renowned artist Hideshi Hino, who anonymously made *Flower of Flesh and Blood*, returns here for a more traditionally structured mood piece in which an art teacher and struggling painter (Shigeru Saiki) discovers a beached mermaid (Mari Somei) in a sewer. He recognises her from a childhood sighting, though now the depletion of rivers has left her to hide underground. He takes her home and keeps her in a bathtub while he determines to only paint her portrait, a process which becomes more difficult once multiple sores begin to infest her body. Withdrawing from everyday life to the consternation of his neighbours, the artist eventually resorts to using the mermaid's multi-coloured, infected fluids to complete his canvas... but things go even further downhill. Complete with slithering worms, dismemberment, and an especially nasty finale, this is not for anyone even remotely squeamish and definitely marks a step up from the previous entry. At 63 minutes, it's also one of the longer instalments in the series and feels the most like a complete film.

Then we switch gears to goofball comedy with *He Never Dies*, whose title sums up the entire conceit. Flatly shot on what appears to be very cheap video equipment, this oddball piece documents a depressed Japanese businessman's attempt to commit suicide after being dumped by his girlfriend. In gruesome detail he slits his wrists but doesn't even feel weak. Realizing he cannot die, the grinning loony resorts to driving pens through his hand, slashing his throat, and eventually earning revenge against his girlfriend and a romantic rival by... well, it isn't pretty. While the wrist-cutting is horrifically effective, the rest of the effects are graphic but more playful than anything else, buoyed by the quirky music and the lead's gleeful mugging to the camera. Unfortunately the amateurish photography severely counteracts what appears to be an attempt at a hardcore splatter version of a situation comedy, though the jokey end credits sequence is definitely one-of-a-kind.

Considering they were shot on video, the *Guinea Pig* episodes translate to DVD surprisingly well. Image quality is faithful to the original scrappy visual scheme (grain, lens flares, and bad focus are in evidence now and then), while detail is razor sharp and several generations above the VHS editions so prevalent for over ten years. *Android* fares the best overall as it was shot with a much slicker visual texture and features some striking colour compositions. Unfortunately, *Mermaid* suffers the most from some distracting compression errors during the fog-ridden sewer opening and some darker passages, but otherwise these look much better than those dupey videos. The optional subtitles are also welcome, as they at least offer some semblance of structure for what used to be rambling studies in depravity. The disc of *Flower* is the slickest of the bunch, with striking motion menus and an array of extras including two interviews with director Hideshi Hino, a gallery replication of his original *Flower of Flesh and Blood* manga (which boasts a far more elaborate narrative set up), a photo gallery, a text history of the series, and seven trailers. Viewers with PAL compatible players can also pick up the entire set from Germany in a region free boxed edition (limited to 3000 copies), which comes with a T-shirt and poster. Choose your poison carefully!

G

GUNS

Colour, 1990, 96m. / Directed by Andy Sidaris / Starring Erik Estrada, Roberta Vasquez / Malibu Bay Films (US R0 NTSC), Laser Paradise (Germany R2 PAL)

After splitting up his female agents in *Savage Beach*, boobs 'n' bombs guru Andy Sidaris paired up LETHAL vixen Donna with a new partner, Nicole Justin (Roberta Vasquez, in a completely different role from *Picasso Trigger*), for *Guns*, a more James Bond-style adventure right down to the video cover art. Most significant here is the casting of *CHiPs* star Erik Estrada as a bad guy, namely murderous gunrunner Juan Degas. Known as the Jack of Diamonds because of the playing card he leaves at the scene of a crime, he's now the target of LETHAL and tangles with the ladies in a series of explosions, near misses, and gunfights. Apparently he's trying to smuggle in deadly Chinese superweapons for a nefarious scheme.

Okay, that's about it for the plot, really; the fun of *Guns* lies as usual in those zany incidentals, like a cross-dressing, gun-toting henchman. The film moves at an unusually zippy clip, which would be a good thing except you get less time to savour the nudity, locales (much of it takes place in Vegas, not exactly a visual oasis), and goofy comedy; instead this one lives up to its title by cramming in an economic action sequence every couple of minutes. No wonder this was a perennial cable favourite; just be sure to shift gears going in and you'll have a fine time indeed.

Sidaris's first stereo surround film sounds terrific, and while the Vegas sequences feature some atypically drab cinematography, the bulk of the film looks marvellous and crystal clear. The Sidaris clan and Julie Strain pop up again for a commentary, a documentary, and the usual sundry goodies from the Sidaris vaults. As with *Do or Die* (also covered here), the U.S. disc promptly went out of circulation but was tweaked for a German release as part of a 10-disc Sidaris box set, with the extras sliced up into nine shorter, slightly different featurettes and the commentary dropped entirely.

GURU THE MAD MONK

Colour, 1970, 56m. / Directed by Andy Milligan / Starring Neil Flanagan, Paul Lieber, Judith Israel, Jaqueline Webb, Jack Spencer / Retromedia (US R1 NTSC)

"*Warning: Eyes Gouged Out with Sticks!*"(from the DVD cover). The setting is Central Europe during the Middle Ages. At the Lost Souls Church on the remote island of Mortavia, all the dregs of society are sent to be tortured, blessed by the Mother Church and then cruelly executed. God works in mysterious ways indeed! This grimly named establishment is run by a shifty priest named Father Guru (Neil Flanagan in an ill-fitting Beatles wig). Carl (Paul Lieber), the none-too-bright jailer, carries out dubious work for him, no questions asked. A woman named Nadja (Judith Israel), Carl's ex-girlfriend, is falsely charged with murdering her baby, and Father Guru does a deal with the lunkhead jailer to help her escape the chopping block. With the help of the weird old gypsy woman Olga (Jaqueline Webb), a potion renders Nadja apparently dead. The plan works and Nadja is hidden within the church. Her problems then begin anew however, as it's a case of out of the frying pan... Father Guru is increasingly growing crazed, talking to himself in the mirror. A battle between Good and Evil is raging within his split person-ality, and Evil seems to be gaining the upper hand. Down in the dungeon, a screaming woman has her plastic hands cut off, a peeping Tom gets knitting needles driven through his boiled-egg eyes, and another poor sap is decapitated (off-camera...). Olga, who is in fact a vampire, comes crawling in and avidly slurps the congealing gore from the chopping block! Nadja wants out of the church, growing terrified of some of the suspicious things she's seen from her window but Carl, confirming his dimwitted nature, trusts Father Guru. An attempt by his superiors to remove the mad monk from office ends in bloody mayhem.

Warning: Eyes Glazing Over with Boredom... Nadja tries to win the trust of Father Guru's hunchback Igor (Jack Spencer), not difficult as he is slavishly devoted to her. Guru attempts to rape Nadja, but Igor hears her cries of distress and intervenes. As a punishment, Father Guru and Olga crucify the unfortunate hunchback to a wall, cutting out his tongue with an inordinately large pair of scissors for good measure. Guru decides to run away, impaling Olga on her own dagger when she tries to stop him leaving her. Igor frees himself from the wall and, along with Carl, chases the maniacal monk upstairs. Cornered like a rat, Guru stabs the hobbling hunchback to death before Carl hangs the crazed cleric from a bell-rope noose. This frenetic finale plays out like a deranged end chase sequence from *The Benny Hill Show*! Which brings us to... *The End*. Mercifully...

Warning: Eyes Propped Open with Matchsticks... Some proclaim that the lurid gorefests peddled by low budget Staten Island filmmaker Andy Milligan are the work of a tortured "genius," a maverick auteur to rival that other famous experimental director/artist Andy Warhol. Others believe, just as fervently, that Milligan should have been tortured to death before inflicting his shoddy shockers on any audience, drive-in or otherwise. Both views are debatable, at least one understandable. True, both Milligan and Warhol had the same first name, surrounded themselves with "street people"

whom they stuck in front of film cameras to "star" in their personal visions, and both favoured long-held static shots of poorly-miked dialogue scenes. However, Andy Warhol surrounded himself with a galaxy of hunky gay studs, transvestites, punky musicians and gorgeous Euro-babes who had genuine charisma and rough talent to spare. Andy Milligan found himself the hub of a gaggle of dreary homosexual has-beens and drugged-out weirdos who seemed more likely to be sporting scabies, terminal acne, BO and any number of sexually transmitted diseases... we're talking rough trade here, not rough talent! Small wonder that the Velvet Underground chose to hang around the Factory rather than Staten Island. However, many whose film interests fall outside the mainstream are strangely drawn to Milligan's OTT *oeuvre*. In 1969's *The Ghastly Ones* (aka: *Blood Rites*, still banned in the U.K. as a video nasty) he did actually create a half-decent film, and hilarious tosh like *Torture Dungeon* is actually quite fun to watch if only to find out what a "tri-sexual" is. Flitting between Staten Island, where the bulk of his films were lensed, and England (!), like Hammer Milligan chose to make all his films costume-heavy period pieces, all the better to stop them dating so badly. A pity then that he didn't tell his actresses (using the term advisedly) to ditch their trowelled-on mascara, false eyelashes and contemporary hairstyles. Oh well, it all adds to the crude charm.

Titled to cash in on one of Hammer's lesser films, *Rasputin the Mad Monk*, *Guru the Mad Monk* is indeed a (very) bad film by the general standards of film criticism, but as with H.G. Lewis and Doris Wishman, one has to step sideways into a different mind-set to appreciate and judge Milligan's filmic universe. *Guru* was actually Milligan's first film to be shot on 35mm stock, though you'd hardly know it. It looks like a Super 8 home movie most of the time, rather like a doting parent's lensing of a primary school play. Shot on location in St. Peter's Church,

Manhattan, which was also supposedly used as a Black Panthers bolthole, this film is a little less gory than some of Milligan's other horrors, and the camera-work leans towards the lethargic. The music comes from stock records so scratched you keep expecting them to jump or stick. In one hilarious scene a choir is heard over a scene of Father Guru and his minimal entourage (two altar boys who struggle to hold their crosses upright!) walking down the church aisle – apart from them the church is empty, and there is no sign of a single choirboy, let alone the full chorus belting it out on the soundtrack!

The acting is abysmal, though Flanagan is pretty amusing as the titular "mad monk"; check out that ridiculous rug on his head. He's no Christopher Lee, to be sure. Likewise Lieber, as the hunky hero, is so bad that he makes Warhol's own plank of wood Joe Dallesandro look like Oscar-worthy material in comparison (no mean feat). In some scenes the interplay between Flanagan and Lieber is so poor that more entertainment can be found in the 1960s furniture clearly visible behind them. And more than a little irritation comes from Milligan's fetish for having a grimacing hunchback lollop into frame in just about all his films... The best that can be said is that *Guru the Mad Monk* is by no means Milligan's worst film. In comparison to sad and sorry sadistic slop like *The Rats Are Coming, the Werewolves Are Here*, it's *Henry V*. Strangely, *Guru* did very well for him, though the fact that some of his new business partners were Times Square hucksters meant that he saw little of the healthy profits. By the late '80s Milligan's style of underground gore was well past its sell-by date. Diagnosed with AIDS, the director died in 1991, penniless and forgotten. Well, almost forgotten, because his *filmbrut* offerings live on to taunt and depress the unwary or the curious, first through video and now the magic of DVD. Who would have thought it possible?

We have Fred Olen Ray's company, Retromedia Entertainment Inc., to thank for this print, which forms part of their hit and miss "Drive-In Theatre" series. Undoubtedly the best this film is ever going to look (though that's not saying much), the print is presented full-frame. Though mastered from original elements, the print is hideously marred by scratches, missing frames etc., which reduce the already short running time by several minutes! There seems to have been censor-snipping in several places. Too bad this stuff could not have been restored. The poster art's boast of the film's "blood-dripping colour" would be more impressive if there was actually much blood dripping in the first place. In any other film by nearly any other director, these kind of visual imperfections would matter; here they just merge into the atmosphere of unrelenting tedium and general weirdness that permeates every (surviving) frame. Extras on the disc boil down to the original trailer and a documentary presented by Thomas Vozza, "Remembering Andy," which may or may not change your opinion of Milligan as a director and human being. It's also available as part of their "Blood Flood" triple feature, too. For masochists only...

– NB

HANDS OF THE RIPPER

Colour, 1971, 84m. / Directed by Peter Sasdy / Starring Eric Porter, Angharad Rees, Dora Bryan, Marjie Lawrence, Lynda Baron, Derek Godfrey, Keith Bell, Jane Merrow / Carlton, Network (UK R2 PAL), Anolis (Germany R2 PAL) / WS (1.66:1) (16:9)

 A terrified young child witnesses her mother's barbarous slaying by her own father, Jack the Ripper. Several years pass and the girl, Anna (Angharad Rees), is rescued from a life of abuse at the hands of her guardian (Dora Bryan) by eminent psychiatrist Dr. John

Pritchard (Eric Porter). He discovers that whenever Anna falls into a trance – triggered by a combination of sparkling light and any display of affection towards her – she turns into a malevolent killer, seemingly possessed by the spirit of the Ripper. Afterwards she has no recollection of what she has done, believing the flashes of violence that flutter through her mind to be remnants of bad dreams. Pritchard is convinced he can cure her condition but as people around him begin to die horribly it appears as if it's a decision he will regret.

The simplest of ideas can often spawn the most interesting of films. The premise for this 1971 Hammer offering was indeed simple: what if Jack the Ripper had a child, a daughter who grew up with her father's murderous streak burned deep into her psyche? What if the legacy of evil that terrorised London during the autumn months of 1888 continued through her? Despite ensuring a goodly measure of Hammeresque violence, with *Hands of the Ripper* director Peter Sasdy (*Countess Dracula*) fabricated a story that isn't so much frightening as it is sad, at times almost overwhelmingly so. This turns expectation on its head, after all, why would one feel sorry for a mass murderer? The fact is that the Ripper's daughter, Anna (endearingly cast in the fragile form of Angharad Rees), is not only unwitting of her actions, she is also so frail and pretty that the audience is rendered helplessly sympathetic towards her. The girl's childlike innocence evokes pity where there should be loathing, for her acts of murder are monstrous. Dora Bryan as Anna's avaricious guardian has a poker driven into her with such force that it passes through both her and the door behind; the housemaid Dolly (Marjie Lawrence) has her throat slashed with a shard of glass from a broken mirror; prostitute Long Liz (Lynda Baron), who rescues Anna from the streets, is rewarded for playing good Samaritan with a handful of hat-pins shoved through her eyeball. Even Pritchard pays the price for dancing with the devil and the harrowing

sequence in which he tries to remove the sword with which Anna has perforated his torso by hooking the grip over a door handle brings tears to your eyes. For all its brutality, *Hands of the Ripper* is wreathed in a downward spiral of melancholy, masterfully intensified by Christopher Gunning's exquisite score.

Eric Porter (who later became the most despicable Moriarty ever, opposite Jeremy Brett's Sherlock Holmes) is wonderfully dour as Pritchard, not so much wicked as misguided. Much like the character of Anna he toys with the viewer's emotions and we teeter between caring and contempt. Although he purports to be helping the poor child – and indeed, he affords her the only true happiness she experiences in her short life – his motives are purely self-serving. Anna's traumas are a professional challenge and unwittingly she becomes his guinea pig, placing her trust in a man who cruelly betrays her. Derek Godfrey is the despicable womanising rake Dysart, with Dora Bryan her usual entertainingly twittery self as the rapacious Mrs. Golding. Scripter L.W. Davidson (whose work is based on an original story by Edward Spencer Shrew) introduces a sub-plot involving Pritchard's son Michael (Keith Bell) and his blind fiancée Laura (Jane Merrow) which paves the way for a moving finale high up in the Whispering Gallery at St. Paul's Cathedral. Now Anna realises that everything Pritchard convinced her was the product of her nightmares has in fact been real and, as her fingers close around Laura's throat, the Ripper's voice echoes chillingly from her lips: "Whose darkness do we meet in Laura? Your darkness or mine?" Momentarily regaining her self-control, as the voices of the Cathedral choir swell on the soundtrack, Anna spots Pritchard down below. Climbing onto the balcony to get to him she plunges to her death. Butchered for American television in the late 1970s in a version that the passage of time has fortunately seen lost, the only way to view *Hands of the Ripper* is as Sasdy intended. His film is one of the most uniquely satisfying in Hammer's vast library, without question a high point in his own career, and essential viewing for Hammerphiles.

First released only on Region 2 format DVD as part of a boxed set from Carlton entitled "The Horror Collection" – which also includes wildly inferior Brit-terrors *The Uncanny* and *The Monster* (aka I *Don't Want to Be Born*) – *Hands of the Ripper* is presented in 1.66:1 format (with 16:9 enhancement) and is accompanied by its theatrical trailer. A subsequent special edition reissue from Network sports a similarly handsome presentation along with a commentary by Kim Newman, Stephen Jones and Rees, who covers the basics of making the film from her perspective. It's interesting from a British horror filmmaking standpoint, with the two writers filling in some Hammer history for good measure. The other extra is Rees's appearance on Brian Clemens's marvellous *Thriller*; alas, "Once the Killing Starts" is one of the weaker episodes, with Patrick O'Neal cracking up as a self-absorbed murderer. The German PAL release is basically superfluous by comparison.

– TG

HÄNSEL UND GRETEL

Colour, 1954, 37m. / Directed by Fritz Genschow / Starring Uwe Witt, Heidi Ewert, Erika Petrick, August Spillner, Werner Stock, Erika Kruse, Wulf Rittscher / VCL (Germany R2 PAL)

 Fritz Genschow's 1954 *Hänsel und Gretel* has generally been considered one of the more elusive children's films from the 1950s, for a variety of reasons. In fact as far as non-German speaking territories were concerned it was to all intents a 'lost' film. In any case it only

survives to this day in a severely compromised edit, the story of which is almost as incredible as the folk tale upon which it draws. Due to an act of carelessness in the 1960s the original negative was lost when loaned to the late Florida-based entrepreneur K. Gordon Murray for U.S. release to the "Kiddie Matinee" market he had spearheaded successfully, and subsequently only about 37 minutes of the original 87 minutes long feature film remain! Missing in action is the bulk of a black and white-lensed book-ending storyline set in then-contemporary Germany and featuring two children called "Hans" and "Greta", which purportedly closely mirrored the fairytale section which was presented in glowing Agfacolor for maximum contrast. Presumably Murray had no truck with such Euro-artiness and scissored this material from the negative for the version he then had struck... Philistine! This part of the movie vanished along with the entire negative, and is presumed gone for good. Only film prints remain, but none of these contain the lost footage.

However, what is left is a tidy condensing of the original Grimm Brothers tale (which I assume all readers are familiar with so won't make *précis* of unduly here), which moves briskly through its simple plot, helped along by some truly inspired and often hallucinogenic imagery that will stick in your mind long after you've seen this film. The cast is great, with Uwe Witt and Heidi Ewert the perfect Hänsel and Gretel respectively. Elsewhere Erika Petrick and August Spillner are suitably tormented as the desperate parents of these two winsome waifs, forced to abandon their offspring in the Black Forest in order to survive starvation... desperate measures for desperate times! It's not all totally bleak though, as comic relief is doled out at regular intervals, with Hänsel and Gretel's cheery neighbours Michel (Werner Stock) and Lene (Erika Kruse) lightening the tone with jolly japes involving glove puppets and an amusing contest between themselves and capitalistic rival Kaufmann Klos (Wulf Rittscher) at the Herzberg market.

It's the sequences of the children lost deep in the tenebrous forest, and their encounter with the cannibalistic witch that most people will focus on though, and here the film goes into fantasy overdrive. For starters there's the bizarre dream that Hänsel and Gretel have after the 'Sandman' sends them to sleep, in which the hungry children find themselves watching a gluttonous magical feast attended by costumed dwarves and hosted by 'Good King Appetite'! The next day, the children come across the Gingerbread House and... well, you know the rest. However familiar this folk tale is to most people, Genschow imbues the proceedings with some unique visual quirks, as in the creepy gingerbread figures that stand like weird scarecrows in front of the witch's house, their eyes following the two children's every move. These are the previous child victims of Elizabeth Ilna's gnarled witch, who emerges from her cottage to ensnare the starving siblings. Outwitted by Hänsel, and pushed into her own oven by Gretel, the witch's fiery demise frees the captured village children who, after a quick song and dance of celebration, and clutching magic bread handed out by Hänsel, wend their merry way down the hillside and into town where of course they are greeted with jubilation by their parents.

There's much to love about this film. Though all the voices seem to have been dubbed in later (all too obviously at times) the songs (many sung by children) are suitably charming. The authentic Black Forest locations help immensely of course, and the photography by Gerhard Huttula is inspired and oft-times lyrical. The gap-toothed witch is scary by any standards too, especially when she does her demented-dervish dance, sweeping Gretel before her with her broomstick... A few endearing anachronisms that betray the film's low budget are to be glimpsed; take a good look at several scenes at the Herzberg market where brightly coloured 1950s cafe umbrellas can be seen quite clearly amongst the milling period costumed extras!

The current Region 2 German DVD on VCL opens with all that survives of the original black and white footage, with the circular "Fritz Genschow Film" logo (which features Genschow's daughter and her teddy bear inset) and full title credits, and then reverts to Agfa-Color for the story itself. Very simple but undeniably effective. The full-frame 1.33:1 print, apparently struck from the only surviving internegative, shows a little wear (a few speckles and scratches) but is in remarkable shape with generally vivid colour. The DVD picture quality is quite good, with only one barely noticeable transfer glitch, and the German-only soundtrack is clear and strong (Dolby Digital mono). The print runs for 37m 26s at PAL speed. There is what may be a newly generated "Ende" title before it fades to black. This DVD was produced for the domestic market so no English subtitles are supplied, but the story is so simple and well known that this is surely no real obstacle to enjoyment. Other Fritz Genschow titles advertised in this DVD series ("Die Schönsten Märchenfilme der Gebrüder Grimm") include *Aschenputtel* (*Cinderella*), *Frau Holle* (*Mother Holly*) and *Tischlein Deck Dich* (*Table, Donkey and Stick*) (the latter two also marketed by K. Gordon Murray in the States). All pretty essential in my book!

– NB

HAPPINESS OF THE KATAKURIS

Colour, 2000, 113m. / Directed by Takashi Miike / Starring Kenji Sawada, Keiko Matsuzaka, Shinji Takeda, Naomi Nishida, Tetsuro Tamba, Kiyoshiro Imawano / Chimera, Eastern Star (US R0 NTSC) / WS (1.85:1) (16:9), Tartan (UK R0 PAL) / WS (1.85:1) (16:9) / DD5.1, Fortex (HK R3 NTSC) / WS (1.85:1) / DD5.1

An upbeat musical from prolific Japanese shockmaster Takashi Miike might seem wholly absurd, at least until you figure in all the dancing corpses, experimental claymation and escalating body count. A pitch black comedy ideally suited for midnight movie viewings, *Happiness of the Katakuris* (*Katakuri-ke no kôfuku*) is a loving and utterly insane salute to Japanese pop kitsch, zombie horror romps, and avant-garde animation. If that sounds like a bizarre stew, well, wait until you see the actual movie.

Determined to help his financially struggling family, Masao Katakuri (Kenji Sawada) decides to open an inn located in a mountainous region of Japan. The whole clan is enlisted to run the establishment: wife Terue (former pop queen and renowned actress Keiko Matsuzaka), rebellious son Masayuki (Shinji Takeda), lovelorn daughter Shizue (Naomi Nishida), and doddering grandfather Jinpei (*You Only Live Twice*'s Tetsuro Tamba). Unfortunately the first customer winds up committing suicide in his room on the first night, so to avoid any possible damage to business, the body is disposed of in a nearby shallow grave. Then along come a huge sumo wrestler and his underage paramour, both of whom meet particularly grotesque ends. Meanwhile Shizue wanders into town and is swept off her feet, literally, by a "half-English" naval officer, Richard (punk singer Kiyoshiro Imawano), who speaks in broken Japanese and bears a suspiciously shaggy haircut. And then there's the nearby volcano that keeps threatening to erupt...

Cult movie fans lucky enough to stumble upon *Katakuris* should find enough to enjoy from Miike's visuals alone: the Brothers Quay-inspired opening involving soup and a torn epiglottis, a *Thriller*-inspired dance sequence involving funky undead strutters, a riotous Karaoke interlude, and best of all, Richard and Shizue's "I love you" musical centrepiece which transforms into a *Moulin Rouge*-style riot of colour and design. Fortunately there's enough of a plot to back up the schizoid shifts in tone, with some wonderfully clever dialogue included to keep the brain occupied even while the eyes are overloaded. Richard gets most of the funniest bits, including a soliloquy involving his royal heritage and his relationship to the late Lady Di that should go down in the camp cinema history books. Not easily forgotten, this is "family viewing" of the oddest, goofiest kind.

The Happiness of the Katakuris was first released on Hong Kong DVD in a skimpy edition containing only the theatrical trailer. Apart from a dynamic 5.1 mix, the disc is largely missable thanks to the mediocre non-anamorphic transfer and unwieldy English subtitles punctuated with a large number of errors. The U.S. disc from Chimera (later reissued through Eastern Star) is a much more satisfying addition to their line of Miike releases. The 16:9 transfer is a beauty with razor sharp detail, in many ways even more eye-catching than the repertory theatrical prints. The optional English subtitles (very legible, spell checked, and in yellow) are quite satisfying, and the 5.1 audio is even punchier than the HK edition. The disc comes loaded with extras including the usual Chimera trailers and a 61-minute documentary, "White Lovers' Guest House", which focuses primarily on the rehearsals and execution of the various musical numbers along with peeks at the costuming process and the staging of the frenetic climax. Miike also appears for a 33-minute interview at a sound mixing board, discussing the film's status as a Japanese "New Year" film (see the liner notes by Patrick Macias for more info on this subgenre) and his approach to pulling off such a technically audacious, non-commercial project. On top of that, Miike also contributes a feature-length audio commentary, in original Japanese on one track or with an English translator on a third audio track. Much of the information is expanded or rephrased from Miike's other appearances on the disc, but he also offers several new nuggets of information including some notes about how the film registers within his amazing, highly diverse body of work. The packaging indicates TV spots for the film, but none appear to be included. There is a TV spot on the British release from Tartan however, and this fully-loaded disc also incorporates all the same extras as are found on the Chimera edition, but improves on that disc's presentation of the Japanese language commentary track by offering an English language translation as an extra subtitle option. Additional extras include a short (5m 30s) look behind the scenes at the film's animators at work, interviews with Miike and five other key personnel and a trailer reel for six Miike films: *Rainy Dog*, *Ley Lines*, *The City of Lost Souls*, *Shinjuku Triad Society*, *Dead or Alive: Final* and *Audition*.

HAPPY TREE FRIENDS: FIRST BLOOD / SECOND SERVING / THIRD STRIKE / WINTER BREAK / OVERKILL / SEASON 1

Mondo Mini Shows/StudioWorks (US R1 NTSC), Revolver (UK R2 PAL) / DD2.0

 Even in the currently burgeoning realm of shock animation, *Happy Tree Friends* is the sort of warped concoction that manages to make even jaded viewers stop in their tracks. Sort of a more unhinged cousin to the likes of *South Park*, *Ren & Stimpy* and "The Itchy and Scratchy Show", this gore-drenched collection of vignettes would seem horribly diseased if it weren't so achingly funny.

The first volume (appropriately subtitled "First Blood") contains a main program of 14 episodes, each running about a minute and a half each. Each skit begins with the horrifyingly catchy theme song and opens with a collection of cute, fuzzy animal characters jabbering in cartoonspeak, then embarking on a seemingly innocent activity that invariably results in graphic carnage and dismemberment. Characters include Handy (a beaver missing his two front paws), Flippy (a Vietnam-traumatized critter prone to gory games of hide and seek), Sniffles (an aardvark who suffers a particularly heinous fate at the hands of some vengeance-driven ants), Lumpy (a stupid and oft-abused moose), and Disco Bear (who consigns his unwilling dance partners to a gory end). Standout episodes include "Spin Fun Knowing You" (in which a merry-go-round romp turns deadly), "Treasure These Idol Moments" (a *Brady Bunch*-inspired bit in which a cursed idol decimates the entire cast), "Nuttin' but the Tooth" (dental surgery gone horribly wrong), and "House Warming" (Handy's finest moment).

But that's not all, kids! You also get a new pirate character introduced in the previously unseen episodes, "Whose Line Is It Anyway", along with a silly pop-up video version of "Spin Fun", a character gallery done trading card-style with amusingly banal "fun facts", an earlier short from the same creators, and a gallery of character designs including numerous unused characters. The twisted minds behind these poisonous goodies appear for a separate commentary edition of the shorts, which unspool alongside storyboard versions; it's a party atmosphere all the way with everyone cramming in to get their anecdotes heard. Perhaps the sickest extra of all is a collection of "Smoochies", in which four characters are put into Sim-like survival situations entitled "Original Cuddles", "Valentine's Day", "Happy Easter" and "Party Smoochie". For example, choosing "sleep" for a character results in a barrage of tranquilizer darts turning its head into a pincushion, while "bathe" turns the screen into a deadly flood of water.

Video quality is excellent all around; all of the shorts were originally shown on the Internet as streaming video, but here you can savour every nasty little detail to your heart's content. The surround audio is quite active, allowing that damn theme song to pump out of your speakers. Every hack, squish and spurt also sounds perfectly clear. The other discs are essentially more of the same and have gone out of print through most retailers, but you can savor their greatest hits all together in one set with *Season 1*, a handy overview of mayhem and bloodshed served up in one cute, fuzzy package. The U.K. saw releases of each volume as well through Revolver in 2005.

HARD HUNTED

Colour, 1992, 93m. / Directed by Andy Sidaris / Starring Dona Speir, Roberta Vasquez, R.J. Moore [Geoffrey Moore] / Malibu Bay Films (US R0 NTSC), Laser Paradise (Germany R2 PAL)

After Andy Sidaris roped Erik Estrada and Pat Morita into his intoxicating world of tropical gals and guns, more oddball celeb casting reared its head in *Hard Hunted*, a more-or-less sequel to *Do or Die*, which features another villain named Kane – or is it really supposed to be the same one? – played by one "R.J. Moore", alias Roger "007" Moore's son, Geoffrey. This time he's gotten his slimy hands on a nuclear device (in the form of a jade trinket) capable of worldwide blackmail and terrorism. Thanks to secret messages sent by scantily-clad undercover radio hosts, the LETHAL team learns of Kane's plot and sends an operative to stop him. Unfortunately it all goes very wrong thanks to an

evil sidekick working for Kane, and soon Donna and Nicole (along with their usual male cohorts) trek to Arizona to infiltrate Kane's headquarters, retrieve the valuable artefact, and blow up everything in sight. Unfortunately Donna falls into enemy hands and seems to fall in love with the other side... or does she? Stay tuned and find out!

Probably the prize winner for most explosions in a Sidaris film, *Hard Hunted* features some lush jungle locales and looks terrific in this digital transfer, which is decked out with the usual avalanche of Sidaris-related extras including commentary, gallery, location and film school featurettes, and trailers for the Sidaris collection. As with other titles in the series, it also went out of print and become quite collectible on the U.S. market, with Germany subsequently releasing it as part of their ten-title Sidaris set, which chops up the featurette material differently into eight smaller, bite-sized morsels ranging from one to eleven minutes each.

HARD TICKET TO HAWAII

Colour, 1987, 96m. / Directed by Andy Sidaris / Starring Ronn Moss, Hope Marie Carlton, Dona Speir, Rodrigo Obregon / Malibu Bay Films (US R0 NTSC), Laser Paradise (Germany R2 PAL)

The success of Sidaris's *Malibu Express* on the drive-in and video circuit naturally inspired a sequel two years later, *Hard Ticket to Hawaii* (the first Sidaris title released on DVD). In the weird postmodern Sidaris universe, *Hard Ticket* takes place both within and outside the world of its predecessor, where hero Cody Abilene has taken off to become a Hollywood actor (with a *Malibu Express* poster adorning one character's houseboat boudoir). Now we have Rowdy Abilene

(Ronn Moss), sent by the Agency to help out regular crime-fighting duo Donna (Dona Speir) and Taryn (Hope Marie Carlton) after they stumble across a cache of gems being routed to ruthless bar owner and crime kingpin Seth Romero (Rodrigo Obregon). When the ladies aren't too busy hopping in and out of their skimpy costumes, various deadly instruments are used against the bad guys including a gory razor Frisbee trick and, most memorably, a huge killer snake pumped up with toxic chemicals. Oh yeah, and lots of stuff blows up for no reason, and you get loads of Hawaiian travelogue footage to justify Andy's business expense sheet. Pure late night heaven.

Image quality is absolutely striking throughout, with bold, eye-searing colours; the full frame compositions look fine but benefit even more from blow-up to 1.78:1 on anamorphic televisions. Mr. and Mrs. Sidaris turn up again for video extras and a commentary track, with the vivacious Julie Strain tagging along for eye candy; the commentary was dropped but the video material was repurposed for Germany's ten-title Sidaris set (see above) and, for once, the commentary was carried over as well.

HAROLD AND MAUDE

Colour, 1971, 87m. / Directed by Hal Ashby / Starring Bud Cort, Ruth Gordon, Vivian Pickles, Charles Tyner, Tom Skerritt / Paramount (US R1 NTSC, UK R2 PAL) / WS (1.85:1) (16:9)

 In therapy to help him cope with an unhealthy obsession with death, twenty-something Harold Chasen (Bud Cort) stages fake suicides in a cry for attention from his overbearing, under-attentive mother, purchases a hearse and religiously attends the funerals of people he didn't even know. On one such occasion

he befriends sprightly septuagenarian Maude (Ruth Gordon). She proves to be the antidote to Harold's maudlin outlook and introduces him to some of the frivolity and fun that life has to offer. As time passes they fall in love and, much to his mother's horror, Harold announces his intention to marry Maude. But the old lady's eightieth birthday looms on the horizon and she has a surprise up her sleeve that will alter Harold's perception of the fragility of life once and for all.

Arguably Hal Ashby's crowning film achievement, *Harold and Maude* is a black comedy unlike anything else you'll ever see. Some of the subject matter – specifically the fulfilling friendship and ultimately sexual alliance between two people with almost sixty years between them – might sound a little quease-inducing, but don't be perturbed. Ashby's approach is so subtly convincing – and it's such a delight to observe the colour gradually eclipsing the deathly pallor on Harold's face as he spends time in the old lady's company – that, by the time the story reaches its sorrowful yet uplifting conclusion, you'll probably have fallen a little bit in love with Maude yourself.

Bud Cort (*Brain Dead*) is perfect as the depressed teenager who stages atrocious, attention-grabbing stunts, which range from putting a bullet through his head as his oblivious mother fills out the application form for a computer dating service to slashing his throat and spraying her bathroom with plasma. When mother goes behind his back and trades in his hearse for a sleek E-Type Jaguar, Harold does the only thing a morbid death-obsessive can – he sets to work with an acetylene torch and transforms it into a mega-nifty flat-top E-Type Hearse. The late Ruth Gordon (*Rosemary's Baby*) gives a career best performance as the concentration camp survivor with little regard for any law that stifles the care-not-a-jot freedom that old age has given her. Whether it be joy-riding in stolen cars or illegally relocating a moribund tree, she wastes not a second of the life she knows is fast drawing to an end. Vivian Pickles too is splendid as Harold's self-occupied mother, while Charles Tyner delivers a nice comic turn as one-armed war veteran Uncle Victor, who lives solely to relate tales of his military glories. Watch out too for an almost unrecognisable Tom Skerritt (*Alien*) – credited as M. Borman and looking like he's just stepped off the stage at a Village People gig – as a befuddled motorcycle cop.

If you've any doubt that a film can be viciously funny, heartbreakingly tragic and sweetly redolent all at once, *Harold and Maude* will put you straight. Writer/producer Colin Higgins's script combines mordant social satire with more drop dead funny moments pro rata than you'll find in a dozen so-billed comedies. The sequence in which Harold scares off a chattery blind date that his mother has set him up with by seeming to set fire to himself is delicious, the icing on the cake following directly on when Cort breaches the third wall by offering the audience a sly sideways smile. Yusuf Islam (better known to the world as hippie Cat Stevens) provides the score, with "Don't Be Shy" (played out over the opening titles as Harold hangs himself), "Where Do the Children Play?" and "If You Want to Sing Out, Sing Out" giving audiences who thought his songs weren't quite their cup of tea the opportunity for a rethink. Hilarious and insightful in equal measure, *Harold and Maude* may look a little dated nowadays, but its overwhelmingly life-affirming message is timeless. Live life to its fullest and don't dwell on the inevitability of death – achieve this and you've truly got it licked.

One must rejoice in the fact that Paramount saw fit to grant this curio a relatively early release on DVD, like versions being available in both R1 and R2 pressings. It must be noted, however, that the colours on the 26-chapter appointed, 1.85:1 matted feature occasionally appear a tad muted, albeit not injuriously so. The only

extra feature is a pair of theatrical trailers, but they unveil so much in the way of alternative takes and unused footage that one can only hope for a *Harold and Maude* special edition at some point in the not too distant future. The British disc offers sound in English, German, Spanish, Italian and French, with subtitling in the same five languages plus Danish, Turkish, Swedish, Norwegian and Dutch. If you're a real completist, the 2007 reissue under the Paramount Originals banner also includes a reproduction of the film poster.
– TG

HAUNTED SCHOOL 4

Colour, 1999, 99m. / Directed by Hideyuki Hirayama / Starring Toyota Mayu, Chouja Yasuyuki, Minagawa Yuuki, Sakai Hideto / Worldtrade (HK R0 NTSC) / WS (2.35:1) / DD2.0

The fourth entry in a popular series of Japanese films from the Toho studios which, like the creepy domestic TV programs of the same name, are based on the book *Gakkou no Kaidan* by Toru Tsunemitsu. In this case the tried and well-tested formula of having a bunch of pre-pubescent Nippon nippers chased around a deserted school by ghoulies, ghosties, long-legged beasties and things that go bump in the night is eschewed for an altogether darker and more serious plotline. Gone are the rubbery – if effective in context – apparitions of the earlier films, along with the *Goonies*-style humour that occasionally jarred the nerves of those viewers intrigued by these curious children's entertainments, the like of which are rarely found in the West (no, *Goosebumps* doesn't come close). Instead the viewer is faced with a genuinely moving story about child-death and the loss of one's school companions, which colours the supernatural storyline a gloomier hue than is usually the case in the *Haunted School* series. Quite why regular scriptwriter Satoko Okudera took this lurch away from slapstick kiddy-comedy into arguably more adult territory is unclear but welcome.

After a dramatic pre-credits sequence sets the tone with a school being overwhelmed by a huge wave (depicted in crisp monochrome by Kozo Shibazaki, whose widescreen camerawork is consistently good throughout), *Haunted School 4* (*Gakkou no Kaidan 4*) jumps to the present day. A couple of Tokyo kids, Yae (Toyota Mayu) and her older brother Kyouichi (Chouja Yasuyuki), visit their Aunt who lives in a coastal town lashed by seasonal typhoons. During their first evening there the lights flicker out due to the battering storm and their cousin Ayumu (Minagawa Yuuki) tells them, "It's done by the ghosts in the sea". It transpires that the town is in the process of celebrating its annual "Ghost Festival", a kind of Summer Halloween in which it is believed that the spirits of those who drowned in past tragedies, like the Tsunami that destroyed their primary school many years before, can return from their watery graves. Yae is fascinated by this dismal tale. The following day the president of the local primary school's children's club, Shuuji (Sakai Hideto), vanishes in bizarre circumstances. Later he returns just as mysteriously, crawling from the surf, muttering dreamily about being forced to play a game of hide and seek in an old-fashioned wooden school. More children vanish as the barriers between life and death seem to weaken... The past appears to bubble up into the present, bringing with it grim reminders like the rotted gym shoe that bobs to the surface of a swimming pool just after a young girl has been dragged under by unseen hands... In particular Kyouichi seems to feel he is being called upon to take part in an unfinished game, one whose rules he doesn't understand. He is drawn repeatedly to an old black and white photo displayed in the school, which shows a group of four children killed by the tidal wave that swept away the old seafront school. Voices whisper his name and his sleep is disturbed by strange dreams. Yae becomes increasingly concerned for him, and when he too vanishes it is up to the brave girl, with the help of a mysterious old man she calls "Uncle Shop", to enter the spirit world to confront and placate the lonely, restless spirits and rescue her brother and the other missing children. In the rotting, creaking remnants of the sunken school, Yae faces a seemingly hopeless task... What will the outcome be?

Haunted School 4 is full of deliciously spooky moments throughout (a peripatetic Buddha statue, a creepy living rag-doll and a real "ghost train" for example), and as noted before is gloomier than the previous entries, rendering it perhaps more adult-friendly (these films were massive family favourites in Japan and the Far East). Some of the images on show are truly effective, such as the scene where the ghosts turn up amongst the happy throng at a bustling fairground, unseen by everyone but Kyouichi, bleached of all colour like their old class photo; this great visual effect is enhanced by the fact they are wearing garish carnival masks. The sequence when the townsfolk, dressed in traditional funerary garments, crowd the nocturnal seafront to release hundreds of glowing floating lanterns to honour their dead is also memorable, and the scene in which the long-dead ghost-children are "found" one by one by Yae and re-united with "Uncle Shop", their erstwhile school friend Kochiyan, the sole survivor from the opening sequence, is quite moving. At several points the film is reminiscent of John Carpenter's *The Fog*, with the central theme of the anniversary of a town's tragedy, a wooden name-board from the lost school bobbing in the surf, a scary sequence set in a lighthouse, and the appearance of glowing mist in some shots. The musical soundtrack is complementary, skipping from childish lightheartedness, through sadness, to jolting frissons from one moment to the next. CGI is used to generally good effect, especially in the scenes set in the waterlogged school, such as shots of the ghosts reconstituting themselves into human form, muscle and skin forming over their bones, and a fish-tank in one of the classrooms still inhabited by the ghostly skeletal remains of its long dead tenant! The end credits feature outtake shots from the film as a pleasant bonus.

The all region NTSC Hong Kong DVD from Worldtrade Entertainment delivers the film in full 2.35:1 Cinemascope, but it is not anamorphically enhanced and the burned in English subtitles are sometimes hard to read. Picture quality is okay but could be better for such a well-shot film. However, this release is now deleted and has been replaced by a non-English-subtitled print on City Connection Ltd (also non-anamorphic). In Japan *Haunted School 4* was released in a lavish (and expensive) five-disc box-set containing all four *Gakkou no Kaidan* films remastered and anamorphically enhanced plus a whole disc of extras, but once again no English subtitles are provided. Hopefully an enterprising U.S. or U.K. DVD company will get around to releasing these movies in due course.

– NB

THE HAUNTED STRANGLER
B&W, 1957, 78m. / Directed by Robert Day / Starring Boris Karloff, Jean Kent, Anthony Dawson
CORRIDORS OF BLOOD
B&W, 1958, 86m. / Directed by Robert Day / Starring Boris Karloff, Betta St. John, Francis De Wolff, Christopher Lee, Francis Matthews, Yvonne Warren [Yvonne Romain] / Image, Criterion (US R1 NTSC)

This pair of blood-and-thunder vehicles for Boris Karloff were shot back-to-back by Robert Day for producer Richard Gordon in the immediate aftermath of the revival of Gothic horror spearheaded by *The Curse of Frankenstein*. Karloff gives *The Haunted Strangler* some class and it has a nice set of period production values. It seems to owe more to the world of Tod Slaughter than Hammer, with a frankly ludicrous plot that allows for a great deal of scenery-chewing, not to mention random exploitation elements like can-can dancers and public executions.

In 1880, twenty years after an innocent one-armed man has gone to the gallows, novelist and humanitarian James Rankin (Karloff) reopens the case of the Haymarket Strangler, a fiend who preyed on women in and around a dubious music hall named the Judas Hole. Certain that a disgraced doctor named Tennant is the missing murderer and that he slipped his scalpel into the executed innocent's coffin, Rankin bribes his way into a prison (allowing for a brutal whipping scene to show the unenlightened nature of 19th Century penal institutions) and has the hanged man's grave dug up. Finding the scalpel, Rankin undergoes a psychological Jekyll-and-Hyde transformation – contorting his face in an unusual manner that is comical and unsettling all at once, he manifests his original personality as the maniac Tennant. More murders ensue and the police (Anthony Dawson, in a rare good guy role) close in, while the film comes up with more excuses to dawdle in the good-time girls' dressing area, and finally even Rankin admits that it's been obvious that he's at once hero and villain.

Also known as *Grip of the Strangler*, this has its dull drawing room patches, but Karloff gives the dual role far more of his talent than was evident in the near-contemporary likes of *Frankenstein 1970* or *Voodoo Island*; maybe a return to the British film industry and the presence of solid supporting players prompted him to pull out a few more stops. Historical nitpickers will note the presence in the archives of Scotland Yard of files labelled "Jack the Ripper" (eight years before those murders took place) and "Constance Kent" (though she killed her brother in Somerset, well off the Yard's patch).

Shot just after *The Haunted Strangler*, *Corridors of Blood* fell through the cracks and wasn't released until 1962. An essay in the comparatively sparse early-days-of-medicine horror filmography and unique in the subgenre in that it isn't a version of the story of Burke and Hare, this spins off a gruesome tale from the development of anaesthesia (treated more seriously in Preston Sturges's *The Great Moment*) with Karloff as Dr. Thomas Bolton, a London physician in 1840 who is sneered at by conservative colleagues and students because he insists that surgery and pain need not be inseparable. After a failed demonstration, Bolton develops a potent opiate to which he becomes addicted, which leads him into the clutches of Black Ben (Francis De Wolff), a scoundrelly inn-keeper in Seven Dials, and his murderous body-snatching sidekick Resurrection Joe (Christopher Lee).

While *The Haunted Strangler* is a Hammer imitation made by people who haven't yet seen *The Curse of Frankenstein*, this gets closer to the mark by giving featured billing to Hammer's new-made horror star Lee and importing Francis Matthews along with several plot elements (the doctor running a free clinic for paupers) from *The Revenge of Frankenstein*. All the anatomy demonstrations and haggling over bodies sold as medical specimens suggests the filmmakers were well aware that *The Flesh and the Fiends* was in the works, though the bulk of the film plays surprisingly as a straight drug addiction story with Karloff reaching for the tincture of opium and see-sawing between cheerful energy and dispirited dishevelment. It may not be *The Man with the Golden Arm*, but the theme was unusual in horror (outside Jekyll and Hyde) and gives some dramatic meat to the slum roistering and drawing room debate. Note, however, that Karloff's fix recipe includes vitriol solely so a bottle can be handy for throwing in Lee's face during the final fight scene.

First available on laserdisc in a double-bill, both films initially came to DVD separately from Image in what looks like a reprise of the laser transfers: nice contrasts in the blacks and white but a little less sharp than they might be, augmented only with the theatrical trailers. Pricier but more satisfying for horror fans, the two are available together on one disc as part of Criterion's *Monsters and Madmen* box set (also containing a second double feature disc with *The Atomic Submarine* and *First Man Into Space*) with improved, high-definition digital transfers from the original negatives, plus fast-paced audio commentaries by Gordon and regular co-commentator Tom Weaver on both films (and a chime-in from co-producer Alex Gordon on *The Haunted Strangler*). Video supplements include filmed interviews with Day, Matthews, Jean Kent, Yvonne Romain (who has a small role in *Corridors* as "Yvonne Warren"), and screenwriter Jan Read, as well as censor cuts deemed too violent by the British authorities, the original trailers and radio spots, hefty stills galleries with production and publicity photographs, and a booklet featuring *Fangoria*'s 1984 interview with producer John Croydon about Karloff and an essay by Maitland McDonagh. – KN

HAUNTING FEAR

Colour, 1990, 85m. / Directed by Fred Olen Ray / Starring Brinke Stevens, Jan-Michael Vincent, Jay Richardson, Delia Sheppard, Karen Black, Robert Quarry, Michael Berryman / Digital Entertainment (UK R2 PAL)

Victoria (played by Brinke Stevens) suffers from a delicate constitution and has started to have nightmares about her late father. She also harbours a mortal dread of being mistaken

for dead and buried alive. Husband Terry (Jay Richardson) isn't much help, more interested in his steamy extra-marital romps with sadomasochist secretary Lisa (Delia Sheppard) than attending to his wife's problems. When Terry comes under pressure to clear a business debt, Lisa urges him to get Victoria to sign over the deeds of the house left her by her father and then to give her a helping hand into an early grave. But neither of them have reckoned on Victoria's resilience.

I have a lot of time for Fred Olen Ray. Ever to be known as the man who gave the world the controversially-titled *Hollywood Chainsaw Hookers* and still shooting movies now, in many respects he was the Ed Wood of the '80s and '90s. At one stage it seemed he was running a cottage industry in popcorn B-graders with plots that wouldn't fill the back of a matchbox, all sprinkled with chills, chuckles (both intentional and otherwise), naked ladies and lashings of the red stuff. Ray has a knack for fashioning relatively glossy looking product out of mega-low budgets and even at his least resourceful he's nothing less than entertaining; a lot of his wares are a notch above any of the rival features in the straight-to-video market. Doggedly enthusiastic about the movies, much like Wood did for Bela Lugosi, he also provides semi-regular work for favourite performers he wants to work with, but whom Hollywood has often left to gather dust. In the case of *Haunting Fear* – which Ray also scripted under the nom de plume Sherman Scott – that meant Karen Black (beneath an unflattering blonde wig as the psychiatrist who ascertains Stevens's fears stem from the fact she's the reincarnation of a woman buried alive several centuries earlier), Robert Quarry (erstwhile Count Yorga, here playing the loan shark after Jay Richardson's hide) and Jan-Michael Vincent (who appeared in some relatively high profile pictures during the 1970s, and pops up as Quarry's debt-collecting crony).

Ray stalwart Jay Richardson proves to be as watchable as ever, playing the scheming husband with the hots for sultry bombshell Delia Sheppard. One of the original Scream Queens, but with notably more talent than some of her peers, Brinke Stevens excels as the tormented wife. The finale, in which she claws her way out of the crate in which Richardson has tricked her into believing she's been interred alive, is worth the price of a rental on its own; brain-frazzled by the experience, her former self takes hold and she emerges, face streaked with blood, hissing and cackling and goes on the rampage with a carving knife.

Haunting Fear is as light on plot as you might expect, but Ray drops in enough low-grade chills – a maggot-spewing skull, a blood-fountain in the bath-tub, and a nightmare sequence with creepy Michael Berryman as a morgue attendant all set to embalm Stevens alive – to keep things bubbling along nicely up to the berserk finish line. It's here that Richardson gets his comeuppance in a *House by the Cemetery* style knife attack and the film draws to a close by pilfering the punchline from *Halloween*. Chuck Cirino, one of the most palatable of the indie composers (and a regular fixture in films by Ray and fellow B-movie guru Jim Wynorski) contributes a typically catchy keyboard-driven score. A modern day take on Edgar Allan Poe's "Buried Alive", Roger Corman and Ray Milland might have handled the premise with more style and atmosphere in 1962's *The Premature Burial*, but *Haunting Fear* is prime Fred Olen Ray – vigorous, violent and bags of fun.

If you already own the VHS release of *Haunting Fear* then the only benefit you'll get from upgrading to Digital Entertainment's DVD is a sharper picture. The full screen transfer has a cleaner soundtrack too, but the 2.0 stereo also highlights inconsistent levels; between exchanges of dialogue it often drops out to complete silence. The 9-chapter encoded presentation is enhanced only by a meagre gallery of blow-up frame-grabs from the film; since you can make your own selections with the pause button, why would they bother, one wonders?

– TG

THE HEARSE

Colour, 1980, 94m. / Directed by George Bowers / Starring Trish Van Devere, Joseph Cotten / Rhino (US R1 NTSC), Digital Entetainment (UK R0 PAL) / WS (1.85:1) (16:9)

This attempt at classy horror from the decidedly non-classy Crown International echoes the previous year's *The Changeling*, right down to star Trish Van Devere as divorcee Jane, who tries to get over a failed relationship by moving out to her dead witch aunt's creepy house, but finds herself stalked by a mysterious hearse. Cashing in on the venerable evil vehicle trend (which also includes such polar opposites as *Duel* and *The Car*) with a little dollop of *Burnt Offerings* for good measure, this is far too light for '70s horror fare but boasts some effective atmosphere, enough to have become a cable staple for years. The "ambiguous" ending is a letdown, but some of the other ghostly antics work well enough and the recurring theme of sexual persecution towards women lends the film a bit more depth than it probably deserved. Also welcome is horror staple Joseph Cotten in one of his last roles, and he acquits himself quite nobly.

Part of a batch of Crown titles released by Rhino, this film gets a surprising anamorphic transfer which may not be any great shakes compared to big studio product but, unlike other video incarnations, at least looks watchable during night scenes. The low-grade photography is rather soft and grainy, so as far as that goes, the disc looks accurate. The only extra is a spoiler-filled trailer. The same transfer was later rehashed as part of Rhino's inappropriately-titled "Horrible Horrors" collection and later appeared in the U.K. as well.

HEART OF GLASS

Colour, 1976, 90m. / Directed by Werner Herzog / Starring Josef Bierbichler, Stefan Güttler / Anchor Bay (UK R2 PAL, US R0 NTSC), Kinowelt (Germany R2 PAL) / WS (1.66:1) (16:9)

Like those William Castle films whose intrinsic features of interest have been obscured by the attention paid to his gimmicks, Werner Herzog's *Heart of Glass* (*Herz aus Glas*) tends to be remembered only as the film in which the director hypnotized the cast – not, as he explains in the commentary track, to impose his will on the actors but to tap into their own dream-state creativity. Herzog's original plan extended to a *Horrors of the Black Museum*-style prologue and epilogue in which he would have appeared onscreen to put the audience under his influence. Made during the director's run of fine features in the 1970s, it lacks the striking central presence of a Klaus Kinski (*Aguirre, the Wrath of God*) or Bruno S (*The Enigma of Kaspar Hauser*) and is deliberately elliptical in its deployment of folklore and anecdote.

Drawing elements from a novel by Herbert Achternbusch, the film is set mostly in a Bavarian village in the late 18th Century. Hias (Josef Bierbichler), a visionary herdsman, constantly recounts prophetic or parable-like stories, while the owner of a glassworks (Stefan Güttler) is in trouble because his senior craftsman has died without passing on the secret of the village's distinctive "ruby glass". Neither of these plot strands really carries the film, which is shot through with deliberately odd, vague little scenes like a ritualized bar fight, the discovery of two bodies (only one dead) by a hysterical servant girl or the prophet's wrestle with an invisible (perhaps imaginary) bear. The muted, inexpressive people (even lines like "the rats will bite your earlobes" are delivered casually) are less important to the film than the landscapes, mostly forested Bavarian hillsides and ravines but with shots of Alaskan wilderness and even Monument Valley (unrecognisable from John Ford's westerns) tipped in, and a finale which soars amazingly over an island "at the edge of the world". The emotional core of the film is in the geography, augmented by a Popol Vuh score that draws on Swiss yodelling and early music. Minimal as narrative, it is involving and emotional as pure cinema. Even in its director's filmography, there is nothing else quite like it.

Anchor Bay's DVD boasts a superb transfer of a very textured film: the opening cuts from pristine shots of Hias on his mountainside to pixilated landscapes deliberately degraded so that they seem to be projected on a ragged sheet, then returns to a misty, muted tone, with glowing red warmth for the glassworks (and the lovely ruby glass) and chill magic hour blue-greens for exteriors. As on DVD releases of *Aguirre*, the image is slightly hard-matted to create a 16:9 frame, which occasionally reduces the headroom but rarely impairs the compositions. Removable English subtitles appear on the frame. Considering that Herzog would soon remake *Nosferatu*, it is interesting that he is already following the style of Murnau, in discovering surreal, magical beauties in landscape, architecture and human faces rather than through artifice – though the performance style perhaps also evokes the Dreyer of *Vampyr*.

The extras are a German-language trailer and a very detailed, informative and satisfying commentary track in which the modest, disarming Herzog is gently quizzed by Norman Hill on his methods and intents; of all 'serious' filmmakers, Herzog is among the best at talking about his own work, striking a fine balance between how-it-was-done and what-it's-all-about without over-explaining or making pompous claims. Sometimes a difficult film even for Herzog's admirers, with its steady (indeed, hypnotic) pace, *Heart of Glass* repays return visits, and this edition goes a long way to making it seem more approachable. Also: a Herzog biography, some stills, and a relevant extract from the book *Herzog on Herzog*.

The German disc from Kinowelt does not include the English subtitles or commentary track but does have a unique German language commentary, which abruptly ends after just 67 minutes to let the pictures speak for themselves. Extras include the short films "Gasherbrum – Der leuchtende Berg" and "Werner Herzog East His Shoe", the latter of which is also available on the Criterion edition of *Burden of Dreams*.

– KN

HELL HOUSE

Colour, 2001, 85m. / Directed by George Ratliff / Plexifilm (US R1 NTSC)

Though it's been going on for years in the American South, the concept of a "Hell House" has remained completely unknown to most of the world. Cleverly designed in order to lure in patrons expecting a traditional haunted house, these evangelical spectacles use melodramatic depictions of various sins and their consequences to warn of the dangers of going to hell, with a tiny taste of heaven shown at the end to reward those who stay on the moral path. Not surprisingly, this extreme approach has come under fire even from within the religious community, and *Hell House* offers one example of how much work and drama goes into the creation of these sociological and horrifically gory curiosities.

The Trinity Assembly of God church in Texas prepares for its next Hell House, which entails extensive casting calls, music design, art direction, and community promotion. Through extensive documentary footage we meet the various teen actors (recruited from within Trinity's private school), eager to act out the gruesome drama of botched abortions, rape, classroom shootings, drug deals gone wrong, and AIDS-related deaths. On the surface it all seems sordid and tasteless enough to make John Waters appear restrained, but the religious angle makes it a far trickier pill to swallow. Staggered throughout the film are testimonials and anecdotes from participants both present and past, putting a continuous human face on this group effort to make the world a holier place.

The fact that the church allowed an outside documentarian to chronicle the creation of a Hell House without any restrictions is quite remarkable, and the result is a surprisingly impartial, God's-eye view of the proceedings leading up to the House itself, where the tableaux themselves and the behind-the-scenes drama receive equal screen time. Attendees react with an understandable mixture of shock and amazement at the combination of sermonizing, histrionic non-acting, and tacky bloodshed, while an outraged band of youths outside provides the film with its single most charged moment. Not surprisingly, the result is highly compelling and extremely well constructed; regardless of one's religious views, this is recommended viewing and a valuable peek into the one of the more extreme corners of the American heartland.

A film festival and TV favourite, *Hell House* has been brought to DVD in a glossy package complete with a beautiful transfer

of the film itself. Presented in its original full frame aspect ratio, the image quality is excellent with stable colours and only some mild grain in the darker scenes near the end. The disc is outfitted with some valuable extras, including a 1999 short by director George Ratliff used to obtain financing for the *Hell House* feature. Entitled "The Devil Made Me Do It", this short takes a similarly detached stance while chronicling Trinity's controversial decision to include a recreation of the Columbine massacre in one of its Hell Houses, resulting in a local uproar. The Columbine skit is shown in its jaw-dropping entirety and is perhaps the single most shocking thing on this disc; no wonder financiers were willing to fund an even longer case study. Also included are the theatrical trailer, a deleted sequence involving a discussion of demons, Trinity's "awards" ceremony to honour the Hell House participants, and a radio broadcast from *This American Life* detailing the film itself and offering a quick history of the Hell House phenomenon.

HENRY:
PORTRAIT OF A SERIAL KILLER

Colour, 1986, 82m. / Directed by John McNaughton / Starring Michael Rooker, Tom Towles, Tracy Arnold / Dark Sky (Blu-ray) (US RA NTSC) / WS (1.78:1) (16:9), Dark Sky (US R1 NTSC) / DD2.0, Cult Epics (Holland R0 NTSC), Optimum (UK R2 PAL)

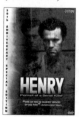

Henry: Portrait of a Serial Killer is exceptionally well acted and shot for a zero-budget movie and resolutely unexploitative in approach. It's loosely based on the disputed confessions of real-life convicted mass murderer Henry Lee Lucas. Like *The Honeymoon Killers* and *The Driller Killer*, it is an unflinching portrait not only of its eponymous killer but also of the world that at once turns him into what he is and allows him to get away with it. The product of an unspecified childhood trauma whose details change each time he recalls it, Henry (Michael Rooker), whose behaviour has not been modified by a spell in jail, drifts from job to job (he's an exterminator), murdering women whenever the mood takes him. In the powerful opening, the camera pans across the bodies of Henry's latest victims while their torture murders are heard on the soundtrack. Meanwhile, we see Henry going through the banal motions of everyday life: complementing a greasy spoon waitress on her smile, returning to the grim Chicago apartment he shares with fellow ex-con Otis (Tom Towles), showing gentlemanly instincts by putting up on the couch while ceding his bedroom to Otis's sister, Becky (Tracy Arnold).

The minimal plot unnervingly bears out Elliott Leyton's musing in *Hunting Humans*, the definitive anthropological study of the phenomenon of serial killers, that the stresses which produce such aberrant behaviour are so widespread that it is surprising so few serial killers stalk America's streets. Henry, the shell-shocked compulsive who can switch off the feelings of empathy he initially seems to display towards Becky and commit crimes even a film as intense as this can't bring itself to act out, is compared constantly with Otis. The cackling lout's increasing delight in all-round depravity shocks and disturbs even Henry, perhaps because his verminous presence gives the lie to Henry's neutral sham of decency, forcing the killer to recognise his own monstrousness (the most explicit murder in the film is that of Otis, his eye burst and his head sawed off) and serving as a reminder to the audience that, though Henry sometimes seems dangerously sympathetic, he truly is beyond the pale. Otis's primarily sexual degeneracy, expressed through rape, incest and necrophilia, conflicts with Henry's almost respectful, joyless recreations of the murder of his mother.

Unlike such flamboyant thrillers as *Manhunter* and *The Silence of the Lambs*, with their mad geniuses, *Henry* takes care to fit its characters in with the real social-psychological profile of most actual serial killers. Henry and Otis kill above their class, selecting victims whose clothes and homes mark them as more established members of society. The most deeply disturbing moments are perhaps the quieter sequences that bracket the killings, as when Henry pulls Otis out of the shock that follows their first, swift murders by offering him coffee and fries and bringing him back to a resolutely ordinary life. However, the strongest, hardest-to-sit-through sequence is a videotaped home invasion which, when the image becomes static because Henry has dropped the camera on its side so he can kill an interloping son, strongly recalls *A Clockwork Orange* as it adopts the same angle on the torture, murder and sexual abuse that the Patrick Magee character had in Kubrick's film. The impact of this scene depends on an audience's instinctive wish to turn away from the material Henry and Otis blankly view on television, the most horrific moment being Otis's line "I wanna see it again", which leads him to reshow on frame-advance the sequence of images an audience must be relieved to think is over. McNaughton's camera homes threateningly on the television image, holding it for a horrifying few seconds before the tactful fade to the film's one calming-down scene.

Like Norman Bates, Henry – who develops genuine if peculiar relationships – seems to be the most normal, well-balanced person in the film, but he is made even more chilling by his matter-of-fact explanations of his lifestyle. After the horrors of the home invasion and Otis's killings, McNaughton is even able to pull off an ambiguous but shattering finale that references the finish of *Five Easy Pieces* as Henry literally dumps the girl who might have been his only chance for normality by the roadside and disappears into the American vacuum to kill and kill again (in the needless *Henry*

Portrait of a Serial Killer 2: Mask of Sanity). *Henry*'s compulsive horrors render it far too disturbing, threatening and emotionally confusing a picture for many audiences, its conscious incorporation into its own strategy of the viewer's inevitable reactions against what is on screen proving a more challenging, uncomfortable and honourable approach to real-life horrors than any attempt to dress up the psychological or sociological subject matter of *Henry* with the generic elements of a thriller or horror movie might have been.

MPI Home Video's fullscreen DVD is afforded 16 chapters and has optional subtitles in English, Spanish and French. The transfer is excellent (which brings out a few tiny on-set flaws like corpses visibly breathing and blinking), revealing that while shot cheaply and with a deliberately seedy look, the film has a genuine eye (courtesy of cinematographer Charlie Lieberman): note the orange-clayey *Videodrome* colour of the motel bathroom where Henry gazes into the mirror in the most-reproduced still (also on the sleeve) and the significant neon signs he walks past twice in the ruthless last reel. Especially welcome is the Dolby stereo mix, which brings out the sparse but strong music score (by Robert McNaughton, Ken Hale and Steven A. Jones) and the terrifying sounds heard in Henry's memory or (tinnily) on the killers' television. (On some early DVD player models, the sound on this disc may slide a second or two out of synch, so beware.) The extras include "factoids" (compiled by someone unaware that the expression means "repeated lies", not "facts"), trailers for *Henry* and the sequel, filmographies for the director and lead cast and (most notably) a half-hour videotaped interview with McNaughton about his early career and the production of the film.

The Dutch Cult Epics disc hosts a very grainy print, and marked the first appearance of the McNaughton commentary track, but is now deleted. The Region 2 disc from Optimum is the first ever uncut release of this film in the U.K., and as such

one of its extras is a censorship history timeline. Also present and correct is the expected commentary from director John McNaughton and two insightful interviews, again with McNaughton. McNaughton's commentary later reappeared for Dark Sky's Region 1 reissue (with a sharper but sadly interlaced-encoded transfer) which adds a second DVD of extras including the worthwhile documentary "Portrait: The Making of *Henry*", as well as the "Henry Lee Lucas" episode of the series *The Serial Killers* (available separately as a complete set); not surprisingly, it's a raw and chilling look at the most prolific killer in American history. A reel of outtakes and deleted scenes (sans production audio but with McNaughton commentary) shows some material dropped from the final assembly, mostly to tighten the film; it's not a big loss but interesting to see at least once. A lengthy sampling of storyboards rounds out the disc. The Dark Sky reissue is also the basis for their Blu-ray edition, which controversially blows the film up to an anamorphic 1.78:1 presentation; the combination of scruffy 16mm and HD doesn't look as flattering as, say, Anchor Bay's *Evil Dead* release, but it's about as good as you could expect and at least isn't interlaced anymore.

– KN

HERCULES IN THE HAUNTED WORLD

Colour, 1961, 82m. / Directed by Mario Bava / Starring Reg Park, Christopher Lee, Giorgio Ardisson, Leonora Ruffo / Fantoma (US R1 NTSC) / WS (2.35:1) (16:9)

Though *Black Sunday* lifted the black and white horror film to new levels of visual artistry, Mario Bava wildly swerved into new territory the following year with *Hercules in*

the Haunted World, a blazingly colourful mixture of Gothic horror and peplum fantasy which stands as one of the most memorable entries in the often derided sword and sandal genre. A stylish concoction of luminous landscapes, ghoulish monsters, and eccentric plot twists, this is miles away from your standard Steve Reeves bodybuilding opus. And it has Christopher Lee as a villain, too!

After performing labours abroad, Hercules (Reg Park) is reunited with his best friend, the lothario Theseus (Giorgio Ardisson). Unfortunately Hercules's true love, Deianira (Leonora Ruffo), has passed into a strange trance and no longer recognises the world around her. The shifty King Lico (Christopher Lee) advises Hercules to seek help from an oracle, who reveals that the only cure for Deianira lies in the underworld, specifically the powerful golden Apple of the Hesperides, which provides access to the coveted Stone of Forgetfulness. Along with the bumbling Telemachus, Hercules (who has relinquished his immortality) and Theseus set off to the other side where they encounter a land of eternal night, filled with rock monsters, bubbling pools of lava, and deadly flying bloodsuckers. However, the greatest threat is yet to come...

Thanks to his extensive experience as a cinematographer, Bava brings a fully formed sensibility to his first colour film and lays out the visual motifs, which would later reach full bloom in such classics as *Planet of the Vampires*. Using a minimal budget and limited sets to his advantage, Bava turns his soundstages and miniatures into delirious whirlpools of colour and texture, pitting his actors against a seemingly endless array of imaginative obstacles. The heroes' climb over bubbling lava, for example, is an expertly rendered example of a special effects set piece created from the barest elements possible, while the forest and tomb sequences bring the established environments of *Black Sunday* into a new context, splashed with unnatural waves of red and blue light. The actors can't help but pale against such settings, but Park makes for one of the more interesting and intelligent Italian musclemen, while Lee as usual makes for an imposing figure despite his relatively limited screen time. A subplot involving Theseus's infatuation with Persephone, the mythical daughter of Pluto, is also imaginatively handled and fits in nicely with the doom-laden romances of Bava's subsequent work.

Most widely seen in a laughably dubbed U.S. version from Woolner Brothers which omits and reshuffles several chunks of footage, *Hercules in the Haunted World* finds much of its dignity restored with this long overdue, definitive treatment of the original, undoctored edition. Boasting the European English language title of *Hercules at the Centre of the Earth* on the actual print, this transfer contains the original opening title sequence (against a stony tomb) and thankfully preserves both the dopey English dub track and the original Italian version which, while less faithful to the actors' actual lip movements, adds some desperately needed gravity to the potentially silly storyline. The optional English subtitles translate the Italian dialogue directly, which makes for a fascinating comparison against the more simplistic English dub. Generations of bad prints and worse PD videotapes have offered only a hint of the visual glories to be found in Bava's second film; the DVD offers the original scope framing (or at least most of it – the precise aspect ratio has been the subject of guesswork for years) as well as a wonderfully saturated colour presentation which puts this up there with the finest of the Bava home video releases available. As with other European films of this vintage, the film stock betrays some signs of graininess and instability at times, but this is miles ahead of how the film has looked on television before. The disc also includes some nicely conversational liner notes by Tim Lucas (who pulls out some wonderfully odd trivia in the last paragraph), a ragged looking U.S. trailer, and an extensive photo and poster gallery. While Bava fanatics and fans of European horror will find this purchase a given, even those who avoid sword and sandal films should find this stellar entry more than worthwhile.

THE HIDEOUS SUN DEMON

B&W, 1959, 75m. / Directed by Robert Clarke / Starring Robert Clarke, Nan Peterson, Bill Hampton, Patrick Whyte, Patricia Manning, Peter Similuk, Xandra Conkling / Image (US R0 NTSC)

 The gimmick of this fondly-remembered 1959 s-f creature feature is that it is the negative image of a werewolf movie – the scientist protagonist turns into a lizard-scaled monster (with unlikely fangs) under direct sunlight, but reverts to his guilt-ridden self when night falls. Put together entirely by star Robert Clarke, who had made it through the likes of *The Astounding She-Monster* and felt he could do better on his own, it has its interesting moments but few ideas about putting them together. Unlike most '50s features, it opens on a moment of pre-credits excitement action, with a ringing alarm bell at an atomic installation and Dr. Gilbert McKenna (Clarke) rushed from a lab accident in an ambulance ("this guy's been soaked with radiation"). Then it slips into dragginess as the crucial "origin" scene (soon to be redone for any number of Marvel Comics characters) is conveyed by one scientist (Bill Hampton) sitting on a desk and talking about what has happened ("whisky and soda mix, not whisky and science") with another expert (Patrick Whyte) and Gil's assistant/girlfriend Ann Lansing (Patricia Manning) – as opposed to showing it to the audience. Some abrupt transitions come about because the film has

to skimp on effects; the budget stretched to a monster suit but not to Lon Chaney Jr-style lap dissolve transformations.

Because so much of the picture is stiff actors in rooms talking through poorly-written exposition, its better moments stand out. The initial glimpse of the monster is especially potent, though it is also contrived because the money wasn't there for a metamorphosis. Left to recuperate on a sun-bed on the hospital roof, the radiation-dosed Gil changes into the sun demon while the camera is on a gossipy old lady who then screams as he runs off; the creature dashes into the building, shot so we can see its claws, and its frightening face is first shown in a mirror which is immediately smashed. Unfortunately, this monster suit works better in brief flashes than in prolonged exposure. Clarke's character, a hard-drinking lech who might have caused his plight by fooling with isotopes while hung-over, has a few regulation hysterical human scenes, but drifts out of the scientific plot to get mixed up in some skid row noir business with bottle blonde Trudy (Nan Peterson), a "singer" who warbles a number called "Strange Pursuit", and her nasty protector (Peter Similuk) before rampaging around Los Angeles. Several exciting incidents are reported to the police, who talk about them back at headquarters, but not shown, though we do go through some business derived from *The Quatermass Experiment* as the down-and-out, unshaven Gil makes friends with an annoying little blonde girl (Xandra Conkling). In the end, Gil is cornered in a factory by a single cop, scurries up the ladders of a giant tank (à la *White Heat*, but without the explosion) and is shot, taking a traditional Kong tumble to his death.

Image's DVD showcases a fullscreen print that is in rough shape in the early stretches, but improves markedly as the film wears on – maybe it's taken from a film print more people started watching than managed to finish. It has a nice, luridly coloured box image, and a relevant extract from Clarke's autobiography (written with Tom Weaver), *To "B" or Not to "B"*, on the reverse of the cardboard cover. The only extra is the traditional Paul Frees-narrated trailer, which promises "Thermo-Dynamic Horror from outer space" (presumably, referring to the sun rather than the demon).

– KN

THE HILLS HAVE EYES

Colour, 1977, 89m. / Directed by Wes Craven / Starring Michael Berryman, Susan Lanier, Robert Houston, Russ Grieve, Virginia Vincent, Martin Speer, Dee Wallace, James Whitworth, Lance Gordon, Janus Blythe / Anchor Bay (US R1 NTSC, UK R2 PAL) / WS (1.85:1) (16:9) / DTS-ES 6.1/DD5.1 EX

As much defence as Wes Craven's *The Last House on the Left* has earned over the years, no one could ever argue that it was a model of how to maintain a consistent tone. In fact, it's hard to imagine a film that induces a harder case of cinematic whiplash, intercutting footage of the two vulnerable, female leads being tortured and raped with clumsy slapstick courtesy of two inept cops. Fortunately Craven learned a lot in the intervening five years before he returned to horror with *The Hills Have Eyes*, one of the finer entries in '70s drive-in cinema. Here Craven seems to have a firm, cheeky grasp of the film's absurdity but still manages to shred the viewers' nerves with scenes of unexpected, gruelling horror.

Not many could claim to genuinely "enjoy" Craven's inaugural film, but no such apologies are necessary here; from a German Shepherd hellbent on avenging his murdered mate to a clan of desert cannibals salivating over a newborn baby snack, this is prime entertainment for the whole mutant family. Blond, tear-prone Bobby (Robert Houston) discovers the grisly remains of one of the family dogs, leaving its mate to wander the hills. By nightfall the first to go is the Carter patriarch, Bob (Russ Grieve), who gets trussed to a cactus in the first of many harrowing scenes. The mother, Ethel (Virginia Vincent), is left alone with the younger generation: couple Doug (Martin Speer) and Lynne (Dee Wallace), and fair-haired brother and sister Brenda (Susan Lanier) and Bobby. Led by crazy-eyed dad Jupiter (James Whitworth), the mutant family includes such charmers as the leering, dog-killing, baby-munching Pluto (Michael Berryman), wild-haired Mars (Lance Gordon), and emotionally torn Ruby (Janus Blythe), whose desire to join the real world figures heavily in the brutal, civilization vs. cannibals climax.

With its deliberately paced opening act, *The Hills Have Eyes* demands a certain amount of patience lacking in many recent horror films. Craven builds a mounting atmosphere of tension by keeping the villains largely offscreen until the attack in the middle of the film, relying instead on the viewer's imagination to fill in the shuddery gaps. Fortunately the payoff is more than worth it, as the first showdown in the family camper is a truly terrifying piece of business in which literally *any* character can die, anytime. The "who are the real savages?" schtick from *Last House* is repeated in the final moments here to equally potent effect, along with that film's attack-and-revenge three act structure; however, few will be interested in the deeper sociological implications of the film, which intends first and foremost to scare the crap out of the audience.

Though the bald Berryman is easily the most memorable aspect of the film (he and Craven reteamed for the underrated *Deadly Blessing*), most of the performers do a fine job with their meaty roles; even Wallace, a relative newcomer whose only previous experience was a religious film and a mostly deleted turn in *The Stepford Wives*, shows what a powerful actress she can be with the right material. The most challenging role belongs to Houston, who freely admits elsewhere on the disc that he wasn't Craven's first choice; the character is virtually impossible to perform, a sniveling crybaby who turns into a "Mad Max" avenger in the closing reel, so it's to Houston's credit that he at least maintains some semblance of credibility. That said, his pouty tantrums never fail to raise howls from an audience whenever this unspools in theatres.

From start to finish, *The Hills Have Eyes* ranks with *Scream* as Craven's most accomplished and completely satisfying horror film. (*A Nightmare on Elm Street* would qualify if it weren't for that damned last scene.) While all of his genre work displays brilliant flourishes of imagination and technique, he either sabotages the story at some point with his own errors in judgment (*Shocker*, *Deadly Friend*) or, more tragically, is undermined by the guys in control of the cash (*The Serpent and the Rainbow*). Here he strikes the perfect balance between the macabre and wryly amusing, the gritty and the absurd; the film moves along like a perfectly oiled piece of machinery, building inevitably to the booby trap-packed finale (a recurring motif in many of his films) which pays off beautifully from all the vignettes preceding it. As usual, Craven's literate knack for symbolism and visual doubling is well used here (the mutants' violence dominates at night, while the Carters are vicious during the following daylight hours; the parents, children, and animals all have doppelgangers); though many critics dismissed it as trash, the film is unquestionably a work of intelligence and commitment which has lost little of its ferocious impact.

As anyone who has suffered through a theatrical showing of this film during the past decade or so can attest, it has not fared well over the years. The few surviving prints looked wretched, with pinkish or faded colour and a sandstorm of scratches

and other debris. The only watchable option was the laserdisc, back in the days of Magnum Entertainment; though colours were unnaturally heightened, it was a decent presentation from elements which seemed to disappear afterwards. Fortunately Anchor Bay's DVD presents the film on its best behaviour in an edition better than most theatrical audiences have ever experienced. While fans used to smooth, immaculate presentations of their horror product may be jarred by the amount of grain on display here (comparable to MGM's *Last House*), this is a startling presentation of a title that bordered on becoming lost forever. A restoration demonstration offers examples of the work performed on the best surviving element, similar to the efforts performed on the *Blue Sunshine* DVD; however, Craven's film is certainly not a visually flashy piece of work, and the subdued appearance here seems accurate. Despite the relatively thin audio mix, *The Hills Have Eyes* fares remarkably well with a souped-up DTS mix. Surrounds are used sparingly, with Don Peake's atmospheric music often grumbling in the rear channels and occasional ambient effects (screeching tyres, thudding rocks, etc.) popping off to the left or right. A much better and smoother job than Anchor Bay's ill-advised remix of *The Last House on the Left*, which just induces headaches. For purists, the mono track is also included (and yes, it is the real mono track) as well as a straight surround version of the remix.

Spread out over two discs, this package of *The Hills Have Eyes* is a horror fan's dream come true. The first disc is reserved for the film itself, along with an audio commentary by Craven and producer Peter Locke. As usual Craven makes for a fine commentator (how he can talk about all of his films in such depth and never run out of things to say is amazing), and Locke joins him all the way for an in-depth discussion of how the film came to be and was shot using such a low budget. Craven offers a few bits of textual insight here and there, but this is a bit less English-class-style than usual for him.

Disc two kicks off with one of Anchor Bay's finest documentaries to date, "Looking Back on *The Hills Have Eyes*", a 55-minute retrospective with most of the living partici-pants. Craven starts off with yet another retread of his "horror audiences must first be afraid of the director" observations, but fortunately it's all fresh and interesting afterwards. Locke also returns along with Berryman, Blythe, Houston, Lanier, Wallace, and cinematographer Eric Saarinen, with each participant getting in several fun anecdotes. (For example, Blythe was originally up for Wallace's part but wanted to play the "wild girl", and the nice, fan-friendly Berryman has at least 25 birth defects. And that's just for starters.) A second documentary is actually the Wes Craven episode of *The Directors*, previously issued separately on DVD from Winstar. Sort of a greatest hits package of Craven's best moments, it also features actors from several of his films. This documentary is absent from the otherwise-identical double disc release from Anchor Bay U.K., but in its place is Adam Simon's highly regarded documentary *The American Nightmare* (71m). The less time-demanding bonus material includes a dupey-looking alternative ending that appeared on some TV prints back in the 1980s; it's an interesting re-edit of the entire climax of the film and concludes with a bit of additional "happy" footage to send viewers off on a more sedate note.

Other extras include U.S. and German trailers, as well as a wealth of U.S. and U.K. TV spots. You also get a behind-the-scenes photo gallery, posters and ad art (the European design is pretty wild), storyboards, a Craven bio, and for you DVD-Rom users, the original screenplay (as a .pdf file) and two screensavers. Special mention as well to the striking spotlight-style menus and thick, illustrated insert booklet, containing liner notes from DVD Maniacs's Jon Putnam.

HITCH-HIKE

Colour, 1977, 104m. / Directed by Pasquale Festa Campanile / Starring Franco Nero, Corinne Clery, David Hess / Blue Underground, Anchor Bay (US R1 NTSC, UK R0 PAL) / WS (1.85:1) (16:9)

 A burned out, alcoholic journalist called Walter Mancini (Franco Nero) and his browbeaten wife Eve (Corinne Clery) are on a trip across America with caravan in tow. Theirs is a tempestuous relationship and when Eve spots a stranded motorist at the roadside she stops to pick him up simply because Walter doesn't want her to. Unbeknownst to them their hitchhiker, Adam Konitz (David Hess), is an escapee from a mental institute now on the run after a bank robbery that has netted him $2 million in cash. Forced at gunpoint to drive Konitz to the border, Walter and Eve's predicament worsens when the madman's double-crossed compatriots show up to claim the money for themselves.

With a wicked sting in its tail, the violent and gritty *Hitch-Hike* (aka *Autostop rosso sangue*) is the ultimate nightmare road movie. A plot which on paper may sound unremarkable is made compelling thanks to a taut script (co-written by director Pasquale Festa Campanile, Aldo Crudo and Ottavio Jemma) and strong performances from the three central characters. If only the Mancinis had seen *The Last House on the Left* they'd have driven past Konitz so fast that you'd not have seen them for dust... but they hadn't and, my word, do they suffer for the oversight.

As Adam Konitz, David Hess may not be given anything as remotely insidious to do as when he played the bent out of shape Krug in Wes Craven's *Last House*, but he still gives his victims a pretty bumpy ride. Franco Nero (*Django*) is Walter, an uncompromis-ingly chauvinistic and abusive swine who verbally and physically humiliates his wife at every opportunity. Perversely, an antagonistic bond develops between Mancini and the psychotic Konitz; bastards clearly thrive in each other's company. Betwixt the classic erotica of *Story of O* and big budget double-0 with *Moonraker*, Corinne Clery is at her most exquisitely sultry as Eve, sporting a sensuous tattoo of a bluebird on her foot in an era long before it became commonplace for women to adopt body art as a fashion accessory. As the only character the viewer can begin to root for, even Eve seems to have an unspoken agenda; she passes up several opportunities to strike back with a hunting rifle stashed in the caravan and her resistance to Konitz's physical intrusions, though evident, is never sufficient enough to be convincing. One gets the distinct impression she sees Konitz as a potential passport out of her unbearable marriage. The power struggle between the trio twists and turns and every time it appears as if Mancini will gain the upper hand Konitz outwits him.

From the word go Campanile adroitly grabs your attention and hangs on with an iron grip, ratcheting up the sexual tension to its unbearable apex when Mancini is trussed up and, eyes red-rimmed and seething with hatred, watches Konitz assault his wife. And if you think the story is all set to wrap when Konitz bites the inevitable bullet, keep watching – fate has mapped out a dastardly and ugly twist just around the next bend in the road. Ennio Morricone's string and percussion biased score (complemented by an unlikely but fitting upbeat "flower power" ballad) strikes all the right notes, travelling the spectrum of mood from lazy afternoon siesta through pulsing carnal desire, peaking in the latter when Konitz rapes Eve, the hypnotic thump building to a pounding crescendo as passion engulfs her and she submits to the moment. *Hitch-Hike* (not to be confused with the 1974 Cloris Leachman/ Cameron Mitchell TV movie *Hitchhike!*) is a road trip from hell you'll not forget in a hurry. Take it for a spin if you have the nerve.

Anchor Bay's DVD release is a jewel (later ported over identically by Blue Underground during a rights leap), housing a print so clean that only the questionable fashion choices divulge the fact that the film wasn't shot last week – there's nary a scratch on it! Sprinkled with a liberal 25 chapter points, it's presented in 16:9 enhanced, 1.85:1 theatrical ratio. The pleasure to be derived from the feature presentation is equalled in a splendid 17-minute retrospective documentary from that team of miracle-workers over at Blue Underground. Entitled "The Devil Thumbs a Ride", it features invaluable reminiscences from Nero, Hess and Clery (who speaks in Italian, subtitles provided). The package is rounded out with a theatrical trailer.

– TG

THE HOLE

Colour, 2001, 98m. / Directed by Nick Hamm / Starring Thora Birch, Desmond Harrington, Embeth Davidtz, Keira Knightley, Laurence Fox, Daniel Brocklebank / Pathé (UK R2 PAL), Buena Vista (US R1 NTSC) / WS (2.35:1) (16:9) / DD5.1

A young girl (Thora Birch), bruised and streaked with blood, stumbles along a country lane. Dazed, she manages to get to a phone. Desperately snatching up the receiver she dials 999... and utters an ear-shattering scream. The girl is Liz and she's spent the past 18 days with three friends, imprisoned in a disused WWII bunker. The story she recounts is terrifying. But is it the product of a twisted rewriting of the facts to mask a truth even more ghastly? Investigating psychiatrist Philippa Horwood (Embeth Davidtz) thinks so and sets about coaxing the facts out of the seemingly traumatized Liz.

Evidence, as if it were really needed, that given the opportunity and the latitude British filmmakers can compete with the best that Hollywood has to offer, the premise of *The Hole* is simple but very effective. A group of school friends dodge a boring field trip to Wales by hiding out in a vast bunker in the woodland behind the school, but three days later when they attempt to get out the door is jammed shut and they're trapped without food or water.

Director Nick Hamm started out in theatre before moving on to sporadic television work and he turns an assured hand to Ben Court and Caroline Ip's screenplay. With the principal activities taking place on one set, *The Hole* would actually work as a stage piece itself, and Hamm skilfully layers on the stomach-squalling anguish as friendships turn sour, grievances are aired, contention erupts and paranoia sets in. Director of photography Denis Crossan makes excellent use of the expansive playground interior of the bunker which, as the jape goes rotten, switches to a choking, claustrophobic iron tomb. Of the four protagonists – Liz (Birch), Mike (*Wrong Turn*'s Desmond Harrington), Frankie (Keira Knightley) and Geoff (Laurence Fox) – only Birch was particularly familiar at the time, which added considerably to their credibility as irksome, cosseted public school types; since *The Hole* relative unknowns Knightley and Harrington have gone on to expand their CVs with considerable success. As the scheming, mildly psychotic Liz, American actress Birch (daughter of adult actors Carol Connors and Jack Birch) is exemplary, and her British accent is right on the money. Starting out in her formative years with saccharine pap like *Parenthood* and *All I Want for Christmas*, she has ascended via more recent films such as *Ghost World* and *American Beauty* to emerge as a talent to be reckoned with. Harrington (*Ghost Ship*'s wicked spook), as the object of Liz's libidinous desires, is also admirable, and there's stimulating support from a slutty Knightley and nice-but-dim Fox. A special word too for Daniel Brocklebank, excellent as Liz's chum Martin, the lad who may or may not be responsible for the teenagers' ordeal. Embeth Davidtz is police psychiatrist Philippa Horwood, whose job it is to reveal the truth. Although *The Hole* was released theatrically, substitute therapist Horwood for forensic scientist Sam Ryan and skew the perspective to amplify the role of the investigator, and it could easily have played as a story in TV's *Silent Witness* series. But don't let that put you off. The conclusion is rather contrived and unlikely, giving it an unsatisfactory – though admittedly unpredictable – twist, but up to that juncture the narrative is involving and original enough to warrant one's time.

The Region 2 DVD of *The Hole*, released in the U.K. by Pathé, presents the movie in a 23-chapter punctuated, 2.35:1 widescreen format with 16:9 enhancement. Colours are stable, blacks are solid – and there's plenty of black down in that bunker – and there's no discernible trace of artefacting. Sound options are English and French, with subtitling accessible in the same two languages as well as Dutch. Along with a feature commentary from director Hamm, there are nine deleted/alternative scenes, two trailers and text filmographies for the key members of the cast. The much-postponed Region 1 release carries over the same presentation and is geared heavily towards promoting Knightley, whose nudity in the film has since made it a regular rental favourite.

– TG

THE HOLY MOUNTAIN

Colour, 1973, 114m. / Directed by Alejandro Jodorowsky / Starring Alejandro Jodorowsky, Zamira Saunders, Horácio Salinas / Anchor Bay (US R1 NTSC), Tartan (UK R2 PAL) / WS (2.35:1) (16:9) / DD5.1, Raro Video (Italy R0 PAL), SPO (Japan R2 NTSC) / WS (2.35:1)

Mad cult director Alejandro Jodorowsky's arguable piece de resistance was made shortly after the success release of his pioneering midnight movie, *El Topo*, which encouraged producer/Apple Records guru Allen Klein to finance a strikingly ambitious follow-up feature. Lensed in gorgeous Cinemascope and featuring a far more luxurious wealth of locations and sets, *The Holy Mountain* goes far beyond the metaphysical spaghetti western theatrics of its predecessor, offering itself a barrage of startling imagery and a tantalizing discourse melding every major religion in the world.

Awakening from a comatose sleep and covered in insects, a bearded thief (Horácio Salinas) wanders into a town populated by freaks, fascists, hookers, and religious fanatics, where skinned, crucified livestock are paraded down the street, costumed frogs and lizards bloodily re-enact the Spanish invasion of South America, and soldiers rape peasant women for the photographic amusement of tourists. Our hero is then used as a body mould to create hundreds of kitschy, edible Christ statues, after which he returns to the street and, courtesy of a handful of balloons, ascends to a secret tower. In this isolated realm he encounters an alchemist (Jodorowsky), who demonstrates his knowledge by transforming the thief's excrement into crystals and gold. The alchemist then leads him to a chamber containing the naked, shaved bodies of six wealthy people of learning, all of them preparing for the next step in their spiritual awakening. One by one we learn their stories, ranging from a sexually-bent bedmaker to a craftsman of pop culture religious weaponry. Led by the Alchemist, these nine souls in total then ascend "the holy mountain" where, they believe, nine wise masters reside and must be replaced.

Along the way they encounter more sights, including a chicken massacre and an old man who shoots tiger breast milk.

With its interjection of deliberate humour and a mixture of abstract and modern urban settings, *The Holy Mountain* is a markedly different animal from *El Topo*. Here Jodorowsky seems to be assimilating the quirks of Fellini, Buñuel, and especially Dusan Makavejev, tossing them together with a number of holy texts for one deeply mindbending cinematic stew. (Fellini would later crib *The Holy Mountain*'s jokey metaphysical ending for *And the Ship Sails On*, though one could argue both men were more than a little inspired by Mario Bava's *Black Sabbath*.) The plaintive Morricone-on-acid score of *El Topo* here gives way to a tantalizing aural mixture of religious instrumentation and funky pop compositions, while Jodorowsky's first time out in scope results in some of the most remarkable images of his career. Obviously not a film for everyone, but the synopsis alone should tell you that.

Since it wasn't the midnight cult hit Klein was evidently aiming for, *The Holy Mountain* languished in obscurity for years before turning up on Japanese laserdisc from Nikkatsu. The letterboxed image was good for its time and the soundtrack preserved the original (heavily accented) English language dialogue, but optical censorship of the abundant full frontal nudity ruined more than a few sequences. A subsequent reissue by Amuse on laserdisc (with a dramatically inferior cover) was little better, while a PAL VHS release in the U.K. offered a somewhat fuzzier transfer with the same annoying censor blobs. Despite Klein's apparent intention to keep both of his Jodorowsky films buried, *The Holy Mountain* resurfaced again on Italian DVD of questionable legality, sporting a watchable if unexceptional (and comparatively colourless) transfer from a muddied and bleached print, with a tendency to turn brownish. The disc contains a subtitled interview with Italian Jodorowsky scholar Massimo Monteleone, as well as a bilingual Jodorowsky filmography, biography and critical anthology contained in the fairly thick insert booklet. (Amusingly, the back sleeve notes this is "presented in a letterbox widescreen format preserving the 2.35:1 aspect ratio of the original theatrical exhibition. Enhanced for 4:3 widescreen Tvs" [sic].) On a more controversial note, the disc also represents a re-edited Italian cut of the film, with fleeting trims made to a number of incidental shots (including the castration sequence) for no discernible reason, often amounting to a few frames.

After Jodorowsky and Klein buried the hatchet, *The Holy Mountain* finally saw a legitimate, restored release which feels far more vibrant and, well, randy than ever before with its pop-art colour schemes and succession of glittering, wholly unique pictorial compositions. The English soundtrack is presented in its original mono mix or a satisfying, spacious 5.1 remix that could seriously affect viewers not in a completely straight frame of mind. Also, the film is totally uncut with all of its casual full-frontal imagery intact. Jodorowsky contributes another enlightening and wholly eccentric commentary track (Spanish with optional English subs) in which he covers his own mystical influences on the film and its unorthodox release history; luckily *The Holy Mountain* DVD eschews the video interview from its *El Topo* companion release in favour of some minor deleted footage, an instruction piece on the Tarot, the great theatrical trailer, and a stills gallery. Also available as part of the Jodorowsky box set in the U.S. and U.K.; see the *El Topo* review for more details.

HOME MOVIES

Colour, 1979, 90m. / Directed by Brian De Palma / Starring Kirk Douglas, Nancy Allen, Keith Gordon, Gerrit Graham, Mary Davenport, Vincent Gardenia / Westlake (US R1 NTSC)

One of the more peculiar by-products of the film school generation during the 1970s, Brian De Palma's *Home Movies* finds the suspense maestro pooling his money back to the source by funding a film whose crew consisted of Sarah Lawrence film students. A goofy throwback to his earlier comedies like *Greetings* and *Hi, Mom!*, this domestic comedy gone haywire mines humour from such bizarre subjects as staged sex acts with stuffed rabbits, underage male molestation, suicide attempts, and blackface voyeurism, among others. How funny viewers find the results will be a matter of taste.

An "extra in his own life", young Denis Byrd (Keith Gordon) lives in the shadow of his god-like older brother, James (Gerrit Graham), who's engaged to the beautiful, formerly wayward Kristina (Nancy Allen). Meanwhile Denis's mother (Mary Davenport) is driven to despair over the philandering ways of her husband (Vincent Gardenia), but things get really odd when Denis is repeatedly harassed by the Maestro (Kirk Douglas), a possibly supernatural director who tries to turn the lad into a star in his own life instead.

Wildly inconsistent, *Home Movies* hits the mark enough to be interesting thanks to De Palma's directorial flourishes (including Allen's nocturnal run through a forest) and some spirited performances; Graham in particular steals all of his scenes with his outrageously stupid "Spartanetics" speeches. Allen and Gordon make such an appealing couple they re-teamed the next year for *Dressed to Kill*, and Pino Donaggio contributes perhaps his wildest score, working *The Barber of Seville* into his main theme over the animated opening credits. Too bad the DVD itself is an utter disappointment, ripped badly from the Vestron/Image laserdisc, which was already a bland, colourless transfer to begin with. The problem is worsened by hideous digital compression that renders the darker scenes a mess of digital blocks and blobs. The cover art is also hideous and looks like it was done with Crayons. Even at the budget price, this disc really should have been better.

L'HOMME BLESSÉ

Colour, 1983, 109m. / Directed by Patrice Chéreau / Starring Jean-Hughes Anglade, Vittorio Mezzogiorno, Armin Mueller-Stahl, Annick Alane / Studio Canal (France R2 PAL), WS (1.66:1) (16:9), DD5.1, Cinevista (US R1 NTSC), WS (1.66:1)

 Long before he startled the worldwide film-going community with *Queen Margot* (*La Reine Margot*) and the graphic *Intimacy*, director Patrice Chéreau was already a master of the psycho-drama thanks to his first film, the Charlotte Rampling vehicle *Flesh of the Orchid*, and this stark look at urban gay life, whose title translates as "The Wounded Man".

Future cult favourite Jean-Hughes Anglade (*Betty Blue*, *La femme Nikita*) takes centre stage as Henri, a timid young man who leaves home for the city life and promptly finds himself witnessing a mugging. He intervenes and tries to stop the attacker, who plants a kiss on his mouth. Instantly Henri realizes he's attracted to men and hooks up with Jean (the late Vittorio Mezzogiorno), a streetwise hustler who becomes the unrequited object of Henri's affections. The two begin a co-dependent relationship that quickly spirals into obsession and violence as Henri's passions bubble to the surface.

Featuring a solid supporting cast including Armin Mueller-Stahl (*Shine*) and veteran actress Annick Alane, *L'homme*

blessé is a gritty, visually stark response to the increasing flashiness of French cinema inaugurated two years earlier with *Diva*. While Chereau's pacing lags at times and his treatment of the characters becomes wildly inconsistent, the actors carry the film through and enact its theme of *amour fou* with remarkable conviction.

Unfortunately, what little polish the film has is rendered moot by Cinevista's overpriced DVD, a shoddy presentation riddled with digital artefacts and mismatched black levels. Even their earlier VHS tapes were better than this substandard presentation; the fact that the movie never earned a laserdisc release but went to DVD in this condition must surely count as a minor tragedy. The burned-in subtitles are small and difficult to read, a flaw exacerbated by the bleary transfer. The bare bones menu contains no chapter stops, only a trailer reel for other Cinevista titles.

Luckily for anyone who can cope without an English language translation, the Studio Canal edition not only offers a superior anamorphic transfer, but also has a enough extras to fill a second disc: a 3-minute Jane Birkin music video "Et quand bien même" by Patrice Chéreau; a 25-minute documentary about Chéreau by Raymond Depardon "1983, la sortie à Cannes"; a 15-minute interview with Hervé Guibert (writer and AIDS sufferer) from the French television series "Apostrophes"; plus 45 minutes of interviews with people involved with the film: Jean-Hugues Anglade (actor), Caroline de Vivaise (costume designer), Renato Berta (cinematographer) and Patrice Chéreau (writer and director).

THE HONEYMOON KILLERS

B&W, 1970, 107m. / Directed by Leonard Kastle / Starring Shirley Stoler, Tony Lo Bianco, Doris Roberts, Mary Jane Higby / Criterion (US R1 NTSC), Metrodome (UK R2 PAL) / WS (1.85:1) (16:9)

The perfect antidote for any viewer numbed by exposure to an excess of romantic comedies, *The Honeymoon Killers* offers the opposite of a "meet cute" relationship. The film's leading lady, Martha Beck (Shirley Stoler), is an overweight nurse stuck at home with her overbearing mother. Raymond Fernandez (Tony Lo Bianco) is a Spanish huckster who bilks lonely, innocent women out of their savings. The two collide when Martha decides to write in to a Lonely Hearts club at the suggestion of her friend Bunny (Doris Roberts, star of – what else? – *Everybody Loves Raymond*), only to have the dreamy Ray love her and leave her after a quick one-nighter. Problem is, they're crazy about each other; Martha doesn't even care about her paramour's true occupation. So it's off to the nursing home for mom as the two hit the road, hitting up middle-aged women for cash with Martha improbably posing as Ray's sister. Ray promises to never sleep with any of their victims, and for a while things go well enough (apart from one unlucky lass who gets nosy and, dying from an overdose of sleeping pills, gets dumped onto a bus out of town). The first signs of trouble appear when they start a long-term scam to rip off Janet Fay (Mary Jane Higby), a sixtysomething Catholic widow with an aversion to pills and a penchant for asking far too many questions in the middle of the night.

Based with extreme fidelity on a true story, this sole directorial effort for opera composer Leonard Kastle ranks up there with Charles Laughton's *The Night of the Hunter* in the one-shot wonder horror hall of fame. The moody monochrome photography, stark use of Gustav Mahler music, and pitch-perfect performances make this a powerful, harrowing experience even decades later; in her first role, Stoler simply couldn't be better as the vicious but pitiable Martha and, despite an over-reliance on future roles as jail wardens, went on to a worthy career in films like *The Deer Hunter* and, most memorably, *Seven Beauties*. Lo Bianco (*God Told Me To*) matches her every step of the way in a tricky part, often cajoling Martha into doing his murderous dirty work without coming off as a completely unsympathetic jerk. While the violence is still shocking (including two harrowing murders that rival *Henry: Portrait of a Serial Killer*), Kastle wisely focuses instead on the humour and pathos of Martha and Ray's relationship; their utter lack of resemblance to each other becomes a great source of comedy, and their claustrophobic encounters with their victims-to-be contain some priceless moments of witty dialogue and staging. Though the film became something of a critical favourite (even earning oft-quoted kudos from François Truffaut), it still hasn't quite earned the fame it deserves; however, one need only look at the early films of John Waters, Brian De Palma, and Martin Scorsese to see how much of an impact it had on the following decade.

Given that it was shot for peanuts with woefully inadequate sound recording, *The Honeymoon Killers* fares well on its DVD incarnations. The first out of the gate was the Metrodome release, with a reasonable but sometimes muddy anamorphic transfer and a small gallery of poster and tie-in art. Much more lavish is the Criterion disc, which contains sharper detail and much clearer dark scenes. While the audio is still muffled on both (this film makes *Pink Flamingos* sound like state of the art THX), the Criterion disc thankfully contains optional English subtitles, which come in handy throughout the running time.

The Criterion extras are all rewarding, kicking off with a 26-minute video interview with Kastle in which he discusses his musical background and the circumstances under which the project was created. Most interestingly, he mentions its genesis as a response to the glamorized, antiseptic crime spree of *Bonnie and Clyde*, itself intended of course as a more realistic response to Hollywood gangster films. "Dear Martha" (the film's original shooting title), an extensive illustrated essay by Scott Christianson, covers the actual Beck/ Fernandez murder spree in surprising detail, illustrating how closely the actors matched their real life counterparts (right down to Lo Bianco's temple scar and hairpiece). Apart from one significant change (Beck actually walked out on her children, not her mother), the history and film go hand in hand until the prison finale; that's where the essay really gets interesting, detailing Ray and Martha's final months and capping off with a horrific account of Martha's bizarre fate in the electric chair. Also included are the original theatrical trailer and a booklet essay by Gary Giddins.

HORROR

Colour, 2002, 77m. / Directed by Dante Tomaselli / Starring Danny Lopes, The Amazing Kreskin, Lizzy Mahon, Vincent Lamberti, Christie Sanford / Elite (US R1 NTSC) / WS (1.85:1) / DD5.1

Outside a snowy farmhouse, a young girl, Grace (Lizzy Mahon), burns her hand while hanging up Christmas lights, then gets spooked by a sinister-looking goat standing near the woods. While running inside, she's suddenly accosted by a demonic-looking man in preacher's garb. Cut to a van carrying a group of teens just escaped from rehab after accidentally shooting one of the guards. The driver, Luck (Danny Lopes), steers them to the country home of a drug-pushing preacher, Salo (Vincent Lamberti), the same kidnapper from the opening scene. Upon arrival they discover

Grace, who is actually Salo's daughter and is living in mind-controlled captivity under the watch of her father's creepy Satanist wife (Christie Sanford). Hallucinatory terrors are immediately unleashed, including more goat appearances, a melting doll, flashbacks (or visions) involving Salo's spiritualist father (The Amazing Kreskin), a horde of shuffling zombies, torture on a rack, blood vomiting, and jack-o-lantern acid trips.

This ghoulish, stream-of-consciousness freak-out on film from *Desecration* director Dante Tomaselli is even more disorienting than his first effort, and its refusal to play by the narrative rules may result in more than a few viewers scratching their heads or staring at their DVD player in confusion. However, more adventurous souls with a taste for the surreal will find plenty of juicy material here as the story giddily skips from one Gothic image to another with only the thinnest of connective narrative tissue. Tomaselli certainly has his visual skills down pat, with the evocative snowbound setting evoking obscure '70s chillers such as *You'll Like My Mother*, while the more outrageous flights of fancy include some absolutely nightmarish visuals of Sanford (in a genuinely skin-crawling performance) looming towards the camera with a devilish grin on her face. That's really how most of the film works; it creeps you out way under the skin if you let it, even though the reasons why may not be immediately clear. This isn't a "scary" movie in the way many audiences now regard the term; this is much closer to Jodorowsky and David Lynch than Wes Craven. That said, after these early outings it would be interesting to see Tomaselli cutting his teeth on a script with a co-writer; his baroque visual talents might meld well with a less personal storyline that could be devoured by a wider horror audience. At least his sense of narrative control is obviously being refined, as *Horror* closes with a deliberately open but tantalizing final scene more effective than the nihilist dead end that closed *Desecration.*

Elite's special edition includes several worthy extras, kicking off with a Tomaselli commentary track in which he excitedly discusses the process of creating and shooting the film without giving away too much in the way of a literal reading of the story. Other goodies include an extended *Horror* trailer (really more of a promo reel), a *Desecration* trailer, a sometimes hilarious stills gallery with plenty of FX shots, footage of The Amazing Kreskin performing his feats on the set (which brings to mind the hypnotism used on Werner Herzog's *Heart of Glass* set), a 10-minute reel of behind-the-scenes footage, and a snippet from the original *Desecration* short film (different from the one included on the DVD for that feature). As for the film itself, the transfer is a bit problematic; shot on Super 16, the overall appearance is usually fine with sharp but deliberately grainy detail. However, there's also a substantial amount of chroma noise visible on some white, cream and yellow areas; fortunately the snowy scenes are largely unaffected, but bright doorways and lightbulbs jitter with colourful video noise. Perhaps this was an intentional effect as the flaw is wildly inconsistent, but whatever the reason, it's an unfortunate distraction. Audio is solid, boasting a Dolby Digital 5.1 track that's only marginally more aggressive than the already paranoia-inducing 2.0 mix on *Desecration*. Split surrounds are very limited but overall the ambience is spacious and contributes greatly to the film's mood of unease. Watch it alone in a dark room with rear speakers nearby, if you dare.

HORROR OF DRACULA (DRACULA)

Colour, 1958, 82m. / Directed by Terence Fisher / Starring Peter Cushing, Christopher Lee, John Van Eyssen, Carol Marsh, Melissa Stribling, Michael Gough / Warner (US R1 NTSC, UK R2 PAL) / WS (1.78:1) (16:9)

Though it plays as loose and easy with the Bram Stoker novel as any of its competitors, Hammer's first attempt to bring Dracula to the screen remains in many respects the consummate adaptation. Shot in voluptuous Technicolor and paced like a speeding train, this film is the one most responsible for kick-starting the Hammer horror avalanche which continued for the next two decades, and while subsequent films in the series managed to outdo this one in terms of both style and bloodshed (*Brides of Dracula* hits the perfect balance), it is *Horror of Dracula* that continues to stand the test of time with admirable grace.

Jonathan Harker (John Van Eyssen) travels to the remote castle of Count Dracula (Christopher Lee) under the guise of some harmless library cataloguing, but in reality he intends to put an end to the bloodsucker's reign of terror. Unfortunately the genteel Englishman is lured in by a mysterious female guest and falls prey to the vampire's feeding habits, forcing intrepid Professor Van Helsing (Peter Cushing) to investigate. Back in London, Dracula vampirizes the women at the Holmwood estate, including Jonathan's fiancée, Lucy (Carol Marsh), and Mina (Melissa Stribling), the wife of Lucy's brother, Arthur Holmwood (Michael Gough, now best known as Alfred from the *Batman* movies). Will Arthur and Van Helsing come to the rescue? Can the fanged fiend be stopped?

A zippier and more full-blooded film (in every sense) than Hammer's previous outings, *Horror of Dracula* (or simply *Dracula* as it's known everywhere except in the U.S.) benefits greatly from Cushing's confident performance and a number of classic set pieces, namely Harker's ordeal at the castle, the investigation into Lucy's nocturnal activities (which culminates in the best jolt in the Hammer catalogue), and of course the oft-imitated, action-packed finale which plays like a vampiric twist on an Errol Flynn movie. There isn't much room for subtext here, of course, and the film's frequently noted eroticism has been greatly muted over the years, but its status as a top calibre popcorn muncher remains unchallenged. Lee also deserves props for making such a vibrant impression with a comparatively tiny amount of screen time; unfortunately his participation would scarcely grow in future outings, causing him to vocally deride his appearances in these films.

For such a crucial horror title, *Horror of Dracula* has not fared very well on home video. Much of its original lustre has been dulled by muted and cropped video transfers, as well as a notorious laserdisc pressing, which omitted part of a gruesome staking at the 55-minute mark. (For the record, all three stake hits and the blood-spewing are here on the DVD, though upon close analysis the reinstated footage appears to be lifted from a different and slightly more degraded print.) Though the film still betrays its age at times, Warner's anamorphic transfer looks comparatively polished and boasts some wonderfully striking colours; reds are appropriately saturated and balance nicely with director Terence Fisher's skilful incorporation of blue and gold into the set design. Flesh tones are also noticeably improved, and the graininess that has become part of the film's video fabric has been thankfully decreased. Resolution looks impressive on a standard monitor but when blown up to home theatre size, detail can be quite soft in numerous shots, particularly the studio-bound exteriors. As with the theatrical prints, facial details sometimes appear blurred and overall the film will still look dated to those expected a crisp, megabudget Warner restoration on the order of *North By Northwest*. The film elements look clean and free from wear. As with their release of *The Mummy*, the decision to letterbox the film at 1.78:1 will no doubt ruffle a few feathers; the framing lops off as much on the top and bottom as it

adds to the sides, but the compositions look more spacious and evenly composed than the claustrophobic full frame version. However, viewers with 16:9 capability may find the framing awfully tight if their set overscans to 1.85:1, which shears off too much headroom for comfort. The mono audio is limited by the dated materials but sounds robust enough, with James Bernard's thunderous score coming through passably, if lacking the stomach-rumbling bass that characterizes his theme on the CD soundtrack. Considering the past track record of Hammer titles on DVD it wouldn't be outrageous to expect a special edition treatment for a title this important, but alas the only extras are the familiar theatrical trailer (in much better shape than on previous compilations) and a few cursory text supplements hopping through the Hammer-Dracula history. Given Lee's fluctuating opinion on discussing his Dracula appearances, his absence here isn't too surprising, but a few goodies to put the film in context (or even a simple gallery) would have been a welcome gesture. The British DVD is only currently available as part of a three-film box set, which also contains *The Curse of Frankenstein* and *The Mummy*.

THE HOUND OF THE BASKERVILLES

Colour, 1959, 97m. / Directed by Terence Fisher / Starring Peter Cushing, Christopher Lee, André Morell, Marla Landi / MGM (US R1 NTSC, UK R2 PAL) / WS (1.66:1)

Adapted for the screen no less than eighteen times, this reliable murder mystery chestnut remains the most famous Sherlock Holmes adventure of all despite the beloved sleuth spending the entire second act off in the wings, or so it would seem. The storyline passed into public lore long ago, but for those with short memories, Baker Street detective Holmes and his right hand man, Dr. Watson, are pressed into service by one Dr. Mortimer, who reports that a mysterious slaying by a wild animal on the moors may be related to a centuries-old curse placed upon the Baskerville family. The current and possibly last member of this unlucky clan is Sir Henry Baskerville, whose life both in London and back at the family estate appears to be in peril. Watson is sent out to investigate, and a deadly chain of revelations involving a ghostly hound leads to an unexpected climax.

After various silent film adaptations, Hollywood took its first major crack at *The Hound of the Baskervilles* in 1939 as the inaugural venture in its successful series of Basil Rathbone big screen mysteries. Withdrawn for years due to a closing line reference to the sleuth's cocaine habit, this atmospheric, black and white yarn established a cinematic pattern that would continue to hold for two decades. The earliest adaptation to be released on DVD is an entirely different matter, thanks to the involvement of Hammer Studios. During their astonishing spate of monster reinventions, including *The Curse of Frankenstein* and *Dracula*, Hammer and regular director Terence Fisher unleashed their own *Hound* in blazing colour. Steeped in Gothic atmosphere, sexual unease and barely concealed brutality simmering beneath the glossy, oaken veneer of English nobility, this outstanding transposition of Arthur Conan Doyle's novel to the bloody red Hammer universe is perhaps dubious as an adaptation but undeniably successful as a blend of murder mystery and horror. Peter Cushing takes the lead as Holmes, performing so convincingly that he continued to reprise the role well into the mid-1980s. Other Hammer regulars abound, with the able André Morell (*Plague of the Zombies*) making a convincing Watson and Christopher Lee assuming a rare, dignified heroic role as Sir Henry. (Lee would also play Holmes in the above-

average German outing, *Sherlock Holmes and the Deadly Necklace*, and appeared as Mycroft Holmes in Billy Wilder's *The Private Life of Sherlock Holmes*.)

Accompanied by James Bernard's rip-roaring music score, Fisher's version opens with an extended, memorable prologue in which the curse's origin is dramatically staged as a "sins of the fathers" malediction from the outset. Complete with a rare early utterance of the word "bitch" and a pair of gruesome fatalities, this curtain raiser promises an unusual ride for Holmes fanatics and more than delivers by the memorable quicksand finale. The plot experiences quite a few alterations along the way, including an enlarged and sexed-up role for Mrs. Stapleton (played here by buxom Marla Landi).

MGM's DVD carries over their already excellent 1.66:1 transfer from laserdisc, with the once-censored profanity intact. While the studio's refusal to anamorphically encode anything framed less than 1.85:1 remains irritating, owners of 16:9 sets can at least zoom in a bit for a more theatrical-style presentation. Extras include a dandy "Actor's Notebook" interview with Lee, who fondly recalls working with all of the principals and, much in the style of his *Dracula, Prince of Darkness* commentary, gives a solid account of the workings of Hammer Studios in its prime along with providing some enjoyable written excerpts from the source novel. The disc also includes the original B&W theatrical trailer, which completely drowns the film's unusual visual textures.

THE HOUND OF THE BASKERVILLES

Colour, 1978, 75/82m. / Directed by Paul Morrissey / Starring Peter Cook, Dudley Moore, Denholm Elliott, Joan Greenwood, Terry-Thomas, Hugh Griffith, Roy Kinnear, Spike Milligan, Prunella Scales / MGM (US R1 NTSC) / WS (2.35:1) (16:9), CDA (UK R2 PAL) / WS (2.35:1)

Without doubt the most undignified adaptation of Conan Doyle's seminal mystery is the 1978 film of the same name, directed by Andy Warhol disciple Paul Morrissey (*Flesh for Frankenstein*) and starring famed comedy team Peter Cook and Dudley Moore (*Bedazzled*) as Holmes and Watson. Featuring a multitude of half-witted movie parodies (including *The Exorcist*) and a scattershot collection of gags, the film never gels as a whole but features an odd moment here and there to provoke a smile. At least the supporting cast offers some much-needed focus every time the film threatens to wander off, including Denholm Elliott as Stapleton, the wonderful Joan Greenwood, Terry-Thomas (in his final role) as Dr. Mortimer, AIP regular Hugh Griffith (the *Dr. Phibes* films), Roy Kinnear (in drag), Spike Milligan, and *Fawlty Towers*'s Prunella Scales, among others. For Holmes-friendly viewers, however, this may not be much comfort as the familiar tale gets dragged through the wringer.

After the less than warm reception accorded to the U.K. theatrical release, the film was hacked to bits with numerous scenes shuffled around, producing a feature-length jumble that makes your average episode of *Monty Python's Flying Circus* look streamlined in comparison. Fortunately the CDA disc offers both versions, the more widely-seen 75-minute cut (pan and scanned but watchable) and the extended, more satisfying original cut (in its original 2.35:1 Techniscope aspect ratio). Moore fans in particular will enjoy significantly more footage of the comic in action, both as Watson and... as an old woman. The disc also includes the U.K. theatrical trailer. The later MGM edition features only the original Morrissey cut in a richer anamorphic presentation.

THE HOUND OF THE BASKERVILLES

Colour, 1981, 147m. / Directed by Igor Maslennikov / Starring Vasili Livanov, Vitali Solomin / Twister (Russia R0 PAL) / DD5.1

The colour version closest to the spirit of the Basil Rathbone/ Holmes films arrived from the Soviet Union, strangely enough, with a lengthy 1981 television production. Busy actor Vasili Livanov had already etched out a notable career as Russia's Sherlock Holmes, starring in a television series and numerous feature-length productions. A very elegant and "English-looking" actor in both demeanour and facial appearance, he makes a satisfying (if culturally peculiar) Holmes and carries this production quite well.

The Russian countryside makes for a fascinating twist on the usual moors, while the opulent Gothic interiors keep the eye busy while the brain is busy sifting through the details of the plot. Mild debits include a sometimes anachronistic music score more appropriate for a spaghetti western and some dubious fashion choices, including some very heavy, Slavic-looking coats.

Twister's region-free PAL disc presents the Russian soundtrack in a gimmicky, reworked 5.1 mix that ranges from effective to distracting; viewers sensitive to digitized remixes may simply want to channel the sound through their television set rather than a souped-up audio system. The full frame video quality is excellent throughout, with only a few minor compression problems in some of the foggy scenes. The disc includes optional English subtitles, which feature the occasional typo but are generally literate and capture the nuances of Doyle's dialogue.

THE HOUND OF THE BASKERVILLES

Colour, 1983, 100m. / Directed by Douglas Hickox / Starring Ian Richardson, Donald Churchill, Denholm Elliott / Image (US R1 NTSC), ILC Prime (UK R2 PAL)

After his turn in Paul Morrissey's dire effort from 1978, Denholm Elliott returned in a different capacity as Dr. Mortimer in a far more faithful and successful 1983 adaptation, made for British television and directed by Douglas Hickox (*Theatre of Blood*). Extremely well acted and photographed, this is one of the most faithful adaptations. This version also benefits from on-location photography of the moors in Devonshire, which make a suitably damp and ominous setting. Kudos as well to the sterling score by Michael J. Lewis, who provides a soaring orchestral accompaniment worthy of a Hollywood epic. The TV format makes for a few odd stylistic quirks, such as the tacky series-style opening credits, but these are minor debits in a worthy production. Ian Richardson acquits himself well as Holmes, though as far as TV-friendly sleuths go, he would soon be surpassed by Granada's long-running Sherlock, Jeremy Brett.

The Image DVD, one of the earlier titles in their catalogue, features a passable transfer that never really surpasses its early '80s low budget origins. That said, the 35mm photography fares well enough and the source material is mostly free from wear and tear. No extras, which also applies to the later British disc from the same master.

Astonishingly, it took several years before the most accomplished TV Holmes, Jeremy Brett, took a stab at the *Baskervilles* story in 1988. Though less successful overall than the 1983 version, this at least offers the chance to see the always worthwhile actor enacting the famous story. It also provides an opportunity for Brett's second Watson, Edward Hardwicke, to take the narrative reins for much of the running time; it's just as well since Brett seems a bit haggard and tired here, perhaps due to a long-running offscreen illness he was suffering at the time.

Easily the most faithful of the *Hound* adaptations to date, this version may seem a bit dry compared to the blood and thunder of previous efforts, but makes for elegant, refined viewing on its own terms; the horror content is understandably downplayed, while some of the seedier aspects are surprisingly played up (in keeping with the original source). The hound itself is also perhaps the most plausible of this cinematic kennel, resembling something close to the explanation provided by the actual mystery.

The MPI DVD looks grey and flat overall, with fairly washed out contrasts, but this may be in keeping with the original photography. It's watchable but hardly demo material, while the audio is crisper than usual for the Brett series. Likewise, the U.K. disc is feature only and similar in appearance.

THE HOUND OF THE BASKERVILLES

Colour, 1988, 105m. / Directed by Brian Mills / Starring Jeremy Brett, Edward Hardwicke / MPI (US R1 NTSC), Cinema Club (UK R2 PAL)

THE HOUND OF THE BASKERVILLES

Colour, 2002, 100m. / Directed by David Attwood / Starring Richard Roxburgh, Ian Hart, Richard E. Grant, Matt Day / BBC (US R1 NTSC, UK R2 PAL) / WS (1.78:1) (16:9) / DD5.1

One of the most controversial Sherlock Holmes adaptations, which is exactly what it was designed to be, the BBC's 2002 hi-tech version stars Aussie actor Richard Roxburgh (*Moulin Rouge*) as the venerable detective. Rugged and without his trusty deerstalker, this Holmes is paired up with a strikingly randier Watson (Ian Hart) who pursues the distaff Stapleton with energy more akin to an *American Pie* sequel. Complete with dramatic smash cuts, flashy digital video editing effects and a rampaging CGI hound from hell, this outrageous overhaul barely qualifies as a whodunit (barely any attempt is made to conceal the villain) and functions better as a suspenseful period drama with genre-bending flourishes, much closer to *The Brotherhood of the Wolf* than Baker Street. Carrying things even further OTT is a scenery-chewing performance by Richard E. Grant, who still seems to be acting in a Robert Altman film. Undeniably fast-paced and entertaining, this *Hound* makes for a lousy introduction to Holmes but, as cracking entertainment on its own terms, serves as an enjoyable popcorn-muncher.

The extras-laden BBC DVD has a crisp 1.85:1 transfer, anamorphically enhanced and with a thunderous 5.1 audio mix. A "making of" featurette includes interviews with the principals (including Australian character actor Matt Day as Sir Henry), along with footage showing the digital effects masters at work creating the hound; the U.K. edition also includes an audio commentary by director Atwood and producer Christopher Hall.

HOUSE OF CLOCKS

Colour, 1989, 80m. / Directed by Lucio Fulci / Starring Keith Van Hoven, Karina Huff, Paolo Paoloni, Bettine Milne, Carla Cassola, Al Cliver / Shriek Show (US R1 NTSC) / WS (1.85:1) (16:9), VIPCO (UK R2 PAL)

Designed to be part of a four-film series for Italian television entitled *Houses of Doom*, the quasi-metaphysical *House of Clocks* is certainly gorier than most countries' concept of made-for-TV fare and makes for minor but enjoyable late-period Fulci viewing. Wisely kept to a small scale and limited to a single remote country location, this modest effort delivers some gruesome goodies to satisfy hardened Luciophiles.

An elderly couple, Victor (Paolo Paoloni) and Sarah (Bettine Milne), passes the time by collecting clocks, ambling around their nicely appointed country home, and killing off those who prove to be inconvenient, such as the nosy maid (Carla Cassola). Meanwhile three semi-young delinquents stop off to loot the house by pulling a *Clockwork Orange* traffic accident story and then raiding the premises, killing the husband and wife along with the devoted handyman, Peter (*Zombie*'s Al Cliver). However, the guard dogs prevent the homicidal trio from leaving; even worse, all of the clocks begin to turn backwards as time itself reverses, bringing the dead back to life...

Though it makes little to no sense (especially the pointless "gotcha!" final scene), *House of Clocks* ambles along well enough for most of its running time and features some halfway competent dubbing, unlike Fulci's other TV movie, *Sweet House of Horrors*. Naturally the characters are all one-dimensional pawns in a game ultimately proven to have no point, but the central conceit is an intriguing one and makes one ponder what Fulci might have done at the peak of his powers with this material. Some nice Gothic touches like the cadavers stashed in the cellar bounce nicely off the suitably gory effects, including some nasty shotgunnings and an effective nod to the malicious hands-in-the-lawn scene from Mario Bava's *Shock*.

Previously released only in Japan (with lots of hazy-looking bootlegs generated over the intervening years), *House of Clocks* received an unlikely and surprisingly lavish American welcome with Shriek Show's DVD. Considering the preponderance of filters used throughout the film, the transfer looks relatively good with stable colours and only a few compression-generated problems cropping up during some dark hallway scenes in the film's midsection. Extras include a strange, noisy-looking trailer with video-generated text, as well as trailers for *Zombi 3*, *Sweet House of Horrors*, *House on the Edge of the Park*, and *Eaten Alive!*. Paoloni and Cassola turn up for video interviews running 5 and 9 minutes respectively; both seem to have fond memories of working on the low budget production, with the special effects and make-up receiving most of their attention. R. Ian Jane contributes an overview of the *House of Doom* series on the printed insert's reverse side, though the black on dark red type causes more than a little eyestrain. The bare-bones Region 2 release from VIPCO is strictly for PAL-fixated Fulci fans.

HOUSE OF 1000 CORPSES

Colour, 2003, 89m. / Directed by Rob Zombie / Starring Sid Haig, Bill Moseley, Sheri Moon, Karen Black, Tom Towles, Michael J. Pollard / Lionsgate (Blu-ray & DVD) (US R0/R1 HD/NTSC), Tartan (UK R0 PAL) / WS (1.85:1) (16:9) / DD5.1

In 1977, four teens researching roadside attractions in America stop off at a tourist trap run by the clown-faced Captain Spaulding (Sid Haig) on the night before Halloween. After experiencing his "murder ride" devoted to real-life psychopaths, they decide to explore the local story of missing maniac Dr. Satan, who was hanged from a nearby tree. Along the way they pick up a hitchhiker, Baby (Sheri Moon, wife of the director, rocker Rob Zombie), and promptly get a flat tyre. Baby leads them to her family for assistance, but unfortunately her clan turns out to be a band of lunatic cannibals including a bleach-blonde mother (Karen Black) and homicidal Otis (*The Texas Chainsaw Massacre 2*'s Bill Moseley). Meanwhile the town sheriff (*Henry: Portrait of a Serial Killer*'s Tom Towles) searches for one of the missing girls along with his deputy and a concerned father, only to wind up in the clutches of these ghoulish flesh eaters on Halloween.

For all its problems (and they are legion), *House of 1000 Corpses* at least deserves some credit for having its heart in the right place. Zombie includes numerous references (and film clips) from classic Universal horror films, while the movie itself pays homage to the likes of *Tourist Trap*, *Night Tide*, *Suspiria* (check out that gel-happy lighting) and the entire *oeuvre* of Tobe Hooper. (Bonus points for the in-joke character names, which reference everything from the Marx Brothers to composer Jerry Goldsmith.) Unfortunately any attempt at pacing and atmosphere is destroyed by far too much editing (this isn't a music video, Rob), repeated cutaways and transitions involving shaky video footage, and godawful pacing; the greatest sin is the long build-up given to Towles and company, whose fate an hour in proves to be an utter waste of time. The film never even attempts to establish character traits for anyone, so the result comes off as a loud, mean-spirited, overly flashy demo piece with no reason for the audience to become involved. Technically it's fairly interesting and does pack a few chilling moments into its final twenty minutes, including a nifty coffin-in-a-well sequence and a predictable but effective twist at the end. Universal was apparently so jittery about the film's sadistic gore (pretty tame by '70s and '80s standards, which should tell you something) that they eventually unloaded it to Lionsgate, who released it with great fanfare as "the movie the studios don't want you to see." The actual carnage is surprisingly unimaginative, mainly a quick scalping and some moments of knife mayhem that are more unpleasant than shocking. Horror buffs will have fun playing "spot that cast member", with *Spider Baby*'s Haig getting most of the prime moments and sharing a great pre-credits sequence (probably the film's best moment) with Michael J. Pollard discussing self-gratification with *Planet of the Apes* figures. (Also, keep an ear out for an out of left field cameo from the cackling doll in Goblin's *Deep Red* remix.)

Much publicity was garnered over Lionsgate's acquisition of R-rated and unrated cuts of the film, though based on bootlegs which circulated before the theatrical release, the longer cut Zombie offered doesn't seem significantly different. As with their disc of *The Rules of Attraction*, Lionsgate has apparently either lost interest in releasing an uncut version or plans to cash in again with a longer cut somewhere down the road; in any case their DVD of *House of 1000 Corpses* feels more like a half-hearted contractual obligation than a labour of love. The transfer is naturally top notch (except for the intentionally cruddy-looking video inserts), the surround audio sounds great (though there isn't as much Zombie music as you'd expect), and Zombie himself contributes a commentary track and discusses the film's tangled history. Also included are a music-only track (in case you really want to hear "She's a Brick House" twice) and the theatrical trailer. The Tartan release beefs things up a bit with three chaotic but somewhat enjoyable making-of featurettes, a radio spot, five brief interview snippets with the cast, rehearsal footage, and a trio of trailers, not to mention two frivolous

Easter eggs. The same additional extras are carried over to Lionsgate's U.S. Blu-ray release, which as expected looks even better with the added resolution of HD and, more noticeably, will rip your speakers apart with its very lively 7.1 lossless audio mix.

THE HOUSE THAT SCREAMED (LA RESIDENCIA)

Colour, 1969, 99m. / Directed by Chicho Ibáñez-Serrador / Starring Lilli Palmer, Cristina Galbó, John Moulder-Brown, Mary Maude / Divisa (Spain R0 PAL) / WS (2.35:1) / DD5.1, Shout! Factory (US R1 NTSC), Alfa Digital (2.35:1)

Young Theresa (*Let Sleeping Corpses Lie*'s Cristina Galbó) arrives at a remote, sprawling finishing school for girls run by the stern Madame Fourneau (stage and screen vet Lilli Palmer), and tentatively begins a friendship with Fourneau's voyeuristic son, Luis (John Moulder-Brown). Unfortunately disobedient girls tend to get locked away in a large storage closet and whipped by Fourneau's right hand girl, Irene (Mary Maude). One night a student slips out to the nearby greenhouse, and a chain of murder and intrigue begins...

In 1969, Italian audiences saw the rebirth of the horrific murder mystery courtesy of Dario Argento's first film, *The Bird with the Crystal Plumage*. At the same time, Spain unleashed its own Gothic twist on the same themes, *La residencia*, a film that would ironically be cited as a major influence on Argento's *Suspiria*. Both films received notable wide releases abroad (with uncharacteristic PG ratings in America), though while Argento went on to a long and notable career, director Chicho Ibáñez-Serrador only returned to the genre once more with the excellent *Quién puede matar a un niño?* (*Who Could Kill a Child?*), released by AIP as *Island of the Damned.*

Luxuriously paced by today's standards, *La residencia* indulges in a full 45 minutes of character development, flagellation, shower room sexual tension, and peeping Tom antics before the knife-wielding killer finally makes an appearance in one of the most startling pre-slasher killings of Euro cinema. The expert scope photography makes marvellous use of the baroque settings, often filing the girls across the screen with each one's expression perfectly conveying where she lies in the academic food chain. Several reviews, most notably the one in Phil Hardy's *Aurum Encyclopedia*, charged the film with misogyny and termed it "gory", but neither criticism bears up under close study. The film's only significant male character is a seriously dysfunctional, pubescent prat with a mommy complex; the women run the show here, and while some like Fourneau allow their power to run rampant, others like Irene display a fascinating ability to adapt to their circumstances (and often subvert audience expectations). The deaths in the film are comparatively restrained but exquisitely well handled; the second uses a freeze frame to shocking effect, while the third occurs offscreen but offers a nasty punchline. The killer's identity is barely concealed and offers little surprise; instead the film focuses on style and atmosphere, with a beautiful score to keep the ears occupied as well. A classic all round and one of the essential titles that needs to be viewed in order to gain a full appreciation of European horror.

Released by AIP as *The House That Screamed*, this film was shorn of a few throat-slashing frames but otherwise kept its shocks intact. The uncut version became a grey market staple, though the essential widescreen framing was destroyed by full frame or compromised 1.85:1 aspect ratios. The flawed but worthwhile Spanish DVD restores the full anamorphic compositions, essential to savouring the sly wit

and crafty visual manipulations of the film. Unfortunately not 16:9 enhanced, the visual appearance is saddled with noticeable flaws including inconsistent black levels and a colour scheme which veers a little too close to rust. Audio is presented in Spanish only with no subtitles, in either a worthless 5.1 mix (which mostly shoves the audio to the front two speakers with a few knob-twisting, gimmicky effects thrown to the rears) or the genuine, infinitely preferable mono mix. Viewers with tapes of the original English language track will obviously want to keep those for reference, but for fans longing to see this film as it was originally shot, the low-priced DVD is the way to go. The limited extras include a stills gallery and Serrador filmography. Though still imperfect, a bootleg edition from Alfa Digital (since pulled from the market) actually looks better with richer colours and, of course, an English soundtrack, and is likewise uncut. This same edition appears to be the source used for Shout! Factory's version, a double feature with *Maneater of Hydra* hosted by Elvira, Mistress of the Dark. The feature can be played either with or without the hostess's videotaped wisecracks, and while the film itself is uncut, it's still interrupted by artificial fades where her breaks and commercials were originally inserted. It's not an ideal presentation, but it's not bad for a cheap, accessible option.

THE HOUSE THAT SCREAMED

Colour, 2000, 79m. / Directed by John and Mark Polonia / Starring Bob Dennis / Sub Rosa (US R1 NTSC) / DD2.0

Between its derivative title (swiped from the Spanish horror film of the same name) to its storyline cobbled together from various sources including *The Changeling* and *Spirits*

of the Dead, this low-budget horror from the determined Polonia Brothers has a lot of obstacles to overcome but at least represents something of a step up from their previous outings, the well nigh unwatchable *Bad Magic* and *Feeders*. In between spastic montages, we follow our protagonist, depressed horror writer Marty (Bob Dennis), whose wife accidentally killed herself and their child after falling asleep while smoking. Seeking inspiration, Marty decides to shack up at a remote, supposedly haunted house. He meets a full-bodied female neighbour who's prone to saying things like, "I love this house. If it were alive, man or woman, I'd make love to it!" Naturally they jump in the sack, during which Marty experiences a horrific vision. Before long strange things like power outages, writhing naked strippers, hallucinations involving severed heads, and axe-wielding little girls have turned his cure for writer's block into an unending nightmare whose solution might come at a severely high cost.

Shot in the middle of the Pennsylvania woods, *The House That Screamed* musters up some decent atmosphere during its night scenes but stumbles quite a bit along the way. The filmmakers obviously love horror films and try to eke a few scares out of their scenario, but the lethargic pacing and erratic production values undermine what could have been an effective model in style. At least the film has the sense to poke fun at itself, with some amusing horror fiction in-jokes and a funny poke at *Feeders* for good measure. Though saddled with some unwieldy dialogue, Dennis manages to carry the film and proves to be vulnerable and sympathetic enough during the long, non-verbal passages in which he explores the ghostly terrain. Wildly erratic, the transfer for *The House That Screamed* depends entirely on the lighting used from scene to scene. The opening sequence, a wildly gratuitous shower scene followed by a hamfisted crawl explaining the role of ghosts in the year 2000, does not bode

well due to an abundance of noise and grain. Luckily the video quality smoothes out somewhat afterwards, though the film never looks really polished or slick. It's at least watchable, and the stereo sound is well rendered despite some occasionally muffled dialogue.

The DVD extras run almost as long as the feature itself, while the Polonias turn up for a commentary track as well. The discussion is fairly dry, explaining why certain elements were filmed and included (with lip service given to the obligatory nude scenes). Trailers include one for this film, two alternative spots for the sequel (*Hellgate*), and one for the Polonias' *Dweller*. Then we get to the real meat of the disc: an 18-minute "making of" documentary consisting mainly of talking heads (Dennis and the Polonias) discussing the film, a 14-minute reel of raw footage from the last day of shooting, and more questionably, a 15-minute tour of the house that could have probably been wrapped up in about a third of the time. The first two featurettes are quite interesting, however, and Dennis in particular turns out to have some interesting observations about the filming and his character. Last up are a stills gallery and a blooper reel (mostly clowning around and outtakes) accompanied by music snippets.

HOW TO MAKE A MONSTER

B&W/Colour, 1958, 73m. / Directed by Herbert L. Strock / Starring Robert H. Harris, Gary Conway, John Ashley, Gary Clarke, Paul Brinegar / Direct Video (UK R2 PAL), Lionsgate (US R1 NTSC)

One of the earliest exercises in self-reflective horror, made a full forty years before the *Scream* movies elevated in-jokes to an art form. Producer Herman Cohen follows up his hits *I Was a Teenage*

Werewolf and *I Was a Teenage Frankenstein* without making an actual sequel, using the movie business as a backdrop for a horror story, allowing for lots of inside-references but also editorialising about the genre itself. It may well be the first horror film to get sentimental about monsters as cultural icons, ahead of the breaking wave of *Famous Monsters* and Shock Theater.

Many Cohen films feature middle-aged crackpots who exert an unhealthy (gay-tinged?) hypnotic influence over teenage boys. Here, instead of a regulation mad scientist, the villain is Jack Pierce-like make-up artist Pete Dumond (Robert H. Harris), thrown out of work when a new studio regime decides monster movies have had their day and that from now on the specialty will be teenage musicals, as exemplified by John Ashley's delivery of the hilarious non-hit "You've Got to Have Ee-oo". Ironically, a few years later, AIP did start making beach party pictures and Ashley was a fixture in them. The bitter and resentful Dumond uses his drug-laden special greasepaint to turn teen idol actors – Gary Conway, recreating his *Teenage Frankenstein* role, and Gary Clarke taking over from on-to-bigger-things Michael Landon as the Werewolf – into snarling monsters, and programming them to kill off the anti-horror execs. "I'll use the very monsters they mock to bring them to an end", he vows, talking to a wall-load of genuine AIP posters. Even with the studio heads murdered, Dumond is discharged, a few steps ahead of the cops, and invites the teen actors to his home. After killing his incipiently treacherous minion (Paul Brinegar), Dumond tells the teens he will either use them as fall-guys for the murders or add them *House of Wax*-style to his collection of monsters ("my children"). A knocked-over candle produces an instant inferno, like those that would soon engulf AIP's *House of Usher* and many another Poe locale, which means a hurried wind-up.

Harris, a George Zucco look-alike, gives an interesting, surprisingly understated performance and the unusual milieu enlivens the standardised police investigation scenes, but this 73-minute picture isn't free of the dead patches of chat or conventional plot turns that prevent most Cohen movies from being as deliriously bizarre overall as they are by fits and starts. Nevertheless, it's a must for fans of 1950s AIP; part of the fun is the pretence that American International, who in actuality had no backlot, are a Hollywood major, complete with studio tour. In ridiculous on-set scenes, a martinet director drills the cast of *Werewolf Meets Frankenstein* as if refereeing a wrestling match ("Werewolf, meet Frankenstein, shake hands and come out snarling"). Connoisseurs will relish the final scenes (the black and white film turns colour for the last eight minutes) in which Dumond's inner sanctum is decorated with masks from the likes of *Invasion of the Saucer Men*, *It Conquered the World*, *The Beast with a Million Eyes* and *The She Creature*; though some have also lamented the destruction by fire of so many vintage Paul Blaisdell props.

Direct Video's DVD release features an excellent transfer of an unworn print, with solidly noirish black and white shadows; the colour finale is muted and muddy, more like a cheap 1940s process than the lurid glows of Roger Corman's impending AIP Poe cycle (those Blaisdell monsters are less vividly-coloured than audiences or poster artists imagine them), though it is a match for Cohen's *Horrors of the Black Museum* (which gets plugged in the dialogue). The extras are identical to those on the other Arkoff Collection releases: see *Earth vs the Spider* for details. A no-frills edition released later in America pairs up the same blah transfer with *Blood of Dracula* and mattes off rather nicely on 16:9 displays.

– KN

I AM CURIOUS – YELLOW

B&W, 1967, 121m. / Directed by Vilgot Sjöman / Starring Lena Nyman, Börje Ahlstedt / Criterion (US R1 NTSC)

I AM CURIOUS – BLUE

B&W, 1968, 107m. / Directed by Vilgot Sjöman / Starring Lena Nyman, Börje Ahlstedt / Criterion (US R1 NTSC), Second Sight (UK R2 PAL)

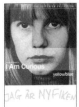

Best known as a cinematic catchphrase for cinematic naughtiness and liberation, "I Am Curious" refers to a pair of semi-experimental features by Swedish director Vilgot Sjöman. A fascinating if uneven stew of radical politics, kitchen sink realism, sexual frankness, and gritty documentary techniques, these films serve as effective celluloid time capsules even now that the shock value has largely dissipated over time.

The first and more notorious instalment, *I Am Curious – Yellow* (*Jag är nyfiken – gul*), conveys the world through the eyes of young Lena (Lena Nyman), a fledgling revolutionary whose budding sexuality and innate curiosity lead her on an eye-opening journey through her country, while the filmmakers and crew are reflected in what amounts to a blurring between art and reality. Lena commences a passionate but troubled relationship with car salesman Börje Ahlstedt (mirrored in the film and real life by a tumultuous triangle with director Vilgot Sjöman), and their experiences range from idyllic weekends together in the country to a far more clinical awakening at a health camp for reactionaries. Lena's story continues with *I Am Curious – Blue* (*Jag är nyfiken – bla*), a far less controversial study of Swedish society via social norms, the penal system, religious doctrine, and domestic relationships, as Nyman and Ahlstedt attempt to ground their lives in an increasing atmosphere of unrest.

Named after the two colours of the Swedish flag, the *I Am Curious* films are especially interesting for their hall of mirrors approach to filmmaking. Newsreel footage of real figures like Martin Luther King Jr. mixes with scribbled onscreen slogans, interviews with common people on the street, and a semblance of a linear narrative. The decidedly unglamorous Lena was something of a shock at the time; her pale and "normal" figure certainly clashes with the ideal of Twiggy and Audrey Hepburn being promoted at the time (to say nothing of where we are today). Sjöman describes the films as concurrent versions of the same story, simply told with different materials; in fact, they were both assembled from one huge mound of film shot in 1966 after the director decided to make an independent project freed from Swedish studio restraints. Of course, few could have predicted the seismic international ramifications of his little cinematic statement; the film was banned in the U.S. and taken all the way to the Supreme Court to be tried for obscenity. Thanks to the legal watersheds inaugurated by this case, many obscenity and pornography laws were lifted, allowing softcore to enter the mainstream. The blurring of documentary and narrative also proved to be influential, as our impressions of the actors versus characters are often unreliable. Ahlstedt turns out to be the father of another woman's child, but we have no idea whether this is fact or part of the film's construct; Nyman is the director's lover but falls for the leading actor, yet we cannot tell where the acting ends and the genuine change of heart begins. As a result the sex scenes have an increased emotional impact, and in *Blue* when they have become domesticated yet remain active in political protests, the viewer is pulled along for the journey as well. Many viewers also associate Swedish cinema with austere, serious subject matter (often unfairly, as Ingmar Bergman actually did several whimsical projects). Here humour is integrated skilfully into the interviews and situations in a realistic fashion; Sjöman also uses effect cutaways to written messages and visual collages to drive his points home with wry aplomb.

Criterion's two-disc boxed set presents each film in its own separate case, with distinct extras relating to each title. Transferred from the original negatives in their intended 1.33:1 aspect ratio, both films look absolutely pristine. Anyone accustomed to battered repertory prints or, even worse, hazy video transfers with unreadable, bleached-out subtitles will be amazed by the visual presentation here. Black levels are dead on, and detail is immaculate and crystal clear. The optional English subtitles are much more literate and easy to follow than earlier versions, which consequently makes the films easier to digest as the imagery whizzes by.

For the *Yellow* disc, supplements include a video interview with publisher Barney Rosset and attorney Edward de Grazia, the two primary figures in the string of legal cases ignited by the film, as well as "The Battle for *I Am Curious – Yellow*, a video document covering the legal skirmishes. Sjöman appears in a newly recorded video introduction, which includes a quick look at the studio where he cut his directorial teeth. He also provides commentary for a variety of scenes, in a manner similar to the M2K Claude Chabrol discs in France. The disc also has an informative essay by Gary Giddins, who rightly points out the film's influence on *Medium Cool* and the work of Dusan Makavejev, among others. The *Blue* disc repeats the Sjöman commentary method and also features a condensed version of *Self Portrait '92*, a Swedish television documentary about the director in which he comes off as something of a crackpot. Other bonuses include a deleted scene (nice but don't except anything revelatory) and text excerpts from a 1968 interview with the director, shortly before the American controversy really broke the following year. Both films are also packed together with forced English subtitles for the cheaper but far less context-heavy U.K. release.

I WILL WALK LIKE A CRAZY HORSE

Colour, 1973, 90m. / Directed by Fernando Arrabal / Starring George Shannon, Hachemi Marzouk / Cult Epics (US R0 NTSC) / WS (1.85:1) (16:9)

Three years after his cinematic bomb *Viva la muerte*, the surrealist film director Fernando Arrabal returned with this more thoughtful, character driven study of nature versus society, though his visuals are no less outrageous. More sexually explicit but less violent than its predecessor, *I Will Walk like a Crazy Horse* (*J'irai comme un cheval fou*) has remained rarely seen since its European debut, making it a jaw-dropping surprise for those brave enough to test its waters.

Haunted by violent, eroticized memories of his domineering mother, businessman Aden (George Shannon from *Sugar Cookies*) retreats in his jeep to the desert where he encounters Marvel (Hachemi Marzouk), a diminutive, shaman-like being who possesses the ability to fly through the air and change day to night. Smitten with his saviour, Aden convinces Marvel to return to the industrialized city, where Marvel experiences a number of bizarre encounters including being rolled around naked in a giant plastic ball. Disillusioned by their environment, the two men return to the desert for a gruesome, transcendent finale, but not before Aden reveals the entire story behind his inner torment.

Typical of avant garde films from the period, *Crazy Horse* studs its mostly linear storyline with a series of peculiar, interstitial-style reveries which comprise some of its most memorable moments: a cross-dressing Aden in a coffin giving birth to a skull, a couple in gas masks making love, and so on. Visually slick and making admirable use of the striking desert locales, Arrabal's film is polished enough to pass for mainstream product even when it's strictly at odds with the content, which is still extreme enough to pack a punch. The Cult Epics DVD sports a spotless anamorphic transfer, with sharp detail and beautifully saturated colours. The French dialogue (with the American Shannon looped by another actor) sounds fine, while the optional English subtitles are always legible and well written. The disc includes extensive liner notes by critic Rayo Casablanca, a trailer for *Viva la muerte* (while that disc contains the trailer for this film), a lobby card gallery, and of course, a video interview with Arrabal, which is even more endearingly irrelevant than its companion piece on the *Viva* DVD. His anecdotes about the two actors are priceless and more than a little puzzling, while he once again resorts to posing with his chair, apparently to prove a point. Also available as part of Cult Epics's "Fernando Arrabal Collection" along with *Viva la muerte* and *The Guernica Tree*.

IDENTITY

Colour, 2003, 89m. / Directed by James Mangold / Starring John Cusack, Ray Liotta, Pruitt Taylor Vince, Alfred Molina, Rebecca De Mornay, Jake Busey, Amanda Peet / Sony (Blu-ray & DVD) (US R0/R1 HD/NTSC, UK R2 PAL) / WS (2.35:1) (16:9) / DD5.1

You have to give 'em credit; for once, the characters in a *Ten Little Indians* knockoff actually get to make reference to the famous Agatha Christie whodunit once they start getting bumped off, and this twisty thriller makes few attempts to disguise its nods to other influential shockers as well. (*Psycho* and *The Sixth Sense* spring to mind most obviously.) The film opens with a hefty bald convict (Pruitt Taylor Vince) awaiting a last minute stay of execution thanks to pleas

from his psychiatrist (Alfred Molina), while elsewhere a dark and violent storm conspires to send ten travellers to seek shelter at a fleabag Nevada motel in the middle of nowhere. Among the strandees are an over the hill actress (Rebecca De Mornay), her chauffeur (John Cusack), a cop (Ray Liotta) escorting a leering criminal (Jake Busey), and a self-respecting hooker (Amanda Peet). Over the course of the evening, they're killed off in order, according to their motel room numbers... but that's just the beginning.

Unlike the increasingly lazy *Scream* sequels and its followers, *Identity* gets points for at least playing fair with its plot conventions and unveiling its twists in a coherent, linear manner that follows directly from preceding events. Interestingly, the big wham-o twist is unveiled barely an hour into the running time; more surprising are the evil little tweaks given to several characters elsewhere in the film, particularly Liotta and a not-too-polite desk clerk. With his portrait stashed in the attic apparently catching up with him at last, Cusack anchors the film well enough with a solid performance; it's amusing that this star of *Being John Malkovich* made a cameo in *Adaptation*, which in turn ridiculed one of the central devices here. The film is far from perfect; De Mornay's fun portrayal is wasted with far too little screen time, and the closing, violent stinger is an unnecessarily nasty and clichéd resolution that pushes audience goodwill just past the breaking point. This is also a textbook example of a horror film that most mainstream critics will refer to as a "suspense thriller", despite the bloody murders piling up left and right at the hands of an unseen killer. The twists might be a tad more metaphysical than your standard *giallo*, but we're still in the same territory.

Sony's DVD offers three different versions of the film: the theatrical cut in widescreen or full frame (the latter slightly opened up per Super 35 procedures but still a headache to watch), or an extended widescreen version with a tad more dialogue and a differently edited denouement, which integrates Vince into the explanatory flashback. (There isn't much difference.) Frustratingly, you have to eject the disc and start all over again if you want to change the version of the film you're watching. The 5.1 audio is a dream for home theatre owners; the thundercracks and bombastic music crash and slam between each speaker in virtually every scene. Director James Mangold (*Girl, Interrupted*) contributes an enjoyable commentary track with nary an empty moment to be found; he makes for good company as he delineates the difficulties of managing a set number of characters in a confined setting for the duration of a film shoot. Also included are four deleted scenes (alternative or longer versions of existing scenes, to be more accurate) with optional Mangold commentary, a fluffy 15-minute featurette made for Starz network, storyboard comparisons, filmographies, and the spoiler-packed theatrical trailer, which blows several key twists if you look closely enough. The bump up to Blu-ray results in an obviously crisper visual presentation and the same roster of extras, though surprisingly, a new audio commentary with screenwriter Michael Cooney is also included and offers enough substance to justify an upgrade beyond the mere technical improvements.

IMAGES

Colour, 1972, 104m. / Directed by Robert Altman / Starring Susannah York, Rene Auberjonois, Marcel Bozzuffi, Hugh Millais, Cathryn Harrison / MGM (US R1 NTSC) / WS (2.35:1) (16:9)

Though most critics will deny that he ever made a full-blown horror film, the wildly erratic Robert Altman certainly toyed with the genre's conventions in *That Cold Day in the Park*, *The Gingerbread Man*, and most notably *Images*, a nerve-jangler usually regarded as a *Repulsion* riff about a woman's violent inability to distinguish between fantasy and reality. The film appropriately opens with a recited fairytale about unicorns – nonexistent creatures, natch – spoken by Cathryn (Susannah York), a woman alone with only a telephone and a come-and-go husband to keep her anchored to the real world. While talking to her friend Joan, she is startled when the voice on the telephone suddenly changes to a different one entirely, warning Cathryn that her husband is off having an affair. When hubby Hugh (Rene Auberjonois) finally returns home, he assures her that it's all just a nasty prank. Unfortunately Cathryn is startled and turns into a screaming wreck when Hugh suddenly turns into her deceased former lover, Rene (Marcel Bozzuffi). Hugh decides it's time to take his wife off to the Irish countryside for a little relaxation, but the vacation proves to be no less traumatic; Cathryn sees a sinister doppelganger of herself, repeatedly encounters Rene, and also runs into another old flame, Marcel (Hugh Millais), whose blonde daughter, Susannah (Cathryn Harrison), is more than a bit eerie herself. Realizing that these visions must be stopped, Cathryn decides to kill off her ghosts... with horrific consequences.

Unlike your standard beautiful-woman-going-crazy melodrama, *Images* elicits its chills through York's often startling reactions rather than the apparitions themselves. We often have to wait for her sudden scream to determine whether what we're seeing is truly unnatural or frightening; as her sanity seems to slide downhill, the viewer is left disoriented by having the one point of view in the film proven to be completely unreliable. In a sense this is closer to the ghost/madness subgenre which also includes *Don't Look Now*, the underrated *A Quiet Place in the Country*, and *Symptoms*, where the film itself becomes a jagged series of hallucinatory visions which the audience must later put together like a nasty jigsaw puzzle. York's excellent performance grounds a film that might otherwise be unbearably flighty, and Altman followers can find plenty of food for thought here.

Sandwiched between *McCabe and Mrs. Miller* and *The Long Goodbye* on his roster of films, *Images* completes what is in essence a trilogy of moody, genre-twisting Altman films with expert, groundbreaking scope photography courtesy of Vilmos Zsigmond. It's a shame the two parted ways afterwards, as their styles fit each other perfectly. The film's elaborate visual scheme is consistently impressive, with mirrors and doubling imagery used to marvellous effect (outdone only by Dario Argento's similarly crafty *Deep Red*); continuing the motif with an especially bizarre stunt, the characters are all named after *different* actors within the film, essentially swapping everyone's identity with someone else of the same gender. Equally vital is the complex and often gut-wrenching sound mix, with an early and highly adventurous score by John Williams (complete with "sounds" by Stomu Yamashta). Good luck finding the extremely scarce soundtrack album; though not exactly accessible, the music works beautifully and obviously inspired Jerry Goldsmith's similar work on *The Reincarnation of Peter Proud* a few years later.

MGM's under-the-radar release is nothing less than a milestone recovery for horror fans with a taste for art house flourishes. Long mentioned as the "lost" Altman film surrounded by rumours of studio suppression, demolished negatives, and legal entanglements, this Hemdale release was first distributed by Columbia but promptly buried without a home video release. Fortunately the DVD finally offers a chance to assess the film in all its widescreen glory, and the results were worth the wait; the spooky Irish scenery and pastoral lighting look wonderful in this anamorphic transfer, which is bright and colourful where it should be and deliberately desaturated

during several interior scenes. Zsigmond's filter-happy photography can be a nightmare even with modern digital know-how (e.g., *Obsession*), but few will find fault here. The disc comes with a handful of welcome supplements, primarily a 24-minute featurette, "Imagining *Images*". Best known as an actors' director, Altman is his usual chatty self and warmly discusses the film without blowing too much of its ambiguity; Zsigmond also pops up for a quick interjection, too. Altman returns for one of those odd "selected scenes" commentary tracks (similar to *What's Up, Doc?*) in which he discusses some of his favourite moments and points out little anecdotes about the production history. The disc closes out with a long, borderline avant-garde theatrical trailer that probably did this film no favours with general audiences.

IMPOSTOR

Colour, 2001, 97m. / Directed by Gary Fleder / Starring Gary Sinise, Madeleine Stowe, Vincent D'Onofrio, Lindsay Crouse, Tony Shalhoub, Mekhi Phifer / Metrodome (UK R2 PAL), Buena Vista (US R1 NTSC) / WS (1.85:1) (16:9) / DD5.1

Impostor has a muddy multi-authored script (by Caroline Case, Ehren Kruger, David Twohy, and Scott Rosenberg), dreadfully edgy direction and an emphasis on botched action over paranoid humour, all of which scupper this promising adaptation of a 1953 Philip K. Dick short story.

In 2079, Earth is a united military state waging perpetual war against "genetically superior" Alpha Centaurans, with a few overpopulated and regimented cities secure under force shield domes and the usual gloomy, rubble-strewn wasteland populated by tough dissidents on the outside. Scientist

Spencer Olham (Gary Sinise), experiencing a few qualms about the super-weapon he has just developed, is hauled from his workplace by security man Hathaway (Vincent D'Onofrio), who claims to have evidence that Spencer is a robot impostor (the script uses the *Blade Runner* term "replicant", which Dick despised) almost indistinguishable from the original but with a heart that turns into a bomb when a specified target is nearby. Hathaway believes Spencer is an assassination weapon aimed at the world's ruler (Lindsay Crouse, barely glimpsed) but Spencer insists a mistake has been made and escapes from the torture/dissection chamber, accidentally gunning down his best friend (Tony Shalhoub) in the process. Spencer tries to get help from his doctor wife (Madeleine Stowe), who might have access to a test that could prove his humanity, but is forced to go outside the dome and enlist the grudging help of a regulation black bald hard-soft freedom fighter (Mekhi Phifer).

The themes of identity and paranoia, central to the Dick canon, ought to suit producer-star Sinise, who can be one of the screen's subtlest actors, but this turns into a formula runabout, with director Gary Fleder adopting an off-putting array of jerky mannerisms and visual gimmicks that still fail to cover up the repetitive run-from-explosions, shootout-with-fascist-cops, computer-hologram-forming-against-the-clock business. Metrodome's DVD looks a little muddy, which is probably a fault of the murky-looking original rather than the transfer. It seamlessly incorporates some minor snippets of footage trimmed from the theatrical cut, but nothing adds much to the picture. Besides the trailer, the only extra is a making-of puff piece.

– KN

[The U.S. DVD contains an extended R-rated cut of the film along with the original, much tighter short film version, originally intended to be part of a three-part science fiction anthology project, "Alien Love Triangle". – ed.]

IN A GLASS CAGE

Colour, 1986, 108m. / Directed by Agustín Villaronga / Starring Günter Meisner, David Sust, Marisa Paredes, Gisela Echevarria / Bildstörung (Germany R2 PAL), Filmax (Spain R2 PAL) / WS (1.85:1) (16:9), Cult Epics (US R1 NTSC) / WS (1.85:1)

Justifiably regarded as one of the most harrowing films ever made, this gruelling yet tremendously accomplished fusion of aesthetic beauty and unbearable cruelty is a nasty antidote to the dozens of Nazi soft porn films generated in Europe during the late 1970s. Initially shown in festivals by some misguided programmers as a gay interest title (with understandably shocked results and mass walkouts), the film was eventually discovered by adventurous horror connoisseurs who quickly placed it alongside *Salò* and *Cannibal Holocaust* in the pantheon of beautifully made cinematic atrocities. However, even among such barbed company, this Spanish production still packs a punch that leaves many viewers reeling long afterwards. Truth be told, anyone who can make it through the opening ten minutes will probably be able to stomach the following hour and a half.

We begin in a crumbling, abandoned building where Klaus (*The Boys from Brazil*'s Günter Meisner), a former Nazi officer spending his twilight years in Spain, contemplates a trussed, heavily bruised young boy before whacking him with a board (mercifully offscreen). Meanwhile an unseen visitor gazes from outside the building and, after Klaus departs to hurl himself off a rooftop, he steals the abuser's scrapbook of photos and scribblings. Flash forward a few months; the suicidal Klaus is now confined to an iron lung as a result of his fall and is tended to by his unhappy wife, Griselda (Pedro Almodóvar regular Marisa Paredes), and their daughter Rena

(Gisela Echevarria). One day their routine is disrupted by the sudden arrival of Angelo (David Sust), a creepy young man who rushes into the house and locks himself in with Klaus, insisting he should be hired as the man's nurse. Despite Griselda's protests, Angelo is hired even though he is apparently unable to properly load a syringe. Even stranger, Angelo spends his private time alone with Klaus by depriving his charge of oxygen, reading entries from Klaus's diaries, and engaging in psychosexual routines; however, when Griselda accidentally trips over the plug to Klaus's iron lung, she awakens less than noble instincts within herself as well. The fragile household soon erupts in violence, and before long Angelo is bringing home victims of his own to dispatch for an audience of one, the confined sadist with whom he shares a mysterious and terrifying bond from the past.

Though it contains more than its share of physical and psychological violence, *In a Glass Cage* (*Tras el cristal*) is less overtly explicit than one might expect; blood is barely glimpsed, with the horror coming instead from the deeply committed performances, which often verge on the unwatchable. A disclaimer thankfully explains that the child actors weren't harmed in any way during the film, which is a relief considering what the viewer is forced to watch; the needle injection bit ranks rather high on the list of scenes to never, ever play in mixed company. Though not normally classified as a horror director, Agustín Villaronga (who went on to make the creepy, highly underrated *99.9*) shows an unerring ability to jar the viewers' nerves while maintaining an aesthetic eye to rival Dario Argento's. Along with reflecting on global events, Villaronga subtly nods at film history as well; the eerie eyeball close-up which begins the film (with a clicking camera shutter to boot) echoes Michael Powell's *Peeping Tom*, while the lush, decaying villa and fluid camera movements recall such masters as Visconti and Ophuls.

Two extended sequences in the middle of the film, Griselda's night walk to the basement, and her subsequent confrontation with Angelo, are magnificent displays of horror filmmaking reminiscent of the finest Italian *gialli*. Not surprisingly, the sadistic narrative device of a psycho intentionally staging his murders as theatrical displays for his "captive audience" was later appropriated by Argento in a more baroque context for *Opera*, but this film never lets its audience forget about the real life violence which underpins the story; from the haunting Holocaust photographs under the opening credits to Angelo's concentration camp redecorating scheme, Villaronga constantly reminds us that the fallout from such intense horror is still lingering no matter how much we'd like to forget it.

Since *In a Glass Cage* was barely exhibited in theatres, most viewers were forced to watch it in a fuzzy, murky VHS transfer from Cinevista. The Cult Epics DVD is a step up in several respects, starting with the far more legible, optional English subtitles. Detail is fairly sharp, and the eerie colour schemes are vivid and well represented. However, the non-anamorphic presentation reveals an uncomfortable amount of debris and compression flaws; this problem can be corrected somewhat by lowering the black levels and contrast on your monitor, as the transfer features the same too-high black level settings found on many Japanese transfers (and DVDs such as *Tomb of Ligeia*). The mono audio sounds fine if a bit thin; crank up the bass to take full advantage of the outstanding music score by Javier Navarette (*The Devil's Backbone*).

A very strangely framed Villaronga appears for a lengthy video interview in which he discusses several aspects of the film, from handling the underage actors (whose scenes were treated as a series of innocent games later manipulated through editing into nightmare material) to the artistic inspirations for the striking, steely blue colour scheme. Unfortunately the striking theatrical trailer created by Cinevista is missing in action. Also, the first pressing (now virtually gone from the market) is slightly out-of-synch in several scenes and can be switched via the distributor.

Entirely non-English friendly are the Italian and Spanish releases, though both feature a better, anamorphic transfer from HD supervised by the director; the former includes a Villaronga audio commentary, a gallery and German trailer, several storyboard sequences including an alternative ending, and a variety of text extras; the Spanish disc carries over the trailer and storyboards but drops the commentary in favour of a photo gallery with director commentary. Both contain the featurette from the Cult Epics disc as well, but again, the lack of English subtitles on the feature or extras will limit the import appeal severely. Very rough stuff; come prepared.

THE INCREDIBLE MELTING MAN

Colour, 1977, 86m. / Directed by William Sachs / Starring Alex Rebar, Burr DeBenning, Edwin Max, Dorothy Love, Janus Blythe, Myron Healey, Cheryl "Rainbeaux" Smith, Jonathan Demme / VIPCO (UK R2 PAL), Raro (Italy R2 PAL), CMV Laservision (Germany R0 PAL) / WS (1.85:1) (16:9)

Three astronauts, while travelling through the rings of Saturn, are exposed to the Sun's rays and a degenerative chemical change assails them. Two die immediately, but the third, Colonel Steve West (Alex Rebar) returns to earth where he's hospitalized with a condition causing his flesh to slide off his skeleton. Deranged, West escapes and turns to cannibalism, quickly realizing that his new diet, though not curative, forestalls the disease that's destroying him. Dr. Ted Nelson (Burr DeBenning) is sent out to catch West

and bring him back, but as the clock ticks down to the next flight to Saturn, the trail of death u-turns towards Nelson's own home...

A deliciously sleazy compote of sci-fi schlock, as '50s Z-grade concept plot copulates with '70s gross out carnage. Director/writer William Sachs, who later brought Dorothy Stratten to the screen in all her glory in *Galaxina*, has uniformly awful players, and the story is wobblier than the titular character's spine. In fact, over the top gore aside, it plays like a failed TV pilot shamelessly padded to feature length; at one point there's a completely superfluous flashback, which replays the entire opening sequence. Arlon Ober (who composed the music for the previous year's *Through the Looking Glass*) submits a score that wouldn't be out of place in an episode of *The Gemini Man*. The dalliance with twisted humour is a misfire too, with an amorous elderly couple (Edwin Max and Dorothy Love) scrumping fruit in a lemon grove, the pair of them subsequently winding up on West's supper plate. Premeditated attempts at the funnies aside, Sachs's crass dialogue – often delivered as if it's been learned phonetically, most jarringly by the talentless DeBenning – occasionally provokes inadvertent sniggers: "Oh God, it's his ear!" exclaims the Doc as he discovers West's radioactive lobe hanging on a bush. And to top things off the plot's suspenseful nucleus is undermined by its own illogicality. West, we learn, must be found before the follow-up mission to Saturn embarks, presumably so it can be aborted; he isn't found and the story concludes with the next rocket leaving the launch pad. Given that the military already know what happened first time out, aside from the fact that West's recapture will ensure the public doesn't find out about it, why the second launch can't just be cancelled is indistinct. All of this paints a pretty unappealing picture doesn't it? Well, believe it or not, I actually like the film. For all its inadequacies, many of which instil unintentional bonus entertainment value, *The Incredible Melting Man* is more fun than a barrel full of monkeys. Why? Because he does exactly what it says on the packet.

After a short establishing sequence in space Sachs lurches into the slimy action as West wakes in hospital, inspects his gelatinous visage in the mirror, blows a fuse and maims a nurse on his way out the door. With *An American Werewolf in London* still three years away, Rick Baker's effects are a tasty *hors d'oeuvre* to his later work and remain among the most impressive of his prodigious career; once seen, those final disgusting shots as irreversible decomposition kicks in and West liquefies into a heap of bloody flesh swimming in fatty deposits are never forgotten. The gruesome goods come thick and fast, the highlights of which include an angler having his head torn off (which then floats down river and over a waterfall with spectacularly squishy results), an eyeball-popping encounter with a little girl in the woods, and a sequence in which almost-victim Janus Blythe strikes back with a handy meat cleaver and West parts company with his arm. The cast of characters are all unsympathetic and most of them end up dead. Of the lukewarm cast Alex Rebar comes off best, which isn't saying much as all he has to do is stumble around and let Baker's marvellously moist effects do the talking. That said, in spite of his anthropophagic habits, you can't help but feel a twinge of pity for the guy come final meltdown. Myron Healey (as ineffectual military man General Perry) is only marginally better than the frightfully inadequate DeBenning. Cheryl "Rainbeaux" Smith is the photographer's model who steps on a hollowed out corpse and Jonathan Demme – a better director than he is an actor – gets served up as one of West's late night snacks. Executive produced by the great Max J. Rosenberg and one of the last films to emerge from the stable of B-Movie giants American Interna-

tional Pictures, I'd go so far as to dub *The Incredible Melting Man* a minor classic. Feel free to despise me for it.

Those hoping that a DVD release of the film would turn up the fabled shot of Alex Rebar chewing on Jonathan Demme might be slightly disappointed with the region free release (under the title *Der Planet Saturn läßt schön grüßen*) from CMV Laservision of Germany; omitted from the release print, this elusive moment remains absent, its atrocity left to be conveyed by a reaction shot from Janus Blythe. Excusing this oversight, it's a largely pleasing disc. The uncut feature, divided by a rather miserly 8 chapter marks, is presented in a 1.85:1 theatrical ratio with garish colours and a pin sharp image. So clean is it in fact that the grainy outer space footage that opens and closes the movie is more conspicuously mismatched than ever before. Sound options are in English and German. While some relatively high profile titles are as bare boned as Steve West at the film's close, it never ceases to amaze how festooned with subsidiary goodies the crummiest titles can be, often boasting more supplemental material than you can believe anyone cared enough to assemble. Gratifyingly *The Incredible Melting Man* is no exception. CMV have decorated this pressing with an original German trailer, which favours the film's gory excesses, and a very presentable music-backed slideshow gallery of original poster art, lobby cards and press stills. One cannot speak so enthusiastically of VIPCO's British disc, inferior to CMV's in every respect, yet all that you might expect of something from their catalogue. The uncut film, a full screen affair, is accompanied by four trailers (not one of them for *Melting Man*, each of them there to promote other VIPCO releases) and a stills gallery which, unsurprisingly, turns out to be a collection of freeze-frame shots lifted from the movie. The Raro release is no better, looking drab and dupey as well.

– TG

INCUBUS

Colour, 2002, 78m. / Directed by Jess Franco / Starring Carina Palmer, Carsten Frank, Fata Morgana, Lina Romay / Sub Rosa (US R1 NTSC) / DD2.0

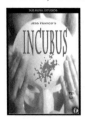 In the inaugural issue of *Video Watchdog* magazine, director Jess Franco protested that his movies could be called anything but silly. Of course, that was before he made *Mari-Cookie and the Killer Tarantula* and this slice of erotic horror hokum, which kicks off with the goofiest rendition of "Rockabye Baby" ever recorded and goes downhill from there.

The story, for lack of a better term, concerns successful, folically-challenged artist Johan (Carsten Frank), whose riches can be attributed to a pact made with the sexy, supernatural Lorna (Fata Morgana), an incubus (err, technically succubus, but whatever...) who gives him fame and fortune in exchange for his daughter when she turns twenty. Coincidentally, said daughter, Lucy (Carina Palmer), returns home and spends her time lolling around naked in bed, reading the Marquis de Sade, and indulging in S&M fantasies. Meanwhile Johan's usually naked wife (Lina Romay) doesn't take too kindly to Lorna's influence on their lives, and when the time comes to pay the devil his due, no one emerges unscathed.

As long-time Franco fans know, the director tends to repeat characters and situations from his earlier films to an obsessive degree. For example, Dr. Orlof has been through innumerable permutations for over four decades, and here Franco revisits the "character" of Lorna, present in 1967's *Succubus* and used again in 1974's *Lorna the Exorcist* (*Les possédées du diable*), of which this is more or less a remake (but minus the crab critters emerging from Romay's nether regions).

Though shot on video, *Incubus* is a bit more visually polished than Franco's other contemporary work; some of his *trompe l'oeil* bits involving mirrors are surprisingly well designed, and apart from the absurd credits, he avoids those tacky digital effects that plagued some of his other video projects. Outside of his hardcore work, this is one of the most nudity-heavy titles in the Franco canon; in virtually every scene there are undraped bodies, both female and male, strolling or writhing in front of the camera. As usual Ms. Romay is the most unabashed of the bunch, which may only appeal to a very select audience. By far the most memorable aspect of the film is its finale, an extended dream-like demon orgy in which a lavish room (by all appearances a hotel lobby) turns into an erotic playground, with a damned, victimized Lucy led on a chain collar by men bearing some very mean strap-ons. And once again Franco recycles Daniel White's music for *Female Vampire*, though the use here is fairly appropriate.

Sub Rosa's DVD does what it can with the limited technology at hand for *Incubus*; the lighting ranges from lush to overly harsh, and edges can look too sharp during daylight scenes. The colour scheme is also muted and earthy throughout. Dialogue ranges from coherent (mostly Frank) to utterly incomprehensible (with la Lina the worst offender, once again). The DVD packaging promises a producer's commentary, which fails to materialise; instead the viewer gets a lengthy documentary, "The Devil's Possessed – Behind The Scenes of *Incubus*", which shows Franco at work during virtually every scene in the film. The footage is presented with the film's score for accompaniment and includes no spoken audio. Also here for some reason are two foreign short films, "Marrakech London" and "The Perfect Taxi Driver", which are interesting and well-shot but not exploitative or related to the main feature.

THE INCUBUS

Colour, 1981, 93m. / Directed by John Hough / Starring John Cassavetes, Kerrie Keane, John Ireland, Duncan McIntosh / Elite (US R0 NTSC) / WS (1.85:1) (16:9)

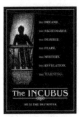

An outrageously sick entry in the slasher sweepstakes from the early '80s, *The Incubus* is comparatively low on graphic bloodshed but makes up for it with dashes of the supernatural, some marvellous small town atmospherics, a few good jolts, and a flood of tasteless dialogue that'll make you choke on your popcorn.

The quiet New England hamlet of Galen finds itself rocked by a string of brutal murders involving the grisly sexual assault of women, with a few unlucky guys dispatched along the way as well. The new doctor in town, Sam Cordell (John Cassavetes, cashing a paycheck for his next directorial effort), teams up with the local police chief (John Ireland) and a glamorous reporter (Kerrie Keane) to find the demented culprit – or perhaps culprits, judging from the amounts of, er, fluid found during the autopsies – behind these ghoulish crimes. Meanwhile Tim (Duncan McIntosh), the boyfriend of Cordell's daughter, suffers from vivid nightmares that seem to coincide with each murder. As it turns out, the town suffers from a history of demonism and mysterious killings that tie in to the mythical incubus, a sexually voracious, nightmare creature that ravages its victims.

Director John Hough had done the offbeat horror routine before, notably in *The Legend of Hell House* and the previous year's *The Watcher in the Woods*, but *The Incubus* is a whole other matter entirely. The shock quotient of the subject matter has been dulled by years of *NYPD Blue* and *Law and Order* covering some of the same general material, but the bizarre hyperbole of characters yammering on about it over and over makes

for strange viewing indeed. The presence of Cassavetes is particularly unsettling, a long way from the urban menace of *Rosemary's Baby*. His influence extends beyond his thespian skills too, as according to John Hough the screenplay of this film was almost entirely rewritten by Cassavetes. The film is professionally mounted and features a solid score by the late Stanley Myers, who wrings tension out of several scenes; however, memorable music honours go to a midnight movie sequence (with a special treat for Iron Maiden fans) in which a young girl is attacked in the theatre bathroom. And watch out for that sick twist ending!

Elite's packaging for this DVD sports a disclaimer on the back: "You may notice occasional film grain in certain scenes in this picture. This grain is inherent in the original film elements used." Naturally alarm bells should go off considering they didn't bother with any kind of warning on their *Popcorn* DVD debacle, but *The Incubus* actually looks surprisingly good. Interestingly, the aforementioned grain turns up during several gritty looking daylight scenes while night scenes are razor sharp, displaying beautiful contrast and shadow delineation. The source appears to be a very clean 35mm print and is a great improvement over the long discontinued Vestron tape, which was simply an unwatchable, colourless mess. While Hough has contributed to some of his past releases, this particular title is threadbare apart from a dupey-looking theatrical trailer (complete with that wonderful early '80s horror narration.) Incidentally, the onscreen title simply reads *Incubus*; perhaps it was changed during promotion to avoid confusion with the rarely seen William Shatner film?

INHABITED

Colour, 2003, 96m. / Directed by Kelly Sandefur / Starring Malcolm McDowell, Megan Gallagher, Sofia Vassilieva, Patty McCormack / Velocity (US R1 NTSC), Watson (UK R2 PAL) / DD2.0

An innocuous but fairly enjoyable addition to the "little creatures in my home" horror subgenre (*Don't Be Afraid of the Dark, Cat's Eye,* etc.), *Inhabited* begins strongly enough, by evoking the fairy tale/ monster tradition as the genesis for its beasties, which are little medieval-clothed monsters that scamper around in the ornate playhouse situated behind the new home of the Russell family. Little Gina (Sofia Vassilieva) enjoys playing with her new "fairy" friends, though of course no one believes her; naturally mother Meg (TV regular Megan Gallagher) reluctantly consults a child psychologist, Dr. Werner (Malcolm McDowell), who happens to be treating a much older patient, Olivia (*The Bad Seed* herself, Patty McCormack), who lived in the same house and also had "invisible" friends responsible for setting a fatal fire.

Surprisingly restrained, this effective fright flick is a throwback to the days of Empire Pictures horrors from the '80s. It has little violence (one human and one animal death, both offscreen), though the monster mayhem is lively and builds to a solid climax capped with a memorable image of dozens of the creatures scampering up the walls of the house. The often mobile camerawork is fluid and frequently better than one would expect from a low budget horror film, and apart from too many failed cheap scares involving the family cat, the pace moves along nicely and the plot throws in some nice twists involving the local handyman. Nothing spectacular, but you could do a lot worse on a slow evening.

The video transfer is acceptable, apparently shot open matte, with accurate but not terribly vivid colours. The surround audio is limited mostly to the typical synth music score.

INNOCENTS WITH DIRTY HANDS

Colour, 1975, 121m. / Directed by Claude Chabrol / Starring Romy Schneider, Rod Steiger, Paolo Giusti, Jean Rochefort / Pathfinder (US R1 NTSC), Arrow (UK R2 PAL), Universal (Germany R2 PAL) / WS (1.66:1)

Arguably the best of Claude Chabrol's English-language films, *Innocents with Dirty Hands* begins with beautiful Julie Wormser (played by Romy Schneider) sunbathing nude and enjoying the company of her lover, Jeff (Paolo Giusti from *Patrick Still Lives*). Unfortunately she's married to a drunken lout, Louis (Rod Steiger), so she and Jeff decide to do away with him. After she whacks Louis on the head and leaves the scene, Julie finds herself in quite a bit of trouble when both her lover and her spouse's body mysteriously disappear, leaving her in the clutches of the law. A slippery attorney (Jean Rochefort, Terry Gilliam's ill-fated Don Quixote) takes care of the legal problems, but that's just the beginning of a highly complicated and startling web of deceit in which murderers turn out to be the most sympathetic people around.

Adapted from *The Damned Innocents*, a thriller by Richard Neely (*The Plastic Nightmare*, later filmed as *Shattered*), this mind-bending chamber piece finds Chabrol in full experimental mode, constantly toying with viewers' sympathies and turning reality upside down with each plot twist. Some uneasy acting aside, the film features a strong lead in Schneider and makes full use of its sunny, decadent, yet strangely claustrophobic setting. There is also time for more than a little humour; as the situation gets increasingly bizarre, the characters make several amusing off-hand remarks, which balance nicely with the tension.

Pathfinder's non-anamorphic DVD looks attractive but a little worn, particularly during the opening titles; colour and detail are fine, though the gauzy photography results in some occasional PAL-conversion artefacting. The film is best viewed with its original English soundtrack, but French and Spanish dubs can also be accessed with optional English subtitles. The film was released on U.S. video in a drastically cut, incoherent 92-minute edition as *Dirty Hands*, but this is the full European version. Extras include a theatrical trailer and stills gallery. The German release (as part of Universal's "Romy Schneider Collection") features the same transfer without the English track option, while the Arrow version is a bit of a compromise as, although the transfer doesn't feature any PAL conversion problems, it only offers the French track with English subtitles, leaving the more appropriate English track missing in action.

INSPECTEUR LAVARDIN

Colour, 1986, 96m. / Directed by Claude Chabrol / Starring Jean Poiret, Jean-Claude Brialy, Jacques Dacqmine, Bernadette Lafont / MK2 (France R2 PAL), Kino (US R1 NTSC), Artificial Eye (UK R2 PAL) / WS (1.66:1) (16:9)

Following the success of 1984's frothy *Poulet au vinaigre*, Chabrol resurrected his unruly cop character, Inspector Lavardin (played by Jean Poiret), for this equally enjoyable and very much recommended follow-up.

When the body of Catholic moralist writer Raoul Mons (Jacques Dacqmine) is discovered on a beach, Lavardin is called in to find the culprit. The widow, Hélène (Bernadette Lafont), turns out to be Lavardin's old girlfriend ("the one that got away"), a situation that complicates the

investigation considerably. The suspects mount as the thuggish Lavardin interrogates his way through an assortment of suspects, including Hélène's gay brother, a colourful troupe of actors, and a teenage girl who may know far more than she lets on.

A slick and witty bonbon of a film, *Inspecteur Lavardin* is one of Chabrol's few genuine sequels, though it differs from its predecessor by making Lavardin the primary focus of attention from the very beginning. Poiret makes the most of his additional time in the spotlight, though it's easy to see why the character didn't catch on like other compromised lawmen; he cuts a bit too close to the bone in his brutish treatment of suspects to be a frivolous figure of fantasy.

The MK2 French disc lives up to the high standards of other titles in the series, though the colour scheme here is among the more muted in the Chabrol canon. The disc includes optional English subtitles, numerous Chabrol trailers (including this title), and Chabrol video commentary for three scenes (no subs). The much later U.S. release from Kino ports over the same transfer but exhibits some PAL-to-NTSC transfer anomalies, while the British one (released a long time after the other two) looks closer to the French one.

IRRÉVERSIBLE

Colour, 2002, 95m. / Directed by Gaspar Noë / Starring Vincent Cassel, Monica Bellucci, Albert Dupontel, Jo Prestia, Philippe Nahon / Studio Canal (France R2 PAL), Tartan (UK R2 PAL), Lionsgate (US R1 NTSC) / WS (2.35:1) (16:9) / DD5.1

The closing credits crawl opens this film, running backwards, then slipping sideways, with the dense block of text hard to read because many letters are printed in reverse, then picks up on the face of Philippe Nahon, still in the character he played in director Gaspar Noë's earlier short *Carne* and feature *Seul contre tous* (*I Stand Alone*), naked on a bed with a clothed man, establishing that he is the same character through some backstory and musing that "time destroys everything". Downstairs from this dingy room is the Rectum, a dark, warren-like gay S&M club, and the film proper begins (or ends) with Marcus (Vincent Cassel) and Pierre (Albert Dupontel) being brought out by ambulance men and the cops, Marcus with his arm broken and Pierre in handcuffs and taunted with the probability of a brutal, sexual life in prison. Then the "story" unwinds in a series of single-take scenes that unfold *Memento*-style backwards, with each giving more context to what we have seen previously. Noë shoots in a hand-held style that most often evokes James Whale's tilted angles than Dogme-like edginess, though as the film recedes from the violence of its opening scenes, the camerawork gets calmer (even if the single most horrifying sequence is shot with a fixed frame that makes it hard to look at). At the end, or the beginning, we get to J.W. Dunne's theories of time and a dizzying spin (signified by a *2001* poster) that allows, if not a happy ending for Marcus's brutalized girlfriend Alex (Monica Bellucci), then a happy beginning.

Each of the scenes depicts actions, dialogue, incident, behaviour and circumstance that any of the leads might have wished didn't happen: from Pierre's fire-extinguisher murder of a thug in the Rectum through Marcus's violent outbursts of racism and homophobia as he drags Pierre on a search through the Paris underworld for a man named la Tenia (the tapeworm) and Alex's encounter in an underpass with a pimp who buggers her and batters her face to pulp, driving her into a coma (even he might wish to take this back: though he shows no remorse or conscience, he is absurdly easy for amateurs to catch so presumably he's liable to suffer too), to

differences of opinion about how to behave at a party, embarrassing public discussions about sex (Pierre turns out to be Alex's ex, who has come along on this evening to make time with her) and the results (ambiguous) of a pregnancy test.

Even tiny details – a woman advising Alex to use the underpass because it's safer, Pierre phoning up and saying his car is broken so they'll have to get to the party by underground station – suggest alternative timelines spinning off in which things happen otherwise, while the single-take format also throws up odd disjunctions and elisions that make it possible that even this string of scenes doesn't belong to the same timeline (it's not like a puzzle in which we gradually realise the set of relationships between the central trio, but as if they were reimagined and rearranged in each scene). Semi-improvised (Cassel introduces himself as Vincent to some party girls, then corrects himself), the scenes all have attack and power, with the later (earlier) conversational sequences suggesting that life isn't all sexual assaults in the dark, and showing equal cinematic imagination.

Arguably not a film people would want to subject themselves to twice in order to perceive its trickier tricks, this is still something that stays in the mind, sparking far more ideas and emotions than most wallow-in-horror pictures. Caveat: like most rape-and-revenge films (*Straw Dogs*, *I Spit on Your Grave*) that aren't *Ms.45*, it's impossible not to feel that the director enjoys humiliating the woman a little too much.

All DVD options offer an anamorphic widescreen transfer that reproduces the theatrical look, initially grainy and dark but calming to pristine beauty, but this is a film whose impact is severely muted on any home viewing format; the scenes in the Rectum, for instance, are merely dark and hard-to-make-out whereas in the cinema they were infernally crowded and nightmarish, while the appalling central scene depends on the viewer being clamped into his or her seat like another Alex in *A Clockwork Orange* as it unreels and is easier to take in circumstances where the eye can look away from the screen. The perfectly acceptable Dolby Digital 5.1 mix needs to be played loud, but still can't be the oppressive force it is in theatrical showings.

The first U.K. Region 2 disc has notes from Hannah McGill and a clutch of trailers, but none of the extra features (audio commentary, deleted scenes, the short *Intoxication*, music videos, soundtrack CD, special effects breakdown) of the French Region 2 edition. The U.S. release contains only the music videos and a trailer, while the advertised featurette on the packaging is missing from the first pressing but can be accessed via the Lionsgate website. A second version from Tartan appeared in 2006 and includes everything from the French disc (contrary to the packaging, the two lead actors do not appear on the commentary) except the deleted scenes (no major loss) with the added bonus of English subtitles for every extra.

– KN

THE ISLE

Colour, 2000, 89m. / Directed by Kim Ki-duk / Starring Suh Jung, Kim Yu-seok / CJ Entertainment (Korea R3 NTSC), Tartan (UK R0 PAL) / WS (1.85:1) (16:9) / DD5.1, First Run (US R1 NTSC), Universe (HK R3 NTSC) / WS (1.85:1) / DD2.0

In an age populated with the gore-drenched fantasias of Takashi Miike, it says a great deal when an Asian film can reduce an audience into a shocked stupor. For better or worse, such is the case with *The Isle* (*Seom*), a deeply troubling and equally beautiful film that will shake the hardiest of souls despite a minimal body count and scant bloodletting.

The poetic setting propels much of the storyline, which follows lost souls Hee-Jin (Suh Jung), an errand girl and occasional prostitute who services a neighbourhood of floating lake homes, and new resident Hyun-Shik (Kim Yu-seok), a quiet, suicidal cop on the run from the law after shooting his girlfriend. When the despondent Hyun-Shik tries to kill himself, the young girl stops him with a well-applied knife poke. She continues to spy on him, and the two silently develop a twisted relationship that escalates when he engages in some self-mutilation involving fishhooks. Add to the mix an accidental death, corpse disposal, more fishhook mayhem, and a lyrical finale, and you have one of the more memorable art-house/shock cinema titles of the past decade.

Though filled with images of sexual mutilation, excretion, and much-discussed animal violence (mainly to fish), *The Isle* is a far cry from an exploitation film; this is deeply felt, melancholy material, a harsh love story between two people beaten down by life and unable to express themselves except through pain. The film also leavens the sombre tone with a few nicely placed sick laughs, often at the expense of the characters' outrageous behaviour, and director Kim Ki-duk (who followed this with the excellent *Bad Guy*) displays an impeccable eye for simple, beautifully composed images. The floating single-room homes over foggy, rippling water are a marvellous, otherworldly visual conceit, though the feeling that the film itself might just float away is indeed fulfilled in the puzzling finale, which unfortunately is about half a minute too long and closes with a *non sequitur* image that undoes much of the climax's power. It's a small blip in an otherwise immaculately constructed film that refuses to play by anyone's rules and stands as another proud example of horror filmmaking as a matter of tone rather than content.

The U.S. and Hong Kong DVD editions of *The Isle* are non-anamorphic affairs with slightly soft but pleasing transfers. The

First Run edition has the slight edge as the HK disc has an overabundance of digital graininess around the edges of some objects, though the latter's English subtitles are removable compared to the burned-in U.S. subs. Both feature wonderfully immersive surround audio tracks, which do justice to the lush, electronic-based music score. In terms of extras the First Run disc wins hands down; included are video interviews with the director and two leads (with subtitles, using text cards to signify questions), seven minutes of behind-the-scenes footage (which eschews any of the nasty stuff), and the moody theatrical trailer. Frustratingly, the U.K. Tartan release sports an anamorphic transfer and both DTS and Dolby Digital 5.1 mixes, but it suffers from almost two minutes of BBFC-mandated cuts that tone down the shock value considerably. The Korean release is also anamorphic but complete, with subtitles in English and Korean. The latter two versions feature mainly the same extras (a music featurette, six interview segments with the cast and crew, and three making-of featurettes, and trailers), with the Korean release also tossing in Cocore's "Insect" music video; however, only the U.K. version offers English subtitles for the special features.

IVANS XTC

Colour, 2002, 91m. / Directed by Bernard Rose / Starring Danny Huston, Peter Weller, Adam Krentzman, Lisa Enos / Tartan (UK R0 PAL) / WS (1.78:1) (16:9) / DD2.0

 Having struggled through a "Hollywood" experience while making a botched version of *Anna Karenina*, Bernard Rose turned his attention to another Tolstoy project, updating the novella *The Death of Ivan Illyich* to mix the writer-director's feelings about the movie business with Tolstoy's universal meditation upon approaching mortality. To stand in for Tolstoy's more obviously "ordinary" Ivan, Rose creates a character based on Hollywood agent Jay Moloney, whose comet-like career ended in suicide while *ivans xtc* was in post-production. Made outside the studio system with minimalist production methods (portable, versatile high-definition video cameras) the film has a distinctive look strikingly different from film but still effective in the creation of the moods desired.

It opens with an off-camera monologue as agent Ivan Beckman (Danny Huston) concludes that all life is shit, then establishes how his sudden death – from cancer, though everyone assumes it's a drugs overdose – shakes up the industry but is swiftly forgotten. Sundry machinations around a greenlit project (the firing of a writer-director, the confirmation of a star) smooth over the hole made by Ivan's passing, with the mourners arguing at his funeral. Then we flash back to the last weeks of Ivan's life, as he charmingly cadges a client (Peter Weller, very creepy as a homophobic, gun-loving movie star) by boosting a script he hasn't even read and pulls strings to put into production a project that has no real reason to exist.

Rose seems to be in the familiar territory of *The Player*, but Rose is attempting portraiture rather than satire and refuses to make his Hollywood power people wittier than they are monstrous, though there is a mordant wit to the way that orgies and funerals are arranged in exactly the same manner as press conferences and premieres. Many of the gloomy faces are played by agents or producers rather than actors (with few of the subgenre's signature self-parody celebrity cameos), and there is quite heroic self-exposure from Rose's agent Adam Krentzman as Ivan's chilled successor and (literally) the film's producer/co-writer Lisa Enos as Ivan's slim but appalling girlfriend.

This is a rare drugs film that genuinely doesn't moralise (after all, Ivan isn't killed by his cocaine intake) and shows the fast-lane lifestyle as emptily unfulfilling but not especially harmful, except in the way that the party hierarchy confirms power relationships between industryites. Because he has the most clout, big star Don West can "direct" who takes what drug or performs which sex act at his penthouse party, emphasising the film's analysis of 'entertainment' as something essentially joyless. As a Hollywood horror movie, this is even more gloomily nightmarish than *Mulholland Dr.*, with the digital look, the carefully selected locations and sharp costuming reducing the visual palette to near-monochrome and excluding anything like warmth.

As a terminal illness drama, this is unsentimental to the point that few who have gone through the death of a contemporary will be able to bear to watch it; in contrast, even *Magnolia* seems indulgent and tear-jerking. The most affecting touch isn't so much that Ivan keeps his illness secret but that he hasn't anyone in his life, including family and girlfriend, interested enough in him to make it worth revealing how sick he is (even his PA says she's too busy to come to the clinic with him) until a call-girl recognises the medicine among his other drugs and he blurts out his fears to a couple of hookers he is partying with. Huston, best-known as a director (*Mr. Corbett's Ghost*, *Mr. North*), is terrific, poised and charming and self-regarding, a snakelike manipulator of the deal who would doubtless have orchestrated the chaos we see in the first reel if he had lived, but also a fragile, sensitive man on the edge. A film much easier to admire than like, this is still a substantial and affecting piece of work.

Tartan's DVD preserves the rough DV look the film had in theatres. Aside from fourteen minutes of rough footage listed as "extended party scene outtakes", star

and director filmographies and notes by Chris Roberts, the disc is bare of extras – even if Rose was unavailable for an audio commentary, it's a shame that his diary of the production (included in the press notes) was left out.

– KN

JACK FROST

Colour, 1996, 89m. / Directed by Michael Cooney / Starring Christopher Allport, Scott MacDonald, Shannon Elizabeth / Simitar (US R0 NTSC) / WS (1.66:1), Film 2000 (UK R2 PAL)

Prisoner Jack Frost (Scott MacDonald) – imprisoned for multiple homicides – is being transported to the site of his execution in the thick of a snowstorm. A road smash en route leaves him doused in a corrosive substance that melts his body to a pulp, but the resultant chemical mush reacts with the snow, crystallizing Frost's molecules and resurrecting him as a living snowman. Now able to melt and reassemble himself at will, Frost heads off to Snomonton on a mission to ice Sheriff Sam Tiler (Christopher Allport), the man responsible for gaoling him.

A movie that could easily pass as early Sam Raimi, *Jack Frost* is every bit as daft as it sounds. Not to be confused with the 1998 Troy Miller/Michael Keaton slush fest of the same name, Michael Cooney's film pipped it to the title by two years and, in spite of its crudely achieved effects and a plot that wouldn't coat the surface of a snowflake, it's by far the better movie. Once you realise that Cooney is aiming squarely for the funny bone, the whole confection becomes even more palatable. The jokes are either in bad taste or just plain bad and the film is loaded with them.

But because the cast never play it less than 100% straight, it just gets even funnier. Example? Finding one of Frost's victims – her face peppered with shards of shattered bauble glass, trussed up with fairy lights and dangling from the Christmas tree – the Sheriff tells his deputy to have the body taken down: "You don't reckon we should leave her up for the twelve days of Christmas?" responds the gormless goon. The laughs are offset by plenty of frosty mayhem. There's a decapitation with the blade of a sledge, an impaling with icicle projectiles, an axe handle rammed down a hapless victim's throat and a wonderfully absurd moment where Frost in snowman form sprouts icicle chompers and chews the head off an FBI agent: "Frost bite", he quips. Told you the jokes were bad. Regrettably Frost himself isn't all that menacing, but given that he's clearly an immobile Styrofoam mannequin from a department store's festive window display, the filmmakers give it their best shot at making him baneful. With a voice like a more crotchety than usual Krusty the Clown, he has small black lumps of coal for soulless eyes, a large carrot for a nose (which substitutes as something more lewd when he rapes Shannon Elizabeth in her bathtub), and twiggy eyebrows, which at least serve to permit the occasional mean frown. With a seasonal score that includes the most menacing spin to age old favourite "Silent Night" since Bob Clark's *Black Christmas*, you could do far worse than to give *Jack Frost* a whirl. But while you're having fun, make a mental note to avoid the belated sequel *Jack Frost 2: Revenge of the Killer Mutant Snowman* like the plague.

Simitar's region-free DVD delivers the film in a widescreen transfer as crisp and clean as a sprinkling of virgin snow, divided into 9 chapters. There are no additional goodies on offer. The later U.K. release is full frame and not as visually pristine.
– TG

JACK THE RIPPER
B&W, 1959, 99m. / Directed by David MacDonald, Frank P. Bibas, George Waggner / Starring Boris Karloff, Niall MacGinnis, Dorothy Alison, Morris Ankrum, Tudor Owen, Harry Bartell, Kay Stewart, Lee Farr, Clifford Evans, Nora Swinburne, Katherine Squire / Rhino, Something Weird (US R1 NTSC)

A phoney feature whipped together from episodes of an aborted TV series called *The Veil*, which traded (as the later, more successful *One Step Beyond* would do) in dramatizations of allegedly authentic (but rarely dramatic) cases of the supernatural. When the show didn't sell, the producers tried repackaging the episodes as anthology-style movies. Most of these efforts were made in Hollywood with genial host Boris Karloff taking a variety of lead roles surrounded by stooges, but with the odd British-made episode distinguished by more imaginative direction and generally better acting. Complete with obvious snips where opening and closing credits would have gone, this feels less like a film than a back-to-back marathon of episodes.

The first three stories here are American-made, and only really have Karloff going for them. The first is a familiar anecdote – done also as a *One Step Beyond* – about a city-dweller (Harry Bartell) who witnesses a murder in a rooming house across the street only to discover the scene of the crime is an unrented apartment. When the crime happens as foreseen, the police suspect the unwitting psychic (a situation that recurs in the final episode) until he can identify the strangling burglar. Next up is a period tale of a contested inheritance, with the ghost of a fellow who had the irritating habit of making successive contradictory wills without telling anyone directing his decent son to find the testament that prevents a villainous brother from selling the family farm and putting Mom in a home. Neither of these add up to much as spook stories, and Karloff simply makes appearances as a decent, concerned psychiatrist or lawyer to deliver exposition.

The star gets more of a work-out in the third story, which casts him in a black wig and sideburns as an EC Comics-style murdering husband, a sea-captain who poisons his nagging wife (Katherine Squire) on a voyage and suffers non-dramatic vengeance from beyond the grave. An unseen ghost repeatedly pulls the cloth off a table and ruins a celebratory dinner, getting the murderer thrown out of the captain's club. Later, offscreen, his ship goes down. It's an ineptly told tale but Karloff gives it the good old villain glower, pretending concern over his ailing wife as he doses her with poison and even expressing genial lechery around a bosomy barmaid (whose appalling cod accent makes her by far the most terrifying thing in the piece).

The film's title comes from the final, Karloff-free episode, a British-made effort that dramatizes an anecdote about the Victorian psychic Robert Lees, who allegedly had visions that enabled the police to track down a distinguished but mad doctor as the Whitechapel Murderer. Though less elaborately staged than *Murder By Decree* and *Jack the Ripper* (1988), which use the real names of the historical characters involved, this benefits from a fine, nervous lead performance by Niall MacGinnis (*Night of the Demon*) as the psychic Lees, here renamed Walter Durst. It may be the first Ripper dramatization to pay attention to details like the correct street locales of the murders, though it drops the most famous killing from the case. It also has a more dramatic shape than the flat anecdotes presented in the other episodes, with an eerie effect as the psychic's hand intrudes into his visions and a disturbing monologue by Mrs. Willowden (Nora Swinburne), the Ripper's

agonised wife, describing the retired and embittered doctor's progression from torturing animals to going out at night and coming home stained with blood.

Rhino's DVD is PD standard, with a murky print and no extras. The film credits only MacDonald (who made the title episode) as director. The whole series is available as *The Veil* in its original form in a visually superior two-disc set (from Something Weird) that includes a couple of episodes of the similar, more lurid *13 Demon Street*.

– KN

JACK THE RIPPER

Colour, 1988, 189m. / Directed by David Wickes / Starring Michael Caine, Armand Assante, Deirdre Costello, Angela Crow, Susan George, Lysette Anthony, Lewis Collins, Jane Seymour, Harry Andrews, Michael Gothard, Ray McAnally, T.P. McKenna, Jonathan Moore, Jon Laurimore, Peter Armitage, Gary Shail, Marc Culwick, Michael Hughes, Richard Morant, Ken Bones, George Sweeney, Kelly Cryer / Anchor Bay (UK R2 PAL) / WS (1.66:1), Warner Archive (US R0 NTSC)

It's the autumn of 1888 and prostitutes in London's East End are falling prey to the knife of serial killer Jack the Ripper. Scotland Yard charges Inspector Frederick Abberline (Michael Caine) with the task of catching the killer, but he must also contend with bureaucracy among his superiors, apathy within the local constabulary and scandal-mongering sensationalism in the press, which is spurring public outrage and widespread belief that the police are impotent to bring the Ripper to justice. As the murders become progressively more brutal, evidence begins to indicate that the killer may be someone of considerable importance...

The passing of time has done little to diminish the public's fascination with the legend of Jack the Ripper. In 1988, marking the centenary of the heinous crimes that blighted Victorian London, this TV film was unleashed amidst ballyhoo claiming it contained information accessed in previously unseen Home Office files which revealed the Ripper's identity. It certainly had the desired effect and a tidal wave of viewers tuned in to see if, between them, director David Wickes and star Michael Caine really would solve the age-old mystery. Opening in the immediate aftermath of the slaying of prostitute Mary Ann Nichols in Bucks Row, *Jack the Ripper* is a sprawling feast of epic proportions, encapsulating the subsequent murders of Annie Chapman (Deirdre Costello), Elizabeth Stride (Angela Crow), Catherine Eddows (Susan George) and Mary Jane Kelly (Lysette Anthony) during those dark months of 1888, and concluding with the (fictional) unmasking of the killer. Aside from a smattering of the red stuff for effect, there's little palpably nasty on display here but the whole show is almost faultlessly staged and charged with a surfeit of atmosphere. From the bustling pomp of the upper class London streets to the squalid, oppressive passageways and squares of Whitechapel, this is Jack the Ripper's milieu to its very core. Co-written, produced and directed by Wickes (who, two years later, helmed *Jekyll & Hyde*, also starring Caine), some of the dialogue is a touch theatrical but it doesn't detract from one of the most satisfying Ripper movies to date. In fact the only bum note arises with the unabated facial transformations of lothario American actor Richard Mansfield (*I, the Jury*'s Assante) on stage in the Lyceum Theatre's presentation of *Dr. Jekyll and Mr. Hyde*. As chilling a bit of business as it makes in terms of film entertainment, isn't it an abuse of verity? Insubstantially explained – and accepted by the police – with Mansfield's casual line, "I observe and I imitate and I do that over and over until I become the person I want

to be", the physically impossible distortion and realignment of his features at will must surely lay open to question the authenticity of some of the film's other assertions (not leastways the identity of the Ripper).

Michael Caine is excellent as the beleaguered Abberline – "Do you want the killer or will anybody do?" he asks his superiors in exasperation – and delivers his often incensed dialogue with discernible tears of rage in his eyes. He and Lewis Collins's Sergeant George Godley make a great team, the veritable Holmes and Watson of true crime, inadequate resources and an almost complete absence of forensic science impeding their investigation at every turn. *Jack the Ripper* is awash with film and television talent, from former Bond squeeze Jane Seymour (as socialite – and Abberline's love interest – Emma Prentiss), Harry Andrews (*Burke and Hare*) and Susan George (*Fright*) to *Scream and Scream Again*'s Michael Gothard (who cuts a menacing swathe as rebel-rousing vigilante George Lusk), Ray McAnally (*Murder in Eden*) and T.P. McKenna (*Straw Dogs*). Smaller roles are made nonetheless pivotal via excellent performances from the likes of Jonathan Moore as oily, muck-raking weasel reporter Ben Bates, Jon Laurimore and Peter Armitage as indolent Inspector Spratling and Sergeant Kerby respectively, and Gary Shail as roughhouse pimp Billy White. All are witnessed behaving extremely furtively at one stage or another; of course, it would be unsporting to reveal who Wickes fingers as the Ripper. Suffice to say that you probably won't guess and, in spite of the hyperbolic claims that the truth would finally be revealed, the director's solution remains neither more nor less believable than the myriad of other hypotheses put forward over the decades. We'll probably never know for sure, but long may the efforts of filmmakers to convince us otherwise continue.

Previously available in the U.K. on disc from Digital Entertainment in an extras-free pressing which ran *Jack the Ripper* from beginning to end in one hit, Anchor Bay's R2 PAL disc delivers it in its original two-part format, matted to 1.66:1, with each instalment allotted its own 16-chapter divide. Episode #1 concludes with the original teaser for the second half of the story, while Episode #2 opens with a recap of events from the first half. Regrettably, mirroring the earlier release, it is slightly cut. On the original television broadcast in 1988 and the Thames video cassette release that followed, after Abberline is seen grilling Netley in the police cells there was a straight scene change to Annette (Cryer) sitting topless in front of her mirror as Godley enters her boudoir. Only after permitting Godley a provocative eyeful does she coyly raise her arms to cover her modesty. In both the Digital Entertainment and Anchor Bay DVD releases – the pair of them, it's safe to assume, sourced from a U.S. television print – a little artifice has discreetly veiled her nudity; a fade-out-fade-in on the transition between the Abberline/Netley and Godley/Annette sequences brings the shot in as the young lady finishes raising her arms. It's a minor grievance to be sure, but a pertinent one just the same. A commentary from director David Wickes accompanies the feature, and it's supplemented by a worthy gallery of production stills and some text biographies. Most interesting of all, however, is the inclusion of a wedge of footage featuring Barry Foster as Abberline, shot over a 10-day period prior to an infusion of U.S. funding which allowed the production to adopt a more ambitiously lavish mantle. Foster is fine in the role but at the insistence of investors was substituted for a bigger name. It has to be noted that in all instances of roles being recast before shooting recommenced, the replacements were sound choices. More importantly, however, these sequences serve to illustrate the magnificent cinematic quality that Alan Hume's photography brought to the party, for had it continued along the same path

it set out on, *Jack the Ripper* would have exhibited the lowly hallmarks of an under-budgeted Brit teledrama, a pale shadow of what instead transpired.

A 2010 release in America via Warner's made-on-demand service offers the title split onto two discs (full frame as originally broadcast) but features no extras.

– TG

JASON X

Colour, 2002, 91m. / Directed by Jim Isaac / Starring Lexa Doig, Lisa Ryder, Kane Hodder, Melyssa Ade, David Cronenberg / New Line (US R1 NTSC), Entertainment In Video (UK R2 PAL), Columbia TriStar (Spain R2 PAL) / WS (1.85:1) (16:9) / DD5.1

It's the year 2010, and Jason Voorhees (Kane Hodder) is still proving to be a thorn in the side of Crystal Lake's tourism department. Frozen cryogenically in the midst of a fresh bout of mayhem, the killing machine and his final victim, Rowan (Lexa Doig), are discovered in the year 2455 by a search party visiting a ravaged Earth. Taken aboard the transport ship Grendel, on course back to Earth II, Rowan's fatal wounds are miraculously healed by modern technology and she is revived. Before she can warn her saviours of the dangers of resuscitating Jason, the natural thawing process takes care of the job and havoc in a hockey mask is unleashed once again.

After New Line took over the reins from Paramount for *Jason Goes to Hell* and resurrected a series in danger of collapse, it was a surprising seven years before everyone's favourite masked maniac clawed his way back before the cameras for *Jason X*, and a further two years before the results were unveiled. But it was certainly worth the wait. The tried and tested formula, like Jason himself at the film's conclusion, gets an upgrade for a hi-tech slice of starscape terror that smells fresh as a daisy and bubbles with wit; "This sucks on so many levels!" screams Janessa (Melyssa Ade) as a loss of cabin pressure propels her out through a fissure in the hull.

Director Jim Isaac kicks off the action with mass carnage wherein a cameoing David Cronenberg gets speared. But it's once we move on some 450 years that it starts firing on all cylinders. The supercilious rapidity with which Doig accepts it's been over four centuries since she lost consciousness is quickly forgotten as Jason de-ices and proves that the passing of time hasn't altered his homicidal habits one iota. Once he's wiped out most of the armed troopers aboard ship we're back in familiar territory with a standard cluster of over-sexed, under-intelligent teens. Well, almost standard. There is one exception: Lisa Ryder as android Kay-Em 14 is a wonderful addition to the saga and every bit the equal of bloodthirsty behemoth Voorhees. Discarding her early attempts to be more feminine – her stick-on nipples hilariously fall off and tinkle to the floor like dropped coins – she gets new circuits installed that transform her into a high-kicking, back-flipping, leather-clad dominatrix with a pair of rapid-fire machine pistols and an attitude to match. But shooting Jason to pieces (literally!) isn't sufficient to keep him down and, when a power surge initiates the remedial process that brought Rowan back to life, he springs into action once again with part-cyborg modifications that render him meaner and more indestructible than ever. Saving the best till last, writer Todd Farmer reintroduces a holographic games room gag that's established earlier in the story, providing the survivors with a diversion that pitches Jason into a holo-recreation of Crystal Lake circa 1980, complete with nubile campers whom he promptly sets about maiming. Arguably the best *Friday* since *Part IV*, *Jason X* could well have paved the way into an interesting new era for the series. Certainly the closing shot hints that, in spite of his fiery impersonation of a comet, Jason has plenty of death-dealing left in him yet, and Earth II seems as fertile a place as any in which to be doing it. However, the avenue ahead took a sharp turn with the long-awaited *Freddy vs. Jason*, in which four-times man behind the mask Kane Hodder was elbowed in favour of someone else.

Mere days after opening theatrically in the U.S. and U.K., *Jason X* premiered on Region 2 DVD in Spain with a rather spiffy disc from Columbia TriStar. A sumptuous, uncut 1.85:1 matted pressing of the movie itself (with English and Spanish sound options and subtitling) heads up the release, divided by a slightly meagre 12 chapter stops. The Dolby Digital surround sound mix piles on the atmosphere with some particularly impressive rear channel activity. A dip into the X-tras division reveals a nice bag of tricks that comprises two trailers, two U.S. TV spots, short interview segments with director Jim Isaac, producer Sean S. Cunningham and players Kane Hodder, Lisa Ryder and Lexa Doig, plus around 18-minutes of entertaining B-Roll behind the scenes footage. The U.S. Region 1 disc in the New Line Platinum Series appeared some four months later with a different (and inferior) array of supplemental features, including two documentaries, a commentary track from Isaac and others, a trailer and an interview with Hodder. Popping the disc into a computer also gives the viewer access to the film's screenplay and the complete Jason X website courtesy of DVD-ROM. Torn *Friday* enthusiasts will doubtless end up purchasing the both the PAL and NTSC editions. Incidentally, there is also a Region 2 PAL edition out in the U.K., from Entertainment In Video, which has the same extras as the Columbia TriStar disc (minus the DVD-ROM content).

– TG

JEWEL THIEF

Colour, 1967, 168m. / Directed by Vijay Anand / Starring Dev Anand, Helen, Vyjayantimala, Ashok Kumar / Eros International (India R0 NTSC) / DD2.0

 A splashy Bollywood musical for '60s pop culture fanatics, *Jewel Thief* updates the old *Prince and the Pauper* identity switch to a Technicolor universe comprised of the filmmaker's fondest bits from James Bond, *The Pink Panther*, and European comic strips, peppered with the usual spirited musical numbers. The result is an irresistible confection, just the kind of thing to throw on at a party to keep the guests' eyes occupied.

A series of high profile jewel thefts have put the city on edge, and sweet-natured Vinay (Dev Anand) has the misfortune of being mistaken for the look-alike culprit, Amar. Even worse, Amar's jilted fiancée, Shalini (Vyjayantimala), accuses Vinay of breaking her heart, and her brother (Ashok Kumar) is out for blood. To get to the bottom of the mystery, Vinay poses as the jewel thief to learn his opponent's next move and tangles with a bevy of beautiful, jewel-spangled women eager for love.

Filled with charming highlights, *Jewel Thief* somehow manages to stretch its unlikely concept to a nearly three hour running time while rarely running out of steam. Apart from the obligatory slow love ballad, the musical numbers are all well integrated into the film and pulled off with great panache, particularly an inspired nightclub act which finds the stunning Helen (of *Gumnaam* fame), decked out in huge feathers and a skimpy showgirl outfit, prancing and belting out a number on a circular stage while another chanteuse mimes her actions for the gentlemen below. Though he occasionally lapses into unfortunate mugging, Anand is a sympathetic and effective hero; he also does

the action routine very well, and while the film could have perhaps done with a couple of additional thriller set pieces (not exactly a Bollywood speciality), the hair-raising climax is more than satisfying. The film proved to be so influential and popular that countless imitations were churned out, with an official sequel starring Anand, *Return of Jewel Thief*, finally appearing in 1996.

The Eros International DVD is a real sparkler, appropriately enough. Despite some noticeable element damage here and there in the form of emulsion scratches, the transfer looks terrific with eye-popping colours in the best Technicolor tradition. Beware the previous, non-Eros DVDs which briefly appeared on the market; they look washed out and ragged, and don't feature English subtitles. The Eros disc features optional subtitles which whiz by a little quickly, so get ready to do some speed reading. The stereo mix (billed as 4.0 surround, which translates to 2.0 really) sounds fine for the film's vintage; separation effects are minimal but the music sounds robust and appropriately loud. The disc includes the usual song search function and a generic reel of coming attractions trailers.

JUBILEE

Colour, 1977, 100m. / Directed by Derek Jarman / Starring Nell Campbell, Toyah Wilcox, Jenny Runacre, David Brandon, Ian Charleson, Jordan, Adam Ant, Richard O'Brien / Criterion (US R1 NTSC) / WS (1.66:1) (16:9), Second Sight (UK R0 PAL)

 While directors like Ken Russell and Julien Temple were giddily overturning the relationship between music and cinema during the 1970s, Derek Jarman entered this tricky arena with his complicated, challenging look at a punked-out, pre-Thatcher England

in *Jubilee*, which groups together an odd assortment of music and theatre personalities for a one of a kind experience.

The story, what little there is, concerns the journey of Queen Elizabeth I (Jenny Runacre) who, thanks to a ghostly white angel (*Stagefright*'s David Brandon), travels through time to a Britain torn apart by gangs and punk anarchy. Violence and sexual decadence are the order of the day for this crumbling land populated by a weird gallery of characters: Mad (pop singer Toyah Wilcox), an aspiring performer with neon orange hair and baby fat who belts out her tunes in a blitzed out Buckingham Palace; Angel (*Opera*'s Ian Charleson, who later disowned the film), a pansexual bleach blond youth; Amyl Nitrate (Jordan), a vicious female gang leader; and Kid (a very young Adam Ant), a leather-clad lad who becomes the object of several characters' fixations. *Rocky Horror* veterans Richard O'Brien (in whacked out period dress) and "Little Nell" Campbell also hop along for the ride, which includes a gruesome sexual asphyxia murder, rampant destruction of public property, a nightclub orgy, and some very catchy tunes.

Though he had dabbled with short films and directed the relatively straightforward *Sebastiane*, Jarman really established his visual style here with a striking visual patchwork of Super 8 inserts, stream of consciousness editing, opulent costumes and sets, and abundant but unsettling nudity. The now legendary soundtrack remains one of the film's biggest selling points, but its chaotic spirit also endeared the film itself to several generations of university students and underground movie fanatics. All others might want to start somewhere else, as this is not the most easily accessible film in the art house canon; the shifts in time and rambling monologues can be daunting to the inexperienced, and those who find Kenneth Anger too heady will no doubt run screaming during the first ten minutes.

Early video editions (especially the one from Mystic Fire) of *Jubilee* were a smeary mess, but here the vivid colour schemes remain in check. The first DVD option to hit the market from the UK's Second Sight offers a generally pleasing fullscreen edition with some element damage (including one nasty splice an hour into the film) evident from time to time, and the Super 8 bits (including one memorable set piece involving a ballerina and a lot of fire) looking appropriately grainy and worn. The disc also contains a "Face to Face" interview with Jarman running a little under half an hour; shot one year before the director's death, this piece offers a thumbnail sketch of his artistic philosophy and makes for an interesting introduction to his work for newcomers wary of jumping into the deep end with the films themselves.

More lavish is the American disc from Criterion, which presents the film in a sharp, appreciably more pristine letterboxed edition, which adds slight information to the sides while trimming some extraneous space from the top and bottom. (On an anamorphic television, which crops 1.66:1 transfers to 1.78:1, however, the headroom is notably tight, so adjust accordingly.) The biggest extra is a half hour documentary, "Jubilee: A Time Less Golden", created by actor Spencer Leigh (who jumped on the Jarman ship with 1986's more sedate *Caravaggio*). Runacre, Wilcox, film writer Tony Rayns, production designer Christopher Hobbs, and filmmakers John Maybury and Lee Drysdale offer their memories and observations about Jarman and this film in particular. Looking warm and wholesome, the charmingly accented Wilcox scores the most memorable points as she recalls her trepidation as an unskilled actress thrown into such a challenging project. Also included is a short 8mm film, which later became the ballerina-and-scissors vision in the film (though minus the feature's nudity), a lengthy gallery of black and white continuity snapshots, various stills and scrapbook titbits, and the raucous original trailer, as well as historical notes by Jarman scholar Tony Peake. The disc also offers optional English subtitles for those having trouble with the hodgepodge of accents.

JUNGLE HOLOCAUST
(LAST CANNIBAL WORLD)

Colour, 1977, 88m. / Directed by Ruggero Deodato / Starring Massimo Foschi, Me Me Lai, Ivan Rassimov / Shriek Show (US R0 NTSC), Minerva (Italy R2 PAL) / WS (2.35:1) (16:9), MIB (Germany R0 PAL), Hardgore (UK R0 PAL) / WS (2.35:1)

 After an inauspicious career directing Italian programmers in the '60s and early '70s, the now infamous Ruggero Deodato hit paydirt in 1977 with his first international hit, *Ultimo mondo cannibale*. Shown in the U.S. as *The Last Survivor* and also known under its more literal translation, *Last Cannibal World*, the film gained far more notoriety among gorehounds as *Jungle Holocaust*, which tied it in more closely with Deodato's second and far more ferocious gut-muncher outing, *Cannibal Holocaust*. More rooted in the pulp yarn tradition than its volatile companion feature, *Jungle Holocaust* is still extremely disreputable by most film standards as it rubs the viewer's nose in animal death scenes (a snake and alligator this time), gory dismemberment and flesh eating, a man's damaged limb consumed by ants, and other charming atrocities. At least this time there's the distance of a traditional narrative to keep the viewer relatively secure, even if the opening does claim the story is based on true events. Uh huh.

While searching for oil in the remote area of Mindanao, a quartet of explorers are involved in a plane crash near an abandoned jungle camp, and soon realize the area is inhabited by cannibalistic natives. Led by anthropologist Rolf (*giallo* regular Ivan Rassimov) and Robert Harper (Massimo Foschi), they find their number dwindling thanks to hungry locals and deadly booby-traps. After a disastrous attempt to sail away to safety, Robert and Rolf are separated, leaving the latter in the hands of the primitive tribe who strip him naked, hoist him in the air by ropes so he can fly like a bird, and then toss him into a homemade underground cage so the cannibal kids can pee on his head. Really. The loveliest of the cannibal women (sexploitation favourite Me Me Lai) takes pity on Robert and helps him escape, but their flight to freedom is hampered by several unexpected complications.

Though Umberto Lenzi's *Man from Deep River* is usually cited as the first real Italian cannibal film, this is the one that truly kicked off the trend worldwide. Even in cut form it enjoyed a wide release and a decent gross-out reputation thanks to frequent reissues from AIP, and relatively speaking, it's still one of the best made of its ilk. The skilful scope photography, atmospheric score, and earnest performances make this a gripping study of survival, while exploitation fans should enjoy the high levels of gore effects (with the most unforgettable set piece saved for the end, which was so effective Lenzi recycled it – along with much of this film's animal atrocity footage – for his ludicrous *Eaten Alive!*). Thematically it's also less didactic than the '80s cannibal films; there isn't any two-faced moralizing along the lines of who the real savages are. More closely akin to survival epics like Cornell Wilde's underrated *The Naked Prey*, this is one of the more tolerable Italian cannibal films for those courageous enough to venture onto such morally treacherous grounds.

Though *Jungle Holocaust* has circulated on home video almost since the format's incarnation, uncut editions have been few and far between. Many store shelves contained copies of the notorious Lettuce VHS edition, titled *Cannibal*, which excised some of the more graphic imagery involving Foschi's manhood and a bunch of curious cannibal guys. Censorship issues have plagued this title ever since it was first released, and the Region 2 disc from the Hardgore label continues the tradition, having shed 2m 46s at the insistence of the BBFC. Away from the confines of British censorship however, Shriek Show came up trumps; at the time of its release their DVD was the first complete, fully widescreen English edition on any home video format. The image quality provoked wildly divergent reactions, mainly concerning the fairly dim black levels and some compatibility problems caused by the PAL-converted master, but the film looked better than any version preciously issued. The letterboxing adds a considerable amount of vital information to the sides, though the uneven and sometimes pasty colour fidelity fluctuates from scene to scene. Subsequent Media Blasters/Shriek Show titles blow this one out of the water by comparison, though, so it does not reflect the superior quality of their other Euro horror titles. Extras are where this disc easily excels; Deodato contributes both a video interview and a commentary track (in Italian with optional English subtitles), while Foschi also appears for a frank video interview. Other goodies include an extensive video gallery of posters and lobbies, trailers for this and other Shriek Show titles, and a batch of international colour lobby card reproductions (à la *Suspiria*). The trailer, under the *Last Cannibal World* title, is especially fascinating as it includes Deodato and crew (dubbed in English) pontificating about the making and importance of the film, intercut with cartoon teeth transitions. Bon appetit!

An uncut version was also released in Germany, but this edition was non-anamorphic. However, the Italian company Minerva issued the most scarce edition (as it swiftly went out of print), which was an uncut anamorphic PAL-mastered print, without the PAL-to-NTSC conversion issues that afflicted Shriek Show's earlier disc.

JUSTINE

Colour, 1969, 119m. / Directed by Jess Franco / Starring Romina Power, Jack Palance, Maria Rohm, Klaus Kinski, Mercedes McCambridge, Akim Tamiroff / Blue Underground (US R1 NTSC), Anchor Bay (UK R2 PAL) / WS (1.85:1) (16:9)

 Made during the alliance of zoom-happy wayward director Jess Franco and "international" producer Harry Alan Towers (aka screenwriter Peter Welbeck), this may not be lavishly-funded by anyone else's standards but seems luxurious next to the average Franco film. An adaptation of de Sade's oft-told and out-of-copyright novel, it recounts the old, old story of orphan sisters Justine (Romina Power) and Juliette (Maria Rohm), who suffer and prosper respectively. Justine's innocence makes her an obvious victim of sundry aristocratic and/or criminal types as she wanders through pre-revolutionary France being robbed, abused, framed, abducted, branded, molested and sacrificed, while the wanton Juliette becomes wealthy and respected through her devotion to vice, theft and murder. A usual drawback to Franco's would-be sexy cinema is his surprising lack of interest in eroticism, but it here meshes with de Sade's own tendencies: the bisexual whore Juliette likes sex no more than the virginal Justine, and is indeed just as disgusted by carnality even as she can turn a profit from it.

With its good-looking costumes, borrowed 18th Century locations (Barcelona subbing for France) and an interesting supporting cast (even if some are robbed of their voices in the dub), this is certainly more like a real film than most Franco efforts, even if there is a general sense of glum continentals trying to ape the boisterousness of *Tom Jones*, and the two hours pass at something of a trudge. Klaus Kinski, well cast as de Sade (replacing the originally-chosen Orson Welles!), has no dialogue but is seen occasionally behind bars, as Franco zooms in and out of his glower (with Bruno Nicolai's score swelling), suggesting that he is dreaming up the whole story as a mental relief from imprisonment. Palance, who does have his own voice, is extremely overwrought as Brother Antonin, the effete master of a group of libertines who pursue "the supreme pleasure" by torturing abducted girls – he also reads a few snatches of voice-over narration that seem to be de Sade's inner monologue. *Touch of Evil* co-stars Mercedes McCambridge and Akim Tamiroff, who might have signed up because of Franco's Welles association, mug enthusiastically as yet more persecutors, while the women just have to look pretty and go topless from time to time.

Anchor Bay's DVD offers a sumptuous anamorphic widescreen transfer of the longest English-language version available (some releases are up to fifteen minutes shorter), with very rich reds and deep blacks as befits a film that at least tries for some Mario Bava-look lighting effects. It's probably the best-looking Franco DVD around, for what it's worth. The only soundtrack option is an English language mix, which is probably as good as any other. The onscreen title has a possessory credit and quotation marks, so it can alternately be listed as *Marquis de Sade's "Justine"*; on video, the film has most often been released as *Deadly Sanctuary*.

Extras include a French trailer (*Les infortunes de la vertu*), a stills gallery and "The Perils and Pleasures of Justine", a featurette including amusingly indiscreet comments from Franco and Towers.

– KN

THE KEY

Colour, 1983, 106/111m. / Directed by Tinto Brass / Starring Stefania Sandrelli, Frank Finlay, Franco Branciaroli, Barbara Cupisti / Cult Epics (US R0 NTSC), Raro (Italy R2 PAL) / WS (1.66:1) (16:9), Arrow (UK R0 PAL) / WS (1.66:1)

In 1983, after a post-*Caligula* hiatus, Tinto Brass returned to Italian films with *The Key*, a visually refined softcore opus that set the pattern for his raunchy epics to come. Starring one of his biggest name actresses, Stefania Sandrelli (who had already worked for Bernardo Bertolucci and went on to appear in international hits like *Jamon Jamon*) and based on a melodramatic novel by Junichirô Tanizaki (*Manji*), this soapy tale follows the sexual adventures of Teresa Rolf, whose much older husband, Nino (British film vet Frank Finlay), encourages his ageing libido by pushing his wife into an affair with their studly future son-in-law, Laszlo (Franco Branciaroli). Needless to say, Nino's naive daughter, Lisa (*Stagefright*'s Barbara Cupisti), is no match in the sack for her lusty mother-in-law.

Arguably the classiest of Brass's post-*Caligula* films, *The Key* sports a lush period setting in pre-World War II Venice, with Mussolini's rise to power mirroring the increasing decadence of the characters. Brass had already explored this area far more viciously with his orgiastic Nazi yarn, *Salon Kitty*, and he would return to the '40s and '50s in his later work with increasingly benign results. The visual slickness is enhanced by Sandrelli, giving her all with an uninhibited and often undraped performance, and a catchy Ennio Morricone score that set the tone for future bouncy Brass music to come.

The film was first available in virtually identical transfers in both the U.S. and U.K., letterboxed at 1.66:1. A big improvement compared to the overmatted, optically censored Japanese version that most fans had to endure for years, this transfer was generally satisfying if a bit on the soft side. For some reason both DVDs claimed to be 16:9 enhanced, but neither actually were. Though the uncut British disc is certainly

K

an improvement over the old VHS release, which was cut by the BBFC, Cult Epics easily surpassed it by offering an anamorphic upgrade that also importantly features yellow English subtitles for the 12 minutes of Italian dialogue during the film, which are left confusingly unsubtitled in the U.K. version. Also, the Cult Epics disc contains a hefty 17-minute video interview with Brass, a photo gallery, filmographies for Brass and Sandrelli, and the original European trailers for this film, *Miranda*, and *All Ladies Do It*, the last of which is mostly a very funny conversation between Brass and his leading lady. Real Brass fanatics may also want to spring for the Raro release from Italy, which adds an additional five minutes of "director's cut" footage (mostly exposition padding, though one of the director's trademark phony phalluses makes a cameo appearance as well). The Raro version is also presented in Italian only with optional English subtitles, and the main extra is a different, 28-minute Brass interview (also subtitled in English).

KILL BY INCHES

Colour, 1999, 79m. / Directed by Diane Donoil-Valcroze and Arthur Flam / Starring Emmanuel Salinger, Myriam Cyr / Wellspring (US R1 NTSC) / WS (1.66:1) / DD2.0

 This peculiar by-product of two directors, French experimental vet Diane Donoil-Valcroze and NYU grad Arthur Flam, belongs to the art-film horror comedy subgenre alongside shaggy tales such as *Curdled* and *Apartment Zero*.

Deeply neurotic tailor Thomas (Emmanuel Salinger) has a problem. His twin sister, Vera (*Gothic*'s Myriam Cyr), has turned up as his rival for the Tailors' Ball Competition Gala, and unlike her brother, she can fit clients without the use of a measuring tape. Driven to fits, the mad tailor viciously takes out his growing homicidal mania on his clients before a final cataclysmic dip into insanity.

The filmmakers wisely focus more on their audacious visuals than the shaky international combination of actors, to the point of eschewing dialogue almost completely; the result feels like a parody of a German expressionist film by way of Dario Argento. Actual terror is confined more to implication than practice, though it's hard not to wince whenever Thomas pulls out his trusty pins and blades for a little cloth slicing. While it's no classic (suffering mainly from an erratic and often sluggish pace), this is well worth checking out by the curious, and deserves a more significant cult following. Unfortunately the biggest hurdle is Wellspring's half-hearted DVD, which features a watchable but mushy-looking widescreen transfer. The striking, neon-lit bar scenes should look much punchier than this, and black levels are too pasty. The only extra is a not terribly gripping U.S. theatrical trailer.

THE KILLER

Colour, 1989, 107m. / Directed by John Woo / Starring Chow Yun-Fat, Danny Lee, Sally Yeh, Kenneth Tsang / Vivendi (Blu-ray & DVD) (US R0 HD/NTSC), Hong Kong Legends (UK R2 PAL), FortuneStar (HK R3 NTSC) / WS (1.85:1) (16:9) / DD 5.1, Wellspring (US R1 NTSC), Media Asia (HK R0 NTSC), Criterion (US R1 NTSC) / WS (1.85:1)

 Though director John Woo, producer Tsui Hark and star Chow Yun-Fat had worked together previously – notably on the gangster drama *A Better Tomorrow* – and each

amassed a body of major work, it was the international success of *The Killer* which established Hong Kong action cinema as a distinct branding. Most of the creatives proceeded to up-and-down Hollywood careers, and Western filmmakers like Robert Rodriguez and Quentin Tarantino began lifting elements of their distinctive style – the popular flat-on-his-back, gun-in-each-hand slide is a favourite Chow Yun-Fat move, often imitated by pretenders – to enliven their own action pictures.

The Killer is a crime melodrama about an honourable, sentimental hit man (Chow) trying to save enough money from a run of assassinations to pay for an operation to restore the sight of a singer (Sally Yeh) accidentally blinded during one of his hits, while a tough cop (Danny Lee) learns to respect the murderer he's required to track down and finally joins with him for a splattery apotheosis. A genocidal film with more corpses than *Total Recall* and *Die Hard* combined, ironic in that the plot hinges on the lack of suitable cornea donors in Hong Kong, this is a literally astonishing mix of stunts, soap and sly humour. The comic book gunplay and violence of the action elements are mixed with an emotional strain that owes something to Douglas Sirk, but the real love story isn't the mild triangle between cop, killer and blind victim but the almost-gay buddyship that works up between the two male leads. The original Chinese title translates as *Bloodshed of Two Heroes*, which represents the film rather better than the export title, emphasising its status as a relationship movie rather than privileging one of its main characters as a solitary figure. It winds up with a scene that establishes Woo's screen personality: a shoot-out in a chapel that sees candles, bullets and bodies flying across the screen as doves flutter (sometimes in snatches of slo-mo) and liturgical music swells, with blotches of blood on bright-white clothes and tears flowing as freely as the gore.

The Hong Kong Legends and FortuneStar DVDs feature a smart anamorphic transfer, which actually has a richer feel than most theatrical prints. Among the extras are in-depth interviews with supporting players Yeh and Kenneth Tsang and cinematographer Peter Pau, a clutch of trailers and a batch of deleted scenes. The audio commentary by expert Bey Logan is very detailed, giving a great deal of information about the filmmakers and covering minutiae (the use of library music from Walter Hill's *Red Heat*), ironies (actually, Hong Kong is remarkably free of guns), the precise body count (120) and glitches (a hospital sign that reads "Scared Heart"). The long unavailable Criterion version (identical on both DVD and laserdisc) featured the deleted scenes and a slew of vintage Woo trailers, too.

The 2010 Ultimate Edition from the Weinsteins' Dragon Dynasty line (via Vivendi) seemed like the answer to fans' prayers until they actually laid eyes on the transfer, which is shockingly soft and mushy for HD (not to mention interlaced on the Blu-ray, though the DVD's progressive transfer actually manages to look even shoddier). At least the English subtitle translation is a huge improvement over the previous Asian editions, and the audio sounds fine. The original announcement indicated this would be the extended Taiwanese cut with deleted sequences reinstated, but thankfully this proved not to be the case; the superfluous scenes (which severely drag down the film's pacing) are instead presented as a separate extra, as usual. Other special features include a 23-minute Woo interview, American Cinematheque talent discussions of this film and *Hard Boiled*, an 8-minute locations featurette, and two original trailers plus additional ones for *A Better Tomorrow*, *Last Hurrah for Chivalry*, and *Hard Boiled*.

– KN

KILLER BARBYS

Colour, 1996, 87m. / Directed by Jess Franco / Starring Mariangela Giordano, Charles S. Chaplin, Santiago Seguera / Hardgore (UK R2 PAL), Shriek Show (US R1 NTSC) / WS (1.85:1) (16:9) / DD2.0

 This minor comeback picture from Franco, his first above-ground credit in nearly a decade, exists purely on the whim of the eponymous Europop group, who wanted to play at being movie stars and came up with a vehicle for themselves even shoddier than the Alice Cooper effort *Monster Dog*. Book-ended by lengthy gig footage from the Killer Barbies (the spelling is different on the title to avoid legal action from the makers of Barbie dolls), complete with Franco's trademark zooms and lyrics on the level of "I love you, I'm going to kill you tonight", the plot has the band's Scooby-Doo style minivan break down in the backwoods. They wander to an old house where demented servants are looking after Olga Lujan (Mariangela Giordano), a bedridden Bathory-type, who grows young after drinking the blood of several band-members only to be thrown naked out of a window and impaled. Santiago Seguera, the hulking star of *The Day of the Beast*, plays the scythe-wielding loon who hangs beheaded corpses up in an out-building and is finally squashed flat under a lawn-roller, while long-time Euro-horror fixture Giordano mostly rants and raves in the role Franco usually assigns to Lina Romay, though she does do some enthusiastic naked and bloody writhing atop one victim. Neither as odd nor inept as the bulk of Franco's work, but pretty much as boring.

Hardgore's DVD (which, on the cover at least, is actually entitled *Vampire Killer Barbies*) offers a 16:9 image that crops a few foreheads but gives the tatty proceedings some added class not provided by overuse of the smoke machine and way too much Killer Barbies music for most people to stand. The soundtrack offered is an appalling English dub, which even translates some light-hearted closing captions aloud; it's a shame that a subtitled Spanish option was not included, though a few dialogue-light scenes play with the cast's original voices (tied to a bed and stabbed, one victim pleads "por favor, por favor"). About the best that can be said for this effort is that it's better than the flood of material (*Lust for Frankenstein*, *Mari-Cookie and the Killer Tarantula*, etc.) Franco has subsequently unleashed. The U.S. disc contains a vastly superior Spanish track with optional English subtitles, as well as video interviews with the cast.

– KN

KILLING ME SOFTLY

Colour, 2002, 100m. / Directed by Chen Kaige / Starring Heather Graham, Joseph Fiennes, Natascha McElhone / Filmauro (Italy R2 PAL), Pathé (UK R2 PAL), MGM (US R1 NTSC) / WS (1.85:1) (16:9) / DD5.1

 Just when you might have thought the erotic thriller had reached the height of silliness with Joe Eszterhas scripts and *Boxing Helena*, along comes this clunky heavy-breathing laugh riot to offer some stiff competition. The first English-language film from director Chen Kaige (*Farewell My Concubine*, *The Emperor and the Assassin*) should have been an elegant, visually sumptuous study in sexual obsession (much like *In the Realm of the Senses*, which this superficially resembles at times), but thanks to dunderheaded plotting and agonizing dialogue, the result comes crashing down within the opening minutes. Fortunately the results are still spectacu-larly entertaining, though perhaps not in the manner its creators intended.

Based on the radically different novel by Sean French, the story is told mostly in flashback by Alice (Heather Graham), a CD-Rom designer (yes, you read that correctly) telling police about her troubled relationship with Adam (Joseph Fiennes), a heroic mountain climber. A naïve American adrift in London, she first meets Adam at a city crosswalk and moments later is having passionate, anonymous sex in his apartment. After a second tryst, she dumps her devoted boyfriend and goes off to Adam's, which it turns out is really the residence of his sister and fellow climber, Deborah (Natascha McElhone). After spending an evening wandering in the snow, Alice finally tracks down her true love. Soon after her purse gets snatched on the street, and a stalking Adam chases the criminal down, smashes his face to ribbons against a glass telephone booth, and proposes marriage to Alice on the spot while the bloody robber twitches in agony at their feet. (Yes, this really happens.) Of course she agrees, and despite a slew of anonymous letters warning her about the man she thinks she knows, Alice goes ahead with the ceremony. To celebrate their honeymoon, Adam drags her for a twelve-hour hike in the woods, leads her into a remote cabin, and forces her into a little sexual asphyxia thanks to some well-tied scarves around her throat. Things get even scarier when it turns out Adam's past girlfriends have a peculiar habit of disappearing, and Alice's amateur sleuthing reveals some nasty secrets about her beau's past.

Replete with symbolic references to oxygen loss (dying mountain climbers, a twitching goldfish, and so on), this pretentious stew of softcore sex and not-very-surprising whodunit mechanics leaps from one howler to another, including one jaw-dropper which finds Graham trussed up on a kitchen table while Fiennes scolds her for not trusting him. Soon after she's fleeing through the strangely empty streets of London in her undies, but the police refuse to offer much help because, after all, everything was consensual. And then there's the shovel-swinging climax in a foggy graveyard, a villain's "why I did it" speech that would seem farfetched even in an Italian *giallo*, and a sad, doe-eyed coda straight out of a Harlequin romance. Surprisingly, the sex scenes (which were trimmed somewhat in the R-rated U.S. DVD edition, though a separate unrated cut is also available) are pretty weak tea and barely cut it as cable fare; Graham's breasts and Fiennes's posterior get almost as much screen time as their faces, but for all of Graham's proud gushing to the press about the actors' refusal to wear crotch covers for their sex scenes, it's hilarious how Kaige's camera swoops and dodges to avoid glimpsing anything too unseemly. The aforementioned scarfing scene tries to outdo a similar bit in *Basic Instinct*, but the results are more humorous than titillating. At least Patrick Doyle's score offers a few nice Hitchcockian flourishes, but the lack of suspense onscreen results in a musical vacuum.

Co-financed with De Laurentiis money, *Killing Me Softly* first hit DVD in an Italian edition with Italian or English audio tracks. The disc includes an Italian trailer, filmographies, and an exclusive 20-minute making-of featurette, including interviews with Fiennes, Graham, and Kaige. While technically uncut, the film frustratingly cuts to black about 30 seconds before the end of the film (!) while credits for the Italian dub roll over the sound of the action; stick with the British or American discs for the complete movie, though they're lighter on supplements. The anamorphic video quality is excellent, making the most of the very few occasions when Kaige indulges in visual flourishes such as Graham's colourful Oriental-style nightgowns. The very active 5.1 audio keeps the rear speakers busy for most of the running time, and the mountain climbing flashbacks are appropriately enveloping.

KILLING SPREE

Colour, 1987, 88m. / Directed by Tim Ritter / Starring Asbestos Felt, Courtney Lercara, Joel D. Wynkoop / Sub Rosa, Camp (US R1 NTSC), Odeon (UK R2PAL)

Back in the early days of homemade horror (circa 1985 to 1990), the game was small with only a few significant players. Brave video explorers could thrill to the zero-budget, hazy delights of 16mm and shot-on-video cardboard terror thanks to *The Ripper*, *BoardingHouse*, and *Gore-Met, Zombie Chef from Hell*, to name but a few. Among such disreputable company, Tim Ritter earned a small but loyal cult reputation thanks to his unorthodox insistence on including such elements as plot, identifiable locations, dark humour, and outrageous gore. For those who have never sampled his homemade dementia, his second opus, *Killing Spree* offers an appropriately insane introduction.

After losing much of his paycheck at work, sad sack Tom (the creatively named Asbestos Felt) suffers from a nasty inferiority complex that extends to his half-year marriage to Leeza (Courtney Lercara). When he finds her diary filled with sexual fantasies involving all of the men in her life, Tom finally snaps and, after indulging in an outrageous fantasy of his own, in which his wife's head turns into a giant, rubbery pair of lips, he hunts down each of the possible cuckolders (with a few other innocent parties mowed down – literally – along the way) en route to a wacko, zombie-filled finale.

Unmistakably a product of the gorehound era, *Killing Spree* is packed with cartoonish, splatter-packed murder scenes involving a spinning-blade ceiling fan, an old woman's face pounded to mush, electrocutions, and more, all designed for an FX artist's greatest hits reel. The acting is very stylized and over the top, which will either delight viewers or grate on their nerves depending on their mood. Felt spends much of his time leering into the camera and pulling faces as he eviscerates the cast, with some deliberately groan-worthy one-liners tossed in for good measure. Featuring an ambience similar to the early efforts of H.G. Lewis (who gets a nod in the closing credits), the film's Florida locales have a seedy, realistic quality that makes the film all the more unique and effective, with some startling mood lighting thrown in to keep the visuals interesting. If you want glossy, sophisticated thrills, forget it; if you want an evening of unapologetic gore and bargain basement fun, slip on your hipboots and get ready to wade in the red stuff.

Looking about as good as it could possibly get, *Killing Spree* was shot on scrappy 16mm with a video history detailed on the disc by director Tim Ritter in the first of two audio commentaries. Ritter exhaustively covers everything you could possibly want to know about the film, including the back-stories of cast members, details about the make-up creations, and much, much more. The second track features actors Felt, Joel D. Wynkoop and R.M. Hoopes, all of whom jokingly recall making the feature and offer alternative stories to the Ritter track. The most astonishing extra is a making-of compilation/feature that runs longer than the film itself, packing in tons of behind the scenes footage and cast interviews, with an intro by horror starlet Debbie Rochon. If you're a Ritter fan, you certainly get your money's worth. The special edition was later reissued by Camp in the U.S., while U.K. audiences were stuck with the bare bones Odeon release (apart from unrelated trailers for *Shatter Dead*, *Realm of Blood*, and *Catwalk Cannibals*).

KISS OF THE TARANTULA

Colour, 1975, 84m. / Directed by Chris Munger / Starring Eric Mason, Suzanne Ling, Beverly Eddins, Herman Wallner / VCI (US R0 NTSC) / WS (16:9)

One of a trickle (see also *Jennifer*, *Stanley*, even *Carrie*) of 1970s "turning worm" movies in which the put-upon central character cracks up and then unleashes vengeance, typically by siccing novelty pets on the sundry overbearing persecutors who litter their lives.

In a flashback prologue, we meet young Susan Bradley, who overhears her lecherous, murderous cop uncle plotting with her trampy, shrewish, spider-hating mother (Beverly Eddins) to kill her beloved mortician father (Herman Wallner). Setting loose her pet spider, Susan causes her mother's mysterious death. The bulk of the film takes place when Susan (Suzanne Ling) is a spooky-looking blonde teenager, now the object of her uncle's unpleasant interest. On Halloween night, three local yahoos invade the funeral home to steal a coffin and harass Susan, killing her favourite tarantula, Jennifer. She tails two of the clods to the drive-in *Dirty Harry* double bill, and finds them necking with their trashy girlfriends. She lets a boxful of spiders loose in their car and, after a protracted sequence of unnoticed crawling, three of the victims meet a fairly deserved end and a marginally innocent girl is left traumatized. The story doesn't really have anywhere to go, but the final tormentor cozies up to Susan to delve into his buddies' death and gets bitten himself and the groping uncle murders a girl who has got suspicious in order to coerce Susan into sex. The lengthy, quite effective finish ditches the spider concept and has the uncle crippled after a fall downstairs, with Susan calmly using the mortuary equipment to heave him into a coffin as he begs for mercy, then mummifying him under the corpse of his victim in order to ensure his burial alive.

It's a leisurely little film, with hectoring performances, trite dialogue ("that's not proof, that's just a strange and tragic coinci-dence") and a notably limited cast – most are in their late twenties but seem to be playing teenagers. The spider scenes might raise a shudder (the alternative title is *Shudder*) with the arachnophobic, but just look like nature movie footage to anyone without that fear, though some of Ling's cooings and strokings show the actress at least had spirit.

VCI's DVD has a nice web and creepy-crawly-motif menu and showcases a widescreen transfer ("from the original 35mm negative") of a quickie most familiar as an ultra-cheap, disposable tape release. There are eighteen chapter-stops, and the DD Mono track is probably about as good as this poorly-recorded, shrilly-acted, droning synth-scored movie ever will sound. The materials aren't in the best shape, with murky, grainy images only a few grades up from VHS though this may again be as much the fault of director Chris Munger and prolific grindhouse cinematographer Henning Schellerup (*Curse of the Headless Horseman*, *Silent Night, Deadly Night*, *Planet of the Dinosaurs*, etc.) as the distributor. The only extras are ropy trailers for *Kiss of the Tarantula*, *Don't Open the Door*, *City of the Dead* and *Horrors of the Black Museum*.

– KN

KNIFE IN THE WATER

B&W, 1962, 94m. / Directed by Roman Polanski / Starring Leon Niemczyk, Jolanta Umecka, Zygmunt Malanowicz / Anchor Bay (UK R2 PAL) / DTS/DD5.1, Criterion (US R1 NTSC), Odeon (UK R2 PAL), Studio Canal (France R2 PAL), Pioneer (Japan R2 NTSC)

One of the key films in the art house movement of the early '60s, this debut feature from Roman Polanski was largely responsible for establishing the cinema of Poland as a force to be reckoned with. Ironically, it also proved to be Polanski's only Polish feature, as subsequent projects took him throughout Europe and the U.S.

Sort of a thematic cousin to Antonioni's *L'avventura*, the film is less plot-driven and more focused on cinematic technique as an expression of character dynamics and a depiction of social order. Here we have a bourgeois couple, Andrzej (Leon Niemczyk) and Krystyna (Jolanta Umecka), who nearly run over a young blond man (Zygmunt Malanowicz) during an afternoon drive. The husband asks the youth to accompany them for a sailboat ride, and over the course of the next few hours, the men become involved in a power struggle for the apparently dissatisfied woman whose loyalty becomes increasingly ambiguous.

Images of sexuality and violence abound in Polanski's three-character nautical drama, though apart from a bit of discreet quasi-nudity, any overt sensationalism is avoided; the rippling water and the young man's beloved switchblade knife make it clear where the story is headed, and the cramped, effective compositions effectively draw attention to various points of dominance achieved by each character. The deliberately open-ended conclusion, later echoed in Adrian Lyne's *Unfaithful* (a Claude Chabrol remake until its final scene), is a haunting decision that left audiences tantalized upon the film's release; even now it's difficult to imagine any other way for the film to end. In a sense this established the first of many elliptical finales in the Polanski canon, from *Cul-de-sac* onward; likewise, the director's skewed sense of humour is well in evidence, particularly in Krystyna's reactions to the macho mind games being conducted for her benefit.

The first DVD release of *Knife in the Water* (*Nóz w wodzie*) came from Japan as part of a series with *Repulsion* and *Cul-de-Sac*, films with which it forms a loose trilogy to be repeated elsewhere in the same format. The presentation in Polish with optional Japanese subtitles left something to be desired, so a tremendously improved master was commissioned and finally released, first through Studio Canal in France as part of a set with the same other two titles. However, that transfer was in Polish with optional French subtitles, leaving English viewers still frustrated.

Virtually simultaneous English editions finally appeared in the U.S. (Criterion) and the U.K. (Anchor Bay), though the differences between them are intriguing. Though taken from the same source, the Criterion transfer is visibly cleaner with less debris and digital noise; it also features smoother blacks. However, at Polanski's request, the viewer cannot fast-forward during the feature; if he and David Lynch ever collaborated on a DVD release, the results could be deadly. While the Criterion disc presents the original mono track, Anchor Bay added surround remixes in DTS and 5.1; the results are extremely mixed, stretching the already thin audio recording past breaking point with artificial rear channel projection that proves to be more of a distraction than an enhancement. (Their other Polanski remixes are considerably more natural, and relatively speaking, the DTS track is preferable.)

The Criterion disc features a 27-minute featurette including exclusive Polanski interview footage alternating with a discussion with his co-writer, Jerzy Skolimowski, who went on to direct the cult favourite *Deep End*. Though some historical context is offered, the documentary is mostly aesthetic, with a detailed breakdown of the rhythms and techniques used to achieve the creators' goals; for example, Skolimowski explains his decision to keep the dialogue to short, pithy chunks during the entire film, and Polanski elaborates on his use of camera placement and editing to create what Polish officials denounced as an unworthy film. Meanwhile the Anchor Bay disc includes the completely different 30-minute "A Ticket to the West", featuring a new interview with Polanski as well as

Niemczyk, Malanowicz, director Andrzej Wajda, and editor Halina Prugar-Ketling (but no Skolimowski). The first portion offers a portrait of Polish filmmaking at the time; it's a solid overview of just how radically different this was than the usual cinematic product of the period. We also learn a bit more about Polanski's film school days and the nervousness felt over his transition to feature films. Along with much political discussion, the documentary also contains some interesting technical revelations including the fact that Umecka, a non-actress, had to be completely dubbed by another actress in post-production. Both discs include extensive galleries culled from Polanski's personal collection of behind-the-scenes photos; many of the rare shots here are astonishing as the actors and crew are seen preparing for some of the most memorable moments in the film. The U.K. reissue from Odeon carries over this featurette along with a Polanski interview from *The Russell Harty Show*.

The Criterion version contains a second disc presenting eight Polanski short films, while the same shorts are available from Anchor Bay exclusively as a bonus fourth disc in their Roman Polanski Collection. The most famous titles here are the oft-screened "Two Men and a Wardrobe", "The Fat and the Lean" (or "The Fat Man and the Thin Man", as it's christened in the U.K., with Polanski as the titular lean), and "The Mammals", all of them little surrealist gems in their own right. (The three were also included on Criterion's mammoth *Repulsion* laserdisc.) All of these are representative of Polanski's flair for off-kilter visual comedy, a trait he exploits far more than most critics seem to acknowledge. Also included are five more obscure titles, each of which is worth watching; significantly, the absence of dialogue makes these among the more fascinating and universally appealing achievements in Polanski's early catalogue. "Murder" begins like a Hitchcockian set up, with a man knifed in bed before a peculiar punchline. The more typical "Teeth Smile"/"Teethful Smile" follows a man spying through a bathroom window on his neighbours, again with a little twist. The bizarre "Break Up the Ball"/"Let's Break the Ball", a sort of rough draft for ideas later explored in *The Fearless Vampire Killers*, depicts an elaborate nocturnal dance disrupted by the arrival of a young gang. The stunning, 20-minute "When Angels Fall", perhaps the greatest discovery on the disc, contrasts stylish black and white footage of an elderly woman attending a crowded men's public urinal with colour imagery of her Hollywood-style fantasies. In "The Lamp", a shop filled with toys and trinkets is demolished by fire, depicted in eerie detail similar to *House of Wax*. All of the shorts look quite good for their age (considering they're student films several decades old), and the mono soundtracks nicely represent the ambitious mixtures of sound effects and music, some by Polanski's regular collaborator, the late and lamented Krzysztof Komeda.

LAKE OF DRACULA

Colour, 1971, 82m. / Directed by Michio Yamamoto / Starring Mori Kishida, Midori Fujita, Sanae Emi, Osahide Takahashi / Artsmagic/Shadow Warrior / (UK R2 PAL) / WS (2.35:1)

 This is the second entry in Michio Yamamoto's "bloodthirsty" trilogy, following up *Legacy of Dracula* (which is also know as *The Bloodthirsty Doll*). The first movie evoked Hammer and Corman's Poe films, but presented a vampire in the image of a Far Eastern ghost girl, a pale-faced, dark-haired malevolent spirit. Secondary characters here conform to that stereotype, but the villain (Mori Kishida) is a Dracula-style fanged predator whose

various attacks and final destruction seem modelled on Christopher Lee's Hammer Count, though the script seems to be less clear than the subtitles as to whether he's the half-Japanese descendant of Dracula himself or merely of some generic "foreign" vampire lineage.

It opens with heroine Akiko's childhood nightmare, later revealed to be an actual experience, of an encounter with a piano-playing dead woman, an ancient Westerner (played by a Japanese actor) and the vampire, whose yellow eyes inspire the grown-up woman (Midori Fujita) to paint a sinister picture of an evil orb. Akiko is a sensitive soul, who lives near the eponymous but underused lake, with her more modern sister Natsuko (Sanae Emi). The Vampire serially seduces and converts women to undeath, and naturally targets the Lucy-like Natsuko – who transforms from mod gear and bobbed hair to the traditional shrouds and hanging curtain – before homing in on the woman he feels is his destined bride. The hero is a sceptical doctor (Osahide Takahashi), who holds out until the last in his belief that the villain is a hypnotist rather than a real monster.

Originally entitled *Noroi no yakata: Chi wo su me* and alternately titled in English *The Bloodthirsty Eyes*, this is perhaps the least distinctive of the trilogy – which was completed by *Evil of Dracula* (aka *The Bloodthirsty Roses*) – with only Akiko and Natsuko emerging as more than stick figure characters and rather a lot of glooming around in the dark to little purpose. However, the film manages striking moments: Kishida's black silhouette with a long white scarf, Emi coming to life on an autopsy table, the vampire tripped by his near-dead father and falling onto a conveniently sharp pole.

Artsmagic's DVD is on a par with their presentation of the other titles in the trilogy: a non-anamorphic widescreen print with optional subtitles below the image – on 16:9 monitors, names are lost from the credits but the dialogue is viewable – and a fairly fuzzy transfer. Extras are a few stills, a portrait gallery and cross-promotional material for other releases.

– KN

THE LAST HOUSE ON DEAD END STREET

Colour, 1977, 77m. / Directed by Victor Janos [Roger Watkins] / Starring Roger Watkins, Ken Fisher / Barrel (US R1 NTSC), Tartan (UK R2 PAL), Eyeless (Germany R2 PAL)

Seven minutes in, *The Last House on Dead End Street*'s Mission Statement is belted out, loud and clear. "I wanna make some films here, some really weird films." And boy, do they ever... Plotwise, things unfold fairly straightforward and simple. Upon release from prison, minor-league pot peddler and all-around sleazebag Terry Hawkins assembles a troupe of misfits and lowlifes to help dole out vengeance to those they feel deserve it – all the while filming their violent misadventures. The premise may sound a bit bland on paper, but watching it play out is a different ballgame entirely. Resembling a strange meshing of art house aesthetics with the hard-edged violence usually found in "roughies" of the previous decade, the unnerving intensity of *Dead End Street* will undoubtedly get under the skin of anyone fostered on the relative safeness of traditional horror cinema. The proceedings could have easily ended up a stereotypical precursor to the slasher outbreak of the '80s, but several elements combine to transform this running sore of nihilism into something far greater than the sum of its parts. From the disquieting marriage of its minimalist score and ambient sound work to the fetishistic sequences of mask-wearing, bizarre pseudo-rituals and the potent climactic frenzy of sadism, segment after segment compound to form a relentlessly bleak worldview that won't be shaken off easily. Mostly an improvised production, *Dead End Street* represents the type of work that simply can't be planned – once in a lifetime, it just *happens*. Ask Tobe Hooper.

Due to its general rarity and the lack of concrete info concerning its history, *Dead End Street*'s reputation has festered to near legendary status over the years. Unseen by most, Barrel Entertainment finally rectified the situation with this double-disc release, which emerges as not only a tribute to a true one-of-a-kind grindhouse classic but also to the fellow who unleashed it onto this world to begin with – late writer / director / star Roger Watkins. For the longest time, nothing was known about the man who was credited on prints as both Victor Janos and Steven Morrison. Misinformation and supposition were easy to come by, but stone cold facts were few and far between. Until the year 2000, that is. Noticing the ridiculous prices the VHS prerecord was getting on eBay, Roger's then-girlfriend Suzanne posted a message on an internet horror newsgroup inquiring about fans of the film. And the rest, as they say, is history. Interviews have been published, appearances have been made... Hell, Watkins even passed out on my hotel room floor watching *The Brainiac*. Based on the incorrect data *still* around, here's a quick refresher course; you may want to take notes...

In December, 1972, a young man named Roger Watkins – who had been associating with the likes of Nicholas Ray, Otto Preminger and Freddie Francis, to name a few – decided to make a no-budget horror flick titled *The Cuckoo Clocks of Hell*. Cognizant of the fact that the only way to get noticed would be to shock audiences out of their seats, he gathered his friends and set out to do just that. Taking his initial inspiration from rumours of Manson family snuff films, the idea later metamorphosed into the entity we know today. Well, sorta.

Watkins's original rough-cut of the film clocked in at an epic 175 minutes, but was later trimmed down to a more acceptable 115 minute length in preparation for a showing at the Cannes Film Festival – a screening which never occurred. Thanks to a fired ex-cast member (who still haunts the film to this day), Roger suddenly found himself and his film ensnared in three years of litigation. Fighting tooth and nail, the case was taken all the way to the New York State Supreme Court, at which point the charges were cleared and the film was given the thumbs-up for distribution. Striking a deal with a company named Warmflash Productions (headed by Robert Warmflash, director of the ghetto-fu curiosity *Death Promise*), everything seemed to finally be working out. Until, of course, it was discovered that they had chopped their acquisition down to 77 minutes, fabricated an entire credits reel, rearranged scenes, re-titled the picture *The Fun House* and added a PC coda! (This version, the only one known to exist today, was later re-released, post-*The Last House on the Left*, under the more familiar *The Last House on Dead End Street* moniker.) Disillusioned by the whole ordeal, Watkins then began to work in the porno industry; at first writing films (for drive-in luminaries including Roberta Findlay) and eventually directing features as Richard Mahler (not, as reported in other sources, Richard Mailer – who made Traci Lords's first film). He also dabbled in some documentary work, spent time scriptwriting, secured an acting gig on an NBC sitcom called *The Doctors* and helmed two semi-mainstream features – a comedy called *Spittoon* and a horror flick titled *Shadows of the Mind*.

The film's home video history is just as confused, since several variants exist – though *any* version is (was) hard to locate. Issued by Sun Video on Beta and VHS in the States and by Marquis in Canada, tapes can be found as both *The Fun House* and *The Last House on Dead End Street*. To make matters worse, some copies were intact while others suffered from a 91-second edit during the film's most graphic set piece – with no way to differentiate by cover art! A longer (and horrible looking) Venezuelan tape surfaced on the bootleg scene with promises of more gore and nudity, but it turned out to be identical, footage-wise, just transferred at a slower speed to accommodate the Spanish subtitles. And then along came Barrel's version, which unquestionably destroys all need for any other inferior release. Originally filmed on 16mm and blown up to 35mm for distribution, this new transfer (from an extremely rare 35mm theatrical print belonging to collector and Fantasia film festival programmer Mitch Davis, who owns the last film elements known to exist) bares all the grainy earmarks of just such a birth. While dirt, scratches and other blemishes certainly appear often enough to warrant mention, this edition boasts much sharper clarity and bolder colours than ever before, especially next to the washed-out and dull Sun tape. This DVD also reveals a more carefully composed film, adding a noticeable amount of picture information to the right, left and top of the 1.33:1 open-matte framing when compared to the old VHS. The (entirely post-dubbed) mono soundtrack is still a bit hissy with the occasional crackle and pop, but it's honestly as good as can ever be expected. Newcomers to the film may complain about these various imperfections, but overall this is a more than acceptable transfer given the circumstances and it's an astonishing improvement on previous versions. (It should be noted that the theatrical print used for this disc was missing the aforementioned 91-second entrail-slingin' sequence. For the sake of completeness it has been composited into Barrel's master from a videotape source, and was colour corrected and digitally stabilized as much as possible. While it's a shame film materials couldn't have been found for this scene, Barrel should be applauded for showing that an uncut release was the top priority. On the plus side, it does help

illuminate the visual differences between this DVD and prior incarnations. It's amazing what we used to put up with.)

It may take a while for them to get things released, but at least Barrel knows their market and doesn't skimp on the supplements. Before you even turn on your DVD player you're treated to original cover art by comic-book legend/film-buff extraordinaire Steve Bissette. Also included with this deluxe package is a 36-page booklet by *Headpress* editor David Kerekes, which details his personal obsession with the film and contains interviews with and reflections from most of the key cast members. Kicking off the discs themselves is a lively commentary track with director Watkins and the late *Deep Red*itor/old hippie Chas. Balun. Though it's a cynical film, the pair remain good humoured throughout, resulting in a surprisingly fun listen. The problems of filming with zero money are addressed, background info (and the real names) of the actors are covered, distribution hassles are recounted and the longer rough cut is discussed. Another audio option is included for play over the film – a 55-minute interview with the director and actor Ken Fisher conducted for a New York radio station in 1973. Sound quality is a bit rough, but the duo remains engaging throughout. Next up is a real treat for fans – close to 19 minutes of hitherto unseen footage culled from a 16mm work print reel that was found in Watkins's basement, of all places. It (silently) showcases several bits exclusive to the missing, longer rough-cut, fleshing out the intro and characters a bit. It's an interesting peek at what could've been, had the fates been kinder. We then get the alternative intro and outro from *The Fun House* release, sourced from videotape. It plays essentially the same as the current print, except with a replaced title card. Also sourced from VHS is the original television spot circa 1979 (provided by underground filmmaker Nathan Schiff of *Long Island Cannibal Massacre* fame). It's rather reminiscent of the U.S. trailer for Argento's *Suspiria*, and according to Roger it's in fact a short, complete sequence from his follow-up horror film, *Shadows of the Mind*. Moving on, we have a 1975 appearance of Watkins and actor / author Paul Jensen on *The Joe Franklin Show* that runs just under 10 minutes. Regrettably focusing more on Jensen's work as a writer than anything else, *The Cuckoo Clocks of Hell* still gets some airtime. For you headbangers there's a Jim Van Bebber directed music video from Necrophagia titled "They Dwell Beneath", which claims to be inspired by the main presentation. I don't see the resemblance, but to each their own. The final supplement on Disc One is a nicely assembled stills collection that actually revolves around Roger Watkins himself more than his work. Hammer fans, take note: included are several behind-the-scenes photos from Roger's on-set visits to films like *Scars of Dracula* and *Horror of Frankenstein*.

With the first disc's extras grouped to appeal to more casual viewers of the film, disc two presents a platter designed specifically for the hardcore fans. First, we are treated to four pre-*Dead End Street* shorts – "Ron Rico", "Requiem", "Masque of the Red Death" and "Black Snow" – totalling almost an hour in length, presented with voiceover commentary from the director. It's an interesting way to see the man honing his skills, sometimes employing the same locations as the feature attraction. Coming up next is a 75-minute audio journal of 40 phone-calls the director recorded while the film was in production. Very entertaining, this extra gives the listener a revealing glimpse into the trials and tribulations of no-budget filmmaking – from organizing shooting locations to talking actresses into nude scenes, not to mention the occasional prank call. Rounding things up, as far as advertised supplements go, is almost 28 minutes worth of amusingly candid footage from an aborted shot-on-video documentary about a day in the life of Roger Watkins,

filmed in 1988. Easter egg hunters will be rewarded with some goofy goings-on from the commentary recording session, along with a dinner gathering of Roger, Jim Van Bebber, Sherri Rickman, David Szulkin and the guys from Barrel – drinking the night away while discussing everything from Spike Lee's *Bamboozled* to the merits of *The Wild Bunch*. The bottom line? A must-see film and a fantastic package.

The much later European releases in Britain and Germany are noticeably compromised in comparison; the German disc only offers a trailer, and the Tartan release features only the Watkins short films and outtakes (following much controversy in which the original label and director tried to assert ownership of the other bonus material, with Tartan wisely opting out of the argument by not including them at all). All are now out of print, but the Barrel version (which naturally commands the highest prices) is the one to look for.

– BH

LAST HOUSE ON HELL STREET

Colour, 2002, 70m. / Directed by Robin Garrels and John Specht / Starring Leah Schumacher, Schmack Virgin / Sub Rosa (US R1 NTSC) / DD2.0

An effective short film dragged, kicking and screaming, to feature length, *Last House on Hell Street* (or more appropriately, *The Only House Around Without a Street in Sight*) incorporates the usual low budget exploitable contents like graphic gore, victimization, and a tiny cast of characters traumatized by unseen evil. However, the end result is more of an art film with gorehound dressing, and if approached as an avant-garde production (or if you prefer, a really long music video without lyrics), it's more satisfying if still deeply flawed.

The skimpy storyline is conveyed almost entirely through narration courtesy of what appears to be a Puritan woman (co-director Robin Garrels), speaking from beyond the grave after being hacked to death by her lover (the other director, John Specht), father of her child, which was "branded by Satan". The same child grows up into Kyle (the unforgettably named Schmack Virgin), who's engaged to willowy nature girl Jessica (Leah Schumacher). Their sylvan romp turns nasty when they camp out near the house where his mother was murdered, and during the night, Jessica has a nightmare in which her husband turns into... someone else. The next morning he tries to "purify her" by waving feathers in her face and, when that fails, dragging her into the basement where he ties her to a table and extinguishes cigars on her chest. Then two of their friends show up, providing more meat for the body count.

Featuring enough visual flourishes to sustain interest, *Last House on Hell Street* is an interesting exercise in surrealist video making but suffers from an ungodly amount of padding, with "atmospheric" views of tree branches consuming nearly a third of the running time. Since the actors are rarely allowed to speak and are established only through the vocally distorted narration, it's impossible to invest much or be traumatized by their plight. Instead the most enjoyment comes from the film's aesthetic accomplishments, including a creepy and skilfully executed music track, dynamically rendered opening credits (which also chomp up a lot of the running time), and a surprisingly effective (if nonsensical) climax, which swerves the story into bizarre Jodorowsky territory. The woodland setting and palpable pagan atmosphere are also highly effective, while the camerawork is often evocative and makes claustrophobic use of the basement setting. As an experimental mood piece this is something of a departure from the same team's more contemporary *Insaniac*, another borderline horror film which ultimately focuses more on psychology and audio-visual disorientation than severed limbs and buckets of gore. All of which is commendable, of course, but next time take it easy with all the tree footage, please?

Video and audio quality are all up to the usual Sub Rosa standards; digital flaws are minimal to absent, while the surround mix keeps your ears perked up throughout. Some of the footage looks grainy and distorted, of course, but that's how it was shot in the first place. Extras are fairly minimal this time around, consisting of a behind the scenes stills gallery, a batch of other Sub Rosa trailers, and two short films, Emily Haack's "Chokehold" (also on the *Scrapbook* DVD) and Jason Christ's creepy B&W sketch, "Vision". Worth checking out, but check any bloodthirsty cravings at the door; this is more akin to Werner Herzog running amok through the Midwest with a DV cam.

THE LAST HOUSE ON THE LEFT

Colour, 1972, 84m. / Directed by Wes Craven / Starring David Hess, Lucy Grantham, Sandra Cassel, Marc Sheffler, Fred J. Lincoln, Jeramie Rain, Martin Kove / MGM (US R1 NTSC), Film-Fradivis (France R2 PAL), Anchor Bay, Metrodome (UK R2 PAL), Dutch FilmWorks (Holland R2 PAL) / WS (1.85:1) (16:9)

 Ranking with *The Exorcist* as the definitive post-Manson generation gap horror film, *The Last House on the Left* is most notable in horror circles for kicking off the careers of Wes Craven (the only director who, love him or hate him, has managed to redefine the entire genre at least once a decade) and Sean Cunningham, who nearly sank the boat entirely with the *Friday the 13th* franchise. Seen today, *Last House* is a thoroughly non-PC film and may seem like a broadcast from another planet to those who think of peace slogans and bra

burnings as distant relics of pop culture. For those a little more tuned in to the tumultuous passage of the past forty years, however, this film will mean a great deal.

On her sixteenth birthday, pretty suburbanite Mari Collingwood (Sandra Cassel) and her more jaded pal, Phyllis (Lucy Grantham), plan a trip to the big city to see a notorious blood and gore rock act. Along the way they try to score some grass from the dim-witted Junior (Marc Sheffler) and wind up captured by his psychopathic father, Krug (David Hess), the ruthless leader of a small criminal gang which also includes the more low-key Weasel (Fred J. Lincoln) and politically inept feminist Sadie (Jeramie Rain). The two girls are taken out to the woods, where much sadistic mayhem ensues. Posing as refined salesmen, the four criminals take refuge in a nearby house which, unfortunately for them, belongs to Mari's parents...

The infamous tag line "To avoid fainting, keep repeating, It's only a movie... only a movie..." got its start here and at least applies to the notorious midsection of the film, which takes the conventions of the already established roughie grindhouse movie (see *The Defilers*) and pushes it into horrific overdrive. Thankfully the syrupy Hess music (eerie opening theme excepted) and the irritating comic relief of two bumbling cops (including future *Cagney & Lacey* star Martin Kove, who was also doing Paul Morrissey stints at the time) make it awfully easy to keep reminding yourself that it's simply fiction. The oft-noted device of borrowing from Ingmar Bergman's *The Virgin Spring* explains the film's basic plot structure, but exploitation films of the time are a much heavier influence. Craven and Cunningham's backgrounds in adult filmmaking, coupled with their shrewd intellectual awareness, made them ideal candidates to demolish the line between "safe" revenge fantasies and dangerous "you are there" documentary-style atrocities; indeed, the formula remains

so effective that the upmarket Miramax art film *In the Bedroom*, made thirty years later, is a barely redressed packaging of the same storyline and narrative tactic. In between the revenge genre has gone through numerous permutations including *I Spit on Your Grave* and *Ms.45*, though the hollow and wrenching feeling evoked by the end of Craven's film has never really been duplicated. It's a highly unpleasant rollercoaster ride which pulverizes the viewer; apart from one expertly timed shock in the woods, the scares come more from the escalating panic and believability of the characters than any tried-and-true horror filmmaking tactics.

The various cuts of this film have become legend over the years, ranging from the standard R-rated version (usually seen in theatres and widely available on VHS) to the "complete" (as far as we know) unrated print originally sourced from Canadian video, which made the bootleg rounds for years. The DVDs all contain the same extended cut (but with closing credit cards missing from the Canadian transfer), with the entrail-pulling and neck-carving bits, which propel the film into the upper ranks of the mainstream cinema of cruelty. (However, the Anchor Bay U.K. disc lost 16 seconds from the "piss your pants" sequence and two bits of knifeplay due to BBFC insanity; the DVD repeatedly and deservedly slaps the face of that maddening institution, even including the deleted footage as a step-by-step gallery!) The initial U.S. and U.K. DVDs contain many (but not all) of the film's notorious outtakes, with some lingering gut-pulling and additional (silent) dialogue scenes; some simulated, medium-shot, forced lesbian action in the woods was left off the disc but appeared in subsequent reissues. The transfer of the film itself is remarkably colourful for a film known for its cruddy visual appearance; shot hard-matted at 1.85:1 in 16mm, the film never looked great in theatres and appears similarly scratchy here, with several permanent in-camera flaws still on display. Medium and long shots are usually on the soft side, consistent with the original film format, but the film has never previously looked this good on home video, comparatively speaking. (Avoid the badly blown up full-frame version on MGM's first disc, which is an atrocity.)

Wes Craven's involvement is a major plus; he prefaces the first MGM disc (the one with the faux skull-cloud and house artwork) with a tongue-in-cheek warning and participates in a commentary track that places the film in its historical context. As with his other DVD appearances, he takes a largely analytical approach to the various symbols and sociological motifs used in his film, with a few production asides to keep things lively. Cunningham appears as well and makes for an engaging conversational partner. They appear in MGM's "It's Only a Movie" documentary too, which also features some of the actors (Hess and Grantham, of course, have the best stories of anyone; also present are Lincoln, Steve Miner, Sheffler, and Kove). Other extras include the unforgettable theatrical trailer and a rundown of the most controversial footage, which previously wound up on several cutting room floors. The U.K. Anchor Bay double-disc set adds 5.1 and DTS audio options, both of which sound disturbingly artificial and very loud, while carrying over the Craven/Cunningham commentary. UK-only exclusives include a David Hess, Fred Lincoln and Marc Sheffler commentary track (which is just as raucous and potentially unsettling as you'd expect), a 10-minute look at David Hess's scoring of the film, radio spots, a German trailer, an alternative U.S. trailer (in very strange surround), a TV combo promo spot with *Don't Open the Window*, an Anchor Bay U.K. TV promo, the interesting but overlong half-hour "Krug Conquers England" (a look at the film's year 2000 revival focusing on Hess's guitar playing and fan base), Wes Craven's 12-minute

unfinished, silent segment from *Tales That'll Tear Your Heart Out* (featuring Hess and later edited into *Dr. Butcher, M.D.*), along with the feature's legendary alternative cut, *Krug and Company*, which features several little differences in editing, dialogue content, establishing shots, and overall pacing. Best of all is a terrific 40-minute "Celluloid Crime of the Century" documentary, which is much more volatile and candid than the MGM doco. Covering the film's porn origins more blatantly and including some disparaging comments from Lincoln, this is fascinating viewing and benefits greatly from the added presence of Rain, who looks stunning and offers some very welcome perspective on the film.

If that's not complicated enough, Metrodome inherited the U.K. video rights in 2008 and finally managed to slip it by completely uncut. Their three-disc version slaps together all of the pre-existing U.K. extras along with the additional recovered lesbian deleted footage, an amusing 21-minute interview with Blue Underground's Carl Daft about the censorship controversy, and an entire disc devoted to *Going to Pieces: The Rise and Fall of the Slasher Film*, available as a separate release in America. Then MGM chimed in again later that same year with a reissue timed to coincide with the theatrical release of the surprisingly good remake, once again misrepresenting the film with baffling cover art straight out of an Italian *giallo*. The cast commentary, scoring featurette, "Celluloid Crime of the Century", extended lesbian footage, and surviving *Tales That'll Tear Your Heart Out* scenes are carried over from the U.K. edition along with a new Craven interview ("Still Standing"), but the director/producer commentary, alternative cut, and older featurettes are missing. In short, the second British and American releases should satisfy most horror fans, but if you have the older versions, they're worth hanging onto as well.

LEGACY OF DRACULA:
THE BLOODTHIRSTY DOLL

Colour, 1970, 71m. / Directed by Michio Yamamoto / Starring Kayo Matsuo, Akira Nakao, Atsuo Nakamura, Yoko Minakaze, Yukiko Kobayashi / Artsmagic (UK R2 PAL) / WS (2.35:1)

 Japan's Toho pictures made three vampire movies in the early 1970s that have been bracketed together (not least by Artsmagic, the company's U.K. DVD distributor) as the "Bloodthirsty Trilogy". Actually, this first entry is a stand-alone, not featuring the Westernised Japanese Dracula figure who appears in *Lake of Dracula* and *Evil of Dracula*; entitled *Chi o suu ningyo* in Japan, its original foreign release handle was *The Vampire Doll*, which has been amended in translation to emphasise its kinship with the other films. Though it features a vampire of sorts, the film seems most like a Japanese take on Roger Corman's Poe films. In an opening that echoes *Fall of the House of Usher*, a young man (Atsuo Nakamura) visits his girlfriend's isolated house because she hasn't been in touch and is told by her strange mother (Yoko Minakaze) that she has died. However, the red-haired, white-faced, green-eyed, bloody-handed Yuko (Yukiko Kobayashi) appears to him, evidently with evil intent. Then we cut to the youth's sensitive sister (Kayo Matsuo), who has been dreaming all this, and she persuades her boyfriend (Nakao) to help her investigate. The set-up turns out to be a complex variant on "The Facts in the Case of M. Valdemar" in that the mass-murdering rapist who fathered Yuko also hypnotised her on the point of death, prompting her to take on a vicious new identity as the "vampire doll". It ends in typical family tragedy fashion with a burst of blood from the villain's throat and the dead girl rotting on the carpet as the survivors inhabit their own light patches in the gloomy widescreen frame.

Kobayashi has a genuinely unsettling presence, stranded between the Western notions of Madeline Usher and Carmilla and the traditional Japanese vengeful girl ghost, and there's an interesting attempt to evoke Western horror films by having the characters live in a house full of European antiques while a harpsichord burbles on the soundtrack. Some elements (a sharp-toothed halfwit minion, lengthy explanatory speeches) are cliché to the point of being comical, and the simple acceptance of the fact that the heroine has dreamed the first act accurately makes the hero's disbelief of other supernatural elements seem unreasonable. It's not a long film, but it has its share of deadweight wandering-in-the-dark material – nevertheless, it's a fascinating genre hybrid.

Artsmagic's DVD presents a widescreen transfer with optional English subtitles under the image but readable on 16:9 monitors set to "cinema" or "subtitle" mode. The image is fairly grainy, thanks to minor source print imperfections and a non-anamorphic transfer that degrades sharp edges; if nothing else, this is a useful demo disc if you ever want to compare "enhanced" with "regular", showing just how much is added to image quality by the now-almost-universal 16:9 enhancement process. The extras are some publicity handouts found also on the *Lake* and *Evil* discs, black and white stills and a useful gallery of portraits that identify the actors and characters. Also: publicity for other Artsmagic releases and a *Zatoichi* promo. The biographies promised on the sleeve don't appear.
– KN

LEGION OF THE DEAD

Colour, 2000, 89m. / Directed by Olaf Ittenbach / Starring Michael Carr, Russell Friedenberg, Matthias Hues, Kimberly Liebe, Hank Stone, Harvey J. Alperin, Christopher Kriesa, Joe Cook / Anchor Bay (UK R2 PAL) / WS (1.85:1) (16:9) / DD5.1/ DTS, Artisan (US R1 NTSC) / WS (1.85:1) (16:9) / DD5.1

Like the Danish *One Hell of a Christmas* and even the Spanish *Perdita Durango*, this German-produced effort is an *echt*-American horror-road-splatter movie that suggests an overdose of the worst aspects of Quentin Tarantino. It has a battle of demonic forces backdrop along the lines of *Tales from the Crypt: Demon Knight* and a generally ramshackle shapeshifters-and-guns-in-a-diner climax which owes too much to *From Dusk Till Dawn*, but is basically a collection of shaggy dog stories assembled so loosely that an all-a-recurring-dream ending can be sprung in order to avoid closure.

Ancient blond baddie Tagao (Matthias Hues) and waitress-cum-lamia Geena (Kimberly Liebe) are locked in a struggle that's hard to follow, while a couple of bickering goons in suits (Hank Stone and Harvey J. Alperin) go around murdering and resurrecting random individuals to join Tagao's ill-defined legion of the dead. Into all this come a couple of lifelong loser buddies (Michael Carr and Russell Friedenberg) who get picked up on the road by a rabid serial killer (Christopher Kriesa), then get rescued by their cowboy-clothed enigmatic buddy Joe (Joe Cook) and wind up with a whole new batch of barely-introduced characters in a demon-besieged diner. It has a lot of gun-pointing, blood-spurting, inept gore slapstick, would-be funny chatter and male bonding, but it's at heart a timid, feeble exercise in third-hand cool, borrowing heavily from filmmakers who were derivative in the first place.

It's a sign of the times that something as marginal as this should score such an extras-packed, luxurious DVD release. Pick your explanation: a) these filmmakers think they really deserve this treatment and insist on slathering their film with a ton of associational stuff, b) the distributors hope you won't notice how bad the movie is if it can get lost in among the special features or c) in the future all DVDs will be like this. Besides an anamorphic transfer, which certainly looks and sounds better than the fullscreen video release, the disc includes the trailer, a 21-minute making-of, nine merciless minutes of deleted scenes, a spasmodic commentary track (not apologetic enough) from Olaf Ittenbach and an unidentified composer (Jaro Messerchmidt? Ralf Wengenmayr?), stills, production notes and the whole script on DVD-ROM. The R1 disc from Artisan is the cut 'R' rated version, and it does not include the audio commentary.
– KN

LEY LINES

Colour, 1999, 105m. / Directed by Takashi Miike / Starring Michisuke Kashiwaya, Kazuki Kitamura, Tomorowo Taguchi, Dan Li, Sho Aikawa, Samuel Pop Aning, Yukie Itou / Tartan (UK R0 PAL), Artsmagic (US R1 NTSC) / WS (1.78:1) (16:9)

Following *Shinjuku Triad Society* and *Rainy Dog*, this completes Takashi Miike's Triad Society (or Japan Black Society) *kuroshakai* trilogy, which melds the themes of Asian criminal underworlds and ethnic outcast figures within Japanese society. As often with Miike, the leads are second-generation Japanese (children and grandchildren of Chinese unwillingly brought to Japan during the War), so marginalised even among their own sub-culture that they dream of escaping by stowing away on a boat bound for Brazil, a country they know only as the home of the samba.

Two brothers (Kazuki Kitamura and Michisuke Kashiwaya) and a flakier friend (Tomorowo Taguchi) flee their rural upbringing after a fracas with a junkyard owner-cum-fence, and wind up in Tokyo, attracting a pathetic hooker (Dan Li) who first robs them but is then co-opted into the group, and getting mixed up in dealing a home-brewed drug. Eventually, the little band sees a way out in robbing the local mob boss, a scheme that might have a better chance of success if everyone around them wasn't ready to steal whatever they steal at a moment's notice. It's a film which lurches between accordion-scored melancholia and authentically messy (but not operatically overblown) violence. The saddest aspect is that in the end the small group of losers can't even stick together, with the most shocking betrayal being the savage beating of the more scholarly younger brother by his hoodlum elder sibling during an argument over how respectfully to dispose of the corpse of their best friend. It ends with an image of fragile hope redolent of '60s art cinema; a couple in a rowing boat on an infinite sea, blood sloshing around their feet.

Tartan's Asia Extreme DVD is their familiar package: a widescreen transfer with optional English subs, preserving some moments of beauty but tending to muddy the waters somewhat with stretches that are murky rather than evocative. It may be that the prolific director is so busy that he's always a dozen films down the line by the time it's ready to prepare a master for the disc release, or it's possible that his fast and loose shooting methods mean that this is the best a home version is ever going to look. Extras: enthusiastic Tom Mes film notes, the trailer, a trailer reel, more extracts from the Miike interview doled out over this whole range of releases, filmographies. The American edition features two different Miike interviews (totalling half an hour), an interview with editor Yasushi Shimamura, and a Tom Mes commentary elaborating on many of the points from his earlier writings about the film.

– KN

LES LIAISONS DANGEREUSES

B&W, 1959, 106m. / Directed by Roger Vadim / Starring Jeanne Moreau, Gérard Philipe, Annette Vadim, Jeanne Valérie, Jean-Louis Trintignant / Wellspring (US R1 NTSC) / WS (1.66:1)

Strangely, this first high profile version of Choderlos de Laclos's scandalous novel is perhaps the farthest removed from its source. While later films such as *Dangerous Liaisons*, *Valmont* and *Cruel Intentions* covered the same territory of scheming, bored aristocrats using sex to commit emotional violence against their enemies both real and imagined, Roger Vadim's rendition is so thoroughly immersed in ultra-chic, New Wave aesthetics that the characters are transformed from ruthless and Machiavellian into a gallery of disaffected, highly photogenic French actors prancing through the Alpine scenery, occasionally bursting into hysterical fits when they're not rolling around naked by the fireplace. Ooh la la!

At a high society party we meet our decadent protagonists, Valmont (Gérard Philipe) and his wife, Juliette (Jeanne Moreau), who survey the guests while plotting battle strategies. Juliette sweet talks her spouse into seducing and abandoning her goody-goody adversary, the ravishing Marianne Tourvel (Annette Vadim), while Valmont has his sights set on the virtuous Cecile (Jeanne Valérie). With all the company gathered at a ski resort, the stage is set for a series of manipulations, double crosses, and emotional entanglements, which result in violence of both an emotional and physical nature.

The choice to make Juliette and Valmont husband and wife is a peculiar one, especially for the libertine Vadim, as it scuttles the corrupt romantic tension that motivates other versions of the story in which Valmont has lusted after his adversary for years. There's no point in Juliette offering her body as a reward, since he's already had it. Fortunately Moreau still makes her scheming viper such a vivid, memorable character that the alteration becomes less damaging than one might suspect, and she's fortunately matched by Philipe, an engaging actor who sadly died the year of this film's release. Annette, who was married to Roger during filming, reunited with the director the following year for the classic *Blood and Roses*, after which the couple split. As usual Vadim transfers his offscreen passion into sensual onscreen visuals, with the camera obviously lingering over her face and body with devoted attention. The supporting cast is no less intriguing, with Jean-Louis Trintignant essentially tweaking his earlier *And God Created Woman* role as the boyish, easily duped Danceny. (Hard to believe Keanu Reeves would essay the same role almost thirty years later!) Of course, one of the most memorable aspects of the film is its vibrant jazz score, most of it provided by the legendary Thelonious Monk. Other cues were provided by an uncredited Duke Jordan, whose work was largely cast aside but later appeared on a soundtrack album all the same. Jazz music in French cinema was all the vogue at the time (e.g., Miles Davis's score for Louis Malle's *L'ascenseur pour l'échafaud*), but no one can top Monk's scorching riffs blasting out over the chessboard opening credits. For all Vadim's liberties with the novel, his version is a highly memorable excursion into familiar territory and offers a least one highly satisfying improvement in the form of Juliette's comeuppance; I wouldn't dream of spoiling it, but the final moments are appropriately sadistic and far more scalding than getting publicly booed at the opera.

Released at the height of Vadim's "respectable" period, *Les liaisons dangereuses 1960* (as it is also sometimes known) later enjoyed a high profile reissue on the art house and home video circuits in the late 1980s. Complete with a hilarious English-language introduction by a beatnik-clad Vadim, filmed for the limited Astor Pictures release in 1961, this latter-day revival successfully cashed in on the Stephen Frears adaptation with Glenn Close and the print has remained widely available since, despite awful white-on-white subtitles, which proved unreadable during outdoor snow scenes. Wellspring's DVD features the original French cut of the film, sans Roger's introduction, and plays far more seriously without it. The 1.66:1 letterboxing appears accurate enough, though it curiously crops some information from the lower text in the opening company title card. Optional yellow subtitles are a tremendous improvement over earlier versions and image quality is excellent, though some noticeable artefacting during mobile camera shots (in the opening party sequence especially) indicates a less than attentive transfer from a PAL source. The only notable extra is a collection of French trailers for the likes of *Jules and Jim*, *Z*, and *Place Vendôme*.

THE LIVING CORPSE

B&W, 1967, 104m. / Directed by Khwaja Sarfaraz / Starring Rehan, Habib, Asad / Mondo Macabro (US R0 NTSC)

Ever since F.W. Murnau ticked off Bram Stoker's estate by turning *Dracula* into the not-terribly-well-disguised *Nosferatu*, that immortal vampire novel has been twisted and turned in almost every country capable of producing motion pictures. The tradition continued in 1967 in Pakistan, which made one of its rare forays into Gothic horror courtesy of *Zinda Laash*, or as it's now known in English, *The Living Corpse*.

The perplexing opening finds a determined scientist, Professor Tabani

(Rehan), furiously toiling away in his laboratory amidst beakers and Bunsen burners. Soon he's concocted a potion capable of conquering "death's domain", which he tests out by promptly swallowing... and dropping dead on the spot. Luckily his buxom assistant finds him soon enough to get his body shuffled down to the crypt, where he's left uncovered long enough for him to rise again from the grave and put the bite on the poor lass. Flash forward to the journey of Dr. Aqil (Habib), a weary traveller who decides to stop for the night at a desolate mansion known to be haunted. The host turns out to be Tabani, now in full vampire-cloak regalia, who offers him a room where he will prove easy prey. That night Aqil is lured downstairs by the vampire bride, who seduces him into a fanged clench by performing a swinging go-go number. Really. With the poor doc now in vampiric clutches, it's up to his brother and friends to track down the fiendish villain who has decided to leave his home and feed on the local populus.

Though structurally indebted to Hammer's 1958 adaptation (and its first sequel), this fascinating exercise lifts many of its visual flourishes from the Universal classics and similar monochromatic offshoots like the Mexican monster films of the 1950s. The fusion of mad scientists, musical numbers, car chases, baby scarfing, and groovy music makes for a wholly unique experience, not unlike what a particularly imaginative child might come up with on a sugar rush after reading a comic version of the Stoker tale. Most of the horror elements are fairly tame by today's standards and certainly pale next to some of the other Eastern horrors unleashed in subsequent decades, but the Gothic mood is skilfully maintained thanks to some very nicely composed camerawork and lighting. The film was apparently strong enough to incur the wrath of the local censor board, who eventually allowed it to be screened for adult audiences only (a rarity in Pakistani

cinema, according to the supplements). Presumably the plentiful neck-biting and cleavage were enough to pull in the audiences and shake up the powers that be; one can only imagine the reaction if the filmmakers had followed through on the implications of the opening scene and gone with a Frankenstein adaptation instead. In any case, it's a respectable result all round; the familiar vampire-hunting climax is pulled off here with real panache, including some startling imagery (the sunlight bit) and one perfectly timed jolt.

Once again Mondo Macabro has salvaged a genuine curiosity from oblivion with this red carpet release, which presents a transfer from the refurbished negative. The image is pin-sharp almost consistently throughout the film, and despite a disclaimer warning about some damage which could not even be repaired with digital aid, there are only a few flawed moments worth mentioning. The picture seems to wobble and shift during a handful of scenes (including one extended warped passage around the 47:00 mark), but most of the drawbacks appear to be printing problems judging by the jagged splices and grainy outdoor/stock footage shots. Optional English subtitles are provided and seem to be both literate and smartly paced.

The plentiful extras kick off with another excellent Mondo Macabro documentary, "South Asian Horror", which offers a mouth-watering look at this strain of *cinema fantastique* with a focus on the '60s through the '90s. Some of the films look borderline goofy or even comedic, but the avalanche of bizarre monsters, lasers, and screwy supernatural voices proves to be quite ingratiating after a few minutes. Topics covered include Pakistani action films, Hindi supernatural/musical epics, and much more.

The film itself is accompanied by an audio commentary with the video label's Pete Tombs and film critic Omar Khan, who explain the cultural state of Pakistani cinema at the time, cover the censorship brouhaha it caused, explain why the vampiric lead imported his fangs from Germany, and provide some welcome context for its entire existence. Also included are an artefact-riddled trailer (which appears to be a newly created promo judging from the digital-looking text copy), a gallery of posters and stills, and another specially created featurette, "Dracula in Pakistan". Focusing entirely on *The Living Corpse*, this nicely crafted 12-minute piece features Habib, Rehan (who had never seen a horror film before), historian Yasin Goreja, and director Khwaja Sarfaraz discussing the genesis of the film, which Habib (also the producer) initiated with great difficulty.

THE LIVING END

Colour, 1992, 92m. / Directed by Gregg Araki / Starring Mike Dytri, Craig Gilmore, Mary Woronov / Strand, Platinum (US R1 NTSC) / DD5.1, Verve (UK R2 PAL)

Billed as "an irresponsible film by Gregg Araki", this vitriolic first effort from the "formerly gay" maverick director remains both his most consistent and memorable work. Effectively capturing the political rage of the gay community in the early 1990s, the film also works as sick entertainment thanks to some unexpected splashes of gore, hilariously nasty dialogue, and a handful of cult-friendly cameos including the always-welcome Mary Woronov.

Morose over his positive HIV status, single guy and self-deprecating film critic Jon (Craig Gilmore) goes about his business in Los Angeles, while nearby, jaded hustler Luke (Mike Dytri) has the ultimate in bad days when he's nearly robbed by two lesbians, then his john (who enjoys being smacked on the butt with a tennis racket) gets hacked to death by his jealous wife.

Teetering on the edge, Luke then unloads a pistol into a trio of gay bashers. Jon passes by and rescues Luke; the two hit it off immediately and become lovers on the lam, peppering their crime spree with socially conscious diatribes against the White House (populated by the first Bush at the time) and other targets of the period. Occasionally Jon returns to reality for short periods by telephoning his best friend, Darcy, but he continues to follow Luke into increasingly despairing and emotionally treacherous terrain, which culminates in one of the decade's most startling, perverse and oddly touching final scenes.

One of the earliest art house hits from indie label Strand Releasing, *The Living End* became a moderate film festival hit and kick-started the bizarre, unpredictable career of Araki, who followed this with *Totally F***ed Up* before moving into more technically slick, celebrity-studded homages to his favourite directors. Even here the cinematic hat-tipping is more than a little obvious, especially when Luke violently blows away his potential assailants and the camera lingers on their bloody T-shirts inscribed with the names of indie hits like *Drugstore Cowboy*. Depending on each viewer's tolerance, the characters will either seem uncompromising, real and erotically charged, or insufferably whiny and self-absorbed; in any case the dialogue is always interesting and punches through to a few areas no other film dared to explore before or since.

Shot on very grainy 16mm and blown up to 35mm for its theatrical engagements, *The Living End* has never looked very slick, to say the least. Its Warholian visual limitations are part of the charm, apparently, and the video transfer originally prepared by Academy in the mid-1990s captures every bit of grit and grime. That said, it's still colourful and sharp enough, and while the film never earned a laserdisc release, the same master was apparently recycled for Platinum's DVD release. The film's most striking aspect, its soundtrack, fares extremely well, and while the music mix may be a little loud for some tastes, Araki's carefully chosen songs from the likes of KMFDM, Coil, Babyland and Braindead Sound Machine contribute greatly to the film's aggressive, caustic, and ultimately unforgettable atmosphere. A "remixed and remastered" version reissued in the U.S. in 2008 and the U.K. in 2009 features an HD restoration that basically pumps up the sound mix to a more professional-sounding level (in 5.1 no less) and features a more vibrant, albeit still grainy and limited transfer. Extras include a director's commentary track, a batch of production photos, a Q&A from the film's special Sundance screening for the restoration, design art concepts, and an insert booklet with the presskit and various photos and promotional images.

LOST IN LA MANCHA

Colour, 2002, 93m. / Directed by Keith Fulton and Louis Pepe / Starring Terry Gilliam, Johnny Depp, Jean Rochefort, Jeff Bridges (narrator) / New Video (US R1 NTSC), Optimum (UK R2 PAL) / DD2.0

One of the nastier aspects of human nature is our fascination – or even love – for disaster. From watching the Capitol building blown to bits by aliens to seeing celebrities on trial for everything from shoplifting to murder, the three-ring circus mentality is always present in mass media. Of course, there's more than a little potential for destruction in the world of film production, where millions of dollars and hard-built careers are at stake on a daily basis. We all know what happens when a jinxed movie finally hits the screen (as any random summer crop of films will demonstrate), but what happens when a film is so cursed it's never even completed? After concocting one of home video's

finest making-of video featurettes ("The Hamster Factor") for Terry Gilliam's *Twelve Monkeys*, filmmakers Keith Fulton and Louis Pepe were brought aboard again to chronicle the making of Gilliam's European production of *The Man Who Killed Don Quixote*. All seemed to go reasonably well at first, with Johnny Depp signing on as a time traveller who becomes an unlikely Sancho Panza to the frail Don Quixote, played by the very frail French actor Jean Rochefort. Depp's wife, pop singer Vanessa Paradis, was slated as the love interest, and the film was intended to include the usual array of Gilliam surrealism and overblown madness, including giants, jousts, and other visual flights of fancy. Unfortunately Rochefort's erratic health, uncooperative weather, disastrous acoustics, and general bad luck conspired to tear the production down, leaving reels of behind-the-scenes footage without a completed film at the centre. With Gilliam's blessing, the results were honed down into a compelling documentary which charts the ill-fated production from start to finish, with a wistful finale indicating that Gilliam's obsession with this cinematic windmill is far from over.

All of the critical hosannas heaped on *Lost in La Mancha* have proven to be a double-edged sword. On the positive side, it's admirable that the filmmakers don't skewer Gilliam (or anyone else, really) for the failure of the production, and the story is cleanly, compellingly laid out from preproduction through the final death throes. Oddly, Depp only appears for about five minutes throughout the film, and Paradis is glimpsed only in costume tests; on the other hand, Rochefort is present throughout, and judging from what was filmed of his performance, it's hard to imagine how on earth Gilliam thought he was a good casting choice. While Rochefort has done a great deal of excellent work in the past, his English here is completely incoherent and his screen presence comes across as utterly dull. While it's tempting to lament the production as some sort of lost, unfinished master-piece, the tattered remains on view suggest that even had the film been completed, its reception would have been less than enthusiastic. Such is the main problem with *Lost in La Mancha* (and its probable roots as a DVD supplement); it's just too genteel. While the legendary *Burden of Dreams* (which chronicled Werner Herzog's lunatic production of *Fitzcarraldo*) stands as the ultimate filmed testament of film directing gone completely off the rails, this "unmaking of a film" is a far gentler affair; aside from some soggy weather, loud planes, and a few bitchy phone calls, nothing really drastic happens. The film just slowly, sadly unravels before your eyes, which is fascinating for Gilliam fans but not exactly the stuff of high drama. This chronicle is still well worth watching and highly recommended, but don't expect an astonishing view of show business excess and disaster. It's a sad little tale about a project that's defeated great directors before (most famously including Orson Welles) and will most likely do so again in the future.

Shot on DV, the film benefits from better postproduction than would normally be accorded to a making-of feature. While the on-location footage can look rough around the edges, the package as a whole has been nicely polished with Gilliam-style animated bits and other postproduction dressing to give this a feature film ambience. It was shown matted to 1.85:1 in some theatres but looks best in its original 1.33:1 aspect ratio, which is nicely preserved here. Contrary to the 5.1 mix indicated on the packaging, this is in 2.0 stereo with some limited separation effects (the jets, rain, background score, etc.). Dialogue sounds clear enough (at least when it's being spoken clearly), and Jeff Bridges's narration comes through well enough. The feature gets the first platter all to itself, except for New Video trailers plugging other features in their line including *Keep the River on Your Right*, *Sound and Fury*, *Don't Look Back*, *Speaking in Strings*, *Fastpitch*, *Regret to Inform*, *Go Tigers!*, *Sophie B. Hawkins: The Cream Will Rise*, *Paul Taylor: Dancemaker*, and *Todd McFarlane: The Devil You Know*.

The extras-packed second disc includes a series of candid, sometimes painful video interviews with the key participants, including Gilliam, Depp, Pepe, Fulton, and producer Lucy Darwin. The extra footage discarded from the film is represented by a sizeable collection of deleted scenes including two alternative openings, a meeting with Almodóvar composer Alberto Iglesias, and most interestingly a bullfight sequence discarded because of its all-too-obvious metaphorical value. Nearly an hour is devoted to a discussion between Gilliam and *fatwa*-plagued writer Salman Rushdie at the 29th Telluride Film Festival; both men are extremely intelligent and engage in lively, passionate conversation about filmmaking as both a process and a gift for fans. Another hour goes to the Independent Film Channel's "IFC Focus on Terry Gilliam", in which Elvis Mitchell interviews Gilliam at the L.A. County Museum of Art (which followed a screening of *Lost in La Mancha* shortly before its theatrical release). Other extras include the theatrical trailer, storyboards, production stills, costume designs, and "soundbites" (random filmmaker observations about aspects of the film). The U.K. disc offers a similar presentation, minus the LACMA and IFC discussions.

LUGOSI: HOLLYWOOD'S DRACULA

Colour/B&W, 2000, 54m. / Directed by Gary D. Rhodes / Narrated by Bob Clarke and Rue McClanahan / Spinning Our Wheels Productions (US R0 NTSC)

This nice two-disc package has enough additional material to make it a worthwhile item for Lugosi fans, even though the under-an-hour-length documentary itself covers material more than familiar to most of the actor's devotees. Like many an A&E Biography or Universal horror DVD making-of, it relies on familiar PD clips (admittedly, creatively edited) and the tiny memories of ageing bit players who once worked with the Great Man or, in the case of the sprightly Audrey Totter, sat opposite him in a studio commissary. Some oft-raised myths are trotted out yet again, such as the yarn about Lugosi 'turning down' the role of the Monster in *Frankenstein* because it was a non-talking part (at that time, Lugosi had trouble with English but was a skilled silent film actor and willing to shoot a test for the role – the inconvenient fact is that James Whale just didn't want him in the film). It's a respectful piece that plays down the tabloid elements (Ed Wood barely gets a mention), though an exclusive interview with Lugosi's last wife, Hope, is shockingly cold in describing the actor's death ("I petted him all over and nothing moved so I thought 'I guess he's dead'"). Of the familiar faces, Richard Gordon has the most to say – though Bela Lugosi Jr. gets surprisingly little footage.

About thirty minutes of deleted scenes are included, as if the main attraction had been cut to fit a TV slot: in this context, it's odd that Lugosi expert Rhodes opted not to present a feature-length version of the documentary. The added material fleshes out the bare bones biography quite a bit, covering whole periods of filmmaking activity, an amusing comment on his only film in colour, *Scared to Death*, and an astonishing 1956 newsreel clip which links Lugosi's obit to footage of the Hungarian uprising. If the footage were spliced back in the film, it would be a more substantial piece of work and the fact that some of the deleted scenes are expanded versions of sequences that are in the film, along with narration and music, suggests that a ninety-minute cut did exist at one point.

Also on the main disc: a 1918 film clip (*The Struggle for Life*) which is the only surviving extract of his Hungarian work, the 1932 short "Intimate Interviews" (familiar from the *White Zombie* DVD), the full *Texaco Star Theatre* TV clip with Milton Berle allegedly confusing Lugosi (though the skit plays better than the version of this anecdote seen in *Ed Wood*), and much longer interviews with Lugosi's friend Richard Sheffield (material excerpted in the film), Gary D. Rhodes (a frank chat about the making of the documentary and how he tried to distinguish it from other, similar efforts) and Hope Lugosi ("he saw a sucker and I was it") than are used in the documentary. In the full-length Hope talk, she mentions that she didn't like Hungarians and explains that the reason she "petted" his corpse was to make sure he wasn't just "crocked".

The second disc is an audio CD of valuable Lugosi radio work: *Baker's Broadcast* (47s, with Ozzie and Harriet, c. 1937-8), *Mystery House* ("The Thirsty Death", a half-hour horror from 1944, with John Carradine), *Texaco Star Theatre* (11m 25s, a radio incarnation, a quite amusing skit with Fred Allen with topical 1943 wartime draft and housing shortage gags), a very crackly eleven-minute 1944 radio interview with William S. Gailmor about the liberation of Hungary and a twenty-six minute Command Performance (1944). "The Thirsty Death", about hydrophobia in the African jungle, is vintage radio spook stuff, with non-stop organ music and hysteria-pitched performances. Command Performance features a fast-paced Superman parody, with Bob Hope and Paulette Goddard as Clark Kent and Lois Lane and Lugosi as the evil Dr. Bikini; prepared for broadcast to the troops rather than general audiences, it has a lot more mildly salacious material than would have been acceptable on any network.

– KN

MACBETH

Colour, 1971, 140m. / Directed by Roman Polanski / Starring Jon Finch, Francesca Annis, Nicholas Selby / Columbia (US R1 NTSC, UK R2 PAL) / WS (2.35:1) (16:9)

Best known for traumatizing generations of teenage literature students, Roman Polanski's savage adaptation of *Macbeth* was his first studio project after the death of his wife, Sharon Tate, at the hands of the Manson family. Not surprisingly, an already grim and disturbing play was turned into a hellish nightmare on film, reeking of corruption, greed, and needless bloodshed. Fortunately it's also one of the director's most brilliant films. Experimenting with scope photography for only the second time, he paints an unforgettable portrait of medieval Scotland as a damp, brooding place in which man's nobler instincts are invariably forced to confront a recurring cycle of evil brought on by politics and financial gain. Even the Christian institution of marriage is portrayed as a breeding ground for insanity and death, as ambitious battle hero Macbeth (Jon Finch) and his wife (Francesca Annis) arrange the gruesome assassination of King Duncan (Nicholas Selby) to speed the young lord's ascent to the throne. Of course, one murder quickly leads to another as Macbeth's reign of terror drags him into paranoia and madness. Spurred on by the prophecy of three witches who foretell his rising power and ultimate downfall, Macbeth struggles to maintain his lofty position while those around him plot a violent revolt.

Turning in a surprisingly versatile and accomplished performance, relative newcomer Finch (who appeared as a more modern antihero the next year in Hitchcock's *Frenzy*) heads a believable cast of characters who perfectly fit the period setting. The financing by Hugh Hefner's Playboy company dictated the injection of nudity and bloody violence, but Polanski turned the financier's expectations around by presenting human flesh as a matter of fact, non-exploitative sight, whether it's the undraped and unappealing coven of witches or Lady Macbeth's legendary nude sleepwalking scene. The level of violence was also astounding for the time and remains quite strong, particularly Duncan's murder and the stunning final death scene (which will remain vague here for the uninitiated). Several other British-based films from '71 also pushed the boundaries of sex and violence (most notably *Straw Dogs*, *The Devils*, and *A Clockwork Orange*), making for one of the more unusual years of big studio entertainment, but *Macbeth* was also remarkably visionary for its time. Watergate broke the following year, making Polanski's depiction of politics as a seemingly endless chain of cover-ups and backstabbing more relevant than ever. Of course, its continued application to the political world today hardly requires any explanation at all.

Due to its relative failure at the box office, *Macbeth* has suffered for years from shoddy, murky pan and scan transfers on VHS and laserdisc which sapped away all of the original schemes and rendered the stylish compositions completely useless. No wonder many students hated to sit through it! Columbia's DVD is a hi-def upgrade of their letterboxed transfer which briefly aired on cable pay channels, often with artificial zooms to conceal frontal nudity. The DVD is completely uncut and uncensored, and apart from the ragged title sequence (which is filled with scratches and scuffs), the print looks magnificent. Colours are bold and nicely saturated, particularly when colours like red and orange suddenly intrude into the background or burst in from the sides of a frame. Detail is smooth and impressive, and the mono audio sounds free of distortion. Credit for the film's unnerving impact must also be given to the eerie score by the Third Ear Band, a concoction of medieval bagpipe music mixed with a few dashes of prog rock.

Though it isn't usually labelled as a horror film, *Macbeth* certainly fits the bill in terms of both sight and sound.

Columbia's DVD is packaged with the same inexplicable cover as their previous editions; too bad they refuse to go back to the excellent original poster art. Skimpy extras include optional English subtitles or subs in Spanish or Portuguese, as well as the theatrical trailer for this and – believe it or not – *Sense and Sensibility*. Apparently there's some connection between Shakespeare and Jane Austen over at the Columbia marketing department.

MAD FOXES

Colour, 1981, 77m. / Directed by Paul Grau (as Paul Gray) / Starring Robert O'Neal [José Gras], Laura Premika, Sally Sullivan, Erik Falk / ABC DVD (Switzerland R0 PAL) / WS (1.85:1) (16:9)

Perturbed about having his make-out session with an 18-year old virgin interrupted by a septet of Nazi bikers, Hal (our "hero", played by Robert O'Neal [José Gras] of *Hell of the Living Dead* fame) puts his Chevy Stingray to good use and runs one of 'em into a parked car. Not a smart move. This act of vehicular manslaughter (!) has some serious repercussions as the filthy fascists later ambush the pair, roughing up our main-man and raping his barely-legal babe. Not one to take this sort of thing lightly, Hal then calls on a local clan of kickboxers (!) who set out to get even with the "gang of hoodlum bastards". The coteries collide at an amphitheatre funeral pyre and engage in *Dolemite*-esque bouts of martial arts, during the climax of which Der Führer is castrated and force-fed his own Bratwurst! And this is literally just the first twenty minutes! Things soon escalate into a full-on blitzkrieg of the senses with good ol' Hal doin' his best Robert Ginty impression as he tries to wipe out the rest of the Wolfpack once and for all.

Bullet-paced and completely indefensible, *Mad Foxes* is one of the most absurd trash-epics ever made. Every single element screams outrageousness – from its tasteless acts of violence and gore to its non-stop slate of sexual shenanigans and nudity (including some startlingly casual male full-frontal shots courtesy of Germany's male version of Lina Romay, Erik Falk). What other film do you know of that includes obscure hair-metal rockers Krokus on the soundtrack? Hilariously vulgar English dubbing only adds to the package. Whether you're a fan of garbage cinema at its finest or just looking for a fun flick to knock back a few bottles with, this 77-minute chunk of celluloid insanity is essential. A Spanish/Swiss co-production partially financed by sleaze magnate Erwin Dietrich, the film was also released internationally as *Los violadores* (which translates to *The Violators* or *The Rapists*), *Stingray 2* and *Desperados op Weilen* (*Desperadoes on Wheels*).

Running afoul of censors in several countries (it was cut in the U.K. and outright refused classification in Australia), *Mad Foxes* strangely never received U.S. theatrical distribution, which is a shame since 42nd St. audiences would have hit the roof watching this sucker play out. On domestic home video it didn't fare any better, and those wanting to see an uncut, English-dubbed copy would either have to settle for a bootleg or track down the rare TechnoFilm PAL tape from the Netherlands. Luckily that's no longer the case as Dietrich's ABC DVD has digitally restored the film to virtual perfection. Their new 1.85:1 transfer looks amazing, instantly impressing with a crystal clear picture and bright, bold colours. Other than one vertical black line that intrudes for about 45 seconds, the print is flawless. The mono soundtrack is equally free of any defects or distractions, which is necessary for proper Krokus appreciation.

M

337

Although it's labelled as a "Special Edition" on the box art, the disc contains very little in the way of supplemental material. The only film-specific extra is a spoiler-laden theatrical trailer that is well worth checking out due to its use of alternative footage. While we're on the subject, the cover sleeve's story synopsis also gives away practically every major plot point! You'd be wise to avoid glancing at either until after you've viewed the feature itself. Other included previews promote additional titles from ABC DVD and consist of *Rolls Royce Baby* (a rare, non-Franco role for a clean-shaven Lina Romay), *Gefangene Frauen* (aka *Island Women*, a sex-filled women-in-prison romp with Brigitte Lahaie) and *Eine Armee Gretchen* (aka *She-Devils of the SS*, a Nazi sex comedy).

– BH

THE MAGIC CHRISTIAN

Colour, 1969, 101m. / Directed by Joseph McGrath / Starring Peter Sellers, Ringo Starr, John Cleese, Graham Chapman, Laurence Harvey, Raquel Welch, Christopher Lee, Yul Brynner, Roman Polanski, Dennis Price, Spike Milligan, Wilfrid Hyde-White, Ferdy Mayne / Artisan (US R1 NTSC), Universal (UK R2 PAL)

 The late 1960s were fertile territory for the late satirist Terry Southern, whose novels *The Magic Christian* and *Candy* were adapted for the screen within a year of each other. Both adaptations sheared away some of Southern's more acidic tendencies in favour of all-star, plotless comedy skits strung together by slender storylines, though the end results are as different as night and day. While *Candy* strives to be a mod, continental exercise in pop sci-fi erotica, this outing instead feels like a celebrity edition of *Monty Python's Flying Circus* gone completely off the rails (which makes sense, as Pythonites John Cleese and Graham Chapman both co-wrote and appeared onscreen), coupled with good old English slapstick (courtesy of Peter Sellers) and a catchy pop soundtrack from Badfinger, an ill-fated band designed to cash in on the popularity of the Beatles. Fortunately their theme song, "Come and Get It" (written by the unmistakable hand of Paul McCartney), is one of the catchiest ever written and kicks the film off in high style, even if the following events don't always live up to it.

While strolling through the park, eccentric millionaire Sir Guy Grand (Sellers) strikes up a friendship with an amiable bum, Youngman (Ringo Starr), whom Guy adopts as his own son. Together they decide to test the limits of human greed by offering money to an increasingly bizarre assortment of characters who debase themselves completely for a little green. After attending a striptease version of *Hamlet* with Laurence Harvey and displaying most un-English bad manners at restaurants and auctions, the father and son wreak pandemonium aboard the maiden voyage of the Magic Christian, a vessel populated by topless slave girls (ordered by "Priestess of the Whip" Raquel Welch), a stampeding vampire (Christopher Lee), and a scary chanteuse (Yul Brynner in drag) hitting on a jittery Roman Polanski. Back on land, humanity is put to one final, scatological test of avarice courtesy of a giant vat of... well, you'll have to see for yourself. Amazingly, this entire final sequence was usually trimmed from U.S. television showings and some theatrical screenings, but it's preserved here on the uncut DVD in all its perverse glory.

This sort of hit and miss celebrity goofiness had already been devoured into the mainstream thanks to the surreal likes of *Casino Royale* (which shares this film's director, Joseph McGrath), though one could probably trace the tradition as far back as *It's a Mad, Mad, Mad, Mad World.* Here the humour goes beyond sheer silliness and into the purely tasteless, most effectively in a sick dog show skit that bears the unmistakable imprint of Cleese and Chapman. Character actor spotters will also have a field day thanks to the likes of Jess Franco regular and *Kind Hearts and Coronets* star Dennis Price (in a very funny boardroom bit), Spike Milligan, Wilfrid Hyde-White, and *The Fearless Vampire Killers*'s Ferdy Mayne, to name but a few. Just don't expect it all to make any sense at the end.

Artisan's DVD looks several notches sharper than their earlier laserdisc edition, though print damage is still in evidence during the opening sequence. The film was shot (very) open matte with plenty of extra headroom and soft matted between 1.66:1 and 1.85:1, depending on the territory in which it played. The transfer plays fine composed at 1.78:1 or so on anamorphic displays, and colours are vivid and stable. Unfortunately the sound is far more problematic; the packaging indicates a Dolby surround mix, though as with past versions it still sounds like poorly recorded mono. The original shoddy mix is largely to blame, with lots of clumsy ADR work in evidence and the music having been recorded at wildly varying levels, but it's a shame something couldn't have been done to bring it closer to normal theatrical standards. The disc includes closed captioning and no extras. Early reports indicated the much later U.K. release would be a new transfer courtesy of Universal, but it doesn't represent much of an improvement at all.

THE MAIDS

Colour, 1975, 95m. / Directed by Christopher Miles / Starring Glenda Jackson, Susannah York, Mark Burns, Vivien Merchant / Kino (US R1 NTSC), Fremantle (UK R2 PAL) / WS (1.85:1) (16:9)

In the mid-1970s, producer Ely Landau concocted an experience called the American Film Theatre (AFT), in which important plays were turned into feature films with top-rung talent and exhibited in the style of theatre, with tickets sold in advance for a limited number of shows. The conceit ran for two "seasons" and included some significant achievements, most notably John Frankenheimer's all-star, four-hour rendition of *The Iceman Cometh* and Ionesco's *Rhinoceros*, which reteamed *The Producers*'s Gene Wilder and Zero Mostel. One of the most fascinating films in the series is an intense adaptation of *The Maids*, a controversial work by notorious novelist/poet/thief Jean Genet (*Querelle*).

Over the opening credits, "Monsieur" (*Juggernaut*'s Mark Burns) is roused from bed by the police and hauled off to prison, where he's indicted for an unspecified crime. Meanwhile in a lavish house, the sneering Solange (Glenda Jackson) serves as a maid for the haughty Claire (Susannah York), who prances around in her elegant gowns and makes degrading demands of her servant. Soon Solange has had enough and finally wraps her hands around her mistress's throat, until a clock alarm suddenly goes off. As it turns out, both women are really the maids for cheerfully oblivious "Madame" (*Frenzy*'s Vivien Merchant), and Solange and Claire pass the time by indulging in sadomasochistic dramas of dominance and servitude climaxing in the ritualistic murder of the tyrannical lady of the house. As it turns out, Monsieur may have witnessed the maids' play-acting, which in turn led to his false imprisonment; even worse, the maids' dementia might be heading on a direct course to murder...

Written in 1945 and first staged in 1947, *The Maids* was based on the 1933 case of the Papin sisters, maids who brutally killed their mother and daughter employers. The story became the French equivalent to the Leopold and Loeb saga, inspiring a number of novels and films including *Sister My Sister* (1994), *Murderous Maids* (2001), and less directly, the Ruth Rendell novel *A Judgment in Stone*, which was filmed as *The Housekeeper* (1986) and, most memorably, Claude Chabrol's *La cérémonie* (1995). *The Maids* is less a straightforward historical depiction than a forum for Genet's typically outrageous writing style, with characters spouting venomous, purple-prosed insults at each other throughout the running time. (No wonder it was a favourite of horror cult favourite Andy Milligan, who staged it throughout his theatrical career.) Jackson is perfectly cast as Solange, her cat-like eyes constantly betraying the insidious thoughts brewing in her head, while Susannah York essentially expands her treacherous, sex-object lesbian role from *The Killing of Sister George* with a few new wrinkles. After the opening sequence, the film stays largely confined to the house where the three leads embark upon extended psychological warfare; while the layers of play-acting don't have quite the same impact on film as they do on the stage, director Christopher Miles (*The Virgin and the Gypsy*) keeps the proceedings intriguing and ambiguous thanks some dazzling, colourful production design worthy of Fassbinder and fluid cinematography by seasoned pro Douglas Slocombe (*The Fearless Vampire Killers*). Laurie Johnson (*The Avengers*, *Captain Kronos – Vampire Hunter*) contributes an appropriately sparse, nerve-jangling score.

Unseen for decades, *The Maids* looks sparkling and clean on Kino's DVD edition, one of their best editions to date. The anamorphic presentation looks crystal clear and colourful, with only some extremely minor print damage visible. Extras are mostly centred around the AFT, with Landau contributing both a new interview and an archival promotional reel about the series,

along with an AFT scrapbook, stills gallery, and "Cinebill". Also included are the film's original theatrical trailer, a bonus trailer for *Murderous Maids*, and an insert containing an essay, "Jean Genet and *The Maids*", by *The Village Voice*'s Michael Feingold. The later U.K. version features a slightly less impressive PAL-converted transfer but compensates with a 19-minute Susannah York interview about performing the play onstage and for the camera.

MALIBU EXPRESS

Colour, 1985, 92m. / Directed by Andy Sidaris / Starring Darby Hinton, Sybil Danning, Niki Dantine / Malibu Bay Films (US R0 NTSC), Laser Paradise (Germany R2 PAL)

Ah, Andy Sidaris. Anyone who's watched late night trash television or browsed through a video store dating back more than five years will recognise many of this man's titles, all plastered across video boxes crammed with bikini-clad babes toting massive firepower. Exotic locations, absurd plots, and debatable acting are just the icing on the cake here while Andy focuses on what these DVDs succinctly refer to as his three "B"s: babes, bombs, and bullets... all given their own icons on the DVD chapter listings to boot. The Sidaris legacy really began with *Malibu Express*, a fun, gender-reversed, semi-remake of his moderately popular '73 drive-in hit, *Stacey!* The mixture of bright locales, ample women (including Sybil Danning as a voluptuous spy/Contessa), buff dudes, and senseless action established an immediate pattern for success, and while there is something resembling a storyline, most viewers have been too distracted by the luscious candy colours, half-naked centrefolds, and giddy explosions to notice.

Here we meet the first of the Abilene detective dynasty, Cody (soap actor Darby Hinton), who is pressed into service to investigate secret international conspiracies involving a computer equipment pipeline to the Soviet Union that threatens to make America's most vulnerable secrets prey for the enemy. His search leads to the hoity toity Chamberlain estate, run by the lady of the house, Lady Lillian (Niki Dantine). Soon the randy butler (who also has a few secrets) winds up dead while Cody's splashing around in the pool; with the bad guys closing in and the super-stacked women piling up, Cody quickly finds himself running out of time. (In case you were wondering, the title comes from the detective's boat.)

Danning fans tend to revere this film, and with good reason; despite her supporting role status, she easily swipes all of her scenes thanks to an eye-popping parade of outfits and a surprisingly funny script, peppered with silly one-liners and bizarre slapstick comedy which makes the plentiful violence impossible to take seriously. The film is also one of Sidaris's slickest on the technical front, with its cheeky '80s fashions, cars, and weaponry captured in razor sharp detail. (Shame about those tacky computer opening credits though!) Even if you're too young to remember the Reagan/Thatcher years, this one offers a time capsule of the era's All-American entertainment.

Trying to explain the appeal of Andy Sidaris's films simply boils down to shrugging and saying, "They are what they are." Despite all the rampant death and ogling of exposed flesh, the tone of his films is persistently upbeat; even the worst actresses (mostly hand picked from *Playboy* magazine) are so chipper and eager to please that it's not hard to laugh along with them. Gorehounds will enjoy some of the more outrageous death schemes, where stage blood pours out after an unlikely gadget finds its target in a baddie's throat

or forehead, and skin fans should find the exposure of bare breasts every five minutes or so to be enough justification to keep watching. (Oddly enough, despite the near-constant peeling and love scenes, there's nary a glimpse of pubic hair to be found.) One of the greatest sources of amusement comes from the increasingly absurd lengths Sidaris goes to in order to keep recycling his favourite locales, namely Hawaii, Texas, and Nevada. Just try to keep track of how many times he uses the same boat and plane, too...

Not surprisingly, the days of early telecine transfers were none too kind to Sidaris's '80s efforts, resulting in washed out, smudgy cable broadcasts and VHS releases that defined the "cheap cable TV" look most closely identified with "after dark" fare. Therefore, it's with both surprise and delight that all of his titles have been given completely new digital overhauls from the original negatives and look markedly different. Though still full frame with extra headroom (as opposed to the matted 1.85:1 transfers during the very brief drive-in runs), the image quality looks quite rich and stunning. Colours during both the scenery shots and interiors are saturated almost to the point of dripping off the TV screen; frankly, these look like they could have been shot yesterday. (Unfortunately that grinding '80s synth music is around to blow that illusion, however.) This particular DVD is lighter in the extras department than most of its successors, but you do get Sidaris, his wife Arlene, and pin-up Julie Strain camping it up in video intros, making-of segments, and a ribald commentary track. Also included are trailers for the entire Sidaris collection, a bonus carried over to all subsequent titles in the collection. Now out of print, the film was later issued in Germany as part of a 10-title Sidaris set that chops up all the existing making-of footage into seven bite-sized featurettes (such as "Film School Action" and "Film School Sexy!") while dropping the commentary.

MALICE@DOLL

Colour, 2001, 74m. / Directed by Keitaro Motonaga / Starring Yukie Yamada (voice) / Artsmagic (UK R2 PAL, US R1 NTSC) / WS (1.78:1) (16:9)

An anime in the common OAV format, splicing together three self-contained episodes, this uses CGI rather than cel animation but is very familiar stuff. It starts out by deploying some Terry Gilliamish eccentric elements in world-building but quickly devolves into the usual tentacle rape borderline paedophile, outright misogynist slop.

In a world where humans have vanished, robot prostitutes are left to their own devices and start mutating into monstrous abusers and waiflike victims. Malice, the heroine, transforms into flesh (CG boob-squeezing demonstrates this), and tries to help out her less lucky friends, who are suffering from wear and tear. There's some tentacle and machine violation of screaming girl-shaped things, and a few bits of warped bio-machinery that evoke Giger and the mutants from *Toy Story*, but it's shrill as drama, rather ugly as animation (despite a lot of detail work – like smudged make-up on a porcelain face) and claustrophobically pointless.

The extras are an interview that finds Keitaro Motonaga and writer Chiaki Konaka (*Evil Dead Trap 2*) in conversation with Yukie Yamada, the voice of Malice, plus character designs and some trailers. Allegedly this is available in fullscreen or anamorphic widescreen: but the duff check discs supplied only play on PCs and seem to contain only the fullscreen version; at least, unlike the duff video review copies, they have optional English subtitles to go with the Japanese language track.

– KN

MAN BITES DOG

B&W, 1992, 95m. / Directed by Rémy Belvaux, André Bonzel & Benoît Poelvoorde / Starring Benoît Poelvoorde, Jacqueline Pappaert, Nelly Pappaert / Criterion (US R1 NTSC) / WS (1.66:1) (16:9), Tartan (UK R0 PAL) / WS (1.66:1)

Possibly the strangest by-product of the serial killer movie fad during the 1990s, *Man Bites Dog* (originally *C'est arrivé près de chez vous*, or *It Happened in Your Neighbourhood*) straddles the art film and exploitation line by passing itself off as a humorous social commentary, albeit packed with brutality stronger than a Lucio Fulci film. Shot in a black-and-white documentary style on 16mm complete with handheld cameras, jump cuts, bad lighting, and negative dirt, the film takes a small band of filmmakers on a harrowing journey with their subject, serial killer Ben (co-director Benoît Poelvoorde). A disturbing mixture of wit, charm, prejudice, and psychopathic behaviour, Ben is soon calling the shots on the production as he dumps bodies, declares his own personal philosophies on every subject in sight, and eventually indicts the cameramen as co-conspirators in his crimes. Victims include everyday folk from all walks of life, with a particularly disturbing Christmas celebration going even further than run of the mill homicide. Eventually an encounter with one of Ben's competitors in the killing and thieving department goes badly, indicating the raconteur/murderer may not be as infallible as he believes.

Despite its enthusiastic critical reception and the largely self-generated controversy (which resulted in the usual watered-down video version for the Blockbuster crowd), *Man Bites Dog* isn't even an especially accomplished film so much as an oddity. Holding a series of fractured mirrors up to a world view that condescendingly celebrates the tortured and the damned, the film fares even better now that real life exploitation has passed from the realm of screeching talk shows into the even more disturbing waters of reality television. Spoofs like *Series 7* and *$lashers* look especially milquetoast compared to this vicious little animal, which isn't much fun to watch but sure makes for a hell of a conversation piece. And while none of the three filmmakers (as of this writing) have gone behind the camera again, it's worth noting that the influence of *Man Bites Dog* lingered far beyond its theatrical and video runs. For proof, just look at that last shot of *The Blair Witch Project*, a bald-faced imitation of the eerie denouement from its nastier and far more effective French cousin.

Criterion's painstakingly upgraded, anamorphic transfer manages to capture every single bit of grain, dirt, and the botched edits in this deliberately scrappy assembly. The optional subtitles improve significantly over previous video editions, not to mention Tartan's U.K. DVD, where the permanent English subs often vanished completely against the blazing white backgrounds. Here the lettering's black outlines make each jaw-dropping line of dialogue perfectly legible. The sound mix is, well, spare and rough as it always has been.

The extras are largely carried over from Criterion's laserdisc, such as a politically incorrect 12-minute short film, "No CC pour Daniel-Daniel", a mock-trailer spy spoof filmed "en Cinemascope 16!" Also on hand is a hand-held video interview with the three directors (speaking English with very thick accents as they wander through a subway tunnel), the nicely edited French theatrical trailer, and a bizarre behind-the-scenes photo gallery, which shows several of the "victims" relaxing between takes.

THE MAN WHO HAUNTED HIMSELF

Colour, 1969, 92m. / Directed by Basil Dearden / Starring Roger Moore, Hildegard Neil, Olga Georges-Picot, Anton Rodgers, Edward Chapman, Thorley Walters, Charles Lloyd Pack, Freddie Jones / Anchor Bay (US R1 NTSC), Cinema Club (UK R2 PAL) / WS (1.85:1) (16:9)

 Harold Pelham (played by Roger Moore) is a stickler for etiquette, a starchy creature of habit who leads his life by the clock. One day he's involved in a car smash in which he almost meets his maker. But fortune smiles on him and he appears to make a full recovery, returning to the routine of everyday life working in the City. However, when friends and colleagues mention things he's done of which he has no recollection and people he's never met before treat him with familiarity, Pelham begins to suspect that someone is impersonating him. As paranoia turns to fear, he begins to question his sanity, and his job, his family, his very life tumble into jeopardy.

Based on Anthony Armstrong's story "The Case of Mr. Pelham" (which was much earlier adapted for an episode of the TV series *Alfred Hitchcock Presents*, with Tom Ewell in the title role), *The Man Who Haunted Himself* is an underrated little nail-biter which, because we don't get to see the "other" Pelham face-on until the final reel, clamps the audience in a state of uncertain suspense right up until the climactic revelation. The script by director Basil Dearden, producer Michael Relph and (uncredited co-producer) Bryan Forbes is a nicely rounded cocktail of suspense and thrills played out against the backdrop of a marriage turning sour. The scenes between Pelham and wife Eve (Shakespearean actress Hildegard Neil) as they discuss their stale relationship strike a chord of acute sadness.

But where the story really excels is in its painstaking build-up of suspense as Pelham becomes obsessed with tracking down his doppelganger, not even sure he really exists. The moment when he phones home from the office to speak to Eve, only to find the man on the end of the phone is himself, makes the hairs on the back of your neck stand up.

The casting is faultless, from headliners Hildegard Neil and Olga Georges-Picot (as the doppelganger's bit on the side) to the solid back-up of Anton Rodgers, Edward ("Mr. Grimsdale!) Chapman, Thorley Walters, Charles Lloyd Pack, and Freddie Jones as Pelham's oddball psychiatrist. But this is 100% Roger Moore's show and his accomplished handling of the two distinctly contrasting roles – the reserved slave to convention Pelham, and the suave, sophis-ticated, impulsive Pelham – makes you step back and reappraise him. Renowned for his re-fashioning of the James Bond character to fit his own tongue in cheek sense of fun – not to mention a habit for making self-effacing jibes about his talents – it wasn't too often that Moore was awarded the opportunity to ply his craft in a serious role, and he's rarely been better than he is here. This is some distance from the Moore whose 007 could snap knicker elastic with the twitch of an eyebrow. His performance as the tortured Pelham is masterful and in the scenes depicting his inevitable breakdown – "Help me, I'm drowning" – looking pale and shaken, eyes brimming with tears, he takes all the critics who ever dared call him wooden by the scruff of the neck and gives them a stinging slap round the chops.

The trick photography when the two Pelhams finally come face to face may look crude and unconvincing by modern CGI standards, but it does its job for the necessary few seconds and certainly doesn't harm Dearden's beautifully conceived denouement. The futility of the situation here as Eve, his children and best friend Alex (Rodgers) side with the impostor is etched in the despair on Pelham's face, and he realizes not only that he has lost everything but also that the man who has installed himself in the marital home has proven to be the antidote to his failed relationship with Eve. *The Man Who Haunted Himself*, with its irritatingly infectious Michael J. Lewis theme tune, is a paranormal gem from a breed of British films tragically long allowed to fall barren.

Available on disc from Anchor Bay in a pristine transfer with 23 chapter points, *The Man Who Haunted Himself* pulls off a coup that eluded even MGM's Special Edition 007 series for years: the first feature length commentary by star Roger Moore. Accompanied by uncredited writer/producer of the film Bryan Forbes, the conversation is relaxed and informative. The only additional offerings are a theatrical trailer and a text bio for Moore. Sound options are provided in English and French. The later U.K. edition is essentially the same package, minus the French track.

– TG

THE MAN WHO KNEW TOO MUCH

B&W, 1934, 72m. / Directed by Alfred Hitchcock / Starring Leslie Banks, Edna Best, Nova Pilbeam, Peter Lorre, Frank Vosper, Pierre Fresnay, Hugh Wakefield / Network, Carlton (UK R2 PAL), Delta (US R1 NTSC)

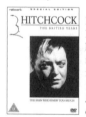 Even though Alfred Hitchcock returned to his earlier works for inspiration many times, for instance refining *The 39 Steps* into *North By Northwest*, he only once chose to mount a remake of material he had done earlier. The 1955 Hollywood version of *The Man Who Knew Too Much* is an expansion of the 1934 British film, but the earlier picture shouldn't be dismissed as a mere rough draft. In some ways, it may be the more satisfying movie,

brisk where the remake is discursive – and the oddly well-spoken but nagging little girl (Nova Pilbeam) who is the victim of kidnap is somehow more appealing (and thus easier to worry about) than the standard American moppet-brat of the 1955 version. Also, this benefits from the very lively, self-amused villainy of a chubby young Peter Lorre, with a fetching white streak in his hair and a childish turn that makes him strangely akin to his intended victim.

It opens with uppercrust Brits Leslie Banks and Edna Best on holiday in Switzerland, and the heroine losing a clay pigeon-shooting contest to an oily-haired bounder with too many teeth (Frank Vosper). Then, during a comic bit at a dance as a knit sweater unravels and wool twines around a whole floorful of couples, a suave French secret agent (Pierre Fresnay) is shot dead, having time only to pass on the location of a vital clue to his English friends. The villains kidnap the couple's daughter and tell them she'll be killed if they reveal anything, and Best and Banks come under pressure from the authorities and the kidnappers. As in many of Hitchcock's spy-themed movies, the premise is sound and emotional, but the plot strings together as many "good bits" as can be crammed in: Banks infiltrating sinister lairs where the villains pose as dentists or sun-worshippers, and thinking fast to turn the situation to his advantage; Best at the Albert Hall as an orchestra performs a piece that climaxes with a cymbal-clash her sharpshooting rival intends to use as cover for the assassination; an extended shoot-out (not in the later film) modelled on the famous siege of Sidney Street as the police put an end to the desperate conspirators.

Hitch originally hashed out this story on the assumption that the lead characters would be Sapper's famous sleuth Bulldog Drummond and his wife Phyllis – but the only trace element of that series is that Banks's hero is partnered by a silly-ass hanger-on (Hugh Wakefield) modelled on Drummond's sidekick Algy.

Carlton's DVD, part of their no-frills Silver Collection, has a fine transfer of a slightly worn print. Though there is a moderate amount of vertical scratching, the contrasts are excellent and the unfussy imagination of Hitch's compositions can be fully appreciated. (The U.S. transfer is comparable.) The only extra is a trailer for the whole collection, though there are optional English subtitles for the hard of hearing. The later U.K. reissue from Network ports over the transfer along with a Charles Barr video intro and a surprisingly juicy 35-minute special, *Aquarius: Alfred the Great*, showing him at work and discussing his craft during the shooting of *Frenzy*.

– KN

THE MANSTER

B&W, 1960, 72m. / Directed by George P. Breakston & Kenneth G. Crane / Starring Peter Dyneley, Jane Hylton, Tetsu Nakamura / Retromedia (US R1 NTSC) **M**

While Japanese cinema was earning acclaim for its classy horror classics like *Ugetsu*, *Onibaba* and *Kwaidan*, they could also get down and dirty with the best U.S. drive-in practitioners as evidenced by *The Manster*, a wonderfully degenerate monster romp co-financed and directed by Americans. Fondly remembered by countless impressionable TV fanatics and the inspiration for films as diverse as *Army of Darkness* and *How to Get Ahead in Advertising*, this one still retains a great deal of its power to startle and amaze.

Starting out as an Asian variation on *The Island of Dr. Moreau*, our tale begins with Dr. Suzuki (*The Human Vapour* and *The H-Man*'s Tetsu Nakamura), a mad scientist first seen gunning down his latest experiment gone awry, a murderous ape-man. Stodgy American reporter Larry Stanford (Peter

345

Dyneley) arrives to interview Suzuki and, before you can say banzai, is guzzling saki and dabbling with geishas. Unfortunately Larry's wife, Linda (Jane Hylton), shows up to put a stop to the doctor's corruptive influence, but not before Suzuki has dosed Larry with a serum designed to alter the entire process of evolution! First Larry's hand becomes clawed and furry (hmm, sense any sexual subtext here yet?), and then an eyeball suddenly appears on his shoulder...

Almost Lovecraftian in its fixation on monstrous, surreal concepts intent on warping the audience's perceptions, *The Manster* is a unique, disturbing achievement well above the standard monster-on-the-loose fare. While the emergence of the eyeball and the climactic "split" are most often cited as the highlights, the whole film seethes with an unhealthy, twisted atmosphere potent from the opening images of a deformed woman frothing and raging inside a cage, with Suzuki looking on in pitied fascination. It's unlikely this one did much for the Japanese tourist trade, but it's a depraved precursor to the gorier terrain the country would soon explore in horrific gems like *Jigoku*. Of course, it also beats the "body in revolt" horror of David Cronenberg by well over a decade; one need only look at films like *Videodrome* and *The Fly* to see how this one scarred filmmakers for life.

A mainstay of public domain home video for years (with a brief detour through MGM thanks to partial funding from United Artists), *The Manster* makes the transition to DVD in a fairly satisfying transfer from the nostalgia junkies at Retromedia. The print is extremely clean and clear apart from the opening credits, and with the exception of some weak contrast in a few shots and occasional soft detail, this is a respectable presentation, far superior to your average PD video. The mono audio sounds clear enough, though dialogue occasionally gets muffled. The disc also includes a fun stills gallery lifted from the film's U.S. promotional press campaign.

MASQUES

Colour, 1987, 96m. / Directed by Claude Chabrol / Starring Philippe Noiret, Robin Renucci, Anne Brochet / Home Vision Entertainment (US R1 NTSC), MK2 (France R2 PAL), Artificial Eye (UK R2 PAL) / WS (1.66:1) (16:9)

When popular television host, former singer and pop culture personality Christian Legagneur ("Bonjour pour tous!") (Philippe Noiret) is approached by up-and-coming journalist Roland Wolf (Robin Renucci) for a new biography, the two retreat to Legagneur's remote country estate. However, the jovial icon in a blood-red smoking jacket provides only superficial, evasive answers to the frustrated reporter's probing questions; furthermore, a gathering of other guests and residents including Legagneur's sickly goddaughter Catherine (Anne Brochet) – with whom Wolf strikes up a peculiar chemistry – provides further distractions. Legagneur asks Wolf to stay away from Catherine and to keep his door shut ("to keep out the mosquitos"), but both men prove to have far more on their minds than a mere puff piece; soon secrets begin to surface and the disarming mask of celebrity slips away before the public eye.

Turning his eye to the theme of celebrity and beginning with a splashy, neon-coloured opening more typical of Claude Lelouch, director Claude Chabrol enjoyed something of a mid-career return to critical acceptance with this cheeky, darkly comic thriller. Often the center of the film's formal compositions, the marvellous Philippe Noiret sinks his teeth into one of his best roles this side of *My New Partner*. Though all the supporting performances are up to the usual high standards, it's really a one-man show as the moustachioed actor dominates each scene while adding layer upon layer (or is he removing layers instead?) as the enigmatic idol. As the younger writer with possible closeted skeletons of his own, clean-cut Renucci (who memorably played the has-been poet father in Bernardo Bertolucci's *The Dreamers*) juggles the obligations of romantic lead and clinical investigator with professional skill.

Meanwhile Chabrol throws in some atypically nudging references to Alfred Hitchcock: a lost woman named Madeleine (*Vertigo*), a tennis challenge (*Strangers on a Train*), a kleptomaniac young woman (*Marnie*), mordant one-liners ("I'll kill my sister for a good pun"), and even the familiar theme music from *Alfred Hitchcock Presents* appropriated for the antihero's own program. Fortunately Chabrol's indelible stamp is still present in every frame, particularly his use of the immaculate bourgeois house – all gold and cream-coloured squares – as the primary visual framing device during the bulk of the film. His usual critique of middle class domestic life is here transformed into a disturbing study of one manipulative but charming man whose path in life eventually runs straight into a dead end, all of his own creation.

Though prescient in its depiction of sweet-faced celebrities concealing their uglier true personalities, *Masques* is one of Chabrol's more benign and sunny thrillers. The characters have a warm, eccentric rapport right down to the casual visitors in the house, and even the most dastardly actions are put in a somewhat sympathetic light during the memorable monologue that closes the film, an actor's showcase that's one of the director and star's best moments.

Unlike some of Chabrol's lesser films from the period, *Masques* inexplicably received little play outside of France and earned its reputation primarily through critical writing and occasional festival and satellite TV screenings. Fortunately an immaculate anamorphic transfer was prepared for release in France under Chabrol's MK2 label and then carried over to the U.S. release from Home Vision Entertainment and the U.K. one from

Artificial Eye (also bundled into their Chabrol box set). It's a solid, colourful transfer that faithfully replicates the gaudy, often saturated colours of Legagneur's Lawrence Welk-style TV program and the softer, more delicate hues of the country scenes. Both versions offer English subtitles, though the HVE disc corrects a few typos present in the French edition. However, Home Vision's disc sports no extras apart from liner notes covering Chabrol's career around the period; the Region 2 French DVD offers a more solid package albeit with little of value for non-French speaking viewers: selected scene commentary by Charol (no subtitles), a video introduction by Joel Magny, and several Chabrol trailers including this film, *Poulet ou vinaigre*, *Madame Bovary*, *Rien ne va plus*, *L'enfer*, and *Betty*.

MAY

Colour, 2002, 94m. / Directed by Lucky McKee / Starring Angela Bettis, Jeremy Sisto, Anna Faris, James Duval, Nichole Hiltz, Bret Roberts / Lionsgate (US R1 NTSC), Media Cooperation One (Germany R2 PAL), Universal (Australia R4 PAL), Mosaic Movies (UK R2 PAL) / WS (1.85:1) (16:9) / DD5.1

A long and proud tradition in horror, the misfit movie ranges all the way from Lon Chaney's *The Hunchback of Notre Dame* through such youth angst classics as *Carrie* and *Willard* (or, on a different plane, *Evilspeak* and *Fear No Evil*). What's most interesting, of course, is that most of these don't feel like horror stories until the final act, when all hell finally breaks loose and lots of people die, horribly. (Or at least get pelted by lots of rats.) To such noble company we may also add *May*, a whimsical yet inherently sad fairy tale for Gothic-minded adults that found its theatrical release hopes sabotaged by one of the most inept marketing strategies in cinema history. A surefire cult item in the making, *May* deserves better on home video and will most likely find its reputation improving via word of mouth once horror fans discover its peculiar charms.

Raised by an apparently dysfunctional mother, young May (Angela Bettis) works as a medical assistant in a veterinary office but only has a creepy doll encased in glass as a friend. Apart from her not terribly articulate doctor boss and the goofy lesbian receptionist (*Scary Movie*'s Anna Faris), May has little contact with the outside world... until she meets Adam (Jeremy Sisto), a Dario Argento disciple with the most beautiful hands May's ever seen. After much reticent stalking she finally lands a couple of dates with the flyblown-haired lothario, but it all ends in tears when he shows her his gory homemade film project and she nearly bites his lip off while they're making out. From there on it's all downhill for poor May, who deals with her intense hunger for friendship in a highly unusual fashion.

Though filled with knowing references to horror films, *May* is certainly an original animal all its own. The three terrific lead performances lend much weight to what could have been a lacklustre Tim Burton or *Heathers* knockoff, and the final act shows an admirable adherence to the classic conventions of horror. (Exactly how we shall not say; it's a series of surprises best experienced cold, though the packaging goes some way towards spoiling that.) Whether combating her lazy eye through contact lenses or having heart to heart rants with her doll, Bettis (who appropriately played *Carrie* in a misbegotten TV remake) never fails to hold the viewer's attention as the film subtly shifts moods from darkly comic to tragic to terrifying. The onslaught of gore, when it comes, is completely earned, though perhaps the most disturbing image comes a bit earlier, which... well, if you've seen the gory

school for the blind scene in *Body Puzzle*, this one takes it several nasty steps further. Also keep an eye out for a strange cameo by wooden indie favourite James Duval, sporting the weirdest hair in recent memory. That's not to say that *May* is entirely perfect; some of the tonal shifts will throw off many viewers, and the final scene, while effective and wholly appropriate, doesn't feel entirely earned; a bit more foreshadowing or perhaps a few additional seconds would have been highly satisfying.

Lionsgate's transfer presents this low budget gem on its best behaviour, with rich bloody reds and solid blacks. Surround audio is limited mostly to the sing-song musical score, which is effective but a tad obvious in spots. The trailer is more than a little spoiler-packed, so approach with caution. Director Lucky McKee provides two different audio commentaries, the first alongside actors Angela Bettis, Nichole Hiltz and Bret Roberts, plus director of photography Steve Yedlin and editor Chris Sivertson. McKee is then joined on the second track by composer Jaye Barnes-Luckett, production designer Leslie Keel and editor Rian Johnson. These extras are carried over to both the German and Australian editions, but the U.K. release from Mosaic only includes the trailer.

MEAT MARKET

Colour, 2001, 91m. / Directed by Brian Clement / Starring Claire Westby, Paul Pedrosa / Sub Rosa (US R0 NTSC), Crypt Keeper (UK R2 PAL) / DD2.0

"From the depths of hell, the dead have returned to walk the earth!" proclaims the tagline for *Meat Market*, a shot-on-video zombie/gore outing whose obvious parallels to *Dawn of the Dead* extend far beyond its ad copy. However, those tired of generic run-of-the-mill homemade horror product will be pleasantly surprised by some of the imaginative flourishes to be found in this skilfully crafted, fast-paced piece of nastiness whose rough edges don't conceal the obvious enthusiasm involved.

A woman is pursued by a horde of zombies in the opening sequence, and is saved by our two gun-toting antiheroes, Shahrokh (Paul Pedrosa) and Argenta (Claire Westby), who toss the near-victim a firearm for protection. The film then breaks down to an origin story beginning with "Week One" in faux-documentary style where, through a series of vignettes (some done in quasi-documentary style which provides a few amusing jabs at news programs and reality TV), we see the undead slowly taking over the city and feeding on the warm flesh available. At first police believe the disease is just a disorder, but soon it turns out the contagion stems from a medical corporation whose experiments have produced ravenous zombies. As society crumbles, the film tosses in a trio of vampiric lesbian gun freaks, sex scenes, some hilarious gratuitous nudity, and a zombie-slaying Mexican wrestler. Honest.

Thanks to its piecemeal construction, the strength of Meat Market lies mostly in its incidentals. When a dialogue or driving scene threatens to overstay its welcome, director Brian Clement (Westby's boyfriend) throws in a quirky touch or surreal image to keep the viewer off balance. The pure zombie imagery works best, include a stunning tracking shot through a nocturnal parking deck under siege, flooded with smoke and shuffling zombies picking off anyone in their way. The standard badass gunplay is really the film's biggest weakness; a longstanding element of post-Tarantino '90s low budget films, the assumption that tossing guns into characters' hands makes them cool is starting to wear pretty thin. Fortunately there are those vampires and the wrestler along for the ride to keep things interesting... Also, bonus points for the most stomach-churning closing credits in recent memory.

In keeping with its commitment to anti-PC underground filmmaking, Sub Rosa presents Meat Market in a squishy special edition containing a transfer about on a par with what you would expect (clear and crisp but dogged by some inconsistent lighting and other flaws in the original elements). For some reason the shades of blood range from red to off-purple, but this also looks carried over from the shooting conditions. Audio is generally well recorded and presented, though the occasional line of dialogue can be muffled. Clement and special effects supervisor Nick Sheehan provide an audio commentary largely concerned with the technical production aspects of the film; they're both fairly low key but keep chatting consistently without any gaps of silence. They also offer a few amusing insights into the themes of the film, some of which seem more reasonable than others. (Check out the dual shower scene commentaries for a chuckle or two.) The disc also contains a trailer and photo gallery, while Easter egg hunters can find an amusing zombie outtake from the film. It's probably worth mentioning that the DVD represents a revised cut of the film compared to an earlier edition, circulated on the fan circuit, which contained an explicit shot of manual male stimulation at the 67 minute mark. The "un-cut" (sort of) U.K. release features only the trailer. The full-strength version of Meat Market later appeared in 2007 as a stripped-down edition with a longer cut of Meat Market 2 from Sub Rosa (see below) in one package.

MEAT MARKET 2

Colour, 2001, 81m. / Directed by Brian Clement / Starring Claire Westby, Alison Therriault, Rob Nesbitt, Chuck DePape, Dustan Roberts, Robin Thomson / Sub Rosa (US R0 NTSC), Crypt Keeper (UK R2 PAL) / DD2.0

While the first *Meat Market* was a scattershot, impressively ambitious attempt to marry *Dawn of the Dead* with a broader social satire, *Meat Market 2* is in essence the same approach welded onto *Day of the Dead*; it's a nastier, grimmer, more claustrophobic piece of work, with the urban guerrilla mentality combined with military tactics and a few jabs at infomercial media culture for good measure. Two survivors from the first film, perpetual warrior Argenta (Claire Westby) and omnisexual bloodsucker Nemesis (Alison Therriault), are caught up in a world slowly being swallowed by the zombie plague. Human society splinters into a number of factions, with the largest one, RCANA, housed in a compound containing military officers and a charismatic motivational speaker, Bill Wilhelm (Rob Nesbitt), whose demonstrations involve zombies on chain leashes. Nemesis can't keep her fangs off an officer or two, but far worse are the *Clockwork Orange*-style brainwashing techniques used by the soldiers and the nutty Dr. Gehlen (Chuck DePape). Meanwhile the undead menace grows until all hell finally breaks loose in an orgy of gut-chomping and explosions.

Once again Brian Clement and his crew make the most of a budget in the area of two thousand dollars, yielding results far above what one might have any right to expect. While the actors have a few awkward moments here and there, the technical aspects of the film are impressive: the grisly make up effects, elaborate camerawork and editing, and expert pacing make for an entirely engrossing experience. The effective, multi-layered soundtrack also helps considerably, giving studio productions a run for their money. But be warned: if you have an aversion to maggots and gushing bodily fluids, approach with caution!

Sub Rosa's DVD carries on the elaborate treatment given to the first film. The transfer looks fine considering the micro-budget origins; the dubious decision to shoot a few hallway scenes under fluorescent lights results in a handful of bleached-out shots, but otherwise colour and detail are pleasing. As with the prior film, some brief shots of aroused genitalia were apparently trimmed but can be seen on a double feature pairing with the first film, albeit shorn of most of the extras. The disc includes two commentary tracks; Clement and Westby take the microphone first along with make-up artist Paul Semande for a fairly technical track, comparing the process of making the sequel to their experience on the first one and explaining the ins and outs of crafting a production with minimal resources. Much looser and goofier is the second "bad guy" commentary with Nesbitt, DePape, and actors Dustan Roberts and Robin Thomson; they seem to be having a lot of fun reliving the film while detailing the process of honing one's thespian craft while surrounding by gunfire and innards. An 18-minute documentary compiles some amusing behind-the-scenes footage, showing the creation of the special effects and climaxing with a funny bit involving one larvae-covered performer chomping on raw meat (and subsequently falling ill, not surprisingly). Other extras include the trailer, a promo for Clement's *Binge and Purge*, a tongue-in-cheek "RCANA Membership Game" featuring multiple-choice questions, a stills gallery, and a rather squishy Easter egg. The U.K. release features the same standard transfer with the trailer.

MERCI POUR LE CHOCOLAT

Colour, 2000, 99m. / Directed by Claude Chabrol / Starring Isabelle Huppert, Jacques Dutronc, Rodolphe Pauly, Anna Mouglalis / First Run (US R0 NTSC) / WS (1.55:1), Artificial Eye (UK R2 PAL) / WS (1.85:1) (16:9), MK2 (France R2 PAL) / WS (1.66:1) (16:9) / DD2.0

The sixth pairing of chameleon-like leading lady Isabelle Huppert with psychological suspense master Claude Chabrol returns the director to his standard territory of sadistic mind games, filled with characters either brimming with psychosis or oblivious to the dangers around them. As with many of his previous thrillers, Chabrol adapts a mannered British literary mystery (in this case, Charlotte Armstrong's *The Chocolate Cobweb*) and transforms it into a work that is undeniably stamped with his eccentric and irresistible personality.

In the Swiss province of Lausanne, elegant chocolate magnate and newly married Mika (Huppert) enjoys a tranquil life with her pianist husband, André (pop star Jacques Dutronc). Also on the scene are Guillaume (Rodolphe Pauly), André's son from a previous marriage (which ended when his first wife died in a violent car accident), and young Jeanne (Anna Mouglalis), a young piano prodigy who learns of a hospital mix-up in which André thought she might be his daughter. Jeanne slowly wiles her way into the maestro's life, much to Mika's frustration; even more strangely, Jeanne begins to suspect that Mika might be tampering with the family's hot chocolate.

Riddled with in-jokes and moments of self-reflexive humour, *Merci pour le chocolat* (shown on the festival circuit as *Nightcap*, a title that never took hold) is primarily a showcase for the always watchable Huppert, who anchors the story with a wry sense of menace which never fully erupts even during the peculiar final scene. Though the film constantly threatens to veer into melodramatic suspense, Chabrol instead tightens the screws in an entirely different manner by keeping the viewer in the dark about character motivations and whether any menace truly exists.

Almost a deadpan comedy, this is certainly lighter Chabrol compared to the explosive viciousness which erupts in, say, *La cérémonie* or *Cry of the Owl*; it's almost quaint in its quirky, stylish focus on a bourgeois family coming apart at the seams due to a few skeletons in the closet.

Merci pour le chocolat first appeared on DVD in a pair of Region 2 PAL releases. The first from MK2, a company responsible for numerous excellent editions of Chabrol's films, features French audio with no subtitles but does boast a sharp, anamorphically enhanced 1.66:1 transfer. On the other hand, the British release from Artificial Eye (also part of their Chabrol box set) is a bit compromised. Though 16:9 enhanced and quite sleek-looking, the 1.85:1 transfer loses significant chunks of information from the top and bottom of the screen, leaving many compositions way out of balance, with characters' faces and eyebrows constantly scraping the edge of the frame. The American disc from First Run is something of a compromise between the two; it's subtitled and more correctly framed, but not 16:9 enhanced. The framing is actually a bit more open than any other transfer, measuring out closer to 1.55:1 than the 1.66:1 stated on the box. The much-needed headroom (and armroom) helps considerably; the U.K. disc displays a sliver more information on the sides, but overall the U.S. framing is much more successful. However, the U.K. disc edges it out for picture quality, so in the end it's really a toss-up depending on the country in which the consumer lives. Subtitles on both the U.K. and U.S. discs are unfortunately burned in, an oddity for such a recent film, but they're clear and always legible. Things get trickier when it comes to the extras. The French and British discs include an interview with Huppert (the latter with optional English subtitles), a 25-minute documentary showing the pipe-puffing Chabrol behind the scenes, Mouglalis's screen test, as well as a bounty of Chabrol-related text extras. The U.S. disc contains

M

a text introduction by Chabrol, bios, and a photo gallery. All three discs include the French theatrical trailer (which is misframed so badly on the U.K. disc that the stars' names vanish off the top of the screen).

METROPOLIS

B&W, 1927, 124/148m. / Directed by Fritz Lang / Starring Brigitte Helm, Alfred Abel, Gustav Fröhlich, Rudolf Klein-Rogge, Erwin Biswanger / Kino (Blu-ray & DVD) (US RA/R1 HD/NTSC), Eureka (Blu-ray & DVD) (UK RB/R2 HD/PAL), UFA (Germany R2 PAL)

 Fritz Lang's epic science fiction tale is many things: the most widely-seen silent film (it has never, in one form or another, been out of circulation for an extended time), the apex (and, arguably, the denouement) of German expressionist cinema, and paradoxically one of the most egregious examples of outside tampering and cutting of the work of a major filmmaker. Kino Video's fine presentation of this meticulously-reconstructed print serves to undo the damage of both time and revisionists, restoring *Metropolis* more closely than previously to the version seen on its initial Berlin premiere in 1927, including the score composed for the film by Gottfried Huppertz.

Based on a serialized novel by Thea von Harbou, Lang's wife at the time, and allegedly inspired by his first view of the contemporary New York skyline, *Metropolis* presents a world where the wealthy elite and their progeny enjoy life amidst a glittering strata of Art Deco-inspired towers. Meanwhile, the poorer, working-class operators of the machinery that keeps the city running are forced to dwell in the Gothic machine rooms and Spartan dwellings deep beneath the city. The story focuses on Freder (Gustav Fröhlich,

of Lang's epic two-part *Die Nibelungen* saga), son of the builder and ruler of Metropolis, Joh Fredersen (Alfred Abel). When Freder sees the beautiful worker-class Maria (Brigitte Helm), he follows her into the depths of the city, realizing for the first time the cost of his life of pleasure, and falling in love with her in the process. Complicating matters considerably, Fredersen finds an uneasy ally in his former romantic rival for the love of Freder's deceased mother, Rotwang (Rudolf Klein-Rogge, of Lang's *Testament of Dr. Mabuse*). Rotwang has created the Machine-Man, a robot which he may endow with human features, and which he has made to replace his lost love. Fredersen convinces Rotwang to give the robot the visage of Maria, so that he can control the workers. The Machine-Maria is presented to the young men of Metropolis, who are driven into a sexual frenzy by her erotic presence, the same dark charisma she uses to lead the workers into revolt, and they destroy the machines that not only power the great city, but also keep the vast reservoirs from flooding their homes. Freder and the real Maria are able to save the workers' children from the floods, and, in the end, Freder unites his father with the workers in the realization of the film's epigram: "The mediator between head and hands must be the heart!"

Even in comparison with Lang's earlier work, *Metropolis* utilizes an astonishing array of special effects, including a number of complex multiple-exposure shots (this being the age before process shots, all of the effects here are done "in camera"), amazingly-fluid stop motion animation, very detailed models and mirrored matte paintings, and animated inter-titles ("MOLOCH!"). Lang manages to tell a fairly conventional, moralistic tale by keeping our attention on his moving images at all times. If you've seen the film before, take note that the camera is almost always stationary; any slight pans (from character to character) or the wild swinging motion during the flood sequence serve as a powerful underlining element.

M

Quite simply, *Metropolis* never looked as good on video as it did until Kino's first delicate reconstruction of the film for DVD (some of which was pieced back together with only cryptic cues from Huppertz's conductor's score). Scenes frequently seen out of sequence or without their joining elements now emerge as clear and entirely necessary elements of the story. As in Giorgio Moroder's often (and unfairly) lambasted 1984 presentation of the film – which, in reconstructing the film in an 87-minute format, drew fire from critics for including original songs performed by Freddie Mercury, Pat Benatar, Bonnie Tyler, and Loverboy, among others – the secondary characters of Josophat and worker 11811 (Erwin Biswanger, with whom Freder trades places) are brought to the fore. The Kino version goes one better, by illustrating the many subplots and motivational elements of von Harbou's story which reveal the characters to be quite a bit more than the flat archetypes which have given so many enthusiasts reason to cringe when introducing *Metropolis* to new viewers. The score by Huppertz, first heard at the Berlin premiere, is, quite simply, among the finest film scores ever written. Surprisingly modern in passages, and very lyrical in others, it is unthinkable that such a work has gone so long unheard. The Moroder version of *Metropolis*, unwisely tinted (with some colourised elements), was briefly made available on VHS and Laserdisc from Vestron, but is long out-of-print and difficult to find. It is however worth a look (and listen).

A preface to the Kino version claimed that a full quarter of Fritz Lang's film must be considered lost forever, but much to everyone's surprise, the missing 25 minutes were recovered in July of 2008 thanks to a surviving print in Buenos Aires. The resulting efforts to piece together the entire film from the best surviving elements resulted in a much richer, deeper presentation of Lang's film, with entire characters

and subplots suddenly merging like never before. The HD-preserved version (available in both the U.S. and U.K., with the latter's "Masters of Cinema" version coming out in a limited, massive package with an enclosed book) betrays the patchwork nature of the source but looks much better than you might imagine, and the original score can't be beaten with a full orchestra and lossless audio. Extras include a 50-minute documentary about the making of the film ("Voyage to Metropolis"), an interview with film curator Paula Felix-Didier, who was involved in the recovery, and the reissue trailer. There's a lot of casual use of the word "masterpiece" today; *Metropolis* certainly earns the title.

– TSG

THE MONSTER (I DON'T WANT TO BE BORN)

Colour, 1975, 89m. / Directed by Peter Sasdy / Starring Joan Collins, Ralph Bates, Donald Pleasence, Caroline Munro, George Claydon, Eileen Atkins, John Steiner / Network, Carlton (UK R2 PAL) / WS (1.85:1) (16:9)

One of the worst British horror films of the 1970s, this is available in a "Classic Horror Collection" box set with director Peter Sasdy's far superior *Hands of the Ripper* and co-star Donald Pleasence's just-as-ropy *The Uncanny*. Considering the low cost of the individual films, the package is worth picking up for *Hands* alone – though connoisseurs of floppy-collared tat might find something amusing in *I Don't Want to Be Born*, presented under its re-release title *The Monster* (in the U.S. it was also known as *The Devil Within Her*).

The obligatory British attempt to ride the possession wave of *The Exorcist*, it also stands as a post-natal depression postscript to the pregnancy paranoia of *Rosemary's Baby*. Ex-stripper Lucy (Joan Collins), married to an understanding Italian businessman Gino (Ralph Bates), has a tough delivery of her first child, prompting the attending obstetrician (Donald Pleasence) to muse that the baby doesn't want to be born, a theme harped on several times in order to justify the original title. The babe (named Nicholas) is soon scratching faces, wrecking his nursery, shoving a baby-sitter into a lake, slipping a dead mouse into the charlady's cup of tea and – though never explicitly shown doing it – hanging, decapitating and stabbing principal characters. The backstory, as Lucy explains to her still-stripping best friend (Caroline Munro), is that Lucy once spurned the advances of Hercules (George Claydon), a lustful dwarf featured in her bizarre gypsy dancer nightclub act. She was then cursed by the little fellow to have a baby "as big as I am small and possessed by the Devil." Also in the mix is Gino's sister, Albana (Eileen Atkins), a nun with scientific qualifications who winds up performing the requisite exorcism, which frees Nicholas of possession and makes Hercules drop dead in the middle of a dance number.

On one level, it's enough that this cast was assembled in a single movie, let alone that they should perform so enthusiastically. In one of her horror diva roles, Collins goes the full nervous breakdown route while Bates and Atkins – among the finest actresses of her generation and in far too few films – struggle with Italian accents. Munro, as usual, is dubbed (here with Barbara Windsor tones) and works in a club with a pay-phone next to the stage so that dull exposition can be delivered with a topless dancer in the background. John Steiner, familiar from disreputable Italian movies, has a sleazy role as the ratty owner of the club where Collins and Munro work, though the actual stripping is handled by professionals. Sasdy might be continuing the trouble-in-the-family themes of his *Taste the Blood of Dracula*, *Countess Dracula* and

Hands of the Ripper here, but can make little of Stanley Price's irredeemably silly, soapy script. A sole touch of class is Ron Grainer's *Tales of the Unexpected*-ish score.

Carlton's no-frills DVD at least offers anamorphic widescreen, while the same transfer popped up again under the Network banner with a theatrical trailer and, God help us, a pdf of the original script. The Rank gong-man's arm is ominously streaky in the logo, but apart from a touch of blue speckling in some of the blacks the transfer is decent, affording a long hard look at the vintage 1975 clothing modelled by Collins and Munro (Atkins, at least, stays wimpled throughout). The shrieking decor is straight out of *Abigail's Party*: the nursery wallpaper seems a more credible explanation for the baby's malevolence than anything in the storyline.

– KN

MOSQUITO

Colour, 1976, 92m. / Directed by Marijan David Vajda / Starring Werner Pochath, Marion Messner / Astro (Germany R0 PAL), Marketing Film (Germany R0 PAL) / WS (1.66:1), Monarex (US R0 NTSC)

This strange precursor to extreme European necrophilia flicks such as *Nekromantik* and *Lucker* shares its era's fascination, as it blends art house aesthetics with repellent subject matter, a trait that arguably reached its zenith with *The Tenderness of Wolves* and *Daughters of Darkness*. Though not as memorable or accomplished as those two films, *Mosquito der Schänder* (better known as *Bloodlust* or simply *Mosquito*) offers a few haunting moments and maintains an eerie mood throughout, with director Marijan David Vajda (who turned almost exclusively to German television afterwards) making the most of his grotesque set pieces.

Still recovering from horrific abuse as a child, a nameless deaf mute accountant (Werner Pochath from *The Cat O' Nine Tails*) develops a fixation with blood spilling across his skin. Brief flirtations with ketchup and red ink seem to satisfy him at first, but soon he develops a taste for the stuff as well. Though he nurses a weird fascination for a neighbour girl who passes the time by dancing on the rooftop, he remains socially withdrawn with his co-workers and can't even find comfort in the arms of a hooker. One night he breaks into the property of the local coffin-maker and ravages the prettiest female corpse. Now addicted, he habitually raids the tombs of the dead and drinks blood from their throats via a spiked, double pronged glass straw. Authorities and citizens are incensed by the crimes and soon begin to cry for the deviant's own blood.

Shot in a staid and carefully composed style, *Mosquito* succeeds more by the perverse impact of its story than the uneven quality of its special effects; even an eyeball removal that would have been riotous in the hands of Lucio Fulci seems more disturbing here in concept than in execution. The camera often lingers on the blood spilling from Pochath's lips over the bodies of pretty girls, but overall it's more pathetic and weirdly poignant than disgusting. Add to that a determinedly irritating organ score, some strangely effective German village scenery out of a depraved fairy tale, and an oddly anticlimactic yet appropriate ending, and you've got one seriously twisted chunk of Eurosleaze.

The German DVDs from Astro and Marketing Film appear to have the same specifications, offering both the original German and English dubbed soundtracks. While the lack of optional subtitles is regrettable, the English track is serviceable enough despite the flatness of the voices. Image quality is absolutely beautiful, struck from a mint source with exceptionally robust colours. Detail is razor sharp throughout, and no element damage is apparent.

Previous versions (including limited U.S. and Japanese VHS editions) were fairly attractive, but these are by far the most satisfying of them all. Extras are limited to a photo gallery and a newly created "trailer" generated for the video release. Definitely unattractive is Monarex's "Customflix" DVD-R release in the U.S. (as *Bloodlust: The Black Forest Vampire*), taken from a full frame tape master with English and Spanish audio options as well as the trailer.

MULHOLLAND DR.

Colour, 2001, 147m. / Directed by David Lynch / Starring Naomi Watts, Laura Elena Harring, Justin Theroux, Ann Miller, Mark Pellegrino, Lafayette Montgomery, Patrick Fischler, Rebekah Del Rio, Lee Grant, Michael J. Anderson, Angelo Badalamenti / Studio Canal (Blu-ray & DVD) (UK RB/R2 HD/PAL, France R2 PAL), Universal (US R1 NTSC, UK R2 PAL), Starmax (Korea R0 NTSC) / WS (1.85:1) (16:9) / DD5.1

Betty Elms (played by Naomi Watts) arrives in Hollywood with dreams of becoming a famous actress. When she encounters a dark-haired woman calling herself Rita (Laura Elena Harring) and learns of an accident that has rendered her an amnesiac, Betty pledges to help Rita determine her true identity. Events take a dark turn when Rita reveals she believes someone is trying to kill her. But is everything really as it appears to be?

There's so much going on here that constructing a coherent *précis* that doesn't uncharitably mar the dramatic twist lurking in the shadows of *Mulholland Dr.* is all but impossible. Understanding a David Lynch film is rarely less than a challenge to the little grey cells, though as any acolyte worth his mettle will attest, probing between the lines is all part of the pleasure to be derived from his work: If it's too linear then it just isn't Lynch. This time, however, he taunts audiences with his most elaborate conundrum yet. Rooted amidst the turmoil of unrequited love, played out against a backdrop where almost everything is something other than it first appears, this is also a twisted sideswipe at Hollywood and its avaricious, self-serving machinations, depicted via the tale of a wannabe actress who experiences the clash between the naive notion of what life in Tinseltown must be like and the harsh reality it accords those for whom aspiration has soured. As the story progresses and suddenly, unpredictably, veers off at a tangent that throws into question everything to which Lynch has had us bear witness, *Mulholland Dr.* becomes a metaphor for the decimation of the archetypal Hollywood Dream of fame and fortune. Anyone approaching it with expectations of having everything spelled out for them and a smiley-smiley payoff is in for a rough ride. A fundamental failure to comprehend the enormity of Lynch's audacity with the aforementioned change of direction at the two hour mark – and the truth as to what's really been going on then being wheeled out in a nimble effusion of information – has had audiences departing the experience scratching their heads and dismissing Lynch's masterpiece as nonsensical tosh. It certainly helps to know that it was forged from an aborted U.S. TV series pilot. As such, what Lynch salvaged and stitched together – blending in some later lensed material to expand the proceedings – is cunning yet some distance from the original vision.

Naomi Watts is nothing short of dazzling as the wide-eyed, devoted innocent and it's hard not to fall just a little bit in love with her; as such, having to deal with the darker side of her psyche when events change direction is very distressing. Laura Elena Harring is a mite less convincing but deliciously provocative as the object of Watts's motherly instincts and libidinous desires. Justin Theroux's self-absorbed movie director and Ann Miller's busybody landlady together provide the predominant support. But there are a myriad of characters (who one assumes were destined for greater things when *Mulholland Dr.* was set to be a TV show) strolling in and out of the tale who leave you wanting to know so much more; Mark Pellegrino's hitman, Lafayette Montgomery's quietly menacing "Cowboy", Patrick Fischler's nightmare-plagued young man, Rebekah Del Rio's nightclub singer, Lee Grant's psychic, and Michael J. Anderson's human embodiment of a corrupt Hollywood, to name but a half dozen. Lynch regular Angelo Badalamenti (who cameos in the film as a mob boss cum coffee connoisseur) submits a score steeped in seductive, brooding menace.

It may seem trivial – indeed in the scheme of things one supposes it is – but the fact that David Lynch chose to digitally obscure the lower half of Laura Elena Harring's brief frontal nude shot for home viewing means that *Mulholland Dr.* is regrettably currently unavailable to collectors in its original form. The R1 disc is a bare bones affair, with only the theatrical trailer and some textual information on the director and his cast by way of accompaniment. The aforementioned anomaly notwithstanding, the presentation of the movie itself – devoid of chapter punctuation (another Lynch importunity) – is without fault. Language and subtitle options are provided in English and French. Lynch's ten clues to understanding the film are accessible as a hidden feature by selecting the first option on the Special Features page, clicking left to highlight a blue key, and hitting the enter button. It's a bit of a superfluous feature since the clues are printed on the inlay card anyway. The first R2 British release, though also without chaptering, offers a little bit more in the way of extras. There's a selection of brief interviews with Lynch, Watts, Harring and Theroux (though most are of the mutual back-slapping variety), and again you get a trailer. It's worth noting, however, that a brighter picture than that on the American release – where the modified shot of Harring gives the impression her crotch is cast in shadow – renders the tampering insultingly conspicuous and leaves her with the anatomically void appearance of a Barbie doll. Studio Canal's R2 French 2-disc Special edition and Optimum's reissue in the U.K. fare better, though they too have their faults. On the second disc there's some lengthy behind the scenes material complemented with on-set interviews, a few location stills, some footage from the Cannes Film Festival press conference, and interviews with producer Mary Sweeney and composer Angelo Badalamenti (who performs a splendid piano rendition of the film's love theme). All these supplementary elements are in English (except for Sweeney, who speaks French and English for separate interviews) but with burnt-in French subtitling for the SC disc. Of equal interest, and to hurl further indecision into the fray, there's also a Region Free Korean disc. The unique facet of this little number is that it's the only version to date to employ decent chapter encoding, there being a total of 20 breaks. (The Optimum reissue has six random chapter breaks, which can only be employed from the menu screen at Lynch's perverse request.) Picture quality on the feature is acceptable, though it's probably the least impressive of the four releases reviewed here, and Miss Harring's big moment remains unsurprisingly obscured. Sound is in English 5.1 surround and there's optional subtitling in English and Korean. A nice assembly of extra features comprise short interview segments with the director and his players, a short – and definitely excess to requirements – collection of "highlights" (why not just pick your own and revisit them in the film itself?), a very scant slideshow gallery of still images, a trailer (with burnt-in Korean subs), and a music video of the toe-tapping "I've Told Every Little Star" performed by Linda Scott and set to a montage of rapid-fire clips from the film. To round things out there are

cast and crew profiles and production notes, though only of use to those able to read Korean. To complicate things even further, Studio Canal's Blu-ray edition (Region B only) features audio in English, French and Italian (with subtitles in Dutch, French or Italian) and a different slate of extras (most shot in HD) including a Thierry Jousse intro, a cryptic "In the Blue Box" featurette about the making and meaning of the film (featuring *Donnie Darko*'s Richard Kelly of all people), "On the Road to Mulholland Drive" (23 mins., incorporating interview footage kept separate on the prior releases), the Sweeney and Badalamenti interviews with an audio-only bonus Badalamenti track, a "Back to Mulholland Drive" critical appraisal featurette with Lynch, and a booklet containing photos and Adam Woodward's liner notes. The actual HD transfer isn't an earth-shaking improvement, but it does sharpen and boost the picture in the right places and makes for a modest upgrade.
– TG

MURDER AT THE BASKERVILLES

B&W, 1937, 65m. / Directed by Thomas Bentley / Starring Arthur Wontner, Ian Fleming, Lyn Harding, John Turnbull, Lawrence Grossmith, Arthur Goullet / Alpha (US R0 NTSC)

This is a U.S. retitling for *Silver Blaze*, the last of five films in which the elderly but spirited Arthur Wontner plays Sherlock Holmes. Taking one of Arthur Conan Doyle's favourite stories – an early example of the murder that turns out to be an unusual accident – the film elaborates logically on the case to make it a sequel to one famous adventure while beefing up the villainy by yoking in a pair of major scoundrels from "The Final Problem" and "The Empty House".

Holmes and Watson are invited to the West Country by Sir Henry Baskerville (Lawrence Grossmith) to commemorate the twentieth anniversary of the *Hound of the Baskervilles* case, and are drawn into a new mystery when Sir Henry's putative son-in-law seems liable to be in the frame for murders connected to a big horse race and the disappearance of the hotly-fancied favourite, Silver Blaze. In an imaginative twist which might have done well for a series of its own, Professor Robert Moriarty (Lyn Harding) has set himself up as a shadow of Holmes, a consulting criminal mastermind hired by nefarious types (in this case, a dodgy bookie) to solve their problems. Moriarty even has a "Watson" in the form of sidekick Colonel Moran (Arthur Goullet), though it seems that merely fixing a horse race is a little below the standard of perfidy we expect from the Napoleon of Crime, even if he does get to commit a murder with powdered opium slipped to a victim in a curry. Like most of the Wontner Holmes movies, it's a low-budget effort and creaks even for its vintage (the integration of racing footage is especially poor) but is redeemed by spirited playing and patches of authentically Doylean dialogue (though the famous exchange about "the dog in the night" is muffed in a bland rewrite).

Alpha's print sounds better than their other Holmes releases, with the odd tiny drop-out but none of the persistent crackle and distortion that mars their issues of *The Triumph of Sherlock Holmes* and *The Sign of Four*, however the battered, blurry print suffers a great deal from flaring whites.
– KN

MY KINGDOM

Colour, 2001, 112m. / Directed by Don Boyd / Starring Richard Harris, Lynn Redgrave, Tom Bell, Emma Catherwood, Aiden Gillen, Louise Lombard, Paul McGann, Jimi Mistry, Lorraine Pilkington, Colin Salmon / Tartan (UK R0 PAL) / WS (1.85:1) (16:9) DD 2.0

This fits into two early turn-of-the-century trends: the renaissance of the British gangster movie and the tendency to dress up Shakespeare plots in modern apparel. Set in Liverpool, this is a close adaptation of *King Lear*, which writer-director Don Boyd tidies up a bit by emphasizing the first reel death of Mandy Sandeman (Lynn Redgrave), wife of gangland patriarch Sandeman (Richard Harris), in a random mugging her hardman husband can't believe isn't part of a plot, thus providing a root cause for the tragic hero's descent into madness beyond just not thinking through the characters of his three daughters. There's a stroke of cleverness in making the gangster one of those crime bosses who has put all his holdings in his wife's name, making it credible that he can so easily be put out on the streets when his nastier daughters get on his case.

Harris, who sadly never gave his real Lear, is fine in the Liverpool Irish early sections, grown into a complacent solitaire-player living in a restored old house outside the city, sure enough of his own untouchable power to take and make mobile phone calls during a concert in Liverpool Cathedral and making credible wrong moves in the aftermath of the disaster; however, he doesn't quite rise to the challenge of the mad scenes, which might be down to the impossibility of finding contemporary language for the soliloquies.

At its best, the film offers a range of interesting actors chances to reimagine the familiar characters: Regan/Kath (Louise Lombard) is an ex-model who has become the scheming madame of a slightly preten-tious but still tatty brothel; Goneril/Tracy (Lorraine Pilkington) is a hair-extended celeb slut who owns a football team and is married to a vicious Sikh (Jimi Mistry) who takes off his turban whenever he tortures anybody (when a victim asks if it isn't a sin to expose his hair, he agrees and says 'that's the point');

and Cordelia/Jo (Emma Catherwood) is the Michael Corleone figure, an ex-junkie who has become a straight student and wants to stay out of the business, even though the mother's will has left everything to her. There's an untidy MacGuffin about cows with golfballs in their stomachs and an incoming drugs shipment, but this is mostly about the fall-out as the crime family collapses. It has some good, big scenes: a wake for the dead mother as the nastier daughters compete, with Tracy one-upping Kath's speech of remembrance by delivering a horrible karaoke take on "Mandy". An interesting gloss on *Lear* is that this is about a father figure who is only a benign influence in his imagination: his criminal empire has wrecked his whole city – to the point when the son of an old friend is a junkie mugger who kills casually – as well as warped his family, and so his downfall has a political dimension rarely acknowledged in Shakespeare productions but definitely rooted in the original text.

The DVD has a scene-specific commentary from Boyd, who is unusually willing to delve into thematic material as well as recount anecdotes about his on-set clashes with the peppery Harris. Also: the trailer, video screen tests for the actresses cast as the daughters, notes by Michael Dwyer and a fifteen-minute making-of with soundbites from the whole cast, which sometimes make an amusing contrast with the revelations in the commentary – Boyd admits that Harris and Lombard didn't get on, but Lombard blithely refers to the star's prickliness as 'refreshing'. The sleeve and the commentary promise deleted scenes, including the mugger's ear being fed to a pig, but they don't seem to have made the cut on the disc.

– KN

MY LITTLE EYE

Colour, 2002, 84m. / Directed by Marc Evans / Starring Jennifer Sky, Kris Lemche, Laura Regan, Stephen O'Reilly, Bradley Cooper / Momentum (UK R2 PAL), Universal (US R1 NTSC) / WS (1.85:1) (16:9) / DD5.1

As if the reality TV craze with the likes of *Big Brother* and *Survivor* were not frightening enough, along comes *My Little Eye*, which takes the inherent cutthroat aspects of those type of shows to their natural conclusion. While the similar *Series 7: The Contenders* and *Kolobos* (and by extension, *The Blair Witch Project*) already mapped out most of this territory, this UK-financed production with American and Canadian actors combines the reality TV format with slasher movie conventions, resulting in a sometimes effective but often frustrating exercise in pop culture commentary.

The set up takes place in a matter of seconds; three twentysomething men and two women are chosen to stay in a remote house for six months, monitored 24 hours a day by a multitude of webcams constantly broadcasting their movements. Now nearing the end of their voluntary tenure, the residents have become weary and anxious in their grim, snowy environment. (Exactly how this is supposed to be entertaining is anyone's guess, as there was only one brief sexual tryst during the whole ordeal and none of the participants are exactly charismatic.) Things get nasty when Emma (Laura Regan) starts noticing menacing messages and bloody objects left in her bed, and while perpetually cynical Rex (Kris Lemche from *Ginger Snaps*) falsely absorbs much of the blame, the others even become more worried. Events become even more mysterious when a studly skier (*The Hangover*'s Bradley Cooper, looking disconcertingly boyish) turns up one night and promptly hops into the sack with busty Charlie (Jennifer Sky), leaving the emotionally unstable Danny (Stephen O'Reilly) more desperate than ever for support. Of course, it's not long before people start dying off... but who's the guilty party? And what's this website really all about?

M

The opening hour of *My Little Eye* is undeniably effective, making excellent use of the wintry setting and the characters' isolation to breed an atmosphere of unease. Unfortunately most of that hard work goes out the window once the film shows its hand, resorting to that old standby of an unkillable slasher villain running around and turning the cast into ground beef. The murders in and of themselves are executed well enough, but the sudden torrent of gore at the end really throws the entire film off balance and leaves a nasty taste in one's mouth. The final moments aim for a deep, meaningful commentary on the predatory nature of modern viewership, but it's a trite, all-too-obvious ploy and was already done better (believe it or not) in the similar "Sick Room" episode of *Cradle of Fear*. The ultimate explanation behind the website is also frankly absurd; try looking back at the rest of the film and figure why on earth they needed *half a year* to accomplish what could have easily been done in a week. In short, once you learn who the villain is, turn the film off and write a better ending in your head.

At least one can't fault the two-disc U.K. DVD set, which takes the digital webcam concept and runs with it. The film can be viewed in either "standard" or "interactive" modes, the latter of which juxtaposes deleted footage within the frame of the film to show what other characters are doing during pivotal events. The same scenes are also accessible in the deleted scenes section for those who want a straightforward viewing experience. The video quality varies of course depending on the camera used, so the images range from pin-sharp to deliberately grainy and muddy. Particularly effective are the green-hued night vision scenes, in which characters' eyes glow like a cat's in the dark. It's a simple but unnerving device and arguably the most memorable thing in the film. The 5.1 audio is fairly spare but uses the surround speakers for a few beautifully executed jolts, such as the scene with a bird in the attic. There's also some highly ill-advised industrial music during the climax, for what it's worth. Naturally there's also a commentary track with Welsh director Marc Evans and producer Jon Finn; they're good natured and offer a few anecdotes about the shooting process, but there's nothing especially eye-opening (ahem) going on. The second disc includes the aforementioned deleted scenes, a half-hour "Making of" featurette (whose highlight is unquestionably a look at the film's test screening on 9/11), a teaser and standard theatrical trailer (both very similar), four TV spots, and a small gallery. (The much later U.S. release carries the extras over onto a single disc, oddly enough, while jettisoning the interactive viewing option.) Worth checking out for horror fans and technology buffs, but don't buy into all the hype.

MYSTERIOUS ISLAND

Colour, 1961, 101m. / Directed by Cy Endfield / Starring Michael Craig, Joan Greenwood, Beth Rogan, Herbert Lom, Percy Herbert, Gary Merrill, Dan Jackson / Columbia (US R1 NTSC, UK R2 PAL) / WS (1.85:1) (16:9)

 Of all the wonderful Saturday matinee pictures made by producer Charles H. Schneer and special effects genius Ray Harryhausen from the 1950s to the 1970s, this is the one that most reminds me of Bart Simpson's enraptured reaction to the Broadway musical version of *Planet of the Apes*, "this show has everything!" An American Civil War prisoner-of-war escape, a storm-tossed trip by balloon, enemies who band together to survive on a South Pacific island paradise, a giant crab, washed-ashore beauty Joan Greenwood, a giant flightless bird, a spooky cave with a suicide's skeleton, Beth Rogan in a goatskin minidress, giant bees, Herbert Lom as Captain Nemo in a diving suit made of huge seashells, a

cavern containing the famous Nautilus, the lushly upholstered interior of the fabulous submersible, an exciting Bernard Herrmann score, pirates, a ruined underwater civilization, a giant genuine nautilus (a kind of mollusc-shelled squid), escape from an exploding volcano. What's not to love?

Jules Verne's novel *L'île mystérieuse* is primarily a sequel to *20.000 lieues sous les mers*, though it was also an early instance of the *Frankenstein Meets the Wolf Man* double sequel in that it picked up a story thread from *Les enfants du capitaine Grant*. Fans of the 1962 Disney film *In Search of the Castaways* will recognise the skeleton in the cave as that of Tom Ayreton, the marooned character played by George Sanders (apparently, Nigel Green was cast in the flesh for this role but his scenes were deleted or never filmed). After the Richard Fleischer smash *20,000 Leagues Under the Sea* and the fortuitous expiry in 1955 of the international copyright on Verne's work, the French author became among the most-adapted of the '50s and '60s and so had enough commercial cachet to warrant a possessory credit; technically, the onscreen title might well be *Jules Verne's Mysterious Island*. The multi-authored screenplay – by John Prebble (*Culloden*), Crane Wilbur (*The Bat*) and Daniel Ullman – evidently went through several rethinks; Harryhausen conceived his trademark monster sequences on the assumption that the nameless island would be home to prehistoric creatures (that bird isn't a giant chicken but a phrocasaurus) but it was then decided that Captain Nemo had been experimenting with *Food of the Gods*-style growth hormones to solve world hunger and thus do away with war.

Whatever, all kids cared about was that the island had monsters! Responding to criticism that previous Schneer-Harryhausen Dynamation features suffered from slackness between the monsters, the team hired McCarthy exile Cy Endfield (*Hell Drivers*, *Zulu*) to handle the direction. The monster scenes still feel like musical numbers spaced throughout a plot that could actually work without them, but the action is non-stop, with a genuinely thrilling balloon escape and good Robinson Crusoe business. Though Percy Herbert's Confederate accent is on the shaky side and the lovely Rogan is justifiably discouraged from saying anything at all, the performances are mostly just what you want: Michael Craig is a stern and resourceful commanding officer (with a pretty good Yankee accent) mildly clashing with Lom's bleached blond humanitarian megalomaniac genius, the wonderfully breathy Greenwood impresses as the resourceful 'best shot in the county' (though, sadly, her rifle misfires on her one chance to be a monster-fighter), Gary Merrill delivers the necessary grumbling as a shipwrecked civilian war correspondent (with far less ham than Henry Hull in the equivalent role in *Master of the World*) and Dan Jackson (*Naked Evil*) is a solid presence as one of the first black characters in adventure cinema to be a regular hero rather than comedy relief (the sort of attitude that got Endfield exiled?).

Columbia TriStar Home Entertainment's "Ray Harryhausen Signature Collection" DVD has "digitally mastered audio and anamorphic video", with 28 chapter-stops and 16:9 widescreen augmentation. The source print has a few grainy moments, but this is almost certainly down to the original elements: note the slight variations in image quality between scenes with and without effects. Some stock shots of tropical birds are so gorgeously flawless they make more-than-acceptable scenes in which they appear seem almost shabby. The extras include the "This Is Dynamation" featurette and the 55-minute documentary "The Harryhausen Chronicles" as seen on other discs in this series, plus a nine-minute illustrated chat from Harryhausen specifically about the making of this picture, galleries of stills, posters and production drawings and trailers for *Mysterious Island* and a pair of Sinbad movies.

– KN

MYSTICS IN BALI

Colour, 1981, 85m. / Directed by H. Tjut Djalil / Starring Ilona Agathe Bastian, Yos Santo / Mondo Macabro (UK R0 PAL, US R0 NTSC) / WS (2.35:1) (16:9)

While vacationing in Indonesia, Kathy, an American girl, decides to author a book on obscure black magic customs and rituals. Making the logical assumption that the best way to unlock their deepest secrets is to learn the dark arts themselves, she turns to her new boy-toy Mahendra for assistance. He informs her that the most powerful local sorcery is known as Leák magic, but warns "a Leák master can change his form at will into anything he wishes, like say an animal. Or a tree." Kathy shortly begins studying under an ancient female practitioner, but after several lessons her blood offerings are no longer payment enough. Needing the fluid to regenerate strength and regain youth, the haggard witch tricks her naïve apprentice into unknowingly performing her bidding – by having Kathy's head sever itself from her body and fly around, entrails a-hangin', to harvest more sanguinary sauce in the most nauseatingly unthinkable way possible! Mahendra, noticing a change in his girlfriend's behaviour (yet not too alarmed by the sight of her vomiting up live mice), calls upon his uncle, a powerful mystic, for help, which sets the stage for an astoundingly berserk climactic showdown where someone willingly transforms into an enormous pig-beast. Yes, you read that correctly.

At one point in the film, a character says, "It's kinda weird, isn't it? It's really unbelievable." Truer words were never spoken. Heavily steeped in territorial lore and legends, *Mystics in Bali* is a perfect antidote for those bored with more standard fare and is an ideal introduction to Indone-sia's unique, wonderful and fantastic filmscape. Though technically unpolished, the outing makes up for its flaws with sheer audacity and outrageous exuberance. It's so unlike anything made by rational humans that it's nearly impossible to avoid its grip. Characters wander about purposelessly, and hardly seem to question the illogical situations that unfold. Time leaps forward in fits and spurts, yet no clue is ever thrown to the audience. Major players metamorphose into serpents, fireballs and the aforemen-tioned porcine monstrosities, and then there's the "Penanggalan". Once seen, a floating, disembodied head with dripping internal organs is not easily forgotten, and the indelible image has become justifiably famous. Xenophobes beware, but those searching for the most off-kilter motion pictures on the planet will find multiple reasons to rejoice with this cinematic oddity.

Based on the novel *Leák Ngakak* by Putra Mada (try finding that one at your grocery store), *Mystics* actually had to be filmed on the island of Java because Bali locals were too superstitious to allow the movie's supposedly-authentic rituals to be performed there. For many years, the only known legit issue was in Japan on Sony's Mount Light arm, which was actually a pretty decent release for the time (it was fully letterboxed and uncut, with the framing raised on the screen to accommodate the foreign subtitles). Thankfully, that impossible-to-find tape has now been trounced by Mondo Macabro's typically excellent effort. Working from an original negative, their U.K. disc (the first on the market by a couple of years) features print damage and some mild grain in darker scenes, but reportedly the elements supplied by Rapi Films were borderline rotten, so the fact that *Mystics* survived for a DVD transfer at all is a minor miracle.

In a continuing effort to introduce and educate slightly bent film-fans to alien cultures, Mondo Macabro has essentially crafted a crash-course in Indonesian exploi-tation history with the supplements on this disc, which seems to go in and out of moratorium like the wind. First we're treated to a 23-minute documentary chronicling the heyday of Indonesian weirdness. Superbly put together, this featurette was originally broadcast on Britain's Channel Four as part of Mondo Macabro's well-received television series. Starring a veritable who's who of the country's jaw-dropping genre picture industry, it mixes interviews with star Barry Prima, members of Parkit and Rapi Films, various actresses, special FX creator El Badrun, etc. with clips from several must-see items like *The Warrior*, *The Devil's Sword*, *Black Magic Terror* and more. Outlining the reasons for their local horror boom and discussing all the main movers and shakers, this is an enlightening, engaging and highly entertaining watch. And if you're not drooling at the mouth for these outlandish titles once the piece is finished, you need to get your priorities straight. In case the TV episode leaves you with a few unanswered queries, we next have a pleasing text essay by Pete Tombs filling in any gaps. Mostly concentrating on *Mystics* and its director, H. Tjut Djalil (who later directed the unbelievable *Lady Terminator* and *Dangerous Seductress*), it's a very informative and thoroughly illustrated read. Fans of the company's namesake tome will be thrilled. Also included is a complete filmography for Djalil. We lastly have lengthy and humorous instructions detailing the steps necessary to become a Leák. Perform at your own risk.

While the U.K. disc looks like it was spliced together with masking tape at certain points, the remastered U.S. disc is one of the most astonishing transfers the company has released to date. It drops the Indonesian featurette (which reappeared on their widely available *Lady Terminator* disc) and represents one hefty leap in quality; culled from the original negative and presented with the utmost care, this is a true feast for the eyes and one of the most psyche-delic experiences you'll ever have in front of a television set. The American disc even tosses in a grungy-looking vintage theatrical trailer, too, which is perfect for confounding guests and relatives. Even if you have the old PAL disc, you shouldn't bat a disembodied eye at upgrading for this one.

– BH

NADA

Colour, 1974, 107m. / Directed by Claude Chabrol / Starring Fabio Testi, Mariangela Melato, Lou Castel / Pathfinder (US R1 NTSC), Arrow (UK R2 PAL) / WS (1.66:1) (16:9)

An outlandish change of pace for the normally restrained Chabrol, this action thriller and caustic political study may come as a shock to those expecting another study of domestic murder. The title (which means "nothing", of course) refers to a group of terrorists, led by the charismatic Diaz (Fabio Testi), who use violent force to abduct the American ambassador to Paris (while he's in the company of prostitutes, no less) and hide him away in the countryside at a remote farmhouse. With the police hot on their trail, the terrorists are stunned as the law demonstrates a callous lack of concern for the hostage and seems more intent on turning the media and the general public against the criminals.

Featuring a pair of *giallo* favourites (*What Have They Done to Solange?*'s Testi and *Paranoia*'s Lou Castel) and the always amazing Mariangela Melato (*Swept Away*, Dino De Laurentiis's *Flash Gordon*), *Nada* feels far more like an Italian crime thriller than a Chabrol effort. In fact, if the director's name were taken off the film, you'd be hard pressed to determine who was behind the camera. His usual technical proficiency is well in evidence, of course, but the brutal action set pieces are a marked change of pace. At least unlike some of his other attempts at other genres (see the disastrous *Quiet Days in Clichy*), Chabrol acquits himself admirably here and delivers his message without any undue preaching or head-smacking.

This film was originally released at 134 minutes, and played in that form in British cinemas. It was later shortened to 111 minutes (probably by Chabrol himself), and this shorter version was released on video in the U.K. by Art House. As the U.S. disc from Pathfinder runs 107 minutes, it would appear that it is probably a PAL transfer. If so, it's a great job; in fact this disc is one of Pathfinder's best, with pristine colours and only the mildest print damage. Since the film was co-financed by France and Italy, the result is at least partially looped no matter how you watch it; the disc contains French, English and Spanish language options (with optional English subtitles), though the French one is the most satisfying of the three. The disc also contains a theatrical trailer (in English, for once) and a stills gallery. The Arrow version (also included in their Chabrol box set) fares considerably worse with a dreary transfer and only the French audio track with subtitles.

NAKED CAME THE STRANGER

Colour, 1975, 72m. / Directed by Henry Paris [Radley Metzger] / Starring Darby Lloyd Rains, Levi Richards, Mary Stuart, Gerald Grant, Alan Marlow / VCA (US R0 NTSC)

In 1969, a torrid book called *Naked Came the Stranger* hit the bestseller charts and joined the ranks of tawdry potboilers from the likes of Harold Robbins and Sidney Sheldon. However, the difference here is that the entire book turned out to be a

gag; the author, "Penelope Ashe", was a pseudonym concocted by a group of writers for *Newsday* who each took a turn writing one chapter. Flash forward six years, when veteran softcore director Radley Metzger was looking for a second project to follow up the original story, *The Private Afternoons of Pamela Mann*, which proved to be his first completely hardcore venture under the name "Henry Paris". Returning to the literary roots of his European erotica films, Metzger latched onto the novelized hoax and tweaked it into another of his urbane, visually stylish studies in the human libido. Fortunately it also turned out to be one of his funniest films, a bubbly and fast-paced trifle that plays like Ernst Lubitsch after a hit of Ecstasy.

Radio hosts and film fanatics Gillian (Darby Lloyd Rains) and William Blake (Levi Richards) enjoy a happy (albeit quirky) marriage, except for one catch – he's having an affair with Phyllis (Mary Stuart), their toothy assistant. Gillian even eavesdrops on one of their afternoon love sessions (one of the film's comic highlights), and afterwards at a bizarre costume party during which she meets several old acquaintances, the noble wife decides to do a little sexual sampling herself. Each of Gillian's affairs appropriately divides the film like a book chapter, the most memorable being her encounter with *Score*'s Gerald Grant, which cleverly plays out like a silent film. Henry Paris regular Alan Marlow also turns up for a daring, no-faking sequence in which he's pleasured by Rains on a double-decker bus as they take a sunny tour of New York. The story moves quickly, and while the sex scenes are probably the mildest of the Paris canon, they still generate some palpable heat. Rains in particular gets to finally break loose in a leading role and proves herself to be a delightful comedienne, often looking quizzically at the camera for maximum effect.

VCA's previous Henry Paris titles have been at least as complete as their VHS counterparts (and in one case even longer), but unfortunately *Naked Came the Stranger* runs almost eleven minutes shorter than the tape. The removal of this footage makes no sense; apart from a comical, fully clothed S&M gag in an office, the cuts appear to be random (including an entire sex scene between Phyllis and William that explains the whole "love bunny" thing). Too bad, really, as the image quality is a much better transfer from the same source tape with more robust colour. Extras include a video intro and commentary from Jim Holliday, who puts the film in its historical context and offers some anecdotes involving '70s porn; he's joined by adult film actress Shayla LaVeaux, who doesn't contribute much aside from admiring the fact that she's never had sex with anyone in the cast. Other extras are devoted mainly to the VHS cover art and a gallery of alternative shots, though the connection between these photo sessions and the movie itself is tenuous at best.

NAKED LUNCH

Colour, 1991, 115m. / Directed by David Cronenberg / Starring Peter Weller, Judy Davis, Ian Holm, Julian Sands, Roy Scheider / Criterion (US R1 NTSC) / WS (1.78:1) (16:9) / DD2.0, Optimum (UK R2 PAL), Video Film Express (Holland R2 PAL) / WS (1.85:1) / DD5.1, GCHTV (France R2 PAL), Asmik Ace (Japan R2 NTSC) / WS (1.78:1) (16:9) / DD5.1

When he first adapted another writer's work in 1983, in the shape of Stephen King's *The Dead Zone*, David Cronenberg was accused by more than a few baffled fans of watering down his distinctive vision in service of Hollywood conventions. However, few lobbied this claim against Cronenberg again when he tackled another book, William S. Burroughs's *Naked Lunch*, and produced

one of the more baffling, incendiary studio films of the 1990s. A compatriot of such beat icons as Jack Kerouac and Allen Ginsberg, Burroughs earned some degree of notoriety by shooting his wife in the head during a William Tell-inspired stunt, only to become a counterculture icon until his death in 1997. Since his explicit, free-associative *Naked Lunch* resists adaptation in the traditional sense, Cronenberg solved the problem by integrating elements of the novel into Burroughs's life and other writings, producing a work representative of both men's philosophies.

Exterminator and former addict Bill Lee (*Robocop*'s Peter Weller) lives with his not-always-faithful wife, Joan (Judy Davis), who has a nasty craving for the bug powder her husband uses on the job. Equipped with breath capable of felling cockroaches on the spot, she draws Bill back into a world of addiction and squalor, which climaxes with the aforementioned bullet accidentally fired into her head. As Bill's dependence on the bug powder increases, his ability to discern between reality and illusion crumbles. His typewriter becomes a twitching, metallic insect, and he receives information from visiting roach-like beings who lure him into the Interzone, a Middle Eastern realm populated by odd characters such as icy Tom Frost (Ian Holm) and the peculiar Yves Cloquet (Julian Sands), who has a penchant for young men. Bill's chemical dependence is further aided by the smiling but shifty Dr. Benway (Roy Scheider), whose role in the Interzone may be more significant than Bill at first realizes.

Initially received with a mixture of confusion and condescension, this challenging, uncompromising film's reputation has grown considerably over the past decade or so thanks to Cronenberg's growing filmography, which places it in a much firmer context. Followed by the likes of *Crash* and *eXistenZ*, this is the obvious blueprint for the next phase in the director's career following the mainstream humanist trilogy of *The Dead Zone*, *The Fly*, and *Dead Ringers*. Here the abrasive relationship between flesh and metal, soul and technology, becomes much more symbiotic, offering a complex and sensual depiction of modern evolution (hinted at in the rejected ending of *Videodrome* but only developed here years later). For Cronenberg newcomers, this film is hardly the ideal entry point; it's a deliberately difficult, off-putting film on first viewing, with multiple layers of meaning depending on one's perspective; it's a story of artistic inspiration, battling with personal demons, succumbing to the alluring addictions which plague everyday life, and of course, very strange creatures engaging in grotesque behaviour. As usual Howard Shore accentuates the visuals with a sly, intricate jazz score, memorably introduced during the stylish opening credits. The actors are all top notch, with seasoned pros Davis and Holm walking off with all of their scenes; Weller has the more difficult task of playing a Burroughs surrogate while remaining a solid identification figure throughout the film, and his ability to convey yearning, confusion, and despair with a simple glance serves Cronenberg well.

Though *Naked Lunch* is one of Cronenberg's more visually rich achievements, most of Fox's sparsely distributed prints were poorly struck and failed to fully convey the burnished colour schemes. All of the DVDs offer a more solid viewing option, with the Criterion, Optimum and pricier Japanese discs the best of the lot thanks to their sterling anamorphic presentations. The Criterion release features the original surround audio, while the Japanese and Dutch editions have a retooled, shaky 5.1 mix with fake split surround effects. As far as extras are concerned, completists may want all of the available variants, but the Criterion double-disc set contains the most thorough and financially sensible option. Cronenberg and Weller appear

for an excellent commentary track, which covers the various stylistic choices, the sources used for the screenplay (including Burroughs's "Exterminator"), a solid rebuttal to common criticism about Cronenberg's treatment of Burroughs's homosexuality, and extensive discussion of the symbolism used throughout the protagonist's journey. All of the extras are confined to the second disc, whose major coup is the *South Bank Show* special, "Naked Making Lunch". Featuring on-location footage and interviews with all of the principals, this 48-minute chronicle is essential viewing for Cronenberg fans and offers considerable insight into the elaborate process of bringing Burroughs to the screen. Other goodies include an annexe of promotional material such as the striking theatrical trailer (featuring a Burroughs sound-alike as narrator), an illustrated essay about the special effects by Jody Duncan, a stills gallery, excerpts of Burroughs reading the original source novel, a black and white gallery of Burroughs photos from various points in his life, and a booklet featuring observations from Janet Maslin, Chris Rodley, Gary Indiana, and a piece by Burroughs himself. The more slimmed-down Japanese and French discs feature a Cronenberg commentary, the TV special, and trailer (with the better-looking French set spread over two platters); while most of the other European discs include only the trailer and an 8-minute video interview with Cronenberg. The Optimum version (the most recent of the bunch) contains the commentary and "Naked Making Lunch" special along with a trailer, photo gallery, and video interview with producer Jeremy Thomas.

NEKROMANTIK 2

Colour, 1991, 104m. / Directed by Jörg Buttgereit / Starring Monika M., Mark Reeder / Barrel (US R1 NTSC), J. & B. (Germany R0 PAL) / DD2.0

How do you outdo one of the most notorious, extreme splatter movies ever made? Simple: make an art film. Though still chock full of the usual body bonking and assorted gross outs, this is a far more elegant and polished piece of work than its predecessor, more concerned with a mood of unease and melancholia than spraying bodily fluids (until the last five minutes, anyway).

Beautiful young nurse and fledgling necrophile Monika (Monika M.) steals into a graveyard and digs up the rotting corpse of Rob, our hero from the first film. She takes his congealed remains home and deposits him in the bathtub, where she does some impromptu prep work and dresses him up to pose for homemade photographs. Of course, our happy couple becomes a love triangle thanks to Mark (Mark Reeder), a nice but slightly kinky guy who makes his living dubbing and providing sound effects (!) for hardcore porn films. When she isn't at home spending quality time with deadbeat Rob, Monika goes with Mark to pretentious art films and watches seal brutality videos, occasionally suspending him naked by his feet. The strain soon takes its toll, however, and Monika devises an ingenious and thoroughly perverse solution for the two suitors in her life.

Best known as the film that finally sent the German censors over the deep end (including a well-publicized theatrical raid), *Nekromantik 2* uses its comparatively lavish running time to develop an ambitious and densely textured narrative. While the corpse scenes are naturally gruesome, there's a strong surrealist sensibility at work that keeps it more curious than repellent. Apart from the aforementioned seal scene, an ill-advised attempt to outdo the bunny footage from the original film, Jörg Buttgereit strangely avoids any graphic bloodshed or nasty latex

dismemberments for most of the running time. Of course, he's really just saving it up for the powerhouse finale, which amazingly outdoes Daktari Lorenz's "climax" from *Nekromantik*. The narrative also has a stronger pull in this case, stopping along the way for some humorous and romantic asides before the ironic final scene. Much credit must also go to the alluring Monika M., a terrific lead who should have gone on to do far more work. (She even chipped in on the lyrical music score, along with five other people!)

As with the film itself, Barrel's meticulous DVD outdoes the original in terms of sheer volume. The transfer itself is quite startling for a 16mm film; colours are extremely vibrant and detail is razor sharp. Some minor blemishes pop up along with the occasional rough splice, but most viewers are unlikely to notice. It's a wonderful-looking presentation, even more miraculous than the overhaul performed on the Super-8 first film. The new stereo mix is mostly confined to the music, while the mono original is retained as well; the optional English subtitles are always legible and well written. Buttgereit returns for another commentary along with co-writer Franz Rodenkirchen and the two lead actors; it's a highly enjoyable and informative track, ranging from discussions of the extensive make-up appliances to the censorship hassles to the camaraderie behind the scenes. "The Making of *Nekromantik 2*" is basically a repurposed version of the half hour of making-of footage from the Buttgereit documentary, *Corpse Fucking Art*; the creation of Rob's corpse is especially interesting to watch and makes one very, very sorry for the poor actor, whose ordeal wouldn't be out of place in a *Jackass* episode. Also included: German radio interviews with Buttgereit and Rodenkirchen (with optional subs); "Rise Up" (a heavy metal music video for The Krupps directed by Buttgereit); "Manne: The Movie", an early Super-8 Buttgereit film apparently done as a lark; a reel of outtakes showing bloopers and the crew at work on the set; a huge stills gallery; trailers for the *Nekromantik* films along with *Schramm* and *Der Tödesking*; a hidden peek at a Buttgereit-designed video game; and of course, the usual filmographies. David Kerekes and Buttgereit contribute liner notes to the extensive booklet, and the first 20,000 units include a second bonus disc, a soundtrack CD containing music from both *Nekromantik* films along with extra tracks (cover and alternative versions). The first handful of tracks are in mono, but have no fear; most of the music from both films is in beautiful stereo and would pass as a particularly odd New Age album on its own terms.

Unfortunately the Barrel release went out of circulation (like all their other titles), though Germany stepped in with a 2003 release carrying over the commentary and making-of along with 11 minutes of outtakes, two "I Can't Let Go" music videos, and Buttgereit's short film, "New York/Paris '86" (none with English subs). A 555-piece limited edition containing the soundtrack and a signed (Buttgereit/Manfred Jelinski) postcard quickly went out of stock as well.

NIGHT OF THE DEMON (CURSE OF THE DEMON)

B&W, 1957, 96/82m. / Directed by Jacques Tourneur / Starring Dana Andrews, Peggy Cummins, Niall MacGinnis / Columbia (US R1 NTSC), MediumRare (UK R2 PAL) / WS (1.66:1) (16:9)

Along with Robert Wise's *The Haunting*, this atmospheric horror classic from Jacques Tourneur is the most notable offering from the disciples of suggestive horror pioneer Val Lewton, the producer of such gems as *Cat People* and *The Seventh Victim*. Here the Lewton principle is applied to a sterling adaptation of "Casting the Runes", a short ghost story by M.R. James skilfully

embellished here with additional characters and situations which never betray the tale's literate approach.

Professional sceptic Dr. Holden (Dana Andrews) arrives in England for a conference on psychology and the paranormal, where he encounters his colleague's niece, Joanna Harrington (*Gun Crazy*'s Peggy Cummins). Distraught over the death of her uncle who died under violent and mysterious circumstances, Joanna believes dark forces may be at work. The chief practitioner of evil appears to be Julian Karswell (Nial MacGinnis), an aristocratic dabbler in the occult who resides with his mother at a remote country estate. Holden scoffs at Karswell's contention that the supernatural is a real, powerful entity, even after Karswell craftily passes to Holden a strange runic parchment which marks him for certain death. As uncanny events accumulate and Holden learns that he only has three days left to live, he and Joanna race against time to unlock the secrets behind Karswell's demonic plans.

Though still obscure by mainstream cinema standards, *Curse of the Demon* has acquired a solid fanbase among the horror crowd since the 1970s and is now regarded as one of our most significant horror classics. Obviously its impact on viewers since the matinee monster movie age has been significant, with the film turning up in pop culture references ranging from *The Rocky Horror Show* to Kate Bush's *The Hounds of Love*. No mere matinee programmer, this is one of the classiest and most intelligent terror films around, even with the presence of a controversial demon (a combination of puppetry and a truly horrific monster make up concoction) which may or may not betray the Lewton aesthetic, depending on which accounts one chooses to believe. In any case it's a crackerjack monster design, but the film has bigger scares up its sleeve on both an intellectual and visceral level. One hypnotism scene offers a wonderfully orchestrated jolt, and Andrews's eerie encounters alone in forests, empty hallways, and desolate farmhouses evoke a wonderfully paranoid atmosphere. The production design by Ken Adam (who notably did many of the James Bond films) is an effective blend of British antiquity and striking modernism, especially in a subdued but effective library sequence. Though not the most consistent of directors, Tourneur operates at full throttle with this film and keeps events moving at a fever pitch.

Columbia's DVD offers both the extended British cut of the film (under its original title, *Night of the Demon*), which has circulated with the U.S. title sequence attached through the home video and repertory theatre circuit for years, along with the long unseen shorter U.S. cut, which truncates much of Karswell's character development (and his mother's as well). The film's moderate 1.66:1 framing has usually fared well on video anyway, but the more generous widescreen presentation here adds subtly to the little visual tricks Tourneur plays on his audience. (The film usually screens at 1.75:1 theatrically, at least with U.S. prints, but the more spacious headroom here is welcome.) While both cuts are certainly enough to justify this disc, it's odd that Columbia didn't see fit to include any ancillary materials – not even the theatrical trailer, which has appeared on numerous public domain compilations. The trailer is similarly absent from the 2010 U.K. release on MediumRare, but it does come with a 24-page booklet written by Marcus Hearn.

NIGHT TRAIN

B&W, 1999, 80m. / Directed by Les Bernstien / Starring John Voldstad, Barry Cutler / Synapse (US R1 NTSC) / DD2.0

Most modern film noirs don't really cut it, but then again, most of them don't use Orson Welles's *Touch of Evil* as their jumping-off point either. In the idiosyncratic and often surprising *Night Train* (which is saddled with a wholly unsurprising title), we meet our flawed protagonist, Joe Butcher (John Voldstad, one of *Newhart*'s Darryls), an ex-convict who crosses the border into Tijuana to find the scum who killed his brother. Faster than you can say "Michael Findlay" this booze-sodden amateur detective finds himself embroiled in a nefarious snuff film conspiracy involving a wide array of colourful characters (including a spicy Mexican señorita and dwarves!), back alley crooks, and a few decapitations for good measure.

Beautifully lensed in black and white, *Night Train* admirably captures the look of its '40s and '50s predecessors. Some of the actors are a bit uneven in their roles, but as embodiments of the surrealist noir aesthetic they work well enough. The film also tips completely into German Expressionism at times, evoking such names as Dreyer and Lang while still maintaining an identity all its own. Oddly enough, perhaps the closest spiritual cousin to this film would be the nightmarish *Dementia* (aka *Daughter of Horror*), a delirious stylistic exercise whose DVD would be a perfect co-feature. (Or perhaps *Singapore Sling*, but that's another story.) The completely looped dialogue makes the experience even more otherworldly, and the extravagant lighting and superimposition effects should make this mandatory film school viewing. Fortunately it's also entertaining as hell.

Synapse's DVD lives up to their painstaking standards with a beautifully rendered full frame transfer (as it was originally intended). Blacks are nice and inky smooth, while the textures are exceptionally film-like. FX specialist-turned-director Les Bernstien appears on the audio commentary track and also contributes a music video "prequel", showing the events that led up to the murderous quest in the main feature. A 22-minute demo version of *Night Train* is also included with much of the same cast, though the setting here is Los Angeles rather than the more colourful Mexican locales of the finished feature.

THE NIGHTCOMERS

Colour, 1972, 94m. / Directed by Michael Winner / Starring Marlon Brando, Stephanie Beacham, Christopher Ellis, Verna Harvey, Thora Hird, Harry Andrews / Momentum (UK R2 PAL), Lionsgate (US R1 NTSC) / WS (1.85:1) (16:9) / DD2.0

 "If you really love someone, sometimes you really want to kill them." Given the improbability of the project and the disparate talents involved, it's remarkable and unfortunate that *The Nightcomers* is such a dreary movie. A prequel to Henry James's *The Turn of the Screw*, then as now most familiar to movie fans as the source of Jack Clayton's *The Innocents*, Michael Hastings's script sets out to fill in the enigmatic ellipses of the narrative. Though the film fudges the viewpoint, we are supposed to see through the eyes of the children, Miles (Christopher Ellis) and Flora (Verna Harvey), as they misunderstand the relationship of the couple destined to become the ghosts who will haunt them, Peter Quint (Marlon Brando) and Miss Jessell (Stephanie Beacham). The story climaxes with the deaths of Quint and Jessell, depicted in a sensationalist manner and with some minor voodoo, but there is no sense of characters strong enough to survive after death. The this-is-where-we-came-in ending dramatises the opening of the James story and the arrival of the new governess but has nothing useful to add to the great question of whether the children really are haunted.

Mounted on the scale of a small British horror film, with familiar supporting actors and a country house locale, the picture is made lopsided by the presence of a glowering, gurning Brando as Quint, who tells apparently-improvised anecdotes in a foine oul Oirish brogue and joylessly ropes up a nude Beacham for silly-looking bondage sessions. Michael Winner, never the subtlest of directors, made this when he was still just about taken seriously on the strength of ambitious efforts like *I'll Never Forget What's 'is Name*, though a slide into standing joke status was soon to come with a clumsy succession of lurid, ham-fisted thrillers and comedies. Here he fails to keep a rein on Brando, does notably poorly by the child actors and rivals Jess Franco in the obsessive use of the zoom lens, a gadget that often has the effect of getting closer to a detail while kicking an audience out of the picture. Typical crudities are an exploding frog and an arrow thunking into the top of Quint's skull, which ought to be upsetting but get laughs. Hastings's script has weak patches but is generally better than the performance and direction allow it to be. The only fully creditable participants are Thora Hird and Harry Andrews as the sensible, small-minded housekeeper and the remote Master of Bly, but Beacham is intermittently interesting: she is squashed in all her scenes with Brando, but plays well off Hird. Though this sort of literary in-filling is a fraught exercise, it can work very well – the novels of *Wide Sargasso Sea* and *Mary Reilly* are excellent, and the films based on them underrated. Here, there's a problem with making literal things intended to be horribly nebulous: we come out with more information but less understanding, and the kids are so broadly-drawn that their "corruption" has no dramatic weight.

Momentum's DVD offers a couple of trailers ("Brando. Brutal. Beautiful.") but not the stills promised unless you count the two tiny ones on the sleeve and some shots of Beacham roped up as menu backgrounds. Optional subtitles in German and Dutch are provided. The anamorphic widescreen image is high quality, showing off pretty, misty countryside (you can spot mismatched shots because the actors' breath fogs to a greater or lesser extent within scenes) and Beacham's exposed flesh tones. Added clarity does Brando's flyaway hair no favours, though. The more interesting

Lionsgate disc (released a couple of years later) looks just as good but also contains a fun, rambunctious commentary with Winner, who talks a lot about Brando and makes one wish he could do this for all of his other films, too.

– KN

NIGHTMARE
(NIGHTMARES IN A DAMAGED
BRAIN)

Colour, 1981, 99m. / Directed by Romano Scavolini / Starring Baird Stafford, Sharon Smith, C.J. Cooke, Kim Patterson, Tammy Patterson, Mik Cribben, Candy Marchese, Danny Ronen / Screen Entertainment (UK R2 PAL) / Digital World (Germany R2 PAL)

 Believing homicidal schizophrenic George Tatum (Baird Stafford) to be successfully cured, doctors release him after several years of incarceration in a New York asylum. Tatum is still a very dangerous individual, however, suffering from torturous nightmares and waking flashbacks of a barbarous slaughter that took place when he was a boy. Even as the medical fraternity realizes its mistake, Tatum is embarking on a murderous spree that will take him back to his hometown in Florida and a confrontation with his estranged family.

A cast iron constitution is beneficial if you want to sit through this one-time video nasty without feeling the bile rise on at least a couple of occasions. Romano Scavolini's *Nightmare*, more widely known under the lurid moniker *Nightmares in a Damaged Brain*, is actually a thinly veiled *Halloween* ("the night He came home") clone, though it's nowhere near in the same class. Scavolini sets the tone for what will follow in the very first scene, which finds Tatum waking to discover a severed head beneath his blood-sodden sheets; suddenly its eyes pop open and stare up at him, upon which he wakes for real in the throes of torment over what turns out to have been a recurring nightmare.

Though rather ponderous for the most part – with much of the narrative centred around the mundane lives of Tatum's ex-wife Susan (Sharon Smith), their three children and her new boyfriend (Mik Cribben) – there are sporadic bursts of the most alarming brutality. And yet, for all the blood-letting (which plunders the ultimate obscenity when Tatum turns cannibal and eats a piece of one of his gutted victims) the most unsettling scenes are derived from his epilepsy. With the drugs designed to suppress his psychotic episodes proving worthless, his body convulses and he foams at the mouth like a rabid stoat. Violent seizures in squalid Times Square peep shows do not make charming viewing.

Often seriously underlit (which, intentional or otherwise, enhances the grimy feel of the film as a whole), its strengths are increased immeasurably by unexpectedly natural performances from the unknown cast. Just look at the sequence in which a police officer quizzes Cooke about the death of his best friend; the proceedings adopt an intimidating fly-on-the-wall documentary feel, in total contrast to the laughably scripted and poorly acted scene you'd expect from your average exploitationer. Baird Stafford is a particular standout. A pretty average looking guy, he runs an energetic gauntlet from sweaty, trembling epileptic spasms through to frighteningly calm and calculated acts of violence; the disturbing expression of menace locked in his eyes when he's about to mutilate a jogger (Candy Marchese) is not easy to forget. A word too for C.J. Cooke, nicely brattish as Tatum's over-imaginative son who, when not mining aberrant pleasure out of playing malicious pranks on his babysitter (Danny Ronen), scares his poor mother witless by smothering himself in tomato ketchup and claiming to have been stabbed by a stranger in the street. In essence his behaviour turns the subsequent events into an age old "cry wolf" morality tale, as he loses the trust of everyone around him to the point that, when Tatum shows up and genuine danger rears its head, no one believes him.

The genesis of Tatum's deranged state of mind is hinted at in fleeting flashback as the story unfolds, disclosed in its entirety only at the conclusion (though still without sufficient explanation as to why he acted as he did), when we learn that, as a child, he hacked up his father and a ladyfriend with an axe upon finding them indulging in some harmless S&M sex games. *Nightmare*'s gruesome effects were originally accredited to splatter guru Tom Savini but, although he later denied responsibility for this work, the goods on show are certainly as realistic and repellent as anything you could wish for.

The general negativity of this review will undoubtedly spur curiosity among those as yet unfamiliar with the film. Just be aware that it's as mean-spirited and depressingly sleazy a serving of bilge as ever felt the warmth of a projection lamp. In fact, by the time the credits roll, you may feel like showering to cleanse yourself of the cloying stench from the cesspool of cruel misogyny in which writer/director Scavolini has immersed you. You have been duly warned.

At the time of writing, a top-tier release of *Nightmare* on DVD seems like an elusive beast. The British disc from Screen Entertainment is cut – though not quite as severely as you might anticipate – with variable picture quality that ranges from just about acceptable to outright poor, blacks often being rendered as murky navy blues. The full screen feature is divided by 9 chapters, and there are a couple of galleries of mixed quality stills (mostly poor blow-ups reproduced from promotional materials and various artworks thrown in. Digital World's German disc, also presented fullscreen and split into 8 chapters, is uncut but it's one of the most heinous abuses of the format I've witnessed to date, a truly grotty

transfer, occasionally almost colourless, severely lacking in definition and with the nastier excesses clearly grafted in from a different print that's in even worse shape. True, such quality is nicely in keeping with the grunginess of the movie, but it's a long way from what one has rightfully come to expect of DVD. Shoddy transfer notwithstanding, the fact that the sound is provided as a German dub without an English subtitling option cements its already questionable acquisition value. In America, Code Red obtained the rights to the film and kept it on their announcement list for years (as well as including the trailer on almost all of their horror releases); the transfer they have is definitely several huge steps up from any other video version, but the best surviving print still has that banged-up, "grindhouse" appearance, especially in the touch-and-go opening reel. The finished product was not pressed at the time of this review, but it's slated to include interviews with Baird Stafford and FX artist Cleve Hall; Scavolini was also interviewed, but the task of preparing the 90-minute, Italian-language chat for a more digestible, format-friendly presentation left its fate in jeopardy.

– TG

THE NUDE PRINCESS

Colour, 1976, 92m. / Directed by Cesare Canevari / Starring Ajita Wilson, Tina Aumont, Luigi Pistilli / Mondo Macabro (UK R0 PAL) / WS (1.85:1) (16:9)

A major problem for this oddly solemn Italian satire/sexploitation item is that its storyline can't compete in strangeness with the real-life inspiration. In the early '70s, President Idi Amin was so ticked off by a former fashion model-turned-politician who refused his offer of a job in his administration because it would also mean becoming his mistress that he cooked up a scandal story that she had sex in the toilets of Orly airport. Amin insisted it run on the front page of the *Uganda Times*, complete with doctored nude photographs. In this loose dramatisation of the anecdote, Princess Mariam (Ajita Wilson) of "Taslamia" actually does have sex in an airport toilet at the climax, in a scene played seriously as a romantic moment with a journalist (Luigi Pistilli) who has done the right thing in not publishing photographs taken of the woman at an orgy. Thus, the film weirdly collaborates with Amin in tarnishing the reputation of its heroine even as it insists she's an admirable figure. Adding to the mixed signals sent out by a film which never settles on a tone is the casting in the lead of Wilson (billed simply as "Ajita"), a voluptuous, striking but somehow asexual black American actress who is alleged to have been born a man.

Though it takes pot-shots at hypocritical, lecherous middle-aged white politicians and the unethical behaviour expected of the Italian press ever since Paparazzo in *La dolce vita*, *The Nude Princess* is essentially another variant on the "Emmanuelle" formula in which a beautiful woman explores her sexuality in a variety of ways couched for titillation – including mild lesbian clinches with co-star Tina Aumont, lingering shower scenes and a very bizarre orgy involving another black woman and her studly midget lover. Wilson and Aumont model a succession of fab outfits, and Wilson experiments with blue and orange feathery afro wigs, while the soundtrack burbles horrible 1970s Europop until your resistance is worn down. Whatever turns the film takes, it can't manage to square a grim dramatisation of Amin-style atrocities as an African leader is seen personally executing a roomful of rebels with bubble-headed comic nonsense about the goings-on in Rome as the princess whips everyone around her into a sexual frenzy without ever changing her

own expression. In the climax, director Cesare Canevari zooms into the heroine's impassive face in the hope of catching a tear that never comes.

Rarely seen in English language territories, the film is given respectful treatment by Mondo Macabro's DVD, which showcases a fine if not lustrous transfer of an Italian-language print (on-screen title: *La princesa desnuda*) with optional English subtitles. The significant extra is "Ten Years in Another Town", an interesting interview featurette with the diffident but charming Tina Aumont, covering her entire Euro-career – though she doesn't seem to have especially vivid memories of this particular gig and expresses only mild surprise at the possibility her co-star in intimate scenes wasn't always a woman. Also: extensive, informative notes on the film and its stars.

– KN

NUTBAG

Colour, 2000, 69m. / Directed by Nick Palumbo / Starring Mack Hail, Renee Sloan / Hardgore (UK R2 PAL), Screen Entertainment/Frightflix (US R1 NTSC)

"Death has been with me ever since I was born." A maudlin, tedious shot-on-video home movie with delusions that it might attain *Henry: Portrait of a Serial Killer*-dom, *Nutbag* spends ten days in the company of a misogynist ("these whores always bleed a lot"), racist, and philosophical ("If I could kill everybody, I wouldn't have these problems") mass murderer (Mack Hail). The bald, big-bearded narrator lives in Las Vegas with his only friend (Heinrich, a dead spider), models of Norman Bates and the Phantom of the Opera and Jack the Ripper-related memorabilia, delivering a non-stop inner monologue between scenes with porno-look harsh women (mostly prostitutes) who tend to end up bloodily naked. The sort of picture shit can look down on, this has that crisp, bright camcorder look you associate with boring holiday videos, and alternately droning or shrill dialogue. The Vegas setting evokes memories of Ray Dennis Steckler, but even the dullest of his efforts has more going for it than this plodding endurance test.

The U.K. release is evidently heavily-cut, but nine minutes of extreme gore would only make it nine minutes longer. Upset at the cutting, the director reclaimed the rights to the film and briefly sold it directly through his own website along with the uncensored version of his subsequent *Murder Set Pieces* (which was heavily trimmed by Lionsgate in the States); however, after an attempt to auction off rights to *Nutbag* and the entire site itself, the film seemed to disappear completely. Not that anyone noticed.

– KN

ONCE UPON A TIME IN THE WEST

Colour, 1968, 165/170m. / Directed by Sergio Leone / Starring Henry Fonda, Claudia Cardinale, Charles Bronson, Jason Robards, Gabriele Ferzetti, Frank Wolff, Woody Strode, Al Mulock, Jack Elam / Paramount (UK R2 PAL, US R1 NTSC, Germany R2 PAL), Italy (CVC R2 PAL) / WS (2.35:1) (16:9) / DD5.1

Once Upon a Time in the West is *The Good, the Bad, the Ugly and the Blonde*. Made after Sergio Leone's lauded "Dollars" trilogy of Italian westerns with Clint Eastwood, this ambitious film is a true epic. Like *High Noon*, the film opens with three caricature bad men (bald, black Woody Strode, scurvy,

beardy Al Mulock and lazy-eyed, sneering Jack Elam) waiting for a train, larger-than-life figures in a stark, desolate, unpeopled landscape. Nearly three hours later, as the film closes, the West and Westerners have changed. The sole survivor (sadly, now in real life also) is Jill McBain (Claudia Cardinale), the ex-whore from New Orleans, last seen at another, different railway station, taking water to the crowds of honest, hard-working, unindividuated labourers toiling, now the shooting is over, to make a town ("Sweetwater") and a future. The left-leaning script, from a story by future directors Bernardo Bertolucci and Dario Argento, loves these decent folk, but isn't about them. Before the town can be built, blood has to be shed.

It takes an hour to get the four main characters (and their memorable Ennio Morricone leitmotifs) introduced, an almost ridiculous exaggeration of the scene-setting of earlier Leone westerns. We spend more than ten minutes with the doomed badmen, watching them cope with dripping water and buzzing flies, before a train chuffs in and pulls out, leaving them face to face with a mystery man, Harmonica (Charles Bronson). In a gag at the expense of Leone's work with Morricone, the opening titles play over natural sound. When the expected theme comes in, the characters in the film hear it – a joke done more elaborately in *Blazing Saddles* – and they swiftly learn the newcomer is as fast with a gun as he is slow with the mouth organ.

The next set-up also brings on characters who don't last long, the family of Brett McBain (Frank Wolff). An outdoor reception is being set up for McBain's new bride, but snipers cut down Brett, his older son and daughter. The younger son, a six-year-old, peers up at the duster-clad killers who stalk out of the wilderness. We see, in astonishment, that blue-eyed Henry Fonda, established as a paragon of Western decency in John Ford movies, is playing

Frank, the cold killer whose first on-screen act is to shoot dead the little boy (later, to confirm his dastardly status, he kicks a cripple's crutch).

Jill shows up at a nearby station and, en route to the homestead, is taken into a dingy bar where she meets the fourth major character, Cheyenne (Jason Robards), a whiskery, life-loving outlaw in the spirit of Eli Wallach's Tuco, and the plot finally kicks in. Frank is working for Morton (Gabriele Ferzetti), the crippled railroad tycoon ("You leave a slime behind you like a snail, two beautiful shiny rails") who is building a coast-to-coast line, and has killed McBain because the man owns a parcel of land which will become a watering station. Frank's gang are wearing those distinctive long coats because they're associated with Cheyenne's bunch, and the outlaw can conveniently take the blame. Harmonica is looking for Frank, intending to avenge (as it turns out) the murder of his brother in a flamboyantly horrid manner revealed in a flashback during the final face-off. He hooks up with Cheyenne and Jill to foil Morton's schemes on the principle that Frank's pretensions to becoming "a business-man" have to be shredded before he can be lured into the Leone-trademarked widescreen duel.

Most westerns we take seriously are novelistic, offering character as well as landscape and unusual or archetypal plotting. Leone's films are more like panoramic paintings – the people are deliberately vague or cartoonish, characterized as much by their clothes and surroundings (Morton's ornate railroad carriage, equipped with a climbing frame the dying man can use to get about) as what they say and do. It's a difficult approach, and Leone found it harder to hit on subjects worth making – he directed only two films in the remaining twenty years of his life – but here it pays off with scene after scene of pictorial beauty invested with real emotion (for which Morricone can take a lot of credit).

The "Dollars" films invented the "spaghetti western", but this is something different. Here, the plains of Spain are augmented by sequences shot in the very homeland of the American western, Ford's beloved Monument Valley, and the iconic Eastwood is set aside in favour of a walking embodiment of the Hollywood West who is not so much cast against type as is allowed to reveal the cruelty and ruthlessness that was always a part of even his most heroic characters. If Henry Fonda can be a child-killer, then the West is indeed consigned to the "once upon a time".

Among the most eagerly-awaited of all DVD releases, this showcases the transfer fans have been waiting for – the longer international version of the film in shimmering widescreen (enhanced for 16:9) which lends full impact to Leone's long-shots of Monument Valley scenery or bustling crowds of activity but also highlights his ultra-close images as Bronson's beady eyes or Cardinale's luscious pout fill the entire screen. A commentary track is mostly by expert Sir Christopher Frayling, with input from other academics (Sheldon Hall), participants (Cardinale) and enthusiasts (John Milius, John Carpenter) – it's good on the detail, and Alex Cox winningly points out that one scene bizarrely can't be reconciled with what happens before or after it. Disc two has four featurettes which add up to a feature-length documentary (presumably split up for arcane reasons) on the film, which overlaps the commentary slightly but has a wealth of further good stuff, especially from the always-pertinent Frayling, and the elegant Cardinale's undiminished smile. Also included in this definitive package: the trailer, notes on the cast, menu screens with generous selections from the score, stills gallery, comparison shots from the film and contemporary snapshots of the locations. You don't have a DVD collection if you don't own this.

Purists should note that the Region 1 disc is the only release to include the film's original mono soundtrack, and completists should note that the German edition is also available in a wooden box, with a four track Ennio Morricone soundtrack CD and a harmonica in a leather pouch! Incredibly, a slightly longer version of undetermined origin later surfaced from Italian label CVC (in Italian with no other language options); it mainly contains a few minor scene extensions (some longer shots held during the opening sequence, several extended reaction shots throughout, a longer version of the final duel with different music extensions); the one significant restoration is actually the closing shot, which now plays out at its intended length with Morricone's music finally in synch and the closing title card appearing at the correct time. The image quality isn't as good as the earlier releases, but it's an interesting variant for Leone fanatics all the same.

– KN

ONE HOUR PHOTO

Colour, 2002, 96m. / Directed by Mark Romanek / Starring Robin Williams, Connie Nielsen, Michael Vartan, Dylan Smith, Erin Daniels, Gary Cole, Eriq La Salle / Fox (US R1 NTSC, UK R2 PAL) / WS (1.85:1) (16:9) / DD5.1

 As a long serving photo lab technician at the SavMart superstore, Seymour "Sy" Parrish (Robin Williams) is obsessed with perfection in his work. He treats most of his customers with familiarity and their photographs as if they were his own. Over the years he has become particularly fond of regular customer Nina Yorkin (Connie Nielsen) and her family, secretly preparing for himself a duplicate set of prints from every roll of film she's ever brought in. A desperately lonely man, Parrish yearns to be part of the seemingly blissful family life he's witnessed

in the Yorkins' photos. But he's gradually losing touch with reality and when, by chance, he finds out that all is not as happy as he thought within the Yorkin household he takes it upon himself to ensure that the sinful are duly punished.

How often have we heard movies hyped with the promise "[Fill in applicable star name] as you've never seen him before!'"? Although Robin Williams has always punctuated his lightweight output with more serious roles, *One Hour Photo* really does lift him to a new plateau. He doesn't just look different; this is genuinely unlike anything he's ever done. For someone who's traded primarily in saccharine comedy the role of Sy Parrish was certainly a courageous one to undertake. An insular, forlorn man whose only human contact is with his customers, his tragic back-story is only sketchily hinted at as the film closes. At first we're uncertain if we should pity him or feel vaguely disturbed by his unhealthy, if seemingly harmless, fixation with the Yorkin clan. As his sanity begins to uncoil and he learns that Nina's husband Will (Michael Vartan) is playing away from home, Parrish's interest in the well being of the woman and her son (Dylan Smith) turns distinctly sinister. Taking a knife to the thousands of their photographs that fill an entire wall in his house, Parrish carefully obliterates Will's face on every one of them and then sets out with an unorthodox solution to hubby's infidelity. The scenes in which he plays out his sadistic and humiliating revenge on Yorkin and his lover Maya (Erin Daniels) are very upsetting; we feel as uncomfortably sorry that the largely good-natured Parrish has gone off the rails as we do sympathy for his victims. The final intimations of childhood abuse which explain his longing to be part of a happy family are sadder yet.

After a slightly hesitant exit from the starting gate, *One Hour Photo* quickly finds its legs and, though it never exactly breaks into a sprint, it canters along engagingly enough to the distressingly downbeat conclusion. Writer/director Mark Romanek manages to turn the antiseptic, brightly illuminated and bustling SavMart where Parrish works into as lonely an environment as his dimly lit, sparsely furnished home. By contrast the comfortingly warm colour schemes of the Yorkin abode embody everything that's missing from Parrish's life. The script includes some nice little observations – delivered in voice over by Williams – about how one can misinterpret people from their photographs. If one were to judge someone else's life solely from the pictures they take, the evidence would surely suggest that they are euphorically happy. But of course that's far too simplistic a conclusion to draw, as no one would take keepsake photos of the unhappy experiences in their life. Romanek also employs some nicely subtle tricks to convey emotion, for example Nina's reaction to the discovery of her husband's adultery, observed by Parrish (who has planted the evidence for her to find) as her car suddenly brakes hard and veers to one side on the highway. Almost out of place, however, are a couple of ultra-violent bursts, most strikingly when Parrish dreams that his eyes are spurting blood.

Williams unsurprisingly dominates the film, though there's strong support from Nielsen and Vartan. Gary Cole (*American Gothic*) plays Parrish's rightfully distrustful boss at SavMart, while Eriq La Salle (*Jacob's Ladder*) is the police detective smart enough to employ a soft approach when our man is apprehended and brought in for malicious harassment. As with most chillers concerning lonely underdogs, *One Hour Photo*'s mapped out route is a fairly familiar one, with only the mode of vengeance holding any vestige of suspense. But it's nevertheless an above average example of its ilk and Williams is a true revelation. If your feelings towards the hirsute comic are less than benevolent, take a look at *One Hour Photo* and discover a talent you never knew existed.

As the trend for offering collectors both fullscreen and widescreen presenta-

tions of their favourite movies on a single platter decreases, 20th Century Fox's Region 1 DVD provides an either/or option with fullscreen and 1.85:1 widescreen formats selling on two separate discs. The quality on the 32-chapter encoded feature is as faultless as one would expect from such a recent production, with vibrant colours and a striking sound mix. Where the disc is rather light on supplementary material, what is here is largely worthwhile. There's a feature length commentary from Mark Romanek and Robin Williams, a trio of TV spots, a trailer and two featurettes. One runs a little under fifteen minutes and proves to be a standard studio promo piece, the second falls just shy of half an hour and takes an interesting look at the construction of the scene in which an awestruck Parrish meets a distinctly indifferent Will Yorkin for the first time. Less interesting is an episode of U.S. TV's *The Charlie Rose Show*, dominated by the loquacious non-wit of Williams (and Rose's embarrassingly feeble attempts to match him), to the detriment of a quietly bemused Romanek. Language choices for the movie are English 5.1 Surround, and French and Spanish Surround, with subtitling supplied in English and Spanish.

– TG

ONE TAKE ONLY

Colour, 2001, 88m. / Directed by Oxide Pang / Starring Pawarith Monkolpisit, Wanatchada Siwapornchai, Chalermporn Paprach, Tok Payathai / Tartan (UK R0 PAL, US R0 NTSC) / WS (1.85:1) (16:9) / DD 5.1

Oxide Pang shot this lowlife romance before achieving international acclaim with his polished ghost story *The Eye*, and it has more in common with the deglamorised, edgy crime drama

Bangkok Dangerous (co-directed by Oxide and Danny Pang), though it concentrates on a criminal stratum even lower than the deaf hit-man of that picture, who is at least involved in big-time conspiracies and assassinations.

Bank (Pawarith Monkolpisit) is a shaggy street hustler, given to fantasies in which he pays back the various people who get the better of him, but more liable to take a beating than dish out retribution. He falls in with Som (Wanatchada Siwapornchai), a young girl who is trying not very hard to get out of the prostitution business, and they dream together of the lives they might lead if they had enough money to buy mobile phones and some nicer clothes.

Tempted by the myth of the "one big score" that enables crooks to settle down to lead an honest life, the couple get out of their depth in a deal and the film's look gets murkier and more unsettling. Things go wrong, as expected, and the lovers remain losers to the last (needing revenge, Bank buys a gun in a jiffy-bag that turns out to be a toy ripped off an arcade video-game), though their dream is passed on along with a symbolic pair of white shoes to a street urchin.

The early stages of the film have jarring fantasised elements delivered by CCTV shots in which Bank pays back for injuries received, an effect that suggests much of the film is providing a subjective reality – the romantic scenes are lushly-coloured, while the descent into messy crime is signalled by a murky, washed-out look that turns blood to brown and gives the world a sickly, late-night blue tone.

Tartan's Asia Extreme DVD uses a transfer which doesn't flatten out the subtly different visual styles used for various sections. The disc has Thai dialogue, with optional English subtitles. Film-specific extras are filmographies for people who don't have many credits (some have only this one), notes by Justin Bowyer and the trailer, though there is also a batch of cross-promotional trailers for other Tartan

titles. For some unknown reason, their American edition tacks on an additional featurette about the making of a completely different Pang Brothers film, "The Making of *Ab-normal Beauty*".

– KN

PANDORA'S BOX

B&W, 1929, 133m. / Directed by G.W. Pabst / Starring Louise Brooks, Fritz Kortner, Krafft-Raschig, Alice Roberts / Criterion (US R1 NTSC), Second Sight (UK R0 PAL)

 A lasting masterpiece from G.W. Pabst, adapted from Frank Wedekind's *Pandora's Box* and *Earth Spirit*, which created an archetypal character in Lulu, an innocent temptress who is possessed of a forthright sexuality that is capable of ruining the lives of everyone around her. Though Pabst was criticized at the time for casting a foreigner in a role which was considered emblematically German, the reason the film is remembered is the performance of American star Louise Brooks. So powerful and sexual a presence that she never made the transition from silent flapper parts to the talkie roles she deserved in a Hollywood dominated by Shirley Temple, Brooks is the definitive gamine vamp, modelling a sharp-banged bobbed haircut known as a "Louise Brooks" or a "Lulu" to this day.

Presented in distinct, theatrical "acts", the story picks up Lulu in a bourgeois Berlin drawing room, where she is the adored mistress of Dr. Schon (Fritz Kortner), a widowed editor, and friendly with her lover's grown-up son Alwa, even on good terms with the gnomish pimp Schigolch, who is either her father or her first "patron". When Schon announces that he is remarrying, Lulu seems to be passed on to a nightclub strongman (Krafft-Raschig) but, piqued when her lover tells his son that "one does not marry" a woman like her, she sets up an incident backstage at music hall where she is dancing that breaks off the editor's engagement and prompts him to marry her though he knows that it will be the death of him. Schon in effect commits suicide, but Lulu winds up convicted of his murder and on the run with Alwa, Schigolch and her lesbian admirer Countess Geschwitz (Alice Roberts), which takes her to an opium-hazed gambling boat on the Seine where she is almost sold to an Egyptian brothel and Alwa is humiliatingly caught cheating, then finally to a Christmassy London stalked by the heroine's last lover, Jack the Ripper.

Pabst surrounds Brooks with startling secondary characters and dizzying settings (the spectacle in the thronged wings of the cabaret eclipses anything taking place on stage), but it is the actress's vibrant, erotic, scary and heartbreaking personality that resonates with a modern audience. Brooks's mix of image and attitude is so strong and fresh that she makes Madonna look like Phyllis Diller, and her acting style is strikingly unmannered for the silent era, unmediated by the trickery of mime or Expressionist make-up and heart-breakingly honest, never playing for easy sentiment as the audience is forced to recognise how destructive Lulu is even as we fall under her spell. Though the original plays are set in 1888, the year of the Ripper murders, Pabst imagines a fantastical but contemporary setting, which seems to begin with the 1920s modernity of Berlin and then travels back in time to a foggy London for a death scene that is the cinema's first great insight into the mindset of a serial killer as Lulu, turned streetwalker so Schigolch can afford a last Christmas pudding, charms the reticent Jack, who throws aside his knife and genuinely tries not to kill again but is overwhelmed by the urge to stab. This tortured, harrowed murderer prefigures Peter Lorre's *M* by a year or two and is a far more resonant figure than the innocent suspect played by Ivor Novello in Hitchcock's contemporary *The Lodger*. Even more startling, perhaps, is the sympathetic portrayal of the mannish Countess who proves that Lulu's effect isn't limited to the male sex; in Roberts's strongest sequence, she has to make up to the brutish Krafft-Raschig and the movie actually presents forced heterosexuality as more perverse than being honestly lesbian.

Second Sight's DVD offers "the restored and uncut version", which runs significantly longer than most previous releases – presented at the proper speed, with a great deal of tidying-up. Though the source print has the inevitable damage of any film of this vintage, especially one that was forgotten for thirty years after its first release, the transfer is relatively fine. Art deco-look intertitles can be played either in English or German. A major extra is *Looking for Lulu*, an hour-long TCM documentary produced by Hugh Hefner and narrated by Shirley MacLaine, which covers Brooks's whole career, from 1920s success through 1930s failure to her re-emergence in later life as a persuasive writer on film. However, the best presentation is the double-disc Criterion release, which features an even more spotless and impressive transfer, four excellent choices of musical scores (including a highly recommended one by Fassbinder composer Peer Raben), audio commentary by film scholars Thomas Elsaesser and Mary Ann Doane, a 1971 Louise Brooks TV interview, new interviews with documentarian Richard Leacock and Pabst's son Michael, a stills gallery, the *Looking for Lulu* documentary, and a huge insert book featuring Kenneth Tynan's 1979 "The Girl in the Black Helmet" essay and copious other written pieces about Brooks and the film.

– KN

PEE-WEE'S BIG ADVENTURE

Colour, 1985, 91m. / Directed by Tim Burton / Starring Pee-wee Herman [Paul Reubens], Elizabeth Daily, Judd Omen, Alice Nunn, Diane Salinger, Jan Hooks / Warner (US R1 NTSC) / WS (1.85:1) (16:9) / DD 5.1

A unique comedy, this is also part of the 1980s trend for giving comedians a shot at seeing if characters developed over a series of sketches or stand-up routines would work in a feature film. The hits of the form include the Blues Brothers and Wayne and Garth; the misses are too numerous to mention. Pee-wee Herman, a squeaky manchild with a Rupert Pupkin suit and a Tintin forelock, was the alter ego of Paul Reubens, who takes onscreen credit here only as co-writer, giving his persona top billing. The stroke of genius that elevates this from the mire inhabited by *It's Pat* and *Stuart Saves His Family* was the signing of Tim Burton, on the strength of his short films, to make his feature debut. It's now hard to separate the elements of *Pee-wee's Big Adventure* that originate with Reubens (and co-writers Phil Hartman and Michael Varhol) from those contributed by Burton. The director's fans will find many obsessions which recur in later Burton films already here: dinosaurs, Japanese monster movies, toys and tricks, oddly asexual outsiders, *non sequitur* anecdotes (cf: "Large Marge"), fractured fairytales, kitsch Americana, subverted Christmases, even the Batmobile.

The plot motor is Pee-wee's overwhelming love for his shiny red bike, which has more gadgets built in than 007's Aston Martin. When this dream machine is stolen at the behest of Pee-wee's rich fat kid rival, he goes into strangulated overdrive to recover his possession. The childish world never gets too sugary, as Reubens makes his character often as obnoxious as he is innocent, ill-treating those around him (like his would-be girlfriend, played by Elizabeth Daily) and so single-minded in his purpose that he keeps making very bad decisions (like yelling at a bar full of bikers to cut the noise because "I'm trying to use the phone"). On his road trip to the Alamo (a psychic has

told him the bike is in the historic site's non-existent basement), Pee-wee runs into an escaped convict (Judd Omen), a ghost trucker (Nunn), a waitress who dreams of escaping to Paris (Diane Salinger), a biker gang who threaten to kill him but are won over by his impromptu bar-dance to "Tequila" and a hilariously perky Texan tour guide (Jan Hooks). It winds up with a relishable silent movie-style chase sequence on the Warners backlot, as Pee-wee is reunited with his bike and pursued by security guards through various sets. One of the most charming notions is the fantasy that a Hollywood studio in 1985 is simultaneously producing a Godzilla picture, a Tarzan movie, a beach party musical, and a Christmas kiddie spectacular. Presumably, there would have been a western except the film already threw in some rodeo gags and gentle digs at Texas. Full of inventive, lunatic comedy, the movie finds room for its own brand of strange beauty – like a desert sunrise seen from the mouth of a giant plaster dinosaur.

Warner has done a super job on this title. Though not advertised as remastered, the transfer is stellar for a medium-budget picture of its vintage. On the commentary track, Burton mentions that one gag – in which Pee-wee pulls an endless chain out of a compartment on his bike – has been improved by the proper framing of this 16:9 edition; earlier standard aperture video releases showed the chain being pulled up through the prop bike. It has a distinctive colour scheme, with everything as primary-colour bright as a toy, and that familiar mid-80s neon fuzzy look is used to good effect in some of the more fantastical sequences. Besides production notes and the trailer, extras include eleven minutes of deleted scenes (including a pay-off for the boomerang bow-tie purchased but never used in the finished version) on poor-quality standard-frame time-coded video and a same-length look at the production drawings narrated by designer David L. Snyder (an innovation that ought to be copied – giving point to a feature that often falls into the glance-at-and-back-to-the-menu category). The track by Reubens and Burton meanders somewhat, but gives a lot of name-checks for walk-ons (a sobering number of those involved have either died or had great personal tragedies). Another usually-skippable feature made to work here is a music-only track that essentially delivers a full soundtrack album with informative, engaging and pointed comments from composer Danny Elfman ("I look upon Bernard Herrmann as my mentor, though we never met and had we ever met he wouldn't have liked me very much") whenever there's no music on screen; Elfman is refreshingly candid in admitting his influences, not only Herrmann but here especially Nino Rota too. – KN

THE PEOPLE UNDER THE STAIRS

Colour, 1991, 102m. / Directed by Wes Craven / Starring Brandon Adams, Everett McGill, Ving Rhames, Wendy Robie / Universal (US R1 NTSC, Brazil R0 NTSC, UK R2 PAL, Germany R2 PAL, Italy R2 PAL) / WS (1.85:1) (16:9) / DD2.0

In retrospect, it's stunning how much genre films got away with during the Reagan and Bush years. With little fanfare, that era bred such amazingly subversive tracts as *They Live*, *The Stepfather*, *Society*, and from horror's most sociologically conscious chronicler, *The People Under the Stairs*. A surprisingly resonant effort from Craven's most difficult period (in which studio and MPAA interference sabotaged nearly all of his post-*Elm Street* efforts), this imperfect but fascinating study of urban blight decked out as a sick fairy tale was an obvious influence on subsequent films including *Trespass* and *Candyman*.

Our story begins as young Fool (Brandon Adams), distressed by his mom's illness and impending eviction, decides to accompany his sister's boyfriend, Leroy (*Pulp Fiction*'s Ving Rhames), on a quest to swipe some rumoured gold coins from the house of their mysterious, money-grubbing landlords, who hold the entire neighbourhood in a state of poverty and despair. Unfortunately it all goes horribly wrong, and Fool winds up trapped in an elaborate, spooky house filled with booby traps and hidden corridors, hunted down by the insane, inbred brother-sister owners (that memorable *Twin Peaks* couple, Everett McGill and Wendy Robie). He also discovers the titular people under the stairs, the mutilated and rejected survivors of children kidnapped in an attempt to breed the perfect offspring.

Featuring such peculiar images as a shotgun-wielding McGill clad head to toe in black studded leather, this bizarre studio project represents Craven at his most imaginative, scooting off in a different direction every twenty minutes or so. There isn't much in the way of explicit violence, but conceptually this is definitely disturbing material; Craven is obviously ticked off at the current state of affairs (one early suspense sequence uses Bush's bombing of Iraq as television accompaniment) and he gets his licks in with admirable skill. Unfortunately the somewhat over-the-top ending gets a bit too preachy, turning Fool into something of a Robin Hood figure with everyone happy and all the scales tipping back into place. Had Craven followed his thesis logically to the end (either as fairy tale or social criticism), the film should have ended on a darker and more ironic note, at least serving up nastier desserts for its villains. What's here is certainly worthwhile and nowhere remotely as compromised as his other films surrounding it; the dark and claustrophobic photography is generally effective, and the trapdoor-laden house makes for a diverting setting

P

capable of knocking the characters and the plot itself around like a pinball machine. Bonus points for the acting, among the strongest of Craven's films.

If ever a Craven film called out for an audio commentary, it's... well, *The Last House on the Left*, which we already have, but surely this one is high up there, given the director's ability to provide literate and illuminating discussion of his work. Unfortunately you'll only get a trailer if you buy this disc outside the US; in America, you don't even get that meagre bonus. While Universal offers a slick and colourful anamorphic transfer, otherwise this smacks of a thoughtless rush job. Technically there's not much to quibble about; black levels look excellent (vital for a film like this) and the surround audio does the job nicely, showing off the dark score by Don Peake (and Graeme Revell, sort of; check out the soundtrack CD for a full explanation of this film's peculiar music history). If *Shocker* can merit a special edition (in Europe at least), certainly *The Serpent and the Rainbow* and this endearing oddity deserve the same treatment.

PERVIRELLA

Colour, 1997, 91m. / Directed by Alex Chandon / Starring Emily Bouffante [Booth], Eileen Daly, Sexton Ming, David Warbeck / Screen Edge (UK R2 PAL)

You can't fault this near-homemade effort for lack of ambition. With extensive model work, panto-level costumes (and performances) and a breadth of reference that extends beyond the usual Russ Meyer-John Waters sleaze to such '60s efforts as *Barbarella*, Hammer's *She* or even *Dr. Dolittle* and *Chitty Chitty Bang Bang*, it gets by from scene to scene on enthusiasm and oddness, even if the actual

jokes ("Don't chew your food so much, I've warned you about the dangers of excessive mastication") are mostly dire.

In Condom, a version of 19th Century England ruled by a decrepit near-immortal Queen Victoria, a baby girl is born who grows up (quickly) to be Pervirella (Emily Booth), a sex-addicted, pink-haired kitten who takes off with her scientist father, Professor Rumphole Pump, on a trip round the world via dirigible, magic carpet and submarine in search of the elixir which sustains the Queen. Along on the expedition is Sexton Ming (himself), the Queen's evil nephew and high priest of the Cult of Perv, who is after the elixir for his own ends. Between charmingly amateur sub-Gerry Anderson/ Harryhausen effects scenes, there's less charming knockabout at various locales with guest stars David Warbeck and Eileen Daly as the rulers of lost civilisations and a surprisingly good score of pastiche '60s music. Though it has its dry spells, mostly as the performers rant at each other in Python wannabe funny voices, the film gets by on its general good nature, even if its sexual aspects never work up the transgressive charge of early John Waters (an obvious influence).

Screen Edge's standard frame DVD has a fine transfer, which makes the best of the super-16mm elements: the image may be a little fuzzy, but the colours are vivid, showing off interesting production design. The film proper is preceded by trailers, which use footage from the main feature but push non-existent movies called *Monarchy of Terror*, *Amicus Reilly Crusade of Doom* (with Warbeck) and *Sins of the Depraved*. The extras are: biographies of director Chandon and producer/writer Josh Collins (which include lengthy trailers for his earlier music-based efforts *Perv Parlour* and *Titten Helga*), notes on the film and its music, and galleries of production stills and Booth pin-up shots.

– KN

PHANTOM SHIP

B&W, 1935, 61m. / Directed by Denison Clift / Starring Bela Lugosi, Shirley Grey, Arthur Margetson, Dennis Hoey, Edmund Willard, Gibson Gowland / Image (US R1 NTSC)

 Despite the presence of imported star Bela Lugosi and its status as a product of an early incarnation of Hammer Films, this is more a maritime adventure than a horror picture. Apparently lost in its original British form, which is twenty minutes longer and tells its story in flashback from a court of inquiry, the movie survives as a trim B picture prepared for American release as *Phantom Ship*. Though some of the narrative is clearly missing – especially in a sub-plot about a doomed sailor who paints a picture of a derelict ship that is the focus of several later scenes – the film makes as much sense as it ever did in its melodramatic solution to the 1872 real-life mystery of the American ship found adrift in the Atlantic abandoned for no apparent reason by its entire crew.

The early stages of the film establish bad omens: Captain Briggs (Arthur Margetson) steals his best friend's girl (Shirley Grey) and unwisely takes her on a voyage, prompting the rejected rival (Dennis Hoey) to order one of his crewmen to sign up on the Mary Celeste and make sure Briggs comes to a bad end. And brutal first mate Bilson (Edmund Willard) resorts to shanghaiing New York dockfront drunks to fill out the crew, which raises bad memories for one-armed Anton Lorenzen (Lugosi), once known as "Handsome Anton" but an embittered wreck of a man since Bilson impressed him into an earlier crew and disciplined him with floggings and a spell as a human anchor (whereupon a shark ate his arm). With the ship under sail, accidents and malign circumstances whittle down the thirteen persons aboard. Star typecasting never puts in doubt

who is responsible for the curse on the ship, but the final stretches as only three mutually suspicious souls are left aboard work up some creaky suspense before the inevitable, somewhat rushed finale as the ship is found a floating derelict.

Image's DVD does its best with the materials available: the print has sustained a lot of wear and tear, but the transfer is more than watchable. The crackle of the soundtrack is diminished enough to allow an appreciation of one of Lugosi's more full-out performances (especially his remorse at the thought of killing one of his fellow men) while Willard and *Greed* veteran Gibson Gowland also work hard as seagoing roughs who snarl their way through salty dialogue and have moments of quivering paranoia. Director-writer Clift had access to a genuine seagoing vessel, "the famous Mary B. Mitchell", which gives the at-sea sequences a more authentic feel than the cramped studio below decks material.

– KN

PHANTOMS (MERIDIAN)

Colour, 1990, 83m. / Directed by Charles Band / Starring Sherilyn Fenn, Charlie Spradling, Malcolm Jamieson, Hilary Mason, Phil Fondacaro / Film 2000 (UK R2 PAL), Full Moon, Echo Bridge (US R0 NTSC)

 An atypical effort from producer-director Charles Band, though it still makes use of his familiar Italian castle and perennial dwarf player Phil Fondacaro; thematically, it might make a good double bill partner with writer Dennis Paoli's later Full Moon credit *Castle Freak*. A steamy fairytale werewolf picture, it is also a fantastical elaboration upon star Sherilyn Fenn's then-recent hit *Two Moon Junction*. Again Fenn plays a repressed aristocratic girl who seeks sexual

satisfaction with a mysterious and perhaps dangerous hunk from a travelling circus; though here, the love interest (Malcolm Jamieson) is under a curse and transforms into a shambling, hairy beast whenever he is smitten.

Making use of a striking garden of monster statues close to Band's usual castle, the film is slower-paced than most Full Moon efforts, with lengthy but mostly tasteful nude love scenes featuring Fenn and ex-model co-star Charlie Spradling (billed simply as "Charlie"), who plays a picture restorer at work on a painting which explains the plot and prophesies the ending. The basic *Beauty and the Beast* business is complicated by the hero's evil twin brother (oddly, their character names are Laurence and Oliver), a nanny who turns out to be a ghost (*Don't Look Now*'s Hilary Mason) and some sinister capering showfolk. Band, never a subtle director, stages a few striking moments – a bizarre mirror effect, a slow-motion procession, a simple stage magic trick involving the twins (Christopher Priest's novel *The Prestige* elaborates this throwaway into a whole premise). A Pino Donaggio score adds to the relatively sumptuous feel, though it's not one of his major efforts; and Greg Cannom's monster is a distant riff on *An American Werewolf in London*, complete with rubbery face-pushed-out effect curtailed presumably because it doesn't look that good.

Full Moon's output has not generally been well-served on DVD, which makes this disc above average though its extras are minimal in comparison with, say, releases from Troma or New Horizons. Film 2000's standard-frame transfer is a little soft and drab, muting the effectiveness of Mac Ahlberg's customary excellent cinematography and hardening the loveliness of the leading ladies. Besides the trailer and brief notes on Jamieson and Fenn, the only extra is a five-minute "making of" puff-piece, which has been cut about a bit to avoid using the original title (also known at some point

as *Kiss of the Beast* or *Meridian: Kiss of the Beast*). Though both *Meridian* and *Phantoms* are meaningless in the plot context, the U.K. release title is additionally problematic in that it creates confusion with the later Joe Chappelle film of Dean Koontz's like-named novel. The film was eventually issued in an equally lacklustre edition for America, first as part of Full Moon's "Charles Band Collection" (alongside *Dr. Mordrid*, *Crash and Burn* and *Head of the Family*) and again from Echo Bridge as a double feature with Charles Band's 2005 monster outing, *Decadent Evil*.

– KN

THE PIANIST

Colour, 2002, 148m. / Directed by Roman Polanski / Starring Adrien Brody, Thomas Kretschmann / Optimum (Blu-ray & DVD) (UK RB/R2 HD/PAL), Universal (US R1 NTSC), TVA (Canada R1 NTSC), Buena Vista (UK R2 PAL) Wild Side (France R2 PAL) / WS (1.85:1) (16:9) / DTS/DD5.1

 One of the more startling cinematic success stories of recent years, Roman Polanski's *The Pianist* finally pulls together the personal and artistic obsessions that had been developing throughout the director's career. Though based on the autobiography of Wladyslaw Szpilman, a Jewish pianist in Poland during the Nazi occupation, the film also reflects many of Polanski's own memories of growing up during World War II. Some critics remarked that *The Pianist* barely felt like a Polanski effort at all, but such is hardly the case; his trademark obsessions with confined living spaces affecting their inhabitants, the terrifying sense of encroaching insanity when one is kept in isolation, and the detached sense of helplessness while watching disaster from afar are all elaborated

here even more fully than in such obvious predecessors as *The Tenant*, *Repulsion* and *Death and the Maiden*.

A successful pianist, Szpilman (Adrien Brody) lives with his family in a respectable area of Warsaw. As the Nazi influence begins to take hold of the city and the Jewish population is forced into increasingly confined living areas, Szpilman stays with his family until all but him are deported by train to labour camps. Alone in a city rapidly crumbling due to Nazi brutality and constant gun and tank fire, Szpilman holes up in a deserted apartment and resorts to desperate measures to survive. However, fate has several more surprises in store for him.

A beautifully executed work of cinema, *The Pianist* never resorts to emotional grandstanding or obvious heart-tugging ploys for an audience response. However the film is deeply moving precisely because of this spare, finely honed approach, in which every shot and line of dialogue serves a distinct purpose. The obvious inclination is to compare this to mainstream Holocaust predecessors like *Schindler's List*, though the two could hardly be more dissimilar in approach. Szpilman is an everyman fighting to make it from one day to the next, without any noble sweeping heroic actions. This is an all too identifiable character, and Brody's remarkable performance (literally wasting away before the viewer's eyes) is essential as all of the events take place from his perspective. Second-billed Thomas Kretschmann (the maniac from Dario Argento's *The Stendhal Syndrome*) also lends solid support in the third act of the film with a subdued, surprisingly emotional turn.

A surprising award winner around the world, *The Pianist* has been served well enough albeit differently in all of its home video incarnations. The most elaborate is the three-disc Canadian set from TVA, packaged in slimline Amaray cases within a slipcase, which contains a solid transfer (albeit PAL-sourced with no speed correction for NTSC) of the film itself allocated to a platter all by itself. The 5.1 and DTS audio is house-shaking, though the film isn't a constant sound effects extravaganza all the way through. The second disc contains a half hour documentary, "A Story of Survival", featuring interviews with all of the principals as well as illuminating biographical information about Szpilman. Also included are a director's statement, a text interview with Polanski, historical notes about Warsaw during WWII, production essays, a soundtrack sample and promo, five TV spots, two theatrical trailers, poster art, and filmographies. The third disc is the original soundtrack CD. (TVA has also issued a two-disc edition, minus the CD, in standard Amaray packaging.) Available in full screen or widescreen editions, the U.S. single disc from Universal contains only the U.S. trailer, the documentary, and the Warsaw overview, not to mention absolutely wretched new cover art ("a riveting adventure story!"). Also packaged with or without the CD, the French DVD (with a very striking cover) contains the documentary, press and festival reactions to the film, and the French trailer, all with obligatory French subtitles (including the feature itself). The first British DVD contains the documentary, U.K. trailer, filmographies, and a photo gallery. The subsequent reissue from Optimum brought the film to Blu-ray in a transfer that looks substantially improved over its standard def counterparts, though some pesky edge enhancement still rears its head during several outdoor scenes. No new extras for that one either, but as BD discs go, it's very affordable.

THE PIANO TEACHER

Colour, 2001, 130m. / Directed by Michael Haneke / Starring Isabelle Huppert, Benoît Magimel, Annie Girardot / Kino (US R1 NTSC) / WS (1.85:1) / DD2.0, Remstar (Canada R1 NTSC) / WS (1.85:1) / DD5.1, Artificial Eye (UK R2 PAL), MK2 (France R2 PAL), Homescreen (Holland R2 PAL), Fox (Italy R2 PAL) / WS (1.85:1) (16:9) / DD5.1

Never afraid to appear unsympathetic, Isabelle Huppert tests audience endurance with this gruelling but fascinating character study from Michael Haneke, best known for the overrated *Funny Games*. Saddled in a deeply dysfunctional relationship with her mother (Annie Girardot), with whom she shares a Vienna apartment, music teacher Erika (Huppert) takes out her suppressed desires by browbeating her piano students, frequenting porn theatres, and engaging in an S&M tryst with a young student, Walter (Benoît Magimel). As with Haneke's other films, this is far from subtle about the buttons it's trying to push; however, at least this time the abuse heaped on his characters can be approached with wry amusement, waiting patiently for the next outrage to erupt onscreen. Huppert's astounding performance makes the film more watchable than it has any right to be, and the supporting cast matches her perfectly.

Despite its pedigree (including a near-sweep at Cannes), several of its DVD editions fall well short of the mark. The best option for English-speaking consumers is the U.K. disc, which boasts a 16:9 transfer, a long Huppert interview, a Haneke interview, and behind-the-scenes featurettes. The even more lavish French edition features longer featurettes but, as with its other continental counterparts, offers no English subtitle options. The U.S. disc (available in both a "director's cut" and must-avoid R-rated version) features a soft, non-anamorphic transfer that looks sick and bleary, with dull colours and weak detail as well as burned-in subtitles, which is insulting for a well-regarded film of this vintage. U.S. extras include the trailer and a shorter, 20-minute interview with Huppert. The Canadian release features the same compromised transfer but, as with all of the other non-US options, at least contains a 5.1 audio track, while the Kino disc is in comparatively pallid 2.0 surround.

PICASSO TRIGGER

Colour, 1988, 99m. / Directed by Andy Sidaris / Starring Steve Bond, Dona Speir, Roberta Vasquez, Rodrigo Obregon / Malibu Bay Films (US R0 NTSC), Laser Paradise (Germany R2 PAL)

The intrepid, buxom spy team of Donna and Taryn proved to be a hit in *Hard Ticket to Hawaii*, so luckily Andy Sidaris and the gang returned the next year with *Picasso Trigger*, featuring our third Agent Abilene, Travis (soap star Steve Bond, one of the better actors to grace the series).

The busty pair are called into action by the Agency after their Hawaii houseboat is blown up, an event which inexplicably ties into a Parisian assassination of the owner (and title character) of a really awful "Picasso triggerfish" painting. Meanwhile Travis puts the moves on fellow agent and former teen flame Pantera (Roberta Vasquez), while the evil Miguel Ortiz (Rodrigo Obregon again) conspires to avenge the death of his brother from the last film. More stuff blows up. Women get naked. And in the film's most infamous scene, Travis hobbles in and confronts Miguel with a bomb-activated crutch. Really.

The fresh digital transfer looks like a million bucks, and the usual Sidaris-related ephemera are included (trailer gallery, commentary, and featurette). Good, clean, disreputable fun, and the perfect lead-in to the girls' next adventure, *Savage Beach*. Unfortunately the disc went out of circulation a few years after its release, and as with its companion Sidaris releases, it was only reissued in Germany as part of a box set. This time the commentary was carried over, and for once the original featurette was left intact instead of getting hacked up into smaller video pieces.

PIN

Colour, 1988, 102m. / Directed by Sandor Stern / Starring David Hewlett, Cyndy Preston, Terry O'Quinn / Anchor Bay (US R1 NTSC), Metrodome (UK R2 PAL) / WS (1.85:1) (16:9) / DD-2.0

 This Canadian-lensed shocker felt out of place in the gore-drenched late '80s horror sweepstakes but fares well now, as it relies more on character-driven chills than visceral shocks. Following the deaths of their parents in a car crash, sheltered siblings Leon (*Stargate: Atlantis*'s David Hewlett) and Ursula (Cyndy Preston) cope with grief quite differently; he finds refuge in his "best friend", a life-size medical dummy named Pin, while she pursues a normal social life at school. Soon the overly possessive Leon goes to deadly lengths to keep little sis at home, with the presence of Pin taking all of the blame.

An obvious influence on *May*, this would barely even qualify as a horror film were it not for the final half hour, which thankfully resists the urge to build up a last minute body count. *The Stepfather*'s Terry O'Quinn offers a good first act turn, while genre regular Hewlett (*Cube*) ekes some sympathy out of a potentially repellent character. Some of the production values swerve towards made-for-TV quality at times (including extremely flat cinematography during daylight scenes), but the film works up an effective mood of sadness and unease, creating a family tragedy balanced with some welcome black humour.

Anchor Bay's DVD looks marvellous, with much-needed 1.85:1 framing restoring the balance of the original compositions, and the 2.0 surround track is fairly aggressive. Extras include a dismal theatrical trailer and a hit-and-miss commentary by director Sandor Stern and journalist Ted Newsom, which is dry but sometimes informative. The later U.K. version only carries over the trailer along with the same transfer.

PIRATES

Colour, 1986, 108m. / Directed by Roman Polanski / Starring Walter Matthau, Cris Campion, Damien Thomas, Charlotte Lewis, Ferdy Mayne, Daniel Emilfork, Anthony Dawson, Roy Kinnear, Sydney Bromley / TF1 (Blu-ray & DVD) (France RB/R2 HD/ PAL), DVD Storm (Italy R2 PAL), Manga (Spain R2 PAL), Concorde (Germany R2 PAL) / WS (2.35:1) (16:9), Force (Australia R4 PAL) / DD5.1

 By far the biggest bomb in Polanski's career and a strong contributor to the capsizing of Cannon Films, this megabudget spectacle has mellowed somewhat with age and, at least for fans of the director, offers a few artistic flourishes worthy of his name.

Walter Matthau stars as Captain Red, an insane, peg-legged seafarer who munches on fishhooks (shades of *The Isle*!) adrift on a raft with a French sailor, the Frog (Cris Campion). The two are retrieved by a Spanish galleon containing a golden Aztec throne, which Red naturally plots to steal. The crew is already mumbling about mutiny under the overbearing Don Alfonso (*Twins of Evil*'s Damien Thomas), so Red manipulates the situation for his own financial gain. Meanwhile Frog develops a crush on the governor's niece, Dolores (Charlotte Lewis, who was in *The Golden Child* the same year... ouch!), and mayhem ensues.

Better as a black comedy than a traditional pirate film, this burgeoning cult item features some spectacular scope visuals (the costly ship is worth a look alone), a stirring score by Philippe Sarde (his last for Polanski), and some funny dialogue here and there. Polanski buffs can have fun spotting riffs on *Knife in the Water* and *The Fearless Vampire Killers* amidst the nautical antics, and the cast sports a delightful array of eccentric talent: horror vet Ferdy Mayne, Daniel Emilfork (*The Devil's Nightmare*), Anthony Dawson (*Dr. No*), Roy Kinnear (*Juggernaut*), and Sydney Bromley (*Dragonslayer*), to name a few. Polanski's odd touches are well in abundance here, from rat-eating and implied cannibalism to an unforgettable scene involving gout. The critical and box office thrashing the film received at the time seems a bit extreme now, given the oddball charm of the finished product; it's no masterpiece but is certainly among the better Cannon releases (for what that's worth).

Shot in lush 70mm and blessed with a six-track Dolby stereo soundtrack, *Pirates* never got anything close to fair treatment on standard DVD. The European discs feature mediocre widescreen versions and are technically 16:9 enhanced, but that's about all they have going for them; the image quality is a mess, resembling a bootleg videotape with digital artefacting and heavy shimmering littering every shot. The soundtracks can be played in dubbed (German, Italian, etc.) 5.1 or English 2.0; both are passable but not overwhelming. The Australian DVD is even worse, a pan and scan nightmare that hacks the compositions to bits. At least it features the English soundtrack in 5.1, but even this sounds like an artificial reprocessing of a 2.0 track. The best version out there (though still imperfect) is found on the French RB Blu-ray and R2 PAL DVDs, both of which look absolutely astonishing; it's even fresher and more impressive than the film looked on the big screen, and the English DTS audio track does full justice to Sarde's magnificent score. Unfortunately you can only play it with forced French subtitles at the bottom of the frame (and yes, they graze over into the actual film) or with the French dub *sans sous-titres. Quel dommage!*

PLAYGIRL KILLER

Colour, 1968, 85m. / Directed by Erick Santamaria / Starring William Kerwin, Jean Christopher / Platinum (US R0 NTSC)

Apparently H.G. Lewis's leading man William Kerwin (or as *Blood Feast* fans know him, under his *nom de sleaze*, "Thomas Wood") was too busy to star in the third and last instalment of the director's notorious Blood Trilogy, *Color Me Blood Red*, but Kerwin later teamed up with his younger brother, Harry, to pen and star in a jaw-dropping twist on the same plot, *Playgirl Killer*. Also known to late night trash TV viewers during the '70s and '80s as *Decoy for Terror* and *Portrait of Fear*, this one doesn't really deliver in the nudity department and only offers a few scant splashes of gore, but don't let that scare you away from this pure, unadulterated slice of Z-grade drive-in heaven.

Struggling artist Bill (Kerwin) is desperate to create his masterpiece, a painted tableau of beautiful women in Greek mythological outfits standing around in a lot of fog. Unfortunately his attempts to translate this vision to canvas are stymied by his first model, whom he drags out for sketches near a mountain lake. She refuses to sit still for long and begins giggling at the would-be Picasso, so he responds by firing a speargun into her chest. After the main titles play out over Bill being chased through the woods, we cut to a nocturnal shindig where bikini-clad girls are go-go dancing their hearts out around the swimming pool while a pudgy Neil Sedaka sings the unforgettable "Waterbug". (Apparently Sedaka was so pleased with his "Jellyfish" theme song in *Sting of Death* three years earlier that he had to encore with another nautical creature ditty.) Here we meet most of our future female victims, including primary target Arlene (Jean Christopher) who's seen snuggling up to the crooner in the film's most terrifying moment. At this happy estate Bill takes a job as a handyman and spends his free time bumping off young ladies, then stashing their bodies in the basement where he continues to paint his heart out.

As if the sight of a goateed, overacting Kerwin doing his crazy artist routine weren't enough, *Playgirl Killer* is stuffed with enough late '60s kitsch to keep trash hounds giddy with delight. The funky lounge score, day-glo outfits, hideously "elegant" decor, and wooden acting all combine for a cheapo delight. The film does work up a few memorable images thanks to the frozen female bodies on view during the finale, which is capped by an amazing comeuppance guaranteed to raise a chuckle or two. It bypassed regular U.S. theatrical venues, but *Playgirl Killer* was trotted around the TV wasteland by New World and eventually turned up on that company's video label in the mid-'80s (with a later reissue by Anchor Bay under the Starmaker label). Though not known for its top of the line transfers, the Platinum DVD offers a surprisingly sharp appearance with some wonderfully bouncy and saturated colours. Like most of the H.G. Lewis films it so closely resembles, this sickie was shot open matte at 1.33:1. (Masked off to 1.78:1 or so on a 16:9 display it still looks fine, however, apart from some tight opening credits.) For the laughably low price tag, this one should be a no-brainer. The disc also contains gushing bios for Kerwin and Sedaka, but the real doozy is New World's howler of a video teaser, consisting of soft focus "erotic thriller" style cheesecake photos and ominous narration, accompanied by Rick Wakeman's theme from *Crimes of Passion*! It's hard to imagine how short-changed video patrons must have reacted when they actually set eyes on the movie itself...

PORNO HOLOCAUST

Colour, 1979, 110m. / Directed by Joe D'Amato / Starring Mark Shannon, George Eastman / Exploitation Digital (US R1 NTSC) / WS (1.85:1) (16:9), Astro (Germany R0 PAL) / WS (1.85:1)

Released the same year as Ruggero Deodato's *Cannibal Holocaust*, this goofy exploitation gem from the prolific Joe D'Amato is the reverse side of the extreme cinema coin. Eschewing gruesome mutilations and animal death in favour of tropical bump and grind footage, this monster mash for the raincoat crowd remains more famous as a title than as an actual film. Furthermore, its odd relationship with D'Amato's similar mix of zombie mayhem and hardcore coupling, *Erotic Nights of the Living Dead* (with which this shares most of the same cast, crew, and locales), has resulted in many filmographies confusing the two. However, while *Erotic Nights* balances the horror and sex about 50/50 thanks to a finale involving roaming zombies (cut from many prints), *Porno Holocaust* dives headlong into the latter category with only a few strange monstrous sex scenes tossed in near the end.

The "plot" doesn't really merit much of a summary, especially since this film has never been legitimately available with any kind of English translation, but the set up is familiar enough. We spend about an hour following the denizens of a sunny Santo Domingo island where scientist George Eastman (aka *Anthropophagous*) recruits perpetually horny captain Mark Shannon to explore a nearby island showing signs of strange radiation. After a series of random sex scenes, they head out along with a handful of insatiable gals and spend most of their time walking up and down the beach. While Shannon continues to explore the native girls in graphic detail, a shuffling zombie with a mutated endowment attacks the infidels one by one.

And that's about it. Amazingly, it takes D'Amato almost two hours to cover territory that would normally be stretched to the breaking point at more than 75 minutes. However, the catchy score by Nico Fidenco (best known for his equally contagious *Black Emanuelle* scores) makes things tolerable when the actors aren't going through the frequently weird and hilarious hardcore motions. By the time the zombie gets in on the action too near the end, most viewers will be rubbing their eyes in disbelief. At least Eastman emerges with his dignity relatively intact; as with *Erotic Nights*, he refrains from the sex scenes and was apparently brought in for whatever marquee value he could muster.

The first DVD on the market, from Germany's Astro, offers a crisp, colourful, and complete transfer of this title, most often seen in dupey grey market editions by curious fans. The disc offers Italian or German language options (both dubbed, obviously), and the mono soundtrack sounds clear enough given the vintage of the film. The letterboxing appears accurate, with a bit more information on the sides than the Italian prerecord (which was approximately 1.78:1). The disc also includes a nifty D'Amato retrospective featurette (without subtitles as well), which was also part of their *Emanuelle in America* disc. However, the Exploitation Digital edition not only looks better but also features optional English subtitles, to help exceptionally slow viewers decipher whatever shreds of plot they may stumble across. Extras include a surprisingly long and in-depth video interview with Eastman, the theatrical trailer, and bonus trailers for the label's other Eurosleaze releases.

POULET AU VINAIGRE

Colour, 1984, 96m. / Directed by Claude Chabrol / Starring Jean Poiret, Stéphane Audran, Lucas Belvaux, Jean-Claude Bouillard, Jean Topart, Michel Bouquet / MK2 (France R2 PAL), Arrow (UK R2 PAL), Kino (US R1 NTSC) / WS (1.66:1) (16:9)

A subdued yet very effective fusion of murder mystery with bitter dark comedy, this sunny countryside yarn from Chabrol revolves around a young postal worker, Louis (played by Lucas Belvaux), who brings the town's mail to be inspected by his nosy mother (Stéphane Audran). This behaviour proves disruptive to the populace, including Gérard Filiol the butcher (Jean-Claude Bouillard), country doctor Morasseau (Jean Topart), and suspicious notary Lavoisier (Michel Bouquet). When a murderer strikes, the people fall under the jurisdiction of highly unorthodox Inspector Lavardin (Jean Poiret), whose radical crime-solving techniques manage to expose the viper in the town's midst.

The punning title (which translates as "Chicken with vinegar") most obviously refers to the nature of the detective himself but could refer to the tone of the film, which seems like an innocuous treat but contains a palpable sting in the tale, so to speak. Lavardin was apparently popular enough to inspire a sequel, *Inspecteur Lavardin*, while the film itself remains a prime example of Chabrol in his more playful mode.

MK2's anamorphic transfer looks excellent, preserving the notably colourful, sun-dappled scenery with admirable, film-like clarity. The disc contains optional English subtitles, as well as the usual MK2 extras (Chabrol video commentary, Joel Magny intro, and Chabrol trailers). The subsequent Kino release drops the Chabrol commentary and is a PAL conversion (looks decent enough, but some definite conversion issues) while the Arrow release (also in their second six-disc Chabrol box set) falls just under the French one in quality and only has the Magny intro.

THE PREMATURE BURIAL

Colour, 1962, 81m. / Directed by Roger Corman / Starring Ray Milland, Hazel Court, John Dierkes, Dick Miller / MGM (US R1 NTSC), Optimum (UK R2 PAL) / WS (2.35:1) (16:9)

THE MASQUE OF THE RED DEATH

Colour, 1964, 89m. / Directed by Roger Corman / Starring Vincent Price, Jane Asher, Hazel Court, Patrick Magee / MGM (US R1 NTSC, UK R2 PAL), Optimum (UK R2 PAL) / WS (2.35:1) (16:9)

 An essential Roger Corman-Hazel Court-Edgar Allan Poe-Charles Beaumont bill, this smartly teams two pictures in which Corman took his Poe series in fresh directions, building on the groundwork laid in his initial entries but trying to get away from the rigid formula.

Premature Burial (as the odd, computer-generated on-screen title reads, in contrast to the original prints and the trailer which blares Edgar Allan Poe's "The Premature Burial") was developed outside AIP, and thus employs Ray Milland rather than Vincent Price as the vivisepulturephobic dilettante Guy Carrell. If Milland's Dr. Xavier (in Corman's *X: The Man with the X-Ray Eyes*) saw too much, this companion character sees too little, obsessing so much on one unlikely fate that he fails to perceive until too late that someone close to him is working a *Diabolique*-style scheme to inherit his wealth. Or maybe not: close textural analysis suggests an alternative possibility that another character might have manipulated the situation to get rid of both impediments to assumption of the family fortune. Milland, addicted to laudanum this time, is a grim protagonist, constantly quarrelling with everyone, only fully alive when spreading neurosis in self-delighted

morbid speeches Beaumont and Ray Russell craft in a perfect echo of Poe's own tendency to rant. With supporting performances that match the star rather than (as often with Price) are intimidated into the background, it's a film whose decay always seems fresh. Nice elements: John Dierkes and Dick Miller as grave-robbers constantly whistling "Molly Malone" (the lyrics are never heard, but you can't help mentally reciting the apt refrain "alive, alive-o"), a throwaway line of dialogue that makes this a crossover with Russell's *Mr. Sardonicus* (whose hero, Robert Cargrave, is supposedly a colleague of the medical characters), and Court's chilly beauty in costumes that reveal more of her character than her dialogue.

The Premature Burial is set in England but was made on a fog-filled California set; *The Masque of the Red Death* is set in Italy but was shot in England, where added studio space, leftover Becket flats and the ingenuity of cinematographer Nicolas Roeg – along with a sterling supporting cast – combine to lend a lavish, expansive feel lacking in the deliberately claustrophobic support feature. Actually, the countryside of *Masque* is as stylised and bare as the *Premature* graveyard, contrasting with the opulence of Prince Prospero's palace and the elaborate costuming of his doomed guests. Especially memorable (to Roeg at least, in that he reworked the move in *The Man Who Fell to Earth*) is a tour of a series of identical rooms each with a different dominant colour (Prospero's father once imprisoned "a friend of his" in the yellow room for three years, and the unfortunate was never able to look at a daffodil again) establishing this as a world of colour-coded Deaths, most of whom show up at the end after the Red Death has ravaged the castle. Price has a tailor-made role as the diabolist prince whose misdeeds are always designed to teach a lesson, savouring dialogue so ripe it's on the point of rotting, arching an eyebrow at lesser villains (Hazel Court, Patrick Magee) who miss the philosophical point of wickedness and display naked self-interest that earns them brutal deaths. There's a touching moment as the devil-worshipper pleads with the Red Death to let the peasant heroine (Jane Asher) go free because she is the only person whose faith is as strong as his own, a grace moment for one of the screen's worst tyrants.

The MGM Midnite Movies double feature presents the films on two sides of a single disc, in glorious 2.35:1 (Fritz Lang's decree that widescreen was good only for funerals comes to mind) and transfers that render the colours as vibrant or gloomy as they should be and do wonders by the skintones of pale, plush Court and red-headed, freckled Asher, with English and French mono tracks (Poe always sounded wonderful in the Beaudelaire translation) and English, French and Spanish subtitle options. The extras are wonderful trailers (*Masque* has the poster-image of Price's red face composed of writhing bodies) and chatty, clip-illustrated interviews with Corman, who is prone to lapses like tagging the Irish Magee as an "English actor" but covers a lot of interesting background material. *The Masque of the Red Death* was issued as a single disc in the U.K. by MGM and later bundled into Optimum's schizophrenic six-disc Roger Corman collection (along with *The Wild Angels*, *Gunslinger*, *Five Guns West*, *The Haunted Palace* and *The Premature Burial*). *The Premature Burial* was later included as part of the U.S. eight-film MGM box set "The Roger Corman Collection" (along with *Bloody Mama*, *A Bucket of Blood*, *Gas-s-s*, *The Trip*, *X: The Man with X-Ray Eyes*, *The Young Racers* and *The Wild Angels*).

– KN

PRINCESS BLADE: SHURA YUKIHIME

Colour, 2002, 93m. / Directed by Shinsuke Sato / Starring Hideaki Ito, Yumiko Shaku / Tartan (UK R0 PAL), ADV (US R1 NTSC), Pioneer (Japan R2 NTSC), Madman (Australia R0 PAL) / WS (1.78:1) (16:9)

Though it has a rather drab, post-breakdown-of-society apocalyptic science fiction setting, this is a basic samurai swordplay picture with more than its share of spaghetti western elements. In a wooded rural area away from decaying cities, the martially superskilled Yuki (Yumiko Shaku), due to become princess of a clan of samurai assassins, learns her legendary mother was murdered by the clan's leader and turns against her supposed friends. Wounded in battle, she seeks refuge with an ex-terrorist (Hideaki Ito), who has retired in disillusion from his own crusade against a corrupt society and is looking after his trauma-tised-into-muteness sister. The girl born to violence and the man driven to violence debate their positions and fall in love, but old feuds intervene and swords are drawn again in the service of revenge and tragedy. As expected, it does not end happily.

With zestful action choreography by Donnie Yen, this engages whenever the fighting starts but is otherwise a paper-thin exercise in posing and pouting, with stick-figure characters glumly trying to deliver meaning to the familiar go-round of duels, battles, murders, betrayals, slicings and deaths. It's a slick, considered piece of work but offers little beyond already-overfamiliar ultra-action business. The most impressive bit of martial choreog-raphy comes in the final duel between Yuki and her mother's murderer as the swordless heroine bests the villain by using a scabbard which she positions so each of his sword-thrusts rams home to the hilt without injuring her.

Tartan Asia Extreme's DVD showcases a letterboxed widescreen transfer which seems a little soft, but perhaps deliberately so since director Sato is going for a muted, colour-drained look. The soundtrack offers Japanese dialogue, with optional English subtitles. Besides the usual trailer reel, the extras are limited to filmographies for three people who haven't actually made many films, and notes from Mark Wyatt. A subsequent American special edition adds some noteworthy extras (three making-of featurettes, outtakes, deleted scenes, cast and crew interviews, and a Donnie Yen interview), while the Australian release features an action sequence audio commentary by Yen. The most lavish version comes from Japan thanks to more extensive interviews with the director and crew, but it has no English-friendly options at all.

– KN

PROJECT A

Colour, 1983, 101m. / Directed by Jackie Chan / Starring Jackie Chan, Sammo Hung, Yuen Biao, Mars, Lee Hoi-san, Dick Wei / Hong Kong Legends (UK R2 PAL), FortuneStar (HK R3 NTSC), Buena Vista (US R1 NTSC) / WS (2.35:1) (16:9) / DD5.1

After becoming a box office draw in the late 1970s with films like *Drunken Master*, Jackie Chan tried to make it big internationally with misfires such as *The Cannonball Run*. Upon returning to Hong Kong, he became more popular than ever thanks to *Project A*, a rip-roaring fantasia of outrageous marital arts which firmly establish what we know today as the Jackie Chan style. Teaming up with the legendary Sammo Hung and Yuen Biao, Chan stars as naval policeman Sgt. Ma, whose failed plot to stop a gang of sea pirates lands him under the command of Captain Tzu (Biao). Another bust gone awry leads Ma to suspect that his superiors are corrupt, so along with sidekick Fei (Hung), Ma sets off on a personal mission to expose the criminals around him.

The blueprint for such future classics as the *Police Story* and *Armour of God* series, *Project A* uses its familiar, rickety plot as a necessary ingredient to justify the explosive series of physical confrontations and pursuits, all executed by Chan (as both director and actor) with boundless energy. From the showstopping teahouse fight to the legendary (and often excerpted) bicycle chase, all three leads have their moment in the spotlight and work spectacularly well together. A sort of early "greatest hits" collection for Hong Kong film fans, this would be essential viewing regardless of the DVD presentation.

Fortunately the Region 2 Hong Kong Legends two-disc set is a superlative edition, boasting one of the best HK film transfers available on standard def home video. Licensed from Media Asia, whose discs tend to feature dodgy image quality at best, this set fortunately sports a brand new anamorphic presentation with Cantonese or English 5.1 audio tracks (with optional English subs). The film is also uncut, as opposed to the slightly trimmed earlier VHS release on U.K. home video. The first disc contains the feature along with an audio commentary by HK scholar Bey Logan, who provides a typically thorough and entertaining history lesson in early '80s Hong Kong filmmaking, as well as the Hong Kong and U.K. promotional trailers and a 15-minute interview with Hong Kong "stunt god" Mars entitled "Dancing with Danger".

The second disc is divided into a number of regions: "The Tea House", "The Schooner", "The Pirate's Cave", and "The Clock Tower". Included here is a wealth of material including "The Elusive Dragon" (a new 18-minute interview with Biao, followed by a trailer for his vehicle, *The Prodigal Son*), "Can't Stop the Music" (an 18-minute chat with composer Michael Lai), an advertising art gallery with text supplements for the actors, "Master Killer" (a 22-minute interview with actor Lee

Hoi-san, a Wing Chun Grandmaster who demonstrates his craft), and "The Pirate's Den" (an entertaining and surprisingly cheery 15-minute interview with Dick Wei, the film's unforgettable villain). The biggest extra here is "*Project A:* A Classic Revisited", a 76-minute documentary hosted by Logan which covers all of the major locales from the film, including visits to the former Marine Police headquarters. Those who prefer their Jackie desecrated can also pick up the U.S. disc of *Project A* from Buena Vista, a typical no-frills hack job best avoided (and it's missing noticeable chunks of footage to boot). The inferior 1987 sequel, *Project A 2* (minus the two co-stars), is also available as a Hong Kong import or a dubbed U.S. disc from Buena Vista. The Hong Kong release (most widely available packaged with *Project A 2*) drops the British extras but does feature some deleted scenes and outtakes, which may make it worth a double-dip for Chan fanatics. The transfer is similar but brighter and with paler black levels, as well as slightly desaturated colours.

THE PROWLER
(ROSEMARY'S KILLER)

Colour, 1981, 89m. / Directed by Joseph Zito / Starring Farley Granger, Vicky Dawson, Lawrence Tierney / Blue Underground (Blu-ray & DVD) (US R0 HD/NTSC), Optimum (UK R2 PAL) / WS (1.85:1) (16:9)

Given the shaft while overseas for WWII, a GI returns home only to promptly pitchfork his ex-gal and her new man-meat at their Graduation Dance. The shindig is cancelled for the next 35 years, until we hit the present day (um, Present Day circa 1981, that is) when the town decides to blow off the past and schedule a new

hop. Surprise, surprise, our psycho soldier comes out of retirement and proceeds to pierce and bayonet the remainder of the cast in hyper-graphic ways.

Filmed under the title *The Graduation* and known overseas as *Rosemary's Killer*, *The Prowler* has garnered a reputation over the years as one of the best entries in the early '80s teen-kill movement, a notoriety probably due more to its previous rarity than its actual merits. That's not to say it's a bad film, as it does prove enjoyable, but plot-wise it's about as cookie-cutter as you can get. The clichés arrive fast and furious (which leads to many jokes on the alternative audio track), without any real twists or turns to help distinguish it from the rest of the splat pack. In all fairness, though, a few noteworthy elements do rear their heads for forgiving fans. First off, we have former Hitchcock actor and Eurojunk fave Farley Granger essaying a small role as the Sheriff. He ain't given much to work with, but he's there – now where are those restored DVDs of *Amuck* and *The Slasher Is the Sex Maniac*? Hollywood tough-ass Lawrence Tierney also makes a tiny appearance, but I'll be damned if he even bothers uttering a syllable. The movie's true *raison d'être*, however, is Tom Savini's gruesome effects. And what grue it is: a knife rammed through a noggin from top to bottom, a super-meaty head detonation via shotgun, a nude body hoisted into the air by a pronged implement of farm labour, etc. Fans of body-count flix and Savini gore groupies *need* this disc.

While the film itself may be relatively typical, Blue Underground's DVD is not. Apparently select prints suffered violence trims for an R rating during Sandhurst Releasing Corp.'s theatrical distribution, but the movie was eventually put out intact on VHS by VCII. Still, *The Prowler* never looked particularly good on home video before. Copies lacked detail and were either too dark or too bright, depending on the tape (VCII actually had two distinct masters – their initial issue and a later version with an altered copyright date and a different set of trailers at the beginning). Needless to say, BU's new disc destroys any necessity to root through the ol' vid stores for an ex-rental copy. Content-wise they're identical but there is a marked improvement when it comes to the picture, though things are still a bit grainy at times. Colours are rendered accurately and are more lifelike, while definition is highly improved (check out that underwater segment). Some scenes appear to have been shot with a rather soft-focus look to them, and contain saturated whites that bloom into the surroundings, while other sequences appear quite crisp – possibly due to the fact that two different directors-of-photography were in charge of the project at separate points. Overall, it's a good-looking disc and a fantastic improvement on the previous presentation. The 1.85:1 framing masks out the barren portions of the picture when compared to the older open-matte release, and looks a tad more carefully composed because of it. The mono sound is nice and clean, with no noticeable problems. Regardless, seasoned vets are a lot more likely to appreciate this quality restoration than newcomers to the film, but who really cares what the rookies think?

Generously doling out supplements, Blue Underground has created a wonderful package. First up is a commentary track with director Joe Zito and make-up man Tom Savini. Having worked with each other on a number of occasions, the duo is perfectly comfortable together and the track is a good, fun listen, with the participants ribbing each other (and the film) while dishing out many on-set anecdotes. Topics range from budget, distribution and scheduling issues, to other projects the pair have collaborated on like *Friday the 13th: The Final Chapter* and *Red Scorpion*. Next we are treated to about 9 minutes of behind-the-scenes gore footage from the vaults of the FX guru himself,

showcasing virtually every murder sequence. The original theatrical trailer is accounted for as well, which does a decent job selling the pic but ruins nearly every dramatic punchline! Last, but not least, we have a 52-image stills gallery featuring ad art and promo materials from around the world, in addition to more of Savini's personal snapshots. Though it's nowhere near as elaborately appointed, this was also released in 2007 uncut for the first time ever in the U.K. from Optimum under the *Rosemary's Killer* title.

Released many years later, the Blu-ray edition offers an equally impressive upgrade as the film benefits tremendously from the increased resolution of HD and the removal of obvious but unavoidable compression hiccups encountered during some of the trickier night scenes. Most of the film looks extremely good, but bear in mind that some scenes (especially the ones with Dawson creeping around dark hallways in the middle third) were obviously shot with very low lighting, which causes a huge boost in the amount of film grain. Thankfully that's been left intact here rather than scrubbing it all away, so the detail is still present and very filmic. This movie will never look sleek or glossy, but this is about as accurate and impressive a presentation as you could possibly get. While the DVD is mono only, the Blu-ray carries over that track along with DTS-HD 7.1 and 5.1 mixes, both of which mainly kick in for the instrumental score, the aforementioned Supertramp-lite performances, and the big band music in the opening scene. It sounds just fine and is tastefully done considering the modest nature of the original source. Apart from the DVD-only image gallery, both releases contain the same extras. Definitely a must-have for slasher fans, this is '80s American horror at its most unflinching and a brilliant example of Savini at his horrific best.

– BH

PSYCH-OUT

Colour, 1968, 89m. / Directed by Richard Rush / Starring Susan Strasberg, Jack Nicholson, Dean Stockwell, Bruce Dern, Henry Jaglom

THE TRIP

Colour, 1967, 79m. / Directed by Roger Corman / Starring Peter Fonda, Susan Strasberg, Bruce Dern, Dennis Hopper, Barboura Morris, Luana Anders / MGM (US R1 NTSC, UK R2 PAL) / WS (1.85:1) (16:9)

 This "Midnite Movies Double Feature" is a surprisingly substantial package, surrounding these two ambitious hippie-era exploitation pictures with a great deal of contextualising material. The jury is still out on AIP's seriousness in tackling drug and youth rebellion themes, but both films play well as nostalgia, documentation and sometimes satire, showcase interesting performers at the beginnings of their careers, and at least try to capture the specific looks and sounds of California, circa 1967-8.

The flipper disc rather oddly presents Roger Corman's better-known, earlier and more-thoroughly-documented *The Trip* on the B-side, by default awarding top-billing to Richard Rush's San Francisco-set *Psych-Out*. It's the simple story of Jenny (Susan Strasberg), a not-quite-innocent deaf girl who arrives in the hippie-dominated Haight-Ashbury district looking for her lost brother, an acid-head visionary who calls himself the Seeker (Bruce Dern). Falling in with a handy rock group, Mumblin' Jim, led by pony-tailed Stoney (Jack Nicholson), Jenny takes a tour of the city, experiencing the highs and lows of the counterculture and winding up with a memorable bad trip as she is dosed by the smugly philosophical guru Dave (Dean Stockwell) and wanders through speeding traffic. With music from the Strawberry Alarm Clock ("Incense and Pepper-mints") and the Seeds and a great deal of rambling, improvised-sounding dialogue ("Warren's freaking out down at the gallery!"), this isn't free from AIP's tendency towards moralising horror stories (tripping artist Henry Jaglom buzzsaws his own hand off) but the cast (especially Strasberg, Dern and Stockwell) play their roles with more depth than is in the script, Stockwell especially finding the infuriating, scheming side of a supposed free-living drop-out.

The version of *Psych-Out* on this disc is presumed to be a TV edit, running 9 minutes shy of the cut on the old VHS release from HBO. The 1.85:1 anamorphic widescreen transfer is smashing, reproducing the wonderfully lurid, candy-coloured look of the film. It doesn't have the full DVD works accorded Rush's *The Stunt* Man or even *The Trip*, but a "Love and Haight" featurette (missing from the U.K. release, alas) has interesting input from Rush, Dern and producer Dick Clark.

Scripted by Nicholson when he wasn't sure whether he wanted to stick with acting, *The Trip* is an unusually simple idea: TV commercials director Paul Groves (Peter Fonda) takes a representative acid trip and spends a few hours hallucinating and exploring his own fractured mind. Free of most of the melodramatic trappings of *Psych-Out*, it cuts between subjective representations of Paul's experiences and objective sequences showing how he appears to the straight world; the former are moderately wild, with inevitable borrowings from Corman's Poe pictures (how many acidheads imagined encounters with Angelo Rossitto?), but the latter (depending on subtle playing from Fonda, LSD guide Dern and bystanders like housewife Barboura Morris, a child played by Corbin Bernsen's sister and waitress Luana Anders) are extremely credible and affecting. An interesting, similarly credible aspect of the movie is that (unlike *Psych-Out*) it features square-dressing and -talking drugs experimenters (Dennis Hopper, breaking the record for the use of the word "man" in a speech, is an exception) rather than flamboyant hippie stereotypes. It also makes fine use of L.A. locations, borrowed hip homes (Dern has a swimming pool in his "living room") and authentic night-spots from clubs to laundromats. It may be that the secret of the film's commercial success was that it served as a substitute for acid to audiences who weren't willing to take the risk, but it probably stands as an honest account, though Corman protested AIP's imposition of a fractured freeze frame to suggest that Paul has been irreparably damaged by his trip.

The Trip extras are a commentary track from Corman (reprising familiar anecdotes about his own research trip), a making-of featurette ("Tune In, Trip Out"), an illustrated account of the psychedelic effects from cinematographer Alan Daviau, a contemporary article on the same from *American Cinematographer*, the trailer, an alternative Spanish language track and a pleasantly reassuring "psychedelic light box" music/images feature. *The Trip* was later included as part of the eight-film MGM box set "The Roger Corman Collection". Only the trailer is included on the U.K. disc, but at least British viewers can now see the film, which was banned until 2002.

– KN

PUMPKINHEAD

Colour, 1987, 83m. / Directed by Stan Winston / Starring Lance Henriksen, Jeff East, Kerry Remsen, Kimberly Ross / MGM (US R1 NTSC), Tartan (UK R0 PAL) / WS (1.85:1) (16:9) / DD2.0

City folks run over backwoodsman Lance Henriksen's kid, and he visits a wizened witch "up on Black Ridge" to have her invoke a hillbilly demon known as Pumpkinhead who slaughters the guilty and the innocent in the name of revenge but demands that the invoker pay a terrible price. Despite elaborate monster effects coordinated by debuting director Winston and some interesting attempts at rural folklore, this is essentially just another *Friday the 13th*-style kill-off-some-teenagers-one-by-one movie. It would like to evoke some of the scary backwoods feel of *Deliverance* or *The Evil Dead*, but this DEG production somehow makes its wildernesses unthreatening. A few mildly dirt-brushed *Waltons* extras stand around, but there's no real charge to the clash between rural and urban America and even the woods aren't filmed in an especially scary manner. Dressed in the worst 1987 fashions (puffy trousers, headbands), the dirtbike-riding city kids seem like refugees from the dreaded second *Hills Have Eyes* movie and of the junior cast only East as the most conscience-stricken of the guys can hold the screen against even a low-wattage Henriksen. The monster resembles a scarecrow version of the *Alien* alien and is an impressive fiend, but the plot plods on in by-the-numbers fashion with the only interesting idea turning up in the last shot, which reveals where pumpkinheads come from.

First released on video in the U.K. as *Vengeance: The Demon*, this release restores the original title. Tartan stretch to EC style menus and a trailer gallery of their 'Tartan terror' product, but there are no other extras. The widescreen transfer looks a tad soft, but the fuzzy colours and speckled darks are fairly typical of medium-budget films made before the digital era and not given a brush-up for DVD release. MGM treated it far worse for years in America, saddling it with a cheap transfer sitting around since the early laserdisc days. In 2008 they finally got around to a more respectful edition with a new (much, much improved) anamorphic transfer and a host of extras. Scott Spiegel moderates a commentary track with co-writer Gary Gerani and FX artists Alec Gillis and Tom Woodruff, Jr., who all return for a massive "Pumpkinhead Unearthed" documentary (chopped into six segments as usual per DVD royalty-dodging guidelines). Henriksen and co-stars Kerry Remsen and Kimberly Ross join in as well for a tour of the entire production from its initial inception to completion and rocky distribution history. Also included is a "Demonic Toys" featurette (about the creation of the popular monster figure), a stills gallery, and a reel of behind-the-scenes footage.

– KN

QUAI DES ORFÈVRES

B&W, 1947, 102m. / Directed by Henri-Georges Clouzot / Starring Suzy Delair, Bernard Blier, Louis Jouvet / Criterion (US R1 NTSC), Optimum (UK R2 PAL)

Though his reputation rests primarily on two films, *Diabolique* and *The Wages of Fear*, director Henri-Georges Clouzot established himself as a consummate professional throughout his career, dabbling in a variety of genres with a consistently skewed, often cynical world view. An exceedingly peculiar entry in the film noir cycle which exploded after World War II, *Quai des Orfèvres* mixes double crosses, sumptuous photography, scheming dames, and musical numbers with energetic glee.

Under the stage name of Jenny Lamour, dance hall performer Margueritte (Suzy Delair from *Rocco and His Brothers*) constantly stokes the passions of her often-jealous husband, Maurice (Bernard Blier, father of director Bertrand). The lecherous patrons of the club display more than a passing interest in the full-figured chanteuse as well, particularly one pawing old man whose elegant jackets disguise a wolf underneath. When Maurice bursts into the old man's home to find a corpse by the fireplace, Inspector Antoine (Louis Jouvet) must get to the bottom of the mystery. Police interrogations and attempted lesbian trysts ensue.

Clouzot's comeback film after his scandalous, politically incendiary *Le corbeau* (*The Crow*), this frenetic mixture of styles and genres is unmistakably the work of a younger, slightly less precise talent than the man who later created indelible art from jungle-traversing truckers and homicidal schoolteachers. It's also one of the most superficially pleasant noir films, with characters who are just as likely to end up happily as dead. With the threat of prison hanging over the entire second half of the film, Clouzot ratchets up the suspense level but still finds time for entertaining ways to appease the crowd, be it a funny throwaway line or an audacious camera move, including some delectable crane shots guaranteed to give film students chills. While Delair (Clouzot's mistress at the time, so the story goes) isn't exactly Marlene Dietrich, she carries her role well enough and keeps viewer sympathies in her camp (even when she's seemingly taunting the poor saps around her); however, it's Blier who really steals the show with his sad-sack but sympathetic spouse who might wind up with a murder rap.

As with Criterion's other titles released in conjunction with Rialto, this is a stunning transfer all around with nary a blemish in sight. Detail level is exquisite, particularly in night scenes that find characters framed in both the foreground and background as reflective lighting and billowing cigarette smoke play across their faces. The comparatively blurry theatrical trailer gives a clear idea of how this must have looked pre-restoration, and the end result is thoroughly satisfying. The optional English subtitles are literate and well-paced, nicely capturing the wildly different speech idioms of the characters from different class levels. Extras include a video interview with Clouzot about the film, the aforementioned trailer, and a stills gallery including some wonderfully atmospheric poster art. Also available in the U.K. (with only the trailer) either solo or as part of the "Henri-Georges Clouzot Collection" (along with *The Wages of Fear* and *Le corbeau*).

QUEEN KONG

Colour, 1976, 87m. / Directed by Frank Agrama / Starring Robin Askwith, Rula Lenska, John Clive, Vicki Michelle, Valerie Leon, Linda Hayden, Carol Drinkwater, Fiona Curzon, Mireille Allonville, Anna Bergman, Marta Gillot / Retromedia (US R1 NTSC) / WS (1.85:1)

Reduced to having to thieve food from market stalls in order to survive, hippie Ray Fay (sex comedy vet Robin Askwith) gets to change his ways when he meets famous film director Luce Habit (Rula Lenska). Habit spirits him away aboard her boat The Liberated Lady to the lost island of Lazanga ("where they do the konga") to shoot a movie that will make him an international star. But the native girls of Lazanga are more interested in making him the sacrificial birthday gift of Queen Kong, a venerated 64-foot tall gorilla that inhabits the isle...

The 1970s: a unique era of British cinema during which filmmakers got dreadful comedies down to a fine art. There were dozens of them, each vying for the most cringe-inducing gags imaginable. A former star of exploitationers such as *Horror Hospital* and *The Flesh and Blood Show*, Robin Askwith appeared in more than his fair share of these groaners. *Queen Kong*, however, had it reached the screen way back then, is the one that would have marked a new lowpoint, even for him. Shot in England during the scorching summer of 1976, *Queen Kong* was the Italian-financed

brainchild of Egyptian director Frank Agrama (probably best known for *Dawn of the Mummy*) and co-writer Ron Dobrin. They felt that they were sufficiently in tune with the British sense of humour to pull off a parody of a Hollywood classic that would have 'em rolling in the aisles. Just how much more wrong could they have been? In hindsight one might question how the throw-everything-at-the-screen-and-something's-sure-to-stick approach could ever have seemed like a good idea to anyone other than Agrama. It obviously did though, for he secured a substantial budget and a cast and crew teeming with Brit-talent of the era. Yet barely had shooting wrapped than Dino De Laurentiis (who was gearing up to unleash his own remake of the 1933 *King Kong*) appeared on the scene and took the production to court for infringement of copyright, the result of which forbade its distribution. Agrama departed for Italy with reel upon reel of film in tow and that was that. No one was more pleased at the verdict in the courts than Robin Askwith and Rula Lenska; they had attended a cast and crew screening in Wardour Street and exited concerned that their careers could be in serious jeopardy if *Queen Kong* ever escaped. An illustrated novelisation by James Moffat did appear briefly in the U.K., but if anything it did the film more harm than good.

You had heard *Queen Kong* was supposed to be awful, hadn't you? Well, awful doesn't begin to cover it. The film – purporting to lampoon the 1933 RKO epic – is a giggle-free zone of outstanding proportions. *Queen Kong* is one of those films during which you find yourself wondering what was going through the minds of the actors as they spouted the gibberish passing for dialogue. Their fees, presumably. And those pay cheques must have accounted for a sizeable part of the budget, because wherever else it went it clearly wasn't spent on special effects. The whole show, particularly a bit of rough and tumble between Kong and a papier-mâché

Q

dinosaur, carries all the hallmarks of an under-rehearsed school pantomime. Lines like "It's disgusting – a travesty!" (Lenska) and "Rubbish!" (a rubber crocodile) seem uncannily well suited in context. On the up side – and we're clutching at straws here – it mimics (I could have said "apes", but thought better of it) the original film's plot pretty religiously, switching the male roles to female and vice versa. And the home run in which Kong storms London – shot at the Tuctonia miniature theme park – is (largely, though not wholly) staged very well. Lenska is an adequate enough lead as dotty filmmaker Luce Habit, while Askwith's Ray Fay is basically Timmy Lee in prissy attire.

There was so much potential to create a marvellous send-up here, but it was squandered thanks to a script so bad that every time you think you've just heard the lamest, most unfunny line imaginable, it delves deeper still and trawls up something even worse. As an example, Habit nicknames the protégé Fay "peach", for no apparent reason beyond a set up for a cringe-worthy gag when she sets out to rescue him from native kidnappers; bending forward in a pair of tight shorts she observes "My peach is just within reach." Yes, folks, that's the level we're working at here. And the less said about the atrocious song and dance numbers the better. Along with feeble skits spoofing then-recent films *Jaws*, *Airport* and *The Exorcist*, Agrama also plays with ideas that can only be described as Pythonesque. Case in point the "prehistoric bagpipe" which Habit encounters in the jungle. You could almost believe that the concept emanated from the minds of Cleese and Palin, except that they'd have written something riotously funny to support the inanity. Agrama and Dobrin's words are puerile and, once again, leave you shaking your head in disbelief. In summation the only fun to be derived from enduring *Queen Kong* is face-spotting. Watch out for John Clive (*Four Dimensions of Greta*), Vicki Michelle (*Virgin Witch*), Hammer ladies Valerie Leon and Linda Hayden (the latter as a singing nun!), Carol Drinkwater (*A Clockwork Orange*), Fiona Curzon (*Frightmare*), and a bevy of Harrison Marks lovelies including Mireille Allonville, Anna Bergman and Marta Gillot.

One has to wonder if Dino De Laurentiis ever got to see *Queen Kong* and, if so, how hard he must have laughed at himself for ever thinking it might harm his own movie. Make no mistake, *Queen Kong* is an abomination. Yet, perversely, that very label makes it an irresistible curio that has to be experienced once, if only to verify for yourself that it deserves its dreadful reputation, then a second time to convince yourself it wasn't all a bad dream. Expect to be dismayed and you'll come away royally rewarded.

26 years after she was canned, *Queen Kong* has been unleashed in all her questionable glory on a Region 1 disc from Fred Olen Ray's Retromedia outfit. It's a 1.85:1 theatrical ratio presentation with (typically for Retromedia) a seriously inadequate 6 chapter marks. The picture quality is generally very clean, with the often misty-looking exterior shots reproducing an ill-conceived aspect of the production's original design. Accompanying the movie is a theatrical trailer more likely to put audiences off seeing it than luring them in. The real bonus here though is a feature-length commentary from director Frank Agrama and Fred Olen Ray. Minutes into their chat you realise with incredulity that Agrama is actually proud of his no-talent effort. He chuckles away at the terrible jokes – often repeating them aloud with evident delight at his own wit – and generally has a fine old time reliving the experience of making the film. His memory appears sharp enough on face value and he recounts plenty of anecdotes worth hearing, but when he makes glaring slip-ups such as claiming it was shot "no later than '72" and citing that the studio work was staged at Pinewood (it was Shepperton) it has the unfortunate effect of casting doubt upon all his recollections. Olen Ray too is

on less than top form; he mistakes Robin Askwith for *When Dinosaurs Ruled the Earth*'s Robin Hawdon (even remarking that "it doesn't look like the same guy" – that's because it isn't, Fred!) and misidentifies Linda Hayden as Jenny Hanley. Hanley's name even features erroneously on Retromedia's packaging. The sound is in English only. Also available as part of Retromedia's "Kong Collection", with *Kong Island*.
– TG

QUEEN OF THE DAMNED

Colour, 2002, 101m. / Directed by Michael Rymer / Starring Stuart Townsend, Aaliyah, Marguerite Moreau, Vincent Perez, Lena Olin, Paul McGann, Matthew Newton / Warner (US R1 NTSC, UK R2 PAL) / WS (1.85:1) (16:9) / DD5.1

 This combines plot elements from the two disappointing-to-dire novels Anne Rice cranked out as the first sequels to *Interview with the Vampire* and contrives to be better than the book it is named after, but not by much. The vampire Lestat (a pale, pretty Stuart Townsend) awakens after a century-long nap and discovers posy metal music, then irritates the vampire community by 'coming out' and courting celebrity while they would prefer to lurk in the shadows. His sub-Marilyn Manson songs interest paranormal-watching human librarian Jesse (Marguerite Moreau), who looks him up in a Mile End Goth club that caters to the undead, but his tunes also awaken Akasha (Aaliyah), eponymous mother of all vampires, who makes him her number one disciple and sets about devastating the world, opposed by a cadre of conservative vampires who include Lestat's sire Marius (Vincent Perez) and Jesse's "aunt" Maharet (Lena Olin).

The plotting is of the one-damn-thing-after-another variety, zipping about the world from New Orleans and London to "Glastonbury, West England" and a huge concert in Death Valley (all locales recreated in Australia) as broody characters exchange solemn but comical dialogue and indulge in fight scenes too swift for the camera to catch. It offers spectacular vampire combustions, but its sado-romance is strictly 15-certificate blood-nuzzling and it's hard to take Lestat himself seriously when Townsend plays him as such a feckless twit. More of a Goth action movie than Neil Jordan's *Interview with the Vampire*, it strays too often into the simply camp and is amazingly overpopulated while still reducing a supposedly epic battle for the fate of humanity and vampirekind to groups of people in large rooms ganging up on a hissing, Cleopatra-suited, very snitty supermodel.

Warner's DVD package shows how much can be added even to the most marginal efforts – the extras don't make you think more fondly of the film, but there are at least a lot of them. Over half an hour of deleted scenes still don't make the story that much clearer or provide anything like a decent role for Paul McGann (as Jesse's human mentor) but do, (a) provide a bad garlic joke and, (b) identify various vampires who are part of the gang at the climax by name (most of them have had sequel novels of their own) and confirming that Armand (played by prettyboy Matthew Newton, who contrives to be amazingly terrible with almost no dialogue) is indeed the character played by Antonio Banderas in *Interview with the Vampire* (with a shrug to get over his apparent death last time out). A commentary track with Australian director Rymer, producer Jorge Saralegui and composer Richard Gibbs is strong on how bits of Rice were changed or stuck in and devolves into a play-by-play that at least serves to explain what is going on when the movie itself is dropping the ball.

Also: full-length versions of three music videos excerpted in the film (one is a *Caligari* parody) and another by Gibbs's band Static X; extended concert sequences (but mercifully not by much); three featurettes, on the vampire effects, the all-Goth soundtrack (Marilyn Manson indeed did some of the session singing) and the late star Aaliyah; a gag reel of on-set larking with funny music to underline its humorousness; the trailer; a sheaf of production photos and artwork; DVD-ROM features that turn out (like 95% of DVD-ROM features) to be web-links for those computer users unfamiliar with the term 'search engine'; a French language alternative track (actually, Quebecois); optional subs in English, French and Spanish.
– KN

RAAZ

Colour, 2002, 151m. / Directed by Vikram Bhatt / Starring Bipasha Basu, Dino Morea, Ashutosh Rana / Tip Top (UK R0 PAL) / WS (2.35:1) (16:9), Tips (India R0 NTSC) / WS (2.35:1) / DD5.1

The strange Bollywood horror parade continues with another tweaked and twisted reinterpretation of American shockers courtesy of *Raaz*. Though it's blatantly designed as a copy of Robert Zemeckis's anaemic *What Lies Beneath* (itself a pastiche of much better Hitchcock and Polanski films), *Raaz* incorporates a flurry of other horror references amidst musical numbers, uneven special effects, and photogenic, fashion-friendly Indian performers.

Things kick off with a bang, as a gang of college students are playing spin the bottle in the woods. One girl refuses to play along and takes off into the darkness, pursued by her male admirer. Upon nearing a desolate house, the girl stops in her tracks and is suddenly attacked by an unseen force, presaged by an eerie gust of wind. Cut to the local hospital hours later, where a skilled parapsychology professor (Ashutosh Rana) is called in to help the now-possessed nymphet, who has broken her boyfriend's arm and does a Linda Blair routine in the isolation ward. The ghost expert exclaims that this is no medical matter but rather "an erratic spirit" of the sort that has taunted mankind for centuries. He then leads the doctors back to the woods, where a sinister black bird swoops by just as the possessed girl expires. "Lightning will strike again", he warns... as we cut to a nightclub complete with monks performing an Enigma-style dance number. Lovely Sanjara (Bipasha Basu) scolds her husband, Aditya (Dino Morea), for ignoring her all night in favour of his business colleagues; they leave the club and continue squabbling in the car, where she insists on a divorce. He angrily leaves, and while driving home, Sanjara is involved in a horrific accident that leaves her near death. Upon her recovery, Sanjara and Aditya agree to repair their marriage by returning to the Swiss-like valley of Ooty, where they first fell in love. Sure enough, they go to the same house where the "erratic spirit" roams. A series of spooky accidents begin to mount involving whispering voices, smoky manifestations in mirrors, and torrents of blood spewing from a chandelier, but Aditya refuses to believe that something is amiss. Distraught and teetering on the verge of insanity, Sanjara enlists the aid of the professor to uncover what will prove to be a deadly mystery in which her husband was directly involved.

Skilfully shot in scope and extremely fast-paced, *Raaz* is an engaging horror confection with a winning lead performance by Basu. Most of the musical numbers (apart from the powerhouse "Shanti Shanti" opener, a catchy song to be sure) are the usual romantic filler which may test the patience of horror buffs unfamiliar with Indian movie fare, but the horrific moments are well handled and feature some wonderfully manipulative split surround audio effects. Though the basic structure echoes Zemeckis's film, this is thankfully a much more confident and memorable effort – and it's pretty to look at, too. The only major drawback is an overly long explanatory flashback to explain the ghost's presence; it could have easily been half the length while conveying the same idea.

Tips's DVD is a technically polished affair, as one might expect from a title this recent. Some exterior scenes display damage, which may be a flaw carried over from the original elements, while interiors are beautifully saturated and appear pristine. The dialogue alternates between Hindi and occasional exclamations in English, which can be disorienting; every fifth line or so appears to be a restatement intended for non-Hindi speaking viewers. In any case there are optional English subtitles, which appear far down in the lower letterbox band (so sorry, no zooming in for 16:9 TV owners). The very active (and loud) 5.1 audio track is just as aggressive as most Indian DVD titles. The disc contains the usual chapter stops and song selections, with an array of trailers for recent theatrical Bollywood titles.

RAINY DOG

Colour, 1997, 95m. / Directed by Takashi Miike / Starring Sho Aikawa, Chen Lian-mei, Gao Ming-jun, He Jian-qin, Tomorowo Taguchi / Tartan (UK R0 PAL), Artsmagic (US R1 NTSC) / WS (1.78:1) (16:9)

The second film in Miike's loose "Triad Society" Trilogy, (the other titles are *Shinjuku Triad Society* and *Ley Lines*), this continues to work his distinctive area of ethnic conflict in the tale of a Japanese mobster (Sho Aikawa) living the low-life in Taipei (watching *Gamera* movies to maintain ties with his homeland). The major plotline is evocative of Takeshi Kitano (especially *Kikujiro*) as the hit-man's life is troubled when an ex-girlfriend dumps on him a mostly-silent boy she claims is his. The child tags along (like the kids who see Gamera as a best friend?), barely batting an eyelid as he watches his father casually execute a gangland victim.

A relationship develops, with a fairly brief idyll of scooter-riding in the countryside scored with Ry Cooder-style guitar licks, but things are unlikely to work out happily in a Miike gangster movie. Another exiled Japanese (Tomorowo Taguchi) is pursuing the hit-man, for reasons that remain obscure, leading to a traumatic face-off that at least spurs the kid to speak. The downbeat punchline is "When you grow up, come and take revenge."

As suggested by the title, the dominant tone of the film is established by Taipei's constant downpour. Early on, a comic vagrant wakes up and urinates on the city – an excuse for a skit on the Japanese practice of fogging genitals as a very large scratch on the emulsion suggests an inhumanly lengthy penis – and sighs "ah, Taipei". Throughout, atmospheric rain comes down in sheets, adding a wash of misery to an already doom-laden scanerio. A single note of optimism at the end is the suggestion that the weather might improve, but most viewers will doubt it. Miike's occasional wild humour and weirdo technical flourishes aren't completely absent (red blots on the screen signify gunshot hits), but this is one of his more controlled, less whimsical efforts – it may be that this seriousness of approach is what sets the trilogy apart from works that otherwise share a great many similarities, like the *Dead or Alive* films or *Ichi the Killer*.

Tartan's DVD is in line with their releases of other Miike titles. The widescreen transfer has an aptly grainy, rainy, muddy look, though its shadows (without true blacks) are a touch too murky. Dialogue is in Mandarin and Japanese, with optional English subtitles. Extras are notes from Tom Mes, trailers for this and other Miike movies and a nine-minute talk with the director, who probes his own themes, aims and achievements in an intriguingly detached manner. The same basic disc is also available in America as part of Artsmagic's box set of the entire Miike trilogy and contains a Mes commentary track as well.

– KN

RAPE OF THE VAMPIRE

B&W, 1967, 91m. / Directed by Jean Rollin / Starring Solange Pradel, Ursulle Pauly, Nicole Romain, Bernard Letrou, Catherine Deville, Jacqueline Sieger

THE LIVING DEAD GIRL

Colour, 1982, 86m. / Directed by Jean Rollin / Starring Francoise Blanchard, Marina Pierro / Encore (Holland R2 PAL), The Dark Side (UK R0 PAL) / WS (1.78:1) (16:9), Image (US R1 NTSC) / WS (1.66:1)

Rape of the Vampire, the first film from French horror director Jean Rollin, is actually a short feature and its sequel edited together with fresh credits in the middle of the action. Most of the director's trademarks are present, including a wayward plot that chops and changes in mid-stream, but this cool black and white effort, performed with earnest if amateur flair, has a primitive feel that's rather winning. It is very much in the French serial tradition, going back even beyond Louis Feuillade to the 19th Century serialised stories of Alexandre Dumas or Eugène Sue, a point made explicit by some duelling and powdered-wig flashbacks. The first part deals with four variously glum vampire sisters and their persecution at the hands of peasant vigilantes, while part two dwells more on the society of vampires, who are ruled by a chic model-look African queen and maintain a clinic to drain their victims without fuss. Already Rollin is playing games on the beach, throwing in doomed love stories, filling the ranks of the undead with provocative non sequitur twins, staging pantomime-show vampire charades, mingling super-science and the Gothic, and making evocative use of provincial French locations. Overpopulated and hectic as it is, the film isn't free from longueurs which seem as much a deliberate attempt to blend in with the late-period of the nouvelle vague as a flaw, tossing off rote Hollywood-style action sequences in the manner of *Alphaville*. The eroticism here is casual, ranging from the perverse spectacle of a naked woman whipped bloody with seaweed to the use of clingy, revealing shroud-nightdresses in inappropriate circumstances (two vampire women fence in these outfits in front of a burning building).

Rape of the Vampire first appeared in the U.S. from Redemption's label (through Image) and in the U.K. as the third value pack release from horror magazine *The Dark Side*. Aside from a "hidden" intro from editor Allan Bryce, along with a catalogue of Dark Side materials available, the major add-on is "Vampire Vault", which consists of trailers for *The Living Dead Girl* and *Rape of the Vampire* (also accessible separately in the film sections), plus *The Bloodsucker Leads the Dance*, *Lips of Blood*, *Vampyres*, *Vampyros Lesbos* and the often-seen but welcome bizarro vox pop spot for *I Dismember Mama/ The Blood Spattered Bride*. Also included is a clip from *Les vampires*: not the Feuillade serial, but an anonymous-ish softcore porn movie. A second U.K. edition appeared shortly afterwards directly from Redemption, which also added on the Rollin short film "Les pays loins" (which is also available on several of his other releases around the world, usually *Les demoniaques*).

We covered Redemption's *Living Dead Girl* release in Volume 1, and this is substantially the same version (down to a minute and a half of Eileen Daly biting a naked girl as a tag-logo). Like the co-feature, it has been anamorphically-enhanced and shown in 1.85:1 – which nicely fills a 16:9 monitor and shows off the beauties of the actresses and the countryside (and the fakiness of some of the gore) but trims the 1.66:1 image, occasionally to skull-clipping effect. The film comes from the latter stages of Rollin's career, when he was blending more explicit sex and violence with his habitual surreal melancholia. Incidentally, on the U.K. menu the titles of the films are scrambled, so that clicking on one leads to the sub-menu for the other. Also included is a selection of stills, rather oddly cropped and pebble-dashed in the presentation. The soundtrack is in French, with optional English subtitles provided.

The best of all available options are the elaborate Dutch releases of the separate films as decked-out special editions, clearly geared to an English-friendly audience. *Rape of the Vampire* features a Rollin audio commentary, a 22-minute featurette ("L'histoire de la nuit des horloges"), three interview featurettes (with Jacqueline Seiger, Alain-Yves Beaujour, and composer François Tusques), a photo gallery, two alternative "censored" scenes, and the theatrical trailer. *The Living Dead Girl* contains Blanchard and Rollin video intros, a Blanchard commentary and interview, additional interviews with actor Jean-Pierre Bouyxou and composer Philippe D'Aram, three alternative scenes, a photo gallery, and a soundtrack CD. As of this writing, Rollin's audio commentary for this film released on laserdisc has yet to see the light of day on DVD.

– KN

RATTLERS
Colour, 1975, 81m. / Directed by John C. McCauley / Starring Sam Chew, Elisabeth Chauvet, Celia Kaye, Dan Priest
SNAKE PEOPLE
Colour, 1968, 91m. / Directed by Juan Ibáñez and Jack Hill / Starring Boris Karloff, Julissa, Tongolele [Yolanda Montes], Rafael Muñoz Santanon, Rafael Bertrand, Carlos East / Something Weird (US R1 NTSC)

This reptile-themed SWV package is essentially a nice platform to release *Rattlers*, a low-key 1975 exploitatio flick remembered mainly for its lurid poster (seen on the cover) of a naked screaming babe in a bathtub full of angry snakes. Of course, the scene in the film is a lot less impressive, with all of two sluggish serpents doing their best to stay away from the flailing, nagging mom victim character (Celia Kaye).

A couple of boys venture into the California desert in search of a 'real-live skeleton' and fall into a pitful of snakes. The sheriff calls in a handsome herpetologist (Sam Chew), who is so underfunded that he has to share a lab and doesn't even own one of those long-handled grabber things real-life snake scientists rely on and which would come in handy in several scenes. The academic is partnered with a women's-libber photographer (Elisabeth Chauvet) who rubs his chauvinist ass the wrong way, though they later bond in the desert as they visit the sites of several horrible deaths (the budget isn't there for make-up snakebites, let alone the bloated corpses described). The human culprit turns out to be an army officer (Dan Priest) with a covert bioweapons program going, who has dumped a leaky canister of nerve gas in a mine: designed to make enemy soldiers turn on each other in a frenzy, the gas has made the snakes aggressive, though the film has no real way of showing this.

We see snakes coiled and hear rattles and hisses, but the wranglers don't get any actual attack footage, so the climax has to involve the renegade Priest going mad and shooting people (including the Atlanta-born cop who has moved West because you never hear of policemen being shot in small desert towns) then blowing himself up with a dropped grenade before he can even get the reward he deserves by being overwhelmed by the rattlers. It has that sunny, casual look of the '70s (Chew models a natty safari jacket) and also that odd lack of urgency exploitation movies had back then. In the third act, the hero and heroine take time out from the snake-hunt for an evening of balancing on fountains in Vegas, while the Sheriff reacts to a rash of deaths by assigning a couple of civilians to poke around and otherwise doing nothing much. SWV's transfer, which can be accessed by highlighting "Start Slithering" or "Choose Your Venom", is a well-above average job, coming from a remarkably damage-free print. It's in glorious standard-frame mono, which is what you'd expect for this sort of thing, and the colour tends slightly to pink in the desert exterior scenes.

Though billed as a *Rattlers* "Special Edition", the disc offers no extras that relate to the main feature but does squeeze in a whole second movie, one of the quartet of quickies ground out in Mexico during 1968, with scenes shot in Los Angeles by Jack Hill featuring Boris Karloff (his last screen work). Originally entitled *La muerta vivente*, it has been around under the aliases *Island of the Snake People* and *Cult of the Dead* but is here presented with minimally-animated credits as *Snake People* (not, as promised, *The Snake People*).

A thinly-plotted effort set on a Caribbean island, this spends a lot of time on orange-lit voodoo ceremonies presided over by a sinister belly-dancer (Tongolele) with a white streak in her hair and an evil glare, and a capering dwarf (Rafael Muñoz Santanon) who decapitates chickens (probably for real) and sometimes belies the film's vague period setting by sporting hippie shades and a daisy decal on his bald head. A French officer (Rafael Bertrand) vows to shut down the cult, while a sceptical outsider (Carlos East) woos a temperance campaigner (Julissa) in a fetching cloche hat. The heroine's uncle is Carl van Molder (Karloff), a white-suited scientist who has devoted his life to the study of voodoo and can move a small mirror with his mind if he concentrates very hard. The cult's rituals involve a black-robed, hatted and goggled Baron Samedi, who also smokes a cigar through a hole in his hood; in any other film, there'd be an attempt to pretend that this villain isn't kindly old Boris in disguise, but here the get-up is mainly so another actor back in Mexico can shoulder some of the menace and murder scenes before van Molder is shown to be Damballah after all (another voice sometimes reads Karloff's wild lines, with no attempt to match his distinctive tones). It's a scrappy, protracted and redundant exercise, which manages to get so confused at the finish that it's hard to tell what exactly has happened and why people have acted as they have.

The transfer is of a very rough-looking, splicy print with hissy, poppy sound, but the Crayola colours are vivid as Hill and Ibáñez try for some Corman lighting effects. It has one priceless line as the priestess discovers a sleazy character in a clinch with a female zombie and decrees "Damballah doesn't like that sort of thing!" Later, the unfortunate lech is attacked by cannibal women for his pains, so at least he gets what he deserves.

The expected Something Weird Video generous package of extras includes: trailers for *Rattlers*, *Attack of the Giant Leeches*, *The Black Cat*, *The Crawling Hand*, *The Crawling Thing/Creature of Evil*, *Creature of the Walking Dead*, *Devil Woman/Dragons Never Die*, *Don't Open the Window*, *The Horror of Party Beach*, *The Killer Shrews*, *Night of the Cobra Woman* and *Spasmitus*

Midnight Thrill Show; the pretty numbing burlesque shorts "Snake Charmer", "Deena Newell, the Cobra Girl", "Esmeralda at the Cafe d'Artist" and "Snake Lover"; the mondo nature short "Snake vs. Snake"; the usual 'ghastly gallery of ghoulish comic cover art with music by the Dead Elvi'; and an easily-accessible "hidden feature" extract in which topless girls are tormented by snakes.

– KN

REAR WINDOW

Colour, 1954, 115m. / Directed by Alfred Hitchcock / Starring James Stewart, Grace Kelly, Thelma Ritter, Raymond Burr, Georgine Darcy / Universal (US R1 NTSC, UK R2 PAL) / WS (1.85:1) (16:9)

 Having been confined to a wheelchair with a leg encased in plaster, magazine shutterbug L.B. "Jeff" Jeffries (James Stewart) is left with empty, sweltering days watching the activities of neighbours visible through the large rear window of his apartment. Despite the advice of his no-nonsense nurse, Stella (Thelma Ritter), Jeff resorts to binoculars and a telephoto lens to spy on one suspicious tenant, Lars Thorwald (Raymond Burr), whose bickering, bedridden wife disappears one rainy night under mysterious circumstances. Jeff's troubled relationship with fashion plate Lisa Freemont (Grace Kelly) gets a much needed jolt when she agrees to help him prove that Thorwald murdered and dismembered his wife, with Stella joining Lisa as a field operative to expose the crime.

Usually classified as an extended metaphor for the act of watching a movie, Alfred Hitchcock's delicious entertainment operates on so many levels that multiple viewings never fail to reap ever-increasing rewards. The potentially sordid subject matter is handled with enough skill and subtlety to make it palatable for viewers of all ages, while the snappy dialogue and pitch-perfect performances are so engaging that the limited confines never feel setbound. The depiction of each neighbour as a different facet of the human impulse and sexual drive (or lack thereof) poses a series of options for Jeff and Lisa's future, together or apart, while offering surprising possibilities for viewers' own lives as well. The immediate need to empathize with the cinematic shadows on the screen makes this experience akin to studying lab samples under a microscope with the sudden realization that these samples could just as easily be watching you. This sense of violation is carried out to its logical conclusion when a shadowy Thorwald steps out of his own apartment and into our own "safe" environment, Jeff's apartment, where we find not a moustache-twirling villain but a confused human being whose life took a disastrous wrong turn.

After a 1961 reissue in the wake of *Psycho*, the Paramount-released *Rear Window* was withdrawn from circulation and remained impossible to see until a 1983 theatrical resurrection along with *The Man Who Knew Too Much*, *Rope*, *The Trouble with Harry*, and *Vertigo*. Robert A. Harris and James Katz, engineers of the touch-and-go restoration of *Vertigo*, then restored the film for a 2000 theatrical reissue. Most exhibitions framed the film at 1.85:1 or opted for the complete filmed image at 1.33:1, though the 1.66:1 framing found on the DVD seems ideal composition-wise. The restoration adjusts the colour and black levels back to their original balance; note those sumptuous sunset hues at several points during the film. Significantly, this restoration also reinstates the memorable opening and closing Paramount logos, unseen for nearly 40 years. The accompanying 55-minute documentary, "*Rear Window* Ethics", is a less satisfying affair; Laurent Bouzareau introduces with his usual gripping montage of highlights, but after that the material would

R

be threadbare for a 15-minute featurette. Pat Hitchcock O'Connell repeats herself many times, recalling her visits to the film set and committing some off-the-cuff factual errors (claiming Cornell Woolrich's real name was William Irish, while the opposite is true). Directors and Hitch buffs Curtis Hanson and Peter Bogdanovich also chime in, with the latter sharing excerpts from his own audio interviews with Hitchcock. Unfortunately this is almost entirely filler, rehashing the basic voyeurism chatter we've heard before. Other subjects include actress Georgine Darcy, assistant director Herbert Coleman, and Harris and Katz for a restoration demo (with the sequence involving the famous Kelly/Stewart kiss providing the documentary's high point). Screenwriter John Michael Hayes contributes a separate video interview as he discusses the process of expanding upon a simple short story, though the literary source's immense legal ramifications on this film's distribution are curiously ignored. Also included is a hilariously overwrought reissue trailer with original narrative footage of Stewart addressing the audience along with a very overexcited narrator, as well as a five-film 1983 reissue trailer with Stewart's voiceover. Other extras include various production photos, poster art, and cast and crew bios. A subsequent "remastered" edition prepared for Universal's "Alfred Hitchcock Masterpieces" collection appears identical, but a two-disc Legacy Series release from the same studio splits everything onto two discs (giving the feature more room for an improved encoding) and adds an audio commentary with Hitchcock author John Fawell, a bonus *Alfred Hitchcock Presents* episode ("Mr. Blanchard's Secret"), "Pure Cinema: Through the Eyes of a Master" (a new featurette featuring influenced filmmakers including Martin Scorsese), excerpts from Hitchcock's legendary interviews with Truffaut about this particular film, and a 25-minute "Breaking Barriers" study of Hitch's innovative use of sound mixing in his films.

RED DAWN

Colour, 1984, 114m. / Directed by John Milius / Starring Patrick Swayze, C. Thomas Howell, William Smith, Harry Dean Stanton, Ron O'Neal, Powers Boothe, Ben Johnson / MGM (UK R2 PAL, US R1 NTSC) / WS (1.85:1) (16:9) / DD2.0

Made at the height of the Reagan Era, with the then-monolithic Soviet Union tagged as "the Evil Empire", *Red Dawn* is at once an ordinary mainstream shoot 'em up action picture and an ideologically demented exercise in paranoid Americana. It opens with captions establishing a near-future in which cataclysmic events (a Green Party Government in Germany instituting nuclear disarmament) have put the Russians (and their Cuban-Nicaraguan allies) in a position to threaten the USA. In Calumet, Colorado, a high school class is being taught about Mongol Hordes when paratroops land on the playing field and set about gunning down innocents and taking over the town. Some kids, mostly members of the loser local football team (the "Wolverines"), stock up on guns, snack food and toilet paper and head for the mountains. Months later, the Russians have occupied a swathe of the country, and the Wolverines become a daring Resistance group, harrying the enemy with well-planned ambushes. The Russians react with mass civilian executions, and then call in a hard man (William Smith) to track down and exterminate the Resistance.

A great deal of this is couched in terms of hard-bitten camp, such as Harry Dean Stanton shouting "avenge me" from behind the wire at the drive-in which has been turned into a "re-education centre", but the *It Happened Here* business of invaders transforming the familiar (*Alexander Nevsky* at the local movie-house, Russian troops in McDonald's) always has a frisson. The most interesting character, and the key to political confusion, is Bella (Ron O'Neal), the Cuban commander who finds it hard to cope with the Wolverines because he has spent his career fighting "on the side of the insurgents" and can't switch tactics to become the oppressor. Weirdly, this plot-strand reveals a chink in the right wing ideology (also found in the *Rambo* movies) in that the wish-fulfilment fantasy is of a world where America stands for freedom-loving rebel guerrillas and the reds are the big bullies crushing the will of the people underlines the fact that the film comes from a time when things are the other way round. To Milius's way of thinking, America needs to be attacked, invaded and overthrown for Americans to regain any sense of purpose – even if it means teenagers becoming mountain men and outright psychopaths. The iconic '80s teen cast perhaps don't rise to the occasion, though the underrated Howell does something almost subtle with the role of the youth who comes to enjoy summarily executing prisoners. Patrick Swayze, in particular, is glum in a role that needs some of the near-mystic presence he brings to *Point Break* or *Road House* and the other kids are upstaged by "guest stars" like Powers Boothe (downed pilot) and Ben Johnson (grandfatherly plot-explainer).

MGM's first stripped-down DVD is acceptable, but no more. The non-anamorphic widescreen is just off 1.85:1, leaving slivers of black top and bottom if viewed on a 16:9 monitor. The presentation also opts to have scenes in Spanish and Russian subtitled below the image, so widescreen viewers have the option of toggling between screen sizes to find out what's going on, or give up and watch windowboxed for the storyline or 1.85:1 for the visuals. The transfer has few actual flaws, but still demonstrates that pre-digital, slightly battered 1980s look; with the puffy hairstyles and dated politics, that's probably appropriate. Dolby Surround tracks are offered in English, French, German, Italian and Spanish, as are subtitles

in a slew of languages (not, unsurprisingly, Russian). The only extra is a trailer that has a duff temp score which makes you appreciate how much Basil Poledouris brings to the table but also affords glimpses of scenes and maybe even sub-plots (a Russian officer dating an American girl?) that didn't make the final cut.

In 2007, MGM revisited the film under its distribution deal with Fox (when talk of a remake began floating around) and offered a new anamorphic transfer that's a significant step up if still very dated in appearance. (The audio remains the same.) Extras for this version are much more substantial: "Red Dawn Rising" (a new featurette with Milius, the late Swayze, Sheen, Howell, Thompson, and Booth, most interesting for the director's own political take on the project), "Building the Red Menace" (a look at the creation of military forces and sets for the film), "Military Training" (with Milius and the film's CIA consultant talking about the rigours used to train the actors), and "WWIII Comes to Town" (with Swayze and Milius revisiting the original New Mexico shooting locations and their residents). Oh, and for the feature itself, there's a silly "carnage counter" (perhaps inspired by the *Twitch of the Death Nerve* DVD) that keeps a body count every time someone snuffs it during the film. Some of the stormy production history (original screenwriter Kevin Reynolds fell out with Milius, and both felt the finished film skewed against their wishes towards simple propaganda) obviously gets glossed over so long after the fact here, but it's still a fascinating film that took a lot time to receive any sort of context on home video.

– KN

THE RED MONKS

Colour, 1988, 85m. / Directed by Gianni Martucci / Starring Lara Wendel, Gerardo Amato, Malisa Longo / Hardgore (UK R0 PAL)

Prefaced by a "Lucio Fulci Presents" tag that predates Wes Craven's habit of getting written into the publicity of films he had little to do with, this conventional bit of castle creepery mostly resembles a Gothic horror make-over for *Rebecca*. Fairly little-known, it's a pleasant watch for fans of Italian genre movies without delivering any major innovations.

It opens in the present day with an aristocrat wandering around a dilapidated ruin where his family used to live and encountering an odd veiled woman who plays the violin and exchanges significant chat with him. Then he enters the crypt-like basement and finds a nude woman standing before an altar, and she spins round with a scythe to chop off his head... prompting a "fifty years earlier" caption and a set-up whereby the saturnine, handsome, secretive master of the castle (Gerardo Amato) hastily woos and marries a sweet young artist (Lara Wendel), exciting the jealousy of his devoted but sinister housekeeper (Malisa Longo). The brooding husband is unable to consummate his marriage, perhaps because the mysterious scarlet-robed and -hooded monks who have a hold over him order that he deliver her to the altar as a virgin sacrifice. The heroine is troubled by her husband's obvious duplicity (not to mention upset when her ooh-la-la French maid's head turns up in a picnic hamper) and somehow gains a pony-tailed, pinstriped rapist as a boyfriend, then visits a know-it-all academic to learn about the history of her new home and the Red Monks. It's clear that a bloody sacrifice is in the offing, but so also are a couple of plot twists that rearrange assumptions about everything that has gone before.

While the 1930s period setting (stronger on cars and clothes than hairstyles) and some mild softcore evoke Joe D'Amato's near-unwatchable late '80s output (*The*

Pleasure, etc.), *I Frati Rossi/The Red Monks* (both the Italian and English titles appear on the print) is mostly an enjoyable horror-mystery with conventional elements thrown together to allow for some genuine surprises.

Hardgore's DVD offers a pristine standard-frame transfer (the film was clearly made with TV and video in mind) which features lovely green landscapes and appropriately vivid reds for the monks' robes and the head-lopping blood-spills. As is too often the case, the only audio option is an English dub that suggests a lacklustre radio play retelling of the same story playing over the original film. Some of the players (Longo, especially) seem to be delivering their dialogue in spitting, venomous Italian and it'd be nice to get the measure of their performances in the original. The extras are a trailer, an image gallery consisting of a poster and two video sleeves, an extensive Lucio Fulci filmography but nothing about the actual makers of the film, and some trailers for the rest of the Hardgore output.
– KN

THE RED SQUIRREL

Colour, 1993, 113m. / Directed by Julio Medem / Starring Emma Suárez, Nancho Novo / Tartan (UK R0 PAL), Sogepaq (Spain R2 PAL) / WS (1.85:1) (16:9) / DD5.1

Poised atop a bridge and despondent over a breakup with his girlfriend, Jota (Nancho Novo) braces himself to plunge over the edge. Suddenly a girl on a motorcycle, Lisa (Emma Suárez), crashes from the bridge onto the beach below. Suffering from amnesia at the hospital, Lisa has no reason to protest when Jota explains that she is his girlfriend and should accompany him on a road trip they had been planning. Together they venture to the Red Squirrel campground, and through flashbacks and mutual discoveries, their darkest secrets erupt during a shattering climax.

The assured second film from Julio Medem (*Sex and Lucia*) draws him into the thriller genre, though as usual he refuses to be restricted by normal cinematic conventions. The intricate characters explore a wide range of emotional reactions to each other and their surroundings, and while the film relies moderately on standard Hitchcockian ploys to generate suspense, this is also a rich character study and rewarding stylistic exercise. The use of dreams and flashbacks adds layers to the already ambiguous narrative, which twists viewer sympathies in a number of surprising directions. Though the set up will remind viewers of such sexy captive dramas as *Tie Me Up! Tie Me Down!*, Medem's *Squirrel* is a wholly original animal that dramatically paved the way for his future masterpieces.

Inexplicably denied a wide international release, *The Red Squirrel* earned a sizeable cult reputation primarily through home video. Though best experienced on the big screen, the film looks quite fine on both the U.K. and Spanish DVD incarnations. The all-important black levels here are dead on, and Medem's unusual colour choices come through with blazing clarity. The pricier Spanish disc gets the edge in terms of extras thanks to a Medem interview and Goya Award coverage, but these are in Spanish only and won't be of much help to English-speaking viewers. Both DVDs offer English subtitles and a collection of Medem trailers.

REIGN IN DARKNESS

Colour, 2002, 90m. / Directed by David W. Allen and Kel Dolen / Starring David W. Allen, John Barresi, Kel Dolen / Hardgore (UK R2 PAL), Madman (Australia R4 PAL), Fox (US R1 NTSC) / WS (2.35:1) (16:9) / DD2.0

"One minute I thought I was working on a cure for HIV, the next minute I find I'm responsible for a new generation of genetically-engineered vampires." Low-budget filmmaking has become more elaborate in the new century: even the cheapest semi-homemade direct-to-video quickie can stretch to widescreen digital camerawork and non-stop action. Sadly, the old bugaboos of marginal cinema – poor scripting and appalling performances – remain as prevalent as ever.

This would-be slick Australian vampire movie has characters walk around in cool shades and black leather trenchcoats, shooting at each other and spilling gore all over the floor, but it's still a nonsensical trudge through over-familiar territory with very few characters (some doing dreadful cod-Yank voices) repeatedly clashing in deserted warehouses and concrete parking structures. The premise is that RVK-17, a drug derived from vampire blood supposedly developed to cure HIV, is being administered to indigents by a sinister organisation. Michael Dorn (Kel Dolen), a government scientist, is accidentally injected and transforms into a hard-to-kill black-eyed blood-drinker who is pursued by a vicious bounty hunter and a bleached blond first-generation vampire through a depopulated urban area, surviving numerous murder attempts. Eventually, Dorn straps on a Kevlar vest that protects his heart and goes up against the originators of the RVK-17 project, "the last of the pure-blood vampires", in order to secure a vaccine which will cure him. The Dracula figure behind it all is Raphael Ravencroft (John Barresi), who swishes a traditional cape and complains at length through fangs about penicillin and pollution, which have all but exterminated vampirekind, while undramatically rehashing the conspiracy-themed storyline. Dolen and David W. Allen, who

411

seem to have done almost everything on the movie, stress posing-with-guns scenes and ominous sneer dialogue.

The U.K. and U.S. DVDs have a trailer. Adventurous souls who want more than just the film can sample Australia's special edition, which also features a commentary by Dolan and Allen and a five-minute behind the scenes featurette. The transfer is sharp, but the film tedious.

– KN

REIGN OF FIRE

Colour, 2002, 102m. / Directed by Rob Bowman / Starring Matthew McConaughey, Christian Bale, Izabella Scorupco, Gerard Butler / Buena Vista (Blu-ray & DVD) (US RA/R1 HD/NTSC, UK R2 PAL) / WS (2.35:1) (16:9) / DTS/DD 5.1

 Audiences reared on the global devastation of blockbuster films such as *Independence Day* and *Armageddon* were disappointed that *Reign of Fire* – which goes further than these epics in actually ending human civilisation – conveys the fall of mankind via a Christian Bale voice-over rather than delivering on the poster promise of thousands of dragons laying waste to major cities. This is less a disaster/invasion story than an essay in the rarer survive-and-reconstruct cycle (e.g.: *The Day of the Triffids, Dawn of the Dead, The Postman*), visiting the traditional post-cataclysm world where tomatoes are impossibly rare but helicopter fuel isn't that hard to come by. The interest is not so much in combating the obvious menace (the dragons) as it is in debating the manner in which civilisation should be preserved and the kind of man who embodies the values of true heroism.

The antagonists are contrasted leaders: Quinn (a bearded Bale) is a British patriarch of something that cross-breeds a feudal castle with an agrarian collective, advocates keeping heads down as the dragons hurry through their specialised and inevitably self-destructive life-cycle, and is identified as a father, a farmer and even a teacher-entertainer (he enchants an audience of children with a fable-like play that turns out to be a remake of *The Empire Strikes Back*); Van Zan (a bald and tattooed Matthew McConaughey) is an American warrior, at the head of a drilled army who obey his every command, fixated on the destruction of the enemy at all costs, a cigar-chewing fanatic who rides a tank as if he were a half-machine centaur, and a visionary who has deduced the dragons' weaknesses (they are especially vulnerable to attack at "magic hour", dusk) and formulated a plan for genocide. Unusually for a Summer action movie, *Reign of Fire* makes the man of peace the protagonist (Quinn even gets the former Bond girl, chopper pilot Izabella Scorupco) rather than a well-intentioned nice guy who has to step aside or become a ruthless killer. *Shane* and *The Magnificent Seven* make gestures towards hailing father-farmers as greater heroes than unattached killers, but they don't mean it; this actually does. In the finale, Quinn temporarily becomes a warrior to save the day, but the thrust of the plot has been to criticise Van Zan's fire-eyed resolution. "Only one thing worse than dragons", Quinn's best pal (Gerard Butler) says as the tanks trundle up to the castle. "Americans!"

Rob Bowman (*The X-Files*) stages a few startling moments with the ragged-winged bat-lizard dragons, but is better with the people: an early scene in which errant castle inhabitants are rescued from a burning tomato patch by firemen in patched asbestos suits is excellent stuff, but the big dragon-catching exercise is too absurd to be really exciting (the gimmick is a free-fall parachutist acting as live bait to draw the monster into the firing line). It sometimes seems as if the spectacle and action have been skimped or trimmed unwisely: the destruction of an entire population of female dragons is tripped over with absurd ease as if a major effects sequence wasn't delivered in time for the release date. Considered as a dragon movie, it one-ups *DragonHeart* and *Dragonworld* by presenting not noble, sympathetic beasts but CGI incarnations of the malignant monsters of legend unseen onscreen since *Dragonslayer*.

Attempts to shoehorn scientific rationalisations (the apparent fire-breathing is due to glands in the mouth that squirt jets of chemical which combust when mixed) are less impressive than Quinn's need to create a new superstition about man's mortal enemy. The traditional line "time to say our prayers" delivered to an audience of grubby children (a cue for maudlin embarrassment in most movies) leads to a chilling survivalist liturgy that replaces "for ever and ever amen" with "and never look back". Though a little too grim to be a crowd-pleaser, suffering from both lacunae and detours, *Reign of Fire* delivers sufficient unconventional and unusual elements to recommend it as an offbeat, provocative science fantasy adventure.

Disney subdivision Touchstone has done a solid but not outstanding job on the DVD and a much more impressive job on the robust Blu-ray (both of which contain identical supplements). The 5.1 soundtrack (in English and version Française) is great on rumbling sound effects, but some of the shouted dialogue tends to get lost in the melee, which might tempt you to the English captions or Spanish subtitles. The extras are the trailer (also a batch of other Touchstone trailers, including a plug for the *Reign of Fire* PS2 game) and three okay featurettes, on the creation of the CGI dragons, the physical on-set pyrotechnics and director Bowman (who has interesting things to say, making it a shame he wasn't on hand for a commentary track). Not quite an extra but almost a covert release for Ed Shearmur's soundtrack are the various music cues that play over the DVD's impressively fiery menus.

– KN

REPULSION

B&W, 1965, 104m. / Directed by Roman Polanski / Starring Catherine Deneuve, Ian Hendry, Yvonne Furneaux, Valerie Taylor / Criterion (Blu-ray & DVD) (US RA/R1 HD/NTSC) / WS (1.66:1) (16:9), Anchor Bay, Odeon (UK R2 PAL) / WS (1.75:1) (16:9) / DTS/DD5.1, Studio Canal (France R2 PAL) / WS (1.75:1) (16:9), Pioneer (Japan R2 NTSC) / WS (1.66:1), EPI, Koch (US R0 NTSC)

The first English-language film for director Roman Polanski, star Catherine Deneuve, and co-writer Gerard Brach, this undisputed horror classic has lost little of its power to unnerve modern viewers. This is also the initial foray into Polanski's series of "apartment horrors", which continued with *Rosemary's Baby*, *The Tenant*, and less directly, *The Pianist*.

Here the tortured protagonist is Carole, a French girl who lives in London with her sister, Hélène (Yvonne Furneaux), and works in a beauty salon. Unlike her more sexually experienced sibling, Carole recoils from the touch of men and furiously brushes her teeth after an unwelcome kiss. With a raw rabbit left to be cooked still sitting fresh in the kitchen, Hélène decides to take off for a few days with her not-so-noble boyfriend, Michael (Ian Hendry), whose amorous activities keep Carole awake at night. Left alone, the fragile beauty slowly goes to pieces... and those unlucky enough to enter the apartment during her breakdown encounter a very nasty surprise.

Part of the great horror upheaval of the 1960s, *Repulsion* was often compared at the time to its closest counterpart, Alfred Hitchcock's *Psycho*; however, Polanski's film has been more fortunate over the years in that, despite a few feeble attempts, it simply cannot be copied or sequelized. The inventive use of disorienting sound (on a par with Robert Wise's *The Haunting*) is the perfect complement to the film's judicious mixture of slow, subtle chills (cracks splitting open the apartment walls, with hands eventually emerging from within) and sudden shocks (the much-touted razor scene, Carole's rape hallucination, the unforgettable wardrobe "jump"). Fresh off her success in *The Umbrellas of Cherbourg*, Deneuve is the perfect choice as Carole; even at her maddest (and most catatonic), she remains sympathetic thanks to those amazing, doe-like eyes. Extra kudos must also go to cinematographer Gilbert Taylor (*Dr. Strangelove*, *The Omen*), whose manipulation of cinematic space and distorting lenses is never less than masterful.

Despite its high profile status, *Repulsion* suffered more than its share of substandard video transfers for decades and was (erroneously) presumed to be public domain for a few years. Early no-frills American DVDs are a fuzzy mess and best avoided, pure and simple. The Japanese DVD (in English with optional Japanese subtitles) is passable, on par with Criterion's letterboxed laserdisc edition. An anamorphic upgrade first came from France courtesy of Studio Canal, while Anchor Bay took the same master and yielded even finer results for their U.K. release. Apart from some extremely mild scratches visible on the far right (especially during the first few minutes), the source material is in excellent shape with strong contrast levels, essential to enjoying the monochromatic imagery. Anchor Bay's decision to include DTS and 5.1 remixes in addition to the original mono track actually makes sense here; while the film should be seen at least once with its original single-channel mix for the sake of historical purity, the surround mixes are extremely effective with notably aggressive surround use during the more horrific scenes. Everything from jangling telephones to thudding footsteps erupt back and forth between the speakers, resulting in an appropriately queasy sonic experience. The Anchor Bay disc is also the only version to include the audio commentary with

Polanski and Deneuve (recorded separately) first released on the Criterion laserdisc; it's an informative and candid discussion, with Polanski discussing many of the film's aspects that dissatisfy him now. Also included is a very informative 23-minute featurette, "A British Horror Film", produced by Blue Underground. Polanski gets the bulk of the screen time here, but he's joined by Taylor, art director Seamus Flannery, and producer Gene Gutowski for a lively look at the film's genesis as one of the more controversial and acclaimed genre efforts in English cinema. (Curiously, the deliberately anti-erotic and mostly implied rape passages were responsible for numerous U.K. censorship hassles over the years, though the DVD is thankfully uncut.) Also included are a gallery of Flannery's designs, an interview with *Eye and Brain* author Professor Richard L. Gregory (one of Polanski's potential collaborators), and a fullscreen theatrical trailer. Odeon reissued the film in the U.K. with the same commentary as well as a 1984 Polanski interview with Clive James (a nice 46-minute chat in a restaurant) and an interview with backup cinematographer Stanley Long. The last release out of the gate, but certainly the most visually impressive, is Criterion's second stab at the film on both Blu-ray and DVD, with the former offering an amazingly textured and rewarding presentation that also happens to be the only anamorphic one in the original aspect ratio. Their audio commentary appears here again along with the Blue Underground featurette, a rare 1964 TV documentary shot on the set, and a booklet with an essay by Bill Horrigan.

RETURN OF THE LIVING DEAD

Colour, 1985, 91m. / Directed by Dan O'Bannon / Starring Clu Gulager, Linnea Quigley, James Karen, Thom Mathews, Don Calfa, Beverly Randolph, Brian Peck, Allan Trautman / MGM (Blu-ray & DVD) (US RA/R1 HD/NTSC), MGM (UK R2 PAL) / WS (1.85:1) (16:9), Tartan (UK R0 PAL)

The legal fallout over 1968's horror classic *Night of the Living Dead* still lingers today, as divergent sequels and other cinematic riffs involving George A. Romero, Tom Savini, John Russo, and a host of others continue to pop up every few years. These can range from worthy (*Dawn of the Dead* and Savini's remake) to insulting (*Children of the Living Dead*), but horror fans had an especially weird situation in 1985 when two distinct sequels-of-sorts appeared on movie screens almost simultaneously. Though hobbled by production cutbacks, Romero's *Day of the Dead* was a haunting and gruelling conclusion to his dead trilogy that brought his beloved zombies into the 1980s with great panache. Meanwhile, Russo and Russ Streiner teamed up with Romero pal Rudy Ricci for a half-funny, half-scary sequel that ignored *Dawn* entirely. *Alien* and *Dead and Buried* scribe Dan O'Bannon was brought in for screenwriting and directing chores, and fortunately he proved to be just the right man for the job. The resulting film took nearly everyone by surprise and became an instant cult classic, propelling naked punker Linnea Quigley to scream queen status and kicking off another line of sequels on its own.

The legendary opening sequence introduces two dim-witted medical supply employees, Frank (James Karen) and Freddy (Thom Mathews). The former tells an elaborate story claiming that *Night of the Living Dead* was actually a bastardized version of a true story, and the real zombies are now stored in the supply warehouse in which both men work. Of course a canister containing one of them is accidentally opened, sending contaminated incineration fumes into the air over a nearby graveyard. A medical corpse promptly comes to life, wreaking havoc on the two numbskulls before finally being dispatched... well, as the characters point out, it doesn't happen like it did in the movie. The company owner (Clu Gulager) and a carload of punks are drawn into the action as well when the dead begin to rise from their graves, loudly demanding "Brains!"

Usually classified as a comedy, *Return of the Living Dead* does contain some wonderfully witty moments (including an unforgettable diagnosis scene involving two major characters) but is, above all, a horror movie through and through. This is not a campy spoof; it treats its subject with reverence and plays fair with the viewer, never condescending and always trying to deliver as many thrills as possible. The result is one of the best horror films of the 1980s, up there with the likes of *Re-Animator*, *Near Dark*, *The Stepfather*, and *A Nightmare on Elm Street*. Gulager and Karen deservedly earned a lot of genre work after this, but the entire cast nails their roles perfectly with a tricky script, which balances a wide variety of tonal shifts. There's also an impeccably chosen punk score (featuring The Cramps, of course) and an unforgettable shocker of an ending that would never, ever fly with today's audiences.

Endless rights entanglements have resulted in *Return of the Living Dead* going in and out of availability to a frustrating degree. Originally shot open matte, the first 1.33:1 transfer shown on cable and available on video from HBO has long been the most widely seen, ported over eventually to a visually mediocre, extras-free DVD release in the U.K. from Tartan (which nevertheless is the only DVD edition to feature the film's original soundtrack). (Ironically, a matted laserdisc was put out as well, only in the U.K.) MGM's first U.S. DVD offers a more generous package, beginning with the option of either open matte or 1.85:1 letterboxed presentations. Both look quite nice, improving dramatically over their predecessors with nicely balanced colour schemes that frequently

R

erupt in surprising splashes of sickly green and blue. The anamorphic widescreen edition loses a hefty amount of interesting visual details from the top and bottom but offers marginally increased clarity on 16:9 displays, so judge accordingly depending on your set up. Interestingly, the full frame version when blown up in 16:9 playback looks quite similar. Bear in mind that, like many mid-'80s titles, this film was shot with a deliberately diffused look in numerous sequences, so that softness in the image (particularly the interiors) was apparently intentional. A couple of night shots (such as the cremation smoke first billowing into the sky) betray some instability in the original elements, with the left side of the image looking noticeably washed out. Overall this is a fine transfer and miles ahead of other renditions, but be aware that the film will always have some inherent problems. The mono audio sounds crystal clear; while a sonic overhaul might have been fun given the nature of the music, this will do just fine. Unfortunately legal SNAFUs (or O'Bannon's artistic decisions, depending on which account you read) resulted in some major music changes, including the deletion of The Damned's "Dead Beat Dance", and an alteration to the tar zombie's voice, so purists may want to hang on to their U.K. discs anyway.

Extras begin with a lively audio commentary from O'Bannon and production designer William Stout, who offer some nice recollections about making the film. They go into great detail about the genesis of the project, the various permutations it experienced (even after filming, as owners of the rare workprint version on video can attest), and the difficulty of creating an entirely new look for a zombie bash. Other extras include a "Designing the Dead" featurette (which covers the special effects and visual sketches used to create the environment and the wide array of zombies on display), Stout's conceptual art for the limited but effective settings, and a handful

of promotional items including the punchy Orion theatrical trailer (both G and R-rated versions) and TV spots.

MGM revisited the film again, first as a U.K. DVD (which only contained two trailers) and then as a second U.S. special edition that carried over all of the extras above along with an absolutely terrible new audio commentary with Stout, Don Calfa, Beverly Randolph, Quigley, Brian Peck, and Allan Trautman, with "zombies" bursting in to kill them every time they die onscreen. It's a lousy concept and even worse in execution, and the omission of most of the lead actors adds to the pointlessness. More palatable is the 20-minute "The Dead Have Risen" featurette, which features Gulager and Karen offering some hilarious anecdotes about the making of the film (though curiously, many of the actors from the featurette don't carry over here). Then we're back to pointlessness again with "The Decade of Darkness", a self-congratulating promo piece for MGM's '80s horror titles padded (literally) with an appearance by Elvira, Mistress of the Dark. The actual transfer carries over the same altered soundtrack and noticeably cooler colour timing, but the actual clarity and print condition is about the same. You also get some "zombie subtitles" that basically waste disc space. This second edition was then ported over MGM for their Blu-ray, which is basically identical in all respects – and alas, this extends to the transfer as well, which barely gets a boost in the jump to HD. If you haven't bought the film already, the cheap Blu-ray is probably the best option but hardly merits an upgrade otherwise.

REVELATION

Colour, 2001, 106m. / Directed by Stuart Urban / Starring James D'Arcy, Natasha Wightman, Terence Stamp, Celia Imrie, Liam Cunningham, Udo Kier, Ron Moody / Metrodome (UK R2 PAL), First Look (US R1 NTSC) / WS (2.35:1) (16:9) / DD5.1

This is a nambitious, religious-themed horror picture that revisits some of the territory of the *Omen* films but with additional emphasis on cutting-edge archaeology, historical conspiracy theory and scientific research. Jake Martel (James D'Arcy), computer hacker son of a mysterious billionaire (Terence Stamp), survives an attack on his father's castle by ninja-like Knights Templar who slaughter a gathering of various experts, making a point by skinning Martel Senior and hanging his hide where his son can find it. After discovering that his mother (Celia Imrie) has been hung upside-down martyr-style over a fire, Jake goes on the run with wild-haired alchemist Mira (Natasha Wightman) and his old prison chaplain Connolly (Liam Cunningham) as the Grand Master (Udo Kier) – who seems to control the Vatican, the EU and the Pentagon – attempts to beat them to the recovery of the Loculus, a sacred relic which, in a neat bit of plotting, is an apparently empty box – only the nails holding it together were used in the crucifixion and are still coated with Jesus Christ's freeze-dried DNA.

The plot unfolds in seemingly random snatches, with a great deal of running about Europe (France, Malta, Patmos, Rome) in search of clues concealed in churches (or the writings of Sir Isaac Newton, played in flashbacks by Ron Moody) that have to do with Biblical prophecy and set up an impossible-to-make sequel about the battle between Christ Reborn raised by the nurturing Mira (more Magdalen than Madonna) and a cloned Antichrist tutored by baddie Kier. It has a strong cast, though D'Arcy is uncertain in a role that doesn't come into focus until he is trapped in a shrine filling slowly with sand, and covers a great deal of genre territory. It makes an interesting contrast with the various American fundamentalist films (*Left Behind*, *The Omega Code*, etc.) that cover pretty much the same prophecies but from a more conservative point of view.

Momentum's DVD looks and sounds fine, though the transfer highlights a few twinkly bits of CGI augmentation that are less magical than the many impressive real-life locales. Writer-director Urban (whose most notable previous credit was the very different *Preaching to the Perverted*) provides a dry commentary track that fills in a lot of the background research and identifies the landmarks used as settings. The extras include a trailer and a clutch of featurettes: a making-of, a look at the various bits of effects work (including a great skinned Stamp), vignettes on alchemy and astrology and (with host duties from genial vicar/paranormal investigator Lionel Fanthorpe, who used to be an unbelievably prolific horror and s-f novelist) on the real-life mysteries of Rennes-le-Chateau and the Knights Templar. The same package with identical extras was later carried over to America via First Look's DVD.

– KN

REVENGE OF FRANKENSTEIN

Colour, 1958, 86m. / Directed by Terence Fisher / Starring Peter Cushing, Francis Matthews, Oscar Quitak, Michael Gwynn, Richard Wordsworth, Eunice Gayson, Lionel Jeffries / Columbia (UK R2 PAL, US R1 NTSC) / WS (1.85:1) (16:9)

R

Three years on from evading his execution at the guillotine, the infamous Baron Frankenstein (played by Peter Cushing) has moved to a new town where he's operating a medical practice as Dr. Stein. His unrivalled success and popularity with patients antagonizes the local medical faculty, for many of their former patients have defected to Stein. One of these doctors, Hans Kleve (Francis Matthews), suspects Stein's true identity but rather than reveal his secret he blackmails him into taking him on as an apprentice. Together they succeed in transplanting the brain of deformed gofer Karl (Oscar Quitak) into a freshly assembled body (Michael Gwynn). But Stein has recklessly disregarded an earlier experiment with a monkey that turned to post-op cannibalism, and when Otto receives a damaging blow to the head his craving for human flesh escalates out of control...

There are those who refuse to hear a word spoken against celebrated Hammer helmer Terence Fisher. It's true that his best work – including *Dracula*, *The Curse of Franken- stein*, *The Devil Rides Out* and *The Mummy* – is exemplary and justifiably earned him his iconic status among Hammer zealots. But even these classics are given to stretches where the pace lags, and his lesser works – *The Stranglers of Bombay* and *Frankenstein and the Monster from Hell* – are practically unwatchable. *Revenge of Frankenstein*, from a wonder- fully cynical Jimmy Sangster screenplay, falls into the former bracket, a spicy brew of stereotypical Frankenstein formula with a nasty dose of cannibalism piped into it. This angle adds atypical vigour to the proceedings and the even more macabre final ten minutes (with the Baron himself yanked back from *la joie de mort*, only to set up yet another practice under the pseudonym Dr. Franck) make this, if nothing else, the most unique entry in Hammer's seven-film Frankenstein series.

After the evil visual monstrosity of Christopher Lee in *The Curse of Franken- stein*, *Revenge*'s Michael Gwynn is likely to prompt initial disappointment, not only because he's the most normal looking of the Baron's creations but also because he's above all an object of pity. That said, the drool dribbling from wild-eyed Gwynn's chin as the cannibal instinct consumes him and paralysis takes a grip, invests a degree of obscenity not fast forgotten. The atmospheric laboratory set is yet another fine example of

the skilled production team circumventing the scant budgets with which they were so often saddled, and the hand-eye co-ordination sequence with a disembodied "living" eyeball peering out of its tank makes for a markedly freakish standout moment.

The urbane Peter Cushing proves yet again that he was tailor-made for the role of the Baron. Francis Matthews (later to cross swords with Dracula and Rasputin for Hammer) and Michael Gwynn (who returned, in the role of a feckless priest, in *Scars of Dracula*) are the icing on a very fine cake. Also featuring Richard Wordsworth (*Quatermass 2*), Eunice Gayson (James Bond's first ever on-screen sexual conquest in *Dr. No*) and Lionel Jeffries as a grubby grave robber, making an early exit via the most theatrical heart attack imaginable.

Columbia's DVD is more or less an anamorphic facsimile of their earlier NTSC laserdisc. Colours are vivid, if slightly unstable on occasion, and there are negligible traces of degradation, speckle and print damage. But this is as good as it's likely to get for a 45-year-old feature. The film enjoys a 28-chapter divide, with sound options in English or German. Subtitling is in the same two languages, plus French and Polish. Additionally there's a well-preserved theatrical trailer, another for *Earth vs. the Flying Saucers*, and a limited step-frame gallery of b&w production stills.
– TG

REVOLVER

Colour, 1973, 109m. / Directed by Sergio Sollima / Starring Oliver Reed, Fabio Testi / Blue Underground (US R0 NTSC) / WS (1.85:1) (16:9)

 After his wife is kidnapped, hard-nosed warden Vito Caprini (legendary lush Oliver Reed) is forced to help petty thief Milo Ruiz (stuntman turned actor Fabio Testi) escape

imprisonment as a hasty ransom exchange. Determined to retrieve his spouse unharmed and discipline those responsible for the insolent deed, our superintendent soon discovers there's more going on than initially meets the eye. Forging an unlikely alliance, the two men are thrust into something much larger than themselves and the clear-cut lines between good and bad quickly get distorted as the pair assimilates each other's traits in their quest for a final, and possibly futile, resolution.

Emphasizing character interaction over car chases and gunfights, fans of standard *poliziotteschi* may at first be disappointed with the slower than usual pace of *Revolver*. Those with some patience, however, will be amply rewarded with fantastic performances from the two leads and several rousing action set pieces that showcase director Sergio Sollima's flair and expertise behind the camera. A thematic throwback to his earlier, politically-charged oaters, Sollima once again creates a work that strays out of its respective genre boundaries, packing more emotional punch than the comparatively complacent fare simultaneously being churned out by others. Impeccably cast, Reed and Testi deliver powerhouse performances so flawless it's impossible to imagine anyone else in their roles (Lino Ventura and Terence Hill were once considered) and their chemistry adds an extra dynamic to the proceedings. Stylish, dramatic and violent with a true kicker of an ending, *Revolver* is a top-notch flick that will hopefully win over some fresh fans with this refurbished DVD edition.

Acquired by drive-in favourites Independent-International Pictures from a third party licensor, *Revolver* was distributed theatrically in 1974 in the States. Initially tested under the title *In the Name of Love* with an ad campaign that played up Ollie's *Women in Love* romantic turn, it soon received a down 'n' dirty exploitation makeover, becoming the more widely-known *Blood in the Streets*. Unfortunately,

the new *Dirty Harry/Death Wish*-inspired marketing still didn't attract customers. According to I-I head honcho Sam Sherman, "The film played a minimum of dates and nobody wanted to book it, I couldn't give it away. *Revolver* did basically nothing for us in the U.S. and was a big waste of time. It didn't play any TV and the home video sales were also very poor. I had to keep drumming it into my head that if I really liked a film I had to stay away, because it would do nothing."

Regardless of numbers, with a little digging the more adventurous VHS collector could turn up copies on I-I's Super Video offshoot. Once a nice addition to the shelf, this 1984 tape has now been officially rendered useless by Blue Underground's sterling DVD release. Put frankly, this is one gorgeous disc – viewing this improved presentation is almost comparable to watching an altogether different film! The picture is remarkably crisp for its vintage with realistically rendered colours and solid, deep blacks, and there's nary a blemish or compression error in sight. The 1.85:1 framing looks perfect and adds an essential amount of visual information to the sides when measured against the previous P&S tape. (compositions set up this carefully, need to be seen in their proper ratio.) The mono soundtrack is clear and concise, without any noticeable background hissing to drown out the dialogue or Ennio Morricone's wonderful and eclectic score. Completists will also be happy to note this new digital version runs approximately 40 seconds longer than the old prerecord (109m31s compared to 108m51s). The main addition is another half-minute of footage at the very onset of the film, as Testi and his wounded partner-in-crime flee a bungled robbery. The remainder of the difference is comprised of various frames previously lost to print damage, including a brief dialogue snippet. It's not much, but it's there nonetheless.

True to form, Blue Underground doesn't disappoint when it comes to supplemental

R

materials, either. First we have a 14-minute featurette consisting of interviews with Sergio Sollima and Fabio Testi. Well-edited and informative, they mainly speak about the production of the film itself with a good bit of Oliver Reed reminiscence. Next we're presented with trailers for the original European release and the domestic *Blood in the Streets* issue. Both efficiently sell the picture and I'm surprised it didn't pull in more money. Two U.S. radio spots are thrown in for good measure. A 58-image stills gallery then rears its head, displaying many promotional photos, posters, newspaper advertisements and the soundtrack album sleeve – but no Super Video cover? Finally come several talent bios detailing the careers of Reed, Testi, Sollima and Morricone. For you remote control jockeys out there, a little fiddling can highlight a pair of Easter egg outtakes from Sollima's talk; one delivers a short anecdote concerning Big Ollie's sense of humour and the other finds him mourning the unfortunate circumstances of the title's Italian theatrical run.

– BH

THE RING

Colour, 2002, 115m. / Directed by Gore Verbinski / Starring Naomi Watts, Martin Henderson, David Dorfman, Brian Cox, Jane Alexander / DreamWorks/Universal (UK R2 PAL) / WS (1.85:1) (16:9) / DD5.1, DreamWorks (US R1 NTSC) / WS (1.85:1) (16:9) / DTS/DD5.1

All the signs foretold disaster: a remake of the Japanese horror film *Ring* (*Ringu*), already considered an instant classic of suggestive horror, directed by the man behind *The Mexican*, written by the screenwriter of the dire *Arlington Road*, and released by the studio that trashed their remake of Robert Wise's *The Haunting*. Despite such odds, this American adaptation, *The Ring*, is a worthy translation of its source and, even for those familiar with the original Asian series, delivers a few jolts and twists of its own.

Busy reporter Rachel Keller (*Mulholland Dr.*'s Naomi Watts) believes she may have stumbled onto an intriguing story when her niece dies under mysterious circumstances, seven days after viewing a cursed videotape, which according to urban legend kills those who watch it. Often leaving her precognitive son (David Dorfman) to the hands of babysitters, Rachel embarks on a sinister journey with her video nut ex-boyfriend, Noah (Martin Henderson), and uncovers a tragic series of events that have now taken on supernatural life through modern technology.

A ghost story for the digital age, *The Ring* respectfully retains the rainy, melancholy atmosphere of its source and, most importantly, resists the temptation to slather its chills with grating pop music or smart-aleck teenagers. Watts proves more than capable of carrying the film (a huge demand considering she's in almost every scene), but able support is provided by a well-chosen supporting cast including the always-effective Brian Cox. While Verbinski's tape montage isn't as spare and nightmarish as the Japanese original, his version offers a few tweaks of its own, including a horrific passage on a commuter ship involving a runaway horse, a more satisfying explanation for the "seven days" of the curse, and a savvy use of subliminal editing (often limited to a single frame) that beats William Friedkin at his own game. The film also offers a few sly nods to Asian horror culture, including an asylum scene lifted from *Ring 2*, a Japanese doctor's evaluation in a vital case history file, and a cameo from that omnipresent Eastern horror, the centipede. Hans Zimmer's score effectively adapts the original's eerie, plaintive textures into a Western tonal format, while Rick Baker provides a few spare but horrific make-up effects, the first of which rarely failed to wrench a scream from the theatrical audience. It's not a perfect film; the new backstory concocted for the curse is far too convoluted for its own good (despite reshoots and various voiceovers tested by DreamWorks) and ultimately can't touch the psychic conference of the original film, and some ludicrous editing nearly derails the film's final, most important scare set piece, which was pulled off in the original without any distracting cutaways to a screeching car and fared all the better for it. In the end, fans are best off watching both films as fascinating variants of a brutally effective story.

The first DreamWorks DVD appears to be a sparse package at first glance, though it does feature a top-notch anamorphic transfer and appropriately loud, well separated DTS and 5.1 tracks. The film is generally either very quiet or very, very loud, and both audio versions serve their purpose well. While the subject matter obviously makes this an ideal title for home viewing, DVD viewers will also enjoy the ability to freeze frame on some of the more devilish editing and visual trickery; for example, note the split second make-up effect which subliminally crawls up during the last shot of Henderson's screaming face. The theatrical trailer is not included, strangely enough, but a promo for it does appear on the DreamWorks edition of the Japanese film (and vice versa, with a *Ringu* promo stuck on this disc). The packaging promises a "short film created by Gore Verbinski exclusively for the video release that reveals more electrifying secrets about the mystery of *The Ring*." Actually, it's a skilfully edited 15 minute reel of alternative and deleted footage seen during the film's various test screenings, presented in anamorphic widescreen with a more polished sound mix to link it all together into one smooth viewing experience. Among the highlights: Watts's original interviews with island residents about the horse farm and Samara (replaced in the

final cut with a different scene featuring Jane Alexander), a bloodier version of the bathtub scene, Henderson's discovery of a grisly fate for the eccentric lodge manager, a nastier extended version of Samara's death (including a rock cracked against her head), and an alternative coda at a video store. For once, there's a good reason the back of the box notes, "Bonus Features Not Rated", as this reel definitely pushes the PG-13 horror film into harder territory. While DVD fanatics may grouse about the lack of a commentary track or featurettes, this fascinating and strangely downplayed extra is the best possible bonus feature. Easter egg hunters will also find a nice little treat hidden in the main menu screen.

A second DreamWorks DVD released only in the U.S. divides everything onto two discs, with the identical first platter and a new second one containing a "Rings" short film (basically a bridge to the second film), cast and crew interviews (basically a glorified PR kit), "The Origin of Terror" featurette about the story's international cycle, the "cursed videos" from the American and first two Japanese films, a trailer for the worthless American sequel, and an Easter egg that plays a longer version of the Samara video.

RIPLEY'S GAME

Colour, 2003, 105m. / Directed by Liliana Cavani / Starring John Malkovich, Dougray Scott, Ray Winstone, Chiara Caselli, Lena Headey / New Line (US R1 NTSC), 01 Distribution (Italy R2 PAL), Entertainment In Video (UK R2 PAL) / WS (1.85:1) (16:9) / DD5.1

One of the great anti-heroes of modern mystery fiction, Patricia Highsmith's character of Tom Ripley has undergone an odd film trend, with a notable European director making an art house version of a novel before it was remade in English decades later. The first entry, *The Talented Mr. Ripley*, became René Clément's *Purple Noon* and then Anthony Minghella's adaptation with Matt Damon under the original title; then Wim Wenders turned *Ripley's Game* into *The American Friend*, followed by this version from Liliana Cavani, again using the book's title. Offering the most accurate and multi-layered cinematic Ripley to date, John Malkovich (who, oddly enough, held together Wenders's sequences in *Beyond the Clouds*) captures the amoral, emotionally austere attraction of this murderous but charming sociopath, who influenced decades of cultivated but disturbed creations leading up logically enough to Hannibal Lecter.

Our tale begins in Italy as Ripley embarks on a shady art deal with the help of none-too-bright Reeves (*Sexy Beast*'s excellent Ray Winstone). Ripley's sudden decision to up his price leads to a murderous payoff, leaving Reeves in the dust but holding a briefcase filled with cash. Three years later, Ripley has retired to the sidelines and lives a married life with harpsichord player Luisa (*Sleepless*'s Chiara Caselli). Reeves arrives on the scene and offers Tom $50,000 to kill off Reeves's underworld rival, a Berlin nightclub owner. Ripley balks, insisting that only an innocent could be recruited to perform such a task. Fortunately Ripley is quickly inspired when he learns that his English neighbour, picture framer Jonathan Trevanny (Dougray Scott), is dying of leukaemia and spending his final days in peace with his wife, Sarah (Lena Headey). Reeves approaches Jonathan with the offer and is quickly refused; however, Ripley decides to double the amount himself for the sheer pleasure of twisting a good, honest man into an assassin.

While Wenders's magnificent film focused on the plight of Jonathan as a sort of metaphor for Germany's political situation at the time, with Dennis Hopper's Ripley functioning as more of a cockeyed supporting character, Cavani's film balances equally between the two men. Shifting the location to Italy from the novel's France, this version benefits greatly from Malkovich's presence; he's in full venomous mode, previously used to good effect in *Dangerous Liaisons* (and in the more compromised *Portrait of a Lady* and *Mary Reilly*). He's most terrifying in the non-violent passages, such as a pivotal early sequence in which he overhears Jonathan's social put-down at a dinner party and immediately dominates the room by simply repeating the word "Meaning?" over and over. Cavani's chilly directorial style suits the material well (despite rumours of trouble during production – Cavani reputedly walked off the set towards the end of production, leaving John Malkovich to direct for the last few days), and while this is nowhere close to the Wenders film as a directorial statement, it is more enjoyable as a luxurious thriller, filled with twists, marvellous scenery, and meaty acting. Ennio Morricone's delicious harpsichord-flavoured score is a jittery treat, and apart from the bumpy opening scene and a few minor stumbles near the end, the script effectively balances mordant wit with gruelling suspense, particularly a tense, *From Russia with Love*-style train sequence that delivers in spades. Co-financed by New Line, this film was first released in Europe but inexplicably dropped from the U.S. release schedule. One can only wonder why, as this is certainly a worthy title and boasts an impressive pedigree.

The glossy Italian DVD was the first on the market by over a year and features 5.1 audio for both the original English and Italian-dubbed audio tracks, with optional English subtitles in both languages as well. The anamorphic picture is pristine and beautiful to behold; the titles are in Italian, but otherwise this is an English-friendly variant. Extras include the Italian trailer (non-anamorphic) and a stills gallery. The much later U.S. release drops the Italian track and substitutes the American trailer prepared for an aborted theatrical release.

It's also the only version with a DTS track, for what that's worth given the restrained sound mix. Last but most substantial is the U.K. disc, which features the trailer, an "On Location" featurette with footage from the set, and interviews with the director and cast.

RONJA RÖVARDOTTER

Colour, 1984, 120m. / Directed by Tage Danielsson / Starring Hanna Zetterberg, Börje Ahlstedt, Dan Hafström, Per Oscarsson, Lena Nyman / Junior/Plazavista (Switzerland R2 PAL) / WS (1.66:1), Svensk Filmindustri (Sweden R2 PAL), Universum (Germany R2 PAL) / WS (1.77:1) (16:9)

 Based on the best selling book from the prolific pen of Sweden's best loved children's author, the late Astrid Lindgren, creator of the enduring "kids' lib" icon Pippi Longstocking, this rather more adult-toned fantasy fable, a canny revival (and renewal) of the once-popular 19th Century Räuber Roman literary genre, borrows freely from William Shakespeare's *Romeo and Juliet* while adding an existentialist twist.

In a mythological Nordic setting, *Ronja Rövardotter* opens with the birth of the titular heroine, as the mountaintop castle lair of father-to-be Mattis (Börje Ahlstedt), fearsome bearded boss of a robber-band, is circled by monstrous cackling, half-human bird-witches, Scandinavian harpies... Moments after the tiny infant is presented to the awestruck father and thence to his fellow thieves, the castle receives a blow from a lightning bolt, which splits it in twain; it's hardly an auspicious blessing for newborn Ronja... Fast-forward 11 years and Ronja (Hanna Zetterberg) is now a fiery, headstrong girl with a penchant for having her own way (she's rather like her literary predecessor Pippi in this respect). She's also prone to getting herself into sticky situations, such as when she falls asleep in the forest and awakens to find herself surrounded by a hairy horde of glowing-eyed grey gnomes from which she's only just rescued in time. But these escapades are as nothing compared with the fall-out from her meeting up with Birk (Dan Hafström), ginger-nutted scion of a rival robber gang led by his father Borka (Per Oscarsson) who have taken up residence in the other half of the bisected castle. Initially wary of this cheeky newcomer, Ronja is soon warming to him, and he to her, calling the young girl his 'sister'. On several occasions the boy has to rescue Ronja from peril (and indeed she herself saved his life on their first meeting, pulling him from a crevice into which he had fallen). When Mattis captures Birk and holds him to ransom an enraged Ronja deliberately surrenders herself to Borka's group, thereby spiking her father's plans. With the correct offspring restored to their rightful families, despite the support of her mother Lovis (Lena Nyman), Ronja finds herself disowned by her once-loving father. Unable to stand this cold-shouldering she runs away into the wilds to be with Birk, who has also left home in disgust at the perpetual fighting between the rival clans. Repeated attempts by family and friends fail to coax Ronja back into the castle, though she is worried increasingly at the prospect of enduring the long northern winter in the abandoned bear's cave that she and Birk have taken over. Eventually Mattis swallows his pride and both Ronja and Birk return home. Following a wrestling match between Mattis and Borka, which is won by Ronja's father, the two clans make their peace. Ronja and Birk foreswear their robber roots and face the future together: gazing over the beautiful wilds that are their heritage Ronja lets out a demented howl of pure animal joy, her 'spring yell', that is taken up by first Birk and then a chorus of local fauna disturbed by the ungodly racket!

R

What we have here is not just a great children's film, but a great fantasy film, period. In the tradition dictated by decades of top-quality filmmaking from the Svensk Filmindustri, director Tage Danielsson (who died in 1985) delivers an exciting film that can be enjoyed by youngsters and adults alike, and without condescending to either (Hollywood take note). The location photography (overseen by Rune Ericson) is at all times superb, evoking the vastness of the wild and lovely Scandinavian landscape which forms an irresistible backdrop to the unfolding storyline (the film's shooting was split between Norway and Sweden), and Björn Isfalt's score is masterly and thoroughly complementary. Hanna Zetterberg is a compelling Ronja, with her brash smile, feminist-friendly confidence and downright spunk providing a winning mix, and the rest of the cast are no slouches either, handling the demanding action and emotional scenes with aplomb. Alongside the very gritty, dirty depiction of the lives led by the rival robber gangs (complete with rousing scenes of drunken dancing and singing) are well-executed fantasy scenes involving creatures taken from Nordic folklore. There are recurring comical interludes involving a family of tiny inquisitive trolls ("rumphobs") who live in a burrow in which puppetry and actors are intermingled seamlessly (I love the scene in which they hang their baby's cradle from Ronja's foot after she puts her boot through their ceiling by mistake). The monstrous harpies are a (not always entirely successful) mix of live action and animation supervised by Per Åhlin, who directed 1974's Swedish live action/cartoon classic *Dunderklumpen*, and the nocturnal gnomes (actually played by heavily costumed children) are also pretty creepy creations that might give some younger viewers a sleepless night. One of the finest moments involves Ronja being lured into the misty forest by a mysterious voice which casts a malign spell over her, a spell that is only broken by Birk's insistent efforts to rouse her from her eerie trance...

Ronja Rövardotter has been available for years on various European video releases, including a maverick "long version" released in Sweden on VHS only that runs over 13 minutes longer than the cinema print that forms the basis for not just one but three different DVDs to date. The first release came from Switzerland on the Junior/Plazavista label, a nice 1.66:1 non-anamorphic print of the film (under the title *Ronja Räubertochter*), attractively packaged with a painting of Ronja and Birk standing in front of the robber-castle, with an Astrid Lindgren biography and a small photo gallery as extras. An insert is provided. The German-only soundtrack is presented in stereo as per the cinema print. The picture quality is very nice overall, though the print utilised shows a little scratching and speckling on occasions. The film runs for 120m 12s in length.

The second release followed from Sweden, courtesy of Svensk Filmindustri, who have done a sterling job remastering this film for the digital medium. The print is anamorphically enhanced for widescreen TVs, presenting the film in a letterboxed ratio of 1.77:1, which crops a little picture information from the top and bottom of the image (this missing picture is visible on non-widescreen TVs though, as the print is hard-matted at nearer 1.66:1). The picture quality is probably the best this film is ever going to look, having been cleaned up digitally from the original negative for a perfect viewing experience. The Swedish-dubbed soundtrack has been given a new 5.1 Surround mix and is equally impressive. The running time is 120m 29s. DVD extras are confined to the original trailer, two "singalong" sequences for the littl'uns (with Swedish undertitles), a (Swedish) text only biography of Astrid Lindgren and a goodly bunch of letter-boxed trailers for the other Lindgren related DVD releases from SF, which include two of the wonderful Inger Nilsson-starring Pippi Longstocking films, the stirring epic *The Brothers Lionheart* and the very wacky *Karlsson on the Roof*. There are no English subtitles, but this film is not hard to follow at all. The packaging is very attractive, featuring a montage painting of scenes from the film, and a little booklet advertising the full range of Astrid Lindgren titles is supplied as an insert. It would have been nice if the extra scenes from the "Long Version" could have been provided amongst the extras, but maybe there will one day be a separate DVD of that extended edit, given its wide availability on several tape releases in Sweden.

The most recent DVD release of *Ronja* hails from Germany, from Universum Film in conjunction with SF. The print appears identical to that used for the Swedish DVD; with the exception of the German title superimposed at the start, all the rest of the onscreen credits are in Swedish. Strangely this print runs the longest at 120m 42s, though I could not notice any obvious difference in the footage presented! In common with the Swedish DVD, the print is anamorphic 1.77:1. There is a choice of either German or Swedish soundtracks, both of which are AC3 stereo. There are no extras offered, not even a trailer. As with the other two DVDs there is an insert provided. The distinctive cover design fits in with the recent slew of Universum Film Lindgren releases on German DVD, which include a few titles not yet available in Sweden on disc at the time of writing, a nice double bill of *Madita* and *Madita und Pim*, and a couple of *Saltkrokan* films (also doubled up on one DVD). Overall the Swedish DVD is probably the one to go for, for its 5.1 remix if nothing else. Whatever print you opt for, it goes without saying that anyone interested in seeing how European directors approach children's fantasy cinema should check out *Ronja Rövardotter*.

– NB

ROTKÄPPCHEN

Colour, 1962, 66m. / Directed by Götz Friedrich / Starring Blanche Kommerell, Helga Raumer, Horst Kube, Friedel Nowack, Jochen Bley, Ernst-Georg Schwill, Harald Engelmann, Werner Dissel / Icestorm (Germany R0 PAL)

Not to be confused with Fritz Genschow's *Rottkäppchen* (1953) or Walter Janssen's *Rotkappchen* (1954), this retelling of the "Little Red Riding Hood" story hails from the East German DEFA-Studio and was directed by Götz Friedrich in 1962. This version adds a few new characters (a friendly rabbit, a grumpy bear, a wily fox), does away with Little Red's many brothers, making her an only child and therefore even more precious to her parents (Helga Raumer and Horst Kube), whilst her Grandmother (Friedel Nowack) becomes a pernickety snuff-addict with a ropy-looking hand-puppet pet squirrel. Overall the full-body animal costumes are a distinct improvement on the earlier films, and the Wolf and Fox in particular are given amazingly realistic fang-snarling masks that must have given the kindergarteners a few sleepless nights back then (the Wolf's full-on look predates *The Howling*'s climactic lycanthropes by several decades). The actors portraying the individual animals are also given specific body movements to further mimic the creatures they are playing, becoming almost balletic on occasion. Little Red's nose-twitching friend Rabbit (Jochen Bley) is a lively, likeable character, and tries to protect her and guide her throughout, which is not easy as the child is as wilful as brave, constantly wandering from the forest pathway and into peril, with her other animal pal, the somewhat slow Bear (Ernst-Georg Schwill), proving more of a hindrance than a help, though he too comes through in the end.

R

An entirely studio-bound production, *Rotkäppchen* is handsomely mounted, with forest sets of stunning intricacy and detail that constantly enchant the viewer, as does Blanche Kommerell's Little Red. She's a tough cookie, seeing off both the crafty Fox (Harald Engelmann) and the fearsome Wolf (Werner Dissel) on two separate occasions before being gobbled up by the lascivious lupine following the traditional verbal exchange we all know and love so well. Cut free from the sleeping Wolf's distended belly by her mother, Little Red is rescued along with her Grandma, and the vicious varmint who caused all the uproar is carted off by her father and Bear, trussed like a turkey, in another break with tradition (usually his split gut is filled with heavy rocks and stitched up, leaving him to die slowly in extravagant agony).

Inventive and consistently visually rewarding, thanks in no small part to Helmut Bergmann's camerawork, and with an effective score by Gerhard Wohlgemuth, *Rotkäppchen* is available in Germany from Icestorm Entertainment GMBH in a lovely looking, brightly coloured full-frame Region-Free PAL transfer. It's in German language with no English subtitles option, but is easy to follow throughout, and runs for just over 66 minutes.

Aimed at children rather than adult film collectors, the only DVD extras offered here are a trailer for *The Golden Goose* and a so-so photo-gallery that serves mainly as a taster for other fairy tales on the label, rather than showing scenes from this film; it's quite a wasted opportunity, as it would have been f more value if they had been able to locate a set of East German lobby stills or some original poster art. However, basic release or not, this little-known gem of European children's cinema comes thoroughly recommended.

– NB

THE RULES OF ATTRACTION

Colour, 2002, 110m. / Directed by Roger Avary / Starring James Van Der Beek, Shannyn Sossamon, Ian Somerhalder, Kip Pardue, Fred Savage, Faye Dunaway / Icon (Blu-ray & DVD) (UK RB/R2 HD/PAL), Lionsgate (US R1 NTSC) / WS (1.85:1) (16:9) / DD2.0, Warner (Australia R4 PAL), Scanbox (Denmark R2 PAL) / WS (1.85:1) (16:9) / DD5.1

The third cinematic attempt to translate the sordid, alarmist prose of Bret Easton Ellis (*Less Than Zero*, *American Psycho*) is technically the most faithful to its source but still more interesting as a study of adapting its era than a literary translation. Eight years after his debut film, the frustrating *Killing Zoe*, Roger Avary continues his fascination with pop violence, disaffected and wayward characters fuelled by drugs and lust, and German Expressionist horror films flickering as wallpaper on televisions. At least *Rules* moves faster and sports a photogenic and able cast, even if the final results aren't as shocking or scintillating as its makers would have you believe.

Set on the trendy Camden campus, *Rules* picks up during an End of the World party where, through a barrage of slo-mo and reverse cinema trickery, we meet our three protagonists: jaded drug dealer Sean Bateman (*Dawson's Creek*'s James Van Der Beek), brittle virgin Lauren (hairdressing casualty Shannyn Sossamon), and manipulative Paul (Ian Somerhalder from *The Vampire Diaries*), who preys on straight boys and has his sights set on Sean. Meanwhile Sean's been getting anonymous love letters and thinks Lauren's responsible, while she's torn between Sean and her absentee boyfriend, Victor (Kip Pardue), who's off carousing in Europe. To stay chaste, she naturally leafs through a book on venereal disease before her weekend partying. Of course, the love triangle plays out badly, with various peripheral characters winding up screwed, dead, or indifferent.

Surprisingly timid considering its subject matter, *Rules* tries to wallow in the sleaze but ultimately proves to have a disappointingly moralist heart at the end. Even the callous Sean gets a few too many doe-eyed moments to entirely shed Van Der Beek's goody-goody image (which would have been obliterated had his long-rumoured footage from Todd Solondz's *Storytelling* ever reached the public); in fact, a disturbing scene involving Fred Savage (*The Wonder Years*) as a college junkie in his skivvies is far more likely to cause distress among regular TV viewers. Sossamon essentially repeats her haughty bitch routine from *A Knight's Tale* and continues to put off audiences, while Somerhalder fares the best of the lot, relatively speaking; apart from some unfortunate cheek rouge, he's a compelling presence and makes the most of his screen time. For some reason advance hype pushed Pardue as a big star here, even though he's in the finished film for all of about four minutes (including a much-ballyhooed speed tour through Europe that pales in comparison to what Russ Meyer's been doing for years). The parade of excess is moderately amusing for a while but ultimately wears thin, about the time Avary trots out a grim suicide scene that feels more technically self-indulgent than necessary to the structure of the film; at least viewers can find some amusement counting the film references, including visual cues lifted from *The Wicker Man* and *Suspiria* of all things. Bonus points for stellar music work by the always-reliable Tomandandy (*The Mothman Prophecies*), essentially an updated riff on Wendy Carlos's *A Clockwork Orange*, coupled with some effectively chosen '80s pop tunes ranging from George Michael to Erasure. And beware of Faye Dunaway's nostrils in this film... they're truly scary.

Lionsgate's DVD is a moderately satisfying presentation, featuring the general release R-rated version of the film (the MPAA demanded some re-editing and a few seconds of cuts, though the final result plays seamlessly). The print is surprisingly dirty for such a technically polished title; debris is evident in several scenes, and the video presentation is colourful but not particularly exceptional. Audio fares better, with an enveloping surround mix that makes effective use of manipulative panning effects; too bad the theatrical 5.1 mix is lost in favour of 2.0 surround, though. The "revolving door" audio commentaries, which feature actors and crew members hopping from one track to another, are fun in a party down, chaotic sort of way but become monotonous after a while; interestingly, Avary's presence on the disc is limited instead to an "Anatomy of a Scene" episode which focuses on a merging split-screen effect halfway into the film. Two rapid-fire teasers are included (one unrated, the other blessed with an MPAA seal) along with the theatrical trailer, which features some footage of *Buffy the Vampire Slayer* villainess Claire Kramer excised from the final print. Finally the "mystery guest" audio commentary actually belongs to the braying Carrot Top; his fans will enjoy his take on the film, while all others will run for cover.

The European and Australian DVDs mercifully drop the Carrot Top commentary while adding 5.1 audio mixes, which seems a fair trade-off. The U.K. release has been cut by the BBFC. According to their website: "A cut was required to a scene in which a teenage girl slits her wrists, on the grounds that the technique used is not widely known and is potentially more likely to result in death than the more common method, in line with the Video Recordings Act 1984, and BBFC Guidelines and Policy." Ironically, all the material cut from the R-rated U.S. disc is included in the U.K. disc, while the material cut from the U.K.

disc is still in the American version. The complete cut finally surfaced on Blu-ray (same extras as the U.K. disc) in both the U.K. and Australia in a greatly improved (albeit still inconsistent) HD transfer with a very immersive DTS soundtrack.

LA RUPTURE

Colour, 1970, 120m. / Directed by Claude Chabrol / Starring Stéphane Audran, Jean-Pierre Cassel, Jean-Claude Drouot / Pathfinder (US R1 NTSC), Arrow (UK R2 PAL) / WS (1.85:1)

 A magnificent and tremendously underrated film from Chabrol that is worthy of being described as a masterpiece, this would rank with the director's more widely esteemed classics from the same period if it were more often screened. The always-wonderful Stéphane Audran returns as Hélène Régnier, who flees to a boarding house after her deranged husband, Charles (Jean-Claude Drouot), attacks her and their son one violent morning. Convinced that Hélène is to blame for their son's mental illness, her in-laws take her to court for custody of the child and then hire the ruthless Paul Thomas (Jean-Pierre Cassel from *The Crimson Rivers*) to destroy her reputation.

Based on *The Balloon Man*, a mystery novel by Charlotte Armstrong (author of *The Chocolate Cobweb*, which became Chabrol's *Merci pour le chocolat*), this film is a dynamic break with the more subdued, slow-building tension of Chabrol's previous output. Here the violence takes centre stage in the opening scene and lingers horribly over the following two hours; the setting is also more volatile and overtly sleazy, as even the bourgeois characters flaunt their corruption on their sleeves. Add to that a rogue's gallery of eccentric characters, a

drug-induced finale complete with a trip sequence, and an unforgettable female sidekick villain with an aversion to clothes.

Pathfinder's DVD is a step up from prior video versions, though the dodgy PAL conversion and subdued colour schemes probably won't seem like a knockout to many viewers. It's an accurate and generally pleasing job, however, and replicates the look of the cinema prints quite nicely. The French audio (or Spanish dubbed, if you prefer) is accompanied by optional English subtitles. Extras include an audio commentary by Howard Rodman, Terry Curtis Fox, and critic F.X. Feeney, all of whom keep going through the lengthy running time with countless bits of historical info about the Chabrol/Audran relationship and the film's creation and critical reception at the time. The bare bones Arrow disc followed later and surprisingly doesn't offer a significantly different visual presentation; it's also available in their hefty eight-disc Chabrol box set.

RUSH WEEK

Colour, 1989, 96m. / Directed by Bob Bralver / Starring Dean Hamilton, Pamela Ludwig, Roy Thinnes, Dominick Brascia, John Donovan, Jay Pickett, Kathleen Kinmont, Gregg Allman / Simitar (US R0 NTSC)

 An ambitious student reporter called Toni Daniels (played by Pamela Ludwig) is intent on grabbing the front page of the college newspaper with her report on Rush Week, the annual coaxing of freshers into campus fraternities and an excuse for much juvenile malarkey. But when she gets a whiff of a better story – the mysterious disappearance of several co-eds – she sets her sights on an article of greater integrity. Learning that

the one thing the missing students shared in common was sidelining for a sleazy amateur photographer who bribed them into posing nude with dead bodies, Toni's investigations take a more sinister turn. And how does the death of the Dean's daughter exactly one year earlier tie in?

If you enjoy formulaic middle-of-the-road slasher films then *Rush Week* will probably appeal. If you prefer something with a bit more meat on its bones it almost certainly won't. It's as clear-cut as that. This is another of those movies where the victim runs away from the killer, while the killer refuses to accelerate beyond walking pace yet still manages to catch up! Released in 1989, when some of the best and worst the genre had to offer had long flowed under the bridge and been mostly forgotten, the first thing you'll notice about *Rush Week* is a lack of blood; even though our resident maniac hacks up his prey with a double headed hatchet there's barely a speck of red in sight. Director Bob Bralver tries to compensate with some brief nudity, but he's pulling the wool over no one's eyes. In fact, cut a few seconds here and there and this could pass comfortably for a Sunday afternoon TV movie, and a second rate one at that. The red herrings swim past in shoals, but the seasoned slasher aficionado shouldn't have too much trouble identifying the guilty party fairly early on. Is it the peeping Tom campus handyman (Dominick Brascia)? Nope. Is it Toni's boyfriend Jeff (Dean Hamilton), who's hiding a secret from his past? Nope. Might it be the refectory chef (John Donovan), who arranges kinky photo shoots for penniless female students? Nope. Is it Dean Grail (*The Invaders*'s Roy Thinnes, who must have been really desperate), disgusted by the sinful behaviour of his young students? Could be. Also featured are Jay Pickett (from TV's *Days of Our Lives*), Kathleen Kinmont (*Bride of Re-Animator* herself) and Rick Wakeman clone Gregg Allman. Paying more heed to the dumb pranks and fraternity rivalry of *Animal House* than the stalking and slashing (which could almost have been grafted on as an afterthought), *Rush Week* is so ghastly that even the fabled Alan Smithee would refuse to have his name associated with it. In fact, to pinch a line from Mike Myers, even stink would say this stinks.

After such a damning overview, quite who would be interested in pursuing *Rush Week* on DVD I'm not sure. The substandard offering on Simitar's region free disc is equally unlikely to tempt the curious. A 9-chapter full screen presentation, the picture quality is acceptable if unremarkable, yet the sound is extraordinarily robust by comparison. There are no extra features of worth, unless you consider "Film Facts" – basically an on-screen reprise of the data on the sleeve – to be interesting.

– TG

SANTO AND BLUE DEMON VS. DOCTOR FRANKENSTEIN

Colour, 1974, 95m. / Directed by Miguel M. Delgado / Starring Santo, Blue Demon, Jorge Russek, Sasga Montenegro / Rise Above (US R1 NTSC)

Dr. Iwin Frankenstein (not "Frankestein" as the subtitles and the box cover have it), 113-year-old grandson of the original mad scientist, has relocated to Mexico and is arrogantly conducting a reign of terror. His latest atrocity is to kidnap two look-alike women and switch their brains; when they die on the operating table, he brings them to half-life with transistor implants and sends them out to throttle their former loved ones. Frankenstein (Jorge Russek) stays young with doses of "factor beta", which he also gives loyal sidekicks (a gimmick from *Santo vs. la hija di Frankestein*), and has on the premises a couple of monsters: the hulking Golem, who has the strength of ten men and is a black giant who has received another giant's brain in a transplant (!), and the scarred fairly traditional Mortis, who gets forgotten and even has to donate his name to his fellow creature for the climax.

Frankenstein wants Santo's brain for Golem, so the monster's strength can be augmented by the hero's wrestling skills, and he sets out to trap the hero by kidnapping the bacteriologist daughter (Sasga Montenegro) of a coach who taught Santo and his tag-team buddy Blue Demon some of their distinctive moves. As in most Santo movies, the plot is at once casual and insane, though Russek at least displays some wry sense that he isn't taking it that seriously. Mixed into the brew are a couple of hefty but glam tough cops who would seem ideal love interests for the heroes but get sidelined in favour of drippy high-class gals who receive only chaste kisses goodnight from the masked ones after a night out. With their distinctive masks and natty sports jackets, the tag team come across as big kids, not that interested in girls but always up for a spot of one-on-one tussling or their traditional tossing-about-a-roomful-of-goons antics. Frankenstein works out of a supervillain lair with gleaming silver-foil corridors and operates with the aid not only of rejuvenated brain surgeons and a clan of pullover-clad goons but also a big boxy computer with plenty of lights and knobs. When thwarted, the mad scientist decides to get even by operating on Golem to change his skin pigmentation (!) and becoming a wrestling manager so the creature can rip Santo apart in the ring. This at least means that the expected wrestling finale has something to do with the main plot, but it's also a conventional toss-about far less fun than the mad science and monster business that has set it up.

Rise Above's Santo Collection DVD uses a mildly worn transfer but brings out the lovely colours, while the audio showcases a pleasantly tuneful easy shivery listening score along with the usual biffs and grunts.

The soundtrack is in Spanish with optional English subtitles, and the extras are some trailers and David Wilt's useful liner notes (though a couple of paragraphs seem to have been transposed). Maybe not El Santo's finest hour, but intermittently endearing.
– KN

SANTO AND BLUE DEMON VS. DRACULA AND THE WOLFMAN

Colour, 1973, 90m. / Directed by Miguel M. Delgado / Starring Santo, Blue Demon, Alfredo Wally Barrón, Aldo Monti, Agustín Martínez Solares / Rise Above (US R1 NTSC)

 This colourful, silly fantasy comes from a period in Mexican exploitation cinema when wrestlers and monsters were doubling up and plots or even entire scripts were being recycled. Though it supposedly exists in a sexed-up version and has moments of bright red gore, the film has the feel of a kiddie matinee serial from the 1940s shot with 1970s colour and will probably play best to younger viewers. Its storyline is crowded, but also very basic: a cackling hunchback (Alfredo Wally Barrón) murders a Professor and uses his blood to revive the villains, Count Dracula (Aldo Monti) and Rufus Rex (Agustín Martínez Solares), "el hombre lobo"; the monsters are out for revenge on the descendants of a magician called Cristaldi who once killed them with a magic dagger; Santo, "the multitude's idol", and tag-team buddy Blue Demon take time out from their wrestling careers to protect the last of the Cristaldis, two young women and a little girl. The good guys (spoiler alert!) win.

It's so lazily thrown together that the film stops twice for lengthy, dully-shot ring scenes (Santo vs. El Angel Blanco and Blue

Demon vs. Renato el Hippie!) and then, after the supposed horror climax, throws in a tag-team bout featuring all four of these worthies that is just as tacked-on and hard-to-take as the country numbers in the last reel of *Hillbillys in a Haunted House*. The most interesting character is Eric the Hunchback, a rare minion who is in the evil business for the money: he dreams of how much Dracula will pay him for the resurrection ritual and is later tempted to murder his bosses and steal their fortunes. The main villains are standard readings of the roles, with Monti arrogant in full evening dress and Solares sometimes sporting a Naschy-look fur face; they swiftly accrue entourages, of red-shifted vampire women and hairy werewolves, though some regular gangsters are also mixed in to give the heroes someone to scuffle with en route to the big battle. The climax involves several characters forced to walk on a teetering plank over a pit of stakes, with a predictable fate for the main villains when Santo gets a hold on their shirtfronts. For such a wild ride, it's something of a plod – as if the promise of the title was enough to make up for the lack of real gutsy action or complex plotting. Delgado directs without much interest, shooting everything with a TV-look brightness that is attractive but means losing the atmospherics of the earlier, monochrome Santo adventures.

Rise Above's "Santo Collection" DVD offers menus in English and Spanish, and a Spanish soundtrack with English subtitles. The transfer is of a slightly worn print which nevertheless has unfaded, bright colour; it's presented fullscreen though extracts in a brief "Best of El Santo" montage of moments from the wrestler's lengthy film career are letterboxed. Compositions seem fine in unmatted form, framing the (endless) wrestling bouts as if from a ringside seat. Also included is a photo gallery which runs black and white stills in the corner of a crowded L of artwork fotobusta-style (missing is the often-seen still of Dracula

and a line of naked lovelies purportedly shot for the more adult-oriented version of the film) and trailers for two other Santo titles but not this one. An insert booklet contains useful liner notes by David Wilt.

– KN

SANTO IN THE TREASURE OF DRACULA

B&W, 1969, 81m. / Directed by René Cardona / Starring Santo, Aldo Monti, Noelia Noel / Rise Above (US R1 NTSC)

This is such an odd item, even by Mexican monster-wrestling standards, that it wouldn't be surprising to learn it was started as a straight period vampire movie and then reworked in mid-shooting as a Santo picture. In support of this is the way a cheapo *Time Tunnel* effect (a bit like *The Spy Who Shagged Me*) is used to send the heroine (Noelia Noel) back in time so she can be menaced by Dracula (Aldo Monti) while the intrepid "Enmascadero de Plata" stays in the present day. The scripted justification for this is that time travel is so gruelling a process that only women can undergo it, but it might also be that the time machine is just a device to tie the story together rather than an actual plot point. Back in the laboratory, Santo and his pals (including a nerdy comedy relief character) use a television set to spy on the past as the heroine gets mixed up in a cut-down of the Dracula story that feels like footage from a previous version. Adding to the bewilderment is the fact that this time out Santo is not only a pro wrestler-cum-superhero but also a genius intent on clearing his name after the scientific community has scoffed at his claims to have invented a practical time machine.

In the past, a handsome Dracula has a confrontation with a Van Helsing type, smashes a mirror while reciting Stoker's line about "a foul bauble of man's vanity", and introduces himself as Count Alucard (prompting a painful bit of mirror writing). He is guarding a Transylvanian treasure transported to a Mexican cave and is accompanied by a gang of plump, silent vampire women in see-through shrouds (though not topless in this version, as seen in stills from the alternative release *El vampiro y el sexo*). He often turns into a flapping toy bat with plenty of mist effects, and is strangely lit (seemingly from inside his cloak) whenever he looms with fangs. The mini-story set in the past comes to an end with Dracula staked; the heroine then returns to the present, where Santo is battling a black-hooded villain who removes Dracula's stake to bring him back to life. This secondary evil mastermind plot is resolved with a sped-up fistfight in a graveyard, a chase in which the film is distorted to make the cars look bigger, and an unmasking. In the actual finish, Santo and his gang are trapped under a net in Dracula's caves but the cavern roof falls on the Count before we get the scene we have a right to expect, in which "el enmascadero de plata" and "el rey de los vampiros" grapple to the finish.

The utter casualness of the time travel angle is bizarre, but there's a disjunction between the Universal-style pantomime of the vampire stuff and the poverty row serial heroics of the Santo business that makes this an even more disorienting experience than the average Mexican wrestling horror picture. Rise Above Entertainment's "Santo Collection" DVD is less good-looking than their colour releases (e.g. *Santo y Blue Demon contra Dracula y el Hombre Lobo*), the transfer being drawn from a slightly worn print and the monochrome cinematography varies between atmospheric for some scenes and flat in others. The feature is offered in Spanish with optional English subtitles, and the extras stretch to familiar trailers and liner notes by David Wilt.

– KN

SANTO IN THE VENGEANCE OF THE MUMMY

Colour, 1971, 87m. / Directed by René Cardona / Starring Santo, Carlos Ancira, Eric del Castillo, Jorge Guzman / Rise Above (US R0 NTSC)

Now here's a real oddity: a Mexican remake of *Death Curse of Tartu*! Well, close enough, anyway; in this Santo outing, the formidable wrestler dons a safari hat and joins a jungle expedition into the ruins of the Opalche Indians. The colourful group of explorers includes blustery Professor Jiménez (Carlos Ancira), macho Sergio (Eric del Castillo), and an insufferably cute kid, Agapito (Jorge Guzman). While the gang is camped out one night by a fire, the professor shares with them the terrifying story (shown in flashback) of Prince Nonoc, whose love for a virgin sacrifice doomed him to an eternity of mummyhood protected by a sacred scroll. Of course the trespassers press on anyway and are soon being picked off by the skull-faced mummy, armed with a bow and arrow.

A heavily padded but enjoyably silly Santo outing, *Santo in the Vengeance of the Mummy* (*Santo en la venganza de la momia*) works best during the aforementioned flashback, obviously inspired by the 1959 Hammer version of *The Mummy*, and the rampage of the mummy who may not be all that he seems. On the other hand, a goofball twist ending is followed by an insane amount of wrestling footage to close out the film, accompanied all the while by Agapito's gleeful reactions to the antics of heroic Santo. As usual director Cardona keeps things moving simply without much in the way of style or character development; this is pure drive-in fodder for the weekend and none the poorer for it.

Rise Above's DVD contains one of the best of their Santo transfers; apart from the damaged opening credits, the film is presented in excellent condition with wonderful colour saturation. Though it doesn't match the later Santo/Blue Demon films in terms of sheer monster excess, this would make a decent introduction for newcomers. Extras are identical to the other Rise Above Santo releases; inexplicably, the sleeves for all of their colour Santo titles only feature black and white stills.

SANTO: INFRATERRESTRE

Colour, 2001, 85m. / Directed by Hector Molinar / Starring El Hijo del Santo, Blue Panther / Rise Above (US R1 NTSC) / WS (1.66:1) / DD2.0

 Though billed as a Santo film, this is actually a vehicle for the Son of Santo ("el Hijo del Santo"), though since they're both muscle-bound wrestlers wearing silver masks and everyone calls him "Santo" anyway, few will be able to tell the difference.

In a CGI-laden opening, we're shown how spiky-faced aliens have long been present on Earth but live deep underground, waiting for the right time for their brethren to arrive and help them rise to the surface. Cut to a remote country road, where young Diego watches in shock as his parents are beamed aboard a spaceship while fixing their truck. Meanwhile Santo Jr. is busy in the ring with his pal Blue Panther, who seems unusually aggressive during the match. Afterwards Santo watches the bout again on video and determines that his friend was actually trying to kill him and may not be himself. Sure enough, Santo and Diego cross paths in a parking garage where the possessed Blue Panther, an alien and a bunch of mind-controlled henchmen show their true colours. Barely escaping in his flying car, Santo must discover a

way to stop these nefarious creatures from taking over Mexico before the sort-of-special effects-filled climax.

Though it has all the ingredients one would expect – wrestling, monsters, lots of fighting, and the silver-masked one himself – *Infraterrestre* is a strangely leaden affair, more reminiscent of cheapo direct to cable fare than a real low budget drive-in outing. The middling CGI effects, clunky techno music and often-murky cinematography are the main culprits, and even by Santo standards, the acting (especially little Diego) is way below par. Still, if you gotta have a Santo fix, this might do the trick on a really slow evening.

Rise Above's elaborate DVD is the most impressively mounted of the Santo collection, featuring a crisp enough transfer with optional English subtitles. The surround audio works well considering the hit and miss nature of the soundtrack itself, and the dialogue sounds nice and clear. Most of the extras aren't English-friendly, but for the record, you get deleted scenes (mostly chatter), a blooper reel, an interview with the director, video footage of a wrestling match between Santo and Blue Demon, a photo gallery, and Rise Above promotional filler.

SANTO VS. FRANKENSTEIN'S DAUGHTER

Colour, 1971, 97m. / Directed by Miguel M. Delgado / Starring Santo, Gina Romand, Roberto Cañedo, Gerardo Cepeda / Rise Above (US R1 NTSC)

 Another enjoyable and daft instalment in the continuing adventures of Mexico's favourite masked wrestler-cum-freelance superhero. The villain this time out is Dr. Freda Frankenstein (Gina Romand), well-preserved daughter of the original mad scientist (though she's dropped

an "n" from her name), who has lived beyond her years thanks to a youth serum she has also used to turn a bunch of old-timers into her red-jerseyed goon squad. She is after El Santo because she has discovered that his in-the-ring indomitability and Wolverine-like increased healing factor is down to a unique factor in his blood which she hopes to use to perfect her youth serum; she also plans on ditching her devoted assistant (Roberto Cañedo) and taking the masked man as her consort. In addition to the ageless gang, Dr. Frankestein's cavern lair is home to two ready-made creatures, both played by Gerardo Cepeda: an ape-faced brute man called Truxón, a dead ringer for the monster Cepeda played in *Night of the Bloody Apes*, and a more traditional patchwork being called Ursus.

The villainess kidnaps Santo's red-headed girlfriend, setting the wrestler and the missing girl's blonde sister on the sleuthing path. Captured by Freda, Santo is even forced to endure an unprecedented humiliation as she rips off his mask while he is chained up and plants a kiss on him – director Miguel M. Delgado films this from behind a post so we don't see the unmasked, and therefore emasculated hero. Santo gets to chain-whip the ape-man, but Ursus (like many Frankenstein monsters) turns out to have a self-sacrificing, decent streak after Santo shows pity and binds his wounds with his own white shirt, an act that prompts the creature to turn against his ranting, utterly rotten mistress. When defeated, Freda naturally undergoes Ayesha-style sped-up ageing and her sub-cemetery lair is blown up in time for the grappler to make his next bout, the somewhat anticlimactic defeat of a commonplace Japanese wrestler so he can claim the world middleweight title.

Typical of the series in the early 1970s, this throws in the usual deadwood wrestling scenes, colourful but basic mad science apparatus, a touch of mystery (thunder-storms in a graveyard), elements from a bunch of familiar *Famous Monsters* classics (including the popular *Bride of Franken-stein* get-out switch in the laboratory that has no function but to blow everything up at the end), mod fashions (check out the heroine's leather miniskirt), Republic serial-style fistfights, pantomime villainy (an eyepatched villain is always upset because acts of violence remind him of the time his eye was gouged out), melodramatic dialogue ("our love is stronger than that woman's wickedness") and an air of unconscious camp all the more appealing for being played utterly straight. Despite the mild gore, this seems pitched at a kiddie matinee level

Rise Above's standard frame transfer prunes letters off the credits; some sources list a 97 minute running time, but the film doesn't seem to have anything missing. Though the cover, spine and poster call the film *Santo contra la hija de Frankestein*, the on-screen title is *Santo vs. la hija de Frankestein*. The print intermittently shows some slight vertical scratching but the colours are vibrant and attractive. The film is presented in Spanish with optional English subtitles. The only extras are a couple of Santo Collection trailers and an insert booklet with useful notes from David Wilt – who points out how frequently the huffily macho Santo was pitted against slinky female master-fiends.

– KN

THE SARAGOSSA MANUSCRIPT

B&W, 1965, 182m. / Directed by Wojciech Has / Starring Zbigniew Cybulski / Image (US R1 NTSC), Mr Bongo (UK R0 PAL) / WS (2.00:1) (16:9)

Impossible to synopsize succinctly, this Polish historical epic, based on a 17th Century novel by Count Jan Potocki, is, in rapid succession, comic, tragic, scary, romantic, bawdy, coy and bloody.

Before reaching its ambiguous conclusion at just over three hours, *The Saragossa Manuscript* becomes one of the most labyrinthine anthology films ever made, beginning with the discovery of the titular tome in a deserted inn during the Napoleonic Wars by a French officer who, with the aid of his Spanish captor, begins to read the large volume aloud, jumping right into the central tale of Alphonse van Worden (Zbigniew Cybulski), whose adventures while trying to find a new short route to Madrid comprise the main thrust of the film's sprawling narrative. If this seems confusing, keep watching. Each character van Worden encounters has either a tale of his own or encourages the hero to recall something of his family's history, taking the story deeper and deeper into tales-within-tales (within tales, within tales). That's not to say that the film is only people talking; visually inventive, Wojciech Has's constantly roving camera delights in revealing everything from a pair of Sapphic beauties (who may be spirits), to bloody duels, to a gouged eyeball. To give away more than this is to spoil the joy of watching each scene unfold and trying to keep track of each new storyteller's revelations, as well as appreciating Cybulski's performance, which maintains an air of comic wonder throughout the film, making him a most agreeable cohort in this puzzle-box of a movie.

The film is shot in "Dyaliscope", a widescreen black and white format that only underlines the ambitious scope of the movie, subtly reinforcing the authenticity of the images, skilfully composed by cinematographer Mieczyslaw Johoda. Image's near-immaculate transfer of the print is beautifully preserved on this DVD (though slightly slicing off the edges to 2.00:1, à la Vittorio Storaro), which was restored to its full length by the Grateful Dead's Jerry Garcia with assistance from both Francis Ford Coppola and Martin Scorsese. Of special interest is the film's musical score, composed by Krzysztof Penderecki, whose compositions were used extensively in Kubrick's *The Shining* and Friedkin's *The Exorcist*. Drawing from well-known themes of Beethoven, Penderecki also utilizes sparse atonal percussive bursts in a way that makes the score as organic as the dusty landscape that comprises the setting for most of the film. Image has isolated this score on a separate track, which, even though only sparingly present, makes for an interesting listening experience. Also indispensable is a detailed booklet of "liner notes" for the film, which provides a detailed history of the production and its exposure to audiences, as well as outlining the late Garcia's appreciation for the film (which helps to explain the baffling presence of the inappropriately psychedelic Haight-Ashbury-flavoured artwork that graces the packaging).

The Image disc is discontinued but fairly easy to find (and fake "Facets" counterfeit discs are rife online), while the much later U.K. disc looks very similar albeit just a notch fuzzier and only features a stills gallery as its lone extra.

– TSG

SATAN'S BREW

Colour, 1976, 106m. / Directed by Rainer Werner Fassbinder / Starring Kurt Raab, Margit Carstensen, Helen Vita, Volker Spengler, Katherina Buchhammer, Ulli Lommel / Wellspring (US R1 NTSC), e-m-s (Germany R2 PAL)

 A neurotic, bratty poet called Walter Kranz (played by *The Tenderness of Wolves*'s Kurt Raab) is having the ultimate bad day. Short on money and stuck in a house with his siren-voiced wife Luise (Helen Vita) and mentally challenged, fly-fixated brother Ernst (Volker Spengler), he seeks escape in the arms of his kinky mistress (Katherina Buchhammer) only to shoot her dead during their sex play.

An oddball assortment of characters arrives, including delusional literary fan Andrea (Margit Carstensen) and a strange policeman (director Ulli Lommel) investigating the murder. Meanwhile Kranz picks up a hooker under the pretence of writing a sociological study and then writes a new poem, only to learn from Luise that it's identical to one written by the great gay poet Stefan George. Naturally Kranz assumes he's a reincarnation of the literary giant and sets about recreating his lifestyle, down to hiring young boys for an appreciative audience and trying to pick up men at the local toilet (with disastrous results). Increasingly desperate for cash, he fleeces his own parents, ignores Luise's rapidly declining health, and faces the prospect that he might even have to start writing again.

A truly depraved comedy, *Satan's Brew (Satansbraten)* is an absurdist change of pace for the normally melodramatic Rainer Werner Fassbinder. Complete with rampant nudity, sexual perversion, utterly despicable characters and a delirious twist ending, this is the closest thing to a German John Waters film you'll ever see. Fassbinder's uncanny visual sense is still on display in every shot; despite the sordid goings-on, this is one terrific-looking film with old cinematography pros Michael Ballhaus and Jürgen Jürges turning the screen into a riot of colour and texture. Filled with malefic energy, Raab is never less than amazing as he verbally lashes everyone else in the room.

Both DVD releases feature the same exceptional transfer, which is mastered from the original negative and is absolutely pristine in appearance. English subtitles are optional on both; while the U.S. disc has no extra features (apart from sketchy filmographies), the German disc adds the trailer and a bonus disc with two short films included on other Wellspring titles, *The City Tramp* (Fassbinder's first short film) and the documentary *Love, Life & Celluloid*.

THE SATANIC RITES OF DRACULA

Colour, 1973, 87m. / Directed by Alan Gibson / Starring Christopher Lee, Peter Cushing, Joanna Lumley, William Franklyn, Michael Coles, Freddie Jones, Valerie Van Ost / Anchor Bay (US R1 NTSC) / WS (1.85:1)

Covert activity by a number of public figures prompts a co-operative investigation by secret service agent Torrence (played by William Franklyn) and Scotland Yard detective Inspector Murray (Michael Coles). Discovering that their subjects have become involved with a black magic coven, the pair enlists the help of occult specialist Lorrimar Van Helsing (Peter Cushing). Before long Van Helsing finds himself once again pitched against his arch-adversary Count Dracula (Christopher Lee) and a conspiracy to invoke Armageddon with the aid of a malignant strain of virus derived from the bubonic plague.

Absurdly over-dramatic dialogue such as "My revenge has spread over centuries, and has just begun!" convey only too well why, by 1973, Christopher Lee had become so disillusioned with the role he had made his own. It's one among barely more than a dozen lines he speaks throughout the entire film. To compound the problem Hammer evidently had no idea where to take the character next; *The Satanic Rites of Dracula*, a last gasp attempt to breathe some death into their stagnating Dracula series, plants the Count in modern day London... as did the previous year's *Dracula A.D. 1972*. There's no faulting its ambitions, but where this was at least a novel approach first time out of the box, the results here are less satisfying. By now Dracula had become a bit-part player in his own films (he doesn't appear until over half an hour into the proceedings), further reflecting Lee's discontent with the part. And let's face it; a Dracula film without a healthy injection of the titular character rather misses the point. The supporting story is not very interesting at all and having the Count conceal himself and his activities by taking on the mantle of Howard Hughes-esque recluse D.D. Denham is about as atypical as it gets.

Director Alan Gibson (who also helmed *Dracula A.D. 1972*, and later "The Silent Scream", one of the better episodes in the *Hammer House of Horror* television series) does manage to serve up a couple of efficient set pieces, the best of which finds Coles set upon in a cellar full of vulpine bloodsuckers whom he dispatches with the running water from an emergency sprinkler system. The finale too is nicely staged, with Dracula falling foul of the barbed limbs of a hawthorn tree, tactfully identified earlier in the film by Van Helsing as the source of Christ's crown of thorns and thus a suitably holy method of slaying vampires.

Whoever thought that William Franklyn would make a good hero type was proven sadly mistaken and, almost as if someone realized it wasn't quite working, he's bumped off halfway through. Michael Coles reprises his detective from *Dracula A.D. 1972* and is marginally more embarrassing than he was first time round. Beneath a mop of bright red hair, Joanna Lumley supplants the previous film's Stephanie Beacham as Van Helsing's granddaughter Jessica. Freddie Jones is the eccentric professor caught up in Dracula's evil machinations. And Valerie Van Ost chips in with a memorable turn as a prim secretary who succumbs to the Count's fanged embrace and transforms into a wanton creature of the night. Unsurprisingly Peter Cushing saves the film from total disaster with a sincere performance that, given the material he had to work with, proves what a real trooper he was. There's a nice bit of business when he forges a silver bullet out of a melted crucifix, though all his efforts are wasted when he fires and misses! All said and done, even a weak Cushing/Lee starrer is a cut above most similar fare of the era and *The Satanic Rites of Dracula* is very much worth a look.

As one of Anchor Bay's earlier ventures into DVD territory, *The Satanic Rites of Dracula* isn't the finest example of their wares, bearing a transfer of a slightly splicy print and suffering from unstable colours. The latter is one of the aspects that collectors defected from VHS to DVD to forget about and its presence gives rise to some disappointment. Compared to Anchor Bay's sumptuous, later-released disc of *Scars of Dracula*, this really is an anti-climax. Nevertheless, there have been far greater abuses of the shiny disc format. Plus it's nice to see Christopher Lee's final spin as the caped Count in its theatrical ratio and (especially for those who've only ever seen Warner's slightly trimmed British tapes) pleasingly intact to boot. The film itself, punctuated by 13 chapter stops, poaches one side of the disc for itself. Flip it over and you're treated to an all-Dracula episode of TV's *World of Hammer* series and two rather ropy looking trailers. One appears under its original title and a second more explicit version bears its ludicrous U.S. release moniker *Count Dracula and His Vampire Bride* which, in the annals of misrepresentation, truly takes the cake: "The king of the undead marries the queen of the zombies!" announces the narrator. Was he watching the right film at the time?

It is surprising that, at the time of writing, Anchor Bay's disc remains the only official DVD release available. Beware of bootlegs! – TG

SATANIK

Colour, 1968, 84m. / Directed by Piero Vivarelli / Starring Magda Konopka, Umberto Raho / Retromedia (US R1 NTSC)

A female Jekyll and Hyde story for the swinging lounge set, *Satanik* (or as the American title card reads, *Satanic*) loosely adapts a semi-popular European comic with a few commercially viable

splashes of blood, nudity and crime. Unlike the traditional superheroes populating American comics of the period, this is dark, morally dubious material, essentially in the same vein as supernaturally tinged graphic novel teases like *Valentina* and *Barbarella*.

Old and scarred Marnie Bannister (Magda Konopka) thinks her best days might be behind her, at least until a colleague demonstrates a new genetic formula capable of regressing the age drive in organisms, albeit with psychologically destructive results. Naturally the old biddy takes a gulp of this youth potion and turns into a sultry blonde vixen, the perfect vehicle for luring wealthy men and stripping them of their fortunes. Unfortunately her first victim, George (*giallo* staple Umberto Raho), catches her mid-transformation and winds up sliced to bits for his trouble. Flip-flopping between appearances thanks to her handy potion, she dons a number of outrageous mod outfits, performs a criminal striptease in a body-hugging black outfit, and eludes the police looking for a homicidal old woman.

As with some other Italian exploitation titles of this vintage, *Satanik* feels deeply conflicted about its attitude toward women, almost pathologically so in this case. While Konopka is a ravishingly beautiful woman, the film coyly avoids any extended nudity and seems to trade in the weird charge of watching her face going through various stages of decay and restoration. Then there's the trademark "poetic justice" ending, which wraps things up with that laziest of judgmental story devices, a handy car crash. (See *Come Together* for an even more outrageous, blatant example of puritanical automotive mayhem.) If you ignore the strange sexual undercurrents, *Satanik* at least delivers a modicum of thrills thanks to its groovy music score, some isolated striking images (the aforementioned stage show in particular), and enough bizarre shifts in tone to keep even Italo-sleaze veterans scratching their heads.

Retromedia's bizarrely designed packaging doesn't really represent this film, from the misleading "booga-booga" Satanic cover to the back copy by Mirek Lipenski, which was probably good at some point but fell victim to the worst copy-editing disaster in the format's history. The colourful transfer is a bit of a step up from the PD prints circulating on VHS for years, though the fullscreen image is still grainy. The cropping from the original theatrical aspect ratio poses problems in a few shots, though the reported 2.35:1 framing of some sources appears questionable; only a marginal amount seems to be missing (and the title cards look fine), so this may have been 1.85:1 originally. Sound is mediocre but tolerable as well. The only notable extra (and it's a doozy!) is a gallery of *Satanik* comic book covers, representing the title character in its male and female incarnations. Also available as part of Retromedia's "Euro Fiends from the Grave" with *The Faceless Monster* and *The Red-Headed Corpse*.

SAVAGE BEACH

Colour, 1989, 92m. / Directed by Andy Sidaris / Starring Dona Speir, Michael Shane, John Aprea, Teri Weigel / Malibu Bay Films (US R0 NTSC), Laser Paradise (Germany R2 PAL)

 Following *Hard Ticket to Hawaii* and *Picasso Trigger*, the foxy LETHAL duo of Donna and Taryn appears one last time for *Savage Beach*, a return of sorts to *Malibu Express* territory (even down to the poster art) and one of Andy Sidaris's most omnipresent home video titles. This time the action centres around the outlying islands of Hawaii, where Donna and Taryn take time out from their fun in the sun to transport a valuable, emergency supply of vaccine via charter

plane, which naturally has to make a crash landing on a mysterious island. They hook up with Captain Andreas (*Matt Houston*'s John Aprea) in a plot to find a sunken World War II ship guarded by the Japanese that has become the target of a gang of villainous fortune hunters. Much bikini-clad mayhem ensues, including a rousing, surprisingly gory finale topped off with some hara-kiri for good measure.

One of Sidaris's most visually accomplished films, *Savage Beach* features even less plot than usual but makes up for it with some amazing on-location footage and a perfectly sculpted cast, including *Playboy* Playmate and future porn actress Teri Weigel. (For the record, it's also one of the rare Sidaris outings with frontal nudity, though it's pretty discreet.) Don't miss the bittersweet ending, either. It's also worth noting that this film introduces yet another Abilene, Shane (played by Michael – what else? – Shane).

The making-of documentary for this disc (which sports the usual top-notch video and audio quality) is a bit more extensive than usual, combining location footage and some generic Strain/Sidaris banter, along with archival interview footage of Roberta Vasquez and other actors hobnobbing with TV personalities like avowed Sidaris fanatic Joe Bob Briggs. The usual good-natured commentary track and trailer collection are included as an added inducement. Like its companion Sidaris titles, this is out of print and tricky to locate now, but Germany provided it later with their collection of the director's films; as usual the commentary's gone, while the documentary footage is lopped into their typical "Film School" video segments.

SAVAGE HARVEST

Colour, 1994, 72m. / Directed by Eric Stanze / Starring Lisa Morrison, Ramona Midgett / Image, Sub Rosa (US R1 NTSC), Crypt Keeper (UK R0 PAL) / DD2.0

The first feature length project for indie director Eric Stanze and his crew, *Savage Harvest* offers an intriguing look at a talent who would improve greatly in just a few years. Strong on atmosphere and gore, the story focuses on fairly traditional monster mayhem with a few interesting wrinkles; though hampered by technical limitations and a handful of uneasy moments, this is definitely not your average first time horror effort. Basically a Native American riff on '80s gore films (in particular *Night of the Demons*), our story begins traditionally enough with a gang of out-of-towner teens arriving at a remote cabin in the middle of the woods for some fun and relaxation. They swap stories to pass the time and, thanks to one youth's uncle on hand, learn the saga of a native curse instigated when, centuries ago, a Cherokee was killed by his tribe for practicing black magic and converting dark powers into a handful of enchanted stones. Naturally one of those stones is on hand now thanks to a recent flood and, when touched, can trigger a demonic transformation in its victim. Naturally it isn't long before said hellish powers are unleashed full force, leaving the survivors to fend off the fanged, forked-tongued fiends from hell.

Right from the beginning Stanze was efficient at finding good, believable actors who can deliver even the toughest dialogue with a straight face. Since the first half is almost devoid of monster mayhem, it's up to the characters and storytelling to carry the weight of entertaining the audience; fortunately everyone is up to the task and aided by some nice, moody nocturnal photography. Though it doesn't quite outdo *Evil Dead* on the red stuff scale, the climax is a rousing piece of work, capped off with a nice twist ending to boot. Compared to Stanze's more severe and outlandish subsequent films, this is almost a quaint and commercial project but it will certainly satisfy horror fans tired of the bloodless, homogenized junk out at the multiplexes.

Shot for scraps on home video, *Savage Harvest* is creatively put together and compositionally savvy. However, it's also almost completely devoid of colour, ranking alongside John Badham's strange desaturation of 1979's *Dracula* as one of the most peculiar colour transfers out there. Even the blood looks dark and grey, which may have been an artistic choice but looks disconcerting all the same.

Considering the grainy limitations of the source material, Sub Rosa's disc looks fine and sports a decent audio track with clear, audible dialogue and some nice sound effects mixing. Stanze and company return again for commentary time; the director turns up on the first track with producer D.J. Vivona for a technically oriented history of the film. It's on par with their other appearances and offers some handy advice about the dos and don'ts of filming under the most strenuous limitations. The five young leads take the microphone for the second track and offer a much looser, goofier commentary, more devoted to the rigors of enduring latex make-up and dealing with not always hospitable location shooting. Also included is a behind the scenes documentary, containing tons of footage from the shoot and interviews with the principals, as well as two *Savage Harvest* trailers, a stills gallery, a Stanze music video, and more Stanze trailers (one each for *Scrapbook* and *Ice from the Sun*). The dark animated menu screens are very disorienting at first, so don't be afraid to punch around on your remote's arrow buttons. The subsequent U.K. disc is bare bones, while a 2006 reissue from Wicked Pixel through Image sports a much more gratifying transfer with actual colours as well as some additional extras like two new commentaries (featuring Stanze and most of the cast) as well as the original Stanze/ Vivona one, two trailers, and an additional making-of segment.

SCARED TO DEATH

Colour, 1947, 68m. / Directed by Christy Cabanne / Starring Bela Lugosi, George Zucco, Joyce Compton, Angelo Rossitto, Nat Pendleton, Douglas Fowley, Gladys Blake / Alpha (US R0 NTSC), Lumivision (US R1 NTSC), Network (UK R2 PAL)

Made just as horror movies were going out of fashion, this frankly desperate little item comes from an outfit (Screen Guild) lower even on the Poverty Row totem pole than Monogram or PRC. The script falls apart even as a cast of B-stalwarts coo and snarl at each other, while a bizarre structure seems to have been imposed in post-production in an attempt to at least get the plot points across. The most unusual aspect is that it is in colour, albeit a garish process a long way off from lustrous Technicolor; it's one of a handful of quickies using colour as a gimmick, as later grindhouse flicks would 3-D or bogus insurance policies.

Prefiguring the original cut of *Sunset Blvd*, the film opens in a mortuary and is narrated by a corpse lying on a slab, though the constant fades in and out of the dead woman (Joyce Compton) get more and more ridiculous, as the former nightclub dancer chattily recounts a story that will wind up with her (as promised) scared to death and incidentally reveals her as a treacherous slut who ratted out her partner to the Nazis in occupied Europe. In the home of psychiatrist Dr. Van Ee (George Zucco), once an insane asylum, the victim is menaced by a green-masked apparition who turns out to be the vengeful partner and sometimes shows up in drag. The bland mask is evidently horrid enough to induce heart attack in the unrepentant villainess, but repeated appearances at the window are mostly seen by no one but the audience, as if random shots of the looming apparition had been cut in to add scary punctuation.

Bela Lugosi is, as so often, a red herring here, a magician/hypnotist with a devoted dwarf sidekick (Angelo Rossitto), and a fair amount of deadening footage is devoted to a lunkhead private eye (played by Nat Pendleton) who lives in the hope that there'll be a murder he can solve so he can get his job on the police back, and a moustached smart-aleck reporter (Douglas Fowley) who gets to the bottom of it. A maid (Gladys Blake) dies but after much manhandling of her corpse turns out to be only hypnotised, suggesting that this was intended to be a black comedy though the laughs come along as rarely as the chills. Zucco and Lugosi, with minimal material, at least try hard and the old spark is occasionally there. However, as with many 1940s Bs, the story will make your head hurt if you try to follow it too closely.

Though the opening titles are battered, this PD item is presented in a fairly decent print; the cheap "Natural Color" process looks surprisingly good, if as much like tinting as ever, and those whose main interest in an otherwise negligible film is seeing Lugosi in colour will find him in the pink, as it were, with a natty scarlet lining to his Dracula-style cape. Unusually for an Alpha Video disc, this has an extra: the trailer. However, Lugosi die-hards may want to spring for the somewhat sharper-looking but scuffed print available from Lumivision with *The Devil Bat* (but without the trailer – or extras of any kind, for that matter). The Alpha version is basically carried over with PAL conversion for the U.K. disc.

– KN

SCARLET DIVA

Colour, 2000, 90m. / Directed by Asia Argento / Starring Asia Argento, Jean Shepard, Vera Gemma / Paramount (France R2 PAL), Media Blasters (US R1 NTSC), MIA (UK R2 PAL) / WS (1.85:1) (16:9) / DD5.1.

Aside from her status as one of Italy's most popular young actresses, Asia Argento has been actively pursuing a directorial career for some time, beginning with an episode of the anthology *De Generazione* in 1994 (made when she was only 19), and continuing with various shorts, music videos, and the "video diary" *Abel (heart) Asia*, a portrait of Abel Ferrara shot while Argento was acting in Ferrara's sublime *New Rose Hotel*. Her feature directorial debut, *Scarlet Diva*, is a remarkable work in which she also plays the lead role, a thinly disguised self-portrait named Anna Battista. What plot there is focuses on Anna's affair with an egotistical musician named Kirk (Jean Shepard in a role originally offered to Vincent Gallo, who asked for too much money, and whose face now adorns a magazine cover on which Anna treads).

Scarlet Diva clearly divides audiences; even Argento has referred to its admirers as "freaks". The film's strengths and flaws are also those of its creator; rarely in today's cinema does one encounter a "commercial" work that is so clearly the product of an individual sensibility, to the extent that getting to know it is much like getting to know another person. Superficially, the film appears to be casual and rambling, but on closer inspection, it becomes clear that not a single detail is superfluous or unrelated to Argento's wider concerns; notice for example how the relationship between the essentially passive Anna and her more active friend Veronica (Vera Gemma) is suggested by the (real) tattoos – depicting, respectively, an eye and a gun – these women have on their backs.

Most reviewers compared *Scarlet Diva* with the work of two significant male directors in Argento's life: her father, Dario Argento, and the director of her finest performance, Abel Ferrara. The influence of the former is clear enough in the garish lighting of a scene wherein Anna is tricked into taking cocaine (not to mention the dream scene in which Anna visits an open-air cinema where Dario's *The Phantom of the Opera* is being screened), while Ferrara might have inspired the opening credits montage (as well as the character of junkie auteur Aaron Ulrich, though Argento now denies this). But this sexist reading suggests that *Scarlet Diva* should conform to a model of filmmaking in which it clearly has no interest. The film only begins to make sense once it is viewed alongside other autobiographical / experimental works by female European directors: Chantal Akerman's *Je tu il elle* and Jackie Reynal's *Deux fois* both uninhibitedly display the filmmakers' own naked bodies in a manner which is neither voyeuristic nor narcissistic, and one need only compare the shot of Argento shaving her armpits with images of Reynal urinating or Akerman and her female lover having sex in order to grasp the tradition in which Argento is working.

Scarlet Diva has previously been available on DVD in France and America. Paramount's French disc offers an excellent 27-minute making of documentary entitled *A's Enigma* (a reference to Dario's *Trauma*, whose working title was *Aura's Enigma*) in which Argento insists that "My images are not intellectual. My film is not intellectual... it's very naive and childish." The American disc from Media Blasters does not include the documentary, but does have an excellent English-language commentary by Argento, who explains exactly how personal much of the film is: I was especially moved to learn that the scene in which Anna releases a rabbit by the side of a road was filmed at the exact spot where Argento's sister, to whom the film is dedicated, died in a motorcycle crash a few years earlier (exactly the kind of information that can deepen one's appreciation of a film). The U.S. disc also contains a 17-minute

interview with Argento (conducted by Maitland McDonagh), and a 30-second introduction (filmed at the same time as the interview) that appears before the film ("You've heard very bad things about it, but it's a good movie"). The commentary and the interview (though, sadly, not the introduction) also appear on MIA's U.K. release, alongside an 8-minute behind the scenes documentary (in Italian with English subtitles, including an interview with Asia's father), quite different from (and frankly inferior to) the one on the French disc: it focuses exclusively on the technology used to shoot *Scarlet Diva*, and seems to have been intended primarily to promote digital video equipment. All three editions contain trailers, with the MIA release adding three TV spots. MIA's DVD offers a good quality letterboxed transfer of the actual film, though, like the American disc (but unlike the French), it displays some noticeable picture break-up during shots of flashing light bulbs. The subtitles on MIA's disc (which runs 86m 33s at 25 fps) are mostly identical to those on the Media Blasters release (the film's dialogue is evenly divided between English and Italian, with a little French), but the American disc adds titles identifying the cities through which Anna travels. Even viewers who require more than a shot of the Eiffel Tower to let them know that they are in Paris must find this annoying, since the various changes of locale are clearly signalled by the dialogue. Thankfully MIA's transfer does not contain these titles.

– BS

SCHIZOPHRENIAC

Colour, 1997, 84m. / Directed by Ron Atkins / Starring John Giancaspro / Cutthroat (US R1 NTSC) / DD2.0

NECROMANIAC

Colour, 1999, 93m. / Directed by Ron Atkins / Starring John Giancaspro, Ron Atkins / Cutthroat (US R1 NTSC) / DD2.0

In the tradition of such fringe atrocities as *Bride of Frank*, *Schramm*, and pretty much everything by Troma, this pair of nutso, shot-on-video efforts chronicles a serial killer's plunge into the depths of dementia. Granted, that's one of the more common themes for low-budget filmmakers, but you have to give these guys credit for not pulling any punches and turning out a body of work that, um, speaks for itself.

After receiving a creepy Howdy Doody ventriloquist doll named Rubberneck from his girlfriend Drew, fledgling serial killer Harry Russo (John Giancaspro) is driven over the edge by ranting voices in his head and goes on a frenetic rampage, beginning with Drew but soon expanding out to anyone within driving distance. While not raping, murdering, dancing to disco music in drag, and leaping around naked in parking lots while screaming at the camera, he takes time out to pee on a neighbour's bushes, shoots up in porno theatres, and drives around endlessly in his car on a one way trip to oblivion.

And that's about it, plot-wise. Best viewed straight through as one film, *Schizophreniac* (which has the demure onscreen subtitle, *The Whore Mangler*) and *Necromaniac* (*Schizophreniac 2*) douse the viewer in a cascading river of video nastiness, with plenty of fast cutting and flashy visual effects to keep the pace moving along briskly. Giancaspro is one seriously fearless actor to say the least, going from shrieking gibberish and gouging gory holes in his victims to borderline hardcore sex in a variety of seedy situations. The packaging dubs these "the vilest piece of filth ever to be filmed", and while that might be debatable

(heck, did they ever see *Forrest Gump*?), it's definitely up there in the shock-for-shock's-sake home video pantheon. Fortunately there's also a lot of sick humour to lighten the experience; one early scene in the first film finds him angrily trying to order a Big Mac at a Wendy's, with profane results.

Both movies come in two-disc special editions (believe it or not), with similar bonus features: deleted scenes (most of them fairly tame and easily expendable), trailers, and video interviews with director Ron Atkins, who also pops up in the second film as Jesus. (Really!) The first film also contains "A Walk with Harry", in which the lead actor goes on a tour of his neighbourhood and reveals a little of his, uh, personality. (Watch it back to back with the "day in the life of Roger Watkins" featurette on *The Last House on Dead End Street* for maximum effect.) The second film also contains a music video, much in the style of those Necrophagia clips. You have been warned, and keep a warm bath handy after viewing.

SCHLOCK

Colour, 1972, 79m. / Directed by John Landis / Starring The Schlockthropus (John Landis), Eliza Garrett [Roberts] / Anchor Bay (US R1 NTSC) / WS (1.85) / (16:9)

A low-budget, comedy riff on Freddie Francis's *Trog*, this was not only John Landis's first feature but also the first sign that a generation reared on *Famous Monsters* would become a significant force in Hollywood. Self-financed and short-scheduled, it has quite a few of the faults you'd expect under the circumstances, not to mention several more that have recurred in bigger-budgeted Landis films. Nevertheless, it scrapes by on a genuine, lively amiability that obviously springs from its creator's personality: not only did Landis write and direct, but he's also in the ape-suit created by a young Rick Baker. Actually, the job Landis does best in the movie is acting, making the misunderstood, comic monster a wholly lovable and winning character. Even when gags are dying all around, the Schlock gets laughs with odd eye-expressions or sudden enthusiasms like a jam session with a blind pianist that is the first expression of the love for black American music which informs much of Landis's later filmography. Also debuting here is the director's very late '60s attitude to the police, who are depicted as pro-establishment idiots and slaughtered for laughs.

It begins with several massacres at which banana skins are the only clue, leading authorities to conclude that an ape-man has revived from hibernation. *Schlock* putters around the sites of the crimes almost unnoticed, even when he rips an arm off a TV news reporter, and drifts into a relationship with a dim blind girl (Eliza Roberts) who at first thinks he's a dog. Most of the film consists of parodies of vintage or then-current movies: *King Kong* (obviously), *2001: A Space Odyssey*, *Elvira Madigan*, *Love Story*, *The Blob* and *Dinosaurus!* (seen spliced together in a cinema scene. Apart from Landis and Roberts, the comic performances are mostly awkward and amateurish and the seventy-nine-minute running time still includes more than a few *longueurs*. Nevertheless, it's a sweet film, and a commentary track by Landis and Baker, full of charming moments as they recognise friends and relations from thirty years ago, captures the lunatic energy of the venture, which both acknowledge as significant in their lives and careers even as they admit its faults. Absolute purists may want to retain battered old videotapes since Landis has made a tiny digital upgrade in the final scene, blanking out his real teeth – which used to be visible behind Schlock's.

Anchor Bay's DVD looks fine, offering a sun-struck transfer from a healthy-looking print. The extras are: an amusing animated menu; a theatrical trailer and four radio spots (in 1972, a major selling point was to promise long-haired audiences "see the police and national guard powerless!"); an extensive gallery of stills, promotional artwork and behind-the-scenes shots; and well-written thumbnail bios of Landis and Baker.
– KN

SCOOBY-DOO

Colour, 2002, 86m. / Directed by Raja Gosnell / Starring Sarah Michelle Gellar, Matthew Lillard, Freddie Prinze Jr., Linda Cardellini, Neil Fanning (voice), Rowan Atkinson, Isla Fisher, Kristian Schmid, Pamela Anderson / Warner (Blu-ray & DVD) (US R0/R1 HD/NTSC, UK R0/R2 HD/PAL) / WS (1.85:1) (16:9) / DD5.1

After a bitter falling out over inequitable credit for their paranormal detective work, the members of Mystery Inc – that's Fred (Freddie Prinze Jr.), Daphne (Sarah Michelle Gellar), Velma (Linda Cardellini), Shaggy (Matthew Lillard) and their faithful hound Scooby-Doo (voiced by Neil Fanning) – go their separate ways. Two years pass and the team are reluctantly reunited when each individually accepts an invitation from Emile Mondavarious (Rowan Atkinson) to solve a problem out at the Spooky Island Theme Park. It seems that college kids are arriving full of beans and ready to party, only to depart like pacified zombies. What can be happening to them in the interim period?

Gags about drugs? Noisy flatulence contests? Bobbling bikini-clad breasts everywhere you look? Zoinks! What's going on? It must be another entry in the irreverent *American Pie* series. Well, no actually. It's

444

the live-action big screen adaptation of cartoon favourite *Scooby-Doo*. Directed by Raja Gosnell, when it was first let off the leash the film underwent a savaging worthy of a rabid Great Dane, by critics and audiences alike. And with good reason too. It's a celluloid mongrel, unsure as to whether it's an homage to or a parody of its source material. The production design and garish cartoon colours lend themselves to the former, but the dialogue soon has you thinking otherwise, at one moment true to the spirit of the cartoon then in the blink of an eye tumbling into the morass of cheap bodily function gags; the low point (or, depending on your sense of humour, possibly the highpoint) arrives with a protracted farting and belching contest between Shaggy and his canine companion.

After a fast and funny opener on the tail end of the gang's latest mystery – which concludes with the mandatory audience-pleaser "I would have gotten away with it too if it weren't for you meddling kids!" – we get to meet the principal characters and almost immediately realise this isn't going to be as much fun as we thought. Scoob himself is amusing to watch but he's a CG creation and looks it; with modern technology what it is, surely they could have come up with something a tad more convincing. Of the human contingent, bleach blond Freddie Prinze Jr. is by far the most woeful piece of casting. If anyone can explain how he continues to find employment, please do so. His Fred is about as far removed from the cartoon original as he could be; an objectionable, parsimonious, preening ponce. To be fair, the script is just as much to blame for this reimagining of the character, but that doesn't make the results any less acrid a pill to swallow. Sarah Michelle Gellar's Daphne is also a reinvention – as a conceited prima donna – and, for no apparent reason other than catering to the obvious, she gets to employ her *Buffy* kick-fighting routine on a muscular miscreant. To her credit Linda Cardellini manages to pull off Velma's

voice, but she's far too attractive – cuter than Gellar in fact – and that's just not right; this is, after all, the bespectacled, roll-neck sweatered plain-Jane brainy member of the team we're talking about here. Nice that they squeezed in the requisite "I can't find my glasses" gag though. One might expect the characters to be more fully fledged than in a 20-minute cartoon show but divorcing them from their roots turns initiative into stupidity. Where they really did get it right, however, is with Matthew Lillard as milquetoast beatnik Shaggy. Not only does he nail the mannerisms and vocal requirements, but his convincing interacting with Scooby almost – I repeat, almost – makes you forget the dumb mutt is a CG confection. Rowan Atkinson chips in with the sort of simpering, twitchy performance he had down pat over twenty years ago in TV's *Not the Nine O'Clock News* and runs rings round most everyone else on screen. Small roles for Isla Fisher (*Home and Away*) and Kristian Schmid (*Neighbours*) reinforce the fact this was shot in Australia, while there's a notable walk-on by surgically-defaced Pamela Anderson (guesting as herself).

With a pretty atrocious rap score and the unforgivable incorporation of Scrappy-Doo (whose absence from the early cartoons, as any Scooby purist will tell you, helps make them the classics they are), there really isn't a great deal to recommend about this one. There are instances, I imagine, where a certain clientele would pay serious money to hear Gellar exclaim, "Oh God, he's peeing on me!" as a stream of amber fluid sprays across her chest; with the source of this genitourinary crudity in *Scooby-Doo* being a rebellious CG Scrappy, it's safe to say that this film is not one of those instances.

Doubtless spurred by the scent of extra cash, the studios have long abandoned those value-for-money double-sided platters that offer both widescreen and full screen viewing options, in their place two separate releases thus endowing the punter with an either/or option. *Scooby-Doo* is just such a case. Whichever one you choose, the transfer on Warner Brothers's Region 1 *Scooby-Doo* DVD is as clean and colourful as you've every right to expect. There are a rather tight-fisted 13 chapter stops and the sound is in English or French, with subtitle options in English, French and Spanish. There are a number of bonus features, the focal point of which is a collection of seven deleted scenes. These include a wisely discarded alternative animated opening titles sequence and some raunchy stuff with Cardellini that leads one to wonder how they ever thought this suited *Scooby-Doo* protocol. Conspicuously truant, however, is the even more inappropriate publicity-spinning excised sequence with Cardellini and Gellar sharing a smooch in order to return their transposed souls to the right bodies. Additionally there's a 20+ minute featurette comprising behind the camera footage and interviews with the cast, an interactive quiz (with the treat for solving it being some backstage footage with Pamela Anderson and a brief interview with the collagen and botox-bloated lady herself), the Outkast promo music video "Land of a Million Drums", and some further behind the scenes footage looking at set design, the Mystery Machine, and the choreography of Gellar's *Buffy*-esque fight scene. You can also choose from two commentary tracks, one with the cast, and the other with the crew. A short trailer for the soundtrack album rounds off the deal. Actual movie trailers (including the clever teaser which spoofs the *Batman* franchise, and which appears on one of Warner's cartoon Scooby disc compilations) are absent from the package. A hidden mini-featurette in which the cast bemoan the adverse weather conditions that struck during filming can be accessed on the main menu page animation; when Scoob drops the Scooby Snack, highlight it and press enter.

The Region 2 disc is virtually identical to the American edition under review, with just one small but significant difference – it has been cut by one second to qualify for a 'PG' rating! According to the BBFC

website, "Distributor chose to remove sight of potentially imitable martial arts techniques (kicks to head) in order to obtain a 'PG'. A '12' uncut was available to the distributor." As expected, the Blu-ray version looks fresher and much sharper with additional CGI detail in nearly every shot, while carrying over all of the extras except for the trivia game.

– TG

SCRAPBOOK

Colour, 1999, 95m. / Directed by Eric Stanze / Starring Emily Haack, Tommy Biondo / Image, Sub Rosa (US R1 NTSC) / DD2.0, Crypt Keeper (UK R0 PAL)

In the increasingly crowded world of shot-on-video horror, it's difficult for many projects to even see the light of day, much less garner any attention. However, that proved to be no obstacle for the ferocious and highly accomplished *Scrapbook*, which has already earned its share of both critical accolades and censorship hassles. The cover warns that it "contains extremely disturbing material", which in this case turns out to be understatement instead of hype.

The viewer is plunged immediately into the environment of a seriously unhinged man named Leonard (played by the film's writer and production designer, Tommy Biondo, who died due to a filming accident on another shoot before he could see the finished product). After a puzzling and effective prologue in which he's taunted by his naked sister and subjected to vicious abuse, we meet his latest captive, Clara (Emily Haack), who's bound to a chair in his kitchen papered with Polaroid snapshots. After brutally raping her, Leonard explains that he maintains a scrapbook filled with the thoughts, scribblings, and cries for help from his victims, and since the book is almost full after twelve years, Clara may be the last one necessary to complete the masterpiece that will make him a media star. Clara's written response doesn't please him, to put it mildly, and punishment is swift. Living in a farmhouse in the middle of nowhere, Leonard has the perfect set up to dispose of his victims in the nearby barn. However, Clara begins to closely analyze the scrapbook, devising a way to prolong her life, explore the mind of her captor, and perhaps even escape.

While many viewers may be tempted to flee in shock from the sucker punches delivered in the opening third, *Scrapbook* is hardly your standard exercise in prurient sadism. Both of the actors deliver impassioned, uncomfortably convincing performances, often naked both physically and emotionally. Haack's modulations between shock, terror, and crafty manipulation are among the best in the rape/revenge subgenre, and the viewer's sympathies rest solidly with her all the way. Also known for his cult favourite *Ice from the Sun*, director Eric Stanze uses the digital video format to his advantage here, creating a smothering atmosphere of claustrophobia and using deliberately distorted, damaged video footage during one harrowing montage in a shower. Interestingly, despite the brutality of the subject matter, the level of onscreen gore is fairly low considering the film's reputation. Most of the shock value comes instead from the horrific intensity of the performances and the gruesome sexual violations of Clara's ordeal, including a brief sojourn into kinda-sorta-hardcore territory that's bound to keep this off the shelves at Blockbuster for all eternity. Fortunately the film does include a few brief glimmers of humour, however dark, including one particular monologue that deserves a place in the sick joke pantheon.

Sub Rosa's impressively mounted DVD edition of *Scrapbook* begins with jittery, tape-shredded menus that nicely capture the ambience of the film itself. The transfer looks extremely good, especially considering the formats involved, and the surround audio (featuring a nerve-jangling electronic/*musique concrète* score) is brutally manipulative. Stanze, Haack, and producer Jeremy Wallace appear on a highly engaging commentary track, in which all of them admit to certain levels of difficulty with making and even watching the film. However, they all have respect for each other and the final product, with several interesting stories about the technical execution. (Of course, be warned that it's also probably the only time you'll hear a horror film's lead actress recall, "We planned the urination. He asked me beforehand, and I said yeah, just don't do it on my face.") A very welcome 15-minute "Making of *Scrapbook*" shows the lighter and more clinical side of things, with an interesting explanation of how the crew participated in the scrapbook's creation and the surprising revelation that one performer had no idea how the final scene would play out while the cameras were rolling. Other extras include two fairly intense *Scrapbook* trailers along with three other Stanze trailers, for *Ice from the Sun*, *I Spit on Your Corpse – I Piss on Your Grave*, and *Savage Harvest*. A small stills gallery and a Biondo remembrance by Stanze round out the obvious extras, but there are also Easter eggs within Easter eggs. *Chokehold* is a grim black and white short film about drug addiction and blurred reality directed by Haack, while *Survive* is a Biondo-directed black and white short about a deranged homeless soldier, featuring Stanze as "the apparition". Stanze's music video for "Slugs Are in My House", by the Ded Bugs, is a heavy metal homage to horror film classics, while "Shooting Slugs" is a nearly 8-minute compilation of behind the scenes footage from the music video shoot. It's fun to watch but not enough to shake off the lingering unease left behind by the main feature. And that's a good thing. The subsequent release from Image when the rights reverted back to Wicked Pixel drops the two short films in favour of a "Shower Cam" featurette (very disturbing) and an extra deleted scene.

Interestingly, the British release on the Crypt Keeper label was initially made available as an uncut release, without official BBFC sanction. After a short time on the market it was inevitably withdrawn from sale then re-issued after cuts, the details of which are described on the BBFC website: "To obtain this category cuts of 15m 24s were required. The cuts were Compulsory. Cuts required to remove sexual assault and humiliation, and sexualised violence, to obtain an '18' in accordance with BBFC guidelines and policy."

SEBASTIANE

Colour, 1976, 85m. / Directed by Derek Jarman and Paul Humfress / Starring Leonard Treviglio, Barney James / Kino (US R1 NTSC), Second Sight (UK R0 PAL) / WS (1.66:1)

After honing his craft with a string of short films while art directing for the likes of Ken Russell, Derek Jarman finally plunged into his first feature length project, a film that seemingly had all the odds stacked against it. Simply put, it's a homoerotic, deliberately paced art house look at the life of St. Sebastian, performed entirely in Latin. Co-directed by BBC helmer Paul Humfress, the film begins with a scene that's pure Jarman: in the Roman court, Emperor Diocletian's minions stage a bizarre orgy complete with body paint and sensual excess. Suddenly we switch to the remote beach outposts of Italy (shot in Sardinia), where the Christian Sebastian (Leonard Treviglio) has been sent to reside with a group of soldiers. The lead centurion, Maximus (Barney James), is displeased with Sebastian's antisocial ways and his conflicting religious views; the fact that most of the men want to bed the new arrival hardly helps matters either. As tensions and libidos mount, the soldiers eventually resort to a violent act of martyrdom that has now become a vital part of Christian iconography.

Beautifully lensed and surprisingly convincing in its evocation of a primal land where the flesh and spirit are the only governing forces, *Sebastiane* is frank for its time (it remains Jarman's most explicit film) but never feels pandering or pornographic. The actors' phonetic readings of their Latin lines sound convincing enough despite the occasional stumble, and for English actors they pass themselves off well as rough Roman soldiers who've spent most of their lives in the sun. Both DVD editions feature a bright (almost *too* bright), fairly crisp transfer, with moderate letterboxing that adds more to the periphery than older video copies. However, one shot of an erect member (which was definitely intentional, according to Jarman's autobiography) has also been matted out for some reason. The U.S. disc only contains a text bio and filmography of Jarman, while the Second Sight disc carries over the *Face to Face* interview (40 mins.) with Jarman from their *Jubilee* platter.

SECRET TEARS

Colour, 2000, 107m. / Directed by Park Ki-Hyung / Starring Kim Seung-Woo, Yoon Mi-Jo / Spectrum (Korea R3 NTSC) / WS (1.85:1) / DD5.1

Bored life insurance salesman Ku-Ho (Kim Seung-Woo) and his two best friends, Hyun-Nam and Do-Kyung, who are somewhat the worse for wear after a boozy night out down the local karaoke bar, accidentally hit a teenage girl on their way home in the cold, autumn rain. Sent flying through the air by the brutal impact of their car, the young girl crashes back to earth in a crumpled heap. Amazingly, after the trio have taken her back to Ku-Ho's house, where they expect her to die from her injuries, the girl appears to be entirely unhurt by the experience, with not even a bruise on her fragile body. Mute and suffering from amnesia, the girl called Mi-Jo (Yoon Mi-Jo) has no clue of her identity or where she has come from. Despite the advice of his concerned friends, Ku-Ho, who blames himself for her condition, takes Mi-Jo under his wing, trying to help her recover her memory. As time passes he finds himself attracted to the minor, to his dismay and the manifest disapproval of his friends and family. As he begins to admit his feelings for Mi-Jo, he discovers he is capable of conversing with her through telepathy, and the bond between them grows deeper and stronger, though it remains on a platonic level. Mi-Jo becomes aware that she has the ability to control objects from a distance. Dismayed with their unconventional relationship, Ku-Ho's friends take it on themselves to delve into the mystery surrounding this enigmatic adolescent and unveil Mi-Jo's terrifying secrets. And as Ku-Ho agonizes over what to do, Mi-Jo unleashes her devastating power to the full...

This atmospheric Korean horror film stretches the definitions of the genre while further consolidating the general superiority of Far Eastern fantasy filmmakers over their Western counterparts. Director Park Ki-Hyung first made waves with 1998's *Whispering Corridors*, a school-set chiller that wowed international festival audiences and Korean cinema-goers alike, and this film did his reputation no harm at all. Based on his own screenplay, *Secret Tears (Bimil)* can be best described as a metaphysical thriller, and has little in common with the horror film as it is looked on in the U.S. in particular, though it has some elements that can be found in European cinema. The final image of the film is deeply haunting, especially

for anyone with a fear of deep water and drowning. The movie is almost completely bereft of gore or violence, aside from a scene where Ku-Ho beats up a customer in a brothel and the moment when Mi-Jo draws the body fluids from one of Ku-Ho's friends, causing him to haemorrhage liberally from every pore.

The Korean release on Spectrum DVD is NTSC, Region 3 and anamorphically enhanced, letterboxed at 1.85:1. It looks and sounds wondrous, which is a necessity given the innovative photography by Moon Yong-Sik, which utilises a lot of slow-motion camerawork, unusual angles, moody shooting through driving rain and murky water, and effective bleeding of the film's muted colour tones in and out of crisp black and white. The disc has a plethora of extras, including cast and crew notes, theatrical trailer, a music video to accompany a featured Sinead O'Connor song, not one but two "making of" clips and, perhaps best of all, Kim Kyu-Yang's beguiling soundtrack music in its entirety, making it a package well worth looking out for. The extras are not given English translations or subtitles however, so brush up your Korean!
– NB

SEDUCTION:
THE CRUEL WOMAN

Colour, 1985, 84m. / Directed by Elfi Mikesch & Monika Treut / Starring Mechthild Grossmann, Udo Kier, Peter Weibel, Carola Regnier, Sheila McLaughlin / First Run (US R1 NTSC)

More or less derived from Leopold von Sacher-Masoch's S&M literary classic, *Venus in Furs*, this oh-so-'80s slice of lesbian chic plays like a Fassbinder film stuck in a universe somewhere between *The Hunger* and *Liquid Sky*. The often-inscrutable plot follows the kinky misadventures of Wanda (*Berlin Alexanderplatz*'s Mechthild Grossmann), a Hamburg dom who engages in mind games and role-playing with her male and female cohorts. For example, a reporter named Mr. Maehrsch (Peter Weibel), gets some first-hand research by licking floors and pretending he's a woman's lavatory (don't ask). Wanda's female lover, high heel fetishist and shoe store owner Caren (Carola Regnier), isn't exactly thrilled when she is tossed aside in favour of the younger and more innocent Justine (Sheila McLaughlin), a Sadean type from America. On top of that, one of Wanda's theatrical slaves, Gregor (cult favourite Udo Kier), begins to fall for the hard-edged mistress when he's not busy being locked up in stocks and trotted around onstage.

A film more about the dynamics of sexual power than the physical mechanics, *Seduction: The Cruel Woman* (or in German, *Verführung: Die grausame Frau*) is a compellingly weird experience with the most extreme use of Dutch angles this side of *Battlefield Earth*. While some of the visuals steer into tacky territory (especially a frenzied climax filled with lesbians in new wave make-up), the bulk of the film is extremely pleasurable to watch and filled with music video-inspired colour schemes. The sexual content is limited to some fairly chaste topless nudity (with nipples covered in black lipstick at one point), so most of the shock value comes from the characters' behaviour and the blurring of lines between genders and sexual orientation. Appropriately, First Run's DVD bears a transfer that will bring back memories of the '80s in more ways than one; the image quality is soft and gauzy, largely a result of the cinematography, though black levels are extremely light and benefit greatly from TV adjustment. Colours are bright, though reds and pinks tend to bleed and smear slightly, and the burned-in English subtitles are legible if not pin-sharp. Co-director Monika

Treut (who also helmed the memorably odd *Virgin Machine*) appears for an English language interview in which she discusses the making of the film, interspersed with bleary film clips from a different source. The package is rounded out with a photo gallery and a handful of not-terribly-Sapphic trailers for other First Run titles, including *Merci pour le chocolat* and *The Twilight Girls*.

SERGE GAINSBOURG: DE GAINSBOURG À GAINSBARRE DE 1958 À 1991

Colour, 2001, 305m. / Starring Serge Gainsbourg, Jane Birkin / Universal (France R2 PAL) / DD2.0

From a groundbreaking, jazz-influenced musical alchemist of the 1960s to the greatest dirty old man in all of pop music history, Serge Gainsbourg enjoyed an astonishing life until his death in 1991. While his own albums would have been enough to ensure his legacy, he also cultivated the recording career of Brigitte Bardot, wrote and produced albums for Catherine Deneuve, Isabelle Adjani, and Vanessa Paradis, and made a star of his wife, Jane Birkin (with whom he had a daughter, Charlotte, now a prominent actress in her own right). Of course he also composed music for numerous films, starred in a variety of cult items including *Cannabis*, *Seven Deaths in the Cat's Eye*, and *The Fury of Hercules*, and even tried his hand at directing with the Birkin/Joe Dallesandro oddity, *Je t'aime moi non plus* (named after his scandalous tune recorded with Bardot, then Birkin). Universal's double-disc DVD set pays homage to the mighty Serge with an overview of his career from his early coffee shop days to his bizarre final years as a hard-drinking, harder-smoking pop culture icon.

Early black and white TV appearances cover the earliest and most "respectable" Gainsbourg period, though the Birkin years garner the most attention. Most of their songs had a sexy edge (after all, they did perform the theme song to *Goodbye Emmanuelle*), and here they perform duets of such tunes as "Sea, Sex and Sun" and "69 année erotique". However, the most scandalous musical entry is undoubtedly Serge's "Lemon Incest", the catchiest song ever written about daughter-lust, performed with Charlotte in a video bound to make viewers either squirm or shut off the DVD player entirely. Music fans also get appearances from Jacques Dutronc (performing "Les roses fanées"), Deneuve, and Screamin' Jay Hawkins (on 1983's "Constipation Blues"), while Serge's bizarre reggae period occupies almost a third of the second disc. All of this is dwarfed by the most jaw-dropping sequence in this set, Serge's infamous talk show appearance with a young, up and coming Whitney Houston. The barely coherent Serge makes an obscene pass at la Whitney, who responds with a squeak and then remarks, "Are you drunk? 'Cause you gotta be!"

This digipack presentation is well organized by menus into distinct time periods, with each video and TV appearance given its own chapter. None of the content includes English subtitles, but it's hardly necessary; the music speaks for itself, and some of the video footage is performed in English. While Gainsbourg fanatics (who are growing in number every year) will find this an essential purchase, adventurous viewers (and listeners) looking into the wilder side of the international music scene will find it illuminating as well.

SEX FRIEND NUREZAKARI (3 BALLS, 1 STRIKE)

Colour, 1999, 58m. / Directed by Rei Sakamoto / Starring Kinako Sato, Tetsuji Sawa, Kuniyuki Sakai, Kiyomi Ito / Screen Edge (US R0 NTSC) / WS (1.65:1)

Ostensibly a sex picture ("pink film"), this literal oddball from Japan is essentially an exercise in whimsical *non sequitur*. Daisuke and his girlfriend are visited by Tsutomu, whom he hasn't seen since they played on the same baseball team as kids. Tsutomu leaves behind a mobile phone, which he later calls up on, asking Daisuke to deliver it to his parents' home. On a trip to the country to perform this errand, the couple run into another couple having mildly kinky sex in the wilds and it turns out that the video-happy male lover, Kentaro, once played against Daisuke and Tsutomu's team in a crucial game and that he too has been lured to Tsutomu's home on a pretext. Tsutomu's parents reveal that their son is dead and another phone call from the ghost summons everyone to a pitch where he plans to recreate the long-ago game in the hope of producing a different outcome.

Enigmatic and thoughtful, with sex scenes shoehorned in rather than integral to the storyline, this may be too thin for its running time in that it has the feel of a protracted short rather than a brief feature. The film has interesting, diffident characters and a formal, appealing shooting style influenced perhaps by Takeshi Kitano, with an unexpected punchline.

Screen Edge's DVD presents a letter-boxed transfer, not augmented for 16:9 – which means a slightly degraded-looking picture. The only extras are notes on the history of "pink" cinema and a brief bio of director Rei Sakamoto that sheds no light on this particular effort. Interesting, but very slight. The sub-title (*3 Balls, 1 Strike*) is far more apt than the meaningless title used for this release – the film doesn't seem to contain a character called Nurezakari. – KN

THE SHAPE OF THINGS TO COME

Colour, 1979, 98m. / Directed by George McCowan / Starring Jack Palance, Carol Lynley, Barry Morse, John Ireland / Blue Underground (US R0 NTSC) / WS (1.66:1) (16:9)

 It's the "tomorrow after tomorrow" and the "great robot wars" have left Earth coated with radioactive fallout. Mankind has been forced to colonize the Moon but unfortunately all is not well in outer space, either. It seems the maniacal Omus (a typically off-his-rocker Jack Palance) has sent an intergalactic kamikaze automaton to wreck some moon-domes in a bid to become emperor. The only fellow that can stop further destruction is Dr. Caball, who heroically dashes aboard his untested super-ship Star-Streak and sets out for Omus's pad on planet Delta Three. Joined by a wacky band of space misfits including his son, the senator's daughter and a comic-relief robot named Sparks (think Robbie the Robot, only less convincing), the future of civilization is now in their hands. But will they be able to stop Crazy Jack and his mechanized pals before it's too late?

Riding the coattails of *Star Wars*'s success, executive producer Harry Alan Towers (responsible for many of Jess Franco's more "refined" works) and director George McCowan (a television director known primarily to Stateside film buffs for the nature-goes-nuts spectacle *Frogs*) really disappoint with *The Shape of Things to Come*. This is matinee kiddie fare at its cheap, unimaginative worst. What can you say about a space opera whose only alien landscapes are the wilds of Ontario and sole extraterrestrial life-forms are simply human children? The casting of several familiar faces (including Carol Lynley, Barry Morse and John Ireland) is nice and a few violent touches near the end (including one dude unexpectedly gettin' brained with a boulder) briefly buoy ones hopes, but nothing can redeem this slow-paced bore. Fans of old-school sci-fi schlock à la *Battlestar Galactica* and *Buck Rogers* may be mildly interested, but all others need not apply.

Sharing its name (but little else) with the 1933 H.G. Wells story (previously brought to the screen by William Cameron Menzies as *Things to Come* (1936)), McCowan's Canadian-filmed attempt was shot in the Fall of 1978 for a little over $2 million. (Where'd the money go?) Receiving decent worldwide distribution in 1979, seasoned exploitation handlers Film Ventures International took care of the chore domestically. Afterwards, the film seemingly disappeared, never gaining an American VHS release. (It was issued north of the border on Astral Video, a probable result of the title's Canadian heritage, but copies were still few and far between.) For better or worse, Blue Underground's DVD marks *The Shape of Things to Come*'s U.S. home video debut. Their 1.66:1 transfer is acceptable if unspectacular (not that the original photography was ever particularly breathtaking), with small blemishes and dirt occasionally appearing throughout. The special effects / miniatures sequences appear very detailed and crisp while the remainder of the footage is shot with the annoying soft-focus look that was so prevalent during the period. Why did any cinematographer ever think this was a good idea? Colours still look dead on, but brights regularly flare out and edges are dulled. The mono soundtrack is problem-free with all dialogue and music remaining clear and distinguishable. (The damned disco theme that's played every ten minutes will be stuck in your head all night. Trust me.) Bonus materials are limited, but not much else could be expected. We are treated to the French theatrical trailer (complete with removable English subtitles), the goofy U.S. TV spot and a 19-image stills collection featuring promotional photos and a few pieces of poster art.

– BH

S

THE SHE-CREATURE

B&W, 1956, 76m. / Directed by Edward L. Cahn / Starring Chester Morris, Marla English, Tom Conway, Lance Fuller, Paul Blaisdell, El Brendel / Direct Video (UK R2 PAL), Lionsgate (US R1 NTSC)

 A high concept monster movie spin-off of the Bridey Murphy craze of the mid-'50s, this AIP picture is directed at such a plod by Edward L. Cahn and played so solemnly by the veteran cast favoured by producer Alex Gordon that it takes a few reels for the absolute dementia of the script to sink in.

Set mostly on a familiar California beach, the plot involves hypnotist con-man Dr. Carlo Lombardi (Chester Morris) taken up by a tycoon (Tom Conway) who thinks he can spin the hustler into a national sensation. Making his name by predicting murders and regressing his glamorous assistant Andrea (Marla English) to a past life as a 17th Century Englishwoman, the hypnotist gets a rivalry going with an academic psychic researcher (Lance Fuller) and generally acts like a smarmy creep. It's almost beside the point, but the villain is somehow manifesting a primeval sea creature that was the original incarnation of the girl, and she slaughters expendables.

Part of the appeal of this film is Paul Blaisdell's beast, a lumbering, thick-middled rubber creature with a snarling cat-face, huge and cracked hooters, teeth in her stomach, anatomically unfeasible vestigial claws and wings and a gait so awkward it's obvious the average victim could outrun the thing if they weren't frozen with fear. Cahn seems to have had doubts about the monster, since he often overlays a glow or makes the creature a disembodied phantom and fails to make use of some of the gruesome aspects (the "lunch-hooks") Blaisdell added to the design. Despite the breasts, the she-creature is clod-hoppingly unfeminine, especially when set beside her supposed avatar, the slinky English. A last-minute switch-around thanks to the loss of original cast members means Morris, a tough guy gangster-type, is weirdly cast as a supposedly suave hypnotist. The upshot is that a conventionally-written smooth baddie comes across as a carny bully whose put-downs of the wealthy or academic come from an interesting grudge. English is lovely, but nobody's idea of an actress; she's okay when drifting ethereally without dialogue, but those regression sessions where she speaks in cod-cockney are embarrassing. The beach scenes have some atmosphere value, but it's mostly a dreary drawing room piece. Swedish comedy relief is handled by El Brendel, one of the reasons *Just Imagine* was a major flop in 1930; he could almost certainly only get work from a nostalgia addict like Gordon, a man who even gave Anna Sten a job.

Direct Video's "Arkoff Film Library" DVD has the same extras as the other titles in the series. The transfer is a couple of generations away from the video master, but grain probably suits the film better than crystal clarity and the shadowed scenes have stable-enough blacks. The same lacklustre transfer was later issued in the U.S. by Lionsgate, paired up with a 4:3 letterboxed (but very oddly-framed) version of *The Day the World Ended*.

– KN

SHEENA

Colour, 1984, 116m. / Directed by John Guillermin / Starring Tanya Roberts, Ted Wass, Trevor Thomas, Elizabeth of Toro, John Forgeham / Columbia Pictures (US R1 NTSC) / WS (2.35:1) (16:9)

 Sent to Africa to shoot a report on royal football star Prince Otwani (played by Trevor Thomas), American TV journalist Vic Casey (Ted Wass) becomes snarled up in a political

conspiracy to steal land from the Zambouli tribe. Fighting the Zambouli's corner is athletic beauty Sheena (*A View to a Kill*'s Tanya Roberts), raised from infancy by their Shaman (Elizabeth of Toro) and able to communicate telepathically with animals. Together Sheena and Casey resolve to take on Otwani and his band of covert mercenaries in a fight to the death.

Were it not for Tanya Roberts's unnecessarily revealing dip in an idyllic jungle pool and a rather grisly moment when a guerrilla Colonel (John Forgeham) gets a spear thrust through his neck, *Sheena* would probably pass for kids' fare – all the more remarkable then that it managed to sneak through with a PG certificate. Certainly in such domain the aforementioned sequence proves as jaw-dropping for audiences as it does for an understandably flustered Ted Wass. The female equivalent of Tarzan, Sheena was first introduced in a comic book, then later to '50s TV audiences in a show starring pin-up favourite Irish McCalla. This 1984 film version might at first seem like a strange entry on the CV of director John Guillermin. His most successful works include '70s mega-blockbusters *The Towering Inferno* and *King Kong*, but delve back a few years and you'll unearth a couple of cheapie Tarzan epics too. So maybe *Sheena* marked a return to roots of sorts, albeit a lacklustre one. Sure, it's a feast for the eyes, with generous employ of the breathtaking Kenyan scenery. Regrettably, however, looking good just isn't enough, not only in the case of the location but equally with regard the film's star. Decked out in a natty chamois-leather bikini, blue-eyed, talent-free Tanya Roberts makes for a strikingly attractive jungle babe, but the moment she opens her mouth you know the film's in trouble. And when she touches her forehead to communicate telepathically with her animal buddies she looks for all the world as if she's struggling to stave off a bitch of a headache. The dialogue (penned by *Superman III*'s David Newman and *Batman*'s Lorenzo Semple Jr.) is so awful you have to wonder if chunks of the script got lost down the back of the photocopier during pre-production, leaving the cast to make it up as they went along. The only convincing performance amidst uniformly sub-average turns comes from Elizabeth of Toro as the tribal Shaman who takes the child Sheena under her wing after the death of her parents.

Richard Hartley's enchanting score serves to make the slothlike pacing a tad less painful, really coming to the fore during a scene when Wass and Roberts get intimate on the riverbank as the sun sets. As passion swells, so does the accompanying music, and an endless tsunami of birdlife takes to the air behind them. It's a beautifully shot sequence, unquestionably the most impressive in the entire film, and one can only marvel at how long it must have taken to co-ordinate the actors embracing, the sun setting and the myriad of birds heading skyward. But Guillermin and late Italian cinematographer Pasqualino De Santis pulled it off with majestic results.

Its wealth of shortcomings aside, *Sheena* has aged remarkably well; it's almost 20 years old and yet it looks as if it were shot yesterday. That's a pretty negligible point to be citing in its favour though, isn't it? If bad acting in a by-the-numbers plot – featuring such unintentionally hilarious fauna as horses painted with stripes to disguise them as zebras and a flock of kamikaze flamingos resembling *Muppet Show* refugees – sounds like a jungle full of fun, *Sheena* is the film for you. And even if it doesn't sound like fun, ignore that little voice urging you to switch off, and see it through if only to delight in its astounding awfulness. Sheena herself was resurrected for TV to similarly unremarkable effect in 2000 with fresh-faced Gina Lee Nolin in the title role.

Perhaps reflecting the lack of value placed on the material at hand, the Columbia Pictures Region 1 DVD of *Sheena* is an affair as scant as Tanya Roberts's loincloth. It's a double-sided disc, offering the film in both 2.35:1 widescreen and severely compromised full screen formats, in a searingly colourful transfer. There are an adequate 28 chapter divisions. The film, however, is all that there is, the "bonus trailers" not even representing *Sheena* itself, rather a couple of other tenuously related Columbia titles. The sound is provided in English Dolby Surround and French, with subtitling in English, French, Chinese, Korean, Thai, Spanish and Portuguese.

– TG

SHINJUKU TRIAD SOCIETY

Colour, 1995, 101m. / Directed by Takashi Miike / Starring Takeshi Caesar, Kyosuke Izutsu / Tartan (UK R0 PAL), Artsmagic (US R1 NTSC) / WS (1.78:1) (16:9)

 The first of Japanese director Takashi Miike's so-called "Triad Society Trilogy", this marks a shift in his prolific career from direct-to-video commercial product to more eccentric, theatrically-targeted material. With an almost classical Warner Brothers gangster-police plot, the film follows an obsessive cop who is out to bring down a mob boss who numbers the hero's lawyer brother among his retinue. What is distinctive is the complex ethnic milieu. The heroes and villains are all scramblings of Japanese and Chinese; the hero was originally one of the despised half-Japanese minority of Taiwan, a legacy of Japan's WWII occupation, who has adopted a full Japanese name and emigrated to his supposed homeland intent on wiping out ethnically Chinese triad criminals who are infiltrating the traditionally yakuza-run Shinjuku district of Tokyo. Also typical of Miike is the extreme sexual and violent content, with brutal buggery an apparently everyday aspect of police interrogations. The cop forms a sado-masochist liaison with a hooker he has personally disfigured

by bashing her face with a chair during yet another interview. Most of the sexual activity is homosexual and power-based, with the younger brother perhaps the lover of the criminal mastermind who is running a black market organ racket and has a doppelganger in a throat-slitting rent boy also mixed up in the (overly) complex scheme.

Even though this was the film Miike intended to be his breakthrough into the theatrical arena, he made little effort to polish or moderate his on-the-fly shooting tactics, maintaining the high energy punctuated by moments of melancholia that characterised much of his huge output. A certain degree of confusion, even to the extent of not quite sorting out who everyone is and how they relate to each other, is a necessary corollary of this, and the extreme punishment all his characters take and dish out (by the end, everyone is dead or scarred) also tends to distract from the subtler relationship and racial politics played out. After all the shock and adrenaline, it may be that the most effective moments of the film come in a low-key three-months-later epilogue that picks up on the battered survivors of the plot just getting on with their lives.

Tartan's Asia Extreme DVD offers an anamorphic 1.85:1 transfer that crops naturally to 1.78:1 on widescreen monitors. In Japanese with optional English subs, the film has razor-sharp editing and slightly rough visuals, probably by design – it could do with blacker blacks, but its look is more likely due to directorial intent rather than mediocre processing. The extras are film notes by Miike biographer Tom Mes, a Miike trailer reel and an extract from a director interview that has been spread among the (many) Miike titles released by Tartan. The follow-ups, also available, are *Rainy Dog* and *Ley Lines*. As with those titles, this was subsequently issued in the U.S., this time with a Mes commentary track, two interviews with Miike (29 and 4 minutes each), and a video interview with editor Yasushi Shimamura.

– KN

SHORT NIGHT OF GLASS DOLLS

Colour, 1971, 92m. / Directed by Aldo Lado / Starring Jean Sorel, Ingrid Thulin, Barbara Bach, Mario Adorf / Anchor Bay (US R1 NTSC), Koch (Germany R2 PAL), Neo (France R2 PAL) / WS (2.35:1) (16:9)

 In 1955, the television series *Alfred Hitchcock Presents* managed to traumatize more than a few impressionable viewers with an episode called "Breakdown", in which businessman Joseph Cotten is paralyzed in a car wreck and left in a state closely resembling death. For the following half hour, we follow the poor sap as he's carted off to the morgue and onto the autopsy table, with the requisite twist ending. Demonstrating he could one-up the master of suspense, first time director Aldo Lado ran with the same concept as the basis for a twist-packed *giallo* in which the protagonist's state of near-death allows the film to flash back and forth in time, gradually revealing details which explain how he came to be in such an uncomfortable predicament.

A speeding ambulance rushes the body of reporter Gregory Moore (the underrated Jean Sorel) to a Prague hospital where he's pronounced dead and plopped onto a steel table. Unfortunately, as his voiceover indicates, he's still very much alive and aware of his surroundings. In flashbacks we see his tender relationship with beautiful Mira (Barbara Bach), who disappears mysteriously one night, and his efforts to investigate with the aid of two colleagues, Jack (Mario Adorf) and Jessica (Ingrid Thulin). Gradually he learns about a nefarious cult (reminiscent of the one in *All the Colors of the Dark*) dedicated to orgies and the violent silencing of anyone who opposes them. How Mira and her obsession with butterflies figure in, however, is a revelation not uncovered until the final act.

With its razor-sharp scope photography, methodical plotting, and icy Ennio Morricone score, this unheralded thriller is the sort of treat die-hard Eurocult excavators enjoy discovering. Straddled somewhere between the mystery and horror genres, it relies more on the viewer's imagination to fill in the grisly gaps in the story without piling on much in the way of explicit sex and gore. Lado also deserves points for some fairly ruthless viewer manipulation, with a memorable climax guaranteed to elicit a gasp. (Interestingly, the '80s revival of *Alfred Hitchcock Presents* remade that "Breakdown" episode but opted for Lado's blacker ending instead of the TV original's.) Sorel, who also appeared in the excellent, remarkably similar *The Double* the same year, once again makes for a solid leading man and carries the film through more than a few potentially confusing story hurdles, and the rest of the cast all fares well enough. The colourful Adorf, who lent support to more than his share of crime thrillers, offers a robust turn nicely balanced by the more austere Thulin (a Visconti regular). Lovely Bach (Mrs. Ringo Starr) doesn't have much to do, but her presence was effectively used to promote this film on video after her fairly successful acting career through the early '80s.

Seen for years only in highly compromised form (the widest letterboxed version barely measured to 1.90:1 during the TV/VHS days), *Short Night of Glass Dolls* looks marvellous on Anchor Bay's DVD. The blue and grey colour schemes look accurate throughout, and the mostly dubbed audio (with English lip movements to match) sounds fine. Lado appears on a solid featurette, the 11-minute "Strange Days of the Short Night", in which he explains the completely irrational title; originally the film was going to be called *Short Night of the Butterflies*, but commercial considerations from a competing project forced a last minute switch. It was also shown as *Malastrana* and, on U.S. video, *Paralyzed* (with a particularly clumsy, video-generated title card). The disc also includes a theatrical trailer and Lado bio/ filmography. The German release features both English and German audio options as well as non-English extras including a featurette on Mario Adorf and a commentary by Jurgen Drews. The French edition (also not English friendly) is even more elaborate, containing a Lado commentary track, a half-hour interview "Portrait" with the director, filmographies, and most surprisingly, a 12-minute interview with Sorel.

SHRIEK OF THE MUTILATED

Colour, 1974, 85m. / Directed by Michael Findlay / Starring Alan Brock, Jennifer Stock / Retromedia (US R1 NTSC)

 After managing to corrupt a great many grindhouse patrons with his notorious "Richard Jennings" trilogy (*Touch of Her Flesh*, *Curse of Her Flesh*, *Kiss of Her Flesh*), crackpot director Michael Findlay and his wife, Roberta (a junk movie auteur in her own right), contributed towards the 1970s trash film legacy by turning towards more mainstream horror fare. Along with the notorious *Snuff*, their most widely seem film is the wonderfully titled *Shriek of the Mutilated*, penned by that incomparable *Invasion of the Blood Farmers* team, Ed Kelleher and Ed Adlum. The result is a Yeti movie unlike any other, stuffed with eye-punishing fashion, twisted violence, loony plot twists, and acting that would make Ed Wood envious.

At a New York university, anthropology expert Dr. Prell (Alan Brock) talks four of his more eager students into a weekend expedition to track down the legendary Yeti, who is apparently stalking one of the area's outlying islands. That night a partygoer issues to them a dire warning about Dr. Prell's field trips, which frequently seem to end in death and dismemberment. Unfortu-

nately the whistle blower meets a nasty end shortly after while trying to kill his wife, in a bravura sequence that could have stepped right out of one of the *Flesh* movies (or Russ Meyer's *Supervixens*). So the students pack up in a Scooby-Doo van (and that's not the only similarity this movie bears to that cartoon) for a remote wooded house, where they meet another scientist and Laughing Crow, the world's hairiest Indian. Before long a fluffy white monster is seen gallivanting in the woods and tearing apart the unfortunate trespassers. However, an even more monstrous secret turns out to be lurking beneath his fanged, furry exterior...

Complete with a sick double-twist ending, *Shriek of the Mutilated* moves along at a fairly brisk clip and, despite its massive technical shortcomings, makes for ideal late night viewing. The seedy upstate locales are well used and evoke memories of the Findlays' other nasty softcore gems, while the loopy dialogue offers some of the choicest flesh-eating one-liners this side of *Cannibal Ferox*. Bonus points for the funky pop soundtrack, which alternates from warbly classical music to lounge-inflected party tunes. Unfortunately the film's signature track, Hot Butter's "Popcorn", was nixed from the DVD due to legal entanglements, but hey, you can always pick up the readily available CD and play it along anyway. That musical hiccup aside, Retromedia's presentation of this, the greatest killer abominable snowman movie of all time, is probably as good as it's ever going to get. An opening disclaimer warns about imperfections inherent in the original elements (hardly surprising since it was shot for pocket change on 16mm); scratches and grain are abundant, but the colour and sharpness are light years ahead of the Lightning and Sinister Cinema tapes (the former of which was a chopped-up TV print, to boot). For some reason the black levels aren't nearly dark enough, but a little adjustment to your set or DVD player can fix that quite easily. More immediately apparent is the improvement in the audio, which offers far more intelligible dialogue than

S

past transfers and captures every shriek with appropriate clarity. The disc also includes a television spot and gushing liner notes by Thorn Sherman which, one hopes, were intended to be sarcastic. A no-frills version is also included in Retromedia's "Bigfoot Terror" collection along with *Search for the Beast*, *Legend of Bigfoot* and *Capture of Bigfoot*.

THE SHUNNED HOUSE

Colour, 2003, 83m. / Directed by Ivan Zuccon / Starring Giuseppe Lorusso, Federica Quaglieri, Emanuele Cerman, Silvia Ferreri, Michael Segal, Cristiana Vaccaro / Salvation (UK R0 PAL), Brain Damage (US R0 NTSC) / WS (1.85:1) / DD2.0

Outside the realm of Stuart Gordon, adapting H.P. Lovecraft is a feat that still confounds most directors as they try to balance out that tricky mixture of unseen dread and grotesque, cosmic beasties. *The Shunned House*, a shot-on-DV Italian horror effort from up-and-coming director Ivan Zuccon, sidesteps this problem by adapting three of Lovecraft's more obtuse, monster-free stores, "The Shunned House", "The Music of Eric Zann", and "The Dreams in the Witch House" (also the basis for the radically different *Curse of the Crimson Altar*). As far as Lovecraft anthologies go, this is more consistent and successful than Brian Yuzna's *Necronomicon* but still misses as often as it hits.

In the moody prologue (which owes more than a tad to *A Blade in the Dark*), a young boy follows his lost ball into a spooky, abandoned house only to find something very nasty inside. Years later he returns as an adult, Alex (Giuseppe Lorusso), a paranormal writer investigating the building, a former inn, along with his mealy-mouthed girlfriend, Rita (Federica Quaglieri). Their exploration of the haunted premises dovetails with two other stories, cutting back and forth over the decades. Mathematician Luigi (Emanuele Cerman) engages in a series of chess games with fellow resident Nora (Silvia Ferreri) as he tries to uncover the perplexing schematics of the building's construction; in the process he becomes the target for supernatural forces, leading to an unnerving sequence in which he strings tiny bells around his bed to alert him if anything nasty tries to pay a visit during the night. In an even earlier tale, writer Marco (Michael Segal) is enchanted by violinist Carlotta (Cristiana Vaccaro), his mute neighbour. Soon he's having unearthly, music-inspired visions of Carlotta slicing herself with razors and another dark figure playing a violin elsewhere in the house. Finally the three narratives tie together for a gory finale, combining a blood-spattered surgeon, a hidden lair filled with candles, and more than a few ghostly twists.

First the positive: *The Shunned House* is a rich-looking affair despite the video format, and Zuccon certainly knows how to use a camera; his rich chiaroscuro lighting and elegant tracking shots create a feeling of poetic apprehension from the opening moments. He also pulls off some very nice scares, including the aforementioned bells scene, and conjures up some nightmarish imagery such as a blonde girl repeatedly knocking her bloody head against a wall. Unfortunately the decision to shoot the film in English was a very bad call; the actors seem extremely uncomfortable with their lines, and their shaky performances are hampered further by the decision to have many scenes delivered in a whisper. At least half the dialogue is completely incomprehensible, which doesn't help the already muddy narrative. The best of the stories by far involves Marco/Carlotta, perhaps because dialogue is kept to a bare minimum; the camera really cuts loose here, telling an almost entirely visual story that caps off with a memorably sick shock ending. (Inexplicably, Carlotta scribbles her thoughts out in

Italian while Marco is speaking English to her.) Gore fans will be pleased at the amount of bodily fluids on display, though the blood-drenched surgeon seems more appropriate for a *Hellraiser* film.

Salvation's DVD does its best to pass this off as a return to form for Italian horror, which is fair enough considering there hasn't been a decent non-Argento pasta horror title in years. Contrary to the packaging, this is not a 16:9 transfer; the presentation looks decent but not exceptional, with some of the darker scenes clogged by dodgy compression and indistinct blacks. The stereo audio is fine, though the wildly inconsistent music tends to drown out the dialogue on more than one occasion. Extras include the U.K. theatrical trailer, an international trailer, a handful of innocuous deleted scenes, a stills gallery, completely unrelated promos for *The Bunker* and *The Playgirls and the Vampire*, essays on Italian horror (blah) and H.P. Lovecraft (better), Philip Ilson's perplexing 10-minute short film "Blood", and more in the usual Salvation vein, a music video for "White Slave" by the Nuns, directed by *Razor Blade Smile*'s Jake West and featuring the usual bevy of leather-clad lesbian vampires. The NTSC disc is missing the unrelated trailers, the short film and the music video.

THE SIGN OF FOUR

B&W, 1932, 73m. / Directed by Graham Cutts / Starring Arthur Wontner, Ian Hunter, Isla Bevan, Graham Soutten, Togo, Roy Emerton, Miles Malleson, Herbert Lomas, Moore Marriott, Kynaston Reeves / Alpha (US R0 NTSC), Classic Entertainment (UK R0 PAL)

 The second most commonly adapted of the Sherlock Holmes tales is here mounted as a vehicle for Arthur Wontner, who'd already played the Great Detective in *The Sleeping Cardinal* and *The Missing*

Rembrandt and would make several more appearances in British films. His Holmes is wryer than most, given to quiet amusement at the presumptions of others and gentle verbal sparring with his Watsons, sundry suspects and the lumpen police. Especially notable here is his look of mock disappointment when someone takes his "elementary" at face value and says a particular deduction doesn't seem that clever when it's explained, and his affectionate, semi-snide remarks as Watson (Ian Hunter) pitches woo at the imperiled heroine (Isla Bevan).

As often with versions of this story, the novel's narrative is rearranged in the adaptation so the complex backstory doesn't tumble out in flashbacks at the end, but is shown in a long set of introductory scenes about the theft of the Agra treasure, the actual sign of the four, a dirty deal struck in a penal colony, the death of a guilty party, the arrival in England of aggrieved Jonathan Small (Graham Soutten) and the mysterious notes to the heroine that bring Holmes into the case. This is a neat bit of storytelling and allows Holmes to dominate the action when he eventually does turn up – but it also lets the audience in early on almost all of the mystery and makes the film an adventure-chase tale rather than an exercise in logical deduction. To make up for this, the script adds a lot of minor clues which Wontner tackles with relish, spinning off deductions from a ship's rope or a hole in the ceiling, and a traditional disguise scene where he impersonates a drunken old sailor.

In addition to Doyle's blowdart-shooting pygmy, played by a regular-sized fellow (Togo) never in frame with anyone else unless perspective is tricked, the film gives Small a hulking minion called the Tattooed Man (Roy Emerton), with whom he has pettish arguments that contrast with the Holmes-Watson banter. As well as the book's river chase, there's a visit to a carnival where, in Tod Browning style, the freakish villains form an Unholy Three. It's crudely-made by Hollywood standards of the time, despite the production supervision of Rowland V. Lee (of *Son of Frankenstein* fame), but eccentric performances (Miles Malleson, Kynaston Lomas, Moore Marriott, Kynaston Reeves) and congenial dialogue make it an intriguing Holmes rarity.

Sadly, it's one of Alpha Video's worst transfers, with an aged, decrepit print in pinkish monochrome and a constant fax machine-like shrilling on the soundtrack. The company also have later Wontner vehicles, *The Triumph of Sherlock Holmes* and *Silver Blaze* (under the title *Murder at the Baskervilles*). The U.K. disc isn't much of a step up, but it does include a copy of the source novel as compensation.

– KN

THE SIGNALMAN

Colour, 1976, 39m. / Directed by Lawrence Gordon Clark / Starring Denholm Elliott, Bernard Lloyd / BFI (UK R2 PAL)

Throughout the 1970s, the BBC offered an annual treat for lovers of the respectably macabre with a series at first titled *A Ghost Story for Christmas*. After five quiet, creepy adaptations of stories by M.R. James, the 1976 episode, which reduced the title to *A Ghost Story*, turned to Charles Dickens and adapted his often-reprinted tale "The Signal-Man". An early instance of the sub-genre of ghost tale (cf: the 'room for one more inside' episode of *Dead of Night*) in which an apparition is not of a spectre from the past but a figure from the future warning of impending disaster, "The Signal-Man" was inspired by Dickens's experience of a bad train wreck – it has a very vivid, still-powerful description of the horrors of "a collision in a tunnel" – and, in a prefiguring of this TV version, was originally published in the 1866 Christmas edition of the author's own periodical *All the Year Round*.

The teleplay by Andrew Davies, later the king of the literary adaptation serial (*Pride and Prejudice*, *Middlemarch*, *Dr. Zhivago*, etc.), is very faithful to the original, using almost all of Dickens's dialogue. Essentially a two-character piece, the set-up is that a nameless traveller (Bernard Lloyd) is drawn to a remote branch line of the railway to befriend the keeper (Denholm Elliott) of a lonely signal-box. Upon his first appearance, the signalman is terrified of the traveller, and later explains that he had mistaken him for a white-faced, waving apparition whose two previous manifestations had presaged ghastly incidents – a major train crash and the death of a bride who fell from a carriage. Director Lawrence Gordon Clark conveys these incidents effectively within a TV budget, with a hallucinatory wander through a hellish tunnel or the striking image of a dead woman in white strewn by the railway line. Elliott, always at his best in roles as terrified little men, uses a soft West Country accent and subtle tremblings. The preservation society steam railway train and signal-box are exploited wonderfully by the production, which manages to avoid puffer-train nostalgia to make things like the Victorian warning bells and telegraph apparatus into sinister artefacts. As in the other short films in the series, the ghost is sparingly seen and yet quite nightmarish: a frozen white mask of fear.

The British Film Institute's DVD (now out of print and fetching absurd prices online) perfectly preserves the soft, almost misty look of 1970s filmed U.K. television. Besides sensitive liner notes from Dick Fiddy, the sole extra is an audio reading of the story by actor John Nettleton (the murderer in *And Soon the Darkness*), who understandably takes a more melodramatic approach than Elliott to the signal-man. The BFI also offer several other outstanding BBC ghost stories: Nigel Kneale's TV play *The Stone Tape*, Jonathan Miller's controversial M.R. James adaptation for

Omnibus ("Whistle and I'll Come to You"), one of Clark's earlier *Ghost Story for Christmas* episodes (James's "A Warning to the Curious") and the reality-TV-themed Stephen Volk-scripted *Ghostwatch*.

– KN

SIGNS

Colour, 2002, 106m. / Directed by M. Night Shyamalan / Starring Mel Gibson, Joaquin Phoenix / Buena Vista (Blu-ray & DVD) (US R0/R1 HD/NTSC, UK R0/R2 HD/PAL) / WS (1.85:1) (16:9) / DD5.1

The opening of *Signs*, which can't help but feel like an *X-Files* teaser, has disillusioned ex-preacher Graham Hess (Mel Gibson) and his family discovering elaborate designs in his cornfield. The rural setting seems to be a break with the world of *The Sixth Sense* and *Unbreakable*, M. Night Shyamalan's previous paranormal dramas, but a caption promptly insists that we are only "forty-five miles from Philadelphia", the city in which the earlier films were set and which the writer-director has turned into his own distinctively haunted territory. Though Gibson replaces Bruce Willis as the family man troubled by a sundered marriage and the paranormal, this third go-round for the MNS formula hits all the beats: soul-revealing conversations in kitchens; adults taught life-lessons by insightful children; nighttime prowling in shadowy houses with the odd sudden scare; an extremely serious treatment of subject matter usually deemed trivial; brilliantly-written and -played unconventional family problems; a highly-significant director cameo ("Is that him?" a child asks); grown men riven by emotions that can't be expressed verbally; apparently off-topic speeches (a musing about the precise freak chain of circumstances that led to Hess's wife's death) that turn out to be plot hinges; a blue-grey colour palette rarely relieved by splashes of colour; a James Newton Howard score. A break with tradition is that the finale seems not to have the sort of kicker twist that were talking points for the earlier films – though, like them, the resolution includes a flashback that forces the hero to reassess his understanding of the universe. The clever title seems to refer to evidence of extra-terrestrial incursion, but actually means those coincidences that suggest the guiding hand of a deity. A problem is that this essentially means that lazy plotting can be written off as evidence of the existence of the divine, while the climax boils down to a rewriting of the last lines of *The War of the Worlds* to the effect that the aliens are defeated by the littlest things that God in his mercy created on Earth – half-drunk glasses of water. A sequence where Graham confronts the possibility of his family's deaths by making them their favourite meals and having a hysterical reaction when they aren't hungry is either a riff on the potato-shaping of *Close Encounters* or weirdly-misjudged comic relief. *Signs* gets as many laughs as gasps, and it's a moot point as to how many are intentional. If the substructure of this piece is shaky, Shyamalan still continues to hone his skills as a suspense/horror filmmaker, and can time a jump almost as well as Wes Craven. The farmhouse besieged by aliens might derive from *Night Skies*, the John Sayles script abandoned by Steven Spielberg in favour of the more amiable *E.T.: The Extra-Terrestrial*, but Shyamalan also incorporates references to *Night of the Living Dead* (the news-dispensing TV set, trundled on when the crisis seems over only to reflect the intruder in a marvellous "reveal") and *The Birds*, upon which the whole script seems structurally modelled.

Disney's DVD is a little less stellar than the job they did with the earlier films, but is still a more-than-adequate represen-

S

tation of a flawed but rewarding film. The transfer is perfectly acceptable, with THX-certified Dolby Digital Surround Sound that reproduces in the home exactly the feeling of being scared you get in the cinema – characters in Shyamalan films all talk softly to lull you for the sudden loud noises that make you jump.

The disc has 21 chapter-stops and an alternative French-language track. Perhaps Shyamalan is writing less fatty scripts, but there are fewer deleted scenes than on the earlier films – and their rougher state suggests they were abandoned at workprint stage. The trims are mostly tiny, like a few seconds noting a dead bird by the roadside, but there's one self-reflexive joke (wisely dropped but worth preserving) as Hess wishes his dead wife were here in the crisis because she was so smart "she always knew how movies would end." A six-part making-of (supervised by the prolific Laurent Bouzereau) goes a lot deeper than the usual puff-piece, and includes an interesting alternative to a commentary track as Shyamalan talks through a *précis* of clips and on-set snippets. The documentary features a bit about marketing that snippets various trailers, but oddly they aren't included on the disc.

Skipping over the inclusion of a multi-angle storyboards feature, a tradition is continued from the *Sixth Sense* and *Unbreakable* discs as Shyamalan presents an extract from *Pictures*, "Night's first alien film", one of his camcordered teenage efforts, in which the future A-list Hollywoodian is menaced by a Halloween-masked tiny robot in what looks like a sub-amateur variation on the Zuni fetish sequence from *Trilogy of Terror*. The same extras appear again for the Blu-ray edition, which features an appreciable uptick in image quality (roughly comparable to the same bump for *The Sixth Sense*) even if it never comes close to the format's more dazzling visual heights.

– KN

SILENT NIGHT, DEADLY NIGHT

Colour, 1984, 83m. / Directed by Charles E. Sellier Jr. / Starring Robert Brian Wilson, Lilyan Chauvin, Linnea Quigley / Anchor Bay (US R1 NTSC), Arrow (UK R2 PAL) / WS (1.85:1) (16:9)

SILENT NIGHT, DEADLY NIGHT 2

Colour, 1987, 88m. / Directed by Lee Harry / Starring Eric Freeman, James Newman, Elizabeth Kaitan / Anchor Bay (US R1 NTSC) / WS (1.85:1) (16:9)

 As every self-respecting slasher fan knows, holidays were big business back in the '80s. We had a heavy-breathing killer for every occasion: Halloween, Valentine's Day, April Fool's Day, Mother's Day... Of course, Christmas slashers were already nothing new; 1972's *Tales from the Crypt* featured Joan Collins stalked by a loony Saint Nick, and Bob Clark's magnificent *Black Christmas* turned a sorority house into a Yuletide slaughterhouse. However, thanks to some canny poster art (an axe-wielding Santa climbing down a chimney) and a catchy title, *Silent Night, Deadly Night* became the most notorious holiday horror film ever, incurring the wrath of parents' groups, nationwide movie critics (including Siskel and Ebert), and sensitive Santa fans everywhere. Naturally, few bothered to actually see the film, which was withdrawn from circulation by TriStar (why didn't they just change the poster?) and shuffled off to a long, profitable shelf life on home video.

Rather than following the standard formula of identifying with the victims-to-be, this film (originally filmed as *Slayride*) charts the development of a mass murderer from early childhood. On Christmas Eve, little Billy and his family go to visit catatonic old grandpa at the nursing home. When everyone else is out of the room, Gramps leans over to impressionable Billy and warns him that Santa only brings presents to good boys and girls; all others better run for their lives because "Christmas Eve is the scariest damn night of the year." Meanwhile a thug in Santa drag robs a convenience store and shoots the clerk, then winds up stranded on the road while making a getaway. Billy's parents stop to help, only to get murdered for their trouble. Billy and his baby brother, Ricky, survive and are shuffled off to a Catholic orphanage where the sadistic Mother Superior (Lilyan Chauvin) teaches Billy that "punishment is good" after he draws pictures of decapitated reindeer and punches out a visiting Santa. She also teaches him that sex is naughty... very, very naughty. Flash forward a few more years, as a pumped-up, eighteen-year-old Billy (soap actor Robert Brian Wilson) gets a job at a local toyshop with the aid of a kindly nun. He's perfectly happy as a stock boy and even develops a crush on one of his co-workers, but things get nastier as Christmas approaches. On Christmas Eve, Billy is forced into playing Santa and, in one of the film's comical highlights, terrorizes one bratty little girl into silence. That night, Billy (still in red and white garb) is told by his drunken boss that he has a long night ahead of him performing Santa duties, so Billy promptly kills all of his co-workers. Soon he's out on the town, yelling "Punish!" while seeking out promiscuous teens. Among the unlucky ones is scream queen Linnea Quigley, playing a topless babysitter having sex on a pool table whose gruesome fate is still "deer" to many horror fans' hearts. (Sorry, couldn't resist.)

Despite its tasteless subject matter, *Silent Night, Deadly Night* isn't really a painfully awful movie so much as it's just rather bland. The camerawork is nailed down and flat in almost every shot, and the actors chomp the scenery without seemingly acting together in the same picture. At least the filmmakers pile on the gore, particularly in this unrated cut; the red stuff flows abundantly in such highlights as a bow and

arrow murder, Quigley's aforementioned demise, and one especially memorable sleigh scene that inspired the original title. Unfortunately the obligatory nudity isn't handled nearly as well; while charges of misogyny are often questionable when it comes to horror films, the label isn't really inappropriate here. With the exception of one nun, women show up just long enough to be portrayed as either hateful bitches or whimpering victims (or both) and often have their shirts ripped open just to offer a quick thrill. The most dismal of these is not one but *two* near-rape scenes, the first of which finds Billy's mother topless before getting her throat slashed by Santa. Ick. Before it descends into typical slasher nonsense, the film does actually offer some novelty with the orphanage sequences, which show a few flickering promises of interesting subtext. Too bad the filmmakers didn't exploit the potential for a *Night of the Hunter*-style Christmas horror film (perhaps with a young Billy still stalked by the first killer Santa, whose fate is never resolved) and went the more obvious route instead.

As with any successful '80s horror film, there had to be a sequel... so direct from the same school that brought you *Boogeyman 2* and *The Hills Have Eyes 2* came *Silent Night, Deadly Night 2*. Horror fans were more than a little surprised when they actually got a comedy stuffed with 39 minutes of footage from the previous film, told in flashback by a now-grown, completely nutty Ricky (*Children of the Corn*'s Eric Freeman) to an asylum shrink (James Newman). Amazingly, Ricky can even recall events from his infancy with perfect clarity, and after the whole exhausting recap is over, he finally dispatches the doc for his trouble. With Ricky now on the streets, the film finally justifies itself with an outlandish series of set pieces that put your average Troma feature to shame: a loan shark getting impaled on an umbrella; Ricky and his girlfriend (Elizabeth Kaitan) attending a screening of the first film (!) with a couple of loudmouths; Ricky using a car battery to kill; and best of all, Ricky strolling through a neighbourhood with a pistol and, in the film's one truly indelible moment, bellowing the immortal words, "Garbage day!" Finally in the last ten minutes he hops into Santa duds and goes after the first film's Mother Superior (now a different actress with weird facial scars), despite the fact that it's obviously not Christmastime. With its locale switch from chilly Utah to sunny L.A., this second entry is a weird, bright-lit attempt to mock its predecessor while still piling on the gore. Freeman's bug-eyed performance is so far off the deep end it can't even be classified as lousy; he's clearly in an orbit all his own. Once again a gratuitous love scene supplies some T&A, but here it's strictly late night cable fare and avoids the ugliness of the first film. Despite the nonexistent budget, the camera even does a few fancy dolly moves here and there, with some fairly ambitious set-ups during the climax (including an amusing and wholly ridiculous nod to William Castle's *Homicidal*). While it's possible that the first film was meant to be scary in some half-assed way, there's no mistaking the comedic tone here; you won't find a fright in sight, but this is the funniest slasher film you'll find without the words "*Student Bodies*" in the title. Note that this also features what could be the single most insane car stunt ever captured on film; try slo-mo during this scene and note how close one actor comes to being plowed right off his feet.

The transfer for *Silent Night, Deadly Night* opens with a disclaimer that this is the most complete version ever released, and had to be culled from different film elements. At least one of them screams '80s one-inch master, judging from the cheese-cloth texture evident in a couple of insert shots, but apart from these minor distractions, the film looks great. The abundant reds are very saturated without bleeding, and detail looks nice and crisp. It's too bad some of the extra gore snippets are taken from lesser material (the "slayride" in particular), as the grue looks dark and murky. Just a minor quibble, though. The second film looks just as good, though the footage from the first feature looks a step down due to the printing process used for the sequel; colours aren't quite as vivid during the rehashed material, but the new footage looks great. Incidentally, the condensed version of the first film also offers a fair approximation of how the R-rated print played on its first release from U.S.A. on VHS, way back when; the unrated version didn't come along until later, and a rather weak transfer eventually wound up on laserdisc from Image. The sequel fared better in both formats and has always looked quite decent. Audio is plain vanilla mono, and none the worse for it. It's also worth mentioning here that, apart from a quick round of "Deck the Halls", the first film features a score of entirely *original* Christmas songs, all of them hysterically awful. There's even a syrupy holiday power ballad, '80s-style, called "The Warm Side of the Door" that will have many unprepared viewers lunging for the nearest pair of earplugs. Also, a big thanks to Anchor Bay for once again including closed captions; it comes in handy during more than a few botched line deliveries.

For some reason the vast amount of Utah talent from the first film remains mostly untapped in the extras here, but director Charles E. Sellier Jr. does turn up for a half-hour audio interview (via telephone) in which he discusses the surprisingly complex story about how the film was financed and brought to completion. He also offers his thoughts about the finished product and the controversy, all with intelligence and good humour. Speaking of which, the ruckus is also covered in a step-through scrapbook containing critical and news blurbs about the film's tumultuous release. Finally, you get a gallery of stills, posters, and video art. The second film gets a more elaborate set of extras, kicking off with a feature-length audio commentary from Newman, director/writer Lee Harry, and co-writer Joseph H.

Earle. In *Mystery Science Theatre* style, they all take potshots at the film and reveal a few nice bits of trivia along the way: the financially impoverished shoot was mostly catered with McDonald's fast food, Newman was one of the higher-paid actors ($150!), and a few frames of gore (including a bit of liver popping out during the umbrella scene) were cut from the film to obtain an R rating and were never reinstated. It would have been nice to have the unrated version restored, of course, but everyone probably gets the general idea. Also included are the uproarious theatrical trailer (which covers most, but not all, of the quotable highlights), a poster and stills gallery, and a DVD-Rom version of the screenplay (in .pdf format) complete with annotations for including scenes from the original film. In 2009 the first film also received its first uncut release ever in the U.K. on DVD, using the same transfer and director interview from the Anchor Bay disc.

SILVER BULLET

Colour, 1985, 95m. / Directed by Daniel Attias / Starring Gary Busey, Corey Haim, Megan Follows, Terry O'Quinn, Everett McGill / Paramount (US R1 NTSC), Momentum (UK R2 PAL), Kinowelt (Germany R2 PAL) / WS (2.35:1) (16:9)

Though Stephen King had dabbled with adapting his stories to the screen in films like *Creepshow* and *Cat's Eye*, the werewolf saga *Silver Bullet* found him finally translating a complete, feature length narrative into script form, with more inconsistent results. Lifting the general storyline of his novella, *Cycle of the Werewolf*, while dropping the twelve-month structure and the whodunit angle, King's adaptation focuses on two teen siblings, Jane Coslaw (Megan Follows) and

her wheelchair-bound little brother, Marty (Corey Haim). Their small town, Traker's Mill, is being torn apart by gruesome monthly deaths in which the victims are found mauled or dismembered. Their alcoholic uncle, Red (Gary Busey), tries to keep the kids under control when Marty expresses a more than passing interest in the crimes, while the sheriff (Terry O'Quinn) and local preacher (Everett McGill from *Twin Peaks*) cope with the townspeople's mounting hysteria... especially when a hairy beast is seen skulking through the woods.

Some good performances and strong scope photography make *Silver Bullet* an enjoyable if largely disposable offering, while some splashy dollops of gore make a valiant attempt to recapture the gruesome tableaux of Berni Wrightson's illustrations for the original text version. As usual, the big problem lies in the fact that King's dialogue simply doesn't translate well to the screen at all. The best adaptations (*The Dead Zone*, *Carrie*, etc.) realized this and tailored his characters in a more realistic fashion, but as with *Pet Sematary* and company, the actors here are saddled with too many unworkable lines and situations (not to mention the soppy narration). Another problem is Jay Chattaway's score, which starts off quite well but annoyingly veers off into grating, mid-'80s synth hell for no particular reason.

The U.S. DVD at least offers the film in its original aspect ratio; considering how crucial the widescreen compositions are to the film's effectiveness (particularly a fogbound werewolf hunt), this is a huge improvement over the dreary laserdisc and VHS tapes. Unfortunately the solid transfer is about all the disc has going for it, as Paramount evidently didn't feel the film was worth any further effort. On the other hand, the European DVDs offer a commentary track by director Daniel Attias and the theatrical trailer. Since these versions also sport an anamorphic transfer, fans with Region 2 players will find their local release a wiser investment.

SILVER SCREAM

Colour, 2003, 98m. / Directed by JimmyO Burril / Starring Justin Alvarez, David Calhoun, Kristen Hudson, JimmyO Burril, Andy Wentsel / Planet X (US R1 NTSC) / WS (1.78:1) / DD5.1

 If you thought the opening "Science Fiction Double Feature" number from *Rocky Horror* wasn't in-jokey enough, take a gander at *Silver Scream*, a Maryland-lensed send-up of horror movies from the silent age through the 1980s. Ah yes, and it's also a musical.

The venerable Saenger Theater is about to be closed down, and its most devoted patrons have gathered for a final midnight movie show. Two doofuses, Tobe (Andy Wentsel) and George (Justin Alvarez), are in attendance with Tobe's busty, blonde sister, Shelley (Kristen Hudson), and soon the threesome find themselves trapped in a world of real-life horror movie madness generated by the theatre itself. Also along for the ride is the wicked owner, Mr. Friedkin (David Calhoun), though the boys find an ally in the form of the Count (director JimmyO Burril), who appears for a song and dance number with his vampire brides. From there the characters are thrust from one cinema-inspired skit to another, with Shelley nearly falling prey over and over again to a number of movie monsters and psychos. Along the way they burst into song with recreations of *Nosferatu*, *Bride of Frankenstein*, *Plan 9 from Outer Space*, *The Texas Chain Saw Massacre*, *Creature from the Black Lagoon*, *Night of the Living Dead*, *Rosemary's Baby*, *Friday the 13th*, *A Nightmare on Elm Street*, *The Wolf Man*, a wild duet version of the shower scene from *Psycho*, and for the grand finale, a jaw-dropping, gore-soaked, all-singing homage to *Carrie* and *Dawn of the Dead*.

Though the opening "real life" segment of this shot-on-video project doesn't look promising, with shaky camerawork and fuzzy picture quality, the body of the film itself is quite impressive. The first hour (prologue excluded) unfolds in skilful black and white, with some Mac-assisted scratches and scuffs added for vintage flavour. The switch to colour (with a go-go dancer/*Blood Feast* number) doesn't cause much of a drop in quality either; the clever manipulation of lighting and colour gels results in some delightful surprises for seasoned horror fans. The music ranges from serviceable to catchy (the beach blanket "Black Lagoon" bit is especially memorable), though the *Bride of Frankenstein* solo number overstays its welcome by a few minutes. Adapted from a local stage production (billed here as "The movie of the musical about other movies"), the tunes are mostly in the vein of '80s alternative pop like Lene Lovich, Book of Love, Siouxsie and the Banshees, and so on; the stripped down electronic arrangements and earthly voices are definitely not your standard musical fare.

The modest but diverting DVD features a fairly splashy transfer, though contrary to the packaging, it's flat widescreen, not anamorphic. The Dolby Digital 5.1 mix sounds very forced and artificial for the most part; when switched over to 2.0 surround playback or run through a TV monitor, it sounds much more agreeable. Extras include a trailer and an inexplicable video feature with "Chainsaw Sally", who stars in the same company's next production.

SITCOM

Colour, 1998, 79m. / Directed by François Ozon / Starring Évelyne Dandry, François Marthouret, Marina de Van, Adrien de Van, Stéphane Rideau, Lucia Sanchez, Jules-Emmanuel Eyoum Deido / Paramount (France R2 PAL), Spectrum (Korea R3 NTSC), New Yorker (US R1 NTSC) / WS (1.66:1) (16:9) / DD2.0

Far less interesting as a meditation on the sitcom format (since one can't really satirize something that's already turned itself into a joke) than as a dry run for more perfectly chiselled cross-genre films from director François Ozon, *Sitcom* is one of the more fascinating debut features in recent memory. Its release earned immediate comparisons to the likes of John Waters and Todd Solondz, though as time has proven, the director had something quite different in mind.

The film begins deceptively with a long shot of a house; a father (François Marthouret) pulls up and enters to hear his family singing "Happy Birthday". Suddenly gunshots ring out... and we flash back months earlier. Siblings Sophie (*See the Sea*'s Marina de Van) and Nicolas (her real life brother, Adrien) prepare for family dinner with their mother (Évelyne Dandry) when the father comes home with a new pet rat, which promptly bites Nicolas's finger. That night at dinner they're joined by Sophie's strait-laced boyfriend, David (*Come Undone*'s Stéphane Rideau), new maid Maria (Lucia Sanchez), and her African husband, a schoolteacher named Abdu (Jules-Emmanuel Eyoum Deido). Before the night is over, Nicolas declares his homosexuality and loses his virginity to Abdu, Sophie hurls herself out of a window to become a dominatrix paraplegic, and the rat continues to spread its peculiar influence through the household. As time passes, events get progressively strange until the bizarre, monster-movie-style climax.

Filled with scattershot gags and hilarious subversions of audience expectations (especially the endless visitors who seem to be pouring into the house for an orgy), *Sitcom* is extremely enjoyable even if its parts don't quite add up to a satisfying whole. The ending feels like more of a stunt to wrap things up than a natural progression of everything that's gone before, but the ride along the way provides enough giggles and shocked gasps to make it worthwhile enough. Though the subject matter often veers into the sordid (with more than a smattering of incest and a flash of a prosthetic member, to name a couple), the film still manages to feel sunny and upbeat.

An incredibly colourful film, this looks marvellous on Paramount's DVD edition, which boasts almost glowing chroma. The surround audio sounds fine, limited mainly to the music, and optional English subtitles are provided. Trailers for the Ozon collection are included along with two non-subtitled short films, "Photo de famille" (1988, 7 mins.) and the truly kinky "Victor" (1993, 14 mins.). The anamorphic Korean release looks fine and has English subtitles but is otherwise featureless; the New Yorker release lives down to the company's dire A/V standards with a muddy, unimpressive PAL-to-NTSC conversion but at least throws in the trailer and "Photo de famille".

SLEEPLESS (NONHOSONNO)

Colour, 2001, 117m. / Directed by Dario Argento / Starring Max von Sydow, Stefano Dionisi, Roberto Zibetti, Chiara Caselli / Medusa (Italy R2 PAL), Arrow, M.I.A. (UK R2 PAL), Dutch FilmWorks (Holland R2 PAL), Free Dolphin (France R2 PAL) / WS (1.85:1) (16:9), Artisan (US R1 NTSC) / DD5.1

S

Following the director's unsuccessful, divisive experiment of *The Phantom of the Opera*, Dario Argento went back to basics for this equally controversial pastiche of his previous *giallo* hits. Long criticized for his unorthodox storytelling (usually dismissed as "weak scripts"), he continued to twist convention by concocting a serial killer yarn in which all of the protagonists are passive, mostly ineffectual figures, bounced around by a helter skelter plot.

In the opening scene, Inspector Moretti (Max von Sydow) investigates a woman's brutal murder in Turin and promises her young son, Giacomo, that the killer will be apprehended. Flash forward a couple of decades, as the same murderer stalks and butchers an especially dim pair of prostitutes on a dark and stormy night at a train station. The retired Moretti is struck by the similarities of the crime to past events, mainly due to his obsession with a macabre children's book, "The Death Farm", whose suicidal dwarf author was fingered for the previous murders. The now grown Giacomo (*Farinelli*'s Stefano Dionisi) returns to Turin and reunites with his old friends, rich asthmatic Lorenzo (Roberto Zibetti, a really awful actor) and pretty harpist Gloria (Chiara Caselli). The murders continue, each modelled on the animal-themed killings from the book, and soon the list of suspects grows...

Even more than the underrated *Trauma*, *Sleepless* cribs bits and pieces from the Argento canon with mixed results: the thunderous opening and ill-fated ballerinas from *Suspiria*, the flawed-memory hero and double-whammy twist ending from *Deep Red*, the pounding rock score from Goblin, and the monstrous parent-child dynamics from *Phenomena* and *Four Flies on Grey Velvet*, to name but a few. One's enjoyment of the film will largely depend on how much one can savour style over content; the wooden performances (von Sydow excepted) and jagged narrative are stumbling blocks as usual, but the film's queasy atmosphere and show-stopping murders are compensating factors. Certain scenes indicate Argento most definitely had his tongue firmly planted in cheek throughout the film: a disorienting location card reading "Rome" while showing a Chinese restaurant with Asian music tinkling in the background; the bizarre dwarf subplot (including a peculiar interrogation scene that parodies *The Bird with the Crystal Plumage*); the hilarious introduction to the rabbit-toothed waitress/murder victim; the naked silicone hooker who quickly drops her clothes and inhibitions when the killer flashes a handful of cash. This growing humorous tendency in Argento's work (already plainly exhibited in *The Phantom of the Opera*) has been a major stumbling block for many of his fans, who understandably have a problem with the fact that Argento is hardly a comedy director and doesn't have the razor-sharp sense of satire blessed upon, say, Brian De Palma. For better or worse, this film finds him continuing to explore and evolve, making a few interesting stumbles along the way.

Even more than the aurally painful *The Stendhal Syndrome*, *Sleepless* (*Nonhosonno*) is a film that suffers dramatically in its English language version. While all of the cast spoke their lines in English, only von Sydow's voice remains on the soundtrack; however, the dubbing and line delivery are so awkward that any Argento fans, even those who didn't warm up to this film in English, should feel obligated to seek out the Italian version, which truly plays like an entirely different film. Therefore the only viable option on DVD for many years was the Italian disc from Medusa, which sports magnificent 5.1 and DTS mixes of the Italian soundtrack with optional English subtitles, or the English version in 5.1. The disc also includes a making-of featurette (in Italian only) and the Italian trailer. Image quality is superb, with a rich, colourful anamorphic transfer that makes mincemeat of the sorry-looking English theatrical prints. The same video transfer is available in several other countries as well, including France (as *Le sang des innocents*, with the French, Italian, and English tracks but no English subs), Holland, and the U.K. (English version only); the latter also includes the featurette (with English subtitles) as well as a bonus disc of *Dario Argento: An Eye for Horror*. This commendable one-hour documentary features interviews with many of the principals from Argento's films, including a scary-looking Daria Nicolodi and some controversial thoughts from Asia Argento about the cinematic abuses she has suffered at her father's hands throughout their collaborations. The second U.K. disc eventually arrived from Arrow, and it features a much better encoding of the anamorphic master and drops the widely available Argento doc in favour of a new featurette, "Murder, Madness and Mutilation", featuring Joe Dante, Tony Timpone, and Sergio Stivaletti dissecting the *giallo* genre and this film in particular. The making-of is repeated here along with a photo gallery and a CD-Rom version of the original screenplay.

Only those completely unable to access either the Italian or British discs will find any reason to seek out the U.S. one from Artisan, which is the worst possible way to make this film's acquaintance. Painfully pan and scanned with a shoddy, muddy transfer, this bad joke of a release is one of the low points of DVD Euro horror; the 5.1 track sounds more like a flimsy, lexiconed version of a 2.0 track than the dynamic mix found on the European releases. More perplexing still, Artisan's early VHS screeners and even the theatrical trailer on the DVD are letterboxed! At least the DVD is uncut, as opposed to the abortive R-rated VHS release, but it should still be avoided if at all possible; the tacky cover art does it no favours either. It isn't quite as agonizing as the home video travesties visited upon *Trauma*, but that's not for lack of trying.

SOFT SKIN ON BLACK SILK

B&W, 1963, 82m. / Directed by José Antonio de la Loma / Starring Agnès Laurent, Armand Mestral, Ira Lewis, Edie Burke, Vicente Parra / First Run (US R1 NTSC)

 Unquestionably the most confusing entry in the Audubon Films erotica catalogue, *Soft Skin on Black Silk* began life as a slightly sexy European co-production called *Tentations* in

France and *Un mundo para mí* in Spain. The cast, headlined by rising sex kitten Agnès Laurent, was made up of French and Spanish actors, and the mixture of mild criminal intrigue and sexy teasing (without any overt nudity) was fairly standard for the time in the wake of 1956's *And God Created Woman*. Flash forward to 1963, when the film made its English language debut in a drastically altered version entitled *Soft Skin on Black Silk*, boasting a new beachside framing narrative and inserted striptease footage with many scenes from the original cut, altered or deleted entirely. The new footage was directed by Audubon founder Radley Metzger, soon to be an acclaimed director in his own right, and the spliced-in actors were appropriately dubbed to match the looping in the body of the film. Billed as "a sexual romance", the film successfully cashed in on the craze for European sauciness and, as far as patchwork cinematic quilts go, it's not half bad.

In the prologue, a young man (Ira Lewis from the Metzger-edited *The Flesh Eaters*) comes across a beautiful woman (Edie Burke) sunbathing topless by the ocean. They strike up a conversation and she learns that he's planning to off the unfaithful woman in his life, so naturally she leads him back to her beach house where they fall into bed. Their antics are intercut with her telling a similar story of dangerous amour, as beautiful French moll Theresa (Laurent) catches the eye of handsome Andre (Vicente Parra) at a nightclub. Unfortunately she's the property of gangster Jean (Armand Mestral), and soon Andre's planning to off his rival to claim the woman who has stolen his heart.

For the most part the Metzger-shot footage integrates smoothly into the rest of the film, as French cast members sit down to watch a show that swiftly turns into a kinkier, stranger performance filmed years later. The beach scenes add some erotic poetry to what is otherwise a standard potboiler, with Laurent providing

S

a couple of fleeting cheesecake shots (such as changing clothes in mid-conversation for no discernible reason) to add *ooh la la* value.

The First Run DVD cobbles together at least three different video sources to assemble the longest cut of *Soft Skin* released to date; the expanded running time results in a few burlesque bits crowding awkwardly against each other but overall this is a more smooth, coherent experience than the edited print which circulated on VHS. Quality-wise the DVD is understandably something of a mixed bag. The footage from the Audubon version fares best, apart from a brief but distracting fluttering at the top of the frame in the opening shot. The inserted French scenes tend to look softer and sport a slight beige hue compared to the pure black and white of the rest of the film; at least it makes it easier to spot the longer scenes. The credits have been newly generated via computer over a static title card, presumably because the older credits wouldn't cut smoothly into the longer cut now. The dubbed English audio sounds fine, though not surprisingly it's more distracting than usual for an Audubon title due to the weird hodgepodge of actors. Extras include the *Tentations* French trailer, the amusing U.S. trailer (with a female narrator repeatedly cooing the title), a photo gallery of production shots of Metzger directing the new scenes, the usual Audubon trailer reel (*The Nude Set*, *The Libertine*, etc.), and for no obvious reason, a comparison of Laurent's alternative shower scenes found in *The Twilight Girls*.

SOLDIER OF ORANGE

Colour, 1977, 147m. / Directed by Paul Verhoeven / Starring Rutger Hauer, Jeroen Krabbe, Derek de Lint, Eddy Habbema, Edward Fox / Tartan (UK R0 PAL), Anchor Bay (US R1 NTSC) / WS (1.85:1) (16:9)

The qualities that give the work of Paul Verhoeven its distinctiveness and force are precisely those which ultimately account for its limitations: a cynical dismissal of all human endeavour, accompanied by an inability (defenders would say refusal) to conceive of human relationships rooted in anything except contempt and mutual exploitation. Verhoeven's fourth feature, *Soldier of Orange* (*Soldaat van Oranje*), follows several Dutch students through the German occupation: Erik (Rutger Hauer) and Guus (Jeroen Krabbe), who join the Resistance, the half-German Alex (Derek de Lint), who joins the SS, and Robby (Eddy Habbema), who becomes an unwilling collaborator.

Whereas *Starship Troopers*'s war was depicted with satirical contempt, the genuine historical events (many of which the director had witnessed first-hand) of the German occupation are here given a more thoughtful treatment, but the two films nevertheless arrive at a similar conclusion: that there is hardly anything to choose between the two sides. Verhoeven's Nazis may be the sadistic *schweinhunds* familiar from American WWII films, but *Soldier of Orange*'s ostensible "heroes" are little better, the German soldiers who push a Jewish man's cart into a river being virtually indistinguishable from the Dutch students who are fond of similar "japes". It is difficult not to admire the audacity of introducing Guus, who will prove to be among the most sympathetic characters, perpetrating an act of gratuitous cruelty during a fraternity initiation ritual, the first in a series of increasingly sadistic assaults which culminate in Guus's death. The initiation sequence functions as a kind of seedbed for the rest of the film, containing numerous images that will be repeated as the "games" played by Guus and Erik become more serious: Guus walks over a "fresher", much as Susan will walk over a solider undergoing basic training in England; Erik hides under a table to escape Guus, while Guus later hides to escape a German roundup; and, in one of the film's subtlest touches, the punishment meted out to Esther, who has her hair forcibly cut following the Liberation, evokes the students' shaved heads. For Verhoeven, the war against fascism is not a struggle between good and evil, but rather the acting out on a wider stage of those destructive impulses which determine all relationships. Violence is seen as rooted in the human personality, the emphasis on excrement (Erik conceals photos of German bunkers in a bucket of faeces, then writes a letter to the prison warden using his own shit, Alex is killed while sitting on the toilet, etc.) suggesting that Verhoeven believes political struggle to be a sublimation of bodily functions. The sexual elements of the male students' relationships are never far from the surface (particularly during the scenes showing Erik and Guus sleeping with Susan), and if Erik's dance with SS officer Alex has the unfortunate effect of conflating homosexuality with fascism, heterosexuality fares little better (as *Basic Instinct* proved, Verhoeven is an equal opportunity offender), being repeatedly equated with impotence and aggression: Erik is distracted from his seduction of Esther by the planes flying overhead ("Are they ours?", "We don't have that many"), and later penetrates Susan from behind while reciting a list of the German cities he intends to bomb.

Although Tartan's DVD presents an excellent quality print of the Dutch-language original, a 41-second sequence is missing immediately after the intermission. The cut scene shows Erik and Guus talking in a cabin of the Swiss ship: they wonder if the ship might be sailing to Russia ("We'll have tea with Stalin"), then see a small boat pulling up alongside. After initially fearing that the boat is German, they hear an English voice asking to see the captain. The DVD cuts straight from the intermission

to Guus and Erik climbing into the boat. The disc's running time is 147 minutes 10 seconds, which is exactly the length of the transfer submitted to the BBFC, so it seems likely that this mistake was made during the mastering process. The deleted footage can be found on Anchor Bay's Region 1 disc (as well as in the print screened by Film Four), which also contains a Verhoeven commentary track. But at least Tartan's version is better than Rank's U.K. cinema/ video release, which was retitled *Survival Run*, dubbed into English, and cut by 33 minutes! Tartan's optional English subtitles are reasonably good, despite consistently misspelling Erik as "Eric" (the correct spelling is clearly seen when Erik writes his name on a wall). Although this translation is similar to the one used by Film Four, various subtitles have been added identifying names, dates and places. The disc includes a Dutch trailer (actually a waste of time teaser trailer, which does nothing except announce the film's forthcoming release) and a hilarious *Survival Run* trailer containing a generous selection of shots from Edward Fox's cameo, thus making him appear to be the co-star.

– BS

SPASMO

Colour, 1974, 94m. / Directed by Umberto Lenzi / Starring Robert Hoffmann, Suzy Kendall, Ivan Rassimov / Shriek Show (US R1 NTSC), Dutch FilmWorks (Holland R2 PAL) / WS (2.35:1) (16:9)

So maddening it almost dares viewers to still classify it in the *giallo* category, this convoluted but strangely effective study in madness gleefully offers a surprising change of pace from the normally commerce-minded Umberto Lenzi. For over an hour, *Spasmo* follows two characters on a dreamlike journey involving murder, vanishing bodies, and jealous lovers, with dialogue and character development so random they would drive David Lynch into fits.

Our nominal "hero" is rich kid Christian (*Grand Slam*'s Robert Hoffmann), who hooks up one night with a cheery but mysterious blonde, Barbara (*Torso*'s Suzy Kendall), whom he had previously encountered on the beach (where she was lying face-down, apparently suffering from memory loss). After he calls her a "sweet, sweet whore", she offers to take him back to her place for a quick one... on the condition that he shave off his beard ("There's a razor at my place; it's big, sharp, and sexy"). Naturally he complies, but before the two can consummate, he's ambushed in the bathroom by a pistol-wielding thug who winds up getting shot in the ensuing scuffle. Without even bothering to see the body, Barbara accepts Christian's word and goes on the lam with him to a friend's house, a desolate villa filled with birds of prey. Unfortunately they're surprised again by a couple renting the propery, but Christian and Barbara are allowed to stay the night (even after explaining why they're hiding from the police). Christian decides to elicit help from his industrialist brother, Fritz (Ivan Rassimov), but the events of the evening and following day put several kinks in his plan. Meanwhile, women in the vicinity are dropping dead thanks to a mysterious killer, and female mannequins with knives in their torsos keep turning up at inopportune moments.

Quite chaste by the genre's standards, *Spasmo* includes only a couple of bloodless gunshots, some mostly offscreen strangulations, and a very quick bit of topless nudity; even compared to its 1960s predecessors, one can only wonder what target audience Lenzi had in mind. What saves the film entirely is its increasing atmosphere of mental disintegration, creating the feeling that the viewer himself is losing his mind. Never one of Euro cinema's stronger actors, Hoffmann is put to good use here as the wide-eyed protagonist;

Kendall doesn't fare quite as well, spending her early scenes spouting cringe-inducing dialogue while modelling a lousy hairstyle, but her looks and acting both improve as the film goes along. Then there's the final act of the film, which essentially redeems all the random nutiness preceding it; if you can get through to this point, the story does pay off. Lenzi has never been much of an aesthetically interesting director, but here he executes some beautiful scope imagery and is helped along by a marvellous Ennio Morricone score (one of his best). The disorienting locales – beachscapes, rocky terrains, forests – in the opening movements effectively give way to more modern, stylized settings for the final stretch, leading to a claustrophobic, oddly resonant coda. No classic, to be sure, but *Spasmo* is better than its reputation might suggest for viewers willing to overlook the absence of flesh and blood.

Shriek Show's DVD presents the essential widescreen framing in a nicely transferred edition, though the audio shows some unfortunate signs of degeneration. Crackling and ambient noise are distracting in quieter scenes, but at least the score sounds robust. Colour and detail look fine, with occasional bursts of red pleasingly vivid.

Extras include the hilarious theatrical trailer ("Spasmo! Spasmo!! Spasmo!!!"), a handful of other Shreik Show trailers, and most significantly, a video interview with the typically unreliable Lenzi. Among his more dubious claims (apparently off the cuff): this film is the final part of a trilogy with *Orgasmo* and *Paranoia*, Hoffmann was a fine and neglected leading man for Visconti, and George Romero should feel disgraced for shooting trashy inserts for *Spasmo*'s U.S. release (footage which seems to have disappeared off into a vault somewhere). Never mind that Lenzi has done more than his share of cinematic cannibalizing in every possible sense. As always he's fun to listen to and offers some good insights into the film, but take it all with more than a few grains of salt. Also available as a no-frills Dutch DVD.

SPIDER-MAN

Colour, 2002, 121m. / Directed by Sam Raimi / Starring Tobey Maguire, Willem Dafoe, Kirsten Dunst, Cliff Robertson, J.K. Simmons, Bruce Campbell, Ted Raimi, Lucy Lawless, Scott Spiegel, Stan Lee / Sony (Blu-ray & DVD) (US R0/R1 HD/NTSC, UK R0/R2 HD/PAL) / WS (1.85:1) (16:9) / DD5.1

In a freak incident during a school trip to the science museum, Peter Parker (Tobey Maguire) is bitten by a radioactive arachnid, whereupon his molecular structure alters, endowing him with the proportionate strength and agility of a spider. From that moment on Parker has to balance a yearning to romance girl-next-door Mary Jane Watson (Kirsten Dunst) with a self-imposed duty to adopt the guise of Spider-Man and cleanse the streets of crime. A blessing in the eyes of many, considered by others as great a menace as the crooks he brings to justice, Parker's powers are put to the ultimate test when a deadly maniac known as the Green Goblin (Willem Dafoe) brings a reign of terror to the city.

Those with a taste for cowled crimefighting capers will find much to applaud in *Spider-Man*. Forget the brave but ultimately rather drab live action TV show of the late '70s (with Nicholas Hammond in the title role); Maguire is Spider-Man, and Sam Raimi's movie – for which his 1992 actioner *Darkman* was the perfect, albeit unwitting, dry run – is truly amazing. The director's affection for the character and the Marvel comics from whence he swung radiates from every frame. Where the TV show got it wrong was in pitching everyone's favourite neighbourhood webslinger against a flaccid collection of petty crooks and con artists, completely overlooking the rich reservoir of villainy offered up by the original comics. A hero is only ever as impressive as the foe against whom he's pitted and Raimi hits the bullseye by employing a fancy bit of fantasy and bringing into play one of Marvel's most infamous bad guys, the Green Goblin, while neatly maintaining a splash of plausibility by setting the action against recognisable New York backdrops.

Those familiar with the genesis of Spider-Man will find themselves in pleasingly familiar territory, as the first third of David Koepp's screenplay adheres closely to Stan Lee's comic strip; wallflower Parker getting bitten by a radioactive spider; the pro-am wresting tournament; the fateful moment when Parker avenges himself against an unscrupulous promoter by allowing a felon to escape justice; the subsequent death of Uncle Ben (the excellent Cliff Robertson); the media scare-mongering against Spider-Man fuelled by testy *Daily Bugle* editor J. Jonah Jameson (J.K. Simmons in fighting form); yes, indeed, the requisite minutiae are all here to mollify the purists. Only after the initial set-up does the story go off at a tangent. There's quite a bizarre spin in that where the comic strip Parker used synthetic webbing ejected from specially designed cartridges worn as wristbands, Koepp's Parker manufactures it bodily and is able to spray it from his wrists, which leads to some humorous moments when he tries to master his new-found feat.

An unexpected choice for the lead, Maguire surpasses all expectation, instantly likeable as good-natured, downtrodden Parker, and remarkably proficient at handling the physical demands once he squeezes into Spidey's lycra costume. There can have been no better choice. There's a substantial amount of computer generated imagery utilised for Spider-Man's acrobatics but it's blended seamlessly into the live action material and only on occasion does it look less than convincing. Willem Dafoe often goes way too far over the top in his portrayal of schizophrenic Norman Osborn (aka the Green Goblin), but there's no disputing that the screen sizzles whenever

S

he shows up. His radically redesigned outfit – which disposes of the cloth Halloween costume of the comic strip original in favour of an intimidating hi-tech suit of armour – is masterful, his helmet bearing the alloy answer to Conrad Veidt's rictus in *The Man Who Laughs*. Kirsten Dunst imbues Mary Jane Watson with an endearing naiveté, but it's a shame they didn't reserve her for a later instalment and use instead Gwen Stacy, Parker's comic strip girlfriend who was murdered by the Goblin. It would have added immeasurable intensity to the climax had Raimi dared to yank the rug from under audience expectancy by killing off his leading lady. Just the same, there's a nicely downbeat wrap when Parker, for his own arcane reasons, doesn't get the girl. Raimi opens the gates for so many cameos by pals and kin – Bruce Campbell, Ted Raimi, Lucy Lawless, Scott Spiegel, even Spidey creator Stan Lee himself gets a look in – that it's hard to keep track of them all.

Uncharacteristically, the score by Danny Elfman (who has penned some exquisite material over the years) feels like a distinctly by-the-numbers affair, boasting none of his usual flair. Although Bryan Singer's outstanding *X-Men* preceded *Spider-Man* by a couple of years, it was the global success of Raimi's movie in 2002 that belatedly kick-started a spate of big screen epics based on Marvel Comics properties, including *Daredevil* and *The Hulk*.

Collectors and completists who count the inclusion of variant trailers as an integral part of a film's DVD release will feel a twinge of disappointment over Sony's double platter *Spider-Man* package. At least four different splashy preview trailers were produced during the build up to the film's release – including the superbly realised and sadly withdrawn World Trade Centre teaser – but there is only one trailer included on this disc (excluding the superfluous half dozen plugs for other studio titles). It may have been wishful thinking to expect to see the WTC one included, but given the presence of no less than eleven different TV spots, it's odd that Sony deigned to include just one of the three remaining theatrical previews. Disregarding this oversight, the double-disc DVD release of *Spider-Man* is a fancy bit of kit but still somehow fails to live up to anticipation. The feature film itself is housed on disc 1 and is, naturally enough, beautifully rendered with dazzling colours and sound. It has been afforded 28 chapter points and makes available either English Dolby Digital or French language options (with subtitling in English, French and Spanish). The bonus materials on the first disc comprise the aforementioned trailer/TV spot selection and a number of "Webisodes", behind the scenes snippets which, irritatingly, can only be accessed via branching during the movie itself. Two separate commentaries cover most aspects of the production. The bulk of the accessories are reserved for disc 2, and it's here that the viewing experience feels a bit empty. What at first look appears to be a wealth of material actually boils down to not a great deal. A fair bit of space has been devoted to delving into the original comic strips – including a documentary, galleries focusing on villains, pivotal events in Spidey's history, etc. – which may be a treat for enthusiasts but not necessarily of much interest for those attracted solely by his movie incarnation. It's worth a once-through, though few but the most ardent will be likely to return for a second helping. The section devoted to the film consists of a couple of chunky behind the scenes featurettes, short but entertaining profiles of director Sam Raimi and composer Danny Elfman, some nice screen-test and costume fitting footage, music videos ("Hero" and "What We're All About"), and a short but largely unfunny blooper reel. A hidden feature, which reveals some CG tests and gags, can be accessed by clicking left on the commentaries menu and pressing enter on the highlighted spider icon. The production designs and conceptual art galleries listed on the sleeve menu do not appear to be on the disc. Finally there's a section of tips for playing the computer game spawned by the movie and an array of DVD-ROM supplements. Also available as a no-frills "SuperBit" version and a 3-disc edition primarily designed to plug *Spider-Man 2* (the movie and video game) with a handful of minor featurettes thrown in on the movie's costume design, spider wrangling, wrestling match and Goblin weapons.

An eventual Blu-ray version was a given (as Sony was the primary force behind the format), and from 2007 until the end of 2010 this was only available as a "Trilogy" set with its two sequels. Not surprisingly, the transfer reveals considerable advances in digital video presentation in the ensuing years as every aspect of the HD version looks considerably more impressive on a large display, and the lossless surround audio couldn't be better. Unfortunately the first film is presented completely bare bones.
– TG

STACY

Colour, 2001, 79m. / Directed by Naoyuki Tomomatsu / Starring Natsuki Kato, Tomoko Hayashi, Yasutaka Tsutsui / Synapse (US R1 NTSC) / WS (1.78:1) (16:9) / DD2.0

When Wes Craven's *Scream* introduced the "postmodern" slasher film, few noted that *Return of the Living Dead* had already done the same trick with zombie films a decade earlier. Now the Japanese have come up with a "post-postmodern" spin on the same idea in the form of *Stacy*, a shot-on-video jawdropper filled with shambling Asian schoolgirls hungry for human flesh. Packed with countless, in-your-face references to Western undead films, this is a treat for horror die-hards but won't make a lick of sense to casual viewers. Of course, who cares what they think?

In the 21st Century (err, now, that is), the world's population has been hit hard by a strange plague. All girls between the ages of 15 to 17 die after a brief state of NDH ("near death happiness") and, covered in a sparkly substance called BTP ("butterfly twinkle powder"), return as zombies called "Stacys". A decidedly unbalanced, Nobel Prize-winning scientist, Dr. Sukekiyo (Yasutaka Tsutsui), proclaims that the only way to kill a Stacy is via "repeat kill", i.e., hacking up the Stacy's body into 165 pieces. Meanwhile residents are instructed by a bunny-eared TV host to off their daughters with the newest hot consumer product, a light, portable, hand-held chainsaw called "Bruce Campbell's Right Hand 2" (though the saw clearly says "Blues Campbell's Right Hand 2"... but never mind). Once a week the Stacy remains are deposited curbside for government pick-up by the Romero Repeat Kill Troop, who are also available to kill Stacys should a family member be unable to do the dirty work himself. However, three girls approaching Stacyhood decide to intercept emergency calls to Romero and start their own business, the Drew Illegal Repeat Kill Troop ("named after Drew Barrymore! We love her!"). And on top of that, the pretty and mysterious Eiko (Natsuki Kato) approaches shy puppetmaker Nozomi (Tomoko Hayashi) with a strange bargain: she'll sleep by his side, and he'll agree to off her when her time comes. All of these elements come together in a very gory climax at a government compound, where an unleashed horde of Stacys, the Romero and Drew squads, and the mad doctor all collide in a frenzy of torn limbs, bloodshed, and twinkle powder.

Got all that? This delirious adaptation of a pulp novel by Kenji Otsuki gleefully tips its hat (perhaps too much) to all the obligatory walking dead films, from *Evil Dead* to *Day of the Dead*, though the more obvious target is actually Japanese pop culture itself. As with *Battle Royale*, this film mocks the overly sentimental, mushy trend in teen entertainment, with heartfelt proclamations of

S

love accompanied by syrupy music disrupted by the occasional swipe of a chainsaw. The bizarre, philosophical ending feels like an unholy collision of Nigel Kneale's Quatermass lore with Hello Kitty, something even stranger to witness than it sounds. On the downside, the puppeteer subplot really wears out its welcome fast; far too much time is spent on Eiko's NDH giggling, which could send viewers lunging for the mute button. Gorehounds will be pleased by the red stuff on display, with body parts and grue flying in every direction, though the budget means some of the effects look a bit less convincing than they probably should.

Synapse's DVD is perhaps the finest-looking presentation of a Japanese DTV title; it's not quite as glossy as a film transfer but closer than one might expect. Colours are rich, with only a deliberately cheap-looking TV interview displaying any shortcomings. The audio is also clear and sharp, doing justice to the bizarre retro-lounge/funk score. Optional yellow English subtitles are clear and easy to read throughout. Extras include the Japanese trailer and thought-provoking liner notes, which pose an interesting theory about the film's underlying statement about the fascination with giggly Japanese school-girls.

STALKER

Colour/B&W, 1979, 155m. / Directed by Andrei Tarkovsky / Starring Aleksandr Kaidanovsky, Alisa Frejndlikh, Anatoli Solonitsyn, Nikolai Grinko / Artificial Eye (UK R2 PAL), Ruscico (R0 NTSC), Kino (US R1 NTSC) / DD5.1

Like Andrei Tarkovsky's earlier *Solaris*, *Stalker* is adapted from a popular Eastern bloc science fiction novel (*Roadside Picnic* by Arkady and Boris Strugatsky) and uses genre trappings,

again a mysterious possibly alien phenomenon that debatably materialises the innermost wishes of flawed investigators, to ask fundamental questions about humanity, memory, desire and desolation.

In an unnamed small country (the book is set in America), a meteorite hit or a visitation from outer space has created the Zone, an abandoned area where the laws of physics and geography are suspended. Though the authorities police the borders of the Zone for the "protection" of the unwary, the title character (Aleksandr Kaidanovsky) is one of a small group of wounded sensitives who smuggle people past the barriers and guide them through the treacherous but magical space. Against the wishes of his wife (Alisa Frejndlikh), who has to care for their physically handicapped but psychically gifted daughter, the Stalker takes two men, a writer in search of inspiration (Anatoli Solonitsyn) and a scientist with a covert mission (Nikolai Grinko), into the Zone, past the rusting remains of a former military expedition and conflicting stories about what became of earlier stalkers and their charges, through perilous and often-changeable pathways to "the Room", where wishes may come true, or which might not exist at all.

It's not unthinkable that the Strugatskys' book might be remade one day as an action movie, but this might more properly be tagged a reflection movie: in the Zone, forward movement as often as not means doubling back. We far more frequently see the travellers at rest, the camera at a respectful, chill distance. Long periods of speechlessness, marked by haunting music and a natural soundscape, are punctuated by intense, challenging, maybe futile debate among the characters. The Zone is one of the cinema's great magical places: damp green and sylvan above-ground giving way to watery, muddy, uninhabited recent ruins as the party nears the perhaps-mythical Room. Like MGM's Oz, the Zone is coloured amid drab, monochrome reality, though the stalker's daughter − allegedly malformed by his exposure to the Zone – has her own colour, notably in a breathtaking final shot that conveys her telekinetic powers with a simplicity as affecting in its own way as the bloody shocks of Brian De Palma in *Carrie* and *The Fury*. Obviously, this has a "not for everybody" stamp all over it, but audiences willing to feel and think for themselves and pay attention should find this among Tarkovsky's most rewarding films.

Artificial Eye's DVD splits the film over two discs, presenting it – as it was originally intended – as a two-part film with an intermission. With menus in Russian, English and French, it offers the Russian language-track (in mono or a wonderful 5.1 mix awash and a-twitter with natural sound) with subtitles in English, French, German, Spanish, Italian, Portuguese, Dutch, Chinese, Swedish, Hebrew, Japanese and Russian. Among the craze for widescreen or even cropped fullscreen-to-create-widescreen transfers, it's refreshing to see a disc that shows how the almost square 4:3 frame allows for poised, affecting, painterly images. It's a film of grassy greens, white mists, scummy water, cast-aside objects and rusted-over tanks, and the transfer reproduces faithfully the muted, seductive colours of the Zone and the harsh, industrial, ever-so-slightly sepia shadows of the crumbling world outside. Among the extras are interviews with cinematographer Aleksandr Kynazhinsky and production designer Rifat Safiulin: Kynazhinsky, filmed on his death-bed, laments that almost the entire crew and cast of the film have died (a close look reveals an ashtray on his bed which suggests one reason why); chain-smoking survivor Safiulin reveals that a Soviet SNAFU meant Tarkovsky shot for a year only to find the negative ruined and undeveloped, forcing him to make both parts of the film with the budget allotted to part two and tells an anecdote to support his contention that the visionary wouldn't countenance 'an unmotivated flower' in one of his perfect frames. Also included are a tiny

short (*Tarkovsky's House*) that uses *Stalker's* music and photographic style to examine the ruin of the filmmaker's childhood home, biographies and filmographies and an extract for the director's diploma film, *The Steamroller and the Violin*. The identical Ruscico disc also contains the 5.1 and mono tracks, though the first international pressing contained a 5.1 track only. Some controversy arose over the decision to alter some of the music cues and sound effects for the surround remix, while the mono mix represents Tarkovsky's original intentions. The subsequent Kino reissue puts the entire feature on one disc and is slightly differently framed but otherwise looks identical and features the same "Memory" short.

– KN

STING OF THE BLACK SCORPION

Colour, 2002, 83m. / Directed by Gwyneth Gibby, Stanley Yung and Tim Andrew / Starring Michelle Lintel, Scott Valentine, Frank Gorshin, Martin Kove, Allen Scotti, Michael J. Anderson / New Concorde (US R1 NTSC)

Firearm (Martin Kove), a psychopath with a prosthetic machine-gun for an arm, declares war on Angel City. Counteracting, the Mayor brings in a task force led by a war veteran who's even more unbalanced than Firearm. Injured in his attempt to get a snapshot of the unmasked Black Scorpion (Michelle Lintel), a photojournalist becomes the vengeance driven Flashpoint (Allen Scotti) and threatens to induce blindness in the entire population of the City with the aid of a powerful laser beam. Released after twenty five years in prison for a crime he didn't commit, Clockwise (Frank Gorshin) plots revenge upon the judge and jury who wrongly sentenced him by using biological devices to prematurely age them. Is Black Scorpion woman enough to take on and defeat three of the most devious master-criminals ever to bring fear to Angel City?

Given that the identification of no less than three directors on the opening credits might pass unnoticed, if *Sting of the Black Scorpion* feels like several unrelated stories bound together that's because it is. Drastic editing has crammed three episodes from Roger Corman's 2001 television series – a spin-off from a couple of mid-90s B-graders – into the combined running time of less than two. This is hardly a new practice, of course; back in the '70s episodes of U.S. TV shows like *Battlestar Galactica* and *Spider-Man* were lashed together for feature length for export to Europe. The odd thing about *Sting of the Black Scorpion* though is that, to date, it has only seen a release Stateside, a territory having already suffered the TV show. Unlike those aforementioned '70s titles, however, the results here are distressingly choppy, doing away with so much exposition that continuity is virtually non-existent, and viewers are left to piece together some semblance of plot amidst the car chases, explosions and bouts of martial arts combat.

Those familiar with the two Joan Severance starrers will almost certainly deem Michelle Lintel an inferior replacement as police detective Darcy Walker by day, vigilante Black Scorpion by night. She certainly looks the business and gets the job done but she lacks Severance's indefinable magnetism. Familiar supporting characters – including Darcy's mechanic Argyle and his lady Tender Lovin', crooked Mayor Artie Worth and crabby Captain Strickland – are on hand (though each is played by a different actor here), but they're mostly relegated to insignificant status in the chronic paring down process. This aside the formula is much as you'd expect, with the Scorpionmobile getting an upgrade and Darcy setting up a secret Scorpion lair in her basement. And what of the episodes from which this feature was cobbled together? The edit of "Armed

and Dangerous" featuring Firearm is the most battle-damaged of the three and gets things off to a shaky start, relying on a surfeit of action and practically no plot. "Blinded by the Light", in which Black Scorpion is pitted against Mr. Freeze look-alike Flashpoint, proves to be a marginal improvement. But the best segment (best not to be interpreted as a recommendation, merely as an indicator of the least painful to endure) is "Crime Time" with the formidable Frank Gorshin as Clockwise and *Twin Peaks*'s diminutive Michael J. Anderson as one of his lackeys. In fashioning these episodes into a movie there's a bit of cost-cutting in evidence; the morphing effects on the Scorpionmobile have been lifted from the first two films, and chunks of Kevin Kiner's original score are recycled and mixed in with David G. Russell's TV material. Given the evidence on hand it's no surprise that the series failed to survive beyond 22 episodes. What is surprising, however, is that it survived beyond two. In summation the curious are best directed towards the 1995 film that started it all – even its own sequel is one to avoid – and *Sting of the Black Scorpion* can be safely ignored with no sense of loss whatsoever.

New Concorde's Region 1 DVD presents this dubious concoction in fullscreen format (no surprise there) with a generous 24-chapter allocation. Picture quality is good, if not outstanding. Sound is in English Dolby Digital with a subtitle option in Spanish only. Supplementary materials comprise a short trailer, cast filmographies and some preview trailers for other New Concorde releases. As is often the case with their output, the sleeve is misleading, this time endowing the movie with an R rating for "brief nudity"; bearing in mind that *Sting of the Black Scorpion* was television sourced, it's not surprising that not only is there no nudity in evidence – brief or otherwise – there's nothing else here to warrant that classification either.

– TG

THE STORY OF RICKY (RIKI-OH)

Colour, 1991, 88m. / Directed by Nam Nai Choi / Starring Fan Siu Wong, Fan Mei Sheng, Ho Kar Kui, Yukari Oshima / Hong Kong Legends (UK R2 PAL) / WS (1.85:1) (16:9) / DD 5.1, Tai Seng (US R0 NTSC) / WS (1.85:1) / DD5.1, Mega Star (HK R0 NTSC) / WS (1.85:1) / DD5.1, Deltamac (HK R0 NTSC) WS

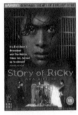 Based on a Japanese comic book, this Hong Kong action picture competes with Peter Jackson's gory epic *Braindead* in its deployment of outrageously gruesome slapstick violence. Never remotely convincing in effects terms and with near-comical face-pulling from the supposedly abused characters, it is at once astonishing and mildly mind-numbing, appalling and inoffensive.

Set in the then-future of 2001, when Far Eastern prisons have been privatised and are run as slave labour businesses, it's a childish melodrama about a hero with amazing, semi-supernatural recuperative powers and unbeatable streetfighting moves. Ricky (Fan Siu Wong) is a Rambo look-alike youth condemned (unjustly?) to a jail where he becomes a hero to the downtrodden by taking a ridiculous amount of punishment (at one point, he is buried alive for a week and survives by eating a raw dog heart a villain has stuffed into his breathing tube) and standing up against the supervillain-look cellblock bullies and the even more grotesque wardens. It's the sort of film where a combatant rips out his own intestines and tries to strangle his opponent or the evil head warden suddenly reveals a hitherto-unhinted ability to transform into a gigantic, fiend-faced Incredible Hulk knock-off to give Ricky some trouble in the climactic fistfight. Most emblematic of all is the triumphant finish in which the hero literally punches a hole in the wall, through which the surviving cons can escape to freedom.

Given that the film doesn't expect to be taken seriously, there's not much point in carping about silly story details or paper-thin characterisations. Like a lot of gross-out movies, it stumbles with the linking material between atrocities, especially when it tries to work up a little sentiment – always a sign that a character is about to get horribly killed to further motivate Ricky. It makes odd decisions, like casting actress Yukari Oshima as a male convict, but there's no sense that this wants to be anything more than fast-paced, ultra-violent rubbish. Some moments suggest a parody of Western action films, but we are supposed to take seriously the hero's ridiculous invulnerability (he even gets better after having razor blades taped into his mouth and being punched in the face) and the campier elements (like the warden's fat obnoxious kid sidekick) are just conventional comic relief.

The Hong Kong Legends DVD is 'totally uncut on DVD for the first time ever'; the transfer is fine for a film that mostly looks drab and cheap (except when the tomato soup is flowing), though the anamorphic widescreen framing is a bit tight, doing some head-chopping of its own on long shots of crowds. Soundtrack options are Cantonese or (badly) dubbed English, with a commentary track from Hong Kong-based critics Jude Poyer and Miles Wood, who contribute a lot of information about the various players and the place of the film in the context of the Hong Kong action industry but aren't overwhelmingly enthusiastic about the picture itself (of whether Ricky will return at the end, the commentary concludes "who cares?"). Other extras are "Rising Star" (a genial 36 minute interview with Fan Siu Wong) and two and a half minutes of the action star working out. An international and domestic trailer are included, the Hong Kong effort stressing the origins of the film in the popular comic, with artwork that segues into live action. Also included are trailers for other Hong Kong Legends titles.

– KN

STRAIGHT ON TILL MORNING

Colour, 1972, 96m. / Directed by Peter Collinson / Starring Rita Tushingham, Shane Briant, Annie Ross, John Clive, Tommy Godfrey, Tom Bell, James Bolam, Katya Wyeth / Anchor Bay (US R1 NTSC), Optimum (UK R2 PAL) / WS (1.85:1) (16:9)

 Leaving home in Liverpool under the phony pretext of being pregnant – anything to get away from her hum-drum life – ugly duckling Brenda Thompson (Rita Tushingham) arrives in London where she engineers a meeting with the handsome Peter (Shane Briant) by stealing his dog. They strike up an unlikely friendship and Peter agrees to give her the baby she wants so badly provided she moves in to look after him, cooking, cleaning and generally acting the part of the dutiful wife. Completely infatuated and anxious to get pregnant, Brenda agrees, unaware that her choice of partner is in fact a homicidal psychotic with an ugliness fixation. It's only because Brenda falls shy of beautiful that he poses her no threat... at least not to begin with.

With its hauntingly melancholy theme song written and performed by Annie Ross (who also appears in the film), *Straight On Till Morning* wasn't the most likely product to crawl out under the Hammer banner, and it subsequently proved to be one of their less successful endeavours. Yet it's still one of their most intriguing, primarily due to the engaging edge-of-sanity interaction between mad-as-a-hatter Briant and mildly unstable Tushingham. That this vulnerable girl isn't alerted to her Prince Charming's instability early in Michael Peacock's story is a bit of a stumbling block in terms of logic, but since she's painted as the most naïve teenager this side of the Mersey, Peacock just about pulls it off. Briant is a devilishly attractive fellow yet, lit in just the right way, his pallid, blank expression and wavy baby-blond hair

lend him the all too convincing *mien* of an A1 mental case. Check out his similar performance in *Demons of the Mind*. Highly respected star of kitchen sink dramas and former British Academy Best Actress award winner (for *A Taste of Honey*), Tushingham seems like improbable casting, but then the film is rife with that: Whoever would expect to find John Clive, Tommy Godfrey, Tom Bell or James Bolam in a movie bearing the Hammer label? More familiar – having previously appeared in *Hands of the Ripper* and *Twins of Evil* – is Katya Wyeth, foolishly deigning to hop between the sheets with Briant, who, as she climaxes, thrusts a Stanley knife between her shoulder blades.

Director Peter Collinson maintains a fairly leisurely pace throughout the twisted tale which, though it never fully draws you in, is sufficiently diverting to command your attention through its ninety-something minutes to the desperately bleak conclusion. Littered with references to J.M. Barrie – our resident lunatic aside, there's a dog called Tinker and Peter insists on addressing Brenda by the name Wendy – *Straight On Till Morning* is certainly the strangest of Hammer's psychological thrillers. Originally punted out as the bottom half of a double bill with the same year's *Fear in the Night*, there's a rather disquieting, cloying aura of morbidity hanging over it and if it's emotional highs you're seeking you really ought to be looking elsewhere.

A quintessential addition to your Hammer library it isn't, but Anchor Bay has treated *Straight On Till Morning* with veneration equal to that afforded anything else in their catalogue. The uncut print used for the transfer is in impeccable health. With a 23-chapter divide, it's accompanied by an optional commentary from star Rita Tushingham, along with the theatrical trailer and a textual biography of director Peter Collinson. With *The Italian Job* being his most popular film, it's a great tragedy that Collinson, who passed away prematurely in 1980, never got to see the quality revival – *Fright* being another notable Anchor Bay release – enjoyed by some of his lesser known work in the wake of the DVD revolution. In 2006 the film finally reached U.K. shelves with the same transfer and extras, first as part of Optimum's 21-disc Hammer box and then as a separate entity.

– TG

STRAW DOGS

Colour, 1971, 118m. / Directed by Sam Peckinpah / Starring Dustin Hoffman, Susan George, David Warner / Criterion (US R1 NTSC), Fremantle (UK R2 PAL), MGM (US R1 NTSC) / WS (1.85:1) (16:9)

 Perhaps the single most incendiary film released in a year notorious for brutal British cinema (along with *A Clockwork Orange*, *The Devils*, etc.), Sam Peckinpah's *Straw Dogs* is perhaps the only step he could have made after the massive, ultraviolent western epic, *The Wild Bunch*. Rapidly becoming a new screen idol after *The Graduate* and *Midnight Cowboy*, Dustin Hoffman made a bizarre but rewarding career choice by taking on the role of David Sumner, an American physicist who moves with his wife, Amy (Susan George), to her childhood home in Cornwall. Her former boyfriend and his cronies are brought in to do handiwork on the Sumner home, and tension immediately mounts as the outsiders are circled and taunted in subtle, brutish ways. However, David's pacifism prevents him from taking action, even when a cat winds up hanged in their closet, and Amy finds herself drifting away from her increasingly passive husband. However, events involving an accused child murder (David Warner) and a bloody brand of vigilante justice force David to confront his inner beast, with horrific results.

In common with allegorical genre films such as *Invasion of the Body Snatchers*, *Straw Dogs* can be read in any number of ways depending upon the viewer. While Peckinpah remains known for his steadfast macho outlook on life, his treatment of the characters in this film and the ultimate collaborative nature of the project make it difficult to evaluate, even today. Much of the controversy centres around an extended, harrowing rape sequence, disturbing more for what it implies from George's reactions than for what it actually shows. Though rarely offered parts which gave her more to do than look kittenish and scream, George is remarkable in this film, expressing tragic depths of emotion which culminate in a finale where her expressions and actions must ultimately be deciphered by looking back at the entire film. Hoffman is no less impressive, transforming subtly as his home comes under fire despite his attempts to keep justice and peace. The much-ballyhooed violence still packs a wallop, with such props as barbed wire, scalding water, and a mantrap put to gruesome use in a final half hour, which has justifiably landed the film in the horror genre in many reference books. If *The Last House on the Left* can be considered a horror film, so can this.

Inexplicably shorn of much crucial footage from the rape scene in the U.S., *Straw Dogs* appeared uncut briefly on VHS before it resurfaced intact again years later on laserdisc from Fox (with an isolated music and effects track) and a featureless DVD from Anchor Bay. The isolated track reappears on both the Criterion and Fremantle DVDs, which sport an improved anamorphic transfer with richer flesh tones and sharper detail than the already excellent Anchor Bay version. The Criterion edition is missing a single, virtually subliminal shot of Susan George being taken from behind during the rape scene. This shot can be found in the U.K. DVD, the American Anchor Bay DVD and the Image laserdisc (as well as the old U.K. VHS release from Guild). The mono soundtrack was never terribly robust to begin with; Jerry Fielding's sparse but haunting score isn't exactly demo material for home theatre enthusiasts but is serviced well enough. (Incidentally, the British DVD also marks the film's first intact appearance for years after countless battles with the BBFC, as the licensor refused to trim a single frame of footage.)

While both the U.S. and U.K. have special editions of the film, the extra features diverge wildly in their content. The Criterion edition contains two discs, the first of which is devoted entirely to the film itself, with an audio commentary by film scholar Stephen Prince. It's a solid track, peppered with useful insights from the very beginning (did you know the first shots were derived from Peckinpah's discarded, original opening for *The Wild Bunch*?). The feature also contains optional English subtitles, a nice plus as this makes it the only captioned edition of the film available.

The second Criterion disc sports a host of extras, with a centrepiece in the form of *Sam Peckinpah: Man of Iron*, an 80-minute documentary featuring interviews, stills, anecdotes, and other ephemera connected to this maverick talent. Actors like Kris Kristofferson offer their own insights, and while many film clips (*Pat Garrett & Billy the Kid*, *The Wild Bunch*, etc.) had to be thrown out for legal reasons, the program serves as a fine primer for the uninitiated and an enlightening resource for the seasoned. Also included is a 7-minute Television South West behind the scenes featurette; shot in black and white, this assemblage of footage offers a fascinating look at the cast and crew at work on location. "On Location: Dustin Hoffman" is a rather pompous educational short film following Hoffman on the set; we see him discussing his role, preparing in the morning by running through his lines, and interacting with Peckinpah and the cast. Video interviews with George and producer

Daniel Melnick are also included; while Melnick offers the most useful technical information, George gives by far one of the most interesting retrospective interviews around. She candidly discusses her experiences on the film, ranging from her unorthodox hiring process to her walking out after coming to verbal blows over the rape scene, which she eventually performed as she saw fit. The disc is rounded out with the theatrical trailer ("Sam Peckinpah, who uncaged *The Wild Bunch*, now unleashes Dustin Hoffman!"), three TV spots, and text of Peckinpah's defensive responses to reviews by Pauline Kael and Richard Schickel.

The Fremantle version contains the George and Melnick interviews (which were originally produced for the U.K. disc) and the Television South West footage but differs in other respects. Two commentary tracks are offered; in the first, Peckinpah biographers Paul Seydor, Garner Simmons and David Weddle practically hold a love-in for the director and pick apart the film in minute detail, while in the second, PA and dialogue director Katy Haber discusses her tempestuous relationship with Peckinpah on the set. Along with the trailer, the disc also includes radio spots, an interview with Peckinpah biographer Garner Simmons, a deleted snippet of footage in the pub, a compilation of script excerpts and stills to show deleted and unfinished scenes, a history of the film's censorship troubles, a stills and posters gallery, various additional Peckinpah correspondence with the likes of Richard Harris and Harold Pinter, and an 8 page booklet with liner notes by Kim Newman. Obviously one's preference will most likely be determined by the country in which they live, but both discs are well worth seeking out and represent worthy editions of a crucial, widely misunderstood film which has lost none of its, er, bite. The limited Criterion version is now somewhat difficult to find, but the same transfer is available from MGM.

STREET OF NO RETURN

Colour, 1989, 89m. / Directed by Samuel Fuller / Starring Keith Carradine, Valentina Vargas, Marc de Jonge, Bill Duke, Andréa Ferréol / Fantoma (US R1 NTSC) / WS (1.85:1) (16:9) / DD5.1

 After the disastrous studio mishandling of *White Dog*, cult auteur Samuel Fuller turned his directorial eye towards European-financed projects like the odd *Thieves After Dark* and the ever-odder *Street of No Return*, a hallucinatory blend of film noir and '80s kitsch based on a novel by David Goodis (*Shoot the Piano Player*). Shot entirely in Portugal with a truly peculiar international cast, this was Fuller's penultimate feature film (he subsequently made *Tinikling or "The Madonna and the Dragon"* in 1989, as well as undertaking some European television work) and offers an unusually hopeful and optimistic vision near the end of one of the cinema's most unorthodox careers.

In the violent opening sequence, a street riot spreading through a nearby prison results in a shocking blow to Michael (Keith Carradine), a shaggy-haired bum who staggers off into the streets. The amnesiac's memories flood back as, in flashback, we learn he was once a successful pop star. While on tour he enters the dangerous world of Celia (*The Name of the Rose*'s perpetually naked Valentina Vargas), a nightclub dancer with whom he ignites a passionate affair. Unfortunately her mobster boyfriend and sponsor, Eddie (Marc de Jonge), doesn't take too kindly to the idea and lures Michael onto a boat, where he leaves the crooner for dead with a slashed throat...

Sporting a colourful array of supporting characters including Bill Duke (cast as a cop, as usual) and the always enjoyable Andréa Ferréol (*A Zed and Two Noughts*), Fuller's film was never released in the United States and has remained something of an odd footnote in his career, rarely seen apart from hazy bootleg tapes. Carradine offers a solid, intriguing performance while typically providing his own singing; his songs have dated rather poorly, but otherwise the film holds him rather well. He and Vargas also go at their love scenes with a sweaty ferocity typical of more continental fare, and the revenge aspect is handled with more romantic aplomb than the following year's strikingly similar goofball Kevin Costner vehicle, *Revenge* (based on another neo-noir novel by Jim Harrison). The low budget's limitations are often evident, but Fuller still conjures up some striking set pieces. In particular, the opening riot and the hallucinatory image of a topless Vargas in showgirl gear astride her horse, trotting through the middle of a deserted city street with Carradine in tow, are among Fuller's strongest visual achievements.

Fantoma's disc offers a razor sharp presentation of a film rarely seen in decent shape. The elements are in beautiful condition, and the Dolby Digital 5.1 remix tweaks the original stereo tracks with some effective split channel effects. The warbling electronic score is spread nicely to the front speakers, while thunderclaps and gunshots split off to the rears with crisp clarity. The biggest extra is a running commentary track with Carradine, who offers numerous recollections of working with Fuller along with some well-observed insights into his directorial method. He also humorously notes the pointed irony of having his bum appearance consist of long, shaggy hair while his rock star style consists of a short, cropped look. Other extras include a disjointed theatrical trailer, a half hour documentary compiled from behind the scenes footage shot during filming, in which we see the various Portuguese settings being handled under the cigar-chomping Fuller's supervision along with extensive interviews with Fuller and Carradine. A text interview with Fuller (excerpted from François

S

Guérif's *Samuel Fuller – Sans espoir de retour*) is also included, while the extensive liner notes by author Lee Server offer a thumbnail overview of Fuller's career and the film's place in his output.

A STUDY IN SCARLET

B&W, 1933, 71m. / Directed by Edwin L. Marin / Starring Reginald Owen, Warburton Gamble, June Clyde, Anna May Wong, Alan Mowbray, Alan Dinehart, J.M. Kerrigan / Alpha (US R1 NTSC)

Evidently made by enthusiasts, this Poverty Row Holmes movie stars Reginald Owen (who had played Dr. Watson a year earlier), who might be a chubby, bland master sleuth but also (with Robert Florey) cobbled together an original screenplay (named after Conan Doyle's novel) with plot elements and character names taken from several different stories.

The "Scarlet Ring", a mysterious tontine-like group presided over by lawyer Merrydew (Alan Dinehart), is awaiting the division of the spoils of a long-ago nefarious enterprise. The Ring is whittled down by murder, each victim found dead with a scrap of doggerel verse about his person (predating Agatha Christie's use of the same rhyme in *Ten Little Indians*). Holmes is brought into the case by curiosity about a coded notice in the newspaper, a need to settle a grudge against outwardly respectable blackmailer Merrydew (who combines the Doyle figures of Professor Moriarty and Charles Augustus Milverton) and, finally, an urge to protect an innocent (June Clyde) on the list of prospective victims. When one corpse is battered beyond recognition but identifiable by a ring and clothes labels, it's not too hard to determine the surprise finish, but there's agreeable crookedness along the way. The slinky (if underused) presence of Anna May

Wong as an oriental femme fatale adds a great deal, and there's an amusing turn as one of the threatened crooks (J.M. Kerrigan) tries to hire Holmes to save his skin.

Far more makeshift than the Basil Rathbone films of a decade later or even the contemporary British series with Arthur Wontner, *A Study in Scarlet* is crowded with good character actors – Warburton Gamble and Alan Mowbray, as Watson and Lestrade, have to jostle to get a look-in – and mysterioso business. A few lines show how long ago 1933 was ("You can't make English gentry out of heathen Chinee", snipes a servant about Wong) but there's a respect for the original material unusual at this budgetary level. Alpha Video's DVD is in line with most of the label's budget-priced PD releases, which is to say a ropy, splicy, beat-up print is ill-served by a transfer that does nothing to alleviate the constant soundtrack rumble and hiss or the bands of faint purple and green over the monochrome image. Still it's a *rara avis*, and the colour-tinted packaging is attractive. The only extra is an extensive onscreen catalogue of other titles.

– KN

SUDDEN FURY

Colour, 1997, 102m. / Directed by Darren Ward / Starring Nick Rendell, Paul Murphy, Andy Ranger, David Warbeck / Sub Rosa, SRS (US R1 NTSC), Boudicca (UK R2 PAL), Dragon (Germany R0 PAL) / WS (1.85:1) / DD2.0

If Quentin Tarantino had directed a remake of Lucio Fulci's *Contraband* as a straight to video project, the results would probably look a lot like *Sudden Fury*, an astonishing frenzy of gangster gore that's still one of the most gruesome British projects ever filmed.

In the opening scene, a crime deal gone wrong results in a back-talking sap getting his head stomped in by crime lord Randall (Paul Murphy), whose henchman Jimmy (Andy Ranger) has a fondness for brutality. Things get worse when two of Randall's men wind up tortured by blowtorch under the hand of a wacko rival kingpin (Fulci regular David Warbeck), who transmits the whole ordeal by cell phone just for kicks. Hungry for payback, Randall hires loose canon hitman Walker (Nick Rendell) for a siege gone very wrong, which results in Walker nearly being taken out by his employer. Soon the two men are out gunning for each other in a frenzied bloodbath, climaxing in a warehouse finale packed with burnings, maimings, and several thousand bullets.

Released one year before Guy Ritchie's *Lock, Stock and Two Smoking Barrels* (which coincidentally uses a lot of stylistic touches found here), *Sudden Fury* is way above your average low budget indie effort. The video format poses a few problems early on, thanks mainly to on-set sound recording that sounds a bit stilted and hollow at times, but once the action really kicks in, these shortcomings quickly fade away. The final half hour is a stunning tour de force, with a single-take, head-through-a-glass-door gag that will have many viewers reaching for the rewind button. The late Warbeck is fun and hammy in one of his final roles, while the other actors do well enough once you get over the fact that clean-cut, college-age English boys are a little implausible as hard-bitten, foul-mouthed drug lords and gangsters. Toss in some gratuitous sex and one of the best final shots you'll ever see, and you've got a great little underdog of a film well worth checking out.

The video transfers for *Sudden Fury* will never surpass the original source, obviously, so even with theatrical-style matting this still looks like a video production. Dropouts and video noise are evident in numerous shots, while contrast varies depending on the lighting. The technical quality improves as the film plays out, and the snappy editing goes a long way to compensating for the erratic video texture found in some of the dialogue scenes. The stereo audio is more consistent and impressive, with music, gunshots, and aggressive foley effects bursting from the speakers at an appropriately loud volume. All DVD editions feature some of the same extras: a trailer, bloopers and brief deleted footage (including a nasty severed arm gag), and an art and photo gallery. The U.K. DVD also tosses in a short film, "Bitter Vengeance", and a preview for *Beyond Fury*, as well as a lengthy reel of behind the scenes make-up footage. Though lacking the make-up reel and short film, the German disc offers an audio commentary with Darren Ward and Rendell, who explain the arduous, years-in-the-making process that resulted in this crimson-soaked labour of love. Regardless of the country of origin, this is a vicious ride well worth taking.

SUNSET BLVD.

B&W, 1950, 110m. / Directed by Billy Wilder / Starring William Holden, Gloria Swanson, Erich von Stroheim, Buster Keaton, H.B. Warner, Anna Q. Nilsson, Cecil B. DeMille, Nancy Olson / Paramount (US R1 NTSC, UK R2 PAL)

This is the definitive Hollywood Gothic. It opens with unemployed screenwriter Joe Gillis (played by William Holden) floating in a swimming pool, face-down and shot in the back, and then has the dead man recount his doomed personal and professional involvement with megalomaniac silent movie queen Norma Desmond (Gloria Swanson). A flapper vampire whose attempts to seem youthful into her fifties paradoxically make her seem a thousand years old, Norma lives in a decaying mansion on Sunset Boulevard, holding a midnight funeral for her pet monkey ("he must have been a very important chimp", muses Joe, "the great grandson of King Kong perhaps"), scrawling an unproducable script and dreaming of an impossible comeback ("I hate that word! This will be a return!") as Salome. In deferential attendance is a sinister butler (Erich von Stroheim) who used to be her favoured director (and, creepily, first husband), who encourages Billy Wilder – usually not a director given to ostentatious visuals – to compositions that evoke both the lair of the Phantom of the Opera and Kane's Xanadu; witness the huge close-up of white-gloved hands playing Bach on a wheezy pipe organ as the trapped gigolo flutters in the background.

Wilder's acidic yet nostalgic traipse through the film industry's haunted house is a film that can be endlessly rewatched even after its influence has seeped into the horror genre (cf: *What Ever Happened to Baby Jane?*) and spun off an Andrew Lloyd Webber stage adaptation, combining strange affection for has-been Norma and never-was Joe with a somewhat sadistic use of such ravaged and frozen silent faces as Buster Keaton, H.B. Warner and Anna Q. Nilsson. An unstressed irony is that Norma can't get away with her insanity ("no one ever leaves a star!") but the industry allows and indeed encourages everyone else to act like a monster; Cecil B. DeMille (playing himself) gently reminds Norma that the picture business has changed, but Wilder concludes his scene by having the camera note his polished riding boots and absurdly outdated on-set strut. Though they recognised their chances for one last blaze of glory, Swanson (who took the role after Mary Pickford turned it down) and von Stroheim (who is forced to watch an extract from *Queen Kelly*, an unfinished 1920s disaster he really did direct Swanson in) understood the cruelty of his vision and the way he made monsters of them.

It's a hard and cynical film which struggles with its doomed but sweet "normal" love affair; in the end, Norma is as terrified that Joe is writing a script ("Untitled Love Story") with D-girl Betty (Nancy "Wholesome" Olson) as she is that he will leave her for a younger rival. Swanson ("I am big; it's the pictures that got small") is vibrant in her madness, sitting on a studio stage and swatting away the hated boom microphone as if it were a bothersome insect, and climaxing with a moment of unforgettable horror-glamour as she vamps towards a newsreel cameraman during her arrest for murder and declares "All right Mr. DeMille, I'm ready for my close-up" even as Wilder pulls back to frame her in a long-shot that emphasizes her isolation in insanity as the big carnival of a celebrity murder scandal begins, pointing the way to Wilder's *Ace in the Hole* and a culture of famous crime that remains horribly alive fifty years on. Hidden inside the film is a struggle between the silents and the talkies, represented by the stylized Swanson and the naturalistic Holden but also by the Gothic, overwrought look of the film and the non-stop verbal patter of the dialogue and even the lengthy passages of voice-over cynical comment (Wilder and co-writers Charles Brackett and D.M. Marshman Jr. don't share Norma's loathing of "words, words, words").

Paramount's Special Collector's Edition of this accepted classic is a first-rate presentation of outstanding materials. An ingenious menu evokes the screening room of Norma Desmond's mansion, and the transfer preserves a gorgeous, flawless academy ratio monochrome print, with 19 chapter-stops and a well-balanced, nuanced Dolby Digital mono track (with a French-language alternative). The extras: a scene-specific commentary by Wilder's biographer Ed Sikov; a retrospective making-of featurette (with Sikov, critic Andrew Sarris, Paramount's A.C. Lyles, Broadway's Norma Glenn Close and sole survivor Olson); a proud trailer; a "Hollywood location map" (inspired perhaps by a similar feature on the *L.A. Confidential* disc) that uses snippets of the film and contemporary footage to highlight the real places Wilder shows in the film; informative little featurettes on costume designer Edith Head and composer Franz Waxman; and two separate drafts of the morgue prologue with some silent footage shot for the scene, which was deleted after a disastrous preview. A "Centennial" Paramount version (the first in the U.K., second in the U.S.) gets a significant visual boost by moving all the extras to the second disc (apart from the commentary, which obviously remains with the feature), giving it more breathing room and maxing out the entire disc. The supplements disc carries over the old extras along with some welcome additions: "*Sunset Boulevard*: The Beginning" covers the inception of the film, "The Noir Side" has crime writer Joseph Wambaugh giving his own take on his involvement in its writing, "*Sunset Boulevard* Becomes a Classic" follows the premiere and its ascent to classic status, "Two Sides of Ms. Swanson" gives the grand dame her due, "Stories of Sunset Boulevard" rattles off a few production anecdotes, "Mad about the Boy" gives a quick overview about Holden, "Recording *Sunset Boulevard*" spotlights the marvellous Franz Waxman score, and "The City of *Sunset Boulevard*" and "Behind the Gates" cover more of the location and studio shooting. Obviously, anyone inclined to double dip wouldn't feel too burned by this one.

– KN

SUPERGIRL

Colour, 1984, 124m./138m. / Directed by Jeannot Szwarc / Starring Helen Slater, Faye Dunaway, Peter O'Toole, Hart Bochner, Peter Cook, Mia Farrow, Simon Ward, Brenda Vaccaro, Marc McClure / Anchor Bay (US R1 NTSC), Warner (US R1 NTSC, UK R2 PAL) / WS (2.35:1) (16:9) / DD5.1

Accidentally placing Argo City in jeopardy by losing its magical power source, the Omegahedron, Kara (Helen Slater) tracks its trajectory from the depths of inner space to the planet Earth. Once there she finds that the difference in gravity accords her incredible powers and she becomes Supergirl. To hide her true identity she adopts the alias of schoolgirl Linda Lee, cousin of Clark Kent (aka Superman). Discovering that the Omegahedron has been found and appropriated by black witch Selena (Faye Dunaway) for her own dark schemes, Supergirl sets out to retrieve it and foil Selena's plans to rule the world.

Directed by Jeannot Szwarc (who made, among others, *Jaws 2*, much maligned but unquestionably the best of the original's sequels), this crack by producers Alexander and Ilya Salkind to cash in on the success of their *Superman* series was savaged by critics from here to the far side of Argo City. Its subsequent failure to set the box office alight buried all notions of a sequel, which is a shame because although *Supergirl* has more than its share of shortcomings, it's nowhere near as dreadful as its denigrators might claim. The problem is that all the good stuff – and there's plenty of it – is smothered by David Odell's extraordinarily feeble script. After a relatively promising start it devolves into a sloth-like, cliché-ridden hotchpotch that seems to lose sight of its premise, all but reducing the narrative to a soap opera love triangle with Supergirl and Selena vying for the affections of handsome but drippy school handyman Ethan (Hart Bochner). The final sprint to the finish line, with Supergirl finally recovering the Omegahedron and returning it to Argo City, feels like a hasty attempt to wrap things up neatly. At times Odell's work is so bad that it makes Akiva Goldsman's horrible efforts on *Batman and Robin* seem positively Shakespearean by comparison.

Saturating the story with a "name" cast might have masked the feeble writing had Dunaway, Peter Cook, Mia Farrow and Simon Ward not proved to be a riper collection of hams than you'd find in a butcher's shop window. In assessment they serve only to compound the problems. Dunaway and Cook are particularly awful, speaking their lines with the authenticity of a couple of two-bit music hall turns. Hart Bochner, equally bad, can be partially forgiven due to his relative inexperience. How ironic then that Helen Slater, a complete unknown at the time, should turn out to be better than all the aforementioned assembled; it's no Oscar worthy performance, but she conveys a convincing and endearing naiveté and in terms of looking the part the makers could not have chosen finer. Peter O'Toole as the sagacious Zaltar and Brenda Vaccaro as Selena's wisecracking sidekick Bianca lend enjoyable support and, in Christopher Reeve's absence (he refused to appear), Mark McClure is on hand as Daily Planet photographer Jimmy Olsen to secure a direct link to the *Superman* franchise.

Made in the pre-CG era, this film boasts effects that stand head and shoulders above those in most of its contemporaries. Some of the flying sequences are startlingly impressive, especially the graceful aerial ballet over the lake when Kara discovers her ability to defy gravity for the first time. You can't get better than the real thing... well, at least as real as a crane and cable/harness rig can make them. The results certainly surpass even the keenest bluescreen work. There are some nice set pieces throughout too, the first encounter between Supergirl and Selena's "Power of Shadow" beast being a pointed highlight, as is Supergirl's later incarceration alongside Zaltar in the Phantom Zone. The indefatigable Jerry Goldsmith contributes a swooping score, as befitting of the material as were John Williams's classic themes for *Superman*. Existing in three different versions – which vary from the shortest to the longest by 33 minutes! – the mid-length cut at 124 minutes is probably the best. The shortest, at 105 minutes, leaves several points in need of clarification, while the longest, at 138 minutes, is just too much catastrophic, rationality-deficient scripting to have to stomach.

Anchor Bay can be heartily commended for assembling more than the most demanding fan of *Supergirl* could hope for in a deluxe limited edition, individually numbered DVD package. The 2-disc set contains both the 124-minute cut and the previously unreleased 138-minute cut (its additional material having apparently been located in a vault inside canisters marked "Do Not Use"). Disc 1 houses the former in a clean and colourful 24-chapter, 2.35:1 widescreen pressing, enhanced for 16:9 viewing, with sound available in Dolby Digital 5.1 and Dolby Surround 2.0. The feature can also be viewed with an optional, very candid commentary from director Jeannot Szwarc and special projects consultant Scott Michael Bosco. A sackful of additional features is headed up by a 50-minute documentary from the time of the film's original release. Hosted by Faye Dunaway, it charts the production from concept to screen and includes plenty of excellent behind camera material and interviews with cast and crew, plus footage of Slater modelling an early, rather awful costume design. Complementing this documentary is a nice collection of stills and artwork, storyboards from half a dozen key sequences, text biographies, 5 trailers and 3 TV spots. Disc 2 contains the 138-minute cut alone, again in 2.35:1 ratio and divided by 24 chapter points. The film was later issued (begrudgingly, by all appearances) in a stripped-down version as part of Warner's *Superman* box set, though they carried over an edited version of the commentary track, which awkwardly hacks out any references to Anchor Bay.

– TG

SUPERVIXENS

Colour, 1975, 105m. / Directed by Russ Meyer / Starring Shari Eubank, Charles Napier, Charles Pitts, Uschi Digard, Stuart Lancaster, Sharon Kelly, John Lazar, Christy Hartburg, Deborah McGuire, Ann Marie, Garth Pillsbury / Arrow (UK R2 PAL), RM Films (US R1 NTSC), DVDY Films (France R2 PAL)

Clint Ramsey (Charles Pitts) is constantly being harangued by his insatiable but possessive wife SuperAngel (Shari Eubank). After a heated row when she thinks Clint is cheating on her, SuperAngel throws him out amid accusations of assault. The only problem is that investigating cop Harry Sledge (Charles Napier) is a psycho with a short fuse. SuperAngel flirts with Sledge but when she invites him into her bed he proves impotent. She tries to help things along by playing the pink oboe but he turns nasty and her mockery at his failure to satisfy her triggers a vicious attack. Trampling her to death in the bathtub, and ensuring she's dead by then dropping an electrical appliance into the water, Sledge takes off, with all the evidence now pointing to hubby as the killer. With little hope of proving his innocence, Ramsey goes on the run, but Sledge is hot on his trail, intent on nailing him at any cost.

We're back in Russ Meyer land and the glory days before silicone enhancement eclipsed natural fleshy curves. It's impossible to take seriously a film whose credits include a C. Unt in its cast of players, and Meyer once again delivers the seriously silly goods with a succession of stupendously endowed women, each with an insatiable craving to copulate. These include Uschi Digard (as SuperSoul, the Austrian mail-order bride of farmer *Faster, Pussycat! Kill! Kill!*'s Stuart Lancaster), Sharon Kelly (as SuperCherry,

hedonistic girlfriend of an acrimonious John *Beyond the Valley of the Dolls* Lazar), Christy Hartburg (as filling station floozy SuperLorna), Deborah McGuire (later Mrs. Richard Pryor, as deaf-mute motelier's daughter SuperEula), and barely glimpsed *Beneath the Valley of the Ultra-Vixens* starlet Ann Marie (as fisherman Garth *Vixen* Pillsbury's wife). The real discovery here though is Shari Eubank in the dual role of spiteful SuperAngel and her sweetiepie reincarnation SuperVixen. It's disheartening that she made only one other film (1975's *Chesty Anderson U.S. Navy*).

"Mighty meaty matey" lovelies aside, all the Meyer trademarks are firmly in place, which is just as it should be. The eclectic, often mismatched musical accompaniment; the outré camera set-ups; the zany, rapid-fire edits, some of the most outrageous shots – Charlie Napier's flaccid penis, its length and girth sufficient to make Dirk Diggler envious – flashing before you so fast that you can't even really be sure you've seen what you think you have. Rest assured, with Meyer you probably have. Once again the ubiquitous participant – he wrote, edited, produced, directed, operated the camera, and even found time for a one-shot cameo (as the bleary-eyed manager of a cheap motel) – Meyer's dabblings with misogyny are more prevalent than ever before. Although he often counteracted the humorous hijinks and eye-popping shots of bountiful chests with short bursts of violence, Sledge's brutal assault on SuperAngel in *Supervixens* is without doubt Meyer's most disagreeable brush with battery and it's extremely difficult to watch. After this, when Sledge kidnaps SuperVixen and stakes her to a rocky outcrop with a stick of fizzing dynamite between her legs, audiences are justified in being fearful of what horrors the director is about to subject them to. Fortunately Sledge's plans backfire and Napier's Oliver Hardy glance into camera as he realizes his number's up is a 24-carat

S

howler. Meyer's habit for throwing every bizarre idea on the screen, regardless of whether it makes any sense or not, is once again in evidence too, most notably when McGuire encounters a leopardskin-clad strongman in the middle of the desert, who steadfastly continues working out with his barbells while the lady gropes, goes down on and eventually straddles him for some up-and-down activity. Bizarre! That said, the shots of McGuire's pendulous assets roaming free as she bounces along through the desert in the back of a dune buggy is a sight once seen, never forgotten. But then doesn't that apply to so much of Meyer's work? *Supervixens* is SuperTrash of the highest order, and if you're just setting out on your exploration his movies, it's as good a place as any to begin.

The French Region 2 edition of *Supervixens* is a full screen average quality presentation, divided by 13 chapter stops. Sound is in English or French, and there's optional French subtitling. As with several other French Meyer titles, this release includes a generic trailer for all his movies and a textual interview / filmography / biography. The American release from RM Films is, as with their other efforts, a half-hearted port of their old master but loaded with compression errors and not even remotely worth the double dip, especially with their ridiculous pricetag. Best of the options by far is the Arrow edition, which features the best compression job, carries over the dynamic Image laserdisc commentary track with Meyer, and adds the original trailer as well as a bounty of other fantastic RM previews.

– TG

SWEET HOUSE OF HORRORS

Colour, 1989, 80m. / Directed by Lucio Fulci / Starring Cinzia Monreale, Pascal Persiano, Jean-Christophe Bretigniere, Lino Salemme / Shriek Show (US R1 NTSC) / WS (1.85:1) (16:9), VIPCO (UK R2 PAL)

This is a made-for-TV companion piece to *House of Clocks*; it is a gory oddity that finds Lucio Fulci returning to the theme of haunted children explored in his more widely seen *The House by the Cemetery* and *Manhattan Baby*, among others. As this is later period work for the director, the film's execution is bumpier than his golden age classics but still bears the unmistakable stamp of his gore-soaked obsessions.

Things start with a bang, literally, as a married couple is slaughtered in their home, with the husband's head pulverized against a wall and the wife viciously knifed. The children of the deceased, Sarah and Marco, become the charges of their aunt and uncle, Marcia (Cinzia Monreale) and Carlo (Jean-Christophe Bretigniere), at the family estate. Unfortunately the grounds seem to be haunted, much to the childrens' delight, and cruel mishaps befall visitors including a real estate agent and the neurotic gardener (*Demonia*'s Lino Salemme). Marcia is terrorized by the ghostly presence, which appears to manifest itself as a glowing, animated swirl of light; however, the spirits turn out to be as protective as they are ruthless, and the true villain is soon unmasked.

Apart from the sadistic opening (which is replayed later for good measure), *Sweet House of Horrors* is a competent but fairly restrained ghost yarn. The murder mystery angle is no great shakes, with the culprit unmasked and dispatched in an offhand manner long before the wind-and-thunder finale. Unlike *House of Clocks*, this film suffers from one of the most grating dubbing jobs in recent memory; though the actors often appear to be speaking English, the looped voices are so disembodied and inappropriate they constantly detract from Fulci's modest visual achievements. The children are a particular embarrassment, voiced by lousy adult voice performers who just yell in a high-pitched tone. It's enough to make the dubbing of Bob in *The House by the Cemetery* almost sound seamless.

VIPCO's Region 2 disc is merely functional, but Shriek Show's DVD sports the usual lavish extras for what once amounted to a throwaway title relegated to the graveyard of Japanese home video and bootleg traders. The letterboxed image quality looks very good overall, and the hazy '80s cinematography (a trademark of most of Fulci's work from the period) registers well enough with only a couple of darker scenes betraying any mild digital flaws. Extras include an introduction from the lovely Monreale (probably shot the same time as her interview from *Beyond the Darkness*, while video interviews go to Bretigniere, Salemme, and actress Pascal Persiano, all of whom offer their own recollections of working with Fulci. (For some reason, Bretigniere is mentioned nowhere on the box's special features.) Salemme has surprisingly little to say considering his oddball genre experience (both *Demons* films, for example), but the others are cheerful and more than forthcoming. Also included are the usual trailers, including an incredibly clumsy, bleary-looking promo for *Sweet House* that could single-handedly account for its lacklustre international distribution.

motorcycle enthusiast – meet at a coffee shop and discuss their unorthodox sex lives. Inoue fondly recalls a tryst on the commuter train that morning, while the biker is still reeling from a retaliatory rape against his unfaithful girlfriend. Together they set out on a nocturnal adventure which, thanks to an O. Henry-style twist, leaves them unaware of how drastically their fates have changed.

A fairly typical example of the Pink genre, *Tandem* is better suited for fans of off-kilter Asian cinema than randy viewers of late night fare, thanks to the restrictions of Japanese cinema; at the time it was made frontal nudity was strictly forbidden, with more oblique thrills delivered through the cultural violation of women. Politically correct it certainly isn't, though the moralistic implications of the ending go some way to redressing these attitudes. The DVD (which sports a misleading running time of one hour on the packaging) for this glorified short film looks fairly ragged with bleary colours, though this appears to have been shot on a very low budget (common for this genre) and transferred rather hastily. Ditto for the audio, which is serviceable but nothing spectacular. The disc contains a text overview of pink cinema and a trailer for *Pervirella*.

TANDEM

Colour, 1994, 43m. / Directed by Toshiki Sato / Starring Hotaru Hazuki, Yuri Ishihara / Screen Edge (UK R0 PAL) / WS (1.66:1)

Sort of a Japanese porn response to the subway scene from *Risky Business*, this later period *pinku eiga* effort mixes furtive commuter sex with art house pretension. Late at night, two men – one a middle-aged businessman, Mr. Inoue, and a young

TAXI ZUM KLO

Colour, 1981, 98m. / Directed by Frank Ripploh / Starring Frank Ripploh, Bernd Broaderup / Pro Fun (Germany R2 PAL) / WS (1.66:1) (16:9), Cinevista (US R1 NTSC)

T

After Nagisa Oshima's *In the Realm of the Senses* opened the floodgates for explicit sexual content in art house films, it was only a matter of time before gay cinema caught up. The first international hit to run with this concept was Germany's *Taxi zum Klo*

(which translates as "Taxi to the Toilet"), a semi-autobiographical portrait directed by and starring the late Frank Ripploh. Often funny, the film presents its more graphic material in a matter of fact style which integrates well with the story; while some may feel it's just shock for shock's sake, the film does have a point to make and swerves into unexpectedly poignant, politically charged pre-AIDS territory in its final third.

A schoolteacher by day, Frank enjoys a rampant sex life and spends his evenings having humorous encounters with his cadre of close friends. He often cruises public toilets for action but decides to change his ways once he starts a relationship with the well-meaning Bernd (Bernd Broaderup). Unfortunately Frank's libido forces him to continue his anonymous sexual encounters, which puts an increasing strain on their relationship. Things go from discomfiting to worse when Frank attends the yearly Queen's Ball in full drag, which has unexpected consequences at work the following morning.

Wholly unapologetic and unashamed, *Taxi zum Klo* goes light years beyond the frank performances of Rainer Werner Fassbinder in his own films. Ripploh puts himself through a number of compromising positions (both emotionally and physically) throughout the film and actually manages to make his cad of a character somewhat sympathetic, even through his various infidelities. It's hard to imagine that a film this extreme actually packed in mainstream audiences during its initial release; the decades of confessional art cinema ever since have done very little to blunt the impact of this unique and highly personal film, which makes up for its technical shortcomings with sheer force of personality.

The German DVD from Pro Fun features a "director's cut" which, in the style of *Picnic at Hanging Rock*, actually runs slightly shorter and shuffles some of the sequencing around. The disc features no English language options but does sport a solid (albeit understandably grainy at times) anamorphic transfer. By comparison the American disc from Cinevista is a lazy job, culled from their ancient video master from the 1980s. Blurry, burned-in English subtitles and the preservation of the original theatrical cut make this the disc's marginal high points, but frankly a videotape would do just as well. No chapter stops, shoddy packaging and a dull menu design add to the air of disinterest.

TEMEGOTCHI

Colour, 1997, 88m. / Directed by Wellson Chin / Starring Law Lan, Ruby Wong, Wong Man Yee, Dayo Wong, Wellson Chin / Universe (HK R3 NTSC) / WS (1.77:1) / DD2.0

This is a reasonably effective and thoroughly entertaining killer-kid/possession movie from Hong Kong, directed by Wellson Chin who specialises in this type of low-budget exploitation and horror film (and who cameos as a policeman in this one).

When little Ting Ting Wang (an impressive debut by Wong Man Yee) fails to turn up for school after a few days, her worried teacher Miss Tsui (the ever-reliable Law Lan) pays a home visit to find out the reason for her absence. What she discovers in the dimly lit coffin shop that is Ting Ting's home sends her over the edge into gibbering, homicidal frenzy and is the beginning of a terrifying series of supernatural events that seem to centre on the orphaned tot, who is taken under the wings of the Hong Kong Social Services. In a state of what appears to be shock-induced muteness, Ting Ting is unable (or unwilling) to help the police or her social worker Sam (the lovely Ruby Wong). A hospital check-up reveals the signs of recent and persistent physical abuse; the girl's fragile body is a mass of bruises and scars. It turns out that her late guardians were responsible for this barbarity. Ting Ting's real parents are both dead, her mother only recently from illness. During a night spent under observation in the hospital a nurse who has been given the run-around by Ting Ting vanishes under mysterious circumstances...

Taken to a local orphanage, Ting Ting's woes continue as she is sexually abused and harassed by an employee nicknamed Uncle Cheung. However he soon dies in a freak accident in which Sam is seemingly implicated, though the orphanage director has reason to suspect that the eerie child is the true cause. In fact all who come into contact with Ting Ting seem to come to sticky ends, including a would-be adoptive family. And that missing nurse has turned up at last... very dead! Sam's police boyfriend Wen (Dayo Wong, also seen in *666: Satan Returns*), annoyed and frustrated at his girlfriend's insistence that Ting Ting is to blame in some way, sets out to clear Sam's name and solve the mystery. However, before long he too lies dead, another victim of the curse that seems to surround the mysterious mite. Released from her cell to identify Wen's body, Sam decides enough is enough and sets off for the orphanage, for a gripping confrontation with Ting Ting and the evil force that protects her.

Temegotchi is a worthy attempt at a sub-*Omen* possession tale, mixing in a doppelganger theme for good measure. This aspect certainly keeps the viewer guessing right up until the final enigmatic moments. The central roles of Sam and Wen are played fairly straight, with minimal humour, allowing for the viewer to sympathise with them more than is sometimes possible in the often slapstick-dominated Hong Kong genre cinema, and Law Lan's Miss Tsui gives good value as the caring teacher who is driven mad by Ting Ting's grim guardian angel (she's also responsible for one of the better 'severed finger' gags to date). As Ting Ting, newcomer Wong Man

Yee is excellent, projecting alternate jolts of fragility and terror to the viewer. The subtext of child abuse is handled with due sensitivity by director Wellson Chin (who refused to direct Category III films), from a well-written script by Laurence Lau, and is not dwelt on long enough to become either preachy or prurient. Interestingly, Ting Ting is ultimately revealed as being a focus for evil rather than the cause of it: no "bad seed" she! Parts of the film show a familiarity with classic Euro-horror cinema. Scenes of Ting Ting playing with her white ball, dressed in white herself, cannot help but remind one of the scenes with ghost girls in Mario Bava's *Kill, Baby... Kill!* and the sublime final Fellini-directed story in *Spirits of the Dead*. The title, spelling changed to avoid Japanese copyright infringement, here refers not to a computerised "pet" but the brightly coloured cassette player that accompanies Ting Ting everywhere, which plays a gentle Chinese lullaby sung by her dead mother, a suitably creepy *leitmotiv* to accompany the prowling Steadicam of DoP Tsang Tat Sze.

This all region NTSC DVD from Hong Kong label Universe is a special edition of sorts. As well as the Category IIB-rated film, which is letterboxed at about 1.77:1 (non-enhanced), there is a choice of either Cantonese or Mandarin soundtracks and removable subtitles in three languages, including English. The transfer is pretty good overall, though some artefacting and digital smearing is at times evident. The English subtitles suffer occasionally from gobbledygook, and offer up some hilarious translations: the doctor diagnosing Ting Ting's trauma refers to the fact she's been tortured and has witnessed two murders, commenting, "It's troublesome for a little girl to have such encounters!" No kidding! We also get the trailer, star files, an interactive interview with Ruby Wong and a lengthy (non-subtitled) clip of the film's Hong Kong Premiere, the highlight of which is Wong Man Yee, clearly over-awed by her surroundings, shyly mumbling her way

through a brief interview, then on request reprising her trademark "sinister scowl!" Now deleted, this DVD can still be found and is well worth picking up for fans of Hong Kong horror or killer-kiddy flicks.
– NB

TEN DAYS' WONDER

Colour, 1972, 105m. / Directed by Claude Chabrol / Starring Orson Welles, Anthony Perkins, Michel Piccoli, Marlène Jobert / Pathfinder (US R1 NTSC) / WS (1.66:1)

Awakening in a delirious haze, rich young Charles Van Horn (Anthony Perkins) finds his hands covered in blood and fears he may have committed a murder. He seeks the aid of rational professor Paul Regis (Michel Piccoli), who goes to Paul's home and encounters a dizzying array of peculiar characters and even more peculiar misdeeds which, by the end of the film, violate each of the Ten Commandments (one for each of the ten days in the story, of course). As it turns out, Paul has been having an illicit affair with Hélène (Marlène Jobert), the young wife of his powerful father, Theo (Orson Welles). Blackmail, murder and jealousy mount in this lavish household, with a surprising unmasking leading to an unexpectedly tragic (but deeply ironic) conclusion.

Nominally based on a book by pseudonymous mystery author Ellery Queen, this audacious and often bewildering film packs as many ideas as Claude Chabrol can manage to stuff into less than two hours. The cultured inhabitants spin out endless observations about philosophy, finance and art, oblivious to the insanity brewing in their midst and incapable of facing their neuroses head on. Most of the international cast fares very well, and Welles has one of his strongest latter day roles as the

betrayed patriarch, alternately imposing and sympathetic. Perkins is his usual twitchy self (and does his only nude scene, for what it's worth), while Piccoli turns in yet another sleek, assured performance.

Pathfinder's disc looks adequate for the most part, though the opening credits and the countdown interstitials look very smudgy and dupey (apparently lifted from another source). Detail is a bit on the dull side, while colours range from bright and eye-popping (especially the brief hallucination sequences) to slightly grungy. The film can be viewed in English (the original track), French or Spanish, with no subtitle options. The usual Chabrol commentary crew, F.X. Feeney, Andy Klein and Wade Major, appear for the alternative audio track; the first half is peppered with some good background information about the creation of the film, but the anecdotes tend to dry out during the second half. Also included are the English trailer, a stills gallery and filmographies.

TEN LITTLE INDIANS

Colour, 1987, 129m. / Directed by Stanislav Govorukhin / Starring Tatyana Drubich, Vladimir Zeldin, Aleksandr Kajdanovsky / CP Digital (Russia R0 NTSC) / DD5.1

You know the routine: ten people are invited to an island for the weekend, an unseen host informs them that they are all criminals who will be executed, and one by one they're killed off, leaving a handful of survivors to deal with the confounding puzzle. This classic Agatha Christie mystery has been filmed both officially and, ahem, unofficially many times; the masterful 1945 version by René Clair remains the one to beat, while subsequent adaptations took place in Switzerland, Iran, and even the savannas of Africa. That's not even counting *Gumnaam*, a Bollywood musical version, or heaven help us, an '80s porno remake (*Ten Little Maidens*). Comparatively speaking, Russia's 1987 version is extremely faithful to its source material and actually feels like the product of a much earlier era. Set in the 1930s and lensed with a moody, grey-tainted palette, this version (originally titled *Desyat negrityat*) drops the witty, tongue in cheek approach which characterizes the other cinematic variations. Here the characters are haunted by their dark secrets, the deaths are shocking and painful, and in a movie first, the story winds up with the original nihilistic coda from Christie's novel, not the happier resolution of her play version, which other directors preferred. The decision to go downbeat is a courageous one and pays off in some interesting surprises, particularly the eerie final shot. Surprisingly this version also ratchets up the exploitation factor; the first death (a poisoning at dinner) climaxes with the victim taking a gory plunge into his place setting, which leaves a smashed plate and wine glass skewered into his face and hands. There's even a discreet but intense love scene between the two nominal heroes, Miss Claythorne (an appealing and lovely Tatyana Drubich) and Mr. Lombard (Aleksandr Kajdanovsky). What would Dame Agatha say?

Previously known only to Russian-speaking audiences, this superior mystery has finally been given its due with an erratic but welcome English subtitled version on DVD. Contrary to the packaging, which promises a 16:9 presentation, the transfer is actually full frame and taken from an obviously worn print. Apart from the debris on the source material, overall the video appearance is acceptable given the deliberately washed out colours. A gimmicky 5.1 track suffers from some distracting audio dropouts and awkward phasing between channels; the 2.0 stereo track is actually superior with a much smoother sound mix. Optional English or Russian subtitles are available; the subtitles convey the essence of the story but suffer from awkward misspellings and clumsy paraphrasing. The packaging and menus retain the politically incorrect original British title of the novel (*Ten Little Niggers*), while retailers tend to stock the film as *Ten Little Indians*. (On the other hand, the subtitle translation refers to the ten title figures as "little Negro boys", which is hardly an improvement.) The menus can be accessed in either Russian or English, and the extras are limited to cast filmographies and a gallery of other titles available from the same DVD company.

THE TENANT

Colour, 1976, 125m. / Directed by Roman Polanski / Starring Roman Polanski, Isabelle Adjani, Shelley Winters, Melvyn Douglas, Rufus, Jo Van Fleet / Paramount (US R1 NTSC, UK R2 PAL) / WS (1.85:1) (16:9)

The first of Roman Polanski's evocative Parisian thrillers, *The Tenant* was widely reviled upon its initial release for what many perceived to be a far too drastic change of pace from the celebrated *Chinatown*. Of course, anyone who could connect the dots further back could see its progression from the similar "apartment living is hell" studies, *Rosemary's Baby* and *Repulsion*; furthermore, the film looks forward in striking ways all the way up to *The Pianist*, which virtually reprises this film in a more compact form during its middle act.

Polanski assumes the lead role of perpetually nervous Trelkovsky, a French citizen originally from Poland who rents a room in a Gothic apartment building populated by a testy concierge (Shelley Winters), cantankerous landlord Monsieur Zy (Melvyn Douglas), and a variety of other eccentrics. The previous tenant,

Simone Choule, committed suicide by leaping from the balcony then suffering for days in the hospital, where Trelkovsky meets Simone's friend, Stella (Isabelle Adjani), with whom he shares a drink and a memorable afternoon at the movies. As the neighbours become increasingly hostile to Trelkovsky by complaining about noise and bullying him for not signing a petition, the man's grip on reality begins to slip. Even worse, these bizarre neighbours (who often spend hours at night standing motionless in the communal toilet) may be conspiring to drive Trelkovsky to follow in Simone's doomed footsteps.

A rich and multi-layered film, *The Tenant* is as pure a distillation of Polanski's technique as one could hope for. The repetition of themes and images can still cause chills after repeated viewings, though often the shudders overlap with skilfully handled black comedy. (Often it's difficult to tell the difference between the two.) The film remains even more relevant now in its study of urbanized human beings as commodities unable to relate to each other on any meaningful level; Trelkovsky and Stella's nervous dates include a few furtive gropes but end with cold farewells or both parties in a drunken stupor. In this world, everyone is identified solely by their outward appearances and how well they conform to expectations; you are the coffee you drink, you are the cigarettes you smoke. The enigmatic Simone Choule is identified as a writer on Egyptology, and indeed her apartment for Trelkovsky becomes a smothering tomb filled with remnants of the dead: make-up, a sole black dress, with the bathroom across the way adorned with hieroglyphics. Choule herself in the hospital is only seen mummified in tight bandages, inarticulate and screaming in horror. This utter disconnect is reinforced by her grieving friend, Georges (Jeunet and Caro regular Rufus), whose raw declaration of love on a postcard of King Tut turns out to be something else entirely. In a world like this it's small wonder an outsider would be

driven mad, and even a pure soul like Stella winds up wounded in this storm of insanity.

As eerie and thematically bewitching as *The Tenant* is, the film is boosted further by highly inventive casting. Adjani is wonderful as always, while Americans Winters, Douglas, and a chilling Jo Van Fleet (as the nasty Madame Dioz) all perform their supporting parts with expert aplomb. Opening with a startling Louma crane credits shot that probably influenced Dario Argento's *Tenebrae*, cinematographer Sven Nykvist (best known for his work on Ingmar Bergman films) performs some of his finest work; there's never a wasted bit of screen space for the entire running time. The film also marked the first of three collaborations between Polanski and composer Philippe Sarde (*Tess, Pirates*), a fruitful union destined to end badly. Be warned, the eerie glass harmonica main theme will stick in your mind long afterward.

Paramount's highly satisfying DVD offers a sterling visual presentation with robust colours and exceptional black levels, essential to appreciating the disturbing final third of the film. Previous transfers were often washed out, but this disc corrects those years of video abuse. Compared to past editions, the disc adds some information to the sides of the image while losing a bit of extraneous headroom from the top; compositions look accurate throughout. The audio has always sounded rather muffled, which unfortunately is the case here as well; prepare to turn up the volume far more than normal. In the English language version, only Polanski, Winters, Douglas and Van Fleet spoke their own performances; everyone else was dubbed afterwards and can be seen speaking a mixture of English and French. The alternative French audio on the disc (which can be viewed with optional English subtitles) is in many ways a more effective and satisfying presentation, as supporting characters who were brash and sloppily dubbed in English come off as far more naturalistic in French. The French track offers the only opportunity to hear Adjani's real voice, while Polanski did dubbing duties for himself as well. Newcomers may want to stick with the English version first, but the alternative audio makes for a rewarding experience as well. And yes, that troublesome *Enter the Dragon* clip with Bruce Lee, which caused more than a few legal headaches and even had to be trimmed out of some U.K. versions, is here in all its glory. The sole extra is the creepy U.S. trailer, which utilizes original footage of Polanski standing in a doorway.

TETSUO: THE IRON MAN

B&W, 1988, 64m. / Directed by Shinya Tsukamoto / Starring Tomorowo Taguchi, Kei Fujiwara, Shinya Tsukamoto / Tartan (UK R0 PAL, US R1 NTSC), Image (US R0 NTSC), Raro (Italy R2 PAL)

Tetsuo, a fairly common Japanese given name, can be written with the characters for "metal" and "man"; whether either or both the male leads are called Tetsuo is open to question since this is the sort of film that gives its characters labels rather than names. The title appears onscreen in English and Japanese, a repetition lost in the export title *Tetsuo: The Iron Man*. This black and white hour-long feature, shot on the cheap with a lot of imagination and enterprise, follows mutating characters through an industrial Japanese Hell. It attracted enough attention to lift its young director out of the semi-underground, though Shinya Tsukamoto has hardly modified his vision for such literally hard-hitting bigger-scale efforts as *Tokyo Fist* and *Tetsuo II: Body Hammer*.

A bespectacled and besuited salaryman (Tomorowo Taguchi) suffers from nightmares of transmutation on the subway and at home, while a scrapheap casualty (director Shinya Tsukamoto) enjoys ramming bits of pipe into his open wounds. It emerges that the salaryman knocked the street kid down in a hit and run accident, then engaged in frenzied sexual congress with his girlfriend (Kei Fujiwara) in front of the apparently dying youth. However, the victim has survived and his techno-infection has passed on. The antagonists transform into hideous half/man, half/machine, all/monster creations, a stainless man of steel and a rusty man of iron, and alternately indulge in even more frenzied (and painful) sexual congress or try to drill, slash, hack and splatter each other to bits. With monster costumes that seem like the X-rated equivalent of the tatty outfits that used to crop up on *Doctor Who* (cf: "The Claws of Axos") or *Lost in Space* (cf: "The Great Vegetable Rebellion"), this features some of the strongest screen stuff of the '80s: at one point, the antihero sprouts a pneumatic drill penis and his girl rides him to a messy death, redecorating the wall; earlier, in a dream, she had turned into a dusky silent movie siren and sodomised him with a mechanical snake appendage.

Painful, funny, pretentious, repetitive and pointed, this evokes the visions of Akira Kurosawa (*Do'des-ka Den*, inspiration also for *Street Trash*), David Cronenberg (the "handgun" of *Videodrome*), Sogo Ishii (the Einstürzende Neubauten video "Halber Mensch") and David Lynch (the industrial fantasyland of *Eraserhead*) but delivers its own shrieking kabuki horror, with especial attention to the clanging, clashing soundtrack. It winds up with a pixilated battle through the city streets, using animation techniques borrowed from Mike Jittlov (*The Wizard of Speed and Time*) and Jan Svankjmajer (*Dimensions of Dialogue*), as two mutants chase and hack each other with Marvel Comics verve, finally achieving both communion and destruction.

Tartan's Asia Extreme DVD offers a fullscreen transfer of a film shot on 16mm, mixing some segments that have a deliberately rough video-grain look with others that offer much lusher contrasts. The full spectrum of light and shade is employed in the film, so the quality of monochrome really matters – paying off in an extremely textured feel, with rust, oil, blood, steel, flesh, sweat, wire and dirt all distinguishable from one another. There are optional Japanese subtitles, though the film has so little dialogue you could easily watch a third of it without realizing you've selected the no-subs choice. The Dolby Digital soundtrack works wonders with material that could just devolve into a lot of noise – rhythmic metal music, industrial grinding sounds, screams of transcendent agony, squelching and tearing, whirring machinery, belching steam and flame. The extras are trailers for both *Tetsuo* films (and others from the Asia Extreme line), filmographies for the creatives and useful notes by Justin Bowyer. *Tetsuo* was also released on U.S. DVD from Image Entertainment but is now discontinued; Tartan's subsequent U.S. edition is, alas, something of a botch, with a badly-compressed transfer that renders the film nearly unwatchable.

Italy's Raro issued a remarkable box set edition, which includes *Tetsuo* along with its sequel and Tsukamoto's experimental forebear, *Denchu Kozo No Boken*, accompanied by a well-illustrated 120-page booklet.

– KN

TETSUO II: BODY HAMMER

Colour, 1992, 81m. / Directed by Shinya Tsukamoto / Starring Tomorowo Taguchi, Kei Fujiwara, Shinya Tsukamoto, Nobu Kanaoka / Tartan (UK R0 PAL), Manga (US R1 NTSC), Raro (Italy R2 PAL)

In this sequel-cum-remake, Tsukamoto ups the budgetary stakes on *Tetsuo* by adding colour, feature-length and a script that supports its primal imagery and spectacular mutations with a proliferation of incident and something approaching a backstory. However, the alterations are cosmetic, serving like the iron shell the protagonist grows to make the project sturdier rather than alter or even extend the subject. Tsukamoto films in colour but deliberately limits the palette to oily blacks, battleship greys and the occasional blotches of blue, green and dark red, giving the effect if not of monochrome then of a minimally tinted comic strip.

The plot is a leftover from *Scanners*, a flesh-twisting sibling conflict between the mutating rival sons of a mad visionary scientist. A suit-and-glasses Japanese urban man (Tomorowo Taguchi) is targeted by an underground movement of mutating skinheads who kidnap and horribly murder his young son. Assaulted with a rivet-gun, Taguchi mutates, sprouting pipe-like guns from his chest and gradually turning into a human tank. An internal coup in the mutant faction brings to power a sleek young monster (Tuskamoto) who enters into personal conflict with Taguchi, his long-lost brother.

The brutal heterosexuality of *Tetsuo* is displaced onto the mutant brothers' father, seen killing his wife while making love in a flashback, while the gay subtext is emphasised more with many scenes of muscular young men penetrating each other with bloody pipes. The emotional register is extended slightly to include Taguchi's grief at the callous slaughter of his son and Nobu Kanaoka's steadfast love for her cyborg husband, but these turn out to be minor tweaks on the machine, which chiefly consists of loving examinations of mutants who seem the illegitimate offspring of surrealist sculptures from Survival Research Laboratories and *kaiju eiga* (Japanese monster movies). With humorous and repulsive special effects, accompanied by an appropriately grinding soundtrack, the film piles more and more debris on Taguchi, finally signalling his continued individuality by leaving his eyes alive in the dead mass of metal meat, as in *The Quatermass Experiment*, but also, in a wittily grotesque touch, allowing him to retain his blinding white and bizarrely expressive human teeth.

Tartan's DVD offers a fullscreen transfer that represents the muted colour well but tends slightly to streak, lacking the b&w subtleties of their *Tetsuo* disc. The Dolby soundtrack highlights the excellent Chu Ishikawa metal score. It has optional English subtitles, a stills gallery, trailers for both *Tetsuo* films and the rest of the Asia Extreme line, and minimal notes by Justin Bowyer.

Viewers who would like to gain a greater insight into Tsukamoto's work are advised to pick up Raro's box set "Il fantasma di ferro", as described at the end of the *Tetsuo* review above.

– KN

THE TEXAS CHAIN SAW MASSACRE

Colour, 1974, 84m. / Directed by Tobe Hooper / Starring Marilyn Burns, Gunnar Hansen, Paul A. Partain, Jim Siedow, Edwin Neal / Dark Sky (Blu-ray & DVD) (US R0/R1 HD/NTSC) / WS (1.85:1) (16:9) / DD5.1, Universal (UK R2 PAL), Pioneer (US R1 NTSC) / WS (1.85:1) / DD2.0

"My family's always been in meat." The sensationalism of Tobe Hooper's low-budget regional horror masterpiece begins with its eye-grabbing, unforgettable title. It takes real guts to be so blatant up-front. More guts, in fact than are spilled in the movie. Nothing could possibly be as bloodily atrocious as title and poster ("Who will survive, and what will be left of them?") imply *The Texas Chain Saw Massacre* will be, so Hooper goes the other way. There are no real close-ups of open wounds (a gore film trademark since H.G. Lewis's *Blood Feast*)

and all limb-lopping happens out of shot (though viewers who cover their eyes and just listen to buzzing and screaming imagine things no non-snuff filmmaker could really put on screen). Instead of the single mummy of *Psycho*, which was also based on the real-life story of Wisconsin ghoul Ed Gein, Hooper has a whole houseful of human and animal remains artistically arranged to freak out the unwary visitor. Rather than Alfred Hitchcock's delicate, suspenseful manipulation, Hooper follows the lead of fellow independents George A. Romero (*Night of the Living Dead*) and Wes Craven (*The Last House on the Left*) and feeds the audience through a mangle of unrelieved horror and violence. Once his film starts, it doesn't let up until the fade-out: other horror films are as frightening, but few are so exhausting.

We begin deep, deep in the heart of Texas, where dead armadillos curl by the roadside, violated corpses are arranged like scarecrows, unfriendly locals snarl in incomprehensible accents and the '70s economic downturn means apparently abandoned farms and disused slaughterhouses. A group of vapid teenagers in a *Scooby-Doo* bus, with a whining cripple (Paul A. Partain) in place of the big dog, take a trip that ends when they unwisely enter an old, dark house. The apparent leading man, a real Freddy type, wanders down a filthy corridor towards a red room walled with animal trophies. Suddenly, without any Hitchcockian overhead shot to pre-empt the shattering shock, Leatherface – a squealing, obese goon in a tanned skin mask – appears from nowhere and smashes in the kid's head with a sledgehammer. Before you've had time really to register what you've just seen, the killer (Gunnar Hansen) slams an unexpected, grating steel shutter across the corridor and finishes off the still-twitching boy out of sight. Leatherface rapidly slaughters three more teen, using a meathook, the sledge, and a buzzing chainsaw. The fleeing Sally (Marilyn Burns), Daphne in white flares, is repeatedly caught in brambles and bushes that the killer easily saws his way through. The girl winds up at the mercy of the down-home cannibal clan, a combination of the Addams Family and the inbred rednecks from *Deliverance*. Out of work since the abattoir shut down, they keep to the old ways by treating passing strangers just how they used to treat beef cattle. The nameless degenerates (they become the Sawyers in the first sequel) are a parody of the sitcom family, with the bread-winning, long-suffering garage proprietor (Jim Siedow) as Pop, the preening, bewigged, apron-wearing Leatherface as Mom, and the rebellious, birthmarked long-haired hitch-hiker (Edwin Neal) as teenage son. The house is a similarly overdone, degraded mirror of the ideal home. Impaled clocks hang from the eaves, an armchair has human arms, and a hen is cooped up in a canary cage. Sally is served up at a family meal, presented to the centenarian half-dead Granpaw, "the best killer of them all..."

The film has outstanding sound effects, art direction and editing, and a clutch of effective, if necessarily one-note, performances. Unlike the notorious and comparable *I Spit on Your Grave*, *Chain Saw* is not a complete turn-off. If Hooper and his collaborators do not make their subject palatable, they at least succeed in justifying their film with sick panache. With its surprising amount of intentional comedy, the film is an important precursor of the horror comic style of Wes Craven's *The Hills Have Eyes*, Sam Raimi's *The Evil Dead* and Stuart Gordon's *Re-Animator*. A parting thought: in Texas, you are allowed to shoot dead someone who steps on your lawn. The kids are trespassing, so this murder spree probably isn't even illegal.

The film has already been issued in several extras-packed editions, and the U.K. DVD ports over features from previous laser and DVD releases while adding substantial new material. The film is presented in slightly too-tight widescreen but the transfer has been spruced up visually and aurally. *The*

Shocking Truth, a 72-minute documentary by David Gregory, separate filmed interviews with Hooper and co-writer Kim Henkel, and a commentary track – with Hooper, Hansen and cinematographer Daniel Pearl – cover the making of the film in exhaustive detail, with surprisingly few overlaps. Also: trailers (for this and all three sequels), deleted and alternative footage, bloopers, on-set test shots, stills, posters, lobby cards and web-links. The Region 1 Pioneer "Special Edition" suffers in comparison to the Region 2 disc due to the absence of the documentary, but the subsequent American edition from Dark Sky picks up the slack and more by including the documentary, a greatly-improved transfer from high-definition, and a spacious 5.1 mix guaranteed to rattle the nerves. (A handful of minor sound effects were somehow lost in the process on the first pressing, an oversight addressed by the company's replacement program.) The feature also contains the original commentary track, a new commentary with the cast and crew (Burns, Allen Danzinger, Paul Partain, make-up artist Robert Burns, and Gregory), two trailers and three TV spots, and a second disc that also contains Mike Felsher's marvellous 72-minute documentary, *Flesh Wounds: Seven Stories of the Saw*, an interview with the president of the film's fan club, footage of the cast and crew reunion, an 8-minute house tour with Gunnar Hansen, and the same deleted footage. Not surprisingly, Dark Sky also pegged this for one of their initial Blu-ray releases, a stunning HD rendering that should be enough to get horror fans to make the format jump by itself. All the extras from their DVD are carried over along with one new featurette, "Off the Hook", with actress Teri McMinn offering her own thoughts about becoming one of the screen's most notorious victims. Completists may want to hang on to the Pioneer release for the "Study in Filmmaking" featurette, but the Dark Sky version should be your first choice without hesitation.

– KN

THAT LITTLE MONSTER

B&W/Colour, 1994, 56m. / Directed by Paul Bunnell / Starring Melissa Baum, Reggie Bannister, Forrest J Ackerman / Elite (US R0 NTSC)

 An oddball roller-coaster ride through pop culture horror from 1930s Universal monster programmers via 1960s *Twilight Zone* surrealism, this hour long cult item garnered some fan word of mouth at festival screenings and through its VHS availability courtesy of Sinister Cinema.

After an amusing prologue, which finds *Famous Monsters* guru Forry Ackerman cautioning sensitive viewers about the nature of this film (à la one particular Universal horror classic), we meet young Jamie (Melissa Baum), a babysitter about to embark on a peculiar voyage thanks to her latest charge, a young infant with a very disturbing secret. The butler, Twelvetrees (*Phantasm*'s Reggie Bannister), cautions her about the danger of both her newest employers and their spawn, but of course she stays around for all the monstrous fun.

Stuck somewhere between a short film and a full feature, *That Little Monster*'s plot treads in the same territory as *Eraserhead* and *It's Alive* while conjuring up some unsettling narrative and visual tricks all its own. Most of the laughs come off quite well, including an unexpected celebrity cameo near the end that will leave many viewers scratching their heads. The camerawork is the real star here, capturing a queasy yet amusing ambience of eccentric terror in which the viewer's eye is given a workout through some amazingly odd cinematic gymnastics. Even at an hour this film can be difficult to take, especially for those who think Tim Burton's enforced weirdness can sometimes wear out its welcome; however, those predisposed to directors who have no idea when to quit will be able to overlook some of its flaws.

Most widely seen on the VHS edition distributed by Sinister Cinema, *That Little Monster* has been upgraded considerably for DVD. Though the source material still looks understandably grainy and overly contrasty at times due to the limited budget and film stock, the appearance here is overall quite satisfying. (And in what may be an odd homage to either Hitchcock's *Spellbound* or Roger Vadim's *Blood and Roses*, the single colour-tinted image is present and accounted for.) The disc also includes a commentary track by director Paul Bunnell with editor and producer Carl Mastromarino; they offer some vivid recollections of working on the film and explain how some of the most audacious visuals were accomplished for very little money. Also included is a 19-minute short film by Bunnell, "The Visitant", another nostalgia-laced horror project. Made in 1981, this mixture of George Romero and *The Twilight Zone* shows how far the director advanced technically in a fifteen-year period but makes for interesting viewing on its own. Finally there's what appears to be a cable access interview with Bunnell, who comes off as hyper and hammy, evidently the effect intended. The interview has a bemused air throughout and offers up a few clips from the film itself for good measure. Incidentally, ignore the unappealing cover art, tagline, and amateurish layout on the back of the box; that old saying about judging books by their covers undoubtedly applies to the DVD world, too.

THEM!

B&W, 1954, 92m. / Directed by Gordon Douglas / Starring James Whitmore, James Arness, Fess Parker, Edmund Gwenn, Joan Weldon / Warner (US R1 NTSC, UK R2 PAL)

An early entry in the 1950s cycle of creature feature pictures, this is the one about hordes of ants who have mutated to giant-size by the after-effects of the first A-bomb test. A very influential picture (see: *The Deadly Mantis*, *Earth vs the Spider*, *Beginning of the End*, etc.), it remains an exciting, persuasive exercise in paranoid science fiction, notably lacking the campier, teen-skewed aspects that came to dominate the big bug sub-genre later in the decade. It exhibits an interesting tension between cautious warning about man's irresponsible tampering with the atom and a Cold War vision of the authorities taking on extraordinary powers to combat a threat to the country (though it's a black and white film, we have to assume these monsters are red ants). When pilot Fess Parker claims to have seen ant-shaped "flying saucers", good guys who know he's sane ensure that he stays locked up in an asylum to prevent panic – perhaps the first instance of a government UFO cover-up in the movies.

It opens as an eerie desert mystery, with a New Mexico cop (James Whitmore) investigating disappearances and deaths – a mobile-home and a general store are crushed as if tanks have rolled over them, a shopkeeper is found dead of massive injuries and a huge injection of formic acid, quantities of sugar have been stolen (the film's sole straight-faced joke) and a catatonic little girl is shocked into shrieking "them, them!" Because one victim was a vacationing FBI agent, a local fed (James Arness) takes charge, and a plaster-cast of a strange imprint sent to Washington summons a father-and-daughter investigative team from the Department of Agriculture, cherubic Dr. Medford (Edmund Gwenn, providing warmth amid so many clipped uniform and fedora roles) and smart-suited professional Pat (Joan Weldon, with one of the masculine character names so often given female scientists in '50s films). There are personal touches – Arness's proprietary romantic interest in the lady entomologist – but this is mostly all business as the various law enforcement, military and scientific experts deduce the nature of the problem and take swift, decisive action to counteract the danger. The reveal of the monster, half an hour in, is textbook: a sandstorm, a high-pitched whine, investigators pottering about the desert, the heroine wandering off to collect samples, a giant anthead looming over a ridge. An educational film clip and a few fairly-sensible scientific bits (these giants didn't sprout overnight, but have come about because successive generations grew bigger than their forebears) might not squash arguments about the plausibility of the monsters' existence, but they do show a rare instance of a big bug film caring about niceties like actual insect behaviour. After a gruesome bit with a stripped-clean human ribcage tossed from monster mandibles onto a strew of other bones, a suspense-scare sequence worthy of Jack Arnold has the gas-masked leads investigate the supposedly wiped-out desert nest, taking flame throwers to the few dangerous survivors among the tunnels and the cyanide-pools. This sets up some fine suspense about two escaped queens ("technically, princesses", notes the boffin) who threaten to establish nests elsewhere. One ends up on a ship at sea, which leads to a nightmarish little vignette of the ants overwhelming a panicky crew, and the other takes refuge in the Los Angeles storm drains. After stern warnings, public announcements, and scenes whose script must read like the minutes of committee meetings, a touch of human eccentricity is provided in an alcoholics ward where a drunk ("make me a sergeant in charge of the booze!") has seen the monsters but assumes that they are hallucinations.

The storm drains finale is well-known and much-homaged (cf: *Point Blank*, *It's Alive*): it's a great use of interesting location, vehicles and extras loaned by the armed forces, and infallible heroism as one of the leads makes the supreme sacrifice to rescue a couple of missing kids. It ends on the regulation ominous note, as Gwenn wonders what future mutations will arise. Director Gordon Douglas, a solid journeyman from *Zombies on Broadway* to some late-'60s Frank Sinatra vehicles, does his most distinctive work here, with the large puppet insects impressively malign and the human cast lending conviction to the wilder passages. Few opticals are used because the film was originally to be shot in 3-D, but the reliance on physical effects makes for some striking imagery as carapaces are studded with bullet-pocks or whole ants are torched by flamethrower jets.

Warner's release of this much-loved title might not be as extras-packed as, say, Universal's *It Came from Outer Space* or *Creature from the Black Lagoon* discs but it does make a nice package. The transfer is smashing, with solid blacks and a nice selection of greys for the eerie underground and sandswept desert scenes – as in the original release prints, but few television or home video editions, the title leaps out in vivid red from an otherwise monochrome film. A witty tabloid menu that makes use of artwork and slogans from the wonderfully lurid 1954 poster (also on the box-cover) affords access to some fascinating alternative take and trim footage of the effects ants and a shrieking hard-sell ballyhoo trailer. The R1 disc has optional subtitles in English, French, Spanish, Portuguese and Japanese.
– KN

THIR13EN GHOSTS

Colour, 2001, 87m. / Directed by Steve Beck / Starring Tony Shalhoub, F. Murray Abraham, Shannon Elizabeth, Alec Roberts, Rah Digga, J.R. Bourne, Matthew Lillard, Shayne Wyler, Shawna Loyer, C. Ernst Harth, Laurie Soper / Warner (Blu-ray & DVD) (US R0/R1 HD/NTSC), Sony (Blu-ray & DVD) (UK R0/R2 HD/PAL) / WS (1.85:1) (16:9) / DD5.1

Recently widowed Arthur Kriticos (Tony Shalhoub) inherits a house from his late Uncle Cyrus (played by F. Murray Abraham), but little does he know what lies in store for him. With daughter Kathy (Shannon Elizabeth), son Bobby (Alec Roberts) and housekeeper Maggie (Rah Digga) in tow, he's escorted to the house by lawyer Ben Moss (J.R. Bourne). Lurking outside is Dennis Rafkin (Matthew Lillard), claiming to be from the power company but in truth Cyrus's highly perceptive psychic consultant; the old man, it seems, collected restless spirits of the dead for a hobby. An amazing edifice constructed entirely from reinforced glass, the house has an auto-locking mechanism which traps the sextet inside, whereupon they discover they're sharing their new abode with a cellar full of Cyrus's ghosts, pent up and decidedly angry about it.

An impressive curtain-raiser in an auto scrapyard as psychic Lillard helps ghost-stalker Abraham seize the malevolent spirit of a sadistic murderer kick-starts this revamp of William Castle's original spooker. Where Castle got audiences to don special specs to reveal the ghosts in his movie, first time director Steve Beck's film reserves this exclusively for the on-screen spectre spectators, which provides a few spine-tingling moments as the protagonists catch first sight of their deceased houseguests. And what a bunch of houseguests they are. In spite of his relatively high profile cast, Beck is smart enough to realise that the true stars of the movie are the ghosts, and he peppers the film with an eclectic bunch of ultra-freaky, wrathful and wretched monstrosities, the best of which are: Ryan Kuhn aka the Jackal (Shayne Wyler, with his caged head and manic gait); Dana Newman aka the Angry Princess (Shawna Loyer, wearing creepy black contact lenses and a disturbing line in self-inflicted all-over body scars); the revoltingly obese Harold Shelburne aka the Great Child (C. Ernst Harth); and diminutive Margaret Shelburne aka the Dire Mother (Laurie Soper).

Distinct highlights include Bourne's lengthways bisection by plate glass door, Elizabeth's unwitting encounter with the Angry Princess and a hair-raising attack by the grotesque Jackal. In spite of the presence of Rah Digga, who provides the fortuitously infrequent sassy comic relief (and also gets vocal for a rudely inappropriate end credits rap number), *Thir13en Ghosts* is played more for chills than chuckles. It's unquestionably an effects-driven piece but still harbours a strong story and sturdy performances from most of the players. Tony Shalhoub in particular, known mainly for comic outings such as TV's *Monk* and films like *Men in Black* and *Galaxy Quest*, is a pleasant surprise as the tortured widower forced to deal with the disfigured spirit of his dead spouse. Only Lillard lets the side down, bringing new dimensions to the term overacting. If you enjoyed the remake of Castle's *House on Haunted Hill* and you're in the mood for something of a similar ilk but with bags more energy, *Thir13en Ghosts* should fill the bill admirably.

The DVD editions do the film proud with a crisp 28-chapter 1.85:1 matted transfer that has bold, bright colours and aggressive use of the 5.1 surround mix. Sound on the U.K. one is available in either English or Italian, with subtitle options in English, Italian, Dutch and Hindi. Additionally there's an audio commentary from director Steve Beck, production designer Sean Hargreaves and FX supervisor Howard Berger on both, a short but interesting behind the scenes documentary, a text bio on William Castle and trailers for this and several other horror titles. The true highlight, however, is a featurette in which Abraham provides background data on the deceased occupants of old Cyrus's basement; it's all fictitious, naturally, but it's presented with plausible sincerity and there's some unsettlingly warped stuff to be found here. The same extras are present on Sony's

U.K. Blu-ray, an early adopter in 2007 that features a beneficial upgrade in quality that SD couldn't handle six years earlier. U.S. fans had to wait much longer until the end of 2010, when a bargain Blu-ray by American rights holder Warner was quietly issued on a double bill with the previously released "remake" of *House of Wax*.

– TG

THIS MAN MUST DIE

Colour, 1969, 107m. / Directed by Claude Chabrol / Starring Michel Duchaussoy, Jean Yanne, Caroline Cellier, Marc Di Napoli / Pathfinder (US R1 NTSC), Arrow (UK R2 PAL) / WS (1.66:1)

Another startling thriller from Chabrol's golden age, *This Man Must Die* (*Que la bête meure*) explores the devastating results when a young boy is killed in a hit and run accident near the shore. The victim's father, children's writer Charles (Michel Duchaussoy), vows revenge on the guilty party, Paul (*Le boucher*'s Jean Yanne). However, the situation is vastly complicated when Charles falls for Hélène (Caroline Cellier), Paul's sister-in-law, and becomes close to Paul's disaffected son, Phillippe (Marc Di Napoli). Charles records his homicidal plans in a diary, but as it turns out, the rest of the family might have even more cause to want Paul dead...

Though many critics compared Chabrol to Alfred Hitchcock throughout his career, few of the French filmmaker's classics really have much in common with Hitch. However, this film comes closest to justifying the Hitchcock comparison thanks to its obsessive meditation on the old transference of guilt theme, which takes on a devastating twist in the finale. Despite the morbid subject matter, the film is surprisingly humane and overflowing with a wide range of emotions;

even the most heartless and scheming of characters couldn't be classified as a villain in the traditional sense, a wonderful realistic trait of Chabrol present in many of his films.

Pathfinder's DVD is a mixed bag, featuring an extremely crisp transfer with better colours than any prior edition; unfortunately the PAL conversion results in some jarring streaking during several motion shots (especially the driving scenes), which can be headache-inducing on larger monitors. The disc includes the original French track (with optional English subtitles), English and Spanish dub tracks, the French trailer (no subs), and a stills gallery. The U.K. disc (also in Arrow's Chabrol box) contains only the French version with subtitles and no extras for what appears to be an identical transfer.

THRONE OF BLOOD

B&W, 1957, 105m. / Directed by Akira Kurosawa / Starring Toshirô Mifune, Isuzu Yamada, Akira Kubo / Criterion (US R1 NTSC), BFI (UK R2 PAL)

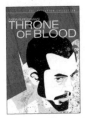

The first of Akira Kurosawa's masterful Shakespeare adaptations (followed by *Ran*), *Kumonosu jo* (known as *Throne of Blood* in English language regions, although the Japanese title actually translates as "Cobweb Castle") is sometimes dismissed as a work sandwiched between his two undisputed masterpieces, *Seven Samurai* and *The Hidden Fortress*. Perhaps the darker, more vicious tone and leaner running time make this film seem less "universal" than its companion features, but his dazzling Japanese twist on *Macbeth* shows the master filmmaker working at the peak of his cinematic powers and features set pieces as striking as anything he ever created. It's also the closest thing to a pure horror film in the Kurosawa catalogue, which makes it especially worthy of a look.

Following a successful battle, celebrated soldiers Taketori Washizu (Toshirô Mifune) and Yoshiteru Miki (monster movie regular Akira Kubo) wander into a forbidding forest, where a weaving woman with flowing white hair portends that both men will become tremendously successful. Spurred on by his ambitious wife (*Yojimbo*'s Isuzu Yamada), Washizu plots to kill the Emperor and usurp his throne, laying blame for the spearing death on the bloody hands of two framed guards. Ensconced in Cobweb Castle with his lust for power growing, Washizu begins to lose his grasp on reality and slaughters both his enemies and friends before a cataclysmic showdown of armies.

Beautifully atmospheric, with images similar to the Italian Gothic horrors of the 1960s, *Throne of Blood* draws influences from Japanese art, medieval army culture, and Elizabethan theatre, creating a wholly unique film which combines Kurosawa's exceptional epic skills with an intimate, terrifying story of human greed and destruction. The humorous or sympathetic Mifune seen in other Kurosawa films is nowhere to be found here; instead we get a grimacing mad dog, intent on climbing up the feudal ladder with an ever-increasing amount of blood on his hands. Yamada's character isn't as forceful as the traditional Lady Macbeth – perhaps due to cultural restraints, but Kurosawa presented far more ferocious women in *Ran*. Here she's more pathetic and insane, though her variation on the familiar "Out! Out, damned spot" mad scene is memorably performed. Like Roman Polanski after him, Kurosawa smudges the play's already precarious line between good and evil by making its nominal hero, Miki/Macduff, equally corruptible: tolerant of violence at his best and horrifically vengeful at his worst. The gruesome and intense finale still packs a punch (even De Palma couldn't quite surpass it in *Scarface*), with a flurry of arrows gory and impressive enough to make Tom Savini stop in his tracks.

T

As with Kurosawa's other black and white output, the original elements of *Throne of Blood* contain some inherent imperfections (grain and the occasional blemish) which will be obvious to those with a taste for digital perfection. That said, Criterion's disc is a sharp-looking piece of work, with beautiful gradation during the night scenes. The foggy opening sequence may not look promising at first, but once the film proper begins, this *Throne* has never looked better. The optional English subtitles are well paced and always legible, with not one but two different translations courtesy of Japanese-film translator Linda Hoaglund and Kurosawa expert Donald Richie. Japanese cinema scholar Michael Jeck contributes an informative commentary track; though it stays on the rehearsed and dry side, he dispenses countless useful bits of information including a detailed study of the Japanese theatre tradition's influence on the deliberately exaggerated acting styles. The package is rounded off with the original Japanese trailer (which spoils most of the highlights) and a text essay by Stephen Prince, who offers an overview of the film's various cultural influences. A movie-only version from Criterion is also out as part of their "Essential Arthouse" line, and a U.K. release from the BFI features a dingier transfer with only a couple of minor extras (text notes, bios, and a *Seven Samurai* trailer).

THROUGH THE LOOKING GLASS

Colour, 1976, 91m. / Directed by Jonas Middleton / Starring Catherine Erhardt, Jamie Gillis, Douglas Wood, Kim Pope, Al Levitsky, Terri Hall / VCX, TVX (US R0 NTSC)

One of the more successful attempts to create a mainstream level production in the adult film genre, the '70s surreal sex flick *Through the Looking Glass* plays like a particularly deviant homage to Federico Fellini, Ken Russell, Roger Vadim, and about a dozen other European directors, all served up in the context of a genuinely creepy horror movie. Our fairy tale gone bad centres around beautiful Catherine (Catherine Erhardt), a wealthy, sexually repressed woman enduring a sexless marriage to Richard (Douglas Wood). At their remote country estate she begins to pass the time by sitting in front of an ornate, antique mirror, which happens to contain a green-skinned demon (Jamie Gillis) who drags her into occasional romps through a series of supernatural realms. From trysting with another woman in a room filled with silver, glittering fabric, to a lavish garden party where the guests enjoy a particularly obscene centrepiece, Catherine loses herself in decadent fantasies which separate her even further from reality. After learning the backstory behind her sexually voracious demon, Catherine is finally torn all the way through the mirror for a nightmarish finale, with a little twist in the tale waiting at the end.

Carefully filmed and paced, *Through the Looking Glass* was released in both hard and soft versions; fortunately the visuals and story are strong enough to support it either way. Far from arousing, the hardcore material simply adds to the surrealism and the terrifying quality of Catherine's experiences, particularly a memorable Gothic sequence during a violent thunderstorm. Apart from Gillis and a turn by porn vet Kim Pope, the film includes a few other familiar faces including Al Levitsky (the guy who gets twigged in George Romero's *Martin*) and the ubiquitous Terri Hall as (what else?) a frisky maid. While '70s porn had flirted with the use of horror conventions before (most notably in *The Devil in Miss Jones*), this is the only film that really succeeds in both genres. Unfortunately director Jonas Middleton apparently retired after a brief grindhouse career; perhaps after this delirious achievement, there simply wasn't anywhere left to go.

If ever a film of this genre and vintage demanded a sparkling new digital transfer, this would be it. Unfortunately VCX's DVD recycles what appears to be the same bleary one-inch master sourced for the long discontinued VHS edition; black levels are especially weak and detail is soft. Colours are generally acceptable and accurate, but that's about it. Compression artefacts are abundant, particularly during the orange-lit finale. Unfortunately this remains the only widely available viewing option for the film, so those who are curious would be advised to watch it for the film itself, not for the DVD quality. The disc contains chapter stops and no extras. Incredibly, the much later reissue from TVX looks even worse!

THUNDERBIRDS ARE GO

Colour, 1966, 89m. / Directed by David Lane / Starring Sylvia Anderson (voice), Shane Rimmer (voice) / MGM (UK R2 PAL, US R1 NTSC) / WS (2.35.1) (16:9)

THUNDERBIRD 6

Colour, 1968, 86m. / Directed by David Lane / Starring Sylvia Anderson (voice), Shane Rimmer (voice) / MGM (UK R2 PAL, US R1 NTSC) / WS (2.35.1) (16:9)

As adjuncts to the luxurious box set of the classic Gerry Anderson *Thunderbirds* television series, the two theatrical spin-off features are available as individual discs with a pleasant smattering of extras. *Thunderbirds Are Go* is larger-scaled but more diffuse, with lots of wonderful sequences but a weak overall storyline. The main thread, which would be continued in the next Anderson series (*Captain Scarlet and the Mysterons*), is the Zero X space program of manned expeditions to Mars. After one test launch ends in the disastrous loss of the ship due to the intervention of a villain never explicitly identified as regular baddie the Hood (though stills show deleted scenes that would have done so), International Rescue are called in to provide security for the Mars shot, and foil a further evil scheme to infiltrate the crew. Then, we get impressive sequences that are still time-outs from the story: a wonderful dream in which Alan goes on a date with Lady Penelope to the Swinging Star orbital night-spot and is entertained by Cliff Richard Jr. and the Shadows (a striking effect is that only the principals are in colour – the background puppets are monochrome) and a creepy sequence on Mars as the Zero X astronauts (a colourless bunch perhaps considered for a spin-off series) encounter some persistently hostile fire-spitting rock snakes. The traditional Thunderbirds business comes into play during the finale, as the Zero X suffers a re-entry malfunction and International Rescue have to deploy their machines to rescue the crew – as was typical in the show, vastly expensive scientific programs are abandoned in an instant (the Zero X crash lands in a small town, with all data from the Mars mission aboard) and human life is paramount.

Thunderbird 6 is more coherent as a story, with Lady Penelope, Parker, Alan and Tin-Tin taking a round-the-world cruise on an anti-gravity airship designed by IR's resident genius Brains as an evil scheme by a villain (The Black Phantom) who looks exactly like a bewigged Hood (but has a different voice because Ray Barrett was unavailable) sets out to lure Thunderbirds 1 and 2 into a trap. It's perhaps lighter in tone, with a caper-style plot and more bizarre *Avengers/ Prisoner*-like sets (themed staterooms in the airship), but carried over from *Captain Scarlet* is a Bondian ruthlessness as we finally see actual deaths resulting from disaster or villainy. Especially striking are shots of Skyship 1 cruising against a sunset as the murdered crew are dumped one by one into the sea. An apparent sub-plot has patriarch Jeff Tracy insisting that Brains design a new Thunderbird but rejecting all his hi-tech designs, with the final wreck of the Skyship prompting the inventor to take to the field in an outmoded biplane, which becomes Thunderbird 6. Perhaps the most exciting "stunt" in the International Rescue canon is Brains's first attempt at landing on the upper hull of the airship, touching down but plunging over the edge. Also striking is a shoot-out amid the revolving metal circles of the anti-gravity engine.

Both films are presented in anamorphic widescreen, a Techniscope process supposedly better for Supermarionation than Panavision – an advantage of the widescreen shape is that it often clips off the visible wires (which are significantly less visible than in the TV show). The first reel of *Thunderbird 6* seems a touch rough-looking, but the rest of the film is as pristine and colourful as the earlier movie, with perhaps even prettier cinematography. The extras for the initial disc are trailers and stills/behind-the-scenes galleries and commentaries from producer-writer-Lady Penelope Sylvia Anderson and director David Lane, which provide a lot of backstage anecdote and some speculation as to the private lives of the puppet characters. Both films were revisited by MGM for special editions available separately or as a two-disc gift set (the second release in the U.K. and first in the U.S.). The first film gets three new featurettes ("History and Appeal", "The Factory of Dolls and Rockets", "Epics in Miniature"), a quote quiz, and an animated photo gallery. The second film also has three new video pieces ("Lady Penelope", "Building Better Puppets", "Tiger Moth"), a "Craft Mission Match-Up" quiz, and another photo gallery. It may be that the more sprawling feature-length was less suited to the Anderson style

than the 25 or 50-minute TV length, but the successive generations who have embraced these characters will still be delighted by the films.

– KN

THE TIME MACHINE

Colour, 2002, 96m. / Directed by Simon Wells and Gore Verbinski / Starring Guy Pearce, Jeremy Irons, Sienna Guillory, Samantha Mumba, Omero Mumba, Phyllida Law, Mark Addy, Alan Young, Orlando Jones / DreamWorks (US R1 NTSC), Warner (UK R2 PAL) / WS (2.35:1) (16:9) / DD5.1

Inconsolable after his fiancée Emma (Sienna Guillory) is shot dead in a mugging incident, scientist Dr. Alexander Hartdegen (Guy Pearce) devotes four years of his life to designing and constructing a fantastical carriage that can transfer its occupant across time. Travelling back to the dreadful night, Emma's fate, though different in its implementation, remains the same. Heartbroken all over again, Hartdegen decides to journey forward to see if the future holds the key to changing history. But an accident catapults him further than intended and he finds himself stranded in a post-apocalyptic 802701, an unrecognisable world with a wretched infrastructure in which mankind has divided into two disparate factions... the hunters and their prey.

Where younger audiences probably approached *The Time Machine* as just another Hollywood special effects extravaganza, those with an affection for George Pal's 1960 version of H.G. Wells's story harboured serious reservations. Well, the new picture isn't as good as the original – no one really ever expected it to be – but it's got more to offer than many anticipated, energised by a strong performance from Guy

Pearce and a cornucopia of show-stopping, eye-popping ILM f/x wizardry. With Simon Wells (great-grandson of H.G.) at the steering wheel, John Logan's screenplay adheres fairly closely to the story with which we're all familiar, while giving Pearce's hero more motivation than predecessor Rod Taylor had for conquering the boundaries of time. The rapacious, anthropophagic Morlocks have also been upgraded from the lumbering, green-skinned troglodytes of the original to a pack of agile and savage predators. Controlled via telepathy by a cerebrally advanced Uber-Morlock whose brain has developed through the back his skull and fused with the upper portion of his spine, they snare the peaceful Eloi and drag them down into the maze of tunnels beneath the Earth's surface. The Uber-Morlock (Jeremy Irons) – whose bizarre, S&M-outfitted appearance is saved for the penultimate act – is a malignant character, yet has a greater understanding of the follies of toying with time than does Hartdegen.

The time machine itself is all finely moulded brass fittings and huge, spinning refractive lenses which irradiate and bend light into a protective bubble that envelops the traveller. Hartdegen's first venture into the future – with the changes of season and then, as he accelerates, more than a century's worth of architectural and scientific progress rapidly taking place around him – is quite breathtaking. Although some of the visuals look a little too much like the computer-generated compositions that they are, others, such as the fragmentation of the Moon after man's disastrous attempt to colonise it, effect imagery that is hard to forget.

Pearce and Irons aside, singer Samantha Mumba equips herself well with a perfor-mance that proves she's got more to offer than an ability to carry a tune. Equally surprising is her little brother Omero, who made this reviewer revise his probably too generalised opinions of child actors. Phyllida Law and Mark Addy are Hartde-gen's housekeeper Mrs. Watchit and best friend David Filby respectively. Even the original film's Filby, Alan Young, shows up in a cameo as a florist, though his big moment is somewhat undermined when the viewer is distracted by the drama unfolding through the window behind him. The only character over whose presence I have mixed feelings is the photonic hologram librarian, Vox (Orlando Jones). First encountered by Hartdegen when he stops off in 2030, Vox is still around 800,000 years later. Although he's a convenient tool of exposition for explaining the circumstances under which the world has changed, he's also clearly intended to bring a splash of comic relief to the party and in this capacity he's most definitely an unwelcome guest. Oliver Scholl's production design is spectacular, from the cliff-hugging dwellings of the Eloi to the labyrinthine lair of the Morlocks, whose cannibalistic proclivities are vividly underscored when Hartdegen stumbles into their slaughter chamber and slips into a pit filled with rotting Eloi carcasses. On his first big budget production Klaus Badelt contributes a wonderfully exuberant, occasionally moving score. Gore Verbinski (*The Ring*), who handled a chunk of the directing chores when Wells was unable to continue, receives only a minor credit in the form of a thank you from the producers on the tail end of the closing credits. Although 2002's *The Time Machine* couldn't hope to match the near perfection of 1960's *The Time Machine*, both films function admirably as fascinating slices of science fiction that prompt conjecture as to just what the future might hold for antagonistic mankind.

The Region 1 DVD of *The Time Machine* (as does its Region 2 counterpart) delivers the film in its 2.35:1 theatrical ratio with a fault-free transfer boasting high levels of detail, colours so ripe they're fit to burst and impressive use of the various sound mixes. The 19-chapter punctuated feature offers sound choices in English DTS Digital, 5.1 Dolby Digital and 2.0 Dolby Surround, French 5.1 and Spanish 2.0.

There are two audio commentaries from director Wells, editor Wayne Wahrman, co-producer David Valdes, f/x supervisor Jamie Price and production designer Oliver Scholl. Supplemental goodies comprise a single five-minute deleted scene (which would have immediately followed the opening credits and slowed the pace immeasurably), four behind-the-scenes featurettes, a bulging gallery of production sketches and conceptual art, three trailers, and text notes on the production, its cast and crew. Subtitling is provided in English and Spanish.

– TG

TO THE DEVIL A DAUGHTER

Colour, 1976, 93m. / Directed by Peter Sykes / Starring Christopher Lee, Richard Widmark, Nastassja Kinski, Denholm Elliott, Isabella Telezynska, Honor Blackman, Anthony Valentine, Eva Maria Meineke, Michael Goodliffe, Lindy Benson, Jo Peters, Zoe Hendry, Bobby Sparrow, Brian Wilde, Francis de la Tour / Optimum (UK R2 PAL), Anchor Bay (US R1 NTSC) / WS (1.66:1) (16:9)

Excommunicated priest Father Michael Rayner (Christopher Lee) has spent years establishing a Satanic cult behind a facade of respectability. Because of a pact between Rayner and craven Henry Beddows (Denholm Elliott), on her eighteenth birthday his daughter Catherine (Nastassja Kinski) is to be subjected to a depraved ritual... and that's now only a matter of days away. With Rayner snapping at his heels, Beddows reneges on the transaction and contacts occult author John Verney (Richard Widmark), promising him information for his new book if he'll take Catherine under his wing. Verney agrees, but locking horns with Rayner takes him into a world of uncharted evil and a battle to protect Catherine from being baptised with the blood of the demon Astaroth, which will transform her into the Devil himself.

Towards the end of *To the Devil a Daughter* Nastassja Kinski fondles a grotesque, sputum-dribbling demon child and gently manipulates it up into her womb. It's a repulsive scene, especially by Hammer's standards, and yet it illustrates perfectly how desperate they were in the early '70s to compete with the big guns who were busily queering their pitch; U.S. product like *The Exorcist* and *The Texas Chain Saw Massacre* had upped the stakes in terror cinema, giving them a trouncing at the box office in the process. Hammer were testing all manner of waters in a bid to stay afloat, producing pictures of mixed merit ranging from spin-offs of lukewarm TV sitcoms (*Nearest and Dearest*) to cerebral thrillers (*Straight On Till Morning*), from responses to the martial arts craze (*Shatter*) to remakes of ageing classics (*The Lady Vanishes*). *To the Devil a Daughter* rode in on the coat-tails of such money-spinning supernatural fare as *Rosemary's Baby* and *The Exorcist*. Composer Paul Glass might easily have been listening to Jerry Goldsmith's stellar score for *The Omen* before lifting his baton. Though the results were somewhat unique for Hammer, in a direct comparison *To the Devil a Daughter* failed to conjure up the miasma of its peers and, based very loosely on a Dennis Wheatley novel, neither does it match the intensity of the company's earlier dabbling with the author's work, *The Devil Rides Out*. In fact Wheatley himself detested the film, which is a shame because, although it might not be faithful to his story, it's an engaging yarn. With Peter Sykes (*Demons of the Mind*) at the steering wheel and more cash in the coffers than usual, the production values went up and it shows, specifically in the extensive location work (with a lack of obvious studio interiors), taking in a beautiful setting on a German lake and some superb aerial shots over

London. Script problems may impede the coherence here and there, and not everything hangs together as well as it should, but the basic story is easy enough to follow and is punctuated by enough perversity to maintain interest. Aside from the aforementioned bit of business between Kinski and the demon child – which, in its debut appearance, looks like a malcontent rubber reject from *The Muppets and the Monster from Hell* (now there's a title with potential!) – Sykes drums up an extremely unpleasant scenario in which Isabella Telezynska has her thighs tightly bound together and endures the pain of labour until she splits. There's also a (very coy) orgy – with Christopher Lee body-doubled by stuntman Eddie Powell for his nude scene – during which eagle-eyed fans of '70s softcore cheapies might spot Lindy Benson, Jo Peters, Zoe Hendry and Bobby Sparrow. Brit sitcom watchers will be equally pleased with cameos from Brian Wilde and Frances de la Tour.

Of the principal players, Lee excels in all his scenes as the smoothly odious defrocked priest, be he foisting mental apparitions upon dishevelled bag of nerves Denholm Elliott, or grinning with malignant glee (when all around him look fit to vomit) as the devil's spawn emerges from its mother's torn womb. In a traditional Hammer pairing one can easily imagine Peter Cushing filling Verney's shoes, but the moneymen needed an American name up front and so we have Richard Widmark. He's actually rather splendid as the slightly crusty, worldly-wise opponent of the black arts. Nastassja Kinski (daughter of Klaus) was still in her teens at the time and although she spends a fair chunk of her scenes hidden beneath a nun's attire, even at this early stage she fostered a mesmerising screen presence. Honor Blackman gets the sharp end of a metal comb shoved through her temple, Anthony Valentine is reduced to a human fireball, Eva Maria Meineke pumps out her own life-blood to provide Lee's protective circle at the film's climax, and Michael Goodliffe

(who took his own life after completing the film) has his head bashed in by Widmark.

I first caught the film as the top half of a double bill and left the cinema rather disappointed, not only because it was the least Hammer-like Hammer film I'd ever seen but more pertinently that its co-feature (Bob Clark's *Black Christmas*) whipped it black and blue in the chills department. Yet with subsequent viewings I've warmed to it and though it's far from Hammer's best (and bears a frustratingly weak conclusion), as their final big screen excursion into horrorland *To the Devil a Daughter* remains a respectable enough swansong for one of the most prodigious and respected film companies of the 20th Century.

Anchor Bay's Region 1 release of *To the Devil a Daughter* is a splendid tribute to the film, offering a nice uncut 1.66:1 ratio transfer punctuated by 24 chapter breaks. The only minor gripe would have to be the detection of sporadically muffled sound during the early part of the film. But the picture quality makes up for that shortcoming: One look at the searing rainbow colours in the opening shot as sunlight pours through the chapel's stained glass window and across the floor, and you know you're in for a treat. A commentary was forsaken with this one, in its place a retrospective documentary. But what a documentary it is. Running 24 minutes, it charts the troubled path trodden by the filmmakers, with input from scripters Christopher Wicking and (uncredited) Gerald Vaughan-Hughes, producer Roy Skeggs, director Peter Sykes, and cast members Anthony Valentine, Honor Blackman and – of course – Christopher Lee. The only possible negative aspect of this fascinating exposé is that for anyone previously unaware of Widmark's unprofessional behaviour on set, the revelations here might tarnish the enjoyment of a subsequent viewing of the feature. Sweetening the deal further there's a British release trailer, a decent gallery of production stills, lobby cards and poster art from across the globe, and text bios for Widmark and Lee. The subsequent Optimum Region 2 release featuring the same excellent transfer adds an onstage video chat with Hammer stuntman Eddie Powell and is included in their recommended "Ultimate Hammer Collection" box set.

– TG

THE TOOLBOX MURDERS

Colour, 1978, 94m. / Directed by Dennis Donnelly / Starring Cameron Mitchell, Pamelyn Ferdin, Tim Donnelly, Wesley Eure, Marianne Walter / Blue Underground (Blu-ray & DVD) (US R0/R1 HD/NTSC) / WS (1.66:1), VIPCO (UK R2 PAL) (16:9)

 A maniac wearing a woolly ski mask is terrorising the residents of an apartment block, slaughtering female tenants with an array of power tools. The police are clueless and landlord Ben Kingsley (Cameron Mitchell) is at a loss to explain how anyone could be doing this in his secure complex. In the wake of a quartet of grisly homicides the perpetrator inexplicably alters his modus operandi and kidnaps young Laurie Ballard (Pamelyn Ferdin)...

Based (without a doubt very loosely) on a true story, The Toolbox Murders is the directorial product of one Dennis Donnelly who, keeping things in the family, cast his brother Tim in the role of the inept investigating detective. As a whodunit, or more precisely a whosdoingit, the film flounders badly since it's patently obvious from the get go that – unless Donnelly is going to pull a previously unseen rabbit out of his hat in the final reel – Kingsley, the owner of the complex, is the killer. As if to acknowledge the narrative's shortcomings, although there are four extremely nasty killings in the first half hour, shortly thereafter Mitchell's

character is unveiled and the pace slows up. It's at this point that the whole show shifts gear and what started out as a slasher film turns to psychological horror for the remainder of its running time with Kingsley, unhinged by the death of his daughter, revealing via a lengthy monologue how he believes he's doing God's work by cleansing the world of easy women. Laurie, it seems, reminds him of his deceased virginal offspring and so he deigns to keep her alive. The twist, if you want to call it that, is that Kingsley's nephew Kent (Land of the Lost's Wesley Eure), whom the audience has pegged as Laurie's potential saviour, turns out to have a trick up his sleeve as well. As an aside, one can't help but wonder whether Oscar-winning Brit thesp Ben Kingsley was ever aware of his insidious namesake in The Toolbox Murders!

Anyone with fond memories of Cameron Mitchell as lovable Buck Cannon in TV's High Chaparral, as well as a whole slew of TV and movie roles, is in for a double shock here; firstly that he should even be appearing in such an unpleasantly sleazy venture, but perhaps more than that how truly awful he is in it. His ineptitude proves contagious to the entire cast, who fail to muster a single convincing performance between them. Having earned most of its notoriety from the nail-gun assault on Marianne Walter (aka adult movie star Kelly Nichols), whom our executioner catches masturbating in the bathtub, this flick is trashy, unrelentingly grim (a facet cemented in by George Deaton's depressingly sombre score) and given to bursts of extremely graphic violence. Which, come to think of it, is probably all the recommendation some will need.

The horrible transfer on Britain's Region 2 disc of The Toolbox Murders (from VIPCO, king of cut cult epics) is so awful that, commensurate with the grimy feel of the film itself, it could almost provoke you to reach for the scrubbing brush and soap after handling it! Not so Blue Underground's eye-popping Region 1 edition, which affords the 23-chapter punctuated film a better clean-up job than it ever deserved, which in turn lends it a glossy sheen of respectability beyond imagination. Where VIPCO's wretched full screen R2 release emulates the dark picture and washed out, muted colours of earlier VHS incarnations (while adding a further handicap to the digital transfer in the form of unstable blacks), Blue Underground's 1.66:1 matted version is bright, colourful and virtually grain-free. It probably looks better than it did back in the late seventies when it toured the provinces on a double bill with Fulci's *Zombie* no less! More pertinent perhaps, where VIPCO's disc is missing a substantial amount of footage from the aforementioned slaying of Marianne Walter, Blue Underground's release is uncut. In the extras department Miss Walter drops in for a retrospective on-screen interview, recalling with good humour the fun she had working on the movie. Also present are a theatrical trailer, a TV spot, a pair of radio spots, a nice (if not particularly extensive) gallery of stills and poster artwork and a Mitchell bio. Producer Tony Didio and DoP Gary Graver team up with lead actress Pamelyn Ferdin for an entertaining audio commentary.

This fine DVD, one of Blue Underground's very first, paved the way for their Blu-ray upgrade, a stellar presentation featuring one of the best catalogue horror transfers around and a stiff competitor with the same company's *New York Ripper* for the most eye-popping presentation of a film you never thought would be treated so well. While the commercial elements of *The Toolbox Murders* are all rendered with startling clarity here (and yes, you can see every bit of detail in Walter's ungroomed nether regions), the film is also much more enjoyable in HD for its most aesthetic quality as a picture-perfect portrait of '70s San Fernando Valley life. Many apartments around Burbank still look the same (even down to the interiors and wall heaters), but the presentation here is a nonstop cavalcade

of tacky carpeting, wall ornamentation, neon-saturated bars, and lo-tech garages. The immaculate image quality might indicate something that was shot yesterday, but the production design clearly gives the game away. Top marks all around. The audio aspect isn't quite as impressive given the very limited nature of the original sound recording (Eure and Beauvy tend to mumble or slur some of their lines, so prepare to flip on those optional English, Spanish or French subtitles from time to time), but the music sounds great and all the screaming comes through loud and clear. The centre-heavy DTS-HD 7.1 mix offers a bit of minor ambient support to the more densely-mixed portions, but it really isn't all that different from the original mono mix (with a third 5.1 option coming somewhere in between). Apart from ditching the DVD's stills gallery, the BD carries over all the extras.
– TG

TRAGIC CEREMONY

Colour, 1972, 88m. / Directed by Riccardo Freda / Starring Camille Keaton, Luciana Paluzzi, Luigi Pistilli / Dark Sky (US R1 NTSC) / WS (1.85:1) (16:9)

Easily the most obscure colour horror effort from Italian horror trailblazer Riccardo Freda, this oddball Gothic potboiler never received much of a release in Europe (or anywhere else). Even in an age filled with neglected titles plucked from the jaws of oblivion, *Tragic Ceremony* (full title: *Tragic Ceremony at Villa Alexander*) may have a tough time winning converts unaccustomed to the bizarre state of Italian horror moving into the 1970s.

A vacation of sailing and exploring for pretty Jane (Camille Keaton, circa *Solange*) and three of her freewheeling young friends takes a turn for the worse when they wind up stranded in the countryside during a dune buggy expedition. They take refuge at a remote palatial estate run by Lord and Lady Alexander (*Twitch of the Death Nerve*'s Luigi Pistilli and *Thunderball*'s Luciana Paluzzi), a peculiar noble couple hosting some friends for the evening. That night Jane finds her sleep interrupted by strange noises, and as she drifts through the mansion by candlelight, she happens upon her hosts engaging in some Satanic devilry, which quickly turns into a potential sacrifice. Much graphic bloodshed ensues, with Jane and company fleeing for their lives into the night. But the nightmare is far from over...

First shown in Italy as *Estratto dagli archivi segreti della polizia di una capitale europea* (or *Taken from the Secret Police Archives of a European Capital*), this film is far more strange and intriguing than its milquetoast monikers would lead you to believe. Lurching between '60s style Gothic atmosphere, Jess Franco-style reality bending and possessions, and trendy gore (including one outrageous cranium splitting), *Tragic Ceremony* doesn't do much to advance its director's artistic growth but does represent a weird collision between the rigorous formalism of his Gothic classics and the surreal nastiness of his last film, *Fear* (*Murder Obsession*). (The same could also be said for Freda's sadistic *giallo* filmed one year earlier, *The Iguana with the Tongue of Fire*.)

Keaton looks beautiful and striking as always, but as with her other European efforts, she's more of a reactor here than an active heroine and barely manages to carry the film. More interesting are pros Paluzzi and Pistilli, though they only have a comparatively limited amount of screen time. Stelvio Cipriani contributes a typically competent score, mixing light pop with his trademark ominous suspense scoring, found at the same time in his work for Mario Bava.

A Spanish prerecord VHS served as the basis for a widely available bootleg edition, but the first authorized DVD comes courtesy of Dark Sky during what now appears to be only a brief flirtation with Euro horror (which also resulted in wild fare like *Ricco the Mean Machine*, *The She Beast*, and a sadly withdrawn special edition of *Kill Baby, Kill!*). The transfer (in Italian with optional English subtitles) looks very pleasing with a solid amount of detail, and extras include the spoiler-packed (and very weird) European trailer and a pleasant 13-minute interview with the personable Keaton ("Camille's European Adventures"), who chats about her unusual career in Italy. Definitely not a title for the Euro-cult newcomer, this is more of an acquired taste but well worth the effort for anyone willing to give it a try.

TRAUMA

Colour, 1993, 102m. / Directed by Dario Argento / Starring Christopher Rydell, Asia Argento, Laura Johnson, James Russo, Brad Dourif, Frederic Forrest, Piper Laurie / Anchor Bay (US R1 NTSC) / WS (2.35:1) (16:9), Optimum (UK R2 PAL) / DD5.1, Tartan (UK R0 PAL) / WS (2.35:1) / DD2.0

After her medium mother (Piper Laurie) is briefly possessed by a recent murder victim at a *Deep Red*-style seance ("the killer is... *present*"), a suicidal anorexic teenager, Aura Petrescu (Asia Argento, the director's daughter), follows her parents into a rainy night and comes upon the aftermath of their murder by a madman who uses a handy-dandy electric decapitator. Aura teams up with ex-junkie sketch artist David (Christopher Rydell, also the son of a director, Mark Rydell) to track down the culprit, whose unhinging springs from the long-ago beheading of Aura's baby brother during a botched delivery and the post-trauma attempt to blot the memory from her mother's mind by dragging her off for electric shock treatment.

Frederic Forrest lurks suspiciously in a neckbrace as an obsessed psychiatrist, while jittery Brad Dourif fits in with the wildly-hamming victims and Tom Savini contributes uncharacteristically fake-looking severed heads for the few gore scenes. A subplot, prompting Pino Donaggio to add some cod-Agatha Christie cheeriness to an otherwise effective score, deals with a *Home Alone* kid living next door to the killer, who shows up with the borrowed guillotine gadget for a desperate *deus ex machina* finale.

A concern for international marketing which briefly gripped Dario Argento (see also *Two Evil Eyes*) before his defiantly Eurocentric *Stendhal Syndrome* and *Sleepless* means that the film is set in Minneapolis. The city is as flatly uninteresting as any nowhere TV series locale, especially in comparison with the style-haunted European cities of Argento's best and even lesser work. Placing a pre-Raphaelite Ophelia picture in a shop window or opening with a toy cut-out French Revolutionary guillotine (accompanied by a sound montage mixing the Marseilleise with judicial murder, used also over the menu) is only an attempt to infuse the film with an aesthetic not found in the suburban streets, drab airport hotel, bland TV station or psychiatric clinic which are the major settings. The triple-authored story, turned into a convoluted screenplay by Argento and novelist T.E.D. Klein, never manages to make any satisfying connection between the investigators' specific neuroses, and the mystery fails to learn the lesson of *Vertigo* – that the wildest plot will play if there's a character through-line for the audience. If the scenes with the kid are supposed to be comical, they fall flat – but too many of the intense, serious moments are frankly silly and provoke unneeded giggles, as when Rydell bends down to hear a severed head repeat a clue before her eyes roll up for the last time.

The first English-friendly DVD of *Trauma* from Tartan serves the film better than previous fullscreen and/or censor-cut video releases, especially the disastrous American and Japanese releases, which hacked huge chunks of visual information off the screen on all sides. Pan-and-scan does special harm to Argento's fondness for windscreen-shaped frames in which odd details might or might not register with the viewer as with the characters, zooming in unsubtly on the clues and removing the air of ambiguity the filmmaker and cinematographer Raffaele Mertes work hard to create with very wide-angle, slightly fisheye-distorted images. Like *The Bird with the Crystal Plumage* and *Deep Red*, the "mystery" hinges on something seen but misunderstood by a witness at a murder site: a fleeing figure in the rain who is *apparently* hiding their face behind a pair of severed heads held up like a brace of grouse. Tartan's DVD is letterboxed to approximately 2.35:1, and has those shimmery top and bottom lines that probably ought to be matted, with a transfer that has adequate colour but tends to get a tad blotchy whenever there's any rapid movement. The "extra features" are a very American fullscreen trailer, a six-frame "behind the scenes gallery", and filmographies for father and daughter. Three text pieces are included: a Billy Chainsaw interview with Asia Argento, an appreciation of the director by Richard Stanley and a listing of BBFC cuts made to earlier video releases but restored here. Incredibly, Optimum snagged the rights to the film in 2005 and reissued it with only the trailer, but at least the transfer was anamorphic this time.

The potential for a far more elaborate special edition was obviously still left unfulfilled, especially given the wealth of behind-the-scenes footage shot on location and the numerous deleted scenes which cropped up on various bootleg videos traded on the fan circuit. Anchor Bay's much-delayed DVD was supposed to contain much of this material, but alas, various changes in the corporate structure resulted in a sadly hobbled product. On the positive side, the transfer is the best to date for this title (though its lack of progressive scan encoding is perplexing given the company's past track record); the compression is at least far better, resulting in smoother, richer blacks and much more satisfying results for Argento's dense, deeply-textured compositions. The 5.1 audio mix is also a huge improvement (particularly during the all-important thunderstorm scenes), a welcome step up from many past video releases which, incredibly enough, presented this Dolby stereo film in mono! Unfortunately the Anchor Bay disc (timed to coincide with their frustrating release of Argento's *The Card Player*) presents only a small portion of the deleted scenes – in Italian with English subtitles, despite the fact that English audio for this footage is widely available. These scenes really would have served the film well by returning to the body of the main feature, particularly a chase sequence which establishes the otherwise head-scratching presence of a reggae band in the closing credits. The theatrical trailer is also included, but if you're interested in anything that happened during the making of the film (which was chronicled with many, many hours of videotaped footage), that will have to wait for another, more comprehensive release somewhere down the road.

– KN

THE TRIUMPH OF SHERLOCK HOLMES

B&W, 1935, 79m. / Directed by Leslie Hiscott / Starring Arthur Wontner, Lyn Harding, Ian Fleming, Charles Mortimer / Alpha (US R0 NTSC)

 Despite an off-page cameo by Professor Moriarty that beefs up a thin story while scuppering the series continuity, Sir Arthur Conan Doyle's *The Valley of Fear* is the least-filmed of the Sherlock Holmes novels. This British vehicle for the fine sleuthing and badinage of Arthur Wontner goes a long way towards explaining why that is.

The Great Detective is on the point of retirement, with Watson (Ian Fleming) planning to move his wife into the Baker Street digs (!) as Holmes heads for the quiet life, and his only regret is that he has never been able to end the criminal career of Moriarty, whom the world believes to be an innocent mathematics professor (though Lyn Harding, whose greatest stage and screen role was as another Sherlockian villain in *The Speckled Band*, plays him as such a glowering, bullying villain it's a wonder he wasn't arrested on general principles years ago). The dense Inspector Lestrade (Charles Mortimer) consults Holmes one last time, on a murder at Birlstone Castle that has baffling features which after a century of mysteries are less baffling than they were. Here's an early instance of the "face destroyed by a shotgun blast but corpse identifiable by his rings and clothes" gambit used in *Laura* and many, many other whodunits to set up a reveal that the supposed victim is still alive and the corpse is someone else entirely.

The backstory comes in an untidy flashback lump that dominates the middle of the film, with the modestly-budgeted British production unable to do much with an American locale or a simplified bit of industrial history about a secret society among Pennsylvania miners (*The Molly Maguires* is a more accurate version of the incidents Doyle tidies up to make a goodies and baddies situation of a complex mess). Things are enlivened once the flashback is over and the movie makes up a final face-off between Holmes and Moriarty on the battlements of an impressively grim tower, with the Napoleon of Crime taking his traditional fall from a high place. "It's the triumph of Sherlock Holmes", says Watson, justifying the title.

Two years later, Wontner's Holmes was out of retirement with Harding's Moriarty alive again for yet another last battle, *Silver Blaze* (aka *Murder at the Baskervilles*). Alpha's transfer is better than some of their releases; the soundtrack is awash with crackle and hiss but is at least audible, and the beat-up print only flares slightly from time to time.

– KN

TUVALU

Colour, 1999, 86m. / Directed by Veit Helmer / Starring Denis Lavant, Chulpan Khamatova, Terrence Gillespie, Philippe Clay / First Run (US R1 NTSC) / WS (1.85:1) / DD2.0, EuroVideo (Germany R2 PAL) / WS (1.85:1) / DD5.1

 A film that wears its influences on its sleeve, the German film *Tuvalu* tosses Lars von Trier's *The Element of Crime* and *Zentropa*, the entire output of Jeunet and Caro, and Charlie Chaplin's *Modern Times* into a blender, resulting in a very peculiar viewing experience best targeted directly at the midnight movie crowd. Using Chaplin-esque babble for dialogue and behavioural tics to convey almost all of the narrative, *Tuvalu* ultimately functions as a visual experience first and a coherent narrative second. Needless to say, those who jumped headfirst into *Delicatessen* will find plenty to enjoy here.

The thin strand of a storyline follows the misadventures of Anton (*Beau travail*'s Denis Lavant), who tries to save his family's doomed bathhouse from the clutches of his scheming brother, Gregor (Terrence Gillespie). Faced with a series of obstacles including threatened closure from the author-ities and the possible disapproval of his blind father, Karl (Philippe Clay), Anton finds life becoming even more complicated with the arrival of Eva (Chulpan Khamatova), a winsome beauty who also catches Karl's eye after she and her father find refuge in this strange, Black Sea village. A treasure hunt involving the island of Tuvalu and other surreal mayhem rapidly ensues.

Shot in black and white and then tinted à la many silent films (along with fleeting use of manipulated colour footage), *Tuvalu* coasts along smoothly on the basis of its sheer oddness and the ability to throw an unexpected, visual treat in the viewer's direction every few minutes. Those looking for substance will have to dig pretty deep, as the film never goes for more than superficial good/bad dichotomies and establishes an order in which cute wins out over ugly every time. So the best way to enjoy the film is simply to sit back, marvel at the production design (apparently a real pool in Bulgaria provides the main setting), and swim along in the cockeyed whimsy of it all.

First Run's DVD of *Tuvalu* offers a peculiar, non-anamorphic transfer which, like the German disc, shifts aspect ratios for no apparent reason, verging closer to 2.20:1 at times depending on the scene. Image quality is acceptable but difficult to evaluate given the deliberate grunge of the visuals, coupled with the often heavily saturated tinting. Detail ranges from pin-sharp to soft and mushy, depending on the source material. The spacious Dolby Digital soundtrack offers plenty of surround activity, and obviously there are no subtitles to contend with for xenophobic viewers. The disc also includes the director's gimmicky 9-minute short film, "Surprise", which plays like a live action *Wallace and Gromit* escapade, as well as a stills gallery.

28 DAYS LATER

Colour, 2002, 112m. / Directed by Danny Boyle / Starring Cillian Murphy, Naomie Harris, Brendan Gleeson, Megan Burns, Christopher Eccleston / Fox (Blu-ray & DVD) (US R0/R1 HD/NTSC, UK R2 PAL) / WS (1.85:1) (16:9) / DD5.1

In his first feature film, *Shallow Grave*, director Danny Boyle demonstrated a knack for combining youthful disaffection along with full-blooded horror. His subsequent films, *Trainspotting*, *A Life Less Ordinary*, and *The Beach*, continued to explore the troubled youth angle, but it took the startling *28 Days Later* to firmly unite the two elements again. A zombie film in spirit if not in scientific fact (technically it's a plague film), this is an inspired post-Gen-X spin on Richard Matheson's *I Am Legend* with the expected George Romero influence thrown in for good measure.

During the jittery prologue, a group of animal activists attempts to free captive monkeys only to unleash "rage", a highly contagious virus (apparently bred by turning hostility into a physical disease) spread through blood contact. 28 days later, Jim (Cillian Murphy) wakes up alone in a deserted hospital, and then stumbles out onto the empty, decimated streets of London. Unfortunately, he isn't quite the only one around; a shambling, red-eyed priest inaugurates an attack of "infected" denizens who nearly do Jim in before the last minute intervention of Selena (Naomie Harris), a tough-willed survivor who teaches him the rules to stay alive. In a nearby high rise they join Frank (Brendan Gleeson) and his daughter, Hannah (Megan Burns), and soon the quartet sets off through the countryside to follow a military aid signal to Manchester. Unfortunately, they do not quite find what they expected.

Featuring the fastest-moving zombies since Umberto Lenzi's *Nightmare City* (with which this shares a few peculiar parallels apart from its obvious nods to *Day of the Triffids*), *28 Days Later* alternates moments of teeth-clenching horror (including one nightmarish tyre-changing sequence in a motorway tunnel) with much-needed moments of lyricism and beauty. As with Romero, the film features unnerving sociological parallels to the evening news; its images of contagion and desolation ring out quite strongly in a post-September 11, SARS/AIDS-riddled age.

Apart from Boyle regular Christopher Eccleston, the cast consists largely of either unknowns or TV character actors and works all the better for it. Murphy is a particular standout, combining moments of necessary brutality with unexpected vulnerability. Of course, he and Gleeson went on to become far better known in several studio blockbusters after this, but at the time they were fresh faces and served the film's needs perfectly.

Though successful theatrically, *28 Days Later* fares better on the small screen thanks to its lensing in digital video. The coarse and grainy 35mm appearance is nowhere to be found here, as the transfer is a real gritty treat in standard def. Boyle's visual flourishes include some striking compositions and bold use of colour, so this anamorphic rendition is really the way to go. The film is also a feast for the ears thanks to a striking, percussive electronic score, quite unlike anything used in a horror film before (but definitely imitated since, including serious overkill in the flawed but sometimes very harrowing sequel, *28 Weeks Later*). The 5.1 mix makes full use of the split surround speakers, with music piping in eerily from each channel and some well-chosen sound effects providing highly effective jolts. (Watch out for that car alarm!) Plentiful extras include a nice commentary track with Boyle and co-writer Alex Garland, who cover everything from the technical shooting aspects to the numerous genre influences on the creation of the film. The half-hour "Pure Rage" is an unusually adept making-of documentary, combining interviews with the major cast and crew with an overview of its scientific basis and a demonstration of how that astonishing "empty London" sequence was achieved. The mostly superfluous deleted scenes lead up to a far more tragic alternative ending, which plays the same dialogue-wise but eliminates one major character. There's yet another alternative ending provided via storyboards, as well as galleries of stills, continuity snapshots, and artwork. Also included are the theatrical teaser and trailer (with male nudity surprisingly intact) and a Jackknife Lee music video. All the supplements are also present on Fox's Blu-ray, which seems like a laughable choice for that format given that it was shot on standard def digital video except for some 35mm segments in the final third. Indeed, this isn't great eye candy on a Blu-ray player hooked to a large screen, but the DTS-HD MA 5.1 track is a real room shaker. (It's also playable in French and Spanish 5.1, with English, Spanish, Cantonese and Korean subtitle options.) No matter how you see it, this remains an essential classic and easily the most influential horror film of the early 2000s.

THE TWILIGHT GIRLS

B&W, 1959, 89m. / Directed by André Hunebelle / Starring Agnès Laurent, Christine Carere, Estella Blain, Henri Guisol, Catherine Deneuve / First Run (US R1 NTSC)

 Released during the heyday of *The Twilight Zone*, this sexy schoolgirl import has nothing to do with Rod Serling's pioneering TV program; in fact, there's nothing remotely uncanny about this girls-loving-girls French romp starring Agnès Laurent, a rival to Brigitte Bardot who made her debut in this film simultaneously with *The Nude Set*, both of which opened in France in 1957. However, *The Twilight Girls* didn't appear in English territories until 1959; the French-language original (entitled *Les collégiennes*) was dubbed, trimmed down, and spiced up with insert shots involving semi-nude schoolgirls touching and flirting with each other at night. This modified version, released by Audubon Films, touched off a scandal when the New York censor board hauled it into court, ensuring plenty of box-office attention for what was originally a fairly mild story of blossoming adolescence.

The story is pretty much business as usual, but for the record, our lady Laurent is Anne-Marie, the new arrival at an exclusive boarding school where the girls apparently spend all their time taking art classes and gossiping when they're supposed to be sleeping in the dorm. Several other girls exchange longing looks at each other during off hours, and soon Anne-Marie becomes the *objet d'amour* for pretty but vaguely masculine Marthe (Estella Blain). To make matters more confusing, the newcomer is also wooed by handsome Christian (*Lola Montes*'s Henri Guisol), while the other girls are busy catfighting in the cafeteria and spreading rumours across the school grounds.

As it now turns out, the biggest casualty of Audubon's editing from the French original was the character of Adelaide, the headmistress's mischievous 13-year-old daughter, played by none other than a prepubescent Catherine Deneuve. Apart from a couple of fleeting background appearances, Deneuve was nowhere to be found in *The Twilight Girls* but has been reinstated for the DVD, with her scenes subtitled in English. Even as a newcomer she's quite charming and funny, and her scenes are a welcome recovery; in fact, with this subplot restored, the film feels considerably less smutty. The DVD as it stands represents something of a composite, containing the deleted Deneuve scenes while retaining the naughtier American bits, with one of the new lesbian students purportedly played by a young Georgina Spelvin (of *The Devil in Miss Jones* fame) with her trademark frizzy hair already in evidence.

If that really is Georgina, she certainly lost a lot of baby fat over the following decade thanks to her stripping career.

Most of *The Twilight Girls* looks quite nice on the DVD, a few notches above past VHS editions, though the French language inserts (with huge permanent subs) are soft and dupey-looking and have a noticeable colour tingle over the footage. This only affects a few minutes of the running time, with the Audubon footage looking stable and, for the most part, crisp. The most interesting bonus is "The Making of the American Version", in which a female narrator explains how certain innocuous shots were expanded and refilmed to introduce lesbian activity where none previously existed; one can only imagine how innocently this film played in its native country. The heavy-breathing theatrical trailer is also included, along with an amusing Deneuve photo gallery showing the actress much further in her career, appearing in the likes of *Tristana* and *The Young Girls of Rochefort*.

TWINS OF EVIL

Colour, 1971, 84m. / Directed by John Hough / Starring Peter Cushing, Madeleine & Mary Collinson, Kathleen Byron, Damien Thomas, Katya Wyeth, Roy Stewart, Dennis Price, Luan Peters, David Warbeck, Isobel Black / Carlton, Network (UK R2 PAL), CIDC (France R2 PAL) / WS (1.78:1) (16:9)

 Recently orphaned teenage twins Maria and Frieda Gellhorn (the Collinsons) arrive in the village of Karnstein to live with their Uncle Gustav Weil (Peter Cushing) and Aunt Katy (Kathleen Byron). Weil is the commander of a band of zealots known as The Brotherhood, preoccupied with burning innocent young girls at the stake while fearfully shirking the responsibility of dealing with their real problem, Count Karnstein (Damien Thomas). Although the twins are physically similar, morally they are worlds apart. Maria is good and pure, but Frieda finds herself drawn to the Count's deviant lifestyle. What she doesn't realise is that Count Karnstein is a vampire...

The final entry in what is widely known as Hammer's Karnstein trilogy, the link between *Twins of Evil* and its predecessors (*The Vampire Lovers* and *Lust for a Vampire*) is a tenuous one. Where the earlier two films were absorbed with the activities of vampiress Carmilla, here the character makes but a fleeting appearance. Regardless of this, the film remains one of the most entertaining in Hammer's latter-day *oeuvre*, probing ever more daringly the sex and violence coalition with which, by 1971, they were becoming synonymous. Peter Cushing's puritanical Gustav Weil is one of his finest screen characterisations, unwilling guardian to his wayward nieces by day, ritually seeking out and burning young girls suspected of witchcraft by night. Weil – not coincidentally pronounced "vile" – is blind in his devotion to duty, his interpretation of good being nothing more than an alternate evil to that being woven by the vampire Count Karnstein; the vigilantism of The Brotherhood achieves nothing more than the death of innocents while generating a source of fear among law-abiding village folk. Director John Hough never once allows the pace to slacken off and events move swiftly to a fast and furious climax in which Weil decapitates one of his own nieces and confronts the Count for the last time. Hough manipulates interesting characters through a choice Tudor Gates story, which falters only once when it eclipses erotica with tactless innuendo as Katya Wyeth ecstatically strokes the shaft of a dripping candle. Wyeth (also in *Straight On Till Morning* and *Dr. Jekyll and Sister Hyde* for Hammer) incidentally went on to pose nude for *Mayfair* magazine in the mid-'70s, as did several of her starlet contemporaries at the time. Roy Stannard's sets are outstanding, particularly the Count's dining room, and Harry Robinson's rousing militaristic titles march pounds out at timely intervals throughout.

The twins of the title are played by Madeleine and Mary Collinson, whose similarity led to a couple of inferior films but most notably earned them a minor place in history as the first twin *Playboy* Playmate centrefolds. Actresses they clearly were not, but any failing in that capacity was balanced with a willingness to shed their diaphanous nightgowns to order. Damien Thomas is a splendidly wicked foil for Cushing's fanatical witchfinder, while Roy Stewart (*Live and Let Die*) is an imposing mountain of a man as his mute manservant Joachim. Dennis Price (whose horror films – the coda of his career – were once described as cheap, worthless and degrading) is a pleasure to watch as the conniving Dietrich. Luan Peters (later to be groped by John Cleese in TV's *Fawlty Towers*) gets chained to a wall and has her bosom nibbled by Madeleine Collinson, who's testing out her new fangs. David Warbeck and Isobel Black's sibling schoolteachers are the anchorpoint of morality counterbalancing the evil perpetrated by Weil and Karnstein. *Twins of Evil* is quite simply a stunner; one of several diamonds in Hammer's heavily jewel-encrusted crown and essential viewing for Hammer buffs and genre aficionados alike.

The British Region 2 DVD from Carlton restores to *Twins of Evil* the sumptuous colours lost on so many of its earlier VHS incarnations, with a 1.78:1 matte split into 8 chapters. There are no additional features offered, and sound and subtitles are in English language alone. *Twins of Evil* is currently available only as part of a box set which also includes *Vampire Circus* and *Countess Dracula*. Later individual releases from Network and CIDC reuse the same excellent transfer.

– TG

TWO EVIL EYES

Colour, 1990, 120m. / Directed by George A. Romero and Dario Argento / Starring Harvey Keitel, Adrienne Barbeau, Ramy Zada, Madeleine Potter, Christine Forrest / Blue Underground (Blu-ray & DVD) (US R0/R1 HD/NTSC) / WS (1.85:1) (16:9) / DTS-ES/DD5.1 EX, Anchor Bay, Arrow (UK R2 PAL) / WS (1.85:1) (16:9) / DD5.1, Creative Axa (Japan R2 NTSC), Laser Paradise (Germany R2 PAL), GCTHV (France R2 PAL) / WS (1.85:1) / DD2.0

 The idea of horror anthologies based on Edgar Allan Poe stories had already been around for decades by the time Dario Argento decided to embark on an ambitious project in which noted directors would each tackle one of the Baltimore scribe's most famous stories. After John Carpenter and Wes Craven proved unavailable for a proposed quartet of tales, Argento teamed up with George Romero for two hour-long adaptations.

Originally interested in "The Masque of the Red Death", Romero changed gears for the more reasonably scaled "The Facts in the Case of M. Valdemar", filmed before in Roger Corman's *Tales of Terror*. Reuniting with Romero after *Creepshow*, Adrienne Barbeau plays another scheming wife, this time married to the much older, much richer, and very comatose Ernest Valdemar. He's being treated by Dr. Hoffman (Ramy Zada), who happens to be Jessica's lover and is using hypnosis to prolong his patient's life. However, together they come up with a plan to induce his premature death without being caught, though of course the scheme winds up failing with quite horrific consequences.

Argento then takes the reins with a loose adaptation of "The Black Cat" (filmed even more loosely in the aforementioned Corman film), with irritable crime photographer Rod Usher (Harvey Keitel) taking not too kindly to the arrival of a new cat in his home. His girlfriend, Annabel (Madeleine Potter), decides to keep the feline, which Rod secretly kills for a series of snuff kitty photos in his next book. However, the cat soon returns again... or does it?

The Romero segment has often been criticized as sluggish and half-hearted, and with good reason; even at an hour it moves along like a crippled turtle and only pays off with a brief, zombified ending that plays more like an episode of his earlier TV show, *Tales from the Darkside*. The actors try their best but an air of lethargy hangs over the proceedings, making it a sad misfire. Fortunately Argento's segment redeems the film as a whole, packing in references to a jaw-dropping number of Poe works ("Berenice", "Annabel Lee", "The Fall of the House of Usher", and "The Pit and the Pendulum", among many others) while integrating several bravura set pieces, violent and otherwise. Fresh off his hyperactive camera experimentation in *Opera*, Argento continues his sweeping POV shots here; the camera swoops around apartment buildings, takes on a cat's perspective, and swings on a pendulum through a bisected corpse; in short, it's one of his most compact, entertaining, and tightly plotted works. The Pino Donaggio score is also a triumph, from the haunting main "Dreaming Dreams" theme to some rousing suspense cues.

Several DVDs of *Two Evil Eyes* have circulated through different countries, most containing the standard two-hour cut which played theatrically and was released on laserdisc by Media. All are letterboxed but only the U.S. and U.K. discs offer anamorphic transfers; not surprisingly for a film of its vintage, the appearance is stellar, with beautiful depth and detail. The U.K. disc has a solid 5.1 mix from the original Dolby Stereo stems, while the U.S. double-disc set goes one better with six channel DTS-ES and 5.1 EX mixes to boot. The difference isn't that radical as the film doesn't have a terribly aggressive mix, but audiophiles

will want to take note. More significantly, the U.S. disc contains a few extra frames during the pendulum sequence, lingering longer on the split torso. It doesn't add up to much more than a second or two, but technically the extra footage is there. However, the U.S. edition is mysteriously missing a line of dialogue at the end of the film, in which the gagging police officer reels back from the opened wall and, beginning to wretch, gasps out, "They're eating her!" (You'll have to see the film to understand what that means.) On the Blue Underground disc, the cop simply turns away and a quick "—er!" is heard on the soundtrack, in each audio mix. Disc one contains the main feature along with an international theatrical trailer (not present on the other discs); apparently the U.S. trailer (which graced a few Fox VHS releases at the time) has disappeared for good, though it's not much of a loss. Also included are the usual well-written talent bios and a poster and stills gallery, which contains *two* shots from the "Murders in the Rue Morgue" sequence, which was written and filmed for the Argento segment but ultimately excised. In this scene, Usher arrives to take photos at a crime scene where two sisters lie on the floor of their home with their necks slashed open. Upon further inspection he discovers animal faeces in the fireplace, indicating the culprit was actually a gorilla. While many sources claim this bit was never actually shot, this DVD proves otherwise (though none of the supplements address its existence).

In the limited two-disc edition, disc two kicks off with "Two Masters' Eyes", a 32-minute featurette including interviews with Romero, Argento, FX supervisor Tom Savini (who seemed to have a *lot* of fun on this film), executive producer Claudio Argento, and the omnipresent Asia Argento. Most interesting is the inclusion of behind the scenes highlights from footage shot during filming by Robert Marcucci, including some amusing shots of Argento in sports-playing mode. Then Savini steps into the spotlight for the 12 minute "Savini's EFX", showing him at work on the pendulum corpse and those memorable kittens. "At Home with Tom Savini" covers many of the props he's kept over the years from his films, a veritable checklist of major gore groundbreakers since the late '70s. Last up are a Barbeau interview segment jettisoned from the original cut of Roy Frumkes's *Document of the Dead* (though she is visible in his later revised video cut), along with an Easter egg containing brief comments from Christine Forrest/Romero about her small role as a nurse.

2010 saw no less than two new editions of the film, with the first coming out on standard DVD from Arrow with a transfer that looks identical to the American version. One disposable but interesting selling point here is the inclusion of the film's alternative Italian soundtrack with optional English subtitles. All of the actors were obviously speaking English on set, but it's intriguing to hear the Argento-supervised Italian version all the same. The extras are far more minor here – the theatrical trailer, Marc Morris's entertaining Argento trailer reel (which is highlighted by a beautiful scope version of the rare American *Four Flies on Grey Velvet* trailer and a subtitled version of the *Five Days of Milan* Italian trailer), and a liner notes booklet.

Most if not all of Blue Underground's extras are carried over for their Blu-ray release, which marks their third trip to the Argento BD well. Obviously the film isn't a visual dazzler on the level of their *Bird with the Crystal Plumage*, but the presentation here is quite admirable and film-like with the edge enhancement which was somewhat visible in their DVD edition subdued into oblivion here. Daylight scenes are very crisp and clean-looking, and while Romero's segment has almost no outstanding visual style to speak of, even the darker scenes in Argento's fare well (note the blood-red lighting in Keitel's darkroom, which is far easier to watch here). The uncompressed audio presented in both Dolby Digital and DTS variants (specifically, Dolby TrueHD 7.1, DTS-HD 7.1 Master Audio, and Dolby Digital 5.1-EX Surround, with optional English, French and Spanish subs) is still restrained for the most part, but the occasional cat yowls and shrieking violin strings certainly sound nice when they do pop up in the ancillary speakers. (The "eating her" line is still absent on all the tracks, by the way.) All of the extras are carried over except the stills gallery (a shame in this case, for obvious reasons) and talent bios; presumably the Easter egg is absent, too, but it'll take a far more savvy Blu-ray hunter than I to verify that for sure. Flaws in the film aside, fans of either director (or both) will find plenty to savour here as this oft-debated film is put into its proper context, and any self-respecting Argento fan should find the Blu-ray an essential purchase.

TWO ORPHAN VAMPIRES

Colour, 1997, 98m. / Directed by Jean Rollin / Starring Alexandra Pic, Isabelle Teboul, Brigitte Lahaie, Tina Aumont, Nathalie Karsenty / Shriek Show (US R1 NTSC), Redemption (UK R0 PAL), X-Rated (Germany R0 PAL) / WS (1.85:1) (16:9)

Loosely inspired by a series of pulp novels penned by director Jean Rollin, *Two Orphan Vampires* marked a comeback of sorts for this idiosyncratic lover of nubile bloodsuckers wafting through the night. Retaining the melancholy poetry which marked his '80s films like *Night of the Hunted* and *The Living Dead Girl*, Rollin concocts a modern fairy tale revolving around his favourite image, a pair of blonde vampires who remain oddly innocent even when they're feasting on the throat of an unlucky passer-by.

Blind teen orphans Henriette (Isabelle Teboul) and Louise (Alexandra Pic) follow the orders of the nuns overseeing their orphanage, and though a kindly doctor attempts to solve what appears to be a case of psychosomatic blindness, he has yet to find a cure. However, at night their sight mysteriously returns, and they flee the orphanage to mingle – sometimes perilously – with the local populace. Occasionally they also lounge around in bed, reading history lessons to each other and speculating about their supernatural heritage. A medicinal trip to Paris with the doctor doesn't seem to help matters, either. In between excursions through the local cemetery, the girls encounter a peculiar menagerie of characters including an ill-fated circus worker (Rollin staple Brigitte Lahaie), a forlorn flesh-eater (Tina Aumont), and even a female werewolf (Nathalie Karsenty).

Though cheaply shot and hampered by an over-reliance on artificial filters, *Two Orphan Vampires* retains many of Rollin's strengths as a director and thematically fits snugly with the rest of his supernatural output. Arguably his most "tasteful" film in ages with nudity and gore kept to an absolute minimum, this is probably not the best place for newcomers to start but it's certainly a goldmine for Rollin diehards. Times have been hard for straight-faced horror films since the 1980s, and therefore *Two Orphan Vampires* often feels like a product made in a completely different era where childish innocence and naive faith in the magical are qualities to be cherished.

The foggy, soft focused appearance of this film would be a nightmare for any DVD compression facility and already resulted in a number of hellish VHS transfers. Unfortunately Shriek Show's DVD cannot overcome the challenges of the source material and, alas, is also plagued by severe motion ghosting, present in every scene. Luckily the characters tend to sit or stand still for long stretches, but it's a crippling flaw in a colourful transfer that should have been

stronger. One major plus is the inclusion of the original French track with optional subtitles; the English dubbed version (to which the disc defaults for some reason) is a laughable, ear-shredding abomination to be avoided at all costs. The audio is crisp enough, though the film itself is hampered by a muddy synthesizer score which greatly diminishes the poetry of the proceedings. Extras include a pair of interviews with the lead actresses, both of whom are charming and enthusiastic despite some very odd, deep suntans (ironic indeed considering their pallid characters onscreen). The disc also includes the entire original score (previously available as a bonus with the highly recommended Rollin book, *Virgins and Vampires*) and a photo gallery, as well as a handful of other Shriek Show trailers. The German release doesn't look much better and features a handmade trailer. Incredibly, it took over a decade for this to get a U.K. release courtesy of Redemption, whose much improved transfer at least doesn't smear all over the screen. Rollin also appears for a new video interview in which he only tangentially touches on this film, talking more about his unique career in general.

THE UMBRELLAS OF CHERBOURG

Colour, 1964, 87m. / Directed by Jacques Demy / Starring Catherine Deneuve, Nino Castelnuovo, Anne Vernon / Arte, Ciné-Tamaris (France R2 PAL) / WS (1.66:1) (16:9), Tartan (UK R0 PAL), Wellspring (US R1 NTSC), Sony (Japan R2 NTSC) / WS (1.66:1) / DD2.0

In the seaside town of Cherbourg, auto mechanic Guy (*Camille 2000*'s Nino Castelnuovo) is secretly in love with and courting beautiful Geneviève (Catherine Deneuve), the daughter of an umbrella shop owner (*Therese and Isabelle*'s Anne Vernon). When Guy is summoned to war, he and the sorrowful Geneviève spend the night together, leaving her pregnant. As the months pass and Geneviève hears nothing from her true love, her mother conspires to resolve the situation by marrying her off to a wealthy jeweller; when Guy finally returns, he finds that the fairy tale setting of his youth has already begun to change and the course of his life changes dramatically.

Still one of the most globally popular of all French films, *The Umbrellas of Cherbourg* is the best-known and most visually stunning achievement of musically inclined director Jacques Demy, who was prone to mixing fantasy and melody in films like *The Pied Piper* and *Donkey Skin*. Though not technically a fantasy as such, this might as well be; the entire real town was painted to colour coordinate with the visual scheme of the film, resulting in a fascinating experience where characters, cars, bicycles, and umbrellas all integrate with the architecture and art direction around them. Furthermore, every single line in the film is sung to catchy music by Michel Legrand, though this isn't really an opera; everything from "You stink of gasoline" to "Guy, I love you!" comes in lilting tones from the gorgeous cast (who were almost all dubbed by professional singers, but who cares?). From the tear-jerking train station sequence to the justifiably famous Christmas finale, everything in the film works perfectly; the simple story moves along with an inevitable grace to an unpredictable fate for all of the characters, a bittersweet resolution far from the traditional wrap-up one would get in a Hollywood production.

After an extensive and very costly restoration, *The Umbrellas of Cherboug* received an international theatrical reissue in the mid-1990s. While the theatrical prints were indeed beautiful to behold, video editions have been a wildly mixed batch. Criterion's surprisingly soft-looking and imperfectly matted laserdisc came first, followed by Wellspring (formerly Fox Lorber) issuing the same transfer with optional English subtitles in the early days of DVD (the only extra was a quick, uninteresting U.S. reissue trailer). The same transfer made the rounds in Japan (with non-removable Japanese subtitles), while the overly bright Tartan DVD utilized a theatrical print with burned-in subtitles. While the framing on the Tartan disc is far too tight on the top and bottom, often losing significant information and headroom, the U.S. and Japanese ones lose information from the sides (especially evident in the opening credits and interstitials identifying the various months of the year). The first satisfactory option was the French DVD, which contains a knockout of a transfer, anamorphic and perfectly framed, with terrifically saturated colours. This two-disc set contains optional English subtitles, the original French theatrical and reissue trailers, and an 87-minute documentary by Agnes Varda, *The Universe of Jacques Demy* (in French with no subtitles, but the film and interview clips are still enjoyable to sample). A condensed single disc edition is also available. The PCM stereo sound on the French disc is full-bodied and very pleasant (better in fact than the reissued double-CD soundtrack), while the other editions sound pinched and tinny in comparison. A much later U.S. reissue features the same excellent new transfer (but not PCM audio), and the Demy documentary is available separately from Wellspring with English subtitles. This also appears in the French "Jacques Demy: Integrale" box set, which is covered in depth in *DVD Delirium Volume 4*.

UNDER THE SAND

Colour, 2001, 92m. / Directed by François Ozon / Starring Charlotte Rampling, Bruno Cremer, Jacques Nolot / Paramount (France R2 PAL), Wellspring (US R1 NTSC), Artificial Eye (UK R2 PAL) / WS (1.85:1) (16:9) / DD5.1

While on vacation at the beach with her husband Jean (Bruno Cremer), professor Marie (Charlotte Rampling) is distraught when Jean abruptly disappears during a quiet afternoon near the water. When his body fails to turn up, Marie reluctantly returns home to Paris only to continuously see her husband appearing in their apartment. She tentatively begins a relationship with Vincent (Jacques Nolot) but finds herself unable to give up her husband, be it a ghost or her own psychological need, and soon the lines between reality and delusion become blurred.

Yet another startling shift in tone for director François Ozon, *Under the Sand* (*Sous le sable*) finds him continuing to coax magnificent performances from his actors and providing viewers with enough ambiguity to allow the film to linger for days after viewing. The emotional, deeply tumultuous final fifteen minutes raise more questions than they answer, but the effect is haunting and quite unlike what one would expect from the preceding events. The scenario could easily turn into a traditional thriller, an erotic melodrama or a tearjerker, but Ozon instead flirts among the three, with Rampling's powerhouse turn lifting it into territory all its own. The director and star later reunited for his first English language film, *Swimming Pool*, and judging from the commentary track they share on both DVD editions, they got along extremely well. Both of them earned their best notices for this film, and with good reason; while it eschews the shock value of prior Ozon films, the unpredictability and keen visual sensibilities are still well in place and continuously honed closer to perfection.

The DVDs share the same crystal clear anamorphic transfer with optional English subtitles; the 5.1 soundtrack is extremely active and spacious throughout, surprising for a film so reliant on dialogue and long moments of silence. The Wellspring disc provides optional English subtitles for the French commentary and includes the U.S. trailer, while the French disc contains interviews with Rampling and Cremer as well as two Ozon short films, "Mes parents un jour d'été" (1990, 12 mins.) and "Les doigts dans le ventre" (1988, 11 mins.) (all non-subtitled). The British disc splits the difference, dropping the commentary but including subtitled versions of both cast interviews as well as bonus text interviews with Rampling and Ozon.

THE UNSEEN

Colour, 1980, 81m. / Directed by Peter Foleg / Starring Stephen Furst, Barbara Bach, Karen Lamm, Lois Young, Sydney Lassick, Lelia Goldoni, Douglas Barr / Digital Entertainment (UK R2 PAL)

A TV news crew – Jennifer Fast (Barbara Bach), her sister Karen (Karen Lamm) and Vicki Thompson (Lois Young) – arrives amidst the community of Solvang in California to report on the annual celebrations of their Dutch ancestry. Unfortunately the girls' hotel reservations have been muddled up and they find themselves out on a limb. But help is on hand as they're offered lodgings by queer little museum manager Ernest Keller (Sydney Lassick), who invites them to stay with himself and his wife Virginia (Lelia Goldoni) at their rambling old house on the outskirts of town. However, Keller isn't the kindly Samaritan he first seems and not only is there unrest in the Keller household, there's also something very nasty lurking in the basement...

This unassuming, competently constructed psychological chiller doesn't have a great deal of originality; in fact anyone with a fondness for the Tyburn opus *The Ghoul* will scent an air of familiarity about *The Unseen*. But for all that – and with the exception of a subplot involving Jennifer's old flame Tony (Doug Barr, from TV's *The Fall Guy*) showing up to try and woo her back – it remains relatively taut throughout its concise duration. Of course, it isn't the occupant of the cellar who's the real monster here; it's Sydney Lassick's childlike, alcoholic bully with a dark secret. The "unseen" himself, kept like an animal, living in squalor in a nest of old rags, is the retarded offspring of Keller's incestuous relationship with Virginia, who isn't actually his wife but his sister. The sight of the bulky thirty-something Junior Keller (Stephen Furst), with the intellect and demeanour of a baby, dressed in a nappy and scampering around the filthy basement waving a threadbare stuffed teddy lives a lot better than it reads, in fact it's fiercely disquieting. With two of the three girls bumped off fairly early on, it leaves Bach to face off against Furst alone, and the sequence in which – too infantile to understand the effect he's having – he innocently terrorises her is horrible to watch. A poorly effected bit of exploitation, with Lassick peeping on Lois Young taking a bath, gives rise to (unintentional) laughter as the shape of the keyhole tracks her movements around the bathroom. Chuckles are quickly stifled, however, with a prolonged attack as Young is dragged down through the ventilation grate in the floor.

Anything with Sydney Lassick – formerly Carrie White's insensitive tutor in *Carrie* – is worth a look, but watching beautiful Barbara Bach go through her paces one can't help but muse over what went wrong with her career; after building a respectable CV in minor genre fare like *Short Night of Glass Dolls* and *Black Belly of the Tarantula*, then headlining in studio blockbusters such as *The Spy Who Loved Me* and *Force 10 from Navarone*, she nose-dived into rubbish like *Island of Mutations*, *The Humanoid* and, most degrading of all, *Caveman*. What a shame. Lelia Goldoni isn't given much to do except look troubled and tearful, but Stephen Furst's subnormal man-child is extremely effective and you can hardly believe it's the same actor who, just a year earlier, was goofing around for John Landis in *Animal House*. Relentlessly grim and vaguely depressing, *The Unseen* is nonetheless atmospheric and well worth a look.

Something of a trip down memory lane for those who remember catching this one in the early days of grotty VHS home cinema, Digital Entertainment have done their utmost to ensure the atmosphere is kept intact with their DVD revival. A cheap and not very cheerful 12-chapter-encoded transfer of a splicy print with hissy sound, damage at the reel change points and evidence of drop-out from its tape source might satisfy your yen for nostalgia, but its hardly the sort of thing one expects from a DVD pressing. The darker sequences also suffer from appalling definition and since 75% of the film takes place at night this is a considerable handicap. The only augmentation – a 12-shot gallery of freeze-frame images from the film – is hardly likely to entice those who already have *The Unseen* in their video collection to invest in this substandard digital rendering. A very different (in terms of transfer and extras) edition subsequently appeared from Code Red in the U.S. and is covered in detail in *DVD Delirium Volume 4*.

– TG

U

UZUMAKI

Colour, 2000, 87m. / Directed by Higuchinsky [Akihiro Higuchi] / Starring Eriko Hatsune, Fhi Fan, Ren Osugi, Keiko Takahashi / Artsmagic (UK R2 PAL), Eastern Star, Elite (US R1 NTSC) / WS (1.77:1) (16:9) / DD 2.0, Universe (HK R3 NTSC) / WS (1.85:1) / DD 2.0

An enigmatic, obsessive horror fantasy about a town cursed by spirals. Kirie (Eriko Hatsune), daughter of a potter, and her best friend (Fhi Fan), whose father (Ren Osugi) collects and obsesses over the shapes, seem to be immune, but everyone else is drawn into the literally spiralling curse. Osugi argues with his wife (Takahashi) about his spiral collection and commits suicide by throwing himself into a concrete mixer, whereupon his widow develops an intense phobia of spirals, even cutting away her fingerprints (her son conceals a medical poster that would reveal that she has spirals in her ears). Meanwhile, at the teenagers' school, several pupils and a teacher gradually transform into giant, slime-covered, spiral-shelled snail-people and the *Heathers*-style bitch queen sprouts a vast Medusa-like hairdo of multiple spirals (these plot threads are conveyed by brief effects shots). Characters die ground around the axles of wheels or against spiral cracks, and when cremated their ashes spiral into the sky as a tornado nears the town.

Director Higuchinsky (real name Akihiro Higuchi) fills the movie with spirals: subtle CGI swirls and natural effects like a potter's wheel or a kind of fish-cake and more outlandish images like the snail-shells sprouting under wet shirts or characters twisted into elongated, spiral-wound corpses. Based, like many anime or live-action films, on the opening instalments of a Japanese manga, this sets up far more mysteries than it can resolve, but it does have an oddly effective, downbeat finish. Also known as *Spiral*, *Vortex* or *Whirlpool*, this should not be confused with *Rasen*, the *Ringu* sequel also released under the title *The Spiral*.

Artsmagic's DVD presents a pristine-looking anamorphic widescreen transfer, with a very satisfyingly creepy 2.0 sound mix full of sinister whispers and quiet drips.

This company always seems to get excellent masters, though they have a tendency to send out duff check discs that will only play on this reviewer's computer monitor – no one has yet reported similar problems with finished copies. A nice but not outstanding extras package runs to a making-of featurette ("Uzumaki Q"), stills (including some from scenes shot but not used), biographies and filmographies and some artwork, plus the usual company cross-promotional stuff. The non-anamorphic Region 3 disc from Universe is moderately grainy, and the only extra offered is a rough-looking, cursory trailer. The anamorphic Elite disc looks fine and features a solid 2.0 mix, but the 5.1 audio option sounds wildly unbalanced and is best avoided; this disc includes only the theatrical trailer. An Eastern Star reissue in the U.S. is much closer to the U.K. version, offering the same transfer and extras as the Elite disc but adding on the making-of featurette and a creepy "Camcorder Footage" reel.
– KN

VACAS

Colour, 1991, 96m. / Directed by Julio Medem / Starring Emma Suárez, Ana Torrent, Kandido Uranga, Carmelo Gómez / Tartan (UK R0 PAL), Sogepaq (Spain R2 PAL) / WS (1.85:1) (16:9), Vanguard (US R1 NTSC) / WS (1.85:1)

The title means "cows" in Spanish, and most of the events in this lush feature debut from director Julio Medem (*Sex and Lucia*, *The Red Squirrel*) involve the presence of bovine creatures in one form or another. Spanning the late 1800s through the 1930s, this epic chronicles two feuding families living in Spain's Basque region. During the Second Carlist War, two soldiers, Carmelo (Kandido Uranga) and Iriguibel (Carmelo Gómez), are torn apart by the latter's cowardice during combat. Decades later their sons (played by the same actors), who have become rival expert log cutters (*aizcolari*), feel the ramifications of this long-running feud when their siblings and children begin a complex dance of romantic entanglements. As the Spanish Civil War approaches, loyalties will be tested as the blood and passion prove to be incompatible partners.

A startling first feature for the consistently fascinating if not always consistent Medem, *Vacas* is a visually sumptuous, often harsh study of Spain's history as a defining force on human destiny. Similar in spirit to Bernardo Bertolucci's *1900*, this multigenerational study spans an even greater length of time and also adds the gimmick of actors portraying three different generations of characters (not unlike Claude Lelouch's *Les uns et les autres*, aka *Bolero*, albeit for wholly different reasons).

The American DVD from Vanguard is a watchable but decidedly mediocre presentation; much like their disc of *Tierra*, this was taken from a flat, highly compromised source with frequently unstable colours. Much more satisfying are the Region 2 Tartan and Sogepaq DVDs, which sport a beautiful anamorphic transfer, optional subtitles, and slightly more spacious widescreen framing. Colours are stable and nicely saturated, essential to appreciating the delicate pastoral photography. Both discs offer further Medem trailers (*Sex and Lucia*, *Tierra*, *Lovers of the Arctic Circle*, and *The Red Squirrel*) and a gallery.

THE VAMPIRE

B&W, 1957, 84m. / Directed by Fernando Mendez / Starring Abel Salazar, Germán Robles, Carmen Montejo, Ariadna Welter

THE VAMPIRE'S COFFIN

B&W, 1957, 82m. / Directed by Fernando Mendez / Starring Abel Salazar, Carlos Ancira, Yerye Beirute / Mondo Macabro (UK R0 PAL), CasaNegra (US R1 NTSC)

Not to be confused with the U.S. science fiction monster movie of the same name also shot in 1957, *The Vampire* is a significant film in the Mexican horror cinema and also an important part of the worldwide revival of Gothic horror that came in the late 1950s. Essentially an attempt to reprise the Universal style of black and white monster picture (owing something plotwise to *Son of Dracula*), it also hits on a couple of innovations (fangs) that would recur a year later in Hammer's *Dracula* and become standard in the vampire subgenre.

It opens with the cloaked Señor Duval (Germán Robles) looming in a courtyard and attacking the heroine's maiden aunt (Carmen Montejo). Then, at a rural railway station, young Marta (Ariadna Welter) meets with nattily-trenchcoated undercover psychologist Dr. Enrique (Abel Salazar) and hitches a lift to the Sycamores, Marta's family estate, with a minion transporting boxes of Hungarian earth to Duval. Most sources list that Duval is an Alucard-style alias for Count Karol de Lavud, the vampire interred in the crypt of the Sycamores, but actually they are separate characters: Duval is the late Count's equally vampiric brother. Duval is out to resurrect his sibling (who never shows up), in addition to the traditional vampire business of drinking the heroine's blood. Aunt Eloise shows up in slinky black as Duval's vampire sidekick and her mad, supposedly dead sister periodically comes out of the cobwebby crypt waving her crucifix and ranting about the vampire threat. As usual, bits of business are parroted from Dracula: vampires not showing up in mirrors, Duval entering the heroine's bedroom via the balcony and biting her neck, physicians puzzling over two small holes in the neck, the vampire in immaculate evening dress sitting up in his coffin.

V

Most familiar in a dubbed version, Mondo Macabro present *El Vampiro* in its original Spanish language, with optional English subtitles. The soundtrack isn't free of crackle and the source print betrays mild wear and tear, but the sharp transfer shows off director Mendez's flair for Universal-look shadowy compositions. An English language track is included for those who can't imagine the film without alien voices, though Robles's hollow Hispanic Lugosi tones are especially distinctive. The extras are the same documentary on Mexican horror found on Mondo Macabro's *Alucarda* DVD and, most interestingly, a translated Mexican photo-novel derived from the film's direct sequel *El Ataud del Vampiro* (*The Vampire's Coffin*) which carries on the story of all the major characters.

The CasaNegra U.S. edition came much later in the game but features the best transfer of the bunch and adds a second disc with *The Vampire's Coffin*. Both feature the English and Spanish-language tracks with optional English subtitles as well as some moderate but welcome extras – radio spots, an audio commentary by Mexican horror expert Robert Cotter, stills galleries, an article on Mexican horror, and a DVD-Rom photo-novel for the second film.
– KN

VAMPIRE BLUES

Colour, 1999, 90/67m. / Directed by Jess Franco / Starring Analía Ivars, Rachel Sheppard, Jess Franco, Lina Romay / Sub Rosa (US R1 NTSC) / DD2.0

Jess Franco whirls out a video generation lesbian remake of his haunting *Female Vampire* in the form of *Vampire Blues*, a free-association romp better appreciated by Franco fans than casual horror viewers. More of an extended music video filled with Franco's trademark directorial quirks and fetishes than a narrative film, this should be familiar terrain for Eurotrash veterans looking for their latest fix from the master of Spanish sleaze.

While lounging topless on the Spanish coast, Rachel (Rachel Sheppard) catches the eye of seductive Countess Irina (Analía Ivars), a vampire prone to hugging trees, dancing behind huge glass bottles, and fondling herself through pink boas. Tormented by dreams of the devilish countess, Rachel is further puzzled when she sees the woman's likeness on a T-shirt peddled by a souvenir salesman (played by Franco, of course). She then takes in a nightclub show where the main attraction, psychic gypsy Magda (Lina Romay) who stays mostly clothed for once) proclaims, "Yew arrrre from New Errrk, New Jeerrsey!" Rachel, her slip-sliding accent notwithstanding, naturally replies, "If you mean Newark, New Jersey, yes." Magda then reveals she knows all about Rachel's visions and has even visited the girl herself in dreams. Furthermore, she knows how to stop the bloodsucker, thanks to the most unorthodox vampire "staking" in movie history.

As with his other shot on video projects like *Tender Flesh* and *Mari-Cookie and the Killer Tarantula*, *Vampire Blues* is saddled with a nonexistent budget and amateurish sound recording, which doesn't help much with the actors' already thick accents. Of course, none of this will matter to Franco fans, who could probably bear anything after wading through sludge like *Lust for Frankenstein*, from which this is definitely several steps up. Fortunately Franco mostly plays to his strengths here and focuses on long, non-dialogue passages scored with funky lounge, jazz, and blues riffs, while the actresses do their thing. It's odd to think that this director once splashed his kinky visions across international cinema screens in lush scope and Technicolor, but at least he's still cranking 'em out well into his days as a senior citizen. As usual Romay is intriguing to watch (especially in her freaky gypsy make-up) and Ivars makes a slinky vampire, but Sheppard gives a clumsy non-performance that would make porn actors wince. She's almost enough to make one pine for Amber Newman.

As with other later Franco titles, *Vampire Blues* is presented in both a streamlined American cut (67 minutes) and a longer European version (90 minutes), the latter basically containing more languorous camerawork and extended crotch shots. Video quality is wholly dependent on how much visual distortion Franco cranks into the picture; scenes are often suffused with chroma effects which turn the screen into a riot of tropical colours. The surround audio sounds fine when the music's playing, at least. The disc also includes a dupey-looking "Vampire Blues" music video by The Ubangis, a candid photo gallery, and the usual Sub Rosa promo reel. The packaging indicates a "behind the scenes", which may have been left off unless it's an exceptionally well-hidden Easter egg.

VAMPIRE CIRCUS

Colour, 1971, 83m. / Directed by Robert Young / Starring Adrienne Corri, Laurence Payne, Domini Blythe, Robert Tayman, Anthony Higgins, Skip Martin, Lynne Frederick, John Moulder-Brown, Lalla Ward, David Prowse, Serena, Milovan / Synapse (Blu-ray & DVD) (US R0 HD/ NTSC) / WS (1.66:1) (16:9), Carlton (UK R2 PAL), Koch (Germany R2 PAL), Filmax (Spain R2 PAL) / WS (1.78:1) (16:9), JVD (Japan R2 NTSC), CVC (Italy R2 PAL)

 Citizens of the plague-ridden village of Schtettel are initially delighted when a travelling circus breaches the quarantine boundaries to take their minds off

their ill fortune. But when children begin to disappear, it looks as if a vile curse is taking its toll, wrought upon them for having slain the vampire Count Mitterhouse fifteen years previous.

With victuals dished out in the form of vampires, stakes-through-the-heart, decapitation, life-saving crucifixes, bare breasts, murder, mayhem and bloodshed by the gallon there's no mistaking that with *Vampire Circus* we're back on well-trodden Hammer stomping-ground. And being Hammer this is no ordinary circus; there's no big top and the sawdust ring is nothing more than a circle of torches stuck in the ground. It differs, however, in that the acrobats, animal trainers and clowns are all vampires. The protracted pre-titles sequence is a mini-epic in its own right, with Domini Blythe (as Anna, wife to Laurence Payne's schoolteacher Albert Mueller) luring a little girl into the clutches of sadistic, silky-voiced vampire Count Mitterhouse (*House of Whipcord*'s Robert Tayman). With the child dead, the couple make love, only to be set upon by angry villagers who overpower and stake Mitterhouse. One has only to scratch the surface of this opening scenario to reveal allusions to child molestation, made even more iffy by Anna's voyeuristic swoon as she watches the Count feed on the child. Fortunately director Robert Young moves the action along swiftly enough that there isn't too much time to dwell on the implications, the focus shifting rapidly to Anna's fate as the villagers loosen their belts and for one horrible moment it appears as if she's going to be gang-raped. It's almost a relief when all they do is administer a thrashing for her collusion with the vampire. And all this before the opening credits roll!

Vampire Circus is a stimulating confection and one of Hammer's few successful attempts at doing something fresh with fatigued themes, and it's right up there with the best of their vampire epics. Although the abduction and murder of children as a plot thread tiptoes on very thin

V

ice, whenever the narrative brushes against it it's quite tactfully handled and avoids a reprise of the more overtly unsavoury tone of the prologue.

The casting is a blend of excellence and folly. Anthony Higgins's sexual predator Emile, Robert Tayman's smoothly arrogant Count and Laurence Payne's world-weary schoolmaster take the honours. Pick of the crop though is Skip Martin, who played the malignant dwarf in *Horror Hospital*, appearing here as a, er... malignant dwarf. The film's most surreal moment occurs when he peels off his clown's mask to reveal a layer of even more sinister clown make-up beneath. But on the other hand we have to put up with Lynne Frederick's irritatingly puny Dora, and an equally ineffectual John Moulder-Brown as young hero Anton, delivering his lines without so much as a hint of conviction. Lalla Ward (one time *Doctor Who* companion and erstwhile Mrs. Tom Baker) pops up as a vampire gymnast. Twice Frankenstein Monster and later Darth Vader, Dave Prowse is the circus strongman.

There are some wonderfully inventive moments scattered throughout the story, such as Emile's metamorphosis into a black panther, whereupon he tears a group of escaping village folk to shreds, strewing the undergrowth with all manner of viscera, brain-matter and eyeballs (all courtesy of Les Bowie and his effects team). There's also a creative decapitation by crossbow wire. The bizarre highlight though is the primal and freakish mock combat between man and tiger woman; as David Whitaker's excellent score reaches a jangling crescendo Serena (bald, naked and coated in black and green striped body paint) is tamed by whip-wielding Milovan the Hunter. Anyone seeking evidence that by the 1970s Hammer's vampire cycle had developed blunt teeth won't find much to support their case in *Vampire Circus*. Slick, exciting, alternately violent and erotic, Young's movie simmers with a surfeit of the Gothic atmosphere for which Hammer knew no peers.

Vampire Circus is available on several different Region 2 discs. Carlton's PAL edition presents the film in an attractive 1.78:1 (16:9 enhanced) format with 8 chapter marks; sound and subtitles are in English only, with the film's theatrical trailer being the sole bonus feature. The disc (technically discontinued but readily available) is a constituent of a Carlton triple box set entitled "The Vampire Collection", which also comprises *Twins of Evil* and *Countess Dracula*. JVD's Region 2 Japanese release is in NTSC format. However, the full screen picture quality on the 9-chapter punctuated feature is not only inferior to the Carlton disc, it's only a marginal step up from video quality. The sound – in English Dolby Digital 2.0 with an option to remove the default Japanese subtitles – is nothing remarkable either. Additional features comprise the same release trailer as the British disc (but with burnt-in Japanese subs), a small but attractive gallery of b&w stills, some textual cast profiles (trust your Japanese is up to par!) and poster artwork. The Italian disc is also a full screen print, while the German and Spanish releases are anamorphic.

Enter Synapse Films, who snagged the rights to this much-requested title along with a couple of other goodies as part of their Hammer Collection line. This one was chosen as their inaugural Blu-ray title, packaged as a combo pack along with the DVD (which features identical bonus features). The HD transfer opens with the MGM logo and appears to be taken from the same source used for HD broadcast, though this time it's 1080p and appears to have undergone some additional colour correction and black level balancing. Most significantly, this marks the first anamorphic transfer in the correct aspect ratio, as the British disc sliced a bit off the top and bottom while the full frame versions lost information on the sides. The opening sequence and some of the later night scenes tend to look a bit murky given the heavy filtering used to simulate a twilight appearance, but after you get past the main credits, it's largely smooth sailing with vivid colours and a nice, film-like appearance with a little bit of natural grain where it should be. The DTS-HD audio is also substantially stronger than previous versions, which is especially obvious during the prologue and Serena's famous bare dance scene. An optional DTS-HD music and effects track is also included. (The DVD features both audio options in standard Dolby Digital.) Incidentally, this also marks the second Hammer Blu-ray in the world, following the UK's excellent *Paranoiac* release from Eureka.

As for extras, the biggie here is the half-hour "Bloodiest Show on Earth: The Making of *Vampire Circus*", an entertaining featurette that manages to pull a surprisingly heavy amount of information together given the difficulty of finding participants for later Hammer titles. Five interview subjects cover the history of the film, with *Flesh and Blood* Hammer doc maker and expert Ted Newsom kicking things off, followed by director Joe Dante, *Video Watchdog*'s Tim Lucas, writer Philip Nutman, and actor Prowse. The featurette is broken down into categories ranging from Hammer's status at the time to scheduling problems to censorship hassles, and everyone gets in several good points about one of Hammer's most unique cult items. (Interestingly, no mention is made of its closest Hammer cousin, the later *Captain Kronos: Vampire Hunter*.) Apart from the annoyingly repetitive calliope music interstitials, it's a great piece and an excellent companion to the main feature. Nutman returns for the 15-minute "Gallery of Grotesqueries: A Brief History of Circus Horrors", which illustrates this peculiar subgenre by covering everything from *The Cabinet of Dr. Caligari* and *Freaks* to, uh, *Carnival of Blood*. Then it's Nutman time again for the 9-minute "Visiting the *House of Hammer*: Britain's Legendary Horror Magazine", which covers the short but interesting heritage of the studio's comic book and

magazine arm, which is followed appropriately by an animated motion version of the *Vampire Circus* comic book (basically the prologue). An animated gallery of stills and posters, and the original UK trailer round out the package, with all extras presented in HD (which is pretty breathtaking when you see some of the razor sharp poster art). Hammer fans, this one has definitely been worth the wait.

– TG

THE VAMPIRE LOVERS

Colour, 1970, 87m. / Directed by Roy Ward Baker / Starring Ingrid Pitt, Peter Cushing, Dawn Addams, Pippa Steel, George Cole, Madeline Smith, Douglas Wilmer, Kate O'Mara, Jon Finch, Ferdy Mayne, Kirsten Betts / MGM (US R1 NTSC) / WS (1.85:1) (16:9), MGM-ILC (UK R2 PAL)

Purportedly summoned to tend a sick friend, the Countess Karnstein (Dawn Addams) asks General Spielsdorf (Peter Cushing) to take care of her daughter Marcilla (Ingrid Pitt) for a few days. Almost immediately people from the nearby village begin dying, but more pressingly for the General his daughter Laura (Pippa Steel) falls ill. He's grateful that Marcilla is there to offer the ailing child comfort. But Laura dies and Marcilla disappears, inveigling herself into the household of Roger Morton (George Cole) and his daughter Emma (Madeline Smith). The pattern of death looks set to repeat itself as Emma falls ill, but now there is talk of vampirism in the village. The General, still grieving over his daughter's unexplained death, turns to his old friend Baron Hartog (Douglas Wilmer). A renowned vampire killer, Hartog tells him they must seek out and destroy Marcilla, who he believes to be a rapacious reincarnation of the long-dead Carmilla Karnstein...

It's not uncommon to hear a song or catch a scent in the street that transports one back to a particular place or time in one's life. The same can happen on occasion with movies. For me *The Vampire Lovers* is one of them. Each time the curtain goes up it's suddenly that warm summer evening when I got to see it for the first time on the late late show. A minor epiphany to be sure, but one never forgotten, and it's a movie I've revisited dozens of times in the intervening years. The late Roy Ward Baker's film is tantamount to manna from heaven for literary vampire aficionados and fans of silver screen bloodsuckers alike, faithful as it is in essence to Joseph Sheridan LeFanu's "Carmilla" while stirring in a liberal helping of the Hammer-esque via Kensington Gore, glistening fangs and diaphanous gowns. In fact, with the possible exception of Gabrielle Beaumont's 1989 mounting of the tale, this remains the most significant page to screen translation – almost verbatim in fact – of LeFanu's masterpiece. Ingrid Pitt's interpretation of the ubiquitous creature of the night makes for one of her most exciting and evocative performances and, in spite of her considerable body of work, it's a role with which many will always associate her. The fact she doesn't quite possess the fresh-faced girlish qualities of LeFanu's invention can be overlooked. Carmilla is a tortured soul, cursed with immortality and empathic to those upon whom she feeds, driven by a bloodlust that sustains life yet preoccupied with the notion of a death that will end her misery. Pitt's performance veers from high passion to melancholy torment while Tudor Gates's juicy script relocates the traditional jugular puncturing a few inches down to more libidinous bodily parts.

The Vampire Lovers draws together more familiar British talent under one roof than almost any other film of the era. Along with Ingrid Pitt and ever-reliable Hammer figurehead Peter Cushing, we have '70s sex-kitten Madeline Smith (also in Hammer's *Taste the Blood of Dracula* and

Frankenstein and the Monster from Hell) as fragile beauty Emma, veteran of film and TV George Cole as her father, and Kate O'Mara (from the same year's *Horror of Frankenstein*) as Mademoiselle Perrodon, riding out a personality change that turns her from genteel governess to passionate, enslaved concubine of the vampire. Douglas Wilmer and former Polanksi leads Jon Finch (*Macbeth*) and Ferdy Mayne (*The Fearless Vampire Killers*) bring their own unique talents to the party.

From its opening sequence as Baron Hartog avenges the murder of his sister by slaying a Karnstein neck-nibbler (Kirsten Betts) to the closing shot of an exquisite oil painting of Carmilla decomposing to a skeletal husk (a nod to Oscar Wilde), *The Vampire Lovers* is a joy to behold. Roy Ward Baker – who had recently shot *Scars of Dracula*, the last of Hammer's Gothic Draculas – manoeuvres the cast around Scott MacGregor's sumptuous period sets with consummate skill. That the film is essential viewing for the genre zealot almost goes without saying. There are certainly better films in Hammer's catalogue of carnage, but neither before nor afterwards did they manufacture one so intensely elegant and appetizingly prurient.

MGM/ILC in the U.K. were the first to push *The Vampire Lovers* out on DVD. With a crisp full screen transfer (awarded just 10 chapter points), it was exciting to discover it included oft-absent footage of Kirsten Betts's decapitation (with the opening credits then playing out over Hartog's bloody sword and her severed head) and Cushing's climactic beheading of Pitt. Regrettably, the disc is completely void of any extras whatsoever. In the U.S. the film received the MGM "Midnite Movies" treatment on a Region 1 disc, doubled-billed with *Countess Dracula*, and complete with an audio commentary by Ingrid Pitt, Roy Ward Baker and Tudor Gates. This disc offers a complete 16:9 widescreen transfer, which is slightly compromised because of

the matting (to about 1.81:1), but it does contain an extra shot lasting just under one and a half seconds, of Ingrid getting out of the bath tub (at 32m 09s). However the feature is exactly the same length as the British ILC disc (after allowing for PAL/NTSC conversion) because there is an insert shot of Madeleine Smith as Ingrid gets up.
– TG

VAMPIRE'S KISS

Colour, 1988, 103m. / Directed by Robert Bierman / Starring Nicolas Cage, Maria Conchita Alonso, Kasi Lemmons, Elizabeth Ashley, Jennifer Beals, Jill Gatsby / MGM (US R1 NTSC, US R2 PAL) / WS (1.85:1) (16:9)

Taking its title from the film-within-a-film found in Brian De Palma's *Body Double*, *Vampire's Kiss* is nothing if not a peculiar addition to the cinematic lore of the undead, poaching an idea or two from *Martin* and then playing like a '70s bizarro big city crack-up comedy – *Who Is Harry Kellermann and Why Is He Saying Those Terrible Things About Me?* or *The Prisoner of Second Avenue* – with seedy psychotic moments lifted from *The Driller Killer* or *Repulsion*.

New York literary agent Peter Loew (Nicolas Cage) is going mad, alienating his girlfriend Jackie (Kasi Lemmons), bullying his assistant Alva Restrepo (Maria Conchita Alonso) and waffling to his psychiatrist Dr. Glaser (Elizabeth Ashley). While drunk, he is interrupted in lovemaking with Jackie by a bat, and finds himself aroused by the creature. The next night, after a day spent harassing Alva over a missing contract, he picks up Rachel (Jennifer Beals), an exotic woman who bites him during sex and whom he fantasises is a vampire. After imaginary encounters with Rachel, Peter begins to think that he is turning into a vampire, and takes to

wearing dark glasses by day, sleeping under his couch, eating cockroaches and shunning crucifixes. When his cruelty to Alva forces her to call in sick, he takes a taxi to her home and apologises, convincing her to come back to the office, although he then turns nasty again and forces her to stay until she locates the contract. When Alva succeeds, Peter claims that it's too late and menaces her. He takes a gun from her, unaware that it's loaded with blanks, and shoots himself, becoming convinced that his transformation into an unkillable monster is now complete. Peter's behaviour becomes even more extreme, extending to rape and murder, but the coherence of his fantasy collapses as he spirals out of control.

There is a familiarity in the use of a yuppie singles bar all night world as a location for vampirism, linking the movie with such '80s bloodsuckers as *Vamp* and *Graveyard Shift*, or even comedy disasters like *Rockula* and *Beverly Hills Vamp*. This is borne out in the early emphasis on the fetishist aspects of vampirism, as a very striking Jennifer Beals does her exsanguinating in black underwear and suspenders, but this then spins off in several directions, almost providing a template for the milieu and narrative approach of *American Psycho* (the novel and the film) as we are presented with horrors of varying levels of reality, from a disco murder (the victim is played by Larry Cohen's daughter) to a truly bizarre left-field diversion as the protagonist briefly escapes into a fantasy of finding the perfect soulmate only to ruin it by imagining the instant collapse of this new relationship into ranting disgust. Given that at least as much of the film's running time is spent on Peter's obsessional terrorising of Alva for her failure to locate the missing contract as it is on his excursion into vampirism, it barely qualifies as the horror movie which appears to be struggling towards birth in the sequences featuring Beals as a slinky vampirette (though she is far better than in her other brush with genre iconography, the

V

1985 Frankenstein adaptation *The Bride*) and settles into the nightmare comic course of screenwriter Joseph Minion's earlier, more sustained *After Hours*.

Robert Bierman, making a big screen debut after his interesting HBO movie *Apology*, works with and around one of Cage's quirkiest, most unrestrained performances. While Griffin Dunne was gradually driven to histrionic despair by his circumstances, Cage's Peter Loew is at the outset suffering from loose-limbed drunkenness by night, tight-ass compulsiveness in the office, and the most bizarre accent all the time. From this, Cage takes off into a hilarious approximation of at least two of the hammiest vampire-related performances of the past, Max Schreck as the scuttling hunchbacked Dracula in *Nosferatu* and Dwight Frye as the wild-eyed, wild-haired, cockroach-eating Renfield in the 1930 *Dracula*. The performance allows for unpredictably effective comedy, especially in the office nit-picking and in Peter's attempts to transform his yuppie environment into a vampire's lair, and extends to a moment of legendary method madness worth setting by the coprophage finale of *Pink Flamingos* as Cage eats a real cockroach.

MGM's American two-sided DVD offers different framings of the film: those with widescreen monitors will prefer the 16:9 enhanced 1.85:1 transfer, which is especially good-looking in scenes that use the city as a panoramic backdrop, but on regular televisions, the full frame version rarely compromises the image and perhaps directs even more attention to the extraordinary central performance. Aside from a trailer and optional subs in English, Spanish and French, the major extra is a commentary track with a reunited Cage and Bierman that reveals this version is slightly expanded from the U.S. release cut. While not entirely free of "this is so great" stroking, the track covers the making of the film in interesting detail, showing that the passions both

brought to the project have not ebbed over the years; neither participant is aware that *Dance of the Vampires* and *The Fearless Vampire Killers* are the same film, but they do show a great awareness of the various precedents they were playing with, to the extent that Cage puts forward the theory that Schreck's vampire performance might have been influenced by John Barrymore's Mr. Hyde while Bierman wonders whether Cage was channelling John Cleese's funny walks. Alas, the international MGM disc released in almost every European country features no extras at all and has one of their irritating non-language menus filled with cryptic symbols to avoid translation costs. – KN

VAMPIRELLA

Colour, 1996, 86m. / Directed by Jim Wynorski / Starring Talisa Soto, Roger Daltrey, Richard Joseph Paul, Angus Scrimm, Lenny Juliano, Peggy Trentini, John Terlesky, Antonia Dorian, Corinna Harney, John Landis, David B. Katz, Forrest J. Ackerman, Jim Wynorski, Gary Gerani / New Concorde (US R1 NTSC)

After massacring the High Elders on the Planet Drakulon, 30 centuries ago renegade vampire Vlad (Roger Daltrey) and his disciples fled to Earth. Intent on avenging the death of her stepfather, one of the Elders, Ella (Talisa Soto) gives chase but is forced to crash-land on Mars where she spends the next 3000 years in stasis. In the year 1996 she manages to hitch a ride to Earth on a space shuttle. Renamed Vampirella, she teams up with Adam Van Helsing (Richard Joseph Paul) to track down Vlad, who has now established himself as Vegas rock star Jamie Blood. Vlad's plans for apocalyptic world decimation are about to come to fruition...

Back in the mid-1970s *Vampirella* was to have been a Hammer Films production with Barbara Leigh in the title role, but insurmountable hurdles prevented it from happening. Travelling one of the rockier roads in pre-production history, it was to be twenty years before the project finally made it from page to screen, albeit some distance from its origins. Lensed for Roger Corman's outfit under Jim Wynorski's direction, *Pumpkinhead* scripter Gary Gerani's story is a bog standard, hi-tech, low-brow thriller with a revenge subplot. The big mistake they made though was substituting the original costume design for something that looks as if it were fashioned from red plastic carrier bags. Soto looked fine wearing the original outfit for a pre-production photo shoot, but when filming commenced she had a change of heart, worried that she might keep slipping out of it. Was Talisa Soto (*Licence to Kill*) such an asset to the production that they couldn't have hired someone who would wear it? Soto is a good actress to be sure, but thespian talent isn't a prerequisite for this particular role. Soto's concerns with regard her modesty may have been valid, but if she'd had an ounce of sense she'd have realised how ridiculous she looked in the substitute and refused to wear that too. Whatever, the decision to make the change alienated a sizeable wedge of the ready-made audience of Vampirella fans who had waited so long for this movie. And quite what Roger Daltrey thought he was doing appearing in this I'm not sure, but according to director Jim Wynorski he hopped aboard by way of a personal tribute to his late friend Keith Moon, who apparently loved Forrest Ackerman's Vampirella comic books. Er... okay. All this aside, *Vampirella* is a standard Wynorski amalgam of bargain basement effects (notably some cartoonish man-to-bat transformations), recycled stock footage from earlier capers, superfluous nudity (no, unsurprisingly not Soto), and occasional infusions of lame humour. Stitched into this blend is a romantic attachment between Vampirella and Van Helsing, the latter having

forsaken the solo, low-key vampire stalking activities of his ancestors to head up an organisation named Purge, dedicated to cleansing the world of bloodsuckers, while cruising around in a Cadillac with the licence plate V HUNT. The less said about the audacity of the monkey-see-monkey-do emulation of *Scars of Dracula*'s climax the better!

Vampirella boasts an eclectic cast, encompassing everyone from the malapropos (Daltrey and Soto) to the charisma-free (Paul), from Wynorski regulars and past cohorts (*Transylvania Twist*'s Angus Scrimm, *Bare Wench Project*'s Lenny Juliano, *Ghoulies IV*'s Peggy Trentini, *Deathstalker II*'s John Terlesky, and *Dinosaur Island*'s Antonia Dorian) to decorous fresh blood (*Playboy* Playmate Corinna Harney). Even director John Landis drops in. There are plenty of in-jokes too: The first character Vampirella meets upon arriving on Earth is a young film buff named Forry Ackerman (David B. Katz), Ackerman himself puts in a one shot cameo, and there are appearances by Wynorski as a newscaster and Gerani as a member of Daltrey's fanged consortium. The final credits are peppered with faux names, among them Peachy Carnehan and Daniel Dravot (characters in John Huston's *The Man Who Would Be King*).

Given his flair for circumventing the constraints of micro-budgets, Wynorksi delivered a fairly glossy looking production – the Vegas location work and climax inside the Hoover dam lend it flash production value – but this fails to compensate for the fact it's just not the *Vampirella* we were all hoping for. While the world continues to wait for both *Death's Dark Avenger* (the sequel promised on the closing titles) and something more in keeping with the character's roots, if you're hankering for Vampi, for the time being this will have to suffice.

New Concorde appear to be tidying up their act, for this Region 1 DVD release of *Vampirella* (presented under the umbrella of their "Vampire Collection") actually

V

includes the trailer promised on the sleeve. As Corman acolytes will be all too aware, there have been occasions in the past where such promises have proven empty ones. In any event, their disc presents the movie in an "original restored version", which reinstates several previously excised sequences, including a fuller version of Daltrey's song "Bleed for Me". It's divided by a generous 18 chapter points. Along with the aforementioned trailer there are also a fistful of previews for other titles in the collection, a selection of cast and crew biographies, plus a jaunty commentary from director Wynorski. Never one to shirk responsibility for his failings, among other things he addresses the costume change controversy, points out moments where the slender budget forced an unhappy compromise and even confesses to his effrontery in the wholesale steal from *Scars of Dracula* (though naturally he refers to it in terms of a tribute).

– TG

VANISHING POINT

Colour, 1971, 94m. / Directed by Richard C. Sarafian / Starring Barry Newman, Dean Jagger, Cleavon Little, Charlotte Rampling / Fox (Blu-ray & DVD) (US R0/R1 HD/NTSC, UK R2 PAL) / WS (1.85:1) (16:9)

This thinly plotted road/action film belongs to the wonderful category of '70s existential chase films where cars take on almost as much personality as the characters. Released the same year as the equally popular *Two-Lane Blacktop* (and with that film the probable inspiration for *Gone in 60 Seconds* and *The Driver* among others), the story follows former cop Kowalski (*The Limey*'s Barry Newman) on a frenetic cross country, speed-fuelled trip after he bets he can race his drive away Challenger from Denver to San Francisco in fifteen hours. Egged on by blind DJ Super Soul (Cleavon Little), Kowalski burns rubber down the highway and encounters a motley crew including a naked female motorbiker, a pair of gay thieves, a faith healer, and plenty of cops.

Featuring a terrific rock soundtrack and whiplash cinematography, *Vanishing Point* is a marvellous sensory experience despite offering very little for the mind. The film was clearly designed to be a counterculture cult item and succeeded mightily, though its dime store philosophy sounds positively silly now. Unlike *Easy Rider* (which despite its continuing importance has dated atrociously from a conceptual point of view), the film at least sticks to a clear agenda, dubious symbolism and all, and moves along at a swift, enjoyable pace.

Best known at the time for a slew of television work, director Richard C. Sarafian encountered numerous problems over the film with Fox, who trimmed it down drastically to remove some of its more outlandish flights of fancy. The U.K. DVD from Fox (also sold throughout Germany and France due to its additional subtitle streams) contains the 94-minute cut most widely seen on video with only the trailer as an extra. The anamorphic transfer looks terrific, with exceptional colour and fine clarity, but the potential for extras seems a bit wasted. Fortunately, the subsequent U.S. release also boasts the slightly longer cut (106 mins.) with an additional sequence in which Kowalski meets and trysts with a beautiful angel of death (Charlotte Rampling) and features the trailer and an interesting but somewhat disjointed commentary by Sarafian. A very good Blu-ray edition carries over the same extras (including both cuts of the film) and captures the feel of watching a mint print in your home; the lossless DTS track seems like overkill considering the limited nature of the sound recording, but it gets the job done well enough. A dire 1996 TV remake with Viggo Mortensen is available from Anchor Bay, if you must watch it.

VERSUS

Colour, 2000, 115/130m. / Directed by Ryuhei Kitamura / Starring Tak Sakaguchi, Hideo Sakaki, Chieko Misaka, Kenji Matsuda / Tartan (UK R0 PAL), Tokyo Shock (Blu-ray & DVD) (US RA/R1 HD/ NTSC) / WS (1.78:1) (16:9) / DD 5.1

 A slickly-shot and edited multi-purpose exploitation movie, this boils down to little more than a mélange of general borrowings from *The Evil Dead, Highlander, Bad Taste* and *Night of the Living Dead*, with specific bits cribbed from *Miller's Crossing* (!) and *Cannibal Apocalypse* (the hole-shot-through-a-torso gag is restaged). It's the sort of film where the action choreographer (Yûji Shimomura) probably deserves equal billing with writer-director Ryuhei Kitamura, and which makes for an exciting trailer but becomes wearying when unreeled at nearly two hours.

After a sylvan period prologue sets the tone as a samurai (Tak Sakaguchi) slices up superior opposition but is bested by a fast-draw sorcerer (Hideo Sakaki), the film returns to the woods in the present day with the nameless hero reincarnated as an escaped prisoner who clashes with New Wave-look yakuza hipsters in a forest where the dead come back to life and the gangsters are therefore troubled by gun-waving zombies rubbed out and buried nearby in shallow graves. After a reel or two of zombie-fu, with guns and swords deployed to re-kill the dead and blood liberally spattered over everyone's face, the sorcerer shows up again, not reincarnated but still alive, and resumes his duel with the hero, over the supposedly magical blood of an undercharacterised heroine (Chieko Misaka). The yakuza fall under the villain's influence, especially a snappily-dressed gay bizarro (Kenji Matsuda) who starts acting like a toad, and a couple of cops (one with a stump where Sakaguchi ripped off his hand during his escape) show up with an unfeasibly large rifle to keep the action coming. Essentially, what happens is that the whole cast of characters dash hysterically around the woods copping John Woo attitudes (the hero is very fond of swishing his long coat) and whirling about to formula techno music doing damage with guns, swords and bare fists. Everyone dies at least once. The most distinctive touch is a "99 years later" epilogue set in a post-holocaust city that finds the antagonists facing each other again and suggests we've misinterpreted the basic good-and-evil set-up of the plot.

Tartan Asia Extreme's DVD showcases a pristine widescreen transfer that, along with the constant camera movement, suggests a healthier budget than was probably available. It has a Japanese language soundtrack with optional English subtitles. The extras include: four interestingly contrasting trailers using the same footage to pitch to different audiences; "Behind *Versus*: The Birth of the Dark Hero", a 25-minute "making-of"; filmographies for a couple of people who haven't made many films; brief notes by Mark Wyatt; and "The Side Show of *Versus*: Nervous", an odd little shot-on-video short (with a serial-like "to be continued" tag) featuring the minor cop characters and perhaps playing an inside joke that will elude most viewers. However, the real labour of love comes from Tokyo Shock, who first issued it in a similar one-disc special edition but then went into overdrive in 2007 with a three-disc set. What do you get? How about a 130-minute extended cut of the film (with massive changes to nearly every sequence in the film!), three audio commentaries with the cast and crew (with optional English subtitles), a DTS version of the Japanese soundtrack (and 6.1 and 2.0 stereo for the English dub), a gallery, five featurettes totalling enough time to fill up the entire second disc ("First Contact: Versus Evolution", "Behind Versus I:

V

Birth of the Dark Hero", "Behind Versus II: Versus the Legend", "Sakigake! Otoko Versus Juku: Making of New Footage", "Deep in the Woods: Behind the Scenes"), 21 minutes of deleted scenes (yes, there are more), a 12-minute editor interview, a Tak Sakaguchi overview featurette, three "Nervous" side stories, six trailers, three film festival clips, and bonus Tokyo Shock trailers. It all comes packed in one of those shiny, heavy steelbook cases, too, just to make sure you get your money's worth. A much cheaper Blu-ray of the director cut is also available, but the extras are stripped down to include the commentaries and a handful of the featurettes.

– KN

VIDOCQ

Colour, 2001, 100m. / Directed by Pitof / Starring Gérard Depardieu, Guillaume Canet, Moussa Maaskri, Ines Sastre, Edith Scob / TF1 Video (France R2 PAL) Seville (Canada R1 NTSC), Lionsgate (US R1 NTSC), Sunfilm (Blu-ray & DVD) (Germany RB/R2 HD/PAL) / WS (1.85:1) (16:9) / DD5.1, Intercontinental (HK R3 NTSC) / DD5.1

As shown by films as different as *Amelie* and *The Brotherhood of the Wolf*, the turn of the 21st Century found French cinema rediscovering a tradition of the imaginative neglected since the era of Méliès. Shot on hi-def video, which gives it an unusual illustrative look, this first feature from the favoured effects man of Jeunet et Caro (Caro contributes some designs) is a fantasy based on the career of the famous French thief-turned-policeman, here played by Gérard Depardieu as a swashbuckling steampunk sleuth.

In the opening sequence, Vidocq pursues a cloaked, mirror-masked murderer through a glassblowing works and is allowed to see the villain's face before falling to his apparent death. In the aftermath, a callow journalist (Guillaume Canet) tries to put together the facts of the case, interviewing Vidocq's partner (Moussa Maaskri) a mock-Chinese dancer/courtesan (Ines Sastre) and assorted witnesses and suspects involved in the great detective's last case, in which gunpowder-impregnated coats and lightning rod-combs concealed in hats were used to combust three establishment worthies. With unrest growing in the Paris of 1830 as Charles X seems about to topple, the journalist in the narrative present and the sleuth in flashbacks pursue the same mystery, which leads to a conspiracy to purchase the virginal daughters of the poor so their blood can be used in the manufacturer of the mask that the murderer known as "the Alchemist" uses to absorb the souls of his victims and keep him eternally young. A very busy film with each scene and setting receiving minute attention, this bustles along messily through a story that is simpler than it seems, with two big reveals – of course, Vidocq turns out to be still alive, with Depardieu plucking off disguise eyebrows with an actorly flourish, but the identity of the supernaturally-powered villain is a delayed (though guessable) surprise. An example of the "cinema du look", this is a circus of a movie, with memorable cameo turns (Franju regular Edith Scob pops up as a ringmistress-cum-brothelkeeper) keeping things lively and fun.

TF1 Video's two-disc edition is a fine way of getting to know this film, which was not widely seen outside France. Disc 1 offers a perfect anamorphic transfer of the film, wonderfully representing the distinctive burnished colour scheme, and – yes – there is an English *sous-titre* option for the non-Francophone, though this sadly doesn't extend to the audio commentary by Pitof and production designer Jean Rabasse. Disc 2, entitled *Le journal de Vidocq*, is so packed with supplementary material that it is almost frustrating to go through: separate quadrants of the main menu highlight five leading characters, affording access to sub-menus that offer featurettes about the characters, filmographies for the performers, costume designs, *un* "making of", trailers, interviews with various creatives (including an hour-long chat with Pitof), *un* "vidéoclip Apocalyptica", a study of the film's poster designs, sketches by Marc Caro, storyboard/film comparisons and much other material. Because this is such a design-intensive work, it's nice to see that the look of the film has been carried over to every aspect of the DVD, from the sleeve through the insert booklet to the menus. There is also a Region 3 disc from Hong Kong, which is full screen and has no extras at all. The Canadian release is no more English friendly, carrying the same extras but without subtitles. At least that's better than the Lionsgate U.S. release entitled *Dark Portals: The Chronicles of Vidocq*, which has only the music video and one trailer. Also available in Germany in two Blu-ray editions(!), a single-disc feature-only version and a two-disc carrying over all of the French extras; alas, even the feature has no subtitle options, making it useful only for those fluent in French or German.

– KN

VIVA LA MUERTE

Colour, 1970, 87m. / Directed by Fernando Arrabal / Starring Mahdi Chaouch, Nuria Espert / Cult Epics (US R0 NTSC) / WS (1.85:1) (16:9)

Along with the notorious Alejandro Jodorowsky and animator Roland Topor (maker of *Fantastic Planet*), the short-lived but scandalous "Panic Movement" in Mexico and Europe was begun by Fernando Arrabal, an artistic renaissance man who began his

film career with *Viva la muerte*, based on his autobiographical novel, *Baal Babylone*. The result is one of the strongest films in the 1970s surrealist movement, fit to be shown in art house theatres but packed with some of the more extreme imagery outside of an Italian cannibal film.

During the Spanish Civil War, young Fando (Mahdi Chaouch) lives with his protective mother (Nuria Espert) and, due to his arrested father, endures the taunts of his schoolmates. Though he loves his mother, Fando begins to indulge in bizarre, sadistic fantasies when he suspects that his father did not kill himself in prison as she claims. In fact, as a discovered letter proves, she herself may have been responsible for his sorry fate. Fando begins to experience perilous health problems as the line between fantasy and reality begins to blur, and his reveries become increasingly violent and depraved.

A technically fascinating film, *Viva la muerte* (*Long Live Death!*) begins with a credit sequence designed over Boschian pen and ink drawings of sexual torture, then proceeds with a mixture of beautifully shot 35mm ("real life") and videotaped footage processed to film and chromatically manipulated (the fantasies), with a little scratchy, real-life surgery footage thrown in at the end for good measure. Arrabal's film would probably make a good double bill with *Spirit of the Beehive* or *The Reflecting Skin*, though the harsh nature of its content will probably limit its appeal to viewers with iron stomachs. Though the human brutality is fairly stylized (human line-ups are gunned down mostly out of frame, eyes are gouged out via jump cuts), the occasional animal brutality is definitely real and provides some of the most upsetting moments: Fando casually slicing up a beetle at his school desk, a lizard's head bitten off at the moment of a woman's sexual climax, and most memorably, a cow's protracted slaughter transformed into a bizarre, surrealist tableau with a man stitched inside the carcass.

V

Cult Epics's beautifully mounted DVD offers a welcome opportunity to finally view this often discussed but rarely seen oddity. The anamorphically enhanced video quality looks terrific, apart from the deliberately dupey-looking video sequences; the bulk of the film boasts razor sharp detail and perfectly balanced colours. The soundtrack was recorded in French (with some dialogue looped later judging from the erratic audio quality), so that first audio option is preferable (with optional English subtitles); however, the dubbed Spanish track is here too for reference. The disc also includes a bizarre, 17-minute interview with Arrabal (in French with optional English subtitles), in which he punctuates his comments by holding up a chair in artistic poses, then later removing his shoe, sniffing it, and observing, "My feet smell good." The offscreen interviewer does not seem to concur, however. In between he offers a thumbnail history of the Panic Movement, argues that his film is not violent or extreme, and explains his own artistic agenda in sometimes rambling detail. The disc also contains a French lobby card gallery, a jaw-dropping trailer for Arrabal's second film, *I Will Walk Like a Crazy Horse*, and an insert essay by *Shock Cinema*'s Rayo Casblanca. If you love Jodorowsky or Spanish surrealism, this disc is a must see. Also available as part of Cult Epic's Arrabal box set with *I Will Walk...* and *The Guernica Tree*.

WAR OF THE COLOSSAL BEAST

B&W/Colour, 1958, 69m. / Directed by Bert I. Gordon / Starring Sally Fraser, Dean Parkin / Direct Video (UK R2 PAL), Lionsgate (US R1 NTSC)

Considering that AIP had so much success in creating memorable screen monsters in the 1950s, they oddly made little effort to develop franchises. Excluding self-referential *Teenage Werewolf* meets *Teenage Frankenstein* in-jokes in *How to Make a Monster*, the only AIP creature to earn a sequel was the Colossal Man. The unfortunate Colonel Glenn Manning, who grew to sixty feet after an Incredible Hulk-style plutonium bomb test mishap, turned out not to be dead after being blown off the top of Boulder Dam, but only mutilated, so a new actor (Dean Parkin) could replace the original Glenn Langan. It's also peculiar that this fairly throwaway effort (aka *The Terror Strikes*) is out on DVD before *The Amazing Colossal Man*, though a lengthy flashback is an excuse to cram in plentiful footage from the original.

The opening reels deal with the mystery of a vanishing truckload of groceries in Mexico, which alerts Manning's sister Joyce (Sally Fraser) that he has survived and is living in the wilderness. With a military stiff in tow, Joyce tracks down the Colossal Man, who lurches into frame to reveal a gruesome skull-face that looks less impressive with further exposure. The plot is slung-together almost at random, with an ineffectual satirical montage in the middle as various government officials pass the buck so as not to take responsibility for the giant serviceman until the Mayor of Los Angeles is browbeaten into stashing the giant in a handy aircraft hangar. There's an attempt to communicate with the amnesiac psychopath, as huge slides of Manning's past are projected on a screen hung over his chained-down form. He escapes, killing a scientist (an exciting sequence that is talked about but never shown) and goes on a nighttime rampage that winds up in Griffith Park. He towers over the observatory where Sal Mineo was gunned down in *Rebel without a Cause*, and Joyce talks him out of smashing a busload of school kids. Coming to his senses, the monster commits suicide – which used to be forbidden by the Hays Code – by grasping high-voltage electric wires, whereupon the black and white film flares into pale, sparkly colour for its final thirty seconds and the Colossal Man just vanishes.

With flatly-delivered dud dialogue ("I'm afraid the world doesn't think of a sixty foot man the way a sister does") and Bert I. Gordon's customary makeshift giant effects, this is among the least-liked of the AIP back-catalogue. Direct Video's DVD at least boasts a decent-looking print and takes the trouble to include the spot of colour at the end. Extras are identical to the other Arkoff Collection releases; see *Earth vs the Spider* for details (with which this film is co-billed with their identical transfers for the U.S. release).

– KN

WAR OF THE PLANETS
Colour, 1977, 87m. / Directed by Alfonso Brescia / Starring John Richardson, Yanti Somer

WAR OF THE ROBOTS
Colour, 1978, 100m. / Directed by Alfonso Brescia / Starring Antonio Sabato, Yanti Somer / Retromedia (US R1 NTSC)

During the 1970s, Italian cinema made no secret of its unabashed attempts to cash in on American blockbusters. *The Exorcist* kicked off a stream of imitators, but that was nothing compared to the avalanche caused by *Star Wars*, whose influence continued to linger for more than a decade. While international audiences were exposed to some of the more amusing examples like *Starcrash* and *The Humanoid*, countless other cash-ins passed under the radar and often went directly to television. Two of the stranger offenders, *War of the Planets* (*Battaglie negli spazi stellari*) and *War of the Robots* (*La guerra dei robot*), were directed back to back by the prolific Alfonso Brescia (under the awkward handle of "Al Bradly"), a jack of all trades best known for *Conqueror of Atlantis* and several spaghetti western and crime yarns. A coherent plot synopsis of either film would be well nigh impossible, given that 90% of their running time consists of costumed actors yammering at control boards and investigating long, loooong planetary caverns and tunnels, with occasional cut-rate special effects thrown in to wake up the audience.

War of the Planets (no relation to the 1966 Antonio Margheriti film, or the Japanese space opera also released in 1977!) stars Eurocult stalwart John Richardson (*Black Sunday*, *Torso*) as arrogant Orion spaceship Captain Hamilton, drawn into mystery in "the Vega Sector" when he and his crew (decked out with airline seatbelts) are pulled to an unstable planet inhabited by strange beings in stranger outfits. The planet may also be related to the mysterious destruction of another ship during a meteor storm (in the pre-credits sequence), while the ship's computer continues to go haywire and astronauts who venture outside the ship seem to be besieged by "mishaps". As it turns out, the planet is inhabited by cave-dwelling, silver-skinned aliens in loincloths driven into hiding by "the Black Peril", a devilish super-computer which ignites a stock-footage-enhanced battle for freedom.

Like its predecessor, *War of the Robots* raids the coffin of Mario Bava's *Planet of the Vampires* more than George Lucas's hit as Brescia floods the screen with gaudy, candy-coloured lighting and cranks up the wonky electronic score whenever things get too slow. Antonio Sabato (Senior, that is) takes the reins as captain this time, investigating a distress signal from a planet which turns out to be inhabited by belligerent, caped aliens (who, yes, still live in caves). As it turns out, this mysterious race is dying and needs American scientists to help preserve them. Oh, but they're also at war against a troop of blonde-wigged robots wearing silver lame jumpsuits. Once again, small-scale mayhem ensues.

Shot with a budget slightly above that of *Hardware Wars*, these sci-fi misfires serve their purpose as amusing '70s-style

W

visual wallpaper, good for scenic design and ambience in your living room but not much use for coherent narrative. Settings and characters are never clearly established, leaving the viewer to grapple with handfuls of interchangeable actors shuffling through the same handful of sets. A large percentage of shots are actually hand held, which makes for a strange aesthetic clash considering the antiseptic sleekness of the locales. Fans of Ken Russell's *Lisztomania* may also be amused to see that film's finale virtually replayed in *War of the Robots*, though arguably to even stranger effect. Oddly, both films share the same supporting casts and a considerable amount of special effects footage, particularly their planet landings and an extended sequence involving a free-floating astronaut repairing a ship's exterior.

Retromedia's handsomely packaged box set of these two titles features some eye-popping cover art that will do any sci-fi serial fan proud. However, the transfers inside are less satisfying, culled from fullscreen masters which lop off information from the sides (originally framed somewhere around 1.85:1) and zooming in to trim the top and bottom as well. Black levels are also too high, resulting in a washed out appearance, but monitor adjustment can solve this problem. For some reason, *War of the Planets* begins with an aspect ratio of 1.85:1 except for some open matte FX inserts, and then reverts to pan and scan a few minutes in. Detail is soft and smudgy, with grain and coarse scratches abounding, though colours are vivid for the most part. Occasional video dropouts can also be spotted. No extras.

The U.S. poster art for this film depicts a snarling punk whose sunglasses reflect a screaming woman's face, with the tagline, "When I go berserk... you're better off dead!" Well, despite the best efforts of the distributor, there's no hiding the fact that this isn't some cheapo knockoff of *Billy Jack* by way of *Death Wish*. It's actually the first *giallo* directed by Antonio Bido, who went on to *The Bloodstained Shadow* before turning his attention to Italian television. An efficient, slick, but ultimately unremarkable entry in the genre, this grisly mystery works mainly thanks to some memorable vicious moments and a great prog rock score by Trans Europa Express firmly in the Goblin tradition. (Bido's next film took this latter aspect even further, but that's another story.)

Driving at night with her director friend Carlo (Lucio Fulci regular Paolo Malco), lovely flamenco dancer Mara (Paola Tedesco) stops for aspirin at a pharmacy and speaks to the raspy-voiced killer who has just slashed the druggist's throat. Her boyfriend Lucas (Corrado Pani) investigates and crosses paths with Giovanni (Fernando Cerulli), a shifty loan shark who seems to be connected with the murder, and his girlfriend who winds up with her face baked in an oven. As the nasty killings begin to pile up, Lucas sorts through an oddball assortment of clues involving a recently released criminal, Nazi atrocities, and felines, due to the killer's weird cat-like eyes.

Originally released as *Il gatto dagli occhi di giada* (*The Cat with Jade Eyes*) and known on U.K. video as *The Cat's Victims*, this thriller strives to imitate *Deep Red* but often gets bogged down in aimless plotting and mindless chitchat. The mobile camerawork slavishly imitates the creepy tracking shots of Argento but conjures up only a small fraction of the style, while the

WATCH ME WHEN I KILL

Colour, 1977, 95m. / Directed by Antonio Bido / Starring Corrado Pani, Paola Tedesco, Paolo Malco, Fernando Cerulli / Shameless (UK R0 PAL) / WS (1.85:1) (16:9), VCI (US R1 NTSC), X-Rated (Germany R2 PAL) / WS (1.85:1)

actors seem to be sleepwalking through their roles without much genuine panic or humour on display. However, Bido certainly knows how to time a scare and pulls off a number of good jolts, some false and others definitely earned. Even when the story veers into sheer silliness at the end (you couldn't count the coincidences on one hand), the possibility of another stylish murder occurring is enough to keep the viewer interested. While the aforementioned oven murder is a half baked (oops) copy of the bathtub scene from *Deep Red*, Bido does come up with one brilliant flourish during a bathtub strangulation set to blaring opera music. Executed with real bravado, it's indisputably the film's highlight and earns it a place in the *giallo* pantheon.

After a number of wonderfully restored Italian horror and mystery titles on DVD, VCI's presentation of this second tier effort – the first DVD version on the market – is a huge disappointment. Culled from a trimmed U.S. print bearing the hokey alternative title and featuring abrupt, doctored opening and closing titles, this suffers from a muddy, grainy transfer. While Bido isn't the most visually stylish director around by any means, the film at least looked better than this on Redemption's tape. Contrary to the packaging, the letterboxed presentation is not 16:9 enhanced. The print itself is in passable condition compared to the old unwatchable U.S. tape, but there are enough scratches and smatterings of dirt to be a distraction. Extras include two marvellous radio spots (30 and 60 seconds) lifted from vinyl, accompanied by ad slicks, as well as trailers for *The Bird with the Crystal Plumage*, *Blood and Black Lace*, and *The Whip and the Body*. Imperfect but far more watchable is the German release (*Stimme des Todes*), which features a much, much nicer transfer from a cleaner and more colourful print (with better framing to boot) as well as the original (better) Italian opening credits, a gallery, and a fake German trailer. The only anamorphic option and by far the most satisfying version of all came along in 2009 with Shameless's release, as lovingly

treated as their other excellent Italian genre titles. The transfer boasts the original Italian credits and looks a notch or two better than the German disc, plus it's 100% complete. Extras include a video intro and 20-minute interview with Bido, an amusing subtitle fact track (a neat device they also employed in other titles like *Oasis of Fear*), the international and American trailers, two alternative title sequences, and of course, a reversible cover. Very nice and highly recommended.

WHAT?

Colour, 1972, 110m. / Directed by Roman Polanski / Starring Marcello Mastroianni, Sydne Rome, Roman Polanski / Severin (UK R0 PAL), Fox (Italy R2 PAL) / WS (2.35:1) (16:9) / DD5.1

Following the death of his wife Sharon Tate in the Charles Manson tragedy, Roman Polanski turned out a double header of blatantly anti-commercial (and antisocial) projects: 1971's *Macbeth* and this peculiar black comedy, which plays like a remake of *Cul-de-Sac* outfitted as a spoof of softcore porn. Frizzy-haired American actress Sydne Rome stars as naïve Nancy, an often-topless tourist in Italy who falls prey one night to a carload of would-be rapists. Her escape leads to a remote seaside villa, where her mere presence sets off a chain of comedic sexual escapades involving lecherous Alex (Marcello Mastroianni) and a colourful cast of supporting characters, including an unbilled, moustachioed Polanski as the gun-toting Mosquito.

For those willing to go along with the free-association plot (which involves fashion-conscious nudists and weird unseen tenants), this is fairly amusing, eccentric viewing, with the cast obviously having fun in an opulent setting. The lazy Mediterranean

W

atmosphere is perfect, while Mastroianni still exudes the effortless charm found in his earlier Fellini outings. The classy score by *Blood for Dracula*'s Claudio Gizzi (incorporating Mozart and Beethoven) keeps things bouncy even in the erratic final act, which finally justifies the title with its concluding lines of shouted dialogue.

Virtually forgotten now, *What?* failed to ignite much box office when it was released in 1972 (with a dubious X rating in the U.S.). Following the success of *Chinatown*, distributor Avco Embassy removed 20 minutes and reshuffled many scenes, marketing the jumpy new product as a sex film called *Diary of Forbidden Dreams*. This edition remained most widely available on home video, but the original cut can be found on the Italian DVD in its much-needed original aspect ratio. The anamorphic transfer looks wonderful apart from the deliberately murky nocturnal opener and was derived from the Italian negative; audio options include a gimmicky 5.1 remix and original mono presentation of the Italian soundtrack, or the original English language version with obligatory (but tiny) Italian subtitles. Extras include a snappily-edited Italian trailer and a new Italian-language interview with Rome, who looks rather unearthly, to put it charitably.

A more elaborate, English-friendly version came down the pike several years later as Severin Films's inaugural U.K. release with what appears to be the same excellent transfer but now without the forced subtitles or phony audio tweaking. Only the English track is included, which is fine considering that's how the film was shot. The disc carries over the same trailer but adds a host of new extras, including a new 16-minute English interview with Rome (who talks about her memories of Polanski, the perception of the film as erotic even though it contains no actual sex scenes, and the gorgeous villa location). Next up, the enigmatic Claudio Gizzi finally appears on camera for "Memories of a Young Pianist",

a 22-minute interview in which he covers everything from his early collaborations with Visconti (including *Death in Venice*) to a thorough dissection of his majestic work for the two Paul Morrissey films, even playing the main theme from *Blood for Dracula* on his piano over the closing credits! Finally, cinematographer Marcello Gatti (*The Battle of Algiers*) appears for the 16-minute "A Surreal Pop Movie"; he focuses mainly on the Polanski shoot and his relationships with the crew while fleetingly touching on some of his other major Italian productions. A very thorough and rewarding package overall for one of Polanski's most obscure, misunderstood works.

WHAT HAVE YOU DONE TO SOLANGE?

Colour, 1971, 107m. / Directed by Massimo Dallamano / Starring Fabio Testi, Cristina Galbó, Camille Keaton / Shriek Show (US R1 NTSC), 01 Distribution (Italy R2 PAL), UFA (Germany R2 PAL) / WS (2.35:1) (16:9), EC (Holland R0 NTSC) / WS (1.85:1)

An assured outing from the golden age of the *giallo*, this twisty murder mystery was the first of two Italian adaptations commissioned from the novels of Edgar Wallace, whose *krimi* had inspired a line of successful German mysteries. Naturally the Italians jazzed up the brew with heady helpings of sex, perversion, and mean-spirited violence, but somehow it all still seems like a first class affair in this expertly rendered whodunit.

While enjoying the lakeside carnal company of her gym teacher Enrico (Fabio Testi), young student Elizabeth (Cristina Galbó) spies a flashing knife in the woods, much to the disbelief of her lover. The next day a girl's body is discovered nearby, and the married Rossini finds himself in hot water when he's suspected of murder and simultaneously may have his dalliances with his students exposed to the public. Soon the boorish hero must put aside his own self-interest and work with the police to expose the criminal, whose vicious activities begin to cut very close to home.

From the ethereal Ennio Morricone theme drifting over slow motion, sepia-tinted opening credits depicting young girls on bicycles, Massimo Dallamano and his cinematographer, Aristide Massaccesi (aka the infamous Joe D'Amato), prove they know how to satisfy their audience while delivering some unexpected subtext and artistry in the mix. Best known at the time for his sexy potboilers like *Dorian Gray* and *Venus in Furs*, Dallamano switched gears here to inaugurate his "schoolgirl trilogy" of shockers, which continued with the police procedural *What Have They Done to Your Daughters?*, and concluded with the disturbing *Red Rings of Fear* (*Trauma*). Already established as a western actor, Testi finally proved his acting chops here and became a genre regular throughout the 1970s as he branched further out to become one of the country's most accomplished thespian/matinee idols. Much of the film's success also lies in its rock solid storyline, which craftily twists Wallace's *The Curse of the Green Pin* (named for a tangential clue) into an early '70s manifesto complete with showering schoolgirls and a depraved climactic resolution, featuring a near-catatonic appearance by Camille Keaton, several years prior to *I Spit on Your Grave*. Props also to the underused but always enjoyable Galbó, one of Eurocult's most striking and engaging actresses, who went on to glory in *Let Sleeping Corpses Lie*. Though comparatively low on sex and splatter when held up to its successors like, say, *Torso*, this remains one of the high points of the *giallo* genre. (Incidentally, the other Italian Edgar Wallace film was the less successful *Seven Bloodstained Orchids*.)

For a film still relatively obscure compared to the likes of Dario Argento, *Solange* has enjoyed a wide number of incarnations under a dizzying array of titles like *The School That Couldn't Scream*, *Who's Next*, and *Terror in the Woods*, all of which not surprisingly correspond as well to substandard video releases over the years.

The first DVD release from EC, transferred from the same master used for Redemption's VHS edition, is a lacklustre affair with weak contrasts. Even worse, the nicely utilized scope framing is hacked down to 1.85:1, lopping characters' faces from the sides of the screen. The anamorphically enhanced Shriek Show disc is a great improvement, with beautifully saturated colours, stable black levels, and admirable detail which manages to sustain a film-like appearance throughout. Even better is the Italian release, a flat-out beautiful presentation that's about as pristine as this film could look outside of high-definition. Curiosity seekers may also want to check out the German edition (included in Volume 8 of UFA's magnificent Edgar Wallace box sets), which contains the English version (similar to the Shriek Show disc) as well as the alternative, shorter German edit, which amazingly recuts the opening sequence to conform to the "Hello, this is Edgar Wallace" credits template.

WHAT'S THE MATTER WITH HELEN?

Colour, 1971, 101m. / Directed by Curtis Harrington / Starring Debbie Reynolds, Shelley Winters, Dennis Weaver, Yvette Vickers, Pamelyn Ferdin, Agnes Moorehead, Michael MacLiammoir / WS (1.85:1) (16:9)

WHOEVER SLEW AUNTIE ROO?

Colour, 1972, 94m. / Directed by Curtis Harrington / Starring Shelley Winters, Mark Lester, Chloe Franks, Michael Gothard, Ralph Richardson, Lionel Jeffries, Rosalie Crutchley / MGM (US R1 NTSC) / WS (1.85:1)

Among the most pleasing of the flipper double-bills offered by the Midnite Movie series of discs is this pair of post-*What Ever Happened to Baby Jane?* horror-nostalgia melodramas made by Curtis Harrington for AIP, affording Shelley Winters a shot at Guignol stardom in two contrasted "mad lady" roles and encouraging the studio to present a classier appearance than that to which they were accustomed. It seems bizarre that DVD should class *The Thing with Two Heads* as an MGM product, but these efforts, with their musical numbers and pastel-pretty bygone days settings, are almost surreally appropriate for the roaring lion logo.

From a story by *Baby Jane*'s Henry Farrell, *Helen* is the more substantial film. Spinning off from the Leopold and Loeb case, the premise is that the mothers of a pair of 1930s psycho killers set themselves up in new identities to escape a vengeful prank-caller and open a Hollywood training school for Shirley Temple wannabes. The vivacious Adelle (Debbie Reynolds) throws herself into their new life and is wooed by a Texan millionaire (Dennis Weaver), while the religious Helen (Winters) suffers hysterical episodes and reacts to imagined or real persecutions with knife-wielding violence. At the heart of the story is a complex co-dependent relationship between the women, both of whom are even stranger than they seem, and Harrington draws outstanding work from his stars, who mix showbiz pizzazz and wild ham with affecting subtleties all the creepier for a refusal to get too explicit about the backstory whereby the sons of these women have resorted to torturing and murdering a woman just like them.

In the light of the character based on her in *Postcards from the Edge*, Reynolds flirts with personal revelation as the glamorous mama who has neglected her weakling son and relishes a chance to strut her stuff in a hideous "kiddystar revue", while Winters gives perhaps the performance of a lifetime as the religious, rabbit-petting lump given to panic attacks, casual atrocities and the most repressed lesbian crush ever depicted in the movies. The film fan director also relishes the letter-perfect period gossip, the satire of ghastly stage mothers (including Yvette Vickers) and horrid moppets (including Pamelyn Ferdin), staging one pre-teen Mae West imitation (using the song "Oh You Nasty Man") that is probably more disturbing than all the film's slasher murders in these paedophilia-conscious times. Agnes Moorehead, a hag movie perennial, has a meaty bit part as a hatchet-faced radio evangelist who doesn't provide the answers Helen is seeking and indirectly leads to the grotesque final act.

Roo, whose multi-authored screenplay has input from Jimmy Sangster, Robert Blees and Gavin Lambert, is set about ten years earlier and in a Christmas card Britain, with Winters doing the showbiz memory bit this time as an over-the-hill music hall artiste obsessed with her dead daughter (whose crumbling mummy is on the premises) and seeking to replace her with an orphan (Chloe Franks) whose brother (Mark Lester) recasts them all in a version of "Hansel and Gretel". After his interesting use of Michael MacLiammoir as a ham called Ham in *Helen*, Harrington relishes the chance to work with a range of plummy British players (Michael Gothard, Ralph Richardson, Lionel Jeffries, Rosalie Crutchley) and the house strewn with magical props and toys is a wonderfully fairytale setting. However, it's a slight anecdote, especially fragile after the intricately-plotted and deeply-felt *Helen*. Subplots about bogus séances, blackmailing servants and the private fantasy world of children ("We've agreed that it's all right to lie to grown-ups but never each other") fill out the running time, but don't serve to disguise the fact that once the fairytale parallel is made explicit in the dialogue the fiery outcome is a foregone conclusion.

MGM's DVD offers widescreen transfers, with English mono (*Helen* has Spanish audio also) and subtitles in English, French and Spanish. *Roo* is good but softer to due the inexplicable lack of anamorphic enhancement, while the crisp *Helen* has odd colour effects (brick-orange skintones) that seem like tinted front-of-house stills and might not reflect the filmmakers' intended look. The only extras are theatrical trailers as heavy on the spoilers as the bizarrely tell-all poster images used as the cover; first-time viewers of *Helen*, in particular, are advised not to look at the packaging before watching the film. Considering that Harrington lent himself to commentary tracks and interview material for earlier (*Night Tide*) and later (*Ruby*) films, it's a shame he remained silent on these important releases.

– KN

WHEN WORLDS COLLIDE

Colour, 1951, 81m. / Directed by Rudolph Maté / Starring Richard Derr, Barbara Rush, John Hoyt / Paramount (US R1 NTSC, UK R2 PAL)

 Because so many fans were exposed to the films of George Pal at a formative age, through matinee screenings and multiple telecasts, his work holds a special place in their affections. He was a rare producer with a commitment to science fiction cinema who had the resources to back up his visions: Paramount may have given him B-level casts, but his special effects work (and gorgeous colour processing) was on a par with any Cecil B. DeMille wrath of God spectacular; the scripts may be littered with awkwardness and melodramatics, but he had a serious devotion to sci-fi as a literature of ideas (most of his films are based on actual books) and some notion of the importance of scientific plausibility. His infectious sense that this flight-into-space/end-of-the-world material was great, magical stuff remains vivid in grown-ups who have maintained a relationship with his work throughout their viewing lives. Actually, most Pal films are easier to love than to admire – the man's heart is in them, but their shortcomings still embarrass and you can't help wishing they were just better. *When Worlds Collide* is a case in point; it deals with the doom of the entire human race (save forty souls), but director Rudolph Maté worked up far more emotion in *D.O.A.*, which followed the last hours of only one doomed man.

Based on a novel by Philip Wylie and Edwin Balmer, this was the first big-scale entry in the end-of-the-world sub-genre since *Deluge* in 1932. It opens with some brisk scientific chat ("if our calculations are proved correct, this could be the most frightening discovery of all time") that establishes the Earth is doomed: a rogue star (Bellus) is on its way, which will cause volcanoes, earthquakes and tidal waves before crushing the planet completely. A few scientists and visionaries see a way out and commit themselves to a space program (as in Pal's *Destination Moon*, a private enterprise effort rather than government-sponsored) to create a sleek silver rocketship ark which can carry a few lucky people to Zyra, a planet revolving around Bellus. We get glimpses of the disaster action, especially an impressive flooding of New York that harks back to *Deluge* and forward to this film's unacknowledged semi-remake *Deep Impact*, but most of the action revolves around the rocket project, which is obviously more urgent than the moonshot of the earlier film. A romance simmers between pilot Richard Derr, who goes from money-grubbing to money-burning and turns altruist in the crisis, and professor's daughter Barbara Rush, who has to cope with another suitor.

W

Quite a lot of plot is provided by crippled, nasty millionaire John Hoyt, who backs the rocket on the understanding that he gets a ticket to live and is the only one cynical enough to suggest the left-behinds will riot and try to get aboard.

It's kid-level social comment, with the existence of similar projects in other countries raised in dialogue and then forgotten and an uncomfortable homogeneity of white bread (indeed white), square-looking, parka-clad Americans among the saved. These are people who take along the Bible and '50s best-seller (and later Irwin Allen movie) *The Story of Mankind* but not Shakespeare or *Robinson Crusoe*. There are *MST3000*-style laughs for the mean-spirited, notably Derr's testing the atmosphere of a new planet with a big inhale ("best air I ever tasted") or a freckle-faced orphan kid's insistence on bringing along a stray dog, but you'll still feel flickers of emotion at some of the big heroic gestures – Derr's rival in love thinking of abandoning him on a roof but coming back in a helicopter, Hoyt kept back from the rocket and standing up to stagger desperately to the closed hatch. Another Pal trait is a vein of religiosity very similar to that of his studio-mate DeMille, and though this isn't as hobbled by Bible-bashing as *Conquest of Space* it does go for a few too many pronouncements and prayers without seriously grappling with the way the imminent end of the world might be greeted by those of various faiths.

Paramount's DVD is a beauty; the standard-frame transfer is lovely to behold, with the steely blues and rich, rich reds of 1950s Technicolor (the looming Bellus is like glowing jam in the sky) captured perfectly. It's so pristine that the matte paintings and miniatures never look like anything but what they are – movie magic, more appealing than mere realism. The only extra is a loud, dramatic trailer, but there are mono soundtracks in English and French plus optional English subs.
– KN

WHERE THE HEART IS

Colour, 1990, 107m. / Directed by John Boorman / Starring Dabney Coleman, Uma Thurman, Suzy Amis, David Hewlett, Dylan Walsh, Sheila Kelley, Crispin Glover, Christopher Plummer / Buena Vista (US R1 NTSC), Cinema Club (UK R2 PAL) / WS (1.85:1) (16:9) / DD2.0

In a fairy tale version of New York, real estate fat cat Stewart McBain (Dabney Coleman) gets his only thrills in life from demolishing buildings. Annoyed by his pampered, post-adolescent children who refuse to leave the nest, McBain finally deposits them one rainy night to live at the Dutch House, a decrepit architectural landmark under McBain's control. "You can't just spoil us and then stop spoiling us whenever it pleases you", complains young Daphne (Uma Thurman), while artistic older sister Chloe (Suzy Amis) finds solace in creating a possibly lucrative calendar from the striking *trompe l'oeuil* tableaux she perfected in art school, creating optical illusions by painting on human bodies and the walls behind them. Young brother Jimmy (David Hewlett) gets to work creating video games, and soon the house is filled with an eccentric assortment of characters: shameless yuppie Tom (*Nip/Tuck*'s Dylan Walsh), sexy speaker-in-tongues Sheryl (Sheila Kelley), gay fashion designer Lionel (Crispin Glover), and a homeless former magician, Shitty (Christopher Plummer, who probably leaves that character name off his résumé). Romance, twists of fate and acts of God result in a narrative whirlwind which places all of the characters under one roof with destinies far removed from those they expected.

Misleadingly promoted as a goofball comedy, this stylish fable from director John Boorman (fresh off his masterful *Hope and Glory*) suffered at the hands of confused critics and went almost directly to cable and video, where it finally amassed a small but devoted cult following. The film is a visual feast throughout, packing each frame with dazzling tricks of light and colour, and fits nicely into the tradition of whimsical morality plays that dot American cinema history dating back to Frank Capra, Ernst Lubitsch and Preston Sturges. Of course modern audiences don't respond well to sincere artifice without irony (see the unjustly maligned *Joe Versus the Volcano*, with which this would make an ideal double bill, or Boorman's similar second film, *Leo the Last*), so this film's effectiveness will depend entirely on the viewer's willingness to go along with its anachronistic tone. The combination of surreal imagery, airy music and mannered performances creates one of Boorman's more accessible films. The end product isn't a classic due to a few stumbles, namely some gratuitous mugging from Coleman and a pat final scene that confusingly shifts several characters' motivations and personalities with no explanation. One could also argue that this tactic is Boorman's nose-thumbing at the convenient wrap-ups found in traditional Hollywood comedies, but for whatever reason, it's only a minor blemish on an otherwise beautiful canvas. Since this was mostly shot in Toronto (which explains why it doesn't really feel like New York), many familiar names from David Cronenberg films turn up, namely cinematographer Peter Suschitzky, production designer Carol Spier, and art director James McAteer; all three work perfectly together to craft a visual look unlike any other. And for you skin watchers, yes, Uma and Suzy spend much of their screen time in their birthday suits, albeit covered in body paint.

If ever a film demonstrated the need for letterboxing an open matte transfer, this is it. Prior full frame editions of this film (VHS, laserdisc, cable) contained all of the exposed film information on each side of the frame, which ruins several carefully mounted images by revealing the edges

of canvases, distracting light fixtures, and other visual ephemera that knocks the compositions off-kilter. The DVD finally restores the original framing and looks quite nice, featuring extremely vivid colours and richer blacks than before. Surrounds are restrained almost entirely to the musical score. The budget-priced disc features no extras and very bland packaging; ditto for the later U.K. release.

WHISTLE AND I'LL COME TO YOU

B&W, 1968, 42m. / Directed by Jonathan Miller / Starring Michael Hordern / BFI (UK R0 PAL)

On a walking holiday on the Norfolk coast, Professor Parkins (played by Michael Hordern) finds a wooden whistle buried in the earth in an overgrown clifftop graveyard. Returning to the modest hotel at which he's staying, he cleans it up and translates an inscription carved on the barrel: Who is this who is coming? Erroneously blowing the whistle, his carefree demeanour undergoes a change, his nights become restless and he's consumed by an indefinable sense of ill ease. As the days pass it becomes ever more apparent that Parkins is sharing his room with an unwelcome guest...

Written and directed for the screen by Jonathan Miller, *Whistle and I'll Come to You* is based on the famous novella by M.R. James, "Oh Whistle, and I'll Come to You, My Lad". It was originally presented as part of BBC television's *Omnibus* series, with 95% of its running time dominated by the delightful Michael Hordern. A simple, largely uneventful tale, it is nonetheless as efficiently engaging today as it was 35 years ago. This is due entirely to Hordern's commanding performance as the insular Cambridge don, one of the most captivating portrayals of eccentric academia ever to grace the screen. It's a tribute to the actor's prowess that he makes even the potentially bland prospect of watching a man eat a grapefruit so infinitely absorbing, and his conveyance of the simple pleasures of solitude in the midst of such an invigorating locale will have you making your hotel reservations post-haste. From a leisurely outset – which establishes Parkins's resolute stubbornness in his refusal to accept the existence of the supernatural – the story escalates into a confounding denouement. Although little that is tangibly frightening occurs, Miller instils the tale with an efficacious sense of foreboding, and whether the climax is truly born of the supernatural or the product of a mental aberration on Parkins's part is up to the individual to decide. Cameraman Dick Bush's masterful black and white compositions of the cinematic winter coastline are beautiful yet also bleak and distressingly foreboding. But the acute aura of apprehensiveness stems primarily from the stunning sound design by Ron Hooper and John Ramsey, climaxing in a haunting dream sequence in which Parkins is pursued along a deserted beach by a dirty, tattered bed sheet that appears to adopt human form. Sounds comical? Seek out *Whistle and I'll Come to You* and have your mind firmly changed. A film no collection should be without.

The BFI, who have been gradually building an impressive library of classic television landmarks on disc, have presented this as a splendid region free platter (out of print and quite pricey now, so snap it up if you can) with a number of subsidiary enticements. The picture quality is remarkably clean given its age and origins, though the picky may quibble over the slightly hissy soundtrack and occasional – albeit negligible – evidence of ghosting and print deterioration. Those unfamiliar with M.R. James's "Oh Whistle, and I'll Come to You, My Lad" but interested in comparing Miller's adaptation with its source are saved the trouble of seeking

it in print form by the inclusion of a reading by Neil Brand. In addition to this there's a rather amateurishly constructed introduction by author Ramsey Campbell, who also reads his own short story, inspired by the works of James, "The Guide".
– TG

WILD SIDE

Colour, 1995, 111m. / Directed by Donald Cammell / Starring Christopher Walken, Anne Heche, Steven Bauer, Joan Chen / Tartan (UK R0 PAL) / WS (1.85:1), Pioneer (US R1 NTSC) / DD2.0

Released years after completion to cash in on the publicity surrounding Anne Heche's lesbian partnership with Ellen DeGeneres, this amusing stab at the erotic thriller genre by director Donald Cammell (*Performance*) was torn to shreds by its distributor, turning the fairly complex narrative into a pandering lesbian thriller. Cammell was so embarrassed by the end product his credit was changed to the pseudonymous Franklin Brauner; his suicide the following year was at least partially a result of the entire ordeal, robbing the cinema world of one of its more valuable talents. Eventually editor Frank Mazzola was allowed to return to the worktable and reconstruct Cammell's original cut (along with a different score by Ryuichi Sakamoto), which is quite a different experience, to say the least.

In Long Beach, California, banker Alex (Heche) spends her evenings as a pricey call girl to pay off her mounting debts. One of her clients, money launderer Bruno (Christopher Walken), is immediately taken with her and decides to continue using her services; however, Bruno's chauffeur, Tony (Steven Bauer), turns out to be an undercover FBI agent and presses Alex into service. On top of that, Alex begins a heated affair with Bruno's wife, Virginia (*Twin Peaks*'s Joan Chen), who's being set up as the fall girl for her husband's crimes. Twist then piles up twist and loyalties change by the minute as Alex tries to find a way out of a very dangerous situation.

By the mid-'90s, some of the more resourceful directors were turning erotic thrillers upside down: Richard Rush with his insane *Color of Night*, Paul Verhoeven with his patently ridiculous *Basic Instinct*, and of course those newcomers, the Wachowski Brothers, with *Bound* (which would make a superb double bill with this film). Cammell's loopy visual style is a bit toned down here (it could almost pass for a slightly glossier Abel Ferrara film), but his zippy editing and stream of consciousness narrative tics are well in place. Walken is, well, Walken, while the other actors are excellent in what appear to be a number of improvised scenes. Of course, interested parties should only go for the U.K. disc, which contains the original director's cut along with a Cammell short film, "The Argument", interviews with Donald Cammell and Anne Heche, and a theatrical trailer (not listed on the packaging). The U.S. DVD is an utter waste of time, a dismal pan and scanned transfer of the bowdlerized cut, which makes nonsense of the character motivations and plot progression.

WILD ZERO

Colour, 2000, 98m. / Directed by Tetsuro Takeuchi / Starring Guitar Wolf, Masashi Endô / Synapse (US R1 NTSC), Rapid Eye Movies (Germany R2 PAL), Artsmagic (UK R2 PAL) / WS (1.66:1) / DD2.0

 If you ever tried to watch a Troma or Full Moon film and thought it would have been a lot better with alien-controlled undead and cross-dressing Japanese men, look no further

than *Wild Zero*, an unrestrained orgy of zombies, flying saucers, hot cars, slicked-back hair, and of course, "rock and roll!"

While aliens prepare to invade the earth, our hero is Ace (Masashi Endô), a nice '50s-culture reject who goes out for some fun by attending a rowdy concert performed by Guitar Wolf (which happens to be both the name of the band and the lead guitarist; appropriately enough, the other members are Drum Wolf and Bass Wolf). When a nasty squabble erupts between the band and the club's crooked manager, Ace intervenes and receives a mystical Guitar Wolf whistle for his efforts. A stop at a gas station brings a new love into Ace's life, along with a horde of shuffling, blue-faced zombies who can only be killed with a gunshot to the head. The aforementioned club owner and a gang of robbers complicate the situation to the point where Ace has no choice but to blow the whistle, leading to a frenzied showdown between flesh-eaters and the leather-clad forces of rock.

Even sillier than that synopsis might lead you to believe, *Wild Zero* never even tries to make sense. From video-generated lightning effects to magical, zombie-killing guitar picks, the film whirls from one madcap idea to another; if you start to worry that all of this might not be holding together, well, don't worry; all the loud music and flashy lighting will keep you distracted. The gore is fairly strong (including the requisite gut-munching) but appropriately cartoonish, and as for the acting... well, one hopes it's this bad on purpose. As far as the "new" Japanese horror wave goes, it's rougher around the edges and more overtly goofy than *Versus*, which is a good or bad thing depending on your taste. Basically this is the sort of film where lots of friends can come by, sit around and talk, and still have no problem getting into the film whenever something insane happens.

In keeping with that philosophy, Synapse has treated *Wild Zero*'s DVD special edition to an innovative, sure-to-be-

W

practiced drinking game, which essentially means that, should you choose, a beer mug pops up on the screen during certain triggers in the film (try it to find out what they are). Not surprisingly, all but the hardiest of constitutions will be on the floor within the first half hour. As for the film itself, the transfer looks fine considering this was a very, very low budget production, shot on 35mm but with post-production effects (lightning, credits, etc.) created afterwards on video (thus, no anamorphic transfer either). The stereo mix is very aggressive and effective, during both musical and flesh-eating interludes. Extras include a funny behind-the-scenes music video (with some bizarre cutaways), a Guitar Wolf bio, a stills gallery, a dupey-looking trailer, and some very, very amusing animated menus. Easter egg hunters will also discover a substantial, hysterical surprise hidden on the bonus features page. Try watching this extra goodie after doing the drinking game; you... will... not... survive.

The PAL edition from Germany's Rapid Eye Movies is the best alternative to the frankly peerless Synapse disc. It similarly presents a non-anamorphic 1.66:1 transfer and the original Japanese language Dolby Digital 2.0 soundtrack as well as a German language variant, and removable subtitle options in German or English. The extras basically consist of a couple of photo galleries and some preparatory sketches. The film's original trailer is also on the disc, accompanied by trailers for other Rapid Eye Japanese releases *Audition*, *Dead or Alive*, *Porno-star* and *Sonatine*.

A WITCH IN THE FAMILY

Colour, 2000, 78m. / Directed by Harald Hamrell / Starring Karin Bogaeus, Bisse Unger, Johan Rheborg, Tintin Anderzon, Rebecca Scheja, Margreth Weivers / Universe (HK R0 NTSC) / WS (1.85:1), Sandrews (Sweden R2 PAL) / WS (1.85:1) (16:9) / DD2.0

Eight-year-old Maria (Karin Bogaeus) has a big problem. Well, actually it's truer to say it's a small problem, namely her bratty little brother Lillen (Bisse Unger) – truly the toddler from Hell! – with whom she shares a bedroom. One morning, after finding her favourite doll has been dunked in a pot of blue paint by Lillen, Maria has just about had it. Once again she begs her parents (Johan Rheborg and Tintin Anderzon) for a room of her own, but to no avail. On her way to school, Maria bumps into new-girl-on-the-block Makka (Rebecca Scheja), who tells her that she has a magic crystal ball from Tibet that can grant wishes; in fact she says she has just wished for a thunderstorm. Maria is sceptical of mouthy Makka (who we have just seen impressing the local toddlers with a bored chant of "Shit, shit, shit, shit...!"), especially as there is no sign of rain, let alone a storm, but decides to give it a try anyway. Climbing into the back of the removals van, the only light coming from Makka's torch, the two girls hunker around the glowing glass orb. Maria wishes she no longer had a little brother. Suddenly the two girls jump as one, as a clap of thunder booms and a lightning flash lights up the van's cluttered interior. Cold rain buckets down... It seems that Makka's wish at least has come true. Arriving at school drenched to the skin, Maria succumbs to a fever and is sent home to recuperate. Her worried parents arrange for a babysitter to stay with her during the next day as neither can get time off work. The only person they can find is an old lady called Gerda. The next day, as Makka is fixing her bike in the street a strange feeling creeps over her; looking up she sees an old woman striding up the path of Maria's house. Birds fly up from the trees as if scared by something... Going up to the door, Makka rings the doorbell.

Gerda answers and Makka, seeing her face, recoils in shock. Rebuffed by the old lady, Makka hurries home to check on something; digging out a book called "Witches and Trolls", she leafs through the pages... Meanwhile, back in Maria's house sinister things are happening. Already startled to see Gerda gulp down a dead wasp, Maria is further scared when the dotty old dear puts on a "shadow-show" for her, especially when the shape of a third hand appears on the wall, the animal it is forming suddenly sprouting sharp fangs! Later Makka shows her new friend illustrations from her ghastly book, pictures that appear to show Gerda, and informs Maria that the elderly sitter has come to steal Lillen away to be eaten. Maria's wish has come true, it would seem, but in the worst possible manner. There is a witch in the house! Can Maria and Makka prove Gerda's true nature and save Lillen from being boiled alive in her cauldron?

Here's a wonderfully spooky Swedish family film with more twists in its plot than are found in the average pig's tail. Coming from a Nordic filmmaking tradition rather than the more familiar (to us at least) North American model works entirely in its favour, as the humour that laces *A Witch in the Family* is dark and not the usual Hollywood inanity. The children are simply great, entirely believable and thoroughly likeable, and cigar-smoking, wasp-eating Margreth Weivers makes for a truly creepy figure, one you are never quite sure about.

Being a Swedish film (made with some input from Norway), it looks good, with effective location photography, especially in the thrilling final scenes set in an old coastal castle, and CGI is used sparingly and to the service of the plot rather than making it a means to an end. The viewer's expectations are always being confounded, and best of all this film doesn't talk down to its target audience. At times the imagery is downright horrific, and the tone is what you would expect from a nation raised on grisly Norse mythology. Undercurrents of infanticide and cannibalism are rife. Director Harald Hamrell has produced a very worthwhile film guaranteed to entertain children and adults alike.

A Witch in the Family is available on Swedish DVD from Sandrews as a non-subtitled, anamorphic release with a few extras, but this review is taken from the bare-bones Hong Kong Universe DVD, letterboxed at approximately 1.85:1 (non-anamorphic sadly) and offering removable English subtitles which are generally well translated and true to the original Swedish. This allows one to enjoy moments like when all the little kids from the street, dressed as witches themselves for Easter, come up to Makka and ask her to say "Shit" for them again! One would imagine that an English-dubbed version would lose such scurrilous but funny dialogue. Also the native dialect is essential in my view to this film, especially in the scenes between Maria and Makka, and it would lose a lot by having British or American accents imposed. It would also render as meaningless the repeated joke that has Lillen calling Gerda "Weirda" (the two words are pronounced almost identical in Swedish)!

Picture quality on the all region Universe disc is very good, with a colourful, detailed image and virtually no artefacting. The soundtrack seems to be a basic Dolby Digital surround mix, but it's fine and supplements the visuals with punchy panache. It's also pretty cool to find a film that utilises Handel's sublime "Ode for St. Cecilia's Day" alongside more obvious classical fare like Orff's "Carmina Burana". There are no extras on the disc, not even a trailer, but where else are you going to find a subtitled print of this film? I'll leave you with a thought from Maria: "But what if there are nice witches?"... *He he he...*

– NB

WITH A FRIEND LIKE HARRY (HARRY, HE'S HERE TO HELP)

Colour, 2000, 116m. / Directed by Dominik Moll / Starring Sergi Lopez, Laurent Lucas, Sophie Guillemin / Buena Vista (US R1 NTSC), Diaphana (France R2 PAL), Eurovideo (Germany R2 PAL), Benelux (Holland R2 PAL) / WS (2.35:1) (16:9) / DD5.1, Artificial Eye (UK R2 PAL) / WS (2.35:1) (16:9) / DD2.0

With Hitchcock homages still cranked out on the cinematic assembly line, it was only a matter of time before someone got around to Claude Chabrol. Virtually a greatest hits homage to the venerable director, *Harry, un ami qui vous veut du bien* (or as it's known in Europe and the U.S. respectively, *With a Friend Like Harry* and the more literal but awkward *Harry, He's Here to Help*) raises several tantalizing possibilities before dropping them abruptly in a play-it-safe finale.

By chance married Michel (Laurent Lucas) and his family cross paths with his old schoolmate, Harry (*Pan's Labyrinth*'s Sergi Lopez), who's on vacation with his sensual girlfriend, Plum (Sophie Guillemin). Michel is busy renovating the family's vacation home (complete with a memorably tacky pink bathroom), and the oppressive presence of his wife and offspring becomes the catalyst for his increasing attraction to the freedom offered by the open, libidinous Harry, who insinuates himself deeply into Michel's life as his more sociopathic character traits come to light.

Half black comedy, *Harry* generates wry smirks from Lopez's memorized recitations of Michel's wretched poetry; in fact, Lopez (who packed on weight for the role) is the primary reason to watch the film. The thriller aspects are more uneven, setting up Michel's family as dead weight best removed but performing a climactic about-face that redeems our dour hero for no particular reason. Had the film stuck to its convictions and pursued the strange, homoerotic bond between the two men to its logical conclusion, this could have been a masterpiece.

Buena Vista's no-frills DVD offers a solid anamorphic transfer with a subdued but nicely mixed 5.1 surround track. Though lacking subtitles, the French DVD offers six minutes' worth of deleted scenes, a trailer, a 12-page booklet, a 36-minute documentary (including interviews with all of the principals), and actor filmographies. The French and German discs also offer a DTS option in addition to Dolby Digital 5.1, while the U.K. edition offers 2.0 surround only. The U.K., German, and Dutch DVDs include the trailer and making-of only as supplemental material.

A WOMAN POSSESSED

Colour, 1975, 95m. / Directed by Mario Mercier / Starring Lisa Livanne, Erica Maaz, Jean-François Delacour / Pathfinder (US R1 NTSC)

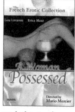

One of the unsung treasures of French '70s horror cinema (a fairly small category, mind you), this feverish stew of witchcraft, sex and screaming bears the influence of Jean Rollin and the various occult movies cleaning up at the box office at the time but still feels like a peculiar animal all its own. Originally released as *La papesse*, this is a cult classic waiting to be discovered.

The madness begins as blonde "Geziale" leads three male disciples in a ritual that involves pouring and lighting a circle of gasoline around a man buried up to the neck, then tossing poisonous snakes around his head. It's downhill from there as married Laurent (Jean-François Delacour) joins the same Satanic cult, which forces him to endure lashings while tied to a cross. In order to become a full member, he must also inaugurate his confused wife, Aline (Lisa Livanne), which leads to nude orgies, sex with clawed demons, catfights and murder.

This thoroughly delirious experience has been packaged as part of Pathfinder's "French Erotic Collection", though it's nothing like the typical softcore '70s shenanigans you'd expect. From the percussive score to the bizarre photography, the film is wildly unpredictable and climaxes in a series of depraved set pieces sure to send most Eurocult fans' heads spinning.

Pathfinder's transfer looks astonishing, which is reassuring for a film with such limited exposure over the years; the clarity of the image is nearly three-dimensional at times, and colours look accurate and striking. The French dialogue is accompanied by optional English subtitles. The feature itself is full frame, but it appears to be open matte compared to the letterboxed (1.78:1) trailer on the disc; the film proper blows up to the same aspect ratio fairly well on a widescreen monitor, but the subtitles are obviously lost in the process. The disc also includes trailers for a handful of other films in the series, including the hallucinatory *Couples of Boulogne* and the extremely dull *Emilienne*.

XANADU

Colour, 1980, 93m. / Directed by Robert Greenwald / Starring Olivia Newton-John, Gene Kelly, Michael Beck, Sandahl Bergman, Matt Lattanzi, Wilfrid Hyde-White (voice), Coral Browne (voice) / Universal (US R1 NTSC, Australia R4 PAL) / WS (1.85:1) (16:9) / DD4.0

If you ever wanted to see Olivia Newton-John and the star of *The Warriors* turn into animated fish while accompanied by Electric Light Orchestra, look no further. Here's a big studio fantasy that could never be made today: a mythological love story on roller skates. From box office bomb to beloved camp classic, this spectacle introduced a generation to the solo animation career of Don Bluth, inspired a successful stage musical, and became the namesake for countless roller rinks in the early '80s. So as you can see, it has a lot to answer for.

In sunny Santa Monica, the life of record album painter Sonny Malone (Michael Beck) is changed forever when he's kissed on the boardwalk by Kira (Newton-John), a mystery girl on roller skates. A disatisfied artist, he makes the acquaintance of beach musician and former big band player Danny McGuire (Gene Kelly) and searches for the enigmatic girl who also appears on an upcoming record cover. Eventually the two cross paths again, and she inspires him to start up a huge roller palace in the middle of Los Angeles, combining the styles of '40s big band and '80s new wave (demonstrated in a truly loopy number featuring the Tubes and few dozen gyrating dancers in spandex). As it turns out, Kira is actually a Greek muse brought to Earth, and when her duty is done, she must return home again. However, a smitten Sonny has other plans.

Featuring one of the most memorable soundtracks of its era (combining Newton-John with the aforementioned ELO), *Xanadu* is one of those films you either love or despise. Its flaws are legion, starting with Beck's awful leading performance (outdone two years later in *Megaforce*), the eye-punishing Bobbie Mannix costumes, and a wholly incoherent story with a knee-jerk happy ending that comes out of nowhere. So what's to like? Well, it's catchy and you can dance to it, there's never a dull moment, and for better or worse, it perfectly captures that confusing time when disco had faded out but alternative and heavy metal music had yet to take over. Celebrity fans can have fun spotting *Conan the Barbarian*'s Sandahl Bergman as a muse, future (and now former) Mr. Newton-John, *My Tutor*'s

X

Matt Lattanzi, in two musical numbers, and the voices of Wilfrid Hyde-White (*The Cat and the Canary*) and Mrs. Vincent Price, Coral Browne (*Theatre of Blood*), as Zeus and Hera! Wow. And to make matters even stranger, the story is an uncredited modernizing of the musical *Down to Earth*, which stars Rita Hayworth who also starred in *Cover Girl*, co-starring Gene Kelly as... a musician named Danny McGuire. For kicks, this would also make a good thematic viewing partner with Harry Kümel's outlandish Greek god horror-art film, *Malpertuis*; it's also highly unlikely you'll ever see that film mentioned in a review for *Xanadu* again.

Universal's first sparsely appointed DVD presents the film much as it appeared in theatres: bright, colourful, and more than a little grainy, which is as it should be. The Dolby surround audio sounds solid enough considering the original mix; those ethereal ELO vocals can sound a little odd in multi-channel playback. The anamorphic framing restores at least a semblance of balance to some of the more bizarre compositions; the "All over the World" number is simply impossible to follow in any other video presentation. The only extra is the feisty original trailer. Apparently someone at Universal went on a sudden nostalgia kick (or noticed the huge sales numbers for the deluxe version of *Grease*) when they started reissuing special editions of their late '70s pop musicals, with *Xanadu* heading up the pack in a "Magical Musical Edition". The new transfer (culled from an HD source used for frequent hi-def airings) isn't a gargantuan leap, but the boost in colour definition is appreciable and the beloved grainy bits are still intact (as are some bits of dirt locked into the original opticals). The 5.1 remix is much more noticeable, pumping the music through speakers at full force far more vividly than the theatrical prints (which might tick off purists, but it's still fun). A French track is also included, with optional subtitles in English, French and Spanish, plus there's a bonus soundtrack sampler CD. The trailer is carried over along with a photo gallery and a new featurette, the 27-minute "Going Back to Xanadu", which doesn't feature any of the lead actors (odd, as Newton-John is still a huge supporter of the film) but does have some fun anecdotes from the participants behind the camera including director Greenwald (who went on to helm several high-profile documentaries attacking the likes of Fox News and Wal-Mart) and choreographer Kenny Ortega. You know you want it; just don't tell anyone.

THE YOUNG GIRLS OF ROCHEFORT

Colour, 1967, 125m. / Directed by Jacques Demy / Starring Catherine Deneuve, Françoise Dorléac, Gene Kelly, George Chakiris, Grover Dale, Jacques Perrin, Danielle Darrieux, Michel Piccoli / Artedis (France R2 PAL), Buena Vista (US R1 NTSC) / WS (2.35:1) (16:9)

If Jacques Demy's all-singing hit *The Umbrellas of Cherbourg* was a musical, some fans wondered, where was the dancing? The answer came three years later with the even more ambitious *The Young Girls of Rochefort* (*Les demoiselles de Rochefort*), a stylized celebration of song and dance set in a seaside town where love and fate have a sly sense of humour. Despite the presence of Gene Kelly (whose French singing was dubbed) and *West Side Story*'s George Chakiris, the film never really caught on like its predecessor but earned a sizeable cult following over the years. A splashy widescreen experience overloaded with outrageous pop-'60s visuals, this is also the only time you'll ever hear an upbeat song about a man chopping his wife to bits with an axe.

Travelling performers Etienne (Chakiris) and Bill (Grover Dale) arrive in the quaint town of Rochefort, where everyone seems to be looking for love. Musically inclined sisters Delphine (Catherine Deneuve) and Solange (Françoise Dorléac, her real-life sibling) teach dance and play instruments, while lovelorn sailor Maxence (Jacques Perrin) spends his time hanging out at the coffee shop and painting his ideal love, who happens to look just like Delphine. The shop's owner, Yvonne (*8 Women*'s Danielle Darrieux), is also the girls' mother and yearns for her long lost love, Simon Dame (Michel Piccoli), whom she abandoned in Mexico because of his silly name. To complicate matters further, American musician Andy Miller (Kelly) crosses paths with Solange but fails to learn her name. These romantically challenged paths finally intersect when the girls appear for a big carnival and talent show at the end, during which destiny finally steps in and sorts everything out.

Teaming up again with composer Michel Legrand, Demy ignores much of the melancholy undercurrent from their previous pairing and instead aims for two hours of unadulterated bliss. He largely succeeds thanks to spirited performances all around (though Kelly seems a little weak, surprisingly enough), and the scope photography is often breathtaking. Demy's trademark use of dazzling colour is well in evidence, while the mobile camerawork is often striking and contains enough visual surprises to reward multiple viewings.

Like *Cherbourg*, the film underwent an extensive restoration thanks to Agnes Varda and looks wonderful on DVD; both editions are culled from the same excellent master and accurately replicate the film's theatrical appearance. Only the French language version is included with optional English subtitles, though it was also simultaneously shot in English; reportedly that latter variant was such a mess that the distributors decided to shelve it. The U.S. disc contains no bonuses besides the usual promo previews, while the flip side of the French disc contains an 87-minute retrospective documentary, in which Varda returns to Rochefort and interviews the surviving principals. It's in French with no subtitle options, but Demy fanatics will find it worth a look anyway for curiosity value. Note that this film was later repurposed as part of France's lavish Jacques Demy box set, which is covered in detail in *DVD Delirium Volume 4*.

ZOMBI 3

Colour, 1988, 96m. / Directed by Lucio Fulci and Bruno Mattei / Starring Deran Sarafian, Beatrice Ring, Ottaviano Dell'Acqua, Massimo Vanni, Marina Loi / Shriek Show (US R1 NTSC), Another World (Denmark R2 PAL) / WS (1.85:1) (16:9), VIPCO (UK R0 PAL) / WS (1.85:1)

As Italian horror began to wane in the late 1980s, word of a sequel to Lucio Fulci's seminal *Zombie* (known as *Zombi 2* in continental Europe and *Zombie Flesh-Eaters* in the U.K.) directed by the maestro himself caused fans to salivate in anticipation. Unfortunately circumstances caused by either ill-health or disinterest forced him to reportedly leave the production, and the, um, idiosyncratic Bruno Mattei took the reins to complete the film. The disbelief with which the final product was met largely sprang from the Fulci name emblazoned on the credits, though if approached as more of an unofficial sequel to Mattei's *Hell of the Living Dead* filtered through the slumming sensibility of late-period Fulci, *Zombi 3* is much easier to, well, digest.

Driven more by gleeful insanity than cinematic skill, *Zombi 3* kicks off with the theft of a top-secret freezer unit via helicopter, which results in a deadly toxin

Z

leaking across the countryside. The military attempts to cover up the potential disaster but, thanks to the handy process of cremation (shades of *Return of the Living Dead*), produces a flock of contaminated birds that spread the contagion. Soon both the military and zombies are rampaging through the jungle while a ragtag band of survivors – namely a trio of G.I.s and some hapless teenage girls – fend for their lives against the flesh-munching dead while a local disc jockey offers profound commentary.

Basically one long chase scene punctuated by outrageously giddy dialogue and such oddball sights as a flying, skin-chomping zombie head, *Zombi 3* falls short when it comes to disposable factors like coherent dialogue and continuity. As with the similarly junky *Nightmare City* and Mattei's previous flesh-muncher favourite, the zombies themselves provide most of the fun as they seem to change behavioural patterns and *raison d'être* every five minutes. They shamble, leap from rafters, craftily hide in haystacks, and jump up at helicopters, much to the audience's amusement. Aside from obviously being affordable, the Philippines shooting location (supposedly in the same village used for *Apocalypse Now*) provides a variety of settings and allows the story to cross-cut to its heart's content even when there's no actual reason for it. Dippy, badly dubbed fun, though the bizarre downplaying of gore is impossible to excuse. There's some munching, hacking, and bullet squibs, to be sure, but given both directors' track records, it's peculiar to see the comparative dryness of the end result. It certainly can't hold a candle to the original and unforgettably moist *Zombie*, a precursor in name only.

Zombi 3 never enjoyed the widespread release of its predecessors. Most fans became acquainted with its dopey charms via bootleg copies and the scarce Japanese edition, which featured a three and a half minute opener detailing the revival of an encased corpse. (It's also the most stylish sequence of the film, drenched in Argento-like reds and

blues.) Other video releases simply kicked in with the main titles, which doesn't do much damage to the already senseless story but feels too abrupt all the same. Shriek Show's DVD grafts a one-inch video edition of the prologue (the only surviving element, apparently) onto a superior anamorphic transfer of the film's interneg. The difference is noticeable of course, especially on larger displays where herringbone patterns plague the video segment, but at least it's there. The rest of the film looks solid and film-like, though the visual dullness of some sequences is a flaw inherent in the original photography. Expect lots of greens and browns here, folks. For some reason a handful of gore shots also appear to be lifted from a one-inch instead of film, including part of the flying head sequence; one can only wonder why. Whether it's considered a late period Fulci or a middle of the road Mattei, *Zombi 3* looks like standard late-'80s low-budget Italian product with its dull cinematography and ham-fisted editing style. The audio sounds fine considering the canned voices, which sometimes match the lip movements and spout one quote-worthy inanity after another. The droning and hilariously dated synth score, which sounds like outtakes from *The A-Team*, is also well rendered for what it is.

The old adage about making lemonade from lemons certainly applies to Shriek Show's DVD, which offers a fascinating and sometimes-hilarious look at how a potential Eurohorror classic could derail so completely. Mattei ("I think all of my films are ugly"), writer/producer Claudio Fragasso, and actors Ottaviano Dell'Acqua, Massimo Vanni, and Marina Loi are all on hand to offer on-camera interviews about their experiences with the film, which was seemingly cursed from its inception. They finally set the record straight about Fulci's involvement; he shot a 70-minute film and declared it completed, but only 50 minutes of his work was usable. When Fulci refused to return for reshoots, Fragasso recruited Mattei for some emergency cinematic surgery. Mattei takes credit for the footage of men in white contamination suits and sundry other details, but apparently the bulk of the film can legitimately be credited to Fulci. Fragasso has the longest interview (18 minutes), while the others range between 6 to 10 minutes each. The actors mainly offer friendly anecdotes about shooting, with Fulci described as alternately witty and monstrous. Other extras include a gallery of posters and lobby cards and the lively theatrical trailer.

Denmark's Another World Entertainment issued the film under the title *Zombie: Hell on Earth*. Scant extras include the film's trailer and some text filmographies. It has none of the interview material found on Shriek Show's edition, but does include a nice booklet by Jesper Moerch and some promo spots for other AWE titles.

ZOMBIE 4: AFTER DEATH

Colour, 1988, 81m. / Directed by Claudio Fragasso / Starring Jeff Stryker, Candice Daly / Shriek Show (US R1 NTSC) / WS (1.85:1) (16:9), X-Rated (Germany R2 PAL) / WS (1.78:1) (16:9), VIPCO (UK R2 PAL)

As the Italian horror industry wound down in the late 1980s, attempts to recapture the glory days (or is that gory days?) of Fulci and Argento resulted in a lot of bizarre genre hybrids, most of which wound up being released only in Europe and Asia. Although Fulci's *Zombi 3* misfired at the box office, that film's writer, Claudio Fragasso (the anti-genius behind *Troll 2*, *Monster Dog*, and *Rats: Nights of Terror*), took over directorial chores for another Filipino-shot romp with the undead, *After Death*. Promoted as *Zombi 4* (but not titled as such in the film itself), this ramshackle outing delivers bucket loads of gore and an equally rich stream of unintentional guffaws.

The goofiness begins full throttle in the obligatory opening set piece, which finds a hyperactive voodoo doctor fending off a gang of white interlopers by turning his drooling, zombie wife loose on them. The sole survivor returns two decades later as pretty Candice Daly, who for no particular reason tags along with a band of mercenaries led by the stoic Chuck (switch-hitting adult star Jeff Stryker, billed as "Chuck Peyton"). Of course, she isn't aware that this is the same island of doom until it's too late, when they're all besieged by the hungry undead. Our heroes run into a band of inept scientists who have accidentally increased the zombie population, resulting in a claustrophobic voodoo showdown strangely reminiscent of the "magic circle" bit from *The Devil Rides Out*, only silly. Eventually it all comes down to a handful of survivors and an ultra-moist finale "borrowed" from the "other" *Zombi 3*, *Burial Ground*.

Not many people are likely to confuse *After Death* with a good movie, but zombie and splatter fans can easily get their jollies here. Faces are torn off in lingering detail, chest cavities are turned into impromptu puppeting devices, bullet squibs burst twenty times wetter than any real gunshot... well, you get the idea. Fans of those agile, gun-toting, kickboxing zombies from *Nightmare City* and *Zombi 3* will find more of the same behaviour here as well. For some reason the two American leads didn't loop their own voices, but the dubbing stays in sync and is better than average for this time period. Ah, and let's not forget the hilarious synth score by Al Festa, the man who went on to perpetrate *Fatal Frames*; the theme song alone is nearly worth the DVD's price tag.

Now here's where things get confusing. Most fans first saw this film via Japanese video as *After Death*; then a passable but somewhat sickly-looking transfer popped up on British DVD as *Zombie Flesh Eaters 3* (since *Zombi 3* was retitled *Zombie Flesh Eaters 2* by VIPCO; got that?). The best

Z

transfer is Shriek Show's edition, which is called *Zombie 4: After Death*. The anamorphic presentation is colourful and features nicely rendered black levels (a first for this title), though the deliberate soft focus photography in some shots translates to an erratic presentation wholly dependent on the original elements. The packaging promises a trailer and an interview with Fragasso, which turns out to be a solid, 17-minute discussion which dovetails directly from his interview on the *Zombi 3* disc. He explains the genesis of the film and the location shooting in great detail and seems to offer a reasonable presentation of the industry during that period. However, a few unadvertised bonuses turn up as well. Daly appears for a very brief on-camera interview; she seems pleasant enough but her recollections are limited. The most unexpected extra turns out to be a 10-minute video interview with Stryker, who looks like he was caught on the way to his car in a Los Angeles parking lot. He explains how he was hired because uncredited producer Werner Pochath (the late, great Eurosleaze character actor from *Mosquito* and *The Cat O' Nine Tails*) was a big fan of his porn work, then repeatedly characterizes his performance as "runnin' around in the jungle, lookin' freaked out!" Along with some liner notes (in illegibly tiny print), the usual Media Blasters tie-in trailers are also included. If that doesn't satisfy you, the insane Germans running the X-Rated Kult label did their own edition which contains both the familiar cut of the film and an extended 88-minute version they dug up from God knows where, in case you want to savour Stryker's dubbing some more. Audio is in English, German or Italian for the standard cut, or English and German for the extended one. Extras include the German, Italian, and English trailers and a bunch of cross-promotional promos. This version comes in four different covers; watch out for the white one – there's only 99 of 'em out there!

INDEX TO DVD DELIRIUM VOLUME 2 REDUX

INDEX TO DVD DELIRIUM VOLUME 2 REDUX

Edited by
Nathaniel Thompson

DVD DELIRIUM

The International Guide to Weird
and Wonderful Films on DVD

Volume 1 Redux

CONTENTS -
THE COMPLETE LIST OF FILMS REVIEWED IN DEPTH IN VOLUME 1:

DEAD, HEMOGLOBIN (BLEEDERS), THE HITCHER, HOLLYWOOD CHAINSAW HOOKERS, HORROR EXPRESS, HORROR HOSPITAL, HORRORS OF SPIDER ISLAND, HOT SUMMER, HOUSE, HOUSE II: THE SECOND STORY, THE HOUSE BY THE CEMETERY, HOUSE OF GAMES, HOUSE OF WHIPCORD, HOUSE OF YES, HOUSE ON HAUNTED HILL, HOUSE ON HAUNTED HILL, THE HOUSE ON SORORITY ROW, HOUSE ON THE EDGE OF THE PARK, THE HUMAN TORNADO, HUMANOIDS FROM THE DEEP, HYPNOSIS (THE HYPNOTIST), I, A WOMAN, I EAT YOUR SKIN, I KNOW WHERE I'M GOING!, I SAW WHAT YOU DID, I SPIT ON YOUR GRAVE, I STILL KNOW WHAT YOU DID LAST SUMMER, I, ZOMBIE, IDLE HANDS, IGUANA, ILSA, HAREM KEEPER OF THE OIL SHEIKS, ILSA, SHE WOLF OF THE SS, ILSA, THE WICKED WARDEN, IMMORAL TALES, IMMORTAL BELOVED, IMMORTALITY (THE WISDOM OF CROCODILES), IMPULSE, IN CROWD, IN DREAMS, IN SEARCH OF DRACULA, IN THE MOOD FOR LOVE, IN THE MOUTH OF MADNESS, IN THE REALM OF THE SENSES, IN THE WOODS, INCUBUS, THE INDIAN TOMB, INFERNO, L'INITIATION, INSEMINOID, INTRUDER, THE INTRUDER, INVASION OF THE BLOOD FARMERS, THE INVISIBLE MAN, THE IRREFUTABLE TRUTH ABOUT DEMONS, J.D.'S REVENGE, JACK BE NIMBLE, JACK THE RIPPER, JACOB'S LADDER, JAIL BAIT, JAM—N JAM—N, JASON GOES TO HELL: THE FINAL FRIDAY, JAWBREAKER, JEWEL OF THE NILE, THE JOHNSONS, JOSIE AND THE PUSSYCATS, JOY HOUSE, JOY RIDE, JURASSIC PARK III, JUST FOR THE HELL OF IT, THE KENTUCKY FRIED MOVIE, KILL, BABY... KILL!, KILLER KLOWNS FROM OUTER SPACE, KING KONG (1976), KISS ME DEADLY, KISS ME MONSTER, KNIGHTRIDERS, KNOCKING ON DEATH'S DOOR, KOLOBOS, KWAIDAN, LABYRINTH, LADY CHATTERLEY, LADY IN WHITE, LADY OF THE LAKE, LAIR OF THE WHITE WORM, LARA CROFT: TOMB RAIDER, THE LAST BROADCAST, THE LAST STARFIGHTER, LAST TANGO IN PARIS, THE LAST WAVE, LAST YEAR AT MARIENBAD, THE LATHE OF HEAVEN, THE LEGEND OF HELL HOUSE, LET SLEEPING CORPSES LIE (THE LIVING DEAD AT MANCHESTER MORGUE), THE LIBERTINE, LICENCE TO KILL, THE LICKERISH QUARTET, LIFE OF BRIAN, LIPS OF BLOOD, LIQUID SKY, LISA AND THE DEVIL, A LITTLE BIT OF SOUL, LITTLE MOTHER, LIVE AND LET DIE, LIVE FLESH, THE LIVING DAYLIGHTS, THE LIVING DEAD GIRL, LOLITA, LORD OF ILLUSIONS, LORD OF THE FLIES, THE LOST CONTINENT, LOST HORIZON, LOST IN SPACE, LUST FOR A VAMPIRE, LUST FOR FRANKENSTEIN, M, MABOROSI, MACABRE, THE MAD BUTCHER, MAHLER, THE MAN WITH THE GOLDEN GUN, THE MAN WITH TWO BRAINS, MANHATTAN BABY, MANIAC, MANJI, MANTIS IN LACE, MARIHUANA, MARNIE, MARTIN, MAY MORNING, THE MEDUSA TOUCH, MEET THE FEEBLES, MEMENTO, MESA OF LOST WOMEN, THE MIGHTY PEKING MAN, MIRANDA, THE MIRROR CRACK'D, MISSISSIPPI MERMAID, MR. SARDONICUS, MR. VAMPIRE, MODERN VAMPIRES, MON ONCLE D'AMERIQUE, MONA LISA, MONKEY SHINES, THE MONSTER OF CAMP SUNSHINE, MONSTERS CRASH THE PAJAMA PARTY, MOONRAKER, THE MOST DANGEROUS GAME, MOTHER'S DAY, MOUNTAIN OF THE CANNIBAL GOD, MS.45 (ANGEL OF VENGEANCE), THE MUMMY, THE MUMMY'S SHROUD, MUTANT, MY BEST FIEND, MYLENE FARMER: MUSIC VIDEOS / MUSIC VIDEOS II & III, NADIE CONOCE A NADIE, THE NAMELESS (LOS SIN NOMBRE), NARCOTIC, NATIONAL LAMPOON'S CHRISTMAS VACATION, NATIONAL LAMPOON'S VACATION, NATURAL BORN KILLERS, NEKROMANTIK, NEVER SAY NEVER AGAIN, NEW ROSE HOTEL, THE NEW YORK RIPPER, NIGHT CALLER FROM OUTER SPACE, NIGHT OF THE BLOODY APES, NIGHT OF THE HUNTED, THE NIGHT OF THE HUNTER, NIGHT OF THE LIVING DEAD, NIGHT OF THE LIVING DEAD, NIGHT OF THE SEAGULLS, THE NIGHT PORTER, NIGHT TIDE, A NIGHT TO DISMEMBER, NIGHTMARE CITY, NIGHTMARES, NIGHTS OF CABIRIA, NIGHTWATCH, THE NINTH GATE, NOSFERATU THE VAMPYRE, NOT OF THIS EARTH, NOTORIOUS, NUDE FOR SATAN, OASIS OF THE ZOMBIES, OCTOPUSSY, THE OLD DARK HOUSE, THE OMEN, OMEN IV: THE AWAKENING, ON HER MAJESTY'S SECRET SERVICE, 100 DAYS, OPEN YOUR EYES (ABRE LOS OJOS), THE OPENING OF MISTY BEETHOVEN, OPERA, ORCA THE KILLER WHALE, ORGAN, ORLOFF AND THE INVISIBLE MAN, ORPHEUS, THE PASSENGER, THE PASSION OF JOAN OF ARC, PECKER, PEEPING TOM, THE PEOPLE THAT TIME FORGOT, PERCY, PERDITA DURANGO, PET SEMATARY, PETEY WHEATSTRAW: THE DEVIL'S SON-IN-LAW, PHANTASM, PHANTOM OF THE OPERA, PHANTOM OF THE OPERA, PHANTOM OF THE OPERA, PHANTOM OF THE PARADISE, PHENOMENA, PICNIC AT HANGING ROCK, PIECES, PIG, THE PILLOW BOOK, PINK FLOYD: THE WALL, PIONEERS IN INGOLSTADT, PIRANHA, PIRATES OF CAPRI, PIT AND THE PENDULUM, THE PIT AND THE PENDULUM, PIT STOP, PITCH BLACK, THE PLAGUE OF THE ZOMBIES, PLAN 9 FROM OUTER SPACE, PLANET OF THE APES, PLANET OF THE VAMPIRES, THE PLAYGIRLS AND THE VAMPIRE, P.O. BOX TINTO BRASS, POISON, POISON IVY, POLA X, PORTRAIT OF JENNIE, POSSESSION, PRACTICAL MAGIC, PREHISTORIC WOMEN, PRETTY AS A PICTURE: THE ART OF DAVID LYNCH, PRINCE OF DARKNESS, THE PRINCESS AND THE CALL GIRL, THE PRISONER, PROPHECY, PSYCHIC KILLER, PSYCHO, PSYCHO III, PSYCHOMANIA, PUPPET MASTER, PUPPET MASTER II, PUPPET MASTER III: TOULON'S REVENGE, PUPPET MASTER 4, PUPPET MASTER 5, QUATERMASS AND THE PIT, QUATERMASS AND THE PIT, QUATERMASS II, QUERELLE, QUILLS, RABID, RABID DOGS, RABID GRANNIES, THE RAGE: CARRIE II, RAINBOW BRIDGE, RASPUTIN THE MAD MONK, RAVENOUS, RAZOR BLADE SMILE, REBECCA, THE RED SHOES, THE RED VIOLIN, REEFER MADNESS (DOPED YOUTH), REPO MAN, THE REPTILE, REQUIEM FOR A VAMPIRE, RESURRECTION, RETRO PUPPET MASTER, RETURN OF THE EVIL DEAD, RETURN OF THE 5 DEADLY VENOMS, RETURN OF THE LIVING DEAD 3, RETURN TO OZ, RICHARD KERN: THE HARDCORE COLLECTION, RING, THE ROCKY HORROR PICTURE SHOW, ROLLERBALL, ROMANCE, ROMANCING THE STONE, ROSEMARY'S BABY, ROUGE, THE RULING CLASS, RUN LOLA RUN, RUNNING TIME, SACRED FLESH, SALEM'S LOT, SALOME'S LAST DANCE, SANJURO, SCARS OF DRACULA, SCHIZO, SCHRAMM, SCORE, SCREAM, SCREAM 2, SCREAM 3, THE SCREAMING SKULL, SCUM OF THE EARTH, SECOND SKIN (SEGUNDA PIEL), SEE THE SEA, THE SENTINEL, 7 FACES OF DR. LAO, THE 7TH VOYAGE OF SINBAD, SEXTETTE, SHE FREAK, SHE KILLED IN ECSTASY, SHE-DEVILS ON WHEELS, SHEBA, BABY, THE SHINING, SHIVER OF THE VAMPIRES, SHIVERS, SHOCK, SHOCK WAVES, SHOGUN ASSASSIN, SHREK, SILENT NIGHT, BLOODY NIGHT, A SIMPLE PLAN, SINBAD AND THE EYE OF THE TIGER, SIRENS, SISTERS, SIX DAYS IN ROSWELL, THE SIXTH SENSE, SKINNER, SLAVE GIRLS FROM BEYOND INFINITY, SLEEPY HOLLOW, THE SLIPPER AND THE ROSE, SLUGS, THE SLUMBER PARTY MASSACRE, SMALL SOLDIERS, SOLARIS, SOMEONE TO WATCH OVER ME, SOMETHING WEIRD, SORORITY HOUSE MASSACRE, SORORITY HOUSE MASSACRE II, SOUTHERN COMFORT, SPACEWAYS, SPELLBOUND, SPIDER BABY, THE SPIRAL STAIRCASE, SPIRITISM, SPIRITS OF THE DEAD, SPLENDOR, THE SPY WHO LOVED ME, STAGEFRIGHT, STARMAN, THE STENDHAL SYNDROME, STOP MAKING SENSE, THE STORY OF O, THE STRAIGHT STORY, STRANGLER OF THE SWAMP, STREET TRASH, THE STUFF, SUBCONSCIOUS CRUELTY, SUCCUBUS, SURRENDER DOROTHY, SUSPIRIA, SWAMP THING, THE SWINGING CHEERLEADERS, SWITCHBLADE SISTERS, TALES OF ORDINARY MADNESS, TALES OF TERROR, A TASTE OF BLOOD, TEENAGE MONSTER, THE TEMPEST, TENDER FLESH, TENDERNESS OF THE WOLVES, TENEBRE, THE 10TH VICTIM, TERROR IS A MAN, TERROR OF FRANKENSTEIN, TERROR TRACT, TESS, THE TESTAMENT OF DR. MABUSE, THE TESTAMENT OF ORPHEUS, THE TEXAS CHAIN SAW MASSACRE, THE TEXAS CHAINSAW MASSACRE 2, THAT OBSCURE OBJECT OF DESIRE, THEATRE OF BLOOD, THEATRE OF DEATH, THERESE AND ISABELLE, THESIS (TESIS), THEY LIVE, THEY SAVED HITLER'S BRAIN, THE THING, THINGS TO COME, THE THIRD MAN, 13 GHOSTS, THE 39 STEPS, THIS NIGHT I'LL POSSESS YOUR CORPSE, THE THOUSAND EYES OF DR. MABUSE, THUNDERBALL, TIE ME UP! TIE ME DOWN!, TIERRA, TIGER BAY, THE TIGER OF ESCHNAPUR, THE TIME MACHINE, THE TINGLER, TOKYO DECADENCE, TOKYO DRIFTER, TOMB OF TORTURE, TOMBS OF THE BLIND DEAD, TOMMY, TOMORROW NEVER COMES, TOMORROW NEVER DIES, TOO MUCH FLESH, TORSO, TOUCH OF EVIL, TOURIST TRAP, TOWER OF EVIL, TRADER HORNEE, THE TRIAL, TRILOGY OF TERROR, TURKISH DELIGHT, THE TWILIGHT PEOPLE, TWITCH OF THE DEATH NERVE, TWO DAYS IN THE VALLEY, TWO LANE BLACKTOP, 2001: A SPACE ODYSSEY, TWO THOUSAND MANIACS!, TWO UNDERCOVER ANGELS, THE UGLY, THE UNBEARABLE LIGHTNESS OF BEING, UNBREAKABLE, THE UNDERTAKER AND HIS PALS, UP!, VALENTINE, VALERIE, VAMPIRES, THE VAMPIRES' NIGHT ORGY, VAMPYRES, VAMPYROS LESBOS, THE VANISHING, VELVET GOLDMINE, VENGEANCE, THE VENGEANCE OF SHE, VENUS IN FURS, VERTIGO, VERY BAD THINGS, VIBRATION, VIDEODROME, A VIEW TO A KILL, THE VIKING QUEEN, THE VIRGIN SUICIDES, VIY (THE VIJ), THE VOYEUR, WATER DROPS ON BURNING ROCKS, WHAT EVER HAPPENED TO AUNT ALICE?, WHAT HAVE THEY DONE TO YOUR DAUGHTERS?, WHEN A STRANGER CALLS, THE WHIP AND THE BODY, WHITE ZOMBIE, WHITY, THE WICKER MAN, WILD THINGS, THE WITCHES, THE WIZARD OF GORE, THE WOLF MAN, THE WOLVES OF KROMER, THE WOMAN IN BLACK, WOMEN IN REVOLT, WONDERWALL, THE WORLD IS NOT ENOUGH, WOYZECK, X - THE MAN WITH THE X-RAY EYES, X THE UNKNOWN, X2000: THE FILMS OF FRANÇOIS OZON, YELLOW SUBMARINE, YOJIMBO, YOU ONLY LIVE TWICE, YOUNG FRANKENSTEIN, ZACHARIAH, A ZED AND TWO NOUGHTS, ZEDER.. ZETA ONE, ZOMBIE FLESH-EATERS (ZOMBIE), ZOMBIE LAKE.

CONTENTS -
THE COMPLETE LIST OF FILMS REVIEWED IN DEPTH IN VOLUME 3:

OF PARTY BEACH, THE HOUSE OF FEAR, HOUSE OF WAX, HOUSE ON BARE MOUNTAIN, THE HOUSE WHERE EVIL DWELLS, HOW TO KILL A JUDGE, HULK, HUSTLE, I AM THE RIPPER, IF YOU WERE YOUNG: RAGE, IMAGES IN A CONVENT, IN A YEAR WITH 13 MOONS, IN THE SOUP, THE INHERITANCE, INSERTS, INUGAMI, INVASION OF THE BEE GIRLS, ISLAND OF THE FISHMEN, IT'S ALIVE, IT LIVES AGAIN, IT'S ALIVE III: ISLAND OF THE ALIVE, THE JACKET, JOE, KANTO WANDERER, KARATE FOR LIFE, KATIEBIRD* CERTIFIABLE CRAZY PERSON, KICHIKU, KILINK ISTANBUL'DA, KILINK STRIP & KILL, KILINK VS. SUPERMAN, THE KILLER MUST KILL AGAIN, THE KILLING CLUB, THE KILLING OF A CHINESE BOOKIE, KING KONG (1933), KISS ME QUICK, LADY EMANUELLE, LADY SNOWBLOOD, LADY TERMINATOR, LARA CROFT: TOMB RAIDER: THE CRADLE OF LIFE, THE LAS VEGAS SERIAL KILLER, THE LEAGUE OF EXTRAORDINARY GENTLEMEN, LEGEND OF THE EIGHT SAMURAI, LEMORA: A CHILD'S TALE OF THE SUPERNATURAL, LES CHIC (1972), LES CHIC (2002), LET ME DIE A WOMAN, LIFEGUARD, LIFESPAN, THE LITTLE GIRL WHO LIVES DOWN THE LANE, LIVING DOLL, LONG WEEKEND, THE LOST BOYS, LOVE AT THE TOP, LOVE RITES, THE LOVELESS, THE LOWER DEPTHS (1936), THE LOWER DEPTHS (1957), MACHINE-GUN KELLY, MAD DOCTOR OF BLOOD ISLAND, MADE IN BRITAIN, MAGIC, MA"TRESSE, MAMMA ROMA, A MAN CALLED MAGNUM, THE MAN FROM DEEP RIVER (DEEP RIVER SAVAGES), THE MAN WHO LAUGHS, MANIACAL, MANIACTS, THE MANITOU, THE MANSION OF MADNESS, THE MANSON FAMILY, MARK OF THE DEVIL, MATANGO, MIDNIGHT BLUE COLLECTION VOLUME 1: THE DEEP THROAT SPECIAL EDITION, MIDNIGHT BLUE COLLECTION VOLUME 2: PORN STARS OF THE 70'S, MIDNIGHT BLUE COLLECTION VOLUME 3: CELEBRITIES EDITION, MILL OF THE STONE WOMEN, MIRROR MIRROR, MIRROR MIRROR 2: RAVEN DANCE, MIRROR MIRROR 3: THE VOYEUR, MIRROR MIRROR 4: REFLECTIONS, MOTORCYCLE GANG, THE MURDER IN THE RED BARN, MURDER SHE SAID, MURDER AT THE GALLOP, MURDER MOST FOUL, MURDER AHOY, MY NAME IS NOBODY, MY OWN PRIVATE IDAHO, THE MYSTERIANS, NAIL GUN MASSACRE, NEON NIGHTS, NIGHT AND THE CITY, THE NIGHT EVELYN CAME OUT OF THE GRAVE, NIGHT TRAIN MURDERS, NIGHTMARES COME AT NIGHT, 9 SOULS, 99 WOMEN, LE NOTTI BIANCHE, THE OBLONG BOX, THE OFFENCE, OLDBOY, OLGA'S GIRLS, THE OMEGA MAN, ONE DEADLY SUMMER (L'ÉTÉ MEURTRIER), ONE FROM THE HEART, ONIBABA, OPEN WATER, OPENING NIGHT, THE ORACLE, THE OTHER, PANIC BEATS, THE PEARL OF DEATH, PENETRATION ANGST, PHONE BOOTH, PHOTOGRAPHING FAIRIES, PICKUP ON SOUTH STREET, PINOCCHIO 964, PIRATES OF THE CARIBBEAN: THE CURSE OF THE BLACK PEARL, THE PLEASURE PARTY, THE POOL (SWIMMING POOL: DER TOD FEIERT MIT), PRETTY POISON, PREY, PRIME CUT, PRISON HEAT, PROMISES! PROMISES!, PURSUIT TO ALGIERS, QUARTET, QUICKSAND, THE RAILROAD MAN, RED COCKROACHES, THE RED QUEEN KILLS SEVEN TIMES, RED SILK, REFORM SCHOOL GIRL, REFORM SCHOOL GIRLS, REVENGERS TRAGEDY, ROADRACERS, ROBINSON CRUSOE, ROCK ALL NIGHT, ROCK & RULE, ROJO SANGRE, ROOTS OF EVIL, RUBBER'S LOVER, RUDE BOY, RUN VIRGIN RUN, RUNAWAY DAUGHTERS, SALVATORE GIULIANO, SATANICO PANDEMONIUM, SATAN'S BLACK WEDDING, SATAN'S BLOOD, SAW, THE SCARLET CLAW, SCHOOL OF THE HOLY BEAST, SCISSORS, LA SCORTA, SCREAM AND SCREAM AGAIN, SCREAM QUEEN HOT TUB PARTY, SCUM (1977), SCUM (1979), SEARCHING FOR THE WRONG-EYED JESUS, SECRETARY, SECRETS OF A CALL GIRL, SECRETS OF A WINDMILL GIRL, THE SEDUCTION OF INGA, SEE NO EVIL, THE SENSUOUS NURSE, SEVEN DEATHS IN THE CAT'S EYE, SEVEN WOMEN FOR SATAN, SEX AND LUCÍA, SEX NURSE, SHADOWS, SHERLOCK HOLMES AND THE SECRET WEAPON, SHERLOCK HOLMES AND THE VOICE OF TERROR, SHERLOCK HOLMES FACES DEATH, SHERLOCK HOLMES IN WASHINGTON, THE SHINING, THE SIGN OF FOUR, SIN CITY, SINGAPORE SLING, LA SIRÈNE ROUGE (RED SIREN), SISTER EMANUELLE, SIXTEEN TONGUES, SKY CAPTAIN AND THE WORLD OF TOMORROW, SLACKER, SMITHEREENS, A SNAKE OF JUNE, THE SOLDIER, SORORITY GIRL, SPELLBOUND, THE SPIDER WOMAN, SPIDER-MAN 2, SQUIRM, SS CAMP: WOMEN'S HELL, SS EXPERIMENT LOVE CAMP, SS GIRLS, THE STAND, STARCRASH, STARSTRUCK, STORY OF A LOVE AFFAIR, STRANGE DAYS, THE STRANGE VICE OF MRS. WARDH, STRAWBERRY ESTATES, STRAY CAT ROCK: SEX HUNTER, STREET LAW, STREET MOBSTER, STRIP NUDE FOR YOUR KILLER, THE STUDENT OF PRAGUE (1913), THE STUDENT OF PRAGUE (1926), SUGAR COOKIES, SUPERSTITION, SUSPICIOUS RIVER, SWAMP WOMEN, SWANN IN LOVE, SWIMMING POOL, SWORD OF DOOM, SYMPATHY FOR MR. VENGEANCE, TAKING LIVES, THE TALENTED MR. RIPLEY, TALES FROM THE CRYPT: FROM COMIC BOOKS TO TELEVISION!, TARKAN VERSUS THE VIKINGS, TASTE THE BLOOD OF DRACULA, TEENAGE CAVE MAN, TEOREMA, TERROR AND BLACK LACE (TERROR Y ENCAJES NEGROS), TERROR BY NIGHT, TEXAS LIGHTNING, THE THREE LIVES OF THOMASINA, 3 NUTS IN SEARCH OF A BOLT, THRILLER: A CRUEL PICTURE (THEY CALL HER ONE EYE), THUNDERBIRDS, TIGRERO, THE TIN DRUM, TINTORERA, THE TIT AND THE MOON, TITANIC, TOMIE, TOMIE: REPLAY, TOMIE: REBIRTH, TONY: ANOTHER DOUBLE GAME, TOOLBOX MURDERS, TOUCH OF DEATH, THE TOXIC AVENGER, TRAILER TRASH, TRANCE (DER FAN), TROUBLE MAN, THE TULSE LUPER SUITCASES: THE MOAB STORY, TWIST AND SHOUT, 2069: A SEX ODYSSEY, THE UGLIEST WOMAN IN THE WORLD, UN DEUX TROIS SOLEIL, THE UNDEAD, THE UNDERTOW, UNDERWORLD BEAUTY, UNKNOWN BEYOND, UNO BIANCA, UTOPIA, VALERIE AND HER WEEK OF WONDERS, VAMPIRE JUNCTION, VENUS IN FURS, VERNON FLORIDA, VIKING WOMEN AND THE SEA SERPENT, VIOLENT MIDNIGHT, THE VIRGIN SPRING, VIRGIN WITCH, VIRGINS FROM HELL, VIRIDIANA, VISITOR Q, VOODOO WOMAN, WALKABOUT, WALLS IN THE CITY, WAR, WARLORDS OF ATLANTIS, WAXWORKS, WELCOME TO ARROW BEACH, WEREWOLVES ON WHEELS, WESTWORLD, A WHISPER IN THE DARK, WHO CAN KILL A CHILD?, WISCONSIN DEATH TRIP, THE WITCH WHO CAME FROM THE SEA, THE WOMAN IN GREEN, A WOMAN UNDER THE INFLUENCE, WOMEN'S PRISON MASSACRE, X-312 FLIGHT TO HELL, YELLOW EMANUELLE, YESTERDAY TODAY AND TOMORROW, YOUNG VIOLENT DANGEROUS, YOUR VICE IS A LOCKED ROOM AND ONLY I HAVE THE KEY, ZAPPA, ZERO FOCUS.

CONTENTS -

THE COMPLETE LIST OF FILMS REVIEWED IN VOLUME 4:

IRON ROSE, ISLE OF THE DAMNED, ITALIAN STALLION, JOE ROCK SUPERSTAR, JOHNNY GRUESOME, JUSTINE & JULIETTE, JUSTINE DE SADE, KADIN DÜSMANI, KARAOKE TERROR, KARATE WARRIORS, KEEP THEM HAPPY AT HOME, THE KILLER LIKES CANDY, KILLER'S DELIGHT, KILLER'S MOON, KILLERS BY NATURE, KILLING CAR, KIZIL TUG, LADY LIBERTINE, LADY OSCAR, THE LAST HORROR FILM, LAST HOUSE ON THE BEACH, THE LAST HUNTER, LAURE, THE LEGEND OF BLOOD CASTLE, LEGENDS OF THE POISONOUS SEDUCTRESS 1: FEMALE DEMON OHYAKU, LEGENDS OF THE POISONOUS SEDUCTRESS 2: QUICK-DRAW OKATSU, LEGENDS OF THE POISONOUS SEDUCTRESS 3: OKATSU THE FUGITIVE, LET THE RIGHT ONE IN, LETHAL FORCE, A LIZARD IN A WOMAN'S SKIN, LOLA, LONDON IN THE RAW, LOOKING GOOD, LOVE CIRCLES, THE LOVE STATUE, LUCKER THE NECROPHAGOUS, MACUMBA SEXUAL, THE MADAM, MADAME O, MADHOUSE, MAHAKAAL, MAID IN SWEDEN, MALABIMBA: THE MALICIOUS WHORE, MALPERTUIS, MAN OF VIOLENCE, MAN WITH A MOVIE CAMERA, MANSION OF THE LIVING DEAD, MARAUDERS, MARK OF THE WITCH, MARQUIS DE SADE'S PROSPERITIES OF VICE, MARTYRS, MASSACRE MAFIA STYLE, MEAN JOHNNY BARROWS, MERCY, MESSIAH OF EVIL, THE MIDNIGHT MEAT TRAIN, MILLIE'S HOMECOMING, MODEL SHOP, MOLLY AND THE GHOST, MOONLIGHTING WIVES, MOTHER OF TEARS, MURDER-ROCK, MY AIN FOLK, MY CHILDHOOD, MY WAY HOME, LA NAISSANCE DU JOUR, NAKED AMAZON, THE NAKED BUNYIP, NAKED FEAR, NATURE MORTE, NECROVILLE, NEXT OF KIN, NIGHT OF DEATH!, NIGHT OF FEAR, NIGHT OF THE WEREWOLF, NIGHTHAWKS, NIGHTMARE CASTLE, NIGHTWATCHING, NUDE IN DRACULA'S CASTLE, THE NUDE VAMPIRE, NURSE SHERRI, OASIS OF FEAR, ÖLÜLER KONU&SCEDIL;MAZKI, OM SHANTI OM, ONE-EYED MONSTER, THE OTHER SIDE OF UNDERNEATH, PACIFIC BANANA, PAPAYA: LOVE GODDESS OF THE CANNIBALS, PARKING, PARTY 7, PATRICK, THE PERFUME OF YVONNE, PERMISSIVE, PERVERSION STORY (ONE ON TOP OF THE OTHER), PETS, PHOENIX, THE PIED PIPER, PLAGUE TOWN, PLAYGIRLS OF MUNICH, PLEASURE PALACE, PORN STARS OF THE 80'S, PORN STARS OF THE 90'S, PORN-O-RAMA, POSED FOR MURDER, POULTRYGEIST: NIGHT OF THE CHICKEN DEAD, POWER PLAY, PRESIDENTIAL PEEPERS, PRIMITIVE LONDON, PRIVATE COLLECTIONS, PRIVILEGE, THE PSYCHIC, PSYCHO KICKBOXER, PSYCHOS IN LOVE, PUNK ROCK, PURANA MANDIR, PURANI HAVELI, QUANDO L'AMORE È SENSUALITÀ, QUEEN OF BLACK MAGIC, RAZORBACK, REFINEMENTS IN LOVE, RICA, RIOT ON 42ND ST., ROCK 'N' ROLL NIGHTMARE, A ROOM IN TOWN, ROSARIGASINOS, ROSELYNE AND THE LIONS, THE RUG COP, RUN LIKE HELL, RUNNING HOT, SACRED FLESH, SACRIFICE OF THE WHITE GODDESS, THE SADIST WITH RED TEETH, SALÒ, OR THE 120 DAYS OF SODOM, SATAN'S BABY DOLL, SATAN'S PLAYGROUND, SATANIC SLUTS: THE BLACK ORDER COMETH, SCHIZO, SCHOOLGIRL REPORT #1: WHAT PARENTS DON'T THINK IS POSSIBLE, SCHOOLGIRL REPORT #2: WHAT KEEPS PARENTS AWAKE AT NIGHT, SCHOOLGIRL REPORT #3: WHAT PARENTS FIND UNTHINKABLE, SCHOOLGIRL REPORT #4: WHAT DRIVES PARENTS TO DESPAIR, SCREAM, SCREWBALLS, THE SECOND COMING OF EVA, SECRETS OF SWEET SIXTEEN, SENSITIVE NEW AGE KILLER, SEPARATION, THE SERPENT'S TALE, SEX MACHINE, THE SEXPERTS, THE SEXPLOITERS, SEXUAL FREEDOM IN DENMARK, SEXUAL LIBERTY NOW, THE SEXUAL STORY OF O, THE SHE BEAST, SHIVER, SHOCK-O-RAMA, SICK GIRL, SILENT SCREAM, SILIP: DAUGHTERS OF EVE, THE SINFUL DWARF, SINS OF SISTER LUCIA, SISTER EMANUELLE, THE SISTER OF URSULA, SISTER STREET FIGHTER, SKIN IN THE FIFTIES, SLASHERS, A SLIGHTLY PREGNANT MAN, SLIME CITY, SLOGAN, SNAKE WOMAN'S CURSE, SNAPSHOT, SO SWEET, SO DEAD, SOLE SURVIVOR, SPIRITUAL EXERCISES, SPLATTER BEACH, SPLATTER DISCO, SPLATTER FARM, STAR, THE STARLETS, STASH, THE STEPFATHER, STEPFATHER II, THE STRANGENESS, STRIP JACK NAKED, STUNT ROCK, SUCCUBUS: THE DEMON, SUMMER PEOPLE, SUMMERFIELD, SUPERMEN DÖNÜYOR, THE SURVIVOR, SUSPECTED DEATH OF A MINOR, SUZIE HEARTLESS, SWEET SIXTEEN, THE SWEET SOUND OF DEATH, SWINGING WIVES, THE SWITCH, OR HOW TO ALTER YOUR EGO, SYLVIA, SYNGENOR, TAHKHANA, TAKE THEM AS THEY ARE, TARZAN ISTANBUL'DA, TERROR CIRCUS (BARN OF THE NAKED DEAD), TERROR EXPRESS, THAT KIND OF GIRL, THIRST, THE THREE TRIALS, TOKYO GORE POLICE, A TOUCH OF GENIE, TRAPPED, TROIS PLACES POUR LE 26, TROMA'S WAR, THE TRUE STORY OF THE NUN OF MONZA, THE UMBRELLAS OF CHERBOURG, UNDYING LOVE, THE UNSEEN, VAMPIRE STRANGLER, VANESSA, VEERANA, VENGEANCE OF THE ZOMBIES, VIDEO VIOLENCE, VIDEO VIOLENCE 2, VIOLENCE AND FLESH, VIOLETTE, VISIONS OF SUFFERING, THE WARRIOR, THE WEEKEND MURDERS, THE WEIRDOS AND THE ODDBALLS, WET WILDERNESS, WHITE SLAVE, WHO CAN KILL A CHILD?, WHO KILLED TEDDY BEAR, WHY DOES HERR R. RUN AMOK?, WINSTANLEY, THE WITCHING HOUR, WOMEN BEHIND BARS, WOMEN IN CELL BLOCK 7, WOODCHIPPER MASSACRE, THE WORLD SINKS EXCEPT JAPAN, THE X-FILES: I WANT TO BELIEVE, THE YOUNG GIRLS OF ROCHEFORT, YOUR WIFE OR MINE?, ZOMBIE BLOODBATH, ZOMBIE BLOODBATH 2: RAGE OF THE UNDEAD, ZOMBIE BLOODBATH 3: ZOMBIE ARMAGEDDON.

More Essential Cinema Books from FAB Press